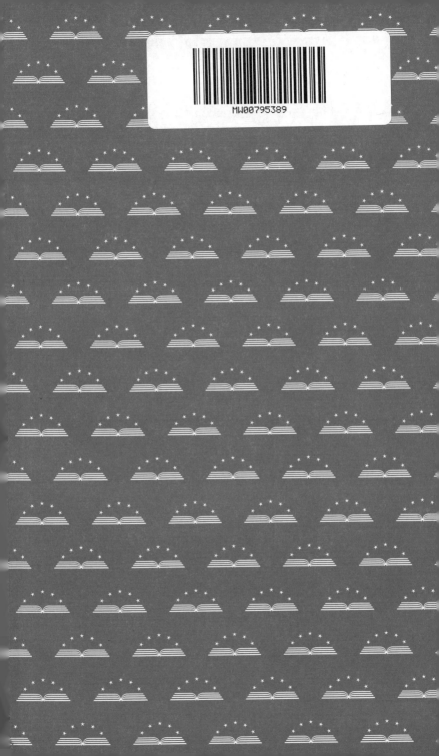

RICHARD HOFSTADTER

RICHARD HOFSTADTER

Anti-Intellectualism in American Life
The Paranoid Style in American Politics
Uncollected Essays 1956–1965

Sean Wilentz, *editor*

THE LIBRARY OF AMERICA

Published in the United States by Library of America.
Visit our website at www.loa.org.

The Paranoid Style in American Politics Copyright © 1952, 1954, 1964, 1965
by Richard Hofstadter. *Anti-Intellectualism in American Life*
Copyright © 1962, 1963 by Richard Hofstadter. Published by arrangement
with Alfred A. Knopf, an imprint of The Knopf Doubleday Publishing
Group, a division of Penguin Random House LLC.

All other texts published by arrangement with the Richard Hofstadter Estate.

This paper exceeds the requirements of
ANSI/NISO Z39.48–1992 (Permanence of Paper).

Distributed to the trade in the United States
by Penguin Random House Inc.
and in Canada by Penguin Random House Canada Ltd.

Library of Congress Control Number: 2019946511
ISBN 978-1-59853-659-1

First Printing
The Library of America—330

Manufactured in the United States of America

Contents

ANTI-INTELLECTUALISM
IN AMERICAN LIFE

To

E. A. H.

1888–1962

Contents

PART I

INTRODUCTION

CHAPTER I

Anti-Intellectualism in Our Time

I

ALTHOUGH THIS book deals mainly with certain aspects of the remoter American past, it was conceived in response to the political and intellectual conditions of the 1950's. During that decade the term *anti-intellectualism*, only rarely heard before, became a familiar part of our national vocabulary of self-recrimination and intramural abuse. In the past, American intellectuals were often discouraged or embittered by the national disrespect for mind, but it is hard to recall a time when large numbers of people outside the intellectual community shared their concern, or when self-criticism on this count took on the character of a nation-wide movement.

Primarily it was McCarthyism which aroused the fear that the critical mind was at a ruinous discount in this country. Of course, intellectuals were not the only targets of McCarthy's constant detonations—he was after bigger game—but intellectuals were in the line of fire, and it seemed to give special rejoicing to his followers when they were hit. His sorties against intellectuals and universities were emulated throughout the country by a host of less exalted inquisitors. Then, in the atmosphere of fervent malice and humorless imbecility stirred up by McCarthy's barrage of accusations, the campaign of 1952 dramatized the contrast between intellect and philistinism in the opposing candidates. On one side was Adlai Stevenson, a politician of uncommon mind and style, whose appeal to intellectuals overshadowed anything in recent history. On the other was Dwight D. Eisenhower, conventional in mind, relatively inarticulate, harnessed to the unpalatable Nixon, and waging a campaign whose tone seemed to be set less by the general himself than by his running mate and the McCarthyite wing of his party.

Eisenhower's decisive victory was taken both by the intellectuals themselves and by their critics as a measure of their repudiation by America. *Time*, the weekly magazine of opinion, shook its head in an unconvincing imitation of concern. Eisenhower's victory, it said, "discloses an alarming fact long suspected: there is a wide and unhealthy gap between the American intellectuals and the people." Arthur Schlesinger, Jr., in a mordant protest written soon after the election, found the intellectual "in a situation he has not known for a generation." After twenty years of Democratic rule, during which the intellectual had been in the main understood and respected, business had come back into power, bringing with it "the vulgarization which has been the almost invariable consequence of business supremacy." Now the intellectual, dismissed as an "egghead," an oddity, would be governed by a party which had little use for or understanding of him, and would be made the scapegoat for everything from the income tax to the attack on Pearl Harbor. "Anti-intellectualism," Schlesinger remarked, "has long been the anti-Semitism of the businessman. . . . The intellectual . . . is on the run today in American society."[1]

All this seemed to be amply justified when the new administration got under way. The replacement, in Stevenson's phrase, of the New Dealers by the car dealers seemed to make final the repudiation of intellectuals and their values—they had already been overshadowed by the courthouse politicians of the Truman years. The country was now treated to Charles E. Wilson's sallies at pure research, to stories about Eisenhower's fondness for Western fiction as reading matter, and to his definition of an intellectual as a wordy and pretentious man. But during the Eisenhower administration the national mood reached a turning point: the McCarthyite rage, confronted by a Republican president, burned itself out; the senator from Wisconsin isolated himself, was censured, and deflated. Finally, in 1957, the launching of the Sputnik by the Soviets precipitated one of those periodic surges of self-conscious national reappraisal to which the American public is prone. The Sputnik was more than a shock to American national vanity: it brought an immense amount of attention to bear on the consequences of anti-intellectualism in the school system and in American life at large. Suddenly the national distaste for intellect appeared to be not just a disgrace but a hazard to survival. After assuming for some years that its main concern with teachers was to examine them for disloyalty, the nation now began to worry about their low salaries. Scientists, who had been saying for years that the growing obsession with security was demoralizing to research, suddenly found receptive listeners. Cries of protest against the slackness of American education, hitherto raised only by a small number of educational critics, were now taken up by television, mass magazines, businessmen, scientists, politicians, admirals, and university presidents, and soon swelled into a national chorus of self-reproach. Of course, all this did not immediately cause the vigilante mind to disappear, nor did it disperse anti-intellectualism as a force in American life; even in the sphere most immediately affected, that of education, the ruling passion of the public seemed to be for producing more Sputniks, not for developing more intellect, and some of the new rhetoric about education almost suggested that gifted children were to be regarded as resources in the cold war. But the atmosphere did change notably. In 1952 only intellectuals seemed much disturbed by the specter of anti-intellectualism; by 1958 the idea that this might be an important and even a dangerous national failing was persuasive to most thinking people.

Today it is possible to look at the political culture of the 1950's with some detachment. If there was then a tendency to see in McCarthyism, and even in the Eisenhower administration, some apocalypse for intellectuals in public life, it is no longer possible, now that Washington has again become so hospitable to Harvard professors and ex-Rhodes scholars. If there was a suspicion that intellect had become a hopeless obstacle to success in politics or administration, it must surely have been put to rest by the new President's obvious interest in ideas and respect for intellectuals, his ceremonial gestures to make that respect manifest in affairs of state, his pleasure in the company and advice of men of intellectual power, and above all by the long, careful search for distinguished talents with which his administration began. On the other hand, if there had ever been an excessive confidence that the recruitment of such talents would altogether transform the conduct of our affairs, time has surely brought its inevitable disenchantment. We have now reached a point at which intellectuals can discuss anti-intellectualism without exaggerated partisanship or self-pity.

2

The political ferment and educational controversy of the 1950's made the term *anti-intellectual* a central epithet in American self-evaluation; it has slipped unobtrusively into our usage without much definition and is commonly used to describe a variety of unwelcome phenomena. Those who have suddenly become aware of it often assume that anti-intellectualism is a new force in this or that area of life, and that, being a product of recent conditions, it may be expected to grow to overwhelming proportions. (American intellectuals have a lamentably thin sense of history; and modern man has lived so long under the shadow of some kind of apocalypse or other that intellectuals have come to look upon even the lesser eddies of social change as though they were tidal waves.) But to students of Americana the anti-intellectual note so commonly struck during the 1950's sounded not new at all, but rather familiar. Anti-intellectualism was not manifested in this country for the first time during the 1950's. Our anti-intellectualism is, in fact, older than our national identity, and has a long historical background. An examination of this background suggests that regard for intellectuals in the United States has not moved steadily downward and has not gone into a sudden, recent decline, but is subject to cyclical fluctuations; it suggests, too, that the resentment from which the intellectual has suffered in our time is a manifestation not of a decline in his position but of his increasing prominence. We know rather little about all this in any systematic way, and there has not been very much historically informed thinking on the subject. A great deal has been written about the long-running quarrel between American intellectuals and their country, but such writings deal mainly with America as seen by the intellectuals, and give only occasional glimpses of intellect and intellectuals as seen by America.[2]

---

[2] The only American historian, to my knowledge, who has concerned himself extensively with the problem is Merle Curti, in his suggestive volume, *American Paradox* (New Brunswick, New Jersey, 1956) and in his presidential address before the American Historical Association, "Intellectuals and Other People," *American Historical Review*, Vol. LX (January 1955), pp. 259–82. Jacques Barzun, in *The House of Intellect* (New York, 1959), has dealt with the

One reason anti-intellectualism has not even been clearly defined is that its very vagueness makes it more serviceable in controversy as an epithet. But, in any case, it does not yield very readily to definition. As an idea, it is not a single proposition but a complex of related propositions. As an attitude, it is not usually found in a pure form but in ambivalence—a pure and unalloyed dislike of intellect or intellectuals is uncommon. And as a historical subject, if it can be called that, it is not a constant thread but a force fluctuating in strength from time to time and drawing its motive power from varying sources. In these pages I have not held myself to a rigorous or narrow definition, which would here be rather misplaced. I can see little advantage in a logically defensible but historically arbitrary act of definition, which would demand singling out one trait among a complex of traits. It is the complex itself I am interested in—the complex of historical relations among a variety of attitudes and ideas that have many points of convergence. The common strain that binds together the attitudes and ideas which I call anti-intellectual is a resentment and suspicion of the life of the mind and of those who are considered to represent it; and a disposition constantly to minimize the value of that life. This admittedly general formulation is as close as I find it useful to venture toward definition.[3]

Once this procedure is adopted, it will be clear that anti-intellectualism cannot be made the subject of a formal history in quite the same way as the life of a man or the development of an institution or a social movement. Dealing as I do with the milieu, the atmosphere, in which American thinking has taken place, I have had to use those impressionistic devices

subject largely in contemporary terms and largely with internal strains within the intellectual and cultural world. An entire number of the *Journal of Social Issues*, Vol. XI, No. 3 (1955), was devoted to discussions of anti-intellectualism by various writers.

[3]For an interesting exercise in definition, see Morton White: "Reflections on Anti-Intellectualism," *Daedalus* (Summer, 1962), pp. 457–68. White makes a useful distinction between the anti-intellectual, who is hostile to intellectuals, and the anti-intellectualist, who is critical of the claims of rational intellect in knowledge and in life. He treats at some length the respective strategies of the two, and their points of convergence.

with which one attempts to reproduce a milieu or capture an atmosphere.

Before giving some examples of what I mean by anti-intellectualism, I may perhaps explain what I do *not* mean. I am not dealing, except incidentally, with the internal feuds or contentions of the American intellectual community. American intellectuals, like intellectuals elsewhere, are often uneasy in their role; they are given to moments of self-doubt, and even of self-hatred, and at times they make acidulous and sweeping comments on the whole tribe to which they belong. This internal criticism is revealing and interesting, but it is not my main concern. Neither is the ill-mannered or ill-considered criticism that one intellectual may make of another. No one, for example, ever poured more scorn on the American professoriat than H. L. Mencken, and no one has portrayed other writers in fiction with more venom than Mary McCarthy; but we would not on this account dream of classing Mencken with William F. Buckley as an enemy of the professors nor Miss McCarthy with the late senator of the same name.[4] The criticism of other intellectuals is, after all, one of the most important functions of the intellectual, and he customarily performs it with vivacity. We may hope, but we can hardly expect, that he will also do it with charity, grace, and precision. Because it is the business of intellectuals to be diverse and contrary-minded, we must accept the risk that at times they will be merely quarrelsome.

[4]These considerations serve as a forcible reminder that there is in America, as elsewhere, a kind of intellectual establishment that embraces a wide range of views. It is generally understood (although there are marginal cases) whether a particular person is inside or outside this establishment. The establishment has a double standard for evaluating the criticism of the intellectuals: criticism from within is commonly accepted as having a basically benign intent and is more likely to be heard solely on its merits; but criticism from outside—even the same criticism—will be resented as hostile and stigmatized as anti-intellectual and potentially dangerous. For example, some years ago many intellectuals were critical of the great foundations for devoting too much of their research money to the support of large-budget "projects," as opposed to individual scholarship. But when the Reece Committee was hot on the trail of the foundations, the same intellectuals were not happy to see the same criticism (among others more specious) pressed by such an agency. It was not that they had ceased to believe in the criticism but that they neither liked nor trusted the source.

It is important, finally, if we are to avoid hopeless confusion, to be clear that anti-intellectualism is not here identified with a type of philosophical doctrine which I prefer to call anti-rationalism. The ideas of thinkers like Nietzsche, Sorel, or Bergson, Emerson, Whitman, or William James, or of writers like William Blake, D. H. Lawrence, or Ernest Hemingway may be called anti-rationalist; but these men were not characteristically anti-intellectual in the sociological and political sense in which I use the term. It is of course true that anti-intellectualist movements often invoke the ideas of such anti-rationalist thinkers (Emerson alone has provided them with a great many texts); but only when they do, and only marginally, is highbrow anti-rationalism a part of my story. In these pages I am centrally concerned with widespread social attitudes, with political behavior, and with middlebrow and lowbrow responses, only incidentally with articulate theories. The attitudes that interest me most are those which would, to the extent that they become effective in our affairs, gravely inhibit or impoverish intellectual and cultural life. Some examples, taken from our recent history, may put flesh on the bare bones of definition.

3

We might begin with some definitions supplied by those most acutely dissatisfied with American intellectuals.

Of course, not only intellectuals do this; it is a common phenomenon of group life. Members of a political party or a minority group may invoke a similar double standard against criticism, depending on whether it originates from inside or outside the ranks. There is, moreover, some justification for such double standards, in historical fact if not in logic, because the intent that lies behind criticism unfortunately becomes an ingredient in its applicability. The intellectuals who criticized the foundations were doing so in the hope (as they saw it) of constructively modifying foundation policies, whereas the line of inquiry pursued by the Reece Committee might have led to crippling or destroying them. Again, everyone understands that a joke, say, about Jews or Negroes has different overtones when it is told within the group and when it is told by outsiders.

Exhibit A. During the campaign of 1952, the country seemed to be in need of some term to express that disdain for intellectuals which had by then become a self-conscious motif in American politics. The word *egghead* was originally used without invidious associations,[5] but quickly assumed them, and acquired a much sharper overtone than the traditional *highbrow*. Shortly after the campaign was over, Louis Bromfield, a popular novelist of right-wing political persuasion, suggested that the word might some day find its way into dictionaries as follows:[6]

> *Egghead:* A person of spurious intellectual pretensions, often a professor or the protégé of a professor. Fundamentally superficial. Over-emotional and feminine in reactions to any problem. Supercilious and surfeited with conceit and contempt for the experience of more sound and able men. Essentially confused in thought and immersed in mixture of sentimentality and violent evangelism. A doctrinaire supporter of Middle-European socialism as opposed to Greco-French-American ideas of democracy and liberalism. Subject to the old-fashioned philosophical morality of Nietzsche which frequently leads him into jail or disgrace. A self-conscious prig, so given to examining all sides of a question that he becomes thoroughly addled while remaining always in the same spot. An anemic bleeding heart.

"The recent election," Bromfield remarked, "demonstrated a number of things, not the least of them being the extreme remoteness of the 'egghead' from the thought and feeling of the whole of the people."

Exhibit B. Almost two years later President Eisenhower appeared to give official sanction to a similarly disdainful view of intellectuals. Speaking at a Republican meeting in Los Angeles

---

[5]The term was taken up as a consequence of a column by Stewart Alsop, in which that reporter recorded a conversation with his brother John. The columnist remarked that many intelligent people who were normally Republicans obviously admired Stevenson. "Sure," said his brother, "all the egg-heads love Stevenson. But how many egg-heads do you think there are?" Joseph and Stewart Alsop: *The Reporter's Trade* (New York, 1958), p. 188.

[6]Louis Bromfield: "The Triumph of the Egghead," *The Freeman*, Vol. III (December 1, 1952), p. 158.

in 1954, he reported a view, expressed to him by a trade-union leader, that the people, presented with the whole truth, will always support the right cause. The President added:[7]

> It was a rather comforting thought to have this labor leader saying this, when we had so many wisecracking so-called intellectuals going around and showing how wrong was everybody who don't happen to agree with them.
>
> By the way, I heard a definition of an intellectual that I thought was very interesting: *a man who takes more words than are necessary to tell more than he knows.*

Exhibit C. One of the issues at stake in the controversies of the 1950's was the old one about the place of expertise in political life. Perhaps the high moment in the case against the expert and for the amateur occurred in 1957 when a chain-store president, Maxwell H. Gluck, was nominated to be ambassador to Ceylon. Mr. Gluck had contributed, by his own estimate, $20,000 or $30,000 to the Republican campaign of 1956, but, like many such appointees before him, was not known for having any experience in politics or diplomacy. Questioned by Senator Fulbright about his qualifications for the post, Mr. Gluck had some difficulty:[8]

FULBRIGHT: What are the problems in Ceylon you think you can deal with?

GLUCK: One of the problems are the people there. I believe I can—I think I can establish, unless we—again, unless I run into something that I have not run into before—a good relationship and good feeling toward the United States. . . .

FULBRIGHT: Do you know our Ambassador to India?

---

[7] White House Press Release, "Remarks of the President at the Breakfast Given by Various Republican Groups of Southern California, Statler Hotel, Los Angeles . . . September 24, 1954," p. 4; italics added. It is possible that the President had heard something of the kind from his Secretary of Defense, Charles E. Wilson, who was quoted elsewhere as saying: "An egghead is a man who doesn't understand everything he knows." Richard and Gladys Harkness: "The Wit and Wisdom of Charlie Wilson," *Reader's Digest*, Vol. LXXI (August, 1957), p. 197.

[8] *The New York Times*, August 1, 1957.

GLUCK: I know John Sherman Cooper, the previous
             Ambassador.
FULBRIGHT: Do you know who the Prime Minister of India
             is?
GLUCK: Yes, but I can't pronounce his name.
FULBRIGHT: Do you know who the Prime Minister of Ceylon
             is?
GLUCK: His name is unfamiliar now, I cannot call it off.

Doubts about Mr. Gluck's preparation for the post he was to
occupy led to the suggestion that he had been named because
of his contribution to the Republican campaign. In a press
conference held July 31, 1957, a reporter raised the question,
whereupon President Eisenhower remarked that an appointment in return for campaign contributions was unthinkable.
About his nominee's competence, he observed:[9]

> Now, as to the man's ignorance, this is the way he was ap-
> pointed: he was selected from a group of men that were recom-
> mended highly by a number of people I respect. His business
> career was examined, the F.B.I. reports on him were all good.
> Of course, we knew he had never been to Ceylon, he wasn't
> thoroughly familiar with it; but certainly he can learn if he is the
> kind of character and kind of man we believe him to be.

It is important to add that Mr. Gluck's service in Ceylon was
terminated after a year by his resignation.

Exhibit D. One of the grievances of American scientists was
their awareness that America's disdain for pure science was a
handicap not only to investigation but also to the progress of
research and development in the Department of Defense. Examining Secretary of Defense Charles E. Wilson in 1954 before the Senate Committee on Armed Services, Senator Stuart
Symington of Missouri quoted earlier testimony in which the
Secretary had said, among other things, that if there was to be
pure research it should be subsidized by some agency other
than the Department of Defense. "I am not much interested,"
Secretary Wilson had testified, "as a military project in why
potatoes turn brown when they are fried." Pressing Secretary

[9] Ibid.

Wilson, Senator Symington pointed to testimony that had been given about the lack of sufficient money for research not on potatoes but on bombers, nuclear propulsion, electronics, missiles, radar, and other subjects. The Secretary replied:[10]

> Important research and development is going on in all those areas. . . .
>
> On the other side, it is very difficult to get these men who are trying to think out ahead all the time to come down to brass tacks and list the projects and what they expect to get. . . . They would just like to have a pot of money without too much supervision that they could reach into. . . .
>
> In the first place, *if you know what you are doing, why it is not pure research*. That complicates it.

Exhibit E. The kind of anti-intellectualism expressed in official circles during the 1950's was mainly the traditional businessman's suspicion of experts working in any area outside his control, whether in scientific laboratories, universities, or diplomatic corps. Far more acute and sweeping was the hostility to intellectuals expressed on the far-right wing, a categorical folkish dislike of the educated classes and of anything respectable, established, pedigreed, or cultivated. The right-wing crusade of the 1950's was full of heated rhetoric about "Harvard professors, twisted-thinking intellectuals . . . in the State Department"; those who are "burdened with Phi Beta Kappa keys and academic honors" but not "equally loaded with honesty and common sense"; "the American respectables, the socially pedigreed, the culturally acceptable, the certified gentlemen and scholars of the day, dripping with college degrees . . . the 'best people' who were for Alger Hiss"; "the pompous diplomat in striped pants with phony British accent"; those who try to fight Communism "with kid gloves in perfumed drawing rooms"; Easterners who "insult the people of the great Midwest and West, the *heart* of America"; those who can "trace their ancestry back to the eighteenth century—or even further" but whose loyalty is still not above suspicion; those

---

[10]U.S. Congress, 84th Congress, 2nd session, Senate Committee on Armed Services: *Hearings*, Vol. XVI, pp. 1742, 1744 (July 2, 1956); italics added.

who understand "the Groton vocabulary of the Hiss-Acheson group."[11] The spirit of this rhetorical *jacquerie* was caught by an editorial writer for the *Freeman*:[12]

> The truly appalling phenomenon is the irrationality of the college-educated mob that has descended upon Joseph R. McCarthy. . . . Suppose Mr. McCarthy were indeed the cad the "respectable" press makes him out to be; would this . . . justify the cataclysmic eruptions that, for almost a year now, have emanated from all the better appointed editorial offices of New York and Washington, D.C.? . . . It must be something in McCarthy's personal makeup. He possesses, it seems, a sort of animal negative-pole magnetism which repels alumni of Harvard, Princeton and Yale. And we think we know what it is: This young man is constitutionally incapable of deference to social status.

McCarthy himself found the central reasons for America's difficulties in areas where social status was most secure. The trouble, he said in the published version of his famous Wheeling speech, lay in[13]

> the traitorous actions of those who have been treated so well by this Nation. It has not been the less fortunate or members of minority groups who have been selling this Nation out, but rather those who have had all the benefits that the wealthiest nation on earth has had to offer—the finest homes, the finest college education, and the finest jobs in Government we can give. This is glaringly true in the State Department. There the bright young men who are born with silver spoons in their mouths are the ones who have been worst.

Exhibit F. The universities, particularly the better-known universities, were constantly marked out as targets by right-wing critics; but according to one writer in the *Freeman* there

---

[11] This mélange of images is taken from the more extended account of the scapegoats of the 1950's in Immanuel Wallerstein's unpublished M.A. essay: "McCarthyism and the Conservative," Columbia University, 1954, pp. 46 ff.

[12] *Freeman*, Vol. XI (November 5, 1951), p. 72.

[13] *Congressional Record*, 81st Congress, 2nd session, p. 1954 (February 20, 1950).

appears to have been only an arbitrary reason for this discrimination against the Ivy League, since he considered that Communism is spreading in all our colleges:[14]

> Our universities are the training grounds for the barbarians of
> the future, those who, in the guise of learning, shall come forth
> loaded with pitchforks of ignorance and cynicism, and stab and
> destroy the remnants of human civilization. It will not be the
> subway peasants who will tear down the walls: they will merely
> do the bidding of our learned brethren . . . who will erase
> individual Freedom from the ledgers of human thought. . . .
>
> If you send your son to the colleges of today, you will cre-
> ate the Executioner of tomorrow. The rebirth of idealism must
> come from the scattered monasteries of non-collegiate thought.

Exhibit G. Right-wing hostility to universities was in part a
question of deference and social status, but in part also a reflection of the old Jacksonian dislike of specialists and experts.
Here is a characteristic assertion about the equal competence
of the common man (in this case the common woman) and
the supposed experts, written by the amateur economist, Frank
Chodorov, author of *The Income Tax: The Root of All Evil,* and
one of the most engaging of the right-wing spokesmen:[15]

> A parcel of eminent economists, called into consultation by
> the Rockefeller Brothers Fund to diagnose the national ailment
> known as recession, came up with a prescription that, though
> slightly condensed, covered the better part of two pages in *The
> New York Times.* The prominence of these doctors makes it pre-
> sumptuous for one who has not "majored" in economics to
> examine the ingredients of their curative concoction. Yet the
> fact is that all of us are economists by necessity, since all of
> us are engaged in making a living, which is what economics is
> all about. Any literate housewife, endowed with a modicum of
> common sense, should be able to evaluate the specifics in the
> prescription, provided these are extracted from the verbiage in
> which they are clothed.

---

[14]Jack Schwartzman: "Natural Law and the Campus," *Freeman,* Vol. II (December 3, 1951), pp. 149, 152.
[15]"Shake Well before Using," *National Review,* Vol. V (June 7, 1958), p. 544.

Exhibit H. Although the following may well be considered by discriminating readers as anti-cultural rather than anti-intellectual, I cannot omit some remarks by Congressman George Dondero of Michigan, long a vigilant crusader against Communism in the schools and against cubism, expressionism, surrealism, dadaism, futurism, and other movements in art:[16]

> The art of the isms, the weapon of the Russian Revolution, is the art which has been transplanted to America, and today, having infiltrated and saturated many of our art centers, threatens to overawe, override and overpower the fine art of our tradition and inheritance. So-called modern or contemporary art in our own beloved country contains all the isms of depravity, decadence, and destruction. . . .
>
> All these isms are of foreign origin, and truly should have no place in American art. . . . All are instruments and weapons of destruction.

Exhibit I. Since I shall have much to say in these pages about anti-intellectualism in the evangelical tradition, it seems important to cite at least one survival of this tradition. These brief quotations are taken from the most successful evangelist of our time, Billy Graham, voted by the American public in a Gallup Poll of 1958 only after Eisenhower, Churchill, and Albert Schweitzer as "the most admired man in the world":[17]

> Moral standards of yesterday to many individuals are no standard for today unless supported by the so-called "intellectuals."
>
> I sincerely believe that partial education throughout the world is far worse than none at all, if we only educate the mind without the soul. . . . Turn that man loose upon the world [who has] no power higher than his own, he is a monstrosity, he is but halfway educated, and is more dangerous than though he were not educated at all.

---

[16] *Congressional Record*, 81st Congress, 1st session, p. 11584 (August 16, 1949); see also Dondero's address on "Communism in Our Schools," *Congressional Record*, 79th Congress, 2nd session, pp. A. 3516–18 (June 14, 1946), and his speech, "Communist Conspiracy in Art Threatens American Museums," *Congressional Record*, 82nd Congress, 2nd session, pp. 2423–7 (March 17, 1952).
[17] William G. McLoughlin, Jr.: *Billy Graham: Revivalist in a Secular Age* (New York, 1960), pp. 89, 212, 213; on the Gallup Poll, see p. 5.

You can stick a public school and a university in the middle of every block of every city in America and you will never keep America from rotting morally by mere intellectual education.

During the past few years the intellectual props have been knocked out from under the theories of men. Even the average university professor is willing to listen to the voice of the preacher.

[In place of the Bible] we substituted reason, rationalism, mind culture, science worship, the working power of government, Freudianism, naturalism, humanism, behaviorism, positivism, materialism, and idealism. [This is the work of] so-called intellectuals. Thousands of these "intellectuals" have publicly stated that morality is relative—that there is no norm or absolute standard. . . .

Exhibit J. In the post-Sputnik furor over American education, one of the most criticized school systems was that of California, which had been notable for its experimentation with curricula. When the San Francisco School District commissioned a number of professional scholars to examine their schools, the committee constituted for this purpose urged a return to firmer academic standards. Six educational organizations produced a sharp counterattack in which they criticized the authors of the San Francisco report for "academic pettiness and snobbery" and for going beyond their competence in limiting the purposes of education to "informing the mind and developing the intelligence," and reasserted the value of "other goals of education, such as preparation for citizenship, occupational competence, successful family life, self-realization in ethical, moral, aesthetic and spiritual dimensions, and the enjoyment of physical health." The educationists argued that an especially praiseworthy feature of American education had been[18]

the attempt to avoid a highly rigid system of education. To do so does not mean that academic competence is not regarded as highly important to any society, but it does recognize that historically, *education systems which stress absorption of accumulated*

[18]*Judging and Improving the Schools: Current Issues* (Burlingame, California, 1960), pp. 4, 5, 7, 8; italics added. The document under fire was William C. Bark et al.: *Report of the San Francisco Curriculum Survey Committee* (San Francisco, 1960).

knowledge for its own sake have tended to produce decadence.
Those who would "fix" the curriculum and freeze educational
purpose misunderstand the unique function of education in
American democracy.

Exhibit K. The following is an excerpt from a parent's report,
originally written in answer to a teacher's complaint about the
lax standards in contemporary education. The entire piece is
worth reading as a vivid statement by a parent who identifies
wholly with the non-academic child and the newer education.
As we shall see, the stereotype of the schoolteacher expressed
here has deep historical roots.[19]

But kindergarten teachers understand children. Theirs is a
child-centered program. School days were one continuous joy
of games and music and colors and friendliness. Life rolled mer-
rily along through the first grade, the second grade, the third
grade . . . then came arithmetic! Failure like a spectre arose to
haunt our days and harass our nights. Father and mother began
to attend lectures on psychology and to read about inferiority
complexes. We dragged through the fourth grade and into the
fifth. Something had to be done. Even father couldn't solve all
the problems. I decided to have a talk with the teacher.

There was no welcome on the mat of that school. No one
greeted the stranger or made note of his coming. A somber
hallway presented itself, punctuated at regular intervals by
closed doors. Unfamiliar sounds came from within. I inquired
my way of a hurrying youngster and then knocked at the for-
bidding threshold. To the teacher I announced my name, smiling as pleasantly as I could. "Oh, yes," she said, as if my business
were already known to her and reached for her classbook, quick
on the draw like a movie gangster clutching for his gun.

The names of the pupils appeared on a ruled page in neat and
alphabetical precision. The teacher moved a bloodless finger
down the margin of the page to my daughter's name. After
each name were little squares. In the squares were little marks,
symbols that I did not understand. Her finger moved across the
page. My child's marks were not the same as those of the other
children. She looked up triumphantly as if there were nothing

more to be said. I was thinking of the small compass into which she had compressed the total activities of a very lively youngster. I was interested in a whole life, a whole personality; the teacher, merely in arithmetical ability. I wished I had not come. I left uninformed and uncomforted.

Exhibit L. The following remarks have already been made famous by Arthur Bestor, but they will bear repetition. After delivering and publishing the address excerpted here, the author, a junior high-school principal in Illinois, did not lose caste in his trade but was engaged for a similar position in Great Neck, Long Island, a post which surely ranks high in desirability among the nation's secondary schools, and was subsequently invited to be a visiting member of the faculty of the school of education of a Midwestern university.[20]

> Through the years we've built a sort of halo around reading, writing, and arithmetic. We've said they were for everybody . . . rich and poor, brilliant and not-so-mentally-endowed, ones who liked them and those who failed to go for them. Teacher has said that these were something "everyone should learn." The principal has remarked, "All educated people know how to write, spell, and read." When some child declared a dislike for a sacred subject, he was warned that, if he failed to master it, he would grow up to be a so-and-so.
>
> The Three R's for All Children, and All Children for the Three R's! That was it.
>
> We've made some progress in getting rid of that slogan. But every now and then some mother with a Phi Beta Kappa award or some employer who has hired a girl who can't spell stirs up a fuss about the schools . . . and ground is lost. . . .
>
> When we come to the realization that not every child has to read, figure, write and spell . . . that many of them either cannot or will not master these chores . . . then we shall be on the road to improving the junior high curriculum.

---

[20]A. H. Lauchner: "How Can the Junior High School Curriculum Be Improved?" *Bulletin of the National Association of Secondary-School Principals*, Vol. XXXV (March, 1951), pp. 299–301. The three dots of elision here do not indicate omissions but are the author's punctuation. The address was delivered at a meeting of this association. See Arthur Bestor's comments in *The Restoration of Learning* (New York, 1955), p. 54.

Between this day and that a lot of selling must take place. But it's coming. We shall some day accept the thought that it is just as illogical to assume that every boy must be able to read as it is that each one must be able to perform on a violin, that it is no more reasonable to require that each girl shall spell well than it is that each one shall bake a good cherry pie.

We cannot all do the same things. We do not like to do the same things. And we won't. When adults finally realize that fact, everyone will be happier . . . and schools will be nicer places in which to live. . . .

If and when we are able to convince a few folks that mastery of reading, writing, and arithmetic is not the one road leading to happy, successful living, the next step is to cut down the amount of time and attention devoted to these areas in general junior high-school courses. . . .

One junior high in the East has, after long and careful study, accepted the fact that some twenty percent of their students will not be up to standard in reading . . . and they are doing other things for these boys and girls. That's straight thinking. Contrast that with the junior high which says, "Every student must know the multiplication tables before graduation."

These exhibits, though their sources and intentions are various, collectively display the ideal assumptions of anti-intellectualism. Intellectuals, it may be held, are pretentious, conceited, effeminate, and snobbish; and very likely immoral, dangerous, and subversive. The plain sense of the common man, especially if tested by success in some demanding line of practical work, is an altogether adequate substitute for, if not actually much superior to, formal knowledge and expertise acquired in the schools. Not surprisingly, institutions in which intellectuals tend to be influential, like universities and colleges, are rotten to the core. In any case, the discipline of the heart, and the old-fashioned principles of religion and morality, are more reliable guides to life than an education which aims to produce minds responsive to new trends in thought and art. Even at the level of elementary education, a schooling that puts too much stress on the acquisition of mere knowledge, as opposed to the vigorous development of physical and emotional life, is heartless in its mode of conduct and threatens to produce social decadence.

4

To avoid some hazards to understanding, it is perhaps necessary to say that a work given single-mindedly to the exploration of such a theme as this must inevitably have the effect
of highlighting its importance in a way that would not be
warranted in a comprehensive history of American culture. I
can only say that I do not suffer from the delusion that the
complexities of American history can be satisfactorily reduced
to a running battle between the eggheads and the fatheads.
Moreover, to the extent that our history can be considered
one of cultural and intellectual conflicts, the public is not simply divided into intellectual and anti-intellectual factions. The
greater part of the public, and a great part even of the intelligent and alert public, is simply non-intellectual; it is infused
with enough ambivalence about intellect and intellectuals to
be swayed now this way and now that on current cultural issues. It has an ingrained distrust of eggheads, but also a genuine yearning for enlightenment and culture. Moreover, a
book on anti-intellectualism in America can hardly be taken as
though it were meant to be a balanced assessment of our culture, any more than a history of bankruptcies could be taken
as a full history of our business life. Although I am convinced
that anti-intellectualism is pervasive in our culture, I believe
that it can rarely be called dominant. Again and again I have
noticed, as I hope readers will, that the more mild and benign
forms of anti-intellectualism prove to be the most widespread,
whereas the most malign forms are found mainly among small
if vociferous minority groups. Again, this is not, as it perhaps
should be, a comparative study: my concentration on anti-
intellectualism in the United States is no more than the result
of a special, and possibly parochial, interest in American society. I do not assume that anti-intellectualism does not exist
elsewhere. I think that it is a problem of more than ordinary
acuteness here, but I believe it has been present in some form
and degree in most societies; in one it takes the form of the
administering of hemlock, in another of town-and-gown riots,
in another of censorship and regimentation, in still another
of Congressional investigations. I am disposed to believe that

anti-intellectualism, though it has its own universality, may be considered a part of our English cultural inheritance, and that it is notably strong in Anglo-American experience. A few years ago Leonard Woolf remarked that "no people has ever despised and distrusted the intellect and intellectuals more than the British."[21] Perhaps Mr. Woolf had not given sufficient thought to the claims of the Americans to supremacy in this respect (which is understandable, since the British have been tired for more than a century of American boasting); but that a British intellectual so long seasoned and so well informed on the cultural life of his own country could have made such a remark may well give us pause. Although the situation of American intellectuals poses problems of special urgency and poignancy, many of their woes are the common experiences of intellectuals elsewhere, and there are some compensating circumstances in American life.

This book is a critical inquiry, not a legal brief for the intellectuals against the American community. I have no desire to encourage the self-pity to which intellectuals are sometimes prone by suggesting that they have been vessels of pure virtue set down in Babylon. One does not need to assert this, or to assert that intellectuals should get sweeping indulgence or exercise great power, in order to insist that respect for intellect and its functions is important to the culture and the health of any society, and that in ours this respect has often been notably lacking. No one who lives among intellectuals is likely to idealize them unduly; but their relation as fallible persons to the vital function of intellect should remind us of the wisdom of the Church, which holds that although the priesthood is vulnerable to the errors and sins of the flesh, the Church itself remains holy. Even here, however, I do not forget that intellect itself can be overvalued, and that reasonable attempts to set it in its proper place in human affairs should not be called anti-intellectual. One does not care to dissent when T. S. Eliot observes that "intellectual ability without the more human attributes is admirable only in the same way as the brilliance of

---

[21]"G. E. Moore," *Encounter*, Vol. XII (January, 1959), p. 68; the context, it should be said, suggests that Woolf was quite aware of the necessary qualifications to this remark.

a child chess prodigy."[22] But in a world full of dangers, the danger that American society as a whole will overesteem intellect or assign it such a transcendent value as to displace other legitimate values is one that need hardly trouble us.

Possibly the greatest hazard of this venture is that of encouraging the notion that anti-intellectualism is commonly found in a pure or unmixed state. It seems clear that those who have some quarrel with intellect are almost always ambivalent about it: they mix respect and awe with suspicion and resentment; and this has been true in many societies and phases of human history. In any case, anti-intellectualism is not the creation of people who are categorically hostile to ideas. Quite the contrary: just as the most effective enemy of the educated man may be the half-educated man, so the leading anti-intellectuals are usually men deeply engaged with ideas, often obsessively engaged with this or that outworn or rejected idea. Few intellectuals are without moments of anti-intellectualism; few anti-intellectuals without single-minded intellectual passions. In so far as anti-intellectualism becomes articulate enough to be traced historically or widespread enough to make itself felt in contemporary controversy, it has to have spokesmen who are at least to some degree competent. These spokesmen are in the main neither the uneducated nor the unintellectual, but rather the marginal intellectuals, would-be intellectuals, unfrocked or embittered intellectuals, the literate leaders of the semi-literate, full of seriousness and high purpose about the causes that bring them to the attention of the world. I have found anti-intellectual leaders who were evangelical ministers, many of them highly intelligent and some even learned; fundamentalists, articulate about their theology; politicians, including some of the shrewdest; businessmen or other spokesmen of the practical demands of American culture; right-wing editors of strong intellectual pretensions and convictions; various marginal writers (*vide* the anti-intellectualism of the Beatniks); anti-Communist pundits, offended by the past heresies of a large segment of the intellectual community; and, for that matter, Communist leaders, who had much use for intellectuals when they could *use* them, but the utmost contempt for what

[22] *Notes towards the Definition of Culture* (London, 1948), p. 23.

intellectuals are concerned with. The hostility so prominent in the temper of these men is not directed against ideas as such, not even in every case against intellectuals as such. The spokesmen of anti-intellectualism are almost always devoted to some ideas, and much as they may hate the regnant intellectuals among their living contemporaries, they may be devotees of some intellectuals long dead—Adam Smith perhaps, or Thomas Aquinas, or John Calvin, or even Karl Marx.

It would also be mistaken, as well as uncharitable, to imagine that the men and women who from time to time carry the banners of anti-intellectualism are of necessity committed to it as though it were a positive creed or a kind of principle. In fact, anti-intellectualism is usually the incidental consequence of some other intention, often some justifiable intention. Hardly anyone believes himself to be against thought and culture. Men do not rise in the morning, grin at themselves in their mirrors, and say: "Ah, today I shall torment an intellectual and strangle an idea!" Only rarely, and with the gravest of misgivings, then, can we designate an individual as being constitutionally anti-intellectual. In any case, it would be of little value in this enterprise—and certainly it is no concern of mine—to classify or stigmatize individuals; what is important is to estimate the historical tendency of certain attitudes, movements, and ideas.[23] With respect to these, some individuals will appear now on one side and now on another. In fact, anti-intellectualism is often characteristic of forces diametrically opposed to each other. Businessmen and labor leaders may have views of the intellectual class which are surprisingly similar. Again, progressive education has had its own strong anti-intellectual element, and yet its harshest and most determined foes, who are right-wing vigilantes, manifest their own anti-intellectualism, which is, though different in style, less equivocal and more militant.

To be confronted with a simple and unqualified evil is no doubt a kind of luxury; but such is not the case here; and if anti-intellectualism has become, as I believe it has, a broadly

---

[23]As a case in point, I have found it desirable to discuss the anti-intellectual implications and the anti-intellectual consequences of some educational theories of John Dewey; but it would be absurd and impertinent to say, on this account, that Dewey was *an* anti-intellectual.

diffused quality in our civilization, it has become so because it has often been linked to good, or at least defensible, causes. It first got its strong grip on our ways of thinking because it was fostered by an evangelical religion that also purveyed many humane and democratic sentiments. It made its way into our politics because it became associated with our passion for equality. It has become formidable in our education partly because our educational beliefs are evangelically egalitarian. Hence, as far as possible, our anti-intellectualism must be excised from the benevolent impulses upon which it lives by constant and delicate acts of intellectual surgery which spare these impulses themselves. Only in this way can anti-intellectualism be checked and contained; I do not say eliminated altogether, for I believe not only that this is beyond our powers but also that an unbridled passion for the total elimination of this or that evil can be as dangerous as any of the delusions of our time.

CHAPTER II

On the Unpopularity of Intellect

I

BEFORE ATTEMPTING to estimate the qualities in our society that make intellect unpopular, it seems necessary to say something about what intellect is usually understood to be. When one hopes to understand a common prejudice, common usage provides a good place to begin. Anyone who scans popular American writing with this interest in mind will be struck by the manifest difference between the idea of intellect and the idea of intelligence. The first is frequently used as a kind of epithet, the second never. No one questions the value of intelligence; as an abstract quality it is universally esteemed, and individuals who seem to have it in exceptional degree are highly regarded. The man of intelligence is always praised; the man of intellect is sometimes also praised, especially when it is believed that intellect involves intelligence, but he is also often looked upon with resentment or suspicion. It is he, and not the intelligent man, who may be called unreliable, superfluous, immoral, or subversive; sometimes he is even said to be, for all his intellect, unintelligent.[1]

Although the difference between the qualities of intelligence and intellect is more often assumed than defined, the context of popular usage makes it possible to extract the nub of the distinction, which seems to be almost universally understood: intelligence is an excellence of mind that is employed within a fairly narrow, immediate, and predictable range; it is a manipulative, adjustive, unfailingly practical quality—one of the

---

[1] I do not want to suggest that this distinction is made only in the United States, since it seems to be common wherever there is a class that finds intellectuals a nuisance and yet does not want to throw overboard its own claims to intelligence. Thus, in France, after the intellectuals had emerged as a kind of social force, one finds Maurice Barrès writing in 1902: "I'd rather be intelligent than an intellectual." Victor Brombert: *The Intellectual Hero: Studies in the French Novel, 1880–1955* (Philadelphia, 1961), p. 25.

most eminent and endearing of the animal virtues. Intelligence works within the framework of limited but clearly stated goals, and may be quick to shear away questions of thought that do not seem to help in reaching them. Finally, it is of such universal use that it can daily be seen at work and admired alike by simple or complex minds.

Intellect, on the other hand, is the critical, creative, and contemplative side of mind. Whereas intelligence seeks to grasp, manipulate, re-order, adjust, intellect examines, ponders, wonders, theorizes, criticizes, imagines. Intelligence will seize the immediate meaning in a situation and evaluate it. Intellect evaluates evaluations, and looks for the meanings of situations as a whole. Intelligence can be praised as a quality in animals; intellect, being a unique manifestation of human dignity, is both praised and assailed as a quality in men. When the difference is so defined, it becomes easier to understand why we sometimes say that a mind of admittedly penetrating intelligence is relatively unintellectual; and why, by the same token, we see among minds that are unmistakably intellectual a considerable range of intelligence.

This distinction may seem excessively abstract, but it is frequently illustrated in American culture. In our education, for example, it has never been doubted that the selection and development of intelligence is a goal of central importance; but the extent to which education should foster intellect has been a matter of the most heated controversy, and the opponents of intellect in most spheres of public education have exercised preponderant power. But perhaps the most impressive illustration arises from a comparison of the American regard for inventive skill as opposed to skill in pure science. Our greatest inventive genius, Thomas A. Edison, was all but canonized by the American public, and a legend has been built around him. One cannot, I suppose, expect that achievements in pure science would receive the same public applause that came to inventions as spectacular and as directly influential on ordinary life as Edison's. But one might have expected that our greatest genius in pure science, Josiah Willard Gibbs, who laid the theoretical foundations for modern physical chemistry, would have been a figure of some comparable acclaim among the educated public. Yet Gibbs, whose work was celebrated in Europe, lived out his life in public and even professional obscurity at Yale, where he taught for thirty-two years. Yale, which led American universities in its scientific achievements during the nineteenth century, was unable in those thirty-two years to provide him with more than a half dozen or so graduate students who could understand his work, and never took the trouble to award him an honorary degree.[2]

A special difficulty arises when we speak of the fate of intellect in society; this difficulty stems from the fact that we are compelled to speak of intellect in vocational terms, though we may recognize that intellect is not simply a matter of vocation. Intellect is considered in general usage to be an attribute of certain professions and vocations; we speak of the intellectual as being a writer or a critic, a professor or a scientist, an editor, journalist, lawyer, clergyman, or the like. As Jacques Barzun has said, the intellectual is a man who carries a brief case. It is hardly possible to dispense with this convenience; the status and the role of intellectuals are bound up with the aggregate of the brief-case-carrying professions. But few of us believe that a member of a profession, even a learned profession, is necessarily an intellectual in any discriminating or demanding sense of the word. In most professions intellect may help, but intelligence will serve well enough without it. We know, for instance, that all academic men are not intellectuals; we often lament this fact. We know that there is something about intellect, as opposed to professionally trained intelligence, which does not adhere to whole vocations but only to persons. And when we are troubled about the position of intellect and the intellectual class in our society, it is not only the status of certain vocational groups which we have in mind, but the value attached to a certain mental quality.

A great deal of what might be called the journeyman's work of our culture—the work of lawyers, editors, engineers, doctors, indeed of some writers and of most professors—though

---

[2]The situation of Gibbs is often mentioned as a consequence of American attitudes. For the general situation it symbolized, see Richard H. Shryock: "American Indifference to Basic Science during the Nineteenth Century," *Archives Internationales d'Histoire des Sciences*, No. 5 (1948), pp. 50–65.

vitally dependent upon ideas, is not distinctively intellectual. A man in any of the learned or quasi-learned professions must have command of a substantial store of frozen ideas to do his work; he must, if he does it well, use them intelligently; but in his professional capacity he uses them mainly as instruments. The heart of the matter—to borrow a distinction made by Max Weber about politics—is that the professional man lives *off* ideas, not *for* them. His professional role, his professional skills, do not make him an intellectual. He is a mental worker, a technician. He may *happen* to be an intellectual as well, but if he is, it is because he brings to his profession a distinctive feeling about ideas which is not required by his job. As a professional, he has acquired a stock of mental skills that are for sale. The skills are highly developed, but we do not think of him as being an intellectual if certain qualities are missing from his work— disinterested intelligence, generalizing power, free speculation, fresh observation, creative novelty, radical criticism. At home he may happen to be an intellectual, but at his job he is a hired mental technician who uses his mind for the pursuit of externally determined ends. It is this element—the fact that ends are set from some interest or vantage point outside the intellectual process itself—which characterizes both the zealot, who lives obsessively for a single idea, and the mental technician, whose mind is used not for free speculation but for a salable end. The goal here is external and not self-determined, whereas the intellectual life has a certain spontaneous character and inner determination. It has also a peculiar poise of its own, which I believe is established by a balance between two basic qualities in the intellectual's attitude toward ideas—qualities that may be designated as playfulness and piety.

To define what is distinctively intellectual it is necessary to be able to determine what differentiates, say, a professor or a lawyer who is an intellectual from one who is not; or perhaps more properly, what enables us to say that at one moment a professor or a lawyer is acting in a purely routine professional fashion and at another moment as an intellectual. The difference is not in the character of the ideas with which he works but in his attitude toward them. I have suggested that in some sense he lives for ideas—which means that he has a sense of dedication to the life of the mind which is very much like a religious commitment. This is not surprising, for in a very important way the role of the intellectual is inherited from the office of the cleric: it implies a special sense of the ultimate value in existence of the act of comprehension. Socrates, when he said that the unexamined life is not worth living, struck the essence of it. We can hear the voices of various intellectuals in history repeating their awareness of this feeling, in accents suitable to time, place, and culture. "The proper function of the human race, taken in the aggregate," wrote Dante in *De Monarchia*, "is to actualize continually the entire capacity possible to the intellect, primarily in speculation, then through its extension and for its sake, secondarily in action." The noblest thing, and the closest possible to divinity, is thus the act of knowing. It is only a somewhat more secular and activist version of the same commitment which we hear in the first sentence of Locke's *Essay Concerning Human Understanding*: "It is the *understanding* that sets man above the rest of sensible beings, and gives him all the advantage and dominion which he has over them." Hawthorne, in a passage near the end of *The Blithedale Romance*, observes that Nature's highest purpose for man is "that of conscious intellectual life and sensibility." Finally, in our own time André Malraux puts the question in one of his novels: "How can one make the best of one's life?" and answers: "By converting as wide a range of experience as possible into conscious thought."

Intellectualism, though by no means confined to doubters, is often the sole piety of the skeptic. Some years ago a colleague asked me to read a brief essay he had written for students going on to do advanced work in his field. Its ostensible purpose was to show how the life of the mind could be cultivated within the framework of his own discipline, but its effect was to give an intensely personal expression to his dedication to intellectual work. Although it was written by a corrosively skeptical mind, I felt that I was reading a piece of devotional literature in some ways comparable to Richard Steele's *The Tradesman's Calling* or Cotton Mather's *Essays to Do Good*, for in it the intellectual task had been conceived as a *calling*, much in the fashion of the old Protestant writers. His work was undertaken as a kind of devotional exercise, a personal discipline, and to think of it in this fashion was possible because it was more than merely workmanlike and professional: it was work at thinking, work done supposedly in the service of truth. The intellectual life has here taken on a kind of primary moral significance. It is this aspect of the intellectual's feeling about ideas that I call his piety. The intellectual is *engagé*—he is pledged, committed, enlisted. What everyone else is willing to admit, namely that ideas and abstractions are of signal importance in human life, he imperatively feels.

Of course what is involved is more than a purely personal discipline and more than the life of contemplation and understanding itself. For the life of thought, even though it may be regarded as the highest form of human activity, is also a medium through which other values are refined, reasserted, and realized in the human community. Collectively, intellectuals have often tried to serve as the moral antennae of the race, anticipating and if possible clarifying fundamental moral issues before these have forced themselves upon the public consciousness. The thinker feels that he ought to be the special custodian of values like reason and justice which are related to his own search for truth, and at times he strikes out passionately as a public figure because his very identity seems to be threatened by some gross abuse. One thinks here of Voltaire defending the Calas family, of Zola speaking out for Dreyfus, of the American intellectuals outraged at the trial of Sacco and Vanzetti.

It would be unfortunate if intellectuals were alone in their concern for these values, and it is true that their enthusiasm has at times miscarried. But it is also true that intellectuals are properly more responsive to such values than others; and it is the historic glory of the intellectual class of the West in modern times that, of all the classes which could be called in any sense privileged, it has shown the largest and most consistent concern for the well-being of the classes which lie below it in the social scale. Behind the intellectual's feeling of commitment is the belief that in some measure the world should be made responsive to his capacity for rationality, his passion for justice and order: out of this conviction arises much of his value to mankind and, equally, much of his ability to do mischief.

2

The very suggestion that the intellectual has a distinctive capacity for mischief, however, leads to the consideration that
his piety, by itself, is not enough. He may live for ideas, as I
have said, but something must prevent him from living for *one
idea*, from becoming obsessive or grotesque. Although there
have been zealots whom we may still regard as intellectuals,
zealotry is a defect of the breed and not of the essence. When
one's concern for ideas, no matter how dedicated and sincere,
reduces them to the service of some central limited preconception or some wholly external end, intellect gets swallowed by
fanaticism. If there is anything more dangerous to the life of
the mind than having no independent commitment to ideas,
it is having an excess of commitment to some special and constricting idea. The effect is as observable in politics as in theology: the intellectual function can be overwhelmed by an excess
of piety expended within too contracted a frame of reference.

Piety, then, needs a counterpoise, something to prevent it
from being exercised in an excessively rigid way; and this it
has, in most intellectual temperaments, in the quality I would
call playfulness. We speak of the play of the mind; and certainly
the intellectual relishes the play of the mind for its own sake,
and finds in it one of the major values in life. What one thinks
of here is the element of sheer delight in intellectual activity.
Seen in this guise, intellect may be taken as the healthy animal
spirits of the mind, which come into exercise when the surplus
of mental energies is released from the tasks required for utility and mere survival. "Man is perfectly human," said Schiller,
"only when he plays." And it is this awareness of an available
surplus beyond the requirements of mere existence that his
maxim conveys to us. Veblen spoke often of the intellectual
faculty as "idle curiosity"—but this is a misnomer in so far as
the curiosity of the playful mind is inordinately restless and
active. This very restlessness and activity gives a distinctive cast
to its view of truth and its discontent with dogmas.

Ideally, the pursuit of truth is said to be at the heart of the
intellectual's business, but this credits his business too much
and not quite enough. As with the pursuit of happiness, the

pursuit of truth is itself gratifying whereas the consummation often turns out to be elusive. Truth captured loses its glamor; truths long known and widely believed have a way of turning false with time; easy truths are a bore, and too many of them become half-truths. Whatever the intellectual is too certain of, if he is healthily playful, he begins to find unsatisfactory. The meaning of his intellectual life lies not in the possession of truth but in the quest for new uncertainties. Harold Rosenberg summed up this side of the life of the mind supremely well when he said that the intellectual is one who turns answers into questions.

This element of playfulness infuses products of mind as diverse as Abelard's *Sic et Non* and a dadaist poem. But in using the terms *play* and *playfulness*, I do not intend to suggest any lack of seriousness; quite the contrary. Anyone who has watched children, or adults, at play will recognize that there is no contradiction between play and seriousness, and that some forms of play induce a measure of grave concentration not so readily called forth by work. And playfulness does not imply the absence of practicality. In American public discussion one of the tests to which intellect is constantly submitted when it is, so to speak, on trial is this criterion of practicality. But in principle intellect is neither practical nor impractical; it is extra-practical. To the zealot overcome by his piety and to the journeyman of ideas concerned only with his marketable mental skills, the beginning and end of ideas lies in their efficacy with respect to some goal external to intellectual processes. The intellectual is not in the first instance concerned with such goals. This is not to say that he scorns the practical: the intrinsic intellectual interest of many practical problems is utterly absorbing. Still less is it to say that he is impractical; he is simply concerned with something else, a quality in problems that is not defined by asking whether or not they have practical purpose. The notion that the intellectual is inherently impractical will hardly bear analysis (one can think so readily of intellectuals who, like Adam Smith, Thomas Jefferson, Robert Owen, Walther Rathenau, or John Maynard Keynes, have been eminently practical in the politician's or businessman's sense of the term). However, practicality is not the essence of his interest in ideas. Acton put this view in rather an extreme form when he said: "I think our studies ought to be all but purposeless. They want to be pursued with chastity, like mathematics."

An example of the intellectual's view of the purely practical is the response of James Clerk Maxwell, the mathematician and theoretical physicist, to the invention of the telephone. Asked to give a lecture on the workings of this new instrument, Maxwell began by saying how difficult it had been to believe, when word first came about it from America, that such a thing had actually been devised. But then, he went on, "when at last this little instrument appeared, consisting, as it does, of parts, every one of which is familiar to us, and capable of being put together by an amateur, the disappointment arising from its humble appearance was only partially relieved on finding that it was really able to talk." Perhaps, then, this regrettable appearance of simplicity might be redeemed by the presence somewhere of "some recondite physical principle, the study of which might worthily occupy an hour's time of an academic audience." But no; Maxwell had not met a single person who was unable to understand the physical processes involved, and even the science reporters for the daily press had almost got it right![3] The thing was a disappointing bore; it was not recondite, not difficult, not profound, not complex; it was not *intellectually* new.

Maxwell's reaction does not seem to me to be entirely admirable. In looking at the telephone from the point of view of a pure scientist, and not as a historian or a sociologist or even a householder, he was restricting the range of his fancy. Commercially, historically, humanly, the telephone was exciting; and its possibilities as an instrument of communication and even of torture surely might have opened vistas to the imagination. But within his self-limited sphere of concern, that of physics, Maxwell was speaking with a certain stubborn daring about the intellectual interest in the matter. For him, thinking as a physicist, the new instrument offered no possibilities for play.

One may well ask if there is not a certain fatal contradiction between these two qualities of the intellectual temperament,

[3] W. D. Niven, ed.: *The Scientific Papers of James Clerk Maxwell* (Cambridge, 1890), Vol. II, p. 742.

playfulness and piety. Certainly there is a tension between them, but it is anything but fatal: it is just one of those tensions in the human character that evoke a creative response. It is, in fact, the ability to comprehend and express not only different but opposing points of view, to identify imaginatively with or even to embrace within oneself contrary feelings and ideas that gives rise to first-rate work in all areas of humanistic expression and in many fields of inquiry. Human beings are tissues of contradictions, and the life even of the intellectual is not logic, to borrow from Holmes, but experience. Contemplate the intellectuals of the past or those in one's neighborhood: some will come to mind in whom the note of playfulness is dominant; others who are conspicuously pious. But in most intellectuals each of these characteristics is qualified and held in check by the other. The tensile strength of the thinker may be gauged by his ability to keep an equipoise between these two sides of his mind. At one end of the scale, an excess of playfulness may lead to triviality, to the dissipation of intellectual energies on mere technique, to dilettantism, to the failure of creative effort. At the other, an excess of piety leads to rigidity, to fanaticism, to messianism, to ways of life which may be morally mean or morally magnificent but which in either case are not the ways of intellect.[4]

Historically, it may be useful to fancy playfulness and piety as being the respective residues of the aristocratic and the priestly backgrounds of the intellectual function. The element of play seems to be rooted in the ethos of the leisure class, which has always been central in the history of creative imagination and humanistic learning. The element of piety is reminiscent of the priestly inheritance of the intellectuals: the quest for and the possession of truth was a holy office. As their legatee, the

[4]It was part of the indictment by Julien Benda in *La Trahison des Clercs* (1927) that so many modern intellectuals had given themselves over to this kind of messianic politics to the grave loss of intellectual values: "Today, if we mention Mommsen, Treitschke, Ostwald, Brunetière, Barrès, Lemaître, Péguy, Maurras, d'Annunzio, Kipling, we have to admit that the 'clerks' now exercise political passions with all the characteristics of passion—the tendency to action, the thirst for immediate results, the exclusive preoccupation with the desired end, the scorn for argument, the excess, the hatred, the fixed ideas." (Translated by Richard Aldington as *The Betrayal of the Intellectuals*, Boston, 1955, p. 32.)

modern intellectual inherits the vulnerability of the aristocrat to the animus of puritanism and egalitarianism and the vulnerability of the priest to anticlericalism and popular assaults upon hierarchy. We need not be surprised, then, if the intellectual's position has rarely been comfortable in a country which is, above all others, the home of the democrat and the antinomian.

It is a part of the intellectual's tragedy that the things he most values about himself and his work are quite unlike those society values in him. Society values him because he can in fact be used for a variety of purposes, from popular entertainment to the design of weapons. But it can hardly understand so well those aspects of his temperament which I have designated as essential to his intellectualism. His playfulness, in its various manifestations, is likely to seem to most men a perverse luxury; in the United States the play of the mind is perhaps the only form of play that is not looked upon with the most tender indulgence. His piety is likely to seem nettlesome, if not actually dangerous. And neither quality is considered to contribute very much to the practical business of life.

3

I have suggested that one of the first questions asked in America about intellect and intellectuals concerns their practicality. One reason why anti-intellectualism has changed in our time is that our sense of the impracticality of intellect has been transformed. During the nineteenth century, when business criteria dominated American culture almost without challenge, and when most business and professional men attained eminence without much formal education, academic schooling was often said to be useless. It was assumed that schooling existed not to cultivate certain distinctive qualities of mind but to make personal advancement possible. For this purpose, an immediate engagement with the practical tasks of life was held to be more usefully educative, whereas intellectual and cultural pursuits were called unworldly, unmasculine, and impractical. In spite of the coarse and philistine rhetoric in which this contention was very often stated, it had a certain rude correspondence to the realities and demands of American life. This skepticism about formally cultivated intellect lived on into the twentieth century. But in our time, of course, American society has grown greatly in complexity and in involvement with the rest of the world. In most areas of life a formal training has become a prerequisite to success. At the same time, the complexity of modern life has steadily whittled away the functions the ordinary citizen can intelligently and comprehendingly perform for himself. In the original American populistic dream, the omnicompetence of the common man was fundamental and indispensable. It was believed that he could, without much special preparation, pursue the professions and run the government. Today he knows that he cannot even make his breakfast without using devices, more or less mysterious to him, which expertise has put at his disposal; and when he sits down to breakfast and looks at his morning newspaper, he reads about a whole range of vital and intricate issues and acknowledges, if he is candid with himself, that he has not acquired competence to judge most of them.

In the practical world of affairs, then, trained intelligence has come to be recognized as a force of overwhelming importance. What used to be a jocular and usually benign ridicule of intellect and formal training has turned into a malign resentment of the intellectual in his capacity as expert. The old idea of the woolly-minded intellectual, so aptly caught in the stereotype of the absent-minded professor, still survives, of course; but today it is increasingly a wishful and rather wistful defense against a deep and important fear. Once the intellectual was gently ridiculed because he was not needed; now he is fiercely resented because he is needed too much. He has become all too practical, all too effective. He is the object of resentment because of an improvement, not a decline, in his fortunes. It is not his abstractness, futility, or helplessness that makes him prominent enough to inspire virulent attacks, but his achievements, his influence, his real comfort and imagined luxury, as well as the dependence of the community upon his skills. Intellect is resented as a form of power or privilege.

It may be said at once that what we really have in mind here is not so much the intellectual as the expert; that many intellectuals are not experts with an important role in public life and that many of them do not impinge very forcefully upon the public consciousness.[5] This is beyond argument; but my point is that the prevailing attitude toward intellectuals is set largely by those intellectuals who do so impinge. In the main, intellectuals affect the public mind when they act in one of two capacities: as experts or as ideologues. In both capacities they evoke profound, and, in a measure, legitimate, fears and resentments. Both intensify the prevalent sense of helplessness in our society, the expert by quickening the public's resentment of being the object of constant manipulation, the ideologue by arousing the fear of subversion and by heightening all the other grave psychic stresses that have come with modernity.

For almost thirty years anyone even moderately informed about public affairs has had to become aware of the machinery through which the expert was making himself felt. At first, during the New Deal the well-publicized brain trust and all the ramifying agencies of control were set up to cope with the depression, and during the war there were the Office of Strategic Services and the Office of Scientific Research and Development. Today the C.I.A., the A.E.C., the Rand Corporation, the President's Council of Economic Advisers, and all the agencies that conduct research on the instruments and strategy of war deal with issues which are beyond the reach of the ordinary man's scrutiny but which can, and often do, determine his fate. A large segment of the public willingly resigns itself to political passivity in a world in which it cannot expect to make well-founded judgments. But in the management of public affairs and private business, where small politicians and small businessmen used to feel that most matters were within their control, these men have been forced, since the days of F.D.R., to confront better educated and more sophisticated

---

[5] A great deal of internal discussion is heard in the intellectual community as to whether the development of expertise is not also dangerous for intellectuals. The question has been asked whether the intellectual's position as an expert does not in fact destroy his intellectual function by reducing him to a mere mental technician. See, for example, H. Stuart Hughes: "Is the Intellectual Obsolete?" in *An Approach to Peace and Other Essays* (New York, 1962), chapter 10. I shall return to this problem in my final chapter.

experts, to their continuing frustration. Along with the general public, such men now take part less vitally and less knowledgeably in the making of important decisions; the less they understand the inner world of power, the more apt they are to share and arouse popular suspicions of the uses to which power is put. The small-town lawyers and businessmen who are elected to Congress cannot hope to expropriate the experts from their central advisory role, but they can achieve a kind of revenge through Congressional investigation and harassment, and, understandably, they carry on this task full of a sense of virtuous mission. There have been, after all, innumerable defeats and failures of expert-initiated policy, and these failures loom in the eyes of millions as the consequences not simply of human error but of cold and cynical manipulation, conspiracy, even treason. The public careers of Alger Hiss and others have given them symbols to which this feeling can be attached, and a few spectacular instances of demonstrated espionage involving scientific knowledge seem to substantiate their image of a world run by the power of secrets and swarming with the stealers of secrets.[6]

The advice of experts in the physical sciences, however suspect many of these experts may be, is accepted as indispensable. Expertise in the social sciences, on the other hand, may be rejected as gratuitous and foolish, if not ominous. One Congressman objected in these words to including the social sciences in the National Science Foundation:[7]

> Outside of myself, I think everyone else thinks he is a social scientist. I am sure that I am not, but I think everyone else seems to believe that he has some particular God-given right to decide what other people ought to do. . . . The average American does not want some expert running around prying into his life and his personal affairs and deciding for him how

[6]The atmosphere in which popular politicians confront experts has been explored with much insight by Edward Shils: *The Torment of Secrecy* (Glencoe, Illinois, 1956).

[7]Testimony before a subcommittee of the Committee on Interstate and Foreign Commerce, House of Representatives, 79th Congress, 2nd session, May 28 and 29, 1946, pp. 11, 13.

he should live, and if the impression becomes prevalent in the Congress that this legislation is going to establish some sort of an organization in which there would be a lot of short-haired women and long-haired men messing into everybody's personal affairs and lives, inquiring whether they love their wives or do not love them and so forth, you are not going to get your legislation.

From the politician's point of view, experts were irritating enough in the time of F.D.R., when they seemed to have free access to the White House while the President kept the politicians at arm's length. The situation has grown worse in the age of the cold war, when matters of the highest public interest are susceptible to judgment only by specialists. All this is the more maddening, as Edward Shils has pointed out, in a populistic culture which has always set a premium on government by the common man and through the common judgment and which believes deeply in the sacred character of publicity. Here the politician expresses what a large part of the public feels. The citizen cannot cease to need or to be at the mercy of experts, but he can achieve a kind of revenge by ridiculing the wild-eyed professor, the irresponsible brain truster, or the mad scientist, and by applauding the politicians as they pursue the subversive teacher, the suspect scientist, or the allegedly treacherous foreign-policy adviser. There has always been in our national experience a type of mind which elevates hatred to a kind of creed; for this mind, group hatreds take a place in politics similar to the class struggle in some other modern societies. Filled with obscure and ill-directed grievances and frustrations, with elaborate hallucinations about secrets and conspiracies, groups of malcontents have found scapegoats at various times in Masons or abolitionists, Catholics, Mormons, or Jews, Negroes or immigrants, the liquor interests or the international bankers. In the succession of scapegoats chosen by the followers of this tradition of Know-Nothingism, the intelligentsia have at last in our time found a place.

If some large part of the anti-intellectualism of our time stems from the public's shock at the constant insinuation of the intellectual as expert into public affairs, much of the sensitiveness of intellectuals to their reputation as a class stems from the awkward juxtaposition of their sacred and profane roles. In his sacred role, as prophet, scholar, or artist, the intellectual is hedged about by certain sanctions—imperfectly observed and respected of course, but still effective: he has his privacy, perhaps his anonymity, in the interstices of modern urban civilization; he commands a certain respect for what seem to be his self-denying qualities; he benefits, if he is an academic, from the imperfectly established but operative principle of academic freedom; he has foundations, libraries, publishing houses, museums, as well as universities, at his service. There is a certain measured and genteel dignity about his life. If, in his capacity as expert, he assumes a profane role by mixing in public affairs, he may be horrified to realize that, having become a public figure, he too is vulnerable to the low ethics of controversy which prevail in our politics and the low regard for privacy which governs our entire society. He may even forget that the malice and slander to which he is exposed are not peculiarly directed against him or his kind but are of the same order as almost any working politician of prominence may experience; even some of our greatest statesmen—among them Jefferson, Lincoln, and Franklin D. Roosevelt—were not immune. As Emerson once asked: "Is it not the first attribute and distinction of an American to be abused and slandered as long as he is heard of?"[8]

4

Compared with the intellectual as expert, who must be accepted even when he is feared, the intellectual as ideologist is an object of unqualified suspicion, resentment, and distrust. The expert appears as a threat to dominate or destroy the ordinary individual, but the ideologist is widely believed to have already destroyed a cherished American society. To understand the background of this belief, it is necessary to recall how consistently the intellectual has found himself ranged in politics against the right-wing mind. This is, of course, no peculiarity of American politics. The modern idea of the intellectuals as constituting a class, as a separate social force, even the term *intellectual* itself, is identified with the idea of political and moral

[8] *Journals* (Boston, 1909–1914), Vol. IX (July 1862), p. 436.

protest. In the broadest signification of the term, there have always been intellectuals, but until the emergence of industrial society and of a kind of market place for ideas, there was little sense of the separateness of the intellectual life as a vocation, and relatively little need for the solidarity, much less for the mobilization, of the intellectuals. Thus, for all that they did in the mid-nineteenth century to prepare the way for the Revolutions of 1848, the liberation of the serfs in Russia, or of the slaves in America, there was still at that time no device widely in use in English to account for them as a group.

The term *intellectual* first came into use in France. It was soon exported—at the time of the Dreyfus case, when so large a part of the intellectual community was aroused to protest against the anti-Dreyfus conspiracy and became involved in an ideological holy war on the French reactionaries.[9] At that time the term came to be used by both sides—by the right as a kind of insult, by the Dreyfusard intellectuals as a proud banner. "Let us use this word," wrote one of them in 1898, "since it has received high consecration." In the following year William James wrote, in a letter referring to the role of the French intellectuals in the Dreyfus affair: "We 'intellectuals' in America must all work to keep our precious birthright of individualism, and freedom from these institutions [church, army, aristocracy, royalty]. *Every* great institution is perforce a means of corruption—whatever good it may also do. Only in the free personal relation is full ideality to be found."[10] It is significant in our own history that this early use of the term—the first in America of which I am aware—should have been made in the context of just such a "radical," utopian, and anti-institutional statement of purpose. At least from the Progressive era onward, the political commitment of the majority of the intellectual leadership in the United States has been to causes that

[9]On the precursors of the term *intellectual*, and its early use in France, see Victor Brombert: *The Intellectual Hero*, chapter 2. The corresponding Russian term, *intelligentsia*, which came into use after the middle of the nineteenth century, originally meant members of the free professions, but it, too, soon took on the connotation of an opponent of the regime. See Hugh Seton-Watson: "The Russian Intellectuals," *Encounter* (September, 1955), pp. 43–50.
[10]*The Letters of William James* (Boston, 1920), Vol. II, pp. 100–1.

might be variously described as liberal (in the American use of
that word), progressive, or radical.[11] (Of course the American
political spectrum is rather foreshortened, and its center lies
considerably to the right of that of France, but the position
of the intellectuals in relation to the center has been similar.)
I am not denying that we have had a number of conservative
intellectuals and even a few reactionary ones; but if there is
anything that could be called an intellectual establishment in
America, this establishment has been, though not profoundly
radical (which would be unbecoming in an establishment), on
the left side of center. And it has drawn the continuing and
implacable resentment of the right, which has always liked to
blur the distinction between the moderate progressive and the
revolutionary.

As long as the progressivism of the intellectual community
remained more or less in harmony with a spirit of protest widely
shared by the general public, as it did notably during the Progressive era and the New Deal, its vulnerability to the extreme
right has been small. But the allegiance of a large part of the
intellectual community to Communism and fellow-traveling in
the 1930's gave hostage to its right-wing enemies. Here it is
important to do justice to a signal element of reality in the
anti-intellectuals' case. It will not do to say that the vulnerability of the intellectuals on this count has already been vastly
overexploited in right-wing propaganda; or that the extent of
Communist sympathies among the intellectuals of the 1930's
has been exaggerated; or even that the most decisively influential intellectuals of the past generation were not Communists
or fellow travelers. All these propositions are true, but the case
that has been so insistently made against the intellectuals rests
on the fact that the appeal of Communism during the 1930's
was stronger among intellectuals than among any other stratum of the population; and that in a few spectacular instances
faith in Communism led to espionage. One must begin, I

[11]On this commitment and its effects, see Seymour M. Lipset: "American
Intellectuals: Their Politics and Status," *Daedalus* (Summer, 1959), pp. 460–
86. Lipset has many pertinent remarks on the position of American intellectuals, but I am not persuaded by his argument that their status can be described,
without qualification, as high.

believe, with the awareness that the intellectual and moral inconsistencies of Communism and fellow-traveling not only put into the hands of the anti-intellectuals a powerful weapon, but that the sense of shame over past credulity and of guilt over past political involvements induced in many intellectuals a kind of paralysis that caused them to be helpless in the face of the Great Inquisition of the 1950's and even at times to indulge in bitter mutual recriminations. One remembers, for example, with some pain and difficulty, that in August 1939, on the eve of the Nazi-Soviet pact, some four hundred liberal intellectuals appended their signatures to a manifesto denouncing the "fantastic falsehood that the U.S.S.R. and the totalitarian states are basically alike," and describing the Soviet Union as a "bulwark" of peace. This document was reproduced in the *Nation* the week that the Hitler-Stalin pact was signed.[12] Intellectuals thus caught out were not in the best historical, moral, or psychological position to make a vigorous response to McCarthyism.

What I believe is important, however, to anyone who hopes to understand the impulse behind American anti-intellectualism is that this grievance against intellectuals as ideologues goes far beyond any reproaches based on actual Communism or fellow-traveling. The practical intellectuals of the New Deal—Rexford Guy Tugwell is the best example—who had nothing to do with the Communists were as objectionable as the fellow travelers. And today, when Communism has been reduced to a negligible quantity in American domestic life, the cry for a revival of this scapegoat is regularly heard in the land, and investigators who are unable to turn up present Communist affiliations have resorted to stirring up the dead husks of fellow-traveling memories or to obscuring as completely as possible the differences between liberals and Communists. The truth is that the right-winger needs his Communists badly, and is pathetically reluctant to give them up.[13] The real function of the Great

---

[12] *Nation*, Vol. 149 (August 19, 1939), p. 228.

[13] This reluctance has been nowhere more candidly and ingratiatingly expressed than by Senator Barry Goldwater, who affirmed in July 1959: "I am not willing to accept the idea that there are no Communists left in this country; I think that if we lift enough rocks, we will find some." Quoted by James Wechsler: *Reflections of an Angry Middle-Aged Editor* (New York, 1960), p. 44.

Inquisition of the 1950's was not anything so simply rational as to turn up spies or prevent espionage (for which the police agencies presumably are adequate) or even to expose actual Communists, but to discharge resentments and frustrations, to punish, to satisfy enmities whose roots lay elsewhere than in the Communist issue itself. This was why it showed such a relentless and indiscriminate appetite for victims and why it seemed happier with respectable and powerful targets than with the occasional obscure Bolshevik it turned up. The McCarthyist fellow travelers who announced that they approved of the senator's goals even though they disapproved of his methods missed the point: to McCarthy's true believers what was really appealing about him were his methods, since his goals were always utterly nebulous. To them, his proliferating multiple accusations were a positive good, because they widened the net of suspicion and enabled it to catch many victims who were no longer, or had never been, Communists; his bullying was welcomed because it satisfied a craving for revenge and a desire to discredit the type of leadership the New Deal had made prominent.

Had the Great Inquisition been directed only against Communists, it would have tried to be more precise and discriminating in its search for them: in fact, its leading practitioners seemed to care little for the difference between a Communist and a unicorn. Real Communists were usually too insignificant to warrant lengthy pursuit; McCarthy did not trouble himself much over an obscure radical dentist promoted by the army when he could use the case to strike at the army itself, and beyond the army at the Eisenhower administration. The inquisitors were trying to give satisfaction against liberals, New Dealers, reformers, internationalists, intellectuals, and finally even against a Republican administration that failed to reverse liberal policies. What was involved, above all, was a set of political hostilities in which the New Deal was linked to the welfare state, the welfare state to socialism, and socialism to Communism. In this crusade Communism was not the target but the weapon, and it is for this reason that so many of the most ardent hunters of impotent domestic Communists were altogether indifferent to efforts to meet the power of international Communism where it really mattered—in the arena of world politics.

The deeper historical sources of the Great Inquisition are best revealed by the other enthusiasms of its devotees: hatred of Franklin D. Roosevelt, implacable opposition to New Deal reforms, desire to banish or destroy the United Nations, anti-Semitism, Negrophobia, isolationism, a passion for the repeal of the income tax, fear of poisoning by fluoridation of the water system, opposition to modernism in the churches. McCarthy's own expression, "twenty years of treason," suggested the long-standing grievances that were nursed by the crusaders, though the right-wing spokesman, Frank Chodorov, put it in better perspective when he said that the betrayal of the United States had really begun in 1913 with the passage of the income-tax amendment.

Clearly, something more is at stake for such people than the heresies of the 1930's and the security problems of the cold war—something more even than the terrible frustration of the Korean War: the McCarthyist era brought to a head several forces engaged in a long-standing revolt against modernity. The older America, until the 1890's and in some respects until 1914, was wrapped in the security of continental isolation, village society, the Protestant denominations, and a flourishing industrial capitalism. But reluctantly, year by year, over several decades, it has been drawn into the twentieth century and forced to cope with its unpleasant realities: first the incursions of cosmopolitanism and skepticism, then the disappearance of American isolation and easy military security, the collapse of traditional capitalism and its supplementation by a centralized welfare state, finally the unrelenting costs and stringencies of the Second World War, the Korean War, and the cold war. As a consequence, the heartland of America, filled with people who are often fundamentalist in religion, nativist in prejudice, isolationist in foreign policy, and conservative in economics, has constantly rumbled with an underground revolt against all these tormenting manifestations of our modern predicament.

One cannot, even if one does not like their responses, altogether withhold one's sympathies from the plight of a people, hitherto so preoccupied with internal material development and in many ways so simple, who have been dragged away from their "normal" concerns, thrust into an alien and demanding world, and forced to try to learn so much in so short a time.

Perhaps the truly remarkable thing about the most common American response to the modern world has been its patience and generosity. Within only two generations the village Protestant individualist culture still so widely observable before the First World War was repeatedly shocked by change. It had to confront modernism in religion, literature, and art, relativity in morals, racial equality as a principle of ethics and public law, and the endless sexual titillation of our mass communications. In rapid succession it was forced to confront Darwinism (*vide* the Scopes trial), Freudianism, Marxism, and Keynesianism, and to submit in matters of politics, taste, and conscience to the leadership of a new kind of educated and cosmopolitan American.

The intellectual as ideologist, having had a leading role in purveying to the country each innovation and having frequently hastened the country into the acceptance of change, is naturally felt to have played an important part in breaking the mold in which America was cast, and in consequence he gets more than his share of the blame. In earlier days, after all, it had been our fate as a nation not to have ideologies but to be one. As European antagonisms withered and lost their meaning on American soil in the eighteenth and nineteenth centuries, the new nation came to be conceived not as sharing the ideologies which had grown out of these antagonisms but as offering an alternative to them, as demonstrating that a gift for compromise and plain dealing, a preference for hard work and common sense, were better and more practical than commitments to broad and divisive abstractions. The great American failure, in this respect, the one capitulation to divisive convictions, resulted in the Civil War; and this had the effect of confirming the belief that it was better to live without too much faith in political abstractions and ideological generalities. Americans continued to congratulate themselves on their ability to get on without the benefit of what are commonly called "foreign isms," just as they had always congratulated themselves on their ability to steer clear of European "corruption" and "decadence."

But in the past few decades the American public has become painfully aware that the breakdown of political and military isolation entails a breakdown of intellectual isolationism, that there are at large in the world powerful forces called ideologies whose consequences we cannot escape, that millions of people are everywhere set in motion by convictions about colonialism, racism, nationalism, imperialism, socialism, communism, and fascism. In all this there is a certain irony that we are ill-equipped to appreciate. The original American hope for the world—in so far as the older America thought about the world at all—was that it might save itself by emulating the American system—that is, by dropping formal ideologies, accepting our type of democracy, applying itself to work and the arduous pursuit of happiness, and by following the dictates of common sense. The irony is that Americans now suffer as much from the victory as from the defeat of their aspirations. What is it that has taken root in the world, if it is not the spirit of American activism, the belief that life can be made better, that colonial peoples can free themselves as the Americans did, that poverty and oppression do not have to be endured, that backward countries can become industrialized and enjoy a high standard of living, that the pursuit of happiness is everybody's business? The very colonial countries that belligerently reject our leadership try to follow our example, and the Russians themselves in the midst of their challenge to American power have not ceased to admire American industrialization. But this emulation has become tinted with ideologies we do not recognize and has brought consequences we never anticipated. The American example of activism has been imitated: what we call the American way of life has not.

To the most insular type of American mind it seemed that only peoples blinded by abstractions and dead to common sense could fail to see and appropriate all the virtues of the American system, and that some fatal complex of moral weaknesses has prevented the systems of foreign societies from working, not least of these being the acceptance of sinister ideologies. But the persistent strength of the Soviet Union, capped by the Sputnik and other triumphs in space, has given a rude shock to this confidence, for the United States is now confronted by a material power strong enough to pose a perpetual and indestructible challenge. What is more, this material power has unmistakably grown up under the stimulus of one of those fatal foreign isms. The American, so ill at ease in this strange, threatening, and seemingly gratuitous world of ideology, sus-pects the intellectual for being at home in it. The intellectual is even imagined to have called it into being—and in a certain sense he has. Inevitably, he has been made to bear some share of the irritation of those who cannot believe that the changes of the twentieth century are consequences of anything but a sin-ister campaign of manipulation and design, or at the very least of a series of fatally stupid errors. Perhaps it is he who has shorn us of the qualities upon which our former strength depended. Certainly he has become a figure in the world just at the time when all these unhappy changes have taken place. If he is not exactly guilty, he will still bear watching.

5

To those who suspect that intellect is a subversive force in so-ciety, it will not do to reply that intellect is really a safe, bland, and emollient thing. In a certain sense the suspicious Tories and militant philistines are right: intellect *is* dangerous. Left free, there is nothing it will not reconsider, analyze, throw into question.[14] "Let us admit the case of the conservative," John Dewey once wrote. "If we once start thinking no one can guarantee what will be the outcome, except that many objects, ends and institutions will be surely doomed. Every thinker puts some portion of an apparently stable world in peril, and no one can wholly predict what will emerge in its place."[15] Further, there is no way of guaranteeing that an intellectual class will be discreet and restrained in the use of its influence; the only assurance that can be given to any community is that it will be far worse off if it denies the free uses of the power of intellect than if it permits them. To be sure, intellectuals, contrary to the fantasies of cultural vigilantes, are hardly ever subversive of a society as a whole. But intellect is always on the move against something: some oppression, fraud, illusion, dogma,

[14]And even, it appears, when not left free; witness the considerable intellectual underground that seems to have grown up in the Soviet Union and its Eastern European satellites.
[15]*Characters and Events* (New York, 1929), p. xi.

or interest is constantly falling under the scrutiny of the intellectual class and becoming the object of exposure, indignation, or ridicule.

In the course of generations, those who have suffered from the operations of intellect, or who have feared or resented it, have developed a kind of counter-mythology about what it is and the role it plays in society. Those who have made their case against intellect in our time have not found it necessary to originate a single new argument, since this mythology is deeply rooted in our historical experience. The chapters that follow illustrate in some detail how this mythology has grown and perpetuated and expressed itself in the United States. But here I should like to state briefly and in general terms what are the perennial assumptions of the anti-intellectualist case, and in what light I think it ought to be regarded.

The case against intellect is founded upon a set of fictional and wholly abstract antagonisms. Intellect is pitted against feeling, on the ground that it is somehow inconsistent with warm emotion. It is pitted against character, because it is widely believed that intellect stands for mere cleverness, which transmutes easily into the sly or the diabolical.[16] It is pitted against practicality, since theory is held to be opposed to practice, and the "purely" theoretical mind is so much disesteemed. It is pitted against democracy, since intellect is felt to be a form of distinction that defies egalitarianism. Once the validity of these antagonisms is accepted, then the case for intellect, and

---

[16]"We always preferred an ignorant bad man to a talented one," wrote B. R. Hall of early Indiana society, "and hence attempts were usually made to ruin the moral character of a smart candidate; since unhappily smartness and wickedness were supposed to be generally coupled, and incompetence and goodness." Baynard R. Hall: *The New Purchase, or Seven and a Half Years in the Far West* (1843; ed. Princeton, 1916), p. 170. This occurred even among the Puritans, for all their rationalism and intellectualism. Cf. John Cotton: "The more learned and witty you bee, the more fit to act for Satan will you bee. . . . Take off the fond doting . . . upon the learning of the Jesuites, and the glorie of the Episcopacy, and brave estate of the Prelates. I say bee not deceived with these pompes, and empty shewes, and faire representations of a goodly condition before the eyes of flesh and blood, bee not taken with the applause of these persons." *The Powring Out of the Seven Vials* (London, 1642), The Sixth Vial, pp. 39–40.

by extension for the intellectual, is lost. Who cares to risk sacrificing warmth of emotion, solidity of character, practical capacity, or democratic sentiment in order to pay deference to a
type of man who at best is deemed to be merely clever and at
worst may even be dangerous?

Of course the fundamental fallacy in these fictional antagonisms is that they are based not upon an effort to seek out the
actual limits of intellect in human life but rather upon a simplified divorce of intellect from all the other human qualities
with which it may be combined. Neither in the development of
the individual character nor in the course of history are problems posed in such a simple or abstract fashion. For the same
reason it would be pointless to accept the form in which the
challenge is put and attempt to make a defense of intellect as
against emotion or character or practicality. Intellect needs to
be understood not as some kind of a claim against the other
human excellences for which a fatally high price has to be paid,
but rather as a complement to them without which they cannot be fully consummated. Few rational men care to deny that
the exercise of intellectual power is one of the fundamental
manifestations of human dignity or that it is at the very least a
legitimate end among the other legitimate ends of life. If mind
is seen not as a threat but as a guide to emotion, if intellect is
seen neither as a guarantee of character nor as an inevitable
danger to it, if theory is conceived as something serviceable
but not necessarily subordinate or inferior to practice, and if
our democratic aspirations are defined in such realistic and
defensible terms as to admit of excellence, all these supposed
antagonisms lose their force. Posed in these rather general
terms, this fact may seem obvious; but historically it has been
obvious to all too few; and the purpose of this book is to trace
some of the social movements in our history in which intellect
has been dissevered from its co-ordinate place among the human virtues and assigned the position of a special kind of vice.

In the first instance, anti-intellectualism must be sought out
in the framework of our religious history. This is not simply
because there is a constant historical tension between rationalism and the requirements of faith—though this in itself is an
enduring human problem—but because the patterns of modern thought, both religious and secular, are prefigured in our

earlier religious history. To the extent that it becomes accepted in any culture that religion is largely an affair of the heart or of the intuitive qualities of mind, and that the rational mind is irrelevant or worse, so far will it be believed that the rational faculties are barren or perhaps dangerous. And to the extent that a society is suspicious of a learned or professional clergy, so far will it be disposed to repudiate or deprive its intellectual class, whether religious or secular. In modern culture the evangelical movement has been the most powerful carrier of this kind of religious anti-intellectualism, and of its antinomian impulse. Of course, America is not the only society whose culture has been affected by evangelicalism. But in America religious culture has been largely shaped by the evangelical spirit, for here the balance of power between evangelicalism and formal religion was long ago overwhelmingly tipped in the direction of the former. To see how much this was true one need only compare the historical development of religion in Britain, where the Establishment was prepared to absorb and domesticate a large part of the evangelical movement, with that of America, where the evangelicals rapidly subverted, outstripped, or overwhelmed the older liturgical churches.

Akin to the spirit of evangelicalism in its effects has been a kind of primitivism which has won extraordinarily wide credence in America and which requires special attention here, in part because I have not dealt with it in this book as a separate force. Primitivism has had its links on one side with Christianity and on another with paganism; and perhaps some of its pervasive appeal may be attributed to the fact that through primitivism one may be a Christian and enjoy the luxury of a touch of paganism; or, contrariwise, that the basically pagan mind may find in primitivism a consoling element of faith. Primitivism has displayed itself in some quarters as a quest for the spirit of primitive Christianity, but also as a demand to recover the powers of "nature" in man; with it one may be close to Nature or to God—the difference is not always wholly clear. But in it there is a persistent preference for the "wisdom" of intuition, which is deemed to be natural or God-given, over rationality, which is cultivated and artificial.

In various guises primitivism has been a constantly recurring force in Western history and in our own national experience.

It is likely to become evident wherever men of the intellectual class itself are disappointed with or grow suspicious of the human yield of a rationally ordered life or when they seek to break away from the routine or apathy or refinement that arise with civilization. In America primitivism has affected the thinking of many men too educated and cultivated to run with the frontier revivalists but sympathetic to their underlying distrust for civilized forms. It is visible in Transcendentalism—which sometimes set itself up as the evangelicalism of the highbrows.[17] It

[17]Cf. George Ripley in his attack of 1839 on Unitarianism and the Harvard faculty of divinity: "I have known great and beneficial effects to arise from the simple exhibition of the truth of the Gospel to the heart and conscience, by earnest men, who trusted to the intuitive power of the soul, for the perception of its divinity. . . . Much as I value a sound logic in its proper place, I am sure it is not the instrument which is mighty through God to the pulling down of the strong holds of sin. It may detect error; but it cannot give so much as a glimpse of the glory of Christ. It may refute fallacies; but it cannot bind the heart to the love of holiness. . . . You maintain, that 'extensive learning' is usually requisite for those who would influence their fellow men on religious subjects. But Jesus certainly did not take this into consideration in the selection of the twelve from the mass of the disciples; he committed the promulgation of his religion to 'unlearned and ignorant' men; the sublimest truths were entrusted to the most common minds; and, in this way, 'God made foolish the wisdom of the world.' . . . Christ . . . saw that the parade of wisdom, which books impart, was as nothing before 'the light that enlighteneth every human mind.' The whole course of his nation's history was an illustration of the fact 'that poor mechanics are wont to be God's great ambassadors to mankind.' . . . Christ established no college of Apostles; he did not revive the school of the prophets which had died out; he paid no distinguished respect to the pride of learning; indeed, he sometimes intimates that it is an obstacle to the perception of truth; and thanks God, that while he has hid the mysteries of the kingdom of Heaven from the wise and prudent, he has made them known to men as ignorant as babes of the lore of the schools." "The Latest Form of Infidelity Examined," *Letters on the Latest Form of Infidelity* (Boston, 1839), pp. 98–9, 111, 112–13.

The argument in this passage is similar to that commonly used by the evangelicals. One begins with the hardly contestable proposition that religious faith is not, in the main, propagated by logic or learning. One moves on from this to the idea that it is best propagated (in the judgment of Christ and on historical evidence) by men who have been unlearned and ignorant. It seems to follow from this that the kind of wisdom and truth possessed by such men is superior to what learned and cultivated minds have. In fact, learning and cultivation appear to be handicaps in the propagation of faith. And since the propagation

is a powerful force in our historical writing from Parkman and Bancroft to Turner.[18] It is a persistent theme in the attitude of American writers toward Indians and Negroes. It runs through the popular legend of frontier figures such as Daniel Boone and Davy Crockett down to the heroes of modern Western stories and detective fiction—embracing all those lonely adventurers whose cumulative mythology caused D. H. Lawrence to say, in one of his harsh, luminous hyperboles, that the essential American soul is "hard, isolate, stoic, and a killer." As a sexual mystique, it has become a powerful moving force in American letters, taking its most exaggerated form in recent years among those writers who have been impressed by the theories of Wilhelm Reich. It has been a force in American politics, and its effects have been visible in the public images of figures as diverse as Andrew Jackson, John C. Frémont, Theodore Roosevelt, and Dwight D. Eisenhower.

All this is hardly surprising: America was settled by men and women who repudiated European civilization for its oppressiveness or decadence, among other reasons, and who found the most striking thing on the American strand not in the rude social forms that were taking shape here but in the world of nature and of savages. The escape from civilization to Arcadia, from Europe to nature, was perpetuated in repeated escapes from the East to the West, from the settled world to the frontier. Again and again the American mind turned fretfully against the encroachments of organized society, which were felt to be an effort to reimpose what had been once thrown off; for civilization, though it could hardly be repudiated in its entirety, was still believed to have something pernicious about it.

---

of faith is the most important task before man, those who are as "ignorant as babes" have, in the most fundamental virtue, greater strength than men who have addicted themselves to logic and learning. Accordingly, though one shrinks from a bald statement of the conclusion, humble ignorance is far better as a human quality than a cultivated mind. At bottom, this proposition, despite all the difficulties that attend it, has been eminently congenial both to American evangelicalism and to American democracy.

[18]On primitivism in Turner, see the penetrating final chapter of Henry Nash Smith: *Virgin Land* (Cambridge, Massachusetts, 1950); there are valuable gleanings on American primitivism in Charles L. Sanford: *The Quest for Paradise* (Urbana, Illinois, 1961).

If evangelicalism and primitivism helped to plant anti-intellectualism at the roots of American consciousness, a business society assured that it would remain in the foreground of American thinking. Since the time of Tocqueville it has become a commonplace among students of America that business activism has provided an overwhelming counterpoise to reflection in this country. Tocqueville saw that the life of constant action and decision which was entailed by the democratic and businesslike character of American life put a premium upon rough and ready habits of mind, quick decision, and the prompt seizure of opportunities—and that all this activity was not propitious for deliberation, elaboration, or precision in thought.[19]

The overwhelming demands of the task of winning a continent and establishing its industries drew men from pursuits where profits and honors were less available. But there was more to it than this: business in America at its highest levels appealed not merely to greed and the lust for power but to the imagination; alluring to the builder, the gamester, and the ruler in men, it offered more sport than hunting and more power than politics. As Tocqueville remarked: "In democracies nothing is greater or more brilliant than commerce," and its devotees engaged in it, "not only for the sake of the profit it holds out to them, but for the love of the constant excitement occasioned by that pursuit."[20] Except in a few older communities, there were no countervailing classes or sets of values—no aristocracy to marry into, no formidable body of national aspirations outside business aspirations. Business not only appealed to vigorous and ambitious men but set the dominant standards for the rest of society, so that members of the professions—law, medicine, schoolteaching, even the ministry—aped businessmen and adapted the standards of their own crafts to those of business. It has in fact been one of the perennial complaints of intellectuals in America that they cannot have much rapport with the professional classes as such, because these have been swung into the business orbit. It was business, finally, that isolated and feminized culture by establishing the masculine legend that men are not concerned with the events of the

[19] *Democracy in America*, Vol. II, pp. 525–6.
[20] Ibid., pp. 642–3.

intellectual and cultural world. Such matters were to be left to women—all too often to the type of women of whom Edith Wharton said that they were so afraid to meet culture alone that they hunted it in packs.

Both our religion and our business have been touched by the pervasive and aggressive egalitarianism of American life, but the egalitarian spirit is still more effective in politics and education.[21] What we loosely call Jacksonian democracy completed the disestablishment of a patrician leadership that had been losing its grip for some time. At an early date, literature and learning were stigmatized as the prerogative of useless aristocracies—and the argument was not pressed any the less firmly because a large part of the American intellectual class actually supported democratic causes. It seemed to be the goal of the common man in America to build a society that would show how much could be done without literature and learning —or rather, a society whose literature and learning would be largely limited to such elementary things as the common man could grasp and use. Hence, early nineteenth-century America was more noted for a wide range of literacy and for the unusual amount of information, independence, self-respect, and public concern possessed by the ordinary citizen than it was for the encouragement of first-rate science or letters or for the creation of first-rate universities.

Again and again, but particularly in recent years, it has been noticed that intellect in America is resented as a kind of excellence, as a claim to distinction, as a challenge to egalitarianism, as a quality which almost certainly deprives a man or woman of the common touch. The phenomenon is most impressive in education itself. American education can be praised, not to

[21]Observers of American academia have often asked with some bitterness why athletic distinction is almost universally admired and encouraged whereas intellectual distinction is resented. I think the resentment is in fact a kind of back-handed tribute democracy pays to the importance of intellect in our affairs. Athletic skill is recognized as being transient, special, and for most of us unimportant in the serious business of life; and the tribute given the athlete is considered to be earned because he entertains. Intellect, on the other hand, is neither entertaining (to most men) nor innocent; since everyone sees that it can be an important and permanent advantage in life, it creates against itself a kind of universal fraternity of commonplace minds.

say defended, on many counts; but I believe ours is the only educational system in the world vital segments of which have fallen into the hands of people who joyfully and militantly proclaim their hostility to intellect and their eagerness to identify with children who show the least intellectual promise. The final segments of this book, though necessarily fragmentary as history, will show how this educational force has been built upon widely accepted premises in our thinking—a narrowly conceived preference for utility and "science," a false variety of egalitarianism, and a primitivist view of the child.

PART 2

THE RELIGION OF THE HEART

CHAPTER III

The Evangelical Spirit

I

THE AMERICAN mind was shaped in the mold of early modern Protestantism. Religion was the first arena for American intellectual life, and thus the first arena for an anti-intellectual impulse. Anything that seriously diminished the role of rationality and learning in early American religion would later diminish its role in secular culture. The feeling that ideas should above all be made to work, the disdain for doctrine and for refinements in ideas, the subordination of men of ideas to men of emotional power or manipulative skill are hardly innovations of the twentieth century; they are inheritances from American Protestantism.

Since some tension between the mind and the heart, between emotion and intellect, is everywhere a persistent feature of Christian experience, it would be a mistake to suggest that there is anything distinctively American in religious anti-intellectualism. Long before America was discovered, the Christian community was perennially divided between those who believed that intellect must have a vital place in religion and those who believed that intellect should be subordinated to emotion, or in effect abandoned at the dictates of emotion. I do not mean to say that in the New World a new or more virulent variety of anti-intellectualist reaction was discovered, but rather that under American conditions the balance between traditional establishments and revivalist or enthusiastic movements drastically shifted in favor of the latter. In consequence, the learned professional clergy suffered a loss of position, and the rational style of religion they found congenial suffered accordingly. At an early stage in its history, America, with its Protestant and dissenting inheritance, became the scene of an unusually keen local variation of this universal historical struggle over the character of religion; and here the forces of enthusiasm and revivalism won their most impressive victories. It is to certain peculiarities of American religious life—above all to its lack of firm institutional establishments hospitable to intellectuals and to the competitive sectarianism of its evangelical denominations—that American anti-intellectualism owes much of its strength and pervasiveness.

The style of a church or sect is to a great extent a function of social class, and the forms of worship and religious doctrine congenial to one social group may be uncongenial to another. The possessing classes have usually shown much interest in rationalizing religion and in observing highly developed liturgical forms. The disinherited classes, especially when unlettered, have been more moved by emotional religion; and emotional religion is at times animated by a revolt against the religious style, the liturgy, and the clergy of the upper-class church, which is at the same time a revolt against aristocratic manners and morals.[1] Lower-class religions are likely to have apocalyptic or millennarian outbursts, to stress the validity of inner religious experience against learned and formalized religion, to simplify liturgical forms, and to reject the idea of a learned clergy, sometimes of any professional clergy whatsoever.

America, having attracted in its early days so many of Europe's disaffected and disinherited, became the ideal country for the prophets of what was then known to its critics as religious "enthusiasm." The primary impulse in enthusiasm was the feeling of direct personal access to God.[2] Enthusiasts did not commonly dispense with theological beliefs or with sacraments; but, seeking above all an inner conviction of communion with God, they felt little need either for liturgical expression or for an intellectual foundation for religious conviction. They felt toward intellectual instruments as they did toward aesthetic forms: whereas the established churches thought of art and music as leading the mind upward toward the divine, enthusiasts commonly felt them to be at best intrusions and at worst

---

[1] Cf. H. Richard Niebuhr: "An intellectually trained and liturgically minded clergy is rejected in favor of lay readers who serve the emotional needs of this religion (i.e., of the untutored and economically disfranchised classes) more adequately and who, on the other hand, are not allied by culture and interest with those ruling classes whose superior manner of life is too obviously purchased at the expense of the poor." *The Social Sources of Denominationalism* (Meridian ed., 1957), p. 30.

[2] I owe much in my remarks on this subject to Msgr. R. A. Knox's *Enthusiasm* (Oxford, 1950).

barriers to the pure and direct action of the heart—though an important exception must be made here for the value the Methodists found in hymnody. The enthusiasts' reliance on the validity of inward experience always contained within it the threat of an anarchical subjectivism, a total destruction of traditional and external religious authority.

This accounts, in some measure, for the perennial tendency of enthusiastic religion toward sectarian division and subdivision. But enthusiasm did not so much eliminate authority as fragment it; there was always a certain authority which could be won by this or that preacher who had an unusual capacity to evoke the desired feeling of inner conviction. The authority of enthusiasm, then, tended to be personal and charismatic rather than institutional; the founders of churches which, like the Methodist, had stemmed from an enthusiastic source needed great organizing genius to keep their followers under a single institutional roof. To be sure, the stabler evangelical denominations lent no support to rampant subjectivism. They held that the source of true religious authority was the Bible, properly interpreted. But among the various denominations, conceptions of proper interpretation varied from those that saw a vital role for scholarship and rational expertise down through a range of increasing enthusiasm and anti-intellectualism to the point at which every individual could reach for *his* Bible and reject the voice of scholarship. After the advent of the higher criticism, the validity of this Biblical individualism became a matter of life or death for fundamentalists.

When America was still a tiny outpost of England on the fringes of Western civilization, movements of religious protest in the mother country began to display qualities that were to become prominent in American religion. As the English religious reformers became convinced that the Reformation had not gone far enough to meet the social or spiritual demands of their followers, successive waves of Millennarians, Anabaptists, Seekers, Ranters, and Quakers assailed the established order and its clergy, preached a religion of the poor, argued for intuition and inspiration as against learning and doctrine, elevated lay preachers to leadership, and rejected the professional clergy as "null and void and without authority." At the time of the Puritan revolution, the preachers of the New Model Army were unsparing in their anti-professional and anti-intellectual broadsides against the clergy, the university teachers, and the lawyers. Most Puritans, to be sure, were heartily in favor of an educated ministry; but the left-wing chaplains, in the line of the Levellers and Diggers, followed Gerrard Winstanley's example in calling the universities "standing ponds of stinking waters," in pointing out that a liberal education did nothing to make men less sinful, and in stirring the egalitarian passions of the poor.[3]

In America the Anglicans, Presbyterians, and Congregationalists, with their severe standards of church organization, and their formally organized and often highly educated clergymen, at first successfully controlled such leveling tendencies. But hardly had these churches been organized when some dissenters began to find fault with them. Many, especially along the Southern frontier, simply drifted away for a time from all church connections. Others criticized and agitated, especially in New England, where religious activism was a major principle of life. For example, before Massachusetts Bay had survived even its first score of years, it was badly shaken by the activities of Mistress Anne Hutchinson, whose hostility to the learned ministers and to university education aroused intense anxiety in the establishment.[4] This unfortunate woman was

[3] On the general aspects of the religion of the disinherited, see Niebuhr: op. cit., chapters 2 and 3. See Leo Solt's suggestive account of "Anti-Intellectualism in the Puritan Revolution," *Church History*, Vol. XXIV (December, 1956), pp. 306–16; and D. B. Robertson: *The Religious Foundations of Leveller Democracy* (New York, 1951), especially pp. 29–40.

[4] As Samuel Eliot Morison has remarked, such hostility among radical Puritans was "an article of faith. Sincere fanatics called the universities 'stews of Anti-Christ,' 'Houses of lies,' that 'stink before God with the most loathsome abomination.'" Edward Johnson saw Anne Hutchinson "and her consorts mightily rayling against learning, perswading all they could to take heed of being spoyled by it." One of her followers had said to him: "Come along with me. . . . I'le bring you to a Woman that Preaches better Gospell then any of your black-coates that have been at the Ninneversity, a Woman of another kinde of spirit, who hath had many Revelations of things to come. . . . I had rather hear such a one that speekes from the meere motion of the spirit, without any study at all, then any of your learned Scollers, although they may be fuller of Scripture." Edward Johnson: *Wonder-Working Providence of Sions Saviour in New England*, ed. by J. F. Jameson (New York, 1910), pp. 127–8.

persecuted in part because of her own courageous intransi-
gence, but largely because the community was persuaded that
she was thoroughly subversive. Not until the time of the Great
Awakening of the eighteenth century did the enthusiasts win
general major victories outside the confines of a single colony.
It was then that they set the precedent on American shores not
only for the repeated waves of nineteenth-century evangelicalism, but also for the tradition of anti-intellectualism itself, in
so far as this tradition was carried within the matrix of religious
belief. But to understand the Awakening, one must look at the
state of the established clergy in the colonies, and here the position of the Puritan clergy is of special interest; for the Puritan
clergy came as close to being an intellectual ruling class—or,
more properly, a class of intellectuals intimately associated with
a ruling power—as America has ever had.

2

Like most intellectual groups, the Puritan ministry had serious faults, and these became dangerous when the ministers wielded power. But what is significant for us—and it
may serve as a paradigm of the situation of the intellectual
in America—is that the Puritan ministry is popularly remembered almost entirely for its faults, even for faults for which
it was less culpable than the community in which it lived. It
is significant, moreover, that this rather odious image of the
Puritan clergy, for which the name of Cotton Mather is a byword, has dominated not only our popular historical lore but
also the historical thinking of our intellectuals. The reputation of this, the first class of American intellectuals, has gone
down in infamy, and subsequent generations of intellectuals
have often led the campaign against them.

It is doubtful that any community ever had more faith in the
value of learning and intellect than Massachusetts Bay. It was
with only slight and pardonable exaggeration that Moses Coit
Tyler wrote, in his history of colonial American literature:[5]

[5] *A History of American Literature, 1607–1765* (Ithaca, New York, 1949), pp. 85–7.

In its inception New England was not an agricultural community, nor a manufacturing community, nor a trading community: it was a thinking community; an arena and mart for ideas; its characteristic organ being not the hand, nor the heart, nor the pocket, but the brain. . . . Probably no other community of pioneers ever so honored study, so reverenced the symbols and instruments of learning. Theirs was a social structure with its corner-stone resting on a book. . . . Only six years after John Winthrop's arrival in Salem harbor, the people of Massachusetts took from their own treasury the fund from which to found a university; so that while the tree-stumps were as yet scarcely weather-browned in their earliest harvest fields, and before the nightly howl of the wolf had ceased from the outskirts of their villages, they had made arrangements by which even in that wilderness their young men could at once enter upon the study of Aristotle and Thucydides, of Horace and Tacitus, and the Hebrew Bible. . . . The learned class was indeed an order of nobility among them.

Among the first generation of American Puritans, men of learning were both numerous and honored. There was about one university-trained scholar, usually from Cambridge or Oxford, to every forty or fifty families. Puritans expected their clergy to be distinguished for scholarship, and during the entire colonial period all but five per cent of the clergymen of the New England Congregational churches had college degrees. These Puritan emigrants, with their reliance upon the Book and their wealth of scholarly leadership, founded that intellectual and scholarly tradition which for three centuries enabled New England to lead the country in educational and scholarly achievement.

It must not be imagined that the earliest generations of Harvard graduates were given nothing but a narrow theological education. The notion has become widespread that Harvard and the other colonial colleges were at their inception no more than theological seminaries—and the fear expressed by the Puritan fathers of the development of an "illiterate ministry" seems to give support to the idea. In fact, however, the Oxford and Cambridge colleges which trained the men who founded Harvard College had long since been thoroughly infused with humanist scholarship. The founding fathers of colonial education saw no difference between the basic education appropriate

for a cleric and that appropriate for any other liberally educated man. The idea of a distinctively theological seminary is
a product of modern specialism, sectarian competition, and of
a reaction to the threat of secularism in the colleges. Such an
idea was outside their ken. They felt the need of learned ministers more acutely than learned men in other professions, but
they intended their ministers to be educated side by side and
in the same liberal curriculum with other civic leaders and men
of affairs. As it turned out, this was precisely what happened;
in Harvard's first two generations, only about half the graduates became ministers and the remainder went into secular
occupations.

Having established a learned and literary class, the Puritan
community gave this class great scope for the realization of
their gifts. The Puritan ministry was well served by the community, and it served the community well in return. As the
country became more settled, the clergy found sufficient leisure to express themselves in writing; the productivity shown
by some of them is astounding. Puritanism, as a religion of
the Book, placed a strong emphasis upon interpretation and
rational discourse and eschewed ranting emotionalism. Puritan
sermons combined philosophy, piety, and scholarship; and it
was one of the aims of Puritan popular education to train a laity
capable of understanding such discourses. In the early days, at
least, this seems to have been achieved.

But a great deal more was achieved. In estimating the intellectual accomplishments of the Puritan colonists it is necessary
to bear in mind that even in 1700, after more than seventy
years of settlement, the population numbered only about
106,000, much of it very thinly spread; that Boston, the largest town, had only about 7,000 souls in 1699; and that during
the 1670's they were ravaged by a serious and costly war with
the Indians in which one of every sixteen men of military age
was killed and half their towns suffered damage. Despite isolation, poverty, and other handicaps, they established a college which graduated scores of civic leaders and ministers, and
whose degrees soon after its founding were accepted *ad eundem gradum* at Oxford and Cambridge. It was a college, too,
where young men learned not merely to read and interpret
the Bible and theological works, but to read Hesiod, Homer,

Sophocles, Aristophanes, and other classical writers. There is every evidence that the learned class of Massachusetts Bay became cultivated men, interested in humane letters as well as theology, and that they successfully brought to the New World much of the best of the heritage of European civilization. In addition to Harvard College, their leaders established a system of grammar and elementary schools, a printing press, and some creditable libraries. The ministers produced a remarkable literature of sermons, histories, and verse, and, in time, a literature of political speculation and controversy which germinated into the political writing of the Revolutionary era. They laid the basis of an educational system and, one might add, of a community morale in matters of study which made New England and the New England mind distinguished in the history of American culture for three centuries. The clergy spread enlightenment as well as religion, fostered science as well as theology, and provided models of personal devotion to things of the mind in tiny villages where such examples might otherwise not have been seen.[6]

The most common modern conception of the Puritan clergy is that they not only shared the faults of their community but also led in its persecutions. This judgment needs severe qualification. It is true that theirs was, by the standards of the enlightened modern mind, an intolerant age, and that the clergy shared its intolerances. Moreover, the clergy displayed, especially in the first generation, a weakness to which intellectuals are prone at times in political affairs—that is, they imagined that they might be able to commit an entire civil society to the realization of transcendent moral and religious standards, and that they could maintain within this society a unified and commanding creed. They had risked the Atlantic and the wilderness to show that this was possible; and of course in the end

[6]For a spirited defense and appreciation of these early cultural achievements, see Samuel Eliot Morison: *The Intellectual Life of Colonial New England* (New York, 1956); cf. Thomas G. Wright: *Literary Culture in Early New England* (Cambridge, 1920); Kenneth Murdock: *Literature and Theology in Colonial New England* (Cambridge, 1949).

they failed, after having committed a number of excesses in the attempt to realize their vision.

But the fairest way to assess any intellectual group like the Puritan ministry is not to put them to the test of the most advanced standards of tolerance and enlightenment, but to measure them against their own times, the community in which they lived, and the laymen they served. The modern liberal mind tends to assume that, as leaders of the community the clergy were the prime movers in those acts, like the Salem witchcraft trials, which are most disturbing to our minds; and that the essential responsibility for the excesses of that community rests with them.

The truth is more complex. The clergy were themselves not a homogeneous group, for with the passing of the first generation and the enlargement of the community they had become diversified.[7] Perhaps the most important points of diversity were those of generation and of location. The older clergy, and especially those in the more remote rural communities, clung to the hard orthodoxies in which the Puritan community had begun. But by the end of the seventeenth century there had also arisen a group of young clergymen who were cosmopolitan in outlook, relatively liberal in religious tendency, and conversant with the latest intellectual influences from Europe. Most of these ministered to the growing towns of the seaboard.

There is ample evidence that, as an intellectual class, the members of the more learned and more cosmopolitan clergy (which includes such men as Increase and Cotton Mather) earned their privileged position. Their leadership was far from fully effective or controlling; but such influence as they had they used to encourage greater tolerance, a broader pursuit of learning, the cultivation of science, and the restraint of some of the bigoted tendencies of the leading country laymen, the public, and the less enlightened clergy. By the close of the

[7]On the state of the clergy during the period 1680–1725, see Clifford K. Shipton: "The New England Clergy of the 'Glacial Age,'" *Colonial Society of Massachusetts Publications*, Vol. XXXII (Boston, 1937), pp. 24–54.

seventeenth century, the leading clergymen were much more liberal in thought than the elderly uneducated laymen who controlled a great many of the rural congregations or the provincial politicians who often invoked religious fundamentalism because it was popular with the growing electorate.

After 1680, the Puritan ministry was more tolerant and more accommodating to dissenters such as Baptists and Quakers than was the Boston public at large; and the influential Boston ministers—including the Mathers—were more liberal in this respect than the older preachers in the countryside. While the cosmopolitan clerics were importing the latest latitudinarian books from England and year by year making more departures from the harsher traditions of Calvinism, leading laymen were often resisting these changes. So far as the encouragement of science is concerned, this was almost entirely in clerical sponsorship before about the middle of the eighteenth century (Harvard had its first lay scientist in Professor John Winthrop, who began to teach in 1738). In the most controversial and stirring of all scientific questions of the day, that of the adoption of inoculation for smallpox, outstanding clerical intellectuals once again took the lead in defending innovation. Not least of them was Cotton Mather, who held to his position even though a bomb was thrown into his study by anti-inoculation agitators. Even with respect to the much-mooted witchcraft trials, the record of the clergy, though mixed, is better than that of the lay judges and the public. Most of the clerics gave credence to the idea of witchcraft itself—as did some of the distinguished minds of the Western world—but they were strongly opposed to the extremely loose criteria of evidence that were admitted in the terrible Salem trials, and many clerics exercised a restraining influence.[8]

[8]After the first hanging had taken place and when many suspects were awaiting trial, a group of clergymen wrote to the governor and council pointing to the "need of a very critical and Exquisite *Caution*, lest by too much *Credulity* for Things received only on the Devils Authority, there be a Door opened for a long Train of miserable Consequences." When the lay authorities ignored this protest and went on accepting what was called "spectral evidence" against suspects, leading ministers continued to complain, and fourteen of them petitioned Governor Phips. At their insistence Phips began to call a halt to the proceedings. Shipton: "The New England Clergy," p. 42.

Toward the end of the seventeenth century, certain strains were already evident in Puritan religious sensibility which affected the lives and the position of the ministry. Puritanism had always required a delicate balance between intellect, which was esteemed as essential to true religion in New England, and emotion, which was necessary to the strength and durability of Puritan piety. This balance proved to be precarious, and there developed a tendency toward a split in the religious community itself. One side of the church tended to be socially correct, and sophisticated, liberal, and latitudinarian in its intellectual outlook, but religiously cold and formal. The other side, which was to prove vulnerable to revivalism, was moved both by ideas and by religious fervor; but its partisans, in their most fervent moments, turned antinomian and anti-intellectual. Jonathan Edwards stood out almost alone among the leading clergymen as exemplifying the old intellectualism and piety of New England and combining with them the ability to deal creatively with new ideas. By the middle of the eighteenth century, the religion of New England, like that of the other colonies, was ripe for an awakening that would have profound consequences for the position of the learned clergy.

3

The first major episode in which the educated clergy was roundly repudiated came during the Great Awakening of the mid-eighteenth century. These religious revivals, to be sure, did not have an unambiguously bad effect on intellect and learning; but they set an important precedent for later attacks upon the learned clergy and for movements to make religion less formal and its leadership less professional.

The American Awakening was a counterpart of similar religious changes in Europe, notably the rise of German pietism and English Methodism, but America was especially ripe for religious reawakening. Large numbers of Americans either were dissenters—Baptists, for instance, living restively under established Anglican or Congregational churches—or were unchurched, without affiliations or the habit of church attendance. The population had moved beyond the reach of the ministry, either geographically or spiritually. In some areas, notably in Virginia, a large portion of the Anglican clergy was especially remote and ineffective. Even the religion of New England had cooled. By the 1730's and 1740's the Congregational churches of New England (and often the Presbyterian churches of the Middle Colonies and elsewhere) had lost much of their pristine morale and had settled into dull repositories of the correct faith of the established classes. Abstract and highly intellectual in their traditions, they had lost the power to grip simple people; the Reformation controversies out of which the doctrinal commitments of these churches had grown had lost much of their meaning.[9] The zealots of the first Puritan generation and their well-schooled sons had long since gone to their graves. The ministers themselves had lost much of the drive, and therefore the prestige, of their earlier days. They were highly civilized, often versatile men; but they were in some cases too civilized, too versatile, too worldly, to play anything like their original role. Their sermons, attended by sleepy congregations, were often dull and abstruse exercises in old dogmatic controversies. As the Awakener, George Whitefield, said, "the reason why Congregations have been so dead is because dead Men preach to them."[10] From Massachusetts southward to Virginia and beyond, the latent religious energies of the people thus lay ready for any preacher who had the skill to reach them.

The Great Awakenings began in 1720, when the members of the Dutch Reformed Church in New Jersey began to be aroused by the sermons of a young preacher, Theodore Frelinghuysen, who had come to the New World inspired by English and Dutch Puritanism. His revival in New Jersey led to a second among the Scotch-Irish Presbyterians of the Middle Colonies. In 1726 one of them, William Tennent, established at Neshaminy, Pennsylvania, his "Log College," a sort of rudimentary theological school, and there, for the next twenty

[9]Perry Miller has written a brilliant account of the institutional and doctrinal aspects of this decline in *The New England Mind: From Colony to Province* (Cambridge, Massachusetts, 1953).
[10]Quoted by Edwin Scott Gaustad: *The Great Awakening in New England* (New York, 1957), p. 27.

years, he trained about a score of young men to carry the revivalist spirit into the Presbyterian ministry. In 1734 revivalism
appeared independently in New England. Jonathan Edwards,
a unique figure among the awakening preachers, combined the
old Puritan regard for doctrine and the Puritan custom of the
written sermon with the passion and religious zeal of the revivalists. Edwards's revival sermons, though they inflamed the
town of Northampton and the surrounding country during
1734 and 1735, were limited in their reach compared with those
of George Whitefield, an eloquent young associate of the Wes-
leys in England, who came to America on evangelistic missions
in 1738 and 1739. His second campaign began in Georgia and
twice brought him northward; he finally came to New England
in the fall of 1740. Whitefield, who, David Garrick said, could
send an audience into paroxysms by pronouncing "Mesopota-
mia," met with a wildly enthusiastic response to his preaching
in America. Thousands flocked from the countryside to the
towns where he chose to talk, and great numbers were seized
with a realization of sin and experienced spiritual rebirth.
Whitefield's first visit to New England was followed by that
of William Tennent's son, Gilbert, who brought the revival to
a degree of frenzy distasteful to many persons who had welcomed the earlier signs of a spiritual awakening.

Representative of the more enthusiastic antics of revivalism
was the work of James Davenport, a Long Island minister and
a graduate of Yale, who toured Connecticut and Massachusetts
in 1742 and 1743, pouring such invective upon the established
ministers and committing such other outrages upon decorum
(singing, for example, on his way to meeting) that he fell afoul
of the authorities. In the summer of 1742 he was tried in Connecticut for breach of the peace under the guise of holding religious meetings, but was charitably spared graver punishment
than deportation from the province because he was deemed
"disturbed in the rational Faculties of his Mind." A few months
later he turned up in Boston, where he was jailed for slander-
ing the ministers, but was again released as *non compos mentis*,
and returned to Long Island to be tried for neglecting his own
parish. After one more gaudy episode in New London, Connecticut, he was at last persuaded to quit, and in 1744 he wrote

a somewhat inconsistent testimonial of repentance. The fact that Davenport was repudiated and sharply condemned by Gilbert Tennent, whose preachings had helped to unsettle him in the first place, suggests that the middle-of-the-road awakeners were almost as much alarmed by the barking and howling that the movement had unleashed as were the regular ministers.[11]

As for the regular ministers, at first the overwhelming majority of them welcomed the itinerant revivalists as agents who would bring a warmer spirit to the religion of their parishioners; this welcome was extended even by such outstanding liberal highbrows as Benjamin Colman of Boston. It was only after the Awakening was well under way that the regular ministers began to realize that the awakeners did not regard them as fellow workers in a common spiritual task but as competitors —and very inferior ones at that.

Gilbert Tennent expressed the revivalists' view of the older clergy (those "orthodox, Letter-learned and regular Pharisees") in a sermon on *The Danger of an Unconverted Ministry*; he attacked them as crafty, cruel, cold-hearted, bigoted, faithless hypocrites who held the people in contempt. Tennent found the motives and the piety of the unawakened ministers suspect, and he regarded them not as co-workers but as enemies. ("If they coud help it, they wo'dn't let one faithful Man come into the Ministry; and therefore their Opposition is an encouraging Sign.") Tennent's approach was hardly ingratiating, but he believed that he was raising a real issue, and it would be hard to deny that what he was advocating could be called religious democracy. If, under existing church organization, a congregation had a cold and unconverted minister, and if it was forbidden to receive an awakened one except with the consent of the unconverted, how would the congregation ever win access to "a faithful Ministry"?[12] Like a true Protestant, Tennent was once again addressing himself to a major problem—how the

---

[11]On Davenport see Gaustad: op. cit., pp. 36–41. Edwards himself, in his *Treatise Concerning Religious Affections* (1746), expressed at length his disapproval of such manifestations.

[12]Gilbert Tennent, *The Danger of an Unconverted Ministry Considered in a Sermon on Mark VI, 34* (Boston, 1742), pp. 2–3, 5, 7, 11–13.

faith could be propagated under conditions of religious monopoly. To the standing ministry, the problem presented itself
in quite another guise: how, under the conditions to which
they were bound by inherited church principles, could they
compete with inspired preachers like Tennent and Whitefield,
if these men took it into their heads to treat the regular ministry as foes?

In truth, the established ministers found it difficult to cope
with the challenge of the awakeners. The regular ministers,
living with their congregations year in and year out under
conditions devoid of special religious excitement, were faced
with the task of keeping alive the spiritual awareness of their
flocks under sober everyday circumstances. Confronted by
flaming evangelists of Whitefield's caliber, and even by such
lesser tub-thumpers and foot-stampers as Gilbert Tennent and
Davenport, they were at somewhat the same disadvantage as
an aging housewife whose husband has taken up with a young
hussy from the front line of the chorus. The revivalists, with
the prominent exception of Edwards, who was an intellectual
largely out of rapport with his own congregation, felt little or
no necessity to work upon the reason of their audiences or
to address themselves to knotty questions of doctrine. They
dispensed (again one must except Edwards) with written sermons, and confronted their listeners with the spontaneity of
direct intercourse. They dealt directly with the ultimate realities of religious experience—the sense of sin, the yearning for
salvation, the hope for God's love and mercy—and rarely hesitated to work upon the sensibilities of the audience; the fits and
seizures, the shrieks and groans and grovelings, the occasional
dementia characteristic of later revivalism made their appearance. Tennent, for instance, commonly frightened his listeners
into conversions, as he stamped up and down and finally lapsed
into incoherence. Performances like his were evidently in demand; on his three-months' tour of New England, when he
often preached in foot-deep snow, he sent his converts grovel-
ing to the ground. As Timothy Cutler, a rather prejudiced Anglican witness, reported it: "After him [Whitefield] came one
Tennent—a monster! impudent and noisy—and told them all
they were *damned, damned, damned!* This charmed them; and

in the most dreadful winter I ever saw, people wallowed in snow, night and day, for the benefit of his beastly brayings; and many ended their days under these fatigues."[13]

Before long, it became clear that the extreme exponents of revivals were challenging every assumption of the settled churches, whether Congregational, Dutch Reformed, Presbyterian, or Anglican. The Congregationalists of New England, and their Presbyterian counterparts elsewhere, had assumed, as I have said, that ministers must be learned professional men. Traditionally their ministers had commanded respect not merely for their learning but also for their piety and their spiritual qualities. But learning was held to be essential because learning and the rational understanding of doctrine were considered vital to religious life. Moreover, the regular churches were conducted in an orderly fashion. Ministers had to be invited and commissioned; their relations with their congregations were stable, solemn, orderly marriages. Unlicensed preachers were not to be thought of, and uninvited preaching simply was not done.

All these assumptions were now challenged. The most extreme revivalists were undermining the dignity of the profession by their personal conduct; they were invading and dividing the allegiances of the established ministers' congregations; they were trying to discredit the standing ministry by denouncing it as cold and unregenerate;[14] many of them were preaching that not learning but the spirit was important to salvation; and finally (despite the disapproval of some awakeners like Tennent),

---

[13] L. Tyerman: *The Life of the Rev. George Whitefield* (London, 1847), Vol. II, p. 125. See Eugene E. White: "Decline of the Great Awakening in New England: 1741 to 1746," *New England Quarterly*, Vol. XXIV (March, 1951), p. 37.

[14] Charles Chauncy compiled a catalogue of some of the epithets Gilbert Tennent used against the established ministry: "Hirelings; Caterpillars; Letter-Learned Pharisees; Men of the craft of Foxes, and the Cruelty of Wolves; plaistered Hypocrites; Varlets; seed of the Serpent; foolish Builders, whom the Devil drives into the Ministry; dry Nurses; dead Dogs that cannot bark; blind Men; dead Men; Men possessed of the Devil; Rebels and Enemies of god; Guides that are Stone-blind and Stone deaf; children of Satan . . . murderous Hypocrites." *Seasonable Thoughts on the State of Religion in New England* (Boston, 1743), p. 249. Most of these examples appear to have been taken from Tennent's *Danger of an Unconverted Ministry.*

they were threatening to undermine the professional basis of the ministry by commissioning laymen—lay exhorters, as they were called—to carry on the work of conversion. Before long many congregations were split in two; and major denominations like the Congregationalists and Presbyterians were divided into quarreling factions. Plainly the thing had got out of hand. As Ezra Stiles recalled nearly twenty years later: "Multitudes were seriously, soberly and solemnly out of their wits."[15]

4

It was not long before the awakeners wore out their welcome from the established ministry. By 1743 the ministers themselves had fallen out—not over such extravagances as the commissioning of laymen or the uninvited invading of parishes, acts which were defended by no one of consequence, but over the meaning of the Awakening itself. A strong minority (perhaps as many as a third) held that, for all its defects, it was "a happy revival of religion," but the majority had come to look upon it as a fit of superstitious enthusiasm, an anti-intellectualist uprising against traditional and rational authority. The most extensive tract against the awakeners was written by one of their most intransigent foes, Charles Chauncy, a somewhat stuffy but liberal-minded leader of the Boston clergy. His *Seasonable Thoughts on the State of Religion in New England*, published in 1743, shows his outrage at the *insolence* of the upstarts from miscellaneous occupations who had come to challenge the ministry—men totally unqualified but of overweening pride and assertiveness. The revivals had opened the door, he complained, to lay exhorters: "Men of all Occupations who are vain enough to think themselves fit to be Teachers of others; Men who, though they have no Learning, and but small Capacities, yet imagine they are able, and without Study too, to speak to the spiritual Profit of such as are willing to hear them."[16]

"Without study too"! Here we are close to one of the central issues of the Great Awakening. An error of "former Times" was now being revived, Chauncy asserted, the error of the heretics

[15]Gaustad: op. cit., p. 103.
[16] *Seasonable Thoughts*, p. 226.

and popular preachers who said that "they needed no Books but the Bible." "They pleaded there was no Need of Learning in preaching, and that one of them could by the SPIRIT do better than the Minister by his Learning; as if the SPIRIT and Learning were Opposites." This, Chauncy thought, was the fundamental error of the revivalists:[17]

> Their depending on the Help of the SPIRIT as to despise Learning. To this it is owing, that so many speak slightly of our Schools and Colleges; discovering a Good-Will, were it in their Power, to rase them to their Foundations. To the same Cause it may be ascrib'd, that such Swarms of Exhorters have appear'd in the Land, and been admir'd and run after, though many of them could scarce speak common Sense . . . and to the same Cause still it must be attributed that so many Ministers preach, not only without Book, but without Study; and justify their doing so, lest, by previous Preparation, they should stint the Spirit.

To the exponent of a religion of the book, for whom a correct reading of the Bible was a vital concern, this was the ultimate heresy: that one who was possessed of the Spirit could, without study and without learning, interpret the word of God effectively enough to be an agent of the salvation of others. And here we have the nub of the difference between the awakeners and the spokesmen of establishments: whether it was more important to get a historically correct and rational understanding of the Book—and hence of the word of God—or to work up a proper emotion, a proper sense of inner conviction and of relation to God.

An association of revivalist ministers put their case in these terms:[18]

> That every brother that is qualified by God for the same has a right to preach according to the measure of faith, and that the essential qualification for preaching is wrought by the Spirit of God; and that the knowledge of the tongues and liberal sciences are not absolutely necessary; yet they are convenient, and

[17]Ibid., pp. 256–8.
[18]Leonard W. Labaree: "The Conservative Attitude toward the Great Awakening," *William and Mary Quarterly*, 3rd ser., Vol. I (October, 1944), pp. 339–40, from Tracy: *Great Awakening*, p. 319.

will doubtless be profitable if rightly used, but if brought in to supply the want of the Spirit of God, they prove a snare to those that use them and all that follow them.

Conservatives found in this a complete repudiation of the role of learning in religion; and in the emotional kind of religion that came from the preaching of men so disposed, they saw the destruction of all rationality in religious life. "As none but rational creatures are capable of religion," wrote a Southern opponent of evangelism,[19]

> so there is no true religion but in the use of reason; there will always be these two things in the former, which the latter must judge of, namely the *Truth* and the *Meaning.* The virtue of our religion must consist in the inward persuasion of our mind, for if we owe our religion to birth, humor, interest, or any external circumstances or motive whatever, we bring all religions upon a level; and though by the happiness of education we should pro-fess the true religion, yet if we do not make it our own by un-derstanding the reasons for it, it will not be profitable to us; we offer to God the *Sacrifice of Fools*, in which he has no pleasure.

Understandably, many of the conservative ministers in the affected colonies, who had at first expected good results for re-ligion from the revivals, soon began to abhor them as a threat to their own position, to the churches themselves, and to all true religion. Fundamental tenets were being neglected, the organized ministry was being bypassed and traduced. Extem-porized preaching threatened to dissolve all rational elements in religion, for many of the evangelists admitted that their preaching came by "the immediate impression of the Holy Ghost putting a long chain of thoughts into their minds and words into their mouths." Conservatives considered this bad practice even in a properly educated minister, but it was much more dangerous in the lay exhorters, who were "private per-sons of no education and but low attainment in knowledge and in the great doctrines of the Gospel."[20] Finally, not only had these irruptions created divisions and quarrels within a great many congregations, but the established ministers feared that

[19]Quoted by Labaree: op. cit., p. 345, from *South Carolina Gazette* (September 12–19, 1741).
[20]Ibid., p. 336.

the evangelists would strike at the very source of the educated ministry by circumventing the colleges and the usual process of ministerial training.

The fear was exaggerated, but the revivalists had tried to bully the colleges and at a few moments of extremism they had gone in for book-burning. Even the moderate Whitefield had urged that certain books be burned and had succeeded in persuading some of his followers to commit them to the flames. In March 1743, James Davenport urged the people of New London to collect for burning their jewelry and objects of personal luxury, as well as books and sermons written by Increase Mather, Benjamin Colman, Charles Chauncy, and other regular ministers. And one Sunday morning a large pyre was consumed on the town wharf while Davenport and his followers sang *Gloria Patri* and *Hallelujah* and chanted this invocation: "The smoak of the torments of such of the authors . . . as died in the same belief, as when they set them out, was now ascending in hell in like manner, as the smoak of these books rise."[21]

The immediate effects of the Awakening on education were mixed. In an organization like the Presbyterian Church, manned as it was by many well-trained ministers from the Scottish universities, even a revivalist was likely to be sensitive to the charge that his work was hostile to learning. William Tennent trained a number of capable scholars at his "Log College," and his son Gilbert was not the ignorant lout that has often been pictured. More important, the revivalist Presbyterians established the College of New Jersey (later Princeton) in 1746, to assure that they would have their own center of learning; and in time other institutions—Brown, Rutgers, and Dartmouth —were founded by men influenced by the revivals. Only later did the revivalist tradition become consistently hostile to education. It must be added, however, that the effect of the Awakening was to subordinate education to religious factionalism and to consolidate the tradition of sectarian control of colleges. What the ardent religious factionalists wanted most of all were not centers of learning, but *their own* instruments of teaching;

21White: op. cit., p. 44.

they pushed doctrinal and pietistic considerations forward, at the expense of humane learning. Even the learned Jonathan Edwards once attacked Harvard and Yale for failing to be "nurseries of piety" and for taking more pains "to teach the scholars human learning" than to educate them in religion.[22]

Whitefield himself, another responsible evangelist, was also dissatisfied with the two New England colleges. The light of these colleges, he complained, had become "darkness, darkness that may be felt." When he returned to New England in 1744, most of the ministers who had opened their pulpits to him on his first visit now kept them resolutely closed, and the faculties of both Yale and Harvard issued pamphlets denouncing him, denying his charges against the colleges, and submitting a bill of countercharges. There is no reason to accept the view of some of Whitefield's more suspicious opponents that he intended to "vilify and subvert" the colleges of New England in order to overthrow its established ministers and create wholly new ways of training their successors. But at a time when scores of local pastors were being denounced to their own congregations by awakeners as lacking in true piety, if not as agents of the devil, the fear of thoroughgoing subversion was an understandable response.[23]

The burning of books and the baiting of colleges, to be sure, were examples not of the characteristic behavior of the awakeners, but of their excesses. The awakeners had not started out to divide the churches, attack the colleges, or discredit intellect and learning; in so far as they did so, it was only to serve their fundamental purpose, which was to revive religion and bring souls to God. And, for all the tart animadversions of men like Chauncy, the anti-intellectual effects of the New England and Middle Colony Awakenings, taking place as they did within the framework of the powerful Congregational and Presbyterian respect for learning and rationality, were distinctly limited. But the Great Awakening, even in New England, revealed the

[22] *Works* (New York, 1830), Vol. IV, pp. 264–5.
[23] On the reaction of the New England colleges to the Awakening, see Richard Hofstadter and Walter P. Metzger: *The Development of Academic Freedom in the United States* (New York, 1955), pp. 159–63.

almost uncontrollable tendency of such revivals toward extremes of various kinds. Opponents, with Chauncy, said that
the emotional fevers and the anti-intellectualism of the Awakening were its essence, but the friends of revival thought these
things were merely the incidental defects of a fundamentally
good movement toward Christian conversion. In the short
run, and in the restrained milieu of the New England churches,
the friends of the Awakening were probably right; but their
opponents divined more correctly what the inner tendency and
future direction of such revivals would be—especially when revivalism got away from the traditions and restraints of New
England into the great American interior. The most recent
historian of the New England Awakening, who writes of it
with evident sympathy, still concludes that it "demonstrated
the feasibility of and made fashionable a fervent evangelism
without intellectual discipline," and observes that "the dis-
crediting of 'human learning,' characteristic of only a minority
during the Awakening, later became typical of a majority of
Protestantism."[24]

There can be little doubt that the conventional judgment is
right: by achieving a religious style congenial to the common
man and giving him an alternative to the establishments run by
and largely for the comfortable classes, the Awakening quickened the democratic spirit in America; by telling the people
that they had a right to hear the kind of preachers they liked
and understood, even under some circumstances a right to
preach themselves, the revivalists broke the hold of the establishments and heightened that assertiveness and self-sufficiency
which visitor after visitor from abroad was later to find characteristic of the American people. Moreover, the impulse given
to humanitarian causes—to anti-slavery and the conversion of
slaves and Indians—must also be chalked up to the credit of
the Great Awakening. There was no soul to whose welfare the
good awakener was indifferent. But the costs (in spite of the
newly formed colleges) to the cause of intellect and learning in
religion must also be reckoned. The awakeners were not the
first to disparage the virtues of mind, but they quickened anti-
intellectualism; and they gave to American anti-intellectualism

24Gaustad: op. cit., pp. 129, 139.

its first brief moment of militant success. With the Awakenings, the Puritan age in American religion came to an end and the evangelical age began. Subsequent revivals repeated in an ever larger theater the merits and defects of the revivals of the eighteenth century.

5

As later revivalism moved from New England and the Middle Colonies and from the Congregational and Presbyterian denominations out into the saddlebag and bear-meat country of the South and West, it became more primitive, more emotional, more given to "ecstatic" manifestations. The preachers were less educated, less inclined to restrain physical responses as an instrument of conversion; and the grovelings, jerkings, howlings, and barkings increased. From the beginning, Whitefield's work had been effective in the Southern colonies; the evangelical movement, spurred by his preaching and by the overflow of Middle-Colony Presbyterian revivalists, spread into Virginia, North Carolina, and the deeper South in the 1740's and 1750's. There revivalists found a large unchurched population; and there, where the rusticated Anglican clergymen sometimes went to seed, the grounds for an indictment of the established ministry were considerably better than they had been in the North. There also, because the Anglican establishment was linked with the upper classes, the democratic and dissenting implications of revivalism were sharper. In the South, despite the activity of such a distinguished Presbyterian preacher as Samuel Davies, later to be president of Princeton, a major part was played by Baptists and later by Methodists, groups less committed than the Presbyterians and Congregationalists to a learned ministry. There only weak obstacles stood in the way of such revival phenomena as unpaid itinerant ministers, laymen preaching to the people, and denunciations of the established clerics.

The Southern revivalists carried the light of the gospel to a people who were not only unchurched but often uncivilized. The Reverend Charles Woodmason, an Anglican minister who traveled extensively in the Carolina back-country during the 1760's and 1770's left a chilling picture of the savagery of the life he found there and a suggestive if rather jaundiced record of "these roving Teachers that stir up the Minds of the People against the Establish'd Church, and her Ministers—and make the Situation of any Gentleman extremely uneasy, vexatious, and disagreeable."

> Few or no Books are to be found in all this vast Country, beside the Assembly, Catechism, Watts Hymns, Bunyans Pilgrims Progress—Russells—Whitefields and Erskines Sermons. Nor do they delight in Historical Books or in having them read to them, as do our Vulgar in England, for these People despise Knowledge, and instead of honouring a Learned Person, or any one of Wit or Knowledge, be it in the Arts, Sciences, or Languages, they despise and Ill treat them—And this Spirit prevails even among the Principals of this Province.

Of the revivalist or New Light faction among the Baptists he reported a few years later that they were altogether opposed to authority and, having made successful assaults upon the established church, were now trying to destroy the state. "The Gentlemen of the Law, seem now to engage their Attention: Like *Straw* and *Tyler*, of old [John Rackstraw and Wat Tyler of the English Peasants' Revolt of 1381], they want for to demolish all the Learned Professions. Human Learning being contrary to the spirit of God."[25]

What Woodmason observed on the Carolina frontier in the eighteenth century was an example, somewhat exaggerated, of the conditions in which the shifting population increasingly found itself. As the people moved westward after the Revolution, they were forever outrunning the institutions of settled society; it was impossible for institutions to move as fast or as constantly as the population. The trans-Allegheny population, which was about 100,000 in 1790, had jumped to 2,250,000 thirty years later. Many families made not one but two or three moves in a brief span of years. Organizations dissolved; restraints disappeared. Churches, social bonds, and cultural institutions often broke down, and they could not be reconstituted

[25]Richard J. Hooker, ed.: *The Carolina Backcountry on the Eve of the Revolution* (Chapel Hill, 1953), pp. 42, 52–3, 113, on cultural conditions in the Southern back-country. See also Carl Bridenbaugh: *Myths and Realities: Societies of the Colonial South* (Baton Rouge, 1952), chapter 3.

before the frontier families made yet another leap into the wilderness or the prairie. Samuel J. Mills, later one of the chief organizers of the American Bible Society, took two companions on Western trips during 1812–15 and found community after community which had been settled many years but which had no schools and no churches and little interest in establishing either. In Kaskaskia, the capital of Illinois territory, they could not find a single complete Bible.[26]

John Mason Peck, the first Baptist missionary to work in the Illinois and Missouri region, later recalled "a specimen of the squatter race found on the extreme frontiers" in 1818 in an extremely primitive condition:[27]

About nine o'clock I found the family to which I was directed. As this family was a specimen of the squatter race found on the extreme frontiers in early times, some specific description may amuse the reader, for I do not think a duplicate can now [1864] be found within the boundaries of Missouri. The single log-cabin, of the most primitive structure, was situated at some distance within the cornfield. In and around it were the patriarchal head and his wife, two married daughters and their husbands, with three or four little children, and a son and daughter grown up to manhood and womanhood. The old man said he could read but "mighty poorly." The old woman wanted a *hyme* book, but could not read one. The rest of this romantic household had no use for books or "any such trash." I had introduced myself as a Baptist preacher, traveling through the country preaching the gospel to the people. The old man and his wife were Baptists, at least had been members of some Baptist church when they lived "in the settlements." The "settlements" with this class in those days meant the back parts of Virginia and the Carolinas, and in some instances the older

[26]Colin B. Goodykoontz: *Home Missions on the American Frontier* (Caldwell, Idaho, 1939), pp. 139–43. It was not merely Protestant denominations that suffered this breakdown of religious practice in the process of migration. An Indiana priest wrote in 1849 of Irish immigrants in his vicinity: "They scarcely know there is a God; they are ashamed to attend Catechism, and when they do come they do not understand the instruction." Sister Mary Carol Schroeder: *The Catholic Church in the Diocese of Vincennes, 1847–1877* (Washington, 1946), p. 58.
[27]Rufus Babcock, ed.: *Forty Years of Pioneer Life: Memoir of John Mason Peck, D.D.* (Philadelphia, 1864), pp. 101–3.

sections of Kentucky and Tennessee, where they had lived in their earlier days. But it was "a mighty poor chance" for Baptist preaching where they lived. The old man could tell me of a Baptist meeting he had been at on the St. François, and could direct me to Elder Farrar's residence near St. Michael. The old woman and the young folks had not seen a Baptist preacher since they had lived in the territory some eight or ten years. Occasionally they had been to a Methodist meeting. This was the condition of a numerous class of people then scattered over the frontier settlements of Missouri. The "traveling missionary" was received with all the hospitality the old people had the ability or knew how to exercise. The younger class were shy and kept out of the cabin, and could not be persuaded to come in to hear the missionary read the Scriptures and offer a prayer. There was evidence of backwardness, or some other propensity, attending all the domestic arrangements. . . .

Not a table, chair, or any article of furniture could be seen. These deficiencies were common on the frontiers; for emigrations from the "settlements" were often made on pack-horses, and no domestic conveniences could be transported, except the most indispensable cooking-utensils, bedding, and a change or two of clothing. But the head of the family must be shiftless indeed, and void of all backwoods' skill and enterprise, who could not make a table for family use. There were two fashions of this necessary article in the time to which I refer. One was a slab, or "puncheon," as then called, split from a large log, four feet long, and from fifteen to eighteen inches wide, and hewn down to the thickness of a plank. In this were inserted four legs, after the fashion of a stool or bench, at the proper height. The other was a rough frame, in which posts were inserted for legs, and covered with split clapboards shaved smooth, and fastened with small wooden pins. We found one of these descriptions of tables in hundreds of log cabins where neatness, tidiness, and industry prevailed. . . .

The viands now only need description to complete this accurate picture of real squatter life. The rancid bacon when boiled could have been detected by a foetid atmosphere across the yard, had there been one. The snap-beans, as an accompaniment, were not half-boiled. The sour buttermilk taken from the churn, where the milk was kept throughout the whole season, as it came from the cow, was "no go." The article on which the traveler made a hearty breakfast, past ten o'clock in the morning, was the corn, boiled in fair water.

At times, the missionaries were simply overwhelmed. One wrote of his difficulties in the town of China, Indiana, in 1833:[28]

> Ignorance & her squalid brood. A universal dearth of intellect. Total abstinence from literature is very generally practiced. Aside from br. Wilder and myself, there is not a literary man of any sort in the bounds. There is not a scholar in grammar or geography, or a *teacher capable* of *instructing* in *them*, to my knowledge. There are some neighborhoods in which there has *never been a school* of *any* kind. Parents and children are one dead level of ignorance. Others are supplied a few months in the year with the most antiquated & unreasonable forms of teaching reading, writing & cyphering. Master Ignoramus is a striking facsimile of them. They are never guilty of teaching any thing but "pure *schoolmaster larnin.*" Of course there is no kind of ambition for improvement; & it is no more disgrace for man, woman or child to be unable to read, than to have a long nose. Our own church the other day elected a man to the eldership who is unable to read the bible. I don't know of ten families who take any kind of paper, political or religious, & the whole of their revenue to the Post office department is not as much as mine alone. Need I stop to remind you of the host of loathsome reptiles such a stagnant pool is fitted to breed! Croaking jealousy; bloated Bigotry; coiling suspicion; wormish blindness; crocodile malice! . . .

But men and women living under conditions of poverty and exacting toil, facing the hazards of Indian raids, fevers, and agues, and raised on whisky and brawling, could not afford education and culture; and they found it easier to reject what they could not have than to admit the lack of it as a deficiency in themselves.

Another worker in a nearby Indiana town wrote more sympathetically at about the same time that "the people are poor & far from market labouriously engaged in improving & cultivating their new land." But the cultural conditions he found were somewhat the same:[29]

---

[28] Goodykoontz: op. cit., p. 191.
[29] Ibid., pp. 191–2. For an account of similar conditions in early Indiana, see Baynard R. Hall: *The New Purchase* (1843; ed. Princeton, 1916), p. 120.

> Society here is in an unformed state composed of persons
> from every part of the Union. . . . Religious sects are numer-
> ous & blind guides enough to swallow all the camels in Arabia
> —Some of these cant read—Some labour to preach down the
> Sabbath! & others to rob *Christ of His divinity!* and all harmo-
> niously unite in decrying education—as requisite for a public
> teacher & in abusing the learned clergy who take wages for
> their services. When shall this reign of ignorance & error cease
> in the West?

Of course, to describe the condition of this country is to provide the evangelists with their best defense. It must be said that
they were not lowering the level of a high culture but trying to
bring the ordinary restraints and institutions of a civilized society into an area which had hardly any culture at all. The best
of them were clearly the intellectual and cultural superiors of
their environment, and the poorest of them could hardly have
made it worse. The home missionaries sent out by the religious
organizations were constantly fighting against one manifestation or another of the process of social dissolution—against
the increasing numbers of unchurched and non-religious people, against "marriages" unsanctified in the church, and against
unregulated lives, wild drinking, and savage fighting. Though
often welcomed, they still had to carry on their work under
opposition that at the least came to heckling and at the worst
was really hazardous. The most famous of the circuit-riding
Methodist preachers, Peter Cartwright, reported that camp
meetings were attended by rowdies armed with knives, clubs,
and horsewhips, determined to break up the proceedings. One
Sunday morning, when his sermon was interrupted by toughs,
Cartwright himself had to lead his congregation in a counter-
assault. Those who undertook the hard task of bringing religion westward, as it were, in their saddlebags, would have
been ineffective had they been the sort of pastors who were
appropriate to the settled churches of the East. They would
have been ineffective in converting their moving flocks if they
had not been able to develop a vernacular style in preaching,
and if they had failed to share or to simulate in some degree the
sensibilities and prejudices of their audiences—anti-authority,
anti-aristocracy, anti-Eastern, anti-learning. The various denominations responded in different ways to this necessity: but

in general it might be said that the congregations were raised and the preachers were lowered. In brief, the elite upon which culture depended for its transmission was being debased by the demands of a rude social order. If our purpose were to pass judgment on the evangelical ministers, a good case could be made for them on the counts of sincerity, courage, self-sacrifice, and intelligence. But since our primary purpose is to assess the transit of civilization and the development of culture, we must bear in mind the society that was emerging. It was a society of courage and character, of endurance and practical cunning, but it was not a society likely to produce poets or artists or savants.

CHAPTER IV

Evangelicalism and the Revivalists

I

IT SEEMS evident in retrospect, as indeed it did to some contemporaries, that the conditions of early nineteenth-century
American development created a new and distinctive form of
Christianity in which both the organization of the churches
and the standards of the ministry were unique. For centuries
the first tradition of Christianity had been not the tradition
of multiple religious "denominations" but the tradition of
the Church. But from the beginning the American colonies
were settled by a variety of immigrant groups representing the
wide range of confessional commitments that had grown up in
post-Reformation Europe—the religions of the "left" as well
as those of the "right." It became clear at an early date that the
maintenance on these shores of a monopolistic and coercive
establishment would be extremely difficult; and by the middle
of the eighteenth century the colonials were well on the way
to learning the amenities of religious accommodation and the
peaceful possibilities of a legal policy of toleration.

As religious disunity was followed by religious multiplicity,
Americans uprooted church establishments and embraced religious liberty. Under the broad liberty prevailing in the American
states at the close of the eighteenth century and the beginning
of the nineteenth, religious groups that had begun as dissenting sects developed into firm organizations, less formal than
the churches of the past, but too secure and well-organized
to be considered sects. The promoted sects and the demoted
establishments, now operating more or less on a par in a voluntary and freely competitive religious environment, settled
down into what has come to be called denominationalism.[1]

---

[1]Readers who are familiar with Sidney E. Mead's brilliant essays on American
religious history will recognize my great indebtedness to him in the following
pages, especially to his penetrating account of "Denominationalism: The Shape
of Protestantism in America," *Church History*, Vol. XXIII (December, 1954),
pp. 291–320; and "The Rise of the Evangelical Conception of the Ministry in

The essence of American denominationalism is that churches became *voluntary* organizations. The layman, living in a society in which no church enjoyed the luxury of compulsory membership and in which even traditional, inherited membership was often extraordinarily weak, felt free to make a *choice* as to which among several denominations should have his allegiance. In the older church pattern, the layman was born into a church, was often forced by the state to stay in it, and received his religious experiences in the fashion determined by its liturgical forms. The American layman, however, was not simply born into a denomination nor did he inherit certain sacramental forms; the denomination was a voluntary society which he chose to join often after undergoing a transforming religious experience.

There was nothing fictional about this choice. So fluid had been the conditions of American life toward the end of the eighteenth century, and so disorganizing the consequences of the Revolution, that perhaps as many as ninety per cent of the Americans were unchurched in 1790. In the subsequent decades this astonishing condition of religious anarchy was to a considerable degree remedied. The religious public sorted itself out, as it were, and much of it fell into line in one denomination or another. But in this process the decision to join a church had been made over and over again by countless individuals. And what the layman chose was a religious denomination already molded by previous choices and infused with the American's yearning for a break with the past, his passion for the future, his growing disdain for history. In the American political creed the notion prevailed that Europe represented corruptions of the past which must be surmounted. The Protestant denominations were based on a similar view of the Christian past.[2] It was commonly believed that the historical development of Christianity was not an accretion of valuable institutional forms and practices but a process of corruption and degeneration in

America (1607–1850)," in Richard Niebuhr and Daniel D. Williams, ed.: *The Ministry in Historical Perspectives* (New York, 1956), pp. 207–49.

[2] For a stimulating exploration of the desire to surmount the past in nineteenth-century American letters, see R. W. B. Lewis: *The American Adam* (Chicago, 1955).

which the purity of primitive Christianity had been lost. The goal of the devout, then, was not to preserve forms but to strike out anew in order to recapture this purity. "This is an age of freedom," wrote the distinguished evangelical Presbyterian, Albert Barnes, in 1844, "and men *will* be free. The religion of forms is the stereotyped wisdom or folly of the past, and does not adapt itself to the free movements, the enlarged views, the varying plans of this age."[3]

The objective was to return to the pure conditions of primitive Christianity, to which Scripture alone would give the key. Even those who disliked this tendency in American religion could see how central it was. In 1849 a spokesman of the German Reformed Church remarked that the appeal of the sects to private judgment and to the Bible[4]

> involves, of necessity, a protest against the authority of all previous history, except so far as it may seem to agree with what is thus found to be true; in which case, of course, the only real measure of truth is taken to be, not this authority of history at all, but the mind, simply, of the particular sect itself. . . . A genuine sect will not suffer itself to be embarrassed for a moment, either at its start or afterwards, by the consideration that it has no proper root in past history. Its ambition is rather to appear in this respect *autochthonic*, aboriginal, self-sprung from the Bible, or through the Bible from the skies. . . . The idea of a historical continuity in the life of the Church, carries with it no weight whatever for the sect consciousness.

It is significant, then, that the bond that held most denominations together need not be a traditional, inherited confessional bond—that is, not a historical system of doctrinal belief —but goals or motives more or less newly constituted and freshly conceived. Since there need be only a shadow of confessional unity in the denominations, the rational discussion of theological issues—in the past a great source of intellectual discipline in the churches—came to be regarded as a distraction,

[3]"The Position of the Evangelical Party in the Episcopal Church," *Miscellaneous Essays and Reviews* (New York, 1855), Vol. I, p. 371. This essay is a thoroughgoing attack on religious forms as being inconsistent with the evangelical spirit.
[4]John W. Nevin: "The Sect System," *Mercersburg Review*, Vol. I (September, 1849), pp. 499–500.

as a divisive force. Therefore, although it was not abandoned, it was subordinated to practical objectives which were conceived to be far more important.[5] The peculiar views or practices of any denomination, if they were not considered good for the general welfare or the common mission enterprise, were sacrificed to this mission without excessive regret.[6] And the mission itself was defined by evangelism. In a society so mobile and fluid, with so many unchurched persons to be gained for the faith, the basic purpose of the denominations, to which all other purposes and commitments were subordinated, was that of gaining converts.

The denominations were trying to win to church allegiance a public which, for whatever reason, had *not* been held by the traditional sanctions of religion and which had lost touch both with liturgical forms and with elaborate creeds. It was unlikely that an appeal mediated by such forms and creeds could now regain the people. What did seem to work was a restoration of

[5]This historical background may go far to explain what Will Herberg has found to be such a prominent characteristic of contemporary American religion—a strong belief in the importance of religion-in-general coupled with great indifference to the content of religion. (Cf. Eisenhower in 1952: "Our government makes no sense, unless it is founded in a deeply felt religious faith—and I don't care what it is.") This generalized faith in faith is the product, among other things, of centuries of denominational accommodation. See Herberg: *Protestant, Catholic, Jew* (Anchor ed., New York, 1960), chapter 5, especially pp. 84–90.

[6]Even in 1782 Crèvecoeur found that in America, "if the sectaries are not settled close together, if they are mixed with other denominations, their zeal will cool for want of fuel, and will be extinguished in a little time. Then the Americans will become as to religion what they are as to country, allied to all. . . . All sects are mixed as well as all nations; thus religious indifference is imperceptibly disseminated from one end of the continent to the other; which is at present one of the strongest characteristics of the Americans. Where this will reach no one can tell, perhaps it may leave a vacuum fit to receive other systems. Persecution, religious pride, the love of contradiction, are the food of what the world commonly calls religion. These motives have ceased here; zeal in Europe is confined; here it evaporates in the great distance it has to travel; there it is a grain of powder enclosed, here it burns away in the open air, and consumes without effect." *Letters from an American Farmer* (New York, 1957), pp. 44, 47. Of course, in the decades after 1790 some of the religious enthusiasm was restored, but the passion for distinguishing sectarian differences was restored in nothing like the same manner.

the kind of primitive emotional appeal that the first Christian proselytizers had presumably used in the early days of the faith. Revivalism succeeded where traditionalism had failed. Emotional upheavals took the place of the coercive sanctions of religious establishments. Simple people were brought back to faith with simple ideas, voiced by forceful preachers who were capable of getting away from the complexities and pressing upon them the simplest of alternatives: the choice of heaven or hell. Salvation, too, was taken as a matter of choice: the sinner was expected to "get religion"—it was not thought that religion would get him. Whatever device worked to bring him back into the fold was good. As that indefatigable saver of souls, Dwight L. Moody, once put it: "It makes no difference how you get a man to God, provided you get him there."[7] Long before pragmatism became a philosophical creed, it was formulated, albeit in a crude way, by the evangelists. For the layman the pragmatic test in religion was the experience of conversion; for the clergyman, it was the ability to induce this experience. The minister's success in winning souls was taken as the decisive evidence that he preached the truth.[8]

The ministry itself was metamorphosed by the denominational system and the regnant evangelical spirit. The churches, whatever their denominational form or plan of organization, tended in varying degrees to move in the direction of a kind of congregationalism or localism. The combined forces of localism and revivalism greatly strengthened the hand of the heretic or the schismatic: so long as he could produce results, who could control him? They also strengthened the hand of the layman. The minister, pulled away from the sustaining power of a formidable central church, was largely thrown on his own resources in working out his relationship with his congregation. He did claim and establish as much authority as he could, but the conditions

[7]Quoted in William G. McLoughlin: *Billy Sunday Was His Real Name* (Chicago, 1955), p. 158. A more sophisticated preacher like Washington Gladden could also say that his own theology "had to be hammered out on the anvil for daily use in the pulpit. The pragmatic test was the only one that could be applied to it: 'Will it work?'" *Recollections* (Boston, 1909), p. 163.
[8]One of the chapters in Charles G. Finney's *Lectures on Revivals of Religion* (New York, 1835) is headed: "A Wise Minister Will Be Successful," and cites Proverbs XI, 30: "He that winneth souls is wise."

of American life favored an extraordinary degree of lay control. In the South even the colonial Anglican church, with its traditions of clerical authority, had found that an extraordinary measure of control passed into the hands of its vestrymen. Everywhere the American ministers seemed to be *judged* by the laymen, and in a sense used by them. Even in the eighteenth century, Crèvecoeur had commented on the attitude of the Low Dutchman who "conceives no other idea of a clergyman than that of an hired man; if he does his work well he will pay him the stipulated sum; if not he will dismiss him, and do without his sermons, and let his house be shut up for years."[9]

The ministers, in turn, unable to rely as much as in the Old World upon the authority of their churches and their own positions, became, when they were most successful, gifted politicians in church affairs, well versed in the secular arts of manipulation. Moreover, there was a premium upon ministers capable of a mixed kind of religious and nationalistic statecraft, whose object was to reform the country and win the West for Christianity. Concerning the apparatus of societies devoted to such purposes which sprang up between 1800 and 1850, one minister complained: "The minister is often expected to be, for the most part, a manager of social utilities, a wire-puller of beneficent agencies," whose character was too often judged by "the amount of visible grinding that it can accomplish in the mill of social reform. . . ."[10] As a consequence, Sidney E. Mead has pointed out, "the conception of the minister practically

[9]Crèvecoeur: op. cit., p. 45. This should not be taken as suggesting that the ministers were not respected. They did not *have* respect by virtue of their office, but they could and often did *win* respect. Timothy Dwight said of the early Connecticut clergy that they had no official power but much influence. "Clergymen, here, are respected for what they are, and for what they do, and not for anything adventitious to themselves, or their office." Mead: "The Rise of the Evangelical Conception of the Ministry," p. 236.

[10]Andrew P. Peabody: *The Work of the Ministry* (Boston, 1850), p. 7. It was the patriotic and statesmanlike concern of the Protestant clergy for the Christianization of the West that caused Tocqueville to remark that "if you converse with these missionaries of Christian civilization, you will be surprised to hear them speak so often of the goods of this world, and to meet a politician where you expected to find a priest." *Democracy in America*, ed. by Phillips Bradley (New York, 1945), Vol. I, pp. 306–7.

lost its priestly dimension as traditionally conceived, and became that of a consecrated functionary, called of God, who
directed the purposive activities of the visible church."[11]

Finally, the work of the minister tended to be judged by
his success in a single area—the saving of souls in measurable
numbers. The local minister was judged either by his charismatic powers or by his ability to prepare his congregation for
the preaching of some itinerant ministerial charmer who would
really awaken its members.[12] The "star" system prevailed in religion before it reached the theater. As the evangelical impulse
became more widespread and more dominant, the selection
and training of ministers was increasingly shaped by the revivalist criterion of ministerial merit. The Puritan ideal of the
minister as an intellectual and educational leader was steadily
weakened in the face of the evangelical ideal of the minister as a
popular crusader and exhorter. Theological education itself became more instrumental. Simple dogmatic formulations were
considered sufficient. In considerable measure the churches
withdrew from intellectual encounters with the secular world,
gave up the idea that religion is a part of the whole life of intellectual experience, and often abandoned the field of rational
studies on the assumption that they were the natural province
of science alone. By 1853 an outstanding clergyman complained
that there was "an impression, somewhat general, that an intellectual clergyman is deficient in piety, and that an eminently
pious minister is deficient in intellect."[13]

---

[11]"The Rise of the Evangelical Conception of the Ministry," p. 228.
[12]This reliance upon the charismatic power of the minister has never ceased
to be important. "Truth through Personality," said Phillips Brooks, "is our
description of real preaching." And one of his contemporaries, William Jewett
Tucker, agreed: "The law is, the greater the personality of the preacher, the
larger the use of his personality, the wider and deeper the response of men to
truth." See Robert S. Michaelsen: "The Protestant Ministry in America: 1850
to the Present," in Niebuhr and Williams: op. cit., p. 283.
[13]Bela Bates Edwards: "Influence of Eminent Piety on the Intellectual Powers,"
Writings (Boston, 1853), Vol. II, pp. 497–8. "Are we not apt to dissociate the
intellect from the heart, to array knowledge and piety against each other, to
exalt the feelings at the expense of the judgment, and to create the impression
extensively, that eminent attainments in knowledge and grace are incompatible?" Ibid., pp. 472–3.

2

All the foregoing is in the nature of broad generalization, always somewhat hazardous where American religion is concerned, because of regional differences and the diversity of American religious practices. But I think these generalizations roughly describe the prevalent pattern of American denominational religion, and the characteristic effects of evangelicalism. There were, of course, important conservative churches largely or wholly uninfluenced by the evangelicals. Some of them, like the Roman Catholic Church and the Lutherans, were unaffected except in external ways by the currents of evangelicalism; others, like the Episcopalian, were affected in varying degrees from place to place; others, like the Presbyterian and Congregational, were internally divided by the evangelical movement.

If one compares American society at the close of the Revolution, still largely hemmed in east of the Alleghenies, with the much vaster American society of 1850, when the denominational pattern was basically fixed, one is impressed by the gains of the groups committed to evangelicalism. At the end of the Revolution the three largest and strongest denominations were the Anglicans, the Presbyterians, the Congregationalists. Two of these had once been established in one place or another, and the third had a strong heritage in America. By 1850, the change was striking. The largest single denomination was then the Roman Catholic. Among Protestant groups the first two were now the Methodists and the Baptists, once only dissenting sects. They were followed by the Presbyterians, Congregationalists, and Lutherans, in that order. The Episcopal Church had fallen to eighth place—a significant token of its inability, as an upper-class conservative church, to hold its own in the American environment.[14]

[14]For an excellent statement about the numbers, schismatic divisions, theological commitments, and mutual relations of the various denominations, see Timothy L. Smith: *Revivalism and Social Reform* (New York and Nashville, 1958), chapter 1, "The Inner Structure of American Protestantism." In 1855 all Methodist groups (including North and South) had 1.5 million members; all Baptist groups 1.1 million; all Presbyterian groups 490,000; all Lutheran, German Reformed and similar groups, 350,000. The Congregationalists numbered about 200,000; the Episcopalians, only about 100,000.

By and large, then, the effort to maintain and extend Protestant Christianity, both in the fresh country of the West and in the growing cities, was carried on successfully by the popular, evangelical denominations, not by the liturgical churches. The sweeping gains of the Methodists and Baptists were evidence of their ability to adapt to the conditions of American life. The extent to which the evangelicals had taken over such denominations as the Congregationalists and the Presbyterians is also evidence of the power of the evangelical impulse to transform older religious structures.

The evangelists were the main agents of the spread of Protestant Christianity, religious revival its climactic technique. From the closing years of the eighteenth century, and well on into the nineteenth, successive waves of revivals swept over one or another part of the country. A first wave, running roughly from about 1795 to 1835, was particularly powerful in the New West of Tennessee and Kentucky, then in western New York and the Middle Western states. Its fevers had not long died out when a new wave, beginning about 1840, swept into the towns and cities, demonstrating (as later revivalists like Dwight L. Moody, Billy Sunday, and Billy Graham were to understand) that revivalism need not be only a country phenomenon. This revival reached its climax in the troubled years 1857 and 1858, when great outpourings of the spirit affected New York, Boston, Philadelphia, Cincinnati, Pittsburgh, Rochester, Binghamton, Fall River, and a host of smaller towns.[15]

Revivals were not the sole instruments of this effort. By the third decade of the century, the evangelicals had founded a number of mission societies, Bible and tract societies, education societies, Sunday-school unions, and temperance organizations, most of them organized on interdenominational lines. These agencies were prepared to assist in a crusade whose

[15]My treatment of revivalism owes much to William G. McLoughlin's excellent survey of the whole movement: *Modern Revivalism* (New York, 1959); to Timothy L. Smith's *Revivalism and Social Reform*, already cited, which is particularly good on the period after 1840 and on the urban revivals; to Charles A. Johnson's account of *The Frontier Camp Meeting* (Dallas, 1955), which is especially illuminating with regard to the primitive frontier conditions of 1800–1820; and to Bernard Weisberger's *They Gathered at the River* (Boston, 1958).

first objective would be to Christianize the Mississippi Valley and save it from religious apathy, infidelity, or Romanism, and whose ultimate purpose was to convert every American and then, quite literally, the world. For a long time denominational differences were subordinated in this drive against the common foes of skepticism, passivity, and Romanism. Where denominations did not co-operate as such, the benevolent societies gave scope to individuals who were interested in a common effort; they also offered opportunities for assertive laymen to take the lead in joint benevolent enterprises where clergymen were reluctant. The evangelical groups maintained their co-operation through most of the great revival upsurge of 1795 to 1835. But by about 1837 the common effort had lost its impetus; in part it was checked by resurgent disputes between the sects and by schisms within them; but it declined also because the evangelizing crusade had already succeeded in achieving its main objectives.[16]

Successful it was, by any reasonable criteria. The figures show a remarkable campaign of conversion carried out under inordinately difficult circumstances. In the mid-eighteenth century, America had a smaller proportion of church members than any other nation in Christendom. American religious statistics are notoriously unreliable, but it has been estimated that in 1800 about one of every fifteen Americans was a church member; by 1850 it was one of seven. In 1855 slightly more than four million persons were church members in a population of over twenty-seven million. To the twentieth-century American, accustomed to see a great majority of the population enrolled as church members, these figures may not seem impressive; but it is important to remember that church membership, now bland and often meaningless, was then a more serious and demanding thing; all the evangelizing sects required a personal experience of conversion as well as a fairly stern religious discipline. There were many more church-goers than church members —at least if we are to judge by the twenty-six million church seating accommodations reported in 1860 for a population of

[16]On the common effort of this period, and its recession, see Charles I. Foster: *An Errand of Mercy: The Evangelical United Front, 1790–1837* (Chapel Hill, 1960).

thirty-one million.[17] The most imposing achievements of all the denominations were those of the Methodists and Baptists, who together had almost seventy per cent of all Protestant communicants.

3

As the evangelical tide at first swept westward, and then into the growing cities, it became clear that the religious conquest of America was mainly in the hands of three denominations: the Methodists, the Baptists, and the Presbyterians. A look at these denominations will tell us much about the cultural evangelization of the continent.

Among the evangelical groups, the strongest intellectual tendencies were shown by the Presbyterians, who carried westward the traditions of both New England Congregationalism and colonial Presbyterianism. Under the terms of their Plan of Union of 1801, the Presbyterians and the Congregationalists had co-ordinated their activities in such a way that Congregationalism largely lost its identity outside New England. The Plan of Union was based upon the common Calvinist-derived theology of the two churches; and since most Congregationalists outside of Massachusetts had no profound objection to the Presbyterian form of church organization, Congregational associations in New York and the Middle West tended to be absorbed into Presbyteries. But Congregationalism contributed a distinct cultural leaven and a strong New England flavor to the Presbyterian Church in the Middle West.

The Presbyterians were often fiercely doctrinaire. Appealing to the enterprising and business classes as they did, they also became the elite church among the untraditional

[17]The estimate for 1800 is that of Winfred E. Garrison: "Characteristics of American Organized Religion," *Annals of the American Academy of Political and Social Science*, Vol. CCLVI (March, 1948), p. 20. The figures for 1855 and 1860 are in Timothy L. Smith: op. cit., pp. 17, 20–1. The proportion of the population having church membership rose roughly from about 15 per cent in 1855 to 36 per cent in 1900, 46 per cent in 1926, and 63 per cent in 1958. Will Herberg: *Protestant, Catholic, Jew*, pp. 47–8.

denominations.[18] The Presbyterians were much concerned with fostering an instrumental form of higher education and using it for their sectarian interests. In time they fell victim to their own doctrinal passions and underwent a schism. Much influenced by their Congregational allies and recruits, a portion of the Presbyterian ministry began to preach what was known as the New Haven theology, a considerably liberalized version of Calvinism, which offered a greater hope of divine grace to a larger portion of mankind and lent itself more readily to the spirit and practice of evangelical revivals. The stricter Calvinists of the Old School, more in the Scottish and Scotch-Irish tradition, and based on Princeton College and Princeton Theological Seminary, could not accept the New School ideas. From 1828 to 1837 the church was shaken by controversies and heresy trials. Leaders of Presbyterian evangelism such as Albert Barnes, Lyman Beecher, Asa Mahan, and Lyman Beecher's son Edward were among those charged with heresy. Finally, in 1837, the Old School ousted the New School, and henceforth synods and presbyteries throughout the country had to line up with one or the other of the two factions. Aside from theological differences, the Old School found the New School altogether too sympathetic to interdenominational missionary societies, and in a lesser measure objected to abolitionist sympathizers and agitators, who were strong in New School ranks. Yale, Oberlin College, and Lane Theological Seminary in Cincinnati were the main intellectual centers of New School evangelism. Its great figure was Charles Grandison Finney, the outstanding revivalist in America between the days of Edwards and Whitefield and those of Dwight L. Moody.

The case of Charles Grandison Finney provides a good illustration of the ambiguities of what has been called "Presbygational" evangelism and of the difficulty involved in any facile classification of religious anti-intellectuals. Finney and his associates, being heirs to the intellectual tradition of New England,

---

[18]There is a bit of Protestant folklore which sheds light on the social position of the various churches. A Methodist, it was said, is a Baptist who wears shoes; a Presbyterian is a Methodist who has gone to college; and an Episcopalian is a Presbyterian who lives off his investments.

were often very much concerned with the continuation, if not the development, of learning. The heritage of such excellent transplanted Yankee colleges as Oberlin and Carleton College is a testimony to the persistent vitality of their tradition. It would be difficult to find among other evangelical groups many such literate and intelligent men as Finney, Asa Mahan, or Lyman Beecher; and one may well wonder how many evangelists of the period since the Civil War could have written an autobiography comparable to Finney's *Memoirs*. The minds of these men had been toughened by constant gnawing on Calvinist and neo-Calvinist theology and disciplined by the necessity of carving out their own theological fretwork. But their culture was exceptionally narrow; their view of learning was extremely instrumental; and instead of enlarging their intellectual inheritance, they steadily contracted it.

Finney himself, although now remembered only by those who have a keen interest in American religious or social history, must be reckoned among our great men. The offspring of a Connecticut family which was caught up in the westward movement, he spent his childhood first in Oneida County in central New York and later near the shore of Lake Ontario. After a brief turn at schoolteaching in New Jersey, he qualified for the bar in a small town not far from Utica. His conversion happened when he was twenty-nine. As he tells it, he was praying for spiritual guidance in a darkened law office when he "received a mighty baptism of the Holy Ghost," the first of several such mystical confrontations that he was to have during his life. The following morning he told a client: "I have a retainer from the Lord Jesus Christ to plead his cause, and I cannot plead yours."[19] From that time forward, he belonged entirely to the ministry. In 1824 he was ordained in the Presbyterian church, and from 1825 to 1835 he launched a series of revivals that made him pre-eminent among the evangelical preachers of his time and established him as one of the most compelling figures in the history of American religion.

Finney was gifted with a big voice and a flair for pulpit drama.

---

[19] *Memoirs* (New York, 1876), pp. 20, 24; there is an illuminating account of Finney and enthusiasm in western New York in Whitney R. Cross: *The Burned-Over District* (Ithaca, 1950).

But his greatest physical asset was his intense, fixating, electri-
fying, madly prophetic eyes, the most impressive eyes—except
perhaps for John C. Calhoun's—in the portrait gallery of
nineteenth-century America. The effect upon congregations of
his sermons—alternately rational and emotional, denunciatory
and tender—was overpowering. "The Lord let me loose upon
them in a wonderful manner," he wrote of one of his most
successful early revivals, and "the congregation began to fall
from their seats in every direction, and cried for mercy. . . .
Nearly the whole congregation were either on their knees or
prostrate."[20]

In his theology Finney was a self-made man, an individualistic village philosopher of the sort whose independence
impressed Tocqueville with the capacity of the American to
strike out in pursuit of untested ideas. As a candidate for the
Presbyterian ministry he politely rejected the offer of a group
of interested ministers to send him to Princeton to study theology: "I plainly told them that I would not put myself under
such an influence as they had been under; that I was confident
they had been wrongly educated, and they were not ministers
that met my ideal of what a minister of Christ should be." An
admitted novice in theology, he still refused to accept instruction or correction when it did not correspond with his own
views. "I had read nothing on the subject except my Bible; and
what I had there found upon the subject, I had interpreted
as I would have understood the same or like passages in a law
book." Again: "I found myself utterly unable to accept doctrine on the ground of authority. . . . I had no where to go
but directly to the Bible, and to the philosophy or workings of
my own mind. . . ."[21]

Finney carried from the law into the pulpit an element of
the old Puritan regard for rationality and persuasion (he once
said he spoke to congregations as he would to a jury), which

[20] *Memoirs*, pp. 100, 103.
[21] Ibid., pp. 42, 45–6, 54. This independence persisted, although Finney was
aware that he lacked the learning to interpret the Bible independently. In
time he learned some Latin, Greek, and Hebrew, but he "never possessed so
much knowledge of the ancient languages as to think myself capable of independently criticising our English translation of the Bible." Ibid., p. 5.

he used especially when he confronted educated middle-class congregations. For all his emotional power, he was soon regarded as too rational by some of his evangelical associates, who warned him in 1830 that his friends were asking about him: "Is there not danger of his turning into an intellectualist?"[22] But Finney was proud of his ability to adapt his preaching style to the sensibilities of his public, stressing emotion in the little country villages and adding a note of rational persuasion in more sophisticated Western towns such as Rochester. "Under my preaching, judges, and lawyers, and educated men were converted by scores."[23]

At any rate, there was no danger of Finney's turning into an "intellectualist." In the main, he was true to the revival tradition both in his preaching methods and in his conception of the ministry. He did not admire ignorance in preachers, but he admired soul-winning *results*, no matter how achieved; he scorned the written sermon, because it lacked spontaneity; and he looked upon secular culture as a potential threat to salvation.

Finney had little use for ministerial education or for the kind of preaching he believed the educated clergy were doing. Not having enjoyed, as he said, "the advantages of the higher schools of learning," he was acutely conscious of being regarded as an amateur by the ministry, and he was aware of being considered undignified. Early in his career, he learned that it was widely believed "that if I were to succeed in the ministry, it would bring the schools into disrepute." After some experience in preaching, he became convinced that "the schools are to a great extent spoiling the ministers," who were being given a great deal of Biblical learning and theology but who did not know how to use it. Practice was all: "A man can never learn to preach except by preaching." The sermons of the school-trained ministers "degenerate into literary essays. . . . This reading of elegant literary essays is not preaching. It is gratifying to literary taste, but not spiritually edifying."[24]

[22] McLoughlin: *Modern Revivalism*, p. 55.

[23] *Memoirs*, p. 84; cf. pp. 365–9.

[24] These opinions are all from Finney's *Memoirs*, chapter 7, "Remarks Upon Ministerial Education," pp. 85–97; cf. Finney's *Lectures on Revivals of Religion*, pp. 176–8.

Finney was against all forms of elegance, literary or otherwise. Ornamentation in dress or efforts to improve one's domestic furnishings or taste or style of life were the same to him as the depraved tastes and refinements of smoking, drinking, card-playing, and theater-going. As to literature: "I cannot believe that a person who has ever known the love of God can relish a secular novel." "Let me visit your chamber, your parlor, or wherever you keep your books," he threatened. "What is here? Byron, Scott, Shakespeare, and a host of triflers and blasphemers of God." Even the classical languages, so commonly thought necessary to a minister, were of dubious benefit. Students at Eastern colleges would spend "four years . . . . at *classical* studies and no God in them," and upon graduation such "learned students may understand their *hic, haec, hoc*, very well and may laugh at the humble Christian and call him ignorant, although he may know how to win more souls than five hundred of them."[25] Looking upon piety and intellect as being in open enmity, Finney found young ministers coming "out of college with hearts as hard as the college walls." The trouble with the "seminaries of learning" was that they attempted to "give young men intellectual strength, to the almost entire neglect of cultivating their moral feelings." "The race is an intellectual one. The excitement, the zeal, are all for the intellect. The young man . . . loses the firm tone of spirituality. . . . His intellect improves, and his heart lies waste."[26]

It is difficult to say whether Finney's description of American ministerial education was accurate, but certainly his sentiments represented the prevailing evangelical view. However prosperous the state of intellect was among fledgling ministers, he was against it.

[25]McLoughlin: *Modern Revivalism*, pp. 118–20. The one field in which education had Finney's approval, McLoughlin points out, was science. Like the Puritans of old, he saw science not as a threat to religion but as a means of glorifying God. The Middle Western church colleges have continued this regard for science, and have produced a great many academic scientists. On the reasons for this, see the stimulating discussion by R. H. Knapp and H. B. Goodrich: *Origins of American Scientists* (Chicago, 1952), chapter 19.

[26]*Lectures on Revivals of Religion*, pp. 435–6.

4

I have spoken of Finney at this length because he is a fair representative of the Presbygational evangelical movement: he was neither the most cultivated nor the crudest of its preachers. The effect of the evangelical impulse, of the search for a new religious style to reach the people and save souls, was to dilute the strong intellectual and educational traditions of the Presbyterians and the Congregationalists. The history of the Methodists, the largest church body and one vastly more successful than the Presbyterians in converting the benighted Americans, presents an interesting contrast. The American Methodists began without an intellectualist tradition and with little concern for education or a highly trained ministry; but as time went on, as they lost much of their sectarian spirit and became a settled church, they attracted a membership whose concern for education grew with the years. Before the middle of the nineteenth century, the church was intermittently shaken by controversy between those who looked back nostalgically to the days of the ignorant but effective circuit-riding preachers and those who looked forward to the day when a better-educated clergy would minister to a respectable laity. The history of both the Methodists and the Baptists is an instructive illustration of the divided soul of American religion. On one hand, many of the members of the church gave free expression to a powerfully anti-intellectual evangelism; on the other, in any large church there was always a wing which gave strong voice to a wistful respect for polite, decorative, and largely non-controversial learning. In this regard, that division between the redskin and the paleface which Philip Rahv has characterized as a feature of American letters was prefigured in American religion.

John Wesley himself, an Oxford-trained cleric and a voracious reader, combined in a curious way an extraordinary intellectual vigor with a strong strain of credulity; he had set creditable intellectual standards for Methodism, but his American followers were not vitally interested in sustaining them. The nature of the evangelical spirit itself no doubt made the evangelical revival anti-intellectualist, but American conditions provided a particularly liberating milieu for its anti-intellectual impulse.[27]

Both Wesley himself and Francis Asbury, the first organizer of American Methodism, were itinerant preachers, committed to itinerancy not out of convenience but out of principle. It was their belief that a resident clergy (as in many an English vicarage) tended to go dead and lose its grip on congregations, but itinerants could bring new life to religion. On American soil the practice of itinerancy was a strategic asset that made the Methodists particularly adept at winning the mobile American population back to Christianity. The bulwark and the pride of the early American Methodists were the famous circuit-riding preachers who made up in mobility, flexibility, courage, hard work, and dedication what they might lack in

[27] "It is a fundamental principle with us," Wesley declared in answer to an early detractor of Methodism, "that to renounce reason is to renounce religion, that religion and reason go hand in hand, and that all irrational religion is false religion." R. W. Burtner and R. E. Chiles: *A Compend of Wesley's Theology* (New York, 1954), p. 26. But, as Norman Sykes has remarked, the influence of the evangelical revival was nonetheless intellectually retrograde, for it rose partly from a reaction against the rationalistic and Socinian tendencies that had grown out of the latitudinarian movement in theology. By comparison with the leading theological liberals, Wesley was "almost superstitious in his notions of the special interventions of Providence attendant upon the most ordinary details of his life," Sykes remarks, and "with Whitefield the situation was much worse, for he lacked altogether the education and cultured influence of his colleague. . . ." Norman Sykes: *Church and State in England in the Eighteenth Century* (Cambridge, 1934), pp. 398–9.

A. C. McGiffert writes of the evangelical revival in England: "It turned its face deliberately toward the past instead of toward the future in its interpretation of man and his need. It sharpened the issue between Christianity and the modern age, and promoted the notion that the faith of the fathers had no message for their children. Becoming identified in the minds of many with Christianity, its narrowness and mediaevalism, its emotionalism and lack of intellectuality, its crass supernaturalism and Biblical literalism, its want of sympathy with art and science and secular culture in general, turned them permanently against religion. In spite of the great work accomplished by evangelicalism, the result in many quarters was disaster." *Protestant Thought before Kant* (New York, 1911), p. 175. On the intellectual limitations of early American Methodism, see S. M. Duvall: *The Methodist Episcopal Church and Education up to 1869* (New York, 1928), pp. 5–8, 12.

ministerial training or dignity. These itinerants were justly proud of the strenuous sacrifices they made to bring the gospel to the people. Ill-paid and overworked, they carried out their mission in all weathers and under excruciating conditions of travel. (During a particularly ferocious storm it used to be said: "There's nobody out tonight but crows and Methodist preachers.") Their very hardships seemed testimony enough to their sincerity,[28] and their achievements in reclaiming the unchurched were often truly extraordinary. It was mainly by their efforts that American Methodism grew from a little sect of some 3,000 members in 1775, four years after Asbury's arrival, to the largest Protestant denomination, with over a million and a half members eighty years later.

Whatever claims might be made for the more educated ministry of the high-toned denominations, the circuit-riders knew that their own way of doing things worked. They evolved a kind of crude pietistic pragmatism with a single essential tenet: their business was to save souls as quickly and as widely as possible. For this purpose, the elaborate theological equipment of an educated ministry was not only an unnecessary frill but in all probability a serious handicap; the only justification needed by the itinerant preacher for his limited stock of knowledge and ideas was that he got results, measurable in conversions. To this justification very little answer was possible.

The Methodist leaders were aware, as their critics often observed, that they appealed to the poor and the uneducated, and

[28]One thing these early churchmen understood was how much of their strength lay in the fact that they were not differentiated from the laymen they served either in culture or in style of living. An English visitor, accustomed to the dignity of Anglican bishops, was astounded at his introduction to an Indiana Methodist bishop in 1825. He was surprised to find that the bishop's residence was a common farmhouse. As he waited with some impatience for the bishop to appear, he was told by one of the American ministers that Bishop Roberts was coming. "I see a man there, but no Bishop," he said. "But that is certainly the Bishop," said the American. "No! no! that cannot be, for the man is in his shirtsleeves." Bishop Roberts had been at work on his property. Charles E. Elliott: *The Life of the Rev. Robert R. Roberts* (New York, 1844), pp. 299–300. On the frontier bishop, see Elizabeth K. Nottingham: *Methodism and the Frontier* (New York, 1941), chapter 5.

they proposed to make a virtue of it. Francis Asbury, who was offended by the students at Yale because they were "very genteel," found even the Quakers too "respectable"—"Ah, there is death in that word."[29] In the country at large the Methodists easily outstripped the other denominations in the race for conversions. It was significant that for them New England, where the more settled populace was still somewhat more acquainted with the standards of an educated ministry, presented the stoniest soil, and that they made least headway there. But even there the Methodists began to make incursions upon religious life in the early nineteenth century. At first they ran up their banner in a fashion reminiscent of the New England Awakening: "We have always been more anxious to preserve a *living* rather than a *learned* ministry."[30] Jesse Lee, the leader of New England Methodism, when challenged about his education (a familiar experience there for Methodists competing with the learned clergy), would simply reply that he had education enough to get him around the country.[31] In time, New England became a test case for the adaptability of the Methodists, and they were not found wanting. A process of accommodation to respectability, gentility, and education set in among them which was to herald later and less spectacular adaptations elsewhere.

The Methodists of Norwich, Connecticut, for instance, were described by a pamphleteer of 1800 as being "the most

[29]George C. Baker, Jr.: *An Introduction to the History of Early New England Methodism, 1789–1839* (Durham, 1941), p. 18.

[30]Ibid., p. 14.

[31]Ibid., p. 72. Cf. these words from a Methodist sermon reported to have been delivered in Connecticut: "What I insist upon, my brethren and sisters, is this: larnin isn't religion, and eddication don't give a man the power of the Spirit. It is grace and gifts that furnish the real live coals from off the altar. St. Peter was a fisherman—do you think he ever went to Yale College? Yet he was the rock upon which Christ built his church. No, no, beloved brethren and sisters. When the Lord wanted to blow down the walls of Jericho, he didn't take a brass trumpet, or a polished French horn; no such thing; he took a ram's horn—a plain, natural ram's horn—just as it grew. And so, when he wants to blow down the walls of Jericho . . . he don't take one of your smooth, polite, college learnt gentlemen, but a plain, natural ram's horn sort of a man like me." S. G. Goodrich: *Recollections of a Lifetime* (New York, 1856), Vol. I, pp. 196–7.

weak, unlearned, ignorant, and base part of mankind."[32] But toward the middle of the nineteenth century, a Congregationalist recalled the changes that had taken place in the Methodist church of nearby Ridgefield in words that might have applied widely elsewhere.[33]

> Though, in its origin, it seemed to thrive upon the outcasts of society—its people are now as respectable as those of any other religious society in the town. No longer do they choose to worship in barns, schoolhouses, and by-places; no longer do they affect leanness, long faces, and loose, uncombed hair; no longer do they cherish bad grammar, low idioms, and the euphony of a nasal twang in preaching. . . . The preacher is a man of education, refinement and dignity.

As Methodism diffused throughout the country, along the frontier and into the South, in a milieu less demanding of educational performance, its original dissent from the respectable, the schooled, and the established kept reasserting itself, but its own success again compelled it to wage a battle against the invading forces of gentility. In a more decentralized church, each locality might have been more free to set its own character, but in a denomination with the formidable centralization of the Methodists, the fight over the cultural tone of the church became general. One can follow changing views within the church through one of its highbrow organs, *The Methodist Magazine and Quarterly Review*, and its successor, entitled after 1841 *The Methodist Quarterly Review*. During the early 1830's, it is clear, the Methodists were still acutely aware of being the butt of attacks by the more established religious groups; they were agitated by a difference between those on the one hand who stood for the kind of preaching represented by the itinerants and on the other hand laymen and educated preachers who wanted reforms.[34] In 1834 the controversy was brought to a head by an article by Reverend La Roy Sunderland, which in

---

[32] Baker: op. cit., p. 16.

[33] Goodrich: op. cit., p. 311.

[34] *Methodist Magazine and Quarterly Review*, Vol. XII (January, 1830), pp. 16, 29–68; Vol. XII (April, 1830), pp. 162–97; Vol. XIII (April, 1831), pp. 160–87; Vol. XIV (July, 1832), pp. 377 ff.

effect proposed to undercut the very existence of the itinerants by requiring a good education of all Methodist preachers. "Has the Methodist Church," he asked heatedly,

> any usage or practice in any department of her membership from which one might be led to infer that an education of any kind is indispensably necessary before one can be licensed as a preacher of the Gospel? Nay, are not many of her usages the most directly calculated to give the impression that an education is not necessary? Do we not say in the constant practice of our . . . conferences, that, if one has gifts, grace, and a sound understanding, it is enough?

Sunderland was answered by a spokesman of the old school who said that those who demanded an elaborate theological education were guilty of looking upon preaching as "a 'business,' a trade, a secular profession like '*law* and *medicine*,' requiring a similar 'training.'" The existing ministry was not in fact ignorant, and to say so was merely to "confirm all that our enemies have said." Had not the Methodists opened their own academies, colleges, even their university? "All our young men may now be educated, without having their morals endangered by corrupt and infidel teachers; and without having their Methodism ridiculed out of them, by professors or presidents."[35] As time went on, the periodical itself reflected the victory of the reformers over the old guard, since it ran fewer reminiscences of the old-fashioned itinerant ministers, which had long been a large part of its stock-in-trade, and more essays on fundamental theological subjects and matters of general intellectual interest.

The church, in fact, was in the throes of a significant change during the 1830's and 1840's. The passion for respectability was winning significant victories over the itinerating-evangelical, anti-intellectualist heritage from the previous generations. Again, the policy toward education, both for laymen and for

---

[35]La Roy Sunderland: "Essay on a Theological Education," *Methodist Magazine and Quarterly Review*, Vol. XVI (October, 1834), p. 429. David M. Reese: "Brief Strictures on the Rev. Mr. Sunderland's 'Essay on Theological Education,'" *Methodist Magazine and Quarterly Review*, Vol. XVII (January, 1835), pp. 107, 114, 115.

ministers, was a focal issue. Earlier Methodist efforts in education had been on the whole rather pathetic.[36] In its earliest
days, the church was handicapped in its educational efforts not
only by a lack of numbers but also by a lack of interest which
seemed to pervade it from the lowliest laymen up to Asbury
himself.[37] Most Methodist laymen could not afford to do much
for general education in any case, and theological education
seemed a waste of time for a ministry whose work it would be
to preach a simple gospel to a simple people.

Such early schools as were launched tended to fail for lack
of support. But after the death of Asbury in 1816, a group of
strong-minded educational reformers, mainly from New England, went to work on the increasingly numerous and receptive body of laymen. Their efforts began to bear fruit in the

[36]The fate of the first Methodist "college," Cokesbury College in Abingdon,
Maryland, may serve as an illustration. The project was the pet idea of Dr.
Thomas Coke, Wesley's emissary, who brought to America his alien Oxford-
inspired notions of education and succeeded in persuading the Methodists that
they should found a college, in spite of the objections of Asbury, who would
have preferred a general school such as Wesley had founded at Kingswood.
Founded in 1787, the college was combined at the beginning (as was so often
the case with early American colleges) with a preparatory school, which was far
the more successful of the two. Within a year of its founding, the college lost
all three faculty members by resignation. In 1794 the collegiate department
was closed, leaving only the lower school; plans to re-found the college were
interrupted by two fires in 1795 and 1796, which put an end to the project
altogether. Asbury felt that it had been a waste of time and money. "The Lord
called not Mr. Whitefield nor the Methodists to build colleges. I wished only
for schools. . . ." *The Journal and Letters of Francis Asbury*, ed. by Elmer T.
Clark et al. (London and Nashville, 1958), Vol. II, p. 75. See also Sylvanus M.
Duvall: *The Methodist Episcopal Church and Education up to 1869* (New York,
1928), pp. 31–6. The Virginia Episcopal evangelist, Devereux Jarratt, who knew
something of the educational standards of the Anglican ministry, was appalled
by the Methodist effort at Abingdon: "Indeed, I see not, how any considerate
man could expect any great things from a seminary of learning, while under
the supreme direction and controul of tinkers and taylors, weavers, shoemakers
and country mechanics of all kinds—or, in other words, of men illiterate and
wholly unacquainted with colleges and their contents." *The Life of the Reverend
Devereux Jarratt Written by Himself* (Baltimore, 1806), p. 181.
[37]Nathan Bangs, the first noted historian of the church, remarked that early
Methodist hostility to learning became proverbial, and justly so. *A History of
the Methodist Episcopal Church* (New York, 1842), Vol. II, pp. 318–21.

late 1820's, and Methodists began to sponsor several academies and a few creditable little colleges. Wesleyan in Connecticut, founded in 1831, was followed by Dickinson College (taken over from the Presbyterians in 1833), Allegheny College (1833), Indiana Asbury (founded in 1833, later DePauw), and Ohio Wesleyan (1842), to mention only the most outstanding. From 1835 to 1860 the church started more than two hundred schools and colleges. As in the past, many of the schools were but poorly supported and maintained. The prevailing Methodist view of education was no doubt mainly instrumental—but it represented an advance over the period when learning was not considered to be even of instrumental value to religion. The passion of some of the leading ministers for a more educated clergy, and the growing need to defend their theological position from increasingly subtle critics,[38] finally broke through the Methodist suspicion of a learned ministry. Theological seminaries were still suspect, as fountainheads of heresy; so the first two Methodist seminaries were founded under the name of "Biblical Institutes." Again, the leadership came from New England—not where the Methodists were strongest or most numerous, but where the competing educational standards were most formidable.[39]

The old guard never became reconciled to the newly emerging Methodist church, with its apparatus of academies, colleges, seminaries, and magazines. The most famous of the circuit-riders, Peter Cartwright, included in his remarkable autobiography, written in 1856, a full and forthright statement of the old-fashioned evangelical view of the ministry which deserves quotation at length as a perfect embodiment of the anti-intellectualist position.[40]

[38] Ibid., Vol. III, pp. 15–18.
[39] The first such seminary was not founded until 1847: it was the Methodist General Biblical Institute, organized at Concord, New Hampshire, and later transferred to Boston as the School of Theology of Boston University. It was followed by the Garrett Biblical Institute, at Evanston, Illinois, in 1854. The third such institution, Drew Theological Seminary, awaited the generosity of the famous Wall Street pirate, Daniel Drew; it was founded in 1867.
[40] Charles L. Wallis, ed.: *Autobiography of Peter Cartwright* (New York, 1956), pp. 63–5, 266–8.

Suppose, now, Mr. Wesley had been obliged to wait for a literary and theologically trained band of preachers before he moved in the glorious work of his day, what would Methodism have been in the Wesleyan connection today? . . . If Bishop Asbury had waited for this choice literary band of preachers, infidelity would have swept these United States from one end to the other. . . .

The Presbyterians, and other Calvinistic branches of the Protestant Church, used to contend for an educated ministry, for pews, for instrumental music, for a congregational or stated salaried ministry. The Methodists universally opposed these ideas; and the illiterate Methodist preachers actually set the world on fire (the American world at least) while they were lighting their matches! . . .

I do not wish to undervalue education, but really I have seen so many of these educated preachers who forcibly reminded me of lettuce growing under the shade of a peach-tree, or like a gosling that had got the straddles by wading in the dew, that I turn away sick and faint. Now this educated ministry and theological training are no longer an experiment. Other denominations have tried them, and they have proved a perfect failure. . . .

I awfully fear for our beloved Methodism. Multiply colleges, universities, seminaries, and academies; multiply our agencies, and editorships, and fill them with all our best and most efficient preachers, and you localize the ministry and secularize them too; then farewell to itinerancy; and when this fails we plunge right into Congregationalism, and stop precisely where all other denominations started. . . .

Is it not manifest that the employing so many of our preachers in these agencies and professorships is one of the great causes why we have such a scarcity of preachers to fill the regular work? Moreover, these presidents, professors, agents, and editors get a greater amount of pay, and get it more certainly too, than a traveling preacher, who has to breast every storm, and often falls very far short of his disciplinary allowance. Here is a great temptation to those who are qualified to fill those high offices to seek them, and give up the regular work of preaching and trying to save souls. . . .

Perhaps, among the thousands of traveling and local preachers employed and engaged in this glorious work of saving souls, and building up the Methodist Church, there were not fifty men that had anything more than a common English education, and scores of them not that; and not one of them was ever trained in a theological school or Biblical institute, and yet hundreds of them preached the Gospel with more success and had more seals to their ministry than all the sapient, downy D.D.'s in modern times, who, instead of entering the great and wide-spread harvest-field of souls, sickle in hand, are seeking presidencies or professorships in colleges, editorships, or any agencies that have a fat salary, and are trying to create newfangled institutions where good livings can be monopolized, while millions of poor, dying sinners are thronging the way to hell without God, without Gospel. . . .

I will not condescend to stop and say that I am a friend to learning, and an improved ministry, for it is the most convenient way to get rid of a stubborn truth, for these learned and gentlemanly ministers to turn about and say that all those ministers that are opposed to the present abuses of our high calling, are advocates for ignorance, and that ignorance is the mother of devotion. What has a learned ministry done for the world, that have studied divinity as a science? Look, and examine ministerial history. It is an easy thing to engender pride in the human heart, and this educational pride has been the downfall and ruin of many preeminently educated ministers of the Gospel. But I will not render evil for evil, or railing for railing, but will thank God for education, and educated Gospel ministers who are of the right stamp, and of the right spirit. But how do these advocates for an educated ministry think the hundreds of commonly educated preachers must feel under the lectures we have from time to time on this subject? It is true, many of these advocates for an improved and educated ministry among us, speak in rapturous and exalted strains concerning the old, illiterate pioneers that planted Methodism and Churches in early and frontier times; but I take no flattering unction to my soul from these extorted concessions from these velvet-mouthed and downy D.D.'s; for their real sentiments, if they clearly express them, are, that we were indebted to the ignorance of the people for our success.

This was, no doubt, exactly the sentiment that some of the critics of the itinerants meant to express; but Cartwright might well have seen fit to concede that there was some truth in their case. Not all his evangelical brothers would have denied it. As one group of evangelical workers had put it years earlier to

Finney: "It is more difficult to labour with educated men, with cultivated minds and moreover predisposed to skepticism, than with the uneducated."[41]

5

In many respects the history of the Baptists recapitulates that of the Methodists; but since the Baptists were much less centralized, still more uncompromising, still more disposed to insist on a ministry without educational qualifications and even without salary, they yielded to change later and less extensively than the Methodists. As William Warren Sweet observes: "Among no other religious body was the prejudice against an educated and salaried ministry so strong as among the Baptists, and this prejudice prevailed not only among frontier Baptists, but pretty generally throughout the denomination in the early years of the nineteenth century."[42]

The Baptists, of course, had had bitter experiences with educated ministers and established churches, both in Congregational Massachusetts and Anglican Virginia, where they had been much persecuted. Characteristically, they supplied their ministry from the ranks of their own people. The Baptist preacher might be a farmer who worked on his land or a carpenter who worked at his bench like any other layman, and who left his work for Sunday or weekday sermons or for baptisms and funerals. He had little or no time for books. Such hard-working citizens did not relish competition from other preachers, and they resisted with the most extraordinary ferocity even the home missionary societies which attempted to join with them in spreading the gospel throughout the hinterland. In this resistance to "outside" interference and centralized control they indoctrinated their followers. The word went out

[41]Charles C. Cole: *The Social Ideas of Northern Evangelists, 1826–1860* (New York, 1954), p. 80. Sam Jones, one of the most successful revivalists of the Gilded Age, later said that he preferred to work in the South: "I find the people further South are more easily moved. They haven't got the intellectual difficulties that curse the other portions of the country." McLoughlin: *Modern Revivalism*, pp. 299–300.

[42]*Religion in the Development of American Culture* (New York, 1952), p. 111.

that anyone who had to do with the missionary societies would not be welcomed into the Baptist Associations. "We cannot receive into fellowship either churches or members who join one of those unscriptural societies," declared a Kentucky Baptist Association. And an Illinois group, manifesting in its almost paranoid extreme a suspicion against authority, declared in a circular letter: "We further say to the churches, have nothing to do with the Bible Society, for we think it dangerous to authorize a few designing men to translate the holy Bible. Stand fast in the liberty wherewith Christ has set you free, and be not entangled with the yoke of bondage."[43] One should, I think, check one's impulse to wonder whether the Bible was to be translated by a national convention, and remember that Baptist suspicions had been kept alive by the memory of early persecutions and cruel ridicule.[44]

Baptists opposed missions in good part because they opposed the centralization of authority. Any concession to central church organization, they felt, would be a step toward "the Pope of Rome and the Mother of Harlots." Their uneducated and unsalaried ministers inevitably resented the encroachments of a better-educated and better-paid ministry. It was easy for an unpaid preacher to believe that the educated missionaries from the East were working only for the money it brought them.[45] A contemporary observer concluded that the uneducated preachers were thoroughly aware of their own limitations. But "instead of rejoicing that the Lord had provided better gifts to promote the cause, they felt the irritability of wounded pride, common to narrow and weak minds." This diagnosis was confirmed by the candid retort of a Baptist preacher to a moderator who pointed out that, after all, no one was compelled to

[43]W. W. Sweet, ed.: *Religion on the American Frontier—The Baptists, 1783–1830* (New York, 1931), p. 65n.
[44]Cf. an early Virginia version of the Baptists: "Some of them were hair-lipped, others were blear-eyed, or hump-backed, or bow-legged, or clump-footed; hardly any of them looked like other people." Walter B. Posey: *The Baptist Church in the Lower Mississippi Valley, 1776–1845* (Lexington, Kentucky, 1957), p. 2.
[45]Sweet: *Religion on the American Frontier*, p. 72. "Money and Theological learning seem to be the pride, we fear, of too many preachers of our day." Ibid., p. 65.

listen to missionaries or to give them money unless he chose. "Well, if you must know, Brother Moderator, you know the big trees in the woods overshadow the little ones; and these missionaries will be all great men, and the people will all go to hear them preach, and we shall be all put down. That's the objection."[46]

The Baptists, however, like the old-guard Methodists, could not absolutely resist the pressure for an educated ministry. Here the desire for self-respect and for the respect of others went hand in hand. A Virginia Baptist Association, seeking to found a seminary as early as 1789, gave the following reason:[47]

> Our brethren of other denominations around us Could no longer curse us for not knowing the Law, or discard and Reprobate a great deal of our Teaching for not knowing our Mother tongue, much less the original languages, and if we (in this as we ought in everything), do it with a single eye to The glory of God, and the advancement of the Redeemer's interest Then shall we have sufficient to hope we shall meet with heaven's approbation.

The Baptist laymen were divided between their desire for respectability and their desire for a congenial and inexpensive ministry. By 1830 Baptist leaders had made considerable progress toward providing an educated and salaried ministry, as well as toward raising the educational level of the laity itself. But it was slow work to transform the original bias of the Baptist churches, and it required a constant struggle against entrenched revivalist influences.[48]

6

After the Civil War, important structural changes occurred in the position of the churches. Bringing Christianity to the people of the growing cities became more and more urgent; it became increasingly difficult as well, since the churches had to

[46]Ibid., pp. 73–4. On the intellectual condition of Baptist preachers and the resistance of preachers and laymen to education, see Posey: op. cit., chapter 2.
[47]Wesley M. Gewehr: *The Great Awakening in Virginia, 1740–1790* (Durham, North Carolina, 1930), p. 256.
[48]For efforts in behalf of education, see Posey: op. cit., chapter 8.

find ways of adapting to the sensibilities of the urban worker and of coping with his poverty, as well as holding migrants from the countryside. The interest of revivalists in the cities, which had risen markedly even in the 1840's and 1850's, now took on special urgency. From the time of Dwight L. Moody to that of Billy Graham, success in making conversions in the big cities—and on an international scale—has been the final test of an evangelist's importance. The exhorter whose appeal was limited to the countryside and the small towns was never more than third rate.

Moody was by far the most imposing figure between Finney and Billy Sunday. The son of a poor brickmason in Northfield, Massachusetts, he lost his father at an early age, and was converted at eighteen by a Congregational pastor who had been an itinerant evangelist. In his early twenties Moody was already involved in the religious and welfare activity that had begun in the cities in the decade before the Civil War. Although very successful as a wholesale shoe salesman in Chicago, he decided in 1860 to give up business for independent mission work. During the war he was active in the Y.M.C.A., and soon after the war's end he became president of the Chicago branch. Unschooled since his thirteenth year, he never sought ordination, and never became a minister.

Before 1873, Moody's main achievements were in Y.M.C.A. and Sunday-school work, though he had demonstrated enterprise and curiosity by twice making trips to Great Britain to look into the methods of Christian leaders there. In 1873 he had his first major success when he was invited by British acquaintances to come and conduct a series of evangelical meetings. Taking with him his organist and singer, Ira D. Sankey, he launched in the summer of 1873 upon a two-year series of meetings that brought him to York, Edinburgh, Glasgow, Belfast, Dublin, Manchester, Sheffield, Birmingham, Liverpool, and London. It was estimated that over two and a half millions heard Moody in London alone. Britain had not known such impressive preaching since the days of Wesley and Whitefield. He had left America in obscurity, and he returned in the full blaze of fame; from 1875 to his death in 1899 he was not only the unchallenged leader of a new phase in American evangelism but the greatest figure in American Protestantism.

Moody was quite unlike Finney. Whereas Finney over-whelmed audiences with an almost frightening power, Moody was a benign and lovable man, much happier holding out the promise of heaven than warning of the torments of hell. Short, corpulent, and full-bearded, he resembled General Grant, and the resemblance was more than physical. Like Grant, Moody was inordinately simple, yet of powerful will; and his sieges of souls showed some of the same determined capacity for or-ganization that went into the siege of Vicksburg. Like Grant, he could bring overwhelming superiority in force to bear at the point of weakness, until resistance wore down. Like Grant, he hid his intensity behind an unpretentious façade. Here the resemblance ends. Grant did what he had to do, in spite of an inner lack of confidence; he had been lost in the business world before his war career and he was to be lost again in politics af-terwards. Moody's self-confidence was enormous. He had been well on his way toward a fortune when, still very young, he gave up business for religion; and it is hard to imagine him fail-ing in any practical sphere of life in which endurance, shrewd-ness, decision, simple manliness, and a human touch were the prime requisites. He was immensely ignorant—ignorant even of grammar, as critics of his sermons were forever saying; but he knew his Bible and he knew his audiences. Unsensational, untiring, he repeatedly confronted them with his inevitable question: "Are you a Christian?" and swept them along toward salvation with breathless torrents of words uttered in a voice that easily filled the huge auditoriums in which he flourished.

Moody's message was broad and nondenominational—it is significant that he had the endorsement at one time or another of practically every denomination except the Roman Catholics, the Unitarians, and the Universalists[49]—and he cared not a whit for the formal discussion of theological issues ("My theol-ogy! I didn't know I had any. I wish you would tell me what my theology is.").[50] The knowledge, the culture, the science of his time meant nothing to him, and when he touched upon them at all, it was with a note as acid as he was ever likely to strike. In this respect, he held true to the dominant evangelical tradition.

[49]McLoughlin: *Modern Revivalism*, pp. 219–20.
[50]Gamaliel Bradford: *D. L. Moody: A Worker in Souls* (New York, 1927), p. 61.

Although he had no desire to undermine the established ministry or its training, he cordially approved of laymen in religious
work and felt that seminary-educated ministers "are often educated away from the people."[51] He denigrated all education
that did not serve the purposes of religion—for secular education, he said, instead of telling men what a bad lot they
are, flatters them and tells them "how angelic they are because
they have some education. An educated rascal is the meanest
kind of rascal." Aside from the Bible, he read almost nothing.
"I have one rule about books. I do not read any book, unless
it will help me to understand *the* book." Novels? They were
"flashy. . . . I have no taste for them, no desire to read them;
but if I did I would not do it." The theater? "You say it is part
of one's education to see good plays. Let that kind of education go to the four winds." Culture? It is "all right in its place,"
but to speak of it before a man is born of God is "the height of
madness." Learning? An encumbrance to the man of spirit: "I
would rather have zeal without knowledge; and there is a good
deal of knowledge without zeal." Science? It had become, by
Moody's time, a threat to religion rather than a means for the
discovery and glorification of God. "It is a great deal easier
to believe that man was made after the image of God than to
believe, as some young men and women are being taught now,
that he is the offspring of a monkey."[52]

True to the evangelical tradition in his attitude toward intellect and culture, Moody nevertheless marked for his generation a new departure in the history of revivalism, a departure
not from goals or attitudes but from methods. In the days of
Jonathan Edwards and his contemporaries, it had been customary to look upon revivals as the consequence of divine vis-
itations. Edwards had referred to the Northampton revival, in
the title of his first great work, as a "surprising work of God";
and it was the adjective here that suggested the Northampton
preacher's conception that the affair was not altogether in the
control of human will. Whitefield, one surmises, knew better;
as a veteran promoter of revivals, he must have had more than
an inkling that human will had something to do with it. The

[51]McLoughlin: *Modern Revivalism*, p. 273.
[52]Bradford: *Moody*, pp. 24, 25–6, 30, 35, 37, 64, 212.

preferred theory, none the less, was that divine intervention was the essential active agent and that the human will was relatively passive. By the time of Finney, this notion was in decline, and the voluntarism characteristic of the American evangelical tradition was in the ascendant. "*Religion is the work of man*," Finney insisted. It is true, he admitted, that God interposes his spirit to make men obey His injunctions. But the spirit is always at work—it is, as we would now say, a constant; the human response is the variable. Revivals take place when the human will rises to the occasion. A revival of religion, Finney asserted, "is not a miracle, or dependent on a miracle, in any sense. It is a purely philosophical result of the right use of the constituted means." Hence, it was false and slothful to sit and wait for the miraculous reoccurrence of revivals. "You see why you have not a revival. It is only because you don't want one."[53]

Finney's *Lectures on Revivals of Religion* were wholly devoted to showing what the right means were and how revivals could be produced, so to speak, at will. But it is noteworthy that the means about which Finney was speaking were not simply mechanical; they were not mere techniques; they were a series of instructions as to how the heart, the mind, and the will could all be marshaled to the great end of reviving religion. Here is where Moody and his generation, adapting revivalism to the spirit of the new industrial age, made their departure. It would be impertinent to suggest that a man of Moody's force and sincerity lacked the necessary inward psychic resources; but it is important to note that he added something else—the techniques of business organization. Finney's revivalism belonged to the age of Andrew Jackson and Lyman Beecher; Moody's belonged to the age of Andrew Carnegie and P. T. Barnum.

Finney's revivals, though carefully planned, had been conducted without much apparatus. Moody's brought an imposing machinery into play.[54] Advance agents were sent to

---

[53] *Lectures on Revivals of Religion*, pp. 9, 12, 32. I have hardly done justice to the full range of Finney's argument for the role of human agency in bringing about revivals; it is stated cogently in the first chapter of his book.

[54] See the excellent account of Moody's revival machinery, in McLoughlin: *Modern Revivalism*, chapter 5, "Old Fashioned Revival with the Modern Improvements."

arrange invitations from local evangelical ministers. Advertising campaigns were launched, requiring both display posters
and newspaper notices (the latter inserted in the amusement
pages). Churches, even the largest, could no longer seat the
crowds. Large auditoriums had to be found, and where there
were none they had to be erected. If temporary, they were afterwards sold and scrapped for what they would bring. The
building for Moody's Boston meetings cost $32,000. To defray
his imposing expenses—a series of meetings in one city might
require from $30,000 (New York) to $140,000 (London)
—finance committees were established; through them the
resources of local businessmen could be tapped. But Moody
did not have to depend only upon small businessmen. Cyrus
McCormick and George Armour helped him in Chicago, Jay
Cooke and John Wanamaker in Philadelphia, J. P. Morgan and
Cornelius Vanderbilt II in New York. The meetings required
staffs of local ushers to handle the crowds, staffs of assistants
for follow-ups on the spiritual condition of Moody's converts
in after-sermon "inquiry" sessions. Then there were the arrangements for the music—Sankey's singing and his organ, the
recruitment of teams of local singers for choirs of from 600
to 1,000 persons for each city. Like almost anything else in
business, the results of Moody's meetings became the object of
measurement. At first Moody himself objected to making estimates of the numbers of souls saved—3,000, they said, in London, 2,500 in Chicago, 3,500 in New York—but in later years
he began to use "decision cards" to record systematically the
names and addresses of those who came to the inquiry room.

Finney, we have seen, was proud that some of his legal training carried over into his most rational sermons. Perhaps less
self-consciously, Moody's preaching revealed his early business
experience. At times he talked like a salesman of salvation. He
seemed still to be selling a product when he mounted a chair at
an "inquiry" meeting to say: "Who'll take Christ now? That's
all you want. With Christ you have eternal life and everything
else you need. Without Him you must perish. He offers Himself to you. Who'll take Him?"[55] Or when he was heard to
say: "If a man wants a coat he wants to get the best coat he

[55] Bernard Weisberger: *They Gathered at the River*, p. 212.

can for the money. This is the law the world around. If we show men that religion is better than anything else, we shall win the world," one can only concur with the judgment of Gamaliel Bradford that this is "the dialect of the shoe-trade."[56] The point was not lost on contemporaries. "As he stood on the platform," Lyman Abbott wrote of Moody, "he looked like a business man; he dressed like a business man; he took the meeting in hand as a business man would; he spoke in a business man's fashion."[57]

Whereas Finney had been a radical on at least one major social issue, that of slavery, Moody was consistently conservative; the union between the evangelical and the business mind which was to characterize subsequent popular revivalists was, to a great extent, his work. His political views invariably resembled those of the Republican businessmen who supported him, and he was not above making it clear how useful the Gospel was to the propertied interests. "I say to the rich men of Chicago, their money will not be worth much if communism and infidelity sweep the land." Again: "There can be no better investment for the capitalists of Chicago than to put the saving salt of the Gospel into these dark homes and desperate centers. . . ." But it would be wrong to suggest that he was pandering. His conservatism was a reflection of his premillennialist beliefs, which in him engendered a thoroughgoing social pessimism. Man was naturally and thoroughly bad, and nothing was to be expected of him on earth. "I have heard of reform, reform, until I am tired and sick of the whole thing. It is regeneration by the power of the Holy Ghost that we need." As a consequence, Moody showed no patience for any kind of sociological discussion.[58] Man was, and always had been, a failure in all his works. The true task was to get as many souls as possible off the sinking ship of this world.

[56] Op. cit., p. 243.
[57] Silhouettes of My Contemporaries (New York, 1921), p. 200.
[58] McLoughlin: Modern Revivalism, pp. 167, 269, 278; Bradford: op. cit., pp. 220-1.

7

In one important respect, the revivalism of Moody's era had
to be more controlled than its predecessors. The "enthusiastic" manifestations of the old-time revivals—the shriekings,
groanings, faintings, howlings, and barkings—were now in-
admissible. It was not merely that pietism had grown more
restrained, but that the city revivals took place under the critical
eye of the urban press and nothing could be allowed to happen
that would lose the sympathetic interest of the public. The loss
of control that had been permissible in village churches and at
camp meetings might also have created dangerous scenes in the
huge auditoriums of the big-time revivals. The most intelligent
sympathizers of revivals had always found the extreme manifestations of enthusiasm an embarrassment. Finney, though he
regularly induced them, thought of them as necessary encum-
brances and evils. Moody, determined to have done with them,
would interrupt a sermon to have ushers remove a disturbed
member of the audience. Even an excess of "Amens" or "Hal-
lelujahs" would bring him to call out: "Never mind, my friend,
I can do all the hollering."[59] His successor, Billy Sunday, believing that "a man can be converted without any fuss," held a
stern hand over audiences, and instructed ushers to throw out
disorderly manifestants. "Two can't windjam at once, brother;
let me do it," he once yelled. And on another occasion: "Just
a minute, sister, hold your sparker back and save a little gasoline."[60] Decorum—of a sort—was to be kept; and there must
be no distractions from the performance of the star.

Although the conditions of city evangelism demanded restraint in audiences, they seem to have released the preachers.
For the historian of popular sensibilities, one of the most arresting aspects of the development of evangelicalism is the decline
of the sermon from the vernacular to the vulgar. The conception that preaching should be plain, unaffected, unlearned, and
unadorned, so that it would reach and move simple people,

[59]McLoughlin: *Modern Revivalism*, p. 245; cf. Bradford: op. cit., p. 223.
[60]McLoughlin: *Modern Revivalism*, p. 433–4; also *Billy Sunday Was His Real
Name*, pp. 127–8.

had always been central to pietism. Finney had argued that the truly good sermon, like the truly good life, would be trimmed of elegance and pretense. He had spoken movingly for the vernacular style in sermons, and preferred the extemporaneous to the written sermon because spontaneous utterance would be more direct and closer to common speech. When men are entirely in earnest, he said, "their language is in point, direct and simple. Their sentences are short, cogent, powerful." They appeal to action and get results. "This is the reason why, formerly, the ignorant Methodist preachers, and the earnest Baptist preachers produced so much more effect than our most learned theologians and divines. They do so now."[61]

One can hardly resist the cogency of Finney's pleas for the vernacular sermon. Is there not, after all, an element of the vernacular in most good preaching? One thinks, for example, of Luther visualizing the Nativity for his listeners with the utmost directness and intimacy:[62]

> Bad enough that a young bride married only a year could not have had her baby at Nazareth in her own house instead of making all that journey of three days when heavy with child! . . . The birth was still more pitiable. No one regarded this young wife bringing forth her first-born. No one took her condition to heart. . . . There she was without preparation: no light, no fire, in the dead of night, in thick darkness. . . . I think myself if Joseph and Mary had realized that her time was so close she might perhaps have been left in Nazareth. . . . Who showed the poor girl what to do? She had never had a baby before. I am amazed that the little one did not freeze.

Perhaps, too, the plain style of Finney's own utterance was no more than an inheritance from the best Puritan preaching. Surely the greatest image in the history of American preaching

---

[61] *Memoirs*, pp. 90–1. Finney's conception of preaching is expounded at length in *Lectures on Revivals of Religion*, chapter 12. Among his rules for the manner of ministerial discourse were these: "It should be *conversational*." "It must be in the *language of common life*." It should be parabolical—that is, illustrations should be drawn from real or supposed incidents of common life, and "from the common business of society." It should be repetitious, but without monotony.

[62] Roland H. Bainton: *Here I Stand: A Life of Martin Luther* (New York and Nashville, 1940), p. 354.

was Jonathan Edwards's image of the soul as a spider held over the fire in the kitchen stove, suspended by a silken thread at the mercy of God. And is it not the vernacular note itself which has given American literature much of its originality and distinction?

All true enough, and justification enough for Finney's own conception of the sermon. The problem for later evangelism was to stabilize the vernacular style at some point before it would merely confirm, or even exaggerate, the coarsest side of popular sensibility. A contemporary of Finney's, Jabez Swan, was no doubt merely adding a racy colloquial touch when he described Jonah's fish in these terms:[63]

> The great fish splashed, foamed, and pitched up and down, here and there, and everywhere, to get rid of his burden. At length, growing more and more sick, as well he might, he made for the shore and vomited the nauseous dose out of his mouth.

Moody's preaching, spilled out at 220 words a minute, was colloquial without being coarse, though Moody, as befitted his time, introduced a heavy note of sentimentality that Finney might have found strange. Like Finney, Moody was impatient with what he called "essay preaching." "It is a stupid thing to try to be eloquent," he said.[64] Conventional audiences were put off by his folkish informality ("Everyone is going to be disappointed in these meetings if he ain't quickened himself") and the London *Saturday Review* found him "simply a ranter of the most vulgar type."[65] But in the main, his sermons stopped short of vulgarity. Younger contemporaries, such as Sam Jones, were striking a broader and more aggressive tone: "Half of the literary preachers in this town are A.B.'s, Ph.D's, D.D.'s, LL.D.'s, and A.S.S.'s." "If anyone thinks he can't stand the truth rubbed in a little thicker and faster than he ever had it before, he'd better get out of here."[66] It was this note, and not Moody's, that was to be imitated by Billy Sunday.

[63]McLoughlin: *Modern Revivalism*, p. 140.
[64]Bradford: op. cit., p. 101. On his preaching style, see also McLoughlin: *Modern Revivalism*, pp. 239 ff.; there is a wide range of illustrative matter in J. Wilbur Chapman: *The Life and Work of Dwight L. Moody* (Boston, 1900).
[65]Bradford: op. cit., p. 103.
[66]McLoughlin: *Modern Revivalism*, p. 288.

With the arrival of Billy Sunday, whose career as an evangelist spans the years 1896 to 1935, one reaches the nadir in evangelical rhetoric. By comparison, a contemporary of ours like Billy Graham seems astonishingly proper and subdued. Sunday's career in some ways parallels Moody's. His father had been an Iowa bricklayer who died in the Union Army in 1862. Sunday had a rather poverty-stricken country boyhood, left high school before graduating, and was picked up in 1883 by a scout for the Chicago White Stockings baseball team. From 1883 to 1891, Sunday made his living as a ballplayer. His later career sounds as though one of the ineffable egomaniac outfielders of Ring Lardner's stories had got religion and turned to evangelism. Like Moody, Billy Sunday went into evangelical work through the Y.M.C.A. A convert in 1886, he began to give Y.M.C.A. talks, worked as a Y.M.C.A. secretary after leaving baseball, and started preaching in 1896. Unlike Moody, who accepted his own lay status, Sunday hungered for ordination, and in 1903 faced a board of examiners of the Chicago Presbytery. After a series of answers in the general tenor of "That's too deep for me," the examination was waived on the ground that Sunday had already made more converts than all his examiners, and he was elevated to the ministry without further inquiry.

After 1906 Sunday left the small towns of the Midwest, where he had his early successes, and began to reach the medium-sized towns. By 1909 he was an established big-time evangelist in the major cities, the heir to Moody's mantle. In one way or another, political leaders like Bryan, Wilson, and Theodore Roosevelt gave him their blessings; tycoons opened their coffers to him, as they had to Moody; the respectable world found him respectable; and millions came to hear him. In 1914 the readers of the *American Magazine*, responding to a poll on the question: "Who is the greatest man in the United States?" put him in eighth place, tied with Andrew Carnegie. He conducted his evangelical enterprise in most external respects in a manner similar to Moody's; but there were two important differences. Moody had needed and sought the invitations of local ministers; Sunday went further and often bulldozed reluctant clerics until they fell in line. And Moody had lived comfortably but without great wealth, whereas Sunday became a millionaire, and replied to critics of the cost of his revivals by saying: "What I'm paid for my work makes it only about $2 a soul, and I get less proportionately for the number I convert than any other living evangelist." Both men were immensely businesslike, but Moody's personal indulgence was limited to heavy meals, and Sunday wore ostentatious clothes. With his striped suits, hard collars, diamond pins and studs, shiny patent-leather shoes, and spats, he resembled a hardware drummer out to make time with the girls. Like Moody, he had his musical accompanist, Homer A. Rodeheaver; but Sankey had sung sweetly, and Rodeheaver began to jazz the hymns.[67]

Finney would have marveled at Sunday's style, and at the elements of entertainment in the work of this revivalist, who hired a circus giant as a doorman, broke into broad imitations of his contemporaries (one of Finney's most solemn injunctions had been against levity), shed his coat and vest during a heated sermon, and punctuated his harangues with feats of physical agility on the platform. Sunday was proud of his slanginess. "What do I care if some puff-eyed little dibbly-dibbly preacher goes tibbly-tibbling around because I use plain Anglo-Saxon words? I want people to know what I mean and that's why I try to get down where they live." Literary preachers, he said, tried "to please the highbrows and in pleasing them miss the masses." The language used by Moody, simple though it was, lacked savor enough for Sunday. Moody had said: "The standard of the Church is so low that it does not mean much." Sunday asserted: "The bars of the Church are so low that any old hog with two or three suits of clothes and a bank roll can crawl through." Moody had been content with: "We don't want intellect and money-power, but the power of God's word." Sunday elaborated: "The church in America would die of dry rot and sink forty-nine fathoms in hell if all members were multimillionaires and college graduates."[68]

Classic folkish preaching had tried to treat Biblical stories in realistic intimacy; Sunday had the powers of darkness and light talking in current small-town lingo. In his sermons the Devil

[67]On Sunday's life, see William G. McLoughlin's thorough and perceptive biography: *Billy Sunday Was His Real Name.*
[68]McLoughlin: *Billy Sunday*, pp. 164, 169.

tempted Jesus with these words: "Turn some of these stones into bread and get a square meal! Produce the goods!" and he told the miracle of the loaves in this way:

> But Jesus looked around and spied a little boy whose ma had given him five biscuits and a couple of sardines for his lunch, and said to him, "Come here, son, the Lord wants you." Then He told the lad what He wanted, and the boy said, "It isn't much, Jesus, but what there is you're mighty welcome to it."

Those who were appalled in the 1920's by the vulgarity of Bruce Barton's *The Man Nobody Knows* may not have realized how much Sunday had done to pave the way for Barton's portrayal of Christ as a go-getter: "Jesus could go some; Jesus Christ could go like a six-cylinder engine, and if you think Jesus couldn't, you're dead wrong." He felt it important also to establish the point that Jesus "was no dough-faced, lick-spittle proposition. Jesus was the greatest scrapper that ever lived."[69]

[69]Weisberger: *They Gathered at the River*, p. 248; McLoughlin: *Billy Sunday*, pp. 177, 179. Sunday's language here expresses a new violence of expression, very common among the clergy during the First World War. See Ray H. Abrams: *Preachers Present Arms* (New York, 1933).

CHAPTER V

The Revolt against Modernity

I

BILLY SUNDAY'S rhetorical coarseness was a surface phenomenon, less important for itself than for what it revealed
about the position of evangelism in his time. Underlying the
slang and the vulgarity was a desperately embattled spirit that
would have been quite unfamiliar to Finney or Moody. It is true
that these earlier evangelists were also embattled—embattled
with the forces of hell, and militant in the saving of souls. But
Sunday was embattled in addition—and at times one suspects
even primarily—with the spirit of modernism. Quite aside
from purely personal temperament, which has its importance
too, his tone derives its significance and popularity from the
travail of fundamentalism in a waning phase of its history.

As we move into the twentieth century, we find the evangelical tradition rapidly approaching a crisis. The first part of
this crisis was internal: it was no longer possible to put off or
avoid a choice between the old religious ways and modernism, since the two had come into more open and more universal confrontation. Fundamentalists, both lay and clerical,
were anguished to see a large portion of the great evangelical
denominations, the Baptists and Methodists, succumb at least
in part to modernist ideas, and their resentment against these
defectors added to their bitterness. The second part was external: secular challenges to religious orthodoxy were older than
the nation itself, but the force of Darwinism, combined with
the new urban style, gave such challenges an unprecedented
force. Moreover, the expanding education and the mobility
of the whole country, and the development of a nationwide
market in ideas, made it increasingly difficult for the secular,
liberated thought of the intelligentsia and the scriptural faith of
the fundamentalists to continue to move in separate grooves.
So long as secularism in its various manifestations was an elite
affair, fundamentalists could either ignore it or look upon it as
a convenient scapegoat for militant sermons. But now the two
were thrown into immediate and constant combat—this was

the first consequence for religion of the development of a mass culture, and of its being thrown into contact with high culture.

I do not want to suggest that a kind of quiet religious withdrawal from the mental environment of secular culture ceased to be possible; but for many combative types it ceased to be desirable. Religion, for many individuals or groups, may be an expression of serene belief, personal peace, and charity of mind. But for more militant spirits it may also be a source or an outlet for animosities. There is a militant type of mind to which the hostilities involved in any human situation seem to be its most interesting or valuable aspect; some individuals live by hatred as a kind of creed, and we can follow their course through our own history in the various militant anti-Catholic movements, in anti-Masonry, and a variety of crank enthusiasms. There are both serene and militant fundamentalists; and it is hard to say which group is the more numerous. My concern here is with the militants, who have thrown themselves headlong into the revolt against modernism in religion and against modernity in our culture in general. We are here dealing, then, with an ever smaller but still far from minuscule portion of the whole body of the evangelical tradition—a type which has found that it can compensate with increasing zeal and enterprise for the shrinkage in its numbers.

The two new notes which are evident in a most striking form in Billy Sunday's rhetoric, the note of toughness and the note of ridicule and denunciation, may be taken as the signal manifestations of a new kind of popular mind. One can trace in Sunday the emergence of what I would call the one-hundred per cent mentality—a mind totally committed to the full range of the dominant popular fatuities and determined that no one shall have the right to challenge them. This type of mentality is a relatively recent synthesis of fundamentalist religion and fundamentalist Americanism, very often with a heavy overlay of severe fundamentalist morality.[1] The one-hundred percenter,

---

[1] Very commonly a sexual fundamentalism—thoroughgoing in its fear both of normal sex and of deviation—is linked with the other two. One frequently gets the feeling from later fundamentalist sermons that they were composed for audiences terrified of their own sexuality. It would be instructive in this respect to trace the treatment of dancing and prostitution in evangelical literature.

who will tolerate no ambiguities, no equivocations, no reservations, and no criticism, considers his kind of committedness an evidence of toughness and masculinity. One observer remarked of Sunday that no man of the time, "not even Mr. Roosevelt himself, has insisted so much on his personal, militant masculinity." Jesus was a scrapper, and his disciple Sunday would destroy the notion that a Christian must be "a sort of dishrag proposition, a wishy-washy sissified sort of galoot that lets everybody make a doormat out of him." "Lord save us from off-handed, flabby-cheeked, brittle-boned, weak-kneed, thin-skinned, pliable, plastic, spineless, effeminate ossified three-karat Christianity." Sunday wanted to kill the idea "that being a Christian takes a man out of the busy whirl of the world's life and activity and makes him a spineless, effeminate proposition." He struck a Rooseveltian note in his assertion: "Moral warfare makes a man hard. Superficial peace makes a man mushy"; and he summed up his temper when he confessed: "I have no interest in a God who does not smite."[2]

To assess the historical significance of this growing militancy, let us go back to the earlier history of the evangelical movement. Sidney E. Mead has remarked that, after about 1800, "Americans have in effect been given the hard choice between being intelligent according to the standards prevailing in their intellectual centers, and being religious according to the standards prevailing in their denominations."[3] But this choice was not nearly so clear nor the problem so acute after 1800 as it was after 1860, and particularly after 1900. Up to about 1800 there was, as Mead himself has pointed out, a kind of informal understanding between the pietist and the rationalist mind, based chiefly on a common philanthropism and on a shared passion for religious liberty. One thinks, for example, of Benjamin Franklin listening to Whitefield's preaching in Philadelphia,

Sunday felt that "the swinging of corners in the square dance brings the position of the bodies in such attitude that it isn't tolerated in decent society," and proposed a law preventing children over twelve from attending dancing schools and another prohibiting dancing until after marriage. McLoughlin: *Billy Sunday*, pp. 132, 142.
[2] McLoughlin: *Billy Sunday*, pp. 141–2, 175, 179.
[3] "Denominationalism: the Shape of Protestantism in America," p. 314.

emptying his pockets for the support of one of the Awakener's favored charities, and, after the regular clergy had refused their pulpits to Whitefield, contributing to the erection of a meeting house that would be available to any preacher. This rapprochement between pietism and rationalism reached a peak at the time of Jefferson's presidency, when the dissenting groups, notably the Baptists, gladly threw their support behind a man who, rationalist or not, stood so firmly for religious freedom.[4]

It is true, of course, that in the 1790's, when the influence of Deism reached its peak in America, there was a great deal of frightened talk about the incursions of infidelity. These alarms mainly affected the members of the established denominations whose colleges and defecting believers were involved.[5] It is also true that Voltaire and Tom Paine served as whipping boys for preachers during the revivals that broke out after 1795.[6] But most early evangelists were far too realistic to imagine that a learned and intellectually self-conscious skepticism was a real menace to the simple public they were trying to reach. They knew that the chief enemy was not rationalism but religious indifference, that their most important work was not with people who had been exposed to Tom Paine's assaults on the Bible but

[4]See, for instance, on the Republicanism of New England Baptists, William A. Robinson: *Jeffersonian Democracy in New England* (New Haven, 1916) pp. 128–41.

[5]The most vivid account of the hysteria over revolution and infidelity that followed the French Revolution is that of Vernon Stauffer in *New England and the Bavarian Illuminati* (New York, 1918). Although a gentle variety of philosophical skepticism was indeed widespread among the American elite at the close of the eighteenth century, it was mainly a private creed without any bent toward proselytizing. After the French Revolution and the rise of Jeffersonian democracy, upper-class rationalists were less disposed than ever to propagate their rationalism among the public. A crusading skeptic like Elihu Palmer, who wanted to unite republicanism and skepticism for the middle and lower classes, found it very hard going, though there were a few Deistic societies in New York, Philadelphia, Baltimore, and Newburgh. See G. Adolph Koch: *Republican Religion* (New York, 1933).

[6]Catherine C. Cleveland: *The Great Revival in the West, 1797–1805* (Chicago, 1916), p. 111. Martin E. Marty, in *The Infidel* (Cleveland, 1961), argues that infidelity was much too weak in America to be of grave importance in itself, but that it became important as a scare word in the orthodox sermon and in theological recriminations between the religious groups.

with those who had never been exposed to the Bible. As evangelicals made increasingly impressive gains from 1795 to 1835, and as Deism lapsed into relative quiescence, the battle between pietism and rationalism fell into the background. There was much more concern among evangelicals with rescuing the vast American interior from the twin evils of Romanism and religious apathy than there was with dispelling the rather faint afterglow of the Enlightenment.

After the Civil War, all this changed, and rationalism once more took an important place among the foes of the evangelical mind. The coming of Darwinism, with its widespread and pervasive influence upon every area of thinking, put orthodox Christianity on the defensive; and the impact of Darwinism was heightened by modern scholarly Biblical criticism among the learned ministry and among educated laymen. Finally, toward the end of the century, the problems of industrialism and the urban churches gave rise to a widespread movement for a social gospel, another modernist tendency. Ministers and laymen alike now had to choose between fundamentalism and modernism; between conservative Christianity and the social gospel.

As time went on, a great many clerics—including a substantial number with evangelical sympathies—became liberal.[7] Those who did not found themselves in the distressing situation of having to live in the same world with a small minority of rationalist skeptics, and of seeing constant defections from orthodox Christianity to modernism: from a Christianity essentially bound up with the timeless problem of salvation to one busied with such secular things as labor unions, social settlements, and even the promotion of socialism. By the end of the century it was painfully clear to fundamentalists that they were losing much of their influence and respectability. One can now discern among them the emergence of a religious style shaped by a desire to strike back against everything modern —the higher criticism, evolutionism, the social gospel, rational criticism of any kind. In this union of social and theological

---

[7]On divergent patterns in the ministry, see Robert S. Michaelson: "The Protestant Ministry in America: 1850 to the Present," in H. Richard Niebuhr and D. D. Williams: op. cit., pp. 250–88.

reaction, the foundation was laid for the one-hundred per cent mentality.

The gradual stiffening can be seen in a comparison of Moody and his most prominent successor. Moody's views were akin to those later called fundamentalist, but his religious style had already been formed by the early 1870's, when the incursions of modernism were still largely restricted to highbrow circles. His references to the emerging conflict between fundamentalism and modernism were determined partly by his personal benignity and partly by the general state of the conflict itself in his formative years. The Bible is the inspired word of God, he insisted; there is nothing in it that is not wise, nothing that is not good, and any attempt to undermine any part of it is the Devil's work. "If there was one portion of the Scripture untrue, the whole of it went for nothing." It was still possible simply to dismiss science, and even rational efforts to interpret the Bible—"the Bible was not made to understand." Talk about figurative language and symbolic meanings made him impatient. "That's just the way men talk now and just figure away everything."[8] For all this, there was a notable freedom from bigotry and militancy in Moody's utterances. He preferred to keep peace with those religious liberals whom he respected; he was glad to have them at his Northfield Conferences, and he disliked hearing them called infidels by other conservatives. It is indicative of the character of his inheritance that of the two educational centers founded under his auspices, one, the Moody Bible Institute at Chicago, later became fundamentalist, whereas the other, Northfield Seminary in Massachusetts, became modernist; both claimed that they were carrying on in the spirit of Moody's work.

With Sunday it was quite another matter. He brooked no suggestion that fundamentalism was not thoroughgoing, impregnable, and tough. He turned his gift for invective as unsparingly on the higher criticism and on evolution as on everything else that displeased him. "There is a hell and when the Bible says so don't you be so black-hearted, low-down, and degenerate as to say you don't believe it, you big fool!" Again:

[8]Bradford: op. cit., pp. 58–60; McLoughlin: *Modern Revivalism*, p. 213; on Moody's pragmatic tolerance, see pp. 275–6.

"Thousands of college graduates are going as fast as they can straight to hell. If I had a million dollars I'd give $999,999 to the church and $1 to education." "When the word of God says one thing and scholarship says another, scholarship can go to hell!"[9]

2

The note of petulance became increasingly shrill. The challenge to orthodoxy had grown too formidable and penetrated too many focal centers of social power and respectability to be taken lightly. Presumably, the fundamentalists themselves were afflicted on occasion by nagging doubts about the adequacy of their faith, which was now being questioned everywhere. As Reinhold Niebuhr has remarked: "Extreme orthodoxy betrays by its very frenzy that the poison of skepticism has entered the soul of the church; for men insist most vehemently upon their certainties when their hold upon them has been shaken. Frantic orthodoxy is a method for obscuring doubt."[10]

The feeling that rationalism and modernism could no longer be answered in debate led to frantic efforts to overwhelm them by sheer violence of rhetoric and finally by efforts at suppression and intimidation which reached a climax in the anti-evolution crusade of the 1920's. The time had come, as Sunday himself asserted in a sermon of that decade, when "America is not a country for a dissenter to live in."[11] But unfortunately for the fundamentalists, *they* had become the dissenters; they lacked the power to intimidate and suppress their critics; they were afloat on a receding wave of history. Even within the large evangelical denominations, they had lost much of their grip. Large numbers of Methodists, and of Baptists at least in the North, were themselves taken with religious liberalism. Having

[9]McLoughlin: *Billy Sunday*, pp. 125, 132, 138.
[10]*Does Civilization Need Religion?* (New York, 1927), pp. 2–3. I trust that it will be clear to readers that my discussion deals with fundamentalism as a mass movement and not with the more thoughtful critics of modernism. For an example of the latter, see J. Gresham Machen: *Christianity and Liberalism* (New York, 1923). On the intellectual development of fundamentalism, see Stewart G. Cole: *The History of Fundamentalism* (New York, 1931).
[11]McLoughlin: *Billy Sunday*, p. 278.

lost their dominance over the main body of evangelicism itself, many fundamentalists began to feel desperate.

The 1920's proved to be the focal decade in the *Kulturkampf* of American Protestantism. Advertising, radio, the mass magazines, the advance of popular education, threw the old mentality into a direct and unavoidable conflict with the new. The older, rural and small-town America, now fully embattled against the encroachments of modern life, made its most determined stand against cosmopolitanism, Romanism, and the skepticism and moral experimentalism of the intelligentsia. In the Ku Klux Klan movement, the rigid defense of Prohibition, the Scopes evolution trial, and the campaign against Al Smith in 1928, the older America tried vainly to reassert its authority; but its only victory was the defeat of Smith, and even that was tarnished by his success in reshaping the Democratic Party as an urban and cosmopolitan force, a success that laid the groundwork for subsequent Democratic victories.[12]

One can hear in the anguished cries of the 1920's a clear awareness that the older American type was passé, and the accusation that it was the intelligentsia who were trying to kill it. In 1926 Hiram W. Evans, the Imperial Wizard of the Ku Klux Klan, wrote a moving essay on the Klan's purposes, in which he portrayed the major issue of the time as a struggle between "the great mass of Americans of the old pioneer stock" and the "intellectually mongrelized 'Liberals.'" All the moral and religious values of the "Nordic Americans," he complained, were being undermined by the ethnic groups that had invaded the country, and were being openly laughed at by the liberal intellectuals. "We are a movement," Evans wrote,[13]

---

[12] On this aspect of Smith's achievement, see my essay: "Could a Protestant Have Beaten Hoover in 1928?" *The Reporter*, Vol. 22 (March 17, 1960), pp. 31–3.

[13] "The Klan's Fight for Americanism," *North American Review*, Vol. CCXXIII (March–April–May, 1926), pp. 38 ff. Cf. Gerald L. K. Smith in 1943: "Our people frequently do not express themselves because there are only a few of us who speak with abandon in times like this, but in the hearts of our people are pent-up emotions which go unexpressed because they fear their vocabularies are insufficient." Leo Lowenthal and Norbert Guterman: *Prophets of Deceit* (New York, 1949), p. 110.

of the plain people, very weak in the matter of culture, intellectual support, and trained leadership. We are demanding,
and we expect to win, a return of power into the hands of the
everyday, not highly cultured, not overly intellectualized, but
entirely unspoiled and not de-Americanized, average citizen of
the old stock. Our members and leaders are all of this class—the
opposition of the intellectuals and liberals who hold the leadership, betrayed Americanism, and from whom we expect to
wrest control, is almost automatic.

This is undoubtedly a weakness. It lays us open to the charge
of being "hicks" and "rubes" and "drivers of second-hand
Fords." We admit it. Far worse, it makes it hard for us to state
our case and advocate our crusade in the most effective way, for
most of us lack skill in language. . . .

Every popular movement has suffered from just this
handicap. . . .

The Klan does not believe that the fact that it is emotional
and instinctive, rather than coldly intellectual, is a weakness.
All action comes from emotion, rather than from ratiocination.
Our emotions and the instincts on which they are based have
been bred into us for thousands of years; far longer than reason
has had a place in the human brain. . . . They are the foundations of our American civilization, even more than our great
historic documents; they can be trusted where the fine-haired
reasoning of the denatured intellectuals cannot.

This is not an altogether irrelevant statement of the case,
and not immoderate in tone. The difficulty was to find any but
immoderate means of putting it into action. On this count, the
shabby history of the Klan speaks eloquently. So does the panic
of the fundamentalists. The Georgia assemblyman who said:

This feeling that the American public is sound at heart but that spokesmen
of the old American values somehow lack the means to compete with the
smart-alecks of modernism runs through the utterances of the right wing. Cf.
Senator Barry Goldwater in *The Conscience of a Conservative* (New York, 1960),
pp. 4–5: "Our failure . . . is the failure of the Conservative demonstration.
Though we Conservatives . . . feel sure that the country agrees with us, we
seem unable to demonstrate the practical relevance of Conservative principles
to the needs of the day. . . . Perhaps we suffer from an over-sensitivity to the
judgments of those who rule the mass communications media. We are daily
consigned by 'enlightened' commentators to political oblivion."

> Read the Bible. It teaches you how to act. Read the hymn-book. It contains the finest poetry ever written. Read the almanac. It shows you how to figure out what the weather will be. There isn't another book that it is necessary for anyone to read, and therefore I am opposed to all libraries.

may seem too obscure to be worth notice; but one can hardly say the same of a former Secretary of State and three-time candidate for the presidency who could proclaim, as Bryan did in a speech before Seventh-Day Adventists in 1924: "All the ills from which America suffers can be traced back to the teaching of evolution. It would be better to destroy every other book ever written, and save just the first three verses of Genesis."[14]

It was in the crusade against the teaching of evolution that the fundamentalist movement reached its climax and in the Scopes trial that it made its most determined stand. The trial afforded a perfect dramatization of everything at stake in the confrontation of the fundamentalist and the modernist mind. That the issue centered over the place of evolution in the public high school was itself evidence of the degree to which modernism had been brought down from the level of elite consciousness and made a part of popular experience. The battle over evolution in education had been fought out once before, in the colleges and universities, where conservative clergymen had tried during the three decades after 1860 to stem the tide of Darwinism. But there it had taken place at the elite level, and the inevitable losses sustained by the anti-evolutionists did not touch the vitals of the fundamentalists. Few of the true believers, after all, then attended college, and those who did could still seek out the backwater schools that had been kept pure from the infections of *The Origin of Species*. By the 1920's, however, the teaching of evolution, moving down the educational ladder, had overtaken high schools, and

---

[14] Both quotations are in Maynard Shipley: *The War on Modern Science* (New York, 1927), pp. 130, 254–5. Such remarks are in the main tradition of evangelicalism, but they reflect its increasing shrillness in this period. Cf. the milder expression of the pre-Civil War Methodist preacher, James B. Finley: "I have wondered if the great multiplication of books has not had a deleterious tendency, in diverting the mind from the Bible." *Autobiography* (Cincinnati, 1854), p. 171.

the high schools had begun to reach the people. In the fifteen years before the First World War, the number of high schools had more than doubled, and this growth continued apace after the war. The high-school diploma was clearly becoming the point to which vast numbers of American children would be educated—the point to which they must be educated if they were to be equipped for the scramble for success. Masses of pious and aspiring Americans were now beginning to feel that their children ought to go to high school, and to realize that they were all but certain to be menaced there by evolutionism. It was over the use of an evolutionist textbook, George Hunter's *Civic Biology*, that John T. Scopes came to trial in Tennessee. This book had been adopted by the state textbook commission in 1919 and had been in use in schools of the state as far back as 1909, fifteen years before it was found dangerous.

To the fundamentalists of Tennessee and elsewhere, the effort to stop the teaching of evolution represented an effort to save the religion of their children—indeed, to save all the family pieties—from the ravages of the evolutionists, the intellectuals, the cosmopolitans.[15] If the fundamentalists deserve any sympathy—and I think they do—it must be on this count. A good deal of their ferocity is understandable if one realizes that they saw (and still see) the controversy as a defense of their homes and families. John Washington Butler, the Primitive Baptist Tennessee legislator who introduced the law against the teaching of evolution in that state, did so because he had heard of a young woman in his own community who had gone to a university and returned an evolutionist. This set him to worrying about what would happen to his own five children, and led at last to his success in 1925 in getting his wishes enacted into law in his state. "Save our children for God!" cried a member of the Tennessee Senate in the debate on Butler's

[15] "The greatest menace to the public school system today is . . . its Godlessness," Bryan remarked in *The Commoner*, February, 1920, p. 11. Bryan was disturbed by the reports he kept receiving from parents throughout the country that the state schools were undermining the faith of their children. *Memoirs* (Chicago, 1925), p. 459. On this theme in the anti-evolutionist literature, see Norman F. Furniss: *The Fundamentalist Controversy, 1918–1931* (New Haven, 1954), pp. 44–5.

bill. When Clarence Darrow said at Scopes's trial that "every child ought to be more intelligent than his parents," he was raising the specter that frightened the fundamentalists most. This was precisely what they did *not* want, if being more intelligent meant that children were expected to abandon parental ideas and desert parental ways. "Why, my friend," said William Jennings Bryan during the trial, "if they believe [evolution], they go back to scoff at the religion of their parents. And the parents have a right to say that no teacher paid by their money shall rob their children of faith in God and send them back to their homes, skeptical, infidels, or agnostics, or atheists." "Our purpose and our only purpose," he announced before the trial began, "is to vindicate the right of parents to guard the religion of their children. . . ."[16] To Bryan and his followers it was patent that Darrow was trying to pull apart the skeins of religion and family loyalties. "Damn you," said one Tennessean, shaking his fist under Darrow's nose, "don't you reflect on *my mother's Bible*. If you do I will tear you to pieces."[17]

It was appropriate that the national leadership of the anti-evolution crusade should have fallen to Bryan, a layman who combined in his person the two basic ancestral pieties of the people—evangelical faith and populistic democracy. In his mind, faith and democracy converged in a common anti-intellectualist rationale. On one side were the voices of the people and the truths of the heart; on the other were the intellectuals, a small arrogant elite given over to false science and mechanical rationalism—variously described by him as a "scientific soviet" and a "little irresponsible oligarchy of self-styled 'intellectuals.'"[18] Religion, he pointed out, had never belonged exclusively to an elite: "Christianity is intended for *all*, not for the so-called 'thinkers' only." Mind, being mechanical, needs the heart to direct it. Mind can plan the commission of crimes as well as deeds for the benefit of society. "Mind worship is

[16]Leslie H. Allen, ed.: *Bryan and Darrow at Dayton* (New York, 1925), p. 70; this work is edited from the trial record and other sources.

[17]Italics added here; see Ray Ginger's excellent study of the Scopes trial: *Six Days or Forever?* (Boston, 1958), pp. 2, 17, 64, 134, 181, 206.

[18]Ginger: op. cit., pp. 40, 181; cf. Bryan's *Famous Figures of the Old Testament*, p. 195; *Seven Questions in Dispute*, pp. 78, 154; *In His Image* (New York, 1922), pp. 200–2; *The Commoner*, August, 1921, p. 3; November, 1922, p. 3.

the great sin in the intellectual world today." Only the heart
—which is the province of religion—can bring discipline to the
things of the mind so that they work for good.

Here is the crux of the matter: the juncture between populistic democracy and old-fashioned religion. Since the affairs
of the heart are the affairs of the common man, and since the
common man's intuition in such matters is as good as—indeed
better than—that of the intellectuals, his judgment in matters
of religion should rule. Where there appeared to be a conflict
between religion and science, it was the public, Bryan believed,
and not "those who measure men by diplomas and college degrees," who should decide. As Walter Lippmann observed, the
religious doctrine that all men will at last stand equal before
the throne of God was somehow transmuted in Bryan's mind
into the idea that all men were equally good biologists before
the ballot box of Tennessee. In effect, Bryan proposed to put
the question of evolution to the vote of Christians, and the
issue was metamorphosed into a question of the rights of the
majority.[19]

> The Bible condemns evolution, theistic evolution as well
> as materialistic evolution, if we can trust the judgment of
> Christians as to what the Bible means. Not one in ten of those
> who accept the Bible as the Word of God have ever believed in
> the evolutionary hypothesis as applied to man. Unless there is
> some rule by which a small fraction can compel the substitution
> of their views for the views entertained by the masses, evolution
> must stand condemned as contrary to the revealed will of God.

[19] Bryan: *Orthodox Christianity versus Modernism* (New York, 1923), pp. 14, 26,
29–30, 32, 42; cf. Ginger: op. cit., pp. 35, 40, 181. "The one beauty about the
word of God," said Bryan, "is that it does not take an expert to understand it."
When some metropolitan newspapers suggested that a jury of Dayton residents
might not be competent to pass on the issues at stake, Bryan commented: "According to our system of government, the people are interested in everything
and can be trusted to decide everything, and so with our juries." As he saw it,
the case raised the question, "can a minority use the courts to force its ideas
on the schools?" In this controversy, poor Bryan, so long starved for victory,
made another of his great miscalculations. He appears to have expected to win.
"For the first time in my life," he told a fundamentalist conference, "I'm on the
side of the majority." Ginger: op. cit., pp. 44, 90. For an astute contemporary
statement on the relation between Bryan's version of democracy, his evangelical sympathies, and his anti-intellectualism, see John Dewey: "The American
Intellectual Frontier," *New Republic*, Vol. XXX (May 10, 1922), pp. 303–5.

In Bryan's mind the question of the teaching of evolution in the schools was a challenge to popular democracy. "What right have the evolutionists—a relatively small percentage of the population—to teach *at public expense* a so-called scientific interpretation of the Bible when orthodox Christians are not permitted to teach an orthodox interpretation of the Bible?" Bryan was not convinced, in any case, that the science of the evolutionists was sound; but even so, he said, they ignored "the science of government," in which "rights are determined by the *majority*," except for those rights safeguarded to the minority by the Constitution. To prevent the minority from teaching their doctrines in the *public* schools would not infringe on their rights. "They have no right to demand pay for teaching that which the parents and the taxpayers do not want taught. The hand that writes the paycheck rules the school." Christians had to build their own schools and colleges in which to teach Christianity. "Why should not atheists and agnostics be required to build their own schools and colleges in which to teach their doctrines?"[20] So, if Bryan had had his way, the public schools would have banned evolutionary biology altogether, and the teaching of modern science would have been confined to a small number of secularist private schools. This would have been a catastrophe for American education, but Bryan, who saw no contradiction between sound education and orthodox faith, knew what the choice must be, if it had to be made. An educated man without religion is a ship without a pilot. "If we have to give up either religion or education, we should give up education."[21]

3

Today the evolution controversy seems as remote as the Homeric era to intellectuals in the East, and it is not uncommon to take a condescending view of both sides. In other parts of the country and in other circles, the controversy is still alive. A few years ago, when the Scopes trial was dramatized in *Inherit the Wind*, the play seemed on Broadway more like a quaint

[20]*Orthodox Christianity versus Modernism*, pp. 29, 45–6; cf. "Darwinism in Public Schools," *The Commoner*, January, 1923, pp. 1–2.
[21]Ginger: op. cit., p. 88.

period piece than a stirring call for freedom of thought. But when the road company took the play to a small town in Montana, a member of the audience rose and shouted "Amen!" at one of the speeches of the character representing Bryan. Today intellectuals have bogies much more frightening than fundamentalism in the schools; but it would be a serious failure of imagination not to remember how scared the intellectuals of the 1920's were. Perhaps not quite so much appeared to be at stake as in the McCarthyist crusade of the 1950's, but the sense of oppressive danger was no less real. One need only read Maynard Shipley's contemporary survey of the anti-evolution movement, *The War on Modern Science*, to recapture a sense of the genuine alarm of the intellectuals. The Scopes trial, like the Army-McCarthy hearings thirty years later, brought feeling to a head and provided a dramatic purgation and resolution. After the trial was over, it was easier to see that the anti-evolution crusade was being contained and that the fears of the intellectuals had been excessive. But before the trial, the crusade had gained a great deal of strength in many states, including several outside the South. In the South, as W. J. Cash, who observed it at first hand, remarked, it was, like the Klan, an authentic folk movement, which had the "active support and sympathy of the overwhelming majority of the Southern people," not only among the masses but among influential lay and clerical leaders.[22] If the highbrows had nothing to fear for themselves in their more secure centers of learning, they could fear with some reason that the country's system of secondary education might be ruined. Nor did they altogether have their way in its defense. To this day, the language of most secondary-school biology texts is guarded, and evolution is taught in many places only by indirection. Just a few years ago, in a poll of representative adolescent opinion throughout the country, only about a third of the sample responded affirmatively to the statement: "Man was evolved from lower forms of animals."[23]

[22]W. J. Cash: *The Mind of the South* (New York, 1941), pp. 337–8.
[23]In this poll, 40 per cent checked "No," 35 per cent "Yes," and 24 per cent "Don't know." H. H. Remmers and D. H. Radler: *The American Teenager* (Indianapolis, 1957). Cf. the pressures against the teaching of evolution in the 1930's as reported by Howard K. Beale in *Are American Teachers Free?* (New York, 1936), pp. 296–7.

The evolution controversy and the Scopes trial greatly quickened the pulse of anti-intellectualism. For the first time in the twentieth century, intellectuals and experts were denounced as enemies by leaders of a large segment of the public. No doubt, the militant fundamentalists were a minority in the country, but they were a substantial minority; and their animus plainly reflected the feelings of still larger numbers, who, however reluctant to join in their reactionary crusade, none the less shared their disquiet about the trend of the times, their fear of the cosmopolitan mentality, of critical intelligence, of experimentalism in morals and literature.[24] Bryan's full-throated assaults upon the "experts" were symbolic of the sharply deviating paths being taken by the two sides. It had not always been so. In the Progressive era the intellectuals had felt themselves to be essentially in harmony with the basic interests and aspirations of the people. Now it was evident once more that this harmony was neither pre-established nor guaranteed. The more spiritually earnest the great religious public was, the more violently it might differ from the views of the majority of intellectuals. As for the fundamentalists, it would be a mistake to forget that being routed in the main contest did not cause them to capitulate or disappear. They retired sullenly, some of them looking for other spheres in which modernists might be more vulnerable. They could not eclipse modernism or secularism in the religious controversy itself, but they might find other areas in which to rise and smite again.

The events of the Great Depression gave them scant comfort. Their theological isolation from the main body of the big evangelical churches was doubly oppressive, for the evangelicals in overwhelming numbers now became politically liberal or left.[25] However, the laymen did not go so far as the clergy,

[24]This concern with morals might bear further examination. As fundamentalists saw it, the loss of faith among their children would be only the preliminary to a loss of morals. They had a good deal to say about the "sensuality" inherent in the notion that man has descended from lower forms of life, and their rhetoric suggests to what a degree sexual fears, as well as others, were mobilized in this controversy.

[25]I am indebted here to two excellent studies of the social crosscurrents in American religion: Paul Carter's *The Decline and Revival of the Social Gospel* (Ithaca, 1954) and Robert Moats Miller's *American Protestantism and Social Issues* (Chapel Hill, 1958).

and many conservative laymen felt that the development of a new social-gospel movement had created a new "priestly class" (as one right-wing churchman put it) out of harmony with the sentiments of many people in their congregations. Their heightened sense of isolation and impotence helped to bring many of the dwindling but still numerically significant fundamentalists into the ranks of a fanatical right-wing opposition to the New Deal. The fundamentalism of the cross was now supplemented by a fundamentalism of the flag. Since the 1930's, fundamentalism has been a significant component in the extreme right in American politics, whose cast of thought often shows strong fundamentalist filiations.[26] The spokesmen of this trend in political fundamentalism have kept alive the folkish anti-intellectualism of the evolution controversy. "I do not understand political science, as an authority from an academic viewpoint," one of their leaders proclaimed. "I am not familiar with the artistic masterpieces of Europe, but I do say this tonight: I understand the hearts of the American people." And he went on to denounce their betrayers: "The Scribes and Pharisees of the Twentieth Century . . . [who] provide a nation with its dominant propaganda, including seasonal fashions in politics, religious attitudes, sub-standard ethics and half-caste morals." It is an ancient and indigenous refrain, echoed in the simplest terms by another: "We are going to take this government out of the hands of these city-slickers and give it back to the people that still believe two plus two is four, God is in his Heaven, and the Bible is the Word."[27]

Although no one has ever tried to trace in detail the historic

---

[26]The several authors, including myself, of the essays assessing *The New American Right* (New York, 1955), ed. by Daniel Bell, have either ignored or given only casual attention to the place of fundamentalism in right-wing extremism. But see some of the more recent essays in the new edition, *The Radical Right* (New York, 1963). The most informative work on the subject is Ralph Lord Roy's *Apostles of Discord* (Boston, 1953), which is written in a mood of muck-raking and exposure but has an extensive scholarly documentation. On recent developments, see David Danzig: "The Radical Right and the Rise of the Fundamentalist Minority," *Commentary*, Vol. XXXIII (April, 1962), pp. 291–8.
[27]Leo Lowenthal and Norbert Guterman: *Prophets of Deceit* (New York, 1949), pp. 109–10; the quotations are from Gerald L. K. Smith and Charles B. Hudson.

links between the radical right of the depression and post-depression periods and the fundamentalism of the 1920's, there are some suggestive continuities among the leaders. Many of the leaders of right-wing groups have been preachers, or ex-preachers, or sons of preachers with rigid religious upbringings. Some of the men associated with Billy Sunday in the mid-thirties later turned up as right-wing or quasi-fascist agitators. Gerald Winrod of Kansas, one of the most prominent right-wing prophets of our time, began his career of agitation as a crusading anti-evolutionist. Another, Gerald L. K. Smith, was a minister's son and a preacher for the Disciples of Christ. The late J. Frank Norris, a Southern Baptist preacher in the forefront of the anti-evolution crusade in Texas, later became one of the most colorful right-wing messiahs. Carl McIntire, a leading organizer of contemporary right-wing opposition to modernism, was originally a protégé of the highbrow fundamentalist, J. Gresham Machen.[28] The more recent resurgence of the right wing in the John Birch Society and various "Christian Crusades" has made the fundamentalist orientation of a large segment of the right wing more conspicuous than at any time in the past; the movement has been led, to a great extent, by preachers and ex-preachers. The literature of the extreme right also shows a significant continuity in style —indicative of the degree to which the pattern of fundamentalism has become the pattern of militant nationalism. (It was with an appropriate sense of this continuity that Gerald L. K. Smith named his paper *The Cross and the Flag*.)

It is not mere opportunism that causes the politically minded fundamentalist to gravitate toward the far right. No less than others, fundamentalists like to feel that they have a comprehensive world view, and their minds are more satisfied when religious and political antipathies can be linked together. They have developed a gift for combining seemingly irrelevant animosities so as to make them mutually re-enforcing. For example, just as contemporary fundamentalists have linked their

[28]On Winrod, Smith, Norris, and McIntire, see Roy: op. cit., *passim*; Carter: op. cit., chapter 4; Miller: op. cit., chapter 11; and McLoughlin: *Billy Sunday*, pp. 290, 310. On fundamentalism and the John Birch Society, see *The New York Times*, April 23 and October 29, 1961; Tris Coffin: "The Yahoo Returns," *New Leader*, April 17, 1961.

religious sentiments to the cold war, the fundamentalists of the twenties responded to the issues of the First World War and to residual anti-German feeling. It was one of their most common arguments against the modernists that higher criticism of the Bible has received its strongest impetus from German scholarship; they were thus able to forge a link between the German amorality supposedly revealed by wartime atrocity stories and the destructive moral effects of Biblical criticism. This case was argued at various levels of sophistication, perhaps most simply and informally by Billy Sunday: "In 1895 at the Potsdam Palace the Kaiser called his statesmen together and outlined his plan for world domination, and he was told that the German people would never stand by and endorse it, as it was not in line with the teaching of Martin Luther. Then the Kaiser cried, 'We will change the religion of Germany then,' and higher criticism began."[29]

There seems to be such a thing as the generically prejudiced mind. Studies of political intolerance and ethnic prejudice have shown that zealous church-going and rigid religious faith are among the important correlates of political and ethnic animosity.[30] It is the existence of this type of mind that sets the stage for the emergence of the one-hundred percenter and determines the similarity of style between the modern right wing and the fundamentalist. In fact, the conditions of the cold war and the militant spirit bred by the constant struggle against world Communism have given the fundamentalist mind a new lease on life. Like almost everything else in our world, fundamentalism itself has been considerably secularized, and this process of secularization has yielded a type of pseudo-political mentality

[29]McLoughlin: *Billy Sunday*, p. 281.

[30]The most interesting work I know of on the generically prejudiced mind is that of E. L. Hartley, who asked college students to rate various nations and races according to their acceptability. He had in his list the names of three fictitious ethnic groups, the Daniereans, Pireneans, and Wallonians. There was a high correlation between expressed prejudice against actual ethnic groups and prejudice against these fictitious ones, bespeaking a set of mind that is prepared to react with a certain hostility to anything. See E. L. Hartley: *Problems in Prejudice* (New York, 1946). On the relation between religious orthodoxy and forms of intolerance, see Samuel A. Stouffer: *Communism, Conformity, and Civil Liberties* (New York, 1955), pp. 140–55; and T. A. Adorno et al.: *The Authoritarian Personality* (New York, 1950), chapters 6 and 18.

whose way of thought is best understood against the historical background of the revivalist preacher and the camp meeting. The fundamentalist mind has had the bitter experience of being routed in the field of morals and censorship, on evolution and Prohibition, and it finds itself increasingly submerged in a world in which the great and respectable media of mass communication violate its sensibilities and otherwise ignore it. In a modern, experimental, and "sophisticated" society, it has been elbowed aside and made a figure of fun, and even much of the religious "revival" of our time is genteel and soft-spoken in a way that could never have satisfied the old-fashioned fundamentalist zeal. But in politics, the secularized fundamentalism of our time has found a new kind of force and a new punitive capacity. The political climate of the post-war era has given the fundamentalist type powerful new allies among other one-hundred percenters: rich men, some of them still loyal to a fundamentalist upbringing, stung by the income tax and still militant against the social reforms of the New Deal; isolationist groups and militant nationalists; Catholic fundamentalists, ready for the first time to unite with their former persecutors on the issue of "Godless Communism"; and Southern reactionaries newly animated by the fight over desegregation.

One reason why the political intelligence of our time is so incredulous and uncomprehending in the presence of the right-wing mind is that it does not reckon fully with the essentially theological concern that underlies right-wing views of the world. Characteristically, the political intelligence, if it is to operate at all as a kind of civic force rather than as a mere set of maneuvers to advance this or that special interest, must have its own way of handling the facts of life and of forming strategies. It accepts conflict as a central and enduring reality and understands human society as a form of equipoise based upon the continuing process of compromise. It shuns ultimate showdowns and looks upon the ideal of total partisan victory as unattainable, as merely another variety of threat to the kind of balance with which it is familiar. It is sensitive to nuances and sees things in degrees. It is essentially relativist and skeptical, but at the same time circumspect and humane.

The fundamentalist mind will have nothing to do with all this: it is essentially Manichean; it looks upon the world as an arena for conflict between absolute good and absolute evil, and accordingly it scorns compromises (who would compromise with Satan?) and can tolerate no ambiguities. It cannot find serious importance in what it believes to be trifling degrees of difference: liberals support measures that are for all practical purposes socialistic, and socialism is nothing more than a variant of Communism, which, as everyone knows, is atheism. Whereas the distinctively political intelligence begins with the political world, and attempts to make an assessment of how far a given set of goals can in fact be realized in the face of a certain balance of opposing forces, the secularized fundamentalist mind begins with a definition of that which is absolutely right, and looks upon politics as an arena in which that right must be realized. It cannot think, for example, of the cold war as a question of mundane politics   that is to say, as a conflict between two systems of power that are compelled in some degree to accommodate each other in order to survive—but only as a clash of faiths. It is not concerned with the realities of power —with the fact, say, that the Soviets have the bomb—but with the spiritual battle with the Communist, preferably the domestic Communist, whose reality does not consist in what he does, or even in the fact that he exists, but who represents, rather, an archetypal opponent in a spiritual wrestling match. He has not one whit less reality because the fundamentalists have never met him in the flesh.

The issues of the actual world are hence transformed into a spiritual Armageddon, an ultimate reality, in which any reference to day-by-day actualities has the character of an allegorical illustration, and not of the empirical evidence that ordinary men offer for ordinary conclusions. Thus, when a right-wing leader accuses Dwight D. Eisenhower of being a conscious, dedicated agent of the international Communist conspiracy, he may seem demented, by the usual criteria of the political intelligence; but, more accurately, I believe, he is quite literally out of this world. What he is trying to account for is not Eisenhower's actual political behavior, as men commonly understand it, but Eisenhower's place, as a kind of fallen angel, in the realm of ultimate moral and spiritual values, which to him has infinitely greater reality than mundane politics. Seen in this light, the accusation is no longer quite so willfully perverse, but appears in its proper character as a kind of sublime nonsense. *Credo quia absurdum est.*

4
A NOTE ON AMERICAN CATHOLICISM

In these pages I have been mainly concerned with the relationship between Protestant evangelicism and American anti-intellectualism, simply because America has been a Protestant country, molded by Protestant institutions. It would be a mistake, however, to fail to note the distinctive ethos of American Catholicism, which has contributed in a forceful and decisive way to our anti-intellectualism. Catholicism in this country over the past two or three generations has waxed strong in numbers, in political power, and in acceptance. At the middle of the nineteenth century it was, though a minority faith, the largest single church in the country and was steadily gaining ground despite anti-Catholic sentiment. Today the Church claims almost a fourth of the population, and has achieved an acceptance which would have seemed surprising even thirty years ago.

One might have expected Catholicism to add a distinctive leaven to the intellectual dialogue in America, bringing as it did a different sense of the past and of the world, a different awareness of the human condition and of the imperatives of institutions. In fact, it has done nothing of the kind, for it has failed to develop an intellectual tradition in America or to produce its own class of intellectuals capable either of exercising authority among Catholics or of mediating between the Catholic mind and the secular or Protestant mind. Instead, American Catholicism has devoted itself alternately to denouncing the aspects of American life it could not approve and imitating more acceptable aspects in order to surmount its minority complex and "Americanize" itself. In consequence, the American Church, which contains more communicants than that of any country except Brazil and Italy, and is the richest and perhaps the best organized of the national divisions of the Church, lacks an intellectual culture. "In no Western society," D. W. Brogan has remarked, "is the intellectual prestige of Catholicism lower than in the country where, in such respects as wealth, numbers, and strength of organization, it is so powerful." In the last two decades, which have seen a notable growth of the Catholic middle class and the cultivated Catholic public, Catholic leaders have become aware of this failure; a few years ago, Monsignor John Tracy Ellis's penetrating brief survey of American Catholic intellectual impoverishment had an overwhelmingly favorable reception in the Catholic press.[31]

Two formative circumstances in the development of early American Catholicism made for indifference to intellectual life. First in importance was the fiercely prejudiced Know-Nothing psychology against which it had to make its way in the nineteenth century. Regarded as a foreign body that ought to be expelled from the national organism, and as the agent of an alien power, the Church had to fight to establish its Americanism. Catholic laymen who took pride in their religious identity responded to the American milieu with militant self-assertion whenever they could, and Church spokesmen seemed to feel that it was not scholarship but vigorous polemicism which was needed.[32] The Church thus took on a militant stance that ill accorded with reflection; and in our time, when the initial prejudice against it has been largely surmounted, its members persist in what Monsignor Ellis calls a "self-imposed ghetto mentality." A second determining factor was that for a long time the limited resources of the American Church were pre-empted by the exigent task of creating the institutions necessary to absorb a vast influx of immigrants—almost ten million

[31]These paragraphs owe much to Monsignor Ellis's article, "American Catholics and the Intellectual Life," *Thought*, Vol. XXX (Autumn, 1955), pp. 351–88. Information and quotations not otherwise identified are taken from this essay. See also, among Catholic writers, the discussions of related issues in Thomas F. O'Dea: *American Catholic Dilemma: An Inquiry Into Intellectual Life* (New York, 1958); and Father Walter J. Ong, S. J.: *Frontiers in American Catholicism* (New York, 1957); and, among non-Catholic writers, Robert D. Cross: *Liberal Catholicism in America* (Cambridge, Massachusetts, 1958), which examines at length some of the tensions within the Church caused by adaptation to America.

[32]As Father Ong (op. cit., p. 38) points out, it is all but impossible for American Catholics to understand "how this evident devotion [of educated French Catholics] can be nurtured in the twentieth century without courses in apologetics of the sort which American Catholic Colleges and universities feature but which are quite unknown at the Institut Catholique (Catholic University faculty) in Paris, Toulouse, or elsewhere. American Catholics are lost when they find that the French apologetic tends to train the youthful mind to think *through* modern problems in Catholic ways. . . ."

between 1820 and 1920—and to provide them with the rudiments of religious instruction. So much was taken up by this pressing practical need that little was left over for the higher culture, in so far as there were members of the Church who were concerned with Catholic culture.

Catholicism was, moreover, the religion of the immigrant.[33] To American Catholics, the *true* Church seemed to be in Europe; and they were content to leave the cultivation of intellectual life to the more sophisticated Europeans—all the while developing an exaggerated and unwarranted deference to such Catholic writers as Belloc and Chesterton. Non-English-speaking immigrants showed a high degree of passivity before clerical leadership, as well as before American society as a whole. What is perhaps most important—though it receives less than its proper share of attention from Catholic analysts of the Church's cultural problems here—is the fact that the Irish became the primary catalysts between America and the other immigrant groups. The Irish, taking advantage of their knowledge of English and their prior arrival, constructed the network of political machines and Church hierarchy through which most Catholic arrivals could make a place for themselves in American life. And more than any other group, the Irish put their stamp on American Catholicism; consequently the American Church absorbed little of the impressive scholarship of German Catholicism or the questioning intellectualism of

[33]The immigrant character of the Church brings into focus a problem that has existed for all immigrant faiths and indeed for all upwardly mobile American groups, Protestant or Catholic, immigrant or native. It is that the process of education, instead of becoming a reinforcing bond between generations, constitutes an additional barrier between them and adds greatly to the poignance of parenthood. Within a stable social class, attendance at the same schools can often provide a unifying set of experiences for parents and children. But in a country in which millions of children of almost illiterate parents have gone to high school and millions more whose parents have only modest educations have gone to college, the process of education is as much a threat to parents as a promise. This has added force to the desire to put, so to speak, a ceiling on the quality and range of education. Parents often hope to give their children the social and vocational advantages of college without at the same time infusing in them cultural aspirations too remote from those of the home environment in which they have been reared.

the French Church, and much more of the harsh Puritanism and fierce militancy of the Irish clergy.

Cut off by language and class from easy entrance into the mainstream of Protestant Anglo-Saxon culture, immigrant working-class Catholics were in no position to produce intellectual spokesmen. It is significant that many of the intellectual leaders of the Church in America were not, in national origin, typical of the mass of American Catholics, but were rather native Anglo-Americans converted to the Church, like Orestes Brownson and Father Isaac Hecker. The social origins and cultural opportunities of Church officials were well characterized by Archbishop Cushing in 1947 when he said that "in all the American hierarchy, resident in the United States, there is not known to me one Bishop, Archbishop or Cardinal whose father or mother was a college graduate. Every one of our Bishops and Archbishops is the son of a working man and a working man's wife." The hierarchy, which has been drawn from this culturally underprivileged background, is of course educated, but primarily in a vocational way. As Bishop Spalding pointed out at the Third Plenary Council of Baltimore: "the ecclesiastical seminary is not a school of intellectual culture, either here in America or elsewhere, and to imagine that it can become the instrument of intellectual culture is to cherish a delusion." So, even in this most ancient of Christian churches, the American environment has prevailed and the American problem has reasserted itself in an acute form: culturally one began *de novo*. So lacking in scholarly distinction were American Catholics that when the Catholic University of America was opened by the American hierarchy in 1889, with the hope of remedying this situation, six of its original eight-man faculty had to be recruited from Europe, and the two native members were converts who had been educated outside the folds of the Church.

For a long time the proportion of lay Catholics wealthy enough to give significant patronage to intellectual institutions was small, as compared with other faiths. The emergence of the modern Catholic millionaire has not changed this situation as much as it might have done. Monsignor Ellis remarks, concerning one case in point, that the Catholic University of America received, during the first sixty-six years of its existence, only about ten bequests of $100,000 or more, and only one of these approached the kind of munificence that has made the American private secular university possible. With the increasing upward mobility of a large part of the Catholic population, Catholics, like Protestants, have sent their children to colleges in growing numbers. But both Catholic educators and non-Catholic friends like Robert M. Hutchins have been dismayed to see Catholic schools commonly reproducing the vocationalism, athleticism, and anti-intellectualism which prevails so widely in American higher education as a whole. The intellectual achievement of Catholic colleges and universities remains startlingly low, both in the sciences and in the humanities. Robert H. Knapp and his collaborators, surveying the collegiate origins of American scientists in 1952, remarked that Catholic institutions are "among the least productive of all institutions and constitute a singularly unproductive sample." Their record in the humanities, surprisingly, is worse: "Catholic institutions, though exceptionally unproductive in all areas of scholarship, achieve their best record in the sciences."[34]

As one might have expected, the way of the Catholic intellectual in this country has been doubly hard. He has had to justify himself not only as a Catholic to the Protestant and secular intellectual community but also as an intellectual to fellow Catholics, for whom his vocation is even more questionable than it is to the American community at large. Catholic scholars and writers tend to be recognized belatedly by their co-religionists, when they are recognized at all.[35]

All of this concerns, of course, not so much the anti-intellectualism of American Catholicism as its cultural impoverishment, its non-intellectualism. But it will serve as background for a more central point: a great many Catholics have been as responsive as Protestant fundamentalists to that revolt against modernity of which I have spoken, and they have done perhaps

[34]Robert H. Knapp and H. B. Goodrich: *Origins of American Scientists* (Chicago, 1952), p. 24; Robert H. Knapp and Joseph J. Greenbaum: *The Younger American Scholar: His Collegiate Origins* (Chicago, 1953), p. 99.
[35]Harry Sylvester's article, "Problems of the Catholic Writer," *Atlantic Monthly*, Vol. CLXXXI (January, 1948), pp. 109–13, contains a stimulating discussion of the subject.

more than their share in developing the one-hundred per cent mentality. In no small measure this has been true because their intellectual spokesmen—who are now growing in numbers and influence—have not yet gained enough authority in the Catholic community to hold in check the most retrograde aspects of that revolt, including its general suspicion of mind and its hostility to intellectuals. A great deal of the energy of the priesthood in our time has been directed toward censorship, divorce, birth control, and other issues which have brought the Church into conflict with the secular and the Protestant mind time and again; some of it has also gone into ultra-conservative political movements, which are implacable enemies of the intellectual community. Catholic intellectuals on the whole have opposed the extreme and (from the point of view of the faith) gratuitous aspects of this enmity, but they have been unable to restrain it.[36]

Indeed, one of the most striking developments of our time has been the emergence of a kind of union, or at least a capacity for co-operation, between Protestant and Catholic fundamentalists, who share a common puritanism and a common mindless militancy on what they imagine to be political issues, which unite them in opposition to what they repetitively call Godless Communism. Many Catholics seem to have overcome the natural reluctance one might expect them to have to join hands with the very type of bigoted Protestant who scourged their ancestors. It seems a melancholy irony that a union which the common bonds of Christian fraternity could not achieve has been forged by the ecumenicism of hatred. During the McCarthy era, the senator from Wisconsin had wide backing both from right-wing Protestant groups and from many Catholics, who seemed almost to believe that he was promulgating not a personal policy but a Catholic policy. It mattered not a bit that the organs of Catholic intellectuals, like *Commonweal* and the Jesuits' *America*, vigorously condemned him. More recently the John Birch Society, despite its heavy Protestant fundamentalist aura, has attracted enough Catholics to cause

[36]For evidence that Catholic clergy and laymen alike are unusually hostile to freedom of thought and criticism, even on subjects remote from dogma, see Gerhard Lenski: *The Religious Factor* (New York, 1960), especially p. 278.

at least one member of the hierarchy to warn them against it. For Catholics there is a dangerous source of gratification in the present indiscriminately anti-Communist mentality of the country. After more than a century of persecution, it must feel luxurious for Catholics to find their Americanism at last unquestioned, and to be able to join with their former persecutors in common pursuit of a new international, conspiratorial, un-American enemy with a basically foreign allegiance—this time not in Rome but in Moscow. The pursuit is itself so gratifying that it does not much matter that the menacing domestic Communist has become a phantom. These Catholics will not thank anyone, not even thinkers of their own faith, for interrupting them with such irrelevancies at a time when they feel as though they have Cromwell's men themselves on the run.

PART 3

THE POLITICS OF
DEMOCRACY

CHAPTER VI

The Decline of the Gentleman

I

WHEN THE United States began its national existence, the relationship between intellect and power was not a problem. The leaders *were* the intellectuals. Advanced though the nation was in the development of democracy, the control of its affairs still rested largely in a patrician elite: and within this elite men of intellect moved freely and spoke with enviable authority. Since it was an unspecialized and versatile age, the intellectual as expert was a negligible force; but the intellectual as ruling-class gentleman was a leader in every segment of society—at the bar, in the professions, in business, and in political affairs. The Founding Fathers were sages, scientists, men of broad cultivation, many of them apt in classical learning, who used their wide reading in history, politics, and law to solve the exigent problems of their time. No subsequent era in our history has produced so many men of knowledge among its political leaders as the age of John Adams, John Dickinson, Benjamin Franklin, Alexander Hamilton, Thomas Jefferson, James Madison, George Mason, James Wilson, and George Wythe. One might have expected that such men, whose political achievements were part of the very fabric of the nation, would have stood as permanent and overwhelming testimonial to the truth that men of learning and intellect need not be bootless and impractical as political leaders.

It is ironic that the United States should have been founded by intellectuals; for throughout most of our political history, the intellectual has been for the most part either an outsider, a servant, or a scapegoat. The American people have always cherished a deep historical piety, second only to that felt for Lincoln, for what Dumas Malone has called "the Great Generation," the generation which carried out the Revolution and formed the Constitution. We may well ask how a people with such beginnings and such pieties so soon lost their high regard for mind in politics. Why, while most of the Founding Fathers were still alive, did a reputation for intellect become a political disadvantage?

In time, of course, the rule of the patrician elite was supplanted by a popular democracy, but one cannot blame the democratic movement alone for the decline in regard for intellect in politics. Soon after a party division became acute, the members of the elite fell out among themselves, and lost their respect for political standards. The men who with notable character and courage led the way through the Revolution and with remarkable prescience and skill organized a new national government in 1787–88 had by 1796 become hopelessly divided in their interests and sadly affected by the snarling and hysterical differences which were aroused by the French Revolution.[1] The generation which wrote the Declaration of Independence and the Constitution also wrote the Alien and Sedition Acts. Its eminent leaders lost their solidarity, and their standards declined. A common membership in the patrician class, common experiences in revolution and state-making, a common core of ideas and learning did not prevent them from playing politics with little regard for decency or common sense. Political controversy, muddied by exaggerated charges of conspiracies with French agents or plots to subvert Christianity or schemes to restore monarchy and put the country under the heel of Great Britain, degenerated into demagogy. Having no understanding of the uses of political parties or of the function of a loyal opposition, the Founding Fathers surrendered to their political passions and entered upon a struggle in which any rhetorical weapon would do.

Not even Washington was immune from abuse and slander; however, the first notable victim of a distinctively anti-intellectualist broadside was Thomas Jefferson, and his assailants were Federalist leaders and members of the established clergy of New England. The assault on Jefferson is immensely instructive because it indicates the qualities his enemies thought could be used to discredit him and establishes a precedent for subsequent anti-intellectualist imagery in our politics. In 1796, when it seemed that Jefferson might succeed Washington, the

[1] See Marshall Smelser: "The Federalist Period as an Age of Passion," *American Quarterly*, Vol. X (Winter, 1958), pp. 391–419.

South Carolina Federalist congressman, William Loughton Smith, published an anonymous pamphlet attacking Jefferson and minimizing his qualifications for the presidency. Smith tried to show how unsettling and possibly even dangerous Jefferson's "doctrinaire" leadership would be. Jefferson was a philosopher and, Smith pointed out, philosophers have a way of being doctrinaires in politics—witness Locke's impracticable constitution for the Carolinas, Condorcet's "political follies," and Rittenhouse's willingness to lend his name to the Democratic Society of Philadelphia![2]

> The characteristic traits of a philosopher, when he turns politician, are, timidity, whimsicalness, and a disposition to reason from certain principles, and not from the true nature of man; a proneness to predicate all his measures on certain abstract theories, formed in the recess of his cabinet, and not on the existing state of things and circumstances; an inertness of mind, as applied to governmental policy, a wavering of disposition when great and sudden emergencies demand promptness of decision and energy of action.

What was needed was not intellect but character, and here too Jefferson was found wanting: philosophers, the pamphleteer argued, are extremely prone to flattery and avid of repute, and Jefferson's own abilities "have been more directed to the acquirement of literary fame than to the substantial good of his country." Washington—there was a man, no nonsense about him: "The great WASHINGTON was, thank God, no philosopher; had *he* been one, we should never have seen his great military exploits; we should never have prospered under his wise administration." Smith hit upon a device that was to become standard among the critics of intellect in politics—portraying the curiosity of the active mind as too trivial and ridiculous

[2][William Loughton Smith]: *The Pretensions of Thomas Jefferson to the Presidency Examined* (n.p., 1796), Part I, pp. 14–15. No one wishes to say that he is opposed to "genuine" learning and wisdom but only to an inferior or debased version. Smith thought Jefferson a bogus philosopher, not a "real" one. He had only the external and inferior characteristics of a philosopher, which meant, in politics, "a want of steadiness, a constitutional indecision and versatility, visionary, wild, and speculative systems, and various other defective features." Ibid., p. 16. Those who remember Adlai Stevenson's campaigns will find in these quotations a familiar ring.

for important affairs. He mocked at Jefferson's skills in "impaling butterflies and insects, and contriving turn-about chairs" and also suggested that no real friend of Jefferson, or of the country, would "draw this calm philosopher from such useful pursuits" to plunge him into the ardors of politics. In language almost identical with that used a generation later against John Quincy Adams, Smith suggested that Jefferson's merits "might entitle him to the Professorship of a college, but they would be as compatible with the duties of the presidency as with the command of the Western army."[3]

In Smith's attack, certain other preoccupations appear which foreshadow the tone of later political literature. There was the notion that military ability is a test of the kind of character which is good for political leadership. It was assumed that a major part of civic character resides in military virtue; even today an intellectual in politics can sometimes counteract the handicap of intellect by pointing to a record of military service.

In the campaign of 1800 all inhibitions broke down. The attempt to score against Jefferson on the ground that he was a man of thought and learning was, of course, only one aspect of a comprehensive attack upon his mind and character designed to show that he was a dangerous demagogue without faith or morals—or, as one critic put it, of "no Conscience, no Religion, no Charity." It was charged that he kept a slave wench and sired mulattoes; that he had been a coward during the American Revolution; that he had started the French Revolution; that he had slandered Washington; that he was ambitious to become a dictator, another Bonaparte; that he was a visionary and a dreamer, an impractical doctrinaire, and, to make matters worse, a French doctrinaire.[4]

The campaign against Jefferson became at the same time an attempt to establish as evil and dangerous the qualities of the speculative mind. Learning and speculation had made an atheist of Jefferson, it was said; had caused him to quarrel with the views of the theologians about the age of the earth and to oppose having school children read the Bible. Such vagaries

---

[3]Ibid., pp. 4, 6, 16; Part II, p. 39.
[4]For a summary of the worst assaults on Jefferson, see Charles O. Lerche, Jr.: "Jefferson and the Election of 1800: A Case Study of the Political Smear," *William and Mary Quarterly*, 3rd ser., Vol. V (October, 1948), pp. 467–91.

might be harmless in a closet philosopher, but to allow him to bring these qualities of mind into the presidency would be dangerous to religion and to society.[5] His abstractness of mind and his literary interests made him unfit for practical tasks. He tended always to theorize about government: "All the ideas which were derived from Experience were hooted at."[6] "I am ready to admit," said one Federalist pamphleteer, "that he is distinguished for shewy talents, for theoretic learning, and for the elegance of his *written* style." He went on:[7]

> It was in France, where he resided nearly seven years, and until the revolution had made some progress, that his disposition to theory, and his skepticism in religion, morals, and government, acquired full strength and vigor. . . . Mr. Jefferson is known to be a theorist in politics, as well as in philosophy and morals. He is a *philosophe* in the modern French sense of the word.

Eminent contemporaries agreed. Fisher Ames thought that Jefferson, "like most men of genius . . . has been carried away by systems, and the everlasting zeal to generalize, instead of proceeding, like common men of practical sense, on the low, but sure foundation of matter of fact."[8] The Federalist writer, Joseph Dennie, saw in him a favorite pupil of the "dangerous, Deistical, and Utopian" school of French philosophy. "The man has talents," Dennie conceded,[9]

> but they are of a dangerous and delusive kind. He has read much and can write plausibly. He is a man of letters, and should be a retired one. His closet, and not the cabinet, is his place. In the first, he might harmlessly examine the teeth of a nondescript monster, the secretions of an African, or the almanac of Banneker. . . . At the seat of government his abstract, inapplicable, metaphysicopolitics are either nugatory or noxious.

---

[5][William Linn]: *Serious Considerations on the Election of a President* (New York, 1800).

[6]*Connecticut Courant*, July 12, 1800, quoted in Lerche: op. cit., p. 475.

[7]*Address to the Citizens of South Carolina on the Approaching Election of a President and Vice-President of the United States. By a Federal Republican* (Charlestown, 1800), pp. 9, 10, 15.

[8]Seth Ames, ed.: *The Life and Works of Fisher Ames* (Boston, 1854), Vol. II, p. 134.

[9]*The Lay Preacher*, ed. by Milton Ellis (New York, 1943), p. 174; the essay originally appeared in the *Port Folio*, Vol. I (1801).

Besides, his principles relish so strongly of Paris and are seasoned with such a profusion of French garlic, that he offends
the whole nation. Better for Americans that on their extended
plains "thistles should grow, instead of wheat, and cockle, instead of barley," than that a philosopher should influence the
councils of the country, and that his admiration of the works
of Voltaire and Helvetius should induce him to wish a closer
connexion with Frenchmen.

Charles Carroll of Carrollton thought Jefferson "too theoretical and fanciful a statesman to direct with prudence the affairs
of this extensive and growing confederacy."[10] The implication
seemed clear: the young confederacy must learn to keep men
of intellectual genius out of practical affairs.

The demagogic attacks made on Jefferson by the established
clergy may be explained also by the fact that he had forged a
singular, and to them obnoxious, coalition. Jefferson, although
a Deist and a man of secular learning, had roused many supporters among the evangelical and pietistic denominations,
particularly among the Baptists. Not only were they impressed
by Jefferson's reputation for democratic sentiments, but as dissenters they were also impressed by his espousal of toleration.
They were far less troubled by the charges of infidelity hurled
at him than by the disabilities imposed on themselves by the
established churches. Jefferson and other secular intellectuals
thus joined the pietistic denominations in a curious political alliance based upon common hostility to established orthodoxy.
Both groups appealed to standards of authority alien to the
established churches: the secular liberals to rationalist criticism,
the pietists to intuition. For the moment, under the pressure
of their common dislike of established dogma, the liberals and
pietists chose to ignore their own differences, and to set aside
the fact that the one objected to all dogma and the other to all
establishments.[11]

---

[10] In a letter to Alexander Hamilton, in J. C. Hamilton, ed.: *The Works of Alexander Hamilton* (New York, 1850–51), Vol. VI, pp. 434–5. Hamilton himself
understood that Jefferson, far from being a thoroughgoing doctrinaire, was a
temporizing and opportunistic statesman.

[11] On the nature of this alliance and the consequences of its ultimate dissolution, see Sidney E. Mead's penetrating essay, "American Protestantism during
the Revolutionary Epoch," *Church History*, Vol. XII (December, 1953), pp.
279–97.

To drive a wedge into this alliance, the established clergy tried to demonstrate that Jefferson was a threat to all Christians— a charge that many of them in their partisan anguish no doubt sincerely believed. In time the alliance between the pietists and the enlightened liberals did break up; a gap was opened between the common man and the intellectual which has seldom since been satisfactorily bridged. But at the time of Jefferson's election the alliance between liberal intellect and evangelical democracy still held good. When the break finally occurred, when the upsurging forces of popular democracy were released from the restraining hand of enlightened patrician leadership, the forces of evangelicalism produced an anti-intellectualism every bit as virulent and of far more effect than that employed by the established clergy against Jefferson.

2

The shabby campaign against Jefferson, and then the Alien and Sedition Acts, manifested the treason of many wealthy and educated Federalists against the cultural values of tolerance and freedom. Unfortunately, it did not follow that more popular parties under Jeffersonian or Jacksonian leadership could be counted on to espouse these values. The popular parties themselves eventually became the vehicles of a kind of primitivist and anti-intellectualist populism hostile to the specialist, the expert, the gentleman, and the scholar.

Even in its earliest days, the egalitarian impulse in America was linked with a distrust for what in its germinal form may be called political specialization and in its later forms expertise. Popular writers, understandably proud of the political competence of the free man, were on the whole justifiably suspicious of the efforts of the cultivated and wealthy to assume an exclusive or excessively dominant role in government. Their suspicions did not stop there, however, but led many of them into hostility to all forms of learning. A current of anti-intellectualism can be found in some of the earliest expressions of popular political thought. In the revolutionary era, some popular writers assumed that efforts to limit the power of the rich and well-born would have to include their allies, the learned classes, as well. A rural delegate to the convention elected in Massachusetts to decide on the ratification of the

Constitution in 1788 explained his opposition to the document in these words:[12]

> These lawyers, and men of learning, and moneyed men, that talk so finely, and gloss over matters so smoothly, to make us poor illiterate people swallow down the pill, expect to get into Congress themselves; they expect to be the managers of this constitution, and get all the power and all the money into their own hands, and then they will swallow up all us little folks, like the great *Leviathan*, Mr. President; yes, just as the whale swallowed up *Jonah*. This is what I am afraid of.

We are fortunate to have, from the hands of a plain New England farmer, William Manning of North Billerica, Massachusetts, a political pamphlet showing what one shrewd, militantly democratic American thought when he turned his mind to the philosophy of government. This spirited Jeffersonian document, *The Key of Libberty*, was written in 1798 at a time when party passions were at a high pitch. Noteworthy here is the central place accorded by Manning ("not a Man of Larning my selfe for I never had the advantage of six months schooling in my life") to learning as a force in the political struggle. The opening words of his manuscript proclaim: "Learning & Knowledg is essential to the preservation of Libberty & unless we have more of it amongue us we Cannot Seporte our Libertyes Long."[13] But to Manning learning and knowledge were of interest mainly as class weapons.

At the heart of Manning's philosophy was a profound suspicion of the learned and property-holding classes. Their education, their free time, and the nature of their vocations made it possible, he saw, for the merchants, lawyers, doctors, clergymen, and executive and judicial officers of state to act together in pursuit of their ends, as the laboring man could not. Among these classes there is, he thought, a general dislike of free government: they constantly seek to destroy it because it thwarts their selfish interests.

---

[12]Jonathan Elliot: *Debates* (Philadelphia, 1863), Vol. II, p. 102.
[13]Samuel Eliot Morison, ed.: *The Key of Libberty* (Billerica, Mass., 1922). The work is reprinted in *William and Mary Quarterly*, 3rd ser., Vol. XIII (April, 1956), pp. 202–54, and quotations in the following paragraphs are from pp. 221, 222, 226, 231–2.

To efect this no cost nor pains is spared, but they first unite their plans and schemes by asotiations, conventions & corraspondances with each other. The Marchents asotiate by themselves, the Phitisians by themselves, the Ministers by themselves, the Juditial and Executive Officers are by their professions often called together & know each others minds, & all letirary men & the over grown rich, that can live without labouring, can spare time for consultation. All being bound together by common interest, which is the strongest bond of union, join in their secret correspondance to counter act the interests of the many & pick their pockets, which is efected ondly for want of the meens of knowledg amongue them.

Since learning is an instrument for the pursuit of one's interests, "the few" naturally favor the institutions that serve their own class: "the few are always crying up the advantages of costly collages, national acadimyes & grammer schooles, in ordir to make places for men to live without work and so strengthen their party. But are always opposed to cheep schooles & woman schooles, the ondly or prinsaple means by which larning is spred amongue the Many." In the colleges (Manning no doubt had Federalist Harvard in mind) the principles of republicanism are criticized, and the young are indoctrinated with monarchical notions. Manning also observed that the graduates of these institutions "are taught to keep up the dignity of their professions"—and to this he objected because it made them set too high a value on their services, and thus made religious and educational services expensive to the many: "For if we apply for a preacher or a School Master, we are told the price, So Much, & they cant go under, for it is agreed upon & they shall be disgrased if they take less." As Manning saw it, the schoolmaster ought to become what in fact he did become in America—an inexpensive hired laborer of very low status.

Here, then, is the key to Manning's educational strategy. Education was to be made cheap for the common man; and higher education, such as there was, would be organized simply to serve elementary education—to provide inexpensive instructors for the common schools. "Larning . . . aught to be promoted in the cheepest and best manner possable"—in such a way, that is, that "we should soone have a plenty of school masters & misstrises as cheap as we could hire other labour, &

Labour & Larning would be connected together & lessen the number of those that live without work." It must be said that Manning's prescription, offered at a time when the vaunted common school system of Massachusetts was being neglected, had its point. But in the interests of the lower reaches of the educational system he proposed to strip the upper reaches, to reduce their functions to that of producing cheap academic labor. Advanced learning Manning considered to have no intrinsic value worth cultivating. Academies and classical studies that went beyond what was necessary "to teach our Children a b c" were "ondly to give imploy to gentlemens sons & make places for men to live without worke. For their is no more need for a mans haveing a knowledge of all the languages to teach a Child to read write & cifer than their is for a farmer to have the marinors art to hold plow." Education had been for a long time the instrument of the few; Manning hoped to make it, so far as possible, the instrument of the many. Of its instrumental, and hence subservient, character he had no doubt; nor did he worry about the consequence of his policy for high culture—which was, after all, the prerogative of those who lived without work.

The place of education, in this controversy between the few and the many, is a perfect paradigm of the place of high culture in American politics. Education was caught between a comfortable class only imperfectly able to nourish it, and a powerful, upsurging, egalitarian public chiefly interested in leveling status distinctions and in stripping the privileged of the instruments of privilege. Understandably, the common man wanted to protect his interests and use education to expand his social opportunities; no one seemed able to show him how to do this without damage to intellectual culture itself.

That there was a certain rough justice in Manning's contentions cannot be denied. The Federalists had indeed appropriated Harvard College; why should the democrats not retaliate by appropriating as far as they could the instruments of common education? If they could have their way, there would be no more Harvard Colleges. If a learned class could do nothing but support privilege, there need be no learned class. Almost half a century after Manning wrote his essay, Horace Greeley argued that the American yeoman did in fact appreciate and respect talent and learning; but that all too often he found them "directed to the acquisition of wealth and luxury by means which add little to the aggregate of human comforts, and rather subtract from his own especial share of them."[14] Hence, as the demand for the rights of the common man took form in nineteenth-century America, it included a program for free elementary education, but it also carried with it a dark and sullen suspicion of high culture, as a creation of the enemy.

3

Something was missing in the dialectic of American populistic democracy. Its exponents meant to diminish, if possible to get rid of, status differences in American life, to subordinate educated as well as propertied leadership. If the people were to rule, if they aspired to get along with as little leadership as possible from the educated and propertied classes, whence would their guidance come? The answer was that it could be generated from within. As popular democracy gained strength and confidence, it reinforced the widespread belief in the superiority of inborn, intuitive, folkish wisdom over the cultivated, oversophisticated, and self-interested knowledge of the literati and the well-to-do. Just as the evangelicals repudiated a learned religion and a formally constituted clergy in favor of the wisdom of the heart and direct access to God, so did advocates of egalitarian politics propose to dispense with trained leadership in favor of the native practical sense of the ordinary man with its direct access to truth. This preference for the wisdom of the common man flowered, in the most extreme statements of the democratic creed, into a kind of militant popular anti-intellectualism.

Even Jefferson, who was neither an anti-intellectual nor a dogmatic egalitarian, seemed at times to share this preference. To his nephew, Peter Carr, he wrote in 1787: "State a moral case to a ploughman and a professor. The former will decide

[14] In an address at Hamilton College, January 23, 1844, quoted in Merle Curti: *American Paradox* (New Brunswick, 1956), p. 20; cf. pp. 19–24.

it as well, and often better than the latter, because he has not been led astray by artificial rules."[15] Jefferson was simply expressing a conventional idea of eighteenth-century thinking: the idea that God had given man certain necessary *moral* sentiments. It would not have occurred to him to assert the intellectual superiority of the plowman. But one need only go one step further than Jefferson, and say that political questions were in essence moral questions,[16] to lay a foundation for the total repudiation of cultivated knowledge in political life. For if the plowman understood morals as well as the professor, he would understand politics equally well; and he was likely to conclude (here Jefferson would not have agreed) that he had little to learn from anyone, and had no need of informed leaders. Push the argument just a bit further and it would support the assertion that anyone who had anything of the professor about him made an inferior leader; and that political leaders should be sought from among those who in this respect resembled the untutored citizen. Ironically, Jefferson himself was to suffer from this notion. Later it became one of the rallying cries of Jacksonian democracy.

The first truly powerful and widespread impulse to anti-intellectualism in American politics was, in fact, given by the Jacksonian movement. Its distrust of expertise, its dislike for centralization, its desire to uproot the entrenched classes, and its doctrine that important functions were simple enough to

[15] *Writings*, A. E. Bergh, ed., Vol. VI (Washington, 1907), pp. 257–8, August 10, 1787. Jefferson was advising his nephew on the conduct of his education, and his chief concern was to establish the point that much study of moral philosophy was "lost time." If moral conduct were a matter of science rather than sound impulse, he pointed out, the millions who had no formal learning would be less moral than the few who had. Clearly, God had not left men without a moral sense, and a very small stock of reason or common sense would be needed to implement it. This was, of course, a familiar doctrine. Jefferson may well have been led to it by the writings of Lord Kames. One may wonder, however, if the study of moral philosophy was useless, why Jefferson had read so widely in this field. On the problems created in his thinking by this doctrine, see Adrienne Koch: *The Philosophy of Thomas Jefferson* (New York, 1943), chapter 3.

[16] As, a century after Jefferson, William Jennings Bryan most explicitly did: "The great political questions are in their final analysis great moral questions." Paxton Hibben: *The Peerless Leader* (New York, 1929), p. 194.

be performed by anyone, amounted to a repudiation not only of the system of government by gentlemen which the nation had inherited from the eighteenth century, but also of the special value of the educated classes in civic life. In spite of this, many intellectuals and men of letters, particularly the young, supported the Jacksonian cause—enough, indeed, to belie the common charge that the educated classes regularly withheld their sympathies from movements meant to benefit the common man. It is true that the leading literary quarterlies were devoted to gentility and remained in the hands of the Whig opposition; but when John L. O'Sullivan founded the *Democratic Review* he was able to get contributions from a distinguished roster of writers of varying political persuasions. It is also true that the leading New England Transcendentalists were largely aloof or hostile. But writers like Orestes Brownson, William Cullen Bryant, George Bancroft, James Fenimore Cooper, Nathaniel Hawthorne, James Kirke Paulding, and Walt Whitman supported the new democracy with varying degrees of cordiality and persistence.[17]

The support of such men was welcomed in Jacksonian ranks, and was sometimes greeted with pride, but on the whole, intellectuals were not accorded much recognition or celebrity. The most outstanding exception was George Bancroft, the historian. In Massachusetts the Democrats felt the need of literary and intellectual leadership to counter the distinguished array of talent in the ranks of the opposition, and Bancroft assumed prominence in his party when he was still in his thirties. He was appointed Collector of the Port of Boston, became Secretary of the Navy under Polk (a post also given to Paulding by Van Buren), and was later minister to Great Britain. His influence enabled him to find a job for Hawthorne in the Boston Custom House and for Brownson (to Bancroft's prompt regret) as steward of the Marine Hospital there. The situation of Hawthorne represents the other side of the picture. He was constantly honored with jobs considerably slighter than his merits or his desperate needs would have dictated. In the Custom House he was no more than a weigher and gauger, and the

---

[17]On the relation of Jacksonian democracy and the intellectuals, see Arthur Schlesinger, Jr.: *The Age of Jackson* (Boston, 1945), especially chapter 29.

post (a "grievous thraldom," he called it) was a poor substitute for the position he had actually sought as historian to an expedition to the Antarctic. Later he sought the postmastership of Salem and was made instead surveyor of the port. And finally, after writing a campaign biography of his friend and college classmate, Franklin Pierce, he was awarded a consulate—but at Liverpool. On the whole, the record of Jacksonian democracy in achieving a *rapprochement* between the intellectual or man of letters and the popular mind was inferior to that later achieved by Progressivism and the New Deal.

The contests in 1824 and 1828 between Jackson and John Quincy Adams provided a perfect study in contrasting political ideals. Adams's administration was the test case for the unsuitability of the intellectual temperament for political leadership in early nineteenth-century America. The last President to stand in the old line of government by gentlemen, Adams became the symbol of the old order and the chief victim of the reaction against the learned man. He had studied in Paris, Amsterdam, Leyden, and The Hague, as well as at Harvard; he had occupied Harvard's chair of rhetoric and oratory; he had aspired to write epic poetry; like Jefferson, he was known for his scientific interests; he had been head for many years of the American Academy of Arts and Sciences; and as Monroe's Secretary of State he had prepared a learned scientific report on systems of weights and measures which is still a classic. Adams believed that if the new republic failed to use its powers to develop the arts and sciences it would be "hiding in the earth the talent committed to our charge—would be treachery to the most sacred of trusts." It was his hope—as it had been Washington's, Jefferson's and Madison's—that the federal government would act as the guide and center of a national program of educational and scientific advancement. But in proposing that Washington be developed as a cultural capital, he mobilized against himself the popular dislike of centralization.

In his first annual message to Congress, Adams proposed a system of internal improvements—roads and canals—advantageous to business interests, and also asked for several things desired chiefly by men of the learned classes: a national university at Washington, a professional naval academy, a national observatory, a voyage of discovery to the Northwest to follow upon the expedition of Lewis and Clark, an efficient patent office, federal aid to the sciences through a new executive department.

It was characteristic of Adams to offend the same bumptious popular nationalism to which Jackson so perfectly appealed. Adams pointed out that European countries, though less happily blessed with freedom than America, were doing more for science; and he had the temerity to suggest that some policies of the governments of France, Great Britain, and Russia could well be emulated here. Then, as now, such intellectual cosmopolitanism was unpopular. Having thus flouted national *amour-propre*, Adams went on to flout democratic sentiment by urging generous appropriations for scientific purposes; he even suggested in an inflammatory phrase that Congressional leaders should not "fold up our arms and proclaim to the world that we are palsied by the will of our constituents." Worse still, Adams referred provocatively to the many observatories built under the patronage of European governments as "lighthouses of the skies." Congress snickered at this phrase, and the lighthouses were thrown back at Adams time and again. His own Cabinet saw that the President's program would shock the country—Clay, for instance, found the proposal of a national university "certainly hopeless," and doubted that Adams could get five votes in the House for his proposed executive department—and in the end Adams had to give it up. He represented a kind of leadership which had outlived its time. Hamilton, Washington, even Jefferson, had been interested in a measure of centralization within some kind of national plan, and had expressed the desire common among the gentlemen of the Eastern seaboard to give some order to the expansion of America. But the country grew too fast for them, and would accept no plan and no order. As their type became obsolete in politics, the position of the man of intellect also deteriorated.[18] Adams was the last nineteenth-century occupant of the White

[18]For Adams's program, see J. R. Richardson: *Messages and Papers of the Presidents* (New York, 1897), Vol. II, pp. 865–83, and the comments of A. Hunter Dupree: *Science in the Federal Government* (Cambridge, 1957), pp. 39–43; cf. Samuel Flagg Bemis: *John Quincy Adams and the Union* (New York, 1956), pp. 65–70.

House who had a knowledgeable sympathy with the aims and aspirations of science or who believed that fostering the arts might properly be a function of the federal government.

As Adams embodied the old style, Andrew Jackson embodied the new; and the opposition between these two in the politics of the 1820's symbolized what America had been and what it would become. In headlong rebellion against the European past, Americans thought of "decadent" Europe as more barbarous than "natural" America; they feared that their own advancing civilization was "artificial" and might estrange them from Nature. Jackson's advocates praised him as the representative of the natural wisdom of the natural man. Among his other gifts as a national leader, the hero of New Orleans, the conqueror of the "barbaric" army of cultivated Britain was able to offer reassurances as to the persistence of native vigor and the native style. Jackson, it was said, had been lucky enough to have escaped the formal training that impaired the "vigour and originality of the understanding." Here was a man of action, "educated in Nature's school," who was "artificial in nothing"; who had fortunately "escaped the training and dialectics of the schools"; who had a "judgement unclouded by the visionary speculations of the academician"; who had, "in an extraordinary degree, that native strength of mind, that practical common sense, that power and discrimination of judgement which, for all useful purposes, are more valuable than all the acquired learning of a sage"; whose mind did not have to move along "the tardy avenues of syllogism, nor over the beaten track of analysis, or the hackneyed walk of logical induction," because it had natural intuitive power and could go "with the lightning's flash and illuminate its own pathway."[19]

George Bancroft, who must have believed that his own career as a schoolmaster had been useless, rhapsodized over Jackson's unschooled mind:[20]

> Behold, then, the unlettered man of the West, the nursling of the wilds, the farmer of the Hermitage, little versed in books,

[19]The quotations from Jacksonian literature are from John William Ward: *Andrew Jackson: Symbol for an Age* (New York, 1955), pp. 31, 49, 52, 53, 68. I am much indebted to Professor Ward's brilliant study of Jacksonian imagery.
[20]Ward: op. cit., p. 73.

unconnected by science with the tradition of the past, raised
by the will of the people to the highest pinnacle of honour, to
the central post in the civilization of republican freedom. . . .
What policy will he pursue? What wisdom will he bring with
him from the forest? What rules of duty will he evolve from the
oracles of his own mind?

Against a primitivist hero of this sort, who brought wisdom
straight out of the forest, Adams, with his experience at foreign
courts and his elaborate education, seemed artificial. Even in
1824, when Adams won a freakish four-way election, Jackson
was by far the more popular candidate; when the General returned to challenge him four years later, there could be no
doubt of the outcome. Adams was outdone in every section
of the country but New England, in a battle fought unscrupu-
lously on both sides and described as a contest between

> John Quincy Adams who can write
> And Andrew Jackson who can fight.

The main case made by Jackson's spokesmen against Adams
was that he was self-indulgent and aristocratic and lived a life of
luxury. And, what is most relevant here, his learning and political training were charged up not as compensating virtues but
as additional vices. A group of Jackson's supporters declared
that the nation would not be much better off for Adams's intellectual accomplishments:[21]

> That he is *learned* we are willing to admit; but his *wisdom* we
> take leave to question. . . . We confess our attachment to the
> homely doctrine: thus happily expressed by the great English
> poet:
>
> > That not to know of things remote
> > From use, obscure and subtle, but to know
> > That which before us lies in daily life,
> > Is the prime wisdom.
>
> That wisdom we believe Gen. Jackson possesses in an eminent
> degree.

---

[21] *Address of the Republican General Committee of Young Men of the City and
County of New York* (New York, 1828), p. 41.

Another Jacksonian, speaking of the past record of the two, said: "Jackson made law, Adams quoted it."[22]

Jackson's triumph over Adams was overwhelming. It would be an exaggeration to say that this was simply a victory of the man of action over the man of intellect, since the issue was posed to the voters mainly as a choice between aristocracy and democracy. But as the two sides fashioned the public images of the candidates, aristocracy was paired with sterile intellect, and democracy with native intuition and the power to act.[23]

4

Although the Jacksonians appealed powerfully to both egalitarian and anti-intellectual sentiments, they had no monopoly on either. It was not merely Jacksonianism that was egalitarian —it was the nation itself. The competitive two-party system guaranteed that an irresistible appeal to the voters would not long remain in the hands of one side, for it would be copied. It was only a question of time before Jackson's opponents,

[22]Ward: op. cit., p. 63.

[23]Electoral appeals on both sides were lacking in truth and delicacy; and Adams never repudiated the viler aspersions cast by the Adams propagandists upon Jackson's life with Mrs. Jackson. Adams seems to have been persuaded that these were justified. In 1831 he wrote in his diary that "Jackson lived in open adultery with his wife." Most of the Brahmin world found itself unable to embrace Jackson as President. Harvard did award him an honorary degree of Doctor of Laws at its 1833 commencement, but Adams refused to attend. "I *would not* be present," he wrote, "to see my darling Harvard disgrace herself by conferring a Doctor's degree upon a barbarian and savage who can scarcely spell his own name." Bemis: op. cit., p. 250; see also Adams's *Memoirs*, Vol. VIII (Philadelphia, 1876), pp. 546–7. Adams was told by President Quincy of Harvard that he was well aware how "utterly unworthy of literary honors Jackson was," but that after a degree had been awarded to Monroe it would be necessary to honor Jackson to avoid the show of "party spirit." At the occasion itself, Jackson appears to have charmed the hostile audience. But the rumor went about, and was widely believed by the credulous in Cambridge and Boston, that Jackson had responded to the ceremonies, which were in Latin, by rising and saying: "*Caveat emptor: corpus delicti: ex post facto: dies irae: e pluribus unum: usque ad nauseam: Ursa Major: sic semper tyrannis: quid pro quo: requiescat in pace.*" See the recollections of Josiah Quincy: *Figures of the Past* (Boston, 1926), pp. 304–7.

however stunned by the tactics of his supporters in 1828, would swallow their distaste for democratic rhetoric and learn to use it. Party leaders who could not or would not play the game would soon be driven off the field.

A persistent problem facing party organizers who were linked to men of affairs—to promoters of canals, banks, turnpikes, and manufacturing enterprises—was to manage to identify themselves with the people and to find safe popular issues which they could exploit without risk to their interests. There was a premium on men who could keep touch with the common people and yet move comfortably and function intelligently in the world of political management and business enterprise.[24] Henry Clay was so gifted, and he had many of the qualities of a major public hero as well; but by the beginning of the 1830's he had been on the national scene too long; his views were too well known, and he was too closely associated with the discredited Adams to be of use. Most notable among the new party bosses with a good grasp of the problem was Thurlow Weed, who used the violently egalitarian passions of anti-Masonry to ride into prominence, and who became one of the greatest of the Whig, and then Republican, party organizers. But the anti-Jacksonians, for all they may have learned in 1828, did not find the figure who set quite the right style for them until Davy Crockett bolted from the ranks of the Jacksonians.

Frontiersman, hunter, fighter, and spokesman of the poor Western squatter, Crockett became a major American folk symbol, and his autobiography a classic of American frontier humor. Unembarrassed by wealth or education, Crockett was drawn into politics by the force of his own appeal. When he was about thirty, and newly arrived at a small settlement on Shoal Creek in Tennessee, he was appointed justice of the peace, was soon elected colonel of the militia regiment organized in his district, and then sent to the state legislature. In 1826, after it had been casually suggested to him that he run for Congress, he waged a campaign enlivened by funny stories, and found himself elected. Tennessee now had a representative in

[24]Cf. the analysis of the situation in Glyndon G. Van Deusen: *Thurlow Weed: Wizard of the Lobby* (Boston, 1947), pp. 42–4; and Whitney R. Cross: *The Burned-Over District* (Ithaca, 1950), pp. 114–17.

Congress who could "wade the Mississippi, carry a steam-boat on his back, and whip his weight in wild cats," and who was not afraid, for all his simplicity, to address the House because he could "whip any man in it."

It was Crockett's pride to represent the native style and natural intuition. In his autobiography, published in 1834, Crockett boasted of the decisions he handed down from the Tennessee bench at a time when he "could just barely write my own name." "My judgments were never appealed from, and if they had been they would have stuck like wax, as I gave my decisions on the principles of common justice and honesty between man and man, and relied on natural born sense, and not on law learning to guide me; for I had never read a page in a law book in all my life."[25] This ingenuous confidence in the sufficiency of common sense may have been justified by Crockett's legal decisions, but he was not content to stop here: he had a considered disdain for the learned world. At one point in his Congressional career, Crockett reported:[26]

> There were some gentlemen that invited me to go to Cambridge, where the big college or university is; where they keep ready-made titles or nicknames to give people. I would not go, for I did not know but they might stick an LL.D. on me before they let me go; and I had no idea of changing "Member of the House of Representatives of the United States," for what stands for "lazy lounging dunce," which I am sure my constituents would have translated my new title to be, knowing that I had never taken any degree, and did not own to any, except a small degree of good sense not to pass for what I was not. . . .

Crockett, who had fought under Jackson in the Creek War in 1813–14, first went to Congress as a member of the Jacksonian group from Tennessee and as a representative of the poor Western squatters of the state, whose condition was very much what his had once been. Before long, he found these two loyalties in conflict. A group of Tennesseeans, led by James K.

[25]Hamlin Garland, ed.: *The Autobiography of Davy Crockett* (New York, 1923), p. 90.
[26]Ibid., p. 180. The main butt of the humor here was Andrew Jackson, who had already received his Harvard degree. "One *digniterry*," said Crockett, "was enough from Tennessee."

Polk, was attempting to get the United States to cede to the state some unappropriated Western District lands as an endowment for education. The interests of education and the interests of the poorer classes seemed unfortunately to be thrown into conflict at this time, and Crockett, as the representative of the squatters, naturally looked askance at Polk's land bill. Land warrants held by the University of North Carolina had already caused some of his constituents to lose their homes. Crockett concluded that the proposal to use part of the land proceeds for a college in Nashville would in the same way hurt others. His constituents, he pointed out, would not be compensated by the development of colleges, for none of them could use them. If, he remarked, "we can only get a common country, or as College Graduates sometimes deridingly call it, a B-a school, convenient enough to send our Big Boys in the winter and our little ones all the year, we think ourselves fortunate, especially if we can raise enough Coon-Skins and one little thing or other to pay up the teacher at the end of every quarter."[27]

Explaining in Congress that he was not an opponent of education, Crockett pointed out that he felt obliged, none the less, to defend the interests of the people he represented, who had "mingled the sweat of their brows with the soil they occupied," and who were now to have their "humble cottages" taken away from them by "the Legislature of the State, for the purpose of raising up schools for the children of the rich."[28]

> I repeat, that I was utterly opposed to this, not because I am the enemy of education, but because the benefits of education are not to be dispensed with an equal hand. This College system went into practice to draw a line of demarcation between the two classes of society—it separated the children of the rich from the children of the poor. The children of my people never

[27] Quoted in Charles Grier Sellers, Jr.: *James K. Polk, Jacksonian: 1795–1843* (Princeton, 1957), pp. 123–4. On the land bill, see ibid., pp. 122–8; James A. Shackford: *David Crockett, the Man and the Legend* (Chapel Hill, 1956), pp. 90–9.

[28] *Register of Debates*, 20th Congress, 2nd session, pp. 162–3 (January 5, 1829). In raising the question of the diversion of funds for the use of colleges, Crockett was here using a false issue, since Polk had already attempted to mollify Crockett by inserting a requirement that the proceeds of land sales be used only for common schools.

saw the inside of a college in their lives, and never are likely to
do so. . . . If a swindling machine is to be set up to strip them
of what little the surveyors, and the colleges, and the warrant
holders, have left them, it shall never be said that I sat by in
silence, and refused, however humbly, to advocate their cause.

We hear in this an echo of Manning's idea that common
schools serve the people and colleges the rich. For American
society it was tragic that the interests of higher education and
those of the ordinary citizen should thus be allowed to appear
to be in conflict. But to the Adams-Clay men, always under
severe pressure from the Jackson forces, the split in the ranks of
the Tennessee Jacksonians came as a gift from heaven. Before
long, the astute opposition organizers, realizing that to have
a pioneer democrat in their ranks would give them a magnificent counterpoise to Jackson, approached Crockett and took
advantage of his alienation from the Jackson men in his state
and his long-standing personal resentment of the President
to bring him around to the opposition. This alliance between
Crockett and the national anti-Jackson forces, negotiated by
Matthew St. Clair Clarke, a friend of Nicholas Biddle, the president of the United States Bank, was apparently in the making
as early as 1829 and was clearly consolidated by 1832. Crockett's
Congressional speeches began to be written for him, and various parts of his famous *Autobiography* were also ghost-written,
though they have about them the air of Crockett's own dicta-
tion.[29] In 1835 Crockett published an assault upon Martin Van
Buren that prefigured the full-blown demagogy of the Whig
campaign of 1840.

By 1840 the conquest of the Whig Party by the rhetoric
of populism was complete. Crockett, who was too provincial
and too unreliable to have presidential stature, had gone off to
Texas, had been killed in the defense of the Alamo, and had
begun to be transformed into a demigod; but in the presidential election of 1836 William Henry Harrison, like Jackson
a hero of early Indian campaigns, had been found to have a
similar public appeal. It mattered little that his famous victory

[29]The most satisfactory account of Crockett's *rapprochement* with the Eastern
conservatives and the authorship of his speeches and autobiographical writings
is that of Shackford: op. cit., pp. 122–9.

over Tecumseh's forces at Tippecanoe in 1811 had been something of a fiasco; with skillful publicity and some lapse of memory on the part of the public, it could be glorified into a feat comparable, almost, to Old Hickory's victory at New Orleans. The common touch was supplied in 1840 by the log-cabin and hard-cider theme, although Harrison lived in a rather substantial mansion on the banks of the Ohio. It seems in fact to have been the depression that tipped the scales against Van Buren, but the Whigs tried to assure their victory by using against him the same techniques of ballyhoo and misrepresentation that the Jacksonians had used against John Quincy Adams twelve years earlier. Representative Charles Ogle of Pennsylvania struck the keynote of the campaign in April when he delivered in the House his masterful address on "The Regal Splendor of the President's Palace," which was distributed as a pamphlet in thousands of copies. Speaking against a trifling appropriation of some $3,600 for alterations and repairs in the White House and its grounds, Ogle entertained the House with a fantastic account of the luxurious life of Martin Van Buren, easily eclipsing similar claims that had been made against Adams in 1828. This tirade reached a climax when Ogle denounced Van Buren for having installed in the White House some bathtubs which, in Ogle's opulent phrases, took on the dimensions of the baths of Caracalla.[30]

A Whig banner of 1840 proclaimed, with all too much truth: "WE STOOP TO CONQUER." Cultivated and hitherto fastidious men, once opposed to universal manhood suffrage, now proclaimed themselves friends of the people and gave their consent to the broadest and most irrational campaign techniques. Eminent politicians, raised on the controversies of an earlier and somewhat more restrained era, may have gagged, but they went along with the use of what one newspaper called "The Davy Crockett Line." A reserved and cultivated Southern aristocrat, Hugh Swinton Legaré, swallowed his distaste and went on a speaking tour. Daniel Webster was inspired to say that although he had not had the good fortune to be born in a log cabin, "my elder brother and sisters were. . . . That

[30]Charles Ogle: *The Regal Splendor of the President's Palace* (n.p., 1840), especially p. 28.

cabin I annually visit, and thither I carry my children, that they may learn to honor and emulate the stern and simple virtues that there found their abode. . . ." Anyone who called him an aristocrat was "not only a LIAR but a COWARD," and must be prepared to fight if Webster could get at him. Henry Clay, for his part, said privately that he "lamented the necessity, real or imagined . . . of appealing to the feelings and passions of our Countrymen, rather than to their reasons and judgments," and then did exactly that.

Sensitive men in the Whig ranks may have shrunk from the rhetoric of the log-cabin, hard-cider campaign, but if they wanted to stay in politics they could not shrink too long. The gentleman as a force in American politics was committing suicide. John Quincy Adams, watching the discouraging spectacle from Washington, found in this boisterous election "a revolution in the habits and manners of the people."[31] The process set in motion decades earlier, and poignantly symbolized by his own expulsion from the White House in 1829, had reached its fulfillment. "This appears to be the first time in our history," Morgan Dix commented, "in which a direct appeal was made to the lower classes by exciting their curiosity, feeding the desire for amusement, and presenting what is low and vulgar as an inducement for support. Since that day the thing has been carried farther, until it is actually a disadvantage to be of good stock and to have inherited 'the grand old name of gentleman.'"[32]

5

The withdrawal of the soberer classes from politics went on, hastened by the new fevers aroused by slavery and sectional animosities. As early as 1835 Tocqueville had commented on the "vulgar demeanor" and the obscurity of the members of the House; he would have found the deterioration quite advanced,

[31]For this campaign and the quotations, see Robert G. Gunderson: *The Log-Cabin Campaign* (Lexington, 1957), especially pp. 3, 7, 101–7, 134, 162, 179–86, 201–18.
[32]*Memoirs of John A. Dix* (New York, 1883), Vol. I, p. 165.

had he returned in the 1850's. "Do you remark," wrote Secretary of the Navy John Pendleton Kennedy to his uncle in the 1850's, "how lamentably destitute the country is of men in public station of whom we may speak with any pride? . . . How completely has the conception and estimate of a *gentleman* been obliterated from the popular mind! Whatever of that character we have seems almost banished from the stage."[33] In 1850, Francis Bowen, writing in the *North American Review*, found that both Houses of Congress had been "transformed into noisy and quarrelsome debating clubs."[34]

> Furious menaces and bellowing exaggeration take the place of calm and dignified debate; the halls of the capitol often present scenes which would disgrace a bear-garden; and Congress attains the unenviable fame of being the most helpless, disorderly, and inefficient legislative body which can be found in the civilized world.

Representative Robert Toombs of Georgia concurred. The present Congress, he wrote to a friend, "furnishes the worst specimens of legislators I have ever seen here. . . . There is a large infusion of successful jobbers, lucky serving men, parishless parsons and itinerant lecturers among them who are not only without wisdom or knowledge but have bad manners, and therefore we can have but little hope of good legislation."[35] By 1853 it was deemed necessary to forbid Congressmen by law to take compensation for prosecuting any claim against the government, and to prescribe penalties against bribery.[36] Deterioration reached the point of outright helplessness in 1859, when the House found itself almost unable to agree on a Speaker. Young Charles Francis Adams was in Washington

[33]Henry T. Tuckerman: *Life of John Pendleton Kennedy* (New York, 1871), p. 187.

[34]"The Action of Congress on the California and Territorial Questions," *North American Review*, Vol. LXXI (July, 1850), pp. 224–64.

[35]U. B. Phillips, ed.: *The Correspondence of Robert Toombs, Alexander H. Stephens, and Howell Cobb*, American Historical Association *Annual Report*, 1911, Vol. II, p. 188.

[36]Leonard D. White: *The Jacksonians*, p. 27. On deterioration in Congress and the public service, see pp. 25–7, 325–32, 343–6, 398–9, 411–20.

that year visiting his father, who was then a Congressman. As he later recalled:[37]

> I remember very well the Senate and House at that time. Neither body impressed me. The House was a national bear-garden; for that was, much more than now, a period of the unpicturesque frontiersman and the overseer. Sectional feeling ran high, and bad manners were conspicuously in evidence; whiskey, expectoration and bowie-knives were the order of that day. They were, indeed, the only kind of "order" observed in the House, over which poor old Pennington, of New Jersey, had as a last recourse been chosen to preside, probably the most wholly and all-round incompetent Speaker the House ever had.

In the earlier days of the Republic it had been possible for men in high places to add to their ranks with confidence other men of talents and distinction. This process was not as undemocratic as it may sound, since those who were thus co-opted were often men without advantages of birth and wealth. In 1808 it had been possible, for instance, for President Jefferson to write to William Wirt, a distinguished lawyer and essayist who had been born the son of an immigrant tavern-keeper, the following letter:[38]

> The object of this letter . . . is to propose to you to come into Congress. That is the great commanding theatre of this nation, and the threshold to whatever department or office a man is qualified to enter. With your reputation, talents, and correct views, used with the necessary prudence, *you will at once*

[37] *An Autobiography* (Boston, 1916) pp. 43–4. This was, of course, only a few years after the famous assault on Sumner by Brooks; during the same year a Congressman shot and killed a waiter out of annoyance with hotel dining-room service in Washington. On the state of Congress in the 1850's, see Roy F. Nichols: *The Disruption of American Democracy* (New York, 1948), pp. 2–3, 68, 188–91, 273–6, 284–7, 331–2. On the background of governmental decline, David Donald's Harmsworth Inaugural Lecture, "An Excess of Democracy: The American Civil War and the Social Process" (Oxford, 1960), is most stimulating. The decline of political leadership in the South has been particularly well traced in Clement Eaton: *Freedom of Thought in the Old South* (Durham, 1940), and Charles S. Sydnor: *The Development of Southern Sectionalism, 1819–1848* (Baton Rouge, 1948), especially chapter 12.

[38] *Writings*, edited by Bergh, Vol. XI (Washington, 1904), pp. 423–4; italics are mine.

be placed at the head of the republican body in the House of Rep-
resentatives; and after obtaining the standing which a little time
will ensure you, you may look, at your own will, into the military, the judiciary, the diplomatic, or other civil departments,
with a certainty of being in either whatever you please. And in the
present state of what may be called the eminent talents of our
country, you may be assured of being engaged through life in
the most honourable employments.

A few years after Jefferson's death, the confident assumptions
of this letter were no longer conceivable. The techniques of
advancement had changed; the qualities that put an aspiring
politician into rapport with the public became more important
than those that impressed his peers or superiors. More men
were pushed up from the bottom than selected from the top.

The change in the standards of elected personnel was paralleled by the fate of the public service. The first tradition of the
American civil service, established for the Federalists by Washington and continued by both Federalists and Jeffersonians
until 1829, was a tradition of government by gentlemen.[39] By
contemporary European standards of administration, Washington's initial criteria for appointments to Federal offices, although partisan, had been high. He demanded competence,
and he also placed much emphasis both on the public repute
and on the personal integrity of his appointees, in the hope that
to name "such men as I conceive would give dignity and lustre
to our National Character" would strengthen the new government. The impersonal principle of geographical distribution
of appointments was observed from the beginning, but nepo-
tism was ruled out. By 1792 political allegiance began to play
more of a role in appointments, but it was still a modest role,
as indicated by the remark of Washington's successor, John
Adams, that the first President had appointed "a multitude of

[39] My conclusions with regard to the history of the civil service have followed
Leonard D. White's invaluable histories: *The Federalists* (New York, 1948), *The
Jeffersonians* (New York, 1951), *The Jacksonians*, already cited, and *The Republican Era 1869–1901* (New York, 1958). Paul P. Van Riper, in his *History of the
United States Civil Service* (Evanston, Illinois, 1958), p. 11, remarks: "During
the formative years of the American national government its public service
was one of the most competent in the world. Certainly it was one of the freest
from corruption."

democrats and jacobins of the deepest die."[40] The greatest obstacle to recruitment into public service was that rural opinion
kept federal salaries low, and from the beginning the prestige
of public service was not high enough to be consistently attractive, even to men chosen for cabinet posts. When the Jeffersonians replaced the Federalists, Jefferson tried partly to calm the
political hysteria of the previous years by avoiding wholesale
public-service removals for political reasons alone; the most
outspoken, intransigent, and active Federalist office-holders
were fired, but the quieter ones retained their jobs. The caliber
of public officers remained the same, although Jefferson advanced the idea that the offices should be more or less equally
divided between the parties. The old criteria of integrity and
respectability prevailed, and whatever else may be said about
Jefferson's "Revolution of 1800," it brought no revolution in
administrative practice. Indeed, in this respect, the remarkable
thing was the continuity of criteria for choosing personnel.[41]

In the meantime, however, partisan use of patronage was
becoming standard practice in some states, notably in Pennsylvania and New York. The idea of rotation in office spread
from elective to appointive positions. With the rise of universal
suffrage and egalitarian passions, older traditions of administration gave way during the 1820's to a more candid use of
patronage for partisan purposes. The principle of rotation in
office, which was considered the proper democratic creed, was
looked upon by Jacksonians not as a possible cause of the deterioration of administrative personnel but rather as a social
reform. Jacksonians saw the opportunity to gain office as yet
another opportunity available to the common man in an open
society. The rotation of officeholders, they held, would make it

[40]John Adams: *Works* (Boston, 1854), Vol. IX, p. 87. This was not said in complete disapproval. Adams himself did not propose to proscribe the opposition,
lest he exclude "some of the ablest, most influential, and best characters in the
Union."
[41]Van Riper remarks that, so far as partisanship is concerned, Jefferson pro-
scribed enough public employees to be considered, as much as Jackson, the
founder of the national spoils system, but that, so far as the caliber and social
type of appointees are concerned, neither he nor his chief associates "made
any real indentation on the essentially upper-class nature of the federal civil
service." Op. cit., p. 23.

impossible for an undemocratic, permanent officeholding class to emerge. Easy removals and easy access to vacancies were not considered administrative weaknesses but democratic merits. This conception was expressed most authoritatively by Andrew Jackson in his first annual message to Congress in December, 1829.

Jackson argued that even when personal integrity made corruption unthinkable, men who enjoyed long tenure in office would develop habits of mind unfavorable to the public interest. Among long-standing officeholders, "office is considered as a species of property, and government rather as a means of promoting individual interests than as an instrument created for the service of the people." Sooner or later, whether by outright corruption or by the "perversion of correct feelings and principles," government is diverted from its legitimate ends to become "an engine for the support of the few at the expense of the many." The President was not troubled by the thought of the numbers of inexperienced and untried men that rotation would periodically bring. "The duties of all public officers are, or least admit of being made, so plain and simple that men of intelligence may readily qualify themselves for their performance"; and more would be lost by keeping men in office for long periods than would be gained as a result of their experience. In this, and in other passages, one sees Jackson's determination to keep offices open to newcomers as a part of the democratic pattern of opportunity, and to break down the notion that offices were a form of property. The idea of rotation in office he considered "a leading principle in the republican creed."[42]

The issue was clearly drawn: offices were in fact regarded by all as a kind of property, but the Jacksonians believed in *sharing* such property. Their approach to public offices was a

[42] J. D. Richardson, ed.: *Messages and Papers of the Presidents* (New York, 1897), Vol. III, pp. 1011–12. Several historians have pointed out that the actual number of Jackson's removals was not very great. His administration was perhaps more notable for providing a rationale for removals. In later years, addiction to the spoils system became so acute that it invaded the factions within the parties. In the 1850's the Buchanan Democrats were throwing out the Pierce Democrats.

perfect analogue of their anti-monopolistic position on economic matters. In a society whose energy and vitality owed so much to the diffusion of political and economic opportunities, there may have been more latent wisdom in this than Jackson's opponents were willing to admit. But the Jacksonian conviction that the duties of government were so simple that almost anyone could execute them downgraded the functions of the expert and the trained man to a degree which turned insidious when the functions of government became complex.[43] Just as the gentleman was being elbowed out of the way by the homely necessities of American elections, the expert, even the merely competent man, was being restricted by the demands of the party system and the creed of rotation into a sharply limited place in the American political system. The estrangement of training and intellect from the power to decide and to manage had been completed. The place of intellect in public life had, unfortunately, been made dependent upon the gentleman's regard for education and training and had been linked too closely to his political fortunes. In nineteenth-century America this was a losing cause.

[43] In fact, the principle of rotation could not be quite so fully realized as Jacksonian pronunciamentos suggested. What emerged was what Leonard D. White has called a "dual system," in which a patronage system and a career system existed side by side. Patronage clerks came and went, while a certain core of more permanent officers remained. See *The Jacksonians*, pp. 347–62.

CHAPTER VII

The Fate of the Reformer

I

B Y MID-CENTURY, the gentlemen had been reduced to a marginal role in both elective and appointive offices in the United States, and had been substantially alienated from American politics. For a time the Civil War submerged their discontents. The war was one of those major crises that suspend cultural criticism. It was a cause, a distraction, a task that urgently had to be done, and, on the whole, Northerners of the patrician class rallied to the support of their country without asking whether the political culture they proposed to save was worth saving. Lincoln, as they came to know him, was reassuring, and he pleased them by appointing men of learning and letters to diplomatic posts—Charles Francis Adams, Sr., John Bigelow, George William Curtis, William Dean Howells, and John Lothrop Motley. If American democratic culture could produce such a man, it was possible that they, after all, had underestimated it.

But when the war was over, the failure of the system seemed only to have been dramatized. Hundreds of thousands of lives had been lost to redeem the political failures of the pre-war generation, and during the terrible fiasco of Reconstruction, it became clear that beyond the minimal goal of saving the Union nothing had been accomplished and nothing learned. The new generation of entrepreneurs was more voracious than the old, and politics appeared to have been abandoned to bloody-shirt demagogy, to dispensing the public domain to railroad barons, and to the tariff swindle. The idealistic Republican Party of 1856 had become the party of men like Benjamin F. Butler and Ben Wade, and the creature of the scandalmakers of the Grant administration.

Many reformers saw how the tide of events was running as early as 1868, when Richard Henry Dana, Jr., tried to oust Benjamin F. Butler from his Massachusetts Congressional seat. For them the issue was sharply drawn: in the Bay State, the heart and center of the Brahmin class and the moral and intellectual wellspring of the patrician type, one of their own kind was now trying to remove from the political scene the man who had become the pre-eminent symbol of candid cynicism in politics. This was, *The New York Times* thought, "a contest between the intelligent, sober-minded, reflective men of the district, and the unthinking, reckless, boisterous don't-care-a-damnative portion of the community."[1] It proved also to be a contest between a tiny minority and the overwhelming majority of the immigrants and workers, marked by the almost classic ineptitude of Dana's electioneering techniques.[2] The dismal prospects of men of Dana's kind were harshly clarified by the election; Dana got less than ten per cent of the votes.

The humiliation of Dana was the first of a series of shocks. The reformers' friends were faring badly. Motley, on the strength of a rumor, was forced out of his diplomatic post by Andrew Johnson; reappointed by Grant, he was ditched once again because Grant wanted to strike through him at Sumner. Judge Ebenezer R. Hoar's nomination for the Supreme Court was rejected mainly because the politicians didn't like him. ("What could you expect," asked Simon Cameron, "from a man who had snubbed seventy Senators?") The able economist, David A. Wells, was cut out of his office as special revenue agent because of his free-trade views. Jacob Dolson Cox, a leading advocate of civil-service reform, felt impelled by lack of presidential support to resign as Grant's Secretary of the Interior. By 1870, Henry Adams, explaining why he had left Washington to teach at Harvard, wrote: "All my friends have been or are on the point of being driven out of the government

---

[1] *The New York Times*, October 24, 1868. For years Butler used the Brahmins' hatred of him as a political asset. A supporter in 1884 declared that he won elections because "all the snobs and all the dilettantes hate him, and Harvard College won't make him a doctor of laws." H. C. Thomas: *Return of the Democratic Party to Power in 1884* (New York, 1919), p. 139.

[2] It was in this campaign that Butler, driving a wedge between Dana and working-class constituencies, accused Dana of wearing white gloves. Dana admitted that he did at times wear white gloves and clean clothes, but assured his audience, the workingmen of Lynn, that when he spent two years before the mast as a young sailor, "I was as dirty as any of you." Benjamin F. Butler: *Butler's Book* (Boston, 1892), pp. 921–2.

and I should have been left without any allies or sources of information."[3]

The young men who had hoped that the party of Lincoln and Grant might bring about a reform no longer had any illusions. As the grim shape of the new America emerged out of the smoke of the war, there emerged with it a peculiar American underground of frustrated aristocrats, a type of genteel reformer whose very existence dramatized the alienation of education and intellect from significant political and economic power. The dominant idea of the genteel reformers was public service; their chief issue, civil-service reform; their theoretical spokesman, E. L. Godkin of the *Nation*; their most successful political hero, Grover Cleveland. Their towering literary monument proved to be that masterpiece in the artistry of self-pity, Henry Adams's *Education*.

The historian, looking back upon the genteel reformers and realizing how many grave social issues they barely touched upon and how many they did not touch at all, may be inclined to feel that their blood ran thin, and to welcome the appearance among them in later days of such a bold and distracted figure as John Jay Chapman. But this class represented the majority of the politically active educated men of the community; and the place of mind in American politics, if mind was to have any place at all, rested mainly upon their fortunes. This they understood themselves; it was what Lowell meant when he begged Godkin to protest in the *Nation* against "the queer notion of the Republican Party that they can get along without their brains"—and Charles Eliot Norton when he made his pathetic if rather parochial plaint that "the *Nation* & Harvard & Yale College seem to me almost the only solid barriers against the invasion of modern barbarism & vulgarity."[4]

The reform type was not national or representative. As a rule, the genteel reformers were born in the Northeast—mainly in

[3]Adams to C. M. Gaskell, October 25, 1870, in W. C. Ford, ed.: *Letters of Henry Adams* (Boston, 1930), p. 196.
[4]J. R. Lowell to Godkin, December 20, 1871, in Rollo Ogden, ed.: *Life and Letters of Edwin Lawrence Godkin* (New York, 1907), Vol. II, p. 87; C. E. Norton to Godkin, November 3, 1871, in Ari Hoogenboom: *Outlawing the Spoils* (Urbana, Illinois, 1961), p. 99.

Massachusetts, Connecticut, New York, and Pennsylvania—although a scattered few lived in those parts of the Middle West which had been colonized by Yankees and New Yorkers. Morally and intellectually these men were the heirs of New England, and for the most part its heirs by descent. They carried on the philosophical concerns of Unitarianism and transcendentalism, the moral animus of Puritanism, the crusading heritage of the free-soil movement, the New England reverence for education and intellectualism, the Yankee passion for public duty and civic reform.

They struck the Yankee note, one must add, of self-confidence and self-righteousness; most of the genteel reformers were certain of their own moral purity. "Each generation of citizens," declared the publisher George Haven Putnam, describing them in his autobiography, "produces a group of men who are free from self-seeking and who, recognizing their obligations to the community, are prepared to give their work and their capacities for doing what may be in their power for the service of their fellow-men."[5] This capacity for disinterested service was founded upon financial security and firm family traditions. The genteel reformers were not usually very rich, but they were almost invariably well-to-do. Hardly any were self-made men from obscure or poverty-stricken homes; they were the sons of established merchants and manufacturers, lawyers, clergymen, physicians, educators, editors, journalists, and publishers, and they had followed their fathers into business and the professions. Their education was far above the ordinary: at a time when college diplomas were still rare, there were among them an impressive number with B.A.'s, and most of those who lacked B.A.'s had law degrees. Several were historians, antiquarians, and collectors; others wrote poetry, fiction, or criticism. A high proportion of the college men had gone to Harvard or Yale, or to such outposts of the New England educational tradition as Amherst, Brown, Williams, Dartmouth, and Oberlin. Those whose religious affiliations can be determined belonged (aside from a few independents and skeptics) to the upper-class denominations, and especially those most affected by the New England tradition or those

[5]George Haven Putnam: *Memories of a Publisher* (New York, 1915), p. 112.

which appealed to mercantile patricians—Congregationalists, Unitarians, and Episcopalians.[6]

Politically and morally, as Henry Adams so poignantly demonstrated, the genteel reformers were homeless. They had few friends and no allies. Almost everywhere in American life— in business as well as in politics—an ingenuous but coarse and ruthless type of person had taken over control of affairs, a type Adams found in possession when he returned to Washington from England after the Civil War:[7]

> In time one came to recognize the type in other men [than Grant], with differences and variations, as normal; men whose energies were the greater, the less they wasted on thought; men who sprang from the soil to power; apt to be distrustful of themselves and of others; shy; jealous, sometimes vindictive; more or less dull in outward appearance, always needing stimulants; but for whom action was the highest stimulant—the instinct of fight. Such men were forces of nature, energies of the prime, like the *Pteraspis*, but they made short work of scholars. They had commanded thousands of such and saw no more in them than in others. The fact was certain; it crushed argument and intellect at once.

Wherever men of cultivation looked, they found themselves facing hostile forces and an alien mentality. They resented the new plutocracy which overshadowed them in business and in public affairs—a plutocracy they considered as dangerous socially as it was personally vulgar and ostentatious; for it consisted of those tycoons about whom Charles Francis Adams, Jr., said that after years of association he had not met one that he would ever care to meet again, or one that could be

[6]My generalizations about the reformers are based on an analysis of factors in the careers of 191 men in an unpublished master's essay at Columbia University written by James Stuart McLachlan: *The Genteel Reformers: 1865–1884* (1958). His conclusions are similar to those in Ari Hoogenboom's analysis of civil-service reformers, op. cit., pp. 190–7. Cf. his essay, "An Analysis of Civil Service Reformers," *The Historian*, Vol. XXIII (November, 1960), pp. 54–78. Paul P. Van Riper emphasizes the prior abolitionist sympathies of these reformers, and their preoccupation with individual liberty and political morality; op. cit., pp. 78–86.
[7]*The Education of Henry Adams* (New York: Modern Library edition; 1931), p. 265.

"associated in my mind with the idea of humor, thought or refinement."[8] No less vulgar were the politicians—"lewd fellows
of the baser sort," Godkin called them[9]—who compounded
their vulgarity with inefficiency, ignorance, and corruption.
Henry Adams had not long returned to Washington when a
Cabinet officer told him how pointless it was to show patience
in dealing with Congressmen: "You can't use tact with a Congressman! A Congressman is a hog! You must take a stick and
hit him on the snout!" Everyone in Boston, New England, and
New York agreed in warning Adams that "Washington was no
place for a respectable young man," and he could see for himself that the place had no tone, no society, no social medium
through which the ideas of men of discernment and refinement could influence affairs.[10]

> Society seemed hardly more at home than he. Both Executive
> and Congress held it aloof. No one in society seemed to have
> the ear of anybody in Government. No one in Government
> knew any reason for consulting any one in society. The world
> had ceased to be wholly political, but politics had become less
> social. A survivor of the Civil War—like George Bancroft, or
> John Hay—tried to keep footing, but without brilliant success.
> They were free to do or say what they liked, but no one took
> much notice of anything said or done.

The genteel reformers were as much alienated from the general public as they were from the main centers of power in
the business corporations and the political machines. They had
too much at stake in society to campaign for radical changes
and too much disdain for other varieties of reformers to make
political allies. The discontented farmers, with their cranky enthusiasms and their monetary panaceas, inspired in them only
distaste. Snobbishness and gentility, as well as class interest,
estranged them from the working class and the immigrants.
Charles Francis Adams, Jr., expressed a feeling common to his
class when he said: "I don't associate with the laborers on my

[8]Charles Francis Adams: *An Autobiography* (Boston, 1916), p. 190.
[9]E. L. Godkin: "The Main Question," *Nation*, Vol. IX (October 14, 1869),
p. 308.
[10]Adams: *Education*, pp. 261, 296, 320. Cf. James Bryce: "Why the Best Men
Do Not Go into Politics," *The American Commonwealth* (New York, 1897),
Vol. II, chapter 57.

place"; and he was no doubt doubly right when he added that such association would not be "agreeable to either of us."[11] As for the immigrants, the reformers considered their role in the misgovernment of cities to be one of the chief sources of the strength of the bosses. Reformers were sometimes skeptical about the merits of unrestricted democracy and universal manhood suffrage, and toyed with the thought of education tests or poll taxes that would disfranchise the most ignorant in the electorate.[12]

Thus estranged from major social interests which had different needs from their own, the genteel reformers were barred from useful political alliances and condemned to political ineffectuality. They had to content themselves with the hope that occasionally they could get their way by acting "on the limited number of cultivated minds,"[13] by appealing, as James Ford Rhodes put it, to men of "property and intelligence." "We want a government," said Carl Schurz in 1874, "which the best people of this country will be proud of."[14] What they were really asking for was leadership by an educated and civic-minded elite—in a country which had no use for elites of any

[11] *Autobiography*, pp. 15–16.
[12] See "The Government of our Great Cities," *Nation*, Vol. III (October 18, 1866), pp. 312–13; *North American Review*, Vol. CIII (October, 1866), pp. 413–65; Arthur F. Beringause: *Brooks Adams* (New York, 1955), pp. 60, 67; Barbara M. Solomon: *Ancestors and Immigrants* (Cambridge, Mass., 1956). On the outlook of the reformers, see Geoffrey T. Blodgett's sensitive account of "The Mind of the Boston Mugwump," *Mississippi Valley Historical Review*, Vol. XLVIII (March, 1962), pp. 614–34.
[13] Adams to Gaskell, quoted in Ernest Samuels: *The Young Henry Adams* (Cambridge, Mass., 1948), p. 182. Cf. Putnam's view: "It was our hope that as the youngsters came out of college from year to year with the kind of knowledge of the history of economics that would be given to them by professors like William Graham Sumner of Yale, we should gradually secure a larger hold on public opinion, and through the influence of leaders bring the mass of the voters to an understanding of their own business interests." Putnam: op. cit., pp. 42–3.
[14] Quoted in Eric Goldman: *Rendezvous with Destiny* (New York, 1952), p. 24. One advocate of civil-service reform pointed out that in "the early days of the Republic" all public servants from cabinet officers down to subordinate members "were generally selected from well-known families," and argued that civil-service reform would reintroduce this practice. Julius Bing: "Civil Service of the United States," *North American Review*, Vol. CV (October, 1867), pp. 480–1.

kind, much less for an educated one. "The best people" were outsiders. Their social position seemed a liability; their education certainly was. In 1888 James Russell Lowell complained that "in the opinion of some of our leading politicians and many of our newspapers, men of scholarly minds are *ipso facto* debarred from forming any judgment on public affairs; or if they should be so unscrupulous as to do so . . . they must at least refrain from communicating it to their fellow-citizens."[15]

Aware that their public following was too small to admit of a frontal attack on any major citadel of politics or administration, the genteel reformers were driven to adopt a strategy of independency. The margin of strength between the two major parties was frequently so narrow that, by threatening to bolt, a strong faction of independents might win an influence out of proportion to their numbers.[16] For a short time, the reformers seemed to be poised tantalizingly on the fringes of real influence. At first, they thought they might have some say in the Grant administration, and when Grant disappointed them, most of them took part in the ill-fated bolt of the Liberal Republicans in 1872. Then they were courted so carefully by Hayes that their expectations were aroused, only to be disappointed again. For the most part, they had to content themselves with limited victories, like the reform of the post office and the New York Customs House, or the occasional appointment of such men as Hamilton Fish, E. R. Hoar, William M. Evarts, Carl Schurz, or Wayne MacVeagh, to Cabinet posts. Their happiest moment came in the election of 1884, when they convinced themselves that the Mugwump bolt from the Republican Party had swung the state of New York from Blaine to Cleveland, and with it the election. But their outstanding legislative success was in civil-service reform, with the passage of the Pendleton Act in 1883. This deserves special attention, for civil-service reform, the class issue of the gentleman, was a touchstone of American political culture.

[15]"The Place of the Independent in Politics," *Writings*, Vol. VI (Cambridge, Mass., 1890), p. 190.
[16]On the strategy of independency, see James Russell Lowell: "The Place of the Independent in Politics," pp. 190 ff.; and E. McClung Fleming: *R. R. Bowker, Militant Liberal* (New York, 1952), pp. 103–8.

2

The central idea of the reformers—the idea which they all agreed upon and which excited their deepest concern—was the improvement of the civil service, without which they believed no other reform could be successfully carried out.[17] The ideal of civil-service reform brought into direct opposition the credo of the professional politicians, who put their faith in party organization and party rewards and the practice of rotation in office, and the ideals of the reformers, who wanted competence, efficiency, and economy in the public service, open competition for jobs on the basis of merit, and security of tenure. The reformers looked to various models for their proposals—to the American military services, to bureaucratic systems in Prussia or even China; but principally this English-oriented intellectual class looked for inspiration to England, where civil-service reorganization had been under way since the publication of the Northcote-Trevelyan Report in 1854.

The English civil-service reformers had designed their proposals in full awareness of the organic relation of the civil service to the class structure and to the educational system. They had planned a civil service which, as Gladstone observed, would give the gentlemanly classes "command over all the higher posts" and allot to members of the lower classes the positions that could be filled by persons with more practical and less expensive training.[18] The scheme owed much to the influence of Lord Macaulay, who conceived of "a public service confined in its upper reaches to gentlemen of breeding and culture selected by a literary competition." The higher posts would be filled by gentlemen who had received a rigorous classical training at one of the ancient universities, the lower posts by candidates with a less exalted education—and within each category recruitment by competitive examination would guarantee the merit of those chosen. By 1877, Sir Charles Trevelyan, one of the leading reformers, reported to an American friend that the British changes had been not only successful but

[17] On the centrality of this reform, see Paul P. Van Riper: op. cit., pp. 83–4.
[18] See J. Donald Kingsley: *Representative Bureaucracy: An Interpretation of the British Civil Service* (Yellow Springs, Ohio, 1944), pp. 68–71 and *passim*.

popular. "Large as the number of persons who profited by the former system of patronage were," he observed,

> those who were left out in the cold were still larger, and these included some of the best classes of our population—busy professional persons of every kind, lawyers, ministers of religion of every persuasion, schoolmasters, farmers, shopkeepers, etc. These rapidly took in the idea of the new institution, and they gladly accepted it as a valuable additional privilege.

Moreover, Sir Charles remarked, the same change that had increased the efficiency of the civil and military services "has given a marvellous stimulus to education." Formerly, upper-class boys who intended to go into public service had had no inducement to exert themselves because they were certain to get an appointment. Now they knew that their future depended in some good measure upon their own energies, and "a new spirit of activity has supervened. The opening of the civil and military services, in its influence upon national education, is equivalent to a hundred thousand scholarships and exhibitions of the most valuable kind. . . ."[19]

The appeal of the British reformers to their American counterparts is quite understandable. The concern of the leading American reformers was not, for the most part, self-interested, in so far as most jobs that would be opened in the American civil service, if competitive examinations were adopted, would not be of sufficient rank to attract them.[20] But it was humiliating to know that by the canons of the society in which they lived they were not preferred for office and could not help their friends.[21] What was mainly at issue for them was a cultural and

---

[19]Sir Charles Trevelyan to Dorman B. Eaton, August 20, 1877, in Dorman B. Eaton: *Civil Service in Great Britain: A History of Abuses and Reforms and Their Bearing upon American Politics* (New York, 1880), pp. 430–2.

[20]No doubt many reformers hoped wistfully that the kind of recognition Lincoln had given to literary men might be resumed, but such posts were above and outside the civil-service system. Characteristically, the reformers aspired to elective rather than appointive office. About half of the leading reformers held office at one time or another, but chiefly in elective positions. A few went to Congress, but most of their elected offices were in state legislatures. McLachlan: op. cit., p. 25.

[21]Consider the implications of Henry Adams's letter to Charles Francis Adams, Jr., April 29, 1869: "I can't get you an office. The only members of this Government that I have met are mere acquaintances, not friends, and I fancy

political ideal, a projection of their own standards of purity and excellence into governmental practice. It was the "national character" which was at stake. The principles of freedom and competitive superiority which they had learned in their college courses in classical economics and had applied to the tariff question ought to be applied to public office: open competition on the basis of merit should be the civil-service analogue of fair competition in industry.[22] But to the professional politicians the means of determining merit—the competitive examination—seemed to have about it the aura of the school, and it instantly aroused their hostility to intellect, education, and training. It was, as they began to say, a "schoolmaster's test." Touching the professions directly on a sensitive nerve, the issue brought forth a violent reaction which opened the floodgates of anti-intellectualist demagogy. The professionals denounced the idea of a civil service based upon examinations and providing secure tenure as aristocratic and imitative of British, Prussian, and Chinese bureaucracies; as deferential to monarchical institutions, and a threat to republicanism; and as militaristic because it took as one of its models the examination requirements that had been instituted in the armed services. From the first, the distrust of trained intellect was invoked. When a bill calling for civil-service reform was introduced in 1868 by Representative Thomas A. Jenckes of Rhode Island, it was denounced in the House by John A. Logan of Illinois in these terms:[23]

---

no request of mine would be likely to call out a gush of sympathy. [David Ames] Wells has just about as much influence as I have. He can't even protect his own clerks. Judge Hoar has his hands full, and does not interfere with his colleagues. . . ." *Letters*, p. 157.

[22]There was an assumption on the part of some that social standing would count, however, in the competition for jobs. Carl Schurz once proposed that "mere inquiries concerning the character, antecedents, social standing, and general ability [of a candidate] may be substituted for formal examination." Hoogenboom: op. cit., p. 115.

[23]*Congressional Globe*, 40th Congress, 3rd session, p. 265 (January 8, 1869). It is suggestive that competitive civil service, so often criticized in the United States as undemocratic, was at times assailed in Britain as excessively democratic, and as throwing the aristocracy on the defensive in the competition for posts. Kingsley: op. cit., p. 62. Others felt that this would only raise the morale and tone of the class of gentlemen. Cf. Asa Briggs: *Victorian People* (London, 1954), pp. 116–21, 170–1.

This bill is the opening wedge to an aristocracy in this country. . . . It will lead us to the point where there will be two national schools in this country—one for the military and the other for civil education. These schools will monopolize all avenues of approach to the Government. Unless a man can pass one or another of these schools and be enrolled upon their lists he cannot receive employment under this Government, no matter how great may be his capacity, how indisputable may be his qualifications. When once he does pass his school and fixes himself for life his next care will be to get his children there also. In these schools the scholars will soon come to believe that they are the only persons qualified to administer the Government, and soon come to resolve that the Government shall be administered by them and by none others.

It became clear, as the debate over civil service developed, that the professionals feared the demand for competence and the requirements of literacy and intelligence as a threat to the principles upon which the machines were based, and with this threat before them, there was almost no limit to the demagogy they would exert in behalf of the spoils principle. A Congressman from Indiana held up the frightening prospect that a graduate of, say, Washington College in Virginia, of which Robert E. Lee was president, would do better on a competitive examination than a disabled soldier of some "common school or workshop of the West, who lost a limb at the battle of Chickamauga." The people, he said, "are not quite ready to permit the students of rebel colleges, upon competitive examinations and scholastic attainments, to supersede the disabled and patriotic soldiers of the Republic, who with fewer educational advantages but larger practical experience are much better fitted for the position."[24]

In similar terms, Senator Matthew H. Carpenter of Wisconsin declaimed that during the Civil War,[25]

[24] *Congressional Globe*, 42nd Congress, 2nd session, p. 1103 (February 17, 1872). This form of competition with college-trained men also troubled the veterans' organizations. See Wallace E. Davies: *Patriotism on Parade* (Cambridge, Mass., 1955), pp. 247, 285–6, 311.

[25] *Congressional Globe*, 42nd Congress, 2nd session, p. 458 (January 18, 1872). Many local bosses, of course, were as troubled as the Congressmen about the effect of competitive examinations on their procedures. "I suppose," objected

when the fate of the nation was trembling in the balance, and our gallant youths were breasting the storm of war, the sons of less patriotic citizens were enjoying the advantages of a college course. And now, when our maimed soldiers have returned, and apply for a Federal office, the duties of which they are perfectly competent to discharge, they are to be rejected to give place to those who were cramming themselves with facts and principles from the books, while they were bleeding for their country, because they do not know the fluctuations of the tide at the Cape of Good Hope, how near the moon ever approaches the earth, or the names of the principal rivers emptying into the Caspian Sea.

Suggesting that "admission into the kingdom of heaven does not depend upon the result of a competitive examination," the senator rang the changes on the contrast between formal education and practical intelligence: "The dunce who has been crammed up to a diploma at Yale, and comes fresh from his cramming, will be preferred in all civil appointments to the ablest, most successful, and most upright business man of the country, who either did not enjoy the benefit of early education, or from whose mind, long engrossed in practical pursuits, the details and niceties of academic knowledge have faded away as the headlands disappear when the mariner bids his native land goodnight."

Such comments were not confined to Northerners who were waving the bloody shirt. Representative McKee of Mississippi objected that educational criteria would make it almost impossible for the less educated sections of the country to capitalize on their old privileges under the geographic criterion for appointment. His complaint, quite candidly put, was that if competence

---

the Boston boss, Patrick Macguire, apropos a Massachusetts civil-service law, "that if any one of my boys wants to have a position in any of the departments of Boston, to start with I shall have to send him to Harvard College. It is necessary that he should graduate with the highest honors, and I suppose that the youths who are now studying there can look forward to the brilliant career that waits for them in our metropolis when they shall have been educated up to the proper point where they are able to handle the pick-axe and the shovel, and all others who don't have the good fortune to be well educated must stand aside and look for positions elsewhere." Quoted in Lucius B. Swift: *Civil Service Reform* (n.p., 1885), p. 10.

were to be required he would be unable to get jobs for his Mississippi constituents. "Suppose," he said, "some wild mustang girl from New Mexico comes here for a position, and it may be that she does not know whether the Gulf stream runs north or south, or perhaps she thinks it stands on end, and she may answer that the 'Japan current' is closely allied to the English gooseberry, yet although competent for the minor position she seeks, she is sent back home rejected, and the place is given to some spectacled school ma'am who probably has not half as much native sense as the New Mexican."[26] McKee complained:

> I had a constituent here who knew more than your whole civil service board. He was brought up here from Mississippi and they found him incompetent for the lowest grade of clerkship; and yet he is now cashier or teller of one of the largest banks on the Pacific slope. And they gave the appointment to a spectacled pedagogue from Maine, who, as far as business capacity and common sense was concerned, was not fit to be clerk to a boot-black. [Laughter.] That is the way it has been all along.

For a long time the opponents of civil service succeeded in creating in the public mind a conception of civil-service reform which had very little to do with reality but which appealed formidably to egalitarian sentiments, machine cupidity, and anti-intellectualism. E. L. Godkin once remarked that when reform agitation first appeared, it was greeted as simply another of "the thousand visionary attempts to regenerate society with which a certain class of literary men is supposed to beguile its leisure." In the inner political circles, between 1868 and 1878, it was known, with much mingled disgust and amusement, as "snivel service reform." "The reformers were sometimes spoken of as a species of millennarians, and others as weak-minded people, who looked at political society as a sort of Sunday-school which could be managed by mild exhortation and cheap prizes, and whom it was the business of practical men to humor in so far as it could be done harmlessly, but not to argue with."[27] The professional politicians succeeded in persuading

[26] *Congressional Globe*, 42nd Congress, 3rd session, p. 1631 (February 22, 1873).
[27] E. L. Godkin: "The Civil Service Reform Controversy," *North American Review*, Vol. CXXXIV (April, 1882), pp. 382–3.

themselves that civil-service reform meant favoritism to the college-educated; that it would restrict job-holding to a hereditary college-educated aristocracy; and that all kinds of unreasonable and esoteric questions would be asked on civil-service examinations. (R. R. Bowker protested that "a great deal of nonsense [is] talked and written about asking a man who had to clean streets questions about ancient history, astronomy, and Sanskrit.") The idea of a literate competitive examination filled the anti-reformers with horror, a horror doubtless shared by many potential job applicants. "Henceforth," declared one of the more articular opponents of reform,[28]

> entrance into the civil service is to be through the narrow portal of competitive examination, practically limiting entry to the graduates of colleges, thus admitting a Pierce and excluding a Lincoln; the favored few thus admitted remaining for life; exempt, likewise, from vicissitudes; advancing, likewise, in a regular gradation, higher and higher; a class separate from the rest of the community, and bound together by a common interest and a common subordination to one man, he also the commander-in-chief of the Army—the President of the United States.

In vain did reformers protest that there was nothing undemocratic about tests open equally to all applicants, especially since the American educational system itself was so democratic, even at the upper levels.[29] In vain did they reprint the texts of examinations which already existed in order to show that potential clerks were not expected to be members of the American Philosophical Society or graduates of the Ivy League colleges. In vain did they produce statistics showing that, for instance, in the New York Customs House, where the competitive examination system had been used before 1881, only a very modest proportion of candidates examined or appointed were college graduates.[30] The grim specter of the educated civil servant haunted the professionals to the very end. Even after President Garfield's assassination, when

[28]William M. Dickson: "The New Political Machine," *North American Review*, Vol. CXXXIV (January 1, 1882), p. 42.
[29]Andrew D. White: "Do the Spoils Belong to the Victor?" *North American Review*, Vol. CXXXIV (February, 1882), p. 129–30.
[30]Godkin: "The Civil Service Reform Controversy," p. 393.

public sentiment for civil-service reform rapidly mounted, his successor, Chester A. Arthur, professed to Congress his anxiety that civil-service examinations would exalt "mere intellectual proficiency" above other qualities and that experienced men would be at a disadvantage in competing with immature college youths.[31] Senator George H. Pendleton, steering the civil-service reform bill through Congress, found it necessary to reassure the Senate that the system of examinations did not present only "a scholastic test" unfairly favoring the college-bred.[32] Had it not been for the fortuitous shooting of Garfield, it is likely that the reforms embodied in the Pendleton Act would have been delayed for almost a generation.

3

In the attacks made by the reformers on the professional politicians, one finds a few essential words recurring: *ignorant, vulgar, selfish, corrupt.* To counter such language, the politicians had to have an adequate and appealing answer. It was not merely the conduct of the public debate which was at stake but also their need to salve their own genuine feelings of outrage. Where rapport with the public was concerned, the politicians, of course, had a signal advantage. But if the debate itself were to be accepted in the terms set by the reformers, the politicians would suffer considerably. Like all men living at the fringes of politics, and thus freed of the burdens of decision and responsibility, the reformers found it much easier than the professionals to keep their boasted purity. Most of the reform leaders were men from established families, with at least moderate wealth and secure independent vocations of their own, and not directly dependent upon politics for their livelihood; it was easier for them than for the professionals to maintain the atmosphere of disinterestedness that they felt vital to the public service. Besides, they *were* in fact better educated and more cultivated men.

[31] J. R. Richardson: *Messages and Papers of the Presidents,* Vol. X, pp. 46, 48–9.
[32] *Congressional Record,* 47th Congress, 2nd session, pp. 207–8 (December 12, 1882).

The politicians and bosses found their answer in crying down the superior education and culture of their critics as political liabilities, and in questioning their adequacy for the difficult and dirty work of day-to-day politics. As the politicians put it, they, the bosses and party workers, had to function in the bitter world of reality in which the common people also had to live and earn their living. This was not the sphere of morals and ideals, of education and culture: it was the hard, masculine sphere of business and politics. The reformers, they said, claimed to be unselfish; but if this was true at all, it was true only because they were alien commentators upon an area of life in which they did not have to work and for which in fact they were unfit. In the hard-driving, competitive, ruthless, materialistic world of the Gilded Age, to be unselfish suggested not purity but a lack of self, a lack of capacity for grappling with reality, a lack of assertion, of masculinity.

Invoking a well-established preconception of the American male, the politicians argued that culture is impractical and men of culture are ineffectual, that culture is feminine and cultivated men tend to be effeminate. Secretly hungry for office and power themselves, and yet lacking in the requisite understanding of practical necessities, the reformers took out their resentment upon those who had succeeded. They were no better than carping and hypocritical censors of office-holders and power-wielders. They were, as James G. Blaine once put it, "conceited, foolish, vain, without knowledge . . . of men. . . . They are noisy but not numerous, pharisaical but not practical, ambitious but not wise, pretentious but not powerful."[33]

The clash between reformers and politicians created in the minds of the professionals a stereotype of the educated man in politics that has never died. It is charmingly illustrated in the sayings, recorded (and perhaps dressed up) by a reporter around the turn of the century, of a candid practitioner of

[33]Gail Hamilton: *Biography of James G. Blaine* (Norwich, 1895), p. 491. For a testy attack on literary men and reformers in politics, and their patronizing attitude toward professionals, see Senator Joseph R. Hawley: *Congressional Record*, 47th Congress, 2nd session, p. 242 (December 13, 1882).

metropolitan politics, George Washington Plunkitt of Tammany Hall. If Tammany leaders were "all bookworms and college professors," Plunkitt declared,[34]

> Tammany might win an election once in four thousand years. Most of the leaders are plain American citizens, of the people and near to the people, and they have all the education they need to whip the dudes who part their name in the middle. . . . As for the common people of the district, I am at home with them at all times. When I go among them, I don't try to show off my grammar, or talk about the Constitution, or how many volts there is in electricity or make it appear in any way that I am better educated than they are. They wouldn't stand for that sort of thing.

Again:[35]

> Some young men think they can learn how to be successful in politics from books, and they cram their heads with all sorts of college rot. They couldn't make a bigger mistake. Now, understand me, I ain't sayin' nothin' against colleges. I guess they have to exist as long as there's bookworms, and I suppose they do some good in certain ways, but they don't count in politics. In fact, a young man who has gone through the college course is handicapped at the outset. He may succeed in politics, but the chances are 100 to 1 against him.

It was not enough for the politicians to say that the reformers were hypocritical and impractical. Their cultivation and

---

[34]William L. Riordon: *Plunkitt of Tammany Hall* (1905; ed. New York, 1948), pp. 60–1. One is reminded here of the techniques of the delightful Brooklyn Democratic leader Peter McGuiness. Challenged for the leadership of his district during the early 1920's by a college graduate who maintained that the community should have a man of culture and refinement as its leader, McGuiness dealt with the newcomer "with a line that is a favorite of connoisseurs of political strategy. At the next meeting McGuiness addressed, he stood silent for a moment, glaring down at the crowd of shirtsleeved laborers and housewives in Hoover aprons until he had their attention. Then he bellowed, 'All of yez that went to Yales or Cornells raise your right hands. . . . The Yales and Cornells can vote for him. The rest of yez vote for me.'" Richard Rovere: "The Big Hello," in *The American Establishment* (New York, 1962), p. 36.
[35]Ibid., p. 10.

fastidious manners were taken as evidence that these "namby-pamby, goody-goody gentlemen" who "sip cold tea"[36] were deficient in masculinity. They were on occasion denounced as "political hermaphrodites" (an easy transition from their uncertain location as to political party to an uncertain location as to sex). The waspish Senator Ingalls of Kansas, furious at their lack of party loyalty, once denounced them as "the third sex"—"effeminate without being either masculine or feminine; unable either to beget or bear; possessing neither fecundity nor virility; endowed with the contempt of men and the derision of women, and doomed to sterility, isolation, and extinction."[37]

From the moment the reformers appeared as an organized force in the Liberal Republican movement of 1872, they were denounced by Roscoe Conkling, one of the most flamboyant of the spoilsmen, as a "convention of idealists and professors and sore-heads."[38] Conkling also produced one of the classics of American invective, and spelled out the implications of the charge of deficient masculinity. Conkling's victim was George William Curtis, once a student at the German universities, editor of *Harper's* and a prominent reformer, the friend of such men as Bryant, Lowell, and Sumner, and one of the most prominent advocates of a more aggressive role in politics for educated men. The occasion was the New York State Republican Convention of 1877, at which a battle between bosses and reformers over the party organization came to a head. When Conkling's moment came, he asked: "Who are these men who, in newspapers and elsewhere, are cracking their whips over Republicans and playing school-master to the Republican party and its conscience and convictions?" "Some of them are the

[36] A letter to *The New York Times*, June 17, 1880, quoted by R. R. Bowker: *Nation*, Vol. XXXI (July 1, 1880), p. 10.

[37] *Congressional Record*, 49th Congress, 1st session, p. 2786 (March 26, 1886). "They have two recognized functions," the senator said of the third sex. "They sing falsetto, and they are usually selected as the guardians of the seraglios of Oriental despots."

[38] Matthew Josephson: *The Politicos* (New York, 1938), p. 163. Conkling's words are reminiscent of those of the businessman who objected to economic reformers as "philanthropists, professors, and Lady Millionaires." Edward C. Kirkland: *Dream and Thought in the Business Community* (Ithaca, 1956), p. 26.

man-milliners, the dilettanti and carpet knights of politics," he went on—and the term man-milliners, a reference to the fashion articles that Curtis's magazine had recently started to publish, evoked howls of derisive laughter. After denouncing the reformers for parading "their own thin veneering of superior purity," and ridiculing their alleged treachery and hypocrisy, their "rancid, canting self-righteousness," he closed with the remark: "They forget that parties are not built by deportment, or by ladies' magazines, or by gush. . . ."[39]

What Plunkitt later suggested when he referred to "dudes that part their name in the middle" Conkling here made as clear as it was admissible to do. The cultivated character and precise manners of the reformers suggested that they were effeminate. Culture suggested feminity; and the editorship of a ladies' magazine proved it in Curtis's case. The more recent attacks by Senator McCarthy and others upon the Eastern and English-oriented prep-school personnel of the State Department, associated with charges of homosexuality, are not an altogether novel element in the history of American invective. That the term "man-milliners" was understood in this light by many contemporaries is suggested by the fact that though the New York *Tribune* reported Conkling's speech in full, with the offending word, Conkling's nephew dropped "man-milliners" from his account of this incident in the biography of his uncle and substituted asterisks as though he were omitting an unmistakable obscenity.[40]

What the politicians relied upon, as the basis for an unspoken agreement about the improper character of the reformers, was the feeling, then accepted by practically all men and by most women, that to be active in political life was a male prerogative, in the sense that women were excluded from it, and further, that capacity for an effective role in politics was practically a

[39]Alfred R. Conkling: *Life and Letters of Roscoe Conkling* (New York, 1889), pp. 540–1; for the full account of the incident, see pp. 538–49.
[40]See also the attack on Curtis in the Elmira *Advertiser*, October 6, 1877, as reported in Thomas Collier Platt's *Autobiography* (New York, 1910), pp. 93–5. Here "a smart boy named Curtis, who parted his hair in the middle like a girl" and lived in an exclusively feminine environment, ran afoul of a masculine redhead named Conkling, who beat him up, to the indignation of Curtis's maiden aunts and all the female neighbors.

test of masculinity. To be active in politics was a man's business, whereas to be engaged in reform movements (at least in America) meant constant association with aggressive, reforming, moralizing women—witness the case of the abolitionists. The common male idea, so often heard in the debate over woman suffrage, was that women would soil and unsex themselves if they entered the inevitably dirty male world of political activity, about which Senator Ingalls once said that its purification was "an iridescent dream."

If women invaded politics, they would become masculine, just as men became feminine when they espoused reform. Horace Bushnell suggested that if women got the vote and kept it for hundreds of years, "the very look and temperament of women will be altered." The appearance of women would be sharp, their bodies wiry, their voices shrill, their actions angular and abrupt, and full of self-assertion, will, boldness, and eagerness for place and power. It could also be expected that in this nightmare of female assertion women would actually "change type physiologically, they will become taller and more brawny, and get bigger hands and feet, and a heavier weight of brain," and would very likely become "thinner, sharp-featured, lank and dry, just as all disappointed, over-instigated natures always are."[41]

In compensation for their political disability, women were always conceded to embody a far greater moral purity than men (though this purity was held to be of a frailer variety);[42] and it was conventionally said that they would make it effective in the world through their role as wives and mothers. So long as they stayed out of politics, the realm of ideals and of purity belonged to them. By the same token, the realm of reality and

[41]Horace Bushnell: *Women's Suffrage: The Reform against Nature* (New York, 1869), pp. 135–6. Cf. p. 56: "The claim of a beard would not be a more radical revolt against nature."

[42]Cf. Bushnell: "We also know that women often show a strange facility of debasement and moral abandonment, when they have once given way consentingly. Men go down by a descent—*facilis descencus*—women by a precipitation. Perhaps the reason is, in part, that more is expected of women and that again because there is more expectancy of truth and sacrifice in the semi-christly, subject state of women than is likely to be looked for in the forward, self-asserting headship of men." Ibid., p. 142.

of dirty dealings, in so far as it must exist, belonged to men; and the reformers who felt that they were bringing purer and more disinterested personal ideals into politics were accused by their opponents of trying to womanize politics, and to mix the spheres of the sexes. Just as women unsexed themselves by entering politics, so reformers unsexed themselves by introducing female standards—i.e., morality—into political life. The old byword for reformers—"long-haired men and short-haired women"—aptly expressed this popular feeling.

The notion that the demand for women's suffrage was perversely unsexing, even dehumanizing, was one of the central themes of Henry James's *The Bostonians*. Like Bushnell, James feared that the male world would be undone by the perverse aggressiveness of women and of feminine principles. His Southern hero, Basil Ransom, bursts out:[43]

> The whole generation is womanized; the masculine tone is passing out of the world; it's a feminine, a nervous, hysterical, chattering, canting age, an age of hollow phrases and false delicacy and exaggerated solicitudes and coddled sensibilities, which, if we don't soon look out, will usher in the reign of mediocrity, of the feeblest and flattest and the most pretentious that has ever been. The masculine character, the ability to dare and endure, to know and yet not fear reality, to look the world in the face and take it for what it is—a very queer and partly very base mixture—that is what I want to preserve, or rather, as I may say, recover. . . .

The world that James had in mind as having already been deprived of its masculine character was not, surely, the world of Jim Fisk, Carnegie, Rockefeller, or the railroad barons, nor the world of the Tweed Ring or Roscoe Conkling; rather it was the world of the cultivated man, whose learning had once been linked with masculine firmness to the life of action and assertion, the Eastern society, epitomized by Boston, which in all America James knew best. There seemed to be an almost painful need in this society for the kind of man who could join the sphere of ideas and moral scruples with the virile qualities of action and assertion.

[43] *The Bostonians* (1886; ed. London, 1952), p. 289.

4

Whether or not the reformers fully realized it, the stigma of effeminacy and ineffectuality became a handicap to them, a token of their insulation from the main currents of American politics. One of the first to meet this challenge was Theodore Roosevelt. A recruit from the same social and educational strata as the reform leaders, he decided at an early age that the deficiencies charged against them were real, and that if reform was to get anywhere, their type must be replaced by a new and more vigorous kind of leader from the same class. In his *Autobiography*, he recalled that the reformers were[44]

> gentlemen who were very nice, very refined, who shook their heads over political corruption and discussed it in drawing-rooms and parlors, but who were wholly unable to grapple with real men in real life. They were apt vociferously to demand "reform" as if it were some concrete substance, like cake, which could be handed out at will, in tangible masses, if only the demand were urgent enough. These parlor reformers made up for inefficiency in action by zeal in criticizing. . . .

When T.R. wrote this, he had long since been separated from reformers of Godkin's stripe by an intense and almost obsessive hatred, occasioned on his side by an irritating sense that they thought of him as a moral traitor, and on their side by an incomprehension that a man of his background could have made his moral compromises. But it was one of the major sources of his popularity in the country at large, toward the end of the century, that he could be portrayed as an Easterner, a writer, and a Harvard man from the well-to-do classes who nevertheless knew how to get along with cowboys and Rough Riders.

In spite of the disapproval of his family and friends, Roosevelt entered politics at the bottom in 1880 by joining the Jake Hess Republican Club near his home in New York City. He persisted in playing the political game despite his early distaste for the environment and the rebuffs of the ward heelers. The next year he had won enough support within the

[44] *An Autobiography* (New York, 1920), pp. 86–7.

Republican machine to be sent to the legislature at Albany. When Roosevelt first entered the New York Assembly at twenty-three, he still suffered from the stigma of his fashionable background. As Henry F. Pringle has written: "In addition to his origin among New Yorkers of moderate wealth, he was a Harvard man. He wore eyeglasses on the end of a black silk cord, which was effeminate. In brief, he was a dude; that comic-supplement creation born of American inferiority toward Great Britain. Even Isaac L. Hunt, who was also a new member and who fought at Roosevelt's side in many a battle, was to recall him as 'a joke . . . a dude the way he combed his hair, the way he talked—the whole thing.'" Handicapped, as Pringle observes, by his manners, his grammatical English, and his feeling for clothes, and cursed with a comically high-pitched voice, which he used, as a contemporary said, to address the chairman "in the vernacular of the first families of New York," Roosevelt began his career inauspiciously.[45] His opponents were quick to brand him as a college-bred sissy. Learning that four members of the national collegiate fraternity, Alpha Delta Phi, were on the Assembly Elections Committee, the New York *World* wrote: "Dear! Dear! Brother Roosevelt [is] a trader of positions on an Assembly Committee. Let the Alpha Delta veil the Mother symbol in crepe." "The horny-handed voters of the State will learn with surprise and disgust that some horny-headed legislators and lawyers are introducing 'college politics' into contested elections to the Legislature. The Alpha Delta Phi fraternity no doubt affords an innocent and agreeable recreation for undergraduates, but it is not exactly a safe guide for maturer statesmanship."[46]

In a short time, however, the strong personal image of himself that Roosevelt managed to create began to take hold in the newspapers. His vigor and sincerity began to win a hearty

---

[45] Henry F. Pringle: *Theodore Roosevelt* (New York, 1931), pp. 65–7.

[46] This and subsequent press comments on Roosevelt are taken from a mass of such quotations in two master's essays written at Columbia University in 1947 and based upon an examination of Roosevelt's scrapbooks—Anne de la Vergne: *The Public Reputation of Theodore Roosevelt, 1881–1897*, pp. 9–16, 45–6; and Richard D. Heffner: *The Public Reputation of Theodore Roosevelt: The New Nationalism, 1890–1901*, pp. 21–4, 41–5, 53–4.

response, and he got favorable notices in spite of his education and background. An upstate editor found it "cheering to see an occasional young man of wealth and education who cares for something more than to be a butterfly of society—who is willing to bring the gifts of fortune to the public service." A Boston paper thought that even though he had "aesthetic leanings," he had delivered a "sagacious and level-headed Republican speech." Another decided that although he was "weighed down . . . with a good deal of theory taken aboard in the leading universities of the Old World and the New," he was none the less "really a very bright young man, with some practical ideas." The Springfield *Republican* was troubled about intellectual training that would hinder young men's understanding of the problems of the average citizen, but it conceded that Roosevelt's was "a culture that does not separate him from the cause of the people." By the time Roosevelt became a Civil Service Commissioner, an editor was able to say: "Reform with him will never become either a literary recreation or a hypocritical subterfuge to cover submission to party."

Roosevelt's familiarity with the West and his ranching experiences were a great help in establishing his virility. He was described as a "manly, athletic, vigorous person . . . fond of hunting big game in the Far West [where] he is the owner of great ranches," and as "schooled in the art of self-protection during his early days of *roughing it* in the West." Heroic tales were retold of his experiences with Indians. His skill in hunting became a political asset: "He is capable of showing the same spirit of true sport in following the trail of the spoilsman, as in his pursuit of the grizzly-bear of the Rocky Mountains, and when he opens fire on civic corruption it is a good deal like the action of a magazine-rifle at close range." Roosevelt was the only reformer whose life could have suggested that civil-service reform was analogous to hunting dangerous game.

Against the urban, commercial, cynical, effeminate world, Roosevelt represented the West and the outdoors, the vigorous, energetic, manly style of life, and a "sincere" and idealistic outlook. T.R. himself was aware of his achievement in dramatizing the compatibility of education and reform with energy and virility, and he took it upon himself to bring this message to the rising generation. When he was invited to speak to Harvard undergraduates in 1894, he chose the subject, "The Merit System and Manliness in Politics," and urged his listeners that they be not only "good men but also manly men, that they should not let those who stand for evil have all the virile qualities." During the 1890's he was especially vociferous in exhorting American men to commit themselves to an active, hardy, practical, and yet idealistic engagement in political struggles. "The strenuous life," of which he often spoke, was not simply a matter of nationalism and imperial assertion but of domestic reform politics. The good American, he repeated, would not merely criticize; he would act. He would throw himself into "the rough hurly-burly of the caucus" and bear his part as a man should, not shrinking from association with "men who are sometimes rough and coarse, who sometimes have lower ideals than they should, but who are capable, masterful, and efficient." He should develop "the rougher, manlier virtues, and above all the virtue of personal courage, physical as well as moral," and must be "vigorous in mind and body," possessing the "hardy virtues" which are admired in the soldier, "the virile fighting qualities without which no nation . . . can ever amount to anything." It would be "unmanliness and cowardice to shrink from the contest because at first there is failure, or because the work is difficult or repulsive." The educated and cultivated class had a special obligation not to show "weak good-nature," not to "cease doing their share of the rough, hard work which must be done" or sink into the kind of "dilettanteism" which resembles the position not of the true artist but of the "cultivated, ineffective man with a taste for bric-a-brac."[47]

In the midst of the anxieties aggravated by the severe economic depression of the nineties, this attitude was widely welcomed. "The ardor and strength of prime manhood," wrote a California paper, "is a much needed quality in American

[47] *Harvard Crimson*, November 10, 1894; see especially "The Manly Virtues and Practical Politics" (1894) and "The College Graduate and Public Life" (1894), from which these quotations were taken, in *American Ideals* (New York, 1897), pp. 51–77.

government, especially at this time, when all things political and all things social are in the transition stage."

Roosevelt's preaching of militant nationalism and the strenuous life helped to round out the picture of his aggressiveness. Here was an intellectual-in-politics who had the Jacksonian qualities of militancy and decision, who could never be charged with cowardice, like Jefferson, or academicism like John Quincy Adams, or with the eunuchoid indecisiveness of a Curtis. He was unmistakably a "fighter." "He loves fighting, but all his fighting is for good government. Roosevelt is aggressiveness itself." In 1896, when American imperialism was being criticized by academics like Theodore Woolsey and Hermann von Holst, the Cleveland *World* found in Roosevelt a perfect antidote to timid scholarship. T.R.'s influence was like a "patriotic breeze. . . . Across the alkali plains of non-patriotism where the Woolseys . . . the von Holsts and other professors have been evaporating, comes this fresh welcome breath from a man as well equipped in scholarship as they." If there was anything missing from the picture of virile patriotism and pugnacity, it was supplied by Roosevelt's active and well-publicized services with the Rough Riders in the Spanish War, which made him, beyond question, the national hero. "His popularity comes from certain virile characteristics which most men like," asserted *Harper's Weekly* in 1899. "They are fond of the picture of the man on horseback—whether he is riding after Spaniards or grizzlies or steers, whether he is a soldier, hunter or ranchman." Describing an ovation given Roosevelt in 1900, the Detroit *News* said: "It was for the man who banded together a strangely contrasted crew—college men and cowboys —and swept with them across the page of current history, that men cheered themselves hoarse and women paid dainty tribute." "It is not to be expected," said the Chicago *Journal* the following year, "that anemic, town-bred, stage-door-haunting, dissipated youths can sympathize with a real man of Theodore Roosevelt's sort. But . . . live, vigorous Americans, with red blood coursing through their veins know how to appreciate him."

A citified, commercial civilization, bedeviled by serious depression and troubled for the first time by the fear of decadence, greeted Roosevelt as the harbinger of a new and more vigorous and masculine generation. Roosevelt paved the way for Progressivism by helping to restore prestige to educated patricians who were interested in reform, by reinvesting their type with the male virtues. American men, impelled to feel tough and hard, could respond to this kind of idealism and reform without fearing that they had unmanned themselves. In Roosevelt one finds the archetype of what has become a common American political image: the aspiring politician, suspected of having too gentle an upbringing, too much idealism, or too many intellectual interests, can pass muster if he can point to a record of active military service; if that is lacking, having made the football team may do.

But Roosevelt had accomplished more than the negative service of dispelling the image of the gentleman scholar as effeminate and ineffectual in politics. He had begun to show that this type of man had a useful part to play. In the generation he and his contemporaries were replacing, men of intellect had laid claim to leadership too much on the ground that their social standing and their mental and moral qualities entitled them to it. T.R. and his generation were more disposed to rest their claim on the ground that they performed a distinct and necessary function in the national scheme of things. For them, the role of the scholar in politics was founded upon his possession of certain serviceable skills that were becoming increasingly important to the positive functions of government. The era of the frustrated gentleman-reformer in politics was coming to a close. With the emergence of the Progressive generation, the era of the scholar as expert was about to begin.

CHAPTER VIII

The Rise of the Expert

I

IN THE Progressive era the estrangement between intellectuals and power which had been so frustrating to the reformers of the Gilded Age came rather abruptly to an end. America entered a new phase of economic and social development; the old concern with developing industry, occupying the continent, and making money was at last matched by a new concern with humanizing and controlling the large aggregates of power built up in the preceding decades. The country seems to have been affected by a sort of spiritual hunger, a yearning to apply to social problems the principles of Christian morality which had always characterized its creed but too rarely its behavior. It felt a greater need for self-criticism and self-analysis. The principles of good government that the gentlemen reformers had called for in vain seemed to be closer to realization.

But these principles, too, had begun to change: the civil-service reformers had had a constricted idea of what good government would actually do, and one reason for their small following had been their inability to say very appealingly what good government was good for. Now, in increasing numbers, intelligent Americans began to think they knew. To control and humanize and moralize the great powers that had accumulated in the hands of industrialists and political bosses, it would be necessary to purify politics and build up the administrative state to the point at which it could subject the American economy to a measure of control. Of necessity, the functions of government would become more complex; and as they did so, experts would be in greater demand. In the interests of democracy itself, the old Jacksonian suspicion of experts must be abated. The tension between democracy and the educated man now seemed to be disappearing—because the type of man who had always valued expertise was now learning to value democracy and because democracy was learning to value experts.

The new social order also required exploration and explanation: there was an all but universal awareness that America was standing at the threshold of a new era. The imperative business of national self-criticism stirred ideas into life. Partly as expert, partly as social critic, the intellectual now came back to a central position such as he had not held in American politics for a century. But the recognition of intellect in national affairs was not accorded on the terms anticipated by the gentlemen reformers of the previous decades. In their eyes, the claims of mind had been founded largely on social class and gentility: they had lamented the disuse of intellect partly because they felt it was entitled to greater deference; but their notion of how it ought to be used was altogether conservative. Now, however, the claims of intellect were not based on the social position of the men who exemplified it, but on their usefulness in mobilizing and directing the restless, critical, reforming energies of the country. Intellect was reinstalled not because of its supposed conservative influence but because of its service to change. In this respect, the changes of the Progressive era in social criticism and administrative organization did not look back to the conservative civil service envisaged in the days of Hayes and Garfield but forward to the New Deal welfare state and Franklin D. Roosevelt's brain trust.

Doubtless, the Progressives were more effective in creating a new moral atmosphere than in realizing a new administrative regime. It was the moral and intellectual requirements of the period which put its intellectuals in unprecedented rapport not only with the American public but with the country's political leaders. Some men of intellect were drawn toward politics from the outside: but others emerged directly within the political order, and found there a more secure and honored place than their predecessors. Political life offered prominent roles to men who were interested in ideas and scholarship—men like Theodore Roosevelt, Woodrow Wilson, Henry Cabot Lodge, Albert J. Beveridge, Robert M. La Follette. Among the outstanding political leaders of the Progressive movement, Bryan alone kept alive the anti-intellectualist strain in popular democracy.[1] La Follette enjoys a special place; though less a scholar or an intellectual than some of his contemporaries, he must be credited with the origins of the brain-trust idea, both

---

[1] For a revealing contemporary encounter, see the interview with Bryan reported by John Reed in *Collier's*, Vol. LVII (May 20, 1916), pp. 11 ff.

because of the effective union he achieved, as governor of Wisconsin, between the University of Wisconsin and the state government, and because of the efficient, research-minded staff he brought with him to Washington during his senatorial days. From the very beginning of his political career, La Follette gave the lie to George Washington Plunkitt's assertion that a college background was of no use in practical politics, when he rallied his former classmates for his first campaigns and made them the nucleus of a well-knit political machine. If Roosevelt had shown that intellect was compatible with virility, La Follette showed that intellect could be politically effective.

2

Progressivism moved from local and state levels to national politics. It was in the state governments that the new agencies of regulation first went into operation and that a substantial place for experts in legislation was first created. The trial ground for the role of experts in political life was not Washington but the state capitals, particularly Madison, Wisconsin, which offered the first example of experts in the service of "the people" and the state. In its successes and failures, in the very antagonisms it aroused, the La Follette experiment in Wisconsin was a bellwether for national Progressive politics and a historical prototype for the New Deal brain trust. The Wisconsin experience is particularly instructive because it prefigured an entire cycle in the role of experts and intellectuals in politics which has by now become familiar: first, there was an era of change and discontent which brought a demand for such men; next, the intellectuals and experts became identified with the reforms they formulated and helped to administer; then, an increasing distaste for reforms arose, often in direct response to their effectiveness. This distaste was felt above all by business interests, which arraigned governmental meddling, complained of the costs of reform, and attempted to arouse the public against reformers with a variety of appeals, among them anti-intellectualism. Finally, the reformers were ousted, but not all their reforms were undone.

The first impetus toward what came to be known as "the Wisconsin idea" occurred in 1892, when the new School of Economics, Political Science, and History was set up at the

University of Wisconsin, under the direction of the young economist, Richard T. Ely. Frederick Jackson Turner and President Thomas C. Chamberlain, the leaders of this movement, hoped to make Wisconsin a pioneer among Midwestern states in promoting social science, which they felt had immense potentialities for providing practical guidance to the complex industrial world that had come into being within the past quarter century. As they planned it, the university would become a center of training in administration and citizenship, and would evolve into an efficient practical servant of the state.

The role of the university, it must be emphasized, was to be wholly nonpartisan; it would be impartial between the political parties, and, in a larger sense, it was expected to serve "the people" as a whole, not a particular class interest. It would not offer propaganda or ideologies, but information, statistics, advice, skill, and training. By the same token, it was hoped that the prestige of the university would grow with its usefulness. University leaders did not anticipate any profound challenge to vested interests. In an early letter Turner asked that Ely "briefly indicate to me the practical ways in which such a school, in your opinion, can be made serviceable to the people of Wisconsin. . . . The very novelty of these practical aspects of the School is what will win us support from these hard headed Wisconsin capitalists—if anything will."[2] Turner later expressed this notion of impartial science more clearly:

> By training in science, in law, politics, economics, and history the universities may supply from the ranks of democracy administrators, legislators, judges and experts for commissioners *who shall disinterestedly and intelligently mediate between contending interests*. When the word "capitalistic classes" and "the proletariate" can be used and understood in America, it is surely time to develop such men, with the ideal of service to the State, who may *help to break the force of these collisions*, to find common grounds between the contestants and to possess the respect and confidence of all parties which are genuinely loyal to the best American ideals. The signs of such a development are already plain in the expert commissions of some States; in

[2] Merle Curti and Vernon Carstensen: *The University of Wisconsin* (Madison, 1949), Vol. I, p. 632. This work has a full-bodied account of the role of the university in the "Wisconsin idea."

the increasing proportion of university men in legislatures; in the university men's influence in federal departments and commissions. It is hardly too much to say that the best hope of intelligent and principled progress in economic and social legislation and administration lies in the increasing influence of American universities.

Turner went on to say that he could see the danger to the universities in all this. "Pioneer democracy" had always had scant respect for the expert, and the expert would have to go on contending against the "inherited suspicion" of his kind; but he could overcome it with "creative imagination and personality."[3]

By the end of the century, the university had gathered some distinguished scholars, who were concentrating on social and economic problems, notably on those of the state and the municipality; it had produced a number of excellent monographs. With its extension system it was helping to educate the people of the state. Through its farmers' institutes it had drawn close to the agricultural interests and had done much to raise the technical level of agriculture in Wisconsin. Its program became truly controversial, however, after the election of Robert M. La Follette as governor in 1900. A graduate of the university, fully in sympathy with the aspirations of its idealistic leaders, La Follette was quick to make use of its experts, who were called upon for advice in his program of tax reform, railroad control, and direct primary legislation.

The efforts of the university were soon supplemented by those of another independent agency, the Legislative Reference Service, organized under another recent Wisconsin graduate student, the energetic Charles McCarthy. McCarthy's aspirations for the reference library were like those of Turner for the university: it was to be an impartial service organization. In the age of the railroad, the telephone, the telegraph, and the insurance company, the problems of the state, he remarked, were growing so various and complex that vast amounts of information were necessary for legislators to deal with them

[3] F. J. Turner: "Pioneer Ideals and the State University," a commencement address delivered at the University of Indiana in 1910 and reprinted in *The Frontier in American History* (New York, 1920), pp. 285–6; italics are mine.

intelligently. "The only sensible thing to do is to have experts gather this material." It was not a question of commitment to one side or another of a legislative debate:[4]

> As to our department in Wisconsin, we are not trying to influence our legislators in any way, we are not upon one side or another of any question nor are we for or against anybody or anything; we are merely a business branch of the government. We are not dictating legislation but are merely servants of the able and honest legislators of our state, clerks to gather and index and put together the information that these busy men desire; it is a business proposition.

This ideal may now seem as naïve as it was sincere. La Follette's governorship was on "one side or another" of quite a few questions; it challenged the interests of the "hard headed Wisconsin capitalists" whose support Turner had hoped to win. Moreover, after 1903, when the president of the university was La Follette's friend, Charles P. Van Hise, who believed in making the university an integral arm of the state, the irritation of conservatives mounted. Matters were not eased by the publicity the "Wisconsin idea" got from journalists throughout the country (most of them sympathetic) who came to examine Wisconsin as a model Progressive state in action and went away to write in exaggerated terms about "the university that governs a state."[5]

The publicity inspired by the journalists may have caused progressives in other states to consider a closer imitation of the Wisconsin model, but within the state it contributed to the conviction of the conservatives that the university was part of a conspiracy against them. Actually, the university experts did not think of themselves as radicals, and did not even consider that they had brought a great deal of initiative into government. An examination of university personnel most active in state service shows that it was mainly technicians (engineers, geologists, scientists, and various kinds of agricultural experts) rather than policy advisers who served the state,

[4] Charles McCarthy: *The Wisconsin Idea* (New York, 1912), pp. 228–9.
[5] On political tension in the Van Hise era, see Curti and Carstensen: op. cit., Vol. II, especially pp. 4, 10–11, 19–21, 26, 40–1, 87–90, 97, 100–7, 550–2, 587–92.

and that the university offered far more technical information than ideology. John R. Commons, one of the most outstanding of the Wisconsin social scientists, considered the university faculty itself overwhelmingly conservative, and recalled: "I was never called in except by Progressives, and only when they wanted me. I never initiated anything."[6]

Nevertheless, university men were consulted on taxation and railroad regulation, and on other matters, and their influence was resented. La Follette was proud that for the old-fashioned secret back-room conferences of bosses which prevailed in the days when Wisconsin was run in the interests of private corporations, he had substituted a Saturday lunch club at which he sat down with McCarthy and President Van Hise, with Commons, Edward A. Ross, Ely, and other university professors to discuss the problems of the state.[7] Business interests which suffered from the Progressive policies—and indeed many which suffered from nothing more than fear of further extension of regulation—became convinced that the university and the Legislative Reference Service must be counted among their enemies, along with the Railroad Commission, the Tax Commission, and the Industrial Commission.

In 1914, when the Wisconsin Progressive Republicans were hurt by the nation-wide split in the party, the conservatives saw their opportunity. They defeated La Follette's Progressive successor, and returned to power with Emanuel L. Philipp, a railroad and lumber man. In his campaign Philipp featured anti-intellectualist denunciations of university experts, and called for a reduction in taxes, retrenchment in the university, and an end to its political "meddling." There must be, he said, a thorough house-cleaning at the university; socialism was gaining ground there, and "many graduates are leaving with ideas that are un-American." The employment of experts, he said, would lead to the continuing encroachment of the university upon

[6]John R. Commons: *Myself* (New York, 1934), p. 110. Cf. McCarthy: "As a general rule the professors wait until asked before venturing to give an opinion upon a public question." Op. cit., p. 137; for a list of university personnel in the service of the state, see pp. 313–17.

[7]*Autobiography* (Madison, Wisconsin, 1913), p. 32; on his use of university personnel, see pp. 26, 30–1, 310–11, 348–50.

politics. To turn government over to experts was, in any case, a confession that the duly elected officials were incompetent. If the state reached the point of conceding that all political wisdom was locked up in the university, the rest of the people might as well confess "mental bankruptcy." Philipp's attack included a demand for the abolition of McCarthy's "bill factory," the Legislative Reference Library.

Once elected, Philipp proved more benign toward these institutions than his campaign had promised. Although he did ask the legislature for the abolition of McCarthy's library and for university retrenchment and consolidation, he became increasingly circumspect as time passed. The growth of the university was checked and its influence trimmed, but Philipp, confronted with a formidable and highly respectable opposition among the friends of the university throughout the country, made peace with Van Hise. Even McCarthy escaped: the governor discovered that his claim to impartiality had some foundation, when draftsmen of conservative bills began to use the Legislative Reference Service.[8]

The commitment of the university to Progressivism had never been completely accepted within the institution itself. As Commons remarked, many of its staff were thoroughly conservative. But more than this, many felt that the practical involvement of the university, regardless of its precise political shading, was itself a betrayal of the old-fashioned ideals of pure, disinterested intellectualism. J. F. A. Pyre, writing about the university in 1920, took issue with Van Hise's view that the university should be conceived as "an asset of the state." This, he said, was an excessively materialistic view of its function and downgraded the tradition of disinterested and autonomous learning, to the ultimate cost of the university.[9] But most of the experts at the university would doubtless have accepted the

---

[8]See Robert S. Maxwell: *Emanuel L. Philipp: Wisconsin Stalwart* (Madison, Wisconsin, 1959), chapters 7 and 8, especially pp. 74, 76–9, 82, 91, 92, 96–104. The *Nation* saw a disheartening lesson on American anti-intellectualism in the attack on the university. "Between Demos and the professor," it lamented, "there is a gulf of misunderstanding and ignorance unbridged since the days of Aristophanes." "Demos and the Professor," Vol. C (May 27, 1915), p. 596.

[9]J. F. A. Pyre: *Wisconsin* (New York, 1920), pp. 347–51, 364–5.

pragmatism expressed by McCarthy in his book, *The Wisconsin Idea*. The older thinkers, in fields like economics, he contended, had been "men of doctrinaire theories who had never studied the actual problems of government at first hand." They were being replaced by common-sense experts who looked at economic questions at first hand and could test their theories "by the hard facts of actual events."[10] Hence, while the lay community debated whether it should accept or reject experts, the scholarly community debated whether the serviceable expert or the man of pure learning held the true key to the future of the university.

3

Progressive achievement in the arena of power may have been limited, but the Progressive atmosphere seemed indefinitely expansive; this was immensely heartening to those who were concerned with the place of mind in American society. The horizons of intellect grew wider, it was free and exuberant, and it seemed now to have been put in touch with the higher reaches of power, as well as with the national mood. What Mabel Dodge Luhan said, thinking mainly of arts and letters, was true of every area of American life: "Barriers went down and people reached each other who had never been in touch before; there were all sorts of new ways to communicate, as well as new communications."[11] In this age of the "Little Renaissance" the keynote for arts and letters was liberation; for scholarship it was the enlarged possibilities for influence. Everywhere there was the intoxicant of new interests and new freedom. There was nothing that could not be re-examined, from railway franchises and the misdeeds of the trusts to sexual life and the conduct of education. Muckrakers were in demand to tell the public just how wicked things were, publicists to

[10] *The Wisconsin Idea*, pp. 188–9; cf. p. 138. McCarthy's point of view can best be understood against the background of the development of pragmatism and the rebellion against the older generation of scholars described in Morton G. White's *Social Thought in America: The Revolt against Formalism* (New York, 1949).

[11] *Movers and Shakers* (New York, 1936), p. 39.

interpret the meaning of events, ministers and editors to point the moral, scholars to work out a theoretical rationale for Progressivism in philosophy, law, history, and political science, and technicians of all kinds to emerge from the academies and make detailed factual studies of social and economic problems, even to staff the new regulatory commissions.

This ferment of ideas, however, brought no social revolution; the old masters of America emerged, at the end of the period, almost as fully in control as they had been before it began. But in matters of tone and style there was a powerful uplift, and tone and style are of first importance not only to scholars and men of letters, but to politicians as well. No one benefited more than the intellectuals, whether they were publicists like Walter Lippmann and Herbert Croly or academic scholars like John Dewey and Charles A. Beard. All their work was animated by the heartening sense that the gulf between the world of theory and the world of practice had been finally bridged. Lippmann captured the essence of this feeling in his book, *Drift and Mastery*, published in 1914, in which he found that the new capacity for control, for mastery, was the key to the promise of his generation. The most abstracted of scholars could derive a sense of importance from belonging to a learned community which the larger world was compelled to consult in its quest for adequate means of social control. It was no longer possible to dismiss ideas by calling them "academic," for no one any longer saw a clear boundary between the academy and society. "A newer type of college professor is . . . everywhere in evidence," wrote an observer,[12]

> the expert who knows all about railroads and bridges and subways; about gas commissions and electrical supplies; about currency and banking, Philippine tariffs, Venezuelan boundary lines, the industries of Porto Rico, the classification of the civil service, the control of trusts.

Perhaps most important of all, the skills of such academic experts were not only needed but applauded. A few commentators might worry about the relationship between the expert

[12]B.P.: "College Professors and the Public," *Atlantic Monthly*, Vol. LXXXIX (February, 1902), pp. 284–5.

and democracy,[13] and an occasional businessman, frightened by the costs of regulation, might fulminate against the rising influence of theorists,[14] but on the whole the new experts had a good press and were widely accepted by the public. Brander Matthews thought in 1909 that it was "an evidence of the common sense of the American people that the prejudice against the College Professors, like that against the men of letters, is rapidly dying down, and that there is beginning to be public recognition and public appreciation of the service they are rendering to the Commonwealth. . . . It is partly due to a growing understanding of the real value of the expert and the theorist."[15]

There was a significant acceptance, moreover, among political leaders themselves. It was characteristic of the age that a journalist like Isaac Marcosson should bring Theodore Roosevelt the proofs of a book by a muckraking novelist like Upton Sinclair, and that his doing so would speed the passage of a pure food bill. Quite aside from the presence in the Senate of men like Beveridge and Lodge who prided themselves on their "scholarship," this was the first time since the nation's beginnings that presidents of the United States could be described as intellectuals.

A closer look at both T.R. and Wilson will show that each in his own way provided a kind of living commentary on the limits of the relationship between intellect and power. Their

[13]See Joseph Lee: "Democracy and the Expert," *Atlantic Monthly*, Vol. CII (November, 1908), pp. 611–20.

[14]For example, the Chicago packer, Thomas E. Wilson, who pleaded before a Congressional committee in 1906: "What we are opposed to, and what we appeal to you for protection against is a bill that will put our business in the hands of theorists, chemists, sociologists, etc., and the management and control taken away from the men who have devoted their lives to the upbuilding and perfecting of this great American industry." Lest it be imagined that Wilson was fighting against a proposal to nationalize the packing industry, it should be explained that he was appearing against a pure food and drug measure. House Committee on Agriculture, 59th Congress, 1st session, *Hearings on the So-Called "Beveridge Amendment"* (Washington, 1906), p. 5. On the actual role of experts in the fight for food and drug control, see Oscar E. Anderson, Jr.'s biography of Harvey W. Wiley: *The Health of a Nation* (Chicago, 1958).

[15]"Literary Men and Public Affairs," *North American Review*, Vol. CLXXXIX (April, 1909), p. 536.

presidencies encouraged the belief that ideas had a vital part in government; but at the same time, neither was entirely in sympathy with his intellectual contemporaries, and neither enjoyed their full confidence. T.R., it must be said, took a lively and wide-ranging interest in ideas, enjoyed the company of men like Croly, Lippmann, and Steffens, found a government job for Edwin Arlington Robinson, attracted into public service a vigorous and dedicated type of man not much seen in government for well over a generation—one thinks of Robert Bacon, Charles Bonaparte, Felix Frankfurter, James Garfield, Franklin K. Lane, and Gifford Pinchot—and called upon academic experts for advice on railroad control, immigration, meat inspection, and other issues. In this he did more to restore mind and talents to public affairs than any president since Lincoln, probably more indeed than any since Jefferson. Lord Bryce, commenting on Roosevelt's achievement, thought that he had "never in any country seen a more eager, high-minded and efficient set of public servants, men more useful and creditable to their country, than the men doing the work of the American Government in Washington and in the field."[16] It sounds exactly like the kind of regime the gentleman reformers of the Gilded Age had called for.

Yet Roosevelt was rather quick to turn on his intellectual friends for what might have been considered marginal differences of opinion, and to dress himself as a stuffed-shirt Americanist when confronted with heterodox ideas. He misgauged the significance of many a mild protest—he imagined, for example, that the muckrakers were a dangerous lot who were building up "revolutionary feeling." Although no twentieth-century president has a greater claim to be considered an intellectual, his feeling about the place of intellect in life was as ambivalent as that of the educated strata of the middle class which looked up to him. He admired intellectual ability, just as he admired business ability, and, if anything, his admiration for

[16]Quoted by Paul P. Van Riper: *History of United States Civil Service*, p. 206; cf. pp. 189–207, and John Blum: "The Presidential Leadership of Theodore Roosevelt," *Michigan Alumnus Quarterly Review*, Vol. LXV (December, 1958), pp. 1–9.

intellect was firmer.[17] But what he called "character" he unceasingly placed above both. Indeed, he embodied the American preference for character over intellect in politics and life, and the all but universal tendency to assume that the two somehow stand in opposition to each other. His writings continually return to this contrast: "Character is far more important than intellect to the race as to the individual." "Exactly as strength comes before beauty, so character must stand above intellect, above genius." "Oh, how I wish I could warn all my countrymen . . . against that most degrading of processes, the deification of mere intellectual acuteness, wholly unaccompanied by moral responsibility. . . ."[18] What seems questionable about these repeated adjurations against intellect-without-character is not that they were wrong but that they were pointless unless he actually believed that there was a tendency in American life to exalt intellect at the expense of morals—a curious judgment in the high moral climate of the Progressive era.

Wilson has been said to have brought to the presidency the temper of the scholar, with its faults and virtues; and few students of the man believe that he had the personal qualities best suited to effective political leadership in the United States. The peculiar rigidity of his mind and his lack of bonhomie, however, seem to be more the result of his Presbyterianism than his scholarly vocation, and probably still more constituted distinctively personal qualities. As a scholar and a critical intellect,

[17] Cf. a famous letter of 1908: "I am simply unable to make myself take the attitude of respect toward the very wealthy men which such an enormous multitude of people evidently really feel. I am delighted to show any courtesy to Pierpont Morgan or Andrew Carnegie or James J. Hill; but as for regarding any one of them as, for instance, I regard Professor Bury, or Peary, the Arctic explorer, or Admiral Evans, or Rhodes the historian, or Selous, the big game hunter . . . why, I could not force myself to do it even if I wanted to, which I do not." Elting Morison, ed.: *The Letters of Theodore Roosevelt*, Vol. VI (Cambridge, 1952), p. 1002.

[18] *Works*, Memorial Ed., Vol. XIV, p. 128; *Outlook* (November 8, 1913), p. 527; *Works*, Vol. XVI, p. 484; cf. other statements to the same effect: *Outlook* (April 23, 1910), p. 880; Address, October 11, 1897, at the *Two Hundredth Anniversary of the Old Dutch Reformed Church of Sleepy Hollow* (New York, 1898); *Works*, Vol. XVII, p. 3; XII, p. 623.

he was a creature of the past. His creative intellectual life had almost come to an end by the close of the 1880's, the decade in which he wrote his brilliant book on *Congressional Government* and his more compendious effort, *The State*. In his tastes, his ideas, and his reading he was a somewhat parochial Southern version of a Victorian gentleman, his mind pleasantly fixed in the era just before the United States became a complex modern society. He believed in small business, competitive economics, colonialism, Anglo-Saxon and white supremacy, and a suffrage restricted to men, long after such beliefs had become objects of mordant critical analysis. His first ideas had come from Bagehot and Burke, and he had just missed exposure to the remarkable *fin de siècle* sunburst of critical thought whose impact carried over into the Progressive era. During the 1890's he was busy as a kind of academic man of affairs, bridging the gap between the academic community and the lay world; and while many of his scholarly contemporaries were ripping up the complacent assumptions of the Gilded Age, Wilson was speaking to groups of laymen, dishing out the kind of fare that bankers and industrialists like to have served by university presidents. From the moment he took the presidency of Princeton in 1902, he ceased trying to stay in touch with developments in the world of ideas. In 1916 he candidly confessed: "I haven't read a serious book through for fourteen years."[19] Understandably, then, his style of thought during his active public career was not much affected by the most creative side of American intellectual life, and his mind was hardly the object of unstinted admiration by contemporary intellectuals.

It is true that when Wilson was elected in 1912 he was supported by many intellectuals who were by then disillusioned by T.R. and who responded to the unmistakable note of nobility in Wilson. But Wilson was not disposed, before the war, to make the extensive use of intellectual advisers in politics that his academic background seemed to promise. Moreover, he had a persistent distrust of what he called "experts." Unlike T.R. and La Follette, he did not conceive of experts as likely

---

[19]Arthur Link: *Wilson: The New Freedom* (Princeton, 1956), p. 63; cf. Link's discussion of Wilson's mind, pp. 62–70.

agents or administrators of reform, but rather as hirelings available only to big business and special interests. Whereas most Progressive thinkers contrasted government by big business with a popular government that would employ experts to regulate unacceptable business practices, Wilson thought of big business, vested interests, and experts as a solid combine that could be beaten only by returning government to "the people." As against T.R., he contended that any experts engaged to regulate big business would be controlled by big business. "What I fear," he said during his 1912 campaign,[20]

is a government of experts. God forbid that in a democratic country we should resign the task and give the government over to experts. What are we for if we are to be scientifically taken care of by a small number of gentlemen who are the only men who understand the job? Because if we don't understand the job, then we are not a free people. We ought to resign our free institutions and go to school to somebody and find out what it is we are about. I want to say I have never heard more penetrating debate of public questions than I have sometimes been privileged to hear in clubs of workingmen; because the man who is down against the daily problem of life doesn't talk about it in rhetoric; he talks about it in facts. And the only thing I am interested in is facts.

The picture of Wilson frequenting workingmen's clubs and disdaining rhetoric is refreshingly novel. But on the whole Wilson lived up to the promise of these remarks when he formulated his domestic policies. Inevitably, the role of experts in government grew considerably during his administration,[21]

[20] *A Crossroads of Freedom: The 1912 Campaign Speeches of Woodrow Wilson*, ed. by John W. Davidson (New Haven, 1956) pp. 83–4. Wilson's ideas about experts seem to have been influenced to some extent by the part played by experts in the tariff controversy and also by the fight over pure food practices in T.R.'s administration. Ibid., pp. 113, 160–1; see also the comments on experts in *The New Democracy: Presidential Messages, Addresses, and Other Papers*, ed. by R. S. Baker and W. E. Dodd, Vol. I (New York, 1926), pp. 10, 16.

[21] This was notably true of the Department of Agriculture under the Secretaryship of David F. Houston, the former chancellor of Washington University and president of the University of Texas whom Wilson had appointed upon House's suggestion. During Houston's tenure, the problems of marketing and

as it had for more than a decade. And the president did, of course, solicit a great deal of advice on economic policy from Louis D. Brandeis, whose ideas about business competition coincided with his own predilections. But Wilson bowed to the animus of Back Bay and the business community in keeping Brandeis out of his Cabinet, and in the main he sought advice from different types—from men like his worshipful secretary, Joe Tumulty, who had a good grasp of machine politics and press relations; or his son-in-law, William Gibbs McAdoo, an amply progressive but not highly reflective mind; and above all, from the subtle and intelligent Colonel House, not the least of whose talents was the capacity to feed Wilson's vanity. House, who served among other things as a channel for the views of the wealthy and powerful, was a strong counterpoise to Progressive figures in the Wilson circle such as Brandeis, Bryan, and McAdoo.

Wilson's administration was not overwhelmingly popular among intellectuals in its first few years—especially among those who thought that the Progressive movement should go beyond the effort to realize the old competitive ideals of small businessmen and do something about child labor, the position of Negroes, the condition of workingmen, and the demand

---

distribution received much greater attention than before and the Department of Agriculture became a magnet for able agricultural economists.

There is suggestive information on the growth of expertise in government during the Progressive era in Leonard D. White: "Public Administration," *Recent Social Trends in the United States* (New York, 1934), Vol. II, pp. 1414 ff.

It should be added that Wilson adhered to the venerable tradition of making diplomatic appointments from the ranks of scholars and men of letters. He offered two appointments, both declined, to President Charles William Eliot of Harvard; sent Professor Paul Reinsch, an expert on international affairs, to China, Walter Hines Page (an unfortunate choice) to Great Britain, Thomas Nelson Page (a politically opportune appointment) to Italy, the ineffable Henry Van Dyke of Princeton to the Netherlands, and Brand Whitlock to Belgium. The level of Wilson's ambassadorial appointments was generally considered satisfactory, but they were offset by Bryan's raid upon the competent professional diplomatic corps which had been built up by John Hay, Roosevelt, and Taft. Bryan's raid on ministerial appointments in the interest of "deserving Democrats," to which Wilson consented, has been described by Arthur Link as "the greatest debauchery of the Foreign Service in the twentieth century." *Wilson: The New Freedom*, p. 106.

for women's suffrage.[22] Intellectuals interested in reform were too skeptical about Wilson to welcome unreservedly even the music of his sonorous speeches, which seemed to them to have overtones of a moralistic but unprogressive past, and their skepticism seemed justified by the halting manner in which reforms were pursued. Herbert Croly, who observed that Wilson's mind "is fully convinced of the everlasting righteousness of its own performances and surrounds this conviction with a halo of shimmering rhetoric," complained also that the President's thinking made "even the most concrete things seem like abstractions. . . . His mind is like a light which destroys the outlines of what it plays upon; there is much illumination, but you see very little."[23]

Only by 1916, in response to the recent achievements of the New Freedom and Wilson's success in keeping out of war, did liberal intellectuals swing wholeheartedly to his support. The war itself, ironically, raised many of them to heights of influence as no domestic issue could. Historians and writers were mobilized for propaganda, and experts of all kinds were recruited as advisers. Military Intelligence, Chemical Warfare, the War Industries Board swarmed with academics, and Washington's Cosmos Club was reported to be "little better than a faculty meeting of all the universities."[24] In September 1919

[22] Link: *Wilson: The New Freedom*, chapter 8. A classic statement of this view was made by Walter Lippmann in *Drift and Mastery*, especially chapter 7.

[23] "Presidential Complacency," *New Republic*, Vol. I (November 21, 1914), p. 7; "The Other-Worldliness of Wilson," *New Republic*, Vol. II (March 27, 1915), p. 195. Charles Forcey's *The Crossroads of Liberalism, Croly, Weyl, Lippmann and the Progressive Era, 1900–1925* (New York, 1961) is instructive about the relations of the *New Republic* group with Roosevelt and Wilson. On the impasse the New Freedom seemed to have reached by 1914 and the discouragement of liberal intellectuals, see Arthur Link: *Woodrow Wilson*, and his *The Progressive Era, 1910–1917* (New York, 1954), especially pp. 66–80.

[24] Gordon Hall Gerould: "The Professor and the Wide, Wide World," *Scribner's*, Vol. LXV (April, 1919), p. 466. Gerould thought it would no longer be possible to condescend to the professors after this experience. "The professor," wrote another, ". . . was reputed to be learned, and much to everyone's surprise he has turned out to be *intelligent*." "The Demobilized Professor," *Atlantic Monthly*, Vol. CXXIII (April, 1919), p. 539. Paul Van Dyke thought that the college man had succeeded, during the war, in showing that he was virile and practical, not soft or incompetent. "The College Man in Action,"

238 ANTI-INTELLECTUALISM IN AMERICAN LIFE

Colonel House organized for Wilson the group of scholars
known as The Inquiry (which already had its counterparts in
Great Britain and France). At one time the expert personnel of
The Inquiry numbered 150 persons—historians, geographers,
statisticians, ethnologists, economists, political scientists—and
these, with their assistants and staffs, brought the number of
the whole organization to several hundred. Kept secret until the
Armistice, The Inquiry was then revamped as the Intelligence
Division of the American Commission to Negotiate Peace, and
its staff accompanied Wilson to Paris, where it played a part of
no small importance. There was a certain amount of amused
comment about this group in the press, and a certain skepticism among old-school diplomats about this tribe of political
amateurs, with their three army truckloads of documents.[25] On
the whole, however, considering the passions aroused by the
war, the peace negotiations, and the debate over the treaty and
the League Covenant, what is most remarkable is the general
public acceptance of scholars in their advisory role. A politician
like Senator Lawrence Sherman of Illinois who launched a long
and ferocious diatribe against the expansion of governmental
powers during the war, and particularly against "a government
by professors and intellectuals," stood out as an exception for
his rancorous anti-intellectualism.[26] But he was prophetic of

Scribner's, Vol. LXV (May, 1919), pp. 560–3. It is instructive to compare the
argument of this piece with the earlier utterances of Theodore Roosevelt.
[25]On The Inquiry and its personnel, see the article by its head, Sidney E.
Mezes, in E. M. House and Charles Seymour, eds.: _What Really Happened at
Paris_ (New York, 1921); _Papers Relating to the Foreign Relations of the United
States_, 1919, Vol. I, _The Paris Peace Conference_ (Washington, 1942); J. T. Shot-
well: _At the Paris Peace Conference_, pp. 15–16. On wartime mobilization of
science, see A. Hunter Dupree: _Science in the Federal Government_, chapter 16.
[26]This remarkable speech is replete with the clichés of anti-intellectualism, and
though it can hardly be imagined to have had much influence at the time, it
must be taken as a landmark in anti-intellectualist oratory: ". . . a coterie of
politicians gilded and plated by a group of theorizing, intolerant intellectuals as wildly impractical as ever beat high heaven with their phrase-making
jargon. . . . They appeal to the iconoclast, the freak, the degenerate . . .
essayists of incalculable horsepower who have essayed everything under the
sun . . . a fair sprinkle of socialists. . . . Everything will be discovered. . . .
Psychologists with X-ray vision drop different colored handkerchiefs on a table, spill a half pint of navy beans, ask you in a sepulchral tone what disease

the future, for the reaction against the war liquidated the Progressive spirit.

The public mood changed with stunning abruptness. William Allen White, who in 1919 was still telling the chairman of
the Republican National Committee that the party's "incrusted
old reactionaries" were done for, was lamenting a year later
that "the Pharisees are running the temple" and that the people were not even troubling to object. "What a God-damned
world this is!" he wrote to Ray Stannard Baker in 1920. "If
anyone had told me ten years ago that our country would be
what it is today . . . I should have questioned his reason."[27]
The consequences were fatal for the position of the intellectuals: having tied themselves to Wilson and the conduct of the
war, they had made it certain that they would suffer from the
public reaction against him and everything connected with
him. But, more decisively, they had broken their own morale by the uncritical enthusiasm with which most of them
had entered into the war spirit. With the exception of some
socialists and a few thinkers like Randolph Bourne and the
group behind the *Seven Arts* magazine, the intellectuals were
either engaged in the war or supported it wholeheartedly, and
they entertained the same fervid expectations of triumph and
reform as a result of it that many of them had had with respect to the Progressive movement. The peace left them disappointed, ashamed, guilty. "If I had it to do all over again,"
said Walter Lippmann, "I would take the other side. . . . We
supplied the Battalion of Death with too much ammunition."
And Herbert Croly confessed that he had had no idea "what

Walter Raleigh died of, and demand the number of legumes without counting.
Your memory, perceptive faculties, concentration, and other mental giblets
are tagged and you are pigeonholed for future reference. I have seen those
psychologists in my time and have dealt with them. If they were put out in a
forest or in a potato patch, they have not sense enough to kill a rabbit or dig a
potato to save themselves from the pangs of starvation. This is a government
by professors and intellectuals. I repeat, intellectuals are good enough in their
places, but a country run by professors is ultimately destined to Bolshevism
and an explosion." *Congressional Record*, 65th Congress, 2nd session, pp. 9875,
9877 (September 3, 1918).

[27]Walter Johnson, ed.: *Selected Letters of William Allen White* (New York,
1947), pp. 199–200, 208, 213.

the psychology of the American people would be under the strain of fighting a world war."[28] The *rapprochement* between the intellectuals and the people dissolved even more quickly than it had been made. The public turned on the intellectuals as the prophets of false and needless reforms, as architects of the administrative state, as supporters of the war, even as ur-Bolsheviks; the intellectuals turned on America as a nation of boobs, Babbitts, and fanatics. Those who were young and free enough expatriated themselves; the others stayed home and read Mencken. It would take a depression and another era of reform to overcome this estrangement.

4

During the New Deal the *rapprochement* between intellectuals and the public was restored. Never had there been such complete harmony between the popular cause in politics and the dominant mood of the intellectuals. In the Progressive era, the intellectuals and the public had, by and large, espoused the same causes. In the New Deal era, the causes were still more engaging, and the need for intellectuals to play a practical role was greater than anyone could have anticipated in the days of Wilson and T.R. But the minority that opposed the New Deal did so with a feverish hostility rarely seen in American politics. While the intellectuals were riding high, a rancorous feeling was forming against them that burst out spectacularly after World War II.

In the long run, the intellectuals were to suffer from this intransigent minority almost as much as they profited in the short run from the patronage of the New Deal. But, in its first flush, what patronage it was! Like everyone else, intellectuals had suffered from the depression, sharing in its unemployment and in its shock to morale. The New Deal gave thousands of jobs to young lawyers and economists, who flocked to Washington to staff its newly created agencies of regulation; the research, artistic, and theater projects of the WPA and NYA helped unemployed artists, intellectuals, and college students.

[28]Forcey: op. cit., pp. 292, 301.

Even more important than this practical aid was a pervasive intangible: by making use of theorists and professors as advisers and ideologists, the New Deal brought the force of mind into closer relation with power than it had been within the memory of any living man—closer than it had been since the days of the Founding Fathers. To offer important work to young men emerging from colleges and law schools was in itself an arresting novelty. But to give to academic advisers such importance as the New Deal gave was to aggrandize the role of every professor and of every speculative or dissenting mind. Ideas, theories, criticisms took on a new value, and the place to go for them was to men who were intellectually trained.[29] The economic collapse had demonstrated that such men were needed, but it was the New Deal that showed how they could make themselves felt. Not surprisingly, the New Deal aroused the enthusiasm of all but a small number of conservative intellectuals on one side and a small number of radicals at the other. (Even the Communists, who opposed the New Deal violently from 1933 to 1935, were able, as we now know, both to infiltrate its ranks and to exploit the public mood in which it flourished.)

The primary manifestation of the changed position of intellectuals was the creation of the brain trust, which was almost constantly in the news during the first few years of the New Deal. Conspicuous brain trusters like Raymond Moley, Rexford Guy Tugwell, and Adolph A. Berle, who were most often under attack, were symbols of the hundreds of obscurer men who staffed federal agencies, notably the protégés of Felix Frankfurter who came to Washington from Harvard. In the earliest days of the New Deal President Roosevelt himself enjoyed such prestige that it was psychologically more natural and strategically easier for his opponents to strike at him through those around him by suggesting that he was accepting ideas from sinister or irresponsible advisers. Among other things, the brain trust became useful to the President as a kind

[29]As Paul P. Van Riper points out, this led to a certain privilege in influencing new policies, which he describes as "ideological patronage." Op. cit., pp. 324–8.

of lightning rod. Much invective that might otherwise have fallen directly upon him as the central figure of the New Deal fell instead upon those around him—and they could be shifted, if the going got rough, into more obscure positions.

After the early eclipse of Raymond Moley, Professor Rexford Guy Tugwell became the favorite target for conservative critics of the New Deal. It was Tugwell's misfortune to believe in some forms of planning and to have written several books expounding his ideas. His nomination as Undersecretary of Agriculture in June, 1934 brought a wave of protest against the exaltation of so sinister a theorist. "Cotton Ed" Smith of South Carolina, one of the most implacable mastodons of the Senate, was so insistent in establishing the point that Tugwell was "not a graduate of God's Great University" that the Columbia economist had to go to great lengths to prove himself a true dirt farmer who as a boy had had plenty of mud on his boots. ("Tell Rex," said F.D.R. to Henry A. Wallace, "that I was surprised to hear that he was so dirty.") The diploma needed for agriculture, Smith told the Senate, "is obtained by bitter experience, and no man can solve the problems of agriculture in America but the man who has trodden the wine press of experience in the field." (He was unable to name a single past Secretary of Agriculture who met this requirement.) Roosevelt could appease Smith only by appointing as United States Marshal one of Smith's favored constituents, who had a record of homicide and whom the President described to the Cabinet as Smith's "favorite murderer." On the strength of this trade—one professor for one murderer—Tugwell finally won Senate confirmation by a vote of fifty-three to twenty-four.

The bad press Tugwell got became worse when his ardent sponsorship of pure food and drug legislation caused such influential advertisers as the proprietary drug houses to mobilize the press against him. Even James A. Farley, neither a radical nor an intellectual, winced at publicity so "raw and uncalled for." The picture of Tugwell painted by his most ardent critics was two-faced: on one side he was a totally feckless, academic, impractical theorist (half an inferior pedagogue, Mencken said, and half a "kept idealist of the *New Republic*"); on the other he was an effective, insidious, subversive force, quite capable of wreaking major damage on the fabric of society. Tugwell's patience under fire suggests that the academic man recruited into politics need not necessarily be thin-skinned.[30]

If the brain trust was to serve the opposition as a suitable whipping boy, it was necessary that its significance as a center of power be greatly exaggerated. "The 'brain trust,'" said a writer in the Chicago *Tribune*, "completely overshadows the Cabinet. It is reputed to have more influence with the President. . . . It has taken the professors from various colleges to put the Cabinet members in their places at last—merely department heads, chief clerks. On a routine administrative matter you go to a Cabinet member, but on matters of policy and the higher statesmanship you consult the professoriat."[31] It is true that at the very beginning of the New Deal—during its first hundred days—a panicky Congress quickly and complaisantly passed a great mass of legislation that it did not have the time or the will to scrutinize with the customary care. This left an unusual amount of discretion in legal draftsmanship and even in policy-making to the inner planning circles of the New Deal, in which expert advisers, though never controlling, were decidedly influential. However, the structure of power in the United States makes it impossible for many vital decisions to be made for very long by a small portion of the professoriat without roots in any basic class interest or political constituency. As the mood of panic passed, the normal processes of Congressional scrutiny returned and limited the influence of

[30]Tugwell's reputation and his role in the New Deal are amply accounted for by Bernard Sternsher's unpublished doctoral dissertation: *Rexford Guy Tugwell and the New Deal*, Boston University, 1957. The debate over his appointment is instructive: *Congressional Record*, 73rd Congress, 2nd session, pp. 11156–60, 11334–42, 11427–62 (June 12, 13, 14, 1934). See also Arthur Schlesinger, Jr.: *The Coming of the New Deal* (Boston, 1958), chapter 21; James A. Farley: *Behind the Ballots* (New York, 1938), pp. 219–20; H. L. Mencken: "Three Years of Dr. Roosevelt," *American Mercury* (March, 1936), p. 264. For further insight into the position of New Deal experts, see Richard S. Kirkendall's unpublished doctoral dissertation: *The New Deal Professors and the Politics of Agriculture*, University of Wisconsin, 1958.

[31]*Literary Digest*, Vol. CXV (June 3, 1933), p. 8. In fact, the brain trust, as an identifiable organization, was called into being for the 1932 campaign and ceased to exist when it was over. In speaking of it more loosely, I have followed the usage of contemporaries.

the technical advisers. For the most part, the steps taken under the New Deal which pleased the intellectuals and the experimenters were taken not because the experts favored them but because some large constituency wanted them. The brain trusters served the public—often very well—but they did not govern it. With few exceptions, the more idealistic and experimental schemes of the liberal brain trusters were circumvented, circumscribed, or sabotaged. It is true that the New Deal tried some unsuccessful inflationary monetary experiments advocated by a few academic theorists. But these were backed by immensely powerful inflationist pressures in the Senate, and they were not dear to the hearts of most of Roosevelt's expert advisers. On vital issues, the liberal experts almost invariably lost. The liberal theorists, led by Jerome Frank, who tried to represent the interests of the consumers in the NRA and of sharecroppers in the AAA were soon driven out. Rexford Tugwell's imaginative ideas for rural resettlement were crippled beyond recognition, and Tugwell himself was eventually consigned to the outer regions. Raymond Moley, who fell into conflict with Secretary of State Cordell Hull over the London Economic Conference, lost out to the Cabinet member.[32]

None the less, the notion became widely current that the professors were running things, and a veritable brain-trust war began which reawakened and quickened the old traditions of anti-intellectualism. The professors were not running things —and yet there was some kernel of truth in the popular notion that they were: they did represent something new in the constellation of power in the United States. They did not wield a great deal of power themselves, in the sense that it did not rest with them to make the central decisions. But upon those who did wield power they exercised a pervasive and vital influence, for it had now become a prerogative of experts to set the very terms in which the issues were perceived, to define the contours of economic and social issues. The right-wingers who denounced professors and brain trusters, however cranky their conceptions of the world of power, thus had a sound instinct. And if they did not have the ear of the majority of the public,

[32]For detailed information on the manner in which the proposals of professors were blunted in one area by business power, see the work by Kirkendall already cited.

they did at least have on their side some of the old weapons of popular prejudice, which they soon began to brandish. Moreover, the celebrity the professors enjoyed for a time enabled them to overshadow old-line politicians and businessmen, who found it particularly galling that a class of men hitherto so obscure and so little regarded should eclipse them in the public eye and make their role in society seem so much less significant. With his usual bald exaggeration, H. L. Mencken saw the irony of the transformation: "A few years ago all the New Deal Isaiahs were obscure and impotent fellows who flushed with pride when they got a nod from the cop at the corner; today they have the secular rank of princes of the blood, and the ghostly faculties of cardinal archbishops." The brain trusters, he continued, were so successful that they had begun to believe in their own panaceas. "What would *you* do," he asked,[33]

> if you were hauled suddenly out of a bare, smelly school-room, wherein the razzberries of sophomores had been your only music, and thrown into a place of power and glory almost befitting Caligula, Napoleon I, or J. Pierpont Morgan, with whole herds of Washington correspondents crowding up to take down your every wheeze, and the first pages of their newspapers thrown open to your complete metaphysic?

The critics of the New Deal exaggerated the power of the intellectuals and also portrayed them as impractical, irresponsible, conspiratorial experimentalists, grown arrogant and publicity-conscious because of their sudden rise from obscurity to prominence. Choosing comment almost at random from the *Saturday Evening Post*, an unimpeachable source of anti-intellectualism, one finds them characterized thus:[34]

> A bunch of professors hauled from their classrooms and thrust into the maelstrom of the New Deal. Very self-conscious;

[33] H. L. Mencken: "The New Deal Mentality," *American Mercury*, Vol. XXXVIII (May, 1936), p. 4.
[34] Samuel G. Blythe: "Kaleidoscope," *Saturday Evening Post*, Vol. CCVI (September 2, 1933), p. 7; Blythe: "Progress on the Potomac," *Saturday Evening Post*, December 2, 1933, p. 10; editorials, *Saturday Evening Post*, December 9, 1933, p. 22, and April 7, 1934, pp. 24–5; William V. Hodges: "Realities Are Coming," *Saturday Evening Post*, April 21, 1934, p. 5. See also Margaret Culkin Banning: "Amateur Year," *Saturday Evening Post*, April 28, 1934; Katherine Dayton: "Capitol Punishments," *Saturday Evening Post*, December 23, 1933.

arrogant seekers after publicity for themselves now they have a chance to get it; eager self-expressionists basking like cats before a fireplace in their new distinctions. . . . The men who rush about and ask excitedly: "What's the dollar going to do?" As if it makes the slightest difference to them what the dollar does—not one of them can muster a hundred dollars of any sort. . . . Out came the professorial law, modified of course, here and there by non-professorial meddlers in the halls of Congress, but with plenty of professorial ideas in them at that. . . . No thoughtful man can escape the conclusion that many of the brain trust ideas and plans are based on Russian ideology. . . . Somebody should tell these bright young intellectuals and professors the facts of business life. The stork does not bring profits and prosperity, and sound currency does not grow under cabbages. . . . In the end it must be the farmer and the industrialist, assisted by nature and wisely backed by Government, who cure their own ills. . . .

Are we so silly, so supine as to permit amateur, self-confessed experimentalists to take our social and business fabric apart to see if they cannot reconstruct it in a pattern that is more to their liking? . . . laboratory experiments on the life, liberty and industry of America. . . . There is a vast difference between an experiment made in a test tube and one made on a living nation. That smacks altogether too much of vivisection . . . men untainted with any practical experience . . . government by amateurs—college boys, irrespective of their age —who have drunk deep, perhaps of the Pierian spring, have recently taken some hearty swigs of Russian vodka . . . the theorist, the dreamer of political dreams, rainmakers and presti-digitators. . . . Realistic senators and representatives have no haven but the seclusion of the locker room. . . .

Defenders of the intellectuals tried to arrive at a more reasonable estimate of their actual power, and to point out that they could hardly do worse than the "practical" men they had displaced. Oswald Garrison Villard, writing in the *Nation*, welcomed the "complete rout of the practical men," and pointed out that all over the world "the practical men are utterly at a loss."[35] Jonathan Mitchell, then a liberal journalist and a former

[35]"Issues and Men, the Idealist Comes to the Front," *Nation*, Vol. CXXXVII (October 4, 1933), p. 371. Cf. the same view in the *New Republic*: "The Brain Trust" (June 7, 1933), pp. 85–6.

New Deal adviser, in one of the most thoughtful analyses of the subject, tried to show that Roosevelt's use of academic experts was a natural consequence of the crisis and of the peculiarities of American administrative life. The professors were not in fact setting major policies, he wrote, but simply advising about instrumentalities. In the absence of a class of civil servants trained for such a purpose, the President's sudden resort to men from outside political or administrative circles was almost inevitable.[36] On this count Mitchell was entirely right. Politicians could not handle the issues raised by the depression; civil servants of the right type did not exist to cope with them; and most business leaders seemed worse than useless. As Samuel I. Rosenman advised the President: "Usually in a situation like this a candidate gathers around him a group composed of some successful industrialists, some big financiers, and some national political leaders. I think we ought to steer clear of all those. They all seem to have failed to produce anything constructive to solve the mess we're in today. . . . Why not go to the universities of the country?"[37]

But Mitchell's analysis might well have been taken by foes of the New Deal as inflammatory:

> What Mr. Roosevelt needed was a neutral, someone who didn't smell of Wall Street but who, on the other hand, wouldn't too greatly scare the wealthy. Moreover, he needed someone who would have the brains, competence, and willingness to carry through whatever policies he determined upon. Mr. Roosevelt chose college professors; there is no other group in the country which these specifications fit. . . .
>
> We have in America no hereditary land-owning class from which to recruit our New Deal civil service. Our nearest equivalents are the college professors, and the neutral professor in Washington is the element which will decide the New Deal's success or failure. . . . There was once a time in this country when we did have a class set apart, to whom others submitted their disputes without question. That class was the colonial ministers, particularly of New England. They were generally unconcerned with worldly things; they regulated their communities

[36]Jonathan Mitchell: "Don't Shoot the Professors! Why the Government Needs Them," *Harper's*, Vol. CLXVIII (May, 1934), pp. 743, 749.
[37]Samuel I. Rosenman: *Working with Roosevelt* (New York, 1952), p. 57.

with a sterner hand than Mr. Roosevelt's New Deal is ever likely to employ, and they gave judgment according to the light they had. . . . The New England ministers have long since departed, but the college professors are their collateral heirs. . . . In the future, we shall succeed in building for ourselves a professional American civil service, supported by its own loyalties and tradition.

None of this could have been expected to appease or reassure the businessmen, displaced politicians, and other members of the conservative classes, who felt little need for a professional civil service, who understandably could not believe that the professors were "neutral," who thought that professors did indeed scare the wealthy, and who could only have been alarmed at the thought of having any class to which disputes would be submitted "without question." No answer, not even an answer couched more moderately than Mitchell's, could assuage their basic fear, which was not a fear of the brain trust or the expert, but of the collapse of the world in which they had put their faith. Among such enemies, the prerogatives offered by the New Deal to intellectuals and experts only served to confirm old traditions of anti-intellectualism, and to strengthen them with new suspicions and resentments.

The Second World War, like the first, increased the need for experts, not only the sort the New Deal employed but also men from previously untapped fields of scholarship—even classicists and archaeologists were suddenly thought important because of their knowledge of the Mediterranean area. But when the war ended, the long-delayed revulsion from the New Deal experience and the war itself swept over the country. For this reaction the battle against the brain trust had laid the groundwork. With it, the *rapprochement* between the intellectuals and the popular democracy once more came to an end.

5

In 1952 Adlai Stevenson became the victim of the accumulated grievances against intellectuals and brain trusters which had festered in the American right wing since 1933. Unfortunately, his political fate was taken as a yardstick by which liberal intellectuals measured the position of intellect in American political life. It was a natural mistake to make: Stevenson had the dimensions and the appeal of a major tragic hero, and intellectuals identified his cause with their own. After the embarrassments of the Truman administration, it was refreshing to listen to his literate style. But more decisive were the overwhelming differences between Stevenson's manner and the Eisenhower–Nixon campaign. Strong as the contrast was between Stevenson's flair for the apt phrase (and his evident ability to work with campaign advisers who shared it) and the fumbling inarticulateness of Eisenhower's early political manner, it was heightened by Nixon, with his egregious "Checkers" speech, his sure touch for the philistine cliché, and his crass eulogies of his senior partner. Finally, there was the ugly image of McCarthy, whose contributions to the campaign were all too plainly welcomed by his party. One does not expect American presidential campaigns to set a high tone, but the tone of the Republican campaign of 1952, which by comparison seemed to endow even Truman's shameless baiting of Wall Street with a touch of old-fashioned dignity, was such as to throw into high relief every one of Stevenson's attractive qualities.

Intellectuals embraced Stevenson with a readiness and a unanimity that seems without parallel in American history. Theodore Roosevelt, after all, had had to earn such popularity as he enjoyed among the intellectuals of his day during a long public career; when he took the presidency there were many intellectuals who regarded him with a mixture of suspicion and amusement; his closest rapport with them was indeed achieved only after he left the White House; it was climaxed by the Bull Moose campaign of 1912 and then eclipsed by his wartime jingoism. Woodrow Wilson, for all his style and his academic origins, was treated by a substantial segment of the intellectual community with a cold reserve that matched his own manner; many intellectuals agreed with Walter Lippmann's contemporary diagnosis of the New Freedom as an ill-conceived, backward-looking movement designed mainly for small business interests; and finally, Wilson's reputation suffered badly from the reaction against the mob-mindedness of the war years from which the President himself had not been immune. Franklin D. Roosevelt, for all the publicity given his brain trust, disappointed most intellectuals during his first presidential campaign, and remained an object of distrust and sharp left-wing criticism during the early years of the New Deal. The intellectuals did not greatly warm to him until the very eve of the 1936 campaign, and even then seemed to love him mainly for the enemies he had made. With Stevenson it was different: men who had hardly heard of him as Governor of Illinois, and for whom he was a new star in the firmament at the time of his nomination in 1952, took him to their hearts at once upon hearing his acceptance speech. He seemed too good to be true.

At a time when the McCarthyist pack was in full cry, it was hard to resist the conclusion that Stevenson's smashing defeat was also a repudiation by plebiscite of American intellectuals and of intellect itself. Those intellectuals who drew this conclusion were confirmed by their critics, among whom there was a great deal of solemn head-shaking: American intellectuals, it was said, did not feel for or understand their country; they had grown irresponsible and arrogant; their chastening was very much in order. That many intellectuals were hurt there can be no doubt; but the notion that Stevenson was repudiated by the public because of his reputation for wit and intellect will not bear analysis, and the implications of his defeat on this count have been vastly exaggerated. In 1952, he was hopelessly overmatched. It was a year in which any appealing Republican could have beaten any Democrat, and Eisenhower was more than appealing: he was a national hero of irresistible magnetism whose popularity overshadowed not only Stevenson but every other man on the political scene. After twenty years of Democratic rule, the time for a change in the parties was overdue, if the two-party system was to have any meaning. The Korean War and its discontents alone provided a sufficient issue for the Republicans; and they were able to capitalize on lesser issues like the Hiss case and other revelations of Communist infiltration into the federal government, and the discovery of trifling but titillating corruption in the Truman administration. Stevenson's hopeless position might more readily have been accepted as such if the Republican campaign, in which Nixon and McCarthy seemed more conspicuous than Eisenhower, had not struck such a low note as to stir the will to believe that such men must be rejected by the public.

In retrospect, however, there seems no reason to believe that Stevenson's style and wit and integrity were anything but assets in his campaign, and that if he had not won a reputation for himself on these counts his defeat would have been still more complete. The notion that the greater part of the public was totally immune to the value of his qualities will not bear even a casual examination. If his personal qualities had been so unattractive as some admirers and detractors alike believed, it is hard to understand how he could have won the governorship of Illinois in 1948 by the largest plurality in the state's history, or why the Democratic convention should have drafted him four years later, in spite of his well-publicized reluctance to be nominated, after the merest brief exposure to his eloquent welcoming speech. (It was the first draft since Hughes's in 1916, and perhaps the only draft of a thoroughly reluctant candidate in our political history.)

Even the dimensions of Stevenson's defeat were magnified by the dramatic contrast between his campaign and that of the Republicans. Twelve years earlier, Wendell Willkie, also running against the great political hero of the moment, received almost exactly the same per cent of the popular vote as Stevenson—44.4 to 44.3—and Willkie was considered a leader of exceptionally dynamic qualities. The truth seems to be that both candidates in 1952 were personally strong, and with political excitements running high, both drew the voters to the polls in large numbers. Stevenson in defeat had a larger popular vote than Truman in his victory of 1948 or Roosevelt in 1944 and 1940. And after the election his mail was full of letters from people who had voted for Eisenhower but who expressed their admiration for his campaign and their wish that circumstances had been different enough to justify their supporting him.

This is not to deny that something was missing from the "image"—in the now fashionable jargon—that Stevenson projected. He knew all too well the difficulty of taking over the leadership of the Democratic Party after its twenty years in power. But his reluctance to assume power—though in a certain light it may be taken as creditable—was all too real, and it aroused misgivings. "I accept your nomination—and your program," he said to the Democratic convention. "I should have preferred to hear these words uttered by a stronger, a wiser, a better man than myself." It was not the right note for the times; it made for uneasiness, and many found it less attractive than Eisenhower's bland confidence. Stevenson's humility seemed genuine, but he proffered it all too proudly. One could recognize his ability to analyze public questions with integrity and without deference to the conventional hokum, and yet remain in doubt as to whether he had that imaginative grasp of the uses and possibilities of power which, in recent times, the two Roosevelts had conveyed with the most effective force. (One cannot, however, refrain from commenting on the delusive character of the contrasting impressions given by Eisenhower and Stevenson: Eisenhower's regime had its merits, but the General, in power, failed to unite or elevate his party, whereas Stevenson out of power did a great deal to renew and invigorate his.)

We would be deluded, then, if we attributed Stevenson's defeat to his reputation for intellectuality, or even if we assumed that this reputation was a liability instead of an asset. But for a substantial segment of the public this quality was indeed a liability; and without any desire to exaggerate the size or influence of this group, we must examine it, for these people are of primary interest to any study of anti-intellectual imagery.

The quality in Stevenson that excited most frequent attack was not his intellect as such, but his wit.[38] In this country wit has never been popular in political leaders. The public enjoys and accepts humor—Lincoln, T.R., and F.D.R. used it to some effect—but humor is folkish, usually quite simple, and readily accessible. Wit is humor intellectualized; it is sharper; it has associations with style and sophistication, overtones of aristocracy. Repeatedly Stevenson was referred to as a "comedian" or

[38]For information and for the quoted matter in the following paragraphs, which is taken from editorials and letters to newspapers, I have drawn on George A. Hage's illuminating unpublished study: *Anti-intellectualism in Newspaper Comment on the Elections of 1828 and 1952*, University of Minnesota doctoral dissertation, 1958; see the same writer's "Anti-intellectualism in Press Comment—1828 and 1952," *Journalism Quarterly*, Vol. XXXVI (Fall, 1959), pp. 439–46.

a "clown" and portrayed in cartoons as a jester with fool's cap and bells. Against the somber, angry, frustrating background of the Korean War, his wit seemed to his detractors altogether out of place; Eisenhower's dull but solid sobriety of utterance seemed more in keeping with the hour. It did Stevenson's supporters little good to point out that he did not jest about the Korean War itself or about other matters of solemn moment to the voters. Far from overcoming other handicaps in his public image, his wit seemed to widen the distance between himself and a significant part of the electorate. ("His fluent command of the English language is far above the heads of the ordinary American.") One of the revealing comments of the campaign was made by a woman who wrote to the Detroit *News* that "we should have something in common with a candidate for President, and that's why I'm voting for General Eisenhower."

Stevenson had been a character witness for Alger Hiss and on this account was especially vulnerable to the common tandem association between intellect and radicalism, radicalism and disloyalty. His intellectual supporters were easily tarred with the same brush, and the fact that so many of them came from the East, particularly from Harvard, was significant in the minds of many critics. HARVARD TELLS INDIANA HOW TO VOTE, ran a headline in a Chicago *Tribune* editorial whose argument was that Stevenson was in the hands of the Schlesingers, father and son, and Archibald MacLeish, all of whom were held to have had the most sinister associations. Westbrook Pegler, who had not forgotten Felix Frankfurter's influence on the New Deal, took pains to remind readers that Stevenson, like F.D.R., had had Harvard associations. He had spent a few years at Harvard Law School, where it seemed to Pegler that he must surely have succumbed to Frankfurter's wiles; Stevenson had been, Pegler thought, "a New Deal bureaucrat of the most dangerous type intermittently ever since 1933." Pegler imagined he had noticed an attempt by Stevenson's supporters and biographers to play down his Harvard connections and his supposed left-wing associations; but none of this could conceal from the vigilant Pegler the fact that "the Springfield wonder boy is serving a warmed-over version of the leftist political line." As a consequence of Stevenson's malign Harvard associations, Frankfurter, Hiss, the Schlesingers, and

Stevenson all merged into a single ominous image in right-wing fantasies.

Other university associations were no better. When a large number of Columbia University faculty members published a manifesto praising Stevenson and criticizing Eisenhower, then the university's president, the New York *Daily News* countered with an exposure of alleged "pinko professors" among the signers. A Midwestern newspaper more calmly remarked that the opposition of Columbia students and faculty would work in Eisenhower's favor because everyone knew that university people "have had their minds infiltrated with strong leftist Socialistic ideas, as well as with definite Communistic loyalties." Such support only damned Stevenson. "Stevenson, the intellectual, must share the views of his advisers or he would not have selected them. A vote for Eisenhower, the plain American, is a vote for democracy." Old resentments against the New Deal were everywhere in evidence among writers to whom this argument of disloyalty was significant: "We have strayed far afield from the good old American ways which made this country great. Our colleges are full of leftists, and these 'bright young boys' want to make this country over into a 'bright new world.' May we be protected from another four years of New Deal-Fair Deal."

The association of intellectuality and style with effeminacy which I have remarked on in connection with the reformers of the Gilded Age reappeared in the 1952 campaign. Here Stevenson was sadly handicapped. Since his service in both world wars had been in a civilian capacity, he had nothing to counter Eisenhower's record as a general. Had he been a boxer, hunter, or soldier like T.R., or a football player (Eisenhower had this too to his credit), or an artilleryman like Harry Truman, or a war hero like Kennedy, the impression that he was removed from the hard masculine world of affairs might have been mitigated. But he was only a gentleman with an Ivy League background, and there was nothing in his career to spare him from the reverberations this history set up in the darker corners of the American mind. The New York *Daily News* descended to calling him Adelaide and charged that he "trilled" his speeches in a "fruity" voice. His voice and diction were converted into objects of suspicion—"teacup words," it was said, reminiscent of "a genteel spinster who can never forget that she got an A in elocution at Miss Smith's Finishing School." His supporters? They were "typical Harvard lace-cuff liberals," "lace-panty diplomats," "pompadoured lap dogs," who wailed "in perfumed anguish" at McCarthy's accusations and on occasions "giggled" about their own anti-Communism. Politics, Stevenson's critics were disposed to say, is a rough game for men. The governor and his followers ought to be prepared to slug it out. They would do well to take a lesson from Richard Nixon's "manly explanation of his financial affairs."

Even in quarters where rancor and vulgarity were absent, there was a frequently stated preference for the "proven ability" of Eisenhower as compared with Stevenson, who smacked of the "ivory tower." "On the basis of past performance, I feel we need Eisenhower, the man of outstanding achievement, rather than Stevenson, the thinker and orator." Jefferson and John Quincy Adams might well have found a familiar note in this remark of a partisan: "Eisenhower knows more about world conditions than any other two men in the country, and he didn't obtain his knowledge through newspapers and books either." The theme is unlikely to lose its usefulness. Eight years later, campaigning for Nixon and Lodge, Eisenhower himself said of them: "These men didn't learn their lessons merely out of books—and not even by writing books. They learned these lessons by meeting the day-in, day-out problems of our changing world."[39]

But in the same campaign John F. Kennedy proved what perhaps should not have had to be proved again—that the reading of books, even the writing of books, is hardly a fatal impediment for a presidential aspirant who combines a reputation for mind with the other necessary qualities. Kennedy seems to have brought back to presidential politics the combination of intellect and character shown at the beginning of the century by T.R.—a combination in which a respect for intellectual and cultural distinction and a passion for intelligence and expertise in public service are united with the aggressive and practical virtues. Stevenson as a campaigner had seemed all sensitivity and diffidence and had appealed to the intellectuals'

[39] *The New York Times*, November 3, 1960.

fond obsession with their own alienation and rejection; Kennedy, on the other hand, was all authority and confidence, and he appealed to their desire that intellect and culture be associated with power and responsibility. He had all of Eisenhower's confidence without his passivity; and his victory over Nixon, despite his religion, his youth, and his relative obscurity at the time of his nomination, was in good part attributable to his visibly superior aggressiveness and self-assurance in their television debates—to his show, as T.R. might have said, of the manly virtues.

To most intellectuals, even to many with an ingrained suspicion of the manifestations of power, the mind of the new President seemed to be, if hardly profound, at least alert and capacious, sophisticated and skeptical, and he was quick to convey his belief that in the national concert of interests the claims of intellect and culture ought to have a place. Some highly intelligent Presidents before Kennedy—Hoover, for example —had been utterly impatient with the ceremonial functions of the presidency, which seemed to them only a waste of precious time on trivialities. The Founding Fathers had conceived the office differently. Many of them understood that the chief of state, above all in a republican political order, ought to be a *personage*, and that the communion between this personage and the public is an important thread in the fabric of government. Washington himself, whose very presence contributed to the success of the new government, was a perfect example of the performance of this function. In the twentieth century, the American mania for publicity and the development of the mass media have put a great strain upon the ceremonial and public side of the presidential office. Franklin D. Roosevelt, through skillful use of the radio and the press conference, was the first President to turn the demands of modern publicity into a major asset. Kennedy has been the first to see that intellectuals and artists are now a sufficiently important segment of the public to warrant not simply inclusion in the ceremonial aspects of state but some special effort to command their loyalty by awarding them a kind of official recognition. The President's mansion has thus been restored as a symbol: to the great audience its renovation has been displayed on television; for a smaller but strategic audience it has become once again a center of receptivity to culture—Robert Frost, E. E. Cummings, and Pablo Casals have been welcomed there. And the idea that power may owe some deference to intellect has been reaffirmed many times—perhaps most impressively by a memorable dinner for Nobel laureates given in the spring of 1962, at which the President characteristically remarked that there were now more brains at the White House table than at any time since the days when Thomas Jefferson dined alone.

Of course, all this was merely a ceremonial means of recognizing the legitimacy of a special interest—the kind of ceremonial whose function had long been understood, for example, by Irish politicians who attended Italian festivals or Jewish politicians who went to Irish wakes. Like the ethnic minorities, the intellectuals were to have their place in the scheme of public acknowledgment. The interest and pleasure of the new administration in the ceremonial recognition of culture was less important than its sustained search for talent, which brought the place of expertise in American government to a new high. From time to time the reputation and recognition of intellect in politics may vary, but the demand for expertise seems constantly to rise. The Eisenhower regime, for example, despite its expressed disdain for eggheads and its pique at their opposition, made considerable strategic use of experts; and Republican leaders also showed interest in what they called the "utilization" of friendly academics. The larger question, to which I shall return in my final chapter, concerns the relations between experts who are also intellectuals, of whom there are many, and the rest of the intellectual community; and touches upon the condition of intellectuals when they find themselves on the fringes of power. One of the difficulties in the relation of intellect to power is that certain primary functions of intellect are widely felt to be threatened almost as much by being associated with power as by being relegated to a position of impotence. An acute and paradoxical problem of intellect as a force in modern society stems from the fact that it cannot lightly reconcile itself either to its association with power or to its exclusion from an important political role.

PART 4

THE PRACTICAL CULTURE

CHAPTER IX

Business and Intellect

I

FOR AT least three quarters of a century business has been stigmatized by most American intellectuals as the classic enemy of intellect; businessmen themselves have so long accepted this role that by now their enmity seems to be a fact of nature. No doubt there is a certain measure of inherent dissonance between business enterprise and intellectual enterprise: being dedicated to different sets of values, they are bound to conflict; and intellect is always potentially threatening to any institutional apparatus or to fixed centers of power. But this enmity, being qualified by a certain mutual dependence, need not take the form of constant open warfare. Quite as important as the general grounds that make for enmity are the historical circumstances that have muted or accentuated it. The circumstances of the industrial era in America gave the businessman a position among the foes of mind and culture so central and so powerful that other antagonists were crowded out of the picture.

Some years ago the business journalist, John Chamberlain, complained in *Fortune* that American novelists have consistently done rank injustice to American businessmen. In the entire body of modern American fiction, he pointed out, the businessman is almost always depicted as crass, philistine, corrupt, predatory, domineering, reactionary, and amoral. In a long list of business novels, from Dreiser's Cowperwood trilogy to the present, Chamberlain could find only three books in which the businessman was favorably portrayed: one was by a popular novelist of no consequence; the others were William Dean Howells's *The Rise of Silas Lapham* and Sinclair Lewis's *Dodsworth*.[1] But the very transiency of these two exceptions confirms Chamberlain's complaint. *Silas Lapham* was written in 1885, before novelists and businessmen had become solidly

---

[1]"The Businessman in Fiction," *Fortune*, Vol. XXXVIII (November, 1948), pp. 134–48.

alienated; five years later, Howells published *A Hazard of New Fortunes*, in which one of the characteristically saurian businessmen of fiction appears, and he later wrote some vaguely socialist social criticism. And it was Sinclair Lewis, after all, who in *Babbitt* gave the world its archetype of the small-town, small-business American philistine.

In the main, Chamberlain remarked, the novelists' portrait of the businessman is drawn out of doctrine ("a dry and doctrinaire attitude," he called it) and not out of direct observation of business or out of an intimate knowledge of businessmen. The perverse intent suggested by this charge may be largely a creation of Chamberlain's fancy. Our society has no unitary elites in which writers and businessmen associate on easy terms; and if real live businessmen fail to appear in the American novel, it is partly because the American writer rarely appears in the society of businessmen: chances for close observation are minimal. The hostility is not one-sided but mutual; and it would be an unenviable task to try to show that the businessman lacks the instruments of self-defense or retaliation, or that he has not used them.

But Chamberlain's main point stands: the portrait of the businessman offered in the social novel in this country conveys the general attitude of the intellectual community, which has been at various times populistic, progressive, or Marxist, or often some compound of the three. Since the development of industrialism after the Civil War, the estrangement between businessmen and men of letters has been both profound and continuous; and since the rise of Progressivism and the New Deal, the tension between businessmen and liberal intellectuals in the social sciences has also been acute. In times of prosperity, when the intellectual community has not been deeply engaged with political conflict, it is content to portray businessmen as philistines. In times of political or economic discontent, the conflict deepens, and the businessmen become ruthless exploiters as well. The values of business and intellect are seen as eternally and inevitably at odds: on the one side, there is the money-centered or power-centered man, who cares only about bigness and the dollar, about boosting and hollow optimism; on the other side, there are the men of critical intellect, who distrust American civilization and concern themselves with quality and moral values. The intellectual is well aware of the elaborate apparatus which the businessman uses to mold our civilization to his purposes and adapt it to his standards. The businessman is everywhere; he fills the coffers of the political parties; he owns or controls the influential press and the agencies of mass culture; he sits on university boards of trustees and on local school boards; he mobilizes and finances cultural vigilantes; his voice dominates the rooms in which the real decisions are made.

The contemporary businessman, who is disposed to think of himself as a man of practical achievement and a national benefactor, shouldering enormous responsibilities and suffering from the hostility of flighty men who have never met a payroll, finds it hard to take seriously the notion that he always gets his way. He sees himself enmeshed in the bureaucratic regulations of a welfare state that is certainly no creation of *his*; he feels he is checkmated by powerful unions and regarded suspiciously by a public constantly piqued by intellectuals. He may also be aware that in former days—in the times, say, of Andrew Carnegie—the great business leader, despite some hostility, was a culture-hero. In those days businessmen were prominent national figures in their own right, sages to be consulted on almost every aspect of life. But since the times of Henry Ford —the last of his kind—this heroic image has gone into eclipse. Businessmen figure in the headlines only when they enter politics or public administration. A man like Charles E. Wilson, for example, had ten times as many notices in *The New York Times* when he was Secretary of Defense in 1953 as he had three years earlier as president of General Motors.[2] Rich men may still be acceptable in politics—John F. Kennedy, Nelson Rockefeller, Averell Harriman, Herbert Lehman, G. Mennen Williams— but these are not truly businessmen: they are men of inherited wealth, often conspicuous for their liberal political views.

At times the businessman may think of himself as having been stripped of his prestige by the intellectual and his allies, in a hostile environment created by intellectuals. If so, he overestimates the power of the intellectuals. In fact, the prestige of the businessman has been destroyed largely by his own achievements: it was he who created the giant corporation, an

[2] Mabel Newcomer: *The Big Business Executive* (New York, 1955), p. 7; on the declining prestige of executives, see p. 131.

impersonal agency that overshadows his reputation as it disciplines his career; it was his own incessant propaganda about the American Way of Life and Free Enterprise that made these spongy abstractions into public generalities which soak up and assimilate the reputations of individual enterprisers. Once great men created fortunes; today a great system creates fortunate men.

The tension between intellect and business has about it, however, a kind of ungainly intimacy, symbolized in the fact that so many intellectuals are rebelling against the business families in which they were reared. An uneasy symbiosis has actually developed between business and intellect. In the United States, where government has done far less for the arts and learning than in Europe, culture has always been dependent upon private patronage; it has not been any less dependent in recent decades, when the criticism of business has been so dominant a concern of intellectuals. The position of the critical intellectual is thus a singularly uncomfortable one: in the interests of his work and his livelihood he extends one hand for the institutional largesse of dead businessmen, the Guggenheims, Carnegies, Rockefellers, Fords, and lesser benefactors; but in his concern for high principles and values his other hand is often doubled into a fist. The freedom of intellect and art is inevitably the freedom to criticize and disparage, to destroy and re-create; but the daily necessity of the intellectual and the artist is to be an employee, a protégé, a beneficiary—or a man of business. This ambiguous relationship affects businessmen as well. Sensitive of their reputation, fearful and resentful of criticism, often arrogant in their power, they can hardly help but be aware that the patronage of learning and art will add to their repute. To speak less cynically, they are also the heirs of traditional moral canons of stewardship; they often feel a responsibility to do good with their money. And they are not without a certain respect for mind; under modern technological conditions, they must, in any case, more or less regularly call upon mind for practical counsel. Finally, being rather more human than otherwise, they too have a natural craving for unbought esteem.

The anti-intellectualism of businessmen, interpreted narrowly as hostility to intellectuals, is mainly a political phenomenon. But interpreted more broadly as a suspicion of intellect

itself, it is part of the extensive American devotion to practicality and direct experience which ramifies through almost every
area of American life. With some variations of details suitable
to social classes and historical circumstances, the excessive
practical bias so often attributed only to business is found almost everywhere in America. In itself, a certain wholesome
regard for the practical needs no defense and deserves no dis-
paragement, so long as it does not aspire to exclusiveness, so
long as other aspects of human experience are not denigrated
and ridiculed. Practical vigor is a virtue; what has been spiritually crippling in our history is the tendency to make a mystique
of practicality.

2

If I put business in the vanguard of anti-intellectualism in our
culture, it is not out of a desire to overstate its role. Certainly
the debt of American culture to a small number of wealthy
men, patrons of learning and art, is great enough to be thrown
immediately into the balance as a counterpoise. The main reason for stressing anti-intellectualism in business is not that
business is demonstrably more anti-intellectual or more philistine than other major sections of American society, but simply
that business is the most powerful and pervasive interest in
American life. This is true both in the sense that the claims of
practicality have been an overweening force in American life
and in the sense that, since the mid-nineteenth century, businessmen have brought to anti-intellectual movements more
strength than any other force in society. "This is essentially a
business country," said Warren G. Harding in 1920, and his
words were echoed by the famous remark of Calvin Coolidge:
"The business of America is business."[3] It is this social preponderance of business, at least before 1929, that gives it a claim
to special attention.

One reason for the success of the argument of American
business against intellect is that it coincides at so many points

[3]Warren G. Harding: "Business Sense in Government," *Nation's Business*, Vol.
VIII (November, 1920), p. 13. Coolidge is quoted, from an address at the
December, 1923 meeting of the American Society of Newspaper Editors, by
William Allen White: *A Puritan in Babylon* (New York, 1938), p. 253.

with the conventional folk wisdom. For example, the feeling about intellect expressed in the businessman's statements about higher education and vocationalism was also the popular feeling, as Edward Kirkland has suggested: the people constantly voted on the educational system by taking their children out of school or by not sending them to college. We need not be surprised to find a "radical" labor reformer like Henry George advising his son that since college would fill his head with things which would have to be unlearned, he should go directly into newspaper work to put himself in touch with the practical world; the same advice might have come from a business tycoon.[4]

The fear of mind and the disdain for culture, so quickly evident wherever the prior claims of practicality are urged in the literature of business, are ubiquitous themes. They rest upon two pervasive American attitudes toward civilization and personal religion—first, a widely shared contempt for the past; and second, an ethos of self-help and personal advancement in which even religious faith becomes merely an agency of practicality.

Let us look first at the American attitude toward the past, which has been so greatly shaped by our technological culture. America, as it is commonly said, has been a country without monuments or ruins—that is, without those inescapable traces of the ancestral human spirit with which all Europeans live and whose meanings, at least in their broadest outlines, can hardly be evaded by even the simplest peasant or workman. America has been the country of those who fled from the past. Its population was selected by migration from among those most determined to excise history from their lives.[5] With their minds fixed on the future, Americans found themselves surrounded with ample land and resources and beset by a shortage of labor

[4] Edward Kirkland: *Dream and Thought in the Business Community, 1860–1900* (Ithaca, New York, 1956), pp. 81–2, 87.
[5] "It is not indiscriminate masses of Europe," Emerson thought, "that are shipped hitherward, but the Atlantic is a sieve through which only or chiefly the liberal, adventurous, sensitive, *America-loving* part of each city, clan, family are brought. It is the light complexion, the blue eyes of Europe that come: the black eyes, the black drop, the Europe of Europe, is left." *Journals* (1851; Boston, Riverside ed., 1912), Vol. VIII, p. 226.

and skills. They set a premium upon technical knowledge and inventiveness which would unlock the riches of the country and open the door to the opulent future. Technology, skill—everything that is suggested by the significant Americanism, "know-how"—was in demand. The past was seen as despicably impractical and uninventive, simply and solely as something to be surmounted. It should be acknowledged that the American disdain for the past, as it emerged toward the end of the eighteenth and the beginning of the nineteenth centuries, had some aspects which were at the very least defensible and at best distinctly praiseworthy. What was at stake was not entirely a technological or materialistic barbarianism which aimed merely to slough off all the baggage of history. Among other things, the American attitude represented a republican and egalitarian protest against monarchy and aristocracy and the callous exploitation of the people; it represented a rationalistic protest against superstition; an energetic and forward-looking protest against the passivity and pessimism of the Old World; it revealed a dynamic, vital, and originative mentality.

But certainly in its consequences, if not in its intentions, this attitude was anti-cultural. It stimulated the development of an intellectual style in which the past was too often regarded simply as a museum of confusion, corruption, and exploitation; it led to disdain for all contemplation which could not be transformed into practical intelligence and for all passion which could not be mobilized for some forward step in progress. This view of human affairs lent itself too readily to the proposition that the sum and substance of life lies in the business of practical improvement; it encouraged the complacent notion that there is only one defensible way of life, the American way, and that this way had been willfully spurned or abandoned by peoples elsewhere.[6] Many Americans found the true secret of

[6]Cf. Thomas Paine in *The Rights of Man*: "From the rapid progress which America makes in every species of improvement, it is rational to conclude that, if the governments of Asia, Africa, and Europe had begun on a principle similar to that of America, or had not been very early corrupted therefrom, those countries must by this time have been in a far superior condition to what they are." *Writings*, ed. by Moncure D. Conway (New York, 1894), Vol. II, p. 402.

civilization in the Patent Office. An orator at Yale in 1844 told the undergraduates that they could read the future there:[7]

> The age of *philosophy* has passed, and left few memorials of its existence. That of *glory* has vanished, and nothing but a painful tradition of human suffering remains. That of *utility* has commenced, and it requires little warmth of imagination to anticipate for it a reign lasting as time, and radiant with the wonders of unveiled nature.

Everywhere, as machine industry arose, it drew a line of demarcation between the utilitarian and the traditional. In the main, America took its stand with utility, with improvement and invention, money and comfort. It was clearly understood that the advance of the machine was destroying old inertias, discomforts, and brutalities, but it was not so commonly understood that the machine was creating new discomforts and brutalities, undermining traditions and ideals, sentiments and loyalties, esthetic sensitivities. Perhaps the signal difference between Europe and America on this count is that in Europe there always existed a strong counter-tradition, both romantic and moralistic, against the ugliness of industrialism—a tradition carried on by figures as diverse as Goethe and Blake, Morris and Carlyle, Hugo and Chateaubriand, Ruskin and Scott. Such men counterposed to the machine a passion for language and locality, for antiquities and monuments, for natural beauty; they sustained a tradition of resistance to capitalist industrialism, of skepticism about the human consequences of industrial progress, of moral, esthetic, and humane revolt.

I do not mean to suggest that there were no American counterparts. Some writers did protest against complacent faith in improvement, though one senses among them a poignant awareness of their futility and isolation, of their opposition to the main stream. Nathaniel Hawthorne might complain, as he did in the preface to *The Marble Faun*, of the difficulties of writing in a country "where there is no shadow, no antiquity,

---

[7] Arthur A. Ekirch: *The Idea of Progress in America, 1815–1860* (New York, 1944), p. 126. I am indebted to chapter 4 for its documentation of the American faith in technology, though I feel that the author is slightly amiss in speaking of it simply as faith in science, for it is largely *applied* science which is involved. The whole work is illuminating on the American mentality before the Civil War.

no mystery, no picturesque and gloomy wrong, nor anything but a commonplace prosperity, in broad and simple daylight"; Herman Melville might warn, as he did in *Clarel*, of

> Man disennobled—brutalized
> By popular science

and answer scientific progressivism with: "You are but drilling the new Hun"; Henry Adams might later view the American scene with ironic detachment and detached resignation—but none of these men imagined himself to be a representative spokesman. Thoreau's *Walden* was, among other things, a statement of humane protest, a vision of the dead men, the lost life, buried under the ties of the railroads. He was immune to the American passion for the future; he was against the national preference for movement, expansion, technology, and utility. "The whole enterprise of this nation," he wrote in 1853,[8]

> which is not an upward, but a westward one, toward Oregon, California, Japan, etc., is totally devoid of interest to me, whether performed on foot, or by a Pacific railroad. It is not illustrated by a thought, it is not warmed by a sentiment; there is nothing in it which one should lay down his life for, nor even his gloves—hardly which one should take up a newspaper for. It is perfectly heathenish—a filibustering *toward* heaven by the great western route. No; they may go their way to their manifest destiny, which I trust is not mine.

In a somewhat similar spirit, the conservative classicist and Orientalist, Tayler Lewis, objected that America boasted of its individualism while encouraging "mediocre sameness" in its utilitarian education. "When may we look for less of true originality," he asked, "than at a time when every child is taught to repeat this inane self-laudation, and all distinction of individual thought is lost, because no man has room for anything else than a barren idea of progress, a contempt for the past, and a blinding reverence for an unknown future?"[9] But only a vociferous minority concurred with these protests. Andrew Carnegie, who spoke of "an ignorant past whose chief province

---

[8] *Writings* (Boston, 1906), Vol. VI, p. 210 (February 27, 1853).
[9] Ekirch: op. cit., p. 175.

is to teach us not what to adopt, but what to avoid"; the oil magnate who saw no value in having students "poring over musty dead languages, learning the disgusting stories of the mythical gods, and all the barbarous stuff of the dead past"; James A. Garfield, who did not want to encourage American youth to "feed their spirits on the life of dead ages, instead of the inspiring life and vigor of our own times"; Henry Ford, who told an interviewer that "history is more or less bunk. It's tradition"—such men were in the main stream.[10]

When a representative American voice is raised, there is a good chance that sooner or later this feeling of condescension toward the machineless past, this note of hope in technological progress will assert itself. Mark Twain, whose voice is one of the most authentic of all, is a case in point. Many years ago, in a memorable passage in his brilliant book, *The Ordeal of Mark Twain*, Van Wyck Brooks reproached Mark Twain because "his enthusiasm for literature was as nothing beside his enthusiasm for machinery: he had fully accepted the illusion of his contemporaries that the progress of machinery was identical with the progress of humanity." Quoting Twain's raptures on the Paige typesetting machine, which the writer considered superior to anything else produced by the human brain, Brooks went on to cite the perversity of Twain's letter to Whitman on the poet's seventieth birthday, in which the author congratulated Whitman for having lived in an age of manifold material benefactions, including "the amazing, infinitely varied and innumerable products of coal-tar," but neglected to recognize that the age was remarkable also for having produced Walt Whitman.[11]

In this, as in so many of his other perceptions about Mark Twain, Brooks seems essentially right. But the letter would not have seemed so exceptionable to Whitman himself. More than

[10]Kirkland: op. cit., pp. 86, 106; Irvin G. Wyllie: *The Self-Made Man in America* (New Brunswick, New Jersey, 1954), p. 104. Ford's explanation of his remark was an illuminating one: "I did not say it was bunk. It was bunk to me. . . . I did not need it very bad." Allan Nevins: *Ford: Expansion and Challenge, 1915–1933* (New York, 1957), p. 138.
[11]*The Ordeal of Mark Twain* (New York, 1920), pp. 146–7.

thirty years earlier, Whitman had written, in very much the same vein:[12]

> Think of the numberless contrivances and inventions for our comfort and luxury which the last half dozen years have brought forth—of our baths and ice houses and ice coolers—of our fly traps and mosquito nets—of house bells and marble mantels and sliding tables—of patent ink-stands and baby jumpers—of serving machines and street-sweeping machines—in a word give but a passing glance at the fat volumes of Patent Office Reports and bless your star that fate has cast your lot in the year of our Lord 1857.

Mark Twain is especially interesting in this because he refracted with extraordinary fidelity the concerns of the technocratic mind. I say refracted, not embodied, because he was too much a moralist and a pessimist to imagine that mechanical progress was an all-sufficient end. He was a man of contradictions, and few men have more passionately embraced the values of business industrialism and at the same time more contemptuously rejected them. His most extended commentary on technical progress, *A Connecticut Yankee in King Arthur's Court*, juxtaposes a nineteenth-century technical Yankee mind with a sixth-century society to satirize both civilizations. The moral burden of this tale is that human rascality and credulity will prevail even over mechanical progress; but within the dialectic of the story all the advantages lie with the Connecticut Yankee, who establishes a benevolent dictatorship on the strength of his command of steam power and electricity. "The very first official thing I did, in my administration—and it was on the very first day of it, too—was to start a patent office; for I knew that a country without a patent office and good patent laws was just a crab, and couldn't travel any way but sideways or backways."[13] Of course, Twain was somewhat ambivalent about his Yankee hero; although he may have been, as Henry James tartly remarked, a writer for rudimentary minds, he was not so rudimentary as to be unaware of at

[12] Emory Holloway and Vernolian Schwarz, eds.: *I Sit and Look Out: Editorials from the Brooklyn Daily Times* (New York, 1932), p. 133.
[13] *A Connecticut Yankee* (1889; Pocket Book ed., 1948), p. 56.

least some of the limitations of the industrial tinkerer.[14] None the less, it is the Connecticut Yankee who enjoys mental and moral superiority and with whom we are expected to sympathize. Mark Twain's national *amour-propre* was engaged in the book—he wrote his British publisher that the work was written not for America but for England; that it was an answer to English criticisms of America (particularly, though he did not say so, to those of Matthew Arnold), an attempt to "pry up the English nation to a little higher level of manhood." Such intentions as he may have had to satirize mankind in general and, more particularly, Yankee industrialism were in effect swallowed up in this impulse to justify what later came to be called the American way of life. Despite a few side-swipes at modern American abuses, the book is mainly a response to Europe and the past, to a society characterized entirely by squalor, superstition, cruelty, ignorance, and exploitation. If it was Mark Twain's intention to be equally satirical about sixth-century and nineteenth-century society, his execution was at fault. But it is easier to believe that his animus ran mostly in one direction; this interpretation accords better with his raptures over the Paige machine, which he hoped would make millions but on which he lost thousands. It accords better with the tone of *The Innocents Abroad*, in which the author confessed that he cared more for the railroads, depots, and turnpikes of Europe than for all the art in Italy, "because I can understand the one and am not competent to appreciate the other."[15] It may help, too, to illuminate one aspect of the long, anticlimactic sequence near the end of *Huckleberry Finn*, in which Tom Sawyer, enamored of the outworn heroics of European romances, insists that Nigger Jim be rescued from captivity by what he conceives to be the only proper method, with all its cumbersome rituals, and overrules Huck Finn's

[14]Speaking to Dan Beard about the illustrations for the book, he said: "You know, this Yankee of mine has neither the refinement nor the weakness of a college education; he is a perfect ignoramus; he is boss of a machine shop; he can build a locomotive or a Colt's revolver, he can put up and run a telegraph line, but he's an ignoramus, nevertheless." Gladys Carmen Bellamy: *Mark Twain as a Literary Artist* (Norman, Oklahoma, 1950), p. 314.
[15]*The Innocents Abroad* (1869; New York ed., 1906), pp. 325–6.

untutored common-sense proposals. This extravagant bur-
lesque has been much condemned as a distraction from the
fundamental moral drama of the book, but for Mark Twain
it had a vital importance. Tom Sawyer represents the impracticality of traditional culture, and Huck stands for the native
American gift for coming to grips with reality.

3

Mark Twain gave voice to what was undoubtedly a widespread
American ambivalence. Its main tenet was a robust faith in the
patent office and the future; but a great many Americans, along
with Mark Twain, also felt a certain respectful and wistful regard for the genteel culture that flourished largely in the East.
(Clemens's own desire to "make good" with this culture and
yet somehow to flout it led to one of the most painful confrontations in all our history—the terrible fiasco of his Whittier
birthday speech.) This culture had its limitations, but during
the greater part of Mark Twain's life, it was the only high culture the country knew. To a considerable degree, it leaned
upon the support of a commercial class.

In the absence of either a strong hereditary aristocracy or
state patronage, the condition of art and learning in America
was dependent upon commercial wealth, and on this account
the personal culture of the American business class was always
a matter of special importance to intellectual life. From the beginning, America was, of necessity, a work-bound society, but
even in the middle of the eighteenth century a material basis
for art and learning had been created in the seaboard towns,
and foundations had been laid for a kind of mercantile society
with an interest in culture. As early as 1743 Benjamin Franklin,
outlining a plan for intercolonial co-operation in promoting
science, observed: "The first drudgery of settling new colonies
which confines the attention of people to mere necessaries is
now pretty well over; and there are many in every province in
circumstances that set them at ease, and afford leisure to cultivate the finer arts and improve the common stock of knowledge."[16] In the coastal towns, which were even then among the

[16]Smyth, ed.: *Writings* (New York, 1905–7), Vol. II, p. 228.

largest in the British empire, the mercantile and professional class was seriously interested in the advancement of learning, science, and the arts, and it was this class that established a model for patronage in the New World.

The backbone of this class was mercantile wealth—wealth, it is important to say, in the hands of men who did not invariably consider the pursuit of business and the accumulation of money an all-sufficient end in life. By some businessmen business is considered to be a way of life; by others, a way *to* life, a single side of a many-sided existence, possibly only a means to such an existence. Among the latter, retirement after the accumulation of a substantial fortune is at least a conceivable goal. Andrew Carnegie, an exceptional man among his generation of millionaires, gave lip service to this ideal, even though he did not quite live up to it. At thirty-three, when he was making $50,000 a year, he wrote:[17]

> To continue much longer overwhelmed by business cares and with most of my thoughts wholly upon the way to make more money in the shortest time, must degrade me beyond the hope of permanent recovery. I will resign business at thirty-five.

Severely business-minded men, to whom this would have made no sense, have always existed in America. But the ideal that Carnegie was expressing did have considerable power. The old-fashioned merchant in Boston, New York, Philadelphia, or Charleston was a versatile and often a cosmopolitan man. Mercantile contacts with Europe and the Orient led his mind outward. The slow pace of business transactions in the days of the sailing ship, which was so soon speeded up by the increasing rapidity of mid-nineteenth-century communication, made the successful pursuit of business consistent with a life of dignified leisure. In the relatively stratified society of the late eighteenth century a significant proportion of the upper business classes were men of inherited wealth and position, who brought to

[17]Burton J. Hendrick: *The Life of Andrew Carnegie* (New York, 1932), Vol. I, pp. 146–7. Compare with this the surprise frequently expressed by American businessmen at their European counterparts who hope to accumulate enough to retire as soon as possible. Francis X. Sutton, et al.: *The American Business Creed* (Cambridge, Mass., 1956), p. 102.

their mercantile roles the advantages of breeding, leisure, and education. Moreover, eighteenth-century merchants were often actively involved in politics; their concerns with officeholding, legislating, and administering, as well as business, made for versatility in action and a reflective turn in thought.

The early nineteenth century inherited this ideal of the man of business as a civilized man and a civilizing agent. Spokesmen of this ideal did not feel any inconsistency in preaching at the same time the Puritan values of dedication to work, frugality, and sobriety, and the gentlemanly ideals of leisure, culture, and versatility. This view of life is expressed in the columns of the leading mercantile journal, *Hunt's Merchants' Magazine*.[18] Its publisher and editor, Freeman Hunt, the son of a Massachusetts shipbuilder, had come to his business, like so many other nineteenth-century publishers, from the printer's trade. He combined in his person the intellectualism and mercantile inheritance of New England with the practical experience of the self-made man; his father's death when Hunt was still a child had made it necessary for him to find his own way. The opening issue of Hunt's monthly journal in 1839 portrayed commerce as a high vocation that elevates the mind, enlarges the understanding, and adds "to the store house of general knowledge." "One of our prominent objects," he wrote, "will be, to raise and elevate the commercial character." He stressed the importance of "probity, and that high sense of honor, wanting which, however abounding in

[18]On examining the sketches of businessmen collected in Freeman Hunt's *Worth and Wealth: A Collection of Maxims, Morals, and Miscellanies for Merchants and Men of Business* (New York, 1856), I have been struck by the breadth of qualities sought for in the good merchant, and by the coexistence of three constellations of virtues. The first are the classic Puritan virtues, having to do with the development and discipline of the individual, and expressed in such terms as *ambitious, frugal, economical, industrious, persevering, disciplined, provident, diligent, simple*. The second are the mercantile-aristocratic virtues, having to do with the elevation of business and society, and expressed in such terms as *upright, generous, noble, civilizing, humane, benevolent, veracious, responsible, liberal, suave, gentlemanly, moderate*. The third might be considered categorically good attributes for almost any undertaking: *clear, explicit, decisive, careful, attentive, lively, firm*.

everything else, a man may assume the name, and be totally deficient in all that forms the high and honorable merchant." Commerce, too, was "a profession embracing and requiring more varied knowledge, and general information of the soil, climate, production, and consumption of other countries—of the history, political complexion, laws, languages, and customs of the world—than is necessary in any other. . . ." He took upon himself the duty of maintaining the intellectual and moral level of the trade. "Wherever the minds of the young are to be formed [to take the places of the old merchants] they will find us . . . doing all in our power to aid the incipient merchant in his high and honorable avocation."[19] One of his books was significantly entitled *Wealth and Worth*. Later writers frequently reiterated the idea that "commerce and civilization go hand in hand." For many years Hunt's magazine ran an extensive "literary department" in which books of general intellectual interest were discussed. Lectures delivered under the auspices of the New York Mercantile Library Association were reported. A clergyman's article on "Leisure—Its Uses and Abuses" was considered important enough to publish. An article on "Advantages and Benefits of Commerce" pointed out that "in every nation whose commerce has been cultivated upon great and enlightened principles, a considerable proficiency has been made in liberal studies and pursuits." What is essential here is that the role of the merchant was justified not solely on the ground that he is materially useful, nor even on the honor and probity with which he pursues his vocation, but

[19] *The Merchants' Magazine and Commercial Review*, Vol. I (July, 1839), pp. 1–3; between 1850 and 1860 the title of the periodical was changed to *Hunt's Merchants' Magazine*. For further passages of interest, see Vol. I, pp. 200–2, 289–302, 303–14, 399–413. Jerome Thomases, writing on "Freeman Hunt's America," *Mississippi Valley Historical Review*, Vol. XXX (December, 1943), pp. 395–407, attempts to assess the influence of the magazine, which was considerable. He touches on the theme I have emphasized, but also points out how much the magazine preached the principles of work, practicality, and self-reliance. It seems a significant token of the extent to which the image of the merchant had established itself as an ideal among businessmen that in New York, by 1850, "bankers, capitalists, brokers, commercial lawyers, railroad speculators, and manufacturers referred to themselves as merchants." Philip S. Foner: *Business and Slavery* (Chapel Hill, 1941), p. vii.

also because he is an agent of a more general culture that lies outside business itself.[20]

The old mercantile ideal, with its imposing set of practical, moral, and cultural obligations, may seem to have been difficult to live up to, but enough men, especially in the large seaboard towns, were capable of living up to it to keep it alive and real. One thinks, for example, of the immensely wealthy and powerful Appleton brothers of Boston, Samuel (1776–1853) and Nathan (1779–1861). Samuel, who was active in politics as well as business, chose to retire from business at sixty, and to devote the rest of his life to philanthropy. He patronized colleges and academies, learned societies, hospitals, and museums with an open hand. His brother Nathan, who was actively interested in science, politics, and theology, was helpful to the Boston Athenaeum, the Massachusetts Historical Society, and other cultural organizations; he once said that the $200,000 he had made in trade would have satisfied him had he not gone into the cotton industry by chance. The grandfather of Henry and Brooks Adams, Peter Chardon Brooks (1767–1849), whose three daughters married Edward Everett, Nathaniel Frothingham, and the elder Charles Francis Adams, was sufficiently detached from trade to retire at thirty-six (he returned to it for a few years later on) and devote his time to public offices, philanthropy, and the political careers of two of his sons-in-law. Men like these, though assiduous in business, were capable of detaching themselves from it. The ideal of civilized accomplishment never ceased to glimmer in their minds. Emerson's eloquent tribute to John Murray Forbes (1813–1898), the versatile and cultivated merchant and railroad entrepreneur, is a token of the *rapprochement* that was possible between intellectuals and the best representatives of the mercantile ideal:[21]

---

[20]Sigmund Diamond has observed that the early nineteenth-century entrepreneur was commonly judged by society on the basis of the personal *use* he made of his wealth, whether philanthropic or economic. In the twentieth century it became more common to look at business enterprise *as a system*, and not to judge it by its philanthropic by-products. *The Reputation of the American Businessman* (Cambridge, Mass., 1955), pp. 178–9.

[21]*Letters and Social Aims* (Riverside ed.), p. 201. There are many interesting sidelights on Forbes in Thomas C. Cochran: *Railroad Leaders, 1845–1890* (Cambridge, Mass., 1953).

Wherever he moved he was the benefactor. It is of course that he should ride well, shoot well, sail well, keep house well, administer affairs well; but he was the best talker, also, in the company. . . . Yet I said to myself, How little this man suspects, with his sympathy for men and his respect for lettered and scientific people, that he is not likely, in any company, to meet a man superior to himself. And I think this is a good country, that can bear such a creature as he is.

In New York the pre-eminent example of the mercantile ideal was the famous diarist, Philip Hone (1780–1851). Hone's experience shows how capable a well-knit local aristocracy was of absorbing a gifted newcomer, for no one lived more fully the life of the civilized merchant than this parvenu, who began life as the son of a joiner of limited means. At nineteen Hone went into an importing business with an older brother. At forty he retired with a fortune of half a million and went off upon a grand tour of Europe. Hone had had no schooling beyond the age of sixteen, but unlike the typical self-made man he did not make a virtue of the circumstance. "I am sensible of my deficiency," he wrote in 1832, "and would give half I possess in the world to enjoy the advantages of a classical education."[22] But in his case the lack of formal education was balanced by an enormous appetite for experience. Over the years he collected an extensive library and read widely and intelligently, acquired a small but good collection of works of art, became a patron of the opera and the theater, a preceptor of New York society, a trustee of Columbia, and a sponsor of innumerable philanthropies. His home became a meeting-place for writers, actors, and diplomats, as well as leading politicians. He was active in politics; he served as assistant alderman and for one brief term as mayor of New York, and played a significant role as the host and counselor of Whigs like Webster, Clay, and Seward. His culture, like that of many men of his kind, may have been rather derivative and genteel; but, without the patronage and interest of such men, American cultural and intellectual life would have been considerably impoverished.

[22]Quoted by Allan Nevins in the Introduction to *The Diary of Philip Hone* (New York, 1936), p. x.

4

The lives of merchants like Forbes and Hone may be taken to discount the statement of Tocqueville that "there is no class . . . in America in which the taste for intellectual pleasures is transmitted with hereditary fortune and leisure, and by which the labors of the intellect are held in honor."[23] But for Tocqueville the word "hereditary" was no doubt vital; and it was a matter of consequence that the Hones and the Forbeses were in the main unable to propagate their social type. This had begun to be evident even by the third decade of the nineteenth century, when Tocqueville visited the United States and wrote his great commentary; it became increasingly evident in the subsequent decades. With the relative decline in the importance of commerce and the rise in manufacturing, a smaller part of the business community was exposed to the enlarging, cosmopolitan effects of overseas trade. The American economy and the American mind began to face inward and to become more self-contained. With the rapid inland spread of business into the trans-Allegheny region and the Middle West, cultural institutions and leisured habits of mind were left behind. Men and materials could move faster than institutions and culture. The breakdown of class barriers and the opening of new business opportunities for the common man meant that the ranks of business and society were filling with parvenus, whose tastes and habits tended increasingly to dominate society. In earlier days, especially in the seaboard cities, established local aristocracies had been strong enough to absorb and mold and train parvenus like Hone. In the new cities of the interior, which had been wilderness when thriving cultures were centered in Boston, New York, and Philadelphia, the new men and the descendants of aristocracy mingled on even terms; and in many of them it was the parvenus who leveled the gentlemen down. Of course, some of the inland towns, such as Cincinnati and Lexington, managed in their own way to become cultural centers, but their efforts were relatively feeble. In inland society the newly successful businessmen had less need or opportunity to

[23] *Democracy in America* (1835; New York, 1898), Vol. I, p. 66.

temper themselves and to elevate their children through marriage into an established professional and business aristocracy such as one found in Boston. Everything was new and raw.

It was not only new and raw, but increasingly unstable and hazardous. Even such a man as Hone was hurt by the instability of the times. In the 1830's he lost perhaps as much as two-thirds of his fortune, and after his reverses drove him back into business, he was unable to repeat his earlier successes. Fortunes were easily made and unmade in the uncommonly speculative ethos of American business. The pace of transactions was stepped up; business became increasingly specialized. The between-times leisure often possible in the past for importers whose business was attuned to the pace of Atlantic crossings did not exist for men faced with new threats or new opportunities at almost every turning. Business needed more tending. Men of business withdrew, to some degree, from their previous direct involvement in politics as officeholders, and to a much greater degree from cultural life. In 1859 Thomas Colley Grattan, a British traveler, observed of young American businessmen:[24]

> They follow business like drudges, and politics with fierce ardour. They marry. They renounce party-going. They give up all pretension in dress. They cannot force wrinkles and crow's feet on their faces, but they assume and soon acquire a pursed-up, keen, and haggard look. Their air, manners, and conversation are alike contracted. They have no breadth, either of shoulders, information, or ambition. Their physical powers are subdued, and their mental capability cribbed into narrow limits. There is constant activity going on in one small portion of the brain; all the rest is stagnant. The money-making faculty is alone cultivated. They are incapable of acquiring general knowledge on a broad or liberal scale. All is confined to trade, finance, law, and small, local provincial information. Art, science, literature, are nearly dead letters to them.

At the same time, the cultural tone of business publications fell off. Hunt's magazine, whose literary department had been

---

[24] *Civilized America* (London, 1859), Vol. II, p. 320; see, however, the writer's misgivings, expressed in the same passage.

fairly conspicuous and serious, allowed this feature to dwindle. During and after 1849, the book reviews that had once taken about eight pages in each issue shrank to four or five, then to two and a half pages of perfunctory notices, and finally disappeared altogether from the penultimate volume in 1870. At the end of that year the magazine itself was merged with the *Commercial and Financial Chronicle. Hunt's Merchants' Magazine* had been a monthly; its successor was a weekly. The increasing speed of business communication, the publishers explained in the last issue of the older journal, had made that kind of business monthly out of date.[25] Its successor was also intelligently edited, but such nods as it gave to literature were few and far between.

The more thoroughly business dominated American society, the less it felt the need to justify its existence by reference to values outside its own domain. In earlier days it had looked for sanction in the claim that the vigorous pursuit of trade served God, and later that it served character and culture. Although

[25] *Hunt's Merchants' Magazine*, Vol. LXIII, pp. 401-3. A cultural history of the business magazines might be illuminating. The first article in the first issue of *Hunt's Merchants' Magazine* was entitled "Commerce as Connected with the Progress of Civilization," Vol. I (July, 1839), pp. 3-20; it was written by Daniel D. Barnard, an Albany lawyer and politician who also wrote historical brochures and who later became minister to Prussia. Barnard's essay dwelt on "the humanizing advantages of a growing and extended commerce." Cf. Philip Hone: "Commerce and Commercial Character," Vol. IV (February, 1841), pp. 129-46. Another writer in the opening volume, to be sure, made note of "an opinion [that] very generally prevails among the mercantile classes of the present day, that commerce and literature are at war with each other; that he who is engaged in the pursuit of the one must entirely abandon the pursuit of the other." This writer announced his intention to confute this view and his confidence that "more liberal views . . . are fast growing upon the public mind." "Commerce and Literature," Vol. I (December, 1839), p. 537. This confidence seems hardly justified by the trend in the cultural fare of *Hunt's* itself, which grew thinner during the 1850's. One must, no doubt, be careful not to assume too readily from such evidence that the cultural interests of businessmen were declining. What does seem to be true, however, is that for these men, *in their character as businessmen*, cultural interests no longer seemed so vital; nor did it seem any longer so important to vindicate business by reference to its civilizing influence.

this argument did not disappear, it grew less conspicuous in the business rationale. As business became the dominant motif in American life and as a vast material empire rose in the New World, business increasingly looked for legitimation in a purely material and internal criterion—the wealth it produced. American business, once defended on the ground that it produced a high standard of culture, was now defended mainly on the ground that it produced a high standard of living.[26] Few businessmen would have hesitated to say that the advancement of material prosperity, if not itself a kind of moral ideal, was at least the presupposition of all other moral ideals. In 1888 the railroad executive, Charles Elliott Perkins, asked:[27]

> Have not great merchants, great manufacturers, great inventors, done more for the world than preachers and philanthropists? . . . Can there be any doubt that cheapening the cost of necessaries and conveniences of life is the most powerful agent of civilization and progress? Does not the fact that well-fed and well-warmed men make better citizens, other things being equal, than those who are cold and hungry, answer the question? Poverty is the cause of most of the crime and misery in the world—cheapening the cost of the necessaries and conveniences of life is lessening poverty, and there is no other way to lessen it, absolutely none. History and experience demonstrate

[26]Francis X. Sutton, et al., in their study of *The American Business Creed* find material productivity a dominant theme; see chapter 2 and pp. 255–6. In so far as non-material values are advanced by business, they are the values of "service," personal opportunity, and political and economic freedom. Some businessmen are disposed to argue that success is sufficient justification for more or less complete neglect of "self-improvement." Ibid., p. 276. Small businessmen, though expressing a special proprietorship in freedom and democracy, along with a resentment of big business, seem to have absorbed the general business emphasis on material productivity as a central vindication. See John H. Bunzel: *The American Small Businessman* (New York, 1962), chapter 3.

[27]Edward C. Kirkland: *Dream and Thought in the Business Community, 1860–1900*, pp. 164–5. This conservative economic materialism has its curious parallel today in the thought of radical apologists for dictatorships in backward countries. Let poverty, misery, and illiteracy be conquered, it is held, and the goods of political freedom and cultural development will follow soon enough. This argument was commonly invoked in defense of the Soviet Union in the Stalinist period, and one hears it again today from apologists for Fidel Castro and others.

that as wealth has accumulated and things have cheapened, men have improved . . . in their habits of thought, their sympathy for others, their ideas of justice as well as of mercy. . . . Material progress must come first and . . . upon it is founded all other progress.

Almost a century and a half after Franklin had considered the material foundations of cultural progress to have been established, the necessity of the material prerequisites was thus being asserted with greater confidence than ever.

CHAPTER X

Self-Help and Spiritual Technology

I

As the mercantile ideal declined, it was replaced by the ideal of the self-made man, an ideal which reflected the experiences and aspirations of countless village boys who had become, if not millionaires, at least substantial men of business. Modern students of social mobility have made it incontestably clear that the legendary American rags-to-riches story, despite the spectacular instances that adorn our business annals, was more important as a myth and a symbol than as a statistical actuality.[1] The topmost positions in American industry, even in the most hectic days of nineteenth-century expansion, were held for the most part by men who had begun life with decided advantages. But there were enough self-made men, and their rise was dramatic and appealing enough, to give substance to the myth. And, quite aside from the topmost positions, there were intermediate positions, representing success of a substantial kind; only a few could realistically hope to be a Vanderbilt or a Rockefeller, but many could in a smaller way imitate their success. If life was not a movement from rags to riches, it could at least be from rags to respectability; and the horizons of experience were scanned eagerly for clues as to how this transformation could be accomplished.

Moreover, if the self-made men of America were not self-made in the sense that most of them had started in poverty, they were largely self-made in that their business successes were achieved without the benefits of formal learning or careful breeding. Ideally, the self-made man is one whose success does not depend on formal education and for whom personal culture, other than in his business character, is unimportant. By

---

[1]For a summary and evaluation of the now considerable literature on social mobility in American history, see Bernard Barber: *Social Stratification* (New York, 1957), chapter 16; Joseph A. Kahl: *The American Class Structure* (New York, 1957), chapter 9; Seymour M. Lipset and Reinhard Bendix: *Social Mobility in Industrial Society* (Berkeley, 1959), chapter 3.

mid-century, men of this sort had come so clearly to dominate the American scene that their way of life cried out for spokesmen. Timothy Shay Arthur, the Philadelphia scribbler who is best known to history as the author of *Ten Nights in a Barroom and What I Saw There*, but who was also well known in his day as a moralist and self-help writer, pointed out in 1856 that "in this country, the most prominent and efficient men are not those who were born to wealth and eminent social positions, but those who have won both by the force of untiring personal energy." To them, Arthur insisted, the country was indebted for its prosperity.[2]

> Invaluable, therefore, are the lives of such men to the rising generation. . . . Hitherto, American Biography has confined itself too closely to men who have won political or literary distinction. . . . Limited to the perusal of such biographies, our youth must, of necessity, receive erroneous impressions of the true construction of our society, and fail to perceive wherein the progressive vigor of the nation lies. . . . We want the histories of our self-made man spread out before us, that we may know the ways by which they came up from the ranks of the people.

The idea of the self-made man was not new. It was a historical outgrowth of Puritan preachings and of the Protestant doctrine of the calling. Benjamin Franklin had preached it, but it is significant that his own later life was not lived in accordance with his catchpenny maxims. After making a modest fortune, he was absorbed into the intellectual and social life of Philadelphia, London, and Paris, and interested himself more in politics, diplomacy, and science than in business. The self-made man as a characteristic American type became a conspicuous figure early in the nineteenth century. Apparently the term was first used by Henry Clay in 1832, in a Senate speech on a protective tariff. Denying that the tariff would give rise to

---

[2] Quoted in Freeman Hunt: *Worth and Wealth* (New York, 1856), pp. 350–1. Only a few years earlier the London *Daily News* remarked: "It is time that the *millionaire* should cease to be ashamed of having made his own fortune. It is time that *parvenu* should be looked on as a word of honor." Sigmund Diamond: *The Reputation of the American Businessman* (Cambridge, Mass., 1955), p. 2.

a hereditary industrial aristocracy, he maintained, to the contrary, that nothing could be more democratic; it would give further opportunities for men to rise from obscurity to affluence. "In Kentucky, almost every manufactory known to me is in the hands of enterprising and self-made men, who have acquired whatever wealth they possess by patient and diligent labor."[3] By the time of Clay's death thirty years later, the type was more than recognizable, it was spiritually dominant.

I say spiritually without ironic intent. Irvin G. Wyllie, in his illuminating study, *The Self-Made Man in America*, points out that the literature of self-help was not a literature of business methods or techniques; it did not deal with production, accounting, engineering, advertising, or investments; it dealt with the development of character, and nowhere were its Protestant origins more manifest. Not surprisingly, clergymen were prominent among the self-help writers, and especially Congregational clergymen.[4] Self-help was discipline in character. The self-help literature told how to marshal the resources of the *will*—how to cultivate the habits of frugality and hard work and the virtues of perseverance and sobriety. The writers of self-help books imagined that poverty in early life was actually a kind of asset, because its discipline helped to produce the type of character that would succeed.

The conception of character advocated by the self-help writers and the self-made men explicitly excluded what they loosely called genius. No doubt there was a certain underlying ambivalence in this—who does not desire or envy "genius"? But the prevailing assumption in the self-help literature was that character was necessary and remarkable talents were not; still more, that those who began by having such talents would lack the incentive or the ability to develop character. The average man, by intensifying his good qualities, by applying common sense to a high degree, could have the equivalent of genius, or something much better. "There is no genius required," said one

[3]Daniel Mallory, ed.: *The Life and Speeches of the Hon. Henry Clay* (New York, 1844), Vol. II, p. 31.
[4]Wyllie: *The Self-Made Man in America* (New Brunswick, New Jersey, 1954), chapters 3 and 4.

New York merchant. "And if there were, some great men have said that genius is no more than common-sense intensified." Reliance on outstanding gifts would lead to laziness and lack of discipline or responsibility. "Genius" was vain and frivolous. Speaking on this subject to an audience of young men in 1844, Henry Ward Beecher remarked:[5]

> So far as my observations have ascertained the species, they abound in academies, colleges, and Thespian societies; in village debating clubs; in coteries of young artists and young professional aspirants. They are to be known by a reserved air, excessive sensitiveness, and utter indolence; by very long hair, and very open shirt collars; by the reading of much wretched poetry, and the writing of much, yet more wretched; by being very conceited, very affected, very disagreeable, and very useless:—beings whom no man wants for friend, pupil, or companion.

Through the decades, this suspicion of genius or brilliance rooted itself into the canons of business. Eighty years after Beecher's characterization of genius, an article appeared in the *American Magazine* under the title, "Why I Never Hire Brilliant Men." The writer identified brilliance in business with mercurial temperament, neuroticism, and irresponsibility; his experience as an entrepreneur with men of this type had been disastrous. "Even fine material, carelessly put together, will not make a fine shoe," he remarked. "But if material which is of just average quality is fashioned with special care and attention, it will result in a quite superior article." "So I took most of my raw material from our delivery wagons, or other places right at hand. Out of this hard-muscled, hard-headed stuff I have built a business that has made me rich according to the standards of our locality." Somewhat defensively, the writer anticipated that he might be considered simply a mediocre man without the capacity to appreciate anyone better than himself. This judgment might well be justified, he said candidly,[6]

[5] Ibid., pp. 35–6.
[6] Anon.: "Why I Never Hire Brilliant Men," *American Magazine*, Vol. XCVII (February, 1924), pp. 12, 118, 122.

for I *am* mediocre. But . . . business and life are built upon successful mediocrity; and victory comes to companies not through the employment of brilliant men, but through knowing how to get the most out of ordinary folks. . . .

I am sorry to forego the company of [brilliant] men in my rather dingy building here in the wholesale grocery district. But I comfort myself with the thought that Cromwell built the finest army in Europe out of dull but enthusiastic yeomen; and that the greatest organization in human history was twelve humble men, picked up along the shores of an inland lake.

With all this there went a persistent hostility to formal education and a countervailing cult of experience. The canons of the cult of experience required that the ambitious young man be exposed at the earliest possible moment to what one writer called "the discipline of daily life that comes with drudgery." Formal schooling, especially if prolonged, would only delay such exposure. The lumber magnate, Frederick Weyerhaeuser, concluded that the college man was "apt to think that because he is a college graduate he ought not be obliged to commence at the bottom of the ladder and work up, as the office boy does who enters the office when he is fourteen years of age."[7] It must be said that here the writers of self-help books disagreed with the businessmen: they usually advised more formal schooling, but this part of their prescription was not convincing to the self-made man of business. In the ranks of business, opinion on free common schools was divided between those who felt that such schools would create a more efficient and disciplined working class and those who balked at taxes or believed that education would only make workers discontented.[8]

On two matters there was almost no disagreement: education should be more "practical"; and higher education, as least as it was conceived in the old-time American classical college, was useless as a background for business. Business waged a long, and on the whole successful, campaign for vocational and trade education at the high-school level and did much to

[7]Charles F. Thwing: "College Training and the Business Man," *North American Review*, Vol. CLXVII (October, 1903), p. 599.

[8]On attitudes toward education, see Wyllie: op. cit., chapter 6; Kirkland: *Dream and Thought in the Business Community, 1860–1900* (Ithaca, New York, 1956), chapters 3 and 4; Merle Curti: *The Social Ideas of American Educators* (New York, 1935), chapter 6.

undermine the high school as a center of liberal education. The position of the Massachusetts wool manufacturer who said that he preferred workers with only a common-school education, since he considered that the more learned were only preparing themselves for Congress, and who rejected educated workmen on the ground that he could not run his mill with algebra, was in no way unusual or extreme; nor was the argument of the industrial publicist Henry Carey Baird, the founder of the first publishing firm in America specializing in technical and industrial books. "Too much education of a certain sort," he protested in 1885,[9]

> such as Greek, Latin, French, German, and especially bookkeeping, to a person of humble antecedents, is utterly demoralizing in nine cases out of ten, and is productive of an army of mean-spirited "gentlemen" who are above what is called a "trade" and who are only content to follow some such occupation as that of standing behind a counter, and selling silks, gloves, bobbins, or laces, or to "keep books." . . . Our system of education, as furnished by law, when it goes beyond what in Pennsylvania is called a grammar school, is vicious in the extreme—productive of more evil than good. Were the power lodged with me, no boy or girl should be educated at the public expense beyond what he or she could obtain at a grammar school, except for some useful occupation. "The high school" of today must, as I believe, under an enlightened system, be supplanted by *the technical school*, with possibly "shops" connected with it. . . . We are manufacturing too many "gentlemen" and "ladies," so called, and demoralization is the result.

The extension of classical and liberal studies through the college years was often considered even worse than academic schooling at the high-school level, because it prolonged the youth's exposure to futile studies and heightened his appetite for elegant leisure. One businessman rejoiced that his son's failure in college-entrance examinations had spared the boy all this. "Whenever I find a rich man dying and leaving a large amount of money to found a college, I say to myself, 'It is a pity he had not died while he was poor.'"[10]

---

[9] Kirkland: op. cit., pp. 69–70.
[10] Ibid., p. 101.

Fortunately, many influential businessmen did not wholly share this attitude. Old Cornelius Vanderbilt was often considered the acme of self-satisfied ignorance, and the story is told that when a friend reported to him Lord Palmerston's remark that it was too bad that a man of his ability had not had the advantages of formal education, Vanderbilt replied: "You tell Lord Palmerston from me that if I had learned education I would not have had time to learn anything else." None the less, Vanderbilt's wealth had brought him into a society in which his lack of culture was a staggering handicap (he is reported to have read one book in his life, *Pilgrim's Progress*, and that at an advanced age). "Folks may say that I don't care about education," he confessed to his clergyman, "but I do. I've been to England, and seen them lords and other fellows, and knew that I had twice as much brains as they had maybe, and yet I had to keep still, and couldn't say anything through fear of exposing myself." When his son-in-law entered the room in time to catch this remark, and chided the Commodore for having at last made such an admission, Vanderbilt beat a retreat: "I seem to get along better than half of your educated men." Still, he had said to his minister: "I'd give a million dollars today, Doctor, if I had your education"; and in the end precisely this magnificent sum was extracted from him for the support of what became Vanderbilt University.[11]

Andrew Carnegie, it is reported, once saw the older and much richer Vanderbilt on the opposite side of Fifth Avenue, and mumbled to his companion: "I would not exchange his millions for my knowledge of Shakespeare."[12] But Carnegie shared, at a higher level, the mixture of feelings about education that Vanderbilt had shown. "Liberal education," he once wrote, "gives a man who really absorbs it higher tastes and aims than the acquisition of wealth, and a world to enjoy, into which the mere millionaire cannot enter; to find therefore that it is not the best training for business is to prove its claim to a

---

[11] W. A. Croffut: *The Vanderbilts and the Story of Their Fortune* (Chicago and New York, 1886), pp. 137–8.
[12] Burton J. Hendrick: *The Life of Andrew Carnegie* (New York, 1932), Vol. I, p. 60.

higher domain."[13] Carnegie's munificent gifts to education and his evident pleasure in the company of intellectuals protect him from the charge that such utterances were hypocritical. And yet he took delight in demonstrating how useless higher education was in business; much as he praised "liberal education," he had nothing but contempt for the prevailing liberal education in American colleges. He enjoyed reciting the names of other successful men who had gone through a tough apprenticeship like his own, and in recording the evidences of the superiority of non-college men to college men in business. "College education as it exists seems almost fatal to success in that domain," he wrote.[14] On the classical college curriculum he was unsparing. It was a thing on which men "wasted their precious years trying to extract education from an ignorant past whose chief province is to teach us, not what to adopt, but what to avoid." Men had sent their sons to colleges "to waste their energies upon obtaining a knowledge of such languages as Greek and Latin, which are of no more practical use to them than Choctaw" and where they were "crammed with the details of petty and insignificant skirmishes between savages." Their education only imbued them with false ideas and gave them "a distaste for practical life." "Had they gone into active work during the years spent at college they would have been better educated men in every true sense of that term."[15] Leland Stanford was another educational philanthropist who had no faith in existing education. Of all the applicants for jobs who came to him from the East, the most helpless, he said, were college men. Asked what they could do, they would say "anything," while in fact they had "no definite technical knowledge of anything," and no clear aim or purpose. He hoped that the university he endowed would overcome this by offering "a practical, not a theoretical education."[16]

One must, of course, be careful about the conclusions one draws from anyone's dislike of the classical curriculum as it was taught in the old college; many men of high intellectual

[13] *The Empire of Business* (New York, 1902), p. 113.
[14] Wyllie: op. cit., pp. 96–104.
[15] *The Empire of Business*, pp. 79–81; cf. pp. 145–7.
[16] Kirkland: op. cit., pp. 93–4.

distinction shared this feeling. The old college tried to preserve the Western cultural heritage and to inculcate a respectable form of mental discipline, but it was hardly dedicated to
the vigorous advancement of critical intellect. The rapid advancement of scientific knowledge, the inflexibility of the old
curriculum in the hands of its most determined custodians, and
the dismal pedagogy that all too often prevailed in the classical
college, did more to undermine the teaching of classics than
the disdain of businessmen. To the credit of men like Carnegie,
Rockefeller, Stanford, Vanderbilt, Johns Hopkins, and other
millionaires, it must be added that their support made possible the revamping of the old-time college and the creation of
universities in the United States. But if one looks closely into
business pronouncements on education, one finds a rhetoric
which reveals a contempt for the reflective mind, for culture,
and for the past.

2

Around the turn of the century the attitudes of businessmen
toward formal education as a background for business success
underwent a conspicuous change. The rapid development of
large-scale business in the last two decades of the nineteenth
century had made the characteristic big-business career a bureaucratic career. By their very success the self-made men rapidly made their own type obsolete. However reluctantly, men
began to see that the ideal of the uneducated self-made man,
especially in the most desirable business positions, was coming to have less and less reality. Formal education, it had to
be admitted, was a distinct asset for the more stable careers
now being followed in bureaucratic businesses: the need for
engineering, accountancy, economics, and law grew from the
changes in business organization itself. Hence, although the
"school of experience" and the "college of hard knocks" still
kept their nostalgic appeal for business spokesmen, the need for
formally inculcated skills had to be recognized. "The day has
quite gone by," the *Commercial and Financial Chronicle* recognized in 1916, "when it is sufficient for a young man to begin
at the bottom and, without more training than he can gather
in the daily routine, to grow up to be something more than a

manager of an existing concern, or to acquire that breadth of knowledge and completeness of training which are necessary if he is to be fitted to compete with the expert young business men produced in other countries." The steel magnate, Elbert H. Gary, considered that the more the businessman knew "of that which is taught in schools, colleges and universities of a general character, the better it will be for him in commencing business."[17]

This new acceptance of education was reflected in the background of men who stood at the helm of the great corporations. The generation of corporation executives that flourished from 1900 to 1910 was only slightly better educated than the generation of the 1870's.[18] But the rising young executives of the first decade of the new century were being recruited out of the colleges. In Mabel Newcomer's sample of top business executives, 39.4 per cent of those chosen from 1900 had some college education; but in 1925 this figure rose to 51.4 per cent and in 1950 to 75.6 per cent.[19] In 1950, about one of every

[17] Wyllie: op. cit., p. 113; see pp. 107–15 for a good brief account of changing business attitudes toward education after 1890.

[18] See Frances W. Gregory and Irene D. Neu: "The American Industrial Elite in the 1870's: Their Social Origins," in William Miller, ed.: *Men in Business* (Cambridge, Mass., 1952), p. 203, comparing the generation of the 1870's with that of 1901–1910 encompassed by William Miller in "American Historians and the Business Elite," *The Journal of Economic History*, Vol. IX (November, 1949), pp. 184–208. In the 1870's, 37 per cent of the executives had some college training; in 1901–1910, 41 per cent had. On the emergence of the bureaucratic business career, see Miller's essay: "The Business Elite in Business Bureaucracies," in *Men in Business*, pp. 286–305.

[19] Mabel Newcomer: *The Big Business Executive* (New York, 1955), p. 69. In 1950, the author concludes (p. 77), "it is accepted that the college degree is the ticket of admission to a successful career with the large corporation, even though the initial employment for the college graduate may be manual labor." Joseph A. Kahl has suggestively remarked in his study of *The American Class Structure*, p. 93, that "if one should demand a single oversimplified distinction underlying class differences in contemporary America to replace the outworn one of Marx, the answer would be this: the possession of a college degree."

Employers sometimes still show a certain ceremonial loyalty to the ideal of the self-made man by putting a new employee, clearly destined for an executive position, through a quick ascending series of minor posts. This is called learning the business from the bottom up, and is especially recommended for the sons or sons-in-law of high executives.

five executives had also had some training in a graduate school (mainly in law or engineering).

Although these figures show that the once cherished model of the self-made man was being relinquished, they cannot be taken as showing a rise in esteem for the liberal arts. The colleges themselves, under the elective system, became more vocational. In the nineteenth century, when the well-to-do sent their sons to college, it was a fair assumption that they were sending them not for vocational training but out of a regard both for intellectual discipline and for social advantages (the two are not always easily distinguishable). In the twentieth century, they may send them, rather, for the gains measurable in cold cash which are supposedly attainable through vocational training. (Among male college graduates in 1954–55, the largest single group was majoring in business and commerce; they outnumbered the men in the basic sciences and the liberal arts put together.)[20]

A sign of the increasing vocational character of American higher education was the emergence of both undergraduate and graduate schools of business. The first of these was the Wharton School at the University of Pennsylvania, founded in 1881; the second was founded at the University of Chicago eighteen years later. There followed an efflorescence of such schools between 1900 and 1914. The early business schools were caught between the hostility of the academic faculties and the lingering suspicion of businessmen, who were sometimes still inclined to doubt that any kind of academic training, even that acquired in a business school, could be of practical use. Like almost every other kind of educational institution in America, the business schools quickly became heterogeneous in the quality of their faculties and students and in the degree to which they included the liberal arts in their curriculums. Thorstein Veblen dealt scathingly with these "keepers of the higher business animus," suggesting mischievously that they were on a par with the divinity schools in that both were equally extraneous to the intellectual enterprise which is the true end of the university. Abraham Flexner, acknowledging in his famous survey of the universities that business-school

[20]William H. Whyte, Jr.: *The Organization Man* (Anchor ed., 1956), p. 88.

faculties sometimes recruited distinguished men, considered their heavily vocational curriculums to be in the main beneath the dignity of the academic enterprise.[21] Within the universities, business schools were often non-intellectual and at times anti-intellectual centers dedicated to a rigidly conservative set of ideas. When Dean Wallace Donham of the Harvard Graduate School of Business suggested to one such school in the Middle West that it offer a course on the problems of trade unionism, he was told: "We don't want our students to pay any attention to anything that might raise questions about management or business policy in their minds."[22]

The condition of American business today, as it is reflected in William H. Whyte's celebrated study of the social and cultural aspects of large business organization, displays a pattern recognizably similar to that of the past. Gone is the self-made man, of course. He may be cherished as a mythological figure useful in the primitive propaganda battles of politics, but every sensible businessman knows that in the actual recruitment and training of big business personnel it is the bureaucratic career that matters. Yet in this recruitment and training the tradition of business anti-intellectualism, quickened by the self-made ideal, remains very much alive. It no longer takes the form of ridiculing the value of college or other formal education in preparation for business, but of selective recruiting governed by narrow vocational principles. Here it is important to note, as Whyte does, that top business executives do not characteristically defend these vocational principles. When they make pronouncements on the subject, at commencement exercises or elsewhere, they usually speak of the importance of liberal education, broad training, and imaginative statecraft in the business world. There is little reason to doubt their sincerity. Most of them, although they are enormously hard-working and too

[21]Thorstein Veblen: *The Higher Learning in America* (New York, 1918), p. 204; Abraham Flexner: *Universities: American, English, German* (New York, 1930), pp. 162–72.
[22]Peter F. Drucker: "The Graduate Business School," *Fortune*, Vol. XLII (August, 1950), p. 116. For a general account of these schools and their problems, see L. C. Marshall, ed.: *The Collegiate School of Business* (Chicago, 1928); and Frank C. Pierson et al.: *The Education of American Businessmen: A Study of University-College Programs in Business Administration* (New York, 1959).

preoccupied to keep their own general culture very much alive, are better educated than their subordinates, and they are disposed to lament mildly their own intellectual stagnation. They have begun to organize arts courses for their junior executives and to sponsor meetings between intellectuals and businessmen. In this way, the old mercantile regard for culture as a sanction for business life is beginning to be revived. However, the news about their concern for the liberally educated man does not seem to filter down to the ranks of the personnel men who turn up each year on the college campuses to recruit talent. At this point of leverage, the overwhelming pressure of business on American higher education is severely vocational.

The preference for vocationalism is linked to a preference for character—or personality—over mind, and for conformity and manipulative facility over individuality and talent. "We used to look primarily for brilliance," said one president, who must have been speaking of the past history of an idiosyncratic firm. "Now that much-abused word 'character' has become very important. We don't care if you're a Phi Beta Kappa or a Tau Beta Phi. We want a well-rounded person who can handle well-rounded people." A personnel manager reports that "any progressive employer would look askance at the individualist and would be reluctant to instill such thinking in the minds of trainees." A trainee agrees: "I would sacrifice brilliance for human understanding every time." Mr. Whyte tells us, in a chapter entitled "The Fight against Genius," that even in the field of industrial science this code prevails; that industrial scientists are shackled by the commitment to applied knowledge; that a famous chemical company's documentary film, made to recruit scientists for the firm, shows three of its research men conferring in a laboratory while the narrator announces: "No geniuses here; just a bunch of average Americans working together"; that the creativity of industrial scientists is pathetically low as compared with that of the men in the universities; and that when the word *brilliant* appears, it is commonly coupled with such words as *erratic*, *eccentric*, *introvert*, and *screwball*.[23]

[23]Ibid., pp. 150, 152, 227–8, 233, 235, and chapter 16 *passim*.

3

As late nineteenth-century America became more secular, traditional religion became infused with, and in the end to some
degree displaced by, a curious cult of religious practicality. If
we are to accept the evidence of a long history of best-selling
handbooks, from Russell H. Conwell's "Acres of Diamonds" to
the works of Norman Vincent Peale, this cult has had millions
of devotees. It has become, by all internal evidence and everything we know about its readership, one of the leading faiths
of the American middle class. It is, as I hope to show, a rather
drastically altered descendant of the older self-help literature,
but it affords, in any case, striking evidence of the broad diffusion in American society of the practical motif. Modern inspirational literature takes its stand firmly with the world: what it
has to offer is practical. "*Christianity*," writes Norman Vincent
Peale, "*is entirely practical.* It is astounding how defeated persons can be changed into victorious individuals when they actually utilize their religious faith as a workable instrument."[24]

The literature of inspiration is of course by no means confined to America; it flourishes wherever the passion for personal
advancement has become so intense that the difference between
this motive and religious faith has been obscured. There has always been in Christian civilization a conviction that the world of
business and that of religion must somehow be related, if only
through their hostility or tension, since both have to do with
morals, character, and discipline. At first, the negative relation
was most clear: medieval prohibitions or limitations on usury
expressed the conviction that it was a part of the task of the
Church in the world to restrain economic exploitation. Later,
the Puritan doctrine of the calling suggested another more
positive relationship: diligence in business was one of the ways
of serving God. Success or failure in business might then be a
clue as to an individual's spiritual condition. But over the years
this relationship gradually became reversed. The distinction between service to God and service to self broke down. Whereas
business had been an instrument in religious discipline, one

---

[24] *A Guide to Confident Living* (New York, 1948), p. 55.

of the various means of serving God, religious discipline now became an instrument in business, a way of using God to a worldly end. And whereas men had once been able to take heart from business success as a sign that they had been saved, they now took salvation as a thing to be achieved in this life by an effort of will, as something that would bring with it success in the pursuit of worldly goals. Religion is something to be *used*. Mr. Peale tells his readers that his work demonstrates "a simple, workable technique of thinking and acting." It "emphasizes scientific spiritual principles which have been demonstrated in the laboratory of personal experience." "The best place to get a new and workable idea for your business is in the type of church service described in this chapter." "If you will practice faith, you can be healed of ill-will, inferiority, fear, guilt, or any other block which impedes the flow of recreative energy. Power and efficiency are available to you if you will believe."[25] As H. Richard Niebuhr has remarked, there is a strain in modern American theology which "tends to define religion in terms of adjustment to divine reality for the sake of gaining power rather than in terms of revelation which subjects the recipient to the criticism of that which is revealed." The consequence is that "man remains the center of religion and God is his aid rather than his judge and redeemer."[26]

The older self-help literature, whatever its faults, had some organic relation both to the world of affairs and to the religious life. It assumed that business success is to a very large degree the result of character, and that character is formed by piety. It was in this way a natural, if intellectually simple, response to the historical convergence of Protestant moral imperatives, the doctrines of classical economics, and a fluid, open society. American society, as most modern studies of the subject show, is still fluid; but the conditions of success have changed: success now seems more intimately related to the ability to seize upon formal training than it does to the peculiar constellation of character traits that figured so prominently in the old self-help books. An early nineteenth-century

[25] Ibid., pp. viii, 14, 108, 148, 165.
[26] "Religious Realism in the Twentieth Century," in D. C. Macintosh, ed.: *Religious Realism* (New York, 1931), pp. 425–6.

businessman, queried as to what "discipline" made for success, might well have answered: "The discipline of poverty and the school of hard knocks," or "The discipline of frugality and industriousness." The modern businessman, faced with the same query, is likely to answer: "Well, law is excellent, but engineering is pretty good too."

Modern inspirational literature builds upon the old self-help tradition and bears a general resemblance to it, but it also has major differences. In the old self-help system, faith led to character and character to a successful manipulation of the world; in the new system, faith leads directly to a capacity for self-manipulation, which is believed to be the key to health, wealth, popularity, or peace of mind. On the surface, this may seem to indicate a turning away from the secular goals of the older self-help books, but it actually represents a turning away from their grasp of reality, for it embodies a blurring of the distinction between the realms of the world and the spirit. In the old literature these realms interacted; in the new they become vaguely fused. The process represents, I believe, not a victory for religion but a fundamental, if largely unconscious, secularization of the American middle-class mind. Religion has been supplanted, not, to be sure, by a consciously secular philosophy, but by mental self-manipulation, by a kind of faith in magic. Both religion and the sense of worldly reality suffer. It is easy to believe that rising young businessmen actually turned to the old self-help literature for a kind of rough guidance to the requisites of the business world, however little actual help they may have got. Today the inspirational literature seems to be read mainly by "defeated persons," to use Peale's words, and not as much by men as by women, who, though affected by the practical code of business, do not actually enter business life.

It is what Raymond Fosdick calls "power for daily living" that the success writers purport to give. In the nineteenth century the primary promise of success writers was that religion would bring wealth. Since the early 1930's there has been a growing emphasis on the promise of mental or physical health; inspirational writing has been infused with safe borrowings from psychiatry and has taken on a faint coloration from the existential anxieties of the past twenty years. Although success

literature has given way to a literature of inspiration, its goals
largely remain everyday practical goals. For more than a generation, the metaphorical language of this writing has been infiltrated and coarsened by terms taken from business, technology,
and advertising; one often gets the sense that the spiritual life
can be promoted by good copy and achieved like technological progress by systematic progressive means. Louis Schnei-
der and Sanford M. Dornbusch, in their illuminating study
of the themes of inspirational books, have spoken of this as
"spiritual technology."[27] One success writer tells us that "God
is a twenty-four-hour station. All you need to do is to plug
in." Another that "religious practice is an exact science that
. . . follows spiritual laws as truly as radio follows its laws."
Another that "high octane thinking means Power and Performance" and that readers should "plug into the Power House."
Another that "the body is . . . a receiving set for the catch-
ing of messages from the Broadcasting Station of God" and
that "the greatest of Engineers . . . is your silent partner."
Another that the railroad "saves money by having a Christian
hand on the throttle." Another exhorts readers to "open every
pore of your being to the health of God." Another relates that
a Sinclair gasoline ad provided "the idea for a sermon about
the unused power in our souls." Bruce Barton, in his ineffable
book, *The Man Nobody Knows*, remarked that Jesus "picked
up twelve men from the bottom ranks of business and forged
them into an organization that conquered the world." "Conduct the affairs of your soul in a businesslike way," exhorts Emmet Fox. Prayer is conceived as a usable instrument. "A man,"
says Glenn Clark, "who learns and practices the laws of prayer
correctly should be able to play golf better, do business better,
work better, love better, serve better." "Learn to pray correctly,
scientifically," commands Norman Vincent Peale. "Employ
tested and proven methods. Avoid slipshod praying."

One of the striking things that has occurred in the inspirational literature is that the voluntaristic and subjective impulses which I noted in commenting on the development of
American Protestantism seem to have come into complete

[27] *Popular Religion: Inspirational Books in America* (Chicago, 1958), pp. 16–4;
the quotations in this paragraph may be found on pp. 1, 6, 7, 44, 51n., 58, 61n.,
63, 90, 91n., 106, 107.

possession and to have run wild. There has been a progressive attenuation of the components of religion. Protestantism at an early point got rid of the bulk of religious ritual, and in the course of its development in the nineteenth and twentieth centuries went very far to minimize doctrine. The inspirational cult has completed this process, for it has largely eliminated doctrine—at least it has eliminated most doctrine that could be called Christian. Nothing, then, is left but the subjective experience of the individual, and even this is reduced in the main to an assertion of his will. What the inspirational writers mean when they say you can accomplish whatever you wish by taking thought is that you can will your goals and mobilize God to help you release fabulous energies. Fabulous indeed they are: "There is enough power in *you*," says Norman Vincent Peale in an alarming passage, "to blow the city of New York to rubble. That, and nothing less, is what advanced physics tells us." Faith can release these forces, and then one can overcome any obstacle. Faith is not a way of reconciling man to his fate: it "puts fight into a man so that he develops a terrific resistance to defeat."[28]

Horatio W. Dresser, discussing one of the earlier manifestations of inspirational thinking, the New Thought movement, once remarked that "the tendency of the New Thought . . . has been to make light of the intellect and of 'the objective mind,' as if it were undesirable to become intellectual and as if one could have whatever one wishes by 'sending out a requisition into the great subconscious.'"[29] In the main, however, the anti-intellectualism of the inspirational cults has been indirect: they represent a withdrawal from reality, a repudiation of all philosophies whose business is an engagement with real problems. At the same time, they manifest a paradoxical secularization. Although professing Christians and ministers of the gospel are proud of having written successful inspirational books, the books themselves are likely to strike even secular intellectuals as blasphemous. The religious inheritance of the West seems more in the custody of such intellectuals than in the custody of these hearty advocates of the "utilization" of religion.

[28] *A Guide to Confident Living*, pp. 46, 55.
[29] *Handbook of the New Thought* (New York, 1917), pp. 122–3.

The confusion between religion and self-advancement is perhaps most aptly embodied in the title of Henry C. Link's remarkable book, *The Return to Religion*, a best-seller from 1936 to 1941. I do not think that this singular work could be regarded as entirely representative of inspirational literature, but it deserves special notice here, for it is possibly the most consummate manual of philistinism and conformity ever written in America. Despite its title, it is in no sense a religious or devotional work. Written by a consulting psychologist and personnel adviser to large business corporations, who reports that he found his way back to religion by way of science, this book views religion as "an aggressive mode of life by which the individual becomes the master of his environment, not its complacent victim."[30] The author feels obliged to wage a running battle against both individuality and mind in the interests of the will to conformity.

The issue is not put quite this way. Link's basic polar terms are introversion and extroversion (used in the popular, not the Jungian sense). Introversion, which involves withdrawal, self-examination, individuality, and reflection, is bad. It is in fact merely selfish. For the Socratic maxim, "Know thyself," Link would substitute the injunction, "Behave yourself," because "a good personality or character is achieved by practice, not by introspection." On the other hand, extroversion, which involves sociability, amiability, and service to others, is unselfish and good. Jesus was a great extrovert. One of the functions of religion—and it would appear that Link considers it the main function—is to discipline the personality by developing extroversion. Link goes to church, he reports, "because I hate to go and because I know that it will do me good." Church attendance builds better personalities. So do bridge-playing and dancing and salesmanship—they bring the individual into contact with others whom he must please. The important thing for the individual is to get away from self-analysis and do work which will give him power over things. This, in turn, will lead to power over people, which will heighten self-confidence.

---

[30]Quotations in this and the following paragraphs are in *The Return to Religion* (1936; Pocket Book ed., 1943), pp. 9, 12, 14, 17, 19, 35, 44–5, 54–61, 67, 69, 71, 73, 78–9, 115–16, 147–9, 157.

For all these purposes, the critical mind is a liability. In college it is the intellectuals, the analytical students, who lose their religion; in later life it is thoughtful men who become excessively withdrawn. In a chapter entitled "Fools of Reason," Link argues that intellect and rationality are commonly overvalued.

> Reason is not an end in itself but a tool for the individual to use in adjusting himself to the values and purposes of living which are beyond reason. *Just as the teeth are intended to chew with, not to chew themselves, so the mind is intended to think with, not to worry about. The mind is an instrument to live with, not to live for.*

To believe and act on faith is central. Although religion has been called the refuge of weak minds, the real weakness "lies rather in the failure of minds to recognize the weakness of all minds." "Agnosticism is an intellectual disease, and faith in fallacies is better than no faith at all . . . foolish beliefs are better than no beliefs at all." Even palmistry leads to holding other people's hands, phrenology to studying their heads—and "all such beliefs take the individual out of himself and propel him into a world of greater interests." Anyway, "the idolatry of reason and the intellectual scorn of religion" has left men prey to quackery and pseudo-science and political panaceas. In America there is an unfortunate national tendency to introversion, which, among other things, causes people to shirk their responsibility for the unemployed and to imagine that the federal government should do something about them.

Mind is also a threat to marriage, because introversion undermines marital happiness. Divorced people turn out to have more intellectual interests than the happily married. A liking for philosophy, psychology, radical politics, and for reading the *New Republic* are much less auspicious for marital bliss than a liking for Y.M.C.A. work, Bible study, and the *American Magazine*. In a chapter entitled "The Vice of Education," Link attacks "the creation of a liberal mind" as "probably the most damaging single aspect of education"—a dogma of education as mystical and irrational, he finds, as any dogma of the church ever was. Such education produces "ruthless iconoclasm" and creates a culture for its own sake and a demand for knowledge for its own sake. Liberalism releases a person from the traditions and restraints of the past and substitutes nothing for them. The liberally educated young are disposed to regard parents as old-fashioned, to spend freely, show intellectual scorn for the pieties of their elders, seek intellectual vocations rather than the occupations of their fathers, and deprecate business as a career. A better insight into the abundant life can be found in army and navy barracks, where people face real values and are certain to become more extroverted.

CHAPTER XI

Variations on a Theme

I

THE REFRAIN about the prior virtues of practicality to which businessmen give expression is a refrain they can easily pick up from the folklore of American life, and it is not always certain who is echoing whom. Expressions of the refrain have differed from time to time and from class to class, but its melody has always been distinguishable, as it resounds through a wide range of occupations and in the most disparate political camps. The evidence is abundant, and it is nearly unanimous in its testimony to a popular culture that has been proudly convinced of its ability to get along—indeed, to get along better—without the benefits of formal knowledge, even without applied science. The possession and use of such knowledge was always considered to be of doubtful value; and in any case it was regarded as the prerogative of specialized segments of the population that were resented for their privileges and refinements.

We can begin with the peculiar accents given to the common theme by farmers, simply because the United States was for a long time primarily a nation of farmers. At the end of the eighteenth century, about nine out of ten Americans made their living directly from farming; in 1820, seven out of ten; not until 1880 did persons otherwise employed equal farmers in numbers. In many ways the American farmer was primarily a businessman. He may often have thought of farming as a way of life, but this way of life soon became astonishingly businesslike in its aspirations if not always in its mode of conduct. The vast extent of the American land, the mobile and non-traditional character of American rural life, and the Protestant dynamism of American society made for a commercially minded and speculative style in farming. The farmer was constantly tempted to engross more land than he could economically cultivate, to hold it speculatively for a rise in values, to go in for extensive and careless rather than intensive and careful cultivation, to concentrate on raising a single big commercial crop, to mine and deplete the soil, then to sell out and move. As early as 1813 John Taylor of Caroline, in his *Arator*, found that Virginia was "nearly ruined" for lack of careful cultivation, and begged his countrymen: "Forbear, oh forbear matricide, not for futurity, not for God's sake, but for your own sake." In the 1830's Tocqueville concluded: "The Americans carry their businesslike qualities into agriculture, and their trading passions are displayed in that as in their other pursuits."[1]

Farmers had their own notion of what was practical, most simply expressed in their attitude toward scientific improvement in agriculture and toward agricultural education. Among a busy and hard-working farm community that was seldom very affluent one could hardly expect to find patrons of art and learning; but a receptive state of mind at least toward applied science would have been immensely useful to the farmers themselves. Even this was considered useless. There was, of course, a deviant minority; but the preponderant attitude of dirt farmers toward improvement in their own industry was a crass, self-defeating kind of pragmatism.

Like almost everything else in American life, the farm industry was large and heterogeneous. But there was one basic class division within it that coincided with a cleavage in philosophical outlook—and that was the early nineteenth-century division between the dirt farmers and a small stratum of gentlemen farmers. The gentlemen farmers were large farmers, professional men, college or university scientists, businessmen, or agricultural editors who commonly had incomes from sources outside farming, who were interested in agricultural experimentation, read and on occasion wrote books on the subject, hoped to use scientific knowledge to improve agriculture, formed agricultural societies, and joined or led movements to uplift agricultural education. Distinguished names, recognizable for their achievements in other areas, can be found among the gentlemen farmers. They include such men as the Connecticut preacher Jared Eliot, who wrote his classic *Essay*

[1]John Taylor: *Arator* (Georgetown, 1813), pp. 76–7; Alexis de Tocqueville: *Democracy in America* (New York, 1945), Vol. II, p. 157; I have tried to assess the commercial element in American agriculture in *The Age of Reform* (New York, 1955), chapter 2.

on Field Husbandry in New England between 1748 and 1759, and Eliot's sometime correspondent, Benjamin Franklin, who maintained a farm near Burlington, New Jersey, from which he hoped to reap a profit but which he also used as a terrain on which to pursue his scientific curiosity. Washington, Jefferson, Madison, and John Taylor of Caroline, who belonged to the tradition of the enlightened agriculturists, attempted to import into the practices of Virginia agriculture the benefits of the revolution in eighteenth-century English farming. They were followed by Edmund Ruffin, famous for his experiments with calcareous fertilizers, editor of the *Farmer's Register*, and later a militant sectionalist who fired the first shot at Fort Sumter. Outside Virginia, the most active and impressive center of agitation for agricultural improvement was not in a notable farming community but at Yale College, where an understanding of the needs of agriculture was linked to the study of advanced chemistry. There, academic scientists, beginning with the younger Benjamin Silliman, concerned themselves with soil chemistry, crops, and scientific agriculture; Silliman was followed by John P. Norton, John Addison Porter, and Samuel W. Johnson. Among other things, these men attempted to popularize the work of Justus Liebig in soil chemistry. Jonathan B. Turner of Illinois, also educated at Yale, was one of the leading agitators for improved agricultural education; the inspiration of the Morrill Act has been rather uncertainly credited to him. In New York the self-educated farm editor Jesse Buel preached consistently for higher standards in agriculture. In Pennsylvania Evan Pugh, a brilliant student of plant growth and plant chemistry, became president of the Agricultural College of Pennsylvania and helped promote the Morrill Act before his premature death at thirty-six.

In that they combined scientific curiosity with agricultural practice and a sense of civic responsibility with the pursuit of agricultural profits, such men provided an example of the admirable union of the intellectual and the practical. And they were not altogether without a public. Their work reached a fairly broad class of gentlemen farmers—men who were the backbone of agricultural societies and farm fairs, readers of farm periodicals, proponents of agricultural schools and colleges. A good practical book on agriculture, if successful, might sell from ten to twenty thousand copies. Perhaps one farmer in ten subscribed to an agricultural journal, and on the eve of the Civil War there were more than fifty such journals, in various stages of prosperity or poverty.[2]

But the advocates of agricultural improvement and the gentlemen farmers were resented by dirt farmers. This resentment had in it an element of class feeling: the gentlemen organized and promoted the agricultural activities, and overshadowed the small farmers. At the county fairs, they were likely to turn up with the prize specimens, produced experimentally and without regard to cost; the common farmer could not compete with these.[3] Their preachments also ran up against a state of mind that was conservative, unreceptive, suspicious of innovation, and often superstitious. The American farmer, untraditional though he was about land speculation, about moving from place to place, or about adopting new machinery, was ultra-conservative about agricultural education or the application of science to farming. As a consequence, the professional agriculturists and farm editors felt that they were working in a skeptical, if not hostile, environment. "If the farmers in your neighborhood," wrote Benjamin Franklin to Jared Eliot, "are as unwilling to leave the beaten road of their ancestors as they are near me, it will be difficult to persuade them to attempt any improvement." George Washington wrote apologetically to Arthur Young that American farmers were more eager to take advantage of cheap land than to expend dear labor, and that, as a consequence, "much ground has been *scratched* over and none cultivated or improved as it ought to have been." Edmund Ruffin, who conducted his early experiments under the eyes of mocking neighbors, concluded: "Most farmers are determined *not* to understand anything, however simple it may be, which relates to chemistry." "Our farmers," complained

---

[2] On the number of farm journals, see Albert L. Demaree: *The American Agricultural Press, 1819–1860* (New York, 1941), pp. 17–19; on books and journals, Paul W. Gates: *The Farmer's Age: Agriculture, 1815–1860* (New York, 1960), pp. 343, 356.

[3] On this aspect of the fairs, see Gates: op. cit., pp. 312–15; cf. W. C. Neely: *The Agricultural Fair* (New York, 1935), pp. 30, 35, 42–5, 71, 183; and P. W. Bidwell and J. I. Falconer: *History of Agriculture in the Northern United States* (Washington, 1925), pp. 186–93.

Jesse Buel, "seem generally indifferent or spiritless in regard to the general improvement of our agriculture, either because they mistake their duty and true interest or that, under the influence of a strange fatuity, they fear they shall sink as others rise." The farmers, said the editor of the *American Farmer* in 1831, "will neither take an agricultural paper, read it when given them, nor believe in its contents if by chance they hear it read." Twenty years later the eminent British agricultural scientist, James F. W. Johnston, reported after a lecture tour in America that the farmers were "averse to change, and more averse still to the opinion that they are not already wise enough for all they have to do." In New York they were opposed to an agricultural college, he found, "on the ground that the knowledge to be given in the school is not required, and that its application to the soil would be of doubtful benefit."[4]

In fact, the farmer had a good deal to learn from the agricultural reformers. Even the open-minded farmer was likely to be ignorant of the principles of plant and animal breeding, of plant nutrition, of sound tillage, of soil chemistry. Many farmers were sunk in the superstitions of moon-farming—sowing, reaping, and mowing in accordance with the phases of the moon. Their practices were wasteful and depletive.[5] For the educative efforts of the reformers they had the disdain of the "practical" man for the theorist expressed in the contemptuous term *book farming*. "The men who are farmers by book are no farmers for me," said one. "Give me the man who prefers his hands to books . . . let those who follow husbandry for amusement try experiments. . . . Let learned men attend to cases, genders, moods and tenses: you and I will see to our flocks, dairies, fields and fences."[6] Against this

[4]Carl Van Doren: *Benjamin Franklin* (New York, 1938), p. 178; Bidwell and Falconer: op. cit., p. 119; Avery O. Craven: *Edmund Ruffin, Southerner* (New York, 1932), p. 58; Harry J. Carman, ed.: *Jesse Buel: Agricultural Reformer* (New York, 1947), p. 10; Demaree: op. cit., p. 38; James F. W. Johnston: *Notes on North America: Agricultural, Economic, and Social* (Edinburgh, 1851), Vol. II, p. 281.
[5]Demaree: op. cit., pp. 4–6, 10, 48–9. On wasteful cultivation, see Gates: op. cit., who makes the necessary regional and ethnic qualifications.
[6]Richard Bardolph: *Agricultural Literature and the Early Illinois Farmer* (Urbana, Illinois, 1948), p. 14; cf. pp. 13, 103.

overwhelming prejudice the reformers and farm editors manfully waged a difficult struggle. Jesse Buel complained that in every other sphere—in war and navigation, law and medicine—Americans had thought of formal education as a meaningful aid, indeed as a necessity:[7]

> And yet, in Agriculture, by which, under the blessing of Providence, we virtually "live, and move, and have our being," and which truly embraces a wider range of useful science than either law, medicine, war, or navigation, we have no schools, we give no instruction, we bestow no governmental patronage. Scientific knowledge is deemed indispensable in many minor employments of life; but in this great business, in which its influence would be most potent and useful, we consider it, judging from our practice, of less consequence than the fictions of the novelist. We regard mind as the efficient power in most other pursuits; while we forget that in Agriculture it is the Archimedean lever, which, though it does not *move*, tends to *fill* a world with plenty, with moral health, and human happiness. Can it excite surprise that, under these circumstances of gross neglect, Agriculture should have become among us, in popular estimation, a clownish and ignoble employment?

But "the great bar to agricultural improvement," Buel thought, "is the degrading idea, which too many entertain, that everything denominated science is either useless in husbandry or beyond the reach of the farmer."[8] The continuous exhortations of the farm editors, their constant efforts to overcome the feeling against book farming, seem to bear out his words. Not all the farm journals were impeccable; some of them had their own quackeries to peddle. But, in any case, they found it constantly necessary to explain apologetically that they were not advocating anything ultra-theoretical, that most of their copy was written by practicing farmers. When Liebig's great work on soil chemistry was brought out in an

---

[7]Carman: op. cit., pp. 249–50. See the instructive essay in which these remarks appeared, pp. 234–54, and Buel's remarks "On the Necessity and Means of Improving Our Husbandry," pp. 8–21.

[8]Carman: op. cit., p. 53. For a temperate answer by another editor to the ultra-practical bias of the working farmer, see: "An Apology for 'Book Farmers,'" *Farmer's Register*, Vol. II (June, 1834), pp. 16–19; cf. "Book Farming," *Farmer's Register*, Vol. I (May, 1834), p. 743.

American edition in 1841—this, it must be said, found a receptive and eager public among agricultural reformers and even
among a few dirt farmers—his discoveries were described in
the *Southern Planter* as "new fine-spun theories."9

> Mr. Justus Liebig is no doubt a very clever gentleman and
> a most profound chemist, but in our opinion he knows about
> as much of agriculture as the horse that ploughs the ground,
> and there is not an old man that stands between the stilts of a
> plough in Virginia that cannot tell him of facts totally at vari-
> ance with his finest spun theories.

2

In the light of what has been said about opposition to science and book farming, it will hardly be surprising that there
was great reluctance among farmers to accept the idea that
education (other than a highly practical on-the-farm training)
could do much for their children. Such hopes as the farmers
may have had for agricultural education seems to have been
overweighed by their fear that more schools would only mean
more taxes. An advocate of agricultural schools in the *American Farmer* in 1827 found that farmers themselves had offered
"the warmest opposition to them."10 A correspondent writing
to the *New England Farmer* in 1852, himself an opponent of a
proposed Massachusetts agricultural college, thought that nine
tenths of the practical farmers of the state agreed with him.
In any case, he set forth articulately enough the arguments of
the opposition to the school: farmers would not make use of
it; they would consider it "a grand and expensive experiment"
that did not promise a corresponding return; it would only
give "a few men a rich and lucrative office" that they had no
experience to qualify for; the advocates of the scheme hoped

9Demaree: op. cit., p. 67. On the dirt farmers and the farm press, see pp.
113–16; cf. Sidney L. Jackson: *America's Struggle for Free Schools* (Washington,
1940), pp. 111–14, 142–4. The farmer's favorite secular reading seems to have
been his almanac, and the old farmer's almanac at times catered to his anti-
intellectual sentiments with racy anecdotes or poems about the impracticality
and foolishness of the learned. Jackson: op. cit., pp. 12–13.
10Gates: op. cit., pp. 358–60.

to give the sons of rich men and those in genteel pursuits a knowledge of farming. As to that, "*the art cannot be taught to any advantage, except by practice.*"[11]

This was only a facet of a more general rural reluctance to support educational enterprises. Sidney L. Jackson, in his analysis of attitudes toward the common-school movement, reports that the farmer "was more a hindrance than a help in the struggle for better schools."[12] The various experiments in agricultural colleges that were made in the United States before the passage of the Morrill Act in 1862 were chiefly the work of small, dedicated groups of agricultural reformers—which no doubt accounts in some part for the fact that in a nation overwhelmingly agricultural and desperately in need of agricultural skills[13] so little was done until the federal government intervened. The passage in 1862 of the Morrill Act owed little to popular enthusiasm; once again, it was the achievement of a group of determined lobbyists. Earle D. Ross, in his excellent study of the land-grant movement, observes that "there was no indication of spontaneous public interest." The Morrill Act was hardly noticed, amid the war news, by the general press; the agricultural papers themselves failed to show much enthusiasm, and some did not even take cognizance of its existence.[14]

---

[11]"Agricultural Colleges," reprinted from the *New England Farmer*, n.s. Vol. IV (June, 1852), pp. 267–8, in Demaree: op. cit., pp. 250–2.

[12]Jackson: op. cit., p. 172; cf. pp. 113, 127, *passim.*

[13]Professor John P. Norton of Yale wrote in 1852: "If any six states of the Union were within the present year to make provision for the establishment of state agricultural schools, or colleges, within their respective borders—were to endow them largely in every department, to furnish them with libraries, implements, museums, apparatus, buildings, and lands, they could not find on this continent the proper corps of professors and teachers to fill them." He doubted, in fact, that a single institution in New York could find a faculty of "thoroughly competent men." Demaree: op. cit., p. 245.

For a brief history of efforts to improve education in farming, see A. C. True: *A History of Agricultural Education in the United States, 1785–1925* (Washington, 1929). In 1851 Edward Hitchcock made a survey of agricultural education in Europe for the Massachusetts legislature; in it the work of the American states appeared to great disadvantage when compared with the continental countries, especially Germany and France.

[14]Earle D. Ross: *Democracy's College* (Ames, Iowa, 1942), p. 66.

The law itself, at first, was hardly more than a well-intentioned promise; and the reformers were to find out in the next thirty years how difficult it was to execute meaningfully a reform so far in advance of public opinion. Senator Morrill's notions were sensible enough. The American soil, he recognized, was badly and wastefully cultivated; other countries were doing far more than the United States in the way of agricultural and mechanical education; experiments and surveys were needed; the farmer had to have instruction in new scientific findings; the creation of sound agricultural and mechanical schools, supported by the revenues from the public lands, would be in line with earlier American precedents for aid to education; it would not interfere with the autonomy of the states or with the kind of education then being offered by the classical colleges. For a time, Morrill's proposals ran afoul of sectional politics, and the idea of agricultural land-grant colleges was vetoed by Buchanan in 1859. But Lincoln signed a similar bill three years later. Congress seems to have been more persuaded of the need for reform than the majority of farmers.[15] Unfortunately, however, as Ross remarks, the measure was never discussed on its educational merits. Objections to it were based largely on its alleged unconstitutionality and on trivia—with the consequence that the law, as it emerged from Congress, was inadequate to realize the intentions of its framers.

Once established, the land-grant colleges were beset by all kinds of difficulties, not least among them the jealousy of the existing colleges and the American preference for educational diffusion and dispersion as against concentration of effort. It was inordinately difficult to recruit competent staffs. Old-line educators, reared on the traditions of the classical colleges, often could not really accept the legitimacy of agricultural and mechanical education, and on occasion they sabotaged the

[15]Rather exceptional in the Congressional debates over the land-grant college principles were such echoes of the feeling about book-farming as were uttered by Senator Rice of Minnesota: "If you wish to establish agricultural colleges, give to each man a college of his own in the shape of one hundred and sixty acres of land . . . but do not give lands to the states to enable them to educate the sons of the wealthy at the expense of the public. We want no fancy farmers; we want no fancy mechanics. . . ." I. L. Kandel: *Federal Aid for Vocational Education* (New York, 1917), p. 10.

new colleges from within. On the opposite side, there was the traditional small-minded opposition from farmers and folk leaders, who persisted in believing that science had nothing "practical" to offer farmers. As Ross points out, "the farmers themselves were the hardest to convince of the need and possibility of occupational training." When they did not resist the idea of such education, they resisted proposals that it have any university connections or any relation to experimental science. Separate farm colleges, severely utilitarian in purpose, would do. The Wisconsin Grange argued that each profession should be taught by its practitioners. "Ecclesiastics should teach ecclesiastics, lawyers teach lawyers, mechanics teach mechanics, and farmers teach farmers." Some governors wanted to get as far away as possible from the tradition of liberal education represented by the classical colleges. The governor of Ohio wanted the instruction to be "plain and practical, not theoretically and artistically scientific in character"; the governor of Texas imagined that an agricultural college was "for the purpose of training and educating farm laborers"; the governor of Indiana thought that any kind of higher education would be a deterrent to honest labor.[16]

More decisive than any argument was the fact that not many farmers sent their sons; and when they did, the sons took advantage of their educational opportunities to get out of farming—usually to go into engineering. For years the agricultural colleges had relatively few students, and among these the students of "mechanic arts"—i.e., engineering—outnumbered the students of agriculture from year to year by ratios of two, three, four, or five to one. An improvement in the situation of agricultural science came with the Hatch Act of 1887, which created the system of federal experiment stations working in close co-operation with the agricultural colleges and also made

[16]Ross: op. cit., chapters 5, 6, 7, and pp. 66, 72, 80, 87, 89–90, 96–7, 108–9. One paper called the agricultural colleges "asylums for classical idiots and political professors," and another suggested that the necessary task was "to clean out the smug D.D.'s and the pimply-faced 'Professors,' and put in their places men who have a lively sense of the lacks in learning among men and women who have to grapple daily with the world's work in this busy age." Ibid., pp. 119–20. Cf. James B. Angell: *Reminiscences* (New York, 1912), p. 123: "The farmers . . . were the hardest class to convince that we could be of any help to them."

available expanding research facilities. By the 1890's the colleges of agriculture finally had something of considerable value to offer in the way of scientific training.

Another flaw in the land-grant system was that it had been built from the top down. No provision had been made by Congress to develop a system of rural secondary schools good enough to equip graduates for admission to agricultural colleges. This defect was remedied in 1917 in the Smith-Hughes Act, which made federal subsidies available to secondary vocational education in agriculture. The return of agricultural prosperity after the long deflationary period from 1873 to 1897 also brought a turn in the fortunes of agricultural education. Better profits encouraged farmers to think about business management, animal breeding, soil science, and agricultural economics. The advance of mechanization made it easier for them to spare their sons from the farms. The number of agricultural students rose consistently and rapidly after 1905, and on the eve of the First World War it almost equalled the number of engineers. As M. L. Wilson, Undersecretary of Agriculture under Franklin D. Roosevelt, recalled, the contempt for book farming, almost universal in his Iowa community down to the turn of the century, was overcome only during the years of his youth:[17]

> Shortly after the twentieth century began, science began to work a revolution among the mass of farmers. When I went to Ames to study agriculture in 1902, I was not the first boy in my Iowa neighborhood to go to college, but I was the first boy from that neighborhood to go to an *agricultural* college. Ten or fifteen years later it was becoming an accepted thing for all who could afford it.

I. L. Kandel, surveying the subject in 1917, remarked with ample justification that the land-grant colleges, "intended by Senator Morrill and his supporters for the function primarily of scientific preparation for agricultural pursuits, are only just now, more than fifty years after their foundation, beginning to fulfil the function for which they were established."[18]

---

[17] Milburn L. Wilson, in O. E. Baker, R. Borsodi, and M. L. Wilson: *Agriculture in Modern Life* (New York, 1939), pp. 223–4.
[18] Kandel: op. cit., p. 103; cf. p. 106. On the number of students in agricultural and mechanical courses in these colleges, see p. 102.

The reader, who will be unlikely to think of the agricultural
and mechanical colleges as pre-eminently centers of intellectualism, may question what was accomplished and what is being
asserted here. I have no intention of misstating the character of
the agricultural colleges in this respect: they were meant only
to bring vocational education and applied science into some
kind of fruitful union, which I take to be a useful objective.
The essential point here is that this much-needed fusion was
achieved only after a century of agitation by agricultural reformers in the teeth of a widespread and extremely obstinate
conviction among working farmers that theory has nothing to
offer to practice.

3

Farming could be plausibly portrayed as a "natural" way of
living, whose practitioners might lose far more than they
would gain by attending to sophisticated critics and adopting bookish or scientific ideas. It was quite otherwise with
the industrial working class, whose way of life was considered
unnatural, and who needed to be brought to some level of
self-awareness and organization before they could give expression to any attitude toward their fate. From the outset, the
relationship of intellectual criticism and the labor movement
took on a more complex character than it had among farmers. In his brilliant inquiry into *The Psychology of Socialism*,
Henri de Man remarked: "The labor movement, uninfluenced
by the intelligentsia and its concerns [Intelligenzlermotives],
would be nothing more than a representation of interests intended to turn the proletariat into a new bourgeoisie."[19] There
is in this observation a certain ironic appropriateness for the
American labor movement, which more than any other has
aimed at making the proletariat into a new bourgeoisie. In
the United States, as elsewhere, the labor movement was in a
very real sense the creation of intellectuals. But it was a child
that turned upon its own father in order to forge its distinctive
character. It was not possible to develop labor leadership of
the type that could finally succeed in creating permanent organizations in America until a curious dialectic had been gone

[19]Henri de Man: *Zur Psychologie des Sozialismus* (Jena, 1926), p. 307.

through: first, the influence of intellectuals and their systematic critique of capitalism created an awareness of the necessity for and the possibilities of a labor movement; but then, in successive stages, this influence had to be thrown off before the labor movement could shed distractions and excrescences, devote itself to organizing job-conscious trade unions, and establish itself on a durable and successful footing.

Historically, the American labor movement did not begin with that narrow concentration on the job, the wage bargain, and the strike which eventually became the essence of its character. It was always heavily infiltrated with bourgeois leadership, affected by the aims of reform theorists, and colored by the interest of its members either in achieving a solid place in bourgeois society or in entirely reforming that society. Its early history consists of association with one sweeping reform panacea or another—land reform, anti-monopoly, Greenbackism, producers' co-operatives, Marxism, Henry George's single tax. Not until more than three quarters of a century of such experimentation had left the American labor movement with next to nothing to show in the way of solid permanent organization did it develop any effectiveness, and this only when it was taken over by pragmatic leaders of the order of Samuel Gompers and Adolph Strasser, who brought it to a focus on the job and the wage bargain and on the organization of skilled trades strong enough to hope to monopolize the labor market in their own crafts.

Both Adolph Strasser, who had been a socialist, and Samuel Gompers, the guiding spirit of the A. F. of L. during its first generation of existence, undoubtedly owed a good deal to their own youthful dialogues with the socialists. Gompers paid what was perhaps a reluctant tribute to this early intellectual training in his autobiography, when he pointed out:

> Many of those who helped to lay the foundations of the trade union movement were men who had been through the experience of Socialism and found their way to sounder policies. . . . They were always men of vision. . . . Experiences in Socialism served a constructive purpose if the individual was able to develop beyond the formulas of Socialism, for such carried to their practical duties a quickened insight and an understanding that tangible objectives are merely instrumentalities for reaching a higher spiritual goal.

However, whereas socialism may have taught such men the possibilities of a labor movement, the labor movement itself, once established, taught them the impossibility of socialism in America. From his earliest days in the labor movement, Gompers had to battle with "faddists, reformers, and sensation-loving spirits"—his terms for the ideologues who hovered around the labor movement; and there were times when these ideologues were among his most formidable enemies. It was the socialists who were instrumental in defeating him for the presidency of the A. F. of L. in 1894, the only year when he was not reelected. He was convinced that leadership could be entrusted "only to those into whose hearts and minds had been woven the experiences of earning their bread by daily labor." "I saw the danger of entangling alliances with intellectuals who did not understand that to experiment with the labor movement was to experiment with human life."[20]

Intellectuals were estranged from labor leaders like Gompers because their expectations from the labor movement were altogether different. The intellectuals tended to look upon the labor movement as a means to a larger end—to socialism or some other kind of social reconstruction. They came from outside the labor movement, and were rarely recruited from the working class itself. As a rule, they disdained the middle-class respectability to which most labor leaders, and in fact most rank and file skilled workers, aspired. A bread-and-butter organization like the A. F. of L. never appealed to their idealism, and they persistently looked down upon its leadership. The labor leaders themselves may best be understood, I believe, as a group of self-made men, in this respect not profoundly different from hundreds of such men in industrial corporations. As Strasser said, in a classic encounter: "We are all practical men."[21]

[20]Samuel Gompers: *Seventy Years of Life and Labor* (1925; ed. New York, 1943), Vol. I, pp. 55, 57, 97–8, 180, 382. This distrust of intellectuals in the labor movement was shared by one of the early labor intellectuals, John R. Commons, who felt that the labor movement attracted a type of intellectual who made a poor leader. See John R. Commons: *Myself* (New York, 1934), pp. 86–9; see also his *Industrial Goodwill* (New York, 1919), pp. 176–9.

[21]Senate Committee on Education and Labor, *Relations between Labor and Capital*, Vol. I (Washington, 1885), p. 460. Cf. the equally classic remark of Gompers in 1896: "The trade unions are the business organizations of the

They came from the ranks of the working class, for the most part, and never quite ceased to hope that labor and its leaders would achieve a respectability comparable to that enjoyed by businessmen. They had been exposed to anti-capitalist and anti-monopoly thought, but unlike the intellectuals they were unfamiliar with the thoroughgoing indictments of bourgeois civilization that pervaded avant-garde thought in politics and esthetics. They were good patriots, good family men, in time good Republicans or Democrats.[22] Their early contacts with intellectuals—or what they took to be intellectuals—were of the sort to arouse their suspicion. At first there were the battles with the socialist doctrinaires within the labor movement itself. The labor leaders constantly smarted from the criticism of academic economists,[23] who were for a long time an almost united

---

wage earners." *Report of the Sixteenth Annual Convention of the American Federation of Labor*, 1896, p. 12.

[22]My remarks here have been shaped in part by Selig Perlman's *A Theory of the Labor Movement* (1928; ed. New York, 1949), pp. viii–ix, 154, 176, 182, and chapter 5, *passim*. See C. Wright Mills's provocative remarks about labor leaders as self-made men, in *The New Men of Power* (New York, 1948), chapter 5.

[23]Although the American labor movement was always favorable to the development of the common-school system, it was chronically suspicious of the higher culture and of institutions of higher learning. From time to time labor journals made acid comments about the gifts of millionaires to museums, libraries, and universities, pointing out that these had been wrung out of the wages of the workers—"millions taken from the earnings of the toilers, given to institutions which the workmen and their children can never enter and enjoy." A particular hostility was expressed toward universities and colleges, as places where poor men's sons could never go and where "millions are annually expended in teaching the sons of the wealthy some new brutality in football." Quite understandably the labor editors feared that the universities would be bound by their endowments to teach that the status quo was beyond criticism, and that colleges and universities would become "incubators" for scabs and strikebreakers. What could be expected to be taught at a university endowed by Rockefeller? Would it be the rights of man or the superiority of the wealthy? One writer even suggested in 1905 that the new "theoretical college men" who were replacing the old practical men in the leadership of industry would be more remote from the workers because they had not risen from the ranks. College men "have nothing in common with plain workingmen upon whom they look down with disdain as did the patricians of old upon the plebians, or the slave owners of the South upon the Negroes." In 1914 the *American Federationist* suggested that private endowments were unsuited to the pursuit

phalanx against labor—"the professoriate," as Gompers labeled them, "the open and covert enemies of the workers," and "faddists, theorists and effeminate men." Finally, around the turn of the century, the movement for "scientific management" was regarded by labor as a grave menace; Gompers saw its leaders as "academic observers" and "intellectuals" who merely wanted to get the most out of the energies of workers before sending them to the junkpile. These were not experiences to encourage confidence.[24] The labor movement was in fact struggling to establish itself in an unfriendly environment, and before 1900 the official intellectuals, on balance, contributed to that unfriendliness. Those who were not unfriendly were in any case regarded as unwise and unwelcome allies. It was not until the advent of the Progressive movement that middle-class intellectuals in any great number were notably friendly to the cause of labor, and not until the New Deal era that a strong, if not altogether durable, alliance was forged.[25]

---

of the truth, and were "a menace to free institutions." If they could not be better devoted to the truth, "then they must give way to state institutions supported by public funds." *American Federationist*, Vol. XXI (February, 1914), pp. 120–1. See *Rail Road Conductor* (November, 1895), p. 613; *Typographical Journal* (June 15, 1896), p. 484; *Boilermakers' Journal* (March, 1899), p. 71; *Railway Conductor* (August, 1901), pp. 639–40; *American Federationist*, Vol. X (October, 1903), p. 1033; *The Electrical Worker* (May, 1905), p. 40; *Railroad Trainmen's Journal*, Vol. XXIV (1907), pp. 264–5; (April, 1907), p. 368; *Locomotive Firemen's Magazine*, Vol. XLIV (January, 1908), pp. 86–7.

No doubt the growing social sympathies of American academics did something to overcome this feeling. The *American Federationist* thought in 1913 that colleges and universities were in fact "helping to establish a more sympathetic, democratic understanding of social and industrial problems." Vol. XX (February, 1913), p. 129. Gompers found himself much sought after by the universities as a speaker, and spent considerable time cultivating good relations there. *Seventy Years of Life and Labor*, Vol. I, pp. 437 ff.

[24] See Gompers: *Organized Labor: Its Struggles, Its Enemies and Fool Friends* (Washington, 1901), pp. 3, 4; Gompers: "Machinery to Perfect the Living Machine," *Federationist*, Vol. XVIII (February, 1911), pp. 116–17; cf. Milton J. Nadworny: *Scientific Management and the Unions* (Cambridge, Mass., 1955), especially chapter 4.

[25] On the recent partial dissolution of this alliance, see James R. Schlesinger: "Organized Labor and the Intellectuals," *Virginia Quarterly Review*, Vol. XXXVI (Winter, 1960), pp. 36–45.

Over the years since the time of Gompers, the growth, success, and stabilization of the trade unions has made it increasingly necessary for these big bureaucratic hierarchies to hire experts for legal, actuarial, and economic advice, for research and journalism, for publicity and lobbying, for their own large educational divisions. In this way, the men who lead the country's eighteen million organized workers have become the employers of substantial staffs of intellectuals. But intellectuals in union headquarters have not found a more comfortable home than those in other areas of organized society—they have, in fact, a relationship to the union leaders not altogether unlike that of business intellectuals to corporation heads.

Three pressures, in the main, seem to alienate the intellectual from the union milieu. The first, operative only for some, is a passion for reform, an ideological commitment that may have made the intellectual want to work for a union in the first place. Sooner or later he will come to see that he has not made the labor movement radical—but rather that he himself has been absorbed into the machinery that buttresses the power and prestige of the leaders. Inevitably, the idealism of the union expert is blunted, as he finds himself caught up in a going concern that is ready to use him but unwilling to be bent by his will. (Union experts who come to the job with missionary enthusiasm tend to be paid somewhat less than more self-centered careerists.) The second source of alienation is his professional feeling for research, his disinterested desire for the truth, which on occasion runs up against the necessities of the union as a militant organization or the personal imperatives of a leader. "They're sloppy in their use of data," complains one expert about his union associates.[26]

> They don't give a damn. They're philosophical relativists with no real belief in truth or in scientific objectivity; or at least they think the search for truth is too difficult, so they abandon it and excuse themselves from it by saying, "Who's interested in the

[26]For my argument here, as well as the quotations from labor leaders and labor experts, I am indebted to Harold L. Wilensky: *Intellectuals in Labor Unions* (Glencoe, Illinois, 1956), *passim*, and especially pp. 55, 57, 68, 88–90, 93, 106, 116–20, 132, 260–5, 266n., 267, 273–6. On the limitations of the power of the labor intellectual, see also C. Wright Mills: op. cit., pp. 281–7.

truth, anyway—management?" Basically, it's because they have
a Marxist or a social reform attitude. Everything becomes a
matter of partisan advantage. . . . All they want to do is build
up the prejudices of the leader. . . . I sometimes wish I'd gone
into university teaching.

From time to time, experts seek unwelcome truths or become
the medium through which union leaders are brought face
to face with some unwelcome reality, say in the legal or economic world. In this capacity they are resented, much as they
are needed. The labor editor may aspire to run an intelligent
organ of critical opinion; his union leader may be far more
concerned that the union's journal take the right side in factional disputes. The union educational director may wish to
offer something akin to a liberal education for workers; the
leader may seek only simple indoctrination and ideological
safety.

Finally, there is a type of alienation which is simply personal,
which arises from the education and in some cases the personal
culture of the expert. He is out of place, he is not the right kind
of man, he would not be sought after as a companion if his
services weren't needed. Mumbled complaints pursue him in
the union offices, just as though he were actually on the assembly line—or for that matter at a Rotary Club meeting: "Prima
donna types . . . you can't work together with them. . . .
They aren't liked. . . . They're not the same Joes. They don't
like the same kind of women. . . ."

The attitude of labor leaders toward labor intellectuals displays an ambivalence somewhat similar to that found in the
business community and in society at large. Harold Wilensky
has found in his study of labor experts that the labor leader is
sometimes intimidated or overawed by the specialized knowledge of the intellectual, and often admires it. But he reassures
himself with disdainful remarks about the impracticality of
the expert, if not about his oddities. One high-ranking union
officer who boasted: "I was educated in the school of hard
knocks," voiced these mixed feelings when he said with equal
pride: "I've told my son to take up labor law in college!" In
some areas the non-intellectual is afflicted by a nagging envy of
the expert's job: "Why, that S.O.B., he's got the soft job. . . .
I knock myself out taking crap from the rank and file, I gotta

go out to local meetings night after night while he sits behind a desk and writes up all that stuff." Like the businessman, the union leader loudly praises practical experience—first-hand acquaintance with the workbench or with union organizing activity. "You can't learn it from books. There's no substitute for experience." *He* was in the struggle from the beginning; the expert is an outsider and a Johnny-come-lately who cannot understand the labor struggle or the psychology of the worker because he has not dealt with it at first hand. "Your whole thinking on this matter . . . is fantastic. You are a legal mind; you are from Harvard, or Yale, or some other place like the rest of the guys up there, and you don't understand the thinking of the workers." Under the circumstances, it is not surprising that the experts at times give way to a feeling of self-distrust and adopt a quietistic pose or attempt to camouflage themselves. The atmosphere in which they work may be in many ways stimulating and benign, but, according to a student of experts in the labor bureaucracy, one of its components is a "pervasive anti-intellectualism."[27]

4

It is hardly surprising that the organized labor movement in America, directed as it is toward "bourgeois" goals, has provided intellectuals with an environment that is not thoroughly congenial. It is somewhat more surprising to find similar problems arising in the non-Communist left, and especially in the Socialist Party, whose debt to intellectuals was heavy indeed. It would be altogether misleading to suggest that the Socialist Party in its day was an anti-intellectual force, or that it was inhospitable to intellectuals. From 1900 to 1914, the American Socialist Party attracted a large number of intellectuals whose support was invaluable and whose writings brought it cachet and greatly widened its influence. Among them were not only muckrakers like Upton Sinclair and John Spargo but the authors of stimulating critical books about socialism and various aspects of American life which are still worth reading—men like Louis B. Boudin, W. J. Ghent, Robert Hunter, Algie M.

[27]Wilensky: op. cit., pp. 269, 276.

Simons, and William English Walling. Unlike the later Communist Party, the Socialist Party maintained an intellectual atmosphere that was far from monolithic, and produced a theoretical literature not entirely cramped by Marxian scholasticism. American socialism, pluralistic in its social recruitment, was still free and even adventurous in thought, and some of its supporters brought to it a light-spirited Bohemian touch. "The *Masses*," one of its periodicals advertised, "has a Sense of Humor. . . . Enjoy the Revolution."

But in some quarters even the Socialist Party suffered from the cult of proletarianism. In the party's frequent factional fights, intellectual spokesmen were often branded as middle-class academics and were compared invidiously with the true proletarians who were the bulwark of the movement. (When revolutionary fervor was in question, the intellectuals were found in the left-wing faction much more often than in the right.) Inevitably, the attempt of socialist intellectuals, often from solid middle-class and sometimes from wealthy backgrounds,[28] to declass themselves spiritually and to accommodate to the proletarian ideals of Marxism led to a certain self-depreciation and self-alienation. Hence, the anti-intellectual wing of the party was not without its intellectual spokesmen.[29] One of them, W. J. Ghent, thought that the *Masses*, with its latitudinarian enthusiasms, was far too frivolous to contribute seriously to the fundamental business of converting workers to socialism:

[28]Finley Peter Dunne was much amused by the interest of a few of the rich in socialism. "Mrs. Vanderhankerbilk," said Mr. Dooley, "Give a musical soree f'r th' ladies iv th' Female Billyonaires Arbeiter Verein. . . . Th' meetin' was addhressed be th' well-known Socialist leader, J. Clarence Lumley, heir to th' Lumley millyons. This well-known prolytariat said he had become a Socialist through studyin' his father. He cud not believe that a system was right which allowed such a man to accumylate three hundherd millyon dollars. . . . Th' ladies prisint cud appreciate how foolish th' captains iv industhree are, because they were marrid to them an' knew what they looked like in th' mornin'. . . . Th' meetin' thin adjourned afther passin' a resolution callin' on th' husband iv th' hostess to go an' jump in th' river." Finley Peter Dunne: *Mr. Dooley: Now and Forever* (Stanford, California, 1954), pp. 252–3.
[29]Charles Dobbs, writing on "Brains" in the *International Socialist Review*, Vol. VIII (March, 1908), p. 533, noticed that "it is the 'intellectuals' who are attacking the 'intellectuals' and the 'leaders' who are delivering the mightiest blows at 'leadership.'"

It has found no trouble in mixing Socialism, Anarchism, Communism, Sinn Feinism, Cubism, sexism, direct action, and sabotage into a more or less harmonious mess. It is peculiarly the product of the restless metropolitan coteries who devote themselves to the cult of Something Else; who are ever seeking the bubble Novelty even at the door of Bedlam.

Another intellectual, Robert Rives La Monte, felt that although the party needed brains in abundance, brains should not be identified with the possession of "a conventional bourgeois education," and concluded that the existence of "a reasonable degree of suspicion of Intellectuals and Parlor Socialists" was a "most reassuring sign that the proletariat are approaching maturity as a class."[30] With this a right-wing party wheelhorse like George H. Goebel could agree. When it came to a choice between the intellectual, preacher, or professor and the working man, "that man who is fresh from the ranks of the working class and who in his every day life is in actual contact with the work and the struggle," Goebel said, he was always with the representative of the working class.[31]

The most extreme anti-intellectual position in the party— a veritable proletarian mucker pose—was taken not by the right-wingers nor by the self-alienated intellectuals but by Western party members affected by the I.W.W. spirit. The Oregon wing of the party, one of its strong Western segments, was a good example of this spirit. The story is told that at the party's 1912 convention in Indianapolis the Oregon delegates refused to have dinner in a restaurant that had tablecloths. Thomas Sladden, their

[30]David Shannon: *The Socialist Party of America* (New York, 1955), p. 57; Robert R. La Monte: "Efficient Brains versus Bastard Culture," *International Socialist Review*, Vol. VIII (April, 1908), pp. 634, 636. On intellectuals in the socialist movement, see Shannon: op. cit., pp. 8, 12, 19, 53–8, 281–2; Daniel Bell: "The Background and Development of Marxian Socialism in the United States," in Donald Drew Egbert and Stow Persons, eds.: *Socialism and American Life* (Princeton, 1952), Vol. I, pp. 294–8; Ira Kipnis: *The American Socialist Movement, 1897–1912* (New York, 1952), pp. 307–11, and Bell's review of this work in *The New Leader*, December 7, 1953.
[31]Bell: "Background and Development," p. 294. Cf. the attack by the right-wing leader, Max Hayes, on parlor socialists and theorists in the party convention of 1912. Socialist Party of America, *Convention Proceedings*, 1912 (Chicago, 1912), p. 124.

state secretary, once removed the cuspidors from the Oregon headquarters because he felt that hardboiled tobacco-chewing proletarians would have no use for such genteel devices. It was Sladden, too, who in the *International Socialist Review* wrote an implacable challenge to the intellectuals. As he saw it, the movement belonged to the worker and to no one else. The Socialist Party and the labor unions "must either give way to, or take up arms against 'the man that thinks through his stomach.'" Sladden delineated the true socialist proletarian in these terms:[32]

> He has a language of his own, different from the accepted language of civilization, he is uncultured and uncouth in appearance, he has a code of morals and ethics as yet unrecognized by society, he has a religion unpreached in orthodox and unorthodox churches, a religion of hate. . . . He has an intelligence which passes the understanding of the intellectuals who are born, reared and living outside his sphere.
>
> Like the instinct of the brute in the forest, his vision is clear and he is ever on the alert, his hearing is keen, his nature suspicious, his spirit is unconquerable. . . . With one swoop he will tear away your puny intellectuality, your bogus respectability and as master of all he surveys he will determine what is right and what wrong.
>
> This is the proletarian. . . . He has little education, no manners, and little care for what people think of him. His school has been the hard school of human experience.

Here the cult of proletarianism seems blended with a variety of primitivism of the sort another Westerner, Jack London, tried unsuccessfully to graft onto the socialist movement. More typical of the feelings of non-intellectuals in the Socialist Party was the moderate position of its leader, Eugene V. Debs. Observing that there were many socialists "who sneer at a man of intellect as if he were an interloper and out of place among Socialists," Debs remonstrated that *intellectual* ought not be a term of reproach. The movement needed brains; the party should seek to attract them. What was important to Debs was that normally "officials and representatives, and candidates for

[32] "The Revolutionist," *International Socialist Review*, Vol. IX (December, 1908), pp. 429–30. On Sladden, see Shannon: op. cit., p. 40; for an answer to Sladden by a socialist who considered that the proletariat embraced the intellectuals, see Carl D. Thompson: "Who Constitute the Proletariat?" *International Socialist Review*, Vol. IX (February, 1909), pp. 603–12.

public office, should be chosen from the ranks of the workers. The intellectuals in office should be the exceptions, as they are in the rank and file." Organizations of workers should not be run by intellectuals, just as organizations of intellectuals should not be run by workers. Debs considered that workers had ample ability to fill the official positions themselves. His fear of intellectuals in official posts was consistent with his fear of stratification and bureaucracy within the socialist movement. Like a good Jacksonian, he acknowledged his belief in "rotation in office." "I confess," he said, "to a prejudice against officialism and a dread of bureaucracy."[33]

5

Whereas the Socialist Party had admitted some measure of diversity, the Communist Party was monolithic: it wanted no writers who would not subject themselves to its characteristic rigid discipline. Moreover, the intellectuals who were drawn to the Socialist Party during its most vital period, before the First World War, were mainly thinkers independently acquainted with Marxism, who took over leadership in the party ranks as theorists. The Communist Party attracted a far higher proportion of creative writers and literary critics, who knew little or nothing of Marxism or of the formal social disciplines and were willing, at least for a time, to submit themselves to the tutelage and discipline of the party apparatus. Within the Communist Party, as its intellectual influence widened during the 1930's, certain anti-intellectual tendencies, notably the cult of proletarianism, which had been hardly more than visible in the Socialist Party, became actually dominant. The change in the balance of moral power was dramatic: in Socialist Party circles one senses the discomfort of true proletarians at the thought that the intellectuals among them wielded so much influence; in Communist Party circles one is aware of the anguish of party or fellow-traveling intellectuals because they are not, by occupation or birth, workers themselves.

[33] "Sound Socialist Tactics," *International Socialist Review*, Vol. XII (February, 1912), pp. 483–4. Three years after these remarks Robert Michels published his *Political Parties*, an analysis of oligarchical tendencies in European left-wing parties.

Earlier American radicals, like Edward Bellamy and Henry Demarest Lloyd, had sometimes taken a slightly condescending and custodial attitude toward the working class; but in the 1930's a number of American writers gave way to the fatally maudlin notion that the sufferings and the "historic mission" of the working class endow it with an immense inherent moral superiority over middle-class intellectuals. To atone for their tainted class origins and their middle-class character, many such intellectuals felt they must immolate themselves on the altar of the working class by service of one kind or another to the party. The Communist Party itself, keenly aware of the usefulness of its intellectual converts and at the same time of the danger that might be posed to its discipline by an influx of independent minds, adopted the strategy of exploiting the guilt and self-hatred of intellectuals as a means of keeping them in line. On one hand, it provided them with a creed and gave them a small but growing audience; on the other, it attempted to play upon their psychological vulnerability to prevent them from straying. This policy had mixed results; the most distinguished writers, whose prestige the party particularly coveted—Dreiser, Sinclair, Steinbeck, Hemingway, MacLeish, Dos Passos—proved to be the most refractory, the most unwilling to follow tamely the decrees of obscure party hacks. Lesser writers, less self-confident and more dependent upon the public the party could give them, were more submissive, though not always submissive enough for the party's purposes. Paul Rosenfeld had writers like these in mind when he complained in 1933 that they had renounced their responsibilities as artists and were competing "as to which could most quickly reconcile himself with the philistinism which the Communist party shares with every other party."[34]

If the true spirit of Bolshevik discipline was to be instilled in radical American writers, the Bohemianism that had flowered

[34] Quoted in Daniel Aaron: *Writers on the Left* (New York, 1961), pp. 254–5. I have drawn heavily for my argument and illustrations on this thorough and perceptive study, and the quotations and incidents in the following paragraphs are from pp. 25, 41, 65, 93–4, 132*n*., 162, 163–4, 168, 209, 210–12, 216, 227, 240–2, 254, 308, 337–8, 346, 409, 410, 417, 425. The attitude of the Communist Party toward intellectuals was far more rigid before 1935, when it adopted the "united front" line, than afterwards.

in the days of the *Masses* had to be destroyed. Writers must be made to feel that Bohemianism and all forms of merely personal revolt were unserious, trivial, neurotic. John Reed, once a Bohemian himself, led the way. "This class struggle," he said, "plays hell with your poetry"; and if it did, no doubt poetry would have to go. "Bolshevism," he declared on another occasion, "is not for the intellectuals; it is for the people." "You fellows," he remarked to a Menshevik theorist, "are not living beings; at best you are bookworms always thinking about what Marx said or meant to say. What we want is a revolution, and we are going to make it—not with books, but with rifles." Reed did not live long enough to demonstrate how far he would have carried the implications of this creed. After his death, the role of goad to the intellectuals was assumed by Michael Gold, for many years the party's critical hatchetman. Gold had succeeded more fully than most left intellectuals in declassing and deintellectualizing himself.[35] Floyd Dell, a party sympathizer but an incurable Bohemian, perceived that Gold, as a literary man, "is for some obscure reason ashamed of not being a workingman. . . . And so he is in awe of the workingman when he meets him, and says extravagant things in praise of him." To a generation of writers younger than Dell, the reasons for this shame and awe were not so obscure.

The Communist view of the intellectual's function brought forth certain ironic variations on the themes of practicality, masculinity, and primitivism that run through the national code at large; and it is amusing to see how, with a few changes in terms, the party code is similar to certain attitudes expressed by businessmen. The important task was a ruggedly practical one—to make a revolution. Everything else was subordinate; art and intellect were useless if they could not be put to work. Writers who failed to serve the revolution were accused, in the party's characteristic imagery, of being literary prostitutes to the bourgeoisie: they were "the most ancient and venerable of prostitutes," and (in the language of a young writer

[35]Gold, who was as impeccably anti-Harvard as any McCarthyite of the 1950's, was impelled to deny his brief attendance there. "Certain enemies have spread the slander that I once attended Harvard College. This is a lie. I worked on a garbage dump in Boston, city of Harvard. But that is all."

of impeccable proletarian origins) "literary vermin . . . who play the scented whore, and for thirty pieces of silver, will do the hootchi-kootchi dance, or wriggle their abdomens in imitation of legendary oriental ladies."

The making of revolutions was a task that called not only for greater moral purity but for a kind of heavy masculinity that too many writers lacked. Again, the practical and masculine demands of politics were contrasted with the futility of estheticism. One writer was taken aback when a party leader referred to his poetry and short stories as his "hobby" for after-hours activity—a revealing illustration of the party's conception of letters as fundamentally unserious. Worst of all was the failure of masculinity in writers who would not deal with the hard realities of the class struggle. Party intellectuals differed over the matter, but the most rugged of them were unsparing in their denunciation of what they called, in their crusade against the literary Humanists, "fairy literature." Michael Gold once told Sinclair Lewis that writers of this sort were nursing a "mad jealousy" because they had been "deprived of masculine experiences." In the course of a famous literary vendetta against Thornton Wilder, Gold accused the novelist of propagating a "pastel, pastiche, dilettante religion, without the true neurotic blood and fire, a daydream of homosexual figures in graceful gowns moving archaically among the lilies."

In their most extreme moments, those who tried to formulate a Communist canon for literature called for working-class writers who would supply the "Proletarian Realism" (Gold's phrase) that bourgeois writers allegedly failed to produce. Let the *New Masses*, the party organ, be written and read by "lumberjacks, hoboes, miners, clerks, sectionhands, machinists, harvesthands, waiters—the people who should count more to us than paid scribblers," urged one of these working-class writers. "It might be crude stuff—but we're just about done primping before a mirror and powdering our shiny noses. Who are we afraid of? Of the critics? Afraid that they will say the *New Masses* prints terribly ungrammatical stuff? Hell, brother, the newsstands abound with neat packages of grammatical offal." Such utterances tended to drive writers away from the movement. They were alienated by what one of them called "the affectation of idealized proletarianism, the monotonous strumming on the hard-boiled string, the hostility to ideas on other levels than one, the contempt for modulated writing and criticism, the evasion of discussion."

These differences were indicative of a major problem faced by the party in dealing with writers and other intellectuals: the conflict between its urgent desire to use them and its inability to sustain a tone that would hold them. Even Michael Gold, whose polemical extravagances did as much as anything to keep otherwise sympathetic intellectuals at arm's length from the party, at times grew restless with the attitude of party leaders toward writers. He once admitted that intellectuals were too commonly made to feel that they were outsiders: "The word 'intellectual' became a synonym for the word 'bastard,' and in the American Communist movement there is some of this feeling." Members of the party were not above exploiting this feeling about intellectuals as a weapon in internal struggles: during a factional fight in the twenties, Joseph Freeman has recalled, the Foster group attacked the Lovestone group in a word-of-mouth campaign on the ground, among others, that they were college men, bourgeois, and Jews. The feeling had astonishing consequences. Malcolm Cowley, writing during the Moscow trials from his post as a fellow-traveling editor of a major metropolitan nonparty weekly, said of Trotsky in all seriousness: "I have never liked the big-city intellectuals of his type, with their reduction of every human question to a bald syllogism in which they are always right at every point. . . ."

For a time, if only a brief time in the life of most radical writers, the canons of the party were accepted, and with them the corollary that the intellectuals, and the institutions that had reared them, were no good. "I think we are all of us a pretty milky lot," John Dos Passos wrote during the First World War, "with our tea-table convictions and our radicalism that keeps so consistently within the bounds of decorum. . . . I'd like to annihilate these stupid colleges of ours, and all the nice young men therein, instillers of stodginess—every form of bastard culture, middle class snobism." Genevieve Taggard, deferring to the urgent "practical" task of revolution, felt that writers were useless:

Practical men run revolutions, and there's nothing more irritating than a person with a long vague look in his eye to have around, when you're trying to bang an army into shape, or put over a N.E.P. If I were in charge of a revolution, I'd get rid of every single artist immediately; and trust to luck that the fecundity of the earth would produce another crop when I had got some of the hard work done. Being an artist, I have the sense that a small child has when its mother is in the middle of housework. I don't intend to get in the way, and I hope that there'll be an unmolested spot for me when things have quieted down.

Many writers had entered the movement in the belief that the revolt against the bourgeois world would be, for them at least, a revolt against its disrespect for culture. But whichever world one might choose, there was always a prior practical job to be done—bourgeois industrialization or a New Economic Policy, the quest for individual success or the need to "bang" an army into shape.

PART 5

EDUCATION IN A
DEMOCRACY

CHAPTER XII

The School and the Teacher

I

ANYONE WHO speaks of anti-intellectualism as a quality in American life must reckon with one of the signal facts of our national experience—our persistent, intense, and sometimes touching faith in the efficacy of popular education. Few observers, past or present, have doubted the pervasiveness or sincerity of this faith. Henry Steele Commager, assessing the primary characteristics of the nineteenth-century American, remarks that "education was his religion" though he is quick to add that Americans expected of education what they expected of religion, that it "be practical and pay dividends."[1] The Americans were the first other people in modern history to follow the Prussian example in establishing free common-school systems. Among their earliest statutes were land ordinances setting aside a portion of the public domain to support school systems. Their rapidly proliferating schoolhouses and libraries testified to their concern for the diffusion of knowledge, and their lyceums and Chautauquas showed that this concern, far from ending with the school years, extended to the education of adults.

From the beginning, American statesmen had insisted upon the necessity of education to a republic. George Washington, in his Farewell Address, urged the people to promote "institutions for the general diffusion of knowledge." To the degree that the form of government gave force to public opinion, Washington argued, "it is essential that public opinion should be enlightened." The aging Jefferson warned in 1816: "If a nation expects to be ignorant and free in a state of civilization, it expects what never was and never will be." The young Lincoln, making his first appeal to a constituency, told the voters

---

[1] Henry Steele Commager: *The American Mind* (New Haven, 1950), p. 10; cf. pp. 37–8. Rush Welter: *Popular Education and Democratic Thought in America* (New York, 1962), is an informative study of what Americans expected from education.

of Sangamon County in 1832 that education was "the most important subject which we as a people can be engaged in."[2] The image of the youthful Lincoln lying before a log fire and reading a book by its flickering light has been fixed as an ideal in the minds of millions of school children (who are not, I believe, pressed to consider what he may have been reading). In popular rhetoric it was always good practice for an editor or orator who wanted to take off on an extended flight of idealism to pay tribute to education. "If the time shall ever come," wrote a small-town Midwestern editor in 1836,[3]

> when this mighty fabric shall totter; when the beacon of joy that now rises in pillar of fire . . . shall wax dim, the cause will be found in the ignorance of the people. If our union is still to continue . . . ; if your fields are to be untrod by the hirelings of despotism; if long days of blessedness are to attend our country in her career of glory; if you would have the sun continue to shed his unclouded rays upon the face of freemen, then EDUCATE ALL THE CHILDREN OF THE LAND. This alone startles the tyrant in his dreams of power, and rouses the slumbering energies of an oppressed people. It was intelligence that reared up the majestic columns of national glory; and this and sound morality alone can prevent their crumbling to ashes.

But if we turn from the rhetoric of the past to the realities of the present, we are most struck by the volume of criticism suggesting that something very important has been missing from the American passion for education. A host of educational problems has arisen from indifference—underpaid teachers, overcrowded classrooms, double-schedule schools, broken-down school buildings, inadequate facilities and a number of other failings that come from something else—the cult of athleticism, marching bands, high-school drum majorettes, ethnic ghetto schools, de-intellectualized curricula, the failure to educate in serious subjects, the neglect of academically gifted children. At times the schools of the country seem to be dominated by athletics, commercialism, and the standards of the

[2]Washington, in Richardson, ed.: *Messages and Papers of the Presidents*, Vol. I, p. 220; Jefferson: *Writings*, P. L. Ford, ed., Vol. X (New York, 1899), p. 4; Lincoln: *Collected Works*, Roy P. Basler, ed., Vol. I (New Brunswick, New Jersey, 1953), p. 8.
[3]R. Carlyle Buley: *The Old Northwest Pioneer Period, 1815–1840* (Indianapolis, 1950), Vol. II, p. 416.

mass media, and these extend upwards to a system of higher education whose worst failings were underlined by the bold president of the University of Oklahoma who hoped to develop a university of which the football team could be proud.[4] Certainly some ultimate educational values seem forever to be eluding the Americans. At great effort and expense they send an extraordinary proportion of their young to colleges and universities; but their young, when they get there, do not seem to care even to *read*.[5]

2

That something has always been seriously missing in our educational performance, despite the high promise of our rhetoric, has been evident to the educators who have taken our hopes most seriously. The history of our educational writing poses a formidable challenge to those modern educational critics who yield too readily to nostalgia for good old days that apparently were never too good. The educational writing that has been left to us by men whose names command our respect is to a remarkable degree a literature of acid criticism and bitter complaint. Americans would create a common-school system, but would balk at giving it adequate support. They would stand close to the vanguard among the countries of the world in the attempt to diffuse knowledge among the people, and then engage drifters and misfits as teachers and offer them the wages of draymen.

The history of American educational reformers often seems to be the history of men fighting against an uncongenial environment. The educational jeremiad is as much a feature of our literature as the jeremiad in the Puritan sermons. That this literature should have been one of complaint is not in itself surprising, for complaint is the burden of anyone who aims at improvement; but there is a constant undercurrent of

[4]An impressive brief critique of these failings may be found in Robert M. Hutchins: *Some Observations on American Education* (Cambridge, 1956).
[5]On American reading, in and out of college, see Lester Asheim: "A Survey of Recent Research," in Jacob M. Price, ed.: *Reading for Life* (Ann Arbor, Michigan, 1959); Gordon Dupee: "Can Johnny's Parents Read?" *Saturday Review*, June 2, 1956.

something close to despair. Moreover, one finds it not only on the educational frontiers of the West, or in darkest Mississippi, but in Massachusetts, the state that stood first in the development of the common-school system and has never lost her place among the leading states in education. Yet, in this state, the educational reformer James Gordon Carter warned in 1826 that if the legislature did not change its policies the common schools would be extinct within twenty years.[6]

The criticisms made by Horace Mann about one of the nation's best school systems during his years as secretary of the Massachusetts Board of Education after 1837 are illuminating. Schoolhouses, he said, were too small, and ill-situated; school committees, to save money, had neglected to insure uniformity in the textbooks, with the consequence that a single class might be using as many as eight or ten manuals in a given subject; school committees were neither well paid nor accorded social recognition; one portion of the community was so apathetic about education that it would do nothing for the school system, but the wealthier portion had given up on the common schools and were sending their children to private institutions; many towns neglected to comply with the state's school requirements; there was an "extensive want of competent teachers for the Common Schools," but the existing teachers, however ill-equipped, were "as good as public opinion has demanded"; there was "an obvious want of intelligence in the reading-classes"; "the schools have retrograded within the last generation or half generation in regard to orthography"; "more than eleven-twelfths of all the children in the reading-classes in our schools do not understand the meaning of the words they read." He was afraid that "neglectful school committees, incompetent teachers, and an indifferent public, may go on degrading each other" until the whole idea of free schools would be abandoned.[7]

[6] *Essays upon Popular Education* (Boston, 1826), p. 41.
[7] Horace Mann: *Lectures and Annual Reports on Education*, Vol. I (Cambridge, 1867), pp. 396, 403–4, 408, 413, 422, 506–7, 532, 539. Of considerable interest is Mann's report of 1843, in which he made extensive comparisons with Prussian education. There, he remarked, "the teacher's profession holds such a high rank in public estimation, that none who have failed in other employments or departments of business are encouraged to look upon school-keeping as an ultimate resource." *Life and Works*, Vol. III (Boston, 1891), pp.

The complaints continued, and the plaintive note spread from New England to the country at large. In 1870, when the country was on the eve of a great forward surge in secondary education, William Franklin Phelps, then head of a normal school in Winona, Minnesota, and later a president of the National Education Association, declared:[8]

> They [the elementary schools] are mainly in the hands of ignorant, unskilled teachers. The children are fed upon the mere husks of knowledge. They leave school for the broad theater of life without discipline; without mental power or moral stamina. . . . Poor schools and poor teachers are in a majority throughout the country. Multitudes of the schools are so poor that it would be as well for the country if they were closed. . . . They afford the sad spectacle of ignorance engaged in the stupendous fraud of self-perpetuation at the public expense. . . . Hundreds of our American schools are little less than undisciplined juvenile mobs.

In 1892 Joseph M. Rice toured the country to examine its school systems and reported the same depressing picture in city after city, with only a few welcome exceptions: education was a creature of ward politics; ignorant politicians hired ignorant teachers; teaching was an uninspired thing of repetitive drill.[9] Ten years later, when the Progressive movement was barely under way, the New York *Sun* had a different kind of complaint:[10]

---

266 ff. and especially pp. 346–8. Francis Bowen, Harvard's professor of moral philosophy, concurred with Mann's views; the New England school system, he said, looking backward in 1857, "had degenerated into routine, it was starved by parsimony. Any hovel would answer for a school-house, any primer would do for a text-book, any farmer's apprentice was competent to 'teach school.'" *American Journal of Education*, Vol. IV (September, 1857), p. 14.

[8] *NEA Proceedings*, 1870, pp. 13, 17. For a series of complaints similar to these, and ranging from 1865 to 1915, see Edgar B. Wesley: *N.E.A.: The First Hundred Years* (New York, 1957) pp. 138–43.

[9] *The Public School System of the United States* (New York, 1893).

[10] Marian G. Valentine: "William H. Maxwell and Progressive Education," *School and Society*, LXXV (June 7, 1952), p. 354. Complaints of this order began to emerge at this time as a response to the new education. See the remarks of Lys D'Aimee as quoted in R. Freeman Butts and Lawrence Cremin: *A History of Education in American Culture* (New York, 1953), pp. 385–6.

> When we were boys, boys had to do a little work in school.
> They were not coaxed; they were hammered. Spelling, writing,
> and arithmetic were not electives, and you had to learn. In these
> more fortunate times, elementary education has become in
> many places a vaudeville show. The child must be kept amused,
> and learns what he pleases. Many sage teachers scorn the old-
> fashioned rudiments, and it seems to be regarded as between a
> misfortune and a crime for a child to learn to read.

A generation later, after the nation had developed its great
mass system of secondary education, and education itself had
become highly professionalized, Thomas H. Briggs of Teachers College, delivering his Inglis Lecture at Harvard, assessed
the nation's "great investment" in secondary education and
concluded that it had gone sadly awry. "There has been no
respectable achievement," he observed, "even in the subjects
offered in the secondary school curricula." Performance in
mathematics, he thought, was of the sort which, applied in
business, would lead to bankruptcy or the penitentiary. Only
half the students could find the area of a circle, when given
the value of *pi* and all necessary data. Students of foreign languages acquired neither the ability to read nor the ability to
communicate. Only half the students who had completed a
year's study of high-school French could translate *Je n'ai parlé
à personne*; and only one fifth of the pupils who elected French
took more than two years of the language. In Latin, the results were as bad. A year's study of ancient history yielded students who could not tell who Solon was; and after a year of
American history, students were unable to define the Monroe
Doctrine—even though both subjects were stressed in these
courses. Courses in English failed to produce in the majority
any "permanent taste for what is called standard literature"
and brought results in written English that were "in a large
fraction of the cases shocking in their evidence of inadequate
achievement."[11]

Today we live in the age of systematic surveys, and the evidences of our various educational failures have accumulated

[11]Thomas H. Briggs: *The Great Investment: Secondary Education in a Democracy* (Cambridge, Mass., 1930), pp. 124–8.

to the point at which documentation is futile.[12] The widest range of difference exists with regard to the practical meaning of this evidence. Many professional educationists welcome it as further proof of their contention that the traditional course of studies is unsuited to vast numbers of children in a system of mass education. Critics of the educational system argue that these findings simply show the need to return to higher standards and to improve our educational morale. Concerning the central fact of educational failure there is relatively slight dispute; and the failure itself underlines one of the paradoxes of American life: that in a society so passionately intent upon education, the yield of our educational system has been such a constant disappointment.

3

We may, of course, nourish the suspicion that there is some-thing misleading about these findings and criticisms. Is not the history of constant complaint by school authorities and educational reformers simply a sign of healthy self-criticism? Were not many of these complaints followed by reforms? If the American public educational system is measured not by some abstract standards of perfection but by the goals for which it was originally established, must it not be considered a success? On this count there is undoubtedly much to be said. The American system of common schools was meant to take a vast, heterogeneous, and mobile population, recruited from manifold sources and busy with manifold tasks, and forge it into a nation, make it literate, and give it at least the mini-mal civic competence necessary to the operation of republi-can institutions. This much it did; and if in the greater part of the nineteenth century the United States did not astound the world with its achievements in high culture, its schools at least

[12]My favorite among such surveys is one Los Angeles made of 30,000 of its school children in 1951. Among other things, it showed that almost one of every seven eighth graders could not find the Atlantic Ocean on a map, and that approximately the same proportion of eleventh graders (aged sixteen to eighteen) could not calculate 50 per cent of 36. *Time*, December 10, 1951, pp. 93–4.

helped to create a common level of opinion and capacity that was repeatedly noticed with admiration by foreign observers.

Here no doubt the American educational creed itself needs further scrutiny. The belief in mass education was not founded primarily upon a passion for the development of mind, or upon pride in learning and culture for their own sakes, but rather upon the supposed political and economic benefits of education. No doubt leading scholars and educational reformers like Horace Mann did care for the intrinsic values of mind. But in trying to persuade influential men or the general public of the importance of education, they were careful in the main to point out the possible contributions of education to public order, political democracy, or economic improvement. They understood that the most irresistible way to "sell" education was to stress its role not in achieving a high culture but in forging an acceptable form of democratic society. They adopted and fixed upon the American mind the idea that under popular government popular education is an absolute necessity. To the rich, who were often wary of its cost, they presented popular education as the only alternative to public disorder, to an unskilled and ignorant labor force, to misgovernment, crime, and radicalism. To the people of middle and lower classes they presented it as the foundation of popular power, the door to opportunity, the great equalizer in the race for success.[13]

As to the vast, inarticulate body of the American public, it is impossible to be certain exactly what it expected from the school system, other than an opportunity for the advancement of its children. That the development of intellectual power was not a central concern seems clear, but there is also some evidence that the anti-intellectualism I have already characterized in religion, politics, and business found its way into school practice. There seems to have been a prevailing concern that

[13]The arguments used by educational reformers are discussed by Lawrence Cremin: *The American Common School* (New York, 1951); Merle Curti: *The Social Ideas of American Educators* (New York, 1935); and Sidney L. Jackson: *America's Struggle for Free Schools* (Washington, 1940). One of the most illuminating documents of American social history is Robert Carlton [Baynard Rush Hall]: *The New Purchase, or Seven and a Half Years in the Far West* (1843; Indiana Centennial ed., Princeton, 1916); it is full of information about folk attitudes toward education in the old Midwest.

children should not form too high an estimate of the uses of mind. Ruth Miller Elson's recent researches in the content of nineteenth-century schoolbooks indicate that the compilers of school readers tried to inculcate in the children attitudes toward intellect, art, and learning which, we have already seen, were widely prevalent in adult society.[14] The old school readers contained a considerable proportion of good literature, but even at their best the selections were hardly chosen because they would inculcate the values of creative intellect.

As Mrs. Elson remarks, the primary intellectual value these books embodied was utility. As an early reader said: "We are all scholars of useful knowledge." Jedidiah Morse's famous geography boasted: "While many other nations are wasting the brilliant efforts of genius in monuments of ingenious folly, to perpetuate their pride, the Americans, according to the true spirit of republicanism, are employed almost entirely in works of public and private utility." Authors of schoolbooks were proud of the democratic diffusion of knowledge in America and were quite content to pay the price of not having so many advanced or profound scholars. "There are none of those splendid establishments such as Oxford and Cambridge in which immense salaries maintain the professors of literature in monastic idleness. . . . The People of this country have not yet been inclined to make much literary display—they have rather aimed at works of general utility." A similar pride was expressed that American colleges and universities, unlike those of Europe, were not devoted simply to the acquisition of knowledge but to the moral cultivation of their students. The American college was complacently portrayed as a place designed to form character and inculcate sound principle rather than to lead to the pursuit of truth.

The common school was thought to have been designed for a similar purpose. "Little children," said Alice Cary in a selection used in a third reader of 1882, "you must seek rather to be good than wise." "Man's intellect," said another writer,

[14] I am much enlightened by Mrs. Elson's article, "American Schoolbooks and 'Culture' in the Nineteenth Century," *Mississippi Valley Historical Review*, Vol. XLVI (December, 1959), pp. 411–34; the quotations in the following paragraphs are taken from this essay, pp. 413, 414, 417, 419, 421, 422, 425, 434.

"is not man's sole nor best adorning." The virtues of the heart were consistently exalted over those of the head, and this preference found its way into the hero literature of the school readers. European heroes might be haughty aristocrats, soldiers destructive on the battlefield, or "great scholars who were pensioned flatterers of power, and poets, who profaned the high gift of genius to pamper the vices of a corrupted court." But American heroes were notable as simple, sincere men of high character. Washington, a central figure in this literature, was portrayed in some of the books as an example both of the self-made man and of the practical man with little use for the intellectual life. "He was more solid than brilliant, and had more judgment than genius. He had great dread of public life, cared little for books, and possessed no library," said a history book of the 1880's and 1890's. Even Franklin was not depicted as one of the intellectual leaders of the eighteenth century, or as a distinguished scientist at home in the capitals of the world and among its aristocracies, but rather as an exemplar of the self-made man and the author of catch-penny maxims about thrift and industry.

The highbrow sources anthologized in the readers consisted of materials that would confirm these sentiments. Anti-intellectual quotations from Wordsworth were prominent in the first half of the century, and from Emerson in the second half. A fifth reader of 1884 quoted Emerson's "Goodbye":

> I laugh at the lore and the pride of man,
> At the sophist schools, and the learned clan;
> For what are they all in their high conceit,
> When man in the bush with God may meet?

There was a certain bias, too, against the idea of intellectual pleasure; the standard injunctions against novel-reading were repeated; and the notion was on occasion set forth that reading for pleasure is an altogether bad business: "A book which is torn and mutilated is abused, but one which is merely read for enjoyment is misused." Mrs. Elson concludes, from an intensive analysis of these readers, that "anti-intellectualism is not only not new in American civilization, but that it is thoroughly imbedded in the school books that have been read by generations of pupils since the beginning of the republic."

This downgrading of intellect was not compensated by any high regard for the arts. Music and the fine arts appeared primarily in connection with discussions of the self-made artist or of national monuments or with exaltation of American art. What seemed to be important to the compilers of school readers was not the aesthetic content of an artist's work but his career as evidence of the virtues of assiduous application. Benjamin West was portrayed as having been too poor as a boy to buy paint brushes and as having plucked hairs from his cat's tail to enable himself to paint: "Thus we see that, by industry, ingenuity, and perseverance, a little American boy became the most distinguished painter of his day in England." But if a career in art could be a means of disciplining character, it also had its dangers. An excerpt from the eighteenth-century English moralist, Hannah More, was exhumed to suggest "that in all polished countries an entire devotedness to the fine arts has been one grand source of the corruption of women . . . and while corruption brought on by an excessive cultivation of the arts has contributed its full share to the decline of states, it has always furnished an infallible symptom of their impending fall." The Italians were commonly held up as an example of a people whose distinguished achievements in the arts went hand in hand with an unsound national character. As time went on, it should be said, the school readers showed an increasing disposition to point to the development of American art and letters as an answer to European critics of American culture. Art, linked to national pride and conceived as an instrument, was at least acceptable.

We cannot know, of course, how much impact the content of school readers had on the minds of children. But any child who accepted the attitudes prevalent in these books would have come to think of scholarship and the fine arts as embellishments identified with the inferior society of Europe, would have thought of art primarily with regard to its services to nationality, and would have judged it almost entirely by its contributions to character. As Mrs. Elson puts it, he would grow up "to be honest, industrious, religious, and moral. He would be a useful citizen untouched by the effeminate and perhaps even dangerous influence of the arts or scholarship." The concept of culture presented in his readers had prepared him for "a life devoted to the pursuit of material success and a perfected character, but a life in which intellectual and artistic achievements would seem important only when they could be made to subserve some useful purpose."

These gleanings from the school readers suggest a clearer definition of the American faith in education as it was manifested during the nineteenth century. Perhaps the most touching aspect of this faith was the benevolent determination that education should not be exclusive, that it should be universally accessible. With impressive success this determination was executed: the schools were made into powerful agencies for the diffusion of social and economic opportunities. Americans were somewhat less certain about what the internal, qualitative standards of education should be and, in so far as they could define these standards, had difficulty in implementing them on the large scale on which their educational efforts were conceived. The function of education in inculcating usable skills and in broadening social opportunities was always clear. The value of developing the mind for intellectual or imaginative achievement or even contemplative enjoyment was considerably less clear and less subject to common agreement. Many Americans were troubled by the suspicion that an education of this kind was suitable only to the leisured classes, to aristocracies, to the European past; that its usefulness was less evident than its possible dangers; that an undue concern with the development of mind was a form of arrogance or narcissism which one would expect to find mainly in the morally corrupt.

4

American reluctance to accept intellectual values in the educational process could hardly have been overcome by a strong, respected teaching profession, since such a profession did not exist. Popular attitudes did not call for the development of such a profession, but even if they had, the conditions of American life made it difficult to recruit and train a first-rate professional corps.

The figure of the schoolteacher may well be taken as a central symbol in any modern society. The teacher is, or at least

can be, the first more or less full-time, professional representative of the life of the mind who enters into the experience
of most children; and the feeling the child entertains toward
the teacher, his awareness of the community's regard for the
teacher, are focal points in the formation of his early, rudimentary notions about learning. This is, of course, somewhat less
important in the primary school, where the essential work is
the inculcation of elementary skills, than it is in the secondary
school, where the rapidly awakening mind of the child begins
to be engaged with the world of ideas. At any level, however,
from the primary grades to the university, the teacher is not
merely an instructor but a potential personal model for his (or
her) pupils and a living clue to the attitudes that prevail in the
adult world. From teachers children derive much of their sense
of the way in which the mind is cultivated; from observing how
their teachers are esteemed and rewarded they quickly sense
how society looks upon the teacher's role.

In countries where the intellectual functions of education
are highly valued, like France, Germany, and the Scandinavian
countries, the teacher, especially the secondary-school teacher,
is likely to be an important local figure representing a personal and vocational ideal worthy of emulation. There it seems
worth becoming a teacher because what the teacher does is
worth doing and is handsomely recognized. The intellectually
alert and cultivated teacher may have a particular importance
for intelligent children whose home environment is not highly
cultivated; such children have no alternative source of mental stimulation. All too often, however, in the history of the
United States, the schoolteacher has been in no position to
serve as a model for an introduction to the intellectual life.
Too often he has not only no claims to an intellectual life of
his own, but not even an adequate workmanlike competence
in the skills he is supposed to impart. Regardless of his own
quality, his low pay and common lack of personal freedom have
caused the teacher's role to be associated with exploitation and
intimidation.

That American teachers are not well rewarded or esteemed
is almost universally recognized in contemporary comment.
A few years ago Marion Folsom, then Secretary of Health,

Education, and Welfare, observed that the "national disgrace" of our teachers' salaries reflected "the lack of respect accorded to teaching by the public."[15] Reminders of this situation constantly appear in the press. One day the public learns that a city in Michigan pays its teachers $400 a year less than its garbage collectors; another that a group of teachers in Florida, finding that the governor pays his cook $3,600 a year, have written to point out that the cook is paid more than many of the state's college-educated teachers.[16] Like other Americans, teachers live better in absolute terms than their European counterparts, but their annual salaries, relative to the per capita income of their country, have been lower than those of teachers in every country of the Western world, except Canada. The American teacher's average annual salary in 1949 stood in a ratio of 1.9 to the per capita income; the comparable figure was 2.5 in England, 5.1 in France, 4.7 in the West German Republic, 3.1 in Italy, 3.2 in Denmark, and 3.6 in Sweden.[17]

The status of schoolteaching as an occupation is lower in this country than elsewhere, and it is far lower than that of the professions in the United States. Characteristically, as Myron Lieberman remarks, teachers are recruited "from the top of the lower half of the population." Upper and upper-middle class persons almost universally reject teaching as a vocation. Teachers frequently resort, during the school year or their summer "vacations," to low-status jobs to supplement their teaching incomes; they work as waitresses, bartenders, housekeepers, janitors, farm hands, checkroom attendants, milkmen, common laborers, and the like. They come from culturally constricted lower- or middle-class homes, where the *Saturday Evening Post* or the *Reader's Digest* is likely to be the

[15] *The New York Times*, November 3, 1957.
[16] Ibid., March 24, 1957.
[17] Myron Lieberman: *Education as a Profession* (New York, 1956), p. 383; chapter 12 of this work is informative on the economic position of American teachers. The comparative disadvantage of American teachers registered in these figures does not take into account a variety of valuable non-salaried forms of compensation available elsewhere, like retirement allowances and free medical treatment.

characteristic reading matter.[18] For most teachers, their jobs, inadequate though they are, represent some improvement over the economic position of their parents, and they will, in turn, do still better by their children, who will be better educated than they are.

There is reason to believe, despite the sensationalism of *The Blackboard Jungle* and the obviously chaotic conditions of many urban slum schools, that the personal rapport between teachers and pupils in American secondary schools is good; it is particularly good among middle- and upper-class children, who are responsive to the educational goals of the schools and who tend to be favored by the teachers over lower-class children even when the latter show equal ability. But the important fact is that American adolescents have more sympathy than admiration for their teachers. They know that their teachers are ill-paid and they are quick to agree that teachers should be better paid. The more ambitious and able among them also conclude that schoolteaching is not for them.[19] In this way, the mediocrity of the teaching profession tends to perpetuate itself. In so far as the teacher stands before his pupils as a surrogate of the intellectual life and its rewards, he unwittingly makes this life appear altogether unattractive.

The unenviable situation of the teacher can be traced back to the earliest days of our history. The educational enthusiasm of the American people was never keen enough to dispose them to support their teachers very well. In part this seems to have reflected a common Anglo-American attitude toward the teaching function, which was sharply different from that prevailing

[18]The best brief discussion of the occupational status of teachers is that of Lieberman: op. cit., chapter 14. There are studies indicating that teachers enjoy a higher social status than I have indicated, but they are based upon opinion polling, a technique which in my opinion yields very poor results on matters of status. On the position of teachers, see also the excellent and rather neglected book by Willard Waller: *The Sociology of Teaching* (New York, 1932).
[19]On the attitude of teen-agers toward their teachers, see H. H. Remmers and D. H. Radler: *The American Teenager* (Indianapolis, 1957); on class factors in the relations between teachers and pupils, see August B. Hollingshead: *Elmtown's Youth* (New York, 1949); and W. Lloyd Warner, Robert J. Havighurst, and Martin B. Loeb: *Who Shall Be Educated?* (New York, 1944).

on the European Continent.[20] In any case, the market in qualified labor was always a problem here, and early American communities had intense difficulties in finding and keeping suitable
schoolmasters. In colonial times there was a limited supply of
educated men, and they were blessed with too many opportunities to be content to settle for what the average community was willing to pay a schoolmaster. Various solutions were
tried. Some elementary education was conducted by women in
"dame schools," usually private but sometimes partly or largely
paid for out of public funds; though it was not until well on in
the nineteenth century that American communities generally
turned to women for their supply of schoolteachers. In some
towns the minister doubled as a schoolmaster; or the schoolmaster doubled as a local man of all work, with a variety of
civic and church duties ranging from ringing the church bells
to serving as the local scribe, the town crier, or the town clerk.
Others accepted the fact that a permanent schoolmaster was all
but an impossibility and employed briefly a series of ambitious
young men who were on the way to other careers, perhaps in
the ministry or the law. Thus, many communities were able
temporarily to secure able teachers of good character, but the
very transience of their role seemed to establish the point that
teaching was no better than a way station in life for a man of
real ability and character.

Men permanently fixed in the role of schoolmaster seem
often to have been of indifferent quality and extraordinarily

[20]Presumably the labor market was somewhat different in England in the early
nineteenth century, but the social and economic conditions of teachers in
public education seem less enviable than that of Americans. See Asher Tropp:
The School Teachers (London, 1957). Somewhat revealing in this connection
was the remark of one of Her Majesty's Inspectors, H. S. Tremenheere, on
a visit to the United States in the 1850's. He wrote: "Any one from England
visiting those schools would be also greatly struck with the very high social
position, *considering the nature of their employment*, of the teachers, male and
female. . . ." *Notes on Public Subjects Made during a Tour in the United States
and Canada* (London, 1852), pp. 57–8. I believe the phrase I have italicized
here would have been intelligible to English and American readers and quite
mystifying to most readers on the Continent. For another English observer,
who found the status of American teachers high, though their pay was equally
bad as in England, see Francis Adams: *The Free School System of the United
States* (London, 1875), especially pp. 176–8, 181–2, 194–5, 197–8, 238.

ill-suited for the job. Perhaps it is because only the pathological aspects of a situation usually make historical news that
Willard S. Elsbree, writing about the character of the colonial schoolmaster, in his history, *The American Teacher*, tells
us mainly about drunkenness, slander, profanity, lawsuits, and
seductions.[21] But it is also suggestive that colonial communities
sometimes had to resort to indentured servants for teachers. A
Delaware minister observed, around 1725, that "when a ship
arrives in the river, it is a common expression with those who
stand in need of an instructor for their children, *let us go and
buy a school master*." In 1776 the *Maryland Journal* advertised
that a ship had just arrived at Baltimore from Belfast and Cork,
and enumerated among its products for sale "various Irish
commodities, among which are school masters, beef, pork, and
potatoes." It was about the same time that the Connecticut
press printed an advertisement offering a reward for a runaway
described as "a school-master, of a pale complexion, with short
hair. He has the itch very bad, and sore legs." Disabled men
were frequently turned into schoolteachers for lack of anything
better to do with them. The town of Albany in 1673 added
a local baker to its existing staff of three teachers because, it
said, "he was impotent in his hand."[22] Although such choices
may have been motivated by a misplaced philanthropy, they
also reflected a persistent difficulty in finding qualified men.
Massachusetts alone stood out as having enough educated
men so that a significant proportion of college graduates were
schoolmasters.

Although competent and dedicated schoolmasters could be
found from time to time, the misfits seem to have been so
conspicuous that they set an unflattering image of the teaching
profession. "The truth is," an observer wrote in 1725, "the office and character of such a person is generally very mean and
contemptible here, and it cannot be other ways 'til the public
takes the Education of Children into their mature consideration."[23] The tradition seems to have persisted well on into the

[21] *The American Teacher* (New York, 1939), chapter 2.
[22] Howard K. Beale: *A History of Freedom of Teaching in American Schools*
(New York, 1941), pp. 11–12; Elsbree: op. cit., pp. 26–7, 34.
[23] Beale: op. cit., p. 13.

nineteenth century, when we find this sad confession: "The man who was disabled to such an extent that he could not engage in manual labor—who was lame, too fat, too feeble, had the phthisic or had fits or was too lazy to work—well, they usually made schoolmasters out of these, and thus got what work they could out of them." There was a train of stereotypes of this order: the one-eyed or one-legged teacher, the teacher who had been driven out of the ministry by his weakness for drink, the lame teacher, the misplaced fiddler, and "the teacher who got drunk on Saturday and whipped the entire school on Monday."[24]

The concern of serious educators with the caliber of teachers was general and knew no bounds of geography. James Gordon Carter, describing the Massachusetts schools as they were in 1824, declared that[25] the men teachers could be divided into three classes: (1) Those who thought teaching easier and possibly more remunerative than common labor. (2) Those who were acquiring a good education, and who took up teaching as a temporary employment, either to earn money for necessities or to give themselves time to choose a regular profession. (3) Those who, conscious of weakness, despaired of distinction or even the means of subsistence by other employments: "If a young man be moral enough to keep out of State prison, he will find no difficulty in getting approbation for a schoolmaster."

Some years later President Joseph Caldwell of the University of North Carolina waxed indignant about the recruitment of the schoolteachers of his state:[26]

> Is a man constitutionally and habitually indolent, a burden upon all from whom he can extract support? Then there is one way of shaking him off, let us make him a schoolmaster. To teach school is, in the opinion of many, little else than sitting

---

[24] R. Carlyle Buley: op. cit., Vol. II, pp. 370–1.

[25] James G. Carter: *The Schools of Massachusetts in 1824*, Old South Leaflets No. 135, pp. 15–16, 19, 21.

[26] Beale: op. cit., p. 93; cf. the early treatise on teaching, Samuel Hall's *Lectures on School-Keeping* (Boston, 1829), especially pp. 26–8. On the condition of the teaching profession in the Southwest ("The great mass of our teachers are mere adventurers"), see Philip Lindsley in Richard Hofstadter and Wilson Smith, eds.: *American Higher Education: A Documentary History* (Chicago, 1961), Vol. I, pp. 332–3.

still and doing nothing. Has any man wasted all his property, or ended in debt by indiscretion and misconduct? The business of school-keeping stands wide open for his reception, and here he sinks to the bottom, for want of capacity to support himself. Has any one ruined himself, and done all he could to corrupt others, by dissipation, drinking, seduction, and a course of irregularities? Nay, has he returned from prison after an ignominious atonement for some violation of the laws? He is destitute of character and cannot be trusted, but presently he opens a school and the children are seen flocking into it, for if he is willing to act in that capacity, we shall all admit that as he can read and write, and cypher to the square root, he will make an excellent schoolmaster.

And what, after all, was the dominant stereotype of the schoolmaster in American literature if not Washington Irving's Ichabod Crane?

The cognomen of Crane was not inapplicable to his person. He was tall, but exceedingly lank, with narrow shoulders, long arms and legs, hands that dangled a mile out of his sleeves, feet that might have served for shovels, and his whole frame most loosely hung together. His head was small, and flat at the top, with huge ears, large, green, glassy eyes, and a long, snip nose, so that it looked like a weather-cock perched upon his spindle neck to tell which way the wind blew. To see him striding along the profile of a hill on a windy day, with his clothes bagging and fluttering about him, one might have mistaken him for the genius of Famine descending upon the earth or some scarecrow eloped from a cornfield.

As Irving portrayed him, Ichabod Crane was not altogether a bad fellow. In the course of boarding around, he did what he could to make himself agreeable to the families of the farmers, undertook a wide variety of chores and dandled and petted the young children. Among the women of the community he cut a figure of some importance, being somewhat more cultivated than the bumpkins they ordinarily met. But this "odd mixture of small shrewdness and simple credulity" was no hero to the men, and when Brom Bones in his ghastly masquerade frightened Ichabod out of town and smashed a pumpkin on his credulous head, he was passing the symbolic judgment of the American male community on the old-time schoolmaster.

5

Complaints such as those of Caldwell and Carter, men who hoped to work some educational reform, probably exaggerated the case; but if they did, they only reflected a stereotype of the teacher that had fixed itself in the mind of the country. A vicious circle had been drawn. American communities had found it hard to find, train, or pay for good teachers. They settled for what they could get, and what they got was a high proportion of misfits and incompetents. They tended to conclude that teaching was a trade which attracted rascals, and, having so concluded, they were reluctant to pay the rascals more than they were worth. To be sure, there is evidence that the competent schoolteacher of good character was eagerly welcomed when he could be found, and soon earned a status in the community higher than that of his colleagues elsewhere; but it was a long time before any considerable effort could be made to improve the caliber of teachers generally.

What helped American education to break out of the vicious circle was the development of the graded primary school and the emergence of the woman teacher. The graded school, a response to the educational problems of the largest cities, began to develop in the 1820's and had become prevalent by 1860. In the latter year most cities had such schools, which pupils entered at about six and could leave at fourteen. The graded school, modeled largely on the German system, made possible smaller classrooms holding more homogeneous groups of pupils and did much to put American teaching on a respectable basis. It also increased the need for teachers and opened the trade to women. Until 1830, most teachers had been men, and women had dealt mainly with very small children and summer classes. The notion prevailed that women were inadequate to the disciplinary problems of the schoolroom, especially in large classes and more advanced age groups. The emergence of the graded school provided a partial answer to these objections. Opponents of women teachers were still to be heard in many communities, but they were often easily silenced when it was pointed out that women teachers could be paid one third or one half as much as men. Here was one answer to the great American quest to educate everybody but to do it cheaply. By

1860 women teachers outnumbered men in some states, and the Civil War accelerated the replacement of men. By 1870 it is estimated that women constituted almost sixty per cent of the teaching force, and their numbers were increasing rapidly. By 1900 over seventy per cent of teachers were women, and in another quarter of a century the figure reached a peak of over eighty-three per cent.[27]

Acceptance of the woman teacher solved the problem of character as well as that of cost, since it was possible to find a fair supply of admirable young girls to work at low pay and to keep them at work as teachers only so long as their personal conduct met the rigid and sometimes puritanical standards set by school boards. But it did not altogether solve the problem of competence. The new teachers were characteristically very young and poorly prepared. For a long time there were practically no public facilities to give them specialized training, and private seminaries for the purpose were not numerous. European countries experimented with the training of teachers for more than a century before the United States gave much thought to it. Horace Mann was instrumental in establishing the first public normal school in Massachusetts in 1839; but at the beginning of the Civil War there were only a dozen such institutions. They proliferated rapidly after 1862; yet at the end of the century they were still unable to keep pace with the rapidly growing demand for teachers. In 1898 only a small proportion of new teachers—perhaps about one fifth—was taken from public or private schools of this order.

Moreover, the training these schools offered was not very exalted. Their admissions standards were haphazard, and even as late as 1900 a high-school diploma was seldom considered a prerequisite of entrance. Two years of high-school work, or the equivalent, was usually the prelude to two or three years of normal school. The four-year normal school became prevalent only after 1920, by which time it was beginning to be superseded by the teachers' college. Even in 1930, a survey by the

[27]Elsbree: op. cit., pp. 194–208, 553–4. By 1956 the figure had fallen to seventy-three per cent. Women school teachers received about two thirds the salaries of men in rural areas. In the cities, where pay was higher for both, they tended at first to get only a little more than one third of the salaries of men.

United States Office of Education showed that only eighteen per cent of the country's current graduates of teachers' colleges and normal schools had had four-year courses. Two thirds of them were products of one-year or two-year curricula.[28]

In spite of the considerable effort made by American communities to meet the demand for competent teachers around the turn of the century and afterwards, they were engaged in a taxing race with the explosive growth of the school population; and the excess of demand over supply in the market for teachers militated against efforts to raise standards of preparation. The best estimates for 1919–20 indicate that half of America's schoolteachers were under twenty-five, half served in the schools for not more than four or five years, and half had had no more than four years of education beyond the eighth grade. A period of rapid improvement at least in the quantitative dimension of teacher education ensued in the next several years. But in 1933, when the United States Office of Education published its *National Survey of the Education of Teachers*, it found that only ten per cent of the elementary teachers of the country, and only fifty-six per cent of the junior high-school teachers and eighty-five per cent of the senior high-school teachers, had B.A. degrees. Education beyond the B.A. degree was almost negligible except among senior high-school teachers, of whom a little more than one sixth had taken their M.A.'s. A comparison of teacher education in America and in selected countries of Western Europe showed the United States to be at some considerable disadvantage, significantly behind England and far behind France, Germany, and Sweden. "What inspires grave concern," wrote the authors of the survey, "is the fact that students in general and important groups of teachers in particular were not much more intelligent than a cross-section of the population at large."[29]

[28]Elsbree: op. cit., pp. 311–34.
[29]E. S. Evenden: "Summary and Interpretation," *National Survey of the Education of Teachers*, Vol. VI (Washington, 1935), pp. 32, 49, 89. For later information on the caliber of persons entering education, see Henry Chauncey: "The Use of Selective Service College Qualification Test in the Deferment of College Students," *Science*, Vol. CXVI (July 25, 1952), pp. 73–9. See also Lieberman: op. cit., pp. 227–31.

To what extent able students stayed out of teaching because
of its poor rewards and to what extent because of the nonsense
that figured so prominently in teacher education, it is difficult
to say. That teachers did not have enough training in the subjects they intended to teach was clear enough; but even more
striking was the fact that, however prepared they might be in
the field of their major interest, their chances of teaching in
that field were no better than fair. The survey's collation of
existing studies showed that a high-school teacher with a good
preparation in an academic subject had hardly better than a
fifty per cent chance of being assigned to teach it. In part this
may have been a consequence of administrative negligence, but
mainly it was attributable to the large number of uneconomi-
cally small high schools about which James Bryant Conant was
still complaining in 1959.[30]

As one looks at the history of teacher training in the United
States, one can hardly escape Elsbree's conclusion that "in our
efforts to supply enough teachers for the public schools we
have sacrificed quality for quantity."[31] The prevailing assumption was that everyone should get a common-school education, and on the whole this was realized, outside the South.
But the country could not or would not make the massive
effort that would have been necessary to supply highly trained
teachers for this attempt to educate everybody. The search for
cheap teachers was perennial. Schoolteachers were considered
to be public officers, and it was part of the American egalitarian philosophy that the salaries of public officers should not
be too high. In colonial times salaries of schoolmasters, which
varied widely, seem on the whole to have been roughly on a

---

[30]On the strength of his observations, Conant concluded that "unless a graduating class contains at least one hundred students, classes in advanced subjects
and separate sections within all classes become impossible except with extrava-
gantly high costs." His survey showed that 73.9 per cent of the country's high
schools had twelfth-grade enrollments of less than a hundred, and that 31.8
per cent of the twelfth-grade pupils were in such schools. *The American High
School Today* (New York, 1959), pp. 37–8, 77–85, 132–3. Of course, an important
reason for the failure to make good use of the academic specialities of teachers
was the practice of specifying requirements in education courses for teachers'
certificates but paying insufficient attention to academic requirements.
[31]Op. cit., p. 334.

par with or below the wages of skilled laborers and distinctly below those of professional men. In 1843 Horace Mann, after making a survey of wages of various occupational groups in a Massachusetts community, reported that skilled workers were getting from fifty to a hundred per cent more than was being paid to any of the district schoolteachers of the same town. He found women teachers getting less than women factory workers. A New Jersey school administrator in 1855 believed that although teachers were generally "miserably qualified for their duties," they were "even better prepared than they can afford to be." It was absurd, he pointed out, to expect men of ability and promise to work for a teacher's pay, and chiefly for this reason "the very name of teacher has been, and is yet to some extent, a term of reproach." Many a farmer would pay a better price for shoeing his horse than he would "to obtain a suitable individual to mould and form the character of his child."[32]

Certainly what was lacking in salary was not made up in dignity or status. Moreover, the growing numerical preponderance of the woman teacher, which did so much to cure the teaching profession of the taint of bad character, created a new and serious problem. Elsewhere in the world the ideal prevails —and the actual recruitment of teachers by and large conforms to it—that men should play a vital role in education generally, and a preponderant role in secondary education. The United States is the only country in the Westernized world that has put its elementary education almost exclusively in the hands of women and its secondary education largely so. In 1953 this country stood almost alone among the nations of the world in the feminization of its teaching: women constituted ninety-three per cent of its primary teachers and sixty per cent of its secondary teachers. Only one country in Western Europe (Italy, with fifty-two per cent) employed women for more than half of its secondary-school personnel.[33]

---

[32] Ibid., p. 273; for Mann, see pp. 279–80.
[33] Lieberman: op. cit., p. 244, gives figures for twenty-five countries. Four Western countries, the United Kingdom, France, West Germany, and Canada, ranged from thirty-four per cent female secondary teachers to forty-five per cent—the average being forty-one per cent. In the U.S.S.R., sixty per cent of primary and forty-five per cent of secondary school teachers are women. See ibid., pp. 241–55, for a discussion of this problem.

The point is not, of course, that women are inferior to men as teachers (in fact, at some levels, and particularly in the lower grades of the elementary school, there is reason to think that women teachers are preferable). But in America, where teaching has been identified as a feminine profession, it does not offer men the stature of a fully legitimate male role. The American masculine conviction that education and culture are feminine concerns is thus confirmed, and no doubt partly shaped, by the experiences of boys in school. There are often not enough male models or idols among their teachers whose performance will convey the sense that the world of mind is legitimately male, who can give them masculine examples of intellectual inquiry or cultural life, and who can be regarded as sufficiently successful and important in the world to make it conceivable for vigorous boys to enter teaching themselves for a livelihood. The boys grow up thinking of men teachers as somewhat effeminate and treat them with a curious mixture of genteel deference (of the sort due to women) and hearty male condescension.[34] In a certain constricted sense, the male teacher may be respected, but he is not "one of the boys."

[34] See, for example, the incident recounted by Waller: op. cit., pp. 49–50. "It has been said," Waller remarks, "that no woman and no Negro is ever fully admitted to the white man's world. Perhaps we should add men teachers to the list of the excluded." The problem is somewhat complicated by the aura of sexlessness that hangs over the public image of the teaching profession, and by the long-prevailing prejudice against the married woman teacher. Nineteenth-century America was dominated by a curious conviction, probably somewhat dissipated in the more recent past, that teachers ought to be oddities in their personal lives—a conviction that was easy to enforce in small towns. No doubt the conviction had been quickened by unhappy experiences with the schoolmaster-scamp, but it seems also to have been shaped by the desire to have children schooled by sexual ciphers. This desire lingered to torment many a perfectly innocent girl even in our own time, and where imposed put hopeless restrictions on the lives of well-intentioned schoolmasters. See the touching letter of protest written in 1852 by a schoolmaster against efforts to prevent him from walking to and from school with his female assistant. Elsbree: op. cit., pp. 300–2. Howard Beale's *Are American Teachers Free?* has ample information on the personal restrictions imposed on teachers. I particularly like a pledge forced on all teachers in a Southern community in 1927, in which one of a number of promises was: "I promise not to fall in love, to become engaged or secretly married." Waller: op. cit., p. 43. Even today, Martin Mayer observes: "It is an interesting fact that most European schools are for boys or girls, but the teachers mingle freely, regardless of sex; most American schools

But this question of the maleness of the teacher's role is only a small part of a large problem. In the nineteenth century men had all too often entered schoolteaching either transiently—as a step on the way to becoming lawyers, ministers, politicians, or college professors—or as a final confession of failure in more worthwhile occupations. Even today, surveys show, the ablest men tend to enter teaching in the expectation that they will become educational administrators or leave the field entirely. In recent decades a new area has opened up which may drain able men, and women as well, out of the public secondary school: the emergence of large numbers of heavily attended junior or community colleges has made it possible for enterprising teachers with an extra increment of ability and training to step up from the high school, or sidestep it altogether, in favor of an institution which offers an easier way of life as well as better pay and more prestige. There, however, some of the instruction they offer will be of a kind which could as well be offered in an efficient, first-rate secondary school. Giving the thirteenth and fourteenth years of public education a separate institutional setting may have a variety of advantages, but it does not in itself add to the total store of the country's teaching talents. In its pursuit of an adequate supply of well-trained teachers, the nation is caught in a kind of academic treadmill. The more adequate the rewards become in the upper echelons of education—in the colleges and junior colleges—and the higher the proportion of the young population that attends such institutions, the greater their capacity becomes to pull talent out of the lower levels of the system. It remains difficult to find enough trained talent to educate large masses in a society that does not make teaching attractive.

---

are co-educational, but the teachers are rigidly segregated by sex during their time off." *The Schools* (New York, 1961), p. 4. Finally, the prevailing old-time prejudice against the married woman teacher, commonly carried to the point of compulsory job severance for teachers who marry, used to confine the female side of the profession in many places to spinsters and very young girls. For the reasons usually invoked for barring married women, see D. W. Peters: *The Status of the Married Woman Teacher* (New York, 1934).

CHAPTER XIII

The Road to Life Adjustment

THE APPEARANCE within professional education of an influential anti-intellectualist movement is one of the striking features of American thought. To understand this movement, which has its most significant consequences in the education of adolescents, one must look at the main changes in public education since 1870. It was in the 1870's that this country began to develop free public secondary education on a large scale, and only in the twentieth century that the public high school became a mass institution.

Here certain peculiarities of American education are of the first importance—above all, its democratic assumptions and the universality of its aims. Outside the United States it is not assumed that all children should be schooled for so many years or so uniformly. The educational systems of most European countries were frankly tailored to their class systems, although they have become less so in our time. In Europe children are generally schooled together only until the age of ten or eleven; after that they go separate ways in specialized schools, or at least in specialized curricula. After fourteen, about eighty per cent are finished with their formal education and the rest enter academic pre-university schools. In the United States children must be in school until the age of sixteen or more, and a larger portion of them are sent to college than in European countries are sent to academic secondary schools. Americans also prefer to keep their secondary-school children in school under a single roof, usually the comprehensive community high school, and on a single educational track (though not in a uniform curriculum). They are not, ideally, meant to be separated, either socially or academically, according to their social class; though the relentless social realities of poverty and ethnic prejudice intervene to preserve most of the class selectivity that our democratic educational philosophy repudiates. In any case, the decision as to a child's ultimate vocational destiny does not have to be made so early in this country as elsewhere, if only because it is not institutionalized by the demands of early educational classification. In the United States specialized preparation even for the professions is postponed to graduate education or at best to the last two years of college. American education serves larger numbers for a longer period of time. It is more universal, more democratic, more leisurely in pace, less rigorous. It is also more wasteful: class-oriented systems are prodigal of the talents of the underprivileged; American education tends to be prodigal of talent generally.

The difference in structure was not always so great, especially in secondary schooling. Before the mass public high school emerged, American practice in secondary education was less in keeping with our democratic theory than with the selective European idea. During the nineteenth century, public education for most Americans ended with the last years of the graded primary school, if not earlier. Free education beyond the primary-school years was established only in the three decades after 1870. Before 1870, the class system, here as well as in Europe, was a primary determinant of the schooling children would get after the age of about thirteen or fourteen. Well-to-do parents, who could afford tuition and who had intellectual or professional aspirations for their children, could send them to private academies, which were often boarding schools. Since the days of Franklin these academies had offered a mixture of the traditional and the "practical": there was a liberal, classical course, founded upon Latin, Greek, and mathematics, commonly supplemented by science and history; but in many schools the students had an option between the "Latin course" and the "English course," the latter being a more "practical" and modern curriculum stressing subjects supposedly useful in business. Academies varied widely in quality, duplicating, in their lowest ranges, some of the work of the common schools and, at their peak, some of the work of the colleges. The best of them were so good that graduates who went on to college were likely to be bored by repetition in the first and even the second college year.[1]

---

[1]It was not necessary to go to an academy to prepare for college; one could also enroll in the "preparatory departments" many colleges maintained to give prospective applicants enough grounding in classics, mathematics, and English

The disparity between the country's moral commitment to educational democracy and its heavy reliance upon private schools for secondary education did not escape the attention of educational critics. On one side there were the generally available public primary schools; on the other, the rapidly proliferating colleges and universities—not free, of course, but cheap and undiscriminating. In between there was an extensive gap, filled by a few pioneering public high schools, but mainly by the private academies, of which it is estimated there were in 1850 about six thousand. As early as the 1830's the academies were denounced as exclusive, aristocratic, and un-American. For a nation already committed to the free common-school system, the extension of this system into the years of secondary education seemed a logical and necessary step. Industry was growing; vocational life was becoming more complex. Skills were more in demand, and it seemed that both utility and equality would be well served by free public education in the secondary years.

Advocates of the public high school had strong moral and vocational arguments, and the legal basis for their proposals already existed in the common-school system. Shortsightedness and mean-spirited tax-consciousness stood in their way, but not for long. The number of public high schools began to rise with great and increasing rapidity after 1860. From 1890 (when usable enrollment figures begin) to 1940, the total enrollment of the high schools nearly doubled every decade. By 1910, thirty-five per cent of the seventeen-year-olds were in school; today the figure has reached over seventy per cent. At this tempo the high school has become an institution which nearly all American youth enter, and from which about two thirds graduate.

Whatever may be said about the qualitative performance of the American high school, which varies widely from place to

---

to enter upon the college course proper. The existence of a large number of such preparatory departments—as late as 1889, 335 of 400 colleges still had them—is testimony of the inadequacy of the secondary schools to prepare for college requirements those who wanted to go to college. Edgar B. Wesley: *N.E.A.: The First Hundred Years* (New York, 1957), p. 95. On the academies, see E. E. Brown: *The Making of Our Middle Schools* (New York, 1903).

place, no one is likely to deny that the free secondary education of youth was a signal accomplishment in the history of
education, a remarkable token of our desire to make schooling
an instrument of mass opportunity and social mobility. Since I
shall have much to say about the high school's curricular problems, it seems important here to stress the positive value of this
achievement, and to note that, in its democratic features, if not
in its educational standards, the American high school has been
to some degree emulated by European school systems in the
last generation.

The development of the high school into a mass institution
drastically altered its character. At the turn of the century the
relatively small clientele of the high school was still highly selective. Its pupils were there, in the main, because they wanted
to be, because they and their parents had seized upon the unusual opportunity the high school offered. It is often said, but
mistakenly, that the high school, sixty or seventy years ago, was
primarily attended by those preparing for college. This was less
true than it has come to be in the past fifteen years. Today approximately half the high-school graduates enter college—an
astonishing proportion. I do not know what proportion of the
high-school graduates actually entered college at the turn of
the century, but there is information as to how many of them
were so *prepared*. In 1891, twenty-nine per cent of the graduates were. By 1910 the portion of those prepared for college
and other advanced institutions was forty-nine per cent. The
figure has fluctuated since.[2]

The great change which has affected the high school is that,
whereas once it was altogether voluntary, and for this reason
quite selective, it is now, at least for those sixteen and under,
compulsory and unselective. During the very years when the
high school began its most phenomenal growth, the Progressives and trade unionists were assailing the old industrial evil of
child labor. One of the most effective devices to counteract this

[2]See John F. Latimer: *What's Happened to Our High Schools?* (Washington,
1958), pp. 75–8. For a penetrating brief account of the place of secondary
education in American society since 1870, see Martin Trow: "The Second
Transformation of American Secondary Education," *International Journal of
Comparative Sociology*, Vol. II (September, 1961), pp. 144–66.

practice was raising the terminal age for compulsory schooling. In 1890, twenty-seven states required compulsory attendance; by 1918 all states had such laws. Legislators also became more exigent in fixing the legal age for leaving school. In 1900 it was set at a mean age of fourteen years and five months in those states which then had such laws. By the 1920's it was close to the figure it has reached today—a mean age of sixteen years and three months. The welfare state and the powerful trade union, moreover, saw to it that these laws were increasingly enforced. The young had to be protected from exploitation; and their elders had to be protected by keeping the young out of the labor market.

Now, in an increasing measure, secondary-school pupils were not merely unselected but also unwilling; they were in high school not because they wanted further study but because the law forced them to go. The burden of obligation was shifted accordingly: whereas once the free high school offered a priceless opportunity to those who chose to take it, the high school now held a large captive audience that its administrators felt obliged to satisfy. As an educational committee of the American Youth Commission wrote in 1940: "Even where a pupil is of low ability it is to be remembered that his attendance at secondary school is due to causes which are not of his making, and proper provision for him is a right which he is justified in claiming from society."[3]

As the years went by, the schools filled with a growing proportion of doubtful, reluctant, or actually hostile pupils. It is a plausible conjecture that the average level of ability, as well as interest, declined. It became clear that the old academic curriculum could no longer be administered to a high-school population of millions in the same proportion as it had been to the 359,000 pupils of 1890. So long as public education had meant, largely, schooling in the primary grades, the American conviction that everyone can and should be educated was relatively easy to put into practice. But as soon as public education included secondary education, it began to be more doubtful that everyone could be educated, and quite certain that not

[3] *What the High Schools Ought to Teach* (Washington, 1940), pp. 11–12.

everyone could be educated in the same way. Beyond a doubt, change was in order.

The situation of school administrators can hardly fail to command our sympathies. Even in the 1920's, to a very large degree, they had been entrusted by the fiat of society with the management of quasi-custodial institutions. For custodial institutions the schools were, to the extent that they had to hold pupils uninterested in study but bound to the school by the laws. Moreover, the schools were under pressure not merely to fulfill the laws, but to become attractive enough to hold the voluntary allegiance of as large a proportion of the young for as long as they could.[4] Manfully settling down to their assignment, educators began to search for more and more courses which, however dubious their merits by traditional educational standards, might interest and attract the young. In time they became far less concerned with the type of mind the high school should produce or with the academic side of the curriculum. (Boys and girls who wanted to go to college would hang on in any case; it was the others they had to please.) Discussions of secondary education became more frequently interlarded with references to a new, decisive criterion of performance—"the holding power of the school."

The need to accept large numbers with varying goals and capacities and to exercise for many pupils a custodial function made it necessary for the schools to introduce variety into their curricula. The curriculum of the secondary school could hardly have been fixed at what it was in 1890 or 1910. But the issue posed for those who would guide public education was whether the academic content and intellectual standards of the school should be made as high as possible for each child, according to his will and his capacities, or whether there was good ground for abandoning any such end. To have striven seriously to keep up the intellectual content of the curriculum would have required a public and an educational profession

---

[4] This was, of course, accentuated by the effects of the great depression and the growing power of the trade unions. But even in 1918 the N.E.A. was advocating that normal children be educated to the age of eighteen. *Cardinal Principles of Secondary Education* (Washington, 1918), p. 30.

committed to intellectual values; it would have demanded much administrative ingenuity; and in many communities it would have called for much more generous financial support than the schools actually had.

But all this is rather in the nature of an imaginative exercise. The problem of numbers had hardly made its appearance before a movement began in professional education to exalt numbers over quality and the alleged demands of utility over intellectual development. Far from conceiving the mediocre, reluctant, or incapable student as an obstacle or a special problem in a school system devoted to educating the interested, the capable, and the gifted, American educators entered upon a crusade to exalt the academically uninterested or ungifted child into a kind of culture-hero. They were not content to say that the realities of American social life had made it necessary to compromise with the ideal of education as the development of formal learning and intellectual capacity. Instead, they militantly proclaimed that such education was archaic and futile and that the noblest end of a truly democratic system of education was to meet the child's immediate interests by offering him a series of immediate utilities. The history of this crusade, which culminated in the ill-fated life-adjustment movement of the 1940's and 1950's, demands our attention; for it illustrates in action certain widespread attitudes toward childhood and schooling, character and ambition, and the place of intellect in life.

2

The rise of the new interpretation of secondary education may be traced through a few examples of quasi-official statements by committees of the National Education Association and the United States Office of Education. These statements were, of course, not obligatory upon local school boards or superintendents. They represent the drift of educational thought without purporting to reflect exactly the changes actually being made in curricular policy.

Toward the close of the nineteenth century, two contrasting views of the purposes of the public high schools were already competing for dominance.[5] The original view, which remained in the ascendant until 1910 and continued to have much influence for at least another decade, might be dubbed old-fashioned or intellectually serious, depending upon one's sympathy for it. The high school, it was believed by those who held this view, should above all discipline and develop the minds of its pupils through the study of academic subject matter. Its well-informed advocates were quite aware that a majority of pupils were not being educated beyond high school; but they argued that the same education which was good preparation for college was good preparation for life. Therefore, the goal of secondary education, even when college was not the child's end-in-view, should be "mind culture," as it was called by William T. Harris, one of the leading advocates of the academic curriculum. Spokesmen of this school were intensely concerned that the pupil, whatever the precise content of his curriculum, should pursue every subject that he studied long enough to gain some serious mastery of its content. (In the continuing debate over education the ideal of "mastery" of subject matter dominates the thinking of the intellectualists, whereas the ideal of meeting the "needs" of children becomes the central conception of their opponents.)

The most memorable document expressing academic views on secondary education was the famous report of the National Education Association's Committee of Ten in 1893. This committee was created to consider the chaos in the relations between colleges and secondary schools and to make recommendations about the high-school curriculum. Its personnel, which reflected the dominance of college educators, compares interestingly with that of later committees set up for similar purposes. The chairman was President Charles William Eliot of Harvard, and the members were William T. Harris, the Commissioner of Education, four other college or university presidents, the headmasters of two outstanding private secondary schools, a college professor, and only one public high-school principal. A series of subsidiary conferences set up by the committee to consider the place of the major academic disciplines

[5]The general outlines of this controversy are sketched in Wesley: *N.E.A.: The First Hundred Years*, pp. 66–77.

in high-school programs also showed college authorities in full control. Although many principals and headmasters took part, there were also university professors whose names are recognizable in American intellectual history—Benjamin I. Wheeler, George Lyman Kittredge, Florian Cajori, Simon Newcomb, Ira Remsen, Charles K. Adams, Edward G. Bourne, Albert B. Hart, James Harvey Robinson, and Woodrow Wilson.

The Committee of Ten recommended to the secondary schools a set of four alternative courses—a classical course, a Latin-scientific course, a modern languages course, and an English course. These curricula varied chiefly in accordance with their relative emphasis on the classics, modern languages, and English. But all demanded, as a minimum, four years of English, four years of a foreign language, three years of history, three years of mathematics, and three years of science. In this respect, the contemporary reader will notice the close similarity between this program and that recently recommended by James Bryant Conant, in his survey of the high schools, as a minimum for "academically talented boys and girls."[6]

The curricula designed by the Committee of Ten show that they thought of the secondary school as an agency for academic training. But they did not make the mistake of thinking that these schools were simply college-preparatory institutions. Quite the contrary, the committee almost exaggerated the opposite point of view when it said that "only an insignificant percentage" of high-school graduates went on to colleges or scientific schools. The main function of high schools, said the committee, was "to prepare for the duties of life" not for college, but if the main subjects were all "taught consecutively and thoroughly, and . . . all carried on in the same spirit . . . all used for training the powers of observation, memory, expression, and reasoning," the pupil would receive an intellectual

[6]Conant recommended four years of mathematics, four years of a foreign language, three years of science, four years of English, and three years of history and social studies. In addition, he thought many academically talented pupils might wish to take a second foreign language or an additional course in social studies. *The American High School Today* (New York, 1959), p. 57. Conant felt that minimum requirements for graduation for *all* students should include at least one year of science, four years of English, and three or four years of social studies.

training that was good for college preparation or for life: "Every subject which is taught at all in a secondary school should be taught in the same way and to the same extent to every pupil so long as he pursues it, no matter what the probable destination of the pupil may be or at what point his education is to cease."[7]

The committee recognized that it would be desirable to find a larger place for music and art in the high schools, but it apparently found these of secondary importance and proposed to leave decisions about them to local initiative. Its members proposed, among other things, that language instruction should be begun in the last four years of the elementary schools, a suggestion that was lamentably ignored. They realized that an improvement in the caliber of secondary-school teachers was necessary to execute their recommendations effectively; they urged that the low standards of the normal schools be raised and suggested that universities might interest themselves more deeply in the adequate training of teachers.

In fact, the high schools had not developed entirely in accordance with the committee's conservative ideal. Even in the 1880's there had been a considerable efflorescence of programs of practical and vocational training—manual training, shop work, and other such studies. Increasingly, those primarily concerned with the management and curricula of high schools became restive about the continuing dominance of the academic ideal, which they considered arose from the high schools' "slavery" and "subjugation" to the colleges. The high schools, they insisted, were meant to educate citizens in their public responsibilities and to train workers for industry, not to supply the colleges with freshmen. The high

[7]For relevant passages, see *Report of the Committee on Secondary School Studies Appointed at the Meeting of the National Education Association, July 9, 1892* (Washington, 1893), pp. 8–11, 16–17, 34–47, 51–5. The committee believed that what pupils learned in high school should permit them to go to college if they should later make that decision. Colleges and scientific schools should be able to admit any graduate of a good secondary course, regardless of his program. At the present time, the committee found, this was impossible because the pupil might have gone through a high-school course "of a very feeble and scrappy nature—studying a little of many subjects and not much of any one, getting, perhaps, a little information in a variety of fields, but nothing which can be called a thorough training."

schools should be looked upon as "people's colleges" and not as the colleges' preparatory schools. Democratic principles, they thought, demanded much greater consideration for the needs of the children who did not go to college. Regard for these needs and a due respect for the principles of child development demanded that the ideal of "mastery" be dropped, and that youth should be free to test and sample and select among subjects, deriving from some what they could retain and use, and passing on to others. To hold children rigorously to the pursuit of particular subjects would only increase the danger of their dropping out of school.

A number of historical forces were working in favor of the new educators. Business, when it was favorably disposed to education, tended to applaud and encourage what they were doing. The sheer weight of growing student numbers increased the appeal of their arguments. Their invocation of democratic principles, which were undergoing a resurgence after 1890, struck a responsive chord in the public. The colleges themselves were so numerous, so competitive, so heterogeneous in quality that in their hunger for more students they were far from vigilant in upholding the admissions standards of the past. They were, moreover, still uncertain about the value of their own inherited classical curriculum, and had been experimenting since about 1870 with the elective system and a broader program of studies. College and university educators were no longer vitally interested in the problems of secondary education, and reformers in that field were left with little authoritative criticism or opposition. The staffs of high schools were increasingly supplied by the new state teachers' colleges; and high-school textbooks, once written by college authorities in their fields, were now written by public-school superintendents, high-school principals and supervisors, or by students of educational methods.

3

The slight concession made by the Committee of Ten to new schools of thought was hardly enough to allay discontent. It had not been able to foresee the extraordinary growth of the high-school population which would soon occur or the increasing heterogeneity of the student body. It quickly became evident that the curricular views of the Committee of Ten were losing ground. By 1908, when the N.E.A. was fast growing in size and influence, it adopted a resolution repudiating the notion that public high schools should be chiefly "fitting schools" for colleges (which, to be sure, had not been the contention of the Committee of Ten), urging that the high schools "be adapted to the general needs, both intellectual and industrial, of their students," and suggesting that colleges and universities too should adapt their courses to such needs.[8] The balance was tipping: the high schools were no longer to be expected to suit the colleges; instead, the colleges ought to try to resemble or accommodate the high schools.

In 1911, a new committee of the N.E.A., the Committee of Nine on the Articulation of High School and College, submitted another report, which shows that a revolution in educational thought was well on its way. The change in personnel was itself revealing. Gone were the eminent college presidents and distinguished professors of the 1893 report; gone, too, were the headmasters of elite secondary schools. The chairman of the Committee of Nine was a teacher at the Manual Training High School of Brooklyn, and no authority on any basic academic subject matter was on his committee, which consisted of school superintendents, commissioners, and principals, together with one professor of education and one dean of college faculties. Whereas the Committee of Ten had been a group of university men attempting to design curricula for the secondary schools, the new Committee of Nine was a group of men from public secondary schools, putting pressure through the N.E.A. on the colleges: "The requirement of four years of work in any particular subject, as a condition of admission to a higher institution, unless that subject be one that may properly be required of all high-school students, is illogical and should, in the judgment of this committee, be immediately discontinued."

The task of the high school, the Committee of Nine argued, "was to lay the foundations of good citizenship and to help in the wise choice of a vocation," but it should also develop unique and special individual gifts, which was "quite as important as the development of the common elements of culture."

[8]N.E.A. *Proceedings*, 1908, p. 39.

The schools were urged to exploit the dominant interests "that each boy and girl has at the time." The committee questioned the notion that liberal education should precede the vocational: "An organic conception of education demands the early introduction of training for individual usefulness, thereby blending the liberal and the vocational. . . ." It urged much greater attention to the role of mechanic arts, agriculture, and "household science" as rational elements in the education of all boys and girls. Because of the traditional conception of college preparation, the public high schools were[9]

> responsible for leading tens of thousands of boys and girls away from the pursuits for which they are adapted and in which they are needed, to other pursuits for which they are not adapted and in which they are not needed. By means of exclusively bookish curricula false ideals of culture are developed. A chasm is created between the producers of material wealth and the distributors and consumers thereof.

By 1918 the "liberation" of secondary education from college ideals and university control seems to have been consummated, at least on the level of theory, even if not yet in the nation's high-school curricula. In that year the N.E.A.'s Commission on the Reorganization of Secondary Education formulated the goals of American schools in a document about which Professor Edgar B. Wesley has remarked that "probably no publication in the history of education ever surpassed this little five cent thirty-two page booklet in importance."[10] This statement, *Cardinal Principles of Secondary Education*, was given a kind of official endorsement by the United States Bureau of Education, which printed and distributed an edition of 130,000 copies. It became the occasion of a nation-wide discussion of educational policy, and some teacher-training institutions regarded it so highly that they required their pupils to memorize essential portions (thus violating a central canon of the new educational doctrines).

The new commission pointed out that more than two thirds of those who entered the four-year high school did not

---

[9]"Report of the Committee of Nine on the Articulation of High School and College," N.E.A. *Proceedings*, 1911, pp. 559–61.
[10]Wesley: op. cit., p. 75.

graduate and that, among those who did, a very large proportion did not go to college. The needs of these pupils must
not be neglected. The old concept of general intellectual discipline as an aim of education must be re-examined. Individual
differences in capacities and attitudes needed more attention.
New laws of learning must be brought to bear to test subject
matter and teaching methods; these could no longer be judged
"primarily in terms of the demands of any subject as a logically
organized science."[11] In short, the inner structure of various
disciplines was to be demoted as an educational criterion and
supplanted by greater deference to the laws of learning, then
presumably being discovered.

Moreover, the child was now conceived not as a mind to
be developed but as a citizen to be trained by the schools.
The new educators believed that one should not be content
to expect good citizenship as a result of having more informed
and intellectually competent citizens but that one must directly
teach citizenship and democracy and civic virtues. The commission drew up a set of educational objectives in which neither the development of intellectual capacity nor the mastery
of secondary academic subject matter was even mentioned. It
was the business of the schools, the commission said, to serve
democracy by developing in each pupil the powers that would
enable him to act as a citizen. "It follows, therefore, that worthy home-membership, vocation, and citizenship demand attention as three of the leading objectives." The commission
went on: "This Commission, therefore, regards the following
as the main objectives of education: 1. Health. 2. Command
of fundamental processes. [It became clear in context that this
meant elementary skills in the three R's, in which the commission, no doubt quite rightly, felt that continued instruction
was now needed at the secondary level.] 3. Worthy home-
membership. 4. Vocation. 5. Citizenship. 6. Worthy use of leisure. 7. Ethical character."

With justice, the commission argued that the traditional high
school had done too little to encourage interests in music, art,
and the drama—but instead of presenting these as a desirable

[11]Quotations in this and the following paragraph are from *Cardinal Principles
of Secondary Education, passim.*

supplement to an intellectually ordered curriculum, it offered them as an alternative. The high school, it said, "has so exclusively sought intellectual discipline that it has seldom treated literature, art, and music so as to evoke right emotional response and produce positive enjoyment." Moreover, the high school placed too much emphasis on intensive pursuit of most subjects. Studies should be reorganized so that a single year of work in a subject would be "of definite value to those who go no further." This would make the courses "better adapted to the needs both of those who continue and of those who drop out of school."

The commission further argued that the colleges and universities should follow the example of the secondary schools in considering themselves obliged to become mass institutions and to arrange their offerings accordingly. "The conception that higher education should be limited to the few is destined to disappear in the interests of democracy," it said prophetically. This meant, among other things, that high-school graduates should be able to go on to college not only with liberal but with vocational interests, and that, once in college, they should still be able to take whatever form of education they can which affords "profit to themselves and to society." In order to accommodate larger numbers, colleges and universities should supplant academic studies to some degree with advanced vocational education. The commission urged that all normal children should be encouraged to stay in school, on full time if possible, to the age of eighteen.

The commission quite reasonably urged that the high-school curriculum should be differentiated to offer a wide range of alternatives; but its way of expressing this objective was revealing:

> The basis of differentiation should be, in the broad sense of the term, vocational, thus justifying the names commonly given, such as agricultural, business, clerical, industrial, fine-arts, and household-arts curriculums. Provision should be made also for those having distinctively academic interests and needs.

Provision should be made also. This reference to the academic side of the high school as being hardly more than incidental to its main purposes captures in a phrase how far the dominant thinking on the subject had gone in the quarter century since the report of the Committee of Ten.

The rhetoric of the commission's report made it clear that the members thought of themselves as recommending not an educational retreat but rather an advance toward the realization of democratic ideals. The report is breathless with the idealism of the Progressive era and the war—with the hope of making the educational world safe for democracy and bringing a full measure of opportunity to every child. Our secondary education, the commission argued, "must aim at nothing less than complete and worthy living for all youth"—thus far had education gone beyond such a limited objective as developing the powers of the mind. Secondary-school teachers were urged to "strive to explore the inner meaning of the great democratic movement now struggling for supremacy." While trying to develop the distinctive excellences of individuals and various groups, the high school "must be equally zealous to develop those common ideas, common ideals, and common modes of thought, feeling, and action, whereby America, through a rich, unified, common life, may render her truest service to a world seeking for democracy among men and nations."

4

The Cardinal Principles of Secondary Education, which set the tone and expressed the ideas current in all subsequent quasi-official statements on secondary-educational policy down to the life-adjustment movement, appeared in the midst of a focal change in the dimensions of the high-school population. Standing at 1.1 million in 1910, it rose swiftly to 4.8 million in 1930. When the document itself was published, all states had adopted compulsory education laws—Mississippi, in 1918, being the last to straggle into line.

The schools, moreover, had been coping for some years, and were to continue to cope for many years more, with the task of educating the children of that vast tidal wave of immigration that had come into the country between 1880 and the First World War. By 1911, for example, 57.5 per cent of the children in the public schools of thirty-seven of the largest cities were of foreign-born parentage.[12] The immigrant children, now entering secondary schools, brought the same problems of class, of language, of Americanization that they had brought to the primary schools. Giving such children cues to American life, and often to elementary hygiene, seemed more important to many school superintendents than developing their minds along the lines of the older education; and it is not difficult to understand the belief that a thorough grounding in Latin was not a primary need, say, of a Polish immigrant's child in Buffalo. Immigrant parents, unfamiliar with American ways, were inadequate guides to what their children needed to know, and the schools were now thrust into the parental role. Moreover, the children, exposed to Yankee schoolmarms in the morning, were expected to become instruments of Americanization by bringing home in the afternoon instructions in conduct and hygiene that their parents would take to heart. Against this background one may better understand the emphasis of the *Cardinal Principles* on "worthy home-membership," "health," and "citizenship." The common complaint that the modern school tries to assume too many of the functions of other social agencies, including the family, derives in good measure from the response of educators to this problem.

Changes in professional education also favored new views of secondary education. The normal schools, which had been at best a kind of stop-gap in teacher education, were now being replaced by teachers' colleges and schools of education. Both the business of training teachers and the study of the educational process were becoming specialized and professional. Unfortunately, as Lawrence Cremin has observed, the schools of education and the teachers' colleges grew up with a high degree of autonomy.[13] Increasingly, the mental world of the professional educationist became separated from that of the academic scholar. The cleavage between Teachers College and the rest of Columbia University—which led to the quip that 120th

[12]See, on this general subject, Alan M. Thomas, Jr.: "American Education and the Immigrant," *Teachers College Record*, Vol. LV (October, 1953–May, 1954), pp. 253–67.
[13]*The Transformation of the School* (New York, 1961), p. 176.

Street is the widest street in the world—became symbolic of a larger cleavage in the structure of American education. Professional educators were left to develop their ideas without being subjected to the intellectual discipline that might have come out of a dialogue with university scholars. In sharp contrast to the days of Eliot, academicians scornfully turned away from the problems of primary and secondary education, which they now saw as the preoccupation of dullards; too many educationists were happy to see them withdraw, leaving the educationists free to realize their own credos in making plans for the middle and lower schools.

At the time the ideas of the *Cardinal Principles* were supplanting those of the Committee of Ten, a new kind of educational orthodoxy was taking form, founded in good part upon appeals to "democracy" and "science." John Dewey was the master of those for whom educational democracy was the central issue; Edward Lee Thorndike of those for whom it was the application to education of "what science tells us." It was not commonly believed that there was any problem in this union of democracy and science, for a widespread conviction existed (not shared, it must be said, by Thorndike) that there must be a kind of pre-established harmony between them—that since both are good, both must serve the same ends and lead to the same conclusions; that there exists, in fact, a kind of science of democracy.[14]

Concerning the use, or misuse, as it may be, of Dewey's ideas, I shall have something to say in the next chapter. Here it is important, however, to say a word about the use of the techniques of testing and the various kinds of psychological and educational research. Much of this research was, of course, valuable, though of necessity tentative. The difficulty was that what should have been simply a continuous inquiry had a way, in the fervent atmosphere of professional education, of being exalted into a faith—not so much by those who were actually doing research as by those who were hungry to find its practical

[14]For a witty analysis of the same blend of science and democracy in recent American political thought, see Bernard Crick: *The American Science of Politics* (London, 1959).

applications and eager to invoke the authority of science on behalf of their various crusades. The American mind seems extremely vulnerable to the belief that any alleged knowledge which can be expressed in figures is in fact as final and exact as the figures in which it is expressed. Army testing in the First World War is a case in point. It was very quickly and very widely believed that the Army Alpha tests had actually measured intelligence; that they made it possible to assign mental ages; that mental ages, or intelligence as reported by tests, are fixed; that vast numbers of Americans had a mental age of only fourteen; and that therefore the educational system must be coping with hordes of more or less backward children.[15] Although such overconfident interpretations of these tests were never without sharp critics—among them John Dewey—the misuse of tests seems to be a recurrent factor in American education. Of course, the credence given to the low view of human intelligence that some people derived from the tests could lead to quite different conclusions. To those not enchanted by the American democratic credo—and Edward Lee Thorndike himself was among them—the effect of mental testing was to encourage elitist views.[16] But for those whose commitment to "democratic" values was imperturbable, the supposed discovery of the mental limitations of the masses only encouraged a search for methods and content in education that would suit the needs of the intellectually mediocre or unmotivated. Paraphrasing Lincoln, the educators-for-democracy might have said that God must love the slow learners because he made so many of them. Elitists might coldly turn their backs on these large numbers, but democratic educators, embracing them as a fond mother embraces her handicapped child, would attempt to build the curriculum upon their supposed needs.

It is impossible here to stress too much the impetus given to the new educational creed by the moral atmosphere of Progressivism, for this creed was developed in an atmosphere of warm

[15]See the good brief account of the early impact of testing in Cremin: *The Transformation of the School*, pp. 185–92.
[16]See, for example, Merle Curti's discussion of the views of Thorndike in *The Social Ideas of American Educators* (New York, 1935), chapter 14.

philanthropy and breathless idealism in which the needs of the less gifted and the underprivileged commanded a generous response. Educators had spent many years discovering a canon and a creed, whose validity seemed now more certain than ever because it seemed to be vindicated morally by the needs of democracy and intellectually by the findings of science. More frequently than ever, the rallying cries of this creed were heard in the land: education for democracy, education for citizenship, the needs and interests of the child, education for all youth. There is an element of moral overstrain and a curious lack of humor among American educationists which will perhaps always remain a mystery to those more worldly minds that are locked out of their mental universe. The more humdrum the task the educationists have to undertake, the nobler and more exalted their music grows. When they see a chance to introduce a new course in family living or home economics, they begin to tune the fiddles of their idealism. When they feel they are about to establish the school janitor's right to be treated with respect, they grow starry-eyed and increase their tempo. And when they are trying to assure that the location of the school toilets will be so clearly marked that the dullest child can find them, they grow dizzy with exaltation and launch into wild cadenzas about democracy and self-realization.

The silly season in educational writing had now opened. The professionalization of education put a premium upon the sober treatment of every mundane problem, and the educators began to indulge in solemn and pathetic parodies of the pedantry of academic scholarship. Not liking to think of themselves as mere advocates of low-grade utilities, they began to develop the art of clothing every proposal, no matter how simple, common-sense, and sound, in the raiments of the most noble social or educational objectives. Was it desirable, for example, for the schools to teach children something about safety? If so, a school principal could read a pretentious paper to the N.E.A., not on the important but perhaps routine business of teaching children to be careful, but on the exalted theme, "The Value of Instruction in Accident Prevention as a Factor in Unifying the Curriculum." It had now become possible to pretend that the vital thing was not to keep youngsters from getting burnt or hit by vehicles but that teaching them about such things infused all learning with higher values—although in this case, at least, the speaker conceded, in closing: "Let me say that instruction in accident prevention serves not only to unify the curriculum but also to reduce accidents."[17]

5

A traveler from a foreign country whose knowledge of American education was confined to the writings of educational reformers might well have envisaged a rigid, unchanging secondary-school system chained to the demands of colleges and universities, fixed upon old ideas of academic study, and unreceptive to the wide variety of pupils it had in charge. The speaker at the N.E.A. meeting of 1920 who lamented that the high schools were still "saturated with college requirement rules and standards" and filled with principals and teachers "trained in academic lore and possessing only the academic viewpoint"[18] sounded a note of complaint that has never ceased to echo in the writings of the new educationists. In fact, the innovators had very considerable success in dismantling the old academic curriculum of the high school. It is hard for an amateur, and perhaps even a professional in education, to know how much of this was justified. But two things it does seem possible to assert: first, that curricular change after 1910 was little short of revolutionary; and second, that by the 1940's and 1950's the demands of the life-adjustment educators for the destruction of the academic curriculum had become practically insatiable.

The old academic curriculum, as endorsed by the Committee of Ten, reached its apogee around 1910. In that year more pupils were studying foreign languages or mathematics or science or English—any one of these—than *all* non-academic subjects combined. During the following forty-year span the academic subjects offered in the high-school curricula fell from about three fourths to about one fifth. Latin, taken in 1910 by 49 per cent of public high-school pupils in grades 9 to 12, fell by 1949 to 7.8 per cent. All modern-language enrollments fell from 84.1 per cent to 22 per cent. Algebra fell from 56.9 per

[17] N.E.A. *Proceedings*, 1920, pp. 204–5.
[18] Ibid., 1920, pp. 73–5.

cent to 26.8 per cent, and geometry from 30.9 per cent to 12.8 per cent; total mathematics enrollments from 89.7 per cent to 55 per cent. Total science enrollments, if one omits a new catch-all course entitled "general science," fell from 81.7 per cent to 33.3 per cent; or to 54.1 per cent if general science is included. English, though it almost held its own in purely quantitative terms, was much diluted in many school systems. The picture in history and social studies is too complex to render in figures, but changing enrollments made it more parochial both in space and in time—that is, it put greater stress on recent and American history, less on the remoter past and on European history.[19]

When the Committee of Ten examined the high-school curricula in 1893, it found that forty subjects were taught, but since of these thirteen were offered in very few schools, the basic curriculum was founded on twenty-seven subjects. By 1941 no less than 274 subjects were offered, and only 59 of these

[19] John F. Latimer, in *What's Happened to Our High Schools?*, has made a useful compilation of Office of Education statistics, and I have followed his presentation of the data; see especially chapters 4 and 7. It is important to note that enrollments thus put in percentages are not meant to conceal the fact that, with the immense growth in the high-school population, a larger number of the *nation's* youth could be studying some of these academic subjects even though a smaller portion of the *high-school* population was pursuing them. However, from 1933 to 1939 there occurred for the first time a drop not merely in the percentages of students studying certain subjects but in the *absolute* enrollments as well.

The consequences in one field, which happens to have been well surveyed, might be examined. During the Second World War the problems of secondary-school education in mathematics became a matter of some official concern. In 1941 the Naval Officers Training Corps reported that, of 4,200 candidates who were college freshmen, sixty-two per cent failed the arithmetic reasoning test. Only twenty-three per cent had had more than one and a half years of mathematics in high school. Later, a 1954 survey reported that sixty-two per cent of the nation's colleges had found it necessary to teach high-school algebra to entering freshmen. See I. L. Kandel: *American Education in the Twentieth Century* (Cambridge, Mass., 1957), p. 62; and H. S. Dyer, R. Kalin, and F. M. Lord: *Problems in Mathematical Education* (Princeton, 1956), p. 23. Many high schools appear to have been approaching the view, widespread among life-adjustment theorists, that foreign languages, algebra, geometry, and trigonometry have "relatively little value except as college preparation or except for a few college curricula," and that "therefore most of the instruction in those fields should be postponed until college." Harl R. Douglass: *Secondary Education for Life Adjustment of American Youth* (New York, 1952), p. 598.

could be classified as academic studies. What is perhaps most extraordinary is not this ten-fold multiplication of subjects, nor the fact that academic studies had fallen to about one fifth the number, but the response of educational theorists: they were convinced that academic studies were still cramping secondary education. In the life-adjustment movement, which flourished in the late 1940's and the 1950's with the encouragement of the United States Office of Education, there occurred an effort to mobilize the public secondary-school energies of the country to gear the educational system more closely to the needs of children who were held to be in some sense uneducable.[20]

   To some degree the life-adjustment movement was a consequence of the crisis in the morale of American youth which has been observable since the Second World War. But it was more than this: it was an attempt on the part of educational leaders and the United States Office of Education to make completely dominant the values of the crusade against intellectualism that had been going on since 1910. Looking at the country's secondary education shortly after the end of the Second World War, John W. Studebaker, then Commissioner of Education, observed that only about seven youths out of ten were entering senior high school (grades 10 to 12), and that fewer than four remained to graduate.[21] Despite the efforts made in the

[20]The term "uneducable" is, of course, not used by life-adjustment educators. It is my translation of what one is asserting about a youth in secondary school when one says that he can neither absorb an academic education nor learn a desirable trade.

[21]*Life Adjustment Education for Every Youth* (Washington, n. d. [1948?]), p. iii. This publication was issued by the Office of Education of the Federal Security Agency and was prepared in the Division of Secondary Education and the Division of Vocational Education. For the Prosser resolution and other statements of purpose in this repetitive document, cited in the following paragraphs, see pp. 2–5, 15*n*., 18*n*., 22, 48–52, 88–90, and *passim.*

   At the same time that the Office of Education was sponsoring life adjustment, the President's Commission on Higher Education was advocating, in its report of 1947, that the colleges themselves should no longer select "as their special clientele persons possessing verbal aptitudes and a capacity for grasping abstractions," and that they should give more attention to cultivating other aptitudes—"such as social sensitivity and versatility, artistic ability, motor skill and dexterity, and mechanical aptitude and ingenuity." *Higher Education for American Democracy: A Report of the President's Commission on Higher Education*, Vol. I (Washington, 1947), p. 32.

preceding forty years to increase the "holding power" of the schools, large numbers of youngsters were still uninterested in completing their secondary education. The effort to enrich the academic curriculum seemed to have failed in one of its main purposes; the suggestion was now made that the curriculum had not been enriched enough.

The life-adjustment movement proposed to remedy the situation by stimulating "the development of programs of education more in harmony with life-adjustment needs of all youth." This would be done by devising an education "which better equips all American youth to live democratically with satisfaction to themselves and profit to society as home members, workers, and citizens." At a national conference held in Chicago in May, 1947, the conferees adopted a resolution drafted by Dr. Charles A. Prosser, the director of Dunwoody Institute of Minneapolis, an agency of industrial education. In its original form (it was later slightly reworded in order "to avoid misinterpretation and misunderstanding"), this resolution expressed the belief of the members of the conference that the needs of the great majority of American youth were not being adequately served by secondary schools. Twenty per cent of them, it was said, were being prepared for college; another twenty per cent for skilled occupations. But the remaining sixty per cent, according to spokesmen for the crusade, were unfit for either of these programs and should be given education for life adjustment. The life-adjustment theorists were explicit about the qualities they attributed to the neglected sixty per cent who needed life-adjustment education. These were mainly children from unskilled and semi-skilled families who had low incomes and provided a poor cultural environment. They began school later than others, continued to be retarded in school, made low grades, scored lower on intelligence and achievement tests, lacked interest in school work, and were "less emotionally mature—nervous, feel less secure."

After having compiled this depressing list of the traits of their clientele, the authors of the Office of Education's first manual on Life Adjustment went on to say that "these characteristics are not intended to brand the group as in any sense inferior." The peculiar self-defeating version of "democracy" entertained by these educators somehow made it possible for them to assert that immature, insecure, nervous, retarded slow learners from poor cultural environments were "in no sense inferior" to more mature, secure, confident, gifted children from better cultural environments.[22] This verbal genuflection before "democracy" seems to have enabled them to conceal from themselves that they were, with breathtaking certainty, writing off the majority of the nation's children as being more or less uneducable—that is, in the terms of the Prosser resolution, unfit not just for the academic studies that prepare for college but even for programs of vocational education leading to "desirable skilled occupations." What kind of education would be suitable for this unfortunate majority? Certainly not intellectual development nor cumulative knowledge, but practical training in being family members, consumers, and citizens. They must be taught—the terms would have been familiar to any reader of the *Cardinal Principles*—"ethical and moral living"; home and family life; citizenship; the uses of leisure; how to take care of their health; "occupational adjustment." Here, as the authors of *Life Adjustment Education for Every Youth* put it, was "a philosophy of education which places life values above acquisition of knowledge." The conception, implicit in this observation, that knowledge has little or nothing to do with "life values," was an essential premise of the whole movement. Repeatedly, life-adjustment educators were to insist that intellectual training is of no use in solving the "real life problems" of ordinary youth.

6

The thinking behind the life-adjustment movement is difficult to exhume from the repetitive bulletins on the subject compiled by the Office of Education in Washington. But before

---

[22]That the capacities of such a large proportion of American youth should be so written off in the name of "democracy" is one of the more perplexing features of the movement. At least one of its supporters, however, faced up to its implications when he said that this neglected group lacks "aroused interests or pronounced aptitudes," but that this fact is "probably fortunate for a society having a large number of jobs to be done requiring no unusual aptitudes or interests." Edward K. Hankin: "The Crux of Life Adjustment Education," *Bulletin* of the National Association of Secondary-School Principals (November, 1953), p. 72. This is a possible point of view and a more realistic assessment of the implications of life-adjustment education. But it is hardly "democratic."

the movement had been so named, its fundamental notions had been set forth by Dr. Prosser himself, an experienced administrator in vocational education, when he delivered his Inglis Lecture at Harvard University in 1939.[23] Although there are in the published lecture occasional traces of the influence of John Dewey's passion for educational democracy, Prosser relied mainly upon psychological research, and he expressed a more fundamental piety for the findings of "science." (Life-adjustment educators would do anything in the name of science except encourage children to study it.) Thorndike and his followers had shown, Prosser imagined, that there is no such thing as intellectual discipline whose benefits can be transferred from one study, situation, or problem to another. "Nothing could be more certain than that science has proven false the doctrine of general education and its fundamental theory that memory or imagination or the reason or the will can be trained as a power." When this archaic notion is abandoned, as it must be, all that is left is education in various specifics. There is no such thing as general mechanical skill; there are only specific skills developed by practice and use. It is likewise with the mind. There is, for example, no such thing as the memory; there are only specific facts and ideas which have become available for recall because we have found use for them.

Contrary, then, to what had been believed by exponents of the older concept of education as the development of intellectual discipline, there are no general mental qualities to be developed; there are only specific things to be known. The usability and teachability of these things go hand in hand; the more immediately usable an item of knowledge is, the more readily it can be taught. The value of a school subject can be measured by the number of immediate, actual life situations to which it directly applies. The important thing, then, is not to teach pupils how to generalize, but to supply them directly with the information they need for daily living—for example, to teach them, not physiology, but how to keep physically fit. The traditional curriculum consists simply of studies that once

[23] *Secondary Education and Life* (Cambridge, Mass., 1939). The argument summarized in this and the following pages is largely in pp. 1–49; especially pp. 7–10, 15–16, 19–21, 31–5, 47–9.

were useful in this way but have ceased to be so. "The general rule seems to be that the younger any school study, the greater is its utilitarian value in affairs outside the schoolroom, and the older the study, the less the usefulness of its content in meeting the real demands of living." Students learn more readily and retain more of what they learn when the transfer of content from school to life is immediate and direct. It is, in fact, the very usefulness of a subject that determines its disciplinary value to the mind. "On all these counts business arithmetic is superior to plane or solid geometry; learning ways of keeping physically fit, to the study of French; learning the technique of selecting an occupation, to the study of algebra; simple science of everyday life, to geology; simple business English, to Elizabethan Classics."

It was an irresistible conclusion drawn from scientific research, said Prosser, that the best teaching material is "the life-adjustment and not the education-for-more education studies." Why, then, had the colleges and universities persisted in fastening unusable and unteachable traditional subjects on the secondary schools? Quite aside from the vested interests of teachers of these subjects, the main reason, he thought, was that the higher institutions had needed some device for selecting the abler pupils and eliminating the others. (The teaching of such subjects as languages and algebra had the function, one must believe, not of educating anyone, but simply of acting as hurdles that would trip up weaker pupils before they got to college.) This outmoded technique required four wasteful and expensive years of futile study in supposedly "disciplinary" subjects. The selection of pupils suited to college, Prosser thought, could now be made with infinitely more economy and accuracy in a few hours of mental testing. Perhaps, then, traditionalists, "as a sporting proposition," could be persuaded to drop at least half the academic curriculum for all students and keep only a few of the older studies in proportion to their surviving usefulness. On this criterion, "all foreign languages and all mathematics should be dropped from the list of required college-preparatory studies" in favor of the more usable subjects—physical science, English, and social studies.

Many new studies of direct-use value should be added to the curriculum: English of a severely practical kind, offering "communication skills"; literature dealing with modern life; science (only "qualitative" science) courses that would give youth "the simple science of everyday life," tell "how science increases our comfort . . . promotes our enjoyment of life . . . helps men get their work done . . . increases wealth"; practical business guidance and "simple economics for youth," supplemented perhaps by material on the "economic history of youth in the United States"; civics, focusing on "civic problems of youth" and on the local community; mathematics, consisting only of varieties of applied arithmetic; social studies, giving attention to "wholesome recreation in the community," amenities and manners, uses of leisure, social and family problems of youth, and the "social history of youth in the United States"; finally, of course, "experiences in the fine arts," and "experiences in the practical arts," and vocational education. In this way, the curriculum could be made to conform to the laws of learning discovered by modern psychological science, and all children would benefit to a much greater degree from their secondary schooling.[24]

In a rather crude form Prosser had here given expression to the conclusion drawn by many educationists from experimental psychology, that "science," by destroying the validity of the idea of mental discipline, had destroyed the basic assumption upon which the ideal of a liberal education was based. Prosser had this in mind when he asserted with such confidence that "*nothing could be more certain*" than that science had proven false the assumptions of general education. Behind this remarkable dogmatism there lies an interesting chapter in the history of ideas. The older ideal of a classical liberal education, as expressed in nineteenth-century America and elsewhere, had been based upon two assumptions. The first was the so-called faculty psychology. In this psychology, the mind was believed to be a substantive entity composed of a number of parts or "faculties" such as reason, imagination, memory, and the like. It was assumed that these faculties, like physical faculties, could be strengthened by exercise; and in

---

[24]For a later, full-scale, authoritative statement of the views of this school on the content of the curriculum, see Harold Alberty: *Reorganizing the High School Curriculum* (New York, 1953).

a liberal education, through constant mental discipline, they were gradually so strengthened. It was also generally believed that certain subjects had an established superiority as agents of mental discipline—above all, Latin, Greek, and mathematics. The purpose of developing competence in these subjects was not merely to lay the foundation for learning more Latin, Greek, or mathematics, but, far more important, to train the powers of the mind so that they would be more adequate for whatever task they might confront.[25]

In good time it was found that the faculty psychology did not hold up under philosophic analysis or the scientific study of the functions of mind. Moreover, with the immense growth in the body of knowledge and the corresponding expansion of the curriculum, the old confidence that the classical languages and mathematics had an exclusive place of honor in mental discipline seemed more and more a quaint parochial conceit.[26]

But most modern psychologists and educational theorists were aware that the decline of the faculty psychology and the classical-mathematical curriculum did not in itself put an end to the question whether such a thing as mental discipline is a realizable end of education. If mental discipline were, after all, meaningless, everything that had been done in the name of liberal education for centuries seemed to have been based on a miscalculation. The question whether the mind can be disciplined, or generally trained, survived the faculty psychology and took on a new, more specific form: can training exercised and developed in one mental operation develop a mental

[25]The classic statement in America of this view of mental discipline was the Yale Report of 1828, which originally appeared in *The American Journal of Science and Arts*, Vol. XV (January, 1829), pp. 297–351. It is largely reprinted in Hofstadter and Smith, eds.: *American Higher Education: A Documentary History*, Vol. I, pp. 275–91.

[26]It was also a conceit that served to justify a good deal of inferior pedagogy. There is overwhelming evidence, for example, that the classical languages were taught in the old-time college in a narrow grammarian's spirit, and not as a means of introducing students to the cultural life of classical antiquity. See Richard Hofstadter and Walter P. Metzger: *The Development of Academic Freedom in the United States* (New York, 1955), pp. 226–30; Richard Hofstadter and C. DeWitt Hardy: *The Development and Scope of Higher Education in the United States* (New York, 1952), chapter I and pp. 53–6.

facility that can be transferred to another? This general question could, of course, be broken down into endless specific ones: can acts of memorization (as William James asked in an early rudimentary experiment conducted on himself) facilitate other memorization? Can training in one form of sensory discrimination enhance other discriminations? Can the study of Latin facilitate the subsequent study of French? If a transfer of training did occur, a cumulation of such transfers over several years of a rigorous liberal education might produce a mind which was better trained *in general*. But if transfer of training did not take place, most of the cumulative academic studies were quite pointless outside the items of knowledge contained in these studies themselves.

At any rate, in the confidence that they could throw light on a question of central importance, experimental psychologists, spurred by Thorndike, began early in the twentieth century to seek experimental evidence on the transfer of training. Anyone who reads an account of these experiments might well conclude that they were focused on such limited aspects of the problem that they were pathetically inadequate; individually and collectively, they did not shed very much light on the grand question to which they were ultimately directed. However, as a consequence of a great many ingenious and often interesting experiments, evidence of a kind did begin to accumulate. Some of it, notably in two papers published by Thorndike in 1901 and 1924, was taken by educational thinkers to be decisive evidence against transfer of training in any degree considerable enough to vindicate the idea of mental discipline. This and similar evidence from other researchers was, in any case, seized upon by some educational theorists. As W. C. Bagley once remarked: "It was inevitable that any theory which justified or rationalized the loosening of standards should be received with favor," by those who, without deliberate intent, distorted experimental findings in the interest of their mission to reorganize the high schools to accommodate the masses.[27]

Actually the accumulating experimental evidence proved contradictory and confusing, and those educators who insisted

[27]W. C. Bagley: "The Significance of the Essentialist Movement in Educational Theory," *Classical Journal*, Vol. XXXIV (1939), p. 336.

that its lessons were altogether clear and that nothing was so certain as what it yielded were simply ignoring all findings that did not substantiate their views. Their misuse of experimental evidence, in fact, constitutes a major scandal in the history of educational thought. If a quantitative survey of the experiments means anything, these educators ignored the bulk of the material, for four of five of the experimental studies showed the presence of transfer under certain conditions. There seems to have been no point at which the preponderant opinion of outstanding experimental psychologists favored the anti-transfer views that were drawn upon by educationists like Prosser as conclusive on what "science has proven." Today, experimental psychology offers them no comfort. As Jerome Bruner summarizes it in his remarkable little book, *The Process of Education*: "Virtually all of the evidence of the last two decades on the nature of learning and transfer has indicated that . . . it is indeed a fact that massive general transfer can be achieved by appropriate learning, even to the degree that learning properly under optimum conditions leads one to 'learn how to learn.'"[28] Presumably, the ideal of a liberal education is still better vindicated by the educational experience of the human race than by experimental psychology; but in so far as such scientific inquiry is taken as a court of resort, its verdict is vastly more favorable to the views of those who believe in the possibility of mental discipline than it was represented to be by the educational prophets of life adjustment.

7

The life-adjustment movement stated, in an extreme form, the proposition toward which professional education had been moving for well over four decades: that in a system of mass secondary education, an academically serious training is an

---

[28]Jerome S. Bruner: *The Process of Education* (Cambridge, Mass., 1960), p. 6. The important consideration, as Bruner points out, is that the learner have a structural grasp of the matter which is learned. For the modern discussion of mental discipline and a brief review of the history of the experimental evidence, see Walter B. Kolesnik: *Mental Discipline in Modern Education* (Madison, 1958), especially chapter 3.

impossibility for more than a modest fraction of the student population. In setting the portion of uneducables with dogmatic certainty at sixty per cent, the spokesmen of this movement were taking such a strong position that some of their critics assumed the figure to be altogether arbitrary. Its source appears again to have been a touching faith in "science." In 1940, when Dr. Prosser, as a member of the National Youth Administration, was in close touch with Washington's view of the problems of youth, the psychologist, Lewis M. Terman, well known for his work in intelligence testing, estimated in a publication of the American Youth Commission, *How Fare American Youth?*, that an IQ of 110 is needed for success in traditional, classical, high-school curricula, and that sixty per cent of American youth rank below this IQ level. There is, in any case, a great discrepancy between this figure and the arithmetic of the life-adjustment educators.[29] But more important is the irresponsibility of trying to base the educational policy of an entire nation on any such finding. Psychologists do not agree (and were still heatedly debating in 1939) whether an individual's IQ is a permanently fixed genetic attribute; and there is now impressive experimental evidence that an individual IQ, given appropriate attention and pedagogy, can often be raised by 15 to 20 points or more. (Results can be particularly impressive when special attention is given to underprivileged children. In New York City's "Higher Horizons" program, many slum children with slightly subnormal or nearly retarded IQ's at the junior high-school level had both their IQ's and their academic performance raised so that they were acceptable in college and some even earned scholarships.) Moreover, the IQ alone would, in no case, be an infallible index to the ceiling of anyone's potential educational achievement; there are other variables, amenable to change, which it does not take into account, such as the caliber of teaching, the amount of schoolwork, and the pupil's morale and motivation. Psychologists and educators are far from being in precise agreement as to the

[29]That is, if Terman's findings are accepted, sixty per cent of American youth might be unfit for an academic high-school curriculum; but of these surely some considerable portion would be fit for the desirable trades mentioned in the Prosser resolution.

proportion of the students in our high schools who, even with today's teaching and low educational morale, can profit from an academic curriculum.[30]

Finally, the plausibility of the life-adjustment movement's view of the educability of the country's youth hinged upon ignoring secondary-educational accomplishments in other countries. It had become a commonplace argument of the new educationists that secondary curricula of the countries of Western Europe, being "aristocratic," class-bound, selective, and traditional, had no exemplary value for the democratic, universal, and forward-looking secondary education of the United States. American educators, therefore, preferred to ignore European educational history as a source of clues to educational policy and looked to "modern science" for practical guidance and to "democracy" for their moral inspiration. European education pointed to the outmoded past; science and democracy looked to the future. This way of thought has been jolted by scientific competition with the Soviet Union. Russian secondary education is neither so universal nor so egalitarian as our own. But it offers the example of an educational system which cannot quite be dismissed as aristocratic or traditional and which is none the less modeled largely upon the secondary systems of Western Europe; it demonstrates in a way that can no longer be conveniently ignored the availability of a demanding academic curriculum to large numbers.

By no means should it be imagined that the life-adjustment educators were content to stop with the assertion that their educational aims should be applied only to the neglected sixty per cent of youth at the bottom of the ladder. Here it would be a mistake to underestimate the crusading idealism

[30]For differing estimates of the distribution of academic ability and its implications for educational policy, see the Report of the President's Commission on Higher Education: *Higher Education for American Democracy*, Vol. I, p. 41; Byron S. Hollinshead: *Who Should Go to College* (New York, 1952), especially pp. 39–40; Dael Wolfle: *America's Resources of Specialized Talent* (New York, 1954); and Charles C. Cole, Jr.: *Encouraging Scientific Talent* (New York, 1956). "I am confident," writes one educational psychologist, "that with better teaching . . . half, or more, of the students in our high schools . . . can profit from it [the classical curriculum]." Paul Woodring: *A Fourth of a Nation* (New York, 1957), p. 49.

of this movement, which is nowhere so well illustrated as in Dr. Prosser's closing remarks to the 1947 Conference on Life Adjustment. "Never in all the history of education," he said, "has there been such a meeting as this . . . a meeting where people were so sincere in their belief that this was the golden opportunity to do something that would give to *all* American youth their educational heritage so long denied. What you have planned," Prosser assured the members, "is worth fighting for—it is worth dying for. . . . God Bless You All."

Accordingly, life-adjustment educators soon became convinced that their high educational ideals should be applied not merely to the neglected sixty per cent: what was good for them would be good for *all* American youth, however gifted. They were designing, as the authors of one life-adjustment pamphlet quite candidly admitted, nothing less than "a blueprint for a Utopian Secondary School"—a school which, they added, "could be operated only by teachers of rare genius."[31] As I. L. Kandel has sardonically remarked, the conviction of life adjustment was "that what is good for sixty per cent of the pupils attending high schools, and, according to reports, deriving no benefit from this stay, is also good for all pupils."[32] These crusaders had thus succeeded in standing on its head the assumption of universality once made by exponents of the classical curriculum. Formerly, it had been held that a liberal academic education was good for all pupils. Now it was argued that all pupils should in large measure get the kind of training originally conceived for the slow learner. American utility and American democracy would now be realized in the education of *all* youth. The life-adjustment movement would establish once and for all the idea that the slow learner is "in no sense" the inferior of the gifted, and the principle that all curricular subjects, like all children, are equal. "There is no aristocracy of 'subjects,'" said the Educational Policies Commission of the N.E.A. in 1952, describing the ideal rural school. "Mathematics

[31] *A Look Ahead in Secondary Education*, U.S. Office of Education (Washington, 1954), p. 76.
[32] *American Education in the Twentieth Century*, p. 156; cf. pp. 173–81. On the universalistic aspirations of the life-adjustment movement, see Mortimer Smith: *The Diminished Mind* (Chicago, 1954), p. 46.

and mechanics, art and agriculture, history and homemaking are all peers."[33]

In the name of utility, democracy, and science, many educators had come to embrace the supposedly uneducable or less educable child as the center of the secondary-school universe, relegating the talented child to the sidelines. One group of educationists, looking forward to the day when "the aristocratic, cultural tradition of education [will be] completely and finally abandoned," had this to say of pupils who showed unusual intellectual curiosity: "Any help we can give them should be theirs, but such favored people learn directly from their surroundings. Our efforts to teach them are quite incidental in their development. It is therefore unnecessary and futile for the schools to attempt to gear their programs to the needs of unusual people."[34] In this atmosphere, as Jerome Bruner puts it, "the top quarter of public school students, from which we must draw intellectual leadership in the next generation, is perhaps the group most neglected by our schools in the recent past."[35] This group has indeed been neglected by many educators and looked upon by some not as the hope or the challenge or the standard of aspiration for the educational system, but as a deviant, a side issue, a special problem, at times even a kind

[33] *Education for All American Youth, A Further Look* (Washington, 1952), p. 140.

[34] Charles M. MacConnell, Ernest O. Melby, Christian O. Arndt, and Leslee J. Bishop: *New Schools for a New Culture* (New York, 1953), pp. 154–5. In partial justification of this curious remark, it should be said that our secondary schools, *as they are now constituted*, often find it relatively difficult to do very much for talented and intellectually curious pupils.

[35] Bruner: op. cit., p. 10. Cf. James B. Conant: "In particular, we tend to overlook the especially gifted youth. We neither find him early enough, nor guide him properly, nor educate him adequately in our high schools." *Education in a Divided World* (Cambridge, Mass., 1948), p. 65; cf. p. 228. On the problems of educating the talented, see Frank O. Copley: *The American High School and the Talented Student* (Ann Arbor, 1961).

In the mid-1950's, about five per cent of the gifted were receiving special, formal attention in American schools. An earlier survey (1948) revealed that about 20,000 pupils were enrolled in special schools or classes for the gifted, about 87,000 in special schools or classes for the mentally deficient. For these and other figures on programs for the gifted, see Cole: *Encouraging Scientific Talent*, pp. 116–19.

of pathology. Possibly I exaggerate; but otherwise it is hard to understand how an official of the Office of Education could have written this insensitive passage:[36]

> A considerable number of children, estimated at about four million, deviate sufficiently from mental, physical, and behavioral norms to require special educational provision. Among them are the blind and the partially seeing, the deaf and the hard of hearing, the speech-defective, the crippled, the delicate, the epileptic, the mentally deficient, the socially maladjusted, *and the extraordinarily gifted.*

8

To ideas such as these, and especially to the claims of their advocates for universality, there has always been a good deal of resistance from parents, school boards, and teachers in many parts of the country. Nevertheless, to fit the views of the new education the curriculum of many a junior and senior high school has been "enriched" with new courses in band, chorus, driver education, human relations, home and family living, "homemaking," and consumer education. It has been possible for an American child to reach his majority in some communities without having had an opportunity to understand that the curricula available in his public high school are not everywhere regarded as an education, and may be wholly unsuited to his own aspirations. A few years ago President A. Whitney Griswold of Yale reported a case of a type altogether familiar to college-admissions officers. An apparently able and otherwise promising youth from a Midwestern city applied for admission to Yale but could not be considered because the academic part of his last two years of high school consisted only of two years of English and one of American history; the rest was made up of two years of chorus, two years of speech,

---

[36]Lloyd E. Blauch, Assistant Commissioner for Higher Education, United States Office of Education, writing in Mary Irwin, ed.: *American Universities and Colleges*, published by the American Council on Education (Washington, 1956), p. 8; italics added. It has been pointed out that the author was, after all, proposing special programs for the gifted, among others, but this consideration does not seem to me to mitigate the implications of this bizarre list of categories.

and one year each of typing, physical education, journalism, marriage and family, and personality problems.[37]

If one examines the character and content of the new courses introduced into the public high school and the rhetoric of the debate between older and newer schools of education, it becomes clear that what was at issue in the argument over life adjustment was in fact the educational aspect of the much more widely debated issue of mass culture. For certainly one of the things at issue in the schools was what kind of character and culture the large masses of high-school children could and should be prepared for. Traditional education had been founded upon a primary conviction about the value of the various subject-matter disciplines and on the assumption that the child, through some degree of mastery of academic subjects, would enlarge his mind for the general ends of life and establish his preparation for the professions or business or other desirable occupations. (It was assumed that vocational education could serve those who could not or would not enter into such competition.) Contrary to the allegations of the new educators, traditional education was not altogether unmindful of the child, but it assumed, on the whole, that he would find some pleasure in the mental activity which was offered him in an academically disciplined education and that he would gain satisfaction from his sense of accomplishment as he moved from stage to stage. In so far as the learning process was irksome to him, it assumed that the self-discipline that came from overcoming irksomeness would at least be a net gain. (No doubt some even went so far as to suggest that there was a high intrinsic value in irksomeness, on the assumption satirized in the remark that it does not matter what a boy studies so long as he doesn't like it; extreme statements of this point of view helped the new educators to draw an unattractive caricature of traditional education.) Politically the older education was conservative, in that it accepted the existing order of society and called upon the child to assert himself within its framework —which was largely that of nineteenth-century individualism. But it was also democratic in that it did not commonly assume,

[37] *Liberal Education and the Democratic Ideal* (New Haven, 1959), p. 29; the case was first reported by Griswold in 1954.

much less rejoice in the idea, that large numbers, from any class in society, were necessarily incapable by native endowment of entering with some degree of hope into the world of academic competition, mastery of subject matter, and discipline of mind and character.

The new education was also at bottom politically conservative, but its warm rhetoric about democracy, its philanthropic approach to the child (not to speak of its having become the object of much harassment by right-wing cranks) made it seem, at least to its advocates, "progressive" or even radical. It prided itself on the realism of recognizing and accepting the intellectual limitations of the masses, and yet on the idealism of accepting, encouraging, and providing for the least able members of the student body. It was founded upon a primary regard for the child, and avoided making large claims upon his abilities. It made no hopeful assumptions about the child's pleasure in intellectual activity, at least where such activity was difficult, or about his satisfaction in achievement. On the contrary, it assumed that the child's pleasure in schooling, which was a primary goal, came from having his needs and interests met; and it was content to posit these interests as the foundation of the educational process. Its spokesmen did not believe that they were neglecting to teach the child to think, but they took an altogether different view from traditional educators as to what he should be encouraged to think about and how much cumulative knowledge and effort might be prerequisite to his thinking effectively. They accepted his world as being, in the first instance, largely definitive for them, and were content to guide his thinking within its terms, however parochial in place and time, and however flat in depth. They did not concede that they were abandoning the task of developing character—but they insisted that they were encouraging a more amply social, sociable, and democratic character.

As one examines the range and content of the new courses the new educators demand—which they have in some measure actually succeeded in installing—one realizes that the new education is indeed trying to educate "the whole child," in that it is trying to shape the character and the personality of its charges; and that what it aims to do is not primarily to fit them to become a disciplined part of the world of production and competition, ambition and vocation, creativity, and analytical thought, but rather to help them learn the ways of the world of consumption and hobbies, of enjoyment and social complaisance—in short, to adapt gracefully to the passive and hedonistic style summed up in the significant term *adjustment*. For this world it is deemed important that the pupil learn, not chemistry, but the testing of detergents; not physics, but how to drive and service a car; not history, but the operation of the local gas works; not biology, but the way to the zoo; not Shakespeare or Dickens, but how to write a business letter. The new education, instead of leaving matters of consumption and personal style to the family and other agencies, converts the family and the home themselves into objects of elaborate study and sometimes offensive re-evaluation ("How can my home be made democratic?"). One life-adjustment educator explained that he wanted children to learn to inquire in school (against, as he put it, the die-hard resistance of some teachers with "a very definite academic slant"): "How can I keep well? How can I look my best? How can I get along better with others? How can hobbies contribute to my social growth?"[38] The aspirations inculcated by the school are intended to conform with adolescent interests, including those inculcated in mass-media advertising. Witness the case of the course in "Home and Family Living" required repetitively in one New York State community in *all* grades from seven to ten. Among the topics covered were: "Developing school spirit," "My duties as a baby sitter," "Clicking with the crowd," "How to be liked," "What can be done about acne?" "Learning to care for my bedroom," "Making my room more attractive." Eighth-grade pupils were given these questions on a true-false test: "Just girls need to use deodorants." "Cake soap can be used for shampooing."[39]

---

[38] Richard A. Mumma: "The Real Barrier to a More Realistic Curriculum: The Teacher," *Educational Administration and Supervision*, Vol. XXXVI (January, 1950), pp. 41–2.

[39] *Bulletin* of the Council for Basic Education (April, 1957), p. 11. The actual exploration of such subjects in the schools is unusual, but their place among the plans of core-curriculum educators is not. See, for instance, the lists of student interests recommended as bases for curricula in Alberty: *Reorganizing the High School Curriculum*, chapter 15.

Today life adjustment as a force in American education has passed its moment of strength and has gone into retreat. In part this may be attributed to certain long-range changes in the function of secondary education in the American social system. As Martin Trow has observed, our secondary education "began as an elite preparatory system; during its great years of growth it became a mass terminal system; and it is now having to make a second painful transition on its way to becoming a mass preparatory system."[40] The situation for which the new educators originally designed their programs no longer exists, and there is no longer such a large receptive audience for their views. From 1900 to the 1930's, most of the parents of high-school children had not gone to high school themselves, and many of them were new to the country and its language. They tended to accept rather passively the findings and the programmatic arrangements of the newly emerging educational specialists. Today the parents of high-school children are very commonly at least high-school graduates, and they have been joined by a large college-educated middle-class generation quite alert to educational problems. This public, which has its own ideas about what a high-school education might be, and which has cultural interests of its own, is less willing to accept as final the doctrines of the new education and has provided a large audience for the growing literature of counter-attack against the ideas of the new education represented by the books of Arthur Bestor and Mortimer Smith. Moreover, the high school is no longer the terminal institution that it was for the earlier generation. The philosophy and program of the high school have to be adapted to the fact that half of its graduates are now going on to some kind of higher education, and that they are being trained for skills and specialities more complex than the ordinary white-collar jobs for which the old high school typically prepared. Parents are increasingly aware of the danger that inadequate local schools will jeopardize the chances of their children for privileged positions in college and university education, and they have become increasingly disposed to put pressure upon school authorities to raise educational standards. Finally, the post-Sputnik educational

[40] "The Second Transformation," p. 154.

atmosphere has quickened the activities of those who demand more educational rigor, who can now argue that we are engaged in mortal educational combat with the Soviet Union. In recent years these counter-pressures have begun to take effect. But the attitudes that gave rise to life adjustment have not by any means disappeared from the educational profession or the public. Professional education is still largely staffed, at the administrative levels and in its centers of training, by people who are far from enthusiastic about the new demand for academic excellence. American education is in a position somewhat like that of a new political regime which must depend for the execution of its mandates upon a civil service honeycombed with determined opponents.

CHAPTER XIV

The Child and the World

I

THE NEW education rested on two intellectual pillars: its use, or misuse, of science, and its appeal to the educational philosophy of John Dewey. Of the two, Dewey's philosophy was much more important, for it embraced within it the belief in the power of science to illuminate educational thought, and yet went beyond this to give educators an inclusive and generous view of the world that satisfied their philanthropic sentiments and their urge to make education useful to democracy. Dewey's contribution was to take certain views of the child which were gaining force around the end of the nineteenth century, and to link them to pragmatic philosophy and the growing demand for social reform. He thus established a satisfying connection between new views of the child and new views of the world.

Anyone concerned with the new education must reckon with its use of Dewey's ideas. To consider this in a study of anti-intellectualism may unfortunately be taken as an attempt to characterize Dewey simply as an anti-intellectual—which hardly seems just toward a man who was so intent on teaching children how to think. It may also be taken as an attempt to locate the "blame" for the failings of American education—and will inevitably take on something of this color—but my purpose is quite otherwise: it is to examine the tendency and consequences of certain ideas to which Dewey gave by far the most influential expression.

An attempt to take account of the limitations and the misuse of these ideas should not be read as a blanket condemnation of progressive education, which, as Lawrence Cremin's discriminating history has shown, contained several streams of thought and a variety of tendencies. Although its reputation suffered unwarranted damage from extremists on its periphery, progressivism had at its core something sound and important. Today, partly because many "conservative" schools have borrowed discriminatingly from progressive innovations, we may

easily forget how dismal and self-satisfied the older conservative pedagogy often was, how it accepted, or even exploited,
the child's classroom passivity, how much scope it afforded to
excessively domineering teachers, how heavily it depended on
rote learning. The main strength of progressivism came from
its freshness in method. It tried to mobilize the interests of the
child, to make good use of his need for activity, to concern the
minds of teachers and educators with a more adequate sense of
his nature, to set up pedagogical rules that would put the burden on the teacher not to be arbitrarily authoritative, and to
develop the child's capacity for expression as well as his ability
to learn. It had the great merit of being experimental in a field
in which too many people thought that all the truths had been
established. In an experimental school, where one can find
picked pupils and teachers and instill in them a special ethos
of dedication and excitement, one is likely to get extraordinary
results, as many progressive schools did and still do.[1] Unfortunately, one cannot expect to make universally applicable the
results, however illuminating, which have been achieved in a
special experimental situation.

The value of progressivism rested on its experimentalism and
its work with younger children; its weakness lay in its efforts to
promulgate doctrine, to generalize, in its inability to assess the
practical limits of its own program, above all in its tendency to
dissolve the curriculum. This tendency became most serious in
the education of older children, and especially at the secondary
level, where, as the need arises to pursue a complex, organized
program of studies, the question of the curriculum becomes
acute. Hitherto I have intentionally spoken not of progressivism in education, but of something still broader and more
inclusive which I prefer to call "the new education." The new
education represented the elaboration of certain progressive
principles into a creed, the attempt to make inclusive claims for

[1] In this respect, the situation of an experimental school may be likened to the
famous Hawthorne experiments in the field of industrial sociology, in which an
attempt to find what working conditions would lead to increased productivity
ended in the discovery that the psychological conditions of the experiment
itself, and not any particular device, was what stimulated a continuing series of
advances in productivity.

their applicability in a system of mass education, their extension from experimental work largely with very young children
into a schematism for public education at all ages, and finally
the development of an attack upon the organized curriculum
and liberal education under the rubric of "progressivism."
For all this, early and late, Dewey's thought was constantly
invoked. His vocabulary and ideas, which were clearly evident
in the *Cardinal Principles* of 1918, seem to appear in every subsequent document of the new education. He has been praised,
paraphrased, repeated, discussed, apotheosized, even on occasions read.

It is commonly said that Dewey was misunderstood, and it
is repeatedly pointed out that in time he had to protest against
some of the educational practices carried on in his name. Perhaps his intent was widely, even regularly violated, but Dewey
was hard to read and interpret. He wrote a prose of terrible
vagueness and plasticity, which William James once characterized as "damnable; you might even say God-damnable." His
style is suggestive of the cannonading of distant armies: one
concludes that something portentous is going on at a remote
and inaccessible distance, but one cannot determine just what
it is. That this style is, perhaps symptomatically, at its worst in
Dewey's most important educational writings suggests that his
great influence as an educational spokesman may have been
derived in some part from the very inaccessibility of his exact
meanings. A variety of schools of educational thought have
been able to read their own meanings into his writings. Although it is tempting to say that Dewey's work was crudely
misread by the most anti-intellectual spokesmen of the new education, it seems fairer to admit that even the life-adjustment
educators could have arrived at their use of Dewey through
an honest and intelligent exegesis of the master. Lawrence
Cremin has observed that, "however tortuous the intellectual
line from *Democracy and Education* to the pronouncements of
the Commission on Life Adjustment, that line can be drawn."[2]

That it is in fact an unduly tortuous line one may be permitted to doubt. Serious faults in style are rarely, if ever, matters of
"mere" style; they embody real difficulties in conception. Far

---

[2] *The Transformation of the School*, p. 239.

more probable than the thesis that Dewey was perversely distorted by obtuse or over-enthusiastic followers is the idea that the unresolved problems of interpretation to which his work gave rise were tokens of real ambiguities and gaps in thought, which themselves express certain difficulties and unresolved problems in educational theory and in our culture. What many of Dewey's followers have done, with or without complete license from the master himself, is to attack the ideas of leadership and guidance, and the values of culture and reflective life, in favor of certain notions of spontaneity, democracy, and practicality. In this respect they repeat in education some of the themes that were sounded by the egalitarians in politics, the evangelicals in religion, and the prophets of practicality in business. Before attempting to see how Dewey's philosophy lent itself to these uses, let us first look at the essential argument of this philosophy and at the intellectual setting in which it emerged.

2

The objectives of Dewey's educational theory, which were closely knit into his general philosophy, comprise a high set of ambitions. In the first instance, Dewey was trying to devise a theory of education—of the development of intelligence and the role of knowledge—which would be wholly consistent with Darwinism. For a thinker born in the year in which *The Origin of Species* was published, and intellectually raised during the flowering of evolutionary science, modern education would be worth nothing if it were not scientific.

Dewey began by thinking of the individual learner as using his mind instrumentally to solve various problems presented by his environment, and went on to develop a theory of education conceived as the growth of the learner. The modern educational system, he saw, must operate in an age of democracy, science, and industrialism; education should strive to meet the requirements of this age. Above all, education should abandon those practices, based upon a pre-democratic and pre-industrial society, which accepted the leisured and aristocratic view that knowledge is the contemplation of fixed verities. Dewey felt that he and his contemporaries must now surmount a series of artificial dualisms inherited from past ages. Primary among these was the dualism between knowledge and action. For Dewey, action is involved in knowledge—not in the sense, as some of his uncomprehending critics charged, that knowledge is subordinated to action and inferior to "practice" but in the sense that knowledge is a form of action, and that action is one of the terms by which knowledge is acquired and used.

Dewey was also trying to find the educational correlates of a democratic and progressive society. How can one construct an educational system that will avoid perpetuating all the flaws of existing society at the root simply by molding children in its own image? If a democratic society is truly to serve all its members, it must devise schools in which, at the germinal point in childhood, these members will be able to cultivate their capacities and, instead of simply reproducing the qualities of the larger society, will learn how to improve them. It was in this sense that he saw education as a major force in social reconstruction. Plainly, if society is to be remade, one must above all look for the regenerative contribution the child is capable of making to society. And this cannot be done, Dewey thought, unless the child is placed at the center of the school, unless the rigid authority of the teacher and the traditional weight of the curriculum are displaced by his own developing interests and impulses. To mobilize these impulses and interests toward learning, under gentle adult guidance, is to facilitate the learning process and also to form a type of character and mind suitable to the work of social reform.

This is an excessively abbreviated statement of Dewey's theory, but it serves at least to show how he stated his problems and to turn attention to the central personage in their solution —the figure of the child. It is here that we may begin, for the conception of the child—no mere intellectual construct but the focus of a set of deep emotional commitments and demands—is at the core of the new education. To anticipate what must subsequently be elaborated at some length, I believe that the conception of the child formed by Dewey and his contemporaries, which later entered into the stream of the new education, was more romantic and primitivist than it was post-Darwinian. This conception of the child, and the related assumptions about his natural growth, made it all the more difficult for Dewey and his followers to resolve those dualisms which he felt should be resolved, and, despite his continuing efforts at clarification, made it difficult also to reconcile the central position of the child with what proved still to be necessary in the way of order and authority in education. Finally, the penumbra of sanctity with which the figure of the child was surrounded made it difficult to discuss with realism the role of democracy in education.

To understand the emotional commitment with which Dewey and his contemporaries approached the child, it is necessary to reconstruct to some extent the intellectual atmosphere around the turn of the century, when his generation began to work its transformation of American education. At this time, both in America and in Europe, there was a quickening of interest in the child and a new turn in sentiment among those professionally concerned with him. It was in 1909 that the Swedish feminist, Ellen Key, wrote her significantly titled book, *The Century of the Child*, which epitomized the expectations of those who felt that the child had been newly rediscovered. But expressions of this order were becoming common coin. In 1900 the state superintendent of public instruction of Georgia presented at the annual meeting of the National Education Association an inspirational paper entitled "What Manner of Child Shall This Be?" In it he declared:[3]

> If I were asked what is to be accounted the great discovery of this century, I would pass by all the splendid achievements that men have wrought in wood and stone and iron and brass. I would not go to the volume that catalogs the printing-press, the loom, the steam-engine, the steamship, the ocean cable, the telegraph, the wireless telegraphy, the telephone, the phonograph. I would not go among the stars and point to either one of the planets that have been added to our solar system. I would not call for the Roentgen ray that promises to revolutionize the study of the human brain as well as the human body. I would pass over all the labor-saving machines and devices by which the work of the world has been marvelously multiplied. Above and beyond all these the index finger of the world's progress, in the march of time, would point unerringly to the little child as the one great discovery of the century now speeding to its close.

[3]See G. R. Glenn: "What Manner of Child Shall This Be?" N.E.A. *Proceedings*, 1900, pp. 176–8, for this and other quotations.

Having thus stated what importance he attached to the discovery of the little child, the school official went on to summarize the progress of the previous century, from the days when, as he imagined, education had been "the exclusive privilege of an autocratic minority" and had been put at the disposal of "an all-powerful democratic majority." Freedom of opportunity had already been given to the American child, but further reforms were still in the making. "Already we Americans have discovered that the old system of education wall not fit his case. . . . We have quit trying to fit the boy to a system. We are now trying to adjust a system to the boy." Turning to religious imagery, the official likened American teachers to Christ, in the sense that they were releasing the American child from shrouds and deathly cerements, as Christ released Lazarus, and turning him loose to grow. In the future, he predicted with remarkable prescience, the Christian challenge to the teacher would rise still higher, for the teacher would be expected to save the humblest of God's children: "Time was when the power of the teacher was measured by what he could do with a bright boy or a bright girl. From the beginning of this new century the power of the teacher will be measured by what he will be able to do with the dull boy, the defective child. More than ever before in the history of this world the real test of teaching power will be measured, not by what can be done with the best, but by what can be done with the worst boy in the school."[4] The new educational psychology will be "the psychology of the prodigal son and the lost sheep." The "great rejoicings" in American life will come when child study is so mastered and the development of schools so perfected that the educational system touches and develops every American boy. "We shall come to our place of rejoicing when we have saved every one of these American children and made every one of them a contributor to the wealth, to the intelligence, and to the power of this great democratic government of ours."

[4] This was, of course, at odds with the conception of more traditional and less evangelical educators like Charles William Eliot, who once wrote that "the policy of an institution of education, of whatever grade, ought never to be determined by the needs of the least capable students. . . ." *Educational Reform* (New York, 1898).

I have chosen these remarks because, though written by a working educator rather than a theorist, they sum up in brief a number of the convictions prevalent in what was then up-to-date educational thinking. They reflect its Christian fervor and benevolence; its sense of the central place of the child in the modern world; its concern with democracy and opportunity as criteria of educational achievement; its conviction of the importance of the dull child and his demands on the educational system; its optimism about educational research and child study; its belief that education is to be defined essentially as growth; and its faith that a proper education, though focused on the self-realization of the individual child, would also automatically work toward the fulfillment and salvation of democratic society.

The Georgia school official may well have been reading the works of leading contemporaries in the field, for his view of the child is largely in accord with what they were then writing. Dewey, who was in his early forties and just beginning his work in education, was of course one of them; but it is desirable also to look for a moment at the influence, then more ponderable, of two older men who preceded him, the educator Francis Wayland Parker and the psychologist G. Stanley Hall. Parker, whom Dewey once called the father of progressive education, was a man of exceptional vitality, a remarkably effective pedagogue, and a distinguished school administrator. In the 1870's he remade the school system of Quincy, Massachusetts, achieving results that, by the most impeccably traditional criteria of educational performance, must be considered brilliant. Not long afterward, he went on to the principalship of the Cook County Normal School in Chicago, where he developed more fully his educational theories and his pedagogical techniques. There he undoubtedly set an important example for John Dewey, who was impressed by the Cook County Normal School before he set up his own "Laboratory School" in 1896, and for G. Stanley Hall, who for a time made annual visits to Parker's school "to set my educational watch."

The terms in which Parker cast his educational theory were in many respects too old-fashioned to be in tune with the new currents of thought. For example, they were altogether pre-Darwinian and had no trace of the more sophisticated functionalist psychology which made Dewey's writings so widely appealing. But Parker's view of the child, which was, to a great extent, patterned after Froebel's, was of capital importance. "The child," he said, "is the climax and culmination of all God's creations," and to answer the question: What is the child? is to approach a knowledge of God. "He put into that child Himself his divinity, and . . . this divinity manifests itself in the seeking for truth through the visible and tangible." "The spontaneous tendencies of the child are the records of inborn divinity," he asserted. "We are here, my fellow-teachers, for one purpose, and that purpose is to understand these tendencies and continue them in all these directions, following nature." If the child was the bearer of divinity and "the fruit of all the past and the seed of all the future," it was natural enough to conclude that "the centre of all movement in education is *the child*." One may hazard the guess that Parker's concern with the spontaneous activities of the child were fruitful rather than stultifying partly because he also conceived of the child as omnivorously curious, as having a natural interest in all subjects, as being a sort of savant in the making, and a born artist and handicraftsman as well. Accordingly, he proposed a rather demanding curriculum, and unlike most later progressives, he believed even in teaching grammar in all grades of the elementary school, since he thought it should be "thoroughly mastered."

As Dewey did later, Parker stressed the school as a community: "A school should be a model home, a complete community and embryonic democracy." Properly used, it could be expected to achieve an extraordinary reformation: "We must believe that we can save *every child*. The citizen should say in his heart: 'I await the regeneration of the world from the teaching of the common schools of America.'"[5]

The era in which these words were written was also the era in which G. Stanley Hall, the leader of the child-study movement, said: "The guardians of the young should strive first of all to keep out of nature's way. . . . They should feel profoundly that childhood, as it comes fresh from the hands of God, is not corrupt, but illustrates the survival of the most

[5]Francis W. Parker: *Talks on Pedagogics* (New York, 1894), pp. 3, 5–6, 16, 23–4, 320–30, 383, 434, 450.

consummate thing in the world. . . . Nothing else is so worthy of love, reverence, and service as the body and soul of the growing child." It was the era in which Dewey himself said that "the child's own instincts and powers furnish the material and give the starting point for all education." Also: "We violate the child's nature and render difficult the best ethical results by introducing the child too abruptly to a number of special studies, of reading, writing, geography, etc., out of relation to [his] social life. The true center of correlation on the school subjects is not science, nor literature, nor history, nor geography, but the child's own social activities."[6]

It will be apparent that the new education was presented to the world not simply as an instrumentality but as a creed, which went beyond the hope of this or that strictly educational result to promise some kind of ultimate salvation for individuals or for the race. We shall presently see, for example, how G. Stanley Hall foresaw that an education designed in accordance with the nature of child growth would rear the superman of the future. Dewey's early view of the possibilities of education were likewise exalted. Education, he said in his well-titled little pamphlet, *My Pedagogic Creed*, "is the fundamental method of social progress and reform." Hence the teacher must be seen as "engaged, not simply in the training of individuals, but in the formation of the proper social life." Every teacher should accordingly think of himself as "a social servant set apart for the maintenance of proper social order and the securing of the right social growth. In this way the teacher always is the prophet of the true God and the usherer in of the true kingdom of God."[7] Plainly, high expectations like these put a staggering burden upon any proposal for educational reform.

This creed, this fighting faith, had to be put forward in the face of much stubborn resistance before it could be established as the reigning creed. Men who feel that they must engage in such a crusade are not likely to be greatly concerned with nuances, or with exploring the limits or dangers of their ideas.

---

[6]G. Stanley Hall: "The Ideal School as Based on Child Study," *Forum*, Vol. XXXII (September, 1901), pp. 24–5; John Dewey: *My Pedagogic Creed* (1897; new ed. Washington, 1929), pp. 4, 9.
[7]*My Pedagogic Creed*, pp. 15, 17.

Unfortunately, what is important in a practical sphere like education is very often not so much the character of a philosophy or creedal commitment as certain questions of emphasis and proportion which arise in trying to execute it; and there is no automatic way of deriving a sense of proportion from a body of ideas. For example, the early spokesmen of the new education demanded that the child be respected, but it was difficult to say where respect might end and a kind of bathetic reverence might begin. Although Dewey himself began to warn in the 1930's against the overuse or the oversimplified use of his theories, he found it difficult to define, even in his later works, the points at which the lines of restraint could or should be drawn without at the same time abandoning certain of his essential commitments.

3

Here perhaps the romantic inheritance, quite as much or more than the appeal of post-Darwinian naturalism, may explain the charm of the concept of the child formulated by Dewey and his generation. The most elaborate statements of this concept come from European writers who applied romantic views to the child—on occasion Dewey referred respectfully to Rousseau, Pestalozzi, and Froebel, as he did to Emerson, whose essay "Culture" foreshadowed many of his ideas. The notion of education advanced at the turn of the century by these pedagogical reformers was romantic in the sense that they set up an antithesis between the development of the individual—his sensibility, the scope of his fancy, the urgency of his personal growth—and the imperatives of the social order, with its demand for specified bodies of knowledge, prescribed manners and morals, and a personal equipment suited to traditions and institutions. Theirs was a commitment to the natural child against artificial society. For them, the child came into this world trailing clouds of glory, and it was the holy office of the teacher to see that he remained free, instead of assisting in the imposition of alien codes upon him. They envisaged a child life engaged more or less directly with nature and with activity, and not with absorbing traditions meaningful only to adults or with reading books and mastering skills set not by the child's desires and interests but by adult society.[8]

This view of education began once again to gain currency among Western thinkers at the turn of the century; the United States provided an unusually receptive soil. This country had always had a strong penchant for child-indulgence—it was an extremely common point of observation for nineteenth-century travelers in America. Moreover, American education, being in a singularly fluid state, offered less resistance to such attractive novelties than the tradition-encrusted educational systems of the European countries. The evangelical climate of this country was also a force: the new educators' rhetoric about "saving" every American child, and their implied promise that the child saved would himself redeem civilization, point to this conclusion. It was decades before even so secular a thinker as Dewey lost the confidence evident in the young educational reformer of 1897 who believed that the good teacher would usher in "the true kingdom of God."

If we attend carefully to the overtones of the new educators' pronouncements, with their stress on such terms as spontaneity, instinct, activity, and nature, we become aware of the way in which the problem of education is posed. The child is a phenomenon at once natural and divine—here post-Darwinian naturalism and the romantic heritage link arms—and the "natural" pattern of his needs and instincts becomes an imperative which it is profane for educators to violate.

We are now prepared to appreciate the significance of the central idea of the new educational thought: that the school should base its studies not on the demands of society, nor on any conception of what an educated person should be, but on the developing needs and interests of the child. This does not mean merely that the nature of the child imposes negative

---

[8]One thinks in this connection of Rousseau in *Émile*: "When I get rid of children's lessons, I get rid of the chief cause of their sorrows, namely their books. Reading is the curse of childhood, yet it is almost the only occupation you can find for children. Émile at twelve years old will hardly know what a book is. . . . When reading is of use to him, I admit he must learn to read, but till then he will only find it a nuisance."

limits on the educational process and that it is vain to try to surmount them: to say this would be superfluous. It means that the nature of the child is a positive guide to educational procedure—that the child himself naturally and spontaneously generates the needs and impulses that should animate the educational process.

In a revealing article of 1901, "The Ideal School as Based on Child Study," G. Stanley Hall attempted to say what this guiding principle would entail. He would try, he said, "to break away from all current practices, traditions, methods, and philosophies, for a brief moment, and ask *what education would be if based solely upon a fresh and comprehensive view of the nature and needs of childhood.*"[9] In short, he would strip away the inherited ideas of what education should be, which are the trappings of an outworn past, and assume that what modern child study has learned is of greater relevance to the purpose. Etymologically, Hall pointed out, the word for school meant leisure, "exemption from work, the perpetuation of the primeval paradise created before the struggle for existence began." Understood in this sense, the school stood for health, growth, and heredity, "a pound of which is worth a ton of instruction."

Because of the natural and sacred character of the child's health, leisure, and growth, every invasion of his time, every demand of the curriculum, must be doubly tried and conclusively justified before we subject him to it:

> We must overcome the fetishism of the alphabet, of the multiplication table, of grammars, of scales, and of bibliolatry, and must reflect that . . . the invention of Cadmus seemed the sowing of veritable dragon's teeth in the brain; that Charlemagne and many other great men of the world could not read or write; that scholars have argued that Cornelia, Ophelia, Beatrice, and even the blessed mother of our Lord knew nothing

[9] Hall: op. cit., p. 24; italics added. For quotations in the following paragraphs, see pp. 25, 26, 30, 39. Compare the views of Francis W. Parker: "I wish to have these words written in italics, we do not claim that nature is the center, neither do we claim that history and literature are the center, *we do claim that the child is the center*, that this being, this highest creation of God, with its laws of body, mind, and soul, determines in itself the very nature and condition of its growth." *Discussions at the Open Session of the Herbart Club, Denver, Colorado,* July 10, 1895 (1895), pp. 155–6.

of letters. The knights, the elite leaders of the Middle Ages, deemed writing a mere clerk's trick beneath the attention of all those who scorned to muddle their wits with others' ideas, feeling that their own were good enough for them.

Of course no one will imagine that Hall, who had received one of the best educations of his generation—and a very traditional one—at Harvard and the German universities, thought that the new education would have as a goal the subversion of literacy.[10] The importance of his views lay in the belief that there is a natural and normal course of child development to which bookish considerations should yield. Some of his particular suggestions were most sensible,[11] and some are still practiced to good effect. It is interesting, too, that just as Parker clung to the value of grammar, Hall did not think that the study of the classical languages had been altogether eliminated by this emphasis on natural development. At least some children might well study languages, Hall thought; what is especially interesting to a contemporary reader, looking back over the span of seventy years, is that Hall felt that he knew quite precisely at what points in a child's development the study of these subjects was "natural." "As to the dead languages, if they are to be taught, Latin should be begun not later than ten or eleven, and Greek never later than twelve or thirteen." A generation later, most proponents of the new education had no use for these languages, and they would have been horrified to see either of them begun in the primary grades.

Hall's hopes for what could be realized in education through the scientific study of the child were avowedly utopian. With a generous grant of funds and five years of experimentation, he had "no shadow of doubt or fear," it would be possible to work out a program that would satisfy educational prophets

[10]The formulation of this goal had to wait for a later generation of educators. See above, chapter 1, Exhibit L.

[11]I find especially perceptive this recommendation: "The children of the rich, generally prematurely individualized or over-individualized, especially when they are only children, must be disciplined and subordinated; while the children of the poor, usually under-individualized, should be indulged." It suggests a greater sensitivity to the social milieu than Hall's commitment to "natural" patterns might imply.

and even persuade conservatives, "because the best things established will be in it."

> But it will be essentially pedocentric rather than scholiocentric; it may be a little like the Reformation which insisted that the Sabbath, the Bible, and the Church were made for man and not he for them; it will fit both the practices and the results of modern science and psychological study; it will make religion and morals more effective; and, perhaps, above all, it will give individuality in the school its full rights as befits a republican form of government, and will contribute something to bring the race to the higher maturity of the superman that is to be, effectiveness in developing which is the highest and final test of art, science, religion, home, state, literature, and every human institution.

It will no doubt seem a far cry from Hall's hopes for ten-year-old Latinists and his call for the superman of the future to the work of the life-adjustment educators with their campaign against disciplinary subjects and their recommended class discussions on "How can I get everyone to participate in the activities at the party?" or "Should I have dates in junior high school?"[12] But utopias have a way of being short-circuited under the very eyes of their formulators.

4

The romantic and Darwinian backgrounds of the new education make it easier to understand why Dewey should have chosen to define education as growth. In Dewey this conception that education is growth is no casual act of definition and no idle metaphor: it represents an attempt to locate and restate the very essence of the educational process. There is a frequently quoted passage in *Democracy and Education* which illustrates at once the disturbing quality of Dewey's style and the importance he attached to the conception of education as growth. There he wrote:[13]

---

[12] The examples are from Alberty: *Reorganizing the High-School Curriculum*, pp. 472–3.
[13] *Democracy and Education* (New York, 1916), pp. 59–62.

We have been occupied with the conditions and implications of growth. . . . When it is said that education is development, everything depends upon *how* development is conceived. Our net conclusion is that life is development, and that developing, growing, is life. Translated into its educational equivalents, this means (*i*) that the educational process has no end beyond itself; it is its own end; and that (*ii*) the educational process is one of continual reorganizing, reconstructing, transforming. . . .

Since in reality there is nothing to which growth is relative save more growth, there is nothing to which education is subordinate save more education. . . . Education means the enterprise of supplying the conditions which insure growth, or adequacy of life, irrespective of age. . . .

Since growth is the characteristic of life, education is all one with growing; it has no end beyond itself. The criterion of the value of school education is the extent in which it creates a desire for continued growth and supplies means for making the desire effective in fact.

The implications of this must be reckoned with: we are not asked to consider that education resembles growth, or has something in common with growth, or may helpfully be thought of as a special form of growth. We are urged to consider that education *is* growth; that growth is life; that life is development; and above all that it is meaningless to try to provide ends for education, since it has no possible further end but more education. "The aim of education is to enable individuals to continue their education."[14]

The idea that education is growth is at first blush all but irresistible. Certainly education is not a form of shrinkage. To say that it is growth seems to assert a desirable connection between the learning process and the world of nature. This concept is refreshingly unmechanical. It does justice to our sense that education is cumulative and self-enlarging and leads toward a mind and character which become larger, more complex, more

[14] Ibid., p. 117. In an earlier work Dewey had said that "the process and the goal of education are the same thing. To set up any end outside of education, as furnishing its goal and standard, is to deprive the educational process of much of its meaning, and tends to make us rely upon false and external stimuli in dealing with the child." *My Pedagogic Creed*, p. 12.

powerful, and yet finer. But several critics have contended that the notion that education is growth was the source of endless difficulties; and I believe that in the hands of some of Dewey's followers this idea became one of the most mischievous metaphors in the history of modern education. Growth is a natural, animal process, and education is a social process. Growth in the child, taken literally, goes on automatically, requiring no more than routine care and nourishment; its end is to a large degree predetermined by genetic inheritance, whereas the ends of education have to be supplied. In contemplating a child's education we are free to consider whether he shall learn two languages, but in contemplating his natural growth we cannot consider whether he shall develop two heads.

Since the idea of growth is intrinsically a biological metaphor and an individualistic conception, the effect of this idea was of necessity to turn the mind away from the social to the personal function of education; it became not an assertion of the child's place in society but rather of his interests as against those of society.[15] The idea of growth invited educational thinkers to set up an invidious contrast between self-determining, self-directing growth from within, which was good, and molding from without, which was bad. Students of Dewey's philosophy might readily object to any portrayal of his educational thought as oriented excessively toward the biological and individual and as insufficiently mindful of the collective and social. What writer on education, it might be asked, ever spoke more positively about the social character of the educational process and about its ultimate social function?

The problem, however, did not arise from any lack of awareness, on Dewey's part, of the social character of education; it arose from the fact that the concept of individual growth became a hostage in the hands of educational thinkers who were obsessed with the child-centered school. Although Dewey himself did not accept the antithesis between the child and society as a finality—indeed, he hoped to achieve a harmonious

[15]Cf. the criticism by Boyd H. Bode in *Education at the Crossroads* (New York, 1938), especially pp. 73 ff. Among the various critiques, I have found this work and I. L. Kandel's *The Cult of Uncertainty* (New York, 1943) most illuminating.

synthesis of the two—the historical effect of the conception of education as growth was to exalt the child and dismiss the problem of society, on the ground that the growth of the child stood for health, whereas the traditions of society (including curricular traditions) stood for outworn, excessively authoritative demands. "The authority of society," wrote a leading psychologist in this tradition, "or of any part of society is not presented to the child as a guide to conduct. Reliance is placed on the experience of each individual child. The experience of the race in discovering what line of conduct works out satisfactorily and what does not is utilized only in so far as the child sees fit to appeal to it."[16]

Dewey himself never argued, as critics and followers have often thought, for a directionless education. On this point at least he was painfully clear. He often said in his early as well as his later educational writings that the child himself, unguided, is not capable of spinning out the proper content of his education; that every superficial act or interest, every stray impulse, of the child is not necessarily valuable; that the teacher must somehow, without imposing "external" ends, guide, direct, and develop those impulses of the child which are moving "forward."[17]

Dewey's difficulty was of another order: having insisted that education, being growth itself, cannot have any end set for it save still more education, he was unable to formulate the criteria by which society, through the teacher, should guide or direct the child's impulses. The teacher was left with a firm mandate to exercise some guidance, to make some discriminations among the child's impulses and needs, but with no directional

[16]Goodwin Watson, as quoted by I. L. Kandel: *The Cult of Uncertainty*, p. 79.
[17]See almost all of *The Child and the Curriculum* (1902; Chicago ed., 1956), but especially pp. 14–18 and the significant passage on pp. 30–1 in which he pleads that there be some kind of continuous interaction between the child's interest and the direction he gets, so that the two will work in some kind of dynamic harmony. See also *Democracy and Education*, pp. 61–2; also p. 133: "The natural, or native, powers furnish the initiating and limiting forces in all education; they do not furnish its ends or aims." At one point, in 1926, Dewey departed from his customarily benign injunctions to say that the studied avoidance of guidance practiced in some progressive schools was "really stupid."

signposts.[18] The child's impulses should be guided "forward" —but in which direction? Such a set of criteria presupposes an educational goal, an adult prevision of what the child should know and what he should be. "Let the child's nature fulfill its own destiny,"[19] Dewey urged, but the suggestion that the child has a destiny implied an end or goal somewhat removed in time and not envisaged by the child. For this reason, what came to be called progressive education, although often immensely fertile and ingenious concerning means, was so futile and confused about ends; much of what it had to say about teaching methods was of the highest value, but it was quite unclear, often anarchic, about what these methods should be used to teach. Remarkably effective beginnings were made at mobilizing the child's interests for learning, but often these interests simply displaced learning. The more certain progressive education was of its techniques, the less explicit it was about its goals—perhaps in this respect it offered a parable on American life.

Dewey's own vagueness about the curriculum is understandable in the light of this conception of education as growth. Naturally, in the course of his career he wrote a good deal about the curriculum; but it is difficult to discover from his major books on education what he thought a good curriculum should be, or rather what the various alternative curricula should be, in the American school system. This absence of curricular commitments was consistent with his proposition that no ends or goals should be formulated for education, since its only legitimate end is the capacity for still further education. By the time he wrote *Democracy and Education*, Dewey had become convinced that "the curriculum is always getting loaded down with purely inherited traditional matter," and that it therefore needs "constant inspection, criticism, and revision." He was concerned, too, that the curriculum "probably represents the values of adults rather than those of children and youth, or those of pupils a generation ago rather than those

[18]"It is as absurd for [the parent or teacher] to set up their 'own' aims as the proper objects of the growth of the children as it would be for the farmer to set up an ideal of farming, irrespective of conditions." *Democracy and Education*, p. 125.
[19] *The Child and the Curriculum*, p. 31.

of the present day." Here he seems to lend his authority to those who believed that the curriculum should be shaped fundamentally in accordance with the expressed desires of children and that it should be largely discontinuous from generation to generation, if not from year to year—for the recommended inspection and revision are not intermittent but "constant."[20]

On one count Dewey was completely forthright: "As long as any topic makes an immediate appeal, it is not necessary to ask what it is good for." Here he favored his readers with one of his rare concrete illustrations: "It is unsound to urge that, say, Latin has a value *per se* in the abstract, just as a study, as sufficient justification for teaching it." Thus far it is easy to give one's assent, but Dewey went on to add that Latin does not need to be justified by having attributed to it some definite use in the future. "When pupils are genuinely concerned in learning Latin, that is of itself proof that it possesses value."[21]

The intention of this was plainly innocent enough, for the context showed that Dewey was simply saying that he set a high value on the spontaneous appreciation by pupils of what they were studying. This did not mean that they were to study whatever was pleasurable. In at least one work he had warned educators against trying to exploit "what is merely pleasure-giving, exciting, or transient."[22] Yet there seems no way of avoiding the conclusion that if the value of every study was to be, as he urged, dependent upon the concrete situation in which the choice of studies was to be made, then the kind of long-range evaluation of subjects which is necessary to the design of curricula becomes inordinately difficult. "In the abstract," said Dewey, "there is no such thing as degrees or order

[20]One is reminded here of the same restless spirit in Francis W. Parker: "Do nothing twice alike. Don't do things you have done before. If the child stood up before, have him sit down now. Whatever you do, do something different. Have no patterns. Uniformity is death—variety is life." N.E.A. *Proceedings*, 1880.
[21]*Democracy and Education*, pp. 283–4.
[22]*The School and Society* (1915; ed. Chicago, 1956), p. 136. The context of this warning was a plea, not for a firm program of academic studies, but rather for a continuous study of what Dewey there called "occupation work." On Dewey's remonstrances against attacks on the orderly organization of subject matter, see Cremin: op. cit., pp. 234–6.

of value." Therefore: "We cannot establish a hierarchy of values among studies."[23]

Again, one may be tempted to agree, if by hierarchy one has in mind the notion that studies are assigned an eternal value equally applicable to all pupils. But it is too easy to conclude from this proposition that any subject is the equal of any other —that, as the N.E.A. later put it, "mathematics and mechanics, art and agriculture, history and homemaking are all peers." A pupil's "genuine concern" to learn Latin was for Dewey sufficient proof of its value. If for "Latin" one substitutes "driver education" or "beauty culture," considering each as justified if it makes "an immediate appeal," one senses the game that later educators played with Dewey's principles. Dewey himself presumably would not have made such substitutions, but in his philosophy there are no barriers against making them.

The effect of Dewey's philosophy on the design of curricular systems was devastating. Even if one is aware of the conditional and limited character of any hierarchy of values one may establish among subjects, one must have such a hierarchy in mind to design a curriculum that runs over the course of several years, for its lower years must be in some measure conceived as the prerequisite to certain choices in the later years. An urgent desire to learn Latin or any other such subject is not a "natural" impulse in any child. Children can become, in Dewey's words, "genuinely concerned" to learn Latin only if adult society decides that it is good for some of them to have that choice and at what age it should be made possible for them, and only if adult society arranges the prior curricular, social, and intellectual experiences of these children in such a way as to make the choice between learning Latin or not learning it possible and meaningful for them. In short, some part of the adult community must have convictions about the curriculum and be willing to organize it accordingly.[24] Such organization, though leaving the child a considerable margin of choice, would go beyond the classroom "guidance" and "direction" which Dewey explicitly allowed for.

[23] *Democracy and Education*, pp. 280–1.
[24] But see Dewey *per contra*: "In education, the currency of these externally imposed aims is responsible for the emphasis put upon the notion of preparation for a remote future and for rendering the work of both teacher and pupil mechanical and slavish." Ibid., p. 129; cf. the whole passage on aims in education, pp. 124–9.

5

The ideal of growth was the primary expression of Dewey's concern with the individual; the ideal of education in the service of
democracy was the expression of his sense of the social function
of education. Although, as I have suggested, the ideal of growth
committed many educators to an anti-societal bias, this was not
Dewey's view of the matter; he felt that individual growth and
the interests of a democratic social order, far from being in any
ineluctable antagonism, were susceptible to a completely harmonious synthesis. In his eyes, the new education was to be
anything but anarchistic or ultra-individualistic. The child, now
released from traditional restraints, would be raised none the
less to accept social responsibilities; but these would be defined
as responsibilities to his peers and to the future. The new education itself would have social responsibilities more demanding
and more freighted with social significance than the education
of the past. Its goal would be nothing less than the fullest realization of the principles of democracy. In setting this aspiration,
Dewey stood firmly within the American tradition, for the great
educational reformers who had established the common-school
system had also been concerned with its potential value to democracy; he was also wholly in tune with his times, for the revival and enlargement of American democracy was one of the
essential aspirations of the Progressives.

Traditional education, Dewey believed, had been founded
upon theories of knowledge and moral development congenial
only to pre-democratic society, and, in so far as it was still operative in democratic society, hampered the realization of the
democratic ideal. Since the time of classical antiquity, the division of society into a leisured and aristocratic class, which was
the custodian of learning, and an enslaved or working class,
which was engaged with work and practical knowledge, had
encouraged a fatal separation of knowledge and action.[25]

In a democratic society, however, where almost everyone
has a function and where there are many shared interests and
objectives, it should be possible to surmount this separation
and arrive at an understanding of knowledge which does full

[25]For Dewey's development of this theme, see *Reconstruction in Philosophy*
(New York, 1920).

justice to the element of social action involved in it. A society which is both democratic and progressive "must have a type of education which gives individuals a personal interest in social relationships and control, and the habits of mind which secure social changes without introducing disorder."[26]

Dewey did not at any time fall victim to the delusion that the whole burden of social change could be put on the educational process. Direct instruction and exhortation, he remarked in *Democracy and Education*, could not in themselves bring about changes in mind and character; such changes would also require changes, of a type he did not clearly specify, in "industrial and political conditions." But education could make a vital contribution: "We may produce in schools a projection in type of the society we should like to realize, and by forming minds in accord with it gradually modify the larger and more recalcitrant features of adult society."[27] This sentence expresses in brief the essence of Dewey's demand on the schools in behalf of democracy, and at the same time shows a central difficulty in his educational philosophy: he was obliged to assume that there is a kind of pre-established harmony between the needs and interests of the child and "the society we should like to realize." Otherwise it would be necessary either to sacrifice the ideal of education as growth or to abandon the goal of "forming minds" in accordance with an adult, and hence externally imposed, vision of the good society.

Dewey's conception of the manner in which education would serve democracy is different from that formulated by earlier educational reformers. They had expected that a common-school system would enlarge opportunities for the common man while at the same time endowing the whole population with those mental and moral qualities which were deemed necessary to a popular form of government. They were traditional, in the sense that they thought of adult society as formulating the ends of education and devising curricula to suit them. But since this was unacceptable to Dewey, he sought for another, more subtle, more pervasive, and yet more "natural" formulation of the relation between democracy and education. One consequence

[26] *Democracy and Education*, p. 115.
[27] Ibid., p. 370.

of this view was that his *Democracy and Education*, for all its generalized discussion of leisure and working classes, had almost nothing to say about the specific class structure of American society, or the relation of educational opportunity to this structure, or the means of extending opportunities to increase social mobility and break down class barriers. In short, his view of the problem of education and democracy was not economic or sociological, or even political, except in the broadest sense of that term; it was largely psychological or social-psychological. In Dewey's theory, the ends of democratic education are to be served by the socialization of the child, who is to be made into a co-operative rather than a competitive being and "saturated" with the spirit of service.

Dewey began with a forceful rejection of systems of education based upon class stratification; for it was the co-existence of a leisured and learned class and an enslaved or working class that led to an unhealthy split between learning and utility. The opposition between learning and utility, between thought and action, can be surmounted only in a democratic educational system which mixes children of varying backgrounds and does not try to reproduce in their schooling the class barriers of their society. A democracy, he argued, "is more than a form of government; it is primarily a mode of associated living, of conjoint communicated experience."[28] The problem of the democratic educator is to make of the school a specialized environment, a miniature community, an embryonic society, which will eliminate so far as possible the undesirable features of the larger environment of society. For an enlightened society will try to transmit not simply the whole of its achievements, but "only such as make for a better future society."[29]

---

[28] *Democracy and Education*, p. 101. While it is quite true that the criterion of democracy can be applied to other social institutions as well as to the apparatus of government, there is much to be lost by encouraging men to think of democracy as a universal and exclusively satisfactory criterion of such institutions as the family and the classroom. I believe Dewey did American education a major disservice by providing what appears to be an authoritative sanction for that monotonous and suffocating rhetoric about "democratic living" with which American educationists smother our discussions of the means and ends of education.

[29] Ibid., pp. 22–4; cf. *The School and Society*, p. 18.

And what would be the characteristics of the democratic school community? The teacher, of course, would no longer be a harsh authority imposing external goals through rigid methods. He would be alert to the spontaneous and natural impulses of the children and would take hold of those that led toward constructive ends, giving gentle direction where necessary. The pupils themselves would take an active part in formulating the purposes of their education and in planning its execution. Learning would not be individual or passive, but collective and active; and in the course of their work the students would learn to share ideas and experiences, would develop mutual consideration and respect, and would acquire a capacity for co-operation. These habits, writ large, would some day reshape the larger society itself; for, as Dewey put it in one of his less fortunate sentences: "In directing the activities of the young, society determines its own future in determining that of the young."[30]

Democratic goals would have profound consequences for content as well as method. As soon as the inherited notion of learning as a leisure-class activity is discarded, the style of education it represented also falls under question, being suited neither to democracy nor to industrialism nor to an age of science. The circulation of learning in modern times has relieved it of its class associations. Intellectual stimuli may be found everywhere. "The merely intellectual life, the life of scholarship and of learning, thus gets a very altered value. Academic and scholastic, instead of being titles of honor, are becoming terms of reproach." But we are still trying to throw off the shackles of a "medieval conception of learning"—a conception "which appeals for the most part simply to the intellectual aspect of our natures, our desire to learn, to accumulate information, and to get control of the symbols of learning; not to our impulses and tendencies to make, to do, to create, to produce, whether in the form of utility or of art."

In fact, the intellectual type of education can be of significance only to a minority: "The simple facts of the case are that in the great majority of human beings the distinctively

[30] *Democracy and Education*, p. 49.

intellectual interest is not dominant. They have the so-called practical impulse and disposition." For this reason, so many youngsters leave school as soon as they have learned the rudiments of reading, writing, and calculating. On the other hand, "if we were to conceive our educational end and aim in a less exclusive way, if we were to introduce into educational processes the activities which appeal to those whose dominant interest is to do and to make, we should find the hold of the school upon its members to be more vital, more prolonged, containing more of culture." Education is already changing in this direction, Dewey remarked, and holds great promise for the future when the new tendencies are put into "complete, uncompromising possession of our school system." "When the school introduces and trains each child of society into membership within such a little community, saturating him with the spirit of service, and providing him with the instruments of effective self-direction, we shall have the deepest and best guaranty of a larger society which is worthy, lovely, and harmonious."[31]

In attempting to realize their social ideals, Dewey and his followers were in time confronted by a certain antagonism between their fear of adult authority and their desire for social reform. Dewey, as I have pointed out, had always endorsed adult guidance in the classroom; what he had opposed was the idea that adults should formulate ends or goals for education, since the principle of growth demanded that it have no end. But the stronger the forces of social reform grew within the ranks of educators, the more evident it became that the ideal of social reform was, after all, an adult end, and that to realize it the co-operation of children could not be automatically counted upon.

---

[31] *The School and Society*, pp. 24–9. Cf. *Democracy and Education*, pp. 9–10, 46–7, 82–3, 88–9, 97–8, 226, 286–90, 293–305. In a characteristic interpretation by a modern educator who is interested in "developing skills in democratic living": "The democratic life of the school shall be so dynamically related to life outside that the students will be led to understand its meaning, and seek to extend it to all situations in which they are involved." Alberty: *Reorganizing the High School Curriculum*, p. 50.

This truth became particularly evident during the reaction to the great depression. By 1938, when Dewey wrote *Experience and Education*, he felt impelled to warn more sharply than ever that the new education had gone too far when it made teachers afraid to offer suggestions in the classroom. He had even heard of cases in which children were surrounded with objects and materials and then left entirely to themselves because the teacher felt it wrong to indicate what might be done with them. "Why, then, even supply materials, since they are a source of some suggestion or other?" Still, it is the function of the teacher to act only as the leader of the group's activities, and to give such directives as he issues only in the interest of the group, and not "as an exhibition of personal power."

The nagging fear of adult authority remains—the fear of forcing "the activity of the young into channels which express the teacher's purpose rather than that of the pupils." The soundest thing in the new education, Dewey reiterated, was its emphasis upon "the participation of the learner in the formation of the purposes which direct his activities in the learning process." Yet, as he also remarked, "the formation of purposes is . . . a rather complex intellectual operation," and, as he did not remark, it was difficult to show how the very young could take much part in such an operation.[32] He was uneasily aware that the progressive schools were having great difficulty in organizing curricula,[33] but it is uncertain whether he saw that this difficulty had something to do with the expectation that young children could enlist in an operation of considerable intellectual complexity.

Dewey's anxiety about adult authority stemmed from his desire to avoid something which we are still trying with much difficulty to avoid—the inculcation of conformist habits in the child. If there was anything he did *not* want, it was to breed conformist character. But he saw the danger of conformity as arising only from adult society and from its surrogate, the teacher. Speaking of traditional education, he wrote:[34]

[32] *Experience and Education*, pp. 84–5; cf. pp. 4, 59, 64, 66, 77, 80.
[33] Ibid., pp. 95–6.
[34] *Democracy and Education*, p. 60. Dewey's version of traditional education seemed at times to be almost as much a caricature as some of the more savage

Since conformity is the aim, what is distinctively individual in a young person is brushed aside, or regarded as a source of mischief or anarchy. Conformity is made equivalent to uniformity. Consequently, there are induced lack of interest in the novel, aversion to progress, and dread of the uncertain and the unknown.

Dewey was so concerned with adult authority as *the* threat to the child that it was hard for him to conceive of the child's peers as also constituting a threat. One can hardly believe that he really intended to liberate the child from the adult world only to throw him into the clutches of an even more omnivorous peer-culture. Yet there was very little place in Dewey's schoolroom for the contemplative or bookish child, for whom schooling as a social activity is not a thoroughly satisfactory procedure. "In social situations," Dewey approvingly wrote, "the young have to refer their way of acting to what others are doing and make it fit in."[35] It was just this kind of activity that provided the participants with a common understanding. Was there not, in his view of the matter, more than a little suspicion of the child who remained aloof or hung back from social activity, who insisted on a singular measure of independence? "Dependence," Dewey wrote,[36]

denotes a power rather than a weakness; it involves interdependence. There is always a danger that increased personal independence will decrease the social capacity of an individual. In making him more self-reliant, it may make him more self-sufficient; it may lead to aloofness and indifference. It often makes an individual so insensitive in his relations to others as to develop an illusion of being really able to stand and act alone—an unnamed form of insanity which is responsible for a large part of the remediable suffering of the world.

---

lampoons of progressivism. Granting that traditional education was frequently rigid and unimaginative, I doubt that Dewey was altogether just in describing it simply as "autocratic" and "harsh," as using "strait-jacket and chain-gang procedures," as opposed entirely to the cultivation of individuality, as offering only "a diet of predigested materials," and as providing a regime under which the individual, while acquiring information, "loses his own soul: loses his appreciation of things worth while, of the values to which these things [items of information] are relative." *Experience and Education*, pp. 2–5, 11, 24, 46, 50, 70.
[35] *Democracy and Education*, p. 47.
[36] Ibid., p. 52.

These words are altogether intelligible against the background of nineteenth-century America. The rampant economic individualism that Dewey could see at work in his formative years had created a personal type which was indeed independent, if not to the point of insanity, at least to the point of being anti-social. And in the schoolroom the older education had given scope to the impulses of occasional teachers who were harshly authoritarian. It would probably be too much to expect anyone in 1916 to anticipate the emergence among children of the kind of peer-group conformity that David Riesman has diagnosed in *The Lonely Crowd*, or the decline in adult authority that is observable both in the classroom and in the regulation of children's lives. Today, when we grow troubled about conformity in children, we are more often troubled about their conformity to the mandates of their peers and to directives from the mass media than we are by their conformity to parents or teachers. We are also aware of the possibility that excessive weakness in adult authority may even create difficulties for children quite as acute as those caused by adult tyranny.

These considerations did not enter into Dewey's world at the time he was formulating his educational theory; but it is possible that his theory itself has helped to bring about a state of affairs which he could hardly have desired. The core-curriculum educators invoke Dewey's principles of immediacy, utility, and social learning when they encourage children to discuss in school "How can I be popular?" or such implicit resistance to parental imperatives as "Why are my parents so strict?" and "What can I do with my old-fashioned parents?" and "Should I follow my crowd or obey my parents' wishes?"[37] Such topics represent the projection of peer-conformity into the curriculum itself in a way that Dewey would surely have found offensive. The problem of conformity and authority was real enough, but it was not solved by reforming the old-fashioned classroom.

Perhaps Dewey somewhat overvalued the social side of learning. He and other thinkers of his generation, notably George

[37]Alberty: op. cit., pp. 470, 474.

H. Mead, were much concerned to establish the intrinsically social character of mind, an effort in which they were eminently successful. In a sense, however, this conception of mind proved almost too much to justify Dewey's view of education. If mental activity is intrinsically social, one may after all claim that the social prerequisites of learning can be met in a wide variety of types of learning, and not merely in the literal social co-operation of the classroom. As the new educators were somewhat reluctant to see, a child sitting alone and reading about Columbus's voyages is engaging in a social experience at least as complex, if of a different kind, from that of a child in the school workshop making model ships with other children. Yet in Dewey's work the important and persuasive idea that a thing gets its meaning from being a social object is at times transmuted into the more questionable idea that all learning has to be overtly shared in social action.[38]

Even more important is a conception of the relationship between the educational process and its outcome which seems excessively mechanical, especially for one who, like Dewey, hoped always to do justice to the dialectical fluidity of life. The notion that the authoritative classroom would of necessity produce the conformist mind and that sociable learning would produce the ideally socialized personality is at first appealing, but there is about it a kind of rigid rationality of the sort that life constantly eludes. Did Dewey, for example, really imagine that traditional education had engendered in America, of all places, a mind notably characterized by "lack of interest in the novel, aversion to progress, and dread of the uncertain and the unknown"? Was it necessarily true that education founded upon authority invariably produces a conformist mind, and that there is a one-to-one relationship between the style of an educational system and the nature of its products? There hardly seems to be any place in Dewey's idea of the educational process for the fact that Voltaire was schooled by the Jesuits, or that the strong authoritative structure of the Puritan family should have yielded a personal type so important to the

[38]See the passage in *Democracy and Education*, pp. 46–8, in which Dewey plays upon the meaning of the term "social."

development of modern democracy. To expect that education would so simply produce a hoped-for personal type was to expect more than past experience warranted.

Finally, there are serious difficulties involved in living up to the idea that education should in no way be looked upon as a preparation for the child's future life—what Dewey always called a "remote future"—but rather as living itself, a simulacrum of life, or a sort of rehearsal in the experiences that make up life. The motive of achieving some continuity between school experience and other experiences seems altogether commendable. But Dewey not only held that education *is* life; he went on to say that the school should provide a *selective* environment for the child, an environment that represents so far as possible what is deemed good in society and eliminates what is bad. Yet, the more successful the school was in this task, the less it could live up to the ideal of representing or embodying life. The moment one admits that it is not all of life which is presented to children in school, one also admits that a selective process has been set up which is determined by some external end; and then one has once again embraced the traditional view that education is after all not a comprehensive attempt to mirror or reproduce life but a segment of life that is specialized for a distinct function.

If the new educators really wanted to reproduce life itself in the classroom, they must have had an extraordinarily benign conception of what life is. To every adult, life brings, in addition to some measure of co-operation, achievement, and joy, a full stint of competition, defeat, frustration, and failure. But the new educators did not accept the idea that these things too would be embodied in the little community that was to be organized for children in the school. Quite the contrary, their strongest impulse was to protect children from too acute an awareness of what their own limitations, under adult conditions, might cost them. They were much closer to the argument of Marietta Johnson, one of the pioneers of "organic education" and a founder of the Progressive Education Association, who said: "No child should ever know failure. . . . The school should *meet* the demands of the nature of childhood, not make demands. Any school system in which one child may fail while another succeeds is unjust, undemocratic, uneducational."[39] In her experimental school at Fairhope, Alabama, which was described with enthusiasm by John and Evelyn Dewey in *Schools of To-Morrow*, there were therefore no examinations, no grading, no failures to win promotion; success was measured not by the amount of subject matter learned or the promotions earned but by the effort and joy of the work itself. This view of education may or may not have better effects on children than the traditional school, but that it bears a closer relation to "life" is eminently questionable.

To this objection the new educators had what they felt was a satisfactory answer: the new education was not trying to raise children to know or fit into the life of the past, with its harsh and selfish individualism, but to know and adapt to the life of the present and future, which was hopefully conceived as more social, more co-operative, more humane—to a life that Dewey thought accorded better with "the scientific democratic society of today."[40]

But this answer could only turn attention to the difficulty of designing education to suit the child's growth and at the same time to form society anew. As time went on, some of the new educators themselves began to doubt that Dewey had made a successful synthesis of the idea of education as the child's growth and education as the reconstruction of society. Boyd H. Bode observed in 1938 that the doctrine of growth in its present form "prevents [the teacher] from discovering that he needs a guiding social philosophy."[41] To believe that Dewey's synthesis was successful required a certain credulity about the pre-established harmony between child nature and democratic culture which not everyone could share. It seemed to some critics that one would have to give up either the emphasis on child nature and spontaneity or the emphasis on educating for democracy. The child, after all, might feel a natural interest in rebelling at some point or other; but it

[39] Marietta Johnson: *Youth in a World of Men* (New York, 1929), pp. 42, 261; cf. the laudatory comment on this feature of her school by John and Evelyn Dewey in *Schools of To-Morrow* (New York, 1915), especially p. 27.
[40] *Schools of To-Morrow*, p. 165.
[41] *Progressive Education at the Crossroads*, p. 78.

was impossible to impute to him a natural interest in the re-construction of society or in having his mind "saturated" with "the spirit of service." During the great depression, the whole school of social reconstructionists tended to recognize quite candidly that this impulse was lacking; that the future good of society required that educators admit that all education em-bodies a measure of indoctrination; and that "external" ends are inevitably imposed in the educational process.[42] Social re-constructionism in education has not been of much lasting interest, but it did render some service in making progressive educators aware that "external"—that is, adult—objectives are unavoidably dominant in the school. For those who expected that education would be, as Dewey had said in 1897, "the fun-damental method of social progress and reform," it would be impossible to leave it as much as he might have hoped in the hands of the child.

6

Dewey's educational theory was formulated in the hope that a proper educational synthesis would overcome certain ancient polarities and dualisms in educational thought. The antitheses between the child and society, interest and discipline, voca-tion and culture, knowledge and action, must all be resolved and ultimately harmonized—as they now supposedly can be in a democratic society which itself has surpassed the aristo-cratic mental framework in which these antitheses originally appeared. This optimism is vital to Dewey's educational argu-ment: he saw these dualisms in education not as a clue to the nature of human problems but as an unfortunate legacy that could be done away with. The world, as he viewed it when he published his earlier and most influential educational books, was indeed progressing. The age of science and democracy, he thought, would be better, more rational, more intelligent than

[42]Some of the political difficulties in Dewey's theory are penetratingly ana-lyzed by Frederic Lilge: "The Politicizing of Educational Theory," *Ethics*, Vol. LXVI (April, 1956), pp. 188–97.

anything man had known in the past; it would be at once the source and the beneficiary of a better kind of education.

There was thus a distinct if rather covert utopianism about Dewey's educational thought—and it was the utopian element that so many educational theorists found appealing. Dewey's utopianism was not based upon some portrait of an ideal educational system. He was too wise to draw a blueprint for a finished world, and the very nature of his thesis that education is the continuous reconstruction of experience argued against it. His utopianism was one of method: he believed that the old polarities and dualisms were not, so to speak, qualities in reality that must be resisted, minimized, managed, and confined; but were miscalculations derived from the false way of conceiving the world that had prevailed in the past. One could do better than merely resolve these polarities in various limited and inevitably unsatisfactory ways; in a higher synthesis one could overcome them altogether.

In this respect Dewey echoes an argument against the past which had been sounded by so many American thinkers before him. His language gives the impression that he saw the entire drama of human experience primarily as a source of errors that must be surmounted. To keep alive any current enterprise like education required that one enable it to peel off the residues of the past. "The present," he wrote in an uncommonly eloquent passage in *Democracy and Education*, "is not just something which comes after the past. . . . It is what life is in leaving the past behind it." For this reason, the study of the cultural *products* of the past will not help us understand the present. It is the *life* of the past that counts, the life of which these cultural products are only dead repositories—and that life itself was at its best also a process of surmounting its own past. "A knowledge of the past and its heritage is of great significance when it enters into the present, but not otherwise." To make the study of the past the main material of education is to lose the vital connection between present and past, "and tends to make the past a rival of the present and the present a more or less futile imitation of the past. Under such circumstances," Dewey goes on, scoring what seems to be the climactic point in his argument, "culture becomes an ornament and solace; a refuge and an asylum."[43] It thus loses its capacity to be a transforming agent, one that can improve the present and create the future.

It is here that we must return again to the child, for the child is the key to the future; he has within himself the resources to liberate the world from the weight of its past. But before he can do this, the child himself must be freed—and under a proper educational regime really *can* be freed—from the oppressions of the world, from everything that is dead about the apparatus of culture, from the constricting effects of society on the school. Dewey himself was realistic enough to see, to assert and reassert, the limits of the child's spontaneous impulses as a guide to this process. But it was precisely these impulses that interested American educators. Since Dewey aimed at freeing the child from the shackles of the past to the point at which the child could make a reconstructive use of past culture, American educators seized upon his theory as having downgraded past culture and its merely ornamental and solacing "products" and as having finally produced a program to liberate the child for unimpeded growth. Having once put the child so firmly at the center, having defined education as growth without end, Dewey had so weighted the discussion of educational goals that a quarter century of clarificatory statements did not avail to hold in check the anti-intellectual perversions of his theory.

Like Freud, Dewey saw the process by which a society inculcates the young with its principles, inhibitions, and habits as a kind of imposition upon them. But Dewey's assumptions led to a more optimistic calculus of possibilities than that offered by Freud. Freud saw the process by which the individual is socialized as making genuinely impairing demands upon his instincts but also as being in some form tragically inevitable. Society, as Dewey saw it, spoiled the "plasticity" of children, which was the source of their "power to change prevailing custom."

---

[43] *Democracy and Education*, p. 88. Here I would refer the reader to John Herman Randall, Jr.'s beautifully conceived and not unsympathetic critique of Dewey's interpretation of the history of philosophy, in which he asks: "Would Dewey dismiss out of hand all that imagination has done to make existence endurable, just because the world has not yet through action been made quite wholly new?" P. A. Schilpp, ed.: *The Philosophy of John Dewey* (Chicago, 1939), pp. 77–102, especially p. 101.

Education, with its "insolent coercions, insinuating briberies, and pedagogic solemnities by which the freshness of youth can be faded and its vivid curiosities dulled," had become "the art of taking advantage of the helplessness of the young,"[44] and education itself an art used by society to choke off the best part of its capacity for self-improvement. For Dewey, the world as a source of misery for the child is largely remediable through the educational process; for Freud the two are fixed in an opposition which, while alterable and even to a degree ameliorable in detail, is insurmountable in substance.[45]

More than a generation of progressive educational experiment confirms Freud's view. Old educational failings have been remedied, often with much success, but other problems have been intensified by the new remedies. Conformity to arbitrary adult wishes has been diminished, but conformity to peers is now seen as a serious problem. The arbitrary authority of the teacher has been lessened, but a subtle manipulation, which requires self-deceit on the part of the teacher and often inspires resentment in the child, has taken its place. The fear of failure in studies has not been removed, but devices introduced to remove it have created frustrations arising from a lack of standards, of recognition, of a sense of achievement.

In his last significant statement on education, Dewey observed that "the drive of established institutions is to assimilate and distort the new into conformity with themselves." While

---

[44] *Human Nature and Conduct* (1922; Modern Library ed., New York, 1929), p. 64.

[45] Like Dewey, Freud's thought has had both good and bad consequences for education. In many quarters the educational implications of Freud's views were even more misconceived than those of Dewey. During the 1920's, Freud's psychology was frequently taken by progressive educators as lending support to a guiding philosophy of instinctual liberation. It also gave rise to a kind of psychologism in education that often diverts attention from the basic instructional task by attempting to make of the educational process an amateur substitute for psychotherapy. It is, of course, hard to draw the line between a legitimate regard for the pupil's psychological needs as a part of the educational process and a tendency to displace pedagogy by psychological concern and even psychological manipulation. The best brief discussion I have seen of Freud's and Dewey's approach to instinct and impulse in their relation to society is in chapter 2 of Philip Rieff's *Freud: The Mind of the Moralist* (New York, 1959).

commenting with some satisfaction on certain improvements introduced by progressive education, he ruefully remarked that the ideas and principles he had helped to develop had also succumbed to this process of institutionalization. "In teachers colleges and elsewhere the ideas and principles have been converted into a fixed subject matter of ready-made rules, to be taught and memorized according to certain standardized procedures. . . ." Memorization and standardized procedures once more! It did all too little good, he said, to train teachers "in the right principles the wrong way." With a hardy courage that can only inspire admiration, Dewey reminded progressive educators, once again and for the last time, that it is the right *method* of training which forms the character of teachers, and not the subject matter or the rules they are taught. Pursue the right methods, and a democratic society might yet be created; follow the "authoritarian principle" and education will be fit only to "pervert and destroy the foundations of a democratic society."[46] And so the quest for a method of institutionalizing the proper anti-institutional methods goes on.

[46]"Introduction" to Elsie R. Clapp: *The Use of Resources in Education* (New York, 1952), pp. x–xi.

PART 6

CONCLUSION

CHAPTER XV

The Intellectual: Alienation and Conformity

ANTI-INTELLECTUALISM IN various forms continues to pervade American life, but at the same time intellect has
taken on a new and more positive meaning and intellectuals
have come to enjoy more acceptance and, in some ways, a
more satisfactory position. This new acceptance sits awkwardly
on their shoulders. Being used to rejection, and having over
the years forged a strong traditional response to society based
upon the expectation that rejection would continue, many of
them have come to feel that alienation is the only appropriate
and honorable stance for them to take. What they have come
to fear is not so much rejection or overt hostility, with which
they have learned to cope and which they have almost come
to regard as their proper fate, but the loss of alienation. Many
of the most spirited younger intellectuals are disturbed above
all by the fear that, as they are increasingly recognized, incorporated, and used, they will begin merely to conform, and will
cease to be creative and critical and truly useful. This is the
fundamental paradox in their position—that while they do re-
sent evidences of anti-intellectualism, and take it as a token
of a serious weakness in our society, they are troubled and divided in a more profound way by their acceptance. Perhaps the
most divisive issue in the intellectual community today arises
over the values to be placed upon the old alienation and the
new acceptance. Let us look first at the way this question has
been posed in recent years and then at the historical position
of the intellectual community for what light it may shed.

For all the popular anti-intellectualism of the 1950's, the intellectuals themselves, especially those of the middle and older
generations, were not disposed, as they had been in the 1920's,
to wage a counterattack upon American values. Instead, they
were ironically engaged in re-embracing their country at the
very moment when they were under the most severe attack
for being constitutionally disloyal. Even McCarthyism did not
quite stop them: the very fear that the senator and his mob

might destroy certain values hitherto taken for granted was a reminder that something about American values in the past had indeed been precious. And certain old-fashioned and eminently conservative senators who stood up to McCarthy were much admired as personal monuments to a venerable American integrity.

In 1952, the editors of the *Partisan Review*, which may be taken as a kind of house organ of the American intellectual community, gave a quasi-official recognition of the new mood of the intellectuals when they devoted several issues to a memorable symposium, significantly entitled "Our Country and Our Culture."[1] "American intellectuals," they explained, "now regard America and its institutions in a new way. . . . Many writers and intellectuals now feel closer to their country and its culture. . . . For better or for worse, most writers no longer accept alienation as the artist's fate in America; on the contrary, they want very much to be a part of American life."

The response of the twenty-five contributors to the editors' questions about the relation of the intellectual to America showed that the overwhelming majority not only shared an awareness of a growing *rapprochement* between the intellectuals and their society but also, for the most part, accepted it. If we omitted their qualifications and the accompanying warnings against an excess of complacency, we would risk exaggerating or caricaturing their acceptance; and we might suggest a complacency that was not there. A composite statement of their views, however, shows how much a once intensely alienated segment of the intellectual class had changed its ideas. The habit of "mere exacerbated alienation," most contributors agreed, no longer seemed defensible. Remarks made by several of them about alienation as an historical phenomenon emphasized that alienation had commonly been an ambivalent feeling, and that the great writers and thinkers of the past had combined with their protests against American society a strong affirmation of many of its values and a profound identification with it—that it was indeed the tension between protest and affirmation that had been most often associated with great achievement.

[1]Reprinted as *America and the Intellectuals* (New York, 1953).

No one doubted that the intellectual's role as a critical non-conformist was of essential value or thought that he ought to give it up to become a mere spokesman or apologist of his society. But it was agreed that American intellectuals no longer look at their country as a cultural desert from which they must flee, or regard it, as one writer put it, with "adolescent embarrassment" when they compare America to Europe. Intellectuals now felt more at home in America than they had twenty or thirty years earlier; they had come to terms with American realities. "We are witnessing a process," wrote one, "that might well be described as the *embourgeoisement* of the American intelligentsia." It was not only intellectuals who had changed; the country had changed too, and for the better. It had matured culturally, and no longer stood in tutelage to Europe. The wealthy and powerful had learned to accept, even defer to, the intellectual and the artist. Accordingly, America had become a reasonably gratifying place in which to carry on intellectual or artistic work, and one in which such pursuits were well rewarded. Even a contributor who found the whole symposium complacent conceded: "The notion that America is uniquely a land of barbarism now seems silly."

2

Among the twenty-five contributors to the symposium, only three—Irving Howe, Norman Mailer, and C. Wright Mills—were entirely at odds with the acquiescent mood of the editors' questions; and a fourth, Delmore Schwartz, thought it important to protest against "the will to conformism which is now the chief prevailing fashion among intellectuals." To these dissenters, this re-embracement of America was simply a surrender to current pressures toward conservatism and patriotism, a capitulation to comfort and smugness. The very idea of "*our* country" and "*our* culture" offended them—"a shrinking deference to the status quo," said C. Wright Mills, "a soft and anxious compliance," and "a synthetic, feeble search to justify this intellectual conduct." What seemed to the older intellectuals, whose adult memories stretched back to the cultural controversies of the thirties and in some cases to the twenties, to be no more than a willingness to abandon an oversimplified commitment to alienation into which they had once been mis-led appeared to somewhat younger men as an incomprehensi-ble moral failure.

The case against the dominant point of view in the *Partisan Review* symposium was put into a formidable statement two years later in the same magazine by one of the dissenting con-tributors, the critic, Irving Howe, then a professor at Brandeis University. In an article on "This Age of Conformity,"[2] Howe asserted that the symposium had been "a disconcerting sign of how far intellectuals have drifted in the direction of cultural adaptation." Capitalism, he said, "in its most recent stage has found an honored place for the intellectuals," who instead of resisting incorporation, have enjoyed returning "to the bosom of the nation." "We are all conformists to one or another de-gree." Even those who still tried to hold a critical stance had become "responsible and moderate. And tame." The prolif-eration of new jobs in the mass-culture industries and in the growing college and university system had helped the intellec-tuals to become absorbed into the permanent war economy. "Intellectual freedom in the United States is under severe at-tack and the intellectuals have, by and large, shown a painful lack of militancy in defending the rights which are a precondi-tion of their existence."

Howe's counter-ideal to this complacent adaptation was an old one: the community of Bohemia. Flaubert had said that Bohemia was "the fatherland of my breed," and Howe believed that it had also been the basic precondition of cultural creativ-ity in the United States. "The most exciting periods of Ameri-can intellectual life tend to coincide with the rise of bohemia," he asserted, and then, as though troubled by the difficulties of this proposition, he added: "Concord too was a kind of bohe-mia, sedate, subversive, and transcendental all at once." Bohe-mia had been a kind of strategy for bringing artists and writers together in their struggle with and for the world, but now its role had disintegrated. "Bohemia gradually disappears as a setting for our intellectual life, and what remains of it seems willed or fake." The breakup of Bohemia had contributed in an important way to "those feelings of loneliness one finds among so many American intellectuals, feelings of damp dispirited isolation which undercut the ideology of liberal optimism." Once young writers faced the world together. Now they "sink into suburbs, country homes and college towns."

It was not, said Howe, a matter of berating anyone for "selling out" or of calling for material asceticism on the part of intellectuals. What was at issue was the "slow attrition which destroys one's ability to stand firm and alone," which is seen in a chain of small compromises. "What is most alarming is that the whole idea of the intellectual vocation—the idea of a life dedicated to values that cannot possibly be realized by a commercial civilization—has gradually lost its allure." The battle against commercial civilization had in his eyes a primary value in its own right. For if the clash between business civilization and the values of art is no longer so urgent as we once thought, he asserted, "we must discard a great deal, and mostly the best, of the literature, the criticism and the speculative thought of the twentieth century."

Howe regretted "the loss of those earlier certainties that had the advantage, at least, of making resistance easy." He was in particular affronted by Lionel Trilling's suggestion in the symposium that the cultural situation of the 1950's, for all its deficiencies, had improved over that of thirty years earlier. "Any comparison," Howe argued, "between the buoyant free-spirited cultural life of 1923 with the dreariness of 1953, or between their literary achievements," was hardly more than a pleasant fantasy. If wealth had accepted the intellectuals, it was only because the intellectuals had become tame, and no longer presumed to challenge wealth, engaging instead in "some undignified prostrations" before it. The intellectuals are more powerless than ever, and most particularly the new realists "who attach themselves to the seats of power, where they surrender their freedom of expression without gaining any significance as political figures." Whenever intellectuals "become absorbed into the accredited institutions of society they not only lose their traditional rebelliousness but to one extent or another *they cease to function as intellectuals.*" Almost any alternative would be preferable to subordination of their talents to the uses of others: "A total estrangement from the sources of power and prestige, even a blind unreasoning rejection of every aspect of our culture, would be far healthier if only because it would permit a free discharge of aggression."

Howe's article was not an entirely personal document, but a kind of manifesto of the intellectuals of the left. Some years later a young historian, Loren Baritz, looking at the social disciplines from a similar point of view, expounded the belief that "any intellectual who accepts and approves of his society prostitutes his skills and is a traitor to his heritage." He asked whether, "by definition, a man of ideas must maintain the posture of the critic, and whether the intellectual who sincerely believes in and approves of the larger movements of his society can reconcile the demands of his mind and those of his society."[3] He called for a principled withdrawal of intellectuals from social institutions, from relevance, responsibility, and power: "Let the intellectual be absorbed into society and he runs the grave risk of permitting himself to be digested by it. . . . When he touches power, it will touch him." The right response is a willed estrangement from social responsibility: "When the intellectual becomes socially, rather than intellectually, responsible his mind must lose at least part of the freedom and resiliency which is part of his most fundamental equipment." If the intellectual withdraws to the ivory tower, it is because of "this need for social irresponsibility, for irrelevancy, for the freedom which comes from isolation and alienation."

3

As one listens first to the dominant mood of the *Partisan Review*'s symposium and then to Mr. Howe and other dissenters, what one hears are the two voices of an old and familiar dialogue. A self-conscious concern with alienation, far from being peculiar to American intellectuals in our time, has been a major theme in the life of the intellectual communities of the Western world for almost two centuries. In earlier ages, when the life and work of intellectuals had been bound up with the Church

---

[3]Loren Baritz: *The Servants of Power* (Middletown, Connecticut, 1960); see also the same writer's article in the *Nation*, January 21, 1961, and my own discussion of the issues, "A Note on Intellect and Power," *American Scholar*, Vol. XXX (Autumn, 1961), pp. 588–98.

or the aristocracy or both, consistent alienation from society was rare. But the development of modern society, from the eighteenth century onwards, created a new set of material and social conditions and a new kind of consciousness. Everywhere in the Western world, the ugliness, materialism, and ruthless human exploitation of early modern capitalism affronted sensitive minds. The end of the system of patronage and the development of a market place for ideas and art brought artists and intellectuals into a sharp and often uncomfortable confrontation with the mind of the middle class. In various ways intellectuals rebelled against the conditions of the new bourgeois world—in romantic assertions of the individual against society, in Bohemian solidarity, in political radicalism.

It is natural, for example, that in looking for a great historic precedent, Mr. Howe should turn to Flaubert, who was a tireless connoisseur of the fatuities of the French bourgeoisie.[4] In England, and in a different manner, Matthew Arnold tried to analyze the new cultural situation in *Culture and Anarchy*. In America, the Transcendentalists were constantly writing about the difficulty which the individual sensibility experienced in coming to terms with modern society.

Each country had its own variation of this general problem, much as each country had its own variety of bourgeois development. The background of alienation in America made an uncompromising position of alienation seem orthodox, axiomatic, and traditional for twentieth-century intellectuals; for in nineteenth-century American society both the accepted, standard writers and the avant-garde writers were likely to be in the one case at least moderately and in the other intensely alienated. One can truly say of this society that by about the middle of the nineteenth century even those who belonged did not altogether belong. Hence, in our own time, those intellectuals whose conception of their role is formed by the history of this society find it strange and even repellent that intellectuals should experience success or have any association with power.

It was not always so. In our earlier days two groups of intellectuals were associated with or responsible for the exercise of

[4]Flaubert, it must be said, saw some dangers in his role. "By dint of railing at idiots," he once wrote, "one runs the risk of becoming idiotic oneself."

far-reaching social power, the Puritan clergy and the Founding
Fathers. Each group in time lost its supremacy, partly because
of its own failings, partly because of historical circumstances
beyond its control. Yet each also left a distinctive legacy. The
Puritan clergy founded the tradition of New England intellectualism; and this tradition, exported wherever New Englanders
settled in large numbers, was responsible for a remarkably large
portion of the country's dynamic intellectual life throughout
the nineteenth century and into the twentieth.[5] The Puritan
founders had their terrible faults, but they had at least the respect for mind and the intensity of spirit which are necessary to
distinguished intellectual achievement. Where it survived, this
intensity often had a wonderfully invigorating effect.

The legacy of the Founding Fathers, itself tinctured by Puritan ideas, was equally important. In the development of new
countries, while the people are engaged in liberating themselves from colonial status and forging a new identity, intellectuals seem always to play an important role. The leaders of the
American Enlightenment did so with signal effectiveness: they
gave the new republic a coherent and fairly workable body of
ideas, a definition of its identity and ideals, a sense of its place
in history, a feeling of nationality, a political system and a political code.

After about 1820, the old republican order in which the Revolution had been carried out and the Constitution adopted,
the order in which both Federalists and Jeffersonians had been
reared, was rapidly destroyed by a variety of economic and social changes. With the settlement of the trans-Allegheny West,
the development of industry, the rise of an egalitarian ethos
in politics, and the submergence of the Jeffersonian South,
the patrician class that had led and in a measure controlled
American democracy became more and more enfeebled. The
laymen and the evangelicals had already dethroned the established clergy. Now a new type of democratic leader with a new

---

[5]In fact, it is too seldom realized how immensely impoverished the intellectual
and cultural life of this large and heterogeneous country would have been, had
it not been for the contributions of three cultural strains: the first was that of
New England, which dominates the nineteenth century; the second and third
are those of the Jews and the writers of the culturally renascent South which
have played an important part in the intellectual life of the twentieth century.

political style was to dethrone the mercantile-professional class from its position of political leadership. Soon a new type of industrialist and promoter would completely overshadow this class in business as well.

What was left was a gentlemanly class with considerable wealth, leisure, and culture, but with relatively little power or influence. This class was the public and the patron of serious writing and of cultural institutions. Its members read the books that were written by the standard American writers, subscribed to the old highbrow magazines, supported libraries and museums, and sent their sons to the old-fashioned liberal-arts colleges to study the classical curriculum. It developed its own gentle tradition of social protest, for it had enough of an aristocratic bias to be opposed to the most vulgar features of the popular democracy that was emerging everywhere and enough of a code of behavior to be opposed to the crass materialism of the new capitalists and plantation lords. The most eloquent tradition of moral protest in America is the creation of a few uncompromising sons of the patrician gentry.

But if one thinks of this class as having inherited the austere traditions of the older republican order, the traditions crystallized by the Founding Fathers, one sees immediately the relative weakness of a type that kept the manners and aspirations and prejudices of an aristocratic class without being able to retain its authority. The mental outlook of the leaders of the old republican order, inherited by subsequent generations of patricians, became transformed into something less spirited and less powerful. The culture of the Founding Fathers was succeeded by what I like to call mugwump culture—and by mugwump I refer not just to the upper-class reform movement of the Gilded Age, which is the conventional usage, but to the intellectual and cultural outlook of the dispossessed patrician class. Throughout the entire nineteenth century this class provided the chief public to which the independent and cultivated American mind expressed itself.[6] The mugwump mind,

[6]I prefer this designation to the term commonly used to evoke this cultural milieu. It is sometimes called Brahmin culture, but this has for my purposes an excessively local New England reference. Santayana's term, the genteel tradition, is more satisfactory, but I believe the expression *mugwump culture* better evokes the broad political implications of this order of society.

in which the influence of New England was again decisive, inherited from the Puritans a certain solemnity and high intent, but was unable to sustain their passion. From the Founding Fathers and the American Enlightenment it inherited in a more direct and immediate way a set of intellectual commitments and civic concerns. In the mugwump ambience, however, the intellectual virtues of the eighteenth-century republican type dwindled and dried up, very largely because mugwump thinkers were too commonly deprived of the occasion to bring these virtues into any intimate or organic relation with experience. It had been essential to the culture of the Founding Fathers that it was put to the test of experience, that it was forced to cope with grave and intricate problems of power; it was characteristic of mugwump culture that its relation to experience and its association with power became increasingly remote.

The mugwump mind reproduced the classicism of the Founding Fathers, their passion for order and respect for mind, their desire to rationalize the world and to make political institutions the embodiment of applied reason, their assumption that social station is a proper fulcrum for political leadership, and their implicit concern for the decorous exemplification of one's proper social role. But having retreated from the most urgent and exciting changes that were taking place in the country, having been edged out of the management of its central institutions of business and politics, and having chosen to withdraw from any identification with the aspirations of the common people, the patrician class produced a culture that became over-refined, desiccated, aloof, snobbish—everything that Santayana had in mind when he identified the genteel tradition. Its leaders cared more that intellect be respectable than that it be creative. What G. K. Chesterton said in quite another connection may be applied to them: they showed more pride in the possession of intellect than joy in the use of it.

Unlike most Americans, these men had a firm sense of tradition, but for them tradition was not so much a source of strength or a point of departure as a fetish. In the inevitable tension between tradition and the individual talent, they weighted the scales heavily against anything assertive or originative in the individual, for it was an essential part of their philosophy that such assertion must be regarded as merely

egoistical and self-indulgent. The tenets of their code of criticism were eminently suited to an entrenched class that is anxious about keeping its position. The business of criticism was
to inculcate "correct taste" and "sound morals"—and taste
and morals were carefully defined in such a way as to establish
disapproval of any rebelliousness, political or esthetic, against
the existing order. Literature was to be a firm custodian of
"morality"; and what was meant by morality was always conventional social morality, not that independent morality of the
artist or thinker which is imposed upon him by the discipline
of artistic form or his vision of the truth. Literature was to be
committed to optimism, to the more smiling aspects of life,
and must not countenance realism or gloom. Fantasy, obscurity, mysticism, individuality, and revolt were all equally beyond the pale.

So it was that Wordsworth and Southey were condemned
by an American critic, Samuel Gilman, in the *North American
Review* in 1823 for their "disinclination to consult the precise
intellectual tone and spirit of the average mass to which their
works are presented." Such writers, Gilman thought, had a de-
served unpopularity: "Theirs is the poetry of soliloquy. They
write apart from and above the world. Their original object
seems to be the employment of their faculties and the gratification of their poetical propensities."[7] Of course, the rejection
of originality that is justified here is not significantly different
from the rejection experienced by many of the best poets of the
nineteenth century in Europe. The difference was that the European environment, despite such critical philosophies as those
of Gilman's European counterparts, was complex enough to
give the writers some room for assertion in its interstices. The
American cultural environment was simpler, more subject to
domination by the outlook of a single, well-meaning, but limited class.

The discomfort this class felt in the presence of true genius
is exemplified at its best and its worst in the relationship of

---

[7] William Charvat: *The Origins of American Critical Thought, 1810–1835* (Philadelphia, 1936), p. 25. The best evocation of the mugwump literary and intellectual atmosphere with which I am acquainted is that of Perry Miller in the
opening chapters of *The Raven and The Whale* (New York, 1956).

Thomas Wentworth Higginson to Emily Dickinson: he, who was so encouraging and so kind to her, even at moments understanding, could never quite rise above thinking of her as another aspiring lady poet and referred to her now and again as "my partially cracked poetess at Amherst." Nor could he resist suggesting to her that she might overcome her loneliness by attending a meeting of the Boston Woman's Club.[8]

For generations, the effort of established criticism was to make writers accede to the sensibilities of a social type which was itself "apart from and above the world." The Puritan intensity of conviction, which had produced fiery dissenters as well as guardians of the laws, was lost; lost too was that engagement with challenging realities and significant power that had helped to form and test the minds of the Founding Fathers. Puritan society, when one pays due regard to its tiny population and its staggering material problems, had laid the foundations for a remarkable tradition of intellectual discipline and had produced a vital literature, first in religion and then in politics. The Founding Fathers, working under exigent political pressures, had given the world a striking example of applied reason in politics, and their generation had made long strides in literature, science, and art as well. Although it drew upon a wealthier society, mugwump culture was notable neither for its political writing nor for its interest in science. It was at its best in history and polite letters, but its coolness to spontaneity and originality disposed it to be a better patron to secondary than to primary talents. It rarely gave the highest recognition to a first-rate writer when a second-rate one was to be found. It passed over the most original native minds—Hawthorne, Melville, Poe, Thoreau, Whitman—and gave its loudest applause to Cooper, its most distinguished figure, and to Irving, Bryant, Longfellow, Lowell, and Whittier. It is easy to yield to the temptation to speak slightingly of the mugwump public, which, after all, provided the support for a large part of the nation's cultural life, but its failure to appreciate or encourage most of the nation's first-rate genius is an ineluctable part of the record.

[8]George Frisbie Whicher: *This Was a Poet* (Ann Arbor, 1960), pp. 119–20.

At any rate, the consequences for American literature of the insulation and deprivation of mind that characterized mugwump culture have long been amply recognized and fervently lamented in American criticism. In 1915 Van Wyck Brooks complained that American literature had suffered from a disastrous bifurcation between the highbrow and the lowbrow; and more recently Philip Rahv, borrowing from D. H. Lawrence, has written of the polarity between the paleface and the redskin, symbolized by Henry James and Walt Whitman. What these critics had in mind was the divorce in American writing and thinking between sensibility, refinement, theory, and discipline on one side and spontaneity, energy, sensuous reality, and the seizure of opportunity on the other—in short, a painful separation between the qualities of mind and the materials of experience. This separation, traceable to mugwump culture, could be followed through American letters in a number of incomplete and truncated minds. Hawthorne might have been complaining not simply for himself but for almost all of well-bred and thoughtful America in the nineteenth century when he wrote: "I have not lived, but only dreamed of living. . . . I have seen so little of the world that I have nothing but thin air to concoct my stories of. . . ."

All this may help us to understand why the case against intellect took the form it did during the nineteenth century. When the spokesmen for hardy, masculine practicality, the critics of aristocratic and feminine and unworldly culture, made their case against intellect, they had some justification for their point of view. But they mistook the paler and more ineffectual manifestations of intellect that they saw around them for intellect as such. They failed to see that their own behavior had in some measure contributed to making intellect what it was, that intellect in America had been stunted in some part by their own repudiation of it—by the arrant populism, the mindless obsession with "practicality" which they had themselves insisted upon. The case of the anti-intellectualist had taken on the character of a self-fulfilling prophecy. Partly by their own fiat, intellect had become associated with losing causes and exemplified by social types that were declining in vigor and influence, encapsulated by an impermeable world.

4

If we turn from consideration of the public to a consideration of American writers themselves, we find that until almost the end of the nineteenth century they were primarily concerned with certain elemental problems of their identity and their craft. They had to find their own national voice, to free themselves from a provincial imitation of English literature and from excessive dependence on English critical judgment, and yet at the same time to steer short of the opposite danger of literary chauvinism. They had to reconcile the aristocratic bias which all but a few of them shared—Cooper was here the most poignant example—with their sympathy for the undeniably appealing energy and hardihood and promise of the American democracy that was developing all around them. The best of them had to come to terms with their own isolation, itself a compelling theme. They had to fashion their own response to the kind of materials which American life offered the creative writer, which were of a different order from the materials available to the European writer. No monuments, no ruins, no Eton, no Oxford, no Epsom, no Ascot, no antiquity, no legends, no society in the received sense of the word—the grievance runs from Hawthorne to Henry James and beyond, though an occasional writer like Crèvecoeur saw merit in being able to dispense with the apparatus of feudalism and oppression, and others like Emerson insisted that only the proper energy of imagination was necessary to see American society in its full potentiality as a literary subject.[9]

[9]America, Emerson wrote in the 1840's, had not yet had the genius who could see in the barbarism and materialism of the times another "carnival of the gods" such as anyone could see in the European past from Homeric times to the struggles of Calvinism. "Banks and tariffs, the newspaper and caucus, Methodism and Unitarianism, are flat and dull to dull people, but rest on the same foundations of wonder as the town of Troy and the temple of Delphi, and are as swiftly passing away. Our log-rolling, our stumps and their politics, our fisheries, our Negroes and Indians, our boats and our repudiations, the wrath of rogues and the pusillanimity of honest men, the northern trade, the southern planting, the western clearing, Oregon and Texas, are yet unsung. Yet America is a poem in our eyes; its ample geography dazzles the imagination, and it will not wait long for metres." *Complete Works* (Boston, 1903–4), Vol. III, pp. 37–8.

There was, again, the sheer necessity of forging a profession for the man of letters (and for the academic too, who taught in colleges which were, most of them, pathetic, libraryless little boardinghouses for drill-masters and adolescent rioters, living under the thumb of this or that sect). Almost no one at first could collect any significant royalties for serious creative work, and in addition to the usual hard economics of authorship, there was the terrible ruthless competition of pirated editions of famous English writers, which, in the absence of an international copyright agreement, unscrupulous reprint houses could pour into the market at low prices. Up to the 1840's, before Longfellow and Whittier struck the public fancy, probably the only authors who made any money to speak of from their creative efforts were Irving and Cooper, but neither of them had much need of his royalties. Practically every man of letters had to have a primary source of income, which his royalties would only supplement, whether it was his patrimony, his wife's trust funds, lectures, college teaching, or an editorial post on a magazine or newspaper, or, as in the case of Thoreau for several years, manual labor.[10]

During these decades, American writers expressed their protest against the more discouraging side of their condition in a variety of ways—withdrawal, expatriation, overt criticism. But they were more disposed to look upon their estrangement as a consequence of the pursuit of other values than as a value in itself. They were on the whole quite free from one of the most pressing difficulties of the modern thinker, the fact that he is to a painful degree the creature of his own self-consciousness. They suffered at the hands of their society, but they were not overwhelmed by their awareness of their own suffering. (One thinks of the wry and melancholy humor with which Thoreau remarked on the seven-hundred-odd unsold copies of an edition of a thousand of his *A Week on the Concord and Merrimac Rivers* which were stacked in his room: "I now have a library

[10] William Charvat has observed, in his interesting study of the economics of authorship, *Literary Publishing in America, 1790–1850* (Philadelphia, 1959), p. 23: "Not a single literary work of genuine originality published in book form before 1850 had any commercial value until much later, and most of our classics were financial failures. . . ."

of nearly nine hundred volumes, over seven hundred of which I wrote myself. Is it not well that the author should behold the fruits of his labor?" What contemporary writer, suffering a comparable disappointment, could refrain from spinning out of it a complete theory of modern culture?) When one compares the situation of American writers to a truly bitter case of estrangement—like that, say, of Joyce from Ireland—it seems less than stark. They were in fact quite ambivalent about their America, and later critics, obsessed by their own alienation, could find in these earlier writers texts that would reinforce their feeling of kinship. It became natural to notice Melville's words, "I feel I am an exile here," and to ignore the feeling of identification he expressed elsewhere: "It is for the nation's sake, and not for her authors' sake, that I would have America be heedful of the increasing greatness among her writers. For how great a shame, if other nations should be before her in crowning the heroes of the pen!" On the whole, one must be persuaded by the observation of Richard Chase, in the *Partisan Review* symposium, that he had never believed "that the great American writers of the past felt half so 'estranged' or 'disinherited' as many modern critics have said they did."

After about 1890, however, American writers and other intellectuals became a more cohesive class than they had been, became restless with the constraints of gentility and conservatism, and took up arms against American society. In the struggle for new freedoms in expression and criticism that occupied them from about 1890 to the 1930's, the idea of their own alienation became a kind of rallying point, a part of their esthetic or political protest. Before this, intellect in America had been mostly associated with the maintenance of old values. Now, both in historical reality and in the public awareness, it was linked with the propagation of novelty—with new ideas in politics and morals, art and literature. Where the American intellectual had been hemmed in during the nineteenth century by safe and genteel idealism, he now rather rapidly established the right, even the obligation, of the intellectual community to talk realistically about corruption and exploitation, sex and violence. Intellect, for so long considered both by its foes and its exponents as passive and futile, came little by little to be involved in and identified once again with power. Once associated by the public with the conservative classes and with a political outlook well to the right of center, the intellectual class emerged after 1890 as a force standing somewhat to the left, and during the great depression much of it moved to the far left.

This brings us to one of the most poignant aspects of the intellectual's position. Anti-intellectualism, as I hope these pages have made clear, is founded in the democratic institutions and the egalitarian sentiments of this country. The intellectual class, whether or not it enjoys many of the privileges of an elite, is of necessity an elite in its manner of thinking and functioning. Up to about 1890, most American intellectuals were rooted in a leisured patrician class which, whatever its limitations on other counts, had no difficulty in accepting its own identity as an elite. After 1890 this was no longer true in the same degree. The problem of identity once again became a difficulty for intellectuals, because, at the very moment when their sensibilities and concerns were deviating more than ever from those of the public at large, they were trying far more than ever to espouse political causes that supposedly represented the case of the people against special interests—it does not matter for this purpose whether these causes were conceived in the populist, progressive, or Marxist traditions.

Intellectuals in the twentieth century have thus found themselves engaged in incompatible efforts: they have tried to be good and believing citizens of a democratic society and at the same time to resist the vulgarization of culture which that society constantly produces. It is rare for an American intellectual to confront candidly the unresolvable conflict between the elite character of his own class and his democratic aspirations. The extreme manifestation of the general reluctance to face this conflict is the writer who constantly assaults class barriers and yet constantly hungers for special deference. Since any alliance between intellectuals and the people is bound to be imperfect, a loyally democratic intellectual class is bound to suffer acute disappointments from time to time. At moments when the political climate is full of hope and vigor—when some democratic cause is flourishing, as it was in the full flush of Progressivism and in the New Deal—these disappointments may be obscured or forgotten, but such moments do not last. Progressivism was followed by the reaction of the 1920's, the New Deal in time by McCarthyism. Sooner or later, when the public fails to meet the political or cultural demands of the intellectuals, the intellectuals are hurt or shocked and look for some way of expressing their feelings without going so far as to repudiate their popular allegiances altogether. The phenomenon of mass culture has given them a vent for their estrangement from the people. The collapse of hope for socialism, and even, for the moment, of any new movement of serious social reform, has eliminated expectations of any new *rapprochement.* One reason for the fascination of so many intellectuals with mass culture —quite aside from the intrinsic gravity of the problem—is that they have found in it a legitimate (that is, non-political) way of expressing their estrangement from democratic society. And it is significant that some of the bitterest indictments of mass culture have come from writers who were, or still are, democratic socialists. The stridency, even the note of inhumanity, which often creeps into discussions of mass culture may be explained in some part by an underlying sense of grievance against a populace that has not lived up to expectations.

Perhaps the most decisive testimony of the changed situation of twentieth-century intellectuals is that after 1890 it became possible for the first time to speak of intellectuals as a class. As the intellectual community began to detach itself from the leisured class, the whole question of the intellectual and society was reopened. The early nineteenth century had known many men of intellect and a few men who were professional intellectuals; but it had not produced institutions that could forge them into a numerous social order with some capacity for cohesion and mutual communication on a national scale. Only at the end of the century did the country develop a system of genuine universities; great libraries suited to advance research; magazines with large circulations, receptive to fresh ideas and able to pay writers well; a considerable number of strong and enterprising publishing houses, operating under the protection of international copyright, alert to the possibilities of native writers, and free from genteel inhibitions; well-organized professional societies in various scholarly disciplines; an array of scholarly journals; expanding governmental bureaucracies with a need for trained skills; and, finally, wealthy foundations to subsidize science, scholarship, and letters. Certain types of intellectual careers that had not existed before now came into being on a national scale. To visualize the scope of the change, one must try to imagine, say, muckraking magazines in the 1830's, or the *Harvard Law Review* in Jackson's time, or Guggenheim Fellowships in the Polk era, or the W.P.A. theater project under Cleveland.

At the very time that intellectuals were beginning to become more numerous and effective and more organically involved in American society, in its institutions and its market place, they were becoming more self-conscious about their estrangement. The older awareness of estrangement had taken shape under the particular conditions of mugwump culture. Its basic sources had been lonely and neglected writers or frustrated patricians, and its most eloquent statement, coming at the end of the mugwump epoch, was Henry Adams's *Education*. Adams's book, written earlier but first available for general public circulation in 1918, was, significantly, seized upon by the intellectuals of the post-war era as a document that spoke for them and expressed their sense of their position in American culture; and it appropriately fell to the same generation to rediscover the merits of the long-forgotten Melville. Clearly, the post-war intellectuals responded so much to Adams, not because they shared any of the circumstances of his singular life or his intensely poignant personal disinheritance, but because his indictment of post-Civil War America as a coarse, materialistic, and mindless society fitted their own sense of America in the 1920's. Although the particular setting of mugwump alienation had been altogether different from the avant-garde alienation of this generation, a common consciousness of estrangement and discomfort, failure and lamentation, established a spiritual link between the two. It began to be evident, at least to some, that the "democratic" intellectual would hardly be any more at home in this society than the patrician intellectual.

There is a certain irony in the fact that alienation became a kind of fixed principle among knowing young intellectuals during the years preceding the war. These were the very years of that "Little Renaissance" in which the literary and political culture of the nation seemed once again so full of originality and energy as to mock all despairing assertions about its past.

Nonetheless, the alienation of the intellectual and the artist, long since a ponderable fact, was beginning to congeal into a sort of ideology, as they fell into a somewhat parochial struggle with their own national inheritance. For American writers what seemed to count was alienation not from modern society in general or modern industrialism or the modern bourgeoisie but specifically from these things as they were manifested *in America*.

The case was best put in Van Wyck Brooks's eloquent early cultural jeremiads, *America's Coming-of-Age* and *Letters and Leadership*, published in 1915 and 1918. There, with a fervor and persuasiveness that he would later regret, Brooks exposed what seemed to be the terrible truth about "a race that has never cultivated life for its own sake." From the beginning, he thought, the American mind, caught between the hopeless imperatives of the Puritan code and the stark realities of business self-assertion, had developed a kind of unwholesome doubleness that militated against the creation or at least the fulfillment of first-rate artists and thinkers. It had forged, on the one side, a world of ideals and abstractions uncommitted to any reality, and, on the other, a world of possession, the soulless accumulation of dollars; caught between them was a thinking class that passed at a frightening pace from youth to middle age and then to slow, relentless decay. A country whose life was "in a state of arrested development," "a national mind that has been sealed against that experience from which literature derives all its values," had given rise to a gallery of wasted, deformed, and unrealized talents:[11]

> Poets, painters, philosophers, men of science and religion are all to be found, stunted, starved, thwarted, embittered, prevented from taking even the first step in self-development, in this amazing microcosm of our society, a society that stagnates for want of leadership, and at the same time, incurably suspicious of the very idea of leadership, saps away all those vital elements that produce the leader.

American experience had not produced an intellectual tradition or a sympathetic soil, and in consequence "we who above

[11] *America's Coming-of-Age* (New York: Anchor ed., 1958), p. 99; cf. pp. 91–110 and *passim*.

all peoples need great men and great ideals have been unable to develop the latent greatness we possess, and have lost [through expatriation] an incalculable measure of greatness that has, in spite of all, succeeded in developing itself." An excessive, rampant individualism had prevented the formation of a collective spiritual life. The pioneering spirit, coarsely bent on acquisition and conquest, had fostered a materialism which was hopelessly opposed to the skeptical or creative imagination; and it had been reinforced by Puritanism, the ideal philosophy for the pioneer, a philosophy whose contemptuous view of human nature simultaneously released the acquisitive side of men and inhibited their esthetic impulses. American business, as it developed in the atmosphere of the pioneer spirit, Puritanism, and frontier opportunities, had indeed become more adventurous and attractive than business elsewhere, but by this very fact it had absorbed and diverted all too much of what was good in the American character. What one had, then, was a society of sorts, but virtually no "organic native culture," and it could hardly be surprising that "our orthodox literary men, whatever models they place before themselves, cannot rise above the tribal view of their art as either an amusement or a soporific."

Brooks's onslaught, which was followed and, in a sense, supposedly documented by his own studies of Mark Twain and Henry James, prefigured the judgment that would be rendered in criticism or literature by writer after writer of his own generation. The same indictment, voiced in more raucous tones and to different ends, ran through the more popular critical diatribes of H. L. Mencken and the literature of Spoon River, Winesburg, and Zenith—those portraits of the mean, stunted, starved lives, the sour little crabapple culture of the American small town, with its inhibitions and its tyrannies.[12] The

[12]What an ancient theme this was! In 1837 even Longfellow had said even of Boston that it was nothing but a "great village," where "the tyranny of opinion passes all belief." And three quarters of a century later John Jay Chapman wrote, along the same lines: "No one who has not been up against it can imagine the tyranny of a small town in America. I believe good old fashioned Medicean, or Papal, or Austrian tyranny is child's play compared to it." Samuel Longfellow, *Life of Henry Wadsworth Longfellow* (Boston, 1886), Vol. I, p. 267; Jacques Barzun, ed.: *The Selected Writings of John Jay Chapman* (New York: Anchor ed., 1959), p. xi.

view of America that had quickened in the pianissimo revolt of the nineties and grown articulate during the Little Renaissance now developed into a fixed conviction, almost an obsession, among the expatriate generation. In 1922, when Harold Stearns edited his volume, *Civilization in the United States*, to which both Brooks and Mencken contributed, the several contributors seemed to be trying to outdo each other to prove that there was no such civilization. They spoke for a generation which was to think of American justice as represented by the Sacco-Vanzetti case, American regard for science by the Scopes trial, American tolerance by the Klan, the American amenities by Prohibition, American respect for law by the metropolitan gangsters, and the most profound spiritual commitment of the country by the stock-market craze.

5

One of the latent premises underlying the cult of alienation was the idea that the cultural problem in America was not a variation, perhaps more acute, of a universal problem of modern societies, but a case of utterly unique pathology. It was as though other nations did not have their own awkward confrontations of bourgeois philistines and rebellious artists, their unappreciated writers or expatriates. The cult of alienation thus inverted the popular approach to the Europe-America antithesis. In the popular mind, Europe had long stood for oppression, corruption, and decadence, whereas America stood for democracy, innocence, and vitality. Among the intellectuals this rather simple view of things was turned upside down: civilized Europe was counterposed to philistine America. Since the days of Benjamin West and Washington Irving, artists and writers had put this notion into action by expatriating themselves from the United States for large parts of their working lives, and in the 1920's a portion of the intellectual community followed suit by taking off for Paris.

But in the 1930's and afterward, this simple Europe-America antithesis broke down. As time went on, it was painfully apparent that this antithesis was less and less valid, and it was now possible also to see that it had never been wholly valid. European countries had become mechanized and had developed mass societies just as the United States had; and although it was possible for pettish Europeans to refer to this as the Americanization or the Coca-Colanization of Europe, as though mass society were nothing but an American exportation or intrusion, wiser interpreters in the tradition of Tocqueville could see that the United States, being in the vanguard of industrialization and mass culture, foreshadowed rather than created events in Europe.

From the 1930's onward, the cultural antithesis between America and Europe was drastically changed. The depression brought the expatriates home, where they found a new America in the making. By the mid-thirties a wholly new moral and social atmosphere was in evidence. The American political intelligence seemed to have been stung into life and awakened from its torpor by the crash. The New Deal, at first an object of suspicion to the intellectuals, ended by winning the loyalty of an overwhelming majority of them. There seemed to be a new need for the brains of the country, and a new respect for them. The resurgent labor movement promised to be not just another interest group but a force for social reconstruction. The people themselves seemed more appealing than they had been before, both in the urgency of their distress and in the signs of their increasing self-assertion against their old rulers. The air was full of protest and rediscovery. The irritations and lighthearted negations of the twenties seemed altogether passé, its disillusionment and moral anarchy quite inadequate to the needs of the battle against domestic reactionaries and foreign fascists. What seemed to be needed now was a positive creed and a usable past.

Once an old mood has evaporated and a new mood has begun to take form, it is truly astonishing how universal the change becomes—how so many thinkers and writers, quite different in their styles, motives, and points of origin, will begin to regroup themselves and converge around a new spiritual focus. There now began a startling resurgence of literary nationalism, whose character has been so well assessed by Alfred Kazin in the closing chapter of *On Native Grounds*. Intellectuals were seized by a passionate desire to look anew at the United States, to report and record and photograph it. Writers took a fresh and more respectful interest in the American past.

For example, whereas a major feature of biographies conceived or written in the twenties had been the task of depreciation— as in W. E. Woodward's cranky assault on Washington, Edgar Lee Masters's merciless assessment of Lincoln, and Van Wyck Brooks's extraordinary critical tour de force on Mark Twain— the characteristic biographical work of the thirties and forties was the type of lavish, tender, full-scale biography whose most massive and sentimental monument was Carl Sandburg's life of Lincoln.

It fell again to Van Wyck Brooks, the eloquent prophet of alienation, to lead the way toward the recapture of America. With *The Flowering of New England* in 1936, he launched one of the most monumental historical labors of our time, his *Makers and Finders* series, which led him to read his way patiently through all the first-, second-, and third-rate figures in American literary history from 1800 to 1915. It seemed now that nothing American was alien to him except his own earlier work, whose strident indictment of the nation's culture he regretted. He had passed from a relentless assertion of the limitations of important writers to an affectionate search for the importance of limited writers. Like a family historian or genealogist, whose insatiable interest in the clan's past endows him with an endless patience for all the family gossip, he reconstructed almost the whole of American literary history, often with striking insight but rarely with his old critical verve.

Brooks, of course, was not alone. Even Mencken, whose red-nosed prose had long since provided a humorous counterpart to Brooks's solemn indictments of America, could not resist nostalgia. True, his sourly reactionary response to the New Deal stamped him indelibly as a figure of the previous era: his irreverence, which had seemed so completely appropriate to the era of Harding and Coolidge, became merely impertinent under Roosevelt, and his comic gift appeared for the moment to have run out. But when he turned at last to writing the three charming volumes of his autobiography, the work was suffused with a gentle nostalgia that matched Brooks's; and no one who knew what an *enfant terrible* Mencken had been could fail to find something benign, after all, in the environment that had given him so much scope for his unique gift of mockery and provided him with so much personal fulfillment. Sinclair Lewis, too, struck a new note in *Dodsworth*, and by 1938 his Americanism became open and even more complacent, in *The Prodigal Parents*, a dismal novel which seemed nothing more than a vindication of American bourgeois values against youthful rebellion. Finally, he announced to an unbelieving European audience what some American critics had begun to suspect, that he had written *Babbitt* not out of hatred but out of love. Even a younger writer like John Dos Passos, who had been the first to express a distaste for American civilization in radical novels, turned in *The Ground We Stand On* to probing the past for virtues that would yield a new political faith.

Some part of this growing Americanism arose from Europe's gradual loss of its old cultural and moral centrality for American intellectuals. The cultural antithesis between them gradually turned on its axis. T. S. Eliot, Gertrude Stein, and Ezra Pound were the last important American expatriates. The tide of expatriation turned, after the Depression brought the American intellectuals home, when fascism sent refugee artists and scholars in their wake. The United States ceased to be a place men fled from and became a place they fled to. European intellectuals began to think of the United States as a place to go to, not always because they were fleeing for their lives but sometimes simply because they found it a comfortable and rewarding place to live. A trickle had begun even before 1933, and it soon grew into a tidal flow: Aldous Huxley, W. H. Auden, Thomas Mann, Einstein, Schoenberg, Stravinsky, Milhaud, Hindemith, and many lesser figures; whole schools of art historians, political scientists, sociologists. Once the industrial leader, the United States now became the intellectual capital of the Western world, in so far as such a capital could be said to exist.[13] From the point of view of many Europeans, the second of these events was the less forgivable. In any case, the America-Europe antithesis lost most of its cultural meaning on both sides of the Atlantic. The old dialogue between Europe

---

[13]Cf. the recent judgment by Sir Charles Snow: "How many Englishmen understand, or want to understand, that during the past twenty years the United States has done something like 80 per cent of the science and scholarship of the entire Western world?" "On Magnanimity," *Harper's*, Vol. CCXXV (July, 1962), p. 40.

and America became less significant than the idea of Western man and Western society as a whole.

In the 1930's Europe lost its political and moral authority. Fascism revealed a political tyranny beyond anything Americans had known, and the appeasement of fascism by the democratic powers showed the chinks in the entire Western political system. The Nazi-Soviet Pact of 1939, which at last made plain to all but the most credulous that the Bolsheviks conducted their foreign policies with the same ruthlessness as the fascist states, punctured the fellow-traveling mentality and made it impossible to keep up the confusion between populist-liberal and Marxist commitments which had reigned for nearly a decade. It was no longer possible to look to any foreign political system for moral or ideological illumination. Even the gravest American failures of decency paled when, at the end of the war, the full horror of the death camps was disclosed. At the same time, Europe's terrible distress put the responsibilities of the United States in a wholly new light. In 1947, the year when America came to Europe's rescue with the Marshall plan, Edmund Wilson, the least provincial of writers, found it possible to say upon returning from Europe that "the United States at the present time is politically more advanced than any other part of the world,"[14] and to speak of our twentieth-century culture as "a revival of the democratic creativeness which presided at the birth of the Republic and flourished up to the Civil War." The twentieth century, he felt, had brought "a remarkable renascence of American arts and letters."

6

Now we have come chronologically full circle to the time of the *Partisan Review* symposium and to the mood expressed there. For the generation of intellectuals for whom the idea of alienation was associated chiefly with certain excesses of the 1920's and 1930's, that idea had played itself out. But a revival of the old commitment to alienation has taken place among dissenting writers, and it has a strong appeal to the rising generation, strongest perhaps to its most vigorous and critical

[14] *Europe Without Baedeker* (New York, 1947), pp. 408–9.

spirits. The new dissenters argue, and with good reason, that at no time has the need for intelligent dissent and free criticism been greater than it is today, and on this count they find the older cult of alienation still meaningful. These writers do not like the present cultural situation or the political state of the world—and who can blame them?—and on the strength of this dislike they have developed their own conception of the role of the thinker, the artist, the intellectual. It is a conception, however, which I believe oversimplifies history and offers a delusive prescription for the conduct of intellectual life.

The issue these writers pose is whether the task of being enlightening about the state of our society is advanced or impaired by accepting alienation as an overwhelming moral imperative. The burden of their argument shows that, in any case, the intellectual's grievance has changed drastically since the thirties. The old complaint that the role and the task of the American scholar or man of letters were not conceived of as important, or even as legitimate, and that in consequence he lacked recognition, encouragement, and a decent income, has not altogether disappeared. Yet an insistent new note has crept into the writing of the past two decades: one hears more and more that the intellectual who has won a measure of freedom and opportunity, and a new access to influence, is thereby subtly corrupted; that, having won recognition, he has lost his independence, even his identity as an intellectual. Success of a kind is sold to him at what is held to be an unbearable price. He becomes comfortable, perhaps even moderately prosperous, as he takes a position in a university or in government or working for the mass media, but he then tailors himself to the requirements of these institutions. He loses that precious tincture of rage so necessary to first-rate creativity in a writer, that capacity for negation and rebellion that is necessary to the candid social critic, that initiative and independence of aim required for distinguished work in science.

It appears, then, to be the fate of intellectuals either to berate their exclusion from wealth, success, and reputation, or to be seized by guilt when they overcome this exclusion. They are troubled, for example, when power disregards the counsels of intellect, but because they fear corruption they are even more troubled when power comes to intellect for counsel. To revert to Professor Howe's language: when bourgeois society rejects them, that is only one more proof of its philistinism; when it gives them an "honored place," it is buying them off. The intellectual is either shut out or sold out.

To anyone who is willfully unsympathetic, these antithetical complaints may seem perverse or amusing. But in truth they epitomize the intellectual's particular version of the tragic predicament that faces any man who is in one way or another caught between his most demanding ideals and his more immediate ambitions and interests. The discomfort the dissenting writers express is engendered by the fact that American society seems to be absorbing its intellectuals just at the moment in history when their services as an independent source of national self-criticism are most desperately needed. They are to be criticized, I think, not for feeling this discomfort, but for a lack of awareness of the tragic predicament that underlies it.

Among the intellectuals of the Western world, the Americans are probably the most prone to such pricks of conscience, possibly because they feel the constant necessity of justifying their role. British and French intellectuals, for example, usually take for granted the worth of what they are doing and the legitimacy of their claims on the community. But today the burden of guilt that has traditionally afflicted American intellectuals is increased by the power this country has taken in the world and by their legitimate alarm at the peculiar irritating mindlessness and sanctimony to which the canons of our political discourse have been given over. (How many of our politicians dare to talk like adults about the problem of Red China?) But perhaps quite as important as all these contemporary considerations is the fact that, not so very long ago, the tradition of alienation turned into a powerful moral imperative. The older generation of intellectuals first came to terms with this imperative by trying to act in accordance with it; but now, feeling they have been misled by it, they find it no longer binding. They have earned their release by more than two decades of disillusioning experience. Having seen the problem of their own moral position from more than one angle of vision, they can no longer think of it as a simple problem; and like anyone who is given to contemplating the complexities of things, they have lost the posture of militancy. The intellectuals of the younger generation, especially those who take their inspiration directly or indirectly from Marxism, find this unforgivable, and they have begun to condemn it in language that partakes both of the natural cruelty of the young and of the artificial puritanism of the political left.

The young intellectual in the United States today very often feels, almost from the outset of his career, the distractions and pressures attendant upon success, the consequences of a new state of affairs in our cultural life, which is encouraging but also exasperating. The battle waged with such enthusiasm by the intellectual generation that flourished between 1890 and 1914 has long since been won: certain esthetic and political free-doms, the claims of naturalism and realism, the right to deal uninhibitedly with sex and violence and corruption, the right to strike out at authority, have been thoroughly established. But the victories have turned sour. We live in an age in which the avant-garde itself has been institutionalized and deprived of its old stimulus of a stubborn and insensate opposition. We have learned so well how to absorb novelty that receptivity itself has turned into a kind of tradition—"the tradition of the new." Yesterday's avant-garde experiment is today's chic and tomorrow's cliché. American painters, seeking in abstract ex-pressionism the outer limits of artistic liberation, find a few years later that their canvases are selling in five figures. Beatniks are in demand on university campuses, where they are received as entertainers and turned into the esoteric comedians of the sophisticated. In social criticism, professional Jeremiahs like Vance Packard become best-sellers; and more serious writers like C. Wright Mills, who compulsively asserted the most thor-oughgoing repudiation of American life in its every aspect, are respectfully reviewed and eagerly read. David Riesman's *The Lonely Crowd*, which can be taken as a depressing account of what the American character has become, is the most widely read book in the history of sociology, and William H. Whyte's mordant analysis of *The Organization Man* is read everywhere by organization men.

It is not hard to understand why many serious minds have come to find these things more discouraging than hopeful. Success that seems to have lost its reality is worse than failure. The large, liberal middle-class audience upon which all this

acceptance depends now brings to the work of the intellectuals a bland, absorptive tolerance that is quite different from a
vital response. To the writer who has just eviscerated their way
of life and their self-satisfying compromises, readers now say
"How interesting!" or even at times "How true!" Such passive
tolerance can only be infuriating to a writer who looks beyond
the size of his royalties and hopes actually to exert some influence on the course of affairs or to strike a note in the moral
consciousness of his time. He objects that serious thinking is
received as a kind of diversion and not as a challenge. Often
he wonders if the fault may perhaps be in himself: whether his
own personal compromises—and invariably he has made them
—have not blunted the force of his message, whether he has
not at bottom become altogether too much like the audience
he condemns.[15]

One might hope that this self-probing honesty would yield
nothing but good; unfortunately, it leads to a kind of desperation, which may in itself command sympathy but which ends
only in the search for a "position" or a pose. Dissenting intellectuals often seem to feel that they are morally on trial for
being intellectuals, and their moral responsibility is then interpreted as a responsibility primarily to repudiation and destruction; so that the measure of intellectual merit is felt to lie not
in imagination or precision, but in the greatest possible degree
of negativism. The responsibility of the intellectual is not seen,
in the first instance, as a responsibility to be enlightening about
society but rather to make an assertion against it—on the assumption that almost any such assertion will presumably be
enlightening, and that in any case it re-establishes the writer's
probity and courage.

The prophets of alienation who speak for the left no doubt
aim to create a basis for some kind of responsible politics of
protest, but when the situation of the intellectual is under
consideration their tone becomes strident, and then one hears
how much better it is to have "blind unreasoning rejection"

---

[15]I do not wish to suggest that this tendency is universal; many writers are simply content to rest with the benefits of the situation. As Alfred Kazin remarks:
"Too many Americans now want to remain fully attached to our social system
and at the same time draw the rewards of a little sophisticated (and wholly
external) criticism of it." *Contemporaries* (New York, 1962), p. 439.

THE INTELLECTUAL 471

than to make moral compromises; the talk is of nostalgia for "earlier certainties that made resistance easy," of the primary need of the intellectual to discharge aggression, of the dangers of becoming a "prostitute" or a "traitor" to the fundamental obligations of the intellectual's role, of the alleged antithesis between social responsibility, which is bad, and intellectual responsibility, which is good. The point here is that alienation in the intellectual is not simply accepted, as a necessary consequence of the pursuit of truth or of some artistic vision, but that a negative stance or posture toward society is prescribed as the only stance productive of artistic creativity or social insight or moral probity. The argument does not rest upon the idea that the intellectual has a primary responsibility to truth or to his creative vision, and that he must be prepared to follow them even when they put him quite at odds with his society. It is rather that he must begin with a primary responsibility to repudiate—in Professor Baritz's term—his society. His alienation is seen not as a risk he must have the integrity to run, but as an obligation which preconditions all his other obligations. Alienation has ceased to be merely a fact of life and has taken on the character of a cure or a prescription for the proper intellectual regimen.

One need follow the cult of alienation only a few steps further to come upon other more demanding exponents of alienation of whom the politically left writers would disapprove at central points but whose dedication to alienation as a leading principle is quite similar—men who are, at best, exponents of romantic anarchism and, at worst, of the adolescent rebellion of the beatniks or of the moral nihilism that has been expressed most eloquently by Norman Mailer. And one of the distinguishing features of this literature of alienation is that while its writers aspire to preserve peace and advance democracy and foster culture and release individuality, their discussions of politics and culture are curiously stark and humorless and inflexible, even at times inhumane.

The voices of the political dissenters express an alienation that is at least politically meaningful, and, whatever their excesses, they have engaged in some kind of dialogue with and feel a responsibility to the rest of the intellectual world. Looming behind them, the beatniks today constitute a very considerable public in their own right and a formidable symptom of our cultural malaise. It is impossible to say that the beatniks are to the left of the political dissenters—they are simply, in the current argot, farther out. In the terms in which I have tried to define the intellectual temperament, the political dissenters are frequently overwhelmed by their own piety, whereas the beatniks have let their playfulness run away with them. In their thinking about society they tend to agree with the dissenters about commercialism, mass culture, nuclear armaments, and civil rights; but on the whole they have withdrawn from serious argument with the bourgeois world. The type of alienation represented by the beatniks is, in their own term, disaffiliated. They have walked out on the world of the squares[16] and for the most part have abandoned that sense of vocation which is demanded both by serious intellectual achievement and by sustained social protest.

In their own way, the beatniks have repudiated the path of intellectualism and have committed themselves to a life of sensation—to put it perhaps too sympathetically, as Lawrence Lipton does in the title of his illuminating book about them, *The Holy Barbarians*, to lives of inverted sainthood, marked by an acceptance of poverty and by their willingness to do without the usual satisfactions of a career and a regular income. Not surprisingly, the beatniks, as even their sympathetic commentators are apt to concede, have produced very little good writing. Their most distinctive contribution to our culture may in the end be their amusing argot. Their experimentation, which seems to consist largely of a relaxation of form, does not seem to offer, as the Dadaists did, a new kind of wit or fantasy, or to promise, as a writer like Gertrude Stein did, to set off a new direction in prose. The movement seems unable to rise above its adolescent inspiration. Somehow, when Jack Kerouac advises: "Remove literary, grammatical, and syntactical inhibition," and suggests "no discipline other than rhetorical exaltation and expostulated statement," one feels that he is less close to these earlier literary experiments in expression than to

---

[16]Here they have on their side the precedent of Thoreau, who said that he did not care to be counted a member of any society which he had not voluntarily joined. (It is interesting how constantly the anti-institutional theme recurs in American thought.) The difference, of course, lies in Thoreau's sense of his vocation as a writer.

the child-indulgent propensities of the lunatic fringe of progressive education. As Norman Podhoretz has remarked, "the primitivism of the Beats serves . . . as a cover for an anti-intellectualism so bitter that it makes the ordinary American's hatred of eggheads seem positively benign."[17]

In their style of withdrawal, the beatniks are in the Bohemian line of succession, but they seem to have far less humor and self-distance than the older Bohemians, and infinitely less regard for individuality. Harry T. Moore has remarked that "individuals of genius have usually been disengaged, yes, particularly in the arts; but mass disengagement is a different matter. Most of the Beats don't have enough formal knowledge of history or political science to see these matters in perspective, but then they wouldn't want to: it's enough for them that they dislike and distrust the world of the Squares. . . ."[18] Their paradoxical creed of mass disengagement and group inaction is reminiscent of the unforgettable words of an undergraduate in a solemn paper on modern culture: "The world will never be saved until the individual comes out of the group *en masse.*" One of the qualities that has so readily subjected the beatniks to mockery in the mass media and the other literature of the squares is this distinctive uniformity—which the beatniks have carried to the point of having their own dress. They have created a new paradox: a conformity of alienation. And in so doing they have caricatured the posture of alienation to a degree that its other exponents find treasonous and unforgivable.

Quite understandably, then, the beatniks are considered, by sterner prophets of alienation, to represent an infantile disorder, and they have been repudiated not only by the angry grandfather of the beat movement, Kenneth Rexroth, but also by such a basically sympathetic critic as Norman Mailer, who has high regard for the beats' search for sensation and orgastic satisfaction, but no patience with their passivity, their lack of assertion. The most forthright case for a really solid kind of estrangement was made a few years ago by Mailer in a famous

[17]"The Know Nothing Bohemians," in Seymour Krim, ed.: *The Beats* (Greenwich, Conn., 1960), p. 119.
[18]In his postscript on the beats, written for the 1960 edition of Albert Parry's *Garrets and Pretenders: A History of Bohemianism in America* (New York: Dover ed., 1960), chapter 30.

piece in *Dissent* entitled "The White Negro: Superficial Reflections on the Hipster." Over the beatnik Mailer would elevate the hipster, whose awareness of the ultimate terrors of life resembles and is derived from that of the Negro, "for no Negro can saunter down a street with any real certainty that violence will not visit him on his walk."

This readiness to live with and face violence and death is now the central virtue, for our collective condition is to face the alternative between instant death by atomic war and "a slow death by conformity." What he admired about the hipster, said Mailer, was his willingness to accept the challenge of death, the challenge "to divorce oneself from society, to exist without roots, to set out on that uncharted journey into the rebellious imperatives of the self. In short, whether the life is criminal or not, the decision is to encourage the psychopath in oneself, to explore that domain of experience where security is boredom and therefore sickness. . . ." The hipster has his own "psychopathic brilliance," not very easily communicable because "Hip is the sophistication of the wise primitive in a giant jungle, and so its appeal is still beyond the civilized man." The importance of hipsters lies not in their numbers—there are, Mailer estimated, not more than a hundred thousand conscious members of the tribe—but in that "they are an elite with the potential ruthlessness of an elite, and [with] a language most adolescents can understand instinctively, for the hipster's intense view of existence matches their experience and their desire to rebel."

If the resulting life proves in fact to be criminal, Mailer makes it clear—if, say, two young hoodlums beat in the brains of a candy-store keeper—the act is not likely to be brave enough to be "very therapeutic," but at least "courage of a sort is necessary, for one murders not only a weak fifty-year-old man but an institution as well, one violates private property, one enters into a new relation with the police and introduces a dangerous element into one's life. The hoodlum is therefore daring the unknown. . . ."[19] Certainly the earlier prophets of alienation in America had never had this much imagination.

[19] *Voices of Dissent* (New York, 1958), pp. 198–200, 202, 205; the essay appears also in *Advertisements for Myself* (New York, 1959), pp. 337–58.

7

The spokesmen of the beatnik, and the hipster, and the left have their own quarrels about the proper style of alienation and the limits of its expression; but they all share a common conviction that there is some proper style or stance or posture to be recommended which will somehow release the individuality and creativity of the artist, or sustain the capacities of the social critic and protect him from corruption. Their conviction that alienation is a kind of value in itself has a double historical root in romantic individualism and in Marxism. For more than a century and a half the position of creative talent everywhere in the bourgeois world has been such as to make us aware of the persistent tension between the creative individual and the demands of society. Moreover, the more self-conscious the artistic and intellectual communities of the Western world have become about their own position, the more acutely aware they are that society cannot have the works of men of genius, or even of distinguished talent, on its own terms but must accept them as they come. The more one looks at great examples of creativity, the more evident it becomes that creative minds are not typically "nice," or well adjusted, or accommodating, or moderate; that genius is often accompanied by some kind of personal disorder and that society must come to terms with this disorder if it wishes to have the benefit of genius—a problem examined most memorably for our time by Edmund Wilson in his discussion of the Philoctetes myth in *The Wound and the Bow*. Our heightened awareness of the alienation of the artist is to a large degree an inheritance from romanticism; the case for the social value of the thinker's alienation was formalized by Marxism, which held that at the focal moment of capitalist crisis the capitalist system would be deserted by many of its intellectuals, who would rather align themselves with the coming movement in history than remain attached to a decaying order.

Once one has accepted the idea that alienation is an inevitable consequence of the assertion of certain artistic or political values, it is easy to slip into the assumption that alienation has a kind of value in itself, much as one may assume that because genius is commonly "temperamental" one can begin to have the manifestations of genius by cultivating temperament. Of course, no one would seriously argue that a young writer, by cultivating, say, a penchant for obsessive gambling, can hope to develop any of Dostoevsky's genius. But so long as such an assumption is not brought into the open, it is easy to drift into the belief that the intellectual cannot fulfill himself unless he cultivates the proper personal style. Just as temperament can be misunderstood as a way to talent, so the proper truculent stance toward the world can be taken as a substitute for the intellectual's critical work. Serious writers on alienation would shrink from defending such a notion, but it asserts itself as a fundamental assumption of their most excited and extreme statements.

Moreover, the culturally constricting aspects of American life have always set American writers upon an imaginative quest for an order of society that could be counterposed to their own as a model, an ideal milieu for intellectual life. Nineteenth-century American academics looked to the German university, artists to French or Italian artistic communities, and writers to the position of the *grand écrivain* in France.[20] For a variety of reasons, these ideals have become tarnished, though they once played a part of real importance in the self-definition and the improvement of American cultural life. Professor Howe is in a very old tradition, then, in his quest for the ideal community in which the writer may find a refuge from his personal battle with society or a fulcrum for self-confident protest. Since Europe will no longer serve, there remains for him the universal country of Bohemia, which he holds up as a model, now unhappily abandoned, which provides a key to freedom and creativity. But about this, too, some objections must be made. No one would care to deny that Bohemian society has considerable intellectual and political value—but does this value not consist mainly in offering the individual a haven in the

[20]Intellectuals outside France still look to that country as an ideal instance of the prestige and influence of the intellectual, but even French intellectuals have their foreign ideals. Once, for Stendhal, it was Italy. Today, for Raymond Aron, it is Britain: "Of all Western countries, Great Britain is probably the one which has treated its intellectuals in the most sensible way." *The Opium of the Intellectuals* (London, 1957), p. 234; cf. his critical comments on the position of the French intelligentsia, pp. 220–1.

earlier transitional phases of his life? For a moment in the life of the young writer or artist, a moment characterized by experimentalism, the search for identity and style, for freedom from responsibility, a Bohemian life can be immensely liberating. But only a small part of the world's important literature has been written by men who were living in Bohemias, and the notion that many intellectuals have spent their mature and productive years there will not stand historical examination. This seems preeminently true of our own national experience. In this country, first-rate writers have been more solitary than lesser ones. Professor Howe's uncomfortable suggestion that Concord was a kind of Transcendentalist Bohemia might be acceptable as a pleasantry, but not as history. Concord was a village refuge from a Boston which Concord intellectuals disliked; but it offered no community of the sort one thinks of in connection with Bohemias, and surprisingly little intellectual society. One need only remember, for example, the truncated relations of Thoreau and Emerson, or of Hawthorne and his neighbors, or Bronson Alcott's lack of organic relations with almost anyone, to realize how true it is that Concord, for all the physical proximity it afforded, hardly constituted an intellectual community.

It is not just that there were no Bohemian revels, which Professor Howe hastens to make clear when he describes Concord's Bohemia as sedate, but that there was very little society. Thoreau reported in his journal that when he "talked, or tried to talk" with Emerson he "lost my time—nay, almost my identity," in a maze of pointless disagreement, and Emerson complained that Thoreau "does not feel himself except in opposition." (Was he aware that since the appearance of "Nature" Thoreau had all but ceased even to read him?) Concerning the Transcendentalists generally, Emerson wrote that "their studies were solitary."[21]

---

[21]Marcus Cunliffe, in his illuminating survey of *The Literature of the United States* (London, 1954), estimates the situation well when he says (pp. 80–1; cf. pp. 90–1):

Loneliness and apartness have characterized the American author, from Poe's day onward. Even the exuberant Americans—Whitman for instance—have had surprisingly few friends with whom to associate, so to speak, professionally.

A certain austere and determined isolation has been more regularly associated with creative work than the distractions of Bohemianism. Solidarity among intellectuals, especially when they are under external pressure, or mutual recognition and encouragement, should not be depreciated; but neither should they be confused with the agreeable face-to-face sociability which is the hallmark of Bohemian life. The truly creative mind is hardly ever so much alone as when it is trying to be sociable. The productive intellectual, rather than relying on Bohemia as a means by which he and others can "face the world together," usually tries to develop the resources by which he can face it alone. Facing the world together is a tactic of politics, but facing it alone seems to be the characteristic creative stance.

Again, for critics concerned with effective political dissent, the history of Bohemia is not encouraging. There was, to be sure, a bright moment in our own history before the First World War when esthetic experimentation, courageous social criticism, and the Bohemian life all seemed to converge —it was represented, for example, by the old *Masses* in Max Eastman's day. But, on the whole, the characteristic Bohemian style has leaned toward personal flamboyance and private rebellion, rather than political effectuality on any considerable scale—and in this respect at least, the beatniks are in the Bohemian tradition. It is dismal to think of doing without Bohemias, but to prescribe a Bohemian life for serious creative or political purposes is to place upon Bohemia a crushing burden of expectation.

In New England, if we except a circle of Bostonians, this has been especially true. . . . Emerson, Thoreau, and Hawthorne lived for a while in the same village, Concord; and they and other personages pop continually in and out of one another's diaries and letters. Yet it would be less accurate to say that they knew one another than that they knew *of* one another. Each stood somewhat aside, a little critical of his companions, a little derisive, reluctant to commit himself. "But how insular and pathetically solitary," Emerson confided to his journal, "are all the people we know!" In the same source he notes that the happy author is the one who, ignoring public opinion, "writes always to *the unknown friend*." Of the known, he remarks that "my friends and I are fishes in our habit. As for taking Thoreau's arm, I should as soon take the arm of an elm tree." After Hawthorne's death, he reflects sadly that he has waited too long in the hope that he "might one day conquer a friendship."

8

The dislike of involvement with "accredited institutions" exhibited by the prophets of alienation bespeaks a more fundamental dislike of the association of intellect with power. The frightening idea that an intellectual ceases altogether to function as an intellectual when he enters an accredited institution (which would at one stroke eliminate from the intellectual life all our university professors) may be taken as a crude formulation of a real problem: there is some discord between the imperatives of a creative career and the demands of the institution within which it takes place. Scholars have long since had to realize that the personal costs of working within institutions are smaller than the costs of living without institutional support. Indeed, they have no real choice: they need libraries and laboratories—perhaps even pupils—which only an institution can provide.

For imaginative writers this problem is more serious. The amenities and demands of academic life do not accord well with imaginative genius, and they make the truly creative temperament ill at ease. Moreover, the conditions of academic life are such as to narrow unduly the range of one's experience; and it is painful to imagine what our literature would be like if it were written by academic teachers of "creating writing" courses, whose main experience was to have been themselves trained in such courses. It would be a waste, too, if poets with primary gifts were to spend time as members of committees on the revision of the freshman composition course—hummingbirds, to resurrect an image of Mencken's, immersed in *Kartoffelsuppe*. Still, the partial or temporary support offered by the academy to writer and artist has proved helpful in many careers, and very often the alternative to such support is the creation of a frustrated cultural lumpenproletariat.

However, for intellectuals in the disciplines affected by the problem of expertise, the university is only a symbol of a larger and more pressing problem of the relationship of intellect to power: we are opposed almost by instinct to the divorce of knowledge from power, but we are also opposed, out of our modern convictions, to their union. This was not always the case: the great intellectuals of pagan antiquity, the doctors of the medieval universities, the scholars of the Renaissance, the philosophers of the Enlightenment, sought for the conjunction of knowledge and power and accepted its risks without optimism or naïveté. They hoped that knowledge would in fact be broadened by a conjunction with power, just as power might be civilized by its connection with knowledge. I have spoken of the terms on which knowledge and power were related in the days of the Founding Fathers as being consonant with this ideal: knowledge and power consorted more or less as equals, within the same social circles, and very often within the same heads. But this was not simply because, as some modern critics seem to imagine, the Founding Fathers were better than we are, though they probably were better. It is not simply that Jefferson read Adam Smith and Eisenhower read Western fiction. The fundamental difference is that the society of the eighteenth century was unspecialized. In Franklin's day it was still possible for a man to conduct an experiment of some scientific value in his woodshed, and for the gifted amateur in politics to move from a plantation to a law office to a foreign ministry. Today knowledge and power are differentiated functions. When power resorts to knowledge, as it increasingly must, it looks not for intellect, considered as a freely speculative and critical function, but for expertise, for something that will serve its needs. Very often power lacks respect for that disinterestedness which is essential to the proper functioning of the expert—the governor of a great state once called several distinguished sociologists into conference to arrange a public-opinion poll on a controversial, current issue, and then carefully outlined for them what this poll was to find.

If the typical man of power simply wants knowledge as an instrument, the typical man of knowledge in modern America is the expert. Earlier I observed that it has been largely the function of expertise which has restored the intellectual as a force in American politics. But the pertinent question is whether the intellectual, as expert, can really be an intellectual —whether he does not become simply a mental technician, to use the phrase of H. Stuart Hughes, working at the call of the men who hire him. Here, as in the case of the university and other accredited institutions, I think the answer is not easy or categorical, and a true answer will almost certainly not be

apocalyptic enough to please the modern intellectual sensibility. The truth is that much of American education aims, simply
and brazenly, to turn out experts who are not intellectuals or
men of culture at all: and when such men go into the service
of government or business or the universities themselves, they
do not suddenly become intellectuals.

The situation of men of real intellectual accomplishment
who may also enter the service of power is much more complicated. Do men distinguished for reflective minds cease to
be intellectuals simply because they become ambassadors to
India or Yugoslavia or members of the President's staff? No
doubt certain intellectual responses are no longer possible for
men who look at the world from an angle of vision that is close
to power and who assume as given those compromises which
have to be made when power is attained. But to me it seems
to be a personal choice, one that cannot be squeezed into the
terms of the forced morality of alienation, whether one is to
sacrifice some of one's range of critical freedom in the hope
that power may be made more amenable to the counsels of intellect, or even for the Faustian urge to learn something about
the world which cannot be so readily learned from the vantage
point of the academy.

The intellectual who has relinquished all thought of association with power understands well—almost too well—that
his state of powerlessness is conducive to certain illuminations.
What he is prone to forget is that an access to power and an involvement with its problems may provide other illuminations.
The critic of power tries to influence the world by affecting
public opinion; the associate of power tries directly to make
the exercise of power more amenable to the thought of the
intellectual community. These functions are not of necessity
mutually exclusive or hostile. Each involves certain personal
and moral hazards, and it is not possible to make the personal
choice of the hazards one cares to run into a universal imperative. The characteristic intellectual failure of the critic of power
is a lack of understanding of the limitations under which power
is exercised. His characteristic moral failure lies in an excessive
concern with his own purity; but purity of a sort is easily had
where responsibilities are not assumed. The characteristic failure of the expert who advises the powerful is an unwillingness

to bring his capacity for independent thought to bear as a source of criticism. He may lose his capacity for detachment from power by becoming absorbed in its point of view. For American intellectuals, so long excluded from places of power and recognition, there is always the danger that a sudden association with power will become too glamorous, and hence intellectually blinding.

What is at stake for individuals is, as I say, a personal choice; but what is important for society as a whole is that the intellectual community should not become hopelessly polarized into two parts, one part of technicians concerned only with power and accepting implicitly the terms power puts to them, and the other of willfully alienated intellectuals more concerned with maintaining their sense of their own purity than with making their ideas effective. Experts there will undoubtedly be, and perhaps also critics capable of stepping mentally outside their society and looking relentlessly at its assumptions, in sufficient number and with sufficient freedom to make themselves felt. Presumably the possibility of debate between them will continue to exist, and the intellectual community will have within it types of minds capable of mediating between the world of power and the world of criticism. If so, intellectual society will avoid the danger of being cut up into hostile and uncommunicative segments. Our society is sick in many ways; but such health as it has lies in the plurality of the elements composing it and their freedom to interact with each other. It would be tragic if all intellectuals aimed to serve power; but it would be equally tragic if all intellectuals who become associated with power were driven to believe they no longer had any connection with the intellectual community: their conclusion would almost inevitably be that their responsibilities are to power alone.

9

A few years ago, in a perceptive historical essay, Marcus Cunliffe suggested designations for two types of mind which had figured in our intellectual achievement: the clerisy (a term first used by Coleridge), consisting of writers sufficiently close to the primary assumptions of their society to act in some degree as its spokesmen, and the avant-garde, who are profoundly alienated from these assumptions.[22] The better part of the creative brilliance and the originative power of our intellectual tradition has come from the avant-garde, but the clerisy has had its eminent figures. Franklin, Jefferson, and John Adams were clerisy; and so were Cooper, Emerson (at least in his mature years), the jurist Holmes, William James, William Dean Howells, and Walter Lippmann. The avant-garde names are more imposing, but such is the variety of interesting minds and major talents that there is an impressive third list composed of figures so mixed in their motives that they are impossible to classify: Mark Twain, for example, who embodied extremes of alienation and acceptance in the same riven mind, and Henry Adams, who in a different fashion did the same. No: it is the elusiveness of major talents rather than their susceptibility to facile classification that in the end impresses us most. And true as this is of the problem of alienation, it is still more true of states of mind and styles of life. Here it is not the presence of a single pattern, whether Bohemian or bourgeois, but the range and variety that is striking: one thinks of Emily Dickinson in her Amherst seclusion, Walt Whitman living his many-faceted and robust life, Wallace Stevens in his insurance executive's office, T. S. Eliot in banking and publishing, William Carlos Williams in medical practice. The futility of trying to prescribe a pattern may be suggested when one compares, say, John Dewey and Charles S. Peirce, Thorstein Veblen and William James, William Dean Howells and Henry James, Oliver Wendell Holmes and Louis D. Brandeis, Mark Twain and Herman Melville, Emerson and Poe, Henry Adams and H. C. Lea, Henry Miller and William Faulkner, Charles A. Beard and Frederick Jackson Turner, Edith Wharton and Ernest Hemingway, John Dos Passos and F. Scott Fitzgerald.

Before any writer or thinker can look upon himself as a potentially productive mind, he has already been born into a particular situation in life and endowed with a character and temperament that are only in limited respects malleable. This is the range that fate gives him, and he must work

[22] "The Intellectuals: The United States," *Encounter*, Vol. IV (May, 1955), pp. 23–33.

within it. To understand this, we may compare, for example, the lives of Oliver Wendell Holmes, Jr., and Thorstein Veblen —contemporaries similar in their passionate and wide-ranging intellectualism and in their gift for ironic detachment, but dissimilar in almost everything else. It would have been futile for either of these men to try to remake himself at the outset of his career—for Holmes to enter some kind of Bohemia and cast off his Brahmin inheritance, or for Veblen to be a good fellow and try to become president of the American Economic Association. Holmes looked at life rather naturally from the standpoint of an historically rooted and socially secure class, and he entered at length into one of our "accredited institutions," where it is generally acknowledged that he did not cease to function as an intellectual or to do useful work in the world. Veblen, reared on the margin between a Yankee culture whose values he could never take seriously and an immigrant Norwegian culture which was not really his own, was fated to remain forever a marginal man, altogether alien to the prevailing American beliefs. As a scholar, he had to pursue a career within accredited institutions if he was to have a career at all, but he succeeded in making himself a source of acute discomfort in every university he worked at. Some kind of instinctive wisdom, I think, caused him to keep the world at arm's length, even when it made friendly gestures. His particular genius, he must have sensed, lay partly in the same perversity that made constant personal trouble for him. We may regard it also as the source of much that is vulnerable in his work, but that perversity kept sharp the biting edge that made him a kind of ponderous sociological Swift, and one of the most original minds of his time.

One of the major virtues of liberal society in the past was that it made possible such a variety of styles of intellectual life —one can find men notable for being passionate and rebellious, others for being elegant and sumptuous, or spare and astringent, clever and complex, patient and wise, and some equipped mainly to observe and endure. What matters is the openness and generosity needed to comprehend the varieties of excellence that could be found even in a single and rather parochial society. Dogmatic, apocalyptic predictions about the collapse of liberal culture or the disappearance of high culture may be right or wrong; but one thing about them seems certain: they are more likely to instill self-pity and despair than the will to resist or the confidence to make the most of one's creative energies. It is possible, of course, that under modern conditions the avenues of choice are being closed, and that the culture of the future will be dominated by single-minded men of one persuasion or another. It is possible; but in so far as the weight of one's will is thrown onto the scales of history, one lives in the belief that it is not to be so.

Acknowledgments

THIS BOOK had its beginning when I was invited to give the first Hayward Keniston Lecture at the University of Michigan on April 27, 1953. That lecture, published in a somewhat expanded form as "Democracy and Anti-Intellectualism in America," *Michigan Alumnus Quarterly Review*, August 8, 1953, left me aware of having raised a variety of unresolved issues, and I found myself impelled to go on with them. It has been helpful to give various parts of the book as lectures: first to a number of undergraduate history societies at Cambridge University, where I was Pitt Professor of American History and Institutions during the academic year 1958–59; then, during the academic year 1961–62, as the Sperry and Hutchinson Lectures at Hiram College, Hiram, Ohio, the Haynes Foundation Lectures at the University of Southern California, and the Ziskind Lectures at Smith College; finally, during the autumn term of 1962–63, when I was Visiting Senior Fellow of the Humanities Council and Class of 1932 Lecturer at Princeton University. To many persons at these institutions I am indebted for their cordial hospitality.

Special aspects of this study were pursued under grants from the Council for Research in the Social Sciences of Columbia University and the program of the Committee on the Role of Education in American History of the Fund for the Advancement of Education. A grant from the Carnegie Corporation made it possible for me to devote a full sabbatical year to this work, and to finish it much earlier and with far more ample research help than I would otherwise have had. Columbia University has been generous in arranging free time, but to mention only this would be insufficient acknowledgment of the many intellectual rewards of my connection with it over a period of twenty-five years, first as a graduate student and then as a member of its department of history.

As always, Beatrice Kevitt Hofstadter has given me textual and substantive criticism of incalculable value. My colleagues, Peter Gay and Fritz Stern, have read the entire manuscript and offered suggestions of vital importance. During the years in which this book was being written, my research assistants, Philip Greven, Jr., Carol Gruber, Neil Harris, and Ann Lane, did resourceful work in original materials. Over a period of several years many friends have helped by discussing my notions, offering suggestions, directing me to new material, or reading drafts of chapters, and I wish to thank Daniel Aaron, Daniel Bell, Lee Benson, John M. Blum, Carl Bridenbaugh, Paul Carter, Lawrence Cremin, Barbara Cross, Robert D. Cross, Marcus Cunliffe, Stanley Elkins, Julian Franklin, Henry F. Graff, Robert Handy, H. Stuart Hughes, Edward C. Kirkland, William E. Leuchtenburg, Eric McKitrick, Henry May, Walter P. Metzger, William Miller, Ernest Nagel, David Riesman, Henry Robbins, Dorothy R. Ross, Irving Sanes, Wilson Smith, Gerald Stearn, John William Ward, C. Vann Woodward, and Irvin Wyllie. Since much of the talk provoked by my ideas took the form of unresolved arguments, it would be especially ironic if any of these persons were assumed to share my views.

An inquiry that covers as much ground as this can be no more satisfactory than the special studies upon which its author must rely. My footnotes indicate, I hope, where my primary obligations rest, but they doubtless fall short of acknowledging the full weight of my indebtedness to contemporary American historical scholarship. In considering the books and articles upon which I have drawn most heavily, I notice that almost all of them were written during the past fifteen or twenty years, and that taken together they constitute a remarkably formidable body of work. Perhaps this, too, should be thrown in the scales when the state of intellectual enterprise in this country is being assayed.

THE PARANOID STYLE IN AMERICAN POLITICS

AND OTHER ESSAYS

To the memory of
Harry J. Carman

Contents

Introduction

THE MOST difficult and delicate task that faces the author of a book of essays is that of writing an introduction that makes his various pieces seem considerably more unified, in theme and argument, than they were in fact when they were written. The best case for gathering essays in a book is simply that it makes them more accessible and more permanent. The best case that can be made for the unity of any such collection is a personal and informal one, and perhaps for that reason is rarely resorted to: it is that the several parts, as the product of a single mind, have a certain stamp upon them; they must be, at least in their style of thought and their concerns, unified by some underlying intellectual intent.

The pieces in this book were written over a span of fourteen years, and during that time I have not always been of the same mind about historical and political matters in general or about some of the particulars dealt with here. Some unresolved tensions undoubtedly remain. It is not, then, a single consistent argument but a set of related concerns and methods that unites these essays. They fall into two groups: one deals with conditions that have given rise to the extreme right of the 1950's and the 1960's, the other with the origins of certain characteristic problems of the earlier modern era when the American mind was beginning to respond to the facts of industrialism and world power. All deal with public responses to a critical situation or an enduring dilemma, whether it is the sudden threat posed by giant business to competition, the panic of the 1890's and the long-standing monetary disputes and sectional animosities it brought to a head, the moral shock of our nascent imperialism, the effects of resurgent fundamentalism on secular politics, the impact of the cold war on the public consciousness.

Since these studies have to do with the style of our political culture as a whole, and with certain special styles of thought and rhetoric that have prevailed within it, they tell more about the milieu of our politics than about its structure. They are more centrally concerned with the symbolic aspect of politics

493

than with the formation of institutions and the distribution of power. They focus on the way large segments of the public respond to civic issues, make them their own, put them to work on national problems, and express their response to these problems in distinctive rhetorical styles. Because my concern is in this sense a bit one-sided, it is necessary to be clear—it is here that the intent of these essays is most likely to be misunderstood—that my reasons for emphasizing milieu rather than structure do not stem from the belief that, of the two, milieu is more important. My case is a more moderate one: it rests—quite aside from the pleasure I take in analyzing styles of thought—on two convictions: first, that our political and historical writing, until recently, has tended to emphasize structure at the cost of substantially neglecting milieu; and second, that an understanding of political styles and of the symbolic aspect of politics is a valuable way of locating ourselves and others in relation to public issues.

The older conception of politics was that it deals with the question: Who gets what, when, how? Politics was taken as an arena in which people define their interests as rationally as possible and behave in a way calculated to realize them as fully as possible. But Harold Lasswell, who made this monosyllabic question the title of a well-known book on the substance of politics, was one of the first in this country to be dissatisfied with the rationalistic assumptions which it implied and to turn to the study of the emotional and symbolic side of political life. It became important to add a new conception to the older one: Who perceives what public issues, in what way, and why? To the present generation of historical and political writers it has become increasingly clear that people not only seek their interests but also express and even in a measure define themselves in politics; that political life acts as a sounding board for identities, values, fears, and aspirations. In a study of the political milieu these things are brought to the surface.

No doubt it is, more than anything else, the events of our time, and among these some of the most ominous and appalling, that have launched students of society upon a restless search for new methods of understanding. But the work of other intellectual disciplines has also made the present generation of historians more conscious of important aspects of behavior which our predecessors left largely in the background. An increasing interest of philosophers, anthropologists, and literary critics in the symbolic and myth-making aspects of the human mind has found its way into historical writing, and with it has come a growing sensitivity to the possibilities of textual analysis. The application of depth psychology to politics, chancy though it is, has at least made us acutely aware that politics can be a projective arena for feelings and impulses that are only marginally related to the manifest issues. The findings of public-opinion polls have made us far less confident than we used to be that the public responds to the issues as they are debated, and more aware that it reacts to them chiefly when they become the object of striking symbolic acts or memorable statements, or are taken up by public figures who themselves have a symbolic appeal. Our enhanced feeling for the non-rational side of politics has thrown into question a whole series of once confidently asserted propositions about the behavior of voters in the past.

People respond, in short, to the great drama of the public scene. But this drama, as it is set before them and as they perceive it, is not identical with questions involving material interests and the possession of power. Even those who exercise power are not immune to the content of the drama. In any case, they are forced to deal, as an element in their calculations, with the emotional life of the masses, which is not something that they can altogether create or manipulate, but something that they must cope with. The political contest itself is deeply affected by the way in which it is perceived and felt.

This does not mean that the material interests of politics can be psychologized away or reduced to episodes in intellectual history. It means only that historians and political scientists have always worked, implicitly or explicitly, with psychological assumptions; that these ought to be made as conscious as possible; and that they should be sophisticated enough to take ample account of the complexity of political action. I have no interest in denying the reality, or even the primacy, of the problems of money and power, but only in helping to define their reality by turning attention to the human context in which they arise and in which they have to be settled.

To accept all this is not to abandon whatever was of value

in the old conception of political history; it suggests that this conception ought to be supplemented by another which amplifies our sense of political life and does justice to the variety of political activity. The intellectual currents stirred by such minds as Freud and Weber, Cassirer and Mannheim, have begun to move American historical writing in exploratory directions. The work of analyzing the significance of intellectual and rhetorical styles, of symbolic gestures, and of the specialized ethos of various subgroups within the population has already produced some remarkable studies. Henry Nash Smith has applied such techniques to the role of the frontier as myth and symbol, Oscar Handlin to the clashing ethos of native and immigrant groups, David Potter to the cultural effects of American wealth, Lee Benson, Marvin Meyers, and John William Ward to the issues of Jacksonian democracy, David B. Davis to the social politics of the middle period, David Donald and Stanley Elkins to the slavery question, Eric McKitrick to Reconstruction, C. Vann Woodward and W. J. Cash to the problems of Southern identity, and Irwin Unger to the contrasting mentalities of money reformers and their opponents.

This volume embodies comparable preoccupations of my own. For many years I have been interested in the conspiratorial mind portrayed in the essay on the paranoid style. Today this mentality is of particular interest as it is manifest on the extreme right wing, among those I have called pseudo-conservatives, who believe that we have lived for a generation in the grip of a vast conspiracy. But this is not a style of mind confined to the right wing. With modulations and differences, it exists today, as it has in the past, on the left, and it has recurred at times in democratic movements from anti-Masonry to populism. "Coin" Harvey's interpretation of American history, for example, sets forth a conspiratorial view of events which has much in common with that of the founder of the John Birch Society, though the first of these men spoke in the interests of the oppressed and downtrodden, while the other is enthralled by rugged individualism.

The mind of "Coin" Harvey illustrates another tendency of our politics which runs through these pieces—the tendency to secularize a religiously derived view of the world, to deal with political issues in Christian imagery, and to color them with the dark symbology of a certain side of Christian tradition. "Coin" Harvey's expectations of this profane world were based on a faith, stated quite explicitly in his later years, that social issues could be reduced rather simply to a battle between a Good and an Evil influence. His almost superstitious Manicheanism, his belief that the Evil influence, if not soon curbed, would bring about a terrible social apocalypse, were not unlike the conceptions prevalent on the extreme right today. (Unfortunately, in our time the views of the extreme right have greater capacity for becoming a self-fulfilling prophecy.) Of course, the power of world communism, which has taken the place of the international bankers' syndicate as the central embodiment of evil, is a far more imposing reality. But my point is that the model on which the world is interpreted contains the same exaggerations, the same crusading mentality, the same sense that all our ills can be traced to a single center and hence can be eliminated by some kind of final act of victory over the evil source. If the warnings of those who diagnose the central treachery are not heeded soon enough, it is argued, we are finished: the world confronts an apocalypse of a sort prefigured in the Book of Revelation.

It is not only in its Manichean and apocalyptic carryovers that the evangelical spirit has entered our thinking about politics. Modern "conservatism" is still pervaded by the spirit of ascetic Protestantism—by the old conviction that economic life, quite as much as religious life, ought to provide a machinery for the disciplining of character. As I have tried to show in my studies of the antitrust movement and of pseudo-conservatism and the Goldwater movement, much of our national anxiety can be traced to the fear that the decline of entrepreneurial competition will destroy our national character, or that the same effect will be brought about by our hedonistic mass culture and by the moral laxity that has grown up with and is charged to our liberal and relativistic intellectual climate.

A further concern which underlies several of the essays is the history of our ethnic animosities, which in America have been at times almost a substitute for the class struggle and in any case have always affected its character. Today we are acutely aware once again of the pressing issue of racial justice. But the especially poignant problem of the American Negro is only the

largest and most difficult of a number of ethnic problems arising out of our polyglot population. Our ethnic mixture has
imposed upon our class structure a peculiar, complex status
system, and has made the achievement of a full American identity a recurrent difficulty which has had profound political effects. The curse of what we call "second-class citizenship" is
perennial in American politics.

Finally, one of these essays deals with the way in which public preoccupations with feelings of outraged humanity and
with aggressive desires have influenced a foreign-policy decision. The public debates over our policy toward Cuba and the
Philippines in the 1890's showed in rapid sequence how the
American sense of mission had its aggressive as well as its benign content. Again, in discussing the Goldwater campaign, I
have tried to show how the contemporary craving for finality
in our foreign policy is related to our national experience, especially to our singular transition from a continental power with
more or less complete hegemony in the Western Hemisphere
to a world power whose aspirations now outrun its reach.

Since so many of these pages deal with the contemporary
right wing and its backgrounds, a word of clarification may be
necessary. The prominence of the right wing reflects a certain
recurrent interest on my part in writing about the historical
background of contemporary events. It does not result from
any disposition to exaggerate the numbers or the representa-
tiveness of our right-wing enthusiasts. As I hope I have made
clear in more than one of these studies, the American right
wing represents only a small portion of the American public.
Anyone whose own observations of our political life still leave
him in doubt about this judgment can put it to the test by
drawing up a list of typical right-wing attitudes and policies
on public questions and comparing them with the responses
of the general public to relevant questions in opinion polls.
The polls, of course, are not infallible, but their findings here,
as in many other situations, can be verified in other ways—for
example, by examining the lengthening list of right-wing senators and other politicians of similar persuasion whose recent
careers have been cut short by the electorate. Nonetheless, the
right wing, from McCarthyism to Goldwaterism, has made itself acutely felt in our time. Its effectiveness rests in part, no

doubt, on plenty of enthusiasm, money, and zealous activity and on increasingly adequate organization. But it rests as well, I believe, on certain points of contact with real problems of domestic life and foreign policy and with widespread and deeply rooted American ideas and impulses. It is against this larger background that I have tried to illuminate some of its themes.

R.H.

June 1965

PART I

STUDIES IN THE
AMERICAN RIGHT

The Paranoid Style in American Politics

This essay is a revised and expanded version of the Herbert Spencer Lecture, delivered at Oxford in November 1963. An abridged text appeared in *Harper's Magazine*, November 1964.

I

ALTHOUGH AMERICAN political life has rarely been touched by the most acute varieties of class conflict, it has served again and again as an arena for uncommonly angry minds. To-day this fact is most evident on the extreme right wing, which has shown, particularly in the Goldwater movement, how much political leverage can be got out of the animosities and passions of a small minority. Behind such movements there is a style of mind, not always right-wing in its affiliations, that has a long and varied history. I call it the paranoid style simply because no other word adequately evokes the qualities of heated exaggeration, suspiciousness, and conspiratorial fantasy that I have in mind. In using the expression "paranoid style," I am not speaking in a clinical sense, but borrowing a clinical term for other purposes. I have neither the competence nor the desire to classify any figures of the past or present as certifiable lunatics. In fact, the idea of the paranoid style would have little contemporary relevance or historical value if it were applied only to people with profoundly disturbed minds. It is the use of paranoid modes of expression by more or less normal people that makes the phenomenon significant.

When I speak of the paranoid style, I use the term much as a historian of art might speak of the baroque or the mannerist style. It is, above all, a way of seeing the world and of expressing oneself. Webster defines paranoia, the clinical entity, as a chronic mental disorder characterized by systematized delusions of persecution and of one's own greatness. In the paranoid style, as I conceive it, the feeling of persecution is central, and it is indeed systematized in grandiose theories of conspiracy. But there is a vital difference between the paranoid spokesman in politics and the clinical paranoiac: although they both tend to be overheated, oversuspicious, overaggressive, grandiose, and apocalyptic in expression, the clinical paranoid sees the hostile and conspiratorial world in which he feels himself to be living as directed specifically *against him*; whereas the spokesman of the paranoid style finds it directed against a nation, a culture, a way of life whose fate affects not himself alone but millions of others. Insofar as he does not usually see himself singled out as the individual victim of a personal conspiracy,[1] he is somewhat more rational and much more disinterested. His sense that his political passions are unselfish and patriotic, in fact, goes far to intensify his feeling of righteousness and his moral indignation.

Of course, the term "paranoid style" is pejorative, and it is meant to be; the paranoid style has a greater affinity for bad causes than good. But nothing entirely prevents a sound program or a sound issue from being advocated in the paranoid style, and it is admittedly impossible to settle the merits of an argument because we think we hear in its presentation the characteristic paranoid accents. Style has to do with the way in which ideas are believed and advocated rather than with the truth or falsity of their content.[2]

A few simple and relatively non-controversial examples may make this distinction wholly clear. Shortly after the assassination of President Kennedy, a great deal of publicity was given to a bill, sponsored chiefly by Senator Thomas E. Dodd of Connecticut, to tighten federal controls over the sale of firearms through the mail. When hearings were being held on the measure, three men drove 2,500 miles to Washington from Bagdad, Arizona, to testify against it. Now there are arguments against the Dodd bill which, however unpersuasive one may

---

[1]There are, of course, exceptions to this rule, particularly among the most outré right-wing agitators—see especially Leo Lowenthal and Norbert Guterman: *Prophets of Deceit: A Study of the Techniques of the American Agitator* (New York, 1949), ch. 9—but their significance is arguable. See, however, the interesting suggestions on the relation between styles of thought and patterns of psychosis in N. McConaghy: "Modes of Abstract Thinking and Psychosis," *American Journal of Psychiatry*, CXVII (August 1960), 106–10.

[2]Milton Rokeach, in *The Open and Closed Mind* (New York, 1960), has attempted to distinguish systematically between the content of ideas and the way in which they are espoused. It is important to bear in mind, however, that while any system of beliefs can be espoused in the paranoid style, there are certain beliefs which seem to be espoused almost entirely in this way.

find them, have the color of conventional political reasoning. But one of the Arizonans opposed it with what might be considered representative paranoid arguments, insisting that it was "a further attempt by a subversive power to make us part of one world socialistic government" and that it threatened to "create chaos" that would help "our enemies" to seize power.[3]

Again, it is common knowledge that the movement against the fluoridation of municipal water supplies has been catnip for cranks of all kinds, especially for those who have obsessive fear of poisoning. It is conceivable that at some time scientists may turn up conclusive evidence that this practice is, on balance, harmful; and such a discovery would prove the anti-fluoridationists quite right on the substance of their position. But it could hardly, at the same time, validate the contentions of those among them who, in characteristic paranoid fashion, have charged that fluoridation was an attempt to advance socialism under the guise of public health or to rot out the brains of the community by introducing chemicals in the water supply in order to make people more vulnerable to socialist or communist schemes.

A distorted style is, then, a possible signal that may alert us to a distorted judgment, just as in art an ugly style is a cue to fundamental defects of taste. What interests me here is the possibility of using political rhetoric to get at political pathology. One of the most impressive facts about the paranoid style, in this connection, is that it represents an old and recurrent mode of expression in our public life which has frequently been linked with movements of suspicious discontent and whose content remains much the same even when it is adopted by men of distinctly different purposes. Our experience suggests too that, while it comes in waves of different intensity, it appears to be all but ineradicable.

I choose American history to illustrate the paranoid style only because I happen to be an Americanist, and it is for me a choice of convenience. But the phenomenon is no more limited to American experience than it is to our contemporaries. Notions about an all-embracing conspiracy on the part

[3] *Interstate Shipment of Firearms*, Hearings before the Committee on Commerce, U.S. Senate, 85th Cong., 1st and 2nd sess. (1964), p. 241; cf. pp. 240–54, passim (January 30, 1964).

of Jesuits or Freemasons, international capitalists, international
Jews, or Communists are familiar phenomena in many countries throughout modern history.[4] One need only think of the
response to President Kennedy's assassination in Europe to be
reminded that Americans have no monopoly of the gift for
paranoid improvisation.[5] More important, the single case in
modern history in which one might say that the paranoid style
has had a consummatory triumph occurred not in the United
States but in Germany. It is a common ingredient of fascism,
and of frustrated nationalisms, though it appeals to many who
are hardly fascists and it can frequently be seen in the left-wing
press. The famous Stalin purge trials incorporated, in a supposedly juridical form, a wildly imaginative and devastating exercise in the paranoid style. In America it has been the preferred
style only of *minority* movements. It can be argued, of course,
that certain features of our history have given the paranoid
style more scope and force among us than it has had in many
other countries of the Western world. My intention here, however, is not to make such comparative judgments but simply
to establish the reality of the style and to illustrate its frequent
historical recurrence.

   We may begin with a few American examples. Here is Senator McCarthy, speaking in June 1951 about the parlous situation of the United States:

   How can we account for our present situation unless we believe that men high in this government are concerting to deliver
   us to disaster? This must be the product of a great conspiracy, a

[4] See Franz Neumann's essay "Anxiety and Politics," in *The Democratic and the
Authoritarian State* (Glencoe, Ill., 1957), pp. 270–300. For two studies in European paranoid styles in widely different settings, see Fritz Stern: *The Politics
of Cultural Despair* (Berkeley, 1961), and Stanley Hoffmann: *Le Mouvement
Poujade* (Paris, 1956).
[5] Conspiratorial explanations of Kennedy's assassination have a far wider currency in Europe than they do in the United States, but no European, to my
knowledge, has matched the ingenuity of Professor Revilo P. Oliver of the
University of Illinois, who suggests that while Kennedy had performed many
services for the Communist conspiracy, he was falling behind in a schedule for
the "effective capture of the United States in 1963" and was "rapidly becoming
a political liability." He therefore had to be shot. *The New York Times*, February 11, 1964.

conspiracy on a scale so immense as to dwarf any previous such venture in the history of man. A conspiracy of infamy so black that, when it is finally exposed, its principals shall be forever deserving of the maledictions of all honest men. . . . What can be made of this unbroken series of decisions and acts contributing to the strategy of defeat? They cannot be attributed to incompetence. . . . The laws of probability would dictate that part of . . . [the] decisions would serve this country's interest.[6]

Now let us turn back fifty years to a manifesto signed in 1895 by a number of leaders of the Populist party:

As early as 1865–66 a conspiracy was entered into between the gold gamblers of Europe and America. . . . For nearly thirty years these conspirators have kept the people quarreling over less important matters, while they have pursued with unrelenting zeal their one central purpose. . . . Every device of treachery, every resource of statecraft, and every artifice known to the secret cabals of the international gold ring are being made use of to deal a blow to the prosperity of the people and the financial and commercial independence of the country.[7]

Next, a Texas newspaper article of 1855:

. . . It is a notorious fact that the Monarchs of Europe and the Pope of Rome are at this very moment plotting our destruction and threatening the extinction of our political, civil, and religious institutions. We have the best reasons for believing that corruption has found its way into our Executive Chamber, and that our Executive head is tainted with the infectious venom of Catholicism. . . . The Pope has recently sent his ambassador of state to this country on a secret commission, the effect of which is an extraordinary boldness of the Catholic Church throughout the United States. . . . These minions of the Pope are boldly insulting our Senators; reprimanding our Statesmen; propagating the adulterous union of Church and state; abusing

[6] *Congressional Record*, 82nd Cong., 1st sess. (June 14, 1951), p. 6602; for a similar passage, see McCarthy's book *McCarthyism: The Fight for America* (New York, 1952), p. 2.

[7] The manifesto is reprinted in Frank McVey: "The Populist Movement," *Economic Studies*, I (August 1896), 201–2; the platform of the Populist party for 1892 asserts: "A vast conspiracy against mankind has been organized on two continents, and it is rapidly taking possession of the world. If not met and overthrown at once, it forbodes terrible social convulsions, the destruction of civilization, or the establishment of an absolute despotism."

with foul calumny all governments but Catholic; and spewing out the bitterest execrations on all Protestantism. The Catholics in the United States receive from abroad more than $200,000 annually for the propagation of their creed. Add to this the vast revenue collected here. . . .[8]

Finally, this from a sermon preached in Massachusetts in 1798:

> Secret and systematic means have been adopted and pursued, with zeal and activity, by wicked and artful men, in foreign countries, to undermine the foundations of this Religion [Christianity], and to overthrow its Altars, and thus to deprive the world of its benign influence on society. . . . These impious conspirators and philosophists have completely effected their purposes in a large portion of Europe, and boast of their means of accomplishing their plans in all parts of Christendom, glory in the certainty of their success, and set opposition at defiance. . . .[9]

These quotations, taken from intervals of half a century, give the keynote of the style of thought. In the history of the United States one finds it, for example, in the anti-Masonic movement, the nativist and anti-Catholic movement, in certain spokesmen for abolitionism who regarded the United States as being in the grip of a slaveholders' conspiracy, in many writers alarmed by Mormonism, in some Greenback and Populist writers who constructed a great conspiracy of international bankers, in the exposure of a munitions makers' conspiracy of the First World War, in the popular left-wing press, in the contemporary American right wing, and on both sides of the race controversy today, among White Citizens' Councils and Black Muslims. I do not propose to try to trace the variations of the paranoid style that can be found in all these movements, but will confine myself to a few leading episodes in our past history in which the style emerged in full and archetypal splendor.

---

[8]Quoted by Sister Paul of the Cross McGrath: *Political Nativism in Texas, 1825–1860* (Washington, 1930), pp. 114–15, from *Texas State Times*, September 15, 1855.

[9]Jedidiah Morse: *A Sermon Preached at Charlestown, November 29, 1798* . . . (Worcester, Mass., 1799), pp. 20–1.

II

A suitable point of departure is the panic that broke out in some quarters at the end of the eighteenth century over the allegedly subversive activities of the Bavarian Illuminati. This panic, which came with the general Western reaction to the French Revolution, was heightened here by the response of certain reactionaries, mostly in New England and among the established clergy, to the rise of Jeffersonian democracy. Illuminism had been founded in 1776 by Adam Weishaupt, a professor of law at the University of Ingolstadt. Its teachings today seem to be no more than another version of Enlightenment rationalism, spiced with an anticlerical animus that seems an inevitable response to the reactionary-clerical atmosphere of eighteenth-century Bavaria. A somewhat naïve and utopian movement which aspired ultimately to bring the human race under the rules of reason, it made many converts after 1780 among outstanding dukes and princes of the German states, and is reported to have had the allegiance of such men as Herder, Goethe, and Pestalozzi. Although the order of the Illuminati was shattered by persecution in its native principality, its humanitarian rationalism appears to have acquired a fairly wide influence in Masonic lodges. It is very easy to believe that it was attractive to some radicals with a conspiratorial cast of mind.

Americans first learned of Illuminism in 1797, from a volume published in Edinburgh (later reprinted in New York) under the title *Proofs of a Conspiracy Against All the Religions and Governments of Europe, carried on in the Secret Meetings of Free Masons, Illuminati, and Reading Societies.* Its author was a well-known Scottish scientist, John Robison, who had himself been a somewhat casual adherent of Masonry in Britain, but whose imagination had been inflamed by what he considered to be the far less innocent Masonic movement on the Continent. Robison's book was a conscientious account, laboriously pieced together out of the German sources, of the origins and development of Weishaupt's movement. For the most part, Robison seems to have made his work as factual as he could, but when he came to estimating the moral character and the political influence of Illuminism, he made the characteristic paranoid leap into fantasy. The association, he thought, was formed, "for the express purpose of ROOTING OUT ALL THE RELIGIOUS ESTABLISHMENTS, AND OVERTURNING ALL THE EXISTING GOVERNMENTS OF EUROPE." The most active leaders of the French Revolution, he claimed, were members; it had become "one great and wicked project fermenting and working all over Europe," and to it he attributed a central role in bringing about the French Revolution. He saw it as a libertine, anti-Christian movement, given to the corruption of women, the cultivation of sensual pleasures, and the violation of property rights. Its members had plans for making a tea that caused abortion, a secret substance that "blinds or kills when spurted in the face," and a device that sounds like a stench bomb—a "method for filling a bed-chamber with pestilential vapours."[10] Robison's credulity was exercised not only on these matters but also on a conviction that the Illuminati, while resolutely anti-Christian, were also heavily infiltrated by the Jesuits.

Almost simultaneously with Robison's book there appeared in London a formidable four-volume work by the Abbé Barruel, a Jesuit who had been expelled from France when that order was suppressed in 1773, under the title *Mémoires pour servir à l'histoire du Jacobinisme*. This work, which was translated into English and published both in England and in the United States, elaborated views similar to Robison's, and traced a "triple conspiracy" of anti-Christians, Freemasons, and Illuminati to destroy religion and order. "We shall demonstrate," wrote Barruel,

> what it is imperative for the nations and their leaders to know. We shall say to them: everything in the French Revolution, even the most dreadful of crimes, was foreseen, contemplated, contrived, resolved upon, decreed; that everything was the consequence of the most profound villainy, and was prepared and produced by those men who alone held the leading threads of conspiracies long before woven in the secret societies, and who knew how to choose and to hasten the favorable moments for their schemes. Although among the day-by-day

[10]Robison: *Proofs of a Conspiracy* (New York, 1798), pp. 14, 376, 311. For a detailed study of the American response to Illuminism, see Vernon Stauffer: *New England and the Bavarian Illuminati* (New York, 1918).

events there were some circumstances which hardly seemed the effects of conspiracies, there existed nonetheless one cause with its secret agents, who called forth these events, who knew how to profit by circumstances or even how to bring them about, and who directed everything towards their main end. The circumstances may have served as pretext and opportunity, but the grand cause of the Revolution, of its great crimes, its huge atrocities, was always independent and self-contained, and it consisted in plots long hatched and deeply premeditated.[11]

These notions were quick to make themselves felt in America, even though it is uncertain whether any member of the Illuminati ever came here. In May 1798, a prominent minister of the Massachusetts Congregational establishment in Boston, Jedidiah Morse, delivered a timely sermon of great import to the young country, which was then sharply divided between Jeffersonians and Federalists, Francophiles and Anglophiles. After reading Robison, Morse was convinced that the United States too was the victim of a Jacobinical plot touched off by Illuminism, and that the country should be rallied to defend itself against the machinations of the international conspiracy. His warnings were heeded throughout New England wherever Federalists brooded about the rising tide of religious infidelity or Jeffersonian democracy. Timothy Dwight, the president of Yale, followed Morse's sermon with a Fourth of July discourse, *The Duty of Americans in the Present Crisis*, in which he held forth against the Antichrist in his own glowing rhetoric.

> The sins of these enemies of Christ, and Christians, are of numbers and degrees which mock account and description. All that the malice and atheism of the Dragon, the cruelty

[11] *Mémoires pour servir à l'histoire du Jacobinisme* (Hamburg, 1803), I, ix–x. In *The Age of the Democratic Revolution: The Struggle* (Princeton, 1964) Robert R. Palmer puts the writings of men like Robison and Barruel in the context of the general reaction to the French Revolution and does justice to the modest element of reality behind their fantasies. See esp. pp. 51–4, 141–5, 163–4, 249–55, 343–6, 429–30, 451–6, 540–3; cf. J. Droz: *L'Allemagne et la Révolution française* (Paris, 1949). On the role of the idea of conspiracy in the background of the American Revolution, see Bernard Bailyn's observations in the Introduction to *Pamphlets of the American Revolution* (Cambridge, Mass., 1965), I, 60–89.

and rapacity of the Beast, and the fraud and deceit of the false Prophet, can generate, or accomplish, swell the list. No personal or national interest of man has been uninvaded; no impious sentiment, or action, against God has been spared. . . . Shall we, my brethren, become partakers of these sins? Shall we introduce them into our government, our schools, our families? Shall our sons become the disciples of Voltaire, and the dragoons of Marat; or our daughters the concubines of the Illuminati?[12]

This note was taken up by others, and soon the pulpits of New England were ringing with denunciations of the Illuminati, as though the country were swarming with them. The prevalence of these denunciations is more intelligible if one remembers that the United States did have, if not any Illuminati, a few Democratic-Republican societies which were widely believed to be Jacobinical and to have instigated the Whiskey Rebellion. It was now "generally believed," as one preacher put it,

that the present day is unfolding a design the most extensive, flagitious, and diabolical, that human art and malice have ever invented. Its object is the total destruction of all religion and civil order. If accomplished, the earth can be nothing better than a sink of impurities, a theatre of violence and murder, and a hell of miseries.[13]

These writers illustrate the central preconception of the paranoid style—the existence of a vast, insidious, preternaturally effective international conspiratorial network designed to perpetrate acts of the most fiendish character. There are, of course, certain ancillary themes which appear less frequently. But before going on to characterize the other motifs in the paranoid style, let us look at a few more historical manifestations.

The anti-Masonic movement of the late 1820's and 1830's took up and extended the obsession with conspiracy. At first blush, this movement may seem to be no more than an extension or repetition of the anti-Masonic theme sounded in the earlier outcry against the Bavarian Illuminati—and, indeed, the works of writers like Robison and Barruel were often cited again as evidence of the sinister character of Masonry.

[12] New Haven, 1798, pp. 20–1.
[13] Abiel Abbot: *A Memorial of Divine Benefits* (Haverhill, Mass., 1798), p. 18.

But whereas the panic of the 1790's was confined mainly to New England and linked to an ultra-conservative argument, the later anti-Masonic movement affected many parts of the northern United States and was altogether congenial to popular democracy and rural egalitarianism.[14] Although anti-Masonry happened to be anti-Jacksonian (Jackson was a Mason), it showed the same fear that opportunities for the common man would be closed, the same passionate dislike of aristocratic institutions that one finds in the Jacksonian crusade against the Bank of the United States.

The anti-Masonic movement, though a product of spontaneous enthusiasm, soon fell victim to the changing fortunes of party politics. It was joined and used by a great many men who did not share its original anti-Masonic feelings. It attracted, for example, the support of several reputable statesmen who had only mild sympathy with its fundamental bias, but who as politicians could not afford to ignore it. Still, it was a folk movement of considerable power, and the rural enthusiasts who provided its real impetus believed in it wholeheartedly.

There must have been some considerable suspicion of the Masonic order to begin with, perhaps a residue of the feeling against Illuminism. At any rate, the movement was precipitated by the mysterious disappearance of one William Morgan in 1826. Morgan was an ex-Mason living in western New York State who was at work on a book exposing the order. There can be no doubt that he was abducted by a small group of Masons, and it was widely and quite understandably believed

---

[14] The status of those who were opposed by these anti movements of the nineteenth century varied widely. Freemasonry was largely an affair of the upper crust of society. Catholics were preponderantly poor immigrants. Mormons drew their strength from the native rural middle class. Ironically, the victims themselves were associated with similar anti sentiments. Freemasonry had strong anti-Catholic associations. Mormons were anti-Catholic, and, to a degree, anti-Masonic. Yet their detractors did not hesitate to couple staunch foes. It was sometimes said, for example, that the Jesuits had infiltrated Freemasonry, and the menace of the Catholicism was frequently compared with the menace of Mormonism. All these movements had an interest for minds obsessed with secrecy and concerned with an all-or-nothing world struggle over ultimate values. The ecumenicism of hatred is a great breaker-down of precise intellectual discriminations.

that he had been murdered, though no certainly identifiable body was ever found. The details of the case need not detain us. Morgan's disappearance was followed by an outbreak of similar charges against Masons, invariably unfounded, of other conspiracies to kidnap or to hold in false imprisonment. Within very short order an anti-Masonic party was making itself felt in the politics of New York State, and the party soon became national. But it is its ideology not its political history that concerns us here.

As a secret society, Masonry was considered to be a standing conspiracy against republican government. It was held to be particularly liable to treason—for example, Aaron Burr's famous conspiracy was alleged to have been conducted by Masons.[15] Masonry was also accused of constituting a separate system of loyalty, a separate imperium within the framework of American and state governments, inconsistent with loyalty to them. Quite plausibly it was argued that the Masons had set up a jurisdiction of their own, with their own obligations and punishments, liable to enforcement even by the penalty of death. Anti-Masons were fascinated by the horrid oaths that Masons were said to take, invoking terrible reprisals upon themselves if they should fail in their Masonic obligations. The conflict between secrecy and democracy was felt to be so basic that other, more innocent societies, such as Phi Beta Kappa, also came under attack.

Since Masons were pledged to come to each other's aid under circumstances of distress, and to extend fraternal indulgence at all times, it was held that the order nullified the enforcement of regular law. Masonic constables, sheriffs, juries, judges, and the like would all be in league with Masonic criminals and fugitives. The press too was held to have been

[15] In his *Anti-Masonic Review* Henry Dana Ward charged in September 1829 that "the private correspondence of that conspiracy was carried on in the *Royal Arch cypher*, which is a proof that the agents were exalted Freemasons. This accounts also for their escaping the vengeance of the law: the evidence of their guilt was chiefly in the mystic characters of Freemasonry, and in Royal Arch breasts, and thus closed against the search of human tribunals by the profane oath, and impious penalty of a Royal Arch Mason's obligations." Leland M. Griffin: *The Anti-Masonic Persuasion*, unpublished doctoral dissertation, Cornell University (1950), pp. 627–8.

so "muzzled" by Masonic editors and proprietors that news of Masonic malfeasance could be suppressed—which was the main reason why so shocking a scandal as the Morgan case had received relatively little publicity. Finally, at a moment when practically every alleged citadel of privilege in America was under democratic assault, Masonry was held to be a fraternity of the privileged classes, closing business opportunities and nearly monopolizing political offices, thus shutting out hardy common citizens of the type the anti-Masonic movement liked to claim for its own.

There may have been certain elements of truth and reality in these views of Masonry, and many distinguished and responsible leaders accepted them, at least in part. Not all of these charges and fears need be dismissed as entirely without foundation. What must be emphasized here, however, is the apocalyptic and absolutist framework in which this hostility to Masonry was usually expressed. Anti-Masons were not content simply to say that secret societies were rather a bad idea. David Bernard, in the standard handbook of anti-Masonic materials, *Light on Masonry*, declared that Freemasonry was the most dangerous institution that ever was imposed on man, "an engine of Satan . . . dark, unfruitful, selfish, demoralizing, blasphemous, murderous, anti-republican and anti-Christian."[16] One of the many anti-Masonic pulpit orators called the order "a work of darkness because IT BEARS DECIDED MARKS OF BEING ONE OF THE CONFEDERATE POWERS OF INIQUITY PREDICTED BY THE APOSTLE JOHN . . . WHICH WOULD COMBINE THE WORLD IN ARMS AGAINST GOD, AND BE OVERCOME AT THE BATTLE OF THE GREAT DAY JUST BEFORE THE MILLENNIUM."[17]

A further aspect of anti-Masonry that is at once arresting and puzzling to the modern mind is its obsession with the character

---

[16] *Light on Masonry* (Utica, 1829), pp. iii, x. *The Address of the United States Anti-Masonic Convention* (Philadelphia, 1830) asserted (p. 17): "The abuses of which we complain involve the highest crimes of which man can be guilty, because they indicate the deepest malice, and the most fatal aim. They bespeak the most imminent danger, because they have proceeded from a conspiracy more numerous and better organized for mischief, than any other detailed in the records of man, and yet, though exposed, maintaining itself, in all its monstrous power."

[17] Griffin: op. cit., pp. 27–8.

of Masonic oaths. Oaths were considered to be blasphemous, since they were profanations of a transaction with God, and contrary to civil order, since they set up a secret pattern of loyalties inconsistent with normal civil obligations. At the first national anti-Masonic convention a committee spent a great deal of time solemnly demonstrating that such oaths were subversive and could not be regarded as binding commitments. Many anti-Masons were particularly fascinated by the penalties invoked if Masons failed to live up to their obligations, and these penalties were ingeniously and bloodily imagined. The mark master mason was alleged to call down upon himself having "my right ear smote off and my right hand chopped off as an imposter," in the event of such a failure. My own favorite is the oath attributed to a royal arch mason who invited "having my skull smote off, and my brains exposed to the scorching rays of the sun."[18] The sanguinary character of Masonry was also thought to be shown by the ritual of the lodges, which supposedly required drinking wine from human skulls—this in temperance communities where drinking wine from any kind of container was considered a sin.

III

Fear of a Masonic plot had hardly been quieted when rumors arose of a Catholic plot against American values. One finds here again the same frame of mind, the same conviction of a conspiracy against a way of life, but now a different villain. Of course, the anti-Catholic movement converged with a growing nativism, and while they were not identical, together they cut such a wide swath in American life that they were bound to embrace many moderates to whom the paranoid style, in its full glory, did not appeal. Moreover, we need not dismiss out of hand as wholly parochial or mean-spirited the desire of Yankee Americans to maintain an ethnically and religiously homogeneous society, nor the particular Protestant commitments to individualism and freedom that were brought into play. But the movement had a large paranoid infusion, and the

[18] *Proceedings of the United States Anti-Masonic Convention* . . . (Philadelphia, 1830), pp. 57, 58.

most influential anti-Catholic militants certainly had a strong affinity for the paranoid style.

Two books which appeared in 1835 described the new danger to the American way of life, and may be taken as expressions of the anti-Catholic mentality. One, *Foreign Conspiracy against the Liberties of the United States*, was from the hand of the celebrated painter and inventor of the telegraph, S. F. B. Morse, who was the son of Jedidiah Morse, the anti-Illuminist. "A conspiracy exists," Morse proclaimed, and "its plans are already in operation . . . we are attacked in a vulnerable quarter which cannot be defended by our ships, our forts, or our armies." In the great war going on in the Western world between political reaction and ultramontanism on one side and political and religious liberties on the other, America was a bastion of freedom, and hence an inevitable target for popes and despots. The main source of the conspiracy Morse found in Metternich's government: "*Austria is now acting in this country.* She has devised a grand scheme. She has organized a great plan for doing something here. . . . She has her Jesuit missionaries travelling through the land; she has supplied them with money, and has furnished a fountain for a regular supply."[19]

"It is an ascertained fact," wrote another Protestant militant,

> that Jesuits are prowling about all parts of the United States in every possible disguise, expressly to ascertain the advantageous situations and modes to disseminate Popery. A minister of the Gospel from Ohio has informed us that he discovered one carrying on his devices in his congregation; and he says that the western country swarms with them under the names of puppet show men, dancing masters, music teachers, peddlers of images and ornaments, barrel organ players, and similar practitioners.[20]

Were the plot successful, Morse said, it would not be long before some scion of the House of Habsburg would be installed as Emperor of the United States. Catholics, working "with the minds and the funds of all despotic Europe," were the only possible channel of this influence. Ignorant, ill-educated immigrants, incapable of understanding the institutions of

[19] Morse: *Foreign Conspiracy* . . . (New York, 1835), pp. 14, 21.
[20] Quoted in Ray Allen Billington: *The Protestant Crusade* (New York, 1938), p. 120.

the United States, would supplement the efforts of wily Jesuit agents. The danger was imminent and must be met at once. "The serpent has already commenced his coil about our limbs, and the lethargy of his poison is creeping over us. . . . Is not the enemy already organized in the land? Can we not perceive all around us the evidence of his presence? . . . We must awake, or we are lost."[21]

Lyman Beecher, the elder of a famous family and the father of Harriet Beecher Stowe, wrote in the same year his *Plea for the West*, in which he considered the possibility that the Christian millennium might come in the American states. Everything depended, in his judgment, upon what influences dominated the great West, where the future of the country lay. There Protestantism was engaged in a life-or-death struggle with Catholicism. Time was already running out. "Whatever we do, it must be done quickly. . . ." A great tide of immigration, hostile to free institutions, was sweeping in upon the country, subsidized and sent by "the potentates of Europe," multiplying tumult and violence, filling jails, crowding poorhouses, quadrupling taxation, and sending increasing thousands of voters to "lay their inexperienced hand upon the helm of our power." Well might we believe, said Beecher, that Metternich knew that there would be a party in the United States willing to hasten the naturalization and enfranchisement of these multitudes and demagogues, a party that would "sell their country into an everlasting bondage." Even so much as a tenth of the voting population, "condensed and wielded by the Catholic powers of Europe, might decide our elections, perplex our policy, inflame and divide the nation, break the bond of our union, and throw down our free institutions."[22] Beecher did not approve violations of the civil rights of Catholics or the burning of convents, but he urged Protestants to a greater militancy and solidarity to fend off a fate that might be waiting for them in a not very distant future.

Anti-Catholicism has always been the pornography of the Puritan. Whereas the anti-Masons had imagined wild drinking bouts and had entertained themselves with fantasies about the

[21]Morse: op. cit., pp. 95–6.
[22]Lyman Beecher: *Plea for the West* (Cincinnati, 1835), pp. 47, 62–3.

actual enforcement of grisly Masonic oaths, the anti-Catholics developed an immense lore about libertine priests, the confessional as an opportunity for seduction, licentious convents and monasteries, and the like. Probably the most widely read contemporary book in the United States before *Uncle Tom's Cabin* was a work supposedly written by one Maria Monk, entitled *Awful Disclosures*, which appeared in 1836. The author, who purported to have escaped from the Hôtel Dieu nunnery in Montreal after a residence of five years as novice and nun, reported her convent life there in elaborate and circumstantial detail. She recalled having been told by the Mother Superior that she must "obey the priests in all things"; to her "utter astonishment and horror," she soon found what the nature of such obedience was. Infants born of convent liaisons were baptized and then killed, she said, so that they might ascend at once to heaven. A high point in the *Awful Disclosures* was Maria Monk's eyewitness account of the strangling of two babies. Her book, hotly attacked and as hotly defended, continued to be read and believed even after her mother, a Protestant living near Montreal, gave testimony that Maria had been somewhat addled ever since childhood when she had rammed a pencil into her head. It was, indeed, read and believed by a dwindling audience even when poor Maria produced a fatherless child two years after the appearance of her book. She died in prison in 1849, after having been arrested in a brothel as a pickpocket.[23]

Anti-Catholicism, like anti-Masonry, mixed its fortunes with American party politics. To trace its political career would take us too far afield, but it did become an enduring factor in American politics. The American Protective Association of the 1890's revived it with ideological variations more suitable to the times—the depression of 1893, for example, was alleged to be an intentional creation of the Catholics, who began it by starting a run on the banks. Some spokesmen of the movement circulated a bogus encyclical attributed to Leo XIII instructing American Catholics on a certain date in 1893 to exterminate

[23]Maria Monk: *Awful Disclosures* (New York, 1836; facsimile ed., Hamden, Conn., 1962); see R. A. Billington's introduction to the 1962 edition and his account in *The Protestant Crusade*, pp. 99–108.

all heretics, and a great many anti-Catholics daily expected a
nation-wide uprising. The myth of an impending Catholic war
of mutilation and extermination of heretics persisted into the
twentieth century.[24]

IV

If we now take the long jump to the contemporary right
wing, we find some rather important differences from the
nineteenth-century movements. The spokesman of those earlier movements felt that they stood for causes and personal
types that were still in possession of their country—that they
were fending off threats to a still well-established way of life
in which they played an important part. But the modern right
wing, as Daniel Bell has put it,[25] feels dispossessed: America has
been largely taken away from them and their kind, though they
are determined to try to repossess it and to prevent the final
destructive act of subversion. The old American virtues have
already been eaten away by cosmopolitans and intellectuals;
the old competitive capitalism has been gradually undermined
by socialist and communist schemers; the old national security
and independence have been destroyed by treasonous plots,
having as their most powerful agents not merely outsiders and
foreigners but major statesmen seated at the very centers of
American power. Their predecessors discovered foreign conspiracies; the modern radical right finds that conspiracy also
embraces betrayal at home.

Important changes may be traced to the effects of the mass
media. The villains of the modern right are much more vivid

---

[24]John Higham: *Strangers in the Land* (New Brunswick, N.J., 1955), pp. 81,
85, 180. Higham, studying Henry F. Bowers, a leader of this later phase of
anti-Catholicism, finds "a mind charged with constant excitement and given
to rigid categorical judgments," moving "in a world of suspicion and imagined
danger. Here a single hostile force explained the trivial events of daily experience, while a sense of grandeur and destiny sustained the struggle against it.
Everywhere Bowers saw evidence of the machinations of a foreign ecclesiastical
conspiracy endowed with immense power." "The Mind of a Nativist: Henry F.
Bowers and the A.P.A.," *American Quarterly*, IV (Spring 1953), 21.
[25]"The Dispossessed," in Daniel Bell (ed.): *The Radical Right* (New York,
1963), pp. 1–38.

than those of their paranoid predecessors, much better known
to the public; the contemporary literature of the paranoid style
is by the same token richer and more circumstantial in personal
description and personal invective. For the vaguely delineated
villains of the anti-Masons, for the obscure and disguised Jesuit
agents, the little-known papal delegates of the anti-Catholics,
for the shadowy international bankers of the monetary conspiracies, we may now substitute eminent public figures like
Presidents Roosevelt, Truman, and Eisenhower, Secretaries of
State like Marshall, Acheson, and Dulles, justices of the Supreme Court like Frankfurter and Warren, and the whole bat-
tery of lesser but still famous and vivid conspirators headed by
Alger Hiss.[26]

Events since 1939 have given the contemporary right-wing
paranoid a vast theater for his imagination, full of rich and
proliferating detail, replete with realistic clues and undeniable
proofs of the validity of his views. The theater of action is now
the entire world, and he can draw on not only the events of
the Second World War but those of the Korean War and the
cold war. Any historian of warfare knows that it is in good part
a comedy of errors and a museum of incompetence; but if for
every error and every act of incompetence one can substitute
an act of treason, we can see how many points of fascinating
interpretation are open to the paranoid imagination: treason in
high places can be found at almost every turning—and in the
end the real mystery, for one who reads the primary works of
paranoid scholarship, is not how the United States has been
brought to its present dangerous position, but how it has managed to survive at all.

The basic elements of contemporary right-wing thought
can be reduced to three: First, there has been the now familiar sustained conspiracy, running over more than a generation,
and reaching its climax in Roosevelt's New Deal, to undermine free capitalism, to bring the economy under the direction
of the federal government, and to pave the way for socialism
or communism. Details might be open to argument among

[26]The appeal of the conspiratorial conception of power is brilliantly and economically set against its historical background by Edward Shils: *The Torment of
Secrecy* (Glencoe, Ill., 1956), esp. Ch. 1.

right-wingers, but many would agree with Frank Chodorov, the author of *The Income Tax: The Root of All Evil*,[27] that this campaign began with the passage of the income tax amendment to the Constitution in 1913.

The second contention is that top government officialdom has been so infiltrated by Communists that American policy, at least since the days leading up to Pearl Harbor, has been dominated by sinister men who were shrewdly and consistently selling out American national interests.

The final contention is that the country is infused with a network of Communist agents, just as in the old days it was infiltrated by Jesuit agents, so that the whole apparatus of education, religion, the press, and the mass media are engaged in a common effort to paralyze the resistance of loyal Americans.

The details of the modern right-wing case are beyond the scope of any brief discussion. Perhaps the most representative

[27]New York, 1954, esp. Ch. 5. For a good brief summary of the history of this alleged conspiracy, see Chesly Manly: *The Twenty-Year Revolution: From Roosevelt to Eisenhower* (Chicago, 1954), which traces all aspects of the "revolution" and finds in the United Nations (p. 179) "the principal instrument of a gigantic conspiracy to control the foreign and domestic policies of the United States, subvert the Constitution, and establish a totalitarian society." A more recent and much more widely read work, particularly popular in the Goldwater movement, is Phyllis Schlafly's *A Choice Not an Echo* (Alton, Ill., 1964), which traces the work of a small group of "secret kingmakers" in New York who have controlled the affairs of the Republican party from 1936 to 1960. The author believes that Republicans have so many issues on their side that (pp. 23, 25–6) "there is no way Republicans can possibly lose *so long as we have a presidential candidate who campaigns on the issues*." However, they have lost four major presidential campaigns because "a small group of secret kingmakers, using hidden persuaders and psychological warfare techniques, manipulated the Republican National Convention to nominate candidates who would sidestep or suppress the key issues." A more substantial contemporary manual of conspiratorial views, which traces ramifications in many areas of American life, is John A. Stormer: *None Dare Call It Treason* (Florissant, Mo., 1964). The writer asks (p. 226): "Is there a conspiratorial plan to destroy the United States into which foreign aid, planned inflation, distortion of treaty-making powers and disarmament all fit?" He answers subtly that it makes no difference whether this is all planned or is merely the work of "misguided idealists. The fact is that the pieces exist. They fit the pattern whether they were planned by the communists or some other secret and mysterious revolutionary group or not. . . . Those who constructed the 'pieces' are few in number, but they exert fantastic control in government, financial circles, the press, unions, schools, etc."

document of its McCarthyist phase was a long indictment of Secretary of State George C. Marshall, delivered in the Senate on June 14, 1951, by Senator McCarthy, and later published in a somewhat different form as *America's Retreat from Victory: The Story of George Catlett Marshall*. McCarthy pictured Marshall as the focal figure in a betrayal of American interests stretching in time from the strategic plans for the Second World War to the formulation of the Marshall Plan. Marshall was associated with practically every American failure or defeat, McCarthy insisted, and none of this was due to either accident or incompetence. There was a "baffling pattern" of Marshall's interventions in the war: "His decisions, maintained with great stubbornness and skill, always and invariably serv[ed] the world policy of the Kremlin." Under his guidance there was conducted at the end of the war "what appeared to be a planned loss of the peace." Marshall's report on his mission to China cannot be understood as the product of incompetence, but appears persuasive and brilliant when it is read as "a propaganda document in behalf of other interests, another country and civilization." Marshall and Acheson were intent on delivering China to Russia. The Marshall Plan was "an evil hoax on the generosity, good will and carelessness of the American people." And, above all, the sharp decline in America's relative strength from 1945 to 1951 did not "just happen," it was "brought about, step by step, by will and intention," the consequence not of mistakes but of a treasonous conspiracy, "a conspiracy on a scale so immense as to dwarf any previous such venture in the history of man." The ultimate aim of this conspiracy was "that we shall be contained and frustrated and finally fall victim to Soviet intrigue from within and Russian military might from without."[28]

Today the mantle of McCarthy has fallen on the retired candy manufacturer Robert H. Welch, Jr., who is less strategically placed but whose well-organized following in the John Birch Society has had a strong influence. A few years ago Welch proclaimed that "Communist influences are now in almost complete control of our Federal Government"—note the care and scrupulousness of that "almost." He has offered a full-scale interpretation of our recent history in which Communists

[28]Joseph R. McCarthy: *America's Retreat from Victory* (New York, 1951), pp. 54, 66, 130, 141, 156, 168, 169, 171.

figure at every turn: They started a run on American banks in 1933 that forced their closure; they contrived the recognition of the Soviet Union by the United States in the same year, just in time to save the Soviets from economic collapse; they have stirred up the fuss over segregation; they have taken over the Supreme Court and made it "one of the most important agencies of Communism." They are winning the struggle for control in "the press, the pulpit, the radio and television media, the labor unions, the schools, the courts, and the legislative halls of America."

Close attention to history wins for Mr. Welch an insight into affairs that is given to few of us. "For many reasons and after a lot of study," he wrote some years ago, "I personally believe [John Foster] Dulles to be a Communist agent." Other apparently innocent figures are similarly unmasked. The job of Professor Arthur F. Burns as the head of Eisenhower's Council of Economic Advisers quite probably was "merely a coverup for Burns' liaison work between Eisenhower and some of his bosses in the Establishment." Eisenhower's brother Milton was "actually [his] superior and boss within the whole Leftwing Establishment." As for Eisenhower himself, Welch characterized him, in words that have made the candy manufacturer famous, as "a dedicated, conscious agent of the Communist conspiracy"—a conclusion, he added, "based on an accumulation of detailed evidence so extensive and so palpable that it seems to put this conviction beyond any reasonable doubt."[29]

The views for which Mr. Welch carefully gathers "detailed evidence" are expressed with less scholarly responsibility by a small but vocal segment of the public. Recently Republican Senator Thomas R. Kuchel, the minority whip of the Senate, revealed that of the 60,000 letters he receives each month, about 10 per cent may be classified as what he calls "fright

[29] *The Politician* (Belmont, Mass., 1963), pp. 222, 223, 229. Quotations from Welch vary slightly because his incredible diatribe against Eisenhower was modified in later editions of this book—for example, Eisenhower was later described as (p. 291) "either a willing agent, or an integral and important part of a conspiracy of gangsters determined to rule the world at any cost." Welch's views are ably summarized by Alan Westin, from a different version of the text, in "The John Birch Society," in Daniel Bell (ed): op. cit., pp. 204–6.

mail"—indignant or anguished letters about "the latest *PLOT!!*
to OVERTHROW America!!!" The imagination of his correspondents is feverishly at work:

> Some of the more memorable "plots" that come to mind
> include these: 35,000 Communist Chinese troops bearing
> arms and wearing deceptively dyed powder-blue uniforms, are
> poised on the Mexican border, about to invade San Diego; the
> United States has turned over—or will at any moment—its
> Army, Navy and Air Force to the command of a Russian colo-
> nel in the United Nations; almost every well-known American
> or free-world leader is, in reality, a top Communist agent; a
> United States Army guerilla-warfare exercise in Georgia, called
> Water Moccasin III, is in actuality a United Nations operation
> preparatory to taking over our country.[30]

V

Let us now abstract the basic elements in the paranoid style.
The central image is that of a vast and sinister conspiracy, a
gigantic and yet subtle machinery of influence set in motion to
undermine and destroy a way of life. One may object that there
are conspiratorial acts in history, and there is nothing paranoid
about taking note of them. This is true. All political behavior
requires strategy, many strategic acts depend for their effect
upon a period of secrecy, and anything that is secret may be
described, often with but little exaggeration, as conspiratorial.
The distinguishing thing about the paranoid style is not that its
exponents see conspiracies or plots here and there in history,
but that they regard a "vast" or "gigantic" conspiracy as *the
motive force* in historical events. History *is* a conspiracy, set in
motion by demonic forces of almost transcendent power, and
what is felt to be needed to defeat it is not the usual methods
of political give-and-take, but an all-out crusade. The paranoid
spokesman sees the fate of this conspiracy in apocalyptic terms
—he traffics in the birth and death of whole worlds, whole
political orders, whole systems of human values. He is always
manning the barricades of civilization. He constantly lives at
a turning point: it is now or never in organizing resistance to

[30] *The New York Times*, July 21, 1963, VI, p. 6.

conspiracy. Time is forever just running out. Like religious millenarians, he expresses the anxiety of those who are living through the last days and he is sometimes disposed to set a date for the apocalypse. "Time is running out," said Welch in 1951. "Evidence is piling up on many sides and from many sources that October 1952 is the fatal month when Stalin will attack."[31] The apocalypticism of the paranoid style runs dangerously near to hopeless pessimism, but usually stops short of it. Apocalyptic warnings arouse passion and militancy, and

[31] *May God Forgive Us* (Chicago, 1952), p. 73. Dr. Fred C. Schwarz of the Christian Anti-Communism Crusade is more circumspect. In his lectures he sets the year 1973 as the date for the Communists to achieve control of the world, if they are not stopped. Most contemporary paranoid spokesmen speak of a "Communist timetable," of whose focal dates they often seem to have intimate knowledge.

Probably the most spectacular American instance of such adventism is the case of William Miller, who flourished in New York in the 1830's. The offspring of a line of Baptist preachers, Miller became preoccupied with millenarian prophecies, and made calculations which indicated that Christ would come at first in 1843, and then on October 22, 1844, and became the leader of an adventist sect with a considerable following. On the appointed day, Millerites gathered to pray, many abandoned their worldly occupations, and some disposed of their property. The Miller movement waned after the fatal day, but other adventists, more cautious about their use of dates, carried on.

A notable quality in Miller's work was the rigorously logical and systematic character of his demonstrations, as was his militant opposition to Masonry, Catholicism, and other seductions. His lieutenants and followers, A. Whitney Cross has remarked, "found the world beyond rescue, legislatures corrupt, and infidelity, idolatry, Romanism, sectarianism, seduction, fraud, murder, and duels all waxing stronger." Cross argues that the Millerite movement was not so far from the mainstream of American Protestantism as some might think: "The Millerites cannot be dismissed as ignorant farmers, libertarian frontiersmen, impoverished victims of economic change, or hypnotized followers of a maniac thrown into prominence by freak coincidences, when the whole of American Protestantism came so very close to the same beliefs. Their doctrine was the logical absolute of fundamentalist orthodoxy, as perfectionism was the extreme of revivalism. . . . All Protestants expected some grand event about 1843, and no critic from the orthodox side took any serious issue on basic principles with Miller's calculations." *The Burned-Over District* (Ithaca, N.Y., 1950), pp. 320–1; see Ch. 17 for a good account of the Millerite movement.

For the story of an interesting contemporary prophetic cult and some sober reflections on the powerful resistance of true believers to overwhelming disconfirmation, see L. Festinger, H. W. Riecken, and S. Schachter: *When Prophecy Fails* (Minneapolis, 1956).

strike at susceptibility to similar themes in Christianity. Properly expressed, such warnings serve somewhat the same function as a description of the horrible consequences of sin in a revivalist sermon: they portray that which impends but which may still be avoided. They are a secular and demonic version of adventism.

As a member of the avant-garde who is capable of perceiving the conspiracy before it is fully obvious to an as yet unaroused public, the paranoid is a militant leader. He does not see social conflict as something to be mediated and compromised, in the manner of the working politician. Since what is at stake is always a conflict between absolute good and absolute evil, the quality needed is not a willingness to compromise but the will to fight things out to a finish. Nothing but complete victory will do. Since the enemy is thought of as being totally evil and totally unappeasable, he must be totally eliminated—if not from the world, at least from the theater of operations to which the paranoid directs his attention.[32] This demand for unqualified victories leads to the formulation of hopelessly demanding and unrealistic goals, and since these goals are not even remotely attainable, failure constantly heightens the paranoid's frustration. Even partial success leaves him with the same sense of powerlessness with which he began, and this in turn only strengthens his awareness of the vast and terrifying quality of the enemy he opposes.

This enemy is clearly delineated: he is a perfect model of malice, a kind of amoral superman: sinister, ubiquitous, powerful, cruel, sensual, luxury-loving. Unlike the rest of us, the enemy is not caught in the toils of the vast mechanism of history, himself a victim of his past, his desires, his limitations. He is a free, active, demonic agent. He wills, indeed he manufactures, the mechanism of history himself, or deflects the normal course of history in an evil way. He makes crises, starts runs on banks, causes depressions, manufactures disasters, and then enjoys and profits from the misery he has produced. The paranoid's interpretation of history is in this sense distinctly personal: decisive events are not taken as part of the stream of history, but as the

[32] "The systems are diametrically opposed: one must and will exterminate the other." Edward Beecher: *The Papal Conspiracy Exposed and Protestantism Defended* (Boston, 1855), p. 29.

consequences of someone's will. Very often the enemy is held to possess some especially effective source of power: he controls the press; he directs the public mind through "managed news"; he has unlimited funds; he has a new secret for influencing the mind (brainwashing); he has a special technique for seduction (the Catholic confessional); he is gaining a stranglehold on the educational system.

This enemy seems to be on many counts a projection of the self: both the ideal and the unacceptable aspects of the self are attributed to him. A fundamental paradox of the paranoid style is the imitation of the enemy. The enemy, for example, may be the cosmopolitan intellectual, but the paranoid will outdo him in the apparatus of scholarship, even of pedantry. Senator McCarthy, with his heavily documented tracts and his show of information, Mr. Welch with his accumulations of irresistible evidence, John Robison with his laborious study of documents in a language he but poorly used, the anti-Masons with their endlessly painstaking discussions of Masonic ritual—all these offer a kind of implicit compliment to their opponents. Secret organizations set up to combat secret organizations give the same flattery. The Ku Klux Klan imitated Catholicism to the point of donning priestly vestments, developing an elaborate ritual and an equally elaborate hierarchy. The John Birch Society emulates Communist cells and quasi-secret operation through "front" groups, and preaches a ruthless prosecution of the ideological war along lines very similar to those it finds in the Communist enemy. Spokesmen of the various Christian anti-Communist "crusades" openly express their admiration for the dedication, discipline, and strategic ingenuity the Communist cause calls forth.[33]

---

[33]This has now become a fashionable trend in more respectable quarters. Stephen Shadegg, known for his success in Senator Goldwater's senatorial campaigns, writes: "Mao Tse-tung . . . has written a valuable book on the tactics of infiltration. In it he says: 'Give me just two or three men in a village and I will take the village.' In the Goldwater campaigns of 1952 and 1958 and in all other campaigns where I have served as a consultant I have followed the advice of Mao Tse-tung." *How to Win an Election* (New York, 1964), p. 106. Writing about cold-war strategy, Goldwater himself declares: "I would suggest that we analyze and copy the strategy of the enemy; theirs has worked and ours has not." *Why Not Victory?* (New York, 1962), p. 24.

David Brion Davis, in a remarkable essay on pre–Civil War "counter-subversive" movements, has commented on the manner in which the nineteenth-century nativist unwittingly fashioned himself after his enemy:

> As the nativist searched for participation in a noble cause, for unity in a group sanctioned by tradition and authority, he professed a belief in democracy and equal rights. Yet in his very zeal for freedom he curiously assumed many of the character- istics of the imagined enemy. By condemning the subversive's fanatical allegiance to an ideology, he affirmed a similarly un- critical acceptance of a different ideology; by attacking the sub- versive's intolerance of dissent, he worked to eliminate dissent and diversity of opinion; by censuring the subversive for alleged licentiousness, he engaged in sensual fantasies; by criticizing the subversive's loyalty to an organization, he sought to prove his unconditional loyalty to the established order. The nativ- ist moved even farther in the direction of his enemies when he formed tightly-knit societies and parties which were often secret and which subordinated the individual to the single pur- pose of the group. Though the nativists generally agreed that the worst evil of subversives was their subordination of means to ends, they themselves recommended the most radical means to purge the nation of troublesome groups and to enforce un- questioned loyalty to the state.[34]

Much of the function of the enemy lies not in what can be imitated but in what can be wholly condemned. The sexual freedom often attributed to him, his lack of moral inhibition, his possession of especially effective techniques for fulfilling his desires, give exponents of the paranoid style an opportu- nity to project and freely express unacceptable aspects of their own minds. Priests and Mormon patriarchs were commonly thought to have especial attraction for women, and hence li- centious privilege. Thus Catholics and Mormons—later Ne- groes and Jews—lent themselves to a preoccupation with illicit sex. Very often the fantasies of true believers serve as strong sado-masochistic outlets, vividly expressed, for example, in the

[34]David Brion Davis: "Some Themes of Counter-Subversion: An Analysis of Anti-Masonic, Anti-Catholic, and Anti-Mormon Literature," *Mississippi Valley Historical Review*, XLVII (September 1960), p. 223.

concern of anti-Masons with the alleged cruelty of Masonic punishments. Concerning this phenomenon, Davis remarks:

> Masons disemboweled or slit the throats of their victims; Catholics cut unborn infants from their mothers' wombs and threw them to the dogs before their parents' eyes; Mormons raped and lashed recalcitrant women, or seared their mouths with red-hot irons. This obsession with details of sadism, which reached pathological proportions in much of the literature, showed a furious determination to purge the enemy of every admirable quality.[35]

Another recurring aspect of the paranoid style is the special significance that attaches to the figure of the renegade from the enemy cause. The anti-Masonic movement seemed at times to be the creation of ex-Masons; it certainly attached the highest significance and gave the most unqualified credulity to their revelations. Similarly anti-Catholicism used the runaway nun and the apostate priest, anti-Mormonism the ex-wife from the harem of polygamy; the avant-garde anti-Communist movements of our time use the ex-Communist. In some part the special authority accorded the renegade derives from the obsession with secrecy so characteristic of such movements: the renegade is the man or woman who has been in the secret world of the enemy, and brings forth with him or her the final verification of suspicions which might otherwise have been doubted by a skeptical world. But I think there is a deeper eschatological significance attached to the person of the renegade: in the spiritual wrestling match between good and evil which is the paranoid's archetypal model of the world struggle, the renegade is living proof that all the conversions are not made by the wrong side. He brings with him the promise of redemption and victory.

In contemporary right-wing movements a particularly important part has been played by ex-Communists who have moved rapidly, though not without anguish, from the paranoid left to the paranoid right, clinging all the while to the fundamentally Manichean psychology that underlies both. Such authorities on communism remind one of those ancient converts from paganism to Christianity of whom it is told that upon

[35]Ibid., p. 221.

their conversion they did not entirely cease to believe in their old gods but converted them into demons.

A final aspect of the paranoid style is related to that quality of pedantry to which I have already referred. One of the impressive things about paranoid literature is precisely the elaborate concern with demonstration it almost invariably shows. One should not be misled by the fantastic conclusions that are so characteristic of this political style into imagining that it is not, so to speak, argued out along factual lines. The very fantastic character of its conclusions leads to heroic strivings for "evidence" to prove that the unbelievable is the only thing that can be believed. Of course, there are highbrow, lowbrow, and middlebrow paranoids, as there are likely to be in any political tendency, and paranoid movements from the Middle Ages onward have had a magnetic attraction for demi-intellectuals. But respectable paranoid literature not only starts from certain moral commitments that can be justified to many non-paranoids but also carefully and all but obsessively accumulates "evidence." Paranoid writing begins with certain defensible judgments. There *was* something to be said for the anti-Masons. After all, a secret society composed of influential men bound by special obligations could conceivably pose some kind of threat to the civil order in which they were suspended. There was also something to be said for the Protestant principles of individuality and freedom, as well as for the nativist desire to develop in North America a homogeneous civilization. Again, in our time innumerable decisions of the Second World War and the cold war can be faulted, and it is easy for the suspicious to believe that such decisions are not simply the mistakes of well-meaning men but the plans of traitors.

The typical procedure of the higher paranoid scholarship is to start with such defensible assumptions and with a careful accumulation of facts, or at least of what appear to be facts, and to marshal these facts toward an overwhelming "proof" of the particular conspiracy that is to be established. It is nothing if not coherent—in fact, the paranoid mentality is far more coherent than the real world, since it leaves no room for mistakes, failures, or ambiguities. It is, if not wholly rational, at least intensely rationalistic; it believes that it is up against an enemy who is as infallibly rational as he is totally evil, and it seeks to match his imputed total competence with its own, leaving nothing unexplained and comprehending all of reality in one overreaching, consistent theory. It is nothing if not "scholarly" in technique. McCarthy's 96-page pamphlet *McCarthyism* contains no less than 313 footnote references, and Mr. Welch's fantastic assault on Eisenhower, *The Politician*, is weighed down by a hundred pages of bibliography and notes. The entire right-wing movement of our time is a parade of experts, study groups, monographs, footnotes, and bibliographies. Sometimes the right-wing striving for scholarly depth and an inclusive world view has startling consequences: Mr. Welch, for example, has charged that the popularity of Arnold Toynbee's historical work is the consequence of a plot on the part of Fabians, "Labour Party bosses in England," and various members of the Anglo-American "liberal establishment" to overshadow the much more truthful and illuminating work of Oswald Spengler.[36]

What distinguishes the paranoid style is not, then, the absence of verifiable facts (though it is occasionally true that in his extravagant passion for facts the paranoid occasionally manufactures them), but rather the curious leap in imagination that is always made at some critical point in the recital of events. John Robison's tract on the Illuminati followed a pattern that has been repeated for over a century and a half. For page after page he patiently records the details he has been able to accumulate about the history of the Illuminati. Then, suddenly, the French Revolution has taken place, and the Illuminati have brought it about. What is missing is not veracious information about the organization, but sensible judgment about what can cause a revolution. The plausibility the paranoid style has for those who find it plausible lies, in good measure, in this appearance of the most careful, conscientious, and seemingly coherent application to detail, the laborious accumulation of what can be taken as convincing evidence for the most fantastic conclusions, the careful preparation for the big leap from the undeniable to the unbelievable. The singular thing about all this laborious work is that the passion for factual evidence does not, as in most intellectual exchanges, have the effect of

[36] *The Blue Book of the John Birch Society* (n.p., 1961), pp. 42–3.

putting the paranoid spokesman into effective two-way communication with the world outside his group—least of all with those who doubt his views. He has little real hope that his evidence will convince a hostile world. His effort to amass it has rather the quality of a defensive act which shuts off his receptive apparatus and protects him from having to attend to disturbing considerations that do not fortify his ideas. He has all the evidence he needs; he is not a receiver, he is a transmitter.

Since I have drawn so heavily on American examples, I would like to emphasize again that the paranoid style is an international phenomenon. Nor is it confined to modern times. Studying the millennial sects of Europe from the eleventh to the sixteenth century, Norman Cohn finds, in his brilliant book *The Pursuit of the Millennium*, a persistent psychological complex that closely resembles what I have been considering—a style made up of certain marked preoccupations and fantasies: "the megalomanic view of oneself as the Elect, wholly good, abominably persecuted yet assured of ultimate triumph; the attribution of gigantic and demonic powers to the adversary; the refusal to accept the ineluctable limitations and imperfections of human existence, such as transience, dissention, conflict, fallibility whether intellectual or moral; the obsession with inerrable prophecies . . . systematized misinterpretations, always gross and often grotesque . . . ruthlessness directed towards an end which by its very nature cannot be realised—towards a total and final solution such as cannot be attained at any actual time or in any concrete situation, but only in the timeless and autistic realm of phantasy."[37]

The recurrence of the paranoid style over a long span of time and in different places suggests that a mentality disposed to see the world in the paranoid's way may always be present in some considerable minority of the population. But the fact that

[37] *The Pursuit of the Millennium* (London, 1957), pp. 309–10; see also pp. 58–74. In the Middle Ages millenarianism flourished among the poor, the oppressed, and the hopeless. In Anglo-American experience, as Samuel Shepperson has observed, such movements have never been confined to these classes, but have had a more solid middle-class foundation. "The Comparative Study of Millenarian Movements," in Sylvia Thrupp (ed.): *Millennial Dreams in Action* (The Hague, 1962), pp. 49–52.

movements employing the paranoid style are not constant but come in successive episodic waves suggests that the paranoid disposition is mobilized into action chiefly by social conflicts that involve ultimate schemes of values and that bring fundamental fears and hatreds, rather than negotiable interests, into political action. Catastrophe or the fear of catastrophe is most likely to elicit the syndrome of paranoid rhetoric.

In American experience, ethnic and religious conflicts, with their threat of the submergence of whole systems of values, have plainly been the major focus for militant and suspicious minds of this sort, but elsewhere class conflicts have also mobilized such energies. The paranoid tendency is aroused by a confrontation of opposed interests which are (or are felt to be) totally irreconcilable, and thus by nature not susceptible to the normal political processes of bargain and compromise. The situation becomes worse when the representatives of a particular political interest—perhaps because of the very unrealistic and unrealizable nature of their demands—cannot make themselves felt in the political process. Feeling that they have no access to political bargaining or the making of decisions, they find their original conception of the world of power as omnipotent, sinister, and malicious fully confirmed. They see only the consequences of power—and this through distorting lenses—and have little chance to observe its actual machinery. L. B. Namier once said that "the crowning attainment of historical study" is to achieve "an intuitive sense of how things do not happen."[38] It is precisely this kind of awareness that the paranoid fails to develop. He has a special resistance of his own, of course, to such awareness, but circumstances often deprive him of exposure to events that might enlighten him. We are all sufferers from history, but the paranoid is a double sufferer, since he is afflicted not only by the real world, with the rest of us, but by his fantasies as well.

[38]L. B. Namier: "History," in Fritz Stern (ed.): *The Varieties of History* (New York, 1956), p. 375.

The Pseudo-Conservative Revolt—1954

In the spring of 1954 I was invited by the directors of the American Civilization Program of Barnard College to speak on some aspect of American dissent. Since the McCarthyist movement was then at its peak, I chose to speak on right-wing or, as I called it, pseudo-conservative dissent. In defining the right-wing movement, which was so fond of designating itself "conservative," as being in some sense a movement of *dissent*, I tried to pose the problem around which my argument was built. The lecture was later published in the Winter 1954–5 issue of *The American Scholar*. I have written nothing else of comparable brevity that aroused more attention or drew more requests for quotation or reprinting.

It soon became apparent that several writers, working independently and simultaneously, were arriving at roughly similar approaches to McCarthyism and related phenomena. Daniel Bell, in *The New American Right* (1955), collected and introduced the relevant pieces, which had been written by David Riesman and Nathan Glazer, Seymour M. Lipset, Talcott Parsons, and Peter Viereck; these essays are now most conveniently available, along with the editor's and authors' afterthoughts and new essays by Alan F. Westin and Herbert H. Hyman, in *The Radical Right* (1963), which puts the earlier analysis into the context of the 1960's. Inevitably, the authors, despite significant differences in their political and social views, have come to be regarded as a school; but in commenting on our convergent ideas in the subsequent essays, I can speak only for myself.

On some counts I no longer hold with what I wrote in 1954. But it proved impossible to take adequate account of the limitations of this essay merely by revising it; and since it serves as a record of how things looked to some of us in 1954 and as a useful way of opening up a dialogue between the present and the recent past, it still seemed desirable to include it here. I therefore reprint it with only minor textual changes and a few added monitory footnotes. The task of correcting and extending it I have left to the two subsequent essays. The first of these restates the issues, and the second shows how pseudo-conservative politics were exemplified in the Goldwater campaign of 1964.

TWENTY YEARS ago the dynamic force in American political life came from the side of liberal dissent, from the impulse

535

to reform the inequities of our economic and social system and to change our ways of doing things, to the end that the sufferings of the Great Depression would never be repeated. Today the dynamic force in our political life no longer comes from the liberals who made the New Deal possible. By 1952 the liberals had had at least the trappings of power for twenty years. They could look back to a brief, exciting period in the mid-1930's when they had held power itself and had been able to transform the economic and administrative life of the nation. After twenty years the New Deal liberals have quite unconsciously taken on the psychology of those who have entered into possession. Moreover, a large part of the New Deal public, the jobless, distracted, and bewildered men of 1933, have in the course of the years found substantial places in society for themselves, have become homeowners, suburbanites, and solid citizens. Many of them still have the emotional commitments to the liberal dissent with which they grew up politically, but their social position is one of solid comfort. Among them the dominant tone has become one of satisfaction, even of a kind of conservatism. Insofar as Adlai Stevenson stirred their enthusiasm in 1952, it was not in spite of but in part because of the air of poised and reliable conservatism that he brought to the Democratic convention. By comparison, Harry Truman's impassioned rhetoric, with its occasional thrusts at "Wall Street," seemed passé and rather embarrassing. The change did not escape Stevenson himself. "The strange alchemy of time," he said in a speech at Columbus, "has somehow converted the Democrats into the truly conservative party of this country—the party dedicated to conserving all that is best, and building solidly and safely on these foundations." What most liberals now hope for is not to carry on with some ambitious new program, but simply to defend as much as possible of the old achievements and to try to keep traditional liberties of expression that are threatened.

There is, however, a dynamic of dissent in America today. Representing no more than a modest fraction of the electorate, it is not so powerful as the liberal dissent of the New Deal era, but it is powerful enough to set the tone of our political life and to establish throughout the country a kind of punitive reaction. The new dissent is certainly not radical—there are hardly any radicals of any sort left—nor is it precisely conservative. Unlike most of the liberal dissent of the past, the new dissent not only has no respect for nonconformism, but is based upon a relentless demand for conformity. It can most accurately be called pseudo-conservative—I borrow the term from *The Authoritarian Personality*, published in 1950 by Theodor W. Adorno and his associates—because its exponents, although they believe themselves to be conservatives and usually employ the rhetoric of conservatism, show signs of a serious and restless dissatisfaction with American life, traditions, and institutions. They have little in common with the temperate and compromising spirit of true conservatism in the classical sense of the word, and they are far from pleased with the dominant practical conservatism of the moment as it is represented by the Eisenhower administration. Their politi cal reactions express rather a profound if largely unconscious hatred of our society and its ways—a hatred which one would hesitate to impute to them if one did not have suggestive evidence both from clinical techniques and from their own modes of expression.

From clinical interviews and thematic apperception tests, Adorno and his co-workers found that their pseudo-conservative subjects, although given to a form of political expression that combines a curious mixture of largely conservative with occasional radical notions, succeed in concealing from themselves impulsive tendencies that, if released in action, would be very far from conservative. The pseudo-conservative, Adorno writes, shows "conventionality and authoritarian submissiveness" in his conscious thinking and "violence, anarchic impulses, and chaotic destructiveness in the unconscious sphere. . . . The pseudo-conservative is a man who, in the name of upholding traditional American values and institutions and defending them against more or less fictitious dangers, consciously or unconsciously aims at their abolition."[1]

[1]Theodor W. Adorno et al.: *The Authoritarian Personality* (New York, 1950), pp. 675–6. While I have drawn heavily upon this enlightening study, I have some reservations about its methods and conclusions. For a critical review, see Richard Christie and Marie Jahoda (eds.): *Studies in the Scope and Method of "The Authoritarian Personality"* (Glencoe, Ill., 1954), particularly the penetrating comments by Edward Shils.

Who is the pseudo-conservative, and what does he want? It is impossible to identify him by social class, for the pseudo-conservative impulse can be found in practically all classes in society, although its power probably rests largely upon its appeal to the less-educated members of the middle classes. The ideology of pseudo-conservatism can be characterized but not defined, because the pseudo-conservative tends to be more than ordinarily incoherent about politics. The lady who, when General Eisenhower's victory over Senator Taft had finally become official in 1952, stalked out of the Hilton Hotel declaiming: "This means eight more years of socialism," was probably a fairly good representative of the pseudo-conservative mentality. So also were the gentleman who, at the Freedom Congress held at Omaha over a year ago by some "patriotic" organizations, objected to Earl Warren's appointment to the Supreme Court with the assertion: "Middle-of-the-road thinking can and will destroy us"; the general who spoke to the same group, demanding "an Air Force capable of wiping out the Russian Air Force and industry in one sweep," but also "a material reduction in military expenditures";[2] the people who a few years ago believed simultaneously that we had no business to be fighting communism in Korea and that the war should immediately be extended to an Asia-wide crusade against communism; and the most ardent supporters of the Bricker Amendment. Many of the most zealous followers of Senator McCarthy are also pseudo-conservatives, although his appeal clearly embraces a wider public.

The restlessness, suspicion, and fear shown in various phases of the pseudo-conservative revolt give evidence of the anguish which the pseudo-conservative experiences in his capacity as a citizen. He believes himself to be living in a world in which he is spied upon, plotted against, betrayed, and very likely destined for total ruin. He feels that his liberties have been arbitrarily and outrageously invaded. He is opposed to almost everything that has happened in American politics in the past twenty years. He hates the very thought of Franklin D. Roosevelt. He is disturbed deeply by American participation in the

[2]On the Omaha Freedom Congress, see Leonard Boasberg: "Radical Reactionaries," *The Progressive*, December 1953.

United Nations, which he can see only as a sinister organization. He sees his own country as being so weak that it is constantly about to fall victim to subversion; and yet he feels that it is so all-powerful that any failure it may experience in getting its way in the world—for instance, in the Orient—cannot possibly be due to its limitations but must be attributed to its having been betrayed.[3] He is the most bitter of all our citizens about our involvement in the wars of the past, but seems the least concerned about avoiding the next one. While he naturally does not like Soviet communism, what distinguishes him from the rest of us who also dislike it is that he shows little interest in, is often indeed bitterly hostile to, such realistic measures as might actually strengthen the United States vis-à-vis Russia. He would much rather concern himself with the domestic scene, where communism is weak, than with those areas of the world where it is really strong and threatening. He wants to have nothing to do with the democratic nations of Western Europe, which seem to draw more of his ire than the Soviet Communists, and he is opposed to all "giveaway programs" designed to aid and strengthen these nations. Indeed, he is likely to be antagonistic to most of the operations of our federal government except congressional investigations, and to almost all its expenditures. Not always, however, does he go so far as the speaker at the Freedom Congress who attributed the greater part of our national difficulties to "this nasty, stinking 16th [income tax] Amendment."

A great deal of pseudo-conservative thinking takes the form of trying to devise means of absolute protection against that betrayal by our own officialdom which the pseudo-conservative feels is always imminent. The Bricker Amendment, indeed, might be taken as one of the primary symptoms of pseudo-conservatism. Every dissenting movement brings its demand for constitutional changes; and the pseudo-conservative revolt, far from being an exception to this principle, seems to specialize in constitutional revision, at least as a speculative enterprise. The widespread latent hostility toward American institutions takes the form, among other things, of a flood of proposals to

[3]See the comments of D. W. Brogan in "The Illusion of American Omnipotence," *Harper's Magazine*, December 1952, pp. 21–8.

write drastic changes into the body of our fundamental law. In June 1954, Richard Rovere pointed out in a characteristically astute piece that Constitution-amending had become almost a major diversion in the Eighty-third Congress.[4] About a hundred amendments were introduced and referred to committee. Several of these called for the repeal of the income tax. Several embodied formulas of various kinds to limit non-military expenditures to some fixed portion of the national income. One proposed to bar all federal expenditures on "the general welfare"; another, to prohibit American troops from serving in any foreign country except on the soil of the potential enemy; another, to redefine treason to embrace not only persons trying to overthrow the government but also those trying to "weaken" it, even by peaceful means. The last proposal might bring the pseudo-conservative rebels themselves under the ban of treason: for the sum total of these amendments could easily serve to send the whole structure of American society crashing to the ground.

As Mr. Rovere points out, it is not unusual for a large number of constitutional amendments to be lying about somewhere in the congressional hoppers. What is unusual is the readiness the Senate has shown to give them respectful consideration, and the peculiar populistic arguments some of its leading members have used to justify referring them to the state legislatures. While the ordinary Congress hardly ever has occasion to consider more than one amendment, the Eighty-third Congress saw six constitutional amendments brought to the floor of the Senate, all summoning simple majorities, and four winning the two-thirds majority necessary before they can be sent to the House and ultimately to the state legislatures. It must be added that, with the possible exception of the Bricker Amendment itself, none of the six amendments so honored can be classed with the most extreme proposals. But the pliability of the senators, the eagerness of some of them to pass the buck and defer to "the people of the country," suggests how strong they feel the pressure to be for some kind of change that will give expression to the vague desire to repudiate the past which underlies the pseudo-conservative revolt.

[4]Richard Rovere: "Letter from Washington," *The New Yorker*, June 19, 1954, pp. 67–72.

One of the most urgent questions we can ask about the United States in our time is: Where did all this sentiment arise? The readiest answer is that the new pseudo-conservatism is simply the old ultra-conservatism and the old isolationism heightened by the extraordinary pressures of the contemporary world. This answer, true though it may be, gives a deceptive sense of familiarity without much deepening our understanding, for the particular patterns of American isolationism and extreme right-wing thinking have themselves not been very satisfactorily explored. It will not do, to take but one example, to say that some people want the income-tax amendment repealed because taxes have become very heavy in the past twenty years: for this will not explain why, of three people in the same tax bracket, one will grin and bear it and continue to support social-welfare legislation as well as an adequate military establishment, while another responds by supporting in a matter-of-fact way the practical conservative leadership of the moment, and the third finds his feelings satisfied only by the angry accusations of conspiracy and extreme demands of the pseudo-conservative.

No doubt the circumstances determining the political style of any individual are complex. Although I am concerned here to discuss some of the neglected social-psychological elements in pseudo-conservatism, I do not wish to appear to deny the presence of important economic and political causes. I am aware, for instance, that wealthy reactionaries try to use pseudo-conservative organizers, spokesmen, and groups to propagate their notions of public policy, and that some organizers of pseudo-conservative and "patriotic" groups often find in this work a means of making a living—thus turning a tendency toward paranoia into a vocational asset, probably one of the most perverse forms of occupational therapy known to man. A number of other circumstances—the drastic inflation and heavy taxes of our time, the imbalance in our party system, the deterioration of American urban life, considerations of partisan political expediency—also play a part. But none of these things seems to explain the broad appeal of pseudo-conservatism, its emotional intensity, its dense and massive irrationality, or some of the peculiar ideas it generates. Nor will they explain why those who profit by the organized movements find such a ready following among a large number of people, and why the rank-and-file janizaries of pseudo-conservatism are so eager to hurl accusations, write letters to congressmen and editors, and expend so much emotional energy and crusading idealism upon causes that plainly bring them no material reward.

Elmer Davis, seeking to account for such sentiment in his recent book *But We Were Born Free*, ventures a psychological hypothesis. He concludes, if I understand him correctly, that the genuine difficulties of our situation in the face of the power of international communism have inspired a widespread feeling of fear and frustration, and that those who cannot face these problems in a more rational way "take it out on their less influential neighbors, in the mood of a man who, being afraid to stand up to his wife in a domestic argument, relieves his feelings by kicking the cat."[5] This suggestion has the merit of both simplicity and plausibility, and it may begin to account for a portion of the pseudo-conservative public. But while we may dismiss our curiosity about the man who kicks the cat by remarking that some idiosyncrasy in his personal development has brought him to this pass, we can hardly help but wonder whether there are not, in the backgrounds of the hundreds of thousands of persons who are moved by the pseudo-conservative impulse, some commonly shared circumstances that will help to account for their all kicking the cat in unison.

All of us have reason to fear the power of international communism, and all our lives are profoundly affected by it. Why do some Americans try to face this threat for what it is, a problem that exists in a world-wide theater of action, while others try to reduce it largely to a matter of domestic conformity? Why do some of us prefer to look for allies in the democratic world, while others seem to prefer authoritarian allies or none at all? Why do the pseudo-conservatives express such a persistent fear and suspicion of *their own government*, whether its leadership rests in the hands of Roosevelt, Truman, or Eisenhower? Why is the pseudo-conservative impelled to go beyond the more or less routine partisan argument that we have been the victims of considerable misgovernment during the past twenty years to the disquieting accusation that we have actually been the

[5]Elmer Davis: *But We Were Born Free* (New York, 1954), pp. 35–6; cf. pp. 21–2 and passim.

victims of persistent conspiracy and betrayal—"twenty years of treason"? Is it not true, moreover, that political types very similar to the pseudo-conservative have had a long history in the United States, and that this history goes back to a time when the Soviet power did not loom nearly so large on our mental horizons? Was the Ku Klux Klan, for instance, which was responsibly estimated to have had a membership of from 4,000,000 to 4,500,000 persons at its peak in the 1920's, a phenomenon totally dissimilar to the pseudo-conservative revolt?

What I wish to suggest—and I do so in the spirit of one setting forth nothing more than a speculative hypothesis—is that pseudo-conservatism is in good part a product of the rootlessness and heterogeneity of American life and, above all, of its peculiar scramble for status and its peculiar search for secure identity. Normally there is a world of difference between one's sense of national identity or cultural belonging and one's social status. However, in American historical development, these two things, so easily distinguishable in analysis, have been jumbled together in reality, and it is precisely this that has given such a special poignancy and urgency to our status strivings. In this country a person's status—that is, his relative place in the prestige hierarchy of his community—and his rudimentary sense of belonging to the community—that is, what we call his "Americanism"—have been intimately joined. Because, as a people extremely democratic in our social institutions, we have had no clear, consistent, and recognizable system of status, our personal status problems have an unusual intensity. Because we no longer have the relative ethnic homogeneity we had up to about eighty years ago, our sense of belonging has long had about it a high degree of uncertainty. We boast of "the melting pot," but we are not quite sure what it is that will remain when we have been melted down.

We have always been proud of the high degree of occupational mobility in our country—of the greater readiness, as compared with other countries, with which a person starting in a very humble place in our social structure could rise to a position of moderate wealth and status, and with which a person starting with a middling position could rise to great eminence. We have looked upon this as laudable in principle, for it is democratic, and as pragmatically desirable, for it has served many a man as a stimulus to effort and has, no doubt, a great deal to do with the energetic and effectual tone of our economic life. The American pattern of occupational mobility, while often much exaggerated, as in the Horatio Alger stories and a great deal of the rest of our mythology, may properly be credited with many of the virtues and beneficial effects that are usually attributed to it. But this occupational and social mobility, compounded by our extraordinary mobility from place to place, has also had its less frequently recognized drawbacks. Not the least of them is that this has become a country in which so many people do not know who they are or what they are or what they belong to or what belongs to them. It is a country of people whose status expectations are random and uncertain, and yet whose status aspirations have been whipped up to a high pitch by our democratic ethos and our rags-to-riches mythology.[6]

In a country where physical needs have been, by the scale of the world's living standards, on the whole well met, the luxury of questing after status has assumed an unusually prominent place in our civic consciousness. Political life is not simply an arena in which the conflicting interests of various social groups in concrete material gains are fought out; it is also an arena into which status aspirations and frustrations are, as the psychologists would say, projected. It is at this point that the issues of politics, or the pretended issues of politics, become interwoven with and dependent upon the personal problems of individuals. We have, at all times, two kinds of processes going on in inextricable connection with each other: *interest politics*, the clash of material aims and needs among various groups and blocs; and *status politics*, the clash of various projective rationalizations arising from status aspirations and other personal

---

[6]Cf. in this respect the observation of Tocqueville: "It cannot be denied that democratic institutions strongly tend to promote the feeling of envy in the human heart; not so much because they afford to everyone the means of rising to the same level with others as because these means perpetually disappoint the persons who employ them. Democratic institutions awaken and foster a passion for equality which they can never entirely satisfy." Alexis de Tocqueville: *Democracy in America*, ed. by Phillips Bradley (New York, 1945), I, 201.

motives. In times of depression and economic discontent—and by and large in times of acute national emergency—politics is more clearly a matter of interests, although of course status considerations are still present. In times of prosperity and general well-being on the material plane, status considerations among the masses can become much more influential in our politics. The two periods in our recent history in which status politics has been particularly prominent, the present era and the 1920's, have both been periods of prosperity.

During depressions, the dominant motif in dissent takes expression in proposals for reform or in panaceas. Dissent then tends to be highly programmatic—that is, it gets itself embodied in many kinds of concrete legislative proposals. It is also future-oriented and forward-looking, in the sense that it looks to a time when the adoption of this or that program will materially alleviate or eliminate certain discontents. In prosperity, however, when status politics becomes relatively more important, there is a tendency to embody discontent not so much in legislative proposals as in grousing. For the basic aspirations that underlie status discontent are only partially conscious; and, even so far as they are conscious, it is difficult to give them a programmatic expression. It is more difficult for the old lady who belongs to the D.A.R. and who sees her ancestral home swamped by new working-class dwellings to express her animus in concrete proposals of any degree of reality than it is, say, for the jobless worker during a slump to rally to a relief program. Therefore, it is the tendency of status politics to be expressed more in vindictiveness, in sour memories, in the search for scapegoats, than in realistic proposals for positive action.[7]

---

[7] Cf. Samuel Lubell's characterization of isolationism as a vengeful memory. *The Future of American Politics* (New York, 1952), Ch. 7. See also the comments of Leo Lowenthal and Norbert Guterman on the right-wing agitator: "The agitator seems to steer clear of the area of material needs on which liberal and democratic movements concentrate; his main concern is a sphere of frustration that is usually ignored in traditional politics. The programs that concentrate on material needs seem to overlook that area of moral uncertainties and emotional frustrations that are the immediate manifestations of malaise. It may therefore be conjectured that his followers find the agitator's statements attractive not because he occasionally promises to 'maintain the American standard of living'

Paradoxically the intense status concerns of present-day politics are shared by two types of persons who arrive at them from opposite directions. The first are found among some types of old-family, Anglo-Saxon Protestants, and the second are found among many types of immigrant families, most notably among the Germans and Irish, who are very frequently Catholic. The Anglo-Saxons are most disposed toward pseudo-conservatism when they are losing caste, the immigrants when they are gaining.[8]

Consider first the old-family Americans. These people, whose stocks were once far more unequivocally dominant in America than they are today, feel that their ancestors made and settled and fought for this country. They have a certain inherited sense of proprietorship in it. Since America has always accorded a certain special deference to old families—so many of our families are *new*—these people have considerable claims to status by descent, which they celebrate by membership in such

---

or to provide a job for everyone, but because he intimates that he will give them the emotional satisfactions that are denied them in the contemporary social and economic set-up. He offers attitudes, not bread." *Prophets of Deceit* (New York, 1949), pp. 91–2.

[8]Every ethnic group has its own peculiar status history, and I am well aware that my remarks in the text slur over many important differences. The status history of the older immigrant groups like the Germans and the Irish is quite different from that of ethnic elements like the Italians, Poles, and Czechs, who have more recently arrived at the point at which they are bidding for wide acceptance in the professional and white-collar classes, or at least for the middle-class standards of housing and consumption enjoyed by these classes. The case of the Irish is of special interest, because the Irish, with their long-standing prominence in municipal politics, qualified as it has been by their relative non-acceptance in many other spheres, have an unusually ambiguous status. In many ways they have gained, while in others, particularly insofar as their municipal power has recently been challenged by other groups, especially the Italians, they have lost some status and power. The election of 1928, with its religious bigotry and social snobbery, inflicted upon them a status trauma from which they have never fully recovered, for it was a symbol of the Protestant majority's rejection of their ablest leadership on grounds quite irrelevant to merit. This feeling was kept alive by the breach between Al Smith and F.D.R., followed by the rejection of Jim Farley from the New Deal succession. A study of the Germans would perhaps emphasize the effects of uneasiness over national loyalties arising from the Hitler era and the Second World War, but extending back even to the First World War.

organizations as the D.A.R. and the S.A.R. But large numbers of them are actually losing their other claims to status. For there are among them a considerable number of the shabby genteel, of those who for one reason or another have lost their old objective positions in the life of business and politics and the professions, and who therefore cling with exceptional desperation to such remnants of their prestige as they can muster from their ancestors. These people, although very often quite well-to-do, feel that they have been pushed out of their rightful place in American life, even out of their neighborhoods. Most of them have been traditional Republicans by family inheritance, and they have felt themselves edged aside by the immigrants, the trade unions, and the urban machines in the past thirty years. When the immigrants were weak, these native elements used to indulge themselves in ethnic and religious snobberies at their expense.[9] Now the immigrant groups have developed ample means, political and economic, of self-defense, and the second and third generations have become considerably more capable of looking out for themselves. Some of the old-family Americans have turned to find new objects for their resentment among liberals, left-wingers, intellectuals, and the like—for in true pseudo-conservative fashion they relish weak victims and shrink from asserting themselves against the strong.

New-family Americans have had their own peculiar status problem. From 1881 to 1900 over 8,800,000 immigrants came here, and during the next twenty years another 14,500,000. These immigrants, together with their descendants, constitute such a large portion of the population that Margaret Mead, in a stimulating analysis of our national character, has persuasively argued that the characteristic American outlook is now a third-generation point of view.[10] In their search for new lives and new nationality, these immigrants have suffered much, and they have been rebuffed and made to feel inferior by the "native stock," commonly being excluded from the better

---

[9]One of the noteworthy features of the current situation is that fundamentalist Protestants and fundamentalist Catholics have so commonly subordinated their old feuds (and for the first time in our history) to unite in opposition to what they usually describe as "godless" elements.

[10]Margaret Mead: *And Keep Your Powder Dry* (New York, 1942), Ch. 3.

occupations and even from what has bitterly been called "first-class citizenship." Insecurity over social status has thus been mixed with insecurity over one's very identity and sense of belonging. Achieving a better type of job or a better social status and becoming "more American" have been practically synonymous, and the passions that ordinarily attach to social position have been vastly heightened by being associated with the need to belong.[11]

The problems raised by the tasks of keeping the family together, disciplining children for the American race for success, trying to conform to unfamiliar standards, protecting economic and social status won at the cost of much sacrifice, holding the respect of children who grow American more rapidly than their parents, have thrown heavy burdens on the internal relationships of many new American families. Both new and old American families have been troubled by the changes of the past thirty years—the new because of their striving for middle-class respectability and American identity, the old because of their efforts to maintain an inherited social position and to realize under increasingly unfavorable social conditions imperatives of character and personal conduct deriving from nineteenth-century Yankee-Protestant-rural backgrounds. The relations between generations, being cast in no stable mold, have been disordered, and the status anxieties of parents have been inflicted upon children.[12] Often

---

[11]Addendum, 1965: Much of the following paragraph now seems to me to be gratuitously speculative, and I think the emphasis on authoritarianism in immigrant as opposed to native families questionable. That the pseudo-conservative mentality is characterized by a disorder in relation to authority, however, still seems to me to be a central point.

[12]See Else Frenkel-Brunswik's "Parents and Childhood as Seen Through the Interviews," in Adorno: op. cit., Ch. 10. The author remarks (pp. 387–8) concerning subjects who were relatively *free* from ethnic prejudice that in their families "less obedience is expected of the children. Parents are less status-ridden and thus show less anxiety with respect to conformity and are less intolerant toward manifestations of socially unaccepted behavior. . . . Comparatively less pronounced status-concern often goes hand in hand with greater richness and liberation of emotional life. There is, on the whole, more affection, or more unconditional affection, in the families of unprejudiced subjects. There is less surrender to conventional rules."

parents entertain status aspirations that they are unable to gratify, or that they can gratify only at exceptional psychic cost. Their children are expected to relieve their frustrations and redeem their lives. They become objects to be manipulated to that end. An extraordinarily high level of achievement is expected of them, and along with it a tremendous effort to conform and be respectable. From the standpoint of the children these expectations often appear in the form of an exorbitantly demanding authority that one dare not question or defy. Resistance and hostility, finding no moderate outlet in give-and-take, have to be suppressed, and reappear in the form of an internal destructive rage. An enormous hostility to authority, which cannot be admitted to consciousness, calls forth a massive overcompensation which is manifest in the form of extravagant submissiveness to strong power. Among those found by Adorno and his colleagues to have strong ethnic prejudices and pseudo-conservative tendencies, there is a high proportion of persons who have been unable to develop the capacity to criticize justly and in moderation the failings of parents and who are profoundly intolerant of the ambiguities of thought and feeling that one is so likely to find in real-life situations. For pseudo-conservatism is among other things a disorder in relation to authority, characterized by an inability to find other modes for human relationship than those of more or less complete domination or submission. The pseudo-conservative always imagines himself to be dominated and imposed upon because he feels that he is not dominant, and knows of no other way of interpreting his position. He imagines that his own government and his own leaders are engaged in a more or less continuous conspiracy against him because he has come to think of authority only as something that aims to manipulate and deprive him. It is for this reason, among others, that he enjoys seeing outstanding generals, distinguished Secretaries of State, and prominent scholars brow-beaten.

Status problems take on a special importance in American life because a very large part of the population suffers from one of the most troublesome of all status questions: unable to enjoy the simple luxury of assuming their own nationality as a natural event, they are tormented by a nagging doubt as to whether they are really and truly and fully American. Since their forebears voluntarily left one country and embraced another, they cannot, as people do elsewhere, think of nationality as something that comes with birth; for them it is a matter of *choice*, and an object of striving. This is one reason why problems of "loyalty" arouse such an emotional response in many Americans and why it is so hard in the American climate of opinion to make any clear distinction between the problem of national security and the question of personal loyalty. Of course, there is no real reason to doubt the loyalty to America of the immigrants and their descendants, or their willingness to serve the country as fully as if their ancestors had lived here for three centuries. Nonetheless, they have been thrown on the defensive by those who have in the past cast doubts upon the fullness of their Americanism. Possibly they are also, consciously or unconsciously, troubled by the thought that since their forebears have already abandoned one country, one allegiance, their own national allegiance might be considered fickle. For this I believe there is some evidence in our national practices. What other country finds it so necessary to create institutional rituals for the sole purpose of guaranteeing to its people the genuineness of their nationality? Does the Frenchman or the Englishman or the Italian find it necessary to speak of himself as "one hundred per cent" English, French, or Italian? Do they find it necessary to have their equivalents of "I Am an American Day"? When they disagree with one another over national policies, do they find it necessary to call one another un-English, un-French, or un-Italian? No doubt they too are troubled by subversive activities and espionage, but are their countermeasures taken under the name of committees on un-English, un-French, or un-Italian activities?

The primary value that patriotic societies and anti-subversive ideologies have for their exponents can be found here. They provide additional and continued reassurance both to those who are of old-American ancestry and have other status grievances and to those who are of recent American ancestry and therefore feel in need of reassurance about their nationality. Veterans' organizations offer the same satisfaction—what better evidence can there be of the genuineness of nationality and *earned* citizenship than military service under the flag of one's country? Of course, such organizations, once they exist, are liable to exploitation by vested interests that can use them as pressure groups on behalf of particular measures and interests. (Veterans' groups, since they lobby for the concrete interests of veterans, have a double role in this respect.) But the cement that holds them together is the status motivation and the desire for an identity.

Sociological studies have shown that there is a close relation between social mobility and ethnic prejudice. Persons moving downward in the social scale, and even upward under many circumstances, tend to show greater prejudice against such ethnic minorities as the Jews and Negroes than commonly prevails in the social strata they have left or are entering.[13] While the existing studies in this field have been focused upon prejudice rather than the kind of hyper-patriotism and hyper-conformism that I am most concerned with, I believe that the typical prejudiced person and the typical pseudo-conservative dissenter are usually the same person, that the mechanisms at work in both complexes are quite the same,[14] and that it is merely the expediencies and the strategy of the situation today that cause groups that once stressed racial discrimination to find other scapegoats. Both the displaced old-American type and the new ethnic elements that are so desperately eager for reassurance of their fundamental Americanism can conveniently converge upon liberals, critics, and nonconformists of various sorts, as well as Communists and suspected Communists. To proclaim themselves vigilant in the pursuit of those who are even so much as accused of "disloyalty" to the United States is a way not only of reasserting but of advertising their own loyalty—and one of the chief characteristics of

[13]Cf. Joseph Greenblum and Leonard I. Pearlin: "Vertical Mobility and Prejudice," in Reinhard Bendix and Seymour M. Lipset (eds.): *Class, Status and Power* (Glencoe, Ill., 1953), pp. 480–91; Bruno Bettelheim and Morris Janowitz: "Ethnic Tolerance: A Function of Personal and Social Control," *American Journal of Sociology*, IV (1949), pp. 137–45.

[14]The similarity is also posited by Adorno: op. cit., pp. 152 ff., and by others (see the studies cited by him, p. 152).

American super-patriotism is its constant inner urge toward self-advertisement. One notable quality in this new wave of conformism is that its advocates are much happier to have as their objects of hatred the Anglo-Saxon, Eastern, Ivy League intellectual gentlemen than they are to have such bedraggled souls as, say, Julius and Ethel Rosenberg. The reason, I believe, is that in the minds of the status-driven it is no special virtue to be more American than the Rosenbergs, but it is really something to be more American than Dean Acheson or John Foster Dulles—or Franklin Delano Roosevelt.[15] The status aspirations of some of the ethnic groups are actually higher than they were twenty years ago—which suggests one reason (there are others) why, in the ideology of the authoritarian right wing, anti-Semitism and other blatant forms of prejudice have recently been soft-pedaled. Anti-Semitism, it has been said, is the poor man's snobbery. We Americans are always trying to raise the standard of living, and the same principle now seems to apply to standards of hating. So during the past fifteen years or so, the authoritarians have moved on from anti-Negroism and anti-Semitism to anti-Achesonianism, anti-intellectualism, anti-nonconformism, and other variants of the same idea, much in the same way as the average American, if he can manage it, will move on from a Ford to a Buick.

Such status strivings may help us to understand some of the otherwise unintelligible figments of the pseudo-conservative ideology—the incredibly bitter feeling against the United Nations, for instance. Is it not understandable that such a feeling might be, paradoxically, shared at one and the same time by an old Yankee-Protestant American, who feels that his social position is not what it ought to be and that these foreigners are crowding in on his country and diluting its sovereignty just as "foreigners" have crowded into his neighborhood, and by a second- or third-generation immigrant who has been trying

---

[15] I refer to such men to make the point that this animosity extends to those who are guilty of no wrongdoing. Of course, a person like Alger Hiss, who has been guilty, suits much better. Hiss is the hostage the pseudo-conservatives hold from the New Deal generation. He is a heaven-sent gift. If he did not exist, the pseudo-conservatives would not have been able to invent him.

so hard to de-Europeanize himself, to get Europe out of his personal heritage, and who finds his own government mocking him by its complicity in these Old World schemes?

Similarly, is it not status aspiration that in good part spurs the pseudo-conservative on toward his demand for conformity in a wide variety of spheres of life? Conformity is a way of guaranteeing and manifesting respectability among those who are not sure that they are respectable enough. The nonconformity of others appears to such persons as a frivolous challenge to the whole order of things they are trying so hard to become part of. Naturally it is resented, and the demand for conformity in public becomes at once an expression of such resentment and a means of displaying one's own soundness. This habit has a tendency to spread from politics into intellectual and social spheres, where it can be made to challenge almost anyone whose pattern of life is different and who is imagined to enjoy a superior social position—notably, as one agitator put it, those in the "parlors of the sophisticated, the intellectuals, the so-called academic minds."

Why has this tide of pseudo-conservative dissent risen to such heights in our time? To a considerable degree, we must remember, it is a response, however unrealistic, to realities. We do live in a disordered world, threatened by a great power and a powerful ideology, a world of enormous potential violence, which has already shown us the ugliest capacities of the human spirit. In our own country there has indeed been espionage, and laxity over security has in fact allowed some spies to reach high places. There is just enough reality at most points along the line to give a touch of credibility to the melodramatics of the pseudo-conservative imagination.

However, a number of developments in our recent history make this pseudo-conservative uprising more intelligible. For two hundred years and more, various conditions of American development—the process of settling the continent, the continuous establishment of new status patterns in new areas, the arrival of continuous waves of new immigrants, each pushing the preceding waves upward in the ethnic hierarchy—made it possible to satisfy a remarkably large part of the extravagant status aspirations that were aroused. There was a sort of

automatic built-in status elevator in the American social edi-
fice. Today that elevator no longer operates automatically, or
at least no longer operates in the same way.[16]

Second, the growth of the mass media of communication
and their use in politics have brought politics closer to the people than ever before and have made politics a form of entertainment in which the spectators feel themselves involved. Thus it
has become, more than ever before, an arena into which private emotions and personal problems can be readily projected.
Mass communications have made it possible to keep the mass
man in an almost constant state of political mobilization.

Third, the long tenure in power of the liberal elements to
which the pseudo-conservatives are most opposed and the wide
variety of changes that have been introduced into our social,
economic, and administrative life have intensified the sense of
powerlessness and victimization among the opponents of these
changes and have widened the area of social issues over which
they feel discontent. There has been, among other things, the
emergence of a wholly new struggle: the conflict between businessmen of certain types and the New Deal bureaucracy, which
has spilled over into a resentment of intellectuals and experts.

Finally, unlike our previous postwar periods, ours has been a
period of continued crisis, from which the future promises no
relief. In no foreign war of our history did we fight so long or
make such sacrifices as in the Second World War. When it was
over, instead of being able to resume our peacetime preoccupations, we were very promptly confronted with another war.
It is hard for a certain type of American, who does not think
much about the world outside and does not want to have to
do so, to understand why we must become involved in such
an unremitting struggle. It will be the fate of those in power
for a long time to come to have to conduct the delicate diplomacy of the cold peace without the sympathy or understanding
of a large part of their own people. From bitter experience,
Eisenhower and Dulles are learning today what Truman and
Acheson learned yesterday.

[16]Addendum, 1965: The substantive point may still be a good one, but it occurs to me that this paragraph might be taken to mean that social mobility in
the United States has been decreasing; the evidence points to the contrary.

These considerations suggest that the pseudo-conservative political style, while it may already have passed the peak of its influence, is one of the long waves of twentieth-century American history and not a momentary mood. I do not share the widespread foreboding among liberals that this form of dissent will grow until it overwhelms our liberties altogether and plunges us into a totalitarian nightmare. Indeed, the idea that it is purely and simply fascist or totalitarian, as we have known these things in recent European history, is to my mind a false conception, based upon the failure to read American developments in terms of our peculiar American constellation of political realities. (It reminds me of the people who, because they found several close parallels between the N.R.A. and Mussolini's corporate state, were once deeply troubled at the thought that the N.R.A. was the beginning of American fascism.) However, in a populistic culture like ours, which seems to lack a responsible elite with political and moral autonomy, and in which it is possible to exploit the wildest currents of public sentiment for private purposes, it is at least conceivable that a highly organized, vocal, active, and well-financed minority could create a political climate in which the rational pursuit of our well-being and safety would become impossible.

Pseudo-Conservatism Revisited—1965

I

THE Goldwater campaign showed that the ultra-right has grown considerably in organization and influence, if not in numbers, over the past ten years, and the effort to understand it has lost none of its urgency. Although a decade of experience and inquiry, climaxed by the Goldwater movement, which is itself almost an ideal test case for the nature of pseudo-conservatism, has confirmed some of the suggestions advanced in "The Pseudo-Conservative Revolt" and similar ventures in explanation, these ideas appear at other points to need revision.

There are four general matters on which I believe my own essay now demands qualification or correction. The first and most complex has to do with the place of status anxieties and status resentments in the right-wing ferment of the McCarthyist era. At the time I wrote, the status factor had been largely ignored and therefore needed emphasizing, but I have no doubt that an essay devoted rather single-mindedly to this one element in a complex situation inevitably had the effect of giving it disproportionate weight. Also, the term "status" was used in an uncommonly wide sense, and needed more definition than it got. But this is not to be taken as a retraction of what I had to say about the importance of status considerations; it is a preface to some refinements of my original statement. The distinction made in the earlier essay between status politics and interest politics seems to me to be of fundamental significance, and to have a general usability in understanding our political history that goes far beyond the issues of the 1950's which it was invoked to explain.

The other points are more easily dealt with. I think that in portraying the pseudo-conservative type, my essay overstressed clinical findings by failing to supplement them sufficiently with a more conventional historical analysis of the rhetoric, arguments, and tactics of the pseudo-conservatives. I hope I have made amends in the next essay, which deals with the Goldwater campaign. Again, I believe now that I overstated the role of certain ethnic minorities in the right wing. To be sure, these were present, as additional data have since shown; but they have turned out to be more a receding than an advancing element, and it is probably the native American side of the right wing that demands our primary attention. Finally—and this point is related to the preceding one—I made only passing reference in a footnote to the role of fundamentalism, and it is plain that this is one of the salient elements in the right wing, an element whose importance has become increasingly evident in the past decade.

The last two points can best be discussed in connection with the significant changes that have recently taken place in the right wing, which, despite some continuity in ideas and in leadership, render any static account of it somewhat misleading. In this respect, my emphasis on ethnic factors in the pseudo-conservatism of 1954 now seems to me analogous to the strategy of generals who are prepared to fight the last war. What was true about it, I believe, is that the extreme right did draw somewhat on the older isolationism, in which the attitudes of German and Irish Americans were important, and also, to a degree, upon the feelings of Americans linked to Eastern European countries under Soviet domination.[1] Our role in the Second World War temporarily stirred the feeling of national dislocation and the Anglophobia of these groups, feelings which were duly exploited by McCarthy. But the radical rightism of the 1960's is predominantly a movement of white Anglo-Saxon Protestant Republicans, with only a fringe of ethnic support. German Anglophobia now appears to be of less consequence than it once was and the election of an Irish Catholic President in 1960 may have helped to quiet the sense of incomplete cultural acceptance that has troubled the American Irish since 1928. In retrospect, it seems that even by 1954 ethnic factors in American pseudo-conservatism were waning, not rising.

Over the past three decades, right-wing movements have appealed to segments of the public which, though overlapping, have been significantly different. In the 1930's the chief vehicle

[1] For some confirmation, see Seymour M. Lipset: "Three Decades of the Radical Right," in Daniel Bell (ed.): *The Radical Right* (New York, 1963), pp. 336–8. In what follows I am much indebted to Lipset's analysis of survey data.

of right-wing discontent was Father Coughlin's Social Justice movement, a depression phenomenon drawing the bulk
of its support from those who suffered most from bad times
—the working class and the unemployed, farmers and some
of the lower middle class. Its tone was more pseudo-radical
than pseudo-conservative. It played on old Populist themes,
attacked international bankers, demanded free silver and other
changes in the money and credit system, and resorted to an
anti-Semitic rhetoric far more virulent than anything the Populists would have dreamed of. It was stronger in rural areas and
small towns than in cities, and much stronger among Catholics, particularly Irish Catholics, than among Protestants. Its
isolationist and Anglophobic note drew support from Germans, both Catholic and Lutheran. It was strongest in two
areas: the West Central states, where its appeal was both ethnic and agrarian, and in New England, where it attracted Irish
Catholics. That Coughlin had little strength in the South is
perhaps an interesting token of surviving religious prejudice;
also, up to the time of Huey Long's assassination, the South
had its own native and more appealing messiah.

Coughlinism died with the war and the subsequent prosperity. The new right wing of the McCarthy era showed both continuity and discontinuity with Coughlinism. McCarthy, as an
Irish Catholic, picked up much of the ethnic and religious following that had once been Coughlin's, as well as some support
from ethnic groups drawn from the "captive" nations of Eastern Europe. But as a phenomenon of prosperity McCarthyism
was almost entirely devoid of economic content and had no
economic program. Since McCarthy appealed both to Republicans who resented their party's continuing domination by its
eastern wing and to those in both parties who were swept up
by the anti-Communist passions of the cold war, his following
was much greater than Coughlin's. On the whole, he received
a measure of support disproportionate to their numbers in the
general population from Catholics and from the ill-educated,
but also from Republicans, Irish Americans, the lower classes,
and the aged. Along with economic issues, McCarthy abruptly
dropped the old right-wing appeal to anti-Semitism.

Part of McCarthy's strength lay in his ability to combine a
mass appeal with a special appeal to a limited stratum of the upper classes. As compared with Coughlin, whose following had

been almost entirely a low-status public, McCarthy was able to win considerable support from the middle and upper ranks of society, mobilizing Republicans who had never accepted the changes brought by the New Deal and whose rage at the long exclusion of the party from presidential power was reaching a peak. There is evidence also that McCarthy had a special appeal to the postwar newly rich. Most prophetic too of the future of the right wing was his strong appeal for fundamentalist-oriented Protestants, who now took a significant place along with their Catholic counterparts.[2]

This is strikingly illustrated by the changing views of Baptists. Probably because of Coughlin's priestly vocation, Baptists had ranked low among the evangelical denominations that supported him, but McCarthy, though a lay Catholic, commanded more support from them than from any other Protestant denomination. It is in the McCarthyist era that the anti-Communist issue becomes so salient for members of this evangelical denomination (and presumably others) that they abandon their traditional anti-Catholic animus in order to take part in right-wing ecumenical anti-Communism.

The right wing of the 1960's, whose leadership has fallen to the John Birch Society, continues to move up the socio-economic ladder. With its strong commitment to ultra-conservative economic ideas, the Birch Society makes little appeal to the economically deprived. It is primarily an organization of well-educated, middle- and upper-status Republicans who are deviants among the educated strata in several

[2]McCarthyism, it must also be remembered, was a phenomenon of much broader significance than the far right itself. During 1953 and 1954, when McCarthy was at the peak of his influence, there was no poll in which less than 34 per cent of the public was found approving him, and at one point, January 1954, the figure rose to 50 per cent. No sensible observer has ever imagined that extreme right-wing ideas command the loyalty of one third, much less one half, of the American public. In July 1964, for example, at a time of great right-wing ferment, a major national poll found that only 4 per cent of the public would be influenced to vote for a presidential candidate because he was endorsed by the John Birch Society, as against 47 per cent who would be more disposed to vote against him; the remainder would have been unaffected or expressed no opinion. *The New York Times*, July 31, 1964. Characteristically, from about 5 to 10 per cent of the public will express approval of the Birch Society (see Bell (ed.): op. cit., pp. 201–2, 349–63), though right-wing positions often receive the endorsement of as much as 15 per cent of the public.

ways—including a greater disposition to ethnic prejudice than the population as a whole.[3] As an elite corps, the Birch Society is, of course, much better educated than the members of other right-wing groups. It has also brought out an interesting polarity within the educated upper classes of American society, which is related to party affiliation. Among Democrats, increasing education is correlated with increasing disapproval of the Birch Society; but among Republicans, increasing education is correlated with increasing support for the society.

Although the Birch Society as a whole draws its most vital public support from affluent Republican Protestants, it has some special appeal, when party affiliation is held constant, to Catholics. Its sociological profile is that of a group enjoying a strong social position, mainly well-to-do and educated beyond the average, but manifesting a degree of prejudice and social tension not customarily found among the affluent and the educated.

Although it is doubtful that extreme rightists in the 1960's are any more numerous than they were in the McCarthyist period, the right wing has learned the secret of organization, which largely accounts for its greater successes. Coughlinism and McCarthyism were largely the creation of astute and voluminous publicity on the radio and in the press, which was not matched by their organizational efforts. Coughlin's organized groups were of relatively little consequence, and McCarthy could barely organize his own files, much less a national movement. The John Birch Society, with only a fraction of McCarthy's support among the public, has won its successes through tightly organized and militant cadres of workers, operating in a manner resembling that of Communist cells, and linked to the Republican party not through publicity but by active work in district, precinct, and community organizations where ideological affinities can be translated into power.

---

[3]Birchite prejudice, it should be said, is directed more significantly against Negroes, Mexicans, and Orientals than it is against Jews. Birchites are a shade *less* prejudiced against Catholics than anti-Birchites. (Lipset: op. cit., p. 361.) Though all polls agree on the relatively high level of formal education among Birchites, they do not provide information about the kind of colleges they attended, and it would be interesting to know to what extent these were the great cosmopolitan universities and colleges or denominational institutions.

At the grass roots the extreme right now draws its primary support from two basic (and at points overlapping) social types: first, the affluent (perhaps newly affluent) suburban educated middle class, largely outside the Northeast, which responds to ultra-conservative economic issues as well as to militant nationalism and anti-communism, and which seeks to win a place in the political structure proportionate to the secure place it has won in society; and second, a large lower middle class, somewhat less educated and less charmed than the first group by old-fashioned economic liberalism but even more fearful of communism, which it perceives rather abstractly in the light of a strong evangelical-fundamentalist cast of thought.

II

The re-emergence of fundamentalism in politics, invigorated by the conditions of the cold war and the stimulus of the affluent society, is a notable development of the past fifteen years. Of necessity I use the term "fundamentalism" in a rather extended way to describe a religious style rather than firm doctrinal commitments, since no one knows how many evangelical right-wingers adhere to a literal view of Scripture and other fundamentalist tenets. Two other qualifications should be made: first, there are large numbers of fundamentalists who interpret their religious commitment as a reason to withdraw from worldly politics, in which they see no more hope than they do in the other things of this world; and second, many fundamentalists have inherited generous views on domestic economic reforms which they do not easily give up. But on certain issues of cultural politics fundamentalists have always been rigid, and when such issues become more salient the fundamentalists become more responsive to the blandishments of pseudo-conservative prophets. Moreover, the Manichean and apocalyptic style of thought prevalent in the fundamentalist tradition can easily be carried over into secular affairs and transmuted into a curiously crude and almost superstitious form of anti-communism.

Not only is the entire right-wing movement infused at the mass level with the fundamentalist style of mind, but the place in its ranks of fundamentalist preachers, ex-preachers, and sons of preachers is so prominent as to underline the mutual congeniality of thought. Leading right-wing spokesmen have brought into politics the methods and the style of the evangelical revivalists, just as many preachers have discovered that they can arouse more fervor and raise more cash by politicizing their message than they can by appealing solely to the religious sensibilities of their audiences.[4]

Under the aegis of right-wing politics, rigid Protestants of a type once intensely anti-Catholic can now unite with Catholics of similar militancy in a grand ecumenical zeal against communism and in what they take to be a joint defense of Christian civilization. The malevolent energy formerly used in the harassment of Catholics can now be more profitably spent in the search for Communists, or even in attacks on the alleged subversiveness of liberal Protestant denominations. The Manichean conception of life as a struggle between absolute good and absolute evil and the idea of an irresistible Armageddon have been thinly secularized and transferred to the cold war. The conflict between Christianity and communism is conceived as a war to the death, and Christianity is set forth as the only adequate counterpoise to the communist credo.

Fundamentalist leaders play a part in right-wing organizations far out of proportion to the strength of fundamentalism in the population at large. Among them are Robert H. Welch, Jr., the founder of the John Birch Society; Dr. Fred

---

[4]This is not the first period in our history in which fundamentalist leaders, anguished over the general repudiation of their beliefs and values, lent their energies to political reaction. During the 1920's they gave heavy support to the Ku Klux Klan, particularly in the South. During the years 1922 to 1928, 26 of 39 anti-Catholic lecturers employed by the Klan were Protestant ministers of the fundamentalist type, and 16 of such ministers were Klan officials. Klansmen were regularly entertained in the homes of such ministers, and churches were used for Klan meetings. The two chief leaders of the new Klan had fundamentalist backgrounds—its initiator, Colonel William J. Simmons, had been a religious camp meeting exhorter, and its most successful promoter, Edward Y. Clarke, went into the fundamentalist movement after giving up his efforts in the Klan. In return, the Klan often fought for passage of the anti-evolution laws. On the relation between the preachers of certain denominations and Klan activities, see Michael Williams: *The Shadow of the Pope* (New York, 1932), pp. 317 ff. On the limitations of this connection and Protestant opposition to the Klan, see Robert Moats Miller: "A Note on the Relation Between the Protestant Churches and the Revival of the Klan," *Journal of Southern History*, XXII (August 1956), 355–68.

C. Schwarz, the head of the Christian Anti-Communism Crusade; and Reverend Billy Hargis, of the Christian Crusade, which flourishes in the Southwest.[5]

A large part of the rise of fundamentalist ultra-conservatism may be linked with the astonishing growth of the Southern Baptist Church, which increased from 2,300,000 members in 1936 to 10,000,000 in 1962. A comparable growth has also been enjoyed by the right-wing Churches of Christ. The increase in these groups has far outstripped that of more moderate Protestant denominations in the same period.[6] Such

[5]Welch, who was raised as a pious fundamentalist Baptist in North Carolina, chose to name his organization after a young fundamentalist Baptist preacher from Macon, Georgia, who was killed by the Chinese Communists. As a prosperous candy manufacturer, once very active in the National Association of Manufacturers, Welch embodies the union of fundamentalist inspiration and small-business parochial conservatism that animates the extreme right. Schwarz is the son of an Australian pentecostal preacher; he had considerable experiences in his native country as a lay preacher before coming to the United States on the invitation of some anti-modernist preachers. He began his American career with an evangelical-style tour. Preachers and ex-preachers figure prominently in the "faculty" he has recruited for his anti-Communist "schools." Hargis moved on from evangelism to right-wing politics in much the same way as such predecessors as Gerald L. K. Smith, Gerald Winrod, and J. Frank Norris. He is the product of Ozark Bible College in Arkansas and of the Disciples of Christ, though his ministry is now independent. Another successful southwestern leader is Dr. George Benson, a former Church of Christ missionary in China, now president of the church-affiliated Harding College in Searcy, Arkansas. This organization still holds forth against Darwin, but its main claim to fame is its role as the source of right-wing political radio broadcasts and films, on the strength of which it has attracted munificent contributions from businessmen. In the East, the Reverend Carl McIntire of the Bible Presbyterian Church in Collingswood, New Jersey, reaches large audiences with his radio broadcasts. A former disciple of the highbrow fundamentalist H. Gresham Machen, McIntire set up on his own after being expelled from the General Assembly of the Presbyterian Church, and he has been vociferous in fighting modernist Christianity and the ecumenical movement. Finally, there is the Church League of America, founded in 1937 to fight liberal Protestantism but now a right-wing organization managed by Edgar Bundy, a minister ordained in the Southern Baptist Convention.

[6]Kenneth K. Bailey: *Southern White Protestantism in the Twentieth Century* (New York, 1964), p. 152. See Chs. 3 and 4 of this work on the fundamentalist background in the South. On internal tensions that have come with this fantastic growth, see Samuel S. Hill, Jr.: "The Southern Baptists," *Christian Century*, LXXX (January 1963), 39–42.

church groups have created a vast religious public, once poor
and depression-ridden but now to a large degree moderately
prosperous, whose members sometimes combine the economic
prejudices of the newly well-to-do with the moral prejudices of
the revolt against modernity.

We know more, of course, about the role of fundamentalist
leaders in right-wing groups than we do about fundamentalism among the mass following. The presence of two kinds of
subcultures in the Christian Anti-Communism Crusade is suggested in a study by Raymond E. Wolfinger and his associates of
a sample of its members in Oakland, California. Their findings
point to a bifurcation between a relatively affluent, educated,
and "sophisticated" wing, concerned most intensely with the
economic content of ultra-conservatism, and a more deeply
religious wing, leaning toward fundamentalism, primarily concerned with religious and moral issues. Among 308 people who
consented to be interviewed, persons belonging to fundamentalist churches constituted 20 per cent (they would be a larger
proportion in southern California). Those who reported that
they came to the "schools" of this right-wing movement because of church influence differed from the whole sample in
important respects: they were more fundamentalist, more active as church members, less affluent, less educated, and less active in politics. They were more favorably disposed than other
respondents to such reforms as medicare and federal aid to
education, and were more willing to accept the legitimacy of
trade unions. Their more intense Christian convictions were
perhaps also reflected in their taking a less sympathetic view
than other members of the South's position on racial integra-
tion. But they were more anti-evolution, more disturbed about
the threat of communism to theistic belief, and more anxious
about the alleged internal threat of communism to the nation.[7]

---

[7] Wolfinger et al.: "America's Radical Right: Politics and Ideology," in David
E. Apter (ed.): *Ideology and Discontent* (Glencoe, Ill., 1964), pp. 281–3. This
study does not purport to be a representative sample. Among other difficulties
was the hostility of a large proportion of members to student interviewers.
Their refusal to be interviewed or to answer mailed questionnaires suggests
that the Wolfinger group's respondents represent the less extreme members of
the movement. The Crusaders were drawn, out of proportion to their numbers in the population, from professional and technical workers and business

An impressionistic study by participant observers of the membership of the same movement in a small midwestern industrial city found the members predominantly Baptist-fundamentalist, educated, with few exceptions, only to the high-school level, aggressively anti-intellectual, anxious about the preservation of the old-fashioned moral virtues, and rather disposed to see the world in the paranoid style.[8]

III

One way of adding to our understanding of the politics of the 1950's and 1960's is to compare it with that of the 1920's. During the 1920's our political life was profoundly affected, and at times dominated, by certain cultural struggles, which were interrupted and deflected by the depression, the New Deal, and the war, but which have in a measure reasserted themselves in the different setting of the postwar decades. Both the 1920's and the postwar years, as periods of relative prosperity, saw some diminution in the force of economic issues and an upsurge in the issues of status politics—issues of religion, morals, personal style, and culture. It is significant that the election campaign which, of all the campaigns in our history, was most completely dominated by status politics was the Smith-Hoover campaign of 1928, conducted when the ill-fated boom of the twenties was nearing its peak. In 1964, again under prosperous conditions, the issues of status politics once more played an unusually significant part.

During the 1920's small-town and rural Protestants were waging a vigorous defense of their cultural values against their rapidly gaining foes—the advancing Catholics and minority ethnic groups on one side and the modernists in religion and secularists in intellectual culture on the other. The Ku

---

managers, from income brackets over $10,000, and from those who had graduated from or attended college. Their average age was also somewhat higher than that of the general population of the Bay area. Their profile bears a fairly close resemblance to those approving the Birch Society in a national sample. See Lipset: op. cit., p. 350.

[8] Mark Chesler and Richard Schmuck: "Participant Observation in a Super-Patriot Discussion Group," *Journal of Social Issues*, XIX (April 1963), 18–30.

Klux Klan, Prohibitionism, the campaign against evolution in the schools, anti-Catholicism and the whispering campaign against Al Smith were all aspects of this struggle. On one count, immigration restriction, the old guard scored an important and permanent victory, and on another, Prohibition, they scored a gratifying if temporary success. But on the others they continued to lose ground. They substantially lost the fight against teaching evolution in the public schools, which exposed them to humiliating ridicule throughout the world. Lost, too, was the fight against modern relaxation in manners, morals, and censorship. Again the effort to contain the influence of immigrants in politics was lost within the Democratic party. The rural Protestant Democrats fought in 1924 to keep their party free of urban ethnic domination, and the two factions nearly tore the Democratic party apart at its 1924 convention. By 1928 the enemy was in control and Smith was nominated. He paid a heavy price for his religion and his defiance of establishment manners and morals, but he did succeed, partly by mobilizing the ethnic Catholic vote, in rehabilitating his party and raising it from the desperate condition it had reached in the two previous elections. The Democratic party became the coalition party of the new urban polyglot America. What Smith had begun, Roosevelt completed; F.D.R.'s consolidation of the ethnic and working-class elements in the country into an effective political force was almost as important as his economic reforms.

The problems of the depression and the Second World War somewhat eclipsed these cultural antagonisms, though they were often visible beneath the surface. Fundamentalist-evangelical America was, in fact, so long divided or quiescent as a political force that many intellectuals have forgotten that it still exists. Nor has it surrendered its commitment to Prohibitionism or its dislike of evolution in popular education.[9] Even as recently as 1959, according to a Gallup poll, 34 per cent of all Protestants favored national Prohibition. Three-fifths of all Protestant farmers and two-fifths of all Protestants living in

[9] I have tried to account for the background of the revolt against modernity in *Anti-Intellectualism in American Life* (New York, 1963), esp. Ch. 5.

towns of less than 10,000 population took this view.[10] Again, only a few years earlier, another survey showed the effects of a resolute if quiet effort being made to protect the young against Darwinism and secularism. In a poll of adolescents based on an unusually large sample, only 35 per cent responded by checking "Yes" alongside the statement: "Man was evolved from lower forms of animals." As many as 40 per cent marked "No," and 24 per cent "Don't know."[11]

Now the point of all this is not to say that the old cultural issues of the 1920's are important manifest issues under present conditions, but rather that ascetic Protestantism remains a significant undercurrent in contemporary America, and that its followers have found newfangled ways of reaffirming some of their convictions. They cannot bring back Prohibition or keep evolution entirely out of the schools. They have been unable even to defend school prayer or prevent *Life* magazine from featuring the topless bathing suit. But they can recriminate against and punish the new America that outrages them, and they have found powerful leaders to echo their views.[12] As the old fight against immigration has waned in significance, the Negro "revolution" has frightened many of them, and has given a new focus to ethnic conflict. The participants in this revolt against modernity are no longer rubes and hicks, and they have gained something both in sophistication and in cohesiveness through modern urbanization. They too live in the cities and the suburbs, at closer and more irritating range to the things that disturb them, but also closer to each other, and more susceptible to organization.

Above all, they have found a fighting issue that helps them to surmount their previous isolation, an issue on which at last they have common ground with all America: they are implacably and consumingly anti-Communist, and in the grand

[10] Seymour M. Lipset: "Religion and Politics in the American Past and Present," in Robert Lee and Martin Marty (eds.): *Religion and Social Conflict* (New York, 1964), pp. 114–15.

[11] H. H. Remmers and D. H. Radler: *The American Teenager* (Indianapolis, 1957).

[12] For example, see below, pp. 598–605.

ecumenicism of their anti-Communist passion they welcome all allies. They are particularly happy to have made terms with the Catholics and to accept members of minority ethnic groups as comrades-in-arms. That the Whore of Babylon now sits in Moscow, not Rome, is to their incalculable advantage, for they have been able to turn a powerful domestic foe, the Church, into an ally, and in its former place they have installed the impotent American Communist. Nor does it trouble them that genuine Communists are all but impossible to find. Liberals, pacifists, beatniks, agitators for racial justice, radicals of other persuasions—what Robert Welch calls "comsymps"—will do as well.

People who share this outlook have a disposition to interpret issues of secular politics as though they were solely moral and spiritual struggles. They are less concerned with the battle against communism in the world theater than they are with the alleged damage it does to politics and morals at home. The cold war serves as a constant source of recriminations about our moral and material failure, but as an objective struggle in the arena of world politics it is less challenging to them than it is as a kind of spiritual wrestling match with the minions of absolute evil, who, as is so often the case with Satanic powers, exercise an irresistible attractiveness. Those who look at the world in this way see their fundamental battle as one to be conducted against other Americans at home, and they respond eagerly to the notion, so pervasive in the right wing, that the worst enemy of American liberties is to be found in Washington. Moreover, whereas in the past only an occasional wealthy crank was interested in subsidizing attacks on Catholicism, the anti-Communist crusade brings lavish outpourings from right-wing foundations and from some of the nation's large business firms.

Though many Americans with fundamentalist leanings have traditionally been sympathetic to economic and social reforms, there is one aspect of right-wing thought that invariably attracts them—the moralistic quality of its economic ideas. Christian economic moralism, to be sure, has often buttressed benevolence and inspired social reform. But it has another side: insofar as economic life is regarded as a sphere for the fulfillment of the ascetic Protestant virtues, Christian moralism has worked for right-wing discontent. One strain in Protestant thinking has always looked to economic life not just for its efficacy in producing goods and services but as a vast apparatus of moral discipline, of rewards for virtue and industry and punishments for vice and indolence. In the past, vocational life was supposed to inculcate prudence, economy, and diligence —and many writers seem to have felt that economic discipline would be more effective in this task than sermons and exhortations. The vocational life was a moral testing ground. Today these assumptions have been flouted. The modern economy, based on advertising, lavish consumption, installment buying, safeguards to social security, relief to the indigent, government fiscal manipulation, and unbalanced budgets, seems reckless and immoral, even when it happens to work. In the intellectual synthesis of contemporary ultra-conservatism, the impulses of Protestant asceticism can thus be drawn upon to support business self-interest and the beautiful mathematical models of neo-classical economists.

IV

We can now return to our original interest: to what extent are the newly affluent, the fundamentalist, and the other constituent elements of the modern American right animated by status resentments and anxieties? This question does not seem to have the same urgency it had ten years ago, because the point which the various authors of *The Radical Right* then sought to make has been widely accepted. At that time we were all struck by a salient fact: the literature of the American right was a literature not of those who felt themselves to be in possession but of those who felt dispossessed—a literature of resentment, profoundly anti-establishment in its impulses.[13] We were all struck by the flimsiness of its pretensions to conservatism, and by its

[13]One is struck also by the disparity between the actual social position of these segments of the population and the intensity of their discontent. As Daniel Bell observes, they come from disparate groups many of which are doing very well. "In identifying 'the dispossessed,' it is somewhat misleading to seek their economic location, since it is not economic interest alone that accounts for their anxieties." Bell (ed.): op. cit., p. 19.

profound hostility to the culture and institutions by which it was surrounded.

If the essays in *The Radical Right* dwelled on status resentments, it was not because the authors thought they had found a final, single explanation of the right-wing line of thought, but because we had come upon a hitherto neglected and unexplained side of the movement. Our ideas were offered as an addition to the store of what was already known about the right wing, not as an attempt to displace the undeniable structural and historical setting in which the right wing arose. We were, in short, not trying to deny the obvious, but to go beyond it.

Our emphasis, then, on certain social and psychological forces at work in American society was not intended to deny the plurality of circumstances that gave birth to the right-wing resurgence—the shock of the Korean War, the failures of our foreign policy, the frustrations of Republicans too long defeated in presidential politics, the traditional irritations of big money, the continued high taxes, the impact of inflation, revelations of Communist espionage and of political corruption, the long-standing pent-up resentment against the New Deal and the social reforms it had established, the dislike of the type of national leadership that it had installed. We were trying to bring to the surface the additional sociological and psychological forces that helped all these circumstances come to a center and find a rhetorical form, and that gave to their anti-establishment animus its particular edge. We were impressed by the way in which the processes of prosperity yield their own kind of discontent, which, if not so widely shared as that of hard times, is nonetheless as bitter.

The emphasis given to status resentments and anxieties in the essays in *The Radical Right* was based partly on inferences from poll data about the socio-economic status and the education of McCarthyists, partly from impressionistic observation of contemporary social changes, and partly from the rhetoric of McCarthyism and the social objects against which its grievances were directed. What seemed important was not only the wrongs the McCarthyist right-wingers thought had been committed but who they thought had committed them; and repeated denunciations of "striped-pants diplomats," Ivy League graduates, high-ranking generals, college presidents, intellectuals, the Eastern upper classes, Harvard professors, and members of Phi Beta Kappa seemed to be serving psychological purposes which had little to do with arriving at a realistic historical account of the nation's difficulties and failures.[14] As McCarthy put it in his famous speech at Wheeling, the nation had been sold out by "those who have had all the benefits that the wealthiest nation on earth has to offer—the finest homes, the finest college education, and the finest jobs in Government. . . . The bright young men who are born with silver spoons in their mouths are the ones who have been worst."[15]

This seemed to voice certain status resentments, but it was hard to gauge them quantitatively or to measure their place among the many forces that were at work. To my knowledge only one study has been made to try to define felt status grievances in such a way as to put the notion to the test, and it reports a modest confirmation of the hypothesis of *The Radical Right*.[16] Other empirical studies have stressed quite correctly the large number of variables that have gone into the making of the right wing, but have not effectively argued that status resentments should be excluded from them.[17]

---

[14] See Immanuel Wallerstein: "McCarthyism and the Conservative," unpublished M.A. essay, Columbia University (1954), pp. 46 ff.

[15] *Congressional Record*, 81st Cong., 2nd sess. (February 20, 1950), p. 1954.

[16] Robert Sokol: "Status Inconsistency," unpublished doctoral dissertation, Columbia University (1961), esp. pp. 87–95, 120–5, 175, 198–200.

[17] The best evaluation, I believe, of available information from various sources remains that of Seymour Lipset in "Three Decades of the Radical Right," esp. pp. 326–48.

The study most frequently cited as having effectively contradicted the status hypothesis is Martin Trow's survey of McCarthyist opinion in Bennington, Vermont, in 1954, "Small Businessmen, Political Tolerance, and Support for McCarthy," *American Journal of Sociology*, LXIV (November 1958), 270–81. Why it is so construed I do not understand. Though it differs clearly enough on a rather marginal point, it puts strong emphasis on the anti-conservative, anti-establishment element in McCarthyism, finds it directed "precisely against the conservative authorities and institutions—the 'big shots,' the 'stuffed shirts,' the 'bureaucrats,'" sees support for McCarthy as "the channeling of certain dissatisfactions with aspects of the social, economic, and political order," finds McCarthyists "angrily confused and deeply resentful of a world that continually offends their deepest values," and reports them animated by

The essays in *The Radical Right* were prompted by a curiosity about certain facts hitherto taken for granted. We wanted to know why Americans who were affected in a similar way by many events reacted to them so differently. Of course, party affiliation, socio-economic status, and geographical region always affect political opinions, but in this case the aggregate of these readily perceptible factors did not yield a satisfactory or exhaustive answer. There was a wide range of reaction to the events of the 1950's, for example, among people in the same social class and in the same political party. People responded to political events, as they always do, not merely with profoundly different opinions about the policies that should be pursued but in strikingly different mental and rhetorical styles. It was understood that the Korean War and the overlong exclusion

---

resentment and indignation that has "no effective and institutionalized channels of expression" and by a "generalized fear of the dominant currents and institutions of modern society"—and in this respect offers an analysis not remarkably dissimilar to that of the authors it is held to refute. See esp. pp. 273, 276, 277. In any case, there was no reason to believe that Bennington was a good or representative place to study McCarthyism, and, as Lipset has pointed out, some of its key findings were not replicated by national data. "Three Decades of the Radical Right," pp. 340–1.

Two of the most valuable studies of the extreme right that have raised serious questions about the status hypothesis are those of Nelson W. Polsby: "Towards an Explanation of McCarthyism," *Political Studies*, VIII (1960), 250–71, and Wolfinger: op. cit. But some of the difficulties of the subject are exemplified in their positive conclusions. Polsby dwells (p. 258) on "the rather heavy evidence supporting the hypothesis that McCarthy succeeded at the grass roots primarily among Republicans," and he is echoed by Wolfinger in his study of right-wing Christian Crusaders of the 1960's, which finds as "the most salient fact about the Crusaders: whatever else they may be, they are not Democrats." The scarcity of Democrats, he says, was "the most striking single characteristic of our sample" (pp. 285, 288). These conclusions—that McCarthy appealed more to Republicans than to Democrats and that the right-wingers of the 1960's are overwhelmingly Republican in partisan affiliation—have the great advantage that they are likely to go ringing down the corridors of time unchallenged and unimpaired. They have an attractive solidity, but they do not offer an arresting new idea to our store of understanding. What would be most pertinent would be to find out just what characteristics divide those Republicans who have joined the extreme right from those who believe that it is a menace to the body politic, and what were the social characteristics of the rather substantial number of Democrats who were pro-McCarthy.

of Republicans from the White House had much to do with the temper of the times, but why did some Republicans welcome the peace in Korea while others branded the Republican President who made it as a traitor? Again, millionaires cannot be expected to like progressive taxation, but how could we account for the political differences between a first- or second-generation oil millionaire in Texas and a third-generation oil millionaire in New York? Why did taxpayers enjoying the same income and belonging to the same political party have such profoundly different views of the social reforms inherited from the New Deal?

I confess to mixed feelings about the term "status politics" as a means of explaining the discontents animated by the right wing. On one hand, I have no desire to overstate the role of status, narrowly defined, in the right wing of the 1950's or of today. There are a large number of factors, social and economic, that enter into the composition of the right wing, and, like any other single explanation, this one is bound to have its limitations. Yet I should be sorry if, because of its limited utility in this context, the fundamental importance of the distinction between status politics and interest politics should be lost. I chose the term "status politics" because I was looking for a way to designate an impulse held in common by a variety of discontented elements. If there is something misleading in the word "status," it is because its meaning is somewhat too specific to account for what it attempts to describe, and takes the part for the whole. Few critics have denied the presence or significance of what is intended, but it has been suggested that such terms as "cultural politics" and "symbolic politics" will serve better.

In my original essay I used the term "status politics" to refer to three things that are related but not identical: first is the problem of American identity, as it is complicated by our immigrant origins and the problems of ethnic minorities; second, the problem of social status, defined as the capacity of various groups and occupations to command personal deference in society; and, finally, the effort of Americans of diverse cultural and moral persuasions to win reassurance that their values are respected by the community at large. The purpose of the term was to heighten our awareness of a constant political struggle arising not out of the real or imagined contest for gain that is familiar in our interest-group politics—that is, the historical struggles for cheap land, cheap credit, higher farm prices, larger profits, market protection of various kinds, more jobs, more bargaining power, economic security—but out of commitments to certain other values, which are taken by the persons who share them to be ultimate moral goals, disinterestedly pursued. Such persons believe that their prestige in the community, even indeed their self-esteem, depends on having these values honored in public. Besides their economic expectations, people have deep emotional commitments in other spheres—religion, morals, culture, race relations—which they also hope to see realized in political action. Status politics seeks not to advance perceived material interests but to express grievances and resentments about such matters, to press claims upon society to give deference to non-economic values. As a rule, status politics does more to express emotions than to formulate policies. It is in fact hard to translate the claims of status politics into programs or concrete objectives (national Prohibition was an exception, though ultimately an unsuccessful one); and for the most part the proponents of such politics, being less concerned with the uses of power than with its alleged misuse, do not offer positive programs to solve social problems. The operative content of their demands is more likely to be negative: they call on us mainly to prohibit, to prevent, to censor and censure, to discredit, and to punish.

The most useful attempt to apply the concept of status politics to an aspect of our history is Joseph R. Gusfield's recent book on the temperance movement, *Symbolic Crusade: Status Politics and the Temperance Movement.* Defining status politics rather sharply as "political conflict over the allocation of prestige," he argues that its importance "lies precisely in identifying non-economic segments as crucial in certain social and political conflicts."[18] Gusfield distinguishes between the political

---

[18] *Symbolic Crusade* (Urbana, Ill., 1963), p. 18. "A political issue becomes one of status when its tangible, instrumental consequences are subordinated to its significance for the conferral of prestige . . . The argument is less over the effect of the proposed measures on concrete actions than it is over the question of whose culture is to be granted legitimacy by the public action of government" (p. 148).

aims of those he calls "cultural fundamentalists" and "cultural modernists"—the fundamentalists having a character more rigidly and exclusively oriented toward production, work, and saving, while the modernists are more concerned with consumption and enjoyment. The fundamentalists are "locals" in Robert Merton's terminology: that is, they take their values from the traditions of local society; the modernists are "cosmopolitans" in that they are more *au courant* with what is going on in the nation-wide mass society, whether or not they approve of it. Both are engaged with politics, but the fundamentalists have a special edge because they want to restore the simple virtues of a bygone age and they feel themselves to be fighting in a losing cause.

This is exemplified by the temperance movement, whose political commitments Gusfield traces from the early days of the Republic to recent times. The temperance movement of the late nineteenth and the early twentieth century, he points out, was often associated with progressive causes—feminism, Christian pacifism, the Progressive movement of the Roosevelt-Wilson era—but as its members have felt an increasing sense of alienation from modernity, and as its more moderate adherents have been drawn away into the orbit of cosmopolitan society, temperance advocates have become more and more embittered. They know that they are regarded as oddities and that the most respectable and honored people no longer support their cause. Since the New Deal—a heavily urban and cosmopolitan administration—gave the *coup de grâce* to national Prohibition, the members of the movement have moved to the political right. The Prohibition party no longer attempts, as it did a generation ago, to appeal to reformers and liberals, but, as Gusfield concludes, "has moved toward an open appeal to the right-wing elements of both major parties."

Gusfield is gratifyingly careful to avoid the reductionist fallacy: he recognizes the profoundly genuine concern of temperance advocates with the moral issues, and does not try to reduce it to a preoccupation with their status. He shows how their moral commitment comes to affect their status, and offers much evidence that in the end they become quite aware of this process. (See esp. Ch. 5.) In his book the concern with status is treated not as something that displaces the substantive purpose of the movement but as an important additional aspect of it. See pp. 57–60.

In many areas of life, the style of status politics has been shaped in large measure by rigid moral and religious attitudes, and those who are moved by the issues of status politics transfer these attitudes to social and economic questions. On many occasions they approach economic issues as matters of faith and morals rather than matters of fact. For example, people often oppose certain economic policies not because they have been or would be economically hurt by such policies, or even because they have any carefully calculated views about their economic efficacy, but because they disapprove *on moral grounds* of the assumptions on which they think the policies rest.

A prominent case in point is the argument over fiscal policy. Deficit spending is vehemently opposed by great numbers of people in our society who have given no serious thought —indeed, are hardly equipped to do so—to the complex questions bearing on its efficacy as an economic device. They oppose it because their personal experience or training in spending, debts, and prudential management leads them to see in deficit spending a shocking repudiation of the moral precepts upon which their lives have been based. As a matter of status politics, deficit spending is an affront to millions who have been raised to live (and in some cases have been forced by circumstances to live) abstemious, thrifty, prudential lives. As a matter of interest politics, deficit spending might work to their advantage; but the moral and psychological effect, which is what they can really understand and feel, is quite otherwise: when society adopts a policy of deficit spending, thrifty small-businessmen, professionals, farmers, and white-collar workers who have been managing their affairs by the old rules feel that their way of life has been officially and insultingly repudiated.

Historians and social critics of the present generation have a particularly urgent need for such an analytical instrument as status politics: it serves to keep their conception of political conflict from being imbued with the excessive rationalism that infused the work of the two preceding generations of historians and political scientists. Under the guidance of such writers as Charles A. Beard, Frederick Jackson Turner, V. L. Parrington, Arthur F. Bentley, and others, we used to think of political man basically as a rational being who reckons as well as he can what his economic interests are, forms pressure groups and parties to advance these interests, and as a citizen casts his vote in order to see them realized.

Of course, the writers of this school understood that men can make miscalculations as to the nature of their interests and the best ways of pursuing them, and they also knew that at times non-economic factors entered significantly into political behavior. But they persisted in seeking fundamental economic motives in almost all political conflict. When they dealt with non-economic factors, as their sense of reality compelled them to do, they tended to discount the significance of these factors and to look upon them as momentary aberrations, and felt no need to develop a theory that would take adequate account of them. They were strongest when writing about those political conflicts that did in fact rest squarely on economic issues, and weakest when other issues came to the foreground. Their conceptions of historical change were least suited to deal with the kind of discontents that have developed during prosperity and which to a significant degree cut across class lines.

This rationalistic bias has very largely broken down in our time, partly under the impact of political events, partly because of what has been learned through public-opinion polling and depth psychology.[19] A conception of politics which dealt with the public largely as a set of economic blocs had no adequate way of coping with the variety of other factors that have entered into our political history—among them the sheer weight of habit and party loyalty, ethnic origins and traditions, religious affiliations and religious styles, racial and ethnic prejudices, attitudes toward liberty and censorship,

---

[19]Even the pollsters, however, were slow to break away from the older pattern of thought. The realization that socio-economic status was a fundamental category was at the very foundation of commercial polling, but the importance of religious affiliation was not realized. George Gallup found it hard to believe when Paul Lazarsfeld first told him that religious affiliation has a powerful and independent relation to voting habits; and even as recently as 1959 Elmo Roper asserted that there is no relation between religious affiliation and voting. Lipset: "Religion and Politics in the American Past and Present," already cited, p. 70. On religion as an independent force in American politics, and on the conservative drive of ascetic Protestantism, see Benton Johnson: "Ascetic Protestantism and Political Preference," *Public Opinion Quarterly*, XXVI (Spring 1962), 35–46.

feelings about foreign policy quite unrelated to commercial goals and of dubious relationship to the national interest. In American history the combined effect of such forces has been singularly large. The wealth of the country and the absence of sharp class-consciousness have released much political energy for expression on issues not directly connected with economic conflict; and our unusually complex ethnic and religious mixture has introduced a number of complicating factors of great emotional urgency.

Significantly, the periods in which status politics has been most strikingly apparent have been the relatively prosperous 1920's and the 1960's. In periods of prosperity, when economic conflicts are blunted or subordinated, the other issues become particularly acute. We have noticed that whereas in depressions or during great bursts of economic reform people vote for what they think are their economic interests, in times of prosperity they feel free to vote their prejudices. In good times, with their most severe economic difficulties behind them, many people feel that they can afford the luxury of addressing themselves to larger moral questions, and they are easily convinced that the kind of politics that results is much superior to the crass materialism of interest politics. They have fewer inhibitions about pressing hard for their moral concerns, no matter how demanding and ill-formulated, as an object of public policy, than they have in pressing for their interests, no matter how reasonable and realistically conceived. In the following essay, I will try to show that Barry Goldwater was one campaigner who saw with considerable clarity the distinction between interest politics and status politics, and went out of his way in his campaign to condemn the immorality of the first and to call for an intensification of the second.

Goldwater and Pseudo-Conservative Politics

I

GOLDWATER'S CAPTURE of the Republican nomination was the triumphal moment of pseudo-conservatism in American politics. One may say that it was an accident, in that it was out of scale with right-wing Republican strength and could happen only because of a series of failures and misadventures among moderate Republicans which are not likely to recur. But in another sense it was far from accidental: it resulted from the chronic, frustrating impotence of the minority party and from the efficient organization that the right wing had quietly built up inside it.

If Goldwater is accepted on his own terms as a conservative, he baffles understanding, but if he is taken as a product of the pseudo-conservative revolt, his ideas fall into place. Questioning his conservatism may seem gratuitous, but there is more at stake here than an empty issue or a suitable label. What is at stake, as Robert J. Donovan puts it, is whether the Republican party can learn to make "a distinction between the conservatism represented by Senator Goldwater and his supporters and the conservatism that conserves."[1]

Unquestionably Goldwater's ideas do retain some shreds and scraps of genuine conservatism, but the main course of his career puts him closer to the right-wing ideologues who were essential to his success, who shaped his tactics, who responded to his line of argument, and whose extremism he chose to defend at the vital moment of his career. Without invoking these formative affiliations, how are we to explain the character of a "conservative" whose whole political life has been spent urging a sharp break with the past, whose great moment as a party leader was marked by a repudiation of our traditional political ways, whose followers were so notable for their destructive and divisive energies, and whose public reputation was marked not with standpattism or excessive caution but with wayward impulse and recklessness?

[1] *The Future of the Republican Party* (New York, 1964), p. 127.

Goldwater's brand of conservatism has its most recognizable American roots in those thinkers, quite numerous in this country, who imagine conservatism to be almost identical with economic individualism. Here he has responded more fervently to the nostalgic reveries and the pronouncements of perennial truths that mark ideological conservatism than he has to the tradition of shrewd and subtle manipulation, concession, and conciliation that has characterized American conservatism in practice. Most conservatives are mainly concerned with maintaining a tissue of institutions for whose stability and effectiveness they believe the country's business and political elites hold responsibility. Goldwater thinks of conservatism as a system of eternal and unchanging ideas and ideals, whose claims upon us must be constantly asserted and honored in full.[2] The difference between conservatism as a set of doctrines whose validity is to be established by polemics, and conservatism as a set of rules whose validity is to be established by their usability in government, is not a difference of nuance, but of fundamental substance.

It is instructive how far Goldwater's devotion to eternal truths brought him beyond the position of such a Republican

[2] "The laws of God, and of nature, have no date-line. The principles on which the Conservative political position is based have been established by a process that has nothing to do with the social, economic, and political landscape that changes from decade to decade and from century to century. These principles are derived from the nature of man, and from the truths that God has revealed about His creation. Circumstances do change. So do the problems that are shaped by circumstances. But the principles that govern the solution of the problems do not. . . . The challenge is not to find new or different truths, but how to apply established truths to the problems of the contemporary world." Barry Goldwater: *The Conscience of a Conservative* (New York, Macfadden ed., 1960), "Foreword," p. 3. (It may be necessary to add, since Goldwater has been exceptionally candid about the extent to which his books were ghost-written, that I have used them on the assumption that he read them carefully before he signed them, and that they do indeed represent his views as of the time that they were written.)

Again: "The basic problems are no different in our times than under Lincoln or Washington. . . . We have merely changed the horse for the tractor, the hand tools for a machine." A speech before the Utah State Convention of the Junior Chamber of Commerce in 1960, quoted in *The New Republic*, March 27, 1961, p. 14.

predecessor as Eisenhower, and how far it took him even beyond the conservatism of Robert A. Taft. Many of Eisenhower's statements both before and after his presidency could lead
one to conclude that his social thinking was more similar to
Goldwater's than different. Eisenhower too spoke often for the
old-fashioned prudential virtues and against growing federal
bureaucracy, and his cabinet incorporated at least two members,
George Humphrey and Ezra Taft Benson, who fully shared the
right-wing philosophy. But in practice Eisenhower was faithful to the opportunistic traditions of American conservatism.
Though a mediocre politician with little enthusiasm for the political game, he was nonetheless so intuitively an "insider" in the
American political tradition that he instinctively took the working politician's approach to the split mentality of American conservatism. He knew that many conservatives yearn for the days
of untrammeled enterprise, uncomplicated foreign problems,
and negligible taxes, but also that they can usually recognize
the complexity of the contemporary world, the difficult obligations the country has taken on, and the irreversibility of the
historical process that has brought us from simple agrarian conditions to the complex conditions of modern urban life and corporate organization. When Eisenhower spoke in philosophical
terms, therefore, he often gave voice to their wistfulness about
old ideals, but in administrative practice he usually bowed to
what he thought were the necessities of the hour.

Here the strategies of three of our leading politicians are
instructive. Eisenhower believed, at least with half his mind, in
the old pieties, but concluded, with whatever misgivings, that
they could not be taken as rules for action. Goldwater not only
believed in them, but believed that they ought to be followed
unerringly. Lyndon Johnson presumably does not believe in
them at all; but understands that since they are widely believed
in by honest men, some symbolic gestures are desirable in order to show such men that he at least respects their values. His
talk of economy, and his much-publicized gesture of turning
out the lights in the White House to save money, are gestures
of this sort. Among cynical men they are naturally taken to be
cynical. But they may also be taken as a humane effort to give
symbolic comfort to those to whom, in the nature of things,
more substantial forms of comfort cannot be given.

In any case, to ultra-conservatives, for whom the old pieties are binding moral principles, the Eisenhower administration was worse than a disappointment, it was a betrayal. It did not repeal the New Deal reforms, do away with high taxes, kill foreign aid, or balance the budget. In fact, its primary historical function seemed to be to legitimate what had been done under Roosevelt and Truman: when it left certain domestic and foreign policies intact, it made them more generally acceptable by passing them, so to speak, through the purifying fire of eight years of Republicanism and thus confirming that they represented, after all, a bipartisan consensus. The right-wing minority saw all this not as a clue to the nature of our national problems but as further evidence that the conspiracy originally set in motion by the Democrats was being carried on by the Eastern Republicans behind Eisenhower. McCarthy, for example, had been quick to strike at Eisenhower and to change his slogan, "Twenty years of treason," to a more inflammatory one: "Twenty-one years of treason." Again, one of Eisenhower's budgets prompted Goldwater to brand his administration as "a dime-store New Deal." On a later occasion he said with fervor: "One Eisenhower in a generation is enough."[3]

Goldwater's deviation from Taft Republicanism also marks him off from the established moderate conservative wing of his party. Unlike Goldwater, Taft came from a family with long seasoning in public affairs; and, again unlike Goldwater, he took an active part on Capitol Hill in framing legislation. His brand of conservatism was modified by several concessions to the demands of expediency and responsibility. Though he had a profound dislike of change and a passionate bias toward fiscal conservatism and decentralized administration, Taft accepted the idea that the federal government should concern itself with "seeing that every family has a minimum standard of decent shelter," should "assist those states desiring to put a floor under essential services in relief, in medical care, in housing, and in education," should underwrite the states in providing "a basic minimum education to every child," sustain minimum-wage laws "to give the unorganized worker some protection"

[3] *Time*, July 24, 1964, p. 27.

comparable to that given to organized workers by the unions, persist in a steeply graduated income tax, maintain minimum farm prices, and through its social security program (which he held to be woefully inadequate) "assure to every citizen 65 years of age and over a living wage."

These commitments, made in various speeches from 1943 to 1951, accept the reality of the welfare state. They stand in sharp contrast to Goldwater's notion that economic individualism can still be ruthlessly applied to American life. Before Goldwater found it necessary to modify a few of his positions for the sake of his primary and presidential campaigns in 1964, his beliefs came straight out of nineteenth-century laissez-faire doctrine and the strictest of strict constructionism. Governmental activities in "relief, social security, collective bargaining, and public housing," he thought, had caused "the weakening of the individual personality and of self-reliance." He asked for "prompt and final termination of the farm subsidy program," declared himself against "every form of federal aid to education," denounced the graduated income tax as "confiscatory," and asserted that the country had "no education problem which requires any form of Federal grant-in-aid programs to the states." The government, he said "must begin to withdraw from a whole series of programs that are "outside its constitutional mandate," including "social welfare programs, education, public power, agriculture, public housing, urban renewal. . . ."[4] Collectively, such statements called for the dismantling of the welfare state. "My aim is not to pass laws but to repeal them," Goldwater once boasted, and on another occasion he said: "I fear Washington and centralized government more than I do Moscow."[5] These are the characteristic accents of the pseudo-conservative agitators, who are convinced that they live in a degenerate society and who see their main enemy in the power of their own government.

[4] *The Conscience of a Conservative*, p. 43; *Congressional Record*, 87th Cong., 1st sess. (June 21, 1961), p. 10971; ibid., 88th Cong., 1st sess. (September 3, 1963), p. 16222; statement to Senate Subcommittee on Education, Senate Committee on Labor and Public Welfare, April 30, 1963 (*Hearings*, I, 279).
[5] *Fortune*, May 1961, p. 139; *Look*, April 21, 1964; cf. *The Conscience of a Conservative*, p. 22.

Goldwater's departure from the Republican pattern was compounded by his position on civil rights. One of the oldest, though hardly the most efficacious, of the traditions of many conservatives in the North—and even to a degree in the South as well—has been a certain persistent sympathy with the Negro and a disposition to help him in moderate ways to relieve his distress. This tradition goes back to the Federalist party; it was continued by the Whig gentry; it infused the early Republican party. By adopting "the Southern strategy," the Goldwater men abandoned this inheritance. They committed themselves not merely to a drive for a core of Southern states in the electoral college but to a strategic counterpart in the North which required the search for racist votes. They thought they saw a good mass issue in the white backlash, which they could indirectly exploit by talking of violence in the streets, crime, juvenile delinquency, and the dangers faced by our mothers and daughters.

Eisenhower, like Goldwater, had been unmoved by noble visions of progress toward racial justice, but he at least gave lip service to the ideal and thought it important to enforce the laws himself and to speak out for public compliance. But Goldwater arrived at the position, far from conservative in its implications, that the decisions of the Supreme Court are "not necessarily" the law of the land.[6] Of course, the decisions of the Court have always had political content and they have often been highly controversial; there is no reason why they should suddenly be regarded with whispered reverence. But it is only in our time, and only in the pseudo-conservative movement, that men have begun to hint that disobedience to the Court is not merely legitimate but is the essence of conservatism.

It is not the authority and legitimacy of the Court alone that the pseudo-conservative right calls into question. When it argues that we are governed largely by means of near-hypnotic manipulation (brainwashing), wholesale corruption, and betrayal, it is indulging in something more significant than the fantasies of indignant patriots: it is questioning the legitimacy of the political order itself. The two-party system, as it has

[6] *The Conscience of a Conservative*, p. 37; cf. *The New York Times*, November 24, 1963.

developed in the United States, hangs on the common recognition of loyal opposition: each side accepts the ultimate
good intentions of the other. The opponent's judgment may
be held to be consistently execrable, but the legitimacy of his
intent is not—that is, in popular terms, his Americanism is not
questioned. One of the unspoken assumptions of presidential
campaigns is that the leaders of both parties are patriots who,
however serious their mistakes, must be accorded the right
to govern. But an essential point in the pseudo-conservative
world view is that our recent Presidents, being men of wholly
evil intent, have conspired against the public good. This does
more than discredit them: it calls into question the validity of
the political system that keeps putting such men into office.

A man like Goldwater, who lives psychologically half in the
world of our routine politics and half in the curious intellectual underworld of the pseudo-conservatives, can neither
wholly accept nor wholly reject such a position. He disdains
and repudiates its manifest absurdities (Eisenhower as a Communist agent), but he lives off the emotional animus that gives
birth to them. This ambiguity makes it more understandable
why, on the night of his defeat, he so flagrantly violated the
code of decorum governing the conduct of losing presidential
candidates. The code requires a message of congratulation,
sent as soon as the result is beyond doubt, so worded that
it emphasizes the stake of the whole nation in the successful
administration of the victor, and reasserts the loser's acceptance of the public verdict. In withholding his congratulations
until the morning after the election, and then in hinting at
Johnson's incapacity to solve the acute problems gratuitously
enumerated in his telegram, Goldwater did something more
than show bad manners. By complying with the code, but
grudgingly and tardily, he expressed his suspicion that the
whole American political system, with its baffling ambiguities
and compromises, is too soft and too equivocal for this car-
nivorous world.

II

Although the ultras usually speak with nostalgia about the
supposed virtues of our remote past, they have a disposition
to repudiate the more recent past, and it was in character for

Goldwater to write off as unacceptable the Republican conservatism of recent years. But in return, he and his followers were unable to win acceptance from the major centers of genuinely conservative power. Businessmen, to be sure, gave Goldwater a narrow margin of support, but they gave him far less than any other Republican in recent history. The press also broke from its normal pattern: for the first time in memory a Democrat was favored by newspapers with an aggregate circulation much larger than those endorsing his opponent. Conservative chains like the Hearst and Scripps-Howard newspapers backed Johnson, as did establishment Republican papers like the New York *Herald Tribune*. Old centers of Republican conservatism such as rural New England turned their backs on Goldwater, and he became the first Republican presidential candidate to lose Vermont. The conservative voters of the normally Republican states of the wheat belt also deserted in large numbers. Repeatedly the pollsters who found Republican voters expressing doubt about Goldwater or open opposition to him noticed a recurrent explanation: "He's too radical for me." The American public is not notably sophisticated about ideological labels, and its use of the term "radical" rarely shows much precision; but this response registers a sounder sense of the situation than that of the highbrow conservatives who acclaimed the Arizonan as their own. Whatever tag Goldwater chose to wear, a large part of the public saw in him an excessively sharp deviation from the pattern of American politics and they found it frightening.

Goldwater's deviation is as much marked in his conduct as in his ideas. American politics is run mainly by professionals who have developed over a long span of time an ethos of their own, a kind of professional code. In emphasizing how completely Goldwater, and even more his followers, departed from the professional code, it is important to be clear that one is not making a substantive criticism of what they stood for but an attempt to compare their ways historically with our normal conservative practice. The professional code is not a binding moral imperative for anyone—not even for politicians. At one time or another most politicians have broken it. On occasion we admire them for breaking it in the interest of what they believe to be a higher principle. Finally, it should be conceded that Goldwater, at certain moments of his career, observed it handsomely, and that he too was victimized at times when the code was broken by others.[7]

The point, however, is that the professional code, for all its limitations, is an American institution embodying the practical wisdom of generations of politicians. It seems ironic that the most unqualified challenge ever made within a major party to this repository of the wisdom of our ancestors should have been made by a self-proclaimed conservative, and that Goldwater's advisers in 1964 brought him as close as any presidential candidate has ever come to subverting the whole pattern of our politics of coalition and consensus.

Professional politicians want, above all, to win, and their conduct is shaped by this pragmatic goal. Moreover, they know that if they win they have to govern; and their behavior in dealing with opposing factions in their own party, with the opposition party, and with the electorate is constantly molded and qualified by the understanding that they have to organize a government capable of coping with the problems of the moment. Both their ideas and their partisan passions are modified by the harsh corrective of reality. They are quite aware, for example, that their promises, which express rather what they think they should offer to do than what they think they can do, cannot be perfectly fulfilled. They are also aware that their denunciation of the opposing party in the conduct of election campaigns must be followed by the attempt to work with the opposition in Washington. Under the heated surface of our political rhetoric, therefore, there exists a certain sobriety born of experience, an understanding that what sounds good on the banquet circuit may not make feasible policy, that statements, manifestos, and polemics are very far from pragmatic programs; that these have to be *translated* into programs for the

[7]For example, Goldwater observed the code conspicuously in his conduct toward Nixon in 1960 and again momentarily in 1964 when he expressed some sympathetic understanding for the position of Republicans who could not afford to be fully identified with him. His opponents broke it at the Cow Palace when they circulated the famous Scranton letter, which, in its denunciation of his ideas and alleged tactics, went far beyond the usual etiquette of intra-party dispute.

On the requirements of American coalition politics as they bear on convention behavior, and on their repudiation by the Goldwater forces, see my essay: "Goldwater & His Party," *Encounter*, XXIII (October 1964), 3–13.

solution of our domestic and foreign problems; and that even then these programs have to undergo still further modification in the legislative mill before they can become reality.

Goldwater's career is distinguished by its lack of training for this code. Before his entry into national politics, his experience had given him responsibility for no national organization and had required an attention to administrative demands no more complex than those of his inherited department store. As a member of the Senate, he assumed no important role, involved himself with no legislation on major national problems. His main business there was simply to vote No. He made no outstanding contributions to debate or to the consideration of legislative details (as, for example, Taft had done); he was not prominent in committee work, and his busy speech-making program made him a frequent absentee. He did not, as a working senator, command the ear of fellow senators, not even of those who shared his views. In the framework of practical politics, he remained an "outsider," and as a presidential candidate he continued to make decisions that reflected the outsider's cast of mind.[8]

But to say this of Goldwater's legislative role is not to deny that he worked hard to earn his position in his party: it is simply that he rose to it not by making contributions to government but through his partisan activity, which for years was dedicated and tireless. He was chairman of the Republican Senatorial Campaign Committee. He was constantly available to fellow Republicans everywhere, giving substantial help to their campaign efforts and their fund-raising. His arduous round of speechmaking on the banquet circuit gave him a chance to bring his "conservative" message to thousands of rank-and-file party workers and to put many party leaders in

[8]For a shrewd statement of the differences between the political mentality of the outsider and that of the insider, see the contrast drawn by Eric L. McKitrick between Andrew Johnson and Abraham Lincoln in *Andrew Johnson and Reconstruction* (Chicago, 1960), esp. Ch. 4.

Oddly enough, the externals of John F. Kennedy's senatorial career correspond with Goldwater's. However, the difference in their cast of mind, not to speak of their intellectual caliber, was beyond reckoning. It was only one aspect of these differences that JFK was, by family training, education, and social position—one suspects also, as it were, by instinct—an insider.

his debt. His role, then, was that of the partisan exhorter and organizer, a speaker and ideologue for whom preaching a sound philosophy was more interesting than addressing himself to the problems of state. But in this role he was constantly speaking to audiences already largely or wholly converted to his point of view, unlike the legislator on Capitol Hill who must constantly deal with shrewd and informed men who differ with him. Resounding applause no doubt confirmed his conviction of the validity and importance of his "conservatism," and persuaded him that an irresistible conservative revival was astir in the country, but it did not enlarge his capacity to conciliate or persuade those who differed with him—still less to learn from an exchange of views. The habits of mind thus shaped were carried into his campaign, during which he once again brought salvation to the already converted.[9]

Goldwater, then, made up for his lack of stature as a legislative leader by his outstanding success as a partisan evangelist who particularly mobilized those Republicans whose discontent was keenest, whose ideological fervor was strongest, those most dissatisfied with the bland and circumspect Eisenhower legacy. At the grass roots large segments of the Republican party were taken over by dedicated enthusiasts, hitherto political amateurs, with a bent for unorthodox ideas and new departures. Reporters at San Francisco were impressed by the preponderance of unfamiliar faces among the Goldwater delegates.[10] Victory won with the help of these new-idea delegates was followed by the creation of a Goldwater staff in which

[9]"With one exception, and that a slip-up apparently, he held no press conferences during the campaign. When he visited the cities he generally avoided the crowds, the slums, and the ghettos and appeared only in halls filled with militant conservatives who needed no persuasion by him. There was precious little effort on the senator's part to take his case to the unconvinced." Donovan: op. cit., p. 55.
[10]Robert D. Novak remarks that these were "not merely the run-of-the-mill party workers under the command and the bidding of regular party leaders. Here was a new breed of delegate, most of whom had never been to a national convention before. . . . They were going there for one purpose: to vote for Barry Goldwater. To woo them away to another candidate would be as difficult as proselytizing a religious zealot." *The Agony of the G.O.P. 1964* (New York, 1965), pp. 345–6.

professionals and cosmopolitans were entirely overshadowed by amateurs and provincials—a staff the press called "the Arizona Mafia."

Goldwater's advisers and enthusiasts, being new to major-party politics, found it easy to abandon the familiar rules of political conduct. Party workers raised on the professional code want above all to find winners, to get and keep office, to frame programs on which they can generally agree, to use these programs to satisfy the major interests in our society, and to try to solve its most acute problems. If they find that they have chosen a loser, they are quick to start looking for another leader. If they see that their program is out of touch with the basic realities, they grope their way toward a new one.

But Goldwater's zealots were moved more by the desire to dominate the party than to win the country, concerned more to express resentments and punish "traitors," to justify a set of values and assert grandiose, militant visions, than to solve actual problems of state. More important, they were immune to the pressure to move over from an extreme position toward the center of the political spectrum which is generally exerted by the professional's desire to win. Their true victory lay not in winning the election but in capturing the party—in itself no mean achievement—which gave them an unprecedented platform from which to propagandize for a sound view of the world.

Since the major parties in the United States have always been coalitions of disparate and even discordant elements, the professional leaders of major parties have always had to forge out of their experience the techniques of consensus politics that are adapted to holding such coalitions together and maintaining within them a workable degree of harmony. The art of consensus politics, in our system, has to be practiced not only in coping with the opposition party but internally, in dealing with one's partisans and allies. The life of an American major party is a constant struggle, in the face of serious internal differences,

---

Cf. Richard Rovere: "They are a new breed. It has been said—quite proudly —by the Goldwater people that this was the first Convention for more than half of them. . . . There was youth on every hand." "Letter from San Francisco," *The New Yorker*, July 25, 1964, p. 80.

to achieve enough unity to win elections and to maintain it long enough to develop a program for government. Our politics has thus put a strong premium on the practical rather than the ideological bent of mind, on the techniques of negotiation and compromise rather than the assertion of divisive ideas and passions, and on the necessity of winning rather than the unqualified affirmation of principles, which is left to the minor parties.

The perennial task of coalition building has resulted in a number of rituals for party conventions, which Goldwater and his followers either ignored or deliberately violated at San Francisco. A candidate who enters a convention with the preponderant and controlling strength that Goldwater had in 1964 has at his disposal a number of effective devices to conciliate and incorporate the opposition. One is to write a conciliatory platform, which makes concessions to the defeated side or which hedges on disputed matters. Party platforms are often vague, they are usually long and tedious, and they remain unread; but their significance lies precisely in showing the ability of all factions and candidates to agree at least on a statement of policy. Their very vagueness proves that party leaders do not consider it necessary to fight issues out or to reach clear statements of principle and policy. Bitter or prolonged platform fights, such as those waged by the Democrats in 1896 and 1924, are always signs of a fatal absence of basic unity.

The winning candidate has other placatory devices available. One is the choice of a running mate: he may pick his leading opponent for this role, as Kennedy did in 1960, or he may turn to someone who represents the main opposing tendency in the party. He may go out of his way to arrive at an understanding, as Eisenhower did with Taft in 1952 or Nixon with Rockefeller in 1960. In his acceptance address he will almost invariably do the graceful thing and dwell upon conciliatory themes, stressing the commitments and sentiments that unite the party rather than those that divide it. In return, some corresponding rituals are expected of the loser: he, or one of his close associates, usually presents a motion to make the nomination unanimous. If he speaks, he minimizes the issues that have divided his party, denounces the opposition party with renewed vigor, and promises to support the victor with all his might. Normally he keeps this promise, as Goldwater himself did for Nixon in 1960.[11]

This traditional placatory ritual was flouted at every point by the Goldwater organization at San Francisco. To begin, their platform in effect repudiated many recent Republican policies. Then, proposed amendments endorsing civil rights, reasserting civilian control over nuclear weapons, and condemning extremist groups were crushed, and in the debate over the last of these, Governor Rockefeller was interrupted unmercifully by booing from the galleries. (The Goldwater managers, disturbed by this outburst, were able to prevent their delegates from persisting in the demonstration but could not stop their partisans in the galleries from giving vent to their feelings.) In the choice of a running mate, Goldwater again had an opportunity to soften the conflict by taking some eminent man from the large moderately conservative middle band of the party who would have been acceptable on all sides, but he settled on an obscure provincial, William E. Miller—professional enough, to be sure, but undistinguished except by belligerent partisanship. The effects of this choice were in no way mollified by the selection of his fellow Arizonan Dean Burch as national chairman—"a politician of limited experience who had never even been a county chairman and who was a complete stranger to hundreds of eminent Republicans around the country."[12] Finally, to top it all, Goldwater's acceptance speech, far from sounding the conciliatory note so necessary after the acrimony of the proceedings, said that "those who do not care for our cause we don't expect to enter our ranks in any case," and flung his famous challenge: "I would remind you that extremism in the defense of liberty is no vice. And let me remind you also that moderation in the pursuit of justice is no virtue!"— a two-sentence manifesto approved by a dozen top members of

---

[11]Goldwater's break with the professional code in 1964 did not come from failure to understand its easily mastered general principles but from his constant gravitation toward the doctrinaires. "We are a big political party," he declared in a speech on September 11, 1963, "and there is all kinds of room for a difference of opinion. But in differing, we need not beat the hides off those we differ with." Novak: op. cit., p. 232. It was this message that got lost at San Francisco.
[12]Donovan: op. cit., p. 92.

his staff and written by a hard-core right-winger whom Gold-water found congenial and kept by his side as a speechwriter throughout the campaign.

Most presidential candidates try to look their best at the strategic moment when their party convention acclaims them. For Goldwater this was impossible. His moment of victory at the Cow Palace found him firmly in the hands of his ecstatic pseudo-conservative followers. For the past few years his own presidential prospects had done much to draw them into active politics, and it was their money and hard work which had built the Goldwater movement. In precinct after precinct and county after county they had fought and ousted old-line Republicans.[13] They were now prominent among his delegates—an official of the John Birch Society claimed that more than a hundred of the Goldwater delegates were Birchites. The Goldwater cam-paign had given focus to the right-wing movement, and had brought into prominence such exponents of the paranoid style as John A. Stormer and Phyllis Schlafly, whose books were sold and given away by the millions, and whose conspiratorial views articulated the mental heat behind pseudo-conservatism more fully than Goldwater's more equivocal utterances. Schlafly's *A Choice Not an Echo* expressed the animus of Midwestern Republicans against "the secret New York kingmakers" who had repeatedly stolen the Republican nomination "to insure control of the largest cash market in the world: the Executive Branch of the United States Government." It was reminiscent of the same bias which a few years earlier had inspired Gold-water to suggest that "this country would be better off if we could just saw off the Eastern Seaboard and let it float out to sea." Stormer's *None Dare Call It Treason*, which took its title from a couplet attributed to Sir John Harrington:

[13]The procedure by which Goldwater and his followers conducted their cam-paign for delegates was not one calculated to develop their talents for concilia-tion. As Novak puts it, Goldwater repealed "the rule of preconvention politics that required a candidate to appease the uncommitted rather than titillate his own committed followers. . . . Rather than appease the uncommitted, Gold-water was destroying them. And this required keeping his own committed fol-lowers in a state of high titillation. . . . He was conquering, not convincing, the Republican party." Op. cit., p. 353.

> Treason doth never prosper, what's the reason?
> For if it prosper, none dare call it treason,

was a masterful piece of folkish propaganda, which continued the McCarthyist and Birchite line of accusation without committing the bizarre verbal indiscretions that have caused people to make fun of Robert Welch. It drew up a thoroughgoing indictment of Eisenhower Republicanism without in so many words calling Eisenhower a traitor.[14]

To be fully faithful to this clientele, Goldwater had to be graceless to many fellow Republicans; yet it would have been graceless too to spurn the people whose work had won his victory. But, in fact, he saw nothing wrong with them. While he could hardly take Robert Welch seriously, he had said more than once that the John Birch Society was a fine organization,[15] and now he would neither repudiate nor offend its members. This meant that the path to the customary procedures of our politics was closed off, since the right-wingers scorned them. The convention showed the nation for the first time how well organized the right-wing movement was, but it also proved, as the subsequent campaign was to prove again, that the right wing, though brilliantly organized for *combat*, was not organized to conciliate or persuade. Having convinced themselves that the forces they were fighting were conspiratorial and sinister, not to say treasonous, they found it impossible to shake off the constricting mental framework of the paranoid

[14]Phyllis Schlafly: *A Choice Not an Echo* (Alton, Ill., 1964), p. 5; John A. Stormer: *None Dare Call It Treason* (Florissant, Mo., 1964), esp. pp. 33–53, 196–8, 224–5. These young writers represent the militant younger generation of conservatives that was attracted to Goldwater. Stormer was chairman of the Missouri Federation of Young Republicans, and Schlafly president of the Illinois Federation of Republican Women and a Goldwater delegate at the Cow Palace.

[15]"A lot of people in my home town have been attracted to the [Birch] society," Goldwater said in 1961, "and I am impressed by the type of people in it. They are the kind of people we need in politics." On another occasion he called them "the finest people in my community," and still later, when it had become clear that they might be a serious campaign liability, he stood by them, insisting that as a group they should not be called extremists. "They believe in the Constitution, they believe in God, they believe in Freedom." *Time*, April 7, 1961, p. 19; ibid., June 23, 1961, p. 16; *The New York Times*, July 18, 1964.

style. The sudden and startling outburst of wild applause, the jeers and fist-shaking at the broadcast booths and press stands, which came when Eisenhower made a mildly hostile reference to some unidentified columnists, was a key to the prevailing mood. Animated by a profound resentment, and now at last on the verge of a decisive victory over their tormentors, the Goldwater zealots were filled with the desire to punish and humiliate, not to appease and pacify.[16] The acceptance speech showed that this desire extended upward into Goldwater's own staff.

The shock inflicted by San Francisco was so severe that some gesture seemed imperative; and for a moment it seemed that Goldwater would make the usual effort at rapprochement when the Hershey Conference was held in August. Indeed he did say there many of the expected things, and some in strong terms; but the damage had been done, and Goldwater's announcement to reporters at the close of the conference that "this is no conciliatory speech at all. It merely reaffirms what I've been saying all through the campaign," canceled much of the conciliatory effect. The wounds had been covered over, not healed, and although Goldwater won the dutiful support of a number of moderates, including his main opponent, Scranton, he went on to conduct a right-wing campaign in which they were inevitably out of key.[17] By now it was not altogether a matter of his being unwilling to offer reassurance. What had happened was that he had been so extreme so long that neither the Republican moderates nor a large, strategic segment of the

---

[16] Cf. Richard Rovere's report from San Francisco (p. 80). For the most part, he found the Goldwater delegates young and affluent, "smartly dressed, well organized, and well spoken. And they were as hard as nails. The spirit of compromise and accommodation was wholly alien to them. They did not come to San Francisco merely to nominate their man and then rally his former opponents behind him; they came for a total ideological victory and the total destruction of their critics. . . . They wished to punish as well as to prevail."

[17] It was impossible after San Francisco to put the pieces together again. Scranton made many strong campaign speeches, as the code required, for Goldwater, and acted as his host at a great rally in Pittsburgh near the end of the campaign. In his introduction he made a casual reference to the fact that he did not always agree with Goldwater. At this he was met by such a chorus of boos from the faithful that he hurried through to a perfunctory and cool conclusion. See Novak: op. cit., p. 5.

electorate had confidence that further reassurances from him would have any meaning.

Overwhelming defeat in the election—a thing which the professional politician always takes as a spur to rethink his commitments and his strategy—had no such effect on the Goldwater camp. His enthusiasts were more disposed to see the event as further evidence of the basic unregeneracy of the country, or worse, of the conspiracy by which they had been thwarted all along. The old right-wing myth, that there was an enormous conservative "silent vote" that would pour out to the polls if the party would only nominate a proper right-winger, was exploded, but it seems to have been replaced by a new one: that Goldwater was defeated so badly largely because he was sabotaged by the party moderates and liberals.[18] It must be conceded that if one's underlying purpose is not to win elections or affect the course of government but to propagandize for a set of attitudes, the right-wing enterprise of 1964 can be considered something of a success. It was so taken by many Goldwater ideologues, and on the far right the post-election mood was one of cheer, if not elation. One of its spokesmen said that the election marked "the defeat not of conservatism but of the Republican party"—a clear confession that the fate of an ideology was taken as being far more important than the well-being of the institution; and Goldwater remarked in a revealing statement: "I don't feel the conservative cause has been hurt. Twenty-five million votes are a lot of votes and a lot of people dedicated to the concept of conservatism."[19]

[18]As is often the case, there is a modest portion of truth in this myth: the battle with the moderates in the primaries and at San Francisco helped to fix an image of Goldwater in the public mind that was never erased. But after San Francisco, it was not true that Goldwater was a loser because the moderates deserted him, but rather that the moderates, with their survival in mind, had to desert him because he was a loser. After the Hershey Conference, most of them were prepared to obey the professional code (as, for example, Scranton handsomely did), but many of those who were running for office found it too dangerous to their chances. This effect was not confined to the moderates. The ultra-conservative senatorial candidate in California, George Murphy, also found it expedient to keep his distance from Goldwater, and this strategy may have been an element in his success.

[19] *The New York Times*, November 5, 1964. Goldwater's figure represented the current state of the vote count, which was not complete.

If one accepts the point of view of political doctrinaires and amateurs, whose primary aim in politics is to make certain notions more popular, this statement has its validity: for a generation, no politician has been able to preach Goldwater's brand of ultra-right-wing individualism and aggressive nationalism to so wide an audience from so exalted a platform. However, a practical conservative politician, more concerned with consequences than with doctrine, might see the matter in a different light. He would observe that Goldwater's overwhelming defeat and the consequent collapse of Republican party strength in Congress have smashed the legislative barriers that for more than twenty-five years have blocked major advances in the welfare state. He would note that the preponderance in Congress has been overwhelmingly shifted toward the liberals, that legislative seniority, the makeup of the House Rules Committee, the composition indeed of all the committees, were so changed that a new flood of welfare legislation of the kind so fervently opposed by Goldwater was made possible; that medicare, a major extension of federal aid to education, a new voting-rights bill, a wider coverage for the minimum-wage act, regional aid for the Appalachian states, and a general anti-poverty program—all policies which the Goldwater forces considered dangerous in the extreme—were brought much closer to enactment; and that beyond these lay the further improved chances of a new immigration act with quota changes, urban transportation measures, the creation of a national arts foundation, even repeal of the "right to work" section of the Taft-Hartley Act.

From this point of view, liberals could be grateful to Goldwater. No other Republican could have made such a startling contribution to the first really significant and general extension of the New Deal since the 1930's. It was his campaign that broke the back of our postwar practical conservatism.

III

The conduct of Goldwater's campaign is no less interesting than his convention strategy. Americans, always ready to forget failure and write off defeat, may be disposed to say that this campaign is dead and should be forgotten, except insofar as it may serve working politicians of all shades of opinion as a model of how not to do things. But it will also serve as a good case history of the pseudo-conservative mentality in action.

On both domestic and foreign policy, Goldwater was encumbered by the many impulsive utterances he had made during the previous years. His campaign engaged him in the unenviable task of trying to disavow the starker implications of these utterances and to give the public some reassurance as to his stability without at the same time sacrificing his entire political identity and the allegiance of his true believers.[20] Although these efforts led to some preposterous inconsistencies, I believe a rigid consistency would in this case have been more discreditable. His inconsistencies represent at least Goldwater's effort—too little, too hesitant, and too late—to transform himself from a right-wing ideologue to a major-party leader in the American tradition, and he would have been more vulnerable to criticism if he had made no effort of this kind.[21] What is most extraordinary about his campaign is not these negative and unsuccessful disclaimers, but his positive strategy, which rested upon an appeal to moral uneasiness and discontent.

In his opening campaign speech at Prescott, Arizona, Goldwater struck his major theme: "There is a stir in the land. There is a mood of uneasiness. We feel adrift in an uncharted and stormy sea. We feel we have lost our way." In later speeches he cited the evidences of this "drift and decay" that had overcome the country: "wave after wave of crime in our streets and in our homes . . . riot and disorder in our cities . . . a breakdown of the morals of our young people. . . . juvenile delinquency. . . . obscene literature. . . . corruption." All these evils had mounted because "the moral fiber of the American people is beset by rot and decay."[22] Decay particularly afflicted

[20]I have tried to establish in a rough way the implications of Goldwater's search for a suitable image at various steps in his career in "A Long View: Goldwater in History," *The New York Review of Books*, October 8, 1964, pp. 17–19.
[21]Goldwater's one significant gesture at refashioning his doctrinaire right-wing posture actually came early in 1961, but he was barraged by protests from the right wing and he withdrew. From that point on his basic commitment never changed. See Novak: op. cit., Ch. 3, for this episode.
[22]Quotations in this and the following paragraphs from Goldwater's campaign speeches are from mimeographed news releases of the Republican National Committee. The speeches I have drawn on are those of September 3 (Prescott),

the young, and this was something more profound and significant than the "normal pranks and rebellion of youth coming of age. . . . something much more fundamental is at work. Something basic and dangerous is eating away at the morality, dignity, and respect of our citizens—old as well as young, high as well as low." And he suggested that this was a poor time in our nation's history "for the Federal Government to ban Almighty God from our school rooms"—a reference to the Supreme Court's school-prayer decision. Not only was the Democratic party platform silent on the question of a constitutional amendment allowing for the restoration of prayer, but "you will search in vain for *any* reference to God or religion in the Democratic platform." Almost his entire speech at Salt Lake City was given over to the theme of religion and "the moral crisis of our time." At Topeka and elsewhere he linked President Johnson to this moral crisis—among other things, he said, Johnson "visited church after church and city after city in a political travesty of the Lord's day" and turned "Sunday into a day of campaign chaos."

Beyond this, however, as Goldwater made clear in a television appearance on October 9, the deterioration of home, family, and community, of law and order and good morals, was "the result of thirty years of an unhealthy social climate. I refer to the philosophy of modern 'liberalism,' the dominant philosophy of the opposition party." It was the modern liberal, he argued, who fosters permissiveness in the school and the home, who regards discipline and punishment as "barbaric relics of a discredited past," who seeks to eliminate religious sentiment from every aspect of public life, who cares more for the criminal than for his victims, who "frowns on the policeman and fawns on the social psychologist." He went on to link these things with modern economics and sociology—their discovery of poverty and unemployment and the equality of human rights, and their well-intentioned but ill-conceived efforts to do something about them. Up to a point, he too was in favor

---

October 7 (Newark), 9 (ABC-TV network), 10 (Salt Lake City), 13 (Topeka and Milwaukee), 15 (Houston), and 16 (Sioux Falls). Where three dots of elision appear, they do not represent omissions from the text but reproduce the punctuation adopted for these releases. Four dots represent cuts of my own.

of such efforts, but what he opposed was the constant expansion of spending, the planning of new controls, the presence of "a government establishment that is preparing to nationalize our society while paying for it with the fruits of private industry." The failures of internal prudence and candor which he saw connected with these policies, he linked to our foreign affairs and the lack of respect with which America is regarded in the world. "I'm talking about the re-establishment of the dignity of the American people . . . the pride of the individual American."

The element, then, that unified Goldwater's foreign and domestic campaign themes was the argument that domestic demoralization, foreign failures, and the decline in our prestige abroad were together the consequence of a failure of the old virtues and the old moral fiber. In response, he urged a twofold stiffening of the moral backbone: first, "take the bureaucratic shackles off," put "our main reliance on individuals, on hard work, on creativity, investment, and incentive"; then, reassert American power overseas. "*Stop the spread of socialism at home and Communism abroad.*"

The rhetoric of these speeches, so far as they dwell on America's internal condition, resounds with the fundamentalist revolt against the conditions of modernity: the call for "hard work, creativity, investment, and incentive," the emphasis on symptoms of "a sickness in our society," "shattered prestige," the demand for "common purpose . . . moral responsibility for our individual actions," the call for "greatness of soul—to restore inner meaning to every man's life in a time too often rushed, too often obsessed by petty needs and material greeds," the fear of "the erosion of individual worth by a growing Federal bureaucracy." The whole election, Goldwater said in his Prescott speech, was not a question of political personalities, or promises or programs: "It is a choice of what sort of people we want to be."

One of Goldwater's many difficulties was that of opposing an incumbent President at a time of high and sustained prosperity. But this difficulty, seen in a larger context, is only one manifestation of a nagging problem confronting ultraright spokesmen. As they see it, we have been committed for many years, for decades, to economic policies which are wrong morally and wrong as expedients, destructive of enterprise, and dangerous to the fabric of free society. At the same time, every informed person recognizes that we have become much richer doing all these supposedly wrong and unsound things than we were when we had hardly begun to do them. Moreover, the portion of the public that responds to appeals to economic discontent is relatively small, and Goldwater knew that the really significant part of that public—the mass of those not sharing in the general prosperity—was already in Johnson's camp. Goldwater's appeal then, like those of the ultra-right generally, had to be addressed to the kind of discontents that appear in an affluent society, and this he did with unusual self-awareness and clarity. He distinguished between interest politics and status politics, and showed why, from his vantage point, the usual practice of interest politics should be regarded as morally discreditable and vastly inferior to status politics.

These matters were best dealt with in his national television program of October 9. He conceded the realities of American affluence: Gross national product was up—so were wages, housing, savings, automobiles. "Yes, more people have more *things* than ever before." But the same thing was true almost everywhere—in England, France, Germany, Nigeria, Japan, even behind the Iron Curtain. The point was that in the United States other things were also up: crime, juvenile delinquency, divorce, illegitimacy, mental illness, school dropouts, drug addiction, pornography, riots, and hoodlumism. These were the terrifying things with which he proposed to deal, and one could infer from this that his campaign on the moral realities was even more significant than anything he had to say about economic policy.

Here he boldly characterized his entire campaign in words that deserve quotation at length:

> You have probably been reading and hearing about some of the unorthodox things I have been doing.
>
> I have gone into the heart of Appalachia . . . and there I have *deliberately* attacked this administration's phony war on poverty.
>
> I have gone into the heart of Florida's retirement country . . . and there I have *deliberately* warned against the outright hoax of this administration's medicare scheme.

I have gone into the heart of our farm area . . . and there
I have *deliberately* called for the gradual transition from a controlled to a free agriculture.

I have gone into an area of rapid urban growth . . . and
there I have *deliberately* leveled against the Supreme Court the
charge that they have no business attempting to draw the map
of our state legislative districts.

I have done all these things *deliberately* . . . for a reason
that is clear in my own mind . . . and I want to make it clear
to you tonight. *I will not attempt to buy the votes of the American people . . . I will not treat any of you as just so many special interests . . . I will not appeal to you as if you were simply
pocketbooks . . . surrounded on all sides by self-serving concerns.*

And of this I am deeply convinced: The American people
won't sell their votes. They won't *sell* their freedom . . . not
for any cheap political appeals.

Having gone thus far to flout the time-honored methods
of American campaigning, which he charged his opponent exemplified in an egregious way, Goldwater went bravely on to
underline the non-political quality of his own politics:

It's not your partisan approval that I'm seeking tonight:
What I want is your undivided attention. Because I want to
ask you this question . . . *What place does politics have in a
campaign for the Presidency?*

You heard me right: What does *politics* . . . the ward heeler
politics of something for everyone . . . have to do with the
American Presidency?

This speech, and the campaign strategy which it correctly
describes, must surely be classed among the most adventurous
episodes in our recent politics, and it underlines the paradox
that if we are in search of tradition-breakers we are most likely
to find them among the ideological conservatives. Old-line
professionals might shake their heads in dismay at a campaigner
who would appear before the old folks and attack medicare,
criticize TVA in the heart of TVA country, and attack the poverty program in Appalachia, but Goldwater was acting in con-
sonance with his belief that interest politics should not merely
be supplemented by status politics but displaced by it. As he
saw it, the venerable tradition of appealing separately to a variety of special interests in the course of a campaign and then

trying to act as broker among them in the actual process of governing was an ignoble kind of politics, vastly inferior to a politics that would address itself to realizing the religious and moral values of the public and to dealing with "the moral crisis of our time." He wanted, in short, to drive the politics out of politics. Goldwater was taking his stand in the hope that the American people (even though their moral fiber was "beset by rot and decay") would somehow reject the kind of interest-appeals they had always responded to in the past and vote for men who could meet the moral crisis.

A vital difficulty, of course, is that Goldwater was not consistent in this effort to surmount interest politics. There is no record, I believe, of his appearing before the National Association of Manufacturers to urge them to be less solicitous about their tax burdens or of his appearing before segregationist audiences to urge that they move over and make some place for the Negro. The abandonment of interest politics, then, is a rather one-sided affair. One need not question Goldwater's sincerity to see that politics, as he practiced it, would leave certain favored interests free to continue to seek their advancement through political action while encouraging large masses of the people to commit themselves entirely to the more abstract effort to fulfill high moral ideals. Confronted with this kind of political imbalance, most Americans, who do not pretend to be as "conservative" as Goldwater, preferred to stay closer to the wisdom of our ancestors, who believed that under the American system a plurality of interests, vigorously pursued, would end by providing a rough counterpoise to each other, which would be more likely to yield satisfactory results than a general appeal to human virtue.

It is important to be clear as to what we find odd and out-of-pattern in Goldwater's campaign appeals. There is nothing singular in believing that there is a moral crisis in our time, or in saying so in a presidential campaign. There is nothing wrong in suggesting that such problems as juvenile delinquency, drug addiction, or crime in the streets might legitimately be made the objects of national discussion or of action by the federal government. Even the view that the moral fiber of the American people is beset by rot and decay is not peculiar to Barry Goldwater—the same view has been regularly expressed by many American intellectuals. What was substantially out of the American political pattern was the concerted attempt to exploit these difficult problems largely for their divisive content (most people understood what Goldwater was getting at when he complained that American women are not safe on the streets).

It is especially odd that they should have been stressed in a presidential campaign by a man whose whole theory of federal-state relations denied that the federal government can or should intervene in the solution of these "local" problems. It was, in short, the non-programmatic character of Goldwater's approach to these issues that stood out as singular. His main solution to the moral crisis, set forth many times during the campaign, was, to put it charitably, ingenuous: he would re-store "domestic tranquillity," as he said in his Newark speech, first of all "by example at the top," because it was the moral ex-ample of the presidency more than anything else that was really at the root of all the evils. Remove from the White House the bad example of Lyndon B. Johnson and such attendant lords as Bobby Baker, Billie Sol Estes, and Matt McCloskey, and the problems of law enforcement would be relatively simple to solve. The arrogance of the suggestion that Goldwater and Miller, by the purity of their superior moral example, would turn the tide, is only incidental. What is important is the style of thought underlying the suggestion: the moral problems in question—which are in fact the great and pervasive social problems of modern industrial urban life and of mass culture —Goldwater saw largely as problems of "law enforcement," and the key to law enforcement he saw in a stiffening of the moral backbone, and the replacement of a bad example by a good example. We are, in short, to lift ourselves up by our moral bootstraps. The conclusion reached by many of us that the problems are intrinsically difficult, that they involve com-plex economic, sociological, and psychological calculations, is swept away—indeed, it was precisely Goldwater's conception that the inquiring and humane spirit behind modern sociology and psychology has not helped to solve but has produced our difficulties.

The root notion here is what linked Goldwater so closely to the fundamentalist right wing and the more paranoid reaches of the pseudo-conservative mentality: it is the same devil theory of social ills found in all the familiar rhetoric about treason and conspiracy. The devil in 1964 was personified by Lyndon B. Johnson, as in earlier years it had been by Truman, Dewey, Acheson, Marshall, Eisenhower, and the Eastern establishment. Ultimately, as this view of the world has it, our problems are only moral; but more than that: the moral life itself is not complex and difficult and full of trial and confusion, it is basically simple. Is this a caricature? Perhaps, but in his Memphis speech Goldwater asserted: "A lot of my enemies call me simple. The trouble with the so-called liberal today is that he doesn't understand simplicity. The answers to America's problems are simple." For Goldwater this was a heartfelt cry. At Salt Lake City he departed from the prepared text of his address to declare with more fervor than grammar: "Many Americans don't like simple things. That is why they are against we conservatives."

It is against the background of this conception of the world that one can best understand the choice of a Goldwater campaign slogan that rests its appeal on simple intuition: "In your heart you know he's right."

IV

Goldwater's views on foreign policy, which were more damaging to him than his views on domestic affairs, required even more strenuous efforts to undo the existing image of him as a reckless adventurer. In his opening speech at Prescott he used the word "peace" twenty times, and for his foreign-policy slogan he adopted the relatively inoffensive "Peace through strength." Many times during the campaign he reiterated that he did not *want* a general war—an assurance which even his critics should have credited but which it was dangerous for a politician to have to offer—and he frequently emphasized the argument that the Republican party had been the historic peace party rather than his own well-known dissatisfaction with some of its recent peaceful policies.

By the autumn of 1964, however, Goldwater was the prisoner of his previous utterances on foreign affairs. The views he had expressed went far beyond what might be called the "hard line" in the cold war. The hard line, which has always been arguable in theory and which has had some successes in practice, views the imperatives of the cold war as an ineluctable challenge, has encouraged a skeptical view of the limits of negotiation, and has placed its primary trust in ample reserves of strength. The pseudo-conservative line is distinguishable from this not alone in being more crusade-minded and more risk-oriented in its proposed policies but also in its conviction that those who place greater stress on negotiation and accommodation are either engaged in treasonable conspiracy (the Birch Society's view) or are guilty of well-nigh criminal failings in moral and intellectual fiber (Goldwater's).

The characteristic note in Goldwater's damaging pre-1964 statements was a certain robust impatience with negotiation and compromise, a resolution to do away with uncertainty and ambiguity, a readiness to believe that large and complex questions of state could somehow be swept off the board by some sudden and simple gesture of violent decision. It was this state of mind that had led him to declare that a policy of coexistence was wholly impossible, to urge on more than one occasion that we withdraw from the United Nations and break off diplomatic relations with Russia and that we flatly declare ourselves against disarmament, to suggest that nuclear defoliation might be considered as a tactic in Vietnam, and to vote against the test-ban treaty.

It can be argued that occasional indiscretions, which were finally qualified or repudiated, were used unfairly to Goldwater's disadvantage. Far more damaging than such indiscretions, however, was the militant conception of the cold war, never repudiated, but embodied in the argument and the title of Goldwater's book *Why Not Victory?* This book denies systematically and articulately a view of the situation that has gradually come to prevail in Washington and Moscow but not in Peking or Phoenix. The prevailing view assumes that in the thermonuclear age the losses in a general war, because it would destroy the peoples and societies on both sides of the Iron Curtain, are monstrously and unacceptably disproportionate to what could conceivably be gained by the military "victory" of either side; and that therefore both sides must conduct the cold war under restraints, both mutually imposed and self-imposed, and hardly less vital for being experimental and ill defined, which it is hoped will prevent conflict in limited theaters from escalating into a general conflict. What makes men circumspect today is their awareness that "victory" gained in such a conflict would be without meaning.

The hope of the peoples of the West has been that the uncomfortable but bearable equipoise made possible by this view will endure, at least until we have reached some less dangerous modus vivendi. And it was the basic message of Goldwater's philosophy of foreign policy that this hope is self-deceptive and cowardly. As he saw it, we are engaged in a relentless life-or-death struggle which makes coexistence meaningless. "Victory is the key to the whole problem," he wrote, "the only alternative is—obviously—defeat." The struggle against communism he saw not simply as the necessary and tragic burden of our time but as the great imperative of our existence; and there were passages in which he appeared to lament the time we find for other things. ("And yet, we still go about our everyday business, being good neighbors, providing comforts for our families, worshiping God, and stubbornly refusing to admit the enormity of the conspiracy which has been created to destroy us.") He was troubled by the thought that "the free world," frightened by nuclear war and too much influenced by unrealistic intellectuals, "is gradually accepting the notion that anything is better than fighting." "A craven fear of death is entering the American consciousness," he wrote in 1960, "so much so that many recently felt that honoring the chief despot himself was the price to pay to avoid nuclear destruction," and he followed this melancholy observation with a strange one-sentence affirmation of faith: "We want to stay alive, of course; but more than that we want to be free." He was among those, he said disquietingly in *Why Not Victory?*, who believe "that armed conflict *may* not be necessary to defeat communism" —the italics are mine.[23]

Goldwater's approach to the world-wide strategic problems of the United States went far beyond the old isolationism, which, arrogant and chauvinist though it could be, was also infused with a strong spirit of pacifism. To the isolationists, our

---

[23] *Why Not Victory?* (New York, Macfadden ed., 1963), pp. 16, 19, 22; *The Conscience of a Conservative*, pp. 90, 94.

withdrawal from a corrupt world was meant at least to serve the interests of our own peace. Goldwater, though taking a dim view of most kinds of foreign aid, stood for the broadest interpretation of our commitments outside our borders. As he once put it, he stood for neither isolationism nor internationalism but for "a new form of nationalism" which underwrites the resistance of free nations to communism and avows as a national goal a final victory over the Communists.[24] Thus far Goldwater was not remote from the American consensus, but his unyielding and unchanging conception of the cold war represented a breach of the continuity that had on the whole pervaded the administrations of Truman, Eisenhower, and Kennedy. Goldwater looked upon the cold war as a series of relentless confrontations between ourselves and the Communists on various fronts throughout the world. If we maintain superior strength we can emerge victorious from all these confrontations, and in time the whole Communist world (which should be treated uniformly as a bloc, whatever its apparent internal differences) will crack under the stress of repeated defeats. The goal of our policies cannot be limited to peace, security, and the extension of our influence, but must

[24] *Why Not Victory?*, pp. 90–1. It was significant that Goldwater, with a certain show of justice, should have denounced Johnson's acceptance speech to the 1964 Democratic convention as "isolationist" because of its failure to deal with the issues of foreign policy. It is also instructive to compare his views with those of Robert A. Taft, which were much affected by the older isolationism. Taft, while hardly deficient in nationalist enthusiasm, was always much more concerned with the prospect that war would completely destroy democracy, local self-government, and private enterprise in America. To the best of my knowledge, this concern has never been expressed by Goldwater in his significant statements on foreign policy. Taft's views, as they had developed to 1951, are stated in his book *A Foreign Policy for Americans* (New York, 1952); but for an excellent factual survey of his changing positions, see Vernon Van Dyke and Edward Lane Davis: "Senator Taft and American Security," *Journal of Politics*, XIV (May 1952), pp. 177–202.

Although Taft's real fear of war and his understanding of its threat to free enterprise have disappeared from most right-wing thinking, there is also a strong point of continuity: Taft himself was among those Republicans who changed the debate on our foreign policy from an argument over political judgment to an argument over "treason." See Richard Rovere: "What's Happened to Taft?" *Harper's Magazine*, April 1952, pp. 38–44.

go on to ultimate total victory, the ideological and political extermination of the enemy. "Our objective must be the destruction of the enemy as an ideological force possessing the means of power. . . . We will never reconcile ourselves to the Communists' possession of power of any kind in any part of the world."[25] Thus to the pseudo-conservative the ambiguous world in which we have lived for twenty years is reduced to a fleeting illusion; what is ultimately real is total victory or total defeat, and it is this upon which we must insist. There can be no middle ground.[26] We are not merely preserving our own security; we are engaged in an attempt to stamp out an idea, in every corner of the globe, by the force of arms.

The question has been repeatedly raised whether the attempt to press every crisis to a victorious solution, especially with the avowed ultimate aim of the utter ideological extermination of the enemy, might not bring on a general war. But to raise this question is felt by right-wingers to be tainted with an unforgivable lack of manhood. Goldwater's answer was to promise that the Soviets, faced with our superiority in weapons, will never strike. But of course this is a promise on which no American can deliver, and for whose fulfillment we must depend upon Moscow, and ultimately Peking. Moreover, there is a curious passage in *Why Not Victory?* in which Goldwater flatly admitted that such fulfillment is not to be expected. The Communist world, he said, is likely to resort to general war only under one of two conditions. One, of course, is if we invite their attack by political weakness and military disarmament. But the other is "if there is a decisive switch in world affairs to the point where it is obvious they are going to lose."[27] And it is, of course, precisely to this point that Goldwater has always urged that they be pushed. The central dilemma of total victory, as expounded by Goldwater, is thus made to seem more ominous and insoluble than the many perplexing dilemmas of coexistence.

It was his casual view of nuclear warfare, and not his occasional indiscretions, that made Goldwater seem dangerous

[25] *Why Not Victory?*, p. 118.
[26] For Goldwater's objection to the idea that total victory cannot be rendered meaningful in our time, see ibid., pp. 106–9.
[27] Ibid., p. 82.

to many conservative Americans. What had become clear by 1964, and what could not be undone in the campaign, was the public impression that Goldwater's imagination had never confronted the implications of thermonuclear war. For a man who was so gravely distressed by violence in the streets, he seemed strangely casual about the prospect of total destruction. The final spiritual Armageddon of the fundamentalists, their overarching moral melodrama, the dream of millennial crusading and decisive conflict, plainly stirred his mind, but the hard realities of the current world seemed more remote. He could no more recognize that nuclear weaponry had created a new age of diplomacy than he could admit that modern urban industrialism had created a new environment. "I do not subscribe to the theory," he wrote, "that nuclear weapons have changed everything. . . . We have in the nuclear bomb an advance in weaponry, and terrible though that advance is, it still is merely a more efficient means of destruction. In a historical and relative sense, it can be compared with the advance made in military operations by the invention and adaption [*sic*] of gunpowder to war-making and the development of aerial warfare and strategic bombing missions."[28]

As a concession to campaign opportunism, Goldwater sometimes soft-pedaled his approach to the problems of foreign policy, contenting himself mainly with appeals to the restlessness of the people over the inability of the country to resolve its foreign crises or maintain its prestige in the world: "Are you proud of our fight for freedom? Are you proud of Panama? Are you proud of the burned effigy in Greece? Are you proud when no country is too small to pull Uncle Sam's whiskers and get away with it? Are you proud of wheat deals with the destroyers of liberty?" An interesting aspect of this appeal, since it sheds light not simply on the pseudo-conservative mentality but on the dynamics of American politics today, is its resemblance to Kennedy's appeal in the campaign of 1960. Like Goldwater, Kennedy had protested that we were seriously underarmed— and his admirers remember the bogus "missile gap" issue with chagrin. Like Goldwater, Kennedy had stressed the theme that the United States had lost prestige abroad, and dwelled on the

[28]Ibid., pp. 83–4.

establishment of Castro in Cuba only ninety miles from our shores.

Thus the Kennedy and Goldwater campaigns were both vigorously nationalist, appealing to public uneasiness over the indecisiveness of the cold war. That two men so different in outlook should have had this much in common as campaigners underlines the force of a persistent issue that opposition candidates will find it hard to resist. Both campaigns signify the deep perplexity of the American public over our foreign policies. The weakness of the pseudo-conservative appeal is that it strikes at only one side of complex public feelings: it shows an utter lack of tenderness for the pervasive American desire to continue in peace. In its appeal to toughness and frontier hardihood and its call for a fundamentalist all-out struggle with absolute evil, it runs up against both the pacific yearnings and the basic hedonism of the public, for which pseudo-conservatives have an ill-concealed contempt. But the strength of the pseudo-conservative position lies in its appeal to the American bafflement before the ambiguities and compromises in our foreign dealings. The American public pays heavy taxes to maintain an immensely expensive military machine with vast and unprecedented powers of destruction and to sustain military and economic operations around the globe; and yet year by year it finds that its expenditures and efforts yield neither decisive victories nor final settlements. The roll of inconclusive negotiations, sorties, and stalemates, symbolized by the names of Yalta, Korea, Berlin, Cuba, and Vietnam, seems to stretch out indefinitely.

All attempts to explain that this frustrating situation is not simply the product of execrable statecraft—not to speak of treason—run up against a fundamental fact of American history and a basic fixture in the American imagination. Many years ago, in an illuminating essay, D. W. Brogan pointed to a state of mind which he called "the illusion of American omnipotence"—defined as "the illusion that any situation which distresses or endangers the United States can only exist because some Americans have been fools or knaves."[29] The

[29]"The Illusion of American Omnipotence," *Harper's Magazine*, December 1952, pp. 21–8.

best illustration, he suggested, was our response to the Chinese Revolution, toward which Americans had neither historical awe nor historical curiosity, preferring to regard it as no more than a problem in our foreign and domestic policy. The oldest civilization in existence, comprising about a fifth of the human race, situated six thousand miles from the Pacific coast of the United States and having a contiguous frontier with Russia, had taken a turn—presumably for reasons deeply rooted in its history and geography, its traditions and problems—which was understandably very unwelcome to Americans. Instead of concluding that this was a response to massive strategic and economic realities largely beyond our control, millions of Americans were apparently convinced that this enormous country had been in our pocket, and had been lost or stolen only because of the mistakes (or treachery) of Roosevelt, Marshall, and Acheson, mistakes which could easily have been rectified by greater statesmen like Walter Judd or Senator Jenner.[30] Roosevelt was anathematized for having "permitted" Russia to become a Pacific power at Yalta, although Russia had been a Pacific power before the United States existed. It was all too lightly assumed, Brogan prophetically remarked, that Russia had "taken over" China as she had taken over Poland. Moreover, the persistent faith that American intervention could have changed Chinese history was accompanied by the faith that this involved nothing more than the choice of a few sound alternative policies, without demanding of the American people the massive sacrifices necessary to sustain a major commitment in China.

The difficulty many Americans have in understanding that their power in the world is not unlimited—a difficulty shared by no other people—Brogan explained by observing that in one very real sense the Americans had only recently been confronted by a situation long since familiar to the rest of the human race. The trying responsibilities and insoluble problems now confronting the United States were, he remarked, "a new story for the United States but . . . an old one for Europe.

---

[30]Cf. Stormer: "About 600-million Chinese were betrayed into communist slavery. It was all done by a handful of American traitors and their liberal dupes." Op. cit., p. 31.

What the American people are enduring now is what the French, the English, the Russian peoples, even the Spanish and Italian peoples, suffered in the process of extending or trying to retain their empires."

The American frame of mind was created by a long history that encouraged our belief that we have an almost magical capacity to have our way in the world, that the national will can be made entirely effective, as against other peoples, at a relatively small price. We began our existence without world-wide territorial aspirations or responsibilities, but as a continental power with basically continental aspirations. From the beginning of our national life, our power to attain national goals on which we were determined was in effect irresistible —*within* our chosen, limited continental theater of action. Our chief foes—Indians, Mexicans, the decaying Spanish Empire—were on the whole easily vanquished. It is true that in fighting the British in 1812 we became engaged with a vastly greater power, but at a time when the British were in mortal combat with Napoleon and their American effort was a sideshow. Even then, though we did rather badly—our invasions of Canada were repulsed, our capital was burned, and our shipping was bottled up—a curious stroke of luck at New Orleans made it possible for us to imagine that the stalemate peace we concluded represented some kind of victory.[31] The only time the American land was truly ravaged by the horrors of war was during our own Civil War when our wounds were self-inflicted. Europe's quarrels, which in the twentieth century have become an American problem, were during the nineteenth an American advantage. The achievement of independence with national boundaries stretching westward to the Mississippi, the bargain purchase of the enormous territory of Louisiana, the easy acquisition of the Floridas without war, the assertion of our place in the world's carrying trade, the annexation of Texas and the seizure of immense

[31]The smashing victory scored by the Americans under Jackson at New Orleans came only after the terms of peace, in which none of our demands was met, were already signed. The news of New Orleans, however, circulated about the country more or less simultaneously with the news of the peace—a fortunate conjuncture for the American imagination.

western territories from Mexico—all these were accomplished at the cost of troubled, preoccupied, or weak nations, and at a minimum expenditure of our blood and treasure. In our own hemisphere, which was our only center of territorial aspirations, our preponderance tempted Secretary of State Olney to say in 1895: "Today the United States is practically sovereign on this continent and its fiat is law on the subjects to which it confines its interposition." A few years later our entry into the imperial game of the nineteenth century came at the expense of a befuddled and bankrupt Spain, incapable of offering us serious opposition.[32]

While expansion was won so cheaply, the United States, thanks largely to its continental position, was enjoying, as C. Vann Woodward has pointed out, virtually free security—which, he suggests, should be given a place among the great shaping forces of our history alongside the free land of our continental interior.[33] Fenced in behind the Atlantic, Pacific, and Arctic oceans, the United States was in a position to spare itself expensive armies and elaborate chains of fortifications. Even naval protection came cheap, since the navy that policed and defended the Atlantic was maintained, to our considerable benefit, by the British. In 1861, as Woodward points out, the United States maintained the second-largest merchant marine in the world without having a battle fleet—there were only 7,600 men in our navy as compared with over ten times that number in the British navy. A luxurious penury also affected our military establishment. At the outbreak of the Civil War the United States army numbered only a few more than 16,000 men, occupied mainly at posts on the Indian frontier. Even by 1914, when the nation had been launched upon its imperial

[32]Goldwater, who is reported to read a good deal in the history and antiquities of Arizona, but not in world history, had a different version of this: "It was this independence—strong, virile, and unafraid—that led us to challenge a much mightier Spain and call her to her account for her tyranny over our Western Hemispheric neighbors." *Why Not Victory?*, p. 54. This is a delusion not shared by any American historian. Nor was it shared by informed American contemporaries. See my essay "Cuba, the Philippines, and Manifest Destiny," below, esp. p. 637.

[33]"This Age of Reinterpretation," *American Historical Review*, XLVI (October 1960), pp. 2–8.

career and had reorganized its military establishment, the proportion of its military appropriations to national income was only one-fourth of that paid by the British people, about one-sixth of that paid by the French, Japanese, and Germans, and about one-eighth of that paid by the Russians.

Free security, easy expansion, inexpensive victories, decisive triumphs—such was almost our whole experience with the rest of the world down to the twentieth century. The First World War, which we entered triumphantly in its closing phases, gave us a glimpse, but only the glimpse of an outsider, of what the rest of the world endured. It was only after the major effort of the Second World War, when we found ourselves not presiding over a pacified and docile world, but engaged in a world-wide stalemate and a costly and indecisive struggle in Korea, that the American people first experienced the full reality of what all the other great nations have long known—the situation of limited power. The illusion of American omnipotence remained, but the reality of American preponderance was gone. It is this shock to the American consciousness to which Goldwater and others appealed when they cried: "Why not victory?" Why not, indeed, when one remembers all those facile triumphs? In this light it becomes possible to understand how Goldwater thought he could promise unremitting victories in the cold war along with balanced budgets and lower taxes.

"Until 1950," Goldwater wrote in *Why Not Victory?*, "America had never lost a shooting war," but within the next ten years we had suffered "repeated defeats."[34] This situation, in his view, is not to be accounted for by the fact that we now have world-wide aspirations going far beyond our early strategic goals or that our free security is gone because of technological changes; it is not because we are for the first time situated, as many peoples have been before us, in a position of limited power, or because we are counterposed to great and numerous peoples with a nuclear weaponry comparable to our own. It is because we have been ruled by the foolish and the incompetent, and perhaps, as his more ardent admirers boldly proclaim, by the treasonous as well. For those who conceive of history not as a sequence of related events but as a moral

[34]Pp. 23-4.

melodrama, such imputations seem plausible enough. And when one ponders how much the world position of America has changed within the past fifty years, what seems most re-markable is not that many should respond wholeheartedly to the pseudo-conservative interpretation of events, but that our statesmanship has been as restrained as it has usually been and that this restraint has won preponderant public support.

V

The right-wing enthusiasts were justified, I believe, in the ela-tion they expressed, even in defeat, over the Goldwater cam-paign. They had less than nothing to show in practical results, but it is not practical results that they look for. They have demonstrated that the right wing is a formidable force in our politics and have given us reason to think that it is a permanent force. Writing in 1954, at the peak of the McCarthyist period, I suggested that the American right wing could best be under-stood not as a neo-fascist movement girding itself for the con-quest of power but as a persistent and effective minority whose main threat was in its power to create "a political climate in which the rational pursuit of our well-being and safety would become impossible."[35] This still seems to be the true potential of the pseudo-conservative right; it is a potential that can be realized without winning the White House, even without again winning the Republican nomination.

That the right-wingers are actually increasing in numbers is doubtful; but their performance in 1964 shows how much leverage they can achieve, whatever their numbers, with dedi-cation and organization. The tally of over 27 million votes for a candidate of pronounced right-wing views is delusive, but to them it is delusive in a heartening and invigorating way. A post-election poll suggested that at the most generous estimate only about 5.4 million Goldwater voters—or one-fifth of the whole —can be counted as hard-core Goldwater enthusiasts, a find-ing which fits roughly with his standing in the pre-nomination Gallup polls and with those primaries in which he was rated by Republican voters against the whole field of moderate and

[35]See above, p. 555.

liberal candidates.[36] But so long as their zeal and gifts for organization are as powerful as they have been in recent years, the
right-wingers still stand in a position to make themselves effective far out of proportion to their numbers. The professionals
who have already repossessed the party apparatus have not yet
had a final reckoning with its right wing. Moreover, Goldwater's views, though far from predominant among the party's
voters, were much more popular among its activist personnel
—among those who do its hard work and supply its funds and
who won him his delegates at the Cow Palace.

The largest single difficulty facing the right wing as a force
within the Republican party is its inability to rear and sustain
national leaders. Most Republican governors belong to the
party's moderate wing. The roll call of the right wing's senatorial heroes is a list of the dead or the departed: Taft, McCarthy,
Knowland, Bricker, Bridges, Jenner, and now Goldwater—and
today not a single right-wing senator remains who is both secure in his seat and well known to the public. Although this is a
serious liability in practical politics, it is less serious in the arena
which the right wing regards as most important, the arena of
"conservative education." At the level of party leadership, the
right-wingers do well. In many parts of the country the most
ardent Republicans are ultra-conservative. Often they are the
heads of small businesses or independent professionals who
can find the time and spend the money to make their views
felt. Moderate Republicans are more likely to be officers or
employees of large corporations whose positions leave them
less time for partisan activity. Hence the party in some sections
of the country has gravitated into the hands of a leadership that

[36] *The New York Times*, December 18, 1964; cf. the pre-election polls and primaries at various stages in the nomination fight, reported in Novak: op. cit.,
pp. 263, 325, 326, 332, 375, 379, 380, 389, 396. Louis H. Bean and Roscoe
Drummond, however, estimate that only 2.5 to 3 million of Goldwater's votes
were those of true believers and that the rest was simply a Republican party
vote. They arrive at this estimate partly by measuring the proportion of Republicans who preferred Goldwater in polls to other Republicans against the total
number of declared Republicans. They have checked this against his actual
performance at the polls, as compared with more typical Republican candidates in the past. See "How Many Votes Does Goldwater Own?" *Look*, March
23, 1965, pp. 75–6.

is considerably more conservative than its voters. The great middle band of the party, which is by far its largest portion, is conservative enough to be susceptible to some of the right-wing notions, even though it does not share the partisan rage and the conspiratorial suspicions of the Goldwaterites.

In the battle for public opinion, the right wing has ample funds at its disposal, and certain advantages that accrue from its rough-and-tumble tactics. The conservative label and the nationalist animus of the far right are handsome advantages: it can wrap itself in the symbols of respectability and Americanism, and yet it has no inhibitions about gaining what it can through intimidation, which it brings to bear with great effectiveness upon schoolteachers and school administrators, librarians, advertisers in the press and mass media, local merchants, and working politicians. It gets a bad press in the sophisticated national media which it so ardently resents, but the journalists and intellectuals in the cosmopolitan centers readily forget how frightening right-wing pressures can be in smaller communities.

Even the seemingly permanent minority position of the Republican party, which in one sense sets a limit to the operations of the far right, is in another sense one of its assets. Over the years the number of American voters who identify themselves in polls as Republicans has shrunk proportionately to a point at which it is now only half as large as the number of Democrats —a situation reflected quite precisely in the present ratio between the two parties in Congress. The Democratic party, with its broad centrist position, has come to embrace so large a part of the American political consensus that moderate Republican leaders find it all but impossible to discover a constructive issue upon which they can forge an independent identity and relieve themselves of the onus of "me-tooism" with which the right wing, on the whole quite correctly, charges them. The very destruction that Goldwater has wreaked within the party has its compensations for the right-wingers. It is true that this immediately cost them the control of the party; but so long as the party continues in its present helpless minority position, the possibility remains that, even without a repetition of the Goldwater takeover, the right-wingers can prevent the moderates from refurbishing the party as a constructive opposition.

But, above all, the far right has become a permanent force in the political order because the things upon which it feeds are also permanent: the chronic and ineluctable frustrations of our foreign policy, the opposition to the movement for racial equality, the discontents that come with affluence, the fevers of the culturally alienated who practice what Fritz Stern has called in another connection "the politics of cultural despair." As a movement, ironically enough, the far right flourishes to a striking degree on what it has learned from the radicals. Their forces, as men like Fred C. Schwarz and Stephen Shadegg have urged, have been bolshevized—staffed with small, quietly efficient cadres of zealots who on short notice can whip up a show of political strength greatly disproportionate to their numbers. The movement now uses the techniques it has taken from the radicals while it spends the money it gets from the conservatives. Finally, it moves in the uninhibited mental world of those who neither have nor expect to win responsibility. Its opponents, as men who carry the burdens of government, are always vulnerable to the discontents aroused by the manifold failures of our society. But the right-wingers, who are willing to gamble with the future, enjoy the wide-ranging freedom of the agitational mind, with its paranoid suspicions, its impossible demands, and its millennial dreams of total victory.

PART II

SOME PROBLEMS
OF THE MODERN ERA

Cuba, the Philippines, and Manifest Destiny

This essay, now considerably revised, was originally written in 1951 as one of a series of fourteen lectures given by various writers at Bennington College and published in 1952 under the editorship of Daniel Aaron in *America in Crisis*. Each of the lecturers undertook to analyze a focal episode in the development of the American public consciousness, in the hope that a common exploration of such episodes would shed some light on the American manner of responding to crises.

My assignment was to analyze the decision made when our entry into and retention of the Philippine Islands after the war with Spain caused the nation to turn from its traditional continental policies and launch itself on a course of world imperialism. What were the issues, what were the consequences for the national mentality, when a democratic country, committed by its creed and its very origins to self-government and self-determination, was confronted with the prospect of taking by conquest distant territory inhabited by an alien and all but unknown people?

The more one looked at it, the clearer it became that the debate set off by the issue of "imperialism" from 1898 to 1900 could not be considered apart from the entire crisis in foreign policy that came with the Spanish-American War. The most striking thing about that war was that it originated not in imperialist ambition but in popular humanitarianism. It started with our desire to free Cuba and ended with our domination over the Philippines. The war was not begun with the intention of taking either Cuba or the Philippines. The Teller Resolution, appended to the declaration of war and adopted without debate, expressly disclaimed any American intention to acquire Cuba, and its promise was kept. As for the Philippines, occupation was never at any time the subject of public discussion or interest, or even of concern among the ruling elites. Before the outbreak of the war no one would have dared to propose the conquest and retention of these islands as an object of national policy. Except for a few naval strategists concerned with a strike at the Spanish navy there, no one thought about the Philippines at all, and Dewey's sudden victory in Manila Bay confronted even policy-makers with an unexpected decision. Little wonder that the people themselves were quickly persuaded that "destiny" had imposed upon them a new and unwelcome duty: destiny or no, they had been confronted with a *fait accompli*.

Yet it was true that the sudden fact of overseas conquest was absorbed by American opinion leaders and by the public itself without extraordinary anguish and by some with enthusiasm. The humanitarian impulse behind the war was strangely coupled with a taste for battle; similarly the imperialist impulse that led to ready acceptance of annexation was also coupled with and softened by much talk of duty and responsibility, which in fact foreshadowed later American policies in the Philippines. Both the humane feelings and the urge to combat and conquest seem to stem from a prevalent state of mind that had come into being in the 1890's, and the primary concern of my essay turned out to be not so much the easily won argument over keeping the islands as the relationship between an observable crisis in the national consciousness and the events of the war. Some readers have been disposed to see in this an attempt to offer a psychological alternative to an economic interpretation of the origins of American imperialism. I consider it less psychological than institutional; less an alternative than a necessary supplement to any economic interpretation that is to avoid running aground on certain stubborn facts. The general depression of the 1890's, the widespread anxieties and discontents of the era, clearly had important bearings on questions of war and empire, and must be seen as major instrumentalities of history.

Two important full-scale studies of the roots of American imperialism have appeared since the original version of this essay was written. Neither is entirely in accord with my analysis, but there is common ground on some points. Walter La Feber, in *The New Empire*, emphasizes—I believe quite rightly—how long and purposeful a preparation the imperialism of the 1890's had, and he looks upon expansion as a response to the industrial revolution of the latter half of the nineteenth century. He stresses the demand for new markets, the propaganda of navalists and expansionists, the creation of the new navy—all of which were well-developed trends before the crisis of the 1890's. He also remarks, however, that "the depression of 1893 acted as the catalyst to these developments of a half century," and it is precisely this catalytic process with which I am concerned. Ernest R. May, whose views of the age likewise differ from mine in significant respects, concurs in finding the source of the war in a crisis of the national consciousness. "The nation," he writes of the 1890's in his *Imperial Democracy*, "was in a state of upset"; and after enumerating some of the sources of this upset, he concludes: "In some irrational way, all these influences and anxieties translated themselves into concern for suffering Cuba. For the people as for the government, war with monarchical, Catholic, Latin Spain had no purpose except to relieve emotion." Whatever else may be said about it, the entire episode is indeed an instructive case study in the dynamics of national emotion.

I

THE TAKING of the Philippine Islands from Spain in 1899 marked a major historical departure for the American people, a breach in their traditions and a shock to their established values. To be sure, from their national beginnings they had constantly engaged in expansion, but almost entirely into contiguous territory. Now they were extending themselves to distant extra-hemispheric colonies. They were abandoning a strategy of defense hitherto limited to the continent and its appurtenances, in favor of a major strategic commitment in the Far East. Thus far their expansion had been confined to the spread of a relatively homogeneous population into territories planned from the beginning to develop self-government; now control was to be imposed by force on millions of ethnic aliens. The acquisition of the islands, therefore, was understood by contemporaries on both sides of the debate, as it is readily understood today, to be a turning point in our history.

To discuss the debate in isolation from other events, however, would be to deprive it of its full significance. America's entrance into the Philippine Islands was a by-product of the Spanish-American War. The Philippine crisis is inseparable from the war crisis, and the war crisis itself is inseparable from a larger constellation that might be called "the psychic crisis of the 1890's."

Central in the background of the psychic crisis was the great depression that broke in 1893 and was still very acute when the agitation over the war in Cuba began. Severe depression, by itself, does not always generate an emotional crisis as intense as that of the nineties. In the 1870's the country had been swept by a depression of comparable acuteness and duration which, however, did not give rise to all the phenomena that appeared in the 1890's or to very many of them with comparable intensity and impact. It is often said that the 1890's, unlike the 1870's, form a "watershed" in American history. The difference between the emotional and intellectual impact of these two depressions can be measured, I believe, not by the difference in severity, but rather by reference to a number of singular events that in the 1890's converged with the depression to heighten its impact upon the public mind.

First in importance was the Populist movement, the free-silver agitation, the heated campaign of 1896. For the first time in our history a depression had created a protest movement strong enough to capture a major party and raise the spec-ter, however unreal, of drastic social convulsion. Second was the maturation and bureaucratization of American business, the completion of its essential industrial plant, and the devel-opment of trusts on a scale sufficient to stir the anxiety that the old order of competitive opportunities was approaching an eclipse. Third, and of immense symbolic importance, was the apparent filling up of the continent and the disappearance of the frontier line. We now know how much land had not yet been taken up and how great were the remaining possibil-ities for internal expansion both in business and on the land; but to the mind of the 1890's it seemed that the resource that had engaged the energies of the people for three centuries had been used up. The frightening possibility suggested itself that a serious juncture in the nation's history had come. As Frederick Jackson Turner expressed it in his famous paper of 1893: "Now, four centuries from the discovery of America, at the end of one hundred years of life under the Constitution, the frontier has gone, and with its going has closed the first period of American history."

To middle-class citizens who had been brought up to think in terms of the nineteenth-century order, the outlook seemed grim. Farmers in the staple-growing region had gone mad over silver and Bryan; workers were stirring in bloody struggles like the Homestead and Pullman strikes; the supply of new land seemed at an end; the trust threatened the spirit of business enterprise; civic corruption was at a high point in the large cities; great waves of seemingly unassimilable immigrants ar-rived yearly and settled in hideous slums. To many historically conscious writers, the nation appeared overripe, like an empire ready for collapse through a stroke from outside or through internal upheaval. Acute as the situation was for all those who lived by the symbols of national power—for the governing and thinking classes—it was especially poignant for young people, who would have to make their careers in the dark world that seemed to be emerging.

The symptomatology of the crisis would record several tendencies in popular thought and behavior that had previously existed only in pale and tenuous form. These symptoms were manifest in two quite different moods. The key to one of them was an intensification of protest and humanitarian reform. Populism, utopianism, the rise of the Christian Social gospel, the growing intellectual interest in socialism, the social settlement movement that appealed so strongly to the college generation of the nineties, the quickening of protest and social criticism in the realistic novel—all these are expressions of this mood. The other mood was one of national self-assertion, aggression, expansion. The motif of the first was social sympathy; of the second, national power. During the 1890's far more patriotic groups were founded than in any other decade of our history; the naval theories of Captain Mahan were gaining in influence; naval construction was booming; there was an immense quickening of the American cult of Napoleon and a vogue of the virile and martial writings of Rudyard Kipling; young Theodore Roosevelt became the exemplar of the vigorous, masterful, out-of-doors man; the revival of European imperialism stirred speculation over what America's place would be in the world of renewed colonial rivalries, and in some stirred a demand to get into the imperial race to avoid the risk of being overwhelmed by other powers. But most significant was the rising tide of jingoism, a matter of constant comment among observers of American life during the decade.

Jingoism, of course, was not new in American history. But during the 1870's and 1880's the American public had been notably quiescent about foreign relations. There had been expansionist statesmen, but they had been blocked by popular apathy, and our statecraft had been restrained.[1] Grant had

[1]See Julius W. Pratt: *America's Colonial Experiment* (New York, 1950), pp. 4–13.

failed dismally in his attempt to acquire Santo Domingo; our policy toward troubled Hawaii had been cautious; in 1877 an offer of two Haitian naval harbors had been spurned. In responding to Haiti, Secretary of State Frelinghuysen had remarked that "the policy of this Government . . . has tended toward avoidance of possessions disconnected from the main continent."[2] Henry Cabot Lodge, in his life of George Washington published in 1889, observed that foreign relations then filled "but a slight place in American politics, and excite generally only a languid interest."[3] Within a few years this comment would have seemed absurd. In 1895, Russell A. Alger reported to Lodge, after reading one of Lodge's own articles to a Cincinnati audience, that he was convinced by the response that foreign policy, "more than anything else, touches the public pulse of today."[4] The history of the 1890's is the history of public agitation over expansionist issues and of quarrels with other nations.

II

Three primary incidents fired American jingoism between the spring of 1891 and the close of 1895. First came Secretary of State Blaine's tart and provocative reply to the Italian minister's protest over the lynching of eleven Italians in New Orleans. Then there was friction with Chile over a riot in Valparaíso in

---

[2] Albert K. Weinberg: *Manifest Destiny* (Baltimore, 1935), p. 252. There is a suggestive similarity to the conditions of the nineties in the circumstances attending the Cuban insurrection of 1868–78. The hostilities were even more bitter and exhausting than those of 1895–8; its latter phases also corresponded with an acute depression in the United States; the case of the *Virginius* offered a pretext for war almost as satisfactory as that of the *Maine*. The public and the press raised a clamor about it. But it did not rise even near to the pitch of overwhelming pressure for war. Several things were supplied in the nineties that were missing in the seventies: among them a psychic crisis that generated an expansionist mood; the techniques of yellow journalism; and an adequate navy that made a war with Spain possible to contemplate. Cf. Samuel Flagg Bemis: *A Diplomatic History of the United States* (New York, 1936), pp. 433–5. In the seventies the country was also too close to the completion of an exhausting internal war of its own.

[3] Samuel Flagg Bemis: op. cit., p. 432.

[4] Walter La Feber: *The New Empire* (Ithaca, 1963), p. 250.

which two American sailors were killed and several injured by a Chilean mob. In 1895 occurred the more famous Venezuela boundary dispute with Britain. Discussion of these incidents would take us too far afield, but note that they all had these characteristics in common: in none of them was national security or the natural interest vitally and immediately involved; in all three American diplomacy was extraordinarily and disproportionately aggressive; in all three the possibility of war was contemplated; and in each case the response of the American public and press was enthusiastically nationalist and almost unanimous.

It is hard to read the history of these events without concluding that politicians were persistently using jingoism to restore their prestige, mend their party fences, and divert the public mind from grave internal discontents. It hardly seems an accident that jingoism and populism rose together. Documentary evidence for the political exploitation of foreign crises is not overwhelmingly abundant, in part because such a motive is not necessarily conscious and where it is conscious it is not always confessed or recorded.[5] The persistence of jingoism in every administration from Harrison's to Theodore Roosevelt's, however, is too suggestive to be ignored. During the nineties the press of each party was fond of accusing the other of exploiting foreign conflict. Blaine was not above twisting the British lion's tail for political purposes; and it is hardly likely that he would have exempted Italy from the same treatment.

---

[5]The most notable case in our earlier history was Seward's fantastic proposal during the crisis of 1861 that Lincoln attempt to reunite the North and South by precipitating a foreign war. A classic expression of the philosophy of this kind of statecraft was made by Fisher Ames in 1802, after the Federalists had been routed by the Jeffersonians. "We need as all nations do," he wrote to Rufus King, "the compression on the outside of our circle of a formidable neighbor, whose presence shall at all times excite stronger fears than demagogues can inspire the people with towards their government." Henry Jones Ford: *The Rise and Growth of American Politics* (New York, 1914), p. 69. One of the signal differences between the 1870's and the 1890's was that there was still a usable domestic enemy in the earlier period. "Our strong ground," wrote Rutherford B. Hayes in 1876, "is a dread of a solid South, rebel rule, etc., etc. . . . It leads people away from 'hard times' which is our deadliest foe." J. F. Rhodes: *History of the United States* (New York, 1906), VII, 220.

Harrison, on the eve of the Chile affair, for the acuteness of which he was primarily responsible, was being urged by prominent Republican politicians who had the coming presidential campaign in mind to pursue a more aggressive foreign policy because it would "have the . . . effect of diverting attention from stagnant political discussions."[6] And although some Democratic papers charged that he was planning to run for re-election during hostilities so that he could use the "don't swap horses in the middle of the stream" appeal, many Democrats felt that it was politically necessary for them to back him against Chile so that, as one of their congressmen remarked, the Republicans could not "run away with all the capital there is to be made in an attempt to assert national self-respect."[7]

Grover Cleveland was a man of exceptional integrity whose stand against pressure for the annexation of Hawaii during 1893–4 does him much credit. But precisely for this act of restraint he was accused by Republican jingoes like Lodge and by many in his own party of being indifferent to America's position in the world. And if Cleveland was too high-minded a man to exploit a needless foreign crisis, his Secretary of State, Richard Olney, was not. The Venezuela affair, which came at a low point in the prestige of Cleveland's administration, offered Olney a rich chance to prove to critics in both parties that the administration was, after all, capable of vigorous diplomacy. That the crisis might have partisan value was not unthinkable to members of Olney's party. He received a letter from a Texas congressman encouraging him to "go ahead," on the ground that the Venezuela issue was a "winner" in every section of the country. "When you come to diagnose the country's internal ills," his correspondent continued, "the possibilities of 'blood and iron' loom up immediately. Why, Mr. Secretary, just think

[6]Donald M. Dozer: "Benjamin Harrison and the Presidential Campaign of 1892," *American Historical Review*, LIV (October 1948), p. 52; A. T. Volwiler: "Harrison, Blaine, and American Foreign Policy, 1889–1893," American Philosophical Society *Proceedings*, Vol. LXXIX (1938), argues plausibly that the imperial mood dawned during Harrison's administration.
[7]Earl W. Fornell: "Historical Antecedents of the Chilean-American Crisis of 1891–92," unpublished M.A. thesis, Columbia University (1950), p. 138; see especially Chs. 11 and 12, for Harrison's exploitation of the war crisis and the intense public reaction.

of how angry the anarchistic, socialistic, and populistic boil appears on our political surface and who knows how deep its roots extend or ramify? One cannon shot across the bow of a British boat in defense of this principle will knock more *pus* out of it than would suffice to inoculate and corrupt our people for the next two centuries."[8]

This pattern had been well established when the Cuban crisis broke out anew in 1895. It was quite in keeping that Secretary Olney should get a letter during the 1896 campaign from Fitzhugh Lee, the American consul in Havana, advising that the conservative faction of Gold Democrats become identified with the strong policy of mediation or intervention in Cuba. Thus, he argued, "the 'Sound Democrats' would get, with the Executive, the credit of stopping the wholesale atrocities daily practised here, the acquisition of Cuba by purchase, or by fighting a successful war, if war there be. In the latter case, the enthusiasm, the applications for service, the employment of many of the unemployed, might do much towards directing the minds of the people from imaginary ills, the relief of which is erroneously supposed to be reached by 'Free Silver.'"[9]

When President McKinley took office he was well aware that nationalist enthusiasm had reached a pitch that made war very likely. A few months earlier, he had told Senator Lodge that he might be "obliged" to go to war as soon as he entered the presidency, and had expressed a preference that the Cuban crisis be settled one way or another in the time between his election and inauguration. Although he had promised Carl Schurz that there would be "no jingo nonsense under my administration," he proved not to have quite enough strength to resist the current. He did not himself partake of the hysteria that was mounting throughout the country, and he was

[8]Alfred Vagts: *Deutschland und die Vereinigten Staaten in der Weltpolitik* (New York, 1935), I, 511; for the domestic roots of administration policy, see Nelson M. Blake: "Background of Cleveland's Venezuela Policy," *American Historical Review*, XLVII (January 1942), 259–77. For a different view, see La Feber: op. cit., pp. 279–83. La Feber considers domestic pressures of minor consequence, and believes that Cleveland and Olney saw important long-range American interests at stake in Venezuela.

[9]Vagts: op. cit., II, 1266 n. Cf. Ernest R. May: *Imperial Democracy* (New York, 1961), pp. 75–6.

concerned that the country was unprepared to wage a war, uncertain even whether war could be confined to a contest with Spain. He soon found himself under incredible pressures for positive action, which he resisted as long as most Presidents would have been able to do. His failure was not in yielding too soon to the war fever but in not taking early initiative to rein it in. Sending the *Maine* to Havana proved to be one of his most vital mistakes, since it gave a hostage to the war party. The act was meant in part to curb the enthusiasm of the jingoes at home, but Cleveland had resisted just such a proposal on the grounds that an inflammatory incident was all too likely. No doubt the actual sinking of the *Maine* on February 16 went even beyond anything that Cleveland or McKinley could have anticipated. From that time onward, the chances of avoiding war seemed slim.

Members of McKinley's own party put a great deal of pressure on him to give the people their war rather than endanger the Republican position. Some of them feared, as an infuriated senator put it to the Secretary of State, that Congress would declare war in spite of him. "He'll get run over and the party with him."[10] For McKinley himself the prospect that Congress might act without him was, by March, a very real fear.[11] It was widely argued that if war was inevitable, as presumably it was, it would be better for the President to lead rather than to be pushed; that resistance to war would be ruinous to the party; that going to war would prevent the Democrats from entering the next presidential campaign with "Free Cuba" and "Free Silver" as their battle cries.[12] After Senator Proctor's moving speech in the Senate on March 17 about conditions in Cuba, the Chicago *Times-Herald*, a McKinley paper, declared that intervention in Cuba, peaceful or forcible, was "immediately inevitable. Our own internal political conditions will not permit

[10] H. Wayne Morgan: *William McKinley and His America* (Syracuse, 1963), p. 370.

[11] Ibid., pp. 369–70.

[12] Vagts: op. cit., II, 1308 n; Samuel Flagg Bemis: *The Latin American Policy of the United States* (New York, 1943), p. 407; Thomas A. Bailey: *A Diplomatic History of the American People* (New York, 1944), pp. 506–8; C. S. Olcott: *The Life of William McKinley* (Boston, 1916), II, 28.

its postponement. . . . Let President McKinley hesitate to rise to the just expectations of the American people, and who can doubt that 'war for Cuban liberty' will be the crown of thorns that Free Silver Democrats and Populists will adopt at the election this fall. . . . The President would be powerless to stay any legislation, however ruinous to every sober, honest interest of the country."[13] "The people want no disgraceful negotiations with Spain," cried the Chicago *Tribune*. "Should the president plunge his administration into that morass, he and his party would be swept out of power in 1900 by a fine burst of popular indignation. An administration which stains the national honor never will be forgiven."[14] Reporting to McKinley on sentiment in Massachusetts, Henry Cabot Lodge wrote in March: "If the war in Cuba drags on through the summer with nothing done, we shall go down in the greatest defeat ever known. . . . I know that it is easily and properly said that to bring on or even to threaten war for political reasons is a crime & I quite agree. But to sacrifice a great party & bring free silver upon the country for a wrong policy is hardly less odious."[15]

In the facing of mounting pressure for war, McKinley was unable to sustain his negotiations with Spain long enough to exhaust the possibilities of a diplomatic solution. By the beginning of April some important demands had been conceded —an end to the *reconcentrado* policy and reparations for the *Maine*. But it is doubtful that a diplomatic solution could have been arrived at, since both the Cuban revolutionaries and the United States were insisting upon full Cuban independence, leaving no face-saving formula for the Spanish government. In the opening days of April, McKinley resolved upon war. On April 10, as he was about to send Congress his war message, word came from his ambassador in Spain, Stewart L. Woodford, that the Spaniards had yielded to the American demand for a prompt armistice, and Woodford also thought, rather optimistically, that even the demand for independence might still be met. This news McKinley incorporated anticlimactically at

[13] Walter Millis: *The Martial Spirit* (New York, 1931), p. 124.
[14] Morgan: op. cit., p. 368.
[15] May: op. cit., p. 146.

the end of the war message, thus passing up his chance for one final statesmanlike act, an appeal for further delay. That such a step could have avoided war, however, is doubtful. Americans seemed to want not merely the freedom of Cuba but a war for the freedom of Cuba. The Spanish government, insofar as it confronted the realities at all, seemed to think that it was preferable to lose the island "honorably," as the consequence of a war, than to back down. McKinley was caught between the aggressive irrationality of his own people and the decadent irrationality of the ancient Latin power.

Historians often say that the war was brought on by sensational newspapers. The press, spurred by the rivalry between Pulitzer and Hearst, aroused sympathy with the Cubans and hatred of Spain and catered to the bellicosity of the public. No one seems to have asked: *Why was the public so fatally receptive to war propaganda?* I believe the answer must be sought in the causes of the jingoism that had raged for seven years before the war actually broke out. The events of the nineties had brought frustration and anxiety to civically conscious Americans. On one hand, as Mark Sullivan has commented, the American during this period was disposed "to see himself as an underdog in economic situations and controversies in his own country";[16] but the civic frustrations of the era created also a restless aggressiveness, a desire to be assured that the power and vitality of the nation were not waning. The capacity for sympathy and the need for power existed side by side. That highly typical American, William Allen White, recalls in his *Autobiography* how during the nineties he was "bound to my idols— Whitman, the great democrat, and Kipling, the imperialist."[17] In varying degrees the democrat and the imperialist existed in the hearts of White's countrymen—the democrat disposed to free Cuba; the imperialist, to vent his spleen on Spain.

I suspect that the readiness of the public to overreact to the Cuban situation can be understood in part through the displacement of feelings of sympathy or social protest generated in domestic affairs; these impulses found a safe and satisfactory discharge in foreign conflict. Spain was portrayed in the press

[16] Mark Sullivan: *Our Times* (New York, 1926), p. 137.
[17] William Allen White: *Autobiography* (New York, 1946), p. 195.

as waging a heartless and inhuman war; the Cubans were portrayed as noble victims of Spanish tyranny, their situation as analogous to that of Americans in 1776.[18] When one examines the sectional and political elements that were most enthusiastic about policies that led to war, one finds them not primarily among the wealthy eastern big-business Republicans who gave McKinley his strongest support and read the dignified conservative newspapers, but in the Bryan sections of the country, in the Democratic party, among western Republicans, and among the readers of the yellow journals.[19] A great many businessmen were known to fear the effects of a war on the prosperity that was just returning, and some thought that a war might strengthen the free-silver movement. During the controversy significant charges were hurled back and forth: conservative peace advocates claimed that many jingoists were hoping for a costly war over Cuba that could be made the occasion of

[18]On the role of the press, see J. E. Wisan: *The Cuban Crisis as Reflected in the New York Press* (New York, 1934); and M. M. Wilkerson: *Public Opinion and the Spanish-American War* (Baton Rouge, 1932). On the evolution of human-interest journalism, see Helen M. Hughes: *News and the Human Interest Story* (Chicago, 1940); and the same author's "Human Interest Stories and Democracy," *Public Opinion Quarterly*, I (April 1937), 73–83.

[19]Wisan (op. cit., p. 445) notes: "It was no mere accident that most of the leading proponents of intervention in Congress represented southern and western states where populism and silver were strongest." Cf. pp. 125–6, 283, 301. A resolution of May 20, 1897, in favor of granting belligerent rights to the Cubans was passed by the Senate, 41–14, with 33 senators not voting. The yeas came from 19 Democrats, 2 Populists, 3 maverick Republicans, and 17 regular Republicans. The nays came from 12 Republicans and 2 Democrats. The 17 Republican votes for recognition broke down as follows: 10 west of the Mississippi, 2 South, 3 Midwest, 2 New England. A New York *Journal* poll of the House in December 1897, on the question of recognizing Cuban belligerency, showed: for, 40 Republicans, 117 Democrats, and 27 Populists, total 184; against, 165 Republicans, 5 Democrats, and 2 Populists, total 172 (Wisan: p. 359); cf. Julius W. Pratt: *Expansionists of 1898* (Baltimore, 1936), pp. 224, 234–6, 242–3. It is noteworthy that dominant sentiment in the labor movement favored recognition of Cuban belligerency from an early date, and that Cleveland's conservative policy was considered to be another instance of the "coldness" toward the underdog that was held to characterize his labor policies. Cf. John C. Appel: "The Relationship of American Labor to United States Imperialism, 1895–1905," unpublished Ph.D. thesis, University of Wisconsin (1950), Ch. 2. Cf. Ernest May: op. cit., pp. 81–2.

a return to free silver; in reply, the inflammatory press often fell into the pattern of Populist rhetoric, declaiming, for example, about "the eminently respectable porcine citizens who —for dollars in the money-grubbing sty, support 'conservative' newspapers and consider the starvation of . . . inoffensive men, women and children, and the murder of 250 American sailors . . . of less importance than a fall of two points in a price of stocks."[20] As Margaret Leech has remarked, peace "had become a symbol of obedience to avarice."[21] In the case of some of the war enthusiasts it is not clear whether they favored action more because they bled for the sufferings of the Cubans or because they hated the materialism and the flaccid pacifism of the *haute bourgeoisie.* Theodore Roosevelt, who was not in the habit of brooding over the wrongs done to the underdog in the United States, expressed some of this when he cried at Mark Hanna: "We will have this war for the freedom of Cuba in spite of the timidity of the commercial interests."[22]

Although imputations of base motives were made by both sides, it is also significant that the current of sympathy and agitation ran strong where a discontented constituency, chagrined at Bryan's defeat, was most numerous. An opportunity to discharge hatred of "Wall Street interests" that were coolly indifferent to the fate of both Cuban *insurrectos* and staple farmers may have been more important than the more rationalized and abstract linkage between war and free silver.[23] The primary significance of this war in the psychic economy of the 1890's was that it served as an outlet for expressing aggressive impulses while presenting itself, quite truthfully, as an idealistic and humanitarian crusade. It had the advantage of expressing in one issue both the hostilities and the generous moral passions of the public. The American public on the whole showed

[20] Wisan: op. cit., p. 394.
[21] Margaret Leech: *In the Days of McKinley* (New York, 1959), p. 179.
[22] H. F. Pringle: *Theodore Roosevelt* (New York, 1931), p. 179.
[23] To say this is not to say that the war "originated" among southern and western farmers, a point on which I have been misunderstood. (Cf. May: op. cit., pp. 75, 145.) The clamor for intervention and war was clearly nation-wide, urban as well as rural. My proposition is that it was much stronger among those who were otherwise discontented than among those who were well off. The agrarians, being particularly discontented, are merely a test case for one side of this proposition, just as the reluctant big-business interests are for the other.

little interest in such material gains as might accrue from an intervention in Cuba. It never dreamed that the war would lead to the taking of the Philippines, of whose existence it was hardly aware. Starting a war for a high-minded and altruistic purpose and then transmuting it into a war for annexation was unimaginable. That would be, as McKinley put it in a phrase that later came back to haunt him, "criminal aggression."

William James, who deplored the war fever from the beginning, correctly diagnosed the popular mood when he wrote to a friend in France: "The basis of it all is, or rather was, perfectly honest humanitarianism, and an absolutely disinterested desire on the part of our people to set the Cubans free. . . . Congress was entirely mad, supposing that the people was in the same condition, as it probably was, in less degree. . . . War . . . was the only possible discharge. We were winning the most extraordinary diplomatic victories, but they were of no use. We were ready (as we supposed) for war and nothing but war must come." Although he reiterated that the American disclaimer of desire for conquest was "*absolutely* sincere" he also shrewdly predicted that once the excitement of military action was aroused, "the ambition and sense of mastery which our nation has will set up new demands," and he accurately forecast that although we would never annex Cuba we might take Puerto Rico and the Philippines.[24]

One might add that inhibitions against going to war were not so strong as they would have been if a major power had been involved. Spain, hardly a formidable foe in a war whose main strategic object was in the Caribbean, had been described by the press as weak, bankrupt, degenerate, and friendless, and her military incompetence was demonstrated by the events in Cuba itself. As T.R. put it to Lodge: "I do not think a war with Spain would be serious enough to cause much strain on this country." Lodge himself had a shrewder estimation than many timid financiers of the bearing of war on the currency question. "If we should have a war," he wrote in March 1898, "we will not hear much of the currency question in the elections."[25]

[24] Ralph Barton Perry: *The Thought and Character of William James* (Boston, 1935), II, 307; William James: *Letters* (Boston, 1935), II, 73–4.
[25] H. C. Lodge (ed.): *Selections from the Correspondence of Theodore Roosevelt and Henry Cabot Lodge* (New York, 1925), I, 243; Morgan: op. cit., p. 369.

III

There is one odd paradox in the evolution of sentiment from a war over freeing Cuba to a peace treaty ratifying the acquisition of the Philippines by conquest. The big-business-conservative-Republican-McKinley element, which was overwhelmingly hostile to this romantic and sentimental war, quickly became interested in the imperialism that grew out of it.[26] The popular Populist-Democratic-Bryanite element, which had been so keen for the war, became the stronghold—although by no means resolute or unbroken—of opposition to the fruits of war. This much, however, must be said of both the populace and the business community: if the matter had been left either to public clamor or to business interests, there would have been no American entrance into the Philippines in 1898.

The dynamic element in the movement for imperialism was a small group of politicians, intellectuals, and publicists, including Senator Henry Cabot Lodge, Theodore Roosevelt, John Hay, Senator Albert J. Beveridge, Whitelaw Reid, editor of the New York *Tribune*, Albert Shaw, editor of the *American Review of Reviews*, Walter Hines Page, editor of the *Atlantic Monthly*, and Henry and Brooks Adams.

Most of these men came from what are known as good families. They were well educated, cultivated, patrician in outlook, of Anglo-Saxon stock, and conservative reformers in politics whose personal goals and standards were non-commercial. Although living in a commercial world, they could not accept business standards for their own careers or become absorbed into the business community. Although they lived in a vulgar democracy, they were not democratic by instinct. They could not and did not care to succeed in politics of the corrupt sort that had become so common in America. They had tried their hands at civic reform, had found it futile, and had become bored with it. When they did not, like Henry Adams, turn away from American life in despair, they became interested in some large and statesmanlike theater of action, broader than American domestic policy. Although there were men of this sort in

[26]Pratt: *Expansionists of 1898*, Ch. 7, has a classic treatment of the business attitude.

the Democratic ranks, like Walter Hines Page, they were most influential within the Republican party, which had become committed to a policy of aggressive commercial diplomacy.[27]

In general, this group of imperialists was inspired by the navalist theories of Mahan and by the practical example of what they on occasion called Mother England. They saw that a new phase of imperialism had opened in the Western world at large, and they were fearful that if the United States did not adopt a policy of expansion and preparation for military and naval struggle, it would be left behind in what they referred to as the struggle for life or the march of the nations. They were much concerned that the United States expand its army and particularly its navy; that it dig an isthmian canal; that it acquire the naval bases and colonies in the Caribbean and the Pacific necessary to protect such a canal; that it annex Hawaii and Samoa. At their most aggressive they also called for the annexation of Canada and the expulsion of European powers from the Western Hemisphere. They were much interested in the Far East as a new theater of political conflict and of possibilities for investment. They were, indeed, more interested than business itself in the Pacific area, particularly in China, as a potential market. As Julius W. Pratt has observed: "The need of American business for colonial markets and fields for investment was discovered not by business men but by historians and other intellectuals, by journalists and politicians."[28]

The central figure in this group was Theodore Roosevelt, who more than any other single man was responsible for our entry into the Philippines. Throughout the 1890's Roosevelt had been eager for a war, whether it be with Chile, Spain, or England. A war with Spain, he thought, would get us "a proper navy and a good system of coast defenses," would free Cuba from Spain, would help to free America from European

---

[27] The best account of the little imperialist elite is in Matthew Josephson: *The President Makers* (New York, 1940), Chs. 1–3; See also Pratt: *Expansionists of 1898*, and Vagts: op. cit., Vol. II, passim.

[28] Pratt: *Expansionists of 1898*, p. 22; for a succinct statement of the outlook of Republican expansionists, see Henry Cabot Lodge: "Our Blundering Foreign Policy," *The Forum*, XIX (March 1895), 8–17; for Mahan's position, see A. T. Mahan: *The Interest of America in Sea Power* (New York, 1898).

domination, would give "our people . . . something to think of that isn't material gain," and would try "both the army and navy in actual practice." Roosevelt feared that the United States would grow heedless of its defense, take insufficient care to develop its power, and become "an easy prey for any people which still retained those most valuable of all qualities, the soldierly virtues." "All the great masterful races have been fighting races," he argued. There were higher virtues than those of peace and material comfort. "No triumph of peace is quite so great as the supreme triumphs of war."[29] Such was the philosophy of the man who obtained for Commodore Dewey his appointment to the Far Eastern Squadron and alerted him before the actual outbreak of hostilities to be prepared to proceed from Hong Kong to engage the Spanish fleet at Manila. These orders were confirmed by McKinley two months later, shortly after war was actually declared.

Our first step into the Philippines presented itself to us as a "defensive" measure. Dewey's attack on the Spanish fleet in Manila Bay was made on the assumption that the Spanish fleet, if unmolested, might cross the Pacific and bombard the west coast cities of the United States. I do not know whether American officialdom was aware that this fleet was so decrepit that it could hardly have gasped its way across the ocean. Next, Dewey's fleet in Manila Bay seemed in danger unless its security were underwritten by the dispatch of American troops to Manila. To be sure, having accomplished his mission, Dewey could have removed this "danger" simply by leaving Manila Bay—and McKinley once remarked to H. H. Kohlsaat that "If Old Dewey had just sailed away when he smashed that Spanish fleet, what a lot of trouble he would have saved us!" However, in war one is always disposed to hold whatever gains have been made, and at Dewey's request American troops were dispatched very promptly after the victory and arrived at Manila in July 1898.

Thus our second step into the Philippines was again a "defensive" measure. The third step was the so-called "capture" of Manila, which was actually carried out in co-operation with the Spaniards, who were allowed to make a token resistance, and in

[29]See Roosevelt: *Works* (New York, 1925), XIV, 182–99; Pringle: op. cit., Ch. 13.

exclusion of the Filipino patriots under Aguinaldo. The fourth step was an agreement, incorporated in the protocol suspending hostilities between the United States and Spain, that the United States would occupy the city, bay, and harbor of Manila pending a final settlement in the peace treaty. The fifth step came much later, on December 21, 1898, when McKinley instructed the War Department to extend the military government already in force at Manila to the entire archipelago. This set off a fierce revolt by the Filipino patriots, who felt that they had been led to expect a much different policy from the American government. Two days before the vote was taken in the Senate on the ratification of the peace treaty, the patriots and the American forces fought their first battle and American soldiers were killed, a fact that seems to have had an important influence on public discussion. Once again, administrative action had given a sharp bias to the whole process of political decision. Tyler Dennett goes so far as to say that by authorizing a campaign of conquest while the Senate was still discussing the issue, McKinley "created a situation . . . which had the effect of coercing the Senate."[30] This is a doubtful conclusion,[31] but there is some reason to believe that the hand of the expansionists was strengthened by the feeling that opposition to the administration's policy would be unpatriotic.

By the time our policy toward the Philippines could be affected by public discussion a great deal had already been accomplished by the annexationists. The argument was already weighted toward staying in simply because we were there. As McKinley put it: "It is not a question of keeping the islands of the East, but of leaving them."[32] It is not an easy thing to persuade a people or a government, at a high pitch of war enthusiasm, to abandon a supposed gain already in hand. Moreover, a great social interest hitherto indifferent to the Philippines, the

---

[30]Tyler Dennett: *Americans in Eastern Asia* (New York, 1922), p. 631.

[31]W. Stull Holt: *Treaties Defeated by the Senate* (Baltimore, 1933), pp. 170–1, concludes that the struggle in the Philippines had no important effects on the debate; see, however, José S. Reyes: *Legislative History of America's Economic Policy toward the Philippines* (New York, 1923), pp. 33–4; cf. Lodge: op. cit., p. 391; and Morgan: op. cit., pp. 421–2.

[32]*Speeches and Addresses of William McKinley from March 1, 1897, to May 30, 1900* (New York, 1900), p. 174.

business community, quickly swung around to an expansionist position. Business began to talk about the Philippines as a possible gateway to the markets of eastern Asia, the potentialities of which were thought to be very large.[33] The Protestant clergy, seeing a possible enlargement of missionary opportunities, also threw in its weight. For the first time the group of imperialists and navalists had powerful allies. Its members took heart and, with the help of navy officers, put increasing pressure upon a rather hesitant administration to follow through.

There seemed four possible ways of disposing of the Philippine problem. The first, returning the islands to Spain, found favor nowhere. The second, selling or otherwise alienating the Philippines to some other power, seemed to invite a general European war; and it would hardly be more justified morally than remaining in possession ourselves. Moreover, we were being encouraged by England to remain in the Philippines, for American possession of those islands was much more palatable to England than possession by any other power. The third possibility, leaving the Philippines to themselves and giving them the independence Aguinaldo's men had been fighting for, was equivalent in the minds of most Americans to leaving them to anarchy or to conquest. It also seemed to be another way of encouraging a scramble among other powers interested in the Far East—flinging, as McKinley put it, "a golden apple of discord among the rival powers."[34] The final possibility was American possession, in the form of a protectorate or otherwise. In the beginning there was much sentiment for merely retaining a naval base and coaling station on the island of Luzon, or perhaps the island of Luzon itself. Second thoughts suggested, however, that such a base would be endangered if the rest of the islands were left open to possible occupation by other nations. The dynamics of the situation suggested an all-or-none policy, and the administration drifted rapidly toward annexation of the entire archipelago. "I didn't want the Philippine Islands," McKinley said in retrospect, "and in the protocol to the treaty I left myself free not to take them; but—in the end there was no alternative."[35] The sincerity of his own doubts

[33]Pratt: *Expansionists of 1898*, pp. 233, 261–78.
[34]Morgan: op. cit., p. 403.
[35]Jacob Gould Schurman: *Philippine Affairs* (New York, 1902), pp. 1–2.

about annexation may be measured by the fact that it took him all of five months to decide that we should take not merely a part but the entire archipelago.

IV

Previously the American public had not been either informed about or interested in the Philippines. In the entire eighty-year period from 1818 through May 1898, only thirty-five articles about the islands had appeared in American magazines.[36] At the moment of Dewey's victory, the press, although given over to encouraging the public jubilation, did not show an immediate interest in taking the islands. However, such sentiment grew with remarkable rapidity. As early as July 1898, the *Literary Digest* noted that the leading Republican papers were pro-expansion. A sample of 65 newspapers taken by the magazine *Public Opinion* in August showed that 43 per cent were for permanent retention of the Philippines, 24.6 per cent were opposed, and 32.4 per cent were wavering. In this case, "wavering" usually meant formerly opposed to expansion but apparently changing views. By December 1898, when the vital debate in the Senate was beginning, the New York *Herald* polled 498 newspapers on the subject of expansion and found that 305, or 61.3 per cent, were favorable. New England and the Middle States showed clear margins in favor of expansion, the West an overwhelming margin. The South alone, by a thin margin, was opposed. The state of press opinion does not *measure* public feeling, but probably does indicate the direction in which public opinion was moving.[37]

[36]A. A. Greenberg: "Public Opinion and the Acquisition of the Philippine Islands," unpublished M.A. thesis, Yale University (1937), pp. 2, 18. What is most impressive is the absence of any conscious commitment of the public to the imperial idea before the outbreak of war. Referring to the failure of proposals of Hawaiian annexation, T.R. wrote as late as January 13, 1898, that he was "a good deal disheartened at the queer lack of imperial instinct that our people show." W. A. Russ, Jr.: *The Hawaiian Republic* (Selinsgrove, Pa., 1961), p. 219.
[37]For the development of press opinion, see surveys cited in *Literary Digest*, XVII (July 1898), 32 ff. (September 10, 1898), 307–8; and, *Public Opinion*, XXV (August 4, 1898), 132–5 (December 29, 1898), 810.

To President McKinley, a benign and far from aggressive man, public sentiment was of great importance, and he studied press opinion assiduously. He was not a man to lead the American people in a direction in which their sympathies were not already clearly bent. There was a current joke: "Why is McKinley's mind like a bed? Because it has to be made up for him every time he wants to use it." However unjust to the President, this does characterize his response to public opinion. He was not by temperament an expansionist, but if his immediate advisers and the public at large were preponderantly for annexation, he was willing to go along, and was thoroughly capable of finding good reasons for doing so. During the fall of 1898 he left Washington for a tour of the West, and made a great many brief speeches sounding out public opinion on annexation of the Philippines, on which he seems to have tentatively been determined in his own mind. He was warmly received and his references to expansion met with an enthusiastic response. Evidently his intent was confirmed by this exposure to public opinion and also by advices concerning the state of the public mind from correspondents and advisers. When he returned to Washington those who were opposed to expansion found him unmovable.[38] The Peace Commission negotiating the treaty in Paris was instructed to ask for all the Philippine Islands, and this provision was included in the peace treaty signed on December 10, 1898.

The debate over the retention of the Philippines then went through two phases. During the first, which lasted from December 1898 to the second week in February 1899, the question was argued both in the Senate and in the forums of public opinion.[39] This phase neared its end when, on February 6, the Senate narrowly voted to ratify the peace treaty; it was definitively closed on February 14, when a resolution sponsored by

[38]Greenberg: op. cit., pp. 84–6. "None of us," said Secretary of the Interior Cornelius Bliss, "have been able to move him since he returned from the west"; Morgan: op. cit., p. 408.

[39]For the debate in the Senate, see *Congressional Record*, 55th Cong., 3rd sess., passim; Reyes: op. cit., Ch. 2; Holt: op. cit., Ch. 8; Marion Mills Miller: *Great Debates in American History* (New York, 1913), III, 245–324; Pratt: *Expansionists of 1898*, pp. 345–60.

Senator Bacon of Georgia, calling for early Philippine independence, was rejected by the preciously narrow margin of one
vote—the vote of the Vice-President, which resolved a 29–29
tie. The second phase of the debate extended throughout 1899
and 1900, when American policy toward the Philippines was a
matter of general public discussion and a partisan issue in the
presidential campaign of 1900.

Who was for and who against annexation? In large measure
it was a party issue. The New York *Herald* poll showed that of
241 Republican papers 84.2 per cent were for expansion, and
of 174 Democratic papers 71.3 per cent were against expansion.
In some degree it was also a young man's movement. Geographically it extended throughout all sections of the country,
and seems to have been predominant everywhere but in the
South, although even there it was strong. We do not have a
clear index of public opinion for the period, but the practical
politicians, whose business it was to gauge public sentiment
in the best way they knew, concluded that the preponderant
feeling was overwhelmingly for annexation.[40]

The debate over the acquisition of the Philippines was perhaps no more than a ceremonial assertion of the values of both
sides. The real decisions were made in the office of Theodore
Roosevelt, in the Senate cloakroom, in the sanctums of those
naval officers from whom the McKinley administration got its
primary information about the Philippines during its period of
doubt over annexation, and, by McKinley's own testimony, in
the privacy of his chambers late at night. The public was, by
and large, faced with a *fait accompli* that, although theoretically
reversible, had the initial impetus of its very existence to carry
it along. The intensity of the public discussion, at any rate,
showed that the conscience of at least some Americans had
really been shocked. No type of argument was neglected on
either side. Those who wanted to take the Philippines pointed
to the potential markets of the East, the White Man's Burden,
the struggle for existence, "racial" destiny, American traditions
of expansion, the dangers of a general war if the Philippines
were left open to a European scramble, the almost parental

[40]For impressive evidence on this point, see Greenberg: op. cit., pp. 35, 42–3,
46–7, 49–50, 60, 67–9, 71, 86.

duty of assuming responsibility for the allegedly childlike Filipinos, the incapacity of the Filipinos for self-government. The
anti-imperialists based their essential appeal on political principle. They pointed out that the United States had come into
existence pledged to the idea that man should not be governed
without his consent. They suggested that the violation of these
political traditions (under which the nation had prospered)
was not only a gross injustice to others, of which we should
feel deeply ashamed, but also a way of tempting Providence
and risking degeneration and disintegration as a sort of punishment for the atrophy of one's own principles. They pointed
also to the expense of overseas dominions, standing armies,
and navalism, and the danger of being embroiled in imperialist
wars, and argued that it would be unwise to try to absorb peoples who were racially incapable of self-government.

Many leading anti-imperialists were men of great distinction;
their ranks included by far the greater part of the eminent figures of the literary and intellectual world. Most of them were,
however, in the unfortunate position of opposing the fruits
of a war that they had either favored or failed to oppose. Unlike the expansionists, they did not have complete control of a
major party (there were more expansionists among the Democrats than there were anti-expansionists among the Republicans). They were hopelessly heterogeneous: Gold Democrats,
Bryan Democrats, New England–conscience Republicans, and
a scattering of reformers and intellectuals.[41]

[41]On the anti-imperialist movement, see Fred H. Harrington: "The Anti-
Imperialist Movement in the United States, 1898–1900," *Mississippi Valley
Historical Review*, XXII (September 1935), 211–30. On the intellectual class
and anti-imperialism, see the same author's "Literary Aspects of American
Anti-Imperialism, 1898–1902," *New England Quarterly*, X (December 1937),
650–67; William Gibson: "Mark Twain and Howells: Anti-Imperialists," *New
England Quarterly*, XX (December 1947), 435–70. Christopher Lasch has
pointed out that the anti-imperialist argument, North and South, was almost
universally based on racist premises; "The Anti-Imperialists, The Philippines,
and the Inequality of Man," *Journal of Southern History*, XXIV (August 1958),
319–31.

They organized late—the Anti-Imperialist League grew up in the months after November 1898—and their political leadership, however ardent in sentiment, pursued a hesitant and uncertain course. Their most eminent political leaders were chiefly old men, and the anti-imperialist movement seems to have had its strongest appeal among the old, high-principled elements in the country, while the imagination of the young was fired far more by the rhetoric of expansionism.[42] It seems clear that the main chance of this minority was to use its position in the Senate to deny the necessary two-thirds approval to the peace treaty by which the islands would be acquired from Spain. Here the opponents of annexation might have delayed it long enough to give themselves a chance to reach the public. But William Jennings Bryan, for reasons that are not altogether clear, persuaded enough members of his party to vote for the treaty to lose the case. Bryan hoped to continue the fight, of course, and grant independence later, but over his conduct and his explanations there hangs a heavy sense of inevitable defeat, stemming from his recognition that the voice of the majority demanded the bold and aggressive policy.[43]

[42]Harrington points out that the average age of the prominent Republican members of the Anti-Imperialist League was 71.1 years; that of the forty-one vice-presidents of the League, 58.3. By contrast, the average age of fourteen leaders of expansionism in 1898 was 51.2. The American consul in London, William M. Osborne, wrote to McKinley: "If what I hear and what I read is true there is a tremendous party growing up for expansion of territory, *especially by the younger and more active elements in the country*." (Italics added.) Quoted by Greenberg: op. cit., pp. 46–7.

[43]Bryan argued that the treaty should be ratified because "a victory won against the treaty would prove only temporary if the people really favor a colonial policy," and because the opponents of the treaty, if they won, "would be compelled to assume responsibility for the continuance of war conditions and for the risks which always attend negotiations with a hostile nation." A minority, he argued, could not permanently thwart annexation. His policy was to appeal to the voters in the election of 1900; but it is impossible to make a presidential election a clear referendum on foreign policy. Bryan found, during the campaign of 1900, that anti-imperialism was not a strong talking point. Cf. Bryan: *The Second Battle* (Chicago, 1900), pp. 126–8; *Bryan on Imperialism* (Chicago, 1900), p. 16. On the election, see Thomas A. Bailey: "Was the Presidential Election of 1900 a Mandate on Imperialism?" *Mississippi Valley Historical Review*, XXIV (June 1937), 43 ff.

V

In the arguments for annexation two essential moral and psychological themes appeared over and over again. These themes were expressed in the words Duty and Destiny. According to the first, to reject annexation of the Philippines would be to fail of fulfilling a solemn obligation. According to the second, annexation of the Philippines in particular and expansion generally were inevitable and irresistible.

The people had entered the war for what they felt to be purely altruistic and humanitarian reasons—the relief and liberation of the Cubans. The idea that territorial gains should arise out of this pure-hearted war of liberation, and the fact that before long the Americans stood in the same relation to the Filipinos as the Spaniards had stood to the Cubans, was most uncomfortable. This situation raised moral questions that the anti-imperialists did not neglect to express and exploit. The imperialists were accused of breaking our national word, of violating the pledge made by McKinley himself that by our moral code forcible annexation would be "criminal aggression." They were also accused of violating the solemn injunctions of the Founding Fathers, particularly the principles of the Declaration of Independence. The rhetoric of Duty was a reassuring answer to this attempt to stir feelings of guilt.

The quick victories won by American arms strengthened the psychological position of the imperialists. The feeling that one may be guilty of wrongdoing can be heightened when the questionable act is followed by adversity.[44] Conversely, it may be minimized by the successful execution of a venture. Misfortune is construed as Providential punishment; but success, as in the Calvinist scheme, is taken as an outward sign of an inward state of grace. One of the most conspicuous things about the war was the remarkable successes achieved by American arms, of which the most astonishing was Dewey's destruction, without losing a single American life, of the entire Spanish Eastern Fleet in Manila Bay. Victories of this sort could readily be interpreted as Providential signs, tokens of divine approval. It was

[44]Cf. Sigmund Freud: *Civilization and Its Discontents* (London, 1930), pp. 110–11.

widely reported in the United States that this was Dewey's own interpretation. "If I were a religious man, and I hope I am," he said, "I should say that the hand of God was in it."[45] This was precisely the sort of reassurance that was needed. "The magnificent fleets of Spain," declared a writer in a Baptist periodical, referring to Spain's senile and decrepit navy, "have gone down as marvelously, I had almost said, as miraculously, as the walls of Jericho went down." The victory, said an editor of the *Christian and Missionary Alliance*, "read almost like the stories of the ancient battles of the Lord in the times of Joshua, David, and Jehosophat."

Furthermore, what might have seemed a sin became transformed into a positive obligation, a duty. The feeling was: *Providence has been so indulgent to us, by giving us so richly of success, that we would be sinful if we did not accept the responsibility it has asked us to assume.* The Protestant clergy, as guardians of the national conscience, did not hesitate to make lavish use of such arguments. "To give to the world the life more abundant both for here and hereafter," reasoned a writer in the *Baptist Missionary Review*, "is the duty of the American people by virtue of the call of God. This call is very plain. The hand of God in history has ever been plain." "If God has brought us to the parting of the ways," insisted a writer in the *Churchman*, "we cannot hold back without rejecting divine leadership."[46] The rhetoric of secular leaders was hardly less inspired. "We will not renounce our part in the mission of our race, trustees under God, of the civilization of the world," said Senator Albert J. Beveridge. "God has not been preparing the English-speaking and Teutonic peoples for a thousand years for nothing but vain and idle self-contemplation and self-admiration. No! He has made us the master organizers of the world to establish system where chaos reigns. He has made us adepts in government that we may administer government among savages and senile peoples."[47]

[45]Louis A. Coolidge: *An Old-Fashioned Senator: Orville H. Platt* (New York, 1910), p. 302.

[46]The quotations are from Pratt: *Expansionists of 1898*, pp. 289–90, 294, 305.

[47]Claude G. Bowers: *Beveridge and the Progressive Era* (New York, 1932), p. 121.

THE PARANOID STYLE

The theme of Destiny was a corollary of the theme of Duty. Repeatedly it was declared that expansion was the result of a "cosmic tendency," that "destiny always arrives," that it was in the "inexorable logic of events," and so on. The doctrine that expansion was inevitable had of course long been familiar to Americans; we all know how often Manifest Destiny was invoked throughout the nineteenth century. Albert Weinberg has pointed out, however, that this expression took on a new meaning in the nineties. Previously destiny had meant primarily that American expansion, *when we willed it*, could not be resisted *by others* who might wish to stand in our way. During the nineties it came to mean that expansion "could not be resisted by Americans themselves, caught, willing or unwilling," in the coils of fate.[48] A certain reluctance on our part was implied. This was not quite so much what we *wanted* to do; it was what we *had* to do. Our aggression was implicitly defined as compulsory—the product not of our own wills but of objective necessity (or the will of God).

"Duty," said President McKinley, "determines destiny." While Duty meant that we had a moral obligation, Destiny meant that we would certainly fulfill it, that the capacity to fulfill it was inherent in us. Ours had been a continuous history of expansion; it had always succeeded before, therefore it was certain to succeed in the future. Expansion was a national and "racial" inheritance, a deep and irresistible inner necessity. Here was a plausible traditionalist answer to the accusation of a grave breach of tradition.

It is not surprising that the public should have found some truth in this concept of inevitable destiny, for the acts that first involved their country with the fate of the Philippines were willed and carried out by others and were made objects of public discussion and decision only *after* the most important commitments had been made. The public will was not freely exercised upon the question, and for the citizens at large, who were in the presence of forces they could not understand or control, the rhetoric of Destiny may have been a

[48]Weinberg: *Manifest Destiny*, p. 254. Appropriately enough, as Weinberg shows (p. 279), when independence was at last granted to the Philippines, it was portrayed not as an act of "destiny" but as an act of "our own free will."

way of softening and ennobling the *fait accompli* with which they were presented. But what of the men whose wills were really effective in the matter? If we examine their case, we find that the manufacturers of inevitability believed deeply in their own product. Indeed, while the extent to which the idea of Destiny was generally accepted is unknown, its wide prevalence among influential politicians, editors, and publicists is beyond argument. When Senator Lodge wrote to Theodore Roosevelt in 1898 that "the whole policy of annexation is growing rapidly under the irresistible pressure of events," when President McKinley remarked in private to his secretary, concerning the taking of Hawaii, "It is manifest destiny," when he declared in his private instructions to the peace commissioners that "the march of events rules and overrules human action"—what was involved was not an attempt to sell an idea to the public but a mode of communication in which the insiders felt thoroughly at home; perhaps a magical mode of thought by which they quieted their own uncertainties. It is easy to say, from the perspective of the twentieth century, that where contemporaries heard the voice of God we think we can discern the carnal larynx of Theodore Roosevelt. But if the insiders themselves imagined that they heard the voice of God, we must be careful of imputing hypocrisy. It is significant that the idea of Destiny was effective even among people who had very grave doubts about the desirability of remaining in the Philippines. Secretary of the Navy John D. Long, who was affectionately regarded by Theodore Roosevelt as an old fuddy-duddy on this score, confided to a friend in 1898 that he would really have preferred the United States to remain what it had been during the first half of the nineteenth century—"provincial," as he expressed it, and "dominated by the New England idea. But," he added, "I cannot shut my eyes to the march of events—a march which seems to be beyond human control."[49]

It would be false to give the impression that only high moral and metaphysical concepts were employed in the imperialist argument. Talk about entry into the markets of Asia was heard often after Dewey's victory; but even those who talked about material gains showed a conspicuous and symptomatic inability

[49]Greenberg: op. cit., p. 89.

to distinguish between interests, rights, and duties. Charles Denby, former minister to China and a member of McKinley's commission to study the Philippines, contributed to *The Forum* two interesting articles full of this confusion. The central business of diplomacy, confessed Denby, was to advance commerce. Our right to hold the Philippines was the right of conquerors. So far, Mr. Denby was all *Realpolitik*. But, he continued, he favored keeping the islands because he could not conceive any alternative to doing so except seizing territory in China, and he did not want to oppress further "the helpless Government and people of China"! Thus a rather odd scruple crept in; but Mr. Denby quickly explained that this was simply because China's strength and prosperity were in America's interest. "We are after markets," he went on, sliding back into *Realpolitik*, "and along with these markets"—sliding back into morality—"will go our beneficent institutions; and humanity will bless us." In a second article Mr. Denby shuttled back to "the cold, hard practical question. . . . Will the possession of these islands benefit us as a nation? If it will not, set them free tomorrow, and let their people, if they please, cut each other's throats." And yet, Mr. Denby made it clear, we did come as benefactors, bringing to our cut-throat friends "the choicest gifts—liberty and hope and happiness."[50]

There was, besides the oscillatory rhetoric of Mr. Denby, a "let's be candid" school, whose views were expressed by the Washington *Post*: "All this talk about benevolent assimilation; all this hypocritical pretense of anxiety for the moral, social, and intellectual exaltation of the natives . . . deceives nobody, avails nothing. . . . We all know, down in our hearts, that these islands . . . are important to us only in the ratio of their practical possibilities, and by no other. . . . Why not be honest?"[51]

There were others who found the primary benefit of our new imperial status in the social cohesion and military spirit that would result when the energies of the country were deflected

[50]Charles Denby: "Shall We Keep the Philippines?" *Forum*, XXVI (October 1898), 279–80; "Why the Treaty Should Be Ratified," ibid., XXVI (February 1899), 644, 647.
[51]Quoted in Grayson L. Kirk: *Philippine Independence* (New York, 1936), p. 25.

from internal to external conflict. "Marse" Henry Watterson, the well-known editor of the Louisville *Courier-Journal*, told a New York reporter: "From a nation of shopkeepers we become a nation of warriors. We escape the menace and peril of socialism and agrarianism, as England has escaped them, by a policy of colonization and conquest. From a provincial huddle of petty sovereignties held together by a rope of sand we rise to the dignity and prowess of an imperial republic incomparably greater than Rome. It is true that we exchange domestic dangers for foreign dangers; but in every direction we multiply the opportunities of the people. We risk Caesarism, certainly; but even Caesarism is preferable to anarchism. We risk wars; but a man has but one time to die, and either in peace or war, he is not likely to die until his time comes. . . . In short, *anything is better than the pace we were going before these present forces were started into life*. Already the young manhood of the country is a goodly brand snatched from the burning, and given a perspective replete with noble deeds and elevating ideas."[52]

Probably the most remarkable statement of the meaning of the war and the whole imperial adventure for American thinking was written by Walter Hines Page in the *Atlantic Monthly* not long after the battle of Manila. Page thought the American people would face graver problems after the war than they had experienced in the preceding years. "A change in our national policy may change our very character," he said, "and we are now playing with the great forces that may shape the future of the world—almost before we know it." Up to then, the nation had been going about the prosaic business of peace, a commercial nation absorbed in problems of finance and administration. Now it had come face to face with the sort of problems connected with the management of world empires, and its isolation was at an end. "Shall we be content with peaceful industry, or does there yet lurk in us the adventurous spirit of our Anglo-Saxon forefathers? And have we come to a time when, no more great enterprises awaiting us at home, we shall be tempted to seek them abroad?"

His own conviction was clear. The Americans had sprung from "a race that for a thousand years has done the adventurous

---

[52] *Literary Digest*, XVII (July 2, 1898), 214; italics added.

and outdoor tasks of the world." Stemming from the English, themselves explorers, conquerors, and founders of states, the Americans had always been engaged with great practical enterprises—fighting Indians, clearing forests, building a new government, extending territory, developing wealth, settling the great issues connected with slavery and the Civil War. These had been "as great enterprises and as exciting, coming in rapid succession, as any race of men has ever had to engage it." The old outdoor spirit of the Anglo-Saxon had thus had wide scope in recent experience.

"But now a generation has come to manhood that has had no part in any great adventure." The chief tasks of domestic politics, like civil service and the reform of the currency and of municipal government, had not been exciting to the imagination, and our politics had been attractive only to petty brigands and second-rate men. In literature too we had fallen into decline. In fact, the three books which had found the most readers and most affected the masses were books of utopian social programs and fantastic philosophy—*Progress and Poverty*, *Looking Backward*, and *Coin's Financial School*. The proliferation of movements for petty social reforms, "societies for the prevention of minor vices and for the encouragement of minor virtues," denoted a lack of adventurous opportunities. It was quite possible that a life of quiet had grown irksome, that it was not "natural" to us. "Is it true that with a thousand years of adventure behind us we are unable to endure a life of occupations that do not feed the imagination?" Perhaps we were still the same old colonizing and fighting race of Anglo-Saxons at heart. "Before we knew the meaning of foreign possessions in a world ever growing more jealous, we have found ourselves the captors of islands in both great oceans; and from our home-staying policy of yesterday we are brought face to face with world-wide forces in Asia as well as in Europe, which seem to be working, by the opening of the Orient, for one of the greatest changes in human history. . . . And to nobody has the change come more unexpectedly than to ourselves. Has it come without our knowing the meaning of it?"[53]

[53] Walter Hines Page: "The War with Spain, and After," *Atlantic Monthly*, LXXXI (June, 1898), pp. 721–7, esp. pp. 725–7.

VI

Since Julius W. Pratt published his *Expansionists of 1898* in 1936, it has been obvious that any interpretation of America's entry upon the paths of imperialism in the nineties in terms of rational economic motives would not fit the facts, and that a historian who approached the event with preconceptions no more supple than those, say, of Lenin's *Imperialism* would be helpless. This is not to say that markets and investments have no bearing; they do, but there are features of the situation that they do not explain at all. Insofar as the economic factor was important, it can be better studied by looking at the relation between the depression, the public mood, and the political system.

The alternative explanation has been the equally simple idea that the war was a newspapers' war. This notion, once again, has some point, but it certainly does not explain the war itself, much less its expansionist result. The New Deal period, when the political successes of F.D.R. were won in the face of overwhelming newspaper opposition, showed that the press is not powerful enough to impose upon the public mind a totally uncongenial view of public events. It must operate roughly within the framework of public predispositions. Moreover, not all the papers of the nineties were yellow journals. We must inquire into the structure of journalistic power and also into the views of the owners and editors to find out what differentiated the sensational editors and publishers from those of the conservative press.

There is still another qualification that must be placed upon the role of the press: the press itself, whatever it can do with opinion, does not have the power to precipitate opinion into action. That is something that takes place within the *political* process, and we cannot tell that part of the story without examining the state of party rivalries, the origin and goals of the political elites, and indeed the entire political context. We must, then, supplement our story about the role of the newspapers with at least two other factors: the state of the public temper upon which the newspapers worked, and the manner in which party rivalries deflected domestic clashes into foreign aggression. Here a perennial problem of politics under the competitive two-party system became manifest again in the 1890's. When there is, for whatever reason, a strong current of jingoism running in the channels of public sentiment, party competition tends to speed it along. If the party in power is behaving circumspectly, the opposition tends to beat the drums. For example, in 1896, with Cleveland still in office, the Republican platform was much more exigent on the Cuba issue. When McKinley came into office and began to show reluctance to push toward intervention, the Democratic party became a center of interventionist pressure; this pressure was promptly supplemented by a large number of Republicans who, quite aside from their agreement on the issue, were concerned about its effect on the fate of their party.

When we examine the public temper, we find that the depression, together with such other events as the approaching completion of the settlement of the continent, the growth of trusts, and the intensification of internal social conflict, had brought to large numbers of people intense frustrations in their economic lives and their careers. To others they had brought anxiety that a period of stagnation in national wealth and power had set in. The restlessness of the discontented classes had been heightened by the defeat of Bryan in 1896. The anxieties about the nation's position had been increased among statesmen and publicists by the revival of world imperialism, in particular by the feeling that America was threatened by Germany, Russia, and Japan. The expansionist statesmen themselves were drawn largely from a restless upper-middle-class elite that had been fighting an unrewarding battle for conservative reform in domestic politics and looking with some eagerness toward a more spacious field of action.

Men often respond to frustration with acts of aggression, and allay their anxieties by threatening acts against others. It is revealing that the underdog forces in American society showed a considerably higher responsiveness to the idea of war with Spain than the groups that were satisfied with their economic or political positions. Our entry into the Philippines then aroused the interest of conservative groups that had been indifferent to the quixotism of freeing Cuba but were alert to the possibility of capturing new markets. Imperialism appealed to members of both the business and the political elites as an enlargement of the sphere of American power and profits; many of the under-dogs also responded to this new note of national self-assertion. Others, however, looked upon our conduct in the Philippines as a betrayal of national principles. Anti-expansionists attempted to stir a sense of guilt and foreboding in the nation at large. But the circumstances of the period 1898–1900—the return of prosperity and the quick spectacular victories in war—made it difficult for them to impress this feeling upon the majority. The rhetoric of Duty and Destiny carried the day. The anti-expansionists had neither the numbers nor the morale of their opponents. The most conspicuous result of their lack of drive and confidence can be seen in the lamentable strategy of Bryan over the ratification of the treaty.

Clearly this attempt to see the war and expansion in the light of social history has led us onto the high and dangerous ground of social psychology and into the arena of conjecture. But simple rationalistic explanations of national behavior will also leave us dissatisfied. What I have attempted here is merely a preliminary sketch of a possible explanatory model. Further inquiry might make it seem more plausible at some points, more questionable at others.

This study has been narrowly focused on a single incident. Other expansionist crises in our own history would show im-portant differences. I have not tried to compare American im-perialism with that of other countries, or to decide how far our behavior is unique to our own country or similar to that which has been found elsewhere. In the history of other nations we can find many parallels to the role of the press and political par-ties in whipping up foreign crises, and to the role of the admin-istration in committing the nation to a foreign policy before it could be made a matter of public discussion. The rhetoric and ideology of expansion also were not singular to us; duty, des-tiny, racism, and the other shibboleths were widespread.

I cannot refrain from adding to these notes on the methods of historical understanding another note on the tragicomic procedure of history itself. It may be of some value to us to be reminded how some of the more grandiose expectations of the nineties were realized. Cuba, to be sure, which might have been freed in peace, was freed in the war—insofar as the little country of Batista, Machado, and Castro can be considered free. The sensational newspapers that had boomed the war lost money on expensive extras, costly war-news coverage, and declining advertising.[54] I do not know whether those silverites who wanted the war really expected that it would remonetize silver, but if they did they were rewarded with McKinley's renewed triumph and the Gold Standard Act of 1900. As for business, the gigantic markets of the East never materialized, and the precise value of the Philippines in getting at them is arguable. The islands themselves proved to be a mildly profitable colony that came to absorb a little over 1 per cent of all United States investments abroad. Yet within a generation the United States had committed itself to restoring independence to the Philippines. When this promise was enacted in 1934 many descendants of Aguinaldo's rebels were unenthusiastic about their new economic and strategic position.[55] Finally, the exact estimation that is to be put on our strategic commitment in the Far East, which began with the Philippines, is still a matter of debate. We should, however, make note of the earlier opinion of one of our most brilliant and farsighted statesmen, who declared in 1907 that the Philippines were the Achilles' heel of our strategic position and should be given "nearly complete independence" at the "earliest possible moment."[56] The author of these remarks was Theodore Roosevelt.

[54] Frank Luther Mott: *American Journalism* (New York, 1947), pp. 537–8.
[55] Pratt: *America's Colonial Experiment*, pp. 243–4, 291–310.
[56] Pringle: *Theodore Roosevelt*, pp. 408–9.

What Happened to the Antitrust Movement?

This essay, which at first carried the subtitle "Notes on the Evolution of an American Creed," was written for a conference on the political and social environment of American business, made possible by the Ford Foundation and held on the Berkeley campus of the University of California in January 1964. The papers, written for the conference by a half-dozen authors, were published in *The Business Establishment* (New York, 1964), edited by Earl Cheit, who organized the conference. The version which appears here is substantially revised. A portion appeared also in *Commentary*, August 1964.

I

THE ANTITRUST movement is one of the faded passions of American reform. Historians have always been interested in the old romance, but with remarkable unanimity and an uncharacteristic lack of realism, they have neglected to tell us what happened when it was over. The writers of our general history books deal with the antitrust issue when they tell of the rise of the great corporations and the passing of the Sherman Act and then, again, in discussing antitrust sentiment in the Progressive era and the enactment of further regulatory laws. Most of them touch on it briefly once more when they take up the New Deal antitrust revival, Thurman Arnold, and the T.N.E.C. Then, for the most part, they drop the subject; the student or the general reader must study law, economics, or business administration to become aware that the antitrust enterprise has more significance in contemporary society than it had in the days of T.R. or Wilson, or even in the heyday of Thurman Arnold.

Presumably the historians drop the subject of antitrust at or around 1938 not because they imagine that it has lost its role in our society but because after that point it is no longer the subject of much public agitation—in short, because there is no longer an antitrust *movement*. The intensity of public concern is, of course, a poor guide for historians, but here their neglect embodies a certain self-protective wisdom. They

ignore antitrust for the same reason the public ignores it: it has
become complex, difficult, and boring. In any case, the intricacies, both legal and economic, of regulating monopoly and
competition are intricacies of a sort the historian is ill equipped
to handle. It is simpler for him to sweep the whole thing under
the carpet, and retire, along with the general public, from the
baffling maze of technical refinements which the lawyers and
economists have created.

Perhaps, at the risk of oversimplifying a little, the source of
the problem can be put in this paradox: once the United States
had an antitrust movement without antitrust prosecutions; in
our time there have been antitrust prosecutions without an
antitrust movement. In its day the antitrust movement had
such consequences for our political and intellectual life that no
historian who writes about the period 1890–1940 can safely
ignore it. But the antitrust enterprise, as an institutional reality, now runs its quiet course without much public attention,
and we lose sight of it. In failing to take more cognizance of
its work, the historians are missing one of the most delicious
minor ironies of our reform history and one of the most revealing facets of our institutional life. In the very years when
it lost compelling public interest the antitrust enterprise became a force of real consequence in influencing the behavior
of business.

For a long time liberal historians held to a kind of mythological history of the antitrust experience which, though it was not
entirely false at any point, ended somehow in being entirely
misleading. Antitrust, as an ideology and a movement of reform, always contrasted so sharply with its actual achievements
in controlling business that it tempted our powers of satire.
The conventional history went something like this: In 1890,
as a largely meaningless and cynical gesture to appease public
sentiment, an ultra-conservative Congress passed the Sherman
Antitrust Act. The act was couched in such vague terms as to
confirm our doubts that those who passed it expected that it
could ever be enforced. Its early history fully warranted such
doubts. From the beginning it was rendered a dead letter by
administrative neglect and judicial hostility. Though it had little effect on the big business firms that were supposed to be

its main object, it was used with greater success against labor unions. By the time Theodore Roosevelt took office, when the Sherman Act was little more than ten years old, it had become all too clearly a charade behind which the consolidation of big business, notably accelerated between 1898 and 1904, went on apace. It was easy and amusing to debunk the reputation of T.R. as a trust-buster when one considered the infrequency and superficiality of his prosecutions, as well as his own doubts about the value of the whole enterprise, and to compare his robust rhetoric with the comic and pathetic image of the Antitrust Division of the Justice Department sallying out against the combined might of the giant corporations with a staff of five lawyers and four stenographers.

Subsequent statutory efforts under Wilson to strengthen regulation of monopolistic conduct, whatever one is to say of their value and the intent behind them, had to be recounted by the historians with a full sense of the denouement in mind. And the denouement required us to say that the antitrust effort went down the drain with the attempt to organize industry for the First World War; that the ensuing saturnalia of reaction during the 1920's, another period of business consolidation, undid the Wilsonian reforms—indeed, that the Federal Trade Commission was converted from an agency to control business into an agency controlled by business. Finally the revival of antitrust under F.D.R., the creation of the Temporary National Economic Commission, and the installation of Thurman Arnold's reforms seemed to be largely a movement of desperation, a return to the old antitrust charade, on the part of an administration which had exhausted its capacity to reform and was having indifferent results in its efforts to bring about recovery. The very appointment of Thurman Arnold as head of the Antitrust Division—a man whose books had effectively ridiculed the antitrust laws as a façade behind which the concentration of American industry could go on unimpeded—seemed to underline perfectly the whole comedy of the antitrust enterprise. And here, for the most part, as I have observed, the standard history of antitrust laws breaks off, perhaps with a few words about the difficulties Arnold confronted, and how his honest efforts were circumvented during the Second World War.

Without attempting to subvert the elements of truth in this version of antitrust history, it seems important to take account of certain additions to the story. First, it seems fair to say that while there was some impatient cynicism present in 1890 when the Sherman Act was passed, there was puzzlement as well, an honest if ineffectual concern with the problems of size and monopoly, and genuine doubts about the proper means of solving them. The general language of the Sherman Act may be looked upon as a broad enabling measure, which at least some men hoped would be followed by statutory and administrative advances. What has customarily been said of the lax enforcement that followed needs little qualification, except to add that the difficulties involved were the difficulties inherent in the subject as well as in the relatively conservative and circumspect attitudes taken by the Progressive Presidents and their advisers. They were living in a society that wanted to reap the benefits of large-scale enterprise, as well as to prevent the evils of monopolization; and on the whole, despite the confident pronouncements they found it desirable to make in political campaigns, men like T.R. and Wilson were aware that they did not know how to arrive at a quick and satisfactory solution to the problem. Whatever else may be said about all the seemingly empty and futile rhetoric about monopoly and bigness in the Progressive era, it did serve to keep alive the salutary American fear of excessive market power.

Something more must also be said about the antitrust revival under Franklin Roosevelt and Thurman Arnold. Viewed in a very flat time perspective, Roosevelt's 1938 message on monopoly capitalism, the T.N.E.C., and Arnold's prosecution may be set down as having originated out of administrative desperation and may be regarded as substantial failures. But in the longer perspective, they mark the true beginning of effective antitrust action, for it was the efforts begun at this time—not to speak of new personnel Roosevelt brought into the federal judiciary—that created the social and legal climate in which something could be done. The 1940's can be seen retrospectively as a watershed in the history of antitrust jurisprudence. Today, anybody who knows anything about the conduct of American business knows that the managers of the large corporations do their business with one eye constantly cast over their shoulders at the Antitrust Division, and that the antitrust enterprise has gone far to make up for its inability to reverse business concentration by considerable successes in affecting business conduct. Antitrust has won its spurs as a useful approach to the problems of large-scale enterprise, and in the Western world as a whole it is gaining acceptance. Its successes in America have aroused some emulation since the Second World War both in Britain and in France, and antitrust enforcement has reached a rudimentary stage in the Common Market.

II

The history of antitrust may be divided into three phases. In the first, from about 1890 to 1914—the era of the founding fathers of antitrust—the opening steps were taken, in statutes and in the courts, to define what form the antitrust efforts of the federal government might take and to see how they would work. The great outburst of business consolidation quickened antitrust sentiment, which was strong throughout the Progressive era. Often a common hostility to big business was the one link that bound together a variety of interest groups that diverged on other issues. The Progressive era, which culminated in 1914 with the passing of the Clayton Act and the creation of the Federal Trade Commission, probably marks the high point of anti-big-business sentiment in our history. As a movement, though hardly as an administrative reality, antitrust was in high gear.

The second phase, lasting from the First World War to about 1937, might be called the era of neglect. Efforts at prosecution during the 1920's were almost minimal, and even the New Deal in its opening years suspended the antitrust laws to accommodate the N.R.A. codes. The present phase, which may be dated from 1937, is the phase of revival, opened by the New Deal's reactivation of the Antitrust Division and the T.N.E.C. investigation. The sharp legal and administrative activity of this period has taken place without any corresponding revival of public sentiment against big business, indeed in the face of a growing public acceptance of the large corporation. Antitrust has become almost exclusively the concern of small groups of

legal and economic specialists, who carry on their work without widespread public interest or support.

Whereas the first of these three phases was marked by tentative efforts at enforcement with nearly negligible results, and
the second by minimal or token enforcement, the comparative
vigor of the third may be measured roughly by the number of
prosecutions. During all the years from 1891 to 1938, the government instituted an average of 9 cases a year. The peak years
of this barren half-century were 1912 and 1913, with 29 and 27
prosecutions respectively. For about thirty years after 1913 the
typical load was about 12 cases, often considerably fewer, and
the objects chosen for prosecution were not often vital points
in American industry. In 1940, with the Roosevelt-Arnold re-
vitalization well on its way, the number of cases jumped to 85
—only two less than the number instituted during the entire
first *two decades* of the Sherman Act. Thereafter the number
of cases, though still fluctuating, stayed at a level considerably
higher than that maintained before 1938.[1] In 1962 the Antitrust
Division, employing 300 lawyers and working with a budget of
$6,600,000, instituted 92 cases. Figures, of course, are crude,
but a qualitative analysis of the legal victories of the antitrust
revival would show that the decisions it has won from the
courts, particularly since 1940, have greatly amplified the possibility of enforcement. Despite the collapse of antitrust feeling both in the public at large and among liberal intellectuals,
antitrust as a legal-administrative enterprise has been solidly
institutionalized in the past quarter-century.

The antitrust movement and its legislation are characteristically American. Perhaps this is attributable to the particularly
flagrant form that monopoly took in America during the early
years of its development. It may also be said that, except for
the Canadians, no other people has taken the principle of economic competition so earnestly as to try to underwrite it by
statute, until recently when some European countries began

[1] On prosecutions to 1940, see Walton Hamilton and Irene Till: *Antitrust in
Action*, T.N.E.C. Monograph No. 16 (Washington, 1940), esp. pp. 135–43; see
also *United States versus Economic Concentration and Monopoly*, a Staff Report
to the Monopoly Subcommittee on Small Business, House of Representatives
(Washington, 1940), pp. 276–89.

to show interest in the American approach to the subject.[2] The idea of competition as a means of social regulation—as an economic, political, and moral force—has grown stronger roots in the United States than elsewhere, partly because it has had little to compete with in the way of aristocratic, militaristic, or labor-socialist theories. Founded to some degree in the common-law tradition, whose injunctions against restraint of trade proved an inadequate basis for the protection of competition, the antimonopoly tradition also rested intellectually upon classical economic theory and upon the pluralism of American democratic thought.

But in America competition was more than a theory: it was a way of life and a creed. From its colonial beginnings through most of the nineteenth century, ours was overwhelmingly a nation of farmers and small-town entrepreneurs—ambitious, mobile, optimistic, speculative, anti-authoritarian, egalitarian, and competitive. As time went on, Americans came to take it for granted that property would be widely diffused, that economic and political power would be decentralized. The fury with which they could be mobilized against any institution that even appeared to violate these expectations by posing a threat of monopoly was manifest in the irrational assault on the Bank of the United States during Jackson's presidency. Their most respected thinkers habitually assured them that their social order was God-ordained or natural, and they probably thought it would last forever.

Then, with extraordinary rapidity as historical time is reckoned, that order was overwhelmed by the giant corporation. In the last three decades of the nineteenth century a wholly new economy came into being. An American born in 1828, the year of Jackson's election, came of age in a society in which

[2]On European developments in antitrust law, see *Antitrust Developments in the European Common Market*, Report of the Subcommittee on Antitrust and Monopoly of the Committee on the Judiciary, U.S. Senate, 88th Cong., 2nd sess. (Washington, 1964), and *Comparative Aspects of Anti-Trust Law in the United States, the United Kingdom, and the European Economic Community*, Supplementary Publication No. 6 of *International and Comparative Law Quarterly* (London, 1963). For a brief and synoptic comparison of antitrust legislation in the United States, Canada, and Britain, see W. Friedmann: *Law in a Changing Society* (London, 1959), Ch. 8.

the old small-enterprise economy, however dynamic and expansive, had kept its fundamental pattern more or less intact. But in his mature years he would have seen that economy fast becoming obsolete, and if he lived as late as 1904, he would have seen industry concentrated to a degree inconceivable not only to his fathers but even to him during most of his adult life. This economic transformation happened so fast that the mind could not easily absorb it. An entire people could hardly be expected to cease overnight to dream the dreams of the small entrepreneur. In 1900 the problem of big business and the threat of monopoly were still so new that it was hard to get one's bearings. Bigness had come with such a rush that its momentum seemed irresistible. No one knew when or how it could be stopped.

It is hardly surprising that the men of the first antitrust generation made some frightening projections into the future. In 1890, and even in 1914, bigness had not yet been domesticated either as a force in the economic world or as a factor in the American imagination. A nation that had gone so fast from competitive small enterprise to corporate giantism might readily go with equal speed from corporate giantism to a system of monopolistic tyranny. Hence, discussions of big business in the last decades of the nineteenth and the opening decade of the twentieth century are full of dark prognostications, most of them plausible enough at the time, however little they have been realized.

Since it had been widely assumed that competition, being "natural," would be largely self-perpetuating, the classical theory had not reckoned with the possible necessity of underwriting competition by statute. But by the 1880's the old confidence in the self-sustaining character of competition was dead, and there seemed no adequate protection for competition in existing law. As soon as it became clear that the common-law tradition against restraints of trade had ceased to have any force and that state laws on the subject were altogether inadequate to the purpose, the demand for federal action arose. George Gunton thought in 1888 that "the public mind has begun to assume a state of apprehension almost amounting to alarm," and that the social atmosphere was "surcharged with an indefinite but almost inexpressible fear of trusts."[3] Senator Sherman warned his colleagues that "the popular mind is agitated with problems that may disturb the social order," singling out inequities of wealth and the formation of combinations of capital so great that they threatened to produce "a trust for every production and a master to fix the price for every necessity of life." Congress must heed the appeal of the voters, he said, "or be ready for the socialist, the communist, and the nihilist. Society is now disturbed by forces never felt before."[4] Historians, like contemporaries, have differed as to how imperative the demand for federal action was. In a careful survey of articulate opinion on the "trust" problem in 1890, Hans B. Thorelli concludes that public demand, though perhaps less than an irresistible tide, was too strong to be ignored by the politicians.

Was the Congress of 1890 cynically offering a sop to public sentiment? The plutocratic character of that Congress lends some credence to this view, as does the observation of Senator Orville Platt, at one point in the debate, that the conduct of the Senate during the previous days was "not in the line of honest preparation of a bill to prohibit and punish trusts" but was merely an effort "to get some bill headed 'A bill to punish trusts' with which to go to the country."[5] These circumstances of its origins have helped to confirm many historians in their suspicion that antitrust was, from beginning to end, only a charade.

---

[3] G. W. Stocking and M. W. Watkins: *Monopoly and Free Enterprise* (New York, 1951), p. 257.

[4] *Congressional Record*, 51st Cong., 1st sess. (March 21, 1890), p. 2460. "Although this body is always conservative," Sherman said hopefully, "yet, whatever may be said of it, it has always been ready to preserve not only popular rights in their broad sense, but the rights of individuals as against associated and corporate wealth and power."

[5] Hans B. Thorelli: *The Federal Antitrust Policy* (Baltimore, 1955), p. 198. There is a mass of information about the antimonopoly aspects of the American tradition in Arthur P. Dudden's unpublished doctoral dissertation, *Antimonopolism, 1865–1890*, University of Michigan (1950). On contemporary views, see also Sanford D. Gordon: "Attitudes towards Trusts prior to the Sherman Act," *Southern Economic Journal*, XXX (October 1963), 156–67.

But there is also reason to believe, on the contrary, that most congressmen thought of the competitive order in business as being the cornerstone of the whole democratic way of life and that they considered themselves to be making the first tentative step in formulating a policy for the control of trusts, which, if it could be put on sound constitutional footing, might serve as the basis for corrective litigation and perhaps subsequent statutory changes. Admittedly, they were breaking new ground. Senator Hoar said that Congress was entering a wholly new field of legislation and that "the opinions of Senators themselves, of able and learned and experienced lawmakers, were exceedingly crude in this matter."[6]

It is true, of course, that Congress emerged with a statute written in the most general terms, which for many years was emasculated by judicial decisions and administrative lethargy. But it is very likely that, with its broadly worded prohibition of conspiracies in restraint of trade and of efforts to monopolize, Congress was attempting to lay down a general declaration of policy that would serve as a guide to future action in much the same flexible way as the Constitution itself had served the country after 1787. Many congressmen doubtless believed that the self-enforcing features of the law would be far more effective than they actually became—that is, that the triple-damage suits authorized for victims of restraints of trade would cause businessmen themselves to carry on a good deal of the policing of the economy. Perhaps the problem confronting Congress can be reconstructed with greater sympathy if we try to imagine whether a drastically different and significantly more effective law would have been passed by a wholly populistic and militantly anti-big-business Congress, and whether such a law could have been expected to receive a more successful implementation than the Sherman Act in the hands of the subsequent administrative officers and judges.

One may say with reasonable assurance that the confusion of Congress over the economic significance of antitrust mirrored a more general confusion in American society. The goals of antitrust were of three kinds. The first were economic; the classical model of competition confirmed the belief that the

[6]*Congressional Record*, 51st Cong., 1st sess. (April 8, 1890), p. 3146.

maximum of economic efficiency would be produced by competition, and at least some members of Congress must have been under the spell of this intellectually elegant model, insofar as they were able to formulate their economic intentions in abstract terms. The second class of goals was political; the antitrust principle was intended to block private accumulations of power and protect democratic government. The third was social and moral; the competitive process was believed to be a kind of disciplinary machinery for the development of character, and the competitiveness of the people—the fundamental stimulus to national morale—was believed to need protection.

Among the three, the economic goal was the most cluttered with uncertainties, so much so that it seems to be no exaggeration to regard antitrust as being essentially a political rather than an economic enterprise.[7] A fundamental difficulty in economic thought, troubling from the very start, arose over the relative claims of combination and competition. The Sherman Act was framed and debated in the pre-expert era, when economists as a professional group were not directly consulted by the legislators. But even if they had been, they would have given mixed and uncertain advice. The profession was split. A few years earlier the American Economic Association had been founded by men in revolt against the classical tradition and laissez-faire doctrines, although, of course, many economists of the older school were still ensconced in universities and colleges. Economists were familiar with the argument that the competitive order, far from being fixed in a permanent, beneficent, self-sustaining equilibrium, might have a strong tendency toward self-liquidation through the disappearance of weaker competitors. One of the early historicists, E. Benjamin Andrews, argued in 1893 that laissez-faire was no more than

---

[7]Hans B. Thorelli, after examining carefully the congressional debates on the Sherman Act, concludes, p. 227, that "the Sherman Act is not to be viewed exclusively as an expression of economic policy," and that in safeguarding the rights of the common man in business it "embodies what is to be characterized as an eminently 'social' purpose." Thorelli believes that Sherman and many of his contemporaries in Congress saw the legislation as "an important means of achieving freedom from corruption and maintaining freedom of independent thinking in political life."

a systematized expression of anarchy, and the following year warned:

> Bills have been brought before half the legislatures of the Union to free competition by making trade syndicates absolutely illegal. To my mind there is no question that such legislation will be vain. The age of competition as we have known it is gone forever. As well try to waken the dead.[8]

The more influential voice of Richard Ely was also raised in protest against the ideal of pure competition. He was among those who insisted that size should not be equated with monopoly, and long before Thurman Arnold he held that antitrust legislation was not only futile but actually encouraging to monopoly, because it caused business leaders to replace "soft" combinations by "hard" combinations in the form of mergers.[9]

No consensus was to be had on the proper line of governmental action on trusts or on the kind of law Congress should pass. Nearly all economists believed that attempts simply to prohibit combinations by law would be futile. There was a growing disposition to consider that both competition and combination needed some measure of control and that neither could be eliminated by law. In this sense, as William Letwin has pointed out, the counsel that was available from the economists, however much attended to or ignored, shared the ambiguity that the legislators themselves could feel as lawyers:

> The economists thought that both competition and combination should play their parts in the economy. The lawyers saw that the common law permitted combination in some instances and prohibited it in others. Congressmen seized on this hidden agreement, and set out to construct a statute which by the use of common-law principles would eliminate excesses but allow "healthy" competition and combination to flourish side by side.[10]

If one gives due regard to the uncertainties of the matter and to the improbability that any attempt at a quick solution would be effective, one may arrive at a more charitable judgment of

[8]Thorelli: op. cit., pp. 112 n., 316.
[9]Ibid., pp. 314–15.
[10]William Letwin: *Law and Economic Policy in America: The Evolution of the Sherman Antitrust Act* (New York, 1965), p. 85; see, in general, Ch. 3 on the intentions of Congress.

the Congress of 1890. Its members were probably trying to lay down general guidelines by means of which their successors might evolve a policy that would give society the advantages of both competition and combination. As Senator Sherman said, "All that we, as lawmakers, can do is to declare general principles."[11] These principles could hardly have been enunciated in more sweeping language than that used in the Sherman Act. Presumably, many congressmen hoped that the courts would find a way of striking at the notoriously unfair methods of competition that had already been used to build such companies as Standard Oil and the National Cash Register Company, without barring useful consolidations or even such restrictive agreements as were intended to eliminate intolerably rigorous competition.

This original uncertainty about the economic rationale for antitrust continued to haunt well-intentioned Progressives in the years before the First World War. The vagueness and inconsistency so often expressed by intelligent and relatively candid political leaders during this era must be taken as a reflection not on the caliber of the leadership but rather on the intrinsic difficulty of the problem.

Theodore Roosevelt represents, on this count, a maximum of shrewdness combined with a minimum of anxiety. With the exception of railroad regulation, Roosevelt was not profoundly interested in the economic issues that agitated the American public during his presidency; indeed, he was quite candid in confessing his reluctance to tackle them head on. When in difficulties, as in 1907, he was disposed to trust to the judgment and the political and financial leadership of the conservatives in the Senate or the economic powers in Wall Street. However, he saw the trust problem as something that must be dealt with on the political level; public concern about it was too urgent to be ignored. He understood how important it was to assure the public that the government of the United States had the will and the power to assert its authority over large corporations. Accordingly, his antitrust prosecutions, although few, were in some cases appropriately spectacular. When he assessed

[11] *Congressional Record*, 51st Cong., 1st sess. (March 21, 1890), p. 2460. Sherman was here conceding the difficulty of defining in law the precise difference between legal and illegal combinations, and expressing a preference for leaving such decisions to the courts in particular cases.

the significance of the Northern Securities case, he did not say that it would open the way to a general assault on bigness, but rather that it was important for showing that "the most power-ful men in this country were held to accountability before the law." His fundamental solution for the problem—that bigness must be accepted as a part of the modern industrial and social order, and that its behavior should be subjected to administra-tive control under full publicity—comes somewhat closer than the views of most of his political contemporaries to anticipat-ing the future course of antitrust procedure.

Roosevelt was accompanied, or perhaps followed, by a school of liberal publicists—among them Charles R. Van Hise, Her-bert Croly, and Walter Lippmann—who accepted his convic-tion that the Sherman Act philosophy was the product of what he called a "sincere rural Toryism" long since outgrown. Lipp-mann, in one of the most penetrating attacks on the antitrust philosophy, characterized it as the philosophy of "a nation of villagers." This school of Progressives saw the Western world as entering upon a new era of organization and specialization for which the old competitive philosophy was hopelessly ret-rograde. Some of them, notably Croly and Van Hise, also saw small-scale business as inadequate to the task of competing in the world's markets, which they believed to be a necessity of the American situation. In retrospect, they appear more so-phisticated and prophetic than those who put great stock in the Sherman Act as a force for actual dissolution. They foresaw the decline of antitrust as a movement, and in some instances recognized that if the Sherman Act persisted it would be as a basis for occasional *ad hoc* regulatory suits rather than as an instrument for dismantling the corporate economy.

Woodrow Wilson spoke more feelingly for the "rural Tory-ism" and the village democracy which seem to have been at the center of popular antitrust feeling; but by the same token he illustrated more clearly than Roosevelt their intellectual dif-ficulties. Speaking in the campaign of 1912, which afforded a full-dress display of the differences between the two schools of thought on trusts, he asserted that he too was not against size as such. He was all for bigness as an inevitable and natural growth, whenever it was the outcome of superior efficiency. But he was against "the trusts," which had grown out of illicit competition. He was never very successful, however, in explaining why a business that had become large through legitimate methods might not become just as menacing to competition as one that had grown large through illicit competition. His statement "I am for big business and I am against the trusts" seems hardly more than an unsatisfactory attempt to evade the argument that there is a self-liquidating threat inherent in competition.[12]

III

The political and social arguments against monopoly were pressed with greater clarity than the economic argument and with hardly less fervor. Antitrust must be understood as the political judgment of a nation whose leaders had always shown a keen awareness of the economic foundations of politics. In this respect, the Sherman Act was simply another manifestation of an enduring American suspicion of concentrated power. From the pre-Revolutionary tracts through the Declaration of Independence and *The Federalist* to the writings of the states' rights advocates, and beyond the Civil War into the era of the antimonopoly writers and the Populists, there had been a perennial quest for a way of dividing, diffusing, and checking power and preventing its exercise by a single interest or by a consolidated group of interests at a single center. Hence, the political impulse behind the Sherman Act was clearer and more articulate than the economic theory. Men who used the vaguest language when they talked about "the trusts" and monopolies, who had not thought through the distinction between size itself and monopolistic practices, who had found no way

[12]For Woodrow Wilson's position on monopoly, see his *The New Freedom* (New York, 1913), pp. 163–222. William Diamond, in *The Economic Thought of Woodrow Wilson* (Baltimore, 1943), makes it clear that in his earlier years, Wilson had been committed to the evolutionist acceptance of size but became more devoted to the competitive principle as he came before the public eye and as he accepted the advice of Brandeis. By 1913 he seems to have been persuaded that dissolution was an essential tactic. "Real dissolution in the case of the trusts is the only thing we can be satisfied with," he wrote privately, and he indicated that this was part of a program necessary "to satisfy the conscience of the country." Ibid., p. 112.

of showing how much competition was necessary for efficiency, who could not in every case say what competitive acts they thought were fair or unfair, or who could not state a rational program that reconciled their acceptance of size with their desire for competition, were reasonably clear about what it was that they were trying to avoid: they wanted to keep concentrated private power from destroying democratic government.

One of the glories of the competitive model had been that it purported to solve the question of market power by denying that such power had any particular location. The decisions of the market were beautifully impersonal, since they were only the averagings of the decisions of thousands of individuals, none of whom enjoyed any decisive power. The market mechanism suggested that power was not really exercised by anyone. With the perfect impersonality of Adam Smith's "invisible hand," the market made decisions that ought not be vested in the hands of any particular man or body of men. Hence, the market mechanism met the desire for the diffusion of power and seemed to be the perfect economic counterpart of American democratic pluralism.

Where power *must* be exercised, it was agreed that it should be located in governmental and not in private hands. But the state governments were inadequate; in sheer mass, business enterprises already overshadowed them. Charles William Eliot pointed out as early as 1888 that the large corporations, considered as units of economic organization, had already begun to tower over the states. A Boston railroad company, for example, employed 18,000 persons and had gross receipts of about $40,000,000 a year, whereas the Commonwealth of Massachusetts employed only 6,000 and had receipts of only $7,000,000.[13] Even individually, some corporations were big enough to dominate state governments, and if they should

[13]C. W. Eliot: "The Working of the American Democracy," *American Contributions to Civilization* (New York, 1907), pp. 85–6. Three-quarters of a century later the T.N.E.C. found that, as economic units, only ten states had assets greater than the two largest corporations, and that more than half the states were completely overshadowed in size by private businesses. *Final Report and Recommendations of the Temporary National Economic Committee* (Washington, 1941), pp. 676–7; David Lynch: *The Concentration of Economic Power* (New York, 1946), pp. 112–13.

combine among themselves, they might come to dominate the federal government as well.

The existence of the industrial combinations and the threat that under one auspice or another—perhaps that of the investment bankers—there would come about some day a combination of the combinations that would be stronger than civil government itself, provoked a fear that haunted the minds of the writers of the industrial era, including many whose social views were as conservative as Eliot's. The fundamental fear of private power was well put by William Jennings Bryan, in a speech delivered at the Chicago Conference on Trusts in 1899:

> I do not divide monopolies in private hands into good monopolies and bad monopolies. There is no good monopoly in private hands. There can be no good monopoly in private hands until the Almighty sends us angels to preside over the monopoly. There may be a despot who is better than another despot, but there is no good despotism.[14]

And the general sense that the dire economic and political consequences of monopoly were as one was incorporated in the Democratic platform of 1900:

> Private monopolies are indefensible and intolerable. . . . They are the most efficient means yet devised for appropriating the fruits of industry to the benefit of the few at the expense of the many, and unless their insatiate greed is checked, all wealth will be aggregated in a few hands and the Republic destroyed.[15]

The most articulate expression of the Progressives' case against the political power of monopoly was made by Woodrow Wilson in 1912. It was the burden of his argument, against T.R., that once the existence of large-scale combinations is accepted, regulation of them by government becomes impossible, because the political power of business combination will be great enough to nullify all attempts at controlling it. Wilson played artfully on the fears and suspicions of the small entrepreneurs. Even some very powerful men, he said, knew that "there is a power somewhere so organized, so subtle, so

---

[14] Thorelli: op. cit., p. 336.
[15] Kirk H. Porter and Donald B. Johnson: *National Party Platforms* (Urbana, Ill., 1956), p. 114.

watchful, so interlocked, so complete, so pervasive, that they
had better not speak above their breath when they speak in
condemnation of it. . . . They know that somewhere, by
somebody, the development of industry is being controlled."[16]
He pictured concentrated capital as being already in control
of the government: "The masters of the government of the
United States are the combined capitalists and manufacturers
of the United States. . . . The government of the United
States at present is a foster-child of the special interests."[17]

Of necessity this would continue to be the state of affairs
until the combinations not only were unseated by the people
but also were dissolved—until "this colossal 'community of
interest'" was disentangled. It was a thing that the laws must
"pull apart, and gently, but firmly and persistently dissect."
Otherwise, under Roosevelt's plan for accepting and regulating monopolies, there would only be a union between monopoly and government: "If the government controlled by the
monopolies in its turn controls the monopolies, the partnership is finally consummated." "If monopoly persists, monopoly
will always sit at the helm of the government. I do not expect
to see monopoly restrain itself. If there are men in this country
big enough to own the government of the United States, they
are going to own it."[18]

The third objective of antitrust action, hardly less important
than the others, was psychological and moral. It sprang from
the conviction that competition has a disciplinary value for character, quite aside from its strictly economic uses. America was
thought to have been made possible by the particular type of
character that was forged by competitive individualism, a type
that had flourished in the United States because competitive opportunities had been so widespread that alert men could hardly
fail to see them, to grasp and use them, and hence, to be shaped
by them. The American male character was believed to have
been quickened and given discipline by the sight and pursuit of
opportunity. For this process to take place it was important that

[16]Wilson: op. cit., pp. 14, 62.
[17]Ibid., pp. 57–8.
[18]Ibid., pp. 118, 207, 286. For a later statement of this view see the dissenting
opinion of Mr. Justice Douglas in *U.S. v. Columbia Steel Co.*, 334 U.S. 495
(1948).

business be carried on fairly—the sporting vocabulary was never far below the surface—and that newcomers be able to enter the game as entrepreneurs on reasonably open terms.

The significance of this faith that competition could be relied upon to form character can be fully grasped only if we bear in mind the Protestant background of our economic thinking. Economists themselves had not been in the habit of analyzing economic relationships in purely mechanical and secular terms, and what may be said of them on this count can be said with greater force about laymen, when they thought about economic issues. Behind the American way of thinking there lay a long Protestant tradition, which tended to identify economic forces with religious and moral forces and which regarded economic processes from the standpoint of their contribution to the discipline and development of character. The economic order was not merely an apparatus for the production of goods and services; it was a set of rules for forging good conduct. Everyone is familiar, I believe, with the proposition that some of the concepts of classical economics were shaped under the influence of a kind of prudential morality in which savings and abstinence were not merely instruments of economic analysis but moral sanctions. In our time we have heard conservatives frankly condemn government fiscal policy that deviates from the prudential rules suitable to a family budget by appealing to the Puritan tradition. Such critics are the legitimate heirs of the men of the nineteenth and the early twentieth century who saw the protection of competition and its incentives as a safeguard of national morale, as a means for mobilizing and rewarding the industrious and the prudent and for penalizing those whom William Graham Sumner called "the poor and the weak, the negligent, shiftless, inefficient, silly, and imprudent . . . the idle, intemperate, and vicious."[19]

Here again one looks to Woodrow Wilson for the most articulate expression of this emphasis on the economic foundations of character and especially to the masterful speeches in 1912 in which he expressed his concern for "the beginner," "the man with only a little capital," "the man on the make," upon whose genius he thought the country had always been built. "The

[19]William Graham Sumner: *What Social Classes Owe to Each Other* (New Haven, 1925), p. 21.

treasury of America," he argued, "lies in those ambitions, those energies, that cannot be restricted to a special favored class." It rests upon the inventiveness and the energy of "unknown men" and would lose its force if the economic order ceased to stimulate such inventiveness and energy. It was possible, he hinted, that under large-scale organization the country would turn its back on its past, which he evoked in poignant terms:

> . . . the ancient time when America lay in every hamlet, when America was to be seen in every fair valley, when America displayed her great forces on the broad prairies, ran her fine fires of enterprise up over the mountainsides and down into the bowels of the earth, and eager men were everywhere captains of industry, not employees; not looking to a distant city to find out what they might do, but looking about among their neighbors, finding credit according to their character, not according to their connections, finding credit in proportion to what was known to be in them and behind them, not in proportion to the securities they held that were approved where they were not known.[20]

The prospect that these "fine fires of enterprise" were about to be quenched suggested that the old kind of character would be destroyed, that the old America was about to die—a reason even more imperative than mere industrial efficiency for seeking out the possibilities of antitrust action.

The inherited belief that small property and opportunity for small business have forged the American character, which might well lose its form without the discipline imposed by a particular variety of entrepreneurial competition, is one that has never died out. Near the end of the Second World War the Small Business Committee of the Senate put this faith clearly when it said that the pursuit of opportunity by the small business owner

> has been a great motive force among our people. It stimulates expression of the fundamental virtues of thrift, industry, intelligence, schooling, home ties, and family pride—in short, those fireside virtues which have counted for so much in developing our strength and character.[21]

[20]Wilson: op. cit., pp. 18–19.
[21]Quoted in John H. Bunzel: *The American Small Businessman* (New York, 1962), p. 84.

The preservation of opportunities for small business, as a member of the S.E.C. put it in 1945, is more important than any economic goal; it is "a goal which transcends economic and political forms and processes as such, and remains fundamentally concerned with the character of the men and women who comprise the nation."[22]

IV

There are two salient differences between the problem of bigness as it was perceived about sixty years ago and the problem as it is perceived now; the first is that it is no longer a new problem, and the second is that the economy has performed in a way hardly dreamed of before the Second World War. In 1965 we are as remote in time from the passage of the Sherman Act as the men of 1865 were from the first term of George Washington. The public has had almost three-quarters of a century of experience in living with big business, and analysts of the big-business problem no longer make the same frightening projections as to its future dangers that could be made with entire plausibility sixty or seventy years ago. At the same time, the public is hardly unaware that the steepest rise in mass standards of living has occurred during the period in which the economy has been dominated by the big corporation. Whatever else may be said against bigness, the conception of monopolistic industry as a kind of gigantic, swelling leech on the body of an increasingly deprived and impoverished society has largely disappeared.

About the change in public attitudes from those prevailing sixty years ago we can make only an educated guess. Today we can check our impressions of the public mind against opinion polls; for the earlier era we have impressions alone. But it is very difficult for anyone who reads widely in the political literature of the period 1890–1914 to believe that public concern today over big business has anything like the sense of urgency that it had then. In 1951 the Institute of Social Research of the University of Michigan published the results of an illuminating survey, *Big Business as the People See It*. Its findings show some

[22]Rudolph L. Weissman: *Small Business and Venture Capital* (New York, 1945), p. 164.

residues of the old popular suspicion of bigness, but the note-worthy thing is public acceptance. Americans have always had to balance their love of bigness and efficiency against their fear of power and their regard for individualism and competition. The survey indicates that this ambivalence has been largely resolved in favor of the big business organization.

A quarter of the population, as represented in the Institute's national sample, showed some concern over big business and an awareness that it had an important effect on their lives. But a substantial majority reacted favorably to big business. Asked to give a general characterization of its social effects, the respondents answered as follows:

The good things outweigh the bad things	76%
They seem about equal	2
The bad things outweigh the good things	10
Don't know	5
Confused; evaluation not ascertainable	7
	100%

Plainly, big business was no longer a scare word to the public at large. Eighty-four per cent of those polled reacted without apparent emotion to the question, and only a small minority reacted unfavorably. Questioned on particulars, respondents spoke with especial favor of the productive powers of big business and its ability to give jobs and keep prices down. The most critical responses about big business dealt mainly with its effect on "the little man" and the destruction of competition. Very little concern was expressed about the power of big business over its workers (it is commonly regarded as a good employer) and surprisingly little about its influence on government.

Whereas fifty years before, fear of an indefinitely continued increase in the political power of big business was common-place, the typical expectation expressed in the poll of 1951 was that the power of big business would decline, and properly so. As in the Progressive era, there was a strong preference for a balance of power and a conviction that wherever there must be a clear preponderance of power it should rest in governmental and not private hands. But the existing state of business power was not widely considered to be dangerous. In fact, big-business power was ranked third among five forces—behind national government and labor unions and ahead of state governments and smaller business. Stronger feeling was shown against labor unions than against big business. There was a fraction of the public that saw big business as more powerful than labor unions and would have liked to see the situation reversed; but there was a fraction almost twice as large that saw the unions as more powerful and would have preferred to see the situation reversed.[23]

The findings of the Michigan group were not widely at variance with those of Elmo Roper, who a few years earlier had collated the responses of the public over a span of fifteen years to questions about business. Roper found that "the public has mixed feelings about big business. There is pride over the achievements of big business but some apprehension over the possible abuses of power inherent in big business." The public was disposed to want a watchdog set upon the amoral and greedy elements in business, but only about a fourth of the respondents were found to believe that the disadvantages of bigness overshadow whatever advantages there might be.[24]

To what can we attribute this public acceptance of big business? Not much, I believe, to the efforts that big-businessmen have made to cultivate a favorable "image" for the large corporation. As the fate of the postwar campaign to sell "free enterprise" suggests, such efforts can miscarry badly when they represent nothing more than an attempt to make the public take seriously the blather with which big business sometimes comforts itself.[25] What has really made bigness palatable more than anything else is the remarkable performance of the economy since the beginning of the Second World War. Something too must be credited to the emergence of countervailing bigness in government and labor, whose effects on public attitudes emerge clearly from the Michigan survey. Moreover, anyone who is aware of the historical circumstances under

[23]Burton R. Fisher and Stephen B. Withey: *Big Business as the People See It* (Ann Arbor, 1951), passim.

[24]Elmo Roper: "The Public Looks at Business," *Harvard Business Review*, XXVII (March 1949), 165–74.

[25]William H. Whyte, Jr., is eloquent on the failure of one such campaign in *Is Anybody Listening?* (New York, 1952).

which hostility to big business flourished must be aware that big business has not lived up to the horrifying billing that it got in the age of the muckrakers. It is not merely that no business treats competitors today as they were treated in the early days of the National Cash Register Company or Standard Oil. What is important is that a whole range of fears that existed in the Progressive era, based largely upon a preoccupation with an unknown future, has vanished. We now live in that future, and although it has fears of its own—nightmarish beyond anything anticipated in the days of Bryan and Wilson—they are of a wholly different origin. Probably the worst of the Populist-Progressive nightmares was the notion—expressed in the Pujo Committee's inquiry, in Brandeis's *Other People's Money*, in Wilson's speeches and in Jack London's *The Iron Heel*—of the formation, under the auspices of the investment bankers, of a giant syndicate, a combination of the combinations, which would rule the country with a tyrannical grip. The self-financing character of the great corporations, the survival of competition in investment banking, and the failure of investment banking to remain a power of the first order after the crash of 1929 have set this specter to rest.

If no sinister central syndicate had to be feared, it did at least seem reasonable at the turn of the century to anticipate a steadily growing concentration of industry that would eventually deprive the country of every advantage of competition. And here, insofar as the antitrust enterprise was directed against size itself or against concentration, it was beaten before it ever got started; American industry was already highly concentrated in 1904, when T.R. was boasting about the lessons of the Northern Securities case. But insofar as the Progressives were worried about what the economists later came to call "workable competition" in industry, they might well have been reassured as time went on. The investigations of such economists as M. A. Adelman, G. Warren Nutter, and George J. Stigler have cast considerable doubt on the idea that either the scope of monopoly or the degree of concentration has, in fact, grown since early in the century. "The extent of concentration," Adelman concluded in an important study, "shows no tendency to grow, and it may possibly be declining. Any tendency either way, if it does exist, must be at the pace of a glacial drift."[26] Measuring monopoly is an undertaking of considerable complexity and the issues are controversial. But it is at least safe to say that no one who has due regard for the difficulties of the problem can any longer raise alarmist cries about the rapid growth of monopoly or concentration without flying in the face of much formidable testimony.

Another cause of concern, very real to many men in the Progressive era and rather quaint from today's perspective, had to do with the progress of industry. "Monopoly," warned Wilson in 1912, "always checks development, weighs down natural prosperity, pulls against natural advance." In the past, he said, competitive America had produced or developed the steamboat, the cotton gin, the sewing machine, the reaper, the typewriter, the electric light, and other great inventions, but the day was at hand when monopoly might end all this. "Do you know, have you had occasion to learn, that there is no hospitality for invention nowadays? There is no encouragement for you to set your wits at work. . . . The instinct of monopoly is against novelty, the tendency of monopoly is to keep in use the old thing, made in the old way." Only a restoration of freedom could unleash American inventiveness again: "Who can say what patents now lying, unrealized, in secret drawers and pigeonholes, will come to light, or what new inventions will astonish and bless us, when freedom is restored?"[27] To two generations that since 1912 have been astonished and blessed almost to death by inventions, such rhetoric can no longer be alarming or inspiring; it is merely a curiosity. Today the public

[26]M. A. Adelman: "The Measurement of Industrial Concentration," *Review of Economics and Statistics*, XXXIII (November 1951), 269–96. See also the discussion by Adelman and others: ibid., XXXIV (May 1952), 156 ff.; G. Warren Nutter: *The Extent of Enterprise Monopoly in the United States, 1899–1939* (Chicago, 1951); and George J. Stigler: *Five Lectures on Economic Problems* (London, 1949), pp. 46–65. However, on the identity of the largest firms and the mobility of firms into positions of leadership, see Norman R. Collins and Lee E. Preston: "The Size Structure of the Largest Industrial Firms," *American Economic Review*, LI (December 1961), 986–1003. Fritz Machlup: *The Political Economy of Monopoly* (Baltimore, 1952), pp. 469–528, is instructive on the difficulties of the subject. See also Edward S. Mason: *Economic Concentration and the Monopoly Problem* (New York: Atheneum ed., 1964), pp. 16–43.
[27]Wilson: op. cit., pp. 265–6, 270.

needs no persuading that it is the large corporations, with their programs of research, that are technologically progressive. As Galbraith has remarked, the showpieces of American industrial progress are, in the main, those dominated by a handful of large firms, and "the foreign visitor, brought to the United States by the Economic Cooperation Administration, visits the same firms as do attorneys of the Department of Justice in their search for monopoly."[28]

Another typical fear expressed in Progressive writing was that the possibility of individual advancement would be frozen out, that the upward social mobility that had refreshed and inspired American development in the past would come to an end, when the business of the country was fully dominated by the large corporation. I know of no very certain information on how the American public regards the prospects for social mobility today, although our concerted scramble for educational position and advantage suggests that the middle-class public, and even much of the working-class public, is rather well aware that mobility still exists; it is also aware of the educational machinery through which it can be pursued. What can be said with greater confidence is that informed observers no longer speak so glibly of the decline of mobility or opportunity.

Indeed, there is strong evidence that the opportunity of middle- or lower-class men to rise to top positions in business has somewhat increased over what it was fifty or sixty years ago,[29] and there is some reason to believe that the increase, or at least the persistence, of occupational opportunity has, in fact, impressed itself on the public mind. In fact, the modern corporation has proved to be a better medium for social mobility and opportunity than the old system of individual and family entrepreneurship, whose openness in this respect was always much exaggerated. Oddly enough, the concentration of capital and the divorce of ownership from the entrepreneurial

[28]John Kenneth Galbraith: *American Capitalism* (Boston, 1952), p. 96; cf. Joseph A. Schumpeter: *Capitalism, Socialism, and Democracy* (New York, 1947), pp. 81–2.
[29]For a good review of the relevant findings, see Seymour M. Lipset and Reinhard Bendix: *Social Mobility in Industrial Society* (Berkeley and Los Angeles, 1960), Ch. 3.

function may prove in the long run to be more conducive to the lowering of social tensions and to political stability than diffused ownership.[30] The ways of achieving occupational advancement and economic success have changed; individual entrepreneurship is a much less sure and satisfactory path as compared with bureaucratic careers. The acquisition of specialized skills has become more important, and with it the seizure and exploitation of educational opportunities.

I do not mean to suggest that the old ideal of self-employment or the old confidence in the entrepreneurial path to success has been entirely abandoned in favor of the bureaucratic career. Although the incidence of self-employment and the number of those who actually live by the competitive ideal have shrunk very considerably in the three-quarters of a century since the Sherman Act, most of this is attributable to the numerical decline of family farmers, who in 1890 still comprised nearly half the population and today comprise about a tenth. The farmers, with their dependence on subsidies and government-administered prices, can hardly be looked upon any more as vigorous exponents of the competitive way of life. But the dream of self-employment that dominated the agrarian-entrepreneurial society of the nineteenth century is still alive. It has been estimated that about 20 to 30 per cent of the American working force has been at some time or other self-employed.[31] The growth of small businesses over the past dozen years or so has roughly kept pace in numbers with the growth of the adult population, and the aspirations of small business have been institutionalized in Senate and House committees as well as in some antitrust activities.

But although small business holds its place as an occupational segment of the economy itself, its role as a sector of society committed to the entrepreneurial ideal has declined. Small business can no longer be idealized for its independence and hardihood or its devotion to competitive principles. It, too, looks to

---

[30]For a shrewd and heretical statement on the political and social effects of the large corporation, see M. A. Adelman: "Some Aspects of Corporate Enterprise," in Ralph Freeman (ed.): *Postwar Economic Trends in the United States* (New York, 1960), pp. 289–308.

[31]Lipset and Bendix: op. cit., pp. 102–3.

government intervention for sustenance, whether in the form of resale price maintenance, anti-chain-store legislation, or the Small Business Administration. Small business, which used to be, as one writer put it,[32] "a symbol of opportunity, enterprise, innovation, and achievement" and of "an independent way of life," has been driven largely into the marginal areas of economic life, where it often tries to maintain itself by waging its own assaults upon the competitive principle. Various segments of small business, in their pressure for support for the Robinson-Patman Act of 1936 and the Miller-Tydings Amendment of 1937, have shown how quickly they can be rallied against competition, when it impinges upon their own interests. Vigorous advocates of the Sherman and Clayton acts where big business is affected, they turn their backs on competitive virility when it suits their purposes. If there is anything rarer than a small-businessman who will question the merits of competition as a principle, it is one who can understand and abide competition when it really afflicts him as a fact.[33]

Not only can the small-businessman not purport, in the eyes of any well-informed observer, to be a vigorous and consistent exemplar of the competitive ideal; he can no longer be idealized by progressive-minded men from other walks of life, as he could, say, in the era when Woodrow Wilson waxed rhapsodical about the new men out of "unknown homes" who had really made America. In the United States and elsewhere, liberal intellectuals now cock a suspicious eye at him, if not as a potential stronghold of support for fascist movements, at least as the backbone of the reactionary wing of the Republican party. An occasional big-business leader may stand out for his enlightenment and urbanity, as compared with the small-businessman, who more often than not proves to be a refractory anti-union employer, a parochial and archaic opponent of liberal ideas, a supporter of vigilante groups and of right-wing cranks.[34] As

[32]Theodore O. Yntema, in the Foreword to A. D. H. Kaplan: *Small Business: Its Place and Problems* (New York, 1948), p. vii.
[33]For an amusing illustration of this incomprehension of competition, see the testimony before the T.N.E.C., quoted in Lynch: op. cit., pp. 155–6.
[34]On the politics of small business, which, of course, still has a liberal minority wing, see Bunzel: op. cit., Ch. 5.

a figure in our economic society, the small-businessman still plays a part of some considerable importance, but as a partner in the American liberal coalition, he has all but disappeared, and with him has gone much of the pristine anti-bigness feeling of the Progressive tradition.

Still, the conviction that American democracy will survive only if small-business enterprise survives to sustain the American character has not disappeared. It has been inherited from the Progressives of yesterday by the conservatives of today. It appears to be, as we shall see, a conviction that flourishes less among the young than among the old, who are often troubled that they cannot persuade their juniors of its importance. "For the development of self-reliance," say two authors of a manual for small-business operation, "for making men as well as money, small business excels."[35] In 1936, when the Robinson-Patman Act was under consideration, this effort to underwrite the middleman was touted by the chairman of the House Committee on the Judiciary as a potential bulwark of the democratic order: "There are a great many people who feel that if we are to preserve democracy in government, in America, we have got to preserve a democracy in business operation. . . . We must make some effort to *maintain the yeomanry in business*."[36]

During the 1940's and 1950's there was evidence of a widespread uneasy conviction that years of war, depression, and bureaucratic expansion had finally drained away the old regard for entrepreneurship among the young, and that the spirit that animated the old competitive ideal had finally succumbed to the world of the large corporation. The signs and portents are numerous, but a memorable article of 1949 in *Fortune* may be taken as a landmark. Surveying "The Class of '49," *Fortune*'s editors pointed out that it was perhaps the most significant college graduating class in our history. It was one of the largest, most mature (with a high proportion of veterans) and responsible; but its distinguishing feature was its aversion to risk, its

[35]Pearce C. Kelley and Kenneth Lawyer: *How to Organize and Operate a Small Business* (Englewood Cliffs, N.J., 1949), p. 11.
[36]Quoted in Merle Fainsod, Lincoln Gordon, and Joseph C. Palamountain, Jr.: *Government and the American Economy* (New York, 1959), p. 549; italics added.

passion for security. "The class of '49," the editors reported, "wants to work for somebody else—preferably somebody big. No longer is small business the promised land. As for the idea of going into business for oneself, the idea is so seldom expressed as to seem an anachronism." Only in the Southwest, which seems socially and intellectually to lag behind the rest of the country, was there any sign of significant exceptions to this generalization. The generation which had been impressionable children during the depression and which had come of age in the shadow of the war rendered a firm verdict in favor of security, service, and the good life (measured in modest income expectations) rather than risk, self-assertion, and the big prizes. The emergent young man, the editors reported, "is not afraid of bigness; where his father of the twenties, fearful of anonymity, was repelled by hugeness in an organization, he is attracted."[37]

This was the response of a generation raised in an economy of giant corporations, educated very often in universities with thousands of students, disciplined by army life, and accustomed to the imperatives of organization, mass, and efficiency. No doubt they often saw in big businesses the promise of laboratories and market research to which the atmosphere of the universities had already accustomed them. Because of its army experiences, the class of 1949 may have been unusually security-minded, but there is no reason to doubt that its acceptance of large organization represented a secular trend. Not long after the *Fortune* piece appeared, the Youth Research Institute Survey put to 4,660 high school and college seniors, recent college graduates, and veterans the question: "Do you feel that you will be able to achieve all of your economic desires by working for someone else?" In reply, 61.1 per cent said yes, 20.4 per cent no, and 18.5 per cent were uncertain.[38] In his essay "The Found Generation," an analysis of the expressed life ideals of the class of 1955, David Riesman found not only a bland acceptance of the large corporation as a place in which to do one's life work but also a depressing complacency about the terms and rewards of the corporate life. The class of 1949

[37] "The Class of '49," *Fortune* (June 1949), pp. 84–7.
[38] William H. Whyte, Jr.: *The Organization Man* (New York, 1957), p. 79 n.

had at least been aware of making a somewhat difficult choice in which their individuality might be at stake. The class of 1955 took the bureaucratic career for granted.[39]

It is this acceptance of the bureaucratic career that, more than anything else, tells us why there is no longer an antitrust movement. It is far more revealing than the law cases or the books on the control of monopoly. It is also a perfect illustration of how the problems of yesterday are not solved but outgrown. Only a few people today are concerned about how to make the large corporations more competitive, but millions are concerned about how they are going to live inside the corporate framework. The existence and the workings of the corporations are largely accepted, and in the main they are assumed to be fundamentally benign. What is questioned, when anything is questioned, is matters of personal style: What can be salvaged, of either individualism or individuality, in an age in which the big corporation has become a way of life? It is this concern that marks the transition from an age in which *The Curse of Bigness* and *Other People's Money* voiced the prevailing anxieties to one in which everyone reads *The Lonely Crowd* and *The Organization Man*.

Long-prevailing systems of values do not usually go under without a fight, and along with the new acceptance there is a good deal of uneasiness about the corporate life. The young may be losing the concern of their elders with the virile prerogatives of enterprise. Certainly they are now much more disposed to ask of the economic order not whether it is raising a nation of enterprising and hardy men but more matter-of-factly whether it is maintaining an adequate level of employment and producing a sufficient increase in the Gross National Product. But there is also a persistent uneasiness, which has its manifestations both on the left and on the right. The left, if it can be called that, rebels in the name of nonconformity and opts out of the whole bourgeois world in the manner of the beatnik and the hipster. The right (in the manner of Barry Goldwater and his enthusiasts) rebels in the name of the older individualism, which believed that economic life should inculcate discipline

[39]David Riesman: "The Found Generation," in *Abundance for What?* (New York, 1964), pp. 309–23.

and character. Though they would hate to admit it, they are both bedeviled in different ways by the same problem; each of them is trying to make its variety of nonconformism into a mass creed—which is a contradiction in terms. The beats opt out of corporate uniformity in their own uniforms and erect themselves into a stereotype. The right-wingers sing their praises of individualism in dreary, regimented choruses and applaud vigilantes who would kill every vestige of genuine dissent.

In politics, of course, it is the right-wingers who really count —it is they who have the numbers, the money, the political leverage. They can also invoke the old American pieties and can appeal to the kind of old-fashioned American who believes that federal fiscal policy is just like the family budget. Much of our conservative writing echoes with concern over the decline of the older kind of economic morale, which it identifies with small entrepreneurship. But conservatives understandably fear to make the large corporation the object of their criticism; this smacks too much of subversion. They have a safer and more congenial outlet for their animus against the organization of modern life in the form of denunciations of big government. In this way, the large corporation escapes its proper share of odium. But, historically, it was the giant corporation far more than government policy that eclipsed the old-fashioned economic morality.

Here conservatives and liberals have all but reversed their former positions. In the main it is conservatives who are disgruntled with the style of contemporary economic life, while liberals complete the paradox by springing to its defense and, in particular, to the defense of bigness. As we have seen, there were always a number of Progressive intellectuals who preferred to accept corporate organization and to whom the possibilities of rationalization and order were more appealing than the competitive ideal. Today it is men of such views who seem to have inherited what is left of American liberalism. Of course, big business still holds a place as a negative symbol in the liberal creed, and the liberal creed still gives a certain ritualistic compliance to the anti-big-business sentiment that was once very close to the heart of progressivism. But by and large, as Carl Kaysen has remarked, "today's liberals have abandoned the symbol of competition without much struggle."[40]

Some of the most striking efforts to reconcile us to the business structure have been written in recent years by liberals who derive from the New Deal tradition. If, in 1953, one read a paean to big business asserting, among other things, that the emotional antagonism to which it was subject was based on "abuses long since corrected"; that the big-business leader is "a man with a strong and practical sense of responsibility to the public, and an awareness of the ethics of present-day business competition"; that "big business has performed economic wonders with one hand tied behind its back"; that it has actually increased competition and multiplied small enterprises; that "size is our greatest single functional asset"; that big business nourishes diversity; that "we are living in what is probably the most highly competitive society men have ever known"; that big-business research has multiplied opportunities for small-business enterprise; that ill-considered antitrust prosecutions have "grave implications for national security"; and that "in Bigness we have the material foundation of a society which can further the highest values known to men, values we describe as spiritual"[41]—one no longer expected to find that one had been reading a speech by a General Motors or A. T. & T. director and was not at all surprised to learn that the author was David E. Lilienthal, once one of the most outspoken democratic idealists of the New Deal bureaucracy and a former disciple of Brandeis.

Lilienthal's innocent rhapsodies to big business may perhaps be taken as the effusions of one who had been reshaped by his experiences in giant public enterprises like the T.V.A. and the A.E.C.[42] But there is also A. A. Berle, Jr., another New Dealer, who held his first job in Brandeis's office and whose

[40]Carl Kaysen: "Big Business and the Liberals, Then and Now," *The New Republic* (November 22, 1954), pp. 118–19.

[41]David E. Lilienthal: *Big Business: A New Era* (New York, 1953), pp. 5, 7, 27, 33, 36, 47, 190, and passim.

[42]For critiques, see Lee Loevinger: "Antitrust and the New Economics," *Minnesota Law Review*, XXXVII (June 1953), 505–68, and Edward S. Mason: *Economic Concentration and the Monopoly Problem* (Cambridge, Mass., 1957), pp. 371–81.

public career was marked by friendships with Robert La Follette, George Norris, and Franklin D. Roosevelt. In his most recent works Berle has been speculating about the possible development of a corporate conscience and arguing that the contemporary business power system is governed by public consensus. In his *Power Without Property* he urged liberals to reconsider their former, and historically justified, antipathy to big business and to judge it in the light of its achievements in increasing income and distributing property.[43] Finally, there is John Kenneth Galbraith, whose book *American Capitalism* has probably done as much as any other work to reconcile the contemporary liberal mind to the diminished role of competition as a force in modern economic society by offering, as an alternative account of the mechanism by which market power is controlled in the public interest, the principle of countervailing power. Of course, neither Berle nor Galbraith advocates doing away with the antitrust laws—Galbraith, in fact, argues that, in the main, federal antitrust policies have helped to produce countervailing power, where it has not emerged spontaneously[44]—but the net effect of their view of our society is to lower the premium on competition and to turn attention to other economic and social mechanisms that promise to control excessive market power.

To be sure, liberal intellectuals have not ceased to be critical of business civilization or, on occasion, of big business. But a variety of other issues—foreign policy, urban development, civil rights, education, and the like—have become more central, and where these issues are concerned, liberals do not always find themselves in a simple antagonistic confrontation with big business, as they did in the past. Their criticisms of business civilization now rest more on cultural than economic grounds. The last thing they are interested in is the restoration of competition as the solution to the evils that they see.[45] Even

---

[43]A. A. Berle, Jr.: *Power Without Property* (New York, 1959), pp. 11–16.
[44]Galbraith: op. cit., p. 151.
[45]Nor are contemporary radicals. The most full-throated indictment of the ruling element in big business that has been written in our time, C. Wright Mills's *The Power Elite*, does not concern itself even fleetingly with the problem of market power. The Sherman and Clayton acts are not listed in its index.

a scandal like the General Electric affair, although it confirms their view of what may be expected from businessmen, no longer excites them very much. In short, that "gale of creative destruction" about which Joseph Schumpeter wrote so eloquently, when he described the progressive character of capitalist technology, has driven both the liberal and the conservative ideologies before it.

V

It is easier to account for the decline of the antitrust movement as a matter of public sentiment than it is to explain the persistence and growth of the antitrust enterprise as a legal and administrative fact. But the fate of antitrust is an excellent illustration of how a public ideal, vaguely formulated and often hopelessly at odds with stubborn realities, can become embodied in institutions with elaborate, self-preserving rules and procedures, a defensible function, and an equally stubborn capacity for survival. Institutions are commonly less fragile than creeds.

The antitrust revival originated in the closing phases of the New Deal. It was a response to the recession of 1937–8, which itself brought about a crisis in the thinking and the political strategy of the New Dealers. The recession gave to the Brandeis liberals, who had always been present in New Deal councils, a chance to reassert their ideas about competition and their suspicion of big business. In 1934, long before the cartelization of the N.R.A. was abandoned, the economist Gardiner C. Means, then economic adviser to the Secretary of Agriculture, had prepared a memorandum on administered prices that provided the economic rationale for a new approach to the depression. Early in 1935 this memorandum was published by the Senate.[46]

[46]Gardiner C. Means: *Industrial Prices and Their Relative Inflexibility*, Senate Document No. 13, 74th Cong., 1st sess. Parts of this document, along with later papers on the same theme, are reprinted in Means's *The Corporate Revolution in America* (New York, 1962). For a critique and some reflections on later interest in the theory, see Richard Ruggles: "The Nature of Price Flexibility and the Determinants of Relative Price Changes in the Economy," in *Business Concentration and Price Policy* (Princeton, 1955), esp. pp. 443–64, and the conflicting views expressed by economists before the Kefauver Committee:

Means contrasted market prices, which were made and remade in the market as the result of interactions between buyers and sellers in the fashion of traditional economic theory, with administered prices, which were set by administrative action and held constant for a considerable period of time. Market prices are flexible and respond readily to a fall in demand; administered prices are rigid. Means considered the disparity between flexible and rigid prices to be an important aggravating force in the depression. Although he did not identify administered prices with monopoly, he focused attention once again on those industries in which market power was sufficiently concentrated to make administered prices possible. Some of his contemporaries seized upon the conception as a rationale for stepping up antitrust activity, and Franklin D. Roosevelt invoked it in his message of 1938, calling for the creation of the T.N.E.C. At the same time, other New Deal theorists, notably Assistant Attorney General Robert Jackson, who was then head of the Antitrust Division of the Department of Justice, and Secretary of the Interior Harold L. Ickes, became convinced that the organized power of big business was attempting to sabotage reform through a "strike of capital" and that a new assault on business power must be undertaken as a basis for further attempts at recovery. The old argument that business power was a threat to democratic government itself thus entered into Roosevelt's T.N.E.C. message.

The new attack on business power took two forms; the first was the elaborate, if inconclusive, T.N.E.C. investigation, which yielded a mass of factual information, much of it new, but no programmatic proposals in which the investigators themselves had any confidence.[47] The second was the

---

Administered Prices, Hearings before the Subcommittee on Antitrust and Monopoly of the Committee on the Judiciary, United States Senate (Washington, 1957).

[47]Early in its *Final Report* (p. 4), the Committee confessed that its members "are not rash enough to believe that they can lay down a program which will solve the great problems that beset the world, but they are convinced that the information which this committee has assembled, when eventually properly analyzed and disseminated, will enable the people of America to know what must be done if human freedom is to be preserved." In short, the Committee did not know what precisely to make of its own data but hoped that in due

stepping up of antitrust activity under the leadership of Thurman Arnold, the new chief of the Antitrust Division. Congress doubled appropriations for Arnold's division in 1939 and then doubled them again in 1940. Between 1938 and 1943 its staff grew almost fivefold.

In retrospect it is instructive to see what results came from uncertain and, at times, ill-considered beginnings. Today the Jackson-Ickes view of the recession seems quite partisan and fanciful; the T.N.E.C. investigation, for all the information it gathered, was from a pragmatic point of view a fiasco; the value of Means's emphasis on administered prices is highly controversial among economists; and Thurman Arnold's experiment with antitrust enforcement can be judged, at least from one angle of vision, a substantial failure. And yet, as in the case of so many of the gropings of the New Deal, there was a valuable outcome, which in this case can best be got at by looking at the core of success wrapped up in Thurman Arnold's frustration.

Arnold's story is replete with ironies. He had written of the antitrust enterprise with a devastating note of mockery, and the appointment of a man with such views, especially by an administration that had only recently resorted to the wholesale cartelization of the N.R.A., was looked at askance by antitrust-minded senators as a possible effort to sabotage the Antitrust Division. But Arnold proceeded to recruit and inspire a splendid staff and to rehabilitate the entire antitrust function. His goal was not to attack bigness or efficient mass production or efficient marketing, but rather to discipline the pricing policies of business at the vital points where abuses seemed most important. Antitrust was thus to become an instrument of social and economic policy, aimed to stop firms from setting prices above reasonable levels, to prevent businesses from holding new processes off the market, and to reduce unemployment. All this was to be achieved not so much by isolated cases or by responding to this or that complaint, but rather by systematic action against whole industries—motion pictures, petroleum, radio broadcasting, drugs, housing.

From a short-run point of view, Arnold's regime could be judged a failure. His program for housing was spiked when the

---

time the public would. See the penetrating critique by two members, Isador Lubin and Leon Henderson: ibid., pp. 51–2.

Supreme Court made it impossible to act effectively against the labor unions, which constituted a linchpin of restraint of trade in that industry; his plan for the food industry lost its point during the war; his program for transportation was put off by the War Production Board.[48] He could not wholly reform a single industry, much less bring about important general structural changes in the economy. And yet he succeeded in demonstrating the usefulness of the antitrust laws. In actually *using* the Sherman Act, thanks to the enlarged staff that Congress had given him, he showed for the first time what it could and could not do. Although it could not alter the fundamental character of the economy or make it less liable to cyclical instability (as Arnold had promised it would in his book *The Bottlenecks of Business*), it could significantly affect the conduct of business within the framework of the existing structure. Arnold's division soon won a number of decisions from the courts—particularly in the Alcoa case of 1945 and the American Tobacco case of the following year—which opened new possibilities for enforcement. It won from Congress a permanent reversal of the former policy of niggardly support. And finally, it put the antitrust enterprise on such a footing that it could flourish under both Democratic and Republican regimes.

The return of the Republicans under Eisenhower did not bring a remission of efforts to use the Sherman Act or a retrenchment of the Antitrust Division. Instead, the Eisenhower administration set up the Attorney General's National Committee to Study the Antitrust Laws, which in 1955 returned a unanimous judgment in favor of antitrust policy and of the current state of case law, under which enforcement had been tightened. Although the Committee did not make any dramatic recommendations for more rigorous enforcement, the effect of its work was to reaffirm the bipartisan character of the antitrust commitment by ratifying the achievements of Democratic administrations in the preceding fifteen years.[49] Nor

[48]See Corwin D. Edwards: "Thurman Arnold and the Antitrust Laws," *Political Science Quarterly*, LVII (September 1943), 338–55.
[49]*Report of the Attorney General's National Committee to Study the Antitrust Laws* (Washington, 1955). For a critique, see Mason: op. cit., pp. 389–401.

should we forget that the most spectacular and revealing case involving a criminal price conspiracy—the General Electric case—took place during the Eisenhower administration.

What makes it possible to institutionalize antitrust activities at the higher plateau that has been maintained since 1938 is not a consensus among economists as to its utility in enhancing economic efficiency, but a rough consensus in society at large as to its value in curbing the dangers of excessive market power. As in the beginning, it is based on a political and moral judgment rather than economic measurement or even distinctively economic criteria. "It must be recognized," says Edward S. Mason, "that there is an element of faith in the proposition that maintaining competition substantially improves the efficiency of resource use." The option for a minimal level of competition to be underwritten by public policy, although it can be backed by substantial economic arguments, "rests basically on a political judgment," write Carl Kaysen and Donald F. Turner in their inquiry into trust policy: "In our democratic, egalitarian society, large areas of uncontrolled private power are not tolerated." "We found," write J. B. Dirlam and A. E. Kahn in their book *Fair Competition*, "that the decisions [of courts and commissions] could not be fully understood or fairly appraised by economic standards alone. Hence we concluded that the appropriate question for economists to ask about antitrust policy is not whether this is the most efficient way of structuring or reorganizing the economy, but the inverted one: Does antitrust seriously interfere with the requirements of efficiency?" "The rationale of antitrust," writes A. D. Neale, a British student of the American experience, "is essentially a desire to provide legal checks to restrain economic power and is not a pursuit of efficiency as such." "For most Americans," concludes John Kenneth Galbraith, "free competition, so called, has for long been a political rather than an economic concept."[50]

In any case, the state of antitrust enforcement seems to correspond with a public consensus. Economists and lawyers

[50] Edward S. Mason in the Preface to Carl Kaysen and Donald B. Turner: *Antitrust Policy* (Cambridge, Mass., 1960), p. xx; ibid., p. 5; J. B. Dirlam and A. E. Kahn: *Fair Competition* (Ithaca, 1954), p. 2; A. D. Neale: *The Antitrust Laws of the U.S.A.* (Cambridge, Eng., 1962), p. 487; Galbraith: op. cit., p. 27.

differ profoundly on how effective the antitrust laws have been
and on how effective they could be if they were more amply
enforced,[51] but there is hardly a major industry that has not
seen a significant lawsuit or two, and in most industries in
which intervention might be thought desirable, government
action has had more than negligible effects.[52] It is also one of
the strengths of antitrust that neither its effectiveness nor its
ineffectiveness can be precisely documented; its consequences
rest on events of unknown number and significance that have
not happened—on proposed mergers that may have died in
the offices of corporation counsel, on collusive agreements that
have never been consummated, on unfair practices contemplated but never carried out. Liberals can support it because
they retain their old suspicion of business behavior, and conservatives support it because they still believe in competition
and they may hope to gain an additional point of leverage in
the battle against inflation. No one seems prepared to suggest
that the antitrust enterprise be cut back drastically, much less
abandoned, and Congress has consistently supported its enlarged staff. The existing state of enforcement conforms to the
state of the public mind, which accepts bigness but continues
to distrust business morals. Even business itself accords to the
principle of antitrust a certain grudging and irritated acceptance, and largely confines its resistance to the courts. Visita-
tions by the Department of Justice are a nuisance, lawsuits are
expensive, and prosecution carries an odious stigma, but the
antitrust procedures can be considered an alternative to more
obtrusive regulation such as outright controls on prices. At any
rate, big business has never found it necessary or expedient to
launch a public campaign against antitrust enforcement; the
pieties at stake are too deep to risk touching.

A final element in antitrust enforcement rests on the fact
that the government itself is now a major consumer, and the
points of exposure of industrial prices to official concern and

---

[51]See, for example, the symposium in Dexter M. Keezer (ed.): "The Effectiveness of the Federal Antitrust Laws," *American Economic Review*, XXXIX (June
1949), 689–724.
[52]See the industry-by-industry survey in Simon N. Whitney: *Antitrust Policies:
American Experience in Twenty Industries*, 2 vols. (New York, 1958).

reaction have been multiplied. One of the reasons for the anti-trust revival in 1938 was the irritation of government officials over the prevalence of what seemed to be collusively priced bids. Thurman Arnold's hope that consumers could be mobilized behind the new antitrust enforcement was out of keeping with the historical passivity and disorganization of American consumers. But the presence of the government as a consumer may supply some of the leverage he was looking for.

Antitrust reform is not the first reform in American history whose effectiveness depended less upon a broad movement of militant mass sentiment than upon the activities of a small group of influential and deeply concerned specialists. In ceasing to be largely an ideology and becoming largely a technique, antitrust has taken its place among a great many other elements of our society that have become differentiated, specialized, and bureaucratized. Since no layman can any longer concern himself with the enormous body of relevant case law or with the truly formidable literature of economic analysis and argument that has come to surround the issue, the potentialities of antitrust action have become almost exclusively the concern of a technical elite of lawyers and economists. Indeed, the business of studying, attacking, defending, and evaluating oligopolistic behavior and its regulation has become one of our lively small industries, which gives employment to many gifted professional men. No doubt this is another, if lesser, reason why antitrust has become self-sustaining: it is not our way to liquidate an industry in which so many have a stake.

If all this is taken as the preface to some unduly optimistic conclusion, my intention will have been misunderstood. My concern is not to suggest that the old problem of market power is on the verge of being solved; it is merely to illustrate how expectations and creeds can change, and how a particular reform, after two generations of noisy but seemingly futile agitation, has been quietly and effectively institutionalized. But it is one thing to say that antitrust has at last begun to fulfill a function, and another to forget how modest that function is. Although the full range of evils anticipated seventy-five years ago from concentration and monopoly has not materialized, the traditional American fear of concentrated power seems hardly less pertinent today. The American economy, whether or not its concentration is still significantly increasing, is extremely concentrated as it stands, and its business structure has brought into being a managerial class of immense social and political as well as market power. This class is by no means evil or sinister in its intentions, but its human limitations often seem even more impressive than the range of its powers, and under modern conditions we have a right to ask again whether we can ever create enough checks to restrain it. The economy over which it presides has had remarkable successes in increasing its production of goods and services, and yet the urban mass society in which these are produced is still not freed from widespread poverty and impresses us again and again with the deepness of its malaise, the range of its problems that stand unsolved, even in some cases pitifully untried. Today our greatest domestic danger lies not in our failure to produce enough goods because we do not have enough competition, but in our failure to render certain humane, healing, humanly productive and restorative social services that are not comprehended at all in the ethos of competition. At its best, big business will not perform such services. At its worst, it can sustain a class of men who will prevent them from being performed.

Free Silver and the Mind of "Coin" Harvey

In 1963 the John Harvard Library republished William H. Harvey's *Coin's Financial School*, the best-selling free-silver tract of the 1890's. Harvey has always been an elusive figure. He left no papers, and it is unlikely that a full biography will ever be written of this man who did as much as any other in our history to give articulate voice to a folk agitation. This essay, now somewhat revised, first appeared as the Introduction to the John Harvard Library edition; it is the most extended account of Harvey that has been written, and it is here set against the complex background of the silver controversy.

I

WHO TODAY can understand without a strenuous effort of imagination the passions once aroused by the cry for free silver? Despite the pointless and long-sustained policy of silver purchases into which the federal government was forced by silver interests in 1934, the once heated issue of the bimetallic standard has been rendered obsolete by modern devices of monetary management. Yet a whole generation of Americans was embroiled from the 1870's to the 1890's in the argument over silver. To the combatants of that era, silver and gold were not merely precious metals but precious symbols, the very substance of creeds and faiths which continued long afterward to have meaning for men living on the echoes of nineteenth-century orthodoxies. In 1933, when Franklin D. Roosevelt took the United States "off gold," Lewis W. Douglas said, at the end of a long and anxious night: "This is the end of Western civilization." From another point of view, Senator Ashurst of Arizona, pressed by Secretary Morgenthau about his obsession with silver, replied: "My boy, I was brought up from my mother's knee on silver and I can't discuss that with you any more than you can discuss your religion with me."[1]

The free-silver campaign of 1896 was one of the stormy, disruptive campaigns of our history, the first since Jackson's day

---

[1] Raymond Moley: *After Seven Years* (New York, 1939), pp. 159–60; John M. Blum: *From the Morgenthau Diaries* (Boston, 1959), p. 186.

when a presidential election hung on a financial issue. Sentiment for free coinage of silver was not strong enough to elect Bryan, but it was strong enough to wrest control of the Democratic party away from President Cleveland, to split the Republicans into two irreconcilable factions, and to transform the new Populist party into a single-issue satellite of Bryan and the Democrats. It was menacing enough to unite all the forces of goldbug respectability behind McKinley, and to spur an election effort without precedent in our history. In defeating silver the goldbugs were not merely defeating a reform, they were stemming a crusade.

The student who tries to recapture the emotions of this crusade reads Bryan's "Cross of Gold" speech as the great document of the silver cause. Yet his speech sums up a case already made; it assumes much and explains little to a reader ignorant of the preceding years of monetary argument. One cannot tell from it how the silver men arrived at their sense of conviction. If Bryan was immediately understood by his audience, it was because he played upon a set of feelings already formed and inflamed by a vast literature of analysis and agitation; and of all this literature, by far the most effective and memorable work was William Hope Harvey's little book of 155 pages, first printed two years before, in June 1894.

Eighteen ninety-four was a grim year. A depression had begun sharply early in 1893. Its effects were heightened by a stock-market panic in May and by the threatened exhaustion of federal gold reserves. By mid-1894 the economy was in its grip. Farmers were frantic over the collapse of wheat and cotton prices. Bank failures and business bankruptcies mounted to unimagined heights. Thousands of men of substance found themselves ruined, as Henry Adams knew when he lamented that his entire generation had had notice to quit. Mills and factories were closing daily, and soon one man of every five in the labor force was unemployed. Long lines of hungry and desperate men tramped the streets and highways. While Harvey was getting *Coin's Financial School* ready for publication, Coxey's "army" of unemployed was marching in protest on Washington, and in the month the book appeared the violent Pullman strike began, which was soon to be smashed by federal troops sent to Illinois by President

Cleveland. By the end of 1894 Cleveland's party was quarreling irreconcilably about his fiscal policies, and the Populist party, which some conservatives looked upon as the vanguard of an anarchistic apocalypse, had made serious inroads on the strength of both major parties in the West and South. No one knew how far the crisis would carry the country from its old ways, or how many institutions were still fated to crumble.

Sufferers from the crisis were crying for a simple solution, and their confusion over its causes only heightened their dogmatism about its cure. The dispute over the government's silver purchases, a central issue since 1890, had fixed everyone's mind on the money question, and the near exhaustion of the Treasury's gold reserves commanded nervous day-by-day attention. Almost everyone was either denouncing the free-silver maniacs of the West and South or scourging the bankers and Shylocks of New York and London. *Coin's Financial School* rode on the wave of an almost unbelievable money mania. A correspondent wrote to Cleveland's secretary in May 1895: "Have been pretty well over the country since we last met, traveling through twenty-four States, more than ten thousand miles, South and West. The people in that section are simply crazy on the money question; they cannot discuss it rationally." A rural editor in Kentucky wrote: "Politics down here has gone mad. Every crank in the country is loose and nothing less than a stone wall will stop them." Kenesaw M. Landis reported from Illinois:

> The God's truth is the Democratic party in Indiana and Illinois is wildly insane on this subject. . . . The farmers are especially unruly. . . . I've got a lot of farmer uncles down in Indiana—good honest and intelligent men as honesty and intelligence go at this day—but utterly wild on the money question. You can't do anything with them—just got to let them go.

A Mississippi congressman wrote to Cleveland's Secretary of War in April 1895: "A little free silver book called 'Coin's Financial School' is being sold on every railroad train by the newsboys and at every cigar store. . . . It is being read by almost everybody."[2]

[2]James A. Barnes: *John G. Carlisle, Financial Statesman* (New York, 1931), pp. 449, 452, 438.

II

For a long time now only a few specialists have read this little tract that was once read by "almost everybody." Although printed in the hundreds of thousands, it is hard to come by, and its yellowing pages crack and crumble as they are turned. No doubt thousands of frail copies were simply read and thumbed to death. But neither Harvey nor his pamphlet can be forgotten. He was the Tom Paine of the free-silver movement, and *Coin's Financial School* was to the silver men of 1896 what *Common Sense* had been to the revolutionaries of 1776. That free silver was a losing cause should not blind us to the importance of *Coin's Financial School* as a basic expression of the American popular imagination.

Bryan remarked of *Coin's Financial School* that it was "the most potent of educational forces at work in behalf of bimetallism. It is safe to say that no book in recent times has produced so great an effect in the treatment of an economic question." No one will ever know how many copies were distributed. Harvey wrote to *The Forum* in 1895 that sales during its first eleven months exceeded 400,000 copies. During the campaign of 1896, the National Silver party bought and distributed 125,000 copies. The most conservative estimate of its sales is 650,000, the most generous is Harvey's of 1,500,000. His widow's more sober guess of 1,000,000 seems closer to the mark, and is by no means implausible.[3] Priced variously at twenty-five cents, fifty cents, and a dollar, published in varying grades of paper and binding, bought in quantities by interested organizations, and widely hawked about by vendors, *Coin's Financial School* was susceptible of a mass circulation reached often in its day by popular magazines but seldom by books.

The literary form chosen for Harvey's presentation of his ideas was simple but effective. "Coin," a young but preternaturally wise little financier, tries to remedy the sufferings of the depression by attacking the intellectual illusions which

---

[3] William Jennings Bryan: *The First Battle* (Chicago, 1896), pp. 153–4, 292; *The Forum*, XIX (July 1895), 573 n.; Frank L. Mott: *Golden Multitudes: The Story of Best Sellers in the United States* (New York, 1947), pp. 170–1. In *Coin's Financial School Up to Date* (Chicago, 1895), p. i, Harvey mentioned sales of 5,000 a day.

have brought it about. He establishes a school in Chicago at the Art Institute, to which he invites the young men of the city for a series of six lectures on the money question. The book reports his lectures, but since he is at times interrupted by friendly or argumentative questions, it takes the form of a monologue broken by occasional dialogues. (Harvey may have been led to this dramatic device by the example of the first book his firm published, Archbishop Walsh's tract on bimetallism, which was presented as an interview with a reporter.) As the lectures go on, the audience supposedly fills with actual persons whom Harvey did not scruple to name; a few are obscure friends of the silver cause, but they are mainly well-known editors, politicians, businessmen, lawyers, and economists. The fictitious Coin thus appears to engage in real encounters, heard attentively by men like Philip D. Armour, Marshall Field, H. H. Kohlsaat, and Senator Shelby Cullom.[4] Gold advocates pose questions which they are confident will trip Coin, but he answers with such a majestic command of fact and theory that they are thrown into confusion. Among those most decisively worsted are the leading Chicago banker, Lyman J. Gage, later to be McKinley's Secretary of the Treasury, and the monetary authority J. Laurence Laughlin, professor of economics at the University of Chicago. The introduction of these contemporaries gave the "school" such an air of reality, despite the patently fictional character of its central figure, that many readers believed that the lectures had actually been given. Laughlin, who was particularly outraged at having been portrayed as worsted by a tyro in economics, found it desirable, along with Gage, Kohlsaat, and some of the others allegedly in attendance at the "school," who had grown tired of answering letters from readers querying them about what they were supposed to have said, to join in a statement that the whole thing was a fiction.

Though Laughlin believed that an amateur work like Harvey's was "not worthy of serious discussion," he found it necessary to answer Harvey in a pamphlet, *Facts about Money*,

---

[4] In an hour spent with contemporary directories one can identify most of the persons named in *Coin's Financial School*. However, there was no such person as "young Medill" (p. 99), and it is possible that a few other names were also erroneous.

and even to debate with him on a public platform. Another of the well-known authors who refuted Harvey was Horace White, the economic journalist of the New York *Evening Post* and the author of a standard work on money and banking, who called his onslaught *Coin's Financial Fool: or The Artful Dodger Exposed. A Complete Reply to Coin's Financial School.* The rage for monetary argument and the extraordinary success of Harvey's little book provoked a host of answers by gold-bug opponents—and the literature mounted to a point which would make a major project for a bibliographer.[5] The answers were written with varying degrees of economic sophistication and provided with titles of varying flippancy or solemnity: for example, George E. Roberts's *Coin at School in Finance*, Edward Wisner's *Cash vs. Coin*, Jay Loring's *Coin's Financial School Exposed and Closed*, Robert F. Rowell's *The Mistakes of Coin*, John A. Frazer and Charles H. Serghel's *Sound Money*, Melville D. Landon's *Money, Gold, Silver, or Bimetallism*, John F. Cargill's *A Freak in Finance*, Stanley Wood's *Answer to "Coin's Financial School,"* W. B. Mitchell's *Dollars or What?*, L. G. Power's *Farmer Hayseed in Town: or, The Closing Days of Coin's Financial School*, Charles Elton Blanchard's *Report of Uncle Sam's Homilies in Finance*, Everett P. Wheeler's *Real Bi-Metallism or True Coin versus False Coin.* Yet not one of these appears to have had even a small portion of the impact of the book it was meant to refute.

These titles evoke the atmosphere of an age of polemics; yet perhaps the most remarkable thing about *Coin's Financial School* is the comparative austerity of its tone. To be sure, it has its flashes of sardonic humor, its strokes of dazzling irrelevancy, and its moments of headlong rhetoric. But on the whole, when one considers Harvey's own mettlesome temperament and re-members the intemperance of a time when the goldbug press

[5]Some of the leading items in this literature were reviewed in Willard Fisher's judicious and valuable essay "'Coin' and His Critics," *Quarterly Journal of Economics*, X (January 1896), 187–208. Harvey wrote a piece about the critics of his book in which he said that they were "slaves set to lash the author of that book and their master is—money." Christ, he said, had been killed at the behest of the money-changers of Judea, and now he, Harvey, was being persecuted by the same "unconquered and relentless" money power. "'Coin's Financial School' and Its Censors," *North American Review*, CLXI (July 1895), 72, 74–5.

frequently described silver senators as "fanatics," "cossacks," "border ruffians," "bandits," "disloyalists," "traitors," and "lunatics," *Coin's Financial School* seems the more remarkable for an air, however delusive, of sticking to the task of rational analysis. It has behind it the fierce logic of the one-idea mind, the firm conviction that complex social issues can be unraveled to the last point and pinned down for good, that social problems can really be solved, and solved by simple means. However amateurish and unsure, it is a rather technical discussion of one of the most intricate of subjects, the monetary standard; and one can only be touched at the thought of the effort of mind that it must have called forth in many of its readers, who hoped that by reading it carefully they might *understand* what had happened. Probably more than any other of our politico-social best sellers, it makes a primarily ratiocinative demand on its readers. Compared with our other popular tracts on social issues, its appeal is hard to comprehend—it lacks the great revolutionary rhetoric of Paine's *Common Sense*, the alluring pornographic overtones of the widely read anti-Catholic pamphlet *Awful Disclosures* by Maria Monk, the human appeal of *Uncle Tom's Cabin*, the major prophetic gifts and sustained analysis of *Progress and Poverty*, the novelistic form and universal significance of *Looking Backward*. It stays close to details of the money problem, relying mainly upon effective cartoons for its emotional impact. For Harvey himself it was the product of a rare moment. Nothing that he wrote afterward was to have anything like its argumentative surge or its show of coherence. Nothing that he had done before gave any hint that he would be known to the world as the author of a book.

III

William Hope ("Coin") Harvey was born in 1851 in the little village of Buffalo, in the western part of Virginia, the fifth child of six born to Robert and Anna Harvey.[6] Robert Trigg Harvey was a Virginian of Scottish and English ancestry, and his wife,

---

[6]Biographical information, except where otherwise indicated, is taken from Jeannette P. Nichols's excellent sketch "Bryan's Benefactor: Coin Harvey and His World," *Ohio Historical Quarterly*, LXVII (October 1958), 299–325.

who had Virginian ancestors traceable to colonial times, was descended also from French stock that had long since peopled the territory around nearby Gallipolis. Almost nothing is known of William Harvey's childhood except that it was disturbed by conflict between the Unionist majority in his region and secessionist sympathizers, among whom were some members of his father's family. One of young Harvey's sisters was sent to a convent for safety's sake during the war and, to the family's distress, became a nun. An older brother was wounded fighting under Lee.

At the war's end, young Harvey began study at the little academy in Buffalo, taught school for a few months at the age of sixteen, and afterward briefly attended Marshall College, then a state normal school offering instruction at the secondary school level. His three months there marked the end of his formal education. He spent a short time reading law, in those days the customary way of preparing for the profession, was admitted to the bar at the age of nineteen, and opened practice in the village of Barboursville, West Virginia, the seat of Cabell County. When the railroad tycoon Collis P. Huntington established a depot for the Chesapeake & Ohio Railroad at the Ohio River town which was named for him, William Hope Harvey made the first of his many adult changes of residence and entered practice in partnership with an older brother in Huntington, West Virginia. The town, which was growing rapidly, was the largest place in which Harvey had lived.

Before long, Harvey's restlessness had him on the move. In 1875, at the age of twenty-four, he moved to Gallipolis, Ohio, a busy spot in the Ohio River valley about forty miles above Huntington, and there met Anna Halliday, whom he married in 1876. The couple soon went to Cleveland, where Harvey tried his hand at law in a major center of commerce and industry and where the first two of their four children were born.[7] After three years in Cleveland, Harvey took his growing family to Chicago, but a little more than a year of Chicago was enough for him, and in 1881 the Harveys, now numbering five,

[7]Since Ohio was a center of Greenback agitation during the 1870's, it is quite possible that Harvey first became interested in the money question during these years.

returned to Gallipolis. Harvey now became attorney for several wholesale houses in Ohio. In 1883 a client's affairs took him to the southwest corner of Colorado, where prospectors had not long before discovered rich deposits of silver, and there, at the age of thirty-two, Harvey had his first experience with the white metal that was to give him his place in history. The following year he took his family, along with a force of ten young workers, to Colorado. There he started working claims near Ouray, and the young entrepreneur's still growing family was housed in a large mountainside cabin. In the cold of winter, his wife and children moved to California, while he stayed at the mines, except for Christmas time, living near his work in a room fashioned out of one corner of an engine house. For three years Harvey worked arduously, and at some cost to his health, superintending the production of the Silver Bell, a mine of considerable yield. But he had entered silver mining at one of its worst moments. High costs of operation were driving out small enterprisers and favoring large producers. The mine fields swarmed with displaced workers, wages fell, and the industry was riven with strikes. Worst of all, silver prices, which had gone down disastrously in the 1870's, were still falling sharply as production rose.

Harvey soon abandoned the mines for the real estate business, which he combined with his law practice. This occupied him for six years successively in Pueblo, Denver, and Ogden, Utah. He was remembered in Colorado for having sold an "Elixir of Life," which was curative of a variety of human ills, and as one of the promoters of an exposition hall in Pueblo, the Mineral Palace, which housed a collection of Rocky Mountain minerals. Opened with a grand fete in the summer of 1890, the palace was the most gaudy and the most successful of the various enterprises with which Harvey had been associated. The taste of success did not overcome Harvey's wanderlust, for his moves to Denver and Ogden followed his ventures in Pueblo. In Ogden he bought and improved a house, perhaps with permanent settlement in mind. He also bought for development a one-mile frontage along Great Salt Lake, and appears to have tried to promote a festival patterned after the New Orleans Mardi Gras, in which local tradition reports that he lost a substantial sum.

In any case, Harvey had enough capital left to move his
brood back to Chicago again in May 1893 and to set up a specialized publishing business dedicated to free silver. At forty-
two he was neither a complete failure nor, in his ambitious
terms, a success. His restless search for wealth had led him to
take up nine residences in the thirteen years since he had begun the practice of law. He had been in Colorado long enough
to feel the anguish and disappointment of the silver miners and
to absorb the historical and monetary lore of the free-silver
advocates, which was as much an orthodoxy in Colorado as the
gold standard was in New York. Untutored in the intricacies
of academic economics, he had absorbed in a bitter school of
experience the convictions that were to bring into focus the
major discontents of his time. "Coin" Harvey was prepared for
his sudden leap onto the stage of history.

IV

"Coin" Harvey was a money crank, one of a type the United
States has produced in substantial numbers. The early demand
for an adequate money supply, the perennial want of an adequate central banking system, the open character of our entrepreneurial economy, the violent upheavals and reversals of
individual fortunes—all these things have produced a great
many economic dissenters and have given their homemade
systems of ideas a wide reception. Each depression has been
a prolific breeder of panaceas, panacea mongers, and monetary pamphleteers. The striking thing about the depression of
the nineties was how rapidly the cry for free coinage of silver
shoved other reform proposals from the center of the stage.

To understand this, one must recall briefly the history of
monetary issues since the Civil War. Before the war, the United
States had been in law (though not, as we shall see, in fact)
on a bimetallic standard. In 1861, wartime demands forced the
country to suspend specie redemption of its currency and to
issue United States notes, the "greenbacks," which were full legal tender, except for the payment of customs duties and interest on the public debt. The nation was now on an inconvertible
paper standard. Its greenbacks circulated at a substantial and
growing discount in terms of gold. A period of hectic inflation

ensued, and when the war was over, many economic and political leaders urged that the greenbacks be retired and that
specie payments be promptly resumed. They met with a good
deal of resistance from farmers and many businessmen, particularly in the West, who remembered wartime inflation for the
prosperity that accompanied it, who had already suffered from
the postwar economic relapse, and who dreaded any further
currency contraction. (There were also some high-tariff businessmen, East and West, who favored inflation because they
thought it would have a protectionist effect.)

Postwar inflationism, then, first took the form of resistance
to the retirement of the greenbacks. Superficially, this movement had a moment of success in 1868, when Congress prohibited the further retirement and cancellation of greenbacks, and
another such moment in 1874, when, under the stress of the
depression, Congress somewhat increased the number of these
bills. Indeed, during the depression that began in 1873, greenback inflationism waxed strong. A new Greenback party arose,
whose candidates amassed a million votes in the congressional
elections of 1878.

But, so far as the price level itself was concerned, the inflationists had been fighting a losing battle since 1865. The men
who directed American policy during these years were following a spartan policy. They believed that the currency would
not be sound or stable until the government returned to specie payments—more specifically, until it restored, at full value,
the gold dollar that had prevailed before the war. In order for
this to be accomplished, it was necessary that the American
price level fall in relation to European price levels—which were
themselves falling. Otherwise, high American prices would
lower exports, increase imports, and cause an outflow of
gold. This would have undermined the policy of the Treasury,
which was to accumulate a gold reserve adequate for ultimate
resumption.

The deflationary policy did not require an actual contraction of the currency—a measure always fraught with political
danger. In fact, thanks largely to an increase in bank deposits
and bank notes, the supply of money in the hands of the public grew steadily from 1870 to 1875 and again after 1878. The
drastic—and to gold-standard strategists satisfactory—fall in

the price level came not from an actual fall in the money supply, as Greenback theorists seemed to think, but from a rapid
rise in real output that outpaced the growth in the money
supply. The American economy was being allowed to grow
into its monetary skin. The contribution of those who controlled monetary policy was simply to resist political demands
for large new issues of greenbacks. Economic growth did the
rest.[8] Meanwhile, the Greenback men in their opposition to
deflation fortified an illusion that the silver movement was to
inherit. In focusing on greenbacks as though they were the
only hope of expanding the money supply, they tended to ignore the sustained increase in the money supply that was being
made available by the activities of the banks, and particularly by
a large increase in demand deposits. The entire overemphasis
on the monetary factor in the business cycle, and the corresponding neglect of other factors, which colored the views of
both sides during the battle of the standards in the 1890's, was
thus strengthened during the Greenback period.

At any rate, many men of otherwise conservative views and
substantial interests were convinced during this period that the
return to gold was being bought at a terrible price. But the
deflationists were successful in realizing their aims: the greenbacks soon began to recover their value in relation to gold.
In 1875 Congress passed the Resumption Act, providing for a
return to specie payments on January 1, 1879. The greenback
dollar itself steadily rose in value until it finally achieved parity
with gold two weeks before the date set for resumption.

Every informed person understood that when specie payments were resumed they would be made in gold alone. Here

[8]On deflation and specie resumption, see James K. Kindahl: "Economic Factors in Specie Resumption in the United States, 1865–70," *Journal of Economic
History*, LXIX (February 1961), 30–48. On the Greenback movement, see the
comprehensive study by Irwin Unger: *The Greenback Era* (Princeton, 1964)
and on the money supply, two essays by J. G. Gurley and E. S. Shaw: "The
Growth of Debt and Money in the United States, 1800–1950: A Suggested Interpretation," *Review of Economics and Statistics*, XLI (August 1959), 250–62,
esp. p. 258, and Ch. 4 of Seymour Harris (ed.): *American Economic History*
(New York, 1961), esp. pp. 111–14. The major work on the whole subject is
Milton Friedman and Anna J. Schwartz: *A Monetary History of the United
States, 1867–1960* (Princeton, 1963).

it may help to bear in mind a distinction between the legal and the actual state of the monetary standard to avoid a confusion that afflicted Harvey and some of his contemporaries. In the beginning, the United States had been legally committed to bimetallism. But in order to have a successful bimetallic standard in fact, a government must be able so to adjust the value of the two metals as to keep them both in circulation. Bimetallism implies that the government will define its monetary unit—in our case, the dollar—as having a certain weight in both metals, maintain their convertibility at a fixed ratio, freely allow their import and export, and buy or coin them in unlimited quantities when they are brought to the mint. It is easy to see how the mechanism of the bimetallic system can be thrown into disorder. The mint ratio of exchange set by the government must correspond very closely with the world market ratio which reflects demand and supply for both monetary and non-monetary uses of the metals. If one of the two metals tends to be worth more in the market than it is at the mint, it is not likely to be brought to the mint for coinage in material amounts.[9] It will go into industrial use or into hoarding, leaving the other metal as the single circulating medium. Thus, if the mint ratio differs significantly from the market ratio, the two metals will circulate together only for a limited time. (Of course, if a number of governments with a sufficient combined demand can concur in a mint ratio, their joint action will tend to stabilize the value of the metals and make possible their simultaneous circulation.)

When the monetary system was organized under Hamilton's guidance, the mint ratio set by Congress at his suggestion was

[9]Or at least so respectable economic theory tells us. Unfortunately the actual behavior of men in the market does not always fully correspond with the theoretical expectations. In American experience the countervailing facts were such that substantial amounts of silver were presented for coinage while gold was overvalued, and even considerable amounts of gold while silver was overvalued. See H. Gordon Hayes's monitory note, "Bimetallism Before and After 1834," *American Economic Review*, XXIII (December 1933), 677–9, and the circumspect account in Neil Carothers: *Fractional Money* (New York, 1930), Ch. 7. While the facts of coinage did not adapt themselves very neatly to the requirements of economic theory, the character of the money in actual circulation did so well enough.

15 to 1—that is, 15 ounces of silver would exchange for 1 ounce of gold. But the commercial market ratio adhered fairly closely to 15.5 to 1—a figure at which it tended to be stabilized because this was the French mint ratio. Since France valued gold more highly in relation to silver than we did, it became profitable for American money brokers to export gold and import silver; after 1800 gold was in circulation only in minuscule amounts, after 1825 not at all. In effect, the nation was on silver.

In 1834, for reasons which need not detain us here, Congress intentionally pushed the pendulum too far in the opposite direction by setting the mint ratio at 16 to 1, expecting that silver would now be displaced by gold. For about a dozen years afterward the two metals circulated together, but at length silver dollars became a rarity. In 1850 the chairman of the House Committee on Ways and Means remarked: "We have had but a single standard for the last three or four years. That has been and now is gold."[10] The *coup de grâce* was given to silver circulation by the mid-century discoveries of gold in California and Australia, which so lowered the value of gold in relation to silver that the silver in a silver dollar became worth about $1.03. It was now worthwhile to melt or export such dollars (and even fractional silver currency), for their bulk silver content, rather than to use them as money.

While still in law committed to bimetallism, the United States had thus been actually on a kind of alternating standard, resting on silver most of the time from 1792 to 1834, and soon after that year on gold. The disappearance of silver from circulation for a generation caused most men to think of gold alone when they thought of the specie standard in the 1870's.

This fact provides the background to the Coinage Act of 1873, which within a few years of its uneventful passage was to become enormously controversial. The Act of 1873 was simply an attempt to codify the coinage practices of the country

[10]J. Laurence Laughlin: *The History of Bimetallism in the United States* (New York, 1885), pp. 78–9; see also pp. 52–74 for the background of the Act of 1834. The best-informed and most perspicuous single work I have found on currency history is Neil Carothers: *Fractional Money*, which of necessity goes beyond the constricted promise of its title.

and to simplify the fractional currency, which was in a chaotic state at the end of the Civil War. But in enumerating the coins that were to be maintained, the framers of the act dropped from the list the long defunct silver dollar. At that moment, the silver in a dollar was still worth $1.03,[11] and silver was not being brought to the mint for coinage in any consequential amount. Although changes were already in motion that would shortly lower the value of silver, only the most foresighted and perspicacious students of money could have foreseen that the value of silver would so soon drop so much. The abandonment of the standard silver dollar, which meant the end of legal bimetallism, was not objected to by any of the representatives of silver states in Congress in 1873 nor by anyone else. But the adoption of the Coinage Act happened to coincide closely with the outbreak of a grave depression and another price collapse, and came just on the eve of a drastic fall in the world price of silver. When the Act of 1873 was followed by the Resumption Act of 1875, it was clear to everyone that in 1879, when specie payments were to be resumed, the United States would be in law as it had earlier been in fact on the gold standard. Now the inflationists, though still stressing the defense of the greenbacks, began to demand the remonetization of silver as a remedy for falling prices. Soon the demand for the free and unlimited coinage of silver at 16 to 1 replaced the greenback issue as the dominant platform of the cheap-money men.

A glance at international price trends from the early 1870's to the middle 1890's will clarify the continuing force of the demand for monetary inflation and the prevalence of worldwide agricultural discontent. The secular downward movement of prices coincided with the formation and spread of the international gold standard, which was considered by many respectable contemporary analysts to be its primary cause. In 1871 (not in 1873, as Harvey dates it) the new German Empire gave

---

[11]While this was true of the silver dollar, it was not true of fractional silver pieces. In 1853 Congress had discovered that fractional coins could be kept in circulation, thus solving a long acute shortage of fractional money, if their silver content was reduced to a point somewhat below face value.

the first of a series of shocks to silver when it resolved to adopt the gold standard, and two years afterward it threw upon the world market substantial supplies of silver realized from melting its old coins. The prospect of absorbing this much silver was too much for the countries of the Latin Union—France, Belgium, Switzerland, Italy, and Greece. In 1873 and 1874 they ceased the free and unlimited coinage of silver, thus removing from the market the primary force that had served to stabilize the value of the white metal. Sweden, Norway, and Holland also followed Germany in adopting the gold standard. These events coincided with the opening of huge new deposits of silver in the American West, which boosted supplies of silver just as demand for its use as money was fast declining in the Western world. At the very time the "Coin" Harveys were sweating to extract more silver from their Silver Bells, the price of the metal was undermined. Standing at $1.32 an ounce in 1872, it fell to $1.11 in 1884 and to 63 cents in 1894.

This fall in the price of silver, though more acute, roughly paralleled the general world price trend from the 1870's to the 1890's. In the United States, the level of prices fell sharply with each depression and rallied only slightly in good times. This price trend was a constant hazard to certain types of new and marginal entrepreneurs, who were dependent on easy credit and especially vulnerable to business shocks; but of course it struck with particular severity those chronic debtors, the farmers. Above all, it was intolerable to those farmers who were producing a large portion of their crops for export into a world market increasingly oversupplied with their products—the growers of wheat and cotton. The swiftness and fatality of the fall in the prices of these two agricultural products outstripped all other. Wheat, which brought $1.37 a bushel in 1870, was down to 56 cents in 1894; raw cotton in the same years went from 23 cents a pound to 7 cents. It is easy to see why Coin, hoping to demonstrate the community of interest of farmers and silver, should have chosen to exhibit a table comparing the price histories of just three products: silver, cotton, and wheat. It is a defensible oversimplification to say that the inflationary movement in politics rested mainly upon the common concern of these three segments of the economy, each confronted with a disastrous oversupply of its product in the world market.

V

When the free-silver men won control of the inflationary
forces, they inherited from the Greenbackers a formidable
body of agitational literature and political folklore. The Greenback movement had succeeded in focusing the dissenting mind
on monetary policy as the primary solution of the nation's ills;
and in its opposition to bond issues and gold accumulation as
the basis for currency contraction, it had already convinced
many people that they were being victimized by a bondholders' conspiracy and that to issue bonds for sale in foreign markets reduced them to "'hewers of wood and drawers of water'
to foreigners." To convert this heritage of agitation to its own
uses, the silver movement had to overcome the prejudice held
by fiat-money men against all forms of specie, including silver.[12]

But as against the Greenbackers, the silver men had some
advantages. The first was intellectual: fiat money seemed unlimited and arbitrary, but hard silver money was tied to a metal
of limited supply, of long historic sanction among the money
systems of the world, and supported by great economists
and statesmen. Legal bimetallism had been traditional in the
United States as well as in many other parts of the world; silver
could be called, with some oversimplification, "the dollar of
our daddies," the staple of the currency system from Washington and Jefferson to Jackson. The second advantage was
political: the silver-producing states had a formidable bloc in
Congress; silver had a good following in both major parties
—in sharp contrast with the Greenback party, which even at its
height in 1878 did not elect a single senator. The silver states,
backed by their allies from the wheat and cotton states, could
not easily be ignored. The final advantage was financial: silver-
mining interests were able to bring to the silver movement

[12]In its first national platform, in 1876, the Greenback party mentioned silver
only to protest against the replacement of paper fractional currency by silver
coins as a policy which "although well calculated to enrich owners of silver mines
. . . will still further oppress in taxation an already overburdened people." By
1880 its platform called for "the unlimited coinage of silver as well as gold." In
1884 its platform boasted: "We forced the remonetization of the silver dollar,"
referring presumably to the Bland-Allison Act. K. H. Porter and D. B. Johnson:
National Party Platforms (Urbana, Ill., 1956), pp. 52, 57, 68.

more financial backing than the Greenback movement ever had. As time went on, the paper-money commitment of the Greenback tradition faded into the background, while its more adaptable sentiments about the world, its hostilities to bankers, bondholders, foreigners, and monopolists, were taken over by the silver spokesmen.

In 1878 the silver men had their first legislative success. Discontents aroused during the years of depression since 1873 had led to a great increase in silver agitation in all sections of the country from Pennsylvania to California, and many manufacturers joined with the silver and agrarian inflationists. Late in 1877 the House passed a bill introduced by "Silver Dick" Bland of Missouri calling for free coinage of silver and full legal tender. The margin was overwhelming: 163 to 34. Secretary of the Treasury John Sherman, still preoccupied with the success of his measures for refunding and resumption, saw that some compromises would have to be made with the forces opposed to monetary contraction. Fortified by the knowledge that free coinage would be blocked by the certain veto of President Hayes, he was able to rally Senate opposition around a compromise finally embodied in the Bland-Allison Act of 1878. This measure required the Secretary of the Treasury to buy and to have coined into dollars having full legal tender not less than $2,000,000 nor more than $4,000,000 worth of silver bullion each month. Although he strongly opposed the legal-tender provision, Sherman resigned himself to accepting it: "In a government like ours, it is always good to obey the popular current, and that has been done, I think, by the passage of the silver bill."[13] Happily the passage of this measure coincided with the return of prosperity, but it stemmed neither the general price decline nor the fall in the price of silver. Although conservative Secretaries of the Treasury consistently bought the minimum required amounts of silver, over $378,000,000 was issued under the provisions of the law, chiefly in the form of silver certificates.

[13]Jeanette P. Nichols: "John Sherman and the Silver Drive of 1877–78: The Origins of the Gigantic Subsidy," *Ohio Archaeological and Historical Quarterly*, XLVI (April 1937), 164; this article provides the most circumstantial account of this compromise.

The demand for silver purchases only increased with the agricultural crisis of the late 1880's. In 1889–90 the silver bloc in Congress received powerful reinforcements when six new Western states committed to silver entered the Union. In 1890, to win needed support for its high-tariff program, the Harrison administration made a new concession to the silver men by stepping up the level of silver purchases. The Sherman Silver Purchase Act of 1890 required the Secretary of the Treasury to buy 4,500,000 ounces of silver each month—an amount equal to the approximate output of domestic silver mines—and again to issue legal-tender Treasury notes in payment for it.

The existence of so large an amount of silver certificates was a threat to the gold reserves of the Treasury which had been so carefully built up by Sherman and his predecessors. Under the Sherman Act, the Secretary of the Treasury was required to maintain the two metals "at a parity," which meant that the silver certificates were to be as good as gold. The government was not committed to keep at par with gold all the old greenbacks still remaining in circulation and the silver dollars and the Treasury notes of 1890. Since the Treasury was required to redeem these obligations in gold, they represented a potential demand against its gold supply. The capacity of the Treasury to stand the strain depended on conditions of general prosperity. Prosperity brought about a substantial Treasury surplus, which left a comfortable margin for the luxury of silver purchases. The gold reserve was also momentarily strengthened by years of big European demand for American crops in 1879–81 and in 1891, which brought inflows of gold.

But even before the crisis of 1893, the Harrison administration had begun to undermine the surplus. Tariff revenues, then the main source of government funds, were cut by some provisions of the tariff of 1890, while an extravagant pension act and other enlarged expenditures made big new demands on federal funds. A growing anxiety in the business community about the state of the Treasury's gold stocks sent gold into hoarding. To meet its expenses the Treasury found that it had to pay out greenbacks and Treasury notes, but as these were soon presented for gold redemption they constituted a potential endless drain on gold supplies. When the central banks of European countries, themselves afflicted by depression and shaken by the failure of the House of Baring in 1890, began to tighten their gold policies, the situation grew worse.

Many years before, $100,000,000 in gold had been set aside as the reserve deemed necessary for the Treasury to hold to assure successful resumption. In time this figure, considered to be the level of a safe Treasury reserve, came to have a kind of magic significance among right-thinking men in the financial community. As Grover Cleveland put it, the figure was regarded "with a sort of sentimental solicitude." Only six weeks after his inauguration in 1893, the gold reserve fell below this figure, and soon afterward there began a headlong financial panic, marked by a stock-market collapse and a run on banks throughout the country. Cleveland was also aware that India was about to close its mints to silver coinage, which would deal another staggering blow to the price of silver. It was no longer possible to pretend that the United States could afford to redeem its silver issues in gold and stay on the gold standard. Accepting the necessity for a showdown with the silver forces, Cleveland called on June 30 for a special session of Congress to repeal the Sherman Silver Purchase Act.

The prosperity that had made it possible to compromise between silver inflationism and the gold standard was now gone, and in consequence the ensuing congressional debate had all the bitterness that occurs when no real accommodation of interests is possible. The gold men attributed the panic almost entirely to the silver purchase policy and to the failure of business confidence that had been created by uncertainty about future values and by threats to foreign trade and investments. They expatiated on the folly of a commitment to silver at a time when the metal was constantly falling in value and when its use as standard money had been abandoned by all the great trading nations of the West.

Silver men saw the panic in quite different terms: again and again they charged that it had been deliberately set off by heartless bankers simply to create conditions of distress under which they could force the repeal of the Sherman Act.[14]

---

[14]Though most of them were ready to admit that the panic had got out of hand. Cf. "Silver Dick" Bland: "Now the panic has come; and those who conspired to bring it about have got more than they bargained for." William V. Byars: *An American Commoner* (Columbia, Mo., 1900), p. 330; cf. the view

As for the Sherman Act itself, they held no brief for it, since what was really needed was the free and unlimited coinage of silver. But they saw it as the line of defense of the silver cause —"the last feeble barrier," a Populist senator from Nebraska called it, "between the patriotic and industrious masses of our people and that hoard of insolent, aggressive, and ravenous money-changers and gamblers of Lombard street and Wall street, who for private gain would . . . turn the world back into the gloom of the Dark Ages with all its attendant evil and misery."[15] When they were told that it was utterly impossible for the United States acting alone to maintain a parity between the two metals and that unlimited coinage was unthinkable at the existing ratio, they tended to fall back upon assertions of the size and grandeur of the United States, aspersions upon the states of Europe, and reminders of the pitiful economic condition of their constituents. In answer to the argument that free coinage would in effect mean silver monometallism, they might assert, as Senator Cockrell of Missouri later did, that this would be so much the better: "They can't exhaust the gold reserves too quickly to suit me. We can go to a silver basis without as much as a ripple in our financial system."[16]

Among those prominent in the congressional debates was William Jennings Bryan, who made a long and stirring speech in the House. In the Senate, where action was delayed by an exhausting filibuster, the silver case was argued by some of its ablest exponents, notably Senator Teller of Colorado, who, in the course of describing the miseries that would befall his own state if repeal passed, broke down in tears, slumped to his desk, and buried his face in his hands. Nothing availed: repeal was finally enacted at the end of October 1893, and the silver men had to rest their hopes on an appeal to the public.[17]

---

of Senator Teller of Colorado, in Elmer Ellis: *Henry Moore Teller* (Caldwell, Idaho, 1941), pp. 222–3.

[15] Senator William V. Allen: *Congressional Record*, 53rd Cong., 1st sess. (August 24, 1893), pp. 788–9.

[16] Barnes: op. cit., p. 367.

[17] On the fight over repeal, see Allan Nevins: *Grover Cleveland* (New York, 1932), Ch. 29, and Jeannette P. Nichols: "The Politics and Personalities of Silver Repeal in the United States Senate," *American Historical Review*, XLI (October 1935), 26–53.

It was here that Harvey found his role. All these climactic events must have absorbed his attention during the eighteen months before the appearance of his book. He moved to Chicago precisely at the outbreak of the panic, and was busy setting up the Coin Publishing Company during the months when the silver debate was nearing its climax. His first publication, a book by Archbishop Walsh of Dublin on *Bimetallism and Monometallism*, appeared two months after the congressional decision on repeal. Although he had shown some interest in bimetallism a few years before, no one knows precisely what silver arguments, beyond Walsh's, he had read.[18] But if he had read even a small part of the hundreds of pages of speeches in the *Congressional Record* taken up by the debate over repeal, he could have found there a basis for all but the most idiosyncratic of his economic arguments for silver, and he could have found confirmation of all his underlying attitudes and convictions.

VI

No doubt the wide currency of these attitudes, which gave the book its rapport with ordinary readers, had as much to do with the success of *Coin's Financial School* as its central economic exposition. Before going on to Harvey's notions about finance, it will be profitable to listen to the tonalities of his work.

Young Coin himself is a suggestive symbol. Though he tackles the most intricate of subjects and offers to solve the most perplexing problems, Coin is not a wise old man but a figure of youth, almost of childhood. He is drawn by Harvey's cartoonist as dressed in tails and carrying a top hat, but his pants are knee breeches, his face is boyish, and he is referred to as "the young financier" and "the little lecturer." In a subsequent book Harvey seemed to push Coin's age back even further by remarking that Coin was only ten years old at the time of these lectures. The choice of such a figure as

[18]Harvey's essay "The Free-Silver Argument," *The Forum*, XIX (June 1895), 401–9, recapitulates the main argument of his book, and documents it with collections of statutes and statistics, as well as the Reports of the Monetary Commissions of 1876 and 1878.

his spokesman implied that the intricacies of economics, once the distracting features of selfishness and self-delusion were set aside, were not too great to be mastered by the acute, simple, and unspoiled mind of a boy, and hence that the intuitions of the common man about the money question were sounder than the complex sophistries of bankers and hireling professors of economics.[19] Harvey took as a congenial Biblical text for the volume Matthew 11:25: "I thank thee, O Father, Lord of heaven and earth, because thou hast hid these things from the wise and prudent, and hast revealed them unto babes."

Throughout Harvey's writings the notion recurs that the old are thoroughly corrupted by selfishness and that the hope of civilization lies in setting youth on the straight path. The school conducted by Coin at the Art Institute is established in the first instance for the youth of Chicago, in the hope that they may be led "out of the labyrinth of falsehoods, heresies, and isms that distract the country." It is only after Coin's first lecture succeeds brilliantly with the young that he is requested to open his school to men of all ages, whereupon it is promptly packed with "middle-aged and old men" who hope to confound the youngster with "knotty questions." Now the big businessmen of Chicago get their comeuppance; it is they, and not Coin, who are befuddled. "They had listened critically, expecting to detect errors in his facts or reasoning. There were none. They were amazed. He was logical . . . That it should come from the lips of a boy they were more surprised." "Coin was like a little monitor in the midst of a fleet of wooden ships. His shots went through and silenced all opposition." The mastery of innocent but well-schooled youth over guileful age is complete. The fathers, by their inept conduct of affairs, had brought the country to the edge of disaster. Coin spoke for the hope that lay in the sons.

---

[19]As Congressman Edward Lane of Illinois said during the House debates on the repeal of the Sherman Silver Purchase Act, "Mr. Speaker, my people do not have to consult Chevalier, John Stuart Mill, Ricardo, or any other writer on finance in order to understand their conditions. They know from personal knowledge that they occupy the garden spot of this whole rich country; that their crops for the last decade have been reasonably abundant, yet their pocketbooks are empty." Barnes: op. cit., p. 268.

Harvey portrayed the departure from bimetallism as a kind of violation of natural order, a willful failure to make use of the *two* metals God had put at man's disposal for use as money, and hence as a kind of disobedience to divine will. "As the two legs are necessary to walk and two eyes to see, so were these two monies necessary to the prosperity of the people." But though both are necessary, they do not have an equal moral or economic significance. Silver, which had historically been the base or component of such small currency units as the ordinary man was likely to see or handle, was held to be the money of the people. Gold was the money of the rich. Silver, which had been abundant, was identified with plenty, gold with niggardliness. The metals were given human characters and fates: poor downtrodden silver was shut out of the mints, while gold, the pampered and petted, was welcomed in. This anthropomorphic treatment of the metals, one of which stood for the downtrodden and neglected masses of farmers and honest working people, was carried out in the cartoons, and found its way into Harvey's language when he spoke of the Act of 1873 as having "deprived silver of its *right* to unrestricted coinage."

Popular animosity in the West and South against the East, and in rural areas against the city, and in folkish tradition against Britain and the monetary power of John Bull and the House of Rothschild, runs through the book and is effectively caught in its cartoons. The United States is seen as having been trapped in "a financial system forced upon us by Europe." This the bankers of the great metropolitan centers accept, but it is destructive almost everywhere else. The mentality of the great centers, preoccupied with personal gain, is narrow and self-deluding. "Cities do not breed statesmen. They breed the specialist. A specialist favors what will tend to promote his business though it may injure the business of others. A statesman must be broad. He must have a comprehensive appreciation of the interests of all the people—especially the poorer classes."

The cartoons, some drawn for the book by H. L. Godall and others borrowed from silver newspapers, reduce these feelings to simple and striking images: gold smiles cruelly at the corpse of silver, assassinated by the pen; the West and the South, duped by the financial traps of the East, finally unite to overthrow the East; a cow feeding in the West is milked in

New York (this was one of the most common of the Populist images); an octopus representing the Rothschilds, centered in England, and labeled "The Great English Devil Fish," grips the entire world in its tentacles; John Bull makes a brutal attack on the female figure of Liberty, while virtuous Silver, helpless in chains, looks on; the British lion is blown out of a cannon by the figure of Uncle Sam; a monstrously rapacious usurer sits clutching his bags of gold.

Yet, for all this, Harvey's language is fairly restrained when he discusses the gold advocates. Harvey made quite a point of the idea that the abuse heaped by the conservative press on silverites was a poor substitute for rational argument, and he preferred to picture Coin as rising nobly above all this. It was, for him, a rare *ad hominem* attack when he described J. Laurence Laughlin as a "professor in a chair of political economy, endowed with the money of bankers, his mental faculties . . . trained with his salary." For the most part, Harvey preferred to picture substantial businessmen as potential friends of silver, willing to listen to reason. The bankers themselves, he said, "as a rule are a patriotic class of men, but they are controlled by a central influence in London and New York."

The stance of rationality and fair play which Harvey struck with most of his contemporaries was possible because silverite hostilities were directed elsewhere—projected backward in time, to the perpetrators of the monstrous Crime of '73, and outward in space, to Britain as the bulwark of the international gold standard and to the House of Rothschild as its financial center. When Harvey discusses the Crime of '73 and the power of Britain, his calm breaks down. The alleged disaster of the demonetization of silver in 1873 was not viewed by Harvey, or by most silverites, as the consequence of a ghastly mistake but as the outcome of a crafty conspiracy. Demonetization, the work of "men having a design to injure business by making money scarce," had accomplished exactly what had been intended: it had created a depression and caused untold suffering. The law of 1873 was passed stealthily, and many of the men who voted for it had no notion of what they were doing. Silver was "demonetized secretly, and since then a powerful money trust has used deception and misrepresentations that have led thousands of honest minds astray." Demonetization is commonly known as the crime of 1873. A crime, because it has confiscated millions of dollars worth of property. A crime, because it has made thousands of paupers. A crime, because it has made tens of thousands of tramps. A crime, because it has made thousands of suicides. A crime, because it has brought tears to strong men's eyes, and hunger and pinching want to widows and orphans. A crime, because it is destroying the honest yeomanry of the land, the bulwark of the nation. A crime, because it has brought this once great republic to the verge of ruin, where it is now in imminent danger of tottering to its fall. [Applause.]

The true center of this criminal conspiracy is, of course, London. Almost every step in Coin's argument is interlarded with a renewal of the old hostility to England, and there are times when one feels that one is back in the atmosphere of 1812. Even the foundations of our monetary system, it is argued, dated from "our revolutionary forefathers, who had a hatred of England, and an intimate knowledge of her designs on this country." Harvey had an important tactical reason for wanting to exploit this feeling. The advocates of unilateral free coinage of silver by the United States were carrying on an argument not only with gold-standard advocates but with the international bimetallists, who believed that the use of both metals in monetary standards was desirable but insisted that the United States could not uphold silver unaided without disaster. The argument of the international bimetallists was in fact one of the most formidable arguments of the opponents of unilateral free silver, and a certain frustration in dealing with it no doubt had something to do with the violent rhetoric in which Harvey put his case.

The climactic passage of *Coin's Financial School* occurs in Coin's sixth and last lecture, in which he spells out defiance to English power. Here he urges that the experiment of monetary independence be tried, and that if the argument of the internationalists should prove correct, one should not capitulate to gold but wage war: "If it is true, let us attach England to the United States and blot out her name from among the nations of the earth. [Applause.]" Coin goes on to say that "a war with England would be the most popular ever waged on the face of the earth," and also the most just, since it would be waged against a power that "can dictate the money of the world, and thereby create world-wide misery." But such a war, he continued, would in fact not be necessary if England were defied in American monetary policy. To hope for her concurrence in international action was futile: she was a creditor nation committed to gold. "Wherever property interests and humanity have come in conflict, England has ever been the enemy of human liberty." To shirk the struggle for unilateral bimetallism "means a surrender to England" and involves the risk that internecine war will arise in the United States that will put an end to the republic. If the present policy is continued, he argued, it will end

> in England owning us body and soul. She is making a peaceable conquest of the United States. What she failed to do with shot and shell in the eighteenth century, she is doing with the gold standard in the nineteenth century. [Applause.] The conservative monied interest furnished the tory friends of England then, and it furnishes her friends now. [Applause.] The business men of New York City passed strong resolutions against the Declaration of Independence in 1776, and they are passing strong resolutions against an American policy now. [Applause.]

VII

While Harvey's was unquestionably the most popular statement of the case for silver, it was far from the best. Indeed it was so much inferior to the speeches of such congressional advocates as Bryan and Teller and to the writings of such American bimetallists as President E. Benjamin Andrews of Brown, President Francis A. Walker of M.I.T., and the silver diplomat and propagandist S. Dana Horton that one is tempted to propound a Gresham's law of popular monetary discussion, by which the weak arguments drive the strong out of circulation. Harvey's case is not developed systematically or logically, and his sense for what is important among the issues is almost touchingly unsure. His greatest failing was his staggering gift for irrelevancy—his readiness to inject into the argument assertions that were either unnecessary to his case or incapable of substantiation. He attached, for example, the highest importance to his assertion that all the gold in the world could be incorporated into a cube of 22 feet; he portrayed Coin's gold-bug auditors as being thrown almost into paroxysms by this revelation, although no one was disposed to deny that gold was a scarce commodity. He tempted the ridicule of economists by insisting that it cost $2.00 an ounce to produce silver, when silver had not brought a price of more than about $1.36 an ounce within the memory of living man—thus implying that the metal had been produced for more than a generation out of philanthropy. He made errors of fact, he distorted statutes and quotations, he invented his own confusing terminology ("redemption money"), he forced side issues or non-issues into the center of attention, he made up a monetary history that was largely fictional, and, all in all, he made himself vastly more vulnerable to his critics than his case required.[20]

Indeed, almost everything about Harvey's book can be argued with except its success. The importance of Harvey's pamphlet for the student of history lies in its popularity, which suggests that Harvey's understanding of the case was close to that held by the ordinary silverite of firm convictions and active intelligence but no special training. Harvey was what Gertrude Stein once called another money crank, Ezra Pound—"a village explainer." Like many another movement, free silver had its lowbrow and highbrow culture. Harvey represents the common man thinking, and the essentials of his argument reproduce a very widespread contemporary view. These essentials may be extracted from his cluttered exposition. They consist of four assertions that are primarily historical in character and four that are primarily programmatic and economic. These historical assertions are that the original unit of American currency was the silver dollar, adopted in 1792; that this was the primary element of a successful bimetallic system down to 1873; that in 1873 silver was "secretly" and stealthily demonetized by a

[20]The most important contemporary critiques, which go at Harvey's argument point by point, are J. Laurence Laughlin's *Facts about Money* (Chicago, 1895) and Horace White's *Coin's Financial Fool* (New York, 1895). Willard Fisher's article "'Coin' and His Critics," already cited, made a scrupulous effort to defend Harvey ("an untrained thinker of considerably more than average ability") at a few points where Fisher felt that Harvey's critics had done him injustice, but also marshaled (pp. 190–2) a brief list of Harvey's most extraordinary and gratuitous errors.

Congress so hypnotized or so corrupted by sinister gold interests that it did not know what it was doing; and that the demonetization of silver in 1873 deprived the country of half the supply of its primary money. The assertions that might be regarded as largely economic are that the depression and misery which the country had endured were simply the consequences of falling prices and the continuing appreciation of gold; that low prices could be remedied by an infusion of new money; that the appropriate source of new money was free and unlimited coinage of silver at 16 to 1; and, finally, that this remedy could be successfully adopted by the United States acting alone and without the cooperation of any foreign country.

Harvey's history of the original American currency system was in fact completely irrelevant to the merits of free coinage of silver as a remedy for the economic conditions of the 1890's. If free silver was good policy in 1894, it mattered not in the least what coinage the Founding Fathers had intended in 1792. After a hundred years of additional experience with currency systems and some advance in economic knowledge, one could hardly expect the currency practices of the founders to have much rational authority for Harvey's contemporaries on either side of the currency issue. But the silver men, like their opponents, cherished their historical lore, and the happy notion that free coinage of silver would restore "the dollar of our daddies" was an important part of it.

Harvey's version of the history of American money could hardly have been more misleading. His elaborate attempt to establish that the original monetary unit was a *silver* dollar, and that gold was "also made money" but that "its value was counted from the silver dollar" is nonsensical, as well as gratuitous. The original monetary unit was simply the dollar, circulated in a variety of pieces of both gold and silver.[21] The dollar was defined as having a certain weight of silver and a certain weight of gold, bearing to each other the proportions of 15 to 1. The fathers did not in fact cherish any preference for silver over gold. Gold was widely preferred as having a more certain

---

[21] The coinage measure of 1792 provided for three gold coins worth $10, $5, and $2.50, for a silver dollar, and for silver half dollars, quarters, dimes, and half dimes, as well as copper pennies and half pennies.

and stable value; but Hamilton, in his report on coinage to Congress in May 1791, recommended a bimetallic unit on the ground that the available quantity of gold was not sufficient to serve as the basis for a money system. If one tries to salvage whatever there may be of fact in Harvey's attempt to claim primacy for silver, it must be simply that gold, being too valuable to serve as common coin, was coined only in units ranging from $2.50 up to the $10 gold eagle, and that the coinage handled by the common man was of silver. ("Gold was considered the money of the rich . . . the poor people seldom handled it, and the very poor people seldom ever saw any of it.")

Harvey's implication that the United States had a smooth-working bimetallic system before the Crime of '73 and that the old American silver dollar had wide circulation in this country was also misleading. In law, as we have seen, bimetallism did exist. In fact, the standard had alternated from silver to gold because Congress failed to set a mint ratio in accord with the world market. This very alternation of standards later persuaded dogmatic gold men to insist—all too glibly—that bimetallism had been proved to be an impossibility. They failed to take into account the fact that it would not have been impossible to arrive at a mint ratio more in harmony with France's if the will to do it had been present in Congress at any time between the days of Hamilton and the Civil War. It is tempting to speculate how much strength international bimetallism might have acquired if Congress had decided soon after 1792 to rectify Hamilton's miscalculation and establish a common ratio with France.

As for the old American silver dollar, Harvey seemed unaware that it had disappeared rapidly from circulation not long after Congress provided for its coinage. This came about because the standard American silver dollar, though lighter in weight than the Spanish silver dollar, was newer, brighter, and less abraded, and thus became more acceptable in certain kinds of foreign trade. Dealers found it profitable to export it in exchange for the Spanish dollars, which were legal tender in the United States, and which became our primary medium of silver circulation. As a consequence of the drainage of the American silver dollar, President Jefferson ordered its coinage discontinued in 1806, and this suspension remained in force for thirty years.

The third of Harvey's historical assertions—that the Coinage Act of 1873 was passed corruptly and in secret at the instance of the gold bankers—was a widespread article of faith among money agitators and had been widely believed for sixteen years. Despite its intrinsic implausibility, gold spokesmen were forced to make elaborate refutations of this charge. No measure could pass Congress in secret, they pointed out, and the Coinage Act had been before Congress almost three years from April 1870 to its passage in February 1873; the chairman of the House Committee of Coinage, Weights and Measures, introducing it to the House, pointed out that it legally established mono-metallism and declared that it had come to him from a Senate committee that had given it "as careful attention as I have ever known a committee to bestow on any measure"; it was printed thirteen times by order of Congress; it had been debated once in the Senate and twice in the House for a total of 144 columns of the *Congressional Globe*; two Directors of the Mint and other experts had pointed out that the bill demonetized the old silver dollar; Samuel Hooper of Massachusetts, who steered the bill through the House, carefully observed that the gold dollar was being established as the standard of value; several senators referred to the cessation of coinage of the silver dollar; and some of the quotations silver men later invoked to show the stealthy passage of the bill were arrived at by misrepresenting congressional debates.[22]

However, when a delusion like that of the Crime of '73 gets to be so widely believed, it is perhaps quite as important to understand how it came about as to repeat elaborate proofs of its falsity. No doubt economic suffering and social resentments had a great deal to do with the formation and spread of the myth. But there was a soupçon of truth out of which the notion of the Crime of '73 grew: it lies in the fact that even the better-informed men in Congress could hardly have had a very

---

[22] For standard refutations by gold advocates, see Laughlin: *Facts about Money*, pp. 57–69, and *The History of Bimetallism in the United States*, pp. 95–102; Horace White: *Coin's Financial Fool*, pp. 44–54; David K. Watson: *History of American Coinage* (New York, 1899), pp. 125–37. By far the most knowledgeable and astute account of the origins of the law of 1873 that I have found is Neil Carothers: *Fractional Money*, Ch. 16, and my estimate of the situation follows his.

keen sense in 1873 of the full implications of what they were doing when they passed the Coinage Act.

This measure was intended in the first instance to codify the coinage laws and to remedy the chaotic and expensive condition in which our fractional currency had been left at the end of the Civil War. After much talk of the need of such action in the late 1860's, John Jay Knox, the Deputy Comptroller of the Currency, was requested by Secretary of the Treasury George Boutwell to prepare such a bill. It was first presented to Congress in 1870, and was much discussed and amended in the three years before its passage. The question of providing for continued coinage of the standard silver dollar was never an issue, and no attentive congressman need have had difficulty in understanding that its coinage was being dropped. The silver dollar, exported before 1806, not coined from 1806 to 1836, and not circulated from 1836 to 1873, was simply an unfamiliar and half-forgotten coin. No one objected to its discontinuance, not because there was any secret about the matter, but because no one cared. The silver interests, who knew that the weight of silver specified for the defunct silver dollar was actually worth a few cents more than a dollar in the open market, had no reason to demand its continued coinage. When the law of 1873 was introduced, Germany had not yet gone on the gold standard, and even when it was passed the effect of German silver sales in the world market had not yet begun to depress the price of the metal.

Seven months after the passage of the Coinage Act the Panic of 1873 began, and the fall in the price of silver began at about the same time. It was natural for money-oriented reformers to connect the two events. As inflationary demands built up, congressmen who found it politic to take up a pro-silver position now began to explain that in voting for the Coinage Act of 1873 they had not known what they were doing—and if one bears in mind the technical character of the law, it becomes evident that in a certain sense most of them were telling the truth. But, at least for a few of them, to join in the general cry about the Crime of '73 required a certain daring mendacity. For example, Representative William D. Kelley of Pennsylvania, the same man who is quoted above as having assured the House how carefully the bill had been weighed in committee, was one of the few who explicitly pointed out the implications of the Coinage Act for silver. He told the House on January 9, 1872: "It is impossible to retain the double standard." Yet six years later Kelley brazenly joined those who insisted that the Coinage Act of 1873 was a fraud, when he said that, "though the chairman of the committee on coinage, I was ignorant of the fact that it would demonetize the silver dollar, or of its dropping the silver dollar from our system of coins."

As for Harvey's contention that the Act of 1873, by demonetizing silver, "destroyed one-half of the redemption money of the United States," his critics were fond of pointing out that a kind of money that was not in circulation at all could hardly have been destroyed, and that it could not conceivably have had any consequences for the depression of 1873–79, since the country was then still on the inconvertible paper standard. They were also fond of pointing out that by the silver acts of 1878 and 1890 silver dollars had in some measure been restored to circulation. In fact more silver dollars or silver certificates having legal-tender status had been put in circulation by 1894 than anyone could have dreamed of in 1873—without having lifted the general price level or the price of silver itself.[23]

The history of our money is full of its own subtle mockeries, and there is one ironic aspect of the law of 1873 that must be noted here: far from having demonetized silver in any operative sense, it actually came close to remonetizing the white metal, despite the intention of its framers. While the old standard silver dollar was dropped from coinage, the law created —largely to facilitate trade with the silver-standard countries of the Orient and to compete with the Mexican dollar—a new silver dollar called the trade dollar. The trade dollar had a silver content slightly greater than the old standard silver dollar and was not expected to circulate within the United States. However, the law provided that the trade dollar was not only to be freely coined but also to be legal tender for payments up to the amount of five dollars within the country. The legal-tender provision was included to bolster the foreign standing of this

[23]By 1894 there were in circulation $326.9 million in silver certificates, $134.6 million in Treasury notes of 1890, and $52.5 million in silver dollars. *Historical Statistics of the United States*, p. 648.

dollar by enhancing its domestic standing. No one thought this dollar would have any actual domestic circulation, because it was at an even greater premium as silver than the lighter standard dollar that had disappeared, and it was not expected to compete for circulation with the then prevailing greenbacks. But the ensuing sudden drop in the value of silver and the rise in that of the greenbacks had the effect of causing the trade dollars to circulate in substantial amounts in this country, in addition to being exported to the Orient. Accordingly, the legal-tender character of the trade dollar was removed by Congress in 1876, and when its circulation persisted, its coinage was discontinued in 1878. Its circulation continued until it was finally redeemed by Congress in 1887. But as Charles R. Whittlesey has observed, the combined provisions for free coinage and legal tender, while they lasted, had the effect of briefly remonetizing silver and, when one takes account of the greater weight of the trade dollar, of remonetizing it at a ratio of about 16⅓ to 1— a ratio which was by no means unfavorable to silver when one considers what was happening to silver prices. But the inflationary forces, failing to see what they had inadvertently gained for their metal by the creation of the trade dollar, showed no great interest in blocking the repeal of its legal-tender power. This may be attributed to their failure to understand its potentialities for remonetization. It would have been far easier, politically, to mobilize the growing silver sentiment against this repeal in 1876 than to regain free coinage of the standard silver dollar. Professor Whittlesey attributes this tactical oversight to "economic illiteracy on the part of the silver interests."[24] But on the whole one is impressed by the sense that all those involved with currency problems in the 1870's were like men groping in the dark.

[24] *Principles and Practices of Money and Banking* (New York, 1954), pp. 206–8. On the trade dollar, see Carothers: op. cit., pp. 233–4, 275–80. In a sense, it is almost anachronistic to speak of the "silver interests" as an organized force in 1876. Sentiment for silver was just crystallizing, and the dominant inflationary rationale was still that of the Greenbackers.

Paul M. O'Leary has revived the idea of the Crime of '73 in a much modified form. He points out that Henry R. Linderman, a special assistant to John Jay Knox, the Comptroller of the Currency and an active figure in the drafting and redrafting of the Coinage Act of 1873, had become aware by

VIII

Let us turn now to the programmatic, as opposed to the historical, side of Harvey's argument. There are two possible ways of looking at the subject. The first is to regard Harvey as though he were a professional economist and to apply to his exposition the same rigorous standards that one would apply to any professional work. In this there is now little point, except by way of establishing the difference between popular agitation and professional analysis. Harvey was an amateur, and his book was at best a caricature of sophisticated bimetallist thought. Of course, it suited contemporary defenders of the gold standard to treat him as though he were a professional, and on this ground they were for the most part unanswerable. He had, after all, presented "Coin" as an expert more authoritative than the experts. J. Laurence Laughlin perhaps spoke with too much personal asperity and failed to reckon with Harvey's honest naïveté when he charged that "the book was

---

November 1872, three months before the passage of the act, that forces at work in the world were about to cause a depreciation in the value of silver. Linderman, who was a strong gold-standard man, did not bring the relevant facts and their implications to the attention of the congressmen who were about to act on the measure, though he did mention them in a report to the Secretary of the Treasury. At least one person, then—and perhaps two if the Secretary of the Treasury was fully cognizant of the implications of Linderman's report—was aware of the impending decline in the value of silver and possibly aware of the future significance of stopping coinage of the old silver dollar.

However, it remains true that because of the acceptance of the trade dollar, and its subsequent circulation in the United States, the inflationary interests were granted a reprise on the issue between 1873 and 1876, when the trade dollar's coinage was discontinued. This opportunity the inflationary forces failed to seize upon; and one can only conclude that, while the considerations raised by O'Leary do indicate gold-standard malice aforethought, at least by one significant actor on the scene, it is of vital consequence that in a time of confusion and changing policies, the interests of cheap money were ineptly defended. Also it is altogether improbable that the *inception* of the Coinage Act of 1873, which dates back to 1870, could have been induced in any way by the expectation of a change in the value of silver. See Paul M. O'Leary: "The Scene of the Crime of 1873 Revisited: A Note," *Journal of Political Economy*, LXVIII (August 1960), 388–92.

intentionally constructed to fit into prevailing prejudices and consciously deceive," but one must bow to the more dispassionate verdict of another contemporary economist, Willard Fisher, who wrote that it was "of no value to those who have been trained to think about monetary problems," and who found it strange "that so crude a product could have created so great a sensation."[25]

But it is also possible to say that complicated issues like money do on occasion have to be made the object of popular discussion in a democracy, and that they must of necessity be discussed in a simplified way. One may then ask whether, disregarding technicalities, there was any substantive economic merit in the demand for inflation as a remedy for the depression of the nineties, and whether the demand for cheaper money did not also have some moral justification. If the issue is looked at in these broad and indulgent terms, Harvey becomes far more defensible—and in a certain way even prophetic, for in some fields of inquiry yesterday's crank may turn out to be closer than yesterday's accepted spokesman to today's dominant views.

The essence of Harvey's programmatic position is summed up on page 175, where he advocates the remonetization of silver in these words: "You increase the value of all property by adding to the number of money units in the land. You make it possible for the debtor to pay his debts; business to start anew, and revivify all the industries of the country, which must remain paralyzed so long as silver as well as all other property is measured by a gold standard." The imprecision of his way of putting things becomes apparent not only in the unintelligible, though charmingly illustrated, conception of business depressions that follows page 147 but also in the assertion on page 203 that cutting the gold dollar in half would "thereby double the value [presumably he meant prices] of all property in the United States, except debts."[26]

[25]Laughlin: "'Coin's' Food for the Gullible," *The Forum*, XIX (July 1895), 577; Fisher: "'Coin' and His Critics," p. 192.
[26]Page references are to the John Harvard Library edition.

Such proposals were so commonly regarded by contemporary conservatives as a form of lunatic radicalism that it is worthwhile to notice the element of

Harvey was, of course, using a rudimentary version of the quantity theory of money. Given stable conditions of demand for money, its value will vary inversely with the quantity available. Hence the general price level varies directly with this quantity. A massive addition to the money supply such as that promised by free coinage of silver would raise the general price level, return inflated debts to a fair level, and reinvigorate the entire economy.

There is a certain danger that we may become so absorbed in the inadequacies of Harvey's case for inflation, and in particular of the quixotic case for free coinage of silver at 16 to 1, that we will ignore the substantial merits of the demand for inflation. Modern economic opinion would treat Harvey's general line of reasoning, especially as applied to the depression of the 1890's which came after a long period of drastic deflation, with much greater respect than dogmatic contemporary professionals. What vitiated Harvey's point of view was his obsession with the bullion basis of the money supply, which in turn reflects his adherence to an old-fashioned view of money, inherited from American agrarian thought. He did not think of money functionally, as a means of payment, but simply as money of account (or, as he would say, a measure of value). He understood "true" money to consist in hard coin. The quantity theory of money, as he employed it (page 188), applied only to "redemption money"—that is, gold or silver. The elaborate apparatus of credit that was growing up in his lifetime he dismissed as irrelevant to the fundamental issue of the monetary standard. The expansion of what he called "credit money" represented

---

latent conservatism in this overwhelming emphasis on the monetary factor in depressions. Harvey and his fellow silverites were not trying to develop a fundamental critique of industrial capitalism; they were merely trying to make it work, and they believed that the device that would do so was essentially a simple one. This premise went unnoticed by their conservative critics, but not by the left wing of the Populist party, whose spokesmen objected to free silver on the ground, among others, that it would not go very far to alleviate the basic ills of American society.

It is perhaps important to point out that in 1933, when the gold content of the dollar was cut to 59 per cent of its previous parity, in the hope of bringing about a proportionate rise in prices, the expedient did not work.

no real addition to the money supply—and its overexpansion he could regard only as dangerous (pages 141–3).

Modern statements of the quantity theory of money measure the money supply by taking into account all the means of payment that are available, including demand deposits—that is, bank deposits subject to withdrawal by check. They also consider the velocity of monetary circulation as a dimension that must be taken into account when the supply of money is estimated for any period of time. The concept of velocity, though an old one, was just beginning to be employed in empirical study in Harvey's time; but the fast-growing use of demand deposits was a familiar and measurable fact to his contemporaries. By the 1890's something like 90 per cent of the volume of business transactions was being carried on by check. Harvey could not be persuaded to take any interest in this fact as having a possible bearing on the demand for money, and he dismissed it (pages 145–7) by saying that while "credit money" was convenient in facilitating transactions, it had nothing to do with the measure of values, which was his only concern.

No doubt Harvey's conception of money stemmed from a kind of business experience, then only recently outmoded, that still fashioned the thinking of many farmers and some businessmen. His views reflected the folkish feeling that pieces of money are not really "good" unless they have a roughly equivalent value for nonmonetary purposes, or are directly redeemable in money that has such value. "Some years ago," E. Benjamin Andrews reported in 1894, "I found a man who for a decade owned and carried on the chief store in a flourishing New England village, ignorant how to draw a check. If this in the East, how slight must be the play of banking methods in the West and South."[27] Men out of such village backgrounds naturally thought of the solution to monetary problems entirely in terms of primary money, and were uninterested in the possibilities that lay in devising more flexible instruments of check credit. Perhaps the most severe stricture that can be made against them was that when the nation finally came to the point of trying to devise a mobile credit structure that would make possible a more adequate response to the kind of evil they had protested against, men like Harvey were too firm

[27] *An Honest Dollar* (Hartford, Conn., 1894), pp. 26–7.

in their anti-bank prejudices to applaud the effort, and were to be found instead sniping at it as nothing more than a new source of profits and power for usurers.

At any rate, Harvey's notion that the appreciation of gold was the primary source of the hardships of his time throughout the price-depressed Western world was a rough popular version of a view of the matter taken by many more sophisticated contemporaries in the United States and Europe, among them distinguished economists and statesmen. Such respectable contemporaries were profoundly disturbed by business instability and unemployment and by the widespread and growing discontent of the agricultural populations of several nations. They put a heavy burden of blame for depressed prices on the formation of the international gold standard. As they saw it, each new Western nation that clambered aboard the gold-standard bandwagon after 1873 added its own needs to the general scramble for a very limited supply of gold. The metal appreciated and prices dropped. And certainly, if price stability was the thing most urgently desired, the record of the gold standard in these years and afterwards was not inspiring.[28] Bimetallism, moreover, was a respectable proposition in economic theory, and it is easy to be persuaded that things might have been somewhat better had the nations, say, in the 1870's or even the early 1880's, successfully arrived at an agreement to put the Western trading community on a bimetallic basis.

It is impossible for the layman to evaluate the merits of this traditional case against the gold standard. But most economists who are familiar with macro-economic developments have tended in recent years to minimize the effect of the bullion basis of money in the secular price decline, as compared with certain long-range changes that came with industrialism and improvements in transportation. The development of industry brought many long-range cost-reducing improvements. Massive investment in railroads and shipping, improvements in transportation facilities, the opening of the Suez Canal—such changes led to the rapid development of great tracts of virgin land throughout the world and the rapid shrinkage of the world into a single market. The effects of these changes

[28]See, on this count, D. H. Robertson: *Money* (4th ed., Chicago, 1959), pp. 117–19.

were felt with special acuteness by the farming populations, which found themselves competing in a crowded international market and victims of a common international agrarian depression. Studies in the history of the real money supply, moreover, indicate that changes in banking during this secular price decline were more and more detaching the real money supply from the rate of growth of the gold supply. The calculations of J. G. Gurley and E. S. Shaw for the United States, which take account of demand deposits and other sources of expansion, show a steady growth in the real per capita money supply for the decades from 1869 to 1899, and an annual rate of growth somewhat higher than in the years before the Civil War.[29] The gold standard may well have aggravated the price decline but it cannot be assigned full blame.

To accept these findings, however, is not to deny the merit of the demand for inflation in the mid-1890's. There was an excellent case, both economic and moral, for a jolt of controllable inflation that would have stimulated enterprise and readjusted the balance between debtors and creditors. The difficulty was to find a mechanism for such inflation that would have achieved the desired price rise without so dislocating foreign trade and investment and so shaking the confidence of the business community that the anticipated benefits would be undone. Under modern conditions of central banking, the

[29]See the two essays by Gurley and Shaw already cited. There is an account of the views of economists on the role of monetary factors in the depression of the 1890's in Rendigs Fels: *American Business Cycles, 1865–1897* (Chapel Hill, N.C., 1959), Chs. 11 and 12. Charles Hoffman, in "The Depression of the Nineties," *Journal of Economic History*, XVI (June 1956), 137–64, concludes that monetary and fiscal policies were secondary aggravating forces. Lee Benson summarizes the literature on the transportation revolution and its international consequences in his essay "The Historical Background of Turner's Frontier Essay," in *Turner and Beard* (Glencoe, Ill., 1960), pp. 42 ff.; and A. E. Musson does the same for the literature on "The Great Depression in Britain, 1873–1896," *Journal of Economic History*, XIX (June 1959), 199–228. On the limitations of the gold standard in accounting for the secular price decline, see J. T. Phinney: "Gold Production and the Price Level," *Quarterly Journal of Economics*, XLVII (August 1933), 647–79, and E. H. Phelps Brown and S. A. Ozga: "Economic Growth and the Price Level," *Economic Journal*, LXV (March 1955), 1–18. Cf. J. M. Keynes: *Treatise on Money* (London, 1930), II, 164–70, and W. T. Layton and Geoffrey Crowther: *An Introduction to the Study of Prices* (London, 1938), Ch. 8.

mechanisms are at hand; in the 1890's this was not the case, and so the debate centered on the monetary standard. From the vantage point of a later age there seems to be something genuinely tragic in the clash of the two hypnotic dogmatisms of gold and silver, neither of whose exponents had an adequate comprehension of the problem nor an adequate program for the relief of economic misery.

It is against this background that the true poignancy of Harvey's willfully amateurish attempt to restate the silver case may be seen. There is, of course, a certain innocent amusement to be had from poking fun at cranks. But when cranks acquire the wide popular following that men like Harvey had, it may be the better part of statesmanship to take their agitations, even if not their ideas, seriously. What was being debated in America and Europe during the 1890's was a major social issue which had its moral as well as its technical economic side. And on the moral side, the defenders of the gold standard often seem as dogmatically sealed within their own premises as the most wild-eyed silver men, and usually less generous in their social sympathies. The right-thinking statesmanship of the era, like its right-thinking economics, was so locked in its own orthodoxy that it was incapable of coming to terms in a constructive way with lasting and pervasive social grievances. The social philosophy of J. Laurence Laughlin and the statecraft of Grover Cleveland cannot, in this respect, command our admiration. They accepted as "natural" a stark, long-range price deflation, identified the interests of creditors with true morality, and looked upon any attempt to remedy the appreciation of debt as unnatural and dishonest, as a simple repudiation of sacred obligations—an attempt, as Laughlin put it in his debate with Harvey, "to transfer from the great mass of the community who have been provident, industrious, and successful a portion of their savings and gains into the pockets of those who have been idle, extravagant, or unfortunate."[30] This attitude, as provocative as it was smug, was not calculated to engender humane statesmanship. Allan Nevins, unstinting though he is

[30] *Facts about Money*, p. 233; cf. his comments about "the less fortunate, the less successful, the less wise," and "the greater prosperity of the successful [that] is due to the possession of superior industrial power," in "'Coin's' Food for the Gullible," pp. 574, 576.

in his admiration for Grover Cleveland's defense of the gold
standard, remarks that the farmers had legitimate grounds for
complaint and that "our history presents few spectacles more
ironic than that of their Eastern creditors taunting them with
dishonesty while insisting upon being repaid in a dollar far
more valuable than had been lent."[31] Laughlin himself put
the case in a fairer light when he said: "The highest justice is
rendered by the state when it extracts from the debtor at the
end of a contract the *same purchasing power* which the creditor
gave him at the beginning of the contract, no less, no more,"
and it is quite understandable why Bryan felt that he was only
echoing Laughlin when he said in his speech against repeal of
the Sherman Silver Purchase Act: "A dollar approaches honesty
as its purchasing power approaches stability."[32]

[31] Nevins: op. cit., p. 594. Any change in the value of money has the effect of
redistributing income among social classes; and changes in the value of money
are the consequences, among other things, of the decisions of governments
—even if they are only decisions *not* to act. One can readily understand the
fury of inflationists, after years of deflationary monetary decisions, at being
told that their proposals to raise prices were unwarranted and dishonest efforts
to interfere with the course of nature. The gold advocates had taken it upon
themselves to define the terms of the controversy in such a way as to make it
impossible for them to be wrong.

[32] Laughlin: *The History of Bimetallism in the United States*, p. 70; Bryan: op.
cit., p. 80. The whole question of the price level as one of both policy and
morality is circumspectly discussed in Ch. 7 of D. H. Robertson's classic exposition, *Money*. See also the grounds for Keynes's conclusion that "it is worse,
in an impoverished world, to provoke unemployment than to disappoint the
rentier"; *Essays in Persuasion* (London, 1931), p. 103.

Milton Friedman and Anna J. Schwartz, in *A Monetary History of the United
States, 1867–1960*, find that the forces making for economic growth over the
course of several business cycles were largely independent of the secular trend
in prices. They suggest that, while generally declining or rising prices had
little effect on the rate of economic growth, "the period of great monetary
uncertainty in the early nineties produced sharp deviations from the longer-
term trend." They also suggest that the abandonment of the gold standard
"might well have been highly preferable to the generally depressed conditions
of the 1890's," but dismiss it only because it was "politically unacceptable."
Concerning the severe deflation that arose from the commitment to the gold
standard, they observe: "In retrospect, it seems clear that either acceptance
of a silver standard at an early stage or an early commitment to gold would
have been preferable to the uneasy compromise that was maintained, with the

The international bimetallists seem to have been on sound ground insofar as they saw the future solution to deflation in supranational arrangements that would enable the trading powers to maintain stable exchange rates and yet keep some freedom in domestic price policies; whereas the dogmatic gold men, who believed that currency was governed by laws so immutable that money was not susceptible to further management, were looking in the wrong direction. Of course, the overwhelming majority of American silver men were not international bimetallists; like Harvey, they were uncompromising advocates of unilateral action. The difference was vital. The international aspect of the problem was the Achilles' heel of the American silver men—and it is no coincidence that when Harvey comes, near the end of *Coin's Financial School,* to the hopeless problem of maintaining bimetallism in one country, he drops his façade of didactic calm and rational argument and breaks into a tirade against England. The idea that the United States, acting alone, could uphold the value of silver and maintain bimetallism, as opposed to adopting silver monometallism, had long been preposterous; the notion that we could coin unlimited amounts of silver at 16 to 1 at a time when the market ratio had dropped to 32 to 1, and still hold to a bimetallic standard, was understandably regarded by its opponents as a form of economic lunacy. For this reason, the "respectable" bimetallists, in the United States as elsewhere, saw the problem of the monetary standard as an international one. On this count they were regarded by the silver nationalists as abject traitors.

The one reality that the silver nationalists would not face was that the course of events since 1871 had so undermined the international position of silver that nothing short of concerted international action could restore it as a standard money. Few of them were candid enough to admit that, because the value of the two metals had so far parted company in the past twenty years, they had in fact become silver monometallists. Today, when we are no longer enthralled by illusions about

---

uncertainty about the ultimate outcome and the consequent wide fluctuations to which the currency was subjected." See Ch. 3, esp. pp. 93, 111, 133–4, and in particular the extended footnote on p. 134, in which they suggest reasons why a silver standard might have been preferable to gold before 1897.

the perfection or inevitability of the gold standard, it may still be possible to argue speculatively, as a few candid silver men did in 1894, that it would have been healthier to restore prices through silver monometallism than to accept the drastic and disheartening fall in prices that was still going on. But the switch to a silver standard might have been self-defeating simply because of its blow to the confidence of the business community. And even if one were to dismiss this intangible, the blows to foreign investment and trade would probably have had repercussions serious enough to delay rather than to hasten recovery. The United States was a debtor nation and an importer of capital; and the effects of a silver standard upon its debt service and the investment market might well have constituted a minor disaster. Abstractly, there was nothing wrong with a silver standard, or for that matter a paper standard, but it does not follow that the shift could have been made without causing, as Senator Cockrell so confidently said, "as much as a ripple in our financial system."[33]

One thing that can be said in the light of historical perspective is that the critical moment for a stand for silver through an international agreement had long since passed. Moreover, the American silver movement itself could be charged with having done its own part to weaken the forces working for such an agreement.

Behind this charge lies a long history of international discussion and negotiation, marked by four international monetary

[33]Most historians who have discussed the battle of the standards have written largely as ideologists. Liberal historians have treated the subject as though the sufferings of the farmers and the broad social sympathies of the silver men were an adequate substitute for sound remedial proposals—somewhat in the spirit of Vachel Lindsay's rhetorical poem "Bryan, Bryan, Bryan, Bryan." On the other hand, most conservative historians who have written at length about the merits of the monetary controversy itself have quietly assumed that the orthodoxies of J. Laurence Laughlin are still untouched. They would have us enter uncritically into the spirit of Grover Cleveland's assertion that if the United States went off gold it "could no longer claim a place among nations of the first class." Actually, it is interesting to speculate on what would have happened if the United States had adopted silver monometallism and had made this the occasion of an aggressive effort to dominate the trade of the silver-using Orient and Latin America.

conferences in 1867, 1878, 1881, and 1892. It is true that Britain had steadfastly refused to abandon her own gold standard, and her unwillingness to do so had been interpreted, rightly or wrongly, by the other great nations as an insuperable obstacle to satisfactory international action on silver. But, partly because of Britain's growing concern for the stability of silver, a concern arising from her trade with India, which was on a silver standard, British spokesmen would have welcomed action taken by the United States, alone or in concert with other nations, that would have successfully sustained the international use and the price of the white metal. In Britain the gold standard was both a habit and a dogma, but it was not considered to be a proselytizing creed eligible for export.

During the many years when the international bimetallic movement was working for an agreement among the nations on the use of silver, the American silver purchase policy, along with the threat that unlimited coinage might soon follow, had hung like a dark cloud over the international conferences. The more reason the European governments had to expect that American silver purchase policies would give them a dumping ground for their silver and an opportunity to strengthen their gold position, the less likely they were to yield to the arguments of their own bimetallists. American Presidents from Hayes to McKinley, sensitive as they were to the political power of silver, had all been interested in efforts to arrive at an international monetary agreement, but their efforts were constantly undermined not only by the success of the silver interests in Congress in 1878 and 1890 but by the indiscreet interventions of silver congressmen in monetary diplomacy.[34]

Probably the most strategic moment for an international agreement was the conference of 1881, when America's gold position was strong and the European powers were suffering a

---

[34]See Jeannette P. Nichols's account of these interventions in "Silver Diplomacy," *Political Science Quarterly*, XLVIII (December 1933), 565–88. Henry B. Russell gives a detailed account of the effects of American silver policies on the international meetings in his *International Monetary Conferences* (New York, 1898); see esp. pp. 192–9, 260, 323–7, 369, 409–10. Concerning the interventions of the silver men and their effects on the prospects of bimetallism, Russell remarks (pp. 324–5): "No doctrine ever stood in such dire need of being delivered from its most officious friends."

serious gold crisis. A great wave of bimetallist sentiment swept Europe, from which Britain was by no means immune, and British representatives came to the conference quite interested in seeing the *other* nations, perhaps the United States and the Latin Union, open their mints to unlimited coinage. But current American silver purchases under the Bland-Allison Act checked the silver impetus almost as much as the British refusal to go off gold.

Eleven years later, the British, led by Alfred de Rothschild, a director of the Bank of England, came to the conference of 1892 still unwilling to change their own standard, but still concerned about the rupee and solicitous about silver.[35] At this meeting they proposed that the Continental nations, together with the United States, should undertake a common program of silver purchases—in support of which the British offered, as their contribution, to raise the amount of silver acceptable as legal tender in England from £2 to £5. This would have been a small price for Britain to pay to relieve the difficulties of her Eastern commerce by inducing the United States to make a firm commitment to silver purchases. British financiers were indeed trying to make use of the resources of the United States—not by forcing this country onto the gold standard, as the American silverites charged, but by getting it pledged to continue the silver purchases of the Sherman Act. The British position was far from disinterested, but it reveals some of the complexities of the economic world that could hardly have been comprehensible to devoted readers of *Coin's Financial School*: "Coin" Harvey, William Jennings Bryan, and Alfred de Rothschild marching arm in arm in a campaign to uphold the American silver purchase policy!

[35]One can only wonder if "Coin" Harvey was aware of the prophetic words of Alfred de Rothschild at this conference, and what he would have made of them: "Gentlemen, I need hardly remind you that the stock of silver in the world is estimated at some thousands of millions, and if this conference were to break up without arriving at any definite result there would be a depreciation in the value of that commodity which it would be frightful to contemplate, and out of which a monetary panic would ensue, the far-reaching effects of which it would be impossible to foretell." Russell: op. cit., p. 385.

IX

The real world of business and finance was complex, but the mental world of the money agitators was beautifully simple. Among its treasured legends was the idea that the gold standard had been stealthily imposed upon the American people by the British banking powers. The anti-British feeling and the conspiratorial view of monetary history expressed in *Coin's Financial School* were dressed out more elaborately in a propagandistic novel, *A Tale of Two Nations*, which Harvey brought out in September 1894, only three months after the appearance of his masterpiece. This work, possibly the only *roman à clef* ever written about the gold standard, deserves attention in its own right. Written more or less at the same time as *Coin's Financial School*, it makes a fuller statement of some of its sentiments, and it must rank in symptomatic significance with Ignatius Donnelly's *Caesar's Column* as a fantasy in fiction that illuminates the populist mind. Harvey himself never lost faith in this novel's importance, for he reprinted it as late as 1931.[36]

A Tale of Two Nations opens in the year 1869, when Baron Rothe (Rothschild), a portly and immensely intelligent banker of an old Jewish house, is discussing his plans with another financier, Sir William T. Cline. The Baron has a daring scheme: if silver can be demonetized in the United States and Europe, gold will double its purchasing power, to the immense advantage of gold owners and holders of debts contracted for payment in gold. Here, he says, is a stroke of policy that will do more for England than a thousand years of conquests by arms. The United States, instead of overshadowing England in world trade, would (in some way not clearly specified) find herself impoverished, her industrial power broken. When his

---

[36] By all accounts it was the second most successful of his writings in popularity. Priced at fifty cents, it was bought eagerly by his public; and while we may not accept his own estimation of a circulation of 500,000, the second edition alone appears to have run to at least one fifth of that figure, and there were further editions. The book had the advantage of being advertised in later editions of *Coin's Financial School* as "the most exciting and interesting novel on American politics ever published." In fact, Harvey appended to such editions the first two chapters of *A Tale of Two Nations* to titillate his readers.

guest demurs that a measure of demonetization amounting to financial suicide would never be enacted by the Congress, Baron Rothe confidently replies that almost no one in Congress knows anything about money, and that a bill framed in sufficiently deceptive terms would go through; its real effects would not be discovered for years. Ruthlessly the Baron outlines his plans: the power of money, skillfully used, would "establish two classes, the rich and the poor. The first to enjoy this world, and the other to live by waiting on the first. We must crush their manhood by making them poor—they then will make good servants and gentle citizens."

The first instrument of this cold-blooded plot is an American senator, John Arnold (John Sherman and Benedict Arnold?), who now visits Baron Rothe in London. Arnold puts up the appearance of noble American statesmanship, but his true character is read by Baron Rothe and by the Baron's beautiful daughter Edith. This dark lady has powers of character diagnosis that are practically occult; she quickly finds that Arnold is a consummate worshipper of the power of money. Baron Rothe has no difficulty in bribing Arnold to use his influence to work for the demonetization of silver. Three years later the conspiracy brings to Washington the young nephew of the Baron, one Victor Rogasner, a darkly handsome cosmopolitan of sybaritic tendencies, whose mission is to forward the final passage of the demonetization measure. Rogasner is aided by a secretary, by two former Scotland Yard men, whose business it is to work on congressmen, and by a passionate and beautiful Russian Jewess who will do anything necessary to advance the projects or achieve the happiness of the man she loves. Rogasner is full of guile and the spirit of vengeance. "In the highest sense I am a military commander," he muses.

> I am here to destroy the United States—Cornwallis could not have done more. For the wrongs and insults, for the glory of my own country, I will bury the knife deep into the heart of this nation. . . . I will crush their manhood. I will destroy the last vestige of national prosperity among them, and humble that accursed pride with which they refer to their revolutionary ancestors, to the very dust. I will set them fighting among each other, and see them cut each other's throats, and carry devastation into each other's homes, while I look on without loss.

In the corrupt atmosphere of the Grant administration, which Harvey fills in with a few hasty strokes, it becomes quite plausible that still another, unknown, scandal, based on the quest for favorable monetary legislation by the gold interests, could actually have taken place. Rogasner has his moments of doubt and suspense, but before long his strategy carries the day —silver is demonetized, the Crime of '73 is a fact. "The greatest crime ever committed in the world—one that was to cause more suffering than all other crimes committed in a century, had been quietly accomplished." The American congressmen do not yet know what they have done, and it takes them three years to discover it. Later Rogasner is instrumental in bringing about the demonetization of silver in Germany (anachronistically) and France. He then returns to the United States to wage a propaganda battle in favor of the gold standard, because silver advocates are now up in arms. But it proves easy to suborn professors of economics and the greater part of the press. The people are "helpless victims in the power of a soulless gold oligarchy."

The story jumps to 1894, and new characters are introduced. The corrupt Senator Arnold has a ward, Grace Vivian; and Rogasner, now a man of great affluence, in his middle years but still handsome, takes a fancy to her. Grace prefers the attentions of John Melwyn, a noble, handsome, well-proportioned, and eloquent young silverite congressman from Lincoln, Nebraska, who resembles William Jennings Bryan. The contest, nonetheless, seems unequal: Rogasner is rich and Melwyn is poor, and, what is more, Rogasner is wily. American innocence is once more at a disadvantage in confronting European duplicity. "The honest heart and frank directness of the younger man; his simple rearing, uneventful, in a sense, furnished few weapons with which to meet the wily diplomacy and cunning, the broad knowledge and teachings of a life of intrigue, possessed by the polished nephew of Baron Rothe." Worst of all, Senator Arnold cannot bear Melwyn's free-silver views. In this contest between the Englishman and the American for a girl "fair and beautiful enough to typify Columbia," the unscrupulous Senator secretly intercepts Melwyn's letters, in order to give Grace the impression that Melwyn has lost interest in her.

The story moves toward its climax against a background of the stirring events of 1894—the suffering brought by the panic, the fear awakened by the march of Coxey's army on Washington, the bitterness aroused by the Pullman strike. Melwyn's brother turns up as a member of Coxey's army, his father too is ruined, and Melwyn himself is plagued by a mortgage he cannot pay, unaware that the long arm of Rogasner is stiffening the demands of his creditors. Rogasner, hardhearted as ever in the midst of all the distress of the depression years, waits for the day when seventy per cent of the people are in distress —at which point, he believes, the political situation will explode, and the present government of the United States will be either supplanted by a monarchy or completely consumed in a revolution. Meanwhile, as the people worry about a variety of unimportant issues, and are thus distracted from the fundamental money question, "we are shooting from ambush, and are perfectly safe. . . . I shall sink this accursed nation; tear it into threads, and leave it bleeding and disrupted, if for no other purpose than to demonstrate the power of our money."

In an interesting passage, Rogasner pursues a line of thought that sheds light on Harvey's conception of the gold conspirators. For Rogasner proves to be a man who understands full well, with the immemorial wisdom and historic consciousness of the Jew ("it takes one of our race [Jesus] to detect this error in our civilization [usury]"), that lending and hoarding since the times of the Medes and Persians have been the root cause of the breakdown of civilizations. He is even clever enough to outline—in private—a Harveyesque scheme for a "perfect civilization" based on the abolition of debt and usury and the heavy taxation of wealth. Still, knowing the path to perfection as he does, he chooses evil. He is an angel of darkness, a Manichean nightmare.[37]

---

[37]Like the other political characters in the book, Rogasner was probably intended to represent an actual person. It was part of the legend subscribed to by many true believers in the silver cause that a London banker, Ernest Seyd, had come to the United States with $500,000 which he used to bribe congressmen to pass the Coinage Act of 1873. The silver men even purported to have an affidavit from a Denver businessman to show that Seyd had later privately confessed to having played such a role. This version of the passage of the Crime of '73 was quite common in silver tracts, and Harvey could hardly

But his personal defeat awaits him. After an assiduous court-
ship he at last hungrily proposes to Grace ("The man's eyes
blazed with the fire of his race in the old days, the fire that
came when David gazed upon Bathsheba, or when the eyes of
Jacob first rested on Rachel at the well"). She politely refuses,
saying that she would just like to be "good friends." Growing desperate, he now reveals to her for the first time his true
identity: he is not an American investment counselor at all, as
his conspiratorial activities have required him to pretend; he
tells her of his aristocratic family and his wealth and prospects,

---

have missed it. (The most ample statement I have seen is in Gordon Clark's
Handbook of Money [n.p., published by the Silver Knight Publishing Company,
1896], pp. 189–206.)

Seyd was in fact a London banker, born in Germany, who had lived in the
United States for many years and had been in business in San Francisco. There
is no reliable evidence that he was in the United States in 1872, but he was consulted by Representative Samuel C. Hooper about the Coinage Act of 1873,
and wrote him a long, technical letter about it, on February 17, 1872, in which
he advised, among other things, the *reintroduction* of the long defunct silver
dollar at what he regarded a more practicable weight, and a firm commitment
to bimetallism. See *Documentary History of the Coinage Act of February 12, 1873*
(Washington, U.S. Government Printing Office, n.d. [1894?]), pp. 95–106; cf.
Seyd's *Suggestions in Reference to the Metallic Coinage of the United States of
America* (London, 1871), and his letter to the Monetary Commission of 1876,
Senate Report 703, 44th Cong., 2nd sess. (1876), *Documents Accompanying
the Report of the U.S. Monetary Commission*, II, 106–35.

Seyd, who died in 1881, was a Fellow of the Royal Statistical Society and one
of the better-known British bimetallists. Most of the silver men who discussed
the subject were aware of Seyd's lifelong advocacy of bimetallism, but in their
view this by no means ruled out the possibility that his fealty to the British gold
power was stronger than his personal convictions. Had they not seen men like
Secretary Carlisle converted from solid bimetallists into defenders of the gold
standard? Like Rogasner, Seyd could know good and do evil. As Gordon Clark
wrote of Seyd: "That very able acquaintance of the Rothschilds—a gentleman
of the same Hebrew blood—was no disburser of bribes, in ordinary circumstances, and was a *sincere bimetallist*. But he was also 'the financial adviser
of the Bank of England,'" and in this capacity "was forced to postpone his
theories when that huge octopus came to see its fat prey in the United States"
(pp. 195–6).

The Seyd story became the object of some discussion on the floor of Congress in 1890 and again in 1893. For the latter year, see *Congressional Record*,
53rd Cong., 1st sess., pp. 474–6, 584–9, 1059.

hoping to appeal to the fortune-hunter or title-hunter that is supposed to lurk in almost every American girl. "I come from one of the oldest and proudest and wealthiest of European families. In fact the oldest and wealthiest in the world. Our millions aid in controlling the affairs of nations. . . . In time I will be a baron."

Rogasner has overplayed his hand; Grace is offended at this attempt to buy her. "You sneer at America and talk of a better civilization of which you say I may be made an ornament. I am proud of being an American woman and I am content with this civilization of which you speak so lightly. It may be barbarous, but I am content." Now Rogasner plays his ace. He goes to Senator Arnold and asks for his intercession. But the Senator, whose one uncorrupted emotion is his affection for his ward, feels that he cannot try to determine her choice of a husband. At home again, Rogasner broods over the possibility of a last resort—blackmailing the Senator with his knowledge of the Senator's corruption. Rogasner's brother, a minor figure in the demonetization conspiracy, chides him for his obsession with Grace: "Are there not women of our own race and faith beautiful enough and with all grace of mind and body to fit them for any man?" But Rogasner is unmoved: "Did not our ancestors, even on Arabian plains, take whatever women of whatever race most pleased their fancy?" Rogasner proceeds to blackmail Senator Arnold, and the threat of exposure reduces the Senator to prostration. Rogasner gloats like the fiend he is—he "was not exactly smiling—he was leering, and he was as happy as Nero was in the death agonies of his mother. The Hebrew was 'harrowing' again." But Grace has overheard his words, and she breaks in on the two men, reproaching her guardian, and upbraiding Rogasner: "You are very shrewd. You are very wise in your way, the commercial way, inbred through generations. The politic, scheming, devious way inbred through generations also. You are as repulsive to me as anything that could exist." As Rogasner arises and approaches her—with who knows what intent—none other than John Melwyn, "the typical American man," breaks in and throws him to the floor.

There is little more to be told. John Melwyn and Grace marry, and Rogasner goes back home to the selfless Jeanne Soutleffsky, "the fair Jewess who had been his agent in so many instances," and who was there to welcome him "like Rebecca solicitous over Ivanhoe." She has patiently endured his pursuit of Grace Vivian, and now "her face was a poem, a great epic poem of the grand old Jewish race." Rogasner needs her: he breaks down and becomes a helpless invalid, and benefits for the rest of his life from her devotion. The book ends on what Harvey's silverite readers must have felt was a chilling note: "On the 29th day of September, 1894, there sailed on the steamer *Paris* from Liverpool a representative of a foreign syndicate to take Rogasner's place."

The mild note of anti-Semitism in Harvey's book will not surprise those who are familiar with the traditional linkage of money crazes and anti-Jewish feeling. In the American silver movement this prejudice was a facet of the far more deeply felt anti-British sentiment; it did not go beyond a kind of rhetorical vulgarity, since no programmatic steps were urged against Jews as such. Like his Populist contemporary Ignatius Donnelly, Harvey had mixed feelings and showed a certain shame about his prejudice which caused him to interlard his anti-Semitic remarks with awkward philo-Semitic amends. In *Coin's Financial School Up to Date* Harvey disavowed prejudice against the Jews—

> the brightest race of people that inhabit the earth, and they treat each other with the greatest fairness as a rule. . . . You should not be prejudiced against any race as a race. . . . Among Jews, many became money changers; it seems to be natural with them, probably on account of their excessive shrewdness. They see that it has advantages not possessed by any other business.[38]

Many Jews, it must be said, might have found Harvey's embraces harder to endure than his slurs.

In the end, Harvey could not untangle himself from the Shylock image, which pervades money crankery from the Greenbackers to Father Coughlin and Ezra Pound, and his later writings are dotted with repetitive citations of prohibitions

---

[38] P. 68. On the similar ambivalence of Ignatius Donnelly, see Martin Ridge: *Ignatius Donnelly* (Chicago, 1962), pp. 263–4, 266 n., 305, 321–3, 336–7, 395–6. C. Vann Woodward has pointed out that the Populists had no monopoly on anti-Semitism in the 1890's. See his remarks in *The Burden of Southern History* (Baton Rouge, La., 1960), pp. 154–5.

against usury on the part of Christian thinkers. In his *Common Sense, or the Clot on the Brain of the Body Politic*,[39] he borrowed a quotation used in Redpath's *History of the World* which stated that the Jew does not work as most men do, contributes nothing to human industry, but "obtains control of the money market, using the same for the exclusive advantage of himself and his people." In spite of the repeated injunctions of the Christian churches against usury down through the ages, Harvey said, the rulers of the Christian churches "ever had a persistent enemy following them and seeking to loan money —taking pledges, binding borrowers to secrecy and adding to their stock of money till by the 17th century their holdings were enough to choke civilization to a favorable concession." Here he quoted the central passage on usury from Deuteronomy 23: 19–20, in which usury within the tribe is forbidden but what he called the "fatal exception" was made: "Unto a stranger thou mayest lend upon usury."[40] This, he declared, "made money-lenders of the Jews. Regarding the Gentiles as 'strangers,' their enemies, they have sought to punish them, to ruin them, with the weapon usury." But there is still hope for the Jews if they will relent and reform:

> A stricken world cries out to them to make public renunciation of usury and to make *restitution* by crowding into the front ranks of reformers against the sin! The Jews come of a noble race, possessing a high order of intelligence, acumen and persistency in a cause; and by recognizing that it is inconsistent with the "brotherhood of man" to wield the Sword of "Usury" against the Gentiles, they will assimilate into the activities of productive civilization, be worthy descendants of their pastoral forefathers, and will become vocationally adapted to the cultivation and rebuilding of their ancient land.

X

During his celebrity as a silver tractarian Harvey was also briefly active in politics. In 1894 he was busy with the affairs of the populist party of Illinois, which, unlike most other state

---

[39] Monte Ne, Ark., 1920, p. 18.
[40] On the historic interpretation of the prohibition in Deuteronomy, see Benjamin F. Nelson: *The Idea of Usury* (Princeton, 1949).

Populist parties, had a strong labor-socialist wing interested in writing a collectivist plank into the party's program. Harvey's sympathies lay with the more conservative agrarian wing of the party, which repudiated collectivism and put its hopes in monetary reform. When the two factions of the Illinois party finally fell out, he joined with the Prohibitionist leader Howard S. Taylor in curbing the radicals. In 1895 he published *Coin's Financial School Up to Date*, in which Coin returns to expound Harvey's financial ideas in a work marked by a long discussion of greed and ignorance as forces in history, and by attacks on British landholders in the United States. During the same year Harvey engaged in a debate on the silver issue with J. Laurence Laughlin and a series of nine debates with former Congressman Roswell G. Horr. He also tried to organize a kind of political fraternal order, open to members of all existing parties, which he hoped to purify. The organization was to be called the Patriots of America, and its lodges were to have their own ritual, somewhat in the fashion of national fraternal orders; there was to be a kind of women's auxiliary, the Daughters of the Republic. Harvey's book *The Patriots of America* was devoted in large part to a proposed constitution for this order, and pending an election, he offered himself as its First National Patriot. *The Patriots of America* suffered from an excess of incoherence that was to envelop Harvey's later writings, and from a striking note of exaggeration, grandiosity, and suspicion. Good and evil were struggling for control of the world, he held, and things had become so bad that "we must make the last stand of freemen for the civilization of the world." Murders, suicides, crime, insanity, and British and railroad landholdings were all strung together as evidence of the pathological state society had reached: "The United States has been honeycombed by foreign influences and our property is rapidly passing into their hands."[41]

Some features of Harvey's proposed Patriots of America, especially its semi-secrecy, worried Bryan and his supporters, who saw in it a possible source of factionalism. Harvey explained that the organization would "give us the finances for a national campaign" against the money power, and that its secrecy and its required pledge that members must vote in conformity with

[41] *The Patriots of America* (Chicago, 1895), pp. 12, 28, 39–40.

majority decisions were intended to foil "cunning and unscrupulous" enemies from working within the ranks. "I love you,"
wrote Harvey to Bryan, "and shall always have your good in
view because I believe you to be one of the first patriots in the
country."[42]

During 1896 Harvey worked fervently for Bryan, giving lectures and speeches and distributing silver badges. Harvey (who
had originally preferred "Silver Dick" Bland of Missouri) was
then a member of the executive committee of the National Silver party, which bought a million copies of Archbishop Walsh's
Bimetallism and Monometallism, half of them in English and
half in a German translation, as well as 125,000 copies of *Coin's
Financial School*.[43] After the campaign Harvey spent some
months lecturing to raise money for the Democrats. His cordial relations with Bryan continued, and as late as 1913 Bryan
was still trying to secure for him a post in the Department of
Agriculture under Woodrow Wilson.[44]

The year 1896 was the zenith of the silver cause. In the following year the tide of depression turned. New gold deposits
and new methods of extraction hastened a rise in prices that
the silver men had thought could come only from the white
metal. It soon became apparent that silver was a lost cause, that
the ground had been cut from under men whose whole intellectual and political lives had hung upon monetary agitation.
Chicago, the scene of his one great success, began to pall for
Harvey. In 1899 he published the last book to appear under the
aegis of the Coin Publishing Company, *Coin on Money, Trusts
and Imperialism*.

Coin, now supposedly a youth of sixteen, returns in this volume for a last effort to stem the tide of reaction. He presents
human history as an arena of struggle between two types of
people—the humane type, which delights in the upbuilding of
mankind without neglecting self, and the selfish type, which
seeks only self-promotion and self-aggrandizement. The first

[42]Nichols: "Bryan's Benefactor," pp. 321–2.

[43]Bryan, op. cit., p. 292.

[44]Much to the irritation of Secretary of Agriculture David F. Houston, who
had always regarded Harvey and his famous book as "huge jokes." D. F. Houston: *Eight Years with Wilson's Cabinet* (New York, 1926), I, 43.

of these forces is now animating the movement for democracy and reform, the second expresses itself in the cry for monarchy and imperialism. Some considerable portion of the book is, of course, given over to Coin's views on money and banking, but it suffers from its lack of concentration on a single theme. It moves on to attack British investors in America and British holders of American land, and then to denounce the British government for permitting moneylenders to shape the laws. Coin then passes on to the trust question, at the time a matter of growing public concern, but Harvey was much less at home with this issue than with money: his main suggestion was that all industrial trusts are nourished by the financial trust, and if the financial trust can be destroyed, the others will disappear with it.

Moving on to imperialism, the great issue of the moment, Coin saw the drive toward imperialism in rather vague moral terms: an evil genius entrenched in the nation's monetary and industrial system naturally sought to extend itself. "A selfish force having despoiled its own people, seeks other people whom it may despoil. Having preyed upon its own people, with an enlarged appetite, it looks about for other peoples to prey upon—which is called *conquest*." What Coin now began to designate in plain Manichean terms as "the Evil influence" was invoked to explain the development of the Spanish-American War into an imperial enterprise. As an act in behalf of a victimized Cuban people against a dissolute Spanish monarchy, Coin, in common with so many Americans, believed the war to be justified. But privileged classes had seized upon it to take the first step toward installing monarchy in the United States by moving into the Philippines and by keeping the United States in Cuba. Many people, Harvey thought, like expansion because they think it will improve business. In fact, there is ample room within the United States for indefinite expansion, and prosperity can be stimulated by improvements at home. He recommended a canal to connect Lake Michigan with Lake Erie and the development of a system of good roads and irrigation ditches.

The emotional climax of the volume occurs at a point at which Coin links American occupation of the Philippines with the British war against the Boers and indicts President

McKinley for showing sympathy for England and following her example. Coin cries:

> I arraign the President *for treason* in waging a war without that war having first been declared by Congress, as required by the Constitution! I arraign him for treason for a *secret alliance* with England against Republics struggling for liberty! I arraign the majority in Congress as the willing puppets of the Evil influence that prompts the President!

This brings the imaginary audience to its feet, cheering and applauding.

One of Harvey's most urgent worries was that expansionism would bring an enlarged standing army of as many as 100,000 men. He believed, as the Founding Fathers had believed, in a citizen soldiery, in state troops. A standing army under national control might well become the instrument of "monarchy," and certainly it would create a mercenary soldiery, dangerous to domestic government and likely to heighten the desire for conquest. Unlike mercenaries, citizen soldiers would refuse to engage in wars of conquest. "Any war that our citizen soldiers will not fight is an unjust war!" The demand for a standing army was only incidental to the struggle that was about to open. "Monarchy is ready to spring at the throat of the Republic!" The privileged few, in their quest for subjugation of the people, have only begun with their demand for a standing army. "If they carry the presidential election in 1900, in four years more, they will disclose openly their desire for a Monarchy! . . . The forces of Evil we are combating are organized, and determined of purpose to enslave America!" Harvey left no doubt about what their instrument was: having failed to take over the Democratic party, they had entrenched themselves among the Republicans. Mark Hanna, the symbol of their intentions, had "a bed in the White House . . . patterned after the style of the bed the Queen of England sleeps in."[45] The crying need of the hour was to keep the Democratic party pure, to tighten its organization, and to rally for victory.

[45] *Coin on Money, Trusts, and Imperialism* (Chicago, 1899), pp. 5–6, 9, 31–41, 78, 107, 135, 142–3, 157, 160–1, 171.

XI

Even before Bryan's second defeat in 1900 it must have become apparent to Harvey that no victory was to be expected. In March the confident Republicans easily put through the Gold Standard Act, which, while it was largely a formal declaration of a fact already established, seemed to drive the last nail in the coffin of the silver issue. Two months later Harvey was preparing to retreat from Chicago. In May 1900 he appeared in the Ozark Mountain town of Rogers, Arkansas, which he had visited in 1894 and 1896 during his campaigns for silver, and rather abruptly bought a tract of 325 acres in a pleasant and well-watered site then called Silver Springs. In the fall he returned with his family, and announced a plan to open an Ozark summer resort outside Rogers. Soon he had renamed his property Monte Ne (which he imagined meant "mountain of waters" in Spanish) and had formed the Monte Ne investment company in concert with two secretaries he had brought from his Chicago enterprises. The following spring the Hotel Monte Ne was opened, and before long it rang with the tunes of oldtime fiddlers whom Harvey had imported in the hope that a revival of old-fashioned rural entertainment would enliven the resort. Visitors arriving at the resort were ferried across the lake by Venetian gondoliers.

Other enterprises followed. A four-mile railroad spur to Lowell was built in 1902 to bring visitors to this isolated resort area. William Jennings Bryan came to speak at its opening. Excursions were planned with the help of the Frisco Railroad, which brought vacationers from Joplin, Fort Smith, and Springfield. With some local entrepreneurs, Harvey organized the Bank of Monte Ne, capitalized at $25,000, and built a white boxlike structure to house it. He also began to build a huge, rambling hotel consisting of a number of ranges of log cottages, and organized a mercantile company to bring supplies into Monte Ne.

For a few years it must have seemed that Harvey might begin a wholly new career in the resort business with capital saved from the silver days. But ill luck, personal and financial, seemed to dog him. His family had hardly been long in Monte Ne before the homestead acquired with the Silver Springs tract

burned down, and Harvey's library, the family piano, silver-
ware, and other household effects brought from Chicago were
destroyed. In 1903 his twenty-three-year-old son Halliday, who
was studying for the law, was killed in a railroad accident. A
campaign Harvey planned to make for Congress in 1904 was
quickly abandoned in the face of obstinate local rebuffs. In
time the Frisco Railroad grew tired of running unprofitable
excursion trains, and it became increasingly difficult to attract
visitors to the splendid isolation of Monte Ne. Harvey's own
little railroad failed, and his bank, with all depositors paid in
full, closed in 1914. Some part of the projected great hotel was
finished, and it was operated with modest success for a period
of years, but, in the words of a local chronicler,

> after the foundation for the big hotel was well under way, Mr.
> Harvey ran into a lot of trouble with union labor organizers,
> and he abandoned the project and left the masonry for future
> generations to ponder over its origin and intent. That labor
> row rather soured Mr. Harvey in his outlook on life and af-
> fected all his later years at Monte Ne. . . . From this time until
> his death, Mr. Harvey's life was filled with financial difficulties,
> legal entanglements over the control of his properties, and the
> numerous changes in his ambitions.[46]

The handicap arising from Monte Ne's isolation stimulated
the last successful effort in Harvey's life, his organization of the
Ozark Trails Association to mark and promote 1,500 miles of
automobile highways, connecting four towns and five million
people in the states of Arkansas, Missouri, Kansas, and Oklahoma. He had seen the railroad fail as a source of transportation for his locality, and it had become evident to any man
of vision by 1910, when he first conceived of the Ozark Trails
Association, that the automobile was America's coming mode
of travel. "My personal interest in the Ozark Trails," Harvey
wrote, "is that they all lead to Monte Ne, where we have a delightful resort." For many years after 1913, when he organized

---

[46] *Rogers Daily News*, July 1, 1950, a local commemorative issue, which contains
news stories, pictures, and reminiscences, is my main source for this last phase
of Harvey's life. Some gleanings are also to be found in his periodical *The
Palladium*, published at intervals in 1920 and 1925, and in Joseph E. Reeve:
Monetary Reform Movements (Washington, 1943).

the Ozark Trails Association at a meeting held in Monte Ne, Harvey gave his energies to the good-roads movement without expectation of immediate profit. In the hope of bringing what he characteristically called "a vast network of modern auto routes into Arkansas," he spent a great deal of time mapping out and actually marking automobile roads, as well as in strenuous efforts to get the backing of businessmen in adjacent cities. For fifteen years Harvey gave unstintingly of his time, receiving in return only the expenses he incurred while actually engaged in travel, road marking, and promotional activities. What was left of his hotel business apparently suffered from the diversion of his energies, but this identification with a thriving cause once again seems to have mobilized the promotional enthusiasm that had always been so strong in him. "When actively in the harness," wrote one of his co-workers in the good-roads movement, "he seemed to be immune to physical discomfort or fatigue. He had an indomitable will, a crusading spirit, and a great reserve of physical power. In the midst of an important campaign, his eyes would burn with the intense fervor of a mystic."[47] This work was largely done by 1920, and Harvey was again free to devote his energy to his agitations.

Harvey's crusading spirit had not been detached from social issues. He never gave up the hope that the world might be induced to listen, that the success of *Coin's Financial School* could somehow be repeated. In 1915 he began publishing again, with a book called *The Remedy*, whose title suggests the hopes he still cherished. *The Remedy* expounded his notion that the forces of good could be strengthened in their battle with evil by a system of character building in the schools. It contained a manual for school instruction in character. In 1920, in his *Common Sense, or The Clot on the Brain of the Body Politic*, he resumed his polemics against selfishness and usury, reviewed the history of money and banking in the United States, and waged a polemic against banking profits under the Federal Reserve system. The Federal Reserve system, he argued, "overshadows the Bank of England, and gives to the money-lenders greater advantage than the

[47]Quoted by Clara B. Kennan: "The Ozark Trails and Arkansas's Pathfinder, Coin Harvey," *Arkansas Historical Quarterly*, VII (Winter 1948), 312–13.

old United States bank did, that General Jackson killed. The money-lenders' organization of the banking system may now be regarded as perfected." In his indiscriminate opposition to banks, Harvey was opposing the creation of credit instruments intended to alleviate the very ills that had originally provoked him into becoming a crusader. In this work the paranoid and apocalyptic note sounds stronger than before. Harvey becomes increasingly concerned not merely with Christian prohibitions against usury but with the terrible and sometimes mysterious fate that overcame early opponents of usurious exploitation. Repeatedly he compares the situation of the United States with that of Rome during the persecutions of the Christians:

> The usurers, the money-power in New York City, Chicago, and the large money-lending cities put out the propaganda based on falsehood and misrepresentation as to what the reformers are teaching—as they did in Rome—till the public mind is poisoned and prejudiced and a fair trial is impossible. By suppressing free speech, free press, peaceable assembly, imprisoning and exiling, *the truth is not heard!*

He had become more and more obsessed with the violence and torture inflicted by the Roman Empire, and warned that it was likely to be repeated. ("The blood of the martyred Christians appeals to the people of the world in this second Crisis!") He saw the persecution of the early Christians as a political event, a response primarily to their protest against usury, and he cited Tacitus to warn of the fate that such protest could expect: "Some were nailed on crosses, others sewn up in the skins of wild beasts and exposed to the fury of dogs; others, again smeared over with combustible materials, were used as torches to illuminate the darkness of the night."[48] It is a melancholy thought that this old man, spending his last years in the quiet of an Ozark village, should have had to be tormented by such nightmares.

In 1924, aroused by the postwar depression and a new collapse in American agriculture, Harvey brought out, through his Mundus Publishing Company, a little book called *Paul's*

[48]The theme of martyrdom, and his own identification with Christ, is apparent as early as 1895 in "'Coin's Financial School' and Its Censors," already cited.

School of Statesmanship, in which another fantastic boy, modeled somewhat after Coin, appears in Monte Ne as Coin had appeared in Chicago, and opens another school. This book, which Harvey said "discloses the most important discovery, relating to civilization and the human race, that has been made in all the history of the world," did not have the reception that its importance warranted. In good part, Paul's was a school of character. He promised a government without taxation or bond issues, in a new society, based on gold, of all things, but whose real source of success was the liberal issue of paper currency. The proper understanding of the function of money, Harvey proposed once again, was the key to civilization, but in spite of his promises of a new civilization based upon the solution of the money question, the book showed that Harvey was more than ever persuaded that a total collapse of civilization would result from the rejection of his views. It was followed six years later by a work entitled, with the simple unaffected confidence of a major prophet, *The Book*, in which Harvey restated many of his old ideas, re-used many of his old quotations, rehearsed the historic Christian opposition to usury, warned against dictatorship, reprinted part of *A Tale of Two Nations*, retold the story of the Crime of '73, and called for a new political party.

By now Harvey's faith in the possibility of social reform had grown dimmer. To quote again the local chronicler of his fortunes: "As he grew older and more bitter in his condemnation of existing laws and conditions, he dropped his wealthy friends of these early [business] experiments at Monte Ne and sought the dimes and quarters of the poorer people." In his sixties, Harvey was returning to the agitational frame of mind in which he had come to Chicago, but without the optimism of his earlier days. A civilization incapable of solving the money question was almost certainly headed for disaster. A new vision, announced as early as 1920, began to form in his brain and grew in obsessive strength with the years: he would build in Monte Ne, at the site of his resort, a great Pyramid, in which he would leave copies of his own books and a variety of artifacts representative of the twentieth-century civilization that he was sure would go to ruin. Thus a future civilization "rising from the ashes" would be able to stumble upon the relics of the past, preserved by "Coin" Harvey. As the years went by, his obsession with the Pyramid grew. It would be 40 feet square at the base and rise to 130 feet in height, and at the top, where it would presumably protrude above the dust of the ages, there would be a plaque, reading: "When this can be read go below and find the cause of the death of a former Civilization." Below, the men of the future would find copies of *Paul's School of Statesmanship*, *The Book*, and the Bible, chemically treated to survive time, along with various volumes on the technical and scientific attainments of twentieth-century civilization, and— a thoughtful precaution—a key to the English language so that the works left there would be the more readily decipherable if found by men of a strange tongue.

To raise money to build such a Pyramid, Harvey solicited contributions from the readers of his books. It would be a boon to a later millennium, he pointed out, and "there will be nothing about it that partakes of self or vanity and no one's name will appear on the outside of it." Construction of the Pyramid was actually begun to Harvey's specifications. To make a secure footing for it, he excavated the hills near his home and built what he liked to call the "foyer" of the Pyramid —"an asymmetrical mass of concrete and stone in the form of seats," as a local reporter described it, "but without any semblance of regular order." In surviving pictures it looks like the village of some strange breed of midget Pueblos with disordered minds. At length, its total cost estimated at $100,000, this project too was abandoned, like Harvey's hotel and his bank and his railroad—but here, at last, he had an unexpected stroke of luck. The "foyer" itself became a kind of curiosity, a substitute for antique ruins, and thousands of visitors were drawn to it, paying admission fees to gaze upon the fragments of Harvey's unrealized dream. They were treated to lectures on financial reform and given the opportunity to buy Harvey's books, old and new, all conveniently displayed.

By the mid-1920's Harvey had given up all business activities and had yielded completely to his messianic dreams. He attempted through his later writings to organize a new national political party, first called the Liberty party and later the Prosperity party. Perhaps he sought advice from "General" Jacob Coxey, who visited him on occasion to discuss old times and bemoan the condition of the world. The Great Depression of the 1930's gave him a last moment of public notice. In 1932 he ran for President and received 800 votes without campaigning. Three years later he reappeared to denounce Roosevelt's policy of silver purchases, which he regarded as absurdly cautious, a "travesty" on silver. In February 1936, forty years after the battle of the standards, Harvey died at the age of eighty-four. To the end he never lost the pride and sense of his importance that had made it possible for him, against all the probabilities, to claim the attention of the world. A photograph taken in his later years shows a slender, hawk-nosed man still erect and alert, his face adorned by a dignified white mustache, his brow slightly furrowed, his mien a little apprehensive and harassed, looking very much the part of the small-town businessman or banker. Though he was only of medium size, an acquaintance said, "he stood and walked so straight he gave the impression of being taller than his real height." It was as though by a sheer effort of will he could add a cubit to his stature.

Acknowledgments

I wish to thank Herbert G. Nicholas, my host on the occasion of the Herbert Spencer Lecture, and many friends who have contributed in a variety of ways to the improvement of these essays. It gives me pleasure to acknowledge the encouragement I have had from Alfred A. Knopf for more than twenty years and to appear on his list in the fiftieth anniversary year of his firm. Thanks are due to Phi Beta Kappa for transferring to me the copyright of "The Pseudo-Conservative Revolt"; to John Wiley & Sons for permission to use a revised version of "What Happened to the Antitrust Movement?"; and to the President and Fellows of Harvard College for permission to reprint "Free Silver and the Mind of 'Coin' Harvey."

R. H.

SELECTED ESSAYS 1956–1965

History and the Social Sciences

THE PROFESSIONAL academic historian suffers in these times from a persistent uncertainty about precisely what he is. Two traditions govern his training and his work. On one side there is the familiar historical narrative, a form of literature for which there is always much demand. On the other is the historical monograph, ideally supposed to approximate a scientific inquiry, which the historian is professionally trained to write. Authors of narrative histories rarely hesitate to retell a story that is already substantially known, adding perhaps some new information but seldom in a systematic fashion or with a clear analytical purpose. Authors of monographs, on the other hand, take it upon themselves to add new information to the fund of knowledge, or to analyze in a new way the meaning of a given sequence of historical events. Many historians, especially the great ones, have combined in single works both sides of this dual tradition, but in the profession as a whole the double function of the historian has been an important cause of the uncertain value of much historical writing. Many a historian feels that it is unsatisfactory merely to repeat with minor modifications what we already know of the past; but many a monograph, though intended to overcome this limitation, leaves its readers, and perhaps even its author, with misgivings as to whether that part of it which is new is truly significant.

This duality is reinforced by the demands made upon the historian. Society and special interests in society call upon him to provide them with memory. The kind of memory that is too often desired is not very different from what we all provide for ourselves—that is, memory that knows how to forget, memory that will rearrange, distort, and omit so much as is needed to make our historical self-images agreeable. In a liberal society the historian is free to try to dissociate myths from reality, but that same impulse to myth-making that moves his fellow men is also at work in him. Society has another, more instrumental task for the historian: to analyze its experience in such a way as to put into its hands workable tools for the performance of certain tasks. In this spirit the military services ask historians to compile the records of previous wars in the hope that such information will be useful in future wars. In the same spirit the Japanese government called upon Charles A. Beard to help with the problems arising out of the Tokyo earthquake of 1923, and wired him, "Bring your knowledge of disaster."

Both advantages and disadvantages arise from this duality of tradition and of function. They bring certain confusions to the historian's role: understandably he may wonder whether he is a writer or a technician, a scientist or a prophet. But there are compensations. The same ambiguities that present him with his problems of method and even of identity give him an opportunity to have valuable interchanges with many kinds of intellectual and practical activity, with politics and public affairs, with journalism and mass media, with literature and criticism, with science, philosophy, and art, and with the social sciences.

I speak of the historian as having contacts with the social sciences rather than as being a social scientist for reasons which I hope to make clear. Although each of the disciplines that study human culture has characteristics that in one way or another set it off from the rest, history is in a still further degree set off from the others by its special constellation of problems, methods, limitations, and possibilities. But the historian's contact with the social sciences is clearly of more importance to the present generation of historians than it has been at any time in the past. Perhaps this closer relationship is in some part attributable to a more receptive frame of mind among historians to inter-disciplinary work; it is more largely due to the fact that in the past quarter century the achievements of the social sciences have been impressive. My interest here is not in the ultimate nature of history of the social sciences or the relations between them, but in the progress of inter-disciplinary work, which I should like to illustrate by reference to some of my own intellectual experiences. What I hope to do, then, is not to deal with philosophical issues but in some measure to clarify an attitude which is becoming fairly widespread among contemporary historians.

Despite what is surely no more than a fragmentary and random acquaintance with the literature of the social sciences, I have found that my interest and gratification in my own discipline have been enormously intensified by what I have been able to take for it from the other disciplines. That I am unable to systematize or formalize what it is that I owe, as a historian, to the social sciences I find puzzling. But I feel sure that in a general way what the social sciences have helped to do is to suggest a new resolution—not a solution, for such problems are never solved—to the problems created by the duality of the historian's role. In brief what they offer him is a host of new insights and new creative possibilities.

When I was first attracted to history as a vocation, it was by a two-fold interest: I was attracted both by what might be called orthodox political history and also by the history of ideas. At first these two seemed parallel rather than converging. Not only did I not have a very clear idea of how the two might be put together, but I had little interest in doing so. As time went on I realized that what I most wanted to write about were things marginal to both political historians and to practitioners of the history of ideas who stem, say, from the severe tradition in which Arthur O. Lovejoy has done such impressive work. My interests lay between the two fields, at the intersection of their perimeters.

I belong to the generation that came of age during the middle thirties. This was a period, of course, of tremendous conflict on a world scale and of intense and lively controversy in American domestic politics. A battle of ideologies roughly similar to that which took place in a world-wide theatre of action could be seen at home as well. For many of us an interest in studying the formation and development of ideologies was a natural intellectual response to the conflict raging around us.[1] But to a detached observer these ideologies were far more interesting for their extraordinary appeal to various types of individuals than they were for their rational or philosophic content. I found myself, therefore, becoming interested in individual and social character types, in social mythologies and styles of thought as they reveal and affect character, and in politics as a sphere of behavior into which personal and private motives are projected.

Such phrases as "styles of thought" and "projective behavior" suggest fundamental influences stemming from Mannheim and from Freud. For me Mannheim provided the link I had been seeking between ideas and social situations. In this

respect too his work has, for the historian, a significance similar to that of the cultural anthropologist: for the anthropologist's feeling for cultural styles and for styles of life is similar to
Mannheim's feeling for styles of thought. All these ideas—of
cultural configuration, of styles of life and thought, and of political style—are filled with significance for the historian, and
he has only begun to sound their potentialities. The influence
of Freud upon the historian, though even more far-reaching,
must of necessity be more indirect than that of a thinker like
Mannheim. Historians may hate to admit it, but they do work
with certain general psychological presuppositions. The intellectual revolution that we associate with Freud is beginning to have some effect, however subtle and unformalized,
upon the way they see their materials. Understandably they
look with caution upon a mechanical or self-confident application of Freudianism, especially of orthodox Freudianism, to
their data. At first the historian has to read Freud more or less
passively; but when he sees the use that such men as Harold
Lasswell or John Dollard make of Freudian concepts in a political context, or observes, say, how David Riesman employs
concepts of character-type in a historical setting, or finds that
social psychologists can shed light on contemporary political
movements, he begins to get an inkling of the possibilities of
psychology for history.

It is here that the social sciences may become particularly
valuable to any historian who shares these concerns. The monograph has been unsatisfactory, most commonly as literature but
often even in the very analytical functions it was designed to
perform. The narrative, while it is sometimes good literature,
has too often disappointed our desire for new understanding.
What his use of the social sciences promises to the historian
is a special kind of opportunity to join these two parts of his
tradition in a more effective way. That the social sciences, with
their striking methodological self-consciousness, should have
something to contribute to the analytical dimension of the historian's work will not surprise us. But our attention may well
be arrested by the likelihood that the literary possibilities of
his work will also be enhanced, that the monograph, without
in the least losing its analytical quality, may take on more of
the literary significance that was previously preeminent in the

historical narrative. The monograph, in short, may yet cease to be a poor imitation of science and may flourish as a kind of exploratory essay which will be a fuller consummation of the mind and spirit of the historian. We may well ask how this could be possible; how the social sciences, whose characteristic practitioners have not usually aspired to distinguish themselves through literary expression, should be able to help to quicken history as a literary art. The answer, I believe, lies largely in this: that it is the achievement of those forms of literature that are most like history that they deal significantly with the problems of human character. History too aspires to deal understandingly with character, and the means for the formal understanding of character have grown enormously in the past half century. Perhaps the most important function which the social sciences can perform for the historian is that they provide means, in some cases indispensable means, by which he can be brought into working relationship with certain aspects of the modern intellectual climate. They bring to him a fresh store of ideas with which to disturb the excessively settled routines of his thought; but they also serve a catalytic function for him: they show him how he may adapt for his own purposes certain modern insights into human behavior and character which he cannot, on his own, immediately and directly appropriate.

The next generation may see the development of a somewhat new historical genre, which will be a mixture of traditional history and the social sciences. It will differ from the narrative history of the past in that its primary purpose will be analytical. It will differ from the typical historical monograph of the past in that it will be more consciously designed as a literary form and will focus on types of problems that the monograph has all too often failed to raise. It will be informed by the insights of the social sciences and at some points will make use of methods they have originated. Without pretending to be scientific, it may well command more reciprocal interest and provide more stimulation for social scientists than a great deal of the history that is now being written. In this genre the work of the historian can best be described as a sort of literary anthropology. His aim will be a kind of portraiture[2] of the life of nations and individuals, classes and groups of men; his approach to every system of culture and sub-culture will be that sympathetic and yet somewhat alien and detached appreciation of basic emotional commitments that anthropologists bring to simpler peoples.

Most discussions of inter-disciplinary work with which I am familiar begin with the assumption that its value rests chiefly upon the exchange or cross-fertilization of methods. For the historian this means that he can acquire new methods with which to tackle his old problems. There are indubitable advantages for the historian in such techniques as panel studies, career-line analysis, content analysis, the comparative method, more sophisticated sampling, an increased use, where it is possible and appropriate, of measurement—all of them methods in which the social sciences have gone far ahead of him.

But to me it is not the formal methods of the social sciences, useful as they may be, that are of central significance, but rather their substantive findings, their intellectual concerns, and their professional perspectives. Taken in this way, their value paradoxically rests not in their ability to bring new methods to bear upon old problems but in their ability to open new problems which the historian has usually ignored. Prompted by the social sciences, the historian begins to realize that matters of central concern to other disciplines force him to enlarge his conception of his task. Questions associated with social status, social mobility, differences and conflicts between generations, child-rearing in its relation to culture, the sociology of knowledge and of the professions, are questions which he might properly take upon himself, and which are interwoven with his traditional concerns. It seems inevitable, too, that some of the discoveries made by modern social research about current mass political behavior and political influence will revise some of the historian's assumptions about political behavior in the past. In short, the other disciplines ask questions about society which the historian has not commonly asked, and collect data which have a bearing, at least by inference and analogy, upon his problems. Even though the historian cannot always answer these questions with the evidence available to him they remain significant for his work.

But it is not necessarily a scientific use that the historian makes of his conceptual borrowings. I have never thought, when approaching a historical problem from a perspective

which I imagine to be rather like that of a sociologist or of
an anthropologist, that I would therefore be able to answer
my questions with greater definiteness and rigor. For me the
fundamental value of these perspectives is in their addition
to the speculative richness of history. The more the historian
learns from the social sciences, the more variables he is likely
to take account of, the more complex his task becomes. The
result may be that his conclusions become more tenuous and
tentative, but this is a result to be welcomed. The closer the
historian comes, with whatever aids, to the full texture of historical reality, the more deeply is he engulfed in a complex
web of relationships which he can hope to understand only in
a limited and partial way.[3] While he may acquire some usable
methods from the social sciences, I doubt that the new techniques that he may acquire will outweigh the new problems
that he will take on. His task has not been simplified; it has
been enlarged. His work has not greater certainty, but greater
range and depth.

Thus far I have spoken only about the value of the social
sciences for the historian. While I should prefer to hear a sociologist speak on the other side of this relationship, I would
not be fair to my own discipline if I did not say that history has
much to offer in return. It is one of the characteristics of our
present-minded and journalistically-minded culture that our
sense of history is very thin. Oddly enough, while our age pays
considerable deference to historians, our capacity to use history to enlarge our understanding is not impressive. Contemporary discussion of mass culture, for instance, is often carried
on as though no previous age had ever presented problems
to specialized intelligence and cultivated sensibility; because
the media of mass communications are new, it is assumed that
the past can teach us nothing about the relationship of artists
and intellectuals to the public. Historians themselves are by
no means immune to the general failing of which this is an
example; the failing is also widespread among social scientists,
not least among social psychologists and sociologists who need
history very much.

While it is the primary business of these disciplines to analyze the relations among special abstracted factors in cultural
situations, it is the distinctive business of the historian to define

the actual situations in which these factors come into play, and
to set the problems of social inquiry in their temporal relations and as nearly in their totality as it is given to the human
mind to be able to do. However impartial and imperfect the
achievement of these objects, it is history's primary gift to the
other cultural disciplines. The historian tries to remind his fellow inquirers that, in the words of Michelet, "He who would
confine his thoughts to present time will not understand present reality."

Most inquiries in sociology or social psychology are of necessity planned in a flat time-dimension. The character of a social-
psychological experiment, or of most of the fruitful empirical
work that has recently been done in mass communications, political behavior, and market research, demands that this be so.
But in the long run and when it deals with the large questions,
inquiry into human affairs must be historical in character, for
the real development of human affairs cannot be sliced out of
time in order to appease our curiosity. The transhistorical generalizations that are made by other disciplines that seek for a
general theory of action—that is, generalizations about human
behavior of such applicability that they cover more than one
historical situation or one culture—have an operational meaning that is different from historical generalizations, in the sense
that the non-historical generalizations are not intended to shed
light upon any historical events, but rather to answer questions
about certain abstracted factors of behavior. Social scientists,
concerned as they are with the dynamics of behavior, are like
the engineers who can tell us about the dynamics of flight. Historians are concerned with such questions as why a particular
scheduled flight has ended in a crash.

It is difficult to show in the abstract how history and the
social sciences complement each other. But when we get away
from abstract discussions of the character and methods of the
disciplines to focus our attentions upon actual problems of
common concern, their mutual interaction and their value to
each other emerge unmistakably. Not long ago a small group
of social scientists and historians met to discuss the resurgence
over the past five or six years of extreme right-wing politics
in this country. We began by talking about the movement in
terms set by the study of *The Authoritarian Personality* by

T. W. Adorno and his co-workers; but as we got deeper into the problem, one of the most interesting aspects of the discussion was the way in which we found ourselves moving quite spontaneously back and forth between social-psychological categories and historical events, because neither approach was for long entirely adequate. There was no need for the historians to take the initiative in pushing the line of argument into the historical frame of reference; for since we were analyzing a problem that had been posed, so to speak, by historical events themselves and were not trying to work out a general theory of behavior, the relevance and mutual helpfulness of both the historical and the social-psychological approaches were immediately apparent to everyone.

There are important and increasingly numerous links between history and the social sciences, but the two are also held apart by real differences. Some of these differences arise out of problems of communication or out of institutional arrangements. Others have intellectual substance and among these probably none is so important as a difference over the scientific ideal, by which I mean the belief that the closer social science gets to the methods of the natural sciences, the more perfect it becomes. The prominence of this commitment to science is expressed in our terminology, for when we grow dissatisfied with "social sciences" we speak of "policy sciences" or "behavioral sciences"—retaining the noun as clear testimony to an enduring ideal.

For many historians the scientific ideal has been a moving faith, since the days when Buckle asserted that he hoped to follow the example of natural science in his *History of Civilization in England.* But in our own time the scientific ideal no longer has quite the same plausibility for historians as it did for their predecessors in the Darwinian age, or as it now has for their colleagues in the social sciences.[4] Most historians continue to feel that they deal with events which, though in some sense comparable, are essentially unique; and that this differentiates history from most branches of natural science, as well as from those branches of social science in which statistical generalization prevails and even some statistical prediction is possible. Formidable criticisms have been written of the familiar distinction between the nomothetic sciences (which

can make general laws about repeatable events) and the ideo-
graphic sciences (which seek to understand unique and nonre-
current events). I am here more concerned with the prevalent
state of mind among historians than with the substance of this
philosophic issue;⁵ and such criticisms, however impressive as
forays in logical analysis, do not succeed in spreading among
historians the conviction that what historians do is in any very
satisfactory sense of the term scientific; and, perhaps what is
still more important, do not affect profoundly the way they go
about their tasks.

Unlike the philosopher of history or the philosopher of science, the working historian is not nearly so much interested in
whether history can, after all, be logically classed with the natural sciences as he is in how far his mode of procedure is in fact
a scientific one or could be changed to resemble it. Certainly,
in the broad sense that he operates from a basis in fact, aspires
to make warrantable assertions, and works in a self-critical discipline, the historian can see that he has something in common
with science. But if the term science has any special meaning, he
sees equally important differences. Since in his work quantification plays so limited a role, and since he cannot conduct experiments, or, strictly speaking, make predictions, he naturally feels
that the difference between his methods and results and those
prevailing in most branches of the natural sciences are of central
importance. I do not forget that there are branches of natural
science which are themselves historical. Perhaps the most notable of these is evolutionary biology; and yet the experience of
some nineteenth-century historians in modelling their conceptions upon this type of scientific work is not such as to inspire
historians today to follow their example. If history falls short
of science, it may help to classify history as a *Wissenschaft*—
no word in English quite conveys this distinction—that is, as
a learned discipline with a firm cognitive element, based upon
verifiable facts and yielding valid knowledge.

We may say, then, that few historians but many social scientists are attracted by the scientific ideal. If we were in a position to inquire into the reasons for this difference, we might
find that somewhat different types of persons are recruited into
the two professions. Aside from this there are institutional reasons. History is an old and established discipline with strong
traditions that weigh heavily against drastic innovation. Since

its traditions have been pre-eminently those of a literary art, it has in the literary ideal a powerful alternative or competitor to the scientific ideal. The social sciences, by contrast, are relatively new, and have had to wage a hard struggle within universities to establish their legitimacy—a struggle which in some parts of the university world, as in Britain, is still going on. Having more rapport than history has with some of the pragmatic demands of a scientific and technological age, they have naturally tended to put themselves on a scientific basis as a means of establishing their case. They have, moreover, found themselves in rapport with the practical world not so much for their broader humanistic interests as for their practical results in social and clinical work, in market research, in poll-taking. Of course the differences are not, with this, entirely explained. Historical data are different from social science data, and the terms upon which the inquirer gains access to them are not at all alike. Important branches of the social sciences can conduct interviews, take projective tests, submit the reactions of large numbers of persons to elaborate analysis, cross-tabulate many kinds of relationships, set up a complicated and sophisticated apparatus for the verification of hypotheses, and emerge with a statistical summation of the evidence. Historians do not have direct access to their subjects. The only questions they can ask with the expectation of getting answers are those questions which happen to be dealt with in surviving documents. While they have an abundance of material in history, they do not have such masses of material focussed upon a given subject as is available to modern sociology. Frequently they are driven to reconstruct partially hypothetical accounts from fragmentary evidence. Rarely if ever do they have enough material to warrant setting up such an elaborate method of processing it as the sociologist frequently does. Working under such limitations, the historian is quickly driven to a kind of agnostic modesty about his own achievement. He may not disparage science, but he despairs of it.

One problem history shares with the social sciences even here. History seems most objective, most definite, most uncontroversial—most "scientific" if you must—in those monographs in which historians exhaustively explore an extremely narrow segment of reality. Similarly social science seems to have the greatest precision where it is focussed on small questions susceptible of careful examination, and is often characterized by great caution in its choice of problems.[6] The answers to small questions sometimes shed bright but narrow beams of light on the larger problems of human behavior and the social process, and it is not unthinkable that they may have some important cumulative result. But there is no reason to think that the answers to all such questions will add up to a comprehensive view of society or of historical processes. The historian stands in somewhat the same relation to his pile of monographs. Monographs are useful, but when put together they do not yield comprehensive answers to the comprehensive questions. No synthesis—at least no "scientific" and commonly acceptable synthesis—can be reached through sheer addition.

At this point the social scientist has, in the scientific ideal, a challenge, but also a refuge and a comfort that is not available to the historian. The history of natural science itself has been the history of cumulative progress, much of it made by very small forward steps. One may therefore get a sense of craftsmanlike satisfaction, if by soundly executing a minute inquiry one feels one is taking a part, however small, in a similar cumulative progression of knowledge. But the historian has before him a discipline which, however industriously it accumulates knowledge, experiences again and again through the generations somewhat the same kind of arguments and disagreements about its matters of central concern. The historian who hopes to achieve important work is unable to rest content with the completion of a small but sound unit of craftsmanship, because the tradition of his profession is not so much to look for the perfection of microscopic units of research as it is to try to cope with certain insistent macroscopic questions. Eventually the historian must deal in such categories as the Reformation, the Renaissance, the Industrial Revolution, with wars and social upheavals, with the great turning points in human experience, still tantalizingly unexplained or half-explained, still controversial.

No historian can do great or lasting work without addressing himself, at least at the margins, to one or another of these major problems. And yet the historian does not approach them with the expectation that he will "solve" them, that the cumulation of knowledge will put him in a position to do what the

entire fraternity of historians has not yet been able to do, or
even that there is any operational way to define the "solution"
of such problems. To appreciate this is to understand the kind
of enterprise the historian must feel himself to be engaged in:
it is to understand that he must see in his own task—so big in
its implications, so hopelessly complex, so triumphant over his
professional forebears, and yet so formidably challenging that
he must again take it on—nothing more nor less than a micro-
cosmic representation of the human situation itself. As soon as
the historian's span of attention becomes sufficiently enlarged
to take in more than a tiny segment of the historic past, he
confronts the precariousness of human effort, sees the passing
not only of great states and powerful institutions but of militant faiths and, most pertinent for him, of the very historical
perspectives that were identified with them. At this point he
is persuaded to accept the imaginative as well as the cognitive
side of his own work, to think of history as being not only the
analysis but the expression of human experience; he sees his
search as a search for clues not simply as to how life may be
controlled but as to how it may be felt, and he realizes more
fully than before how much history is indeed akin to literature.

1956

Notes

1. This no doubt accounts for the surge of interest in the history of ideas
   that has taken place in the United States during the past twenty years. Not
   since the era of the French Revolution has America felt itself to be as much
   involved in the ideological battles of the Western World as it did in the
   mid-thirties.
2. I might almost say caricature rather than portraiture, for most social systems
   are too complex to be portrayed. Caricature may seem an invidious label,
   but I do not intend it to be so. Unlike caricature, good history does not
   attempt to portray through wilful distortion. But caricature has this in common with history, that its effects must be achieved in broad and exaggerated
   strokes that cannot render all the features of the subject. And in good caricature the subject is instantly recognizable.
3. One of the most interesting aspects of this problem has become apparent
   in connection with what I would call the paradox of quantification. The
   essence of this paradox is that the recent use of quantitative methods to
   test historical generalization has resulted in the wholesale destruction of
   categories that previously held sway in the historian's vocabulary without
   supplanting them with new generalizations of comparable significance. See,

for example, D. Brunton and D. H. Pennington, *Members of the Long Par-liament* (London, 1954) and W. O. Aydelotte, "The House of Commons in the 1840's," *History*, n.s., vol. XXXIX (October, 1954), pp. 249–62. Such studies have usually been designed to test the relation between material interest or social status and political behavior. It is, of course, quite conceivable that the uprooted generalizations will be replaced by interpretations having a more social-psychological cast. But in such case it is unlikely that the historian can, with the type of evidence available to him, put these interpretations on any better footing than that of intelligent and partially verified guesses. Should this be true, we might find ourselves in possession of more sophisticated and seemingly more satisfactory explanations which would have to stand largely upon a speculative foundation.

4. At a recent meeting of representative American historians on the problem of relations with the social sciences, it was the consensus that historians "should not point simply in the direction of becoming 'more scientific,'" and that "historians should not consciously attempt to remake history in the social-science image and should not attempt to restore communication with the social sciences simply by adopting social science methods as their own." The meeting is reported by Richard D. Challener and Maurice Lee, Jr. in "History and the Social Sciences: The Problem of Communications," *American Historical Review*, vol. LXI (January, 1956), pp. 331–38.

5. Though I am fully aware of the reductionist trap that awaits all efforts to discuss substantive issues only in terms of their psychological backgrounds, I will confess in this case to being far more interested in knowing why some men feel happier when history is classified with the sciences while others feel that they must resist the idea than I am in the question itself. The valuations attached to the use of the word science suggest important differences in intellectual temperament and styles of thought, and shed direct light on the kind of work men choose to do.

6. To choose at random from some of the social-psychological inquiries cited in the recent volume by Elihu Katz and Paul F. Lazarsfeld, *Personal In-fluence* (Glencoe, Illinois, 1955), characteristic matters of inquiry were questions like these: Do group leaders know that they are leading? What different uses do well socialized and less socialized children make of their radio listening? Does an individual tend to accept the outlook of a group more readily if he is attracted to that group? Is an authoritarian atmosphere more likely to restrict conversation in small groups than a democratic or a laissez-faire atmosphere? Does a planted rumor tend to spread outside the ranks of those who are intimately concerned with its content? Do inexperienced soldiers show greater readiness for combat if they are sent into divisions composed of veterans than if they are sent into divisions composed of other inexperienced soldiers? Do people tend to be more friendly with those who live near them and share their values than with those who live at a distance and have different values? Are children more likely to follow the lead of other children than that of adults in making food choices?

American Higher Education

I HAVE BEEN asked to speak on the past, the present, and the future of American higher education from the standpoint of a historian, and I should like to survey the subject by examining four successive periods in the history of our educational system: the colonial period, which sets the foundations of our institutional pattern; the early national period down to the Civil War, which is the era of the old-time college; the period from the Civil War down to about 1910, which is the age of what we may call the university revolution; and finally the more recent period of quantitative growth and economic crisis. About the future I shall have relatively little to say, for which I can perhaps excuse myself by saying that I am a historian and not a soothsayer.

THE COLONIAL PERIOD

The first American colleges were founded not for the purpose of making educational innovations, but to reproduce, so far as the means and conditions of America made possible, the traditional education of the Old World and particularly of the English universities. It was not possible under colonial conditions to reproduce the "university" as the English then understood it—that is, a loosely associated cluster of undergraduate colleges. But the early American colleges were founded with the English colleges as their models, and they not only took over the standard curriculum but aspired to achieve the same levels of attainment in the study of it. (Indeed, one of the proudest achievements of young Harvard College under its first president, Henry Dunster, was that its undergraduates were accepted in the English universities, *ad eundem gradum*.) The American educational system also took over from the English an educational ideal less familiar outside the Anglo-Saxon countries—the notion that it is the business of institutions of higher education not merely to instill in their graduates intellectual skills but to cultivate character and to impose upon them a certain stamp of moral upbringing. We still speak of educating "the whole man."

American colleges were never theological seminaries nor institutions designed entirely for the rearing of ministers. It was understood from the beginning—even at Harvard, whose founders were particularly troubled at the thought that an "illiterate ministry" would grow up in New England—that the colleges would give education to *all* the leaders of the community, whether their leadership was to be exercised in the church or the state. None the less, it was their goal to educate Christian gentlemen. The inheritance of the colleges was an ecclesiastical inheritance and their sponsors were church bodies, acting through provincial legislatures profoundly influenced by, and at times almost identical with, the organized churches. Education was conceived to have some relation to the affairs of the soul, and to human salvation. While on the secular side it provided leaders for church and state, on the personal side it was thought successful only if it conduced to Christian knowledge and to devout life. Its discipline was thus directed toward those most intimate aspects of character that bear upon the achievement of a state of grace and the capacity to glorify God. Modern colleges and universities consider themselves in some measure custodians of the body and cultivators of the personality; early American colleges tried to be custodians of the soul and nurseries of character. The modern notion that the ability to swim is a necessary requirement for the degree of bachelor of arts would have seemed preposterous to the founding fathers of American education (as indeed it still does to me), but the idea that it was part of the business of the teacher to pray with his students and to regulate, so far as he could, their moral lives was entirely congenial.

AMERICAN SYSTEM EMERGES

During the course of the eighteenth century the major outlines of the American college system became visible. The first colleges were small colleges, usually under the eye of one or more religious sects and of the members of the state legislatures. They were for the most part aristocratic institutions, but not through any rigid or arbitrary principles of closure. They were, in broad respects, governed, or at least interfered with, by boards of absentee trustees who were not teachers. And they were in fact managed, promoted, nursed, made, or unmade by their presidents, who (with a few exceptions) were the only teaching members who enjoyed the full repute of the mature man of knowledge as he was known in European institutions of learning. During the eighteenth century the original sectarian impulse tended to break down, not because the men who controlled colleges were always so wise as to be able to see the educational and social limits of sectarianism, but because the colleges had to have students and student fees to keep going, and most of them could attract ample student bodies only by beginning to tone down their original sectarian commitments. A broadminded man like President Witherspoon made a success of Princeton, and Harvard College made great strides under latitudinarians. A bigot like Thomas Clap nearly ruined Yale. Queens College (later Rutgers) twice had to close its doors under the guardianship of men who aspired to retain a severely sectarian character.

While sectarianism waned, secularization grew. Colleges still aspired to rear Christian gentlemen. But very few of these gentlemen were fated to become clergymen. They showed an increasing interest in the flourishing natural science of the eighteenth century. Science made its way into the curriculum, giving it greater breadth and improving teaching methods. The old curriculum was not abandoned, but it was broadened and improved. Whatever the limitations of the eighteenth-century colleges, the greatest generation of political leaders we have had—the generation that fought the Revolution and framed the Constitution—was in good part educated within their walls and on their classical curriculum.

THE EARLY NATIONAL PERIOD

The outstanding thing that happened to the American college system during approximately the first 50 years of life under the Republic was that that system was diffused throughout the country in an extremely haphazard way. In 1780 there were nine colleges—not an unreasonable number for people of our numbers or a nation of that size. By 1799, 16 more institutions had been added—a total of 25—and still perhaps a number not too much in excess of what sound educational practice might have demanded; for the country had grown and transportation was not cheap or easy. But during the early decades of the nineteenth century the process of founding colleges ran wild. By 1861 a total of 182 permanent colleges had been founded. This figure, large though it may seem, dwindles into insignificance when one counts at least 412 colleges that were founded during this period and did not survive.[1] What this means is that the educational resources of the young republic were squandered in the most indefensible way. There were too many colleges; they were too weak and ill-nourished to survive; they were too small and feeble to have rendered good educational services, most of them, if they had survived.

If we ask why this disastrous diffusion of effort took place, I think we will find that it was only in small part a response to the size of the Union. No doubt the cost of sending boys to distant colleges made more attractive the idea of founding a multitude of colleges close to the grass roots. No doubt, too, social prejudice played a part: the larger and more pretentious institutions were accused of harboring aristocratic prejudices and of serving—as they often did—the sons of gentlemen. Hometown folks were a little cautious of sending their boys to places where they might be looked down on by the sons of fancier gentry; and perhaps, though this is largely conjecture, they were still more frightened at the thought that some of their boys might be accepted and incorporated into a more sophisticated society and thus outgrow their parents, families, and friends. But the chief responsibility for the excessive multiplication and wasteful diffusion of small colleges must be laid at the door of the Protestant denominations, which vied with each other for educational supremacy instead of cooperating with each other for educational achievement. Each denomination capable of doing so insisted on having its own institution in each region, and most of the denominations were more willing to risk total failure than to suppress sectarian pride or

[1]Donald G. Tewksbury, *The Founding of American Colleges and Universities before the Civil War* (New York Teachers College Bureau of Publications, 1932), p. 28.

sacrifice sectarian objectives. In some measure local pride, and indeed even local real estate boosting, entered into the picture; for it was a source of distinction and advantage to a growing community to be the site of a college.

THE "OLD-TIME COLLEGE"

The old-time college has been so much sentimentalized that it may be necessary to explain exactly why the small college was vulnerable to educational criticism. It was not so much that the old-time college itself was small and inadequate—we still have its successors dotting our countryside and not all of them are bad—as it was that the sponsors of such colleges "ganged up" on most attempts to found or maintain large and more adequate institutions. This process was notable not only in the early struggles of the state universities of the South during this period, and in the enthusiastic educational lynching administered to such fine emergent institutions as Transylvania, but also in the difficulties experienced even by some of the more successful institutions like the University of Virginia and the College of South Carolina. The small, low-grade institutions were in the educational market offering something that purported to be college degrees. And if they could agree on nothing else, they could agree to thwart the growth of any major institution looming on the horizon that threatened by comparison to demonstrate their intellectual poverty and to entice their students.[2]

We think today of some of the fine "small" colleges in our country, and are perhaps tempted to assume that the typical old-time college resembled them. At my own college, Columbia, we are proud to think of ourselves as a "small college"—except for Brown, the smallest in the Ivy League—because we have only about 2,400 undergraduates. Many an institution does highly creditable work with half as many. But to visualize the typical old-time college one must think of an institution not of 2,400 or 1,000 or even 500 undergraduates, but of

[2]On the character and social role of the old-time college see Richard Hofstadter and Walter P. Metzger, *The Development of Academic Freedom in the United States* (New York: Columbia University Press, 1955), chaps. 5, 6.

a college like Randolph-Macon with its 98 students in 1839 or the still more typical Kenyon with 55 students. In that year there were only ten bona fide colleges in the entire country having more than 150 students, all of them on or very near to the eastern seaboard. As to the faculty bodies, we must think of faculties not nearly so imposing as Harvard's body of 23 in 1839 or Yale's of the same number or even Dartmouth's 15, but rather, again, of Randolph Macon with its six professors or Kenyon with its six professors and one tutor.[3]

But surely, one may say, the old-time college had a simple curriculum that could be competently taught by a small and dedicated staff. Surely the small size and intimate associations of the college had their advantages, intellectual and social. No doubt such demurrers should have their weight in any estimate we make of the old-time college system. No doubt there has always been, as there is still, a certain proportion of gifted and dedicated men, passionately fond of their subjects or of the art of teaching or of the young, who inspired and successfully educated their charges, even within the limits of the old college system. No doubt the students did much to educate each other, as they always do. There is testimony to this effect; but there is also ample testimony to the effect that the pedagogy of the old-time college was commonly very bad. Modern educational reformers tend to lay the faults of the old college to the old prescribed classical curriculum. No doubt that curriculum was excessively rigid; it changed too slowly; science and modern languages often were unduly neglected. But it was a great curriculum, embracing a course of studies upon which many distinguished minds had been adequately fed.

PEDAGOGICAL DEFECTS

I believe that the difficulty lay only in small part with the curriculum and in very large part with the pedagogy and the pedagogues. Teaching was carried on by the tedious recitation method; it relied excessively upon memory and drudgery. Moreover it was too often administered by men without notable abilities, or notable incentives. Academic salaries were

[3] *American Quarterly Register*, vol. XIII (August, 1840), pp. 110–16.

poor. Tenure was uncertain. There was no system of promotion or rewards for teaching or—God save the mark—research. In most places there *was* no research—and how could there be in college libraries that often had no more than 1,000 or 2,000 volumes at a time when the library at Göttingen had more than 200,000 and when the private library of a scholar like George Ticknor numbered 13,000?[4] The achievement of these poor harassed pedagogues—who presumably suffered even more than their pupils from the tedium of the recitation method— seems to have been a meagre one indeed. It was a classical curriculum, as I have said, that they taught; and yet hear Edward Everett in 1817: "It fills me with indignation that a person may pass through all our schools, academies and colleges, without being taught to speak a Latin sentence. . . . But our poor schoolmasters and preceptors and tutors are not to blame, they cannot teach what they never learned."[5] Hear Andrew D. White discussing his education at Yale—one of the best colleges—in the 1850's: "We were reading . . . the *De Senectute* of Cicero, —a beautiful book; but to our tutor it was neither more nor less than a series of pegs on which to hang Zumpt's rules for the subjunctive mood."[6] Or Brander Matthews on Columbia a few years later: "We were expected to prepare so many lines of Latin and Greek, or so many pages of the textbook in logic or political economy; and in the classroom we were severally called upon to disgorge this undigested information; it was information we were expected to acquire, rather than the ability to turn this to account to think for ourselves."[7] Or John D. Long, a member of the Harvard class of 1857 and later Governor of Massachusetts and Secretary of the Navy: "I recollect no instruction which was not of the most perfunctory and indifferent sort, unless possibly it was that of Professor Cooke in

[4]C. C. Jewett, "Statistics of American Libraries," in *Fourth Annual Report . . . of the Smithsonian Institution . . . during the Year 1849* (Washington, 1850).

[5]Orie William Long, *Literary Pioneers* (Cambridge: Harvard University Press, 1935), p. 71.

[6]Andrew D. White, *Autobiography* (New York: The Century Co., 1914), vol. I, p. 27.

[7]Brother Agathe Zimmer, *Changing Concepts of Higher Education Since 1700* (Washington: Catholic University of America, 1938), p. 37.

Chemistry and Professor Child in English. . . . The element
of personal influence was entirely lacking. . . . No word of
advice or stimulus or encouragement was ever uttered. . . .
It was four years of monotonous routine, going into the classroom, spending an hour, and coming out."[8]

In sum, despite the presence of a few institutions of vitality
and distinction, despite a number of scholars and teachers of
note harbored upon their faculties, and despite the graduates
one could point to as having been to all appearances signally
benefited by their undergraduate experiences, the characteristic achievement of the characteristic old American college was
not quite a collegiate achievement at all. The colleges were,
in fact, as many contemporaries recognized, most commonly
the equivalent of preparatory schools or good academies. An
American college president, F. A. P. Barnard, could speak flatly
in 1858 of "the grade of the German gymnasium—which is precisely our grade of today."[9] He might have added that while
the best colleges went somewhat beyond the gymnasia, the
poorest probably never reached them.

Few Americans readily accept the deficient or the second-
rate when they recognize it as such. As one would expect, there
was a great deal of dissatisfaction with the old-time college
among persons both inside and outside academic life. So far
as I have been able to determine, there were two kinds of reform demands—not entirely different or mutually exclusive,
but with sufficiently different emphases to warrant listing them
separately. The first took the form of dissatisfaction with the
unprogressive character of the classical curriculum and issued
forth in demand for a somewhat more practical and vocational
course of studies, embodying more science, more applied
studies, and more modern languages in place of the ancient.
While this demand seems always to have been present, it is
perhaps also worth noting that the several colleges which did

[8]John D. Long, "Reminiscences of Seventy Years' Education," *Publications of
the Massachusetts Historical Society*, vol. 42 (June, 1909), p. 352.
[9]On dissatisfaction with the old college see Richard J. Storr, *The Beginnings of
Graduate Education in America* (Chicago: University of Chicago Press, 1953).
See also George P. Schmidt, *The Old Time College President* (New York: Columbia University, doctoral dissertation, 1930), pp. 102-5.

experiment with their offerings in the hope of meeting it did not at first fare any better on the whole than the more traditional institutions. The second demand, particularly popular among serious scholars and administrators, was to supplement the college curricula with advanced studies and to develop true universities.

The most striking change that came with the university revolution of the post–Civil War period was in the rising means available to the greater institutions of education. It is hard for us to visualize the poverty of the old colleges, even of those that did not succumb to poverty by disappearing from the face of the earth. Yale, one of the largest of the colleges, counted her receipts from all sources, including tuition, at less than 20,000 dollars in 1831. Indeed, in their famous Report of 1828 the faculty pointed out that Yale's entire income from all sources in the more than a century and a quarter from her founding did not amount to 300,000 dollars. A college like Williams was founded on 14,000 dollars, Amherst on 50,000 dollars. When Princeton launched an ambitious drive for funds during her revivification of the 1830's the goal of the drive was 100,000 dollars, the largest single donation, 5,000 dollars. Compare with this the lavish sums put at the disposal of the university builders of the new era: Ezra Cornell's 500,000 dollars, supplemented by a large amount of land scrip; Vanderbilt's 1,000,000 dollars; Johns Hopkins' 3,500,000 dollars; the 20,000,000 dollars yielded over some years from the Stanford estate; Rockefeller's 30,000,000 dollars for the University of Chicago.

OLD COLLEGES REFORM

With the providing of ample means and the development of the university idea, a great many of the shortcomings of the old colleges were rectified in a great many places, as new standards and new methods filtered down from the universities to many of the colleges. Academic men found themselves better paid and more adequately rewarded for research, more amply assisted in their efforts to develop specialties. The recitation method of teaching did not immediately disappear, but it was supplemented by classes in which undergraduates were

privileged to hear scholars of some distinction and some measure of specialized competence lecture on subjects that commanded their passionate interest; it was supplemented, too, by
the development of graduate education, by seminars, and finally by some courses in which the methods of graduate teaching, with its intimate contact, advanced work, and interplay of
ideas between teachers and pupils, penetrated into undergraduate teaching. The rigidity of the old curriculum was relaxed:
science and modern languages found their place, and a wide
measure of choice was ultimately made available to undergraduates. The whole system of university life, with its ideal of adding to knowledge as well as preserving and diffusing it, with its
areas of choice and assumption of maturity, with its secularism
and even its bureaucratization, became the essential model for
American academic institutions in all but the most backward
places.

Not everything, to be sure, was gain. The old curriculum
had given to American collegiate education a substance and a
style; it had created a community of educated men with some
common cultural experience. It had imposed a recognizable
educational discipline, even though that discipline may have
been excessive. The new education was itself eventually carried to the extreme in many institutions. The elective system
could become so broad that it was possible, especially with the
hodge-podge of practical and trivial courses that became available, to achieve a Bachelor of Arts degree without more than
the smattering of a real education.[10] Moreover, while the old
curriculum had tended to neglect science or to teach it badly,
the new higher education became in good time the victim of
excessive scientism. By this I do not mean to assert that the
natural sciences characteristically occupy a place in our curricula larger than their importance warrants; but simply that the
ideal of scientific work, especially in the post-Darwinian age,
became for a time—and in some areas still is—so overreaching
that even humanistic subjects have been studied and taught as
though the only substantial parts of them were those parts that

[10] George W. Pierson, "The Elective System and the Difficulties of College
Planning, 1870–1940," *Journal of General Education*, vol. IV (April, 1950), pp.
165–74. On the general history of the curriculum in America see R. Freeman
Butts, *The College Charts its Course* (New York: McGraw-Hill Book Co., 1939).

could be reduced to the scientific. Call this scientism or positivism or what you will, there are still areas of our intellectual life that may be overrun and debased by it.

In sum, where the old-time college too often suffered from an excess of the traditional, the classical, the impractical, and the inflexible, the university development, so liberating in so many ways, eventually veered too far in the opposite direction, toward the practical, vocational, scientistic, hyper-experimental.

TWENTIETH-CENTURY DEVELOPMENTS

If one were to delineate the two outstanding developments in American higher education since the turn of the century —that is to say since the period when the university revolution reached its consummation—I suppose that these developments would be: first, the enormous quantitative extension of higher education, with all the consequences attendant upon making higher education *mass* education; and secondly the search, particularly within our better institutions, graduate and undergraduate, collegiate and professional, for a new kind of curriculum which will strike a balance between prescription and election, between professional and vocational preparation and liberal education.

Of these two developments the quantitative expansion in American higher education is the more spectacular though not the more beneficent. From 1900 to 1950 the American population doubled. But enrollment in high schools increased by about 12 times and enrollment in colleges increased by about 10 times. As for graduate enrollments, there were about 5,800 in 1900. In 1950 more than 60,000 Master of Arts degrees and about 7,000 doctorates were conferred. Enrollments in institutions of higher learning have passed the figure of two and a half million. If the recommendations of the President's Commission on Higher Education are followed there will be 4,600,000 students in institutions of higher learning by 1960, and we may anticipate that by 1970 the American population will have in its midst 15 million college graduates.[11]

[11]Seymour E. Harris, *The Market for College Graduates* (Cambridge: Harvard University Press, 1949), pp. 1, 5, 6.

GENERAL EDUCATION PROGRAMS

The second development may be considered in substantial part
a reaction against the excesses of the elective system, which had
reached its peak around 1910. Despite all its initial advantages,
the elective system created a chaos in the curriculum which
several reorganizations had failed entirely to remedy. It opened
the door to excessive vocationalism, to the lowering of standards, to college programs cluttered with the trivial and the
unorganized. With students coming in great numbers to the
colleges there were bound to be many without serious educational purposes; and these were free to load their curricula
with easy courses of slight intellectual merit. Between 1910 and
1930 there was a notable tendency among better institutions to
try to bring greater order and seriousness into their curricula.
During the depression, when the country faced an intellectual
and moral crisis that impelled a certain revaluation of traditional
goals, this movement gained impetus. Between 1920 and 1940
there was a minor revival in the teaching of humanities: at least
30 new general humanities courses were introduced into leading colleges, and others were being planned.[12] The concern in
recent years for general education, and the appearance of such
plans as those of Columbia, Saint John's, Chicago, Minnesota,
and Harvard all manifest a tendency to create core curricula
that would guarantee the achievement of a certain common
minimum of knowledge in the humanities and social sciences
before students launch upon their careers of specialization.

This search for educational poise may unfortunately have
already passed its apogee. Since World War II, students coming to colleges have professed once again an avowed and un-
abashed concern primarily or exclusively with practical and
technical courses that will help them make a living. Thus while
colleges in the years from 1950 to 1953 were able to maintain
their staffs in physics, chemistry, and applied sciences, they cur-
tailed somewhat their ranks in English, foreign languages, and
the humanities.[13] Students have responded to the pressure for

[12] Patricia Beesley, *The Revival of the Humanities in American Education* (New
York: Columbia University Press, 1940).
[13] The *New York Times*, March 9, 1952.

technical skills coming from the military services, war-related industries, and from government itself. The only major qualification one can make concerning this trend is that the graduate professional schools, certainly in engineering (as manifested by the Massachusetts Institute of Technology) and in medicine and law, are themselves beginning to decry the overspecialized students they receive and to call for better-rounded minds. The pressure here, and in the colleges, seems however to come *from* the more responsible educators *to* the students and the community; there is little sign that there is any spontaneous public demand for a strengthening of the humanities. On the side of research, the demands of business and government pull against the humanities even more powerfully than the vocational desires of the public. Of the 350,000,000 dollars spent on research projects by American colleges and universities in 1952–53, 90 per cent was earmarked for the physical or biological sciences.[14] Educational leaders now see in this trend toward the physical sciences a gradual weakening of the humanities and, except in a few favored areas, the so-called social sciences. We are more than ever in danger of creating an educated class with extremely well-developed technical skills but little humanistic understanding.

THE PRESENT PROSPECT

The two problems of which I have spoken—that is, accommodating huge numbers of students and finding a balance in our educational offerings—are interrelated. In the past the chief interest shown by the public and by the students in their system of higher education has been in its vocational advantages.[15] This is likely to be even more true in the future than it has been in the past. I see no reason to believe that the vast numbers of future students anticipated in the report of the President's Commission will include a high proportion of those who have well-developed intellectual interests. It seems far more likely

[14] *Ibid.*, December 7, 1952.
[15] This statement has been documented more than once. Some of the most interesting recent material may be found in Ernest Haveman and Patricia Salter West, *They Went to College* (New York: Harcourt Brace & Co., Inc., 1952).

that the proportion will be lower, and that to a measure even greater than in the past the central goal of higher education will be vocational.

But—and here is the essence of the problem—in the future, higher education is not likely, if Seymour E. Harris is nearly right in his survey,[16] to pay off vocationally with the same frequency as it has in the past. More than ever, Americans go to college today in order to prepare for jobs in the professions and at high skills. But even in 1940, as Professor Harris says, "not more than half of our three million college graduates were in the professions." Millions of students will graduate from college in the future not to become doctors or lawyers, or even underpaid teachers, but to be salesmen, clerks, retail merchants and to enter into a host of similar white collar or small-business positions.[17]

Some educators, among them former President Conant of Harvard, have expressed grave concern lest the United States become the home of a large army of professionals and intelligentsia for whom there will be no work at the positions in society to which they aspire, a situation which has contributed much to political tensions and to authoritarian sentiments in some of the countries of Europe. I am not sure that this is inevitable, but if it is to be avoided, it seems likely that much of the anticipated expansion in higher education must be fended off rather than encouraged. Moreover, those who do enter higher education must be warned, as gravely and as responsibly as the educational world can manage to do, that their purely

[16]Harris, *op. cit.*

[17]Harris is probably not entirely right, for events since the publication of his book do not fully bear out his pessimism. See Dael Wolfle, *America's Resources of Specialized Talent* (New York: Harper & Brothers, 1954), pp. 264–66. But Wolfle agrees with the practical import of Harris's estimates: p. 266. ". . . the student who enters college for its social and economic advantages will find these factors of decreasing value as college training continues to gain in popularity. A prospective college student in whose thinking these factors assume major proportions might be reminded that a well-educated college graduate should have the personal and intellectual resources which would enable him to meet periods of stress—such as those envisaged by Harris—without immediately viewing himself as part of an unemployed intellectual proletariat. Perhaps readiness to bear risks responsibly is an essential part of being well educated."

vocational aspirations in seeking higher education are not altogether realistic. Perhaps the task of issuing such warnings may also be coupled with an important opportunity to do a long-range task of propaganda on behalf of the nonvocational advantages of higher education. To be a college-educated retail salesman whose original aspiration was to become a physician may be a sad role to play. But to be a college-educated salesman whose college education was expected not merely to give him a chance at one of the professions but to provide him with an insight into new ways of enjoying his mind and of managing his life might have many compensations. It would demand a very serious change in our ways of looking at things—a change not easily or quickly accomplished—to put humanistic values and the enjoyment of the mind back in the center of college education, and to order our curricula and our educational arrangements to that end.

Still another aspect of our educational future remains to be touched upon. In the near future our colleges will presumably have to handle students less adequately prepared for advanced education than students have commonly been in the recent past. Our lower schools are overcrowded and understaffed; teachers themselves are all too often ill-chosen, miserably trained, and miserably paid.[18] What I prefer to call pseudo-progressivism in education has helped to undermine intellectual standards and has lowered intellectual achievement. I suspect that many a child who completes junior college today is no better educated—possibly even less educated—than his parents who 40 years ago graduated from sound high schools. Perhaps what this means is that we are educating more slowly as well as more widely than we were a generation ago, and that a good deal of what our colleges and junior colleges are doing is simply repairing in a few extra years of teaching some of the deficiencies of preparatory training. In 1900 only about 25 per cent of our population completed high school. Today we already anticipate the point at which 40 per cent of the relevant age groups will have the equivalent of a junior college

[18]On latest trends in teacher recruitment see Benjamin Fine, "Students Training to Be Teachers Are Rated Lowest in Selective Service Tests," The *New York Times*, February 1, 1953.

education. If a junior college education today is as good as the old high school education—certainly a debatable, but at least possible assumption—then in purely qualitative terms we have not actually lost ground in the past 50 years; we have merely become more leisurely about our educational pace, or if you will, less efficient. With our increasing productivity of labor, it may happen that we will some day hope to keep our young people out of the labor market until they are as old as 20 or 21. We may then do in 16 years of teaching what we used to do in 12.

STANDARDS HAVE DROPPED

If these remarks sound pessimistic or perhaps even morose, I should add that I do not intentionally convey such an impression. My aim is to be neither pessimistic nor optimistic, but realistic. There is little about the cultural situation in America today that, in my opinion, warrants extravagant optimism. For some time we have let educational standards slip and have permitted our education preparations to become too limited for the great wave of students, the so-called demographic bulge that is now in the high schools and will soon be in the colleges, to be as well educated on the average as their fathers were. I do not see how it would be possible any longer to remedy the situation in time to meet the needs of the children of this generation. But in the long run we seem to have, as a people, sufficient resources and sufficient interest to recoup a good deal of what we have lost, and perhaps even in the end to make new gains, as we have in the past. I believe, too, that it would hardly be claiming too much to say that the educational profession shows every sign of providing enough leaders who could point the way out of the trough of the coming educational depression, if the country will but take its cues from them. We do not yet know what the problems of education will be for the generation now in its infancy, sitting bug-eyed before 20 million television sets; but the past history of such innovations as television suggests that neither its most optimistic admirers nor its most ardent detractors will be fully borne out by the course of events.

I will confess to one concern of my own—the concern that in this age of mass culture and of advancing Philistinism, the traditional centers of our finest achievement in the educational field will not permit themselves to be turned aside from their essential task, the task of cultivating the life of the mind. A large part of American education has long since been given over to vocationalism and to triviality (I do not identify the two), and in an age of mass education I can understand why this should have happened and why it cannot, except in some very small proportion, be undone. In an age when practically everyone goes to high school we can hardly expect that the average level of high school achievement will be what it was 50 years ago when a large proportion of high schools dealt mainly with the needs of selected youngsters interested in the liberal arts as a preparation for college. But it would be inexcusable in a country as rich as ours to fail to make adequate arrangements at both the secondary and collegiate levels for the benefit of that priceless minority whose educational goals are genuinely intellectual and whose needs are now being neglected in the public secondary schools. The main tendency of secondary school teaching in the era of "Life Adjustment" education has been to neglect the curricular needs of the student with cultural interests, and even to undersell the cultural capacities of the ordinary student—all in the name of a bogus notion of educational democracy. Literacy itself is going out of fashion.[19] Those who are devoted to the finest traditions of liberal education and to the idea that education is a part of the development of the mind and soul may have to redouble their energies in the near future merely to retain intact the major features of liberal education. If they succeed in maintaining the best standards of the past 60 or 70 years, they will deserve the thanks of generations to come.

1956

[19]See some of the striking evidence in Mortimer B. Smith, *The Diminished Mind* (Chicago: Henry Regnery Co., 1954), Chap. I.

The Political Philosophy of the
Framers of the Constitution

SINCE THE theme of our conference is the United States in the 20th century, it may seem a bit odd that we should begin by going back to the end of the 18th century, to the establishment of the American Republic and the writing and the adoption of the American Constitution. But one of our central themes is American politics, and there is no better point of departure for the study of American politics than the Constitution. I am not going to talk about the Constitution in the spirit of one who is giving you an elementary lecture in American government. I shall rather talk in somewhat abstract terms about the philosophy of those who framed it. Now, when I say philosophy I am not talking essentially about a metaphysic; I am not even talking about an attempt to work out an abstract political philosophy, or a systematic political philosophy, in the tradition of the great figures in the history of political speculation in the Western world; or, for that matter in the manner of such thinkers in the English political tradition as Hobbes or Harrington, or Locke or Sidney, with whom the Americans were so well acquainted. Instead what I shall be talking about will be an attempt to apply a philosophy already formed in European experience and well formulated by English thinkers and inherited from them by the Americans, an attempt to apply a philosophy, the general outlines of which you will be already familiar with, to a practical problem. We have here at once a significant and characteristic trait of American thought and of American political procedure: the philosophy which was being applied was both an eclectic and one whose interest for the Americans was urgently practical. This eclecticism, this interest in the pragmatic, in the practical, is altogether characteristic of the American approach to politics, and I shall have occasion to refer to it again when I talk about Franklin D. Roosevelt.

Now, let me clarify at least one matter of method. Not all the men who framed the American Constitution in 1787, or who favored its adoption in 1787–1788, had exactly the same political ideas on all points, on all particulars. There were differences among them. However, I am concerned here with the *common* political philosophy that I think emanated from the Constitution rather than the differences over marginal matters and particulars which I think should not be your concern or mine here. So we will deal with the way in which the founders of the Constitution on the whole, on the mean average, tend to agree on generalities rather than the extent to which they differed on particulars. We are constructing then, so to speak, an ideal type of the philosophy of the Constitution, a melange of the leading ideas of a considerable number of men. I am going to be rather vague about who the men were. Mr. Johnson, in preceding me, named some of the leading philosophers. I think the only important thing to do is to delineate for you the sources to which any American historian would go in trying to arrive at an idea of what the philosophy was behind the Constitution, and give you some idea of which men he would study most intensively. The reports of the Federal Convention at Philadelphia in 1787, which rest chiefly upon the notes taken at the time by James Madison, are the leading source on what the men said to each other when they talked about how this prospective form of government should be framed. *The Federalist*, written chiefly by Hamilton and Madison, with a few contributions from John Jay, was the leading argumentative statement for the Constitution. The various debates in the separate American states on whether or not the Constitution should be ratified, provide us with another source of information, and these have been systematically collected. At least one other writing of the time, I think, should be mentioned particularly. This was a work by John Adams who, though he was our minister to England at the time and was not present at the framing of the Constitution, wrote a book, "A Defense of the Constitutions of the American States," which was an elaborate statement of the idea of balanced government which lay behind it. These documents together with a few scattered others are the essential sources from which we can compose a kind of ideal picture of what the characteristic idea was behind the Constitution.

Let me say, first, a few things about the generation that framed the Constitution. It was, of course, the same generation that had made the American Revolution and when the Founding Fathers met in Philadelphia in that very hot summer

of 1787 they were sitting down, now not in their capacity as
destroyers, breakers of older political bonds but as the forgers
of new ones. But it is not a totally new group of men, it is not
a totally new philosophical outlook from that of the revolution
that we are examining, but rather the revolutionary outlook,
the revolutionary philosophy, in a new social context. We can,
in fact, however, take two possible views of the relationship between the American revolution and the Constitution between
such a document as the Declaration of Independence, a revolutionary statement, and the Constitution, an embodiment of
institutions, and in that sense a conservative statement. The
first view and one that was for a long time, I think, predominant among American historians was to stress the opposition
between the tradition of the Revolution and the tradition of
the Constitution and to look upon the drawing up and acceptance of the Constitution as a kind of Thermidor. In accordance with this view, one stressed a philosophy of rebellion
and upheaval and innovation and the assertion of human rights
in connection with the Revolution. And then, in connection
with the Constitution, one stressed the philosophy of a conservative reaction that set in after the Revolution had done its
work. Now there is some truth in this idea, I think. There are,
in a certain thin way, two kinds of traditions running down
through American thought: the tradition of radicals who are
most at home with the tradition of the Declaration of Independence, who like its ringing phrases about human rights and
tend to invoke it as the source and the fountain of American
experience and of the American political tradition. Then, on
the other side, there is the tradition, if you will, of the conservatives for whom an appeal to the sacred text of the Constitution is more congenial; and one can, within limits, I think
very legitimately counterpose these two traditions. But if we
are interested in understanding what went on in America at the
end of the 18th century when this remarkable experiment in
Republican government was framed, one is more interested in
stressing the fundamental *continuity* in the American tradition,
and the fundamental unity between the tradition of the Revolution and the tradition of the Constitution. One can find in
them two statements in two different moods and two different

moments of the same political temperament and the same basic common outlook.

Now, of course, if this is true, then we must seek for the elements of stability in the thought and aims of the Revolution to find, if you will, the conservative element, within the revolutionary upheaval; and we must also not forget the elements of progressivism, democracy and innovation that one can find in the more conservative Constitution. I think this is the correct view of the matter. Our main concern, of course, will be to assess the Constitution and the thought behind it, but first let me for the sake of completeness and for the sake of filling in the background of the Constitution say for a moment a few words about the conservative element in the American Revolution. The idea of a conservative Revolution is a paradox, of course, but like many other paradoxes will serve to open up certain truth to us. Now, if you go back to the beginnings of the agitation which led to the American Revolution, you will find that when Americans first began to protest seriously against British regulations and taxes after 1763 and in that long course of agitation which finally, after 12 years in 1775 led to the outbreak of the Revolution, their protests were not made in the name of breaking off old ties with some other country, they were not made in the name of establishing some kind of a new order, not in the name of realizing or claiming human rights that had never been realized or claimed or demanded before. On the contrary, the argument, oddly enough, for this revolutionary movement was a traditionalist argument in its first impulse, and in its first assertions tended largely to invoke not the drastic ultimates of human rights but rather legalistic traditions thoroughly intelligible within the framework of British history, British practice, and British constitutionalism. The colonists said, "You are violating British traditions," when they protested to Parliament; "you are denying old rights which we always have had; merely restore these rights of Englishmen which we were promised, and all will be well between us." So their argument had a legalistic and, in this sense for a revolutional movement, a surprisingly conservative ring. In the first place they appealed to the charters granted to companies and to groups by kings under the authority of which America had been settled. These charters guaranteed the rights of English-men including the right not to be taxed without consent. The colonists in the first instance argued "these Rights may not be infringed by Parliament, these were given us by the King," —hardly a Jacobin point of view, as you can see. Then, going beyond the specific terms of their charters which one might call almost a contractual kind of argument, they appealed to the larger principles of the British constitution. They said: "It has become a principle of the unwritten British constitution that men cannot be taxed without their consent." And what they did here was to take the familiar Natural Rights Philoso-phy of John Locke, the ideas of natural law and natural rights, and read them into the British constitution, assuming that the British constitution was in some sense based upon these ideas. Here they were drawing mainly on the experience of the English Puritan Revolution and the 17th century and a good many Englishmen, while differing with them on particulars, often could accept the notion that the British constitution embodied abstract principles of natural law and certain fun-damental human rights. Finally, but only in desperation, the Americans did go beyond the tradition of their charters and beyond the traditions of British constitutionalism to appeal to the natural rights philosophy in its starkest implications. This led, of course, to the revolutionary assertion of the Declaration of Independence, the assertion that if a government violates certain rights then it is the natural right of the people to over-throw it. And if the British constitution did not in fact observe such fundamental human rights so much the worse for the British constitution.

But the Americans arrived at this rather stark position only after much preliminary ideological maneuvering and were in a sense reluctantly again driven to the revolutionary position by a series of British measures and British arguments. Here another important point must be made. The aim was to shake off taxa-tion by Parliament. The Americans would gladly have accepted fealty to the king and repudiation of all Parliamentary authority over them, if that would have been acceptable to the English. In short, many of their theorists anticipated an arrangement very much like the Commonwealth arrangement as it exists in the British Commonwealth today, an arrangement under which a loyalty to the crown was recognized and accepted but no loyalty, no subordination to government by Parliament. Hardly again a revolutionary position so far as the situation of the crown was concerned and a very un-Jacobin point of view. And it was only when all these ideas and compromises of a more traditional sort failed that the Americans went on to the revolutionary position of the Declaration of Independence in which they repudiated *both* the authority of Parliament and their loyalty to the crown. Even in the Declaration of Independence itself we find Thomas Jefferson saying "Prudence indeed will dictate that governments long established should not be changed for light and transient causes" and he goes on to say that "only a long train of abuses and usurpations" which he alleged showed an intention to reduce the Colonists under absolute despotism, only such a long train of abuses justified the extreme step of revolution. I might add that it would be an interesting thesis to compare the American revolution with the French revolution, stressing that the American revolution in a certain sense was executed in this, if you will, paradoxically conservative temper. There was no reign of terror. There were of course expropriations of the property of "Loyalists" or "Tories," confiscations of their land, and many of them were driven out; others left in haste on their own initiative; but there was no reign of terror. And in a quite characteristically American fashion the American states confiscated the landed property of Loyalists not to distribute it among the poorer classes, such as they were, but rather to resell the land in order to finance the Revolution. I should add that the survivors of the Revolution who later learned of the French revolutionary terror began to refer retrospectively, with pride, to the measure of restraint that had been characteristic of them so far as the treatment of Loyalist sympathizers was concerned. This lays the groundwork for my suggestion that there need not have been too much of a conservative reaction from the Revolution because the Revolution was not such a Jacobin enterprise in the first place.

But in the situation in which they found themselves at the end of the Revolution, and in the years between 1783 and 1787, the Americans and many leaders found themselves unhappy about a number of circumstances. They were living under a government that had been ratified by the states in 1781, the

Articles of Confederation, which was thus far their most significant attempt to solve the problem of federal union and
an attempt which they felt had to a very large degree failed.
The central government under the Articles of Confederation
in addition to its many other deficiencies lacked the power of
the purse. The Americans had a federal union, but from the
standpoint of the innovators who led the movement for the
new Constitution the federal union was too loose. The central
government above all lacked the power to tax citizens directly
and to raise the funds by that means that it needed to carry
out its business. It lacked the power to regulate commerce between and among the states or to prevent commercial quarrel-
ings and mutual tariffs. Simply because it lacked the finances, it
lacked the power to maintain a truly adequate army or navy. It
could not pay the very considerable debts that had been inherited from the Revolution.

So there was a great deal of disillusionment in many quarters
with the performance of the new government. The rhetoric of
American correspondence at this time shows that there was a
great deal of sensitivity among the Americans, almost in the
manner of adolescents who have rebelled against parents and
find that they cannot manage their lives, a sense of being on
trial with these new assertions of Republicanism and liberty and
not making out very well. Quite aside from these psychological
aspects of the problem, there were graver fears. There was a
good deal of talk about dissolving the federal union altogether
and reverting simply to 13 separate states. There was some talk
of forming perhaps two or three smaller confederacies that
might have a stronger central government, but what this raised
for some people was the prospect of the "Balkanization" of the
North American Continent. Of course, it is perfectly true that
at the time, the settlement of the Continent had extended only
about as far as the Appalachian mountains, but at the same
time the peace treaty had given the Americans the control of
the land up to the Mississippi. However, the conception that
instead of having a unified country the Continent might be
settled by various states fighting over land claims, fighting over
tariffs, fighting over other issues, rather than by some kind of
peaceful and harmonious central federal republic, was a genuine threat. There was also a threat that the libertarian and

republican institutions with which Americans were familiar would fail, would collapse. There were quarrels between debtors and creditors in the states. Massachusetts had experienced actual disorder in Shays' Rebellion and in the movement of debtors against the courts to prevent the foreclosures of mortgages. So there was a fear that perhaps after a period of popular disorder there would be a relapse into monarchy or some kind of tyranny. There were even proposals made to Washington that he undertake to set up a dictatorship, proposals which he indignantly rejected. So the Constitution was formed by men who were trying to strike a balance between the populistic currents that were stirring at the bottom of the social scale, among the poorer debtors and the poorer farmers and the adventurous, anti-Republican dictatorial ideas on the other hand, and to steer away from the notion of letting the federal union dissolve altogether. Their problem, then, was to form a government which would be effective as a central government and yet re-assure the deep-seated American suspicions of centralized power, re-assure people that they would not suffer from an excessive concentration of power.

So we come then to one of the two major problems that confronted the founders of the Constitution: I call them the problems of power and the problems of federalism. The framers of the Constitution were caught in a kind of dilemma over this problem of power. They had had very unpleasant experiences under the Articles of Confederation and during the Revolution with the lack of sufficient central power. But at the same time they had a long experience before the Revolution with an excess of power. They had to create a greater central power and yet at the same time satisfy the widespread American suspicion of authority and satisfy themselves that they were not recreating on their own ground the potentialities for the kind of parliamentary absolutism that they thought they had repudiated. They must, they thought, form a government strong enough to govern more effectively than under the Articles of Confederation, but not strongly enough to be tyrannical. Lincoln put the same problem beautifully 75 years later at the time of the American Civil War when he asked: "Must a government of necessity be too strong for the liberties of its own people or too weak to maintain its own existence?" The Founding Fathers thought not and they sat down to try to solve the problem by amplifying the powers of the federal government but setting up effective checks over the way in which this power could be exercised. We will return to this in a moment.

The second problem was, of course, the federal problem, something which does not need, I think, very much explanation or elaboration to a German audience. There had been long American experience with proposals for some type of federal union even before the unsuccessful, or largely unsuccessful, experiment with the Articles of Confederation. Now the essence of this problem was to find an exact balance, an exact way of distributing the powers between a central government and the separate states so that the states would be assured that a significant amount of local authority still existed and yet that the central government had genuine meaning. It was also necessary to satisfy the claims and the suspicions of certain particular states, especially the smaller ones. They thought that they would be swallowed up in a strong central union by the larger states if the larger states had a voice in the central government proportionate to their wealth and population. Some kind of check representing the suspicions and the claims of the small states was necessary. Now this is the practical framework, this is the exigency, this is the crisis to which these ideas had to be adapted.

And now let me say something about the approach of contemporaries like Adams and Madison to this problem. I think the most important thing to say about the Constitution is that it was conceived in anything but a utopian spirit; it was a thoroughly realistic affair. One of the most consistent notes struck in the discussion of human affairs in connection with the framing and adoption of the Constitution was that of a rather grim view of human nature. We are in the habit of accusing the Enlightenment of the late 17th and 18th century of being glibly optimistic, of having a dogmatic faith in progress and human perfectibility. I think we do the 18th century a great injustice in this respect and that if we read its texts carefully we find that the unqualified and rash optimists were very few and that there was a great deal of very hard-headed thinking in the Enlightenment about human affairs. This would, I am certainly prepared to assert, apply to the kind of thinking that went on in the American states.

Government, Madison, Adams, and others said, cannot rely on human goodness, on human restraint, on human checks. One must construct a frame of society that is based upon the worst expectations of man, not upon excessive overdrafts on his virtue. Men, and the collective interests in which they aggregate, are rapacious, ambitious, vindictive, greedy. This is the fundamental position from which they began. Furthermore, now there is a nice impartiality about most of the thinking of these people because although they represented the upper classes, the patrician elite—I think the word aristocracy is too thick and too rich for the American blood and inapplicable, but they did represent a patrician elite—they were quite impartial about the way in which they applied this notion of unchecked human nature. This tendency, this ambition, this capacity for disorder, for overassertion, they said, is true both of the rich and of the poor. There is a danger both that the rich will, if equipped with too much power, push the exploitation of the poorer classes to the utmost and that the rich, if unchecked by a means of expressing the popular will, will despoil the public. Both the rich and the poor will exploit, if they can. The proper equipoise in a balanced society and a balanced government is to check greed with greed, power with power, ambition with ambition, interest with interest, class with class, so that the entire society reaches a kind of equipoise. In a way one can think of the philosophy behind the Constitution as a grand Newtonian metaphor. But how do you find the mechanism, how do you find the proper formula for attraction and repulsion? Here, of course, they resorted to the idea of checks and balances.

The notion of a balanced government which they were adopting and taking over from their predecessors is a very old one which goes back at least as far as Polybius. These were men of a good deal of classical learning and historical sense and they were quite well aware, on the whole, of the historical antecedents of their thought. But what you have here is an attempt to put it into practical application. And there emerged out of this a characteristic American practical insight which I think had not been made by most previous exponents of the idea of

balanced government. The main insight, arising out of American conditions and expressed very clearly by Madison in some
numbers of *The Federalist*, was this: that the goal of balance is
easier in the state and the society of a pluralistic structure, if
there are multiple centers of power and multiple interests—it
is easier to construct this balanced frame than if there are only
a few units in centered power, it is easier to arrive at an equipoise in which they can in some sense cancel each other out so
that no single interest, no single minority group approaches a
position in which it can impose its will upon the whole society.
Now in arriving at this formula the Founding Fathers thought
they had an answer to a very common notion in 18th century
political thought, the notion that a republican form of government was suitable only to a small state, to a city state, and
that if you wanted to create a frame of government adequate
to the governance of a large territory, of an empire, then you
must have something like an imperial form, a more centralized
government on the order of an effective monarchy. What the
Americans were trying to say is that it is precisely the large
state which is consistent with republicanism because in a large
and pluralistic society you can create this kind of equipoise of
variety of interests. This had an element of novelty in it, even
an element of heresy, because most of what men knew then
about republics came from the history of the city-state republics of antiquity and the Italian city-states of the Middle Ages.
The Founding Fathers were very well aware that the history of
these political units had been a history of agitation and disorder
followed by the dissolution of republicanism and the adoption
of tyrannies. They were quite self-consciously trying to make
an asset out of the diversity of American society so as to create
a society, to create a frame of government that would be stable. So you find in the frame of government with which they
emerged an elaborate complex of balances. In the first place, in
the departments of government themselves there is a separation of powers among the executive, legislative and judicial and
an attempt to set the three agencies of the central government
over each other as watch dogs. There is a distribution of powers
between the states and the federal government which leaves
many of the significant functions of the state in the hands of
the state governments and puts the core of essential powers in

the hands of the federal government. There is a balance even within the legislature of social classes. The House of Representatives was expected to be a popular body which would represent the suffrages and the wills of the active political public, which constituted even then a very large portion of the adult male population. The Senate would represent the patrician and the wealthier classes by and large; and these two Houses would, so to speak, have to do business with each other. Over and above them the President was expected to give leadership to both Houses and impose a certain unity upon them. But he too was checked because all his major appointments were subject to confirmation by the Senate and his budget was of course subject to action by Congress.

In order to bring the whole problem of taxation and the raising of funds closer to the people it was required that all measures for raising funds and for levying taxes must originate in the House of Representatives, the popular side of the body. Finally, the Supreme Court was placed in a curious position over this body of executive and legislative authority. Here I think you have another American heresy, another American deviation from the British political tradition. The Americans had always objected in the past in their struggles over parliamentary regulation and parliamentary taxation to the idea of parliamentary supremacy. They felt that if there were a constitution, and if the constitution embodied fundamental law and fundamental human rights and, especially if that constitution were to be written, there must be somewhere in the society an authority which can put its finger upon the point at which an act of the parliament contravenes fundamental law. There is a trap of course in this, because it involves arrogating to a small judicial group an extremely sweeping power, something which we found out later on in our experience with the Supreme Court. But it was a testimony to the sincerity and the passion and the naiveté with which Americans went about trying to incarnate this idea of fundamental law into a written constitution that they should have felt that they could somehow establish a judiciary which would automatically apply the principles of fundamental law to the acts of the legislature, square the acts of the legislature with the requirements of the constitution, and automatically find out which laws were constitutional or unconstitutional. Of course a long series of struggles grew out of this question of the place of the Supreme Court in the political system. But again the court was felt to be a check upon tyrannical exercise of power.

One thing, despite all their political realism, the Fathers left out of the picture: they had no place in their scheme of thought for political parties. This is rather interesting because without the political parties, without the two-party system, it was dubious that their constitutional system for all its ingenuity could have been made operative. They had actually had no experience either from their observations of British politics or from the experience of the American colonies with a working party system. What you tended to have were factions whose achievements were extremely dubious, and the Americans thought of political parties largely as a nuisance, largely as a way in which a particular extremely limited interest goes into the politic arena simply to make a demand in its own behalf. They also thought that instead of having nation-wide parties you would simply have units which represented the interests of particular states; the idea that a party system would coalesce across state lines was not very persuasive to them. However, parties very quickly developed once the Constitution was put into operation and it was the political parties that enabled the President to lead the whole political process, enabled him to formulate a program, to get it through Congress. It was the party system that enabled conflicting interests to arrive at compromises, the necessary compromises of politics, both inside and outside the framework of formal government. I think I will have occasion to talk in the discussion group about this.

One further aspect of the Constitution that I think needs mention before we pass on is its flexibility. Although it was a written constitution many things were left open, many things were left rather deliberately vague. There are large silences in the Constitution and there are huge open clauses which gave many a "field day" for lawyers and judges. For instance, there was a commerce clause which empowered Congress to regulate commerce between and among the states, that opened up endless possibilities as to how far the actual power of Congress over commerce went. After a certain number of specific powers which Congress could exercise was enumerated, there was the "necessary and proper clause" that said that Congress could have all powers necessary and proper to the execution of the enumerated powers, an immense blank check, as it might be made to be, for further expansion of the authority of the central government. Finally, I think we must speak in passing of the Bill of Rights which is another token of the continuity between the thought of the Revolution and the thought of the Constitution. It is of course true that when the Constitution was finally drafted in Philadelphia in 1787 there was no Bill of Rights included, and this matter had been given only the most casual discussion on the floor of the convention. But I think we must not infer from this that there was any intention on the part of the framers to subvert rights or to leave them out. Bills of Rights which guaranteed fundamental freedoms of religion, of press, of assembly, of speech, and so on, had existed in all the state constitutions and somehow the framers felt that these made an adequate supply of guarantees. In fact it had been so under the Articles of Confederation, because under the Articles of Confederation these state governments had been the real agencies of sovereignty and their statements of rights were adequate to the purpose. What the framers forgot—and here they committed a tremendous faux-pas—was that if you were forming a truly firm central government, a reassertion of the Bill of Rights as operative *within that government* would also be necessary to appease the prevailing American suspicion of authority. However, when they got into it, when they sent the Constitution back to the states for ratification and discovered that one of the main objections, one of the profoundest suspicions, of this new instrument which they had proposed was its failure to incorporate such guarantees of rights, they quickly readjusted their strategy. In a few of the strategic states they promised specifically that as soon as the new government was put in operation a Bill of Rights would be added in the form of amendments to the Constitution. This promise was a sincere one and was carried out immediately after the new government was set up. Without such promise of a Bill of Rights the Constitution probably would not have been accepted by enough states to make it operative. But my point here is that the Bill of Rights was not itself an intensely controversial issue. There was no intention to foreclose any of these fundamental rights in the framing of the Constitution and there was no real argument as to whether they should or should not be included. There was a momentary failure of insight in not adopting the Bill of Rights as a part of the original document. The men who framed the Constitution were, here once again, ratifying the continuity of what they were trying to do with the older tradition of protest, with the natural law traditions of the Revolution.

1959

The Economic and Social Philosophy of Franklin D. Roosevelt

I THINK there are few American historians who would be as embarrassed by this subject as I am, largely because I have written a book in which there is a chapter on Franklin D. Roosevelt under the title: "F.D.R. the Patrician as Opportunist." Part of the argument there is that whatever his very considerable merits were, Roosevelt was not a man of extraordinary intellectual interest and had very little consistent or coherent political, economic or social philosophy. I am going to talk about Roosevelt in any case and I will stand by the chapter in my book to some extent—at least to the extent that I will not make too much of the character of his political philosophy. I will still stand with one sentence in it: "At the heart of the New Deal there was not a philosophy but a temperament." I don't, however, wish to suggest any denigration or any failure of appreciation of Franklin Roosevelt. He was one of our great men and I admire him. I do think, however, that while we must be interested in the character of his mind and in the nature of his thoughts, that it is a mind which interests us because he was a great man and not because his was a great mind. His genius was for things other than profound or consistent or systematic, reflective thought. He knew this perfectly well himself. Once when he was asked by a reporter during the New Deal days what his philosophy was, he looked rather startled and said: "I am a Christian and a democrat, that's all." And he, of course, meant "democrat" in this case with a small "d" although he was also a democrat with a capital "D" as well. I suppose if one were to try to characterize the style of his mind, one would perhaps pick out the word "experimentation" more than anything else. Here one of his statements during the 1932 presidential campaign when he was first running for election is most appropriate. He said to the electorate: "It is common sense to take a method and try it. If it fails, admit it frankly and try another, but above all try something." And you can't imagine how pointed this was to a people who had experienced four years of Herbert Hoover. But I shall come to that comparison in a moment. The only part of this quotation that he did not completely live up to was "admit it frankly." That is, perhaps, asking too much. Supreme Court Justice Oliver Wendell Holmes, who was a very old man when he met Franklin D. Roosevelt in Washington in 1932, came away from an interview with him and reported to a friend of Roosevelt's, "A second-class intellect but a first-class temperament." I think this is quite appropriate. Holmes, by the way, had a good deal of experience as a basis on which to make comparisons of Roosevelt with other Presidents. He had seen every President since James Buchanan before the Civil War. He was about ninety when he had his interview with Roosevelt. I think his choice of the word "temperament" is excellent. It isn't quite character although I don't want to suggest that Roosevelt was a man without character or with an excessively deficient character but it is neither mind nor character that is most impressive, but a kind of temperament, a kind of facility, a kind of confidence, a kind of energy, that is truly extraordinary. Perhaps to suggest another dimension of Roosevelt and another encounter with him that illuminates the other side, was his meeting with John Maynard Keynes, the economist, after the New Deal had been launched and at a time when many people were saying that the New Deal was "Keynesian," which I think it was not, at least not quite yet. They had a long talk, Keynes left and Roosevelt said to an intimate of Keynes in a bewildered way, "He must be a mathematician rather than an economist." And Keynes, for his part, confessed to someone to whom he spoke after the interview that he had supposed the President was "more literate, economically speaking." But it is not to this that we should look for Roosevelt nor should we perhaps make the mistake (and I may have made it to some extent in the chapter of my book) of depreciating him excessively because he was not an academic economist.

Now, what I should like to do since the foreground of Roosevelt's thought is of less pressing interest than the thought of, say, James Madison might have been or John Adams or John C. Calhoun, is to spend a good deal more time on the social background of his thought and to get around to his particular kind of reactions after filling in a bit of the background. It's a bit easier to do this after you have listened to Professor

Current this morning and for that I am very grateful. But I think one of the things one perhaps should know is at least the consistent thread of pragmatism running through both the themes of my lectures. I emphasized, in talking about the Founding Fathers in my lecture yesterday, that what they were doing was not thinking out a new abstract political philosophy but applying abstractions that they had inherited from the English to a concrete crisis, a concrete political situation. In Roosevelt's case, one is applying not even abstractions so much, I think here, as certain kinds of intuitions and feelings, certain kinds of political professional "expertise" to a social crisis without nearly as much emphasis on the theoretical inheritance as you would find in the generation of the Founding Fathers. If you had in the Founding Fathers pragmatism, you have in Roosevelt the apotheosis of pragmatism. But Roosevelt becomes important for us because of the New Deal about which I should like to emphasize a few points. The first thing that must be emphasized is the extraordinary severity of the crisis which put Roosevelt into his focal situation. It was a world-wide depression, of course, but I think that the impact of the depression in the United States was as great as in any country of the Western world and probably greater than in many countries. The level of industrial production, for instance, in the summer of 1932, when the election campaign between Roosevelt and Hoover was going on, had fallen to 51% of that of 1929. There were huge masses of unemployed, but more urgently than this, there was the absence, the lack of any institutional palliatives to prevent the acuteness of the suffering that would come with unemployment, the total inadequacy of the relief mechanisms for unemployment. It perhaps intensified the shock of the whole thing that we had just gone through this period of the 1920's during which, as Professor Current pointed out, there was this extraordinary complacency and this extraordinary confidence that the plateau of prosperity would go on. The period of the Twenties was a period of stable prices, of general prosperity, of high level of employment, of the rapid diffusion of certain kinds of consumer goods. The latter were novelties and very interesting and gratifying, household gadgetry, which we Americans love, refrigerators, electrical apparatus, radios and the whole automobile complex. But it was also

the period of the most inequitably distributed wealth in modern American history. I think by all the indices that we have,
the year 1929, which was the peak of our prosperity before the
recent period, was also the peak of inequitable distribution of
wealth in American history. There were a good many people
not sharing actively in this prosperity who began from a very
low base to begin with. When the depression started they were
quickly very conscious of the immense inequities that this, in
some ways superficial prosperity, had covered over. Again,
there had been a great deal of disillusionment with America
among intellectuals during the 1920's which I am sure you
were reminded of in Professor Stavig's talk about the "Protest
Tradition." A tremendous hatred of the clownishness of American politics in the Harding-Coolidge era, a tremendous sense
of injustice in the age of the Sacco and Vanzetti trial, a tremendous revulsion from American Puritanism in the period of prohibition, with revulsion on the part of intellectuals from
intolerance in the period of the Ku Klux Klan. So that all that
was needed to cap this whole sense of discontent among thinking Americans with our own institutions was the additional
shock of the failure of the economic system. I'll get to Roosevelt soon, but I think, too, part of his background and ours was
a tremendous lack of institutional preparation in American
government for the ready handling of a depression of this mag-
nitude. A very important thing, and it is here, I think, that
Roosevelt's flexibility is most outstanding. Now, in many ways
the United States in 1929 was still a loose federal union; this
looseness of the federal union lasted much longer than most
people think, much longer than most Americans think. In
thinking about the nature of our federal union we generally
take the Civil War of 1861–1865 as a breaking point. We say,
before then we had a loose federal union of states more effective, to be sure, than what we had under the Articles of Confederation but still with a great deal of the center of gravity in
the states and a great deal of uncertainty as to where the fundamental center of gravity, of political sovereignty, would come
to rest. And we usually say that we went through this tremendous Civil War and that settled the question of separatism, of
particularism, of state sovereignty, of state rights, and really
located the center of American power in Washington. Formally

yes; but if one looks beneath the formalities and asks, when did this really become a centralized society, one might push it down very readily as far as the late 1880's, after the great industrial developments of the years following the Civil War had economically knit the country together. But in some things, and in the things that affect us and that affected Franklin D. Roosevelt, it was long after that there was still an enormous amount of administrative decentralization—right down to 1929, right down to 1932, to 1933 when Roosevelt took the reins of office. I've been casting around for some way in which I could make this meaningful to you quickly, and it occurred to me that perhaps the best way to do it would be to look at where the money was spent by governmental agencies in the United States. Now, if you compare the size of the budgets of the federal and state and the local governments, you have a rather good index, I think, of where the character of state expenditure is and where the center of gravity is. Now, it is true that during the entire 19th century, except during and immediately after wars, the aggregate finances of state and local governments (that is, you add the expenses of all the state governments and all the local governments together) were always at least roughly *twice* that of the budget of the federal government. Here, you see, you get a sort of crude economic index of the diffusion of administration. And this was the case right up to 1913. It was not very much changed even by the events of Progressivism, of the Progressive Movement, with its tendency toward expanding the federal government. It was of course affected by the First World War. But it is not really until Roosevelt takes the helm that the federal government begins to bulk large as compared with the expenses of the state and local government. Finally, by the year 1939—at the end of the New Deal and after the great period of the domestic reforms had actually taken place and Roosevelt's large budgets had been adopted—the total expenditures of the federal government had reached approximate parity, approximate equality, with those of all the state and local governments put together. The 1950 figure is an index of how rapidly we have moved on since the New Deal toward centralization, if you'll accept this as an index. In 1950 the expenditure of the federal government was approximately a little more than twice as much as the aggregate of state and local government. We have now moved into, you see, the new era even within the span of the period from 1939 to 1950. So that if you go back, then, to 1932 and look at this problem of administrative development and ad-ministrative expenditure from the standpoint of how one is to meet the great national economic emergency the United States was an administrative anachronism when Roosevelt took it over. Of course, as Professor Current said, in the Progressive Era certain concepts—the attempt to control monopolies, the attempt to regulate railroads by national government—had been accepted. But these were only effective in very, very lim-ited areas of activity. In 1932, one veteran corporation lawyer from New York wrote to another in Philadelphia these words: "When you and I first began to practice law," he said, "one hardly needed to know that there was a federal government until one went abroad (meaning till you had to ask for a pass-port)." And, of course, there was good justification for this statement. This was actually still substantially true at the time he wrote except in one very important arena, that of the in-come tax. That was the one great difference between this man's first days at the bar and the moment at which he was writing this letter in 1932. So that when the great depression broke upon America in 1929–32 this was still, to a very large degree, a society governed by state and local government and these agencies were beginning to break down, were proving totally inadequate to the emergency. Far from being able to supply the unemployed and the poverty-stricken with the means of subsistence, many cities were bankrupt and could not even pay their teachers. Now there had been a philosophical equivalent, a philosophical counterpart of all this in politics and in eco-nomic thinking which took the form of what now seems, from the retrospect of the depression generation, a very excessive faith in "localism in government." A belief that this was not only what we had, but a good thing and a necessary thing and all that we needed. Accompanying this was a faith in volun-tarism, that is, an assumption that most of the needs of our society could be met by private, voluntary action and by private enterprise.

   There was also a remarkable persistence in many quarters of what I call the old Yankee-Protestant-Puritan notion, that there is, must be and should be, an inevitable intimate relation between virtue and success. The demand for individual self-reliance had a great effect upon our attitude toward the relief problem. We could not deal with the relief problem as a social emergency in which there were so many people on the job market and so small a number of jobs for them, but rather, to say, you know the hearty, the self-reliant, the virtuous, the careful, the prudent man will take care of himself, *and should.*

The perfect exemplar of this philosophy was Herbert Hoover. Now if our subject were Herbert Hoover and the economic and social philosophy of Herbert Hoover, I could talk to you a great deal more about ideas than I could about Franklin D. Roosevelt. Hoover had a great many ideas, dating in origins from the 16th to the 18th century and very few, I think it not unfair to say, originating after that period. He had studied them well, he was a man of rather remarkable intellectual capacities in his own way, but a terrible doctrinaire. With him individualism was almost an item of religious faith, so that to deviate from it was not something that was open to discussion; it was simply a heresy; it was not to be thought of, it was immoral to suggest. Here the comparison with Franklin D. Roosevelt is very significant. Hoover was an amateur in politics. He had never run for any office of any kind in the capacity of the American people to give, before he ran for President in 1928 when he was elected. His career had been in private business and then in administration as a cabinet officer—Secretary of Commerce in Washington. He had had a good deal of what might be called public experience, but it was all on the level of negotiation with peers rather than dealing with newspaper men and, through them, the public opinion of the country. And his approach to the American public, I think, was what you might call custodial. He knew better, he knew what was right and wrong, he had learned it from the proper books, from the cleverest economists, and he would do his best, as indeed he did with great devotion and energy, to try to execute what was right, to carry it out, and the clamour of the public was simply a distraction and a nuisance on the sidelines. Now, we finally do come to F.D.R., whom we must, I think, compare with Hoover. I don't think that F.D.R. really had, in many ways, an intellect of Hoover's sort, but he was a political

professional from the soles of his feet to his hair. He was prepared for this crisis in which he assumed responsibility, not so
much in terms of philosophy as in terms of his temperament
of which I've spoken and in terms of his political training. So
far as his philosophy was concerned, he had, during the 1920's,
taken his own share in the kind of smug, complaisant and self-
congratulatory atmosphere that prevailed, perhaps not as out-
spokenly or as articulately as Herbert Hoover and certainly not
in as doctrinaire a manner, but nonetheless he had shared in
it. So it was not any greater philosophical training that would
characterize him, but rather greater temperamental flexibility.
But above all, he had been taught by a long career in practical
politics to be a compromiser, a pleaser and a manoeuvrer.

Now I should like to talk about him a bit personally, again, in
terms of his background and history, and return, by this circle,
again to the crisis with which he was dealing. In the first place
he had (I've ruled out the word "aristocratic" for American
experience, I think quite rightly) what you might call a patrician background. He was one of those Americans who were,
perhaps, all too few in number, who have a real proprietary
sense in the country to which they belong, in a sense that he
came from an old family which means very simply a family that
has been in one place for a long time. This gave him a certain
sense of assurance and yet, he had inherited along with this
family confidence, this family sense of real proprietorship in the
country, a sense of responsibility, a sense of *noblesse oblige*. He
had been trained on a vague, but I think nonetheless very real
kind of humane attitude toward those who stood below him in
the social scale. Moreover, unlike Hoover, whose backgrounds
were in the Middle West and the Far West and who was reared
in a rural environment, Roosevelt, despite his up-country home
in the Hudson, was familiar with Eastern urban politics. He
lived all his political life in the Democratic party on the fringes
of the Tammany Hall Machine in New York. He had had a very
close political relationship for quite some time with the hero
and the leader of this machine, Al Smith. And if you wanted
to be in politics in New York State, or if you want to be today,
you must know how to deal with a complex environment, both
rural and urban, and also you have to know how to deal with
the special ethnic needs, groups, susceptibilities and desires of

the Irish, the Italians, the Jews, etc. It's very good training in compromise, in sensitivity for the demands of others. Then, again, there was a special situation in the Democratic party in the 1920's which gave Roosevelt his professional schooling. He had come into prominence on the national basis as Assistant Secretary of the Navy during World War I and then had run for the Vice-Presidency in the very disastrous Democratic campaign of 1920. Then, four years later in the Presidential election of 1924, there was a frightful break in the Democratic party, a terrible split between the rural, Puritanical, prohibitionist element and the urban, anti-prohibition, to a very large extent Catholic and ethnically heterogeneous element that favored Al Smith. And the party had simply fought itself to a standstill at its national convention in 1924 over many of these issues. Roosevelt was the one man who stood out for his ability to maintain genuinely friendly relationships with both sides in this difficult fight, and he became a kind of agency of party reconstruction during this period. He developed a huge correspondence with people from all over the country and developed a sensitivity not only to what was going on within his own party, in its sentiments etc., but an understanding, through the party, of the country as a whole. Furthermore, he had come to learn the importance of one fundamental thing in politics: he understood that in a democratic society, to the true statesman, every interest is prima-facie legitimate, until it can be shown to be otherwise. Every interest, every demand, every grievance is legitimate until one reaches a point to which the grievance can no longer be met, the point at which the demand is too unreasonable, the point at which the interest is overreaching itself. And so he readily conceived the idea of forming what he called a true concert of interests in the early days of the New Deal. He had respect for the business interest, the labor interest, the agricultural interest, the unemployed interest, the Italian, Irish, Jewish, Polish, German interests, for all kinds of special ethnic, regional, economic demands and sensitivities. His first impulse in statecraft, and it could be carried to the point at which it was something of a weakness and a vice but it was also his strong point, was an impulse to satisfy everybody, even if the particular political formula under which it was done might have certain intellectual inconsistencies. A perfect illustration of this occurred during the campaign of 1932 when he was trying to formulate, as he went along, a program which would anticipate for the electorate what he would do when he were elected. His advisers disagreed as to what should be said and done about the tariff. And when the time came for him to make his most important speech on the tariff issue, he was confronted with two separate drafts, manuscripts of speeches which had two quite inconsistent sets of proposals for a solution of the tariff problem. With his characteristic impatience for the intricacies of economic speculation, he leaped through them rather rapidly, got the gist of them in his facile and sometimes superficial way, handed them back to one of the speech-writers and said, "Weave the two together."

Of course, this attitude is not very good when it is necessary to work out a very tight, consistent line in planning, but it is very good at welding together and holding together a political coalition. So, I think the *key* to understanding Roosevelt, and, through him the "New Deal" that we look at through his eyes, is not to call it social planning but social experimentation, not to emphasize its adherence to principle but its adherence to humane concern, not its philosophy but its flair for change, not its economics but its political virtuosity. When Roosevelt was elected you had a perfect instance of what goes on in American politics. Even in the midst of this great crisis, this terrible social breakdown which alerted everyone to political issues perforce, there was no really full-scale discussion of the issues confronting the American public with any clarity. There was no anticipation, if one looks at Roosevelt's utterances, of what the New Deal would do, what the New Deal, which it, already promised in those words, would become. But there was what always goes on in the American political process, a vague groping of the public to find out which they preferred of two types of temperament, two types of style, two types of expression and character, not between two clearly articulated philosophies. Of course, the depression had hurt Hoover so badly that Roosevelt did not have to commit himself very specifically in many things to win. It was easy to win and he did not make the practical mistake of being too specific. But if you look at his 1932 election utterances and try to say, "ah, here is the outline of the coming New Deal," you will at most points not be able to find it. He was extraordinarily vague, and in some respects, particularly in his cry for a balanced budget and a cut on federal expenditures, anticipated exactly the opposite of what came to be. And he was sufficiently vague on other issues so that Walter Lippmann made one of the most famous unfortunate remarks that any intelligent and perceptive man of Lippmann's stature could have made. He said during the 1932 campaign: "Mr. Roosevelt is an amiable man who wants very much to be President but seems to have little other qualifications for the job." He could not have been more wrong and yet, a great many of us felt that way in 1932, and were disquieted, we were disquieted by the vagueness and "lack of muscle" in this campaign. Roosevelt did, however, make one big philosophical commitment during the campaign in a speech he made at the Commonwealth Club in San Francisco. And I want to give you a little bit of that speech before I make my comment on it because the speech is arresting in its argument, it did have a philosophy behind it, but I'm just going to warn you that after I give you the speech with its philosophy there is a frightful anti-climax coming. But first let's see what he said. He said: the nation has now arrived at a great watershed in its development, popular government and a big continent to exploit, had given the United States an unusually favored early history, he said, and then the industrial revolution brought the promise of abundance for everybody. But then this productive capacity had been controlled by ruthless and wasteful men. They had free land, a growing population and needed industrial plant, and so the country had paid a rather heavy price to the great entrepreneurs who were able to develop this industrial plant. They had given the ambitious man unlimited reward provided only that he produced the economic plant so much desired. Then the turn of the tide came with the turn of a century, Roosevelt said, as America reached its last frontiers. The demand of the people for more positive controls of economic life gave rise to the Square Deal of Theodore Roosevelt, the New Freedom of Woodrow Wilson. Now, said Roosevelt, the country is faced squarely with the problem of industrial control, and I quote him verbatim: "A glance at the situation today only too clearly indicates that equality of opportunity, as we have known it, no longer exists. Our industrial plant is built. The problem just now is whether

under existing conditions it is not overbuilt; our last frontier
has long since been reached and there is practically no more
free land. More than half of our people do not live on the farms
or on their lands and cannot derive a living by cultivating their
own property. There is no safety valve in the form of the Western prairie to which those, thrown out of work by the Eastern
economic machines, can go for a new start. We are not able to
invite immigration from Europe to share our endless plenty,
we are now providing a drab living for our own people," and
so on. He also added that, put plainly, we are steering a steady
course toward economic oligarchy, if we are not there already
because of the growth of the big business corporation. Then
he said, clearly "all this calls for a reappraisal of values. A mere
builder of more industrial plants, a creator of more railroad
systems, an organizer of more corporations, is as likely to be a
danger as a help. The day of the great promoter or the financial
titan to whom they granted anything if only he would build or
develop is over. Our task now is not discovery or exploitation
of natural resources or necessarily producing more goods, it is
the soberer less dramatic business of administering resources
and plants already in hand, of seeking to re-establish foreign
markets for our surplus production, of meeting the problem
of under-consumption, of adjusting production to consumption, of distributing wealth and products more equitably, of
adapting existing economic organizations to the service of the
people. The day of enlightened administration has come. As I
see it, the task of government in its relation to business is to
assist the development of an economic Declaration of Rights,
an economic constitutional order." So what you have here is
the whole idea which one can refer to, in short-hand, as the
idea of a mature economy and the necessity for many types
of social and administrative re-adjustments to cope with the
mature economy. However, there is only one trouble with all
this: Roosevelt had never read the text of this speech before he
got up to deliver it at the Commonwealth Club. This is something we have learned only recently with the very interesting recollection by Rexford Guy Tugwell, one of Roosevelt's
"brain-trusters," of these early years. It was written by some of
Roosevelt's advisers; it did represent to be sure their maturely
considered views, but Tugwell himself thinks, and thought at

the time, that it was not really quite as close to Roosevelt's philosophy as it was to theirs, that Roosevelt probably would not have accepted the full line of argument if he'd had the time to work out the text of the speech with his "brain-trust" and his advisers, as he usually did with most speeches.

I won't even try to summarize the major measures of the New Deal because I think Professor Current did it very well this morning in talking about the growth of the American economy in its relation to government. I will just go on to say that the New Deal went through, during its very hectic and interesting life from 1933 to 1939, at least two phases, the emphasis of which was different, and in many cases, the thinking was actually quite different. There was no straight, consistent line of economic philosophy, even after the period of campaigning was over and the period of administering and dealing with financial problems and relief problems and social problems actually began. On the whole, the New Deal was successful in sparing people the greatest incidence of exploitation, oppression and misery of the kind that they endured from 1930 to 1932. It was not so successful in bringing about full recovery because when the war came with the new stimulus to American industry there were still about seven million unemployed. I don't think that one can say that for all the excellent and now obviously durable reforms that originated in the New Deal that it had solved the problems of the American economy in any serious sense. And I would add one thing to what Professor Current said this morning about the two waves of reform that have swept over the American economy in the twentieth century, enumerated as the Progressive Era and then the period of the New Deal. I think in some way, though oddly it was not intended in any sense as an economic reform, one must strangely and paradoxically add the war, because World War II taught us far more about the potentialities of our economy for production and gave us far higher sights for what we could accomplish with it than either the Progressives or the New Dealers had dreamed of. I do think it is important that we went into the war (shall we say out of the framework of the New Deal mentality, the New Deal style, the New Deal sympathy for the public, the New Deal concern with the redistribution of wealth) because we carried on with taxation policies during and after the war that were profoundly affected by the equalitarianism and the Reformist period and this period of the New Deal. And if we had gone into World War II out of, say, a Harding, Coolidge or even Hoover type of mentality, I shudder to think what the United States might have looked like after the war. And I think we owe some of the success of our economy, such as it has been, to the lessons learned from the depression and the lessons mediated by this very free-wheeling kind of experimentation and this experimental mentality that Roosevelt brought to the problems of the country between 1933 and 1939.

1959

Could a Protestant Have
Beaten Hoover in 1928?

M Y GENERATION was raised upon the cliché that no Catholic can be elected to the Presidency. This cliché is based upon one historical experience—Al Smith's losing campaign in 1928, during which the notion that a Catholic cannot be elected was often referred to as an "unwritten law."

Those who are still convinced that the unwritten law exists find the case of Al Smith conclusive. A few undeniable facts fit their argument. In a massive campaign, waged partly in the open and partly at the level of whispers and snickers, Smith's religion was used against him. This intolerance was repudiated by his opponent, but no one doubts that it affected many voters, and that hundreds of thousands, especially in the South and Middle West, voted against Smith partly or largely on this account. He lost the electoral votes of states in the Solid South that no Democratic candidate since the Civil War had ever come close to losing. He was overwhelmed by Hoover at the polls, receiving 40.8 per cent of the total popular vote as compared to Hoover's 58.1 per cent. He had only eighty-seven electoral votes to Hoover's 444, and in this respect no Democrat since the days of Jackson had fared so badly.

Although historians and political scientists have been careful in their generalizations about the role of religion in the outcome of the 1928 campaign, glib conclusions have been drawn in popular legend, and even among the educated public. Only recently William E. Bohn, writing in the *New Leader*, said of Smith: "He was defeated for the worst of reasons—because he was a Catholic." Absurd as it is, this notion has been too seldom challenged in public discussion. A little thoughtful attention to the history of the 1920's will convince almost any student that there was not a Democrat alive, Protestant or Catholic, who could have beaten Hoover in 1928.

The overwhelming character of Hoover's victory should itself suggest to us that the religious issue may not have been decisive. If the election had been very close in a number of

decisive states, it might be easier to believe that the religious
issue had tipped the balance and given the victory to Hoover.
In fact, so far as the electoral vote is concerned, we know only
that religious bias swung the votes of Florida and Texas and
four normally or invariably Democratic states of the upper
South into Hoover's column. But if Smith had won the electoral votes of all these states, he would still have been very far
from winning. Even if he had then also added the few Northern states in which he ran reasonably well (that is, where he had
forty-five per cent or more of the major-party vote), his electoral vote would still have been only half as large as Hoover's.

My contention is not that the religious issue was unimportant in the campaign, but that it worked both ways. The prime
fallacy in the popular view of the 1928 election lies in notic-
ing only what Smith lost from the religious issue and ignoring
what he may have gained. Of course the number of voters who
were decisively influenced by the religious issue is something
that eludes exact measurement. But it is vital to remember that
there are two such imponderables to be considered: not only
the number of voters who voted *against* Smith but also the
number who voted *for* him because of his religion. Smith's
Catholicism, a grave liability in some areas, was a great asset in
others. He made about as good a showing as could have been
expected from any Democrat that year. Taken by itself, his religion proves nothing conclusively about the effect of Catholic
adherence on a future Presidential candidacy.

Perhaps the most helpful way of isolating the significance of
the religious issue in 1928 and chopping it down to size would
be to imagine the difficulties the Democratic nominee would
have had to face that year if he had been a Protestant.

Above all, the Democrats were confronted with the overwhelming fact of prosperity. After seven years of Republican
control, the golden glow was glowing more brightly than ever
before. The business index was approaching its 1929 peak at
the time the election took place, and the number of unemployed, though growing considerably, was only a little more
than three per cent of the total labor force. In the history of
the Presidency since 1892, no incumbent party has been turned
out of power without the jarring effect of a depression, a war,
or—as in 1912—a party split. Polls under Roosevelt, Truman,
and Eisenhower have shown that the popularity of a President

in peacetime tends to fluctuate along with the business cycle. In the autumn of 1928 the business cycle was voting Republican.

A second consideration working against the Democrats—one easily forgotten by Americans who have come to political maturity after 1930—was the immense prestige of Herbert Hoover. The dour, ultraconservative image of Mr. Hoover that is called up in the minds of his critics in both parties today was not the conventional image before the Great Depression. A successful relief administrator during the First World War, Hoover had won universal acclaim as an effective humanitarian. John Maynard Keynes had written of him that he was "the only man who emerged from the ordeal of Paris with an enhanced reputation." Both parties had hoped to have him in their ranks in 1920, much as both would have welcomed Eisenhower in 1948. It is one of the amusing ironies of our history that Franklin D. Roosevelt had hoped to promote him for the Presidency in 1920. "He is certainly a wonder," F.D.R. wrote in January of that year, "and I wish we could make him President of the United States. There could not be a better one."

As Secretary of Commerce, Hoover was one of the Cabinet members who survived the disaster of the Harding administration with a reputation largely untainted and undimmed. Even the liberals, though disappointed by his attitudes on several public questions, still kept an open mind about him, and some thought of him as one of the more progressive leaders of his party. Hoover's record inspired confidence that he would be an excellent custodian of prosperity. He took over the Republican standard from Coolidge with what appeared to be rosy prospects.

A third and strangely unremembered aspect of the 1928 candidacy was the hopeless condition of the Democratic Party when Smith took it over. Since the days of Bryan and McKinley the Democratic Party had been almost a permanent minority party. Between 1896 and 1908, no Democratic Presidential candidate had won more than 45.9 per cent of the total popular vote, and Woodrow Wilson's election in 1912 had been possible only because of the Republican split between Taft and Theodore Roosevelt. Elected as a minority President in 1912, with 41.8 per cent of the popular vote, Wilson was very narrowly re-elected in 1916, partly on the strength of his progressive achievements, and partly because of his success thus far in staying out of the war. Our entry into the war, the unpopularity of the peace, and the sweeping reaction against Wilson and all those associated with him left the postwar Democratic Party in ruins. As measured by the popular vote, the victory recorded by Harding over Cox in 1920 was the most decisive victory ever scored by a Presidential candidate.

Already deprived of the allegiance of almost two-thirds of the voting public in 1920, the Democrats themselves reduced their party to a shambles in 1924. Here the religious issue played a major part, but one that cannot be disentangled from related issues. The Democrats came to their 1924 convention sharply divided between the rural, dry, Protestant anti-Tammany contingent supporting Wilson's son-in-law William G. McAdoo and the urban, immigrant, Catholic, wet contingent supporting Smith. They wrangled furiously over a resolution condemning the Ku Klux Klan, and in the end narrowly failed to adopt it. The Smith and McAdoo forces fell into such an interminable Donnybrook that it became clear that the nomination would be worthless to the man who got it. John W. Davis, who was finally settled upon at the 103rd ballot by an exhausted mob of delegates, was unable in his campaign to exploit effectively even the ghastly scandals of the Harding administration. The support of most liberals that year went to Robert M. La Follette, who polled 4,892,000 votes on an independent ticket. Davis polled only 8,385,000, against Coolidge's 15,718,000.

Although the Democrats still held a respectable contingent in Congress, it seemed that for all practical purposes the two-party system had ceased to function at the level of Presidential politics. The outcome of the mid-term Congressional elections of 1926 confirmed the general impression that the country was overwhelmingly Republican. Normally, the party in power expects to lose a substantial number of seats in these off-year elections. In the five mid-term elections from 1906 to 1922, for instance, the average loss had been sixty seats. In 1926 the Republicans lost only ten seats. In the summer of the following year F.D.R. confided to Josephus Daniels that he thought no Democrat could win in 1928 if "the present undoubted general prosperity continues."

Roosevelt's view was shared by most informed observers. Frank R. Kent, the veteran journalist and historian of the Democratic Party, pointing out that it was "without unity, intelligence, or courage . . . without leaders, without an issue or policy or program," had stated in 1926 that "no one capable of clear political judgment now believes it can be vitalized sufficiently to put up a formidable fight in the next Presidential campaign unless a political miracle occurs." Walter Lippmann observed that the Republicans could go into any campaign "knowing that normally there are enough Republicans to win. They do not have to convert anybody, but merely to prevent about ten per cent of their supporters from backsliding." In 1927 Lippmann thought (quite rightly) that Smith, though a losing candidate, would be the best the Democrats could find, and that "the best way for the Democrats to look at 1928 is to look beyond to 1932." After Smith's nomination, Lippmann remarked that the New Yorker had inherited nothing more than a party label, a small core of electoral votes, "two warring factions bound together by no common ideas," and a party "as nearly bankrupt intellectually as it is possible to be." Smith's task, he said, "is to re-create the Democratic party."

An anonymous "Democrat" writing in the *Century* magazine pointed out that practically every commentator who had written on the subject started from the premise that the Donkey was sick. The Democrats, he said, "know perfectly well that the Donkey can not win," and were thinking only of finding a Presidential candidate who could help their local tickets. He advised that the party give up altogether the goal of winning the Presidency and concentrate for the moment on capturing Congress, where it still had at least a chance. This was the situation that any Democratic nominee had to cope with in 1928.

Finally, it should be remembered that in addition to their other handicaps the Democrats had no good issue. The tariff bores most voters, especially during prosperity. Prohibition did not bore them, and its failure was a usable issue in some areas, but a firm wet stand still seemed likely to lose more votes than it would gain. There were, of course, pockets of economic discontent. The most important of these was among farmers. Unfortunately, the most outspoken defenders of the farmers' interests outside the South were chiefly Republican insurgents in Congress who (with the exception of George W. Norris) were not bolting their party in a winning year.

A Midwestern Democrat might have done better than Smith in the farm areas, but it would have been difficult for any Eastern city Democrat to capitalize on the farm problem. F.D.R. had remarked in 1927 that he did not believe the Western farmers would vote Democratic "in sufficient numbers [for a Democratic victory] even if they are starving." Here his sectional and urban background was quite as much a handicap for Smith as his religion. It was difficult to persuade farmers that the man from the sidewalks of New York understood or felt deeply about their problems. Cartoons of Smith in his brown derby and a gaudy tie peering over a farm fence were more formidable than anything the New Yorker could say on the farm problem. (This was a handicap which F.D.R. was able to overcome four years later, not merely because his upstate residence and his tree farm helped establish the image of a rural squire, but also because he had spent years traveling and cultivating political friendships in the agricultural states.)

If we suppose, then, that a Protestant had been nominated by the Democrats in 1928, what could his supporters realistically have expected? They might have hoped that, aside from helping some local candidacies, he could do three things: hold the minimal areas of Democratic strength, exploit residual areas of discontent to extend Democratic influence, and finally wage his campaign in such spirit and with such effectiveness as to restore the unity of the party and strengthen its morale for future campaigns. Smith did not, of course, succeed in the first of these, since he lost states in the Solid South. His failure here was what showed up on the electoral charts. Relatively unnoticed (though not unnoticed by Smith himself) was that he far exceeded what might have been expected on the second of these objectives, and that he did extremely well on the third.

Smith's showing is impressive when compared with that of his two postwar predecessors. The Democratic Presidential vote, which had been 9,128,000 for Cox and had sunk to 8,385,000 for Davis, was raised by Smith to 15,016,000. Cox had had only 34.1 per cent of the popular vote, Davis 28.8 per cent. After these two disastrous campaigns, the "Happy

Warrior," in restoring his party's percentage to 40.8 per cent, had at least brought it to within hailing distance of the "normal" Democratic minority vote of the prewar years. The fact that he outdistanced his two predecessors by this much should arouse our curiosity about the sources of his gains.

Both 1928 candidates were immensely successful in overcoming voter apathy and bringing the public out to the polls. In 1924 only 51 per cent of the eligible voters had turned out: in 1928 it was 67.5 per cent—a striking show of interest for a year of prosperity. If we compare Smith with his Democratic predecessor and Hoover with his Republican predecessor, we find that the Democratic vote rose by 6,631,000 from Davis to Smith and the Republican vote rose by 5,673,000 from Coolidge to Hoover. Smith thus gained almost a million more votes for his party than Hoover did. He gained seventy-six per cent over Davis's vote and sixty-four per cent over Cox's. By comparison, Hoover gained thirty-six per cent on Coolidge and thirty-two per cent on Harding.

If Smith's religion had hurt him as badly on a nation-wide scale as we are expected to believe, it seems incredible that he should thus have outgained Hoover. In broad outline, what happened seems reasonably clear. There was a Catholic vote as well as a Protestant vote. (Neither, of course, can be isolated and measured with finality, because they were parts of a Catholic-wet-immigrant complex and a Protestant-dry-nativist complex.) Even though the country was two-thirds Protestant, Catholic voters were animated in equal or greater numbers to turn out and vote. Many of them were from the immigrant stocks that had poured into the country by the millions before the First World War, and among them there were large numbers of new citizens who had never before been sufficiently excited by unfamiliar American domestic issues to bring them out to the polls. The number of previously unactivated Smith voters seems to have been much larger than the number of unactivated Hoover voters. But the distribution of the newly activated Protestant-dry voters and Catholic-wet voters was such that Smith lost some Southern votes in the electoral college. This, together with the overwhelming nature of the returns, obscured what he did achieve.

Not the least of Smith's achievements was to unify and re-mold his party. In the recent past the Democratic Party, under the leadership of men like Bryan, Wilson, and Cox, had been based mainly upon strength in the agrarian South and West. The Republican Party, as measured by the distribution of urban seats in Congress and popular votes in Presidential campaigns, had been the dominant metropolitan party. Even in his losing campaign, however, Smith turned the normally huge Republican pluralities in the twelve largest cities into a slender Democratic plurality. He brought into the voting stream of the Democratic Party ethnic groups that had never taken part in politics and others that had been mainly Republican. He extricated his party from its past dependence on agrarian interests and made it known to the great urban populations. He lost a campaign that had to be lost, but in such a way as to restore his party as an effective opposition and to pave the way for the victories of F.D.R. While he had to pay a political price for his religion, it must also be counted among the personal characteristics that made these achievements possible.

1960

Darwinism and Western Thought

HENRY ADAMS, who, like some of his contemporaries, at times confused the idea of evolution with the idea of progress, once suggested that he had a simple disproof of evolution—just a look at the history of the American Presidency from Washington to Grant. We are less likely than Adams' generation to be optimistic about progress, more likely to agree with his pessimism. Someone has appropriately remarked that whereas a hundred years ago we worried about the survival of the fittest, we now worry about the survival of anyone. In some ways it is this grim predicament that causes us to look back with curiosity to see what has been made of evolution in social thinking. I think I should warn you before I get into the substance of my lecture that it marches off in two different directions. The first half of it is devoted to telling what Darwin's generation and the generation that immediately followed him made of his ideas in social theory and why we have good reason to think that they were almost entirely wrong on almost all counts. The second half will attempt to suggest to you that we should not overstress the business of blaming their failures for our present problems.

At any rate, very soon after the publication of *Origin of Species* in 1859, Darwinism acquired such an importance in the intellectual world that every serious thinker felt obliged to reckon with its implications, and such prestige that every ideologist wanted to claim it and make use of it to strengthen his pre-existing ideas. The social thinkers of the late nineteenth century had a powerful impulse to unify knowledge. Their thought was usually aimed at synthesis, at the formation of a grand system in which all knowledge would be comprehended. As early as 1848, Comte declared in his first sentence of *A General View of Positivism* that ". . . the object of all true philosophy is to frame a system which shall comprehend human life under every aspect, social as well as individual." This drive toward synthesis thus predated Darwin's work, but it was strengthened by the sweeping implications of evolutionism. To a significant degree, therefore, social speculation, and what one might call a certain kind of intellectual propaganda, between 1859 and the end of the century, took its course along a path which, it was believed, would finally lead to a completed system of thought in which society would be understood as a segment of nature and social evolution would be understood as an extension of biological evolution. I need hardly make a secret at the outset of my conviction that this path proved in the end to be a blind alley. Many of the social Darwinian thinkers of the late nineteenth century lived long enough to see their hopes disappointed. Their efforts at synthesis were abandoned if not repudiated by their successors. We have ceased in most cases to study them. We no longer honor them. Of course, we enjoy the luxury of hindsight over this episode in modern thought, and we have the great advantage over its contemporaries of knowing, or thinking we know, where it led; but we ought not to be too condescending to the thinkers of the last half of the nineteenth century who felt it necessary to explore the social Darwinian path. The great insights of Darwin had been set before them in all their grandeur and promise. It would have been strange if these thinkers had not been tempted to extract from such insights every possible bit of illumination for the social as well as the natural world. Believing as they did in the unity of knowledge, it would have been remarkable if they had not tried to build upon the most striking idea of contemporary science a unified system of thought.

The thinkers of the late nineteenth century, like thinkers of other eras, were engaged not simply in the pursuit of truth but also in a contest over social and political ideals. The French Revolution had shattered the pattern of the older Europe. The development of industrialism, democracy, and nationalism had given rise to a variety of new competing interests and ideas. The middle classes were asserting themselves against the spokesmen of the old order, and behind the middle classes— peering, as it were, ominously over their shoulders—were aggressive new spokesmen of the proletariat.

While some men from the older nations were establishing the authority and carrying the trade of Europe to far corners of the globe, other men were creating new nations on the European Continent. In 1831, when Darwin was waiting in Plymouth to set out on the momentous voyage of the "Beagle," Parliament was agitated over the Reform Bill, and mob violence broke out in Bristol. During the next few years, while Darwin was sailing around the world, Parliament was trying to cope with the realities of industrialism by passing a new factory act and a new Poor Law. While Darwin was at work on *The Structure and Distribution of Coral Reefs*, which appeared in 1842, England was being rocked by the Chartists' agitations. In 1848, when he had among his papers a completed but unpublished first sketch of the theory of natural selection and was working on the first volume of his *Cirripedia*, the Continent was shaken by the liberal revolution, and Marx and Engels published the *Communist Manifesto*. The year 1859, when *Origin of Species* was published, was also the year of Marx's *Critique of Political Economy*, whose preface brilliantly spelled out the materialist interpretation of history and Marx's own scheme of social evolution. It was also the year of Samuel Smiles's *Self-Help*, a sacred text of competitive capitalism, and of John Stuart Mill's *Essay on Liberty*. In 1871, the year of *The Descent of Man*, the Franco-Prussian War ended, and the German Empire was established. In 1882, the year of Darwin's death, the British Fleet bombarded Alexandria. By that time the nations of Europe had gone far on their way toward the partition of the remaining uncolonized portions of the world.

Darwinism appeared, then, at a time when conservatives were looking for fresh and more authoritative answers to the challenge of democracy and liberalism, when spokesmen of private capitalism were trying to resist the encroachments of the national state, when prophets of nationalism were seeking justifications for national strife, and when imperialists were advocating and justifying expansion. The ideas of evolution and natural selection could thus never develop in a social vacuum but had to be absorbed into Western thought in the midst of arguments over competition and collectivism, laissez faire and state control, democracy and liberty, nationalism and imperialism.

A brief reminder of the main elements in Darwin's theory of natural selection will help us to see how each of these elements was translated into social terms. First, Darwin postulated, as Malthus and Spencer had done before him, that within each species more organisms are constantly generated than can be nourished and supported by their environment. Second, because of the rapid rate at which living forms increase, there takes place a constant struggle for existence, a constant competition for food and other means of survival. Third, some variation of physical type always occurs within a species. Not all organisms are equally equipped for survival. Those whose variations are better adapted to the environment in which they must live are the ones that survive and reproduce themselves. Fourth, the offspring of these survivors inherit their favorable variations. Finally, the accumulation of such small favorable variations over a very long period of time results in the emergence of new species.

Now the key terms in this scheme of thought are "struggle," "survival," "variation," "inheritance," "adaptation," and "environment." When the ideologues of social Darwinism set to work on this scheme, they tried to translate Darwin's main categories into social categories. The struggle for existence became economic competition or, perhaps, war. Survival became economic success or military predominance. The Darwinian emphasis on the inheritance of variations of unequal value in survival was taken as further evidence of the social value of human inequality, whether it be inequality between individuals or between races. Adaptation to environment was elevated to a social as well as a biological value. To adapt was to be superior, and since one adapts, sociologically, to a society, many thinkers identified society with the environment. The whole scheme of development was taken by many thinkers to be a promising analogue of social progress, and many concluded that the mechanisms of natural selection were the chief, or even the only, mechanisms of human progress. Even the conception of geological periods of time, which Darwin believed necessary to bring about new species, was appropriated by some social philosophers. Long periods of time would be necessary to bring about social change, they argued, just as it took eons for the species to develop into the multiple varieties on the earth and to produce the highest forms of animal life. Therefore, all schemes for hasty social reform flew in the face of nature.

The trouble was not that it was difficult to construct such analogies between nature and society but that it was all too easy. The thinkers of the last four decades of the nineteenth

century flung themselves into a Darwinian free-for-all. But
the more speculative elaborations of social evolution (as they
called it) they were able to conceive, the clearer it became that
the precise implications of Darwinism for society were not a
matter upon which men could readily agree. It was easy, for
instance, to see the life of men in society as a constant struggle,
but it was not so easy to interpret the meaning of the struggle. Which, in fact, were the struggling units? Individual men,
groups, business firms, tribes or races, nation-states? It made
a great deal of difference how this question was answered. A
social theory built upon the struggle of individuals would in
practice point to one direction. A social theory based upon
a struggle of groups might point to opposite conclusions. The
struggle of individuals seemed analogous at many points to
economic competition. That of tribes or races seemed analogous to war; but, many writers argued, if war is the true equivalent of the struggle for existence in nature, then solidarity
among the individuals in the warring tribes or nations is necessary for the survival of the group. Yet if solidarity within a
society is the important element in survival, how could one
sanction the principle of struggle among individuals that
would destroy solidarity? Understandably, a whole generation
was thrown into confusion by such problems. Some thinkers,
notably Herbert Spencer, compounded the confusion by trying to have it both ways. In his individualist mood he was all
for competition and the devil take the hindmost. At the same
time he adhered to an organismic theory of the state which
hardly seemed consistent with his individualism. Karl Marx
and his followers complicated matters by arguing that the real
struggle was one between classes. Marx thought that, as he
expressed it, Darwin gave him a basis in natural science for the
class struggle in history. Later social scientists concluded that
the important struggle to take account of was not among individuals or nations but among institutions, habits, and types of
character. But this takes us a long way from Darwin.

Even the ideal of a science of society was affected in an ironic
way. The attempt to translate natural selection into social terms,
oddly enough, did not lead to an era of "social science." That
is to say, it did not bring about the kind of careful, fact-minded
observation, classification, and laborious study and elaborate

notation of endless minute details that we associate with the work of Darwin and the other great naturalists of his era. Darwin gave the world a theoretical scheme which, though revolutionary, was essentially simple; he pulled a light freight of ideas with a powerful engine of fact. He permitted himself a few major theoretical suggestions. The social Darwinian thinkers launched upon an orgy of speculation. Darwin accumulated an elaborate mass of data; his followers usually worked with occasional illustrations, partial clues, and fragmentary observations. He practiced science; they were so devoted to preaching it that they had little time for its practice. Perhaps there is a clue in this to the character of much positivistic thinking. To revere science is not to be scientific. In fact, reverence sometimes gets in the way of science.

Two basic and mutually antagonistic views and uses, I have suggested, were made of Darwinism. First, Darwinism was used in the service of conservatism, industrial capitalism, and laissez faire. This kind of thinking, propagated by Herbert Spencer in England and by William Graham Sumner in the United States, was largely an Anglo-American phenomenon. The development of the Continental economies was such that laissez faire never had such popularity. At any rate, social Darwinism flourished from the 1860's until about the end of the century, when it ceased to be fashionable at the level of serious thinking and passed into the limbo of stale popular clichés. In the 1880's, William Graham Sumner was writing a passage like this: "The millionaires are a product of natural selection, acting on the whole body of men to pick out those who can meet the requirement of certain work to be done. It is because they are thus selected that wealth, both their own and that entrusted to them, aggregates under their hands. They may fairly be regarded as the naturally selected agents of society for certain work." I have other such passages but I will spare you. At the time Sumner wrote these lines, what he said was still acceptable to many thinkers as serious social thought, but a whole generation of intellectual critics and of social reformers hammered away at these notions until the hopeless simplicity as well as the smugness of such utterances became all too evident to reflective men. It is of course true that the high-brow sociology of one generation may become the low-brow sociology of the next. When Robert and Helen Lynd made their second famous investigation of Middletown in the 1930's, they found that individualist social Darwinism had survived as folklore. "You can't make the world all planned and soft," they were told by a Middletown businessman. "The strongest and best survive —that's the law of nature after all—always has been and always will be." I hasten to say that I realize that some serious thinkers still advocate thoroughgoing laissez faire. I have not forgotten the ideas of Hayek, von Mises, Herbert Simon, Milton Friedman, and others who are contemporaries. But such exponents of laissez faire today are the best proof of the obsoleteness of the social Darwinian arguments, for these men disdain to use such arguments. They, too, recognize almost as fully as any advocate of the welfare state that the synthetic philosophies of the social-Darwinian era have not held up. Even Herbert Spencer, the precursor and archangel of the social Darwinian revelation, had sadly admitted it near the close of his lifetime. In his *Principles of Ethics*, published in 1893, he wrote: "The doctrine of evolution has not furnished guidance to the extent I had hoped. Most of the conclusions, drawn empirically, are such as right feelings, enlightened by cultivated intelligence, have already sufficed to establish."

The second phase of social Darwinism was the racist-military phase. This was the main form in which Darwinism was made into a social doctrine on the Continent, though it had influential Anglo-American spokesmen as well. In the years after 1870, as nationalism in Europe passed from an urge toward political and cultural liberation to a climate of mutual hatred, fear, and frustration, and as the imperial colonization of the world once again accelerated, the Darwinian vision of the warfare of nature seemed to become increasingly germane to the contemporary world. Army and navy officers, spokesmen of nationalism and imperialism, could easily refurbish and strengthen their old arguments with new Darwinian metaphors. A new literature of group struggle arose. The argument for national or racial superiority, already widely believed, now seemed to have a natural sanction.

Perhaps, the first of the imperial Darwinians was the English economist, Walter Bagehot, who discussed the pattern of national progress in his *Physics and Politics* in 1872, in which he observed that those nations which are strongest tend to prevail and in certain marked peculiarities the strongest are the best. The historian J. A. Froude saw the victory of Protestant England over Catholic Spain and the domination of England over Ireland as exemplifications of the principle and concluded that the superior part has a natural right to govern; the inferior part has a right to be governed. Nicholas Danilevsky, a Russian pan-Slavist, who later wrote a critical book on Darwinism, found that each group of people or race is like a species. It seems hardly necessary to add that he found the Slavs the superior race.

Social Darwinian interpretations became prominent after the Franco-Prussian War among both victor and vanquished. Even Ernest Renan referred to war in 1871 as "one of the conditions of progress, the cut of the whip which prevents a country from going to sleep."

Ludwig Gumplowicz, a Polish professor of law, began to elaborate a sociological theory based upon a series of unremitting struggles between racial groups, national states, and social classes. Gustav Ratzenhofer, an Austrian field marshal, elaborated a theory of society based upon self-assertion and the mutual hostility of all men. This hostility, he argued, could be submerged only in war or great projects of co-operative labor. Culture and commerce weaken the social structure but struggle and war consolidate it. "War," wrote the victorious Marshal von Moltke, "is an element of the order of the world established by God. Without war the world would stagnate and lose itself in materialism."

In the United States, John Fiske, James K. Hosmer, Albert J. Beveridge, and Josiah Strong predicted the worldwide supremacy of the Anglo-Saxon peoples. John W. Burgess declared that the Teutonic nations were best fitted to exercise the political leadership of the world. Brooks Adams warned that the nations were engaged in a war to the death. And Theodore Roosevelt predicted that if the American people ceased to live the strenuous life and lost what he called the great fighting masterful virtues, "then the bolder and stronger peoples will pass us by and win for themselves the domination of the world." And so it went.

The cruder uses of Darwinism by individualists, racists, and nationalists were hardly unchallenged. Time does not permit the full recounting of the successive poundings to which these notions were subjected from 1870 onward. Having attempted this task for our own climate of opinion in my book on *Social Darwinism in American Thought*, I can testify that tracing the decline of these ideas leads one over a long and tortuous path of argumentation. It may be enough now to say that the counterattack came from a great many sources—reformers; Socialists, Christian and Marxian; anti-imperialists—and was urged from a variety of intellectual perspectives. Lester Frank Ward and his followers in American sociology, British Fabians, economists like Thorstein Veblen, the pragmatic school in American philosophy, exponents of national economics and the welfare state in all countries, Continental writers like Prince Peter Kropotkin and Jacques Novicow—all these added their blows. Over the years these opponents of social Darwinism picked away at it so tellingly that we need hardly wonder at its decline. They pointed out—among them T. H. Huxley—that the fundamental terms of the analogy made no sense, because the struggle that takes place among men in society is not exactly a struggle for existence. In natural selection, less fit organisms do not procreate because they do not survive to maturity. In society, as the eugenists began soon enough gloomily to warn, the so-called unfit classes do survive long enough to procreate and in greater numbers than the so-called fit, and there arose a whole school of thought based upon anxiety over the failure of Vassar girls to have more than 1.6 children per person. But the whole use of biological definitions of fitness in a social setting was soon singled out as preposterous. Perhaps someone was struck by the irony that dyspeptic, neurotic, and even suicidal intellectuals should be preaching the survival of the strong and the hardy.

Once it was accepted that physical characteristics were meaningless for social survival, it became clear that a whole new set of social criteria must be employed. When men began to consider new criteria, the door was open to a reconsideration of the meaningfulness of "nature red in tooth and claw" for social behavior, and to the suggestion—as Lester Ward did suggest—that fitness to survive is something different from real superiority. Ward also stressed the inefficiency of nature in the raw as compared with human techniques of plant and animal culture. It was easy to show that nature was wasteful of organisms, that it brought millions into existence while only hundreds survived, and that human intelligence moved even toward biological goals, not to speak of social ones, in a more direct and economical way. Once it was possible to see that artificial processes are actually superior to natural ones, it was also possible to abandon the absurd worship of nature upon which the mystique of social Darwinism rested. Other critics, like John Fiske in the United States and Henry Drummond in Great Britain, stressed the survival value in human affairs of the non-ferocious qualities, of altruism and love, especially as manifested in the human family, and in this they had a predecessor in Darwin.

But the most satisfactory general critique of social Darwinism, in my opinion, was made by the American pragmatists, who themselves started from a Darwinian standpoint in the sense that they were concerned among other things with the role of mind in survival. The social Darwinians had originated the idea that "society equals environment"; that is to say, what the natural environment is to plants and animals, society is to the human species. When one considers animal life there is little use in questioning the environment as a whole. True, animals modify their environment in small ways—beavers, for instance—and within limits change it when they migrate. But in the subhuman world of nature, the environment is an absolute; it is there, and the creature must adapt. What the pragmatists realized most effectively is that the moment human consciousness appears on the scene, with its capacity for formulating goals and manipulating both the natural and the social environment, the whole game is played differently. Mind, consciousness, is not merely passive or adaptive. When mind begins to change environment, the conditions of biological evolution are not only superseded, they are in a sense reversed. As William James put it:

> The knower is an actor, and a coefficient of the truth on one side, whilst on the other he registers the truth which he helps to create. Mental interests, hypotheses, postulates, so far as they are bases for human action—action which to a great extent transforms the world—help to *make* the truth which they declare. In other words, there belongs to mind, from its birth upward, a spontaneity, a vote. It is in the game and not a mere

looker-on, and its judgments of the *should be*, its ideals, cannot
be peeled off from the body of the cogitandum as if they were
excrescences, or meant, at most, survival.

So when human consciousness operates, survival ceases to be
the all-pervasive and controlling goal of existence and becomes
instead merely an assumption upon which may be based the
formulation of other more complex, more interesting, more
human, and more humane goals. The crude, monistic, positivistic assumption of a continuity of principle between nature and society is thus ruined, and we are free to erect such
understanding of society as we are capable of achieving, on
independent sociological and historical principles. Biology as
a foundation for sociology is in the dust bin; we are free to
realize, even though our academic psychology has been slow
to realize it, that biology will not even take us very far as a
foundation for psychology.

Within thirty years of *The Descent of Man* it was hardly possible for a serious and informed thinker to adhere to the old
hope of a monistic synthesis of all the sciences. Now it was
the qualitative differences between the operative principles of
society and those of nature that were taking the foreground.

Most of us, then, think of social Darwinism as a more or
less closed episode in intellectual history, but there is less
agreement about its meaning. There are two widespread and
intimately related theses on the subject from which I should
like to enter a dissent. I propose to call them the intellectualist fallacy and the obscurantist fallacy. Those who commit
the intellectualist fallacy assume—and indeed at times seem
flatly to assert—that we are ruled by ideas and by little else.
Placing this heavy burden of responsibility upon ideas, they
say that the whole worship of force, so prominent in Europe
between 1870 and 1914, should be laid at the door of the Darwinian, positivistic, mechanistic complex of ideas; and there
was a time, indeed, about fifteen years ago when these ideas
by extension were even made responsible in very great part for
the evils of the two world wars of the twentieth century and
of totalitarianism. The effect of the intellectualist fallacy is to
overplay the influence of such ideas by stripping them out of
the social context in which they were formed and interpreted.

The effect of the obscurantist fallacy is to suggest that the bad influence of the social Darwinian ideas is attributable to the fact that they were naturalistic ideas. They undermine social morality, it is held, because they undermine religious and supernatural sanctions for behavior, leaving no canons but those of nature red in tooth and claw. We can see the intellectualist fallacy in operation when the publishers of the revised 1958 edition of Jacques Barzun's *Darwin, Marx, Wagner* tell us on the jacket that the triumphs of the late nineteenth-century age of materialism "have according to Professor Barzun been *the source* of the 20th century's characteristic problems." Professor Barzun himself is much more careful. In fact, he tells us only that the ideas and methods of materialistic mechanism have been *a* source of real woe in our day. However, his discussion of the issue is such as to make his editors' view of his analysis a reasonable one, and it is certainly one that is commonly made. (I feel a little sensitive about the intellectualist fallacy because, although I don't think I committed it in so many words in my book on social Darwinism, I believe the effect of the book was perhaps to encourage it.) Another writer, John Hallowell, tells us that positivism, by which he means what I mean by social Darwinism, was as important as any other single factor in the decline of liberalism and the victory of fascism. Other writers compound the intellectualist fallacy with a note of obscurantism. "It was boys schooled by the generation of materialism," Carleton J. H. Hayes tells us at the close of his book on *A Generation of Materialism, 1871 to 1900*, "who would grow up to fight the World War and it was some of their sons who would follow supermen into the totalitarian state and into totalitarian war." If this were simply a statement about a chronological sequence of generations, it would be too obvious to be made. But it suggests that the materialist ideas of the generation of materialism were a distinct and special source of what the sons and grandsons of that generation endured. Yet I wonder if it would not be just as fair, and just as unfair, if in a book, say, on the generation from 1520 to 1550, to assert that its members were drunk on religious and theological dispute and that the persecutions of the late sixteenth century and the horrors of the Thirty Years' War must be attributed to the theology of the Reformation. Surely, the victims of the St. Bartholomew's Day massacre and the religious wars could not have found their fate any more pleasant because it was brought on by religious differences rather than by a naturalistic philosophy of struggle. Western man, with centuries of religious militancy and persecution behind him, did not need to stumble on a materialist philosophy to provide him for the first time with a rationale for violence or exploitation. Given the impulse to exploit or persecute, both materialist and non-materialist philosophies can be bent to serve the purpose.

I hope I may succeed in being clear about where the difference of opinion lies. I share the dislike of these writers whom I have quoted for the positivist mentality of the late nineteenth century. I agree that ideas do have effects in history, and I hasten to agree that the crude social Darwinian image of nature as a battlefield and of struggle as the only source of progress had bad effects in so far as it had any effect. I agree, finally, that this experience ought to warn us against simple monistic, mechanistic philosophies and against crude attempts to transfer scientific findings to social thought. My differences hang on these points: First, I object to the implicit assumption which is often made, though few writers seem to care explicitly to defend it, that ideas not merely influence but actually control history. I particularly object to this when it is assumed that influential social ideas develop solely or largely out of their own internal dynamic, more or less unaffected by the demands and the canons of the society from which they emerge. I insist that ideas, though they have consequences, must also be thought of as *being* consequences themselves. Otherwise, we may be in danger of reducing our inquiries into the problems of our time to an exercise in the history of ideas and thus of distracting ourselves from a necessary work of social criticism, for it is institutions as well as ideas that we must scrutinize.

Second, the cruder and more violent philosophies that grew up around Darwinism were not logically inevitable extensions of Darwin's theory or of naturalism, but became dominant notions in some circles because they suited some men's purposes. Alternative uses of the social significance of Darwinism were available to them, and I propose simply that these alternatives,

when they were rejected, were rejected not because of any intrinsic inferiority or lack of substance but rather because they
were less suited to the needs of certain social interests.

Finally, as one with a naturalist and secularist turn of mind, I
object to the imputation that the ill uses that were often made
of Darwinism in social thought could be made simply because
Darwinism gave rise to naturalistic and secularist views. I reject
the inference that there is a logically necessary connection between naturalistic thinking and the immense social mischief of
our time. Philosophies of struggle, violence, ruthless competition, and racism existed long before natural selection was formulated by Darwin. No one, I believe, cares to deny this, or to
assert that Darwinism originated such views. But we must go
back and look at some of the crassest assertions of these views
in pre-Darwinian days to remind ourselves how forceful, how
raw and "Darwinian" they were, in the absence of Darwin.
Carlyle may serve as a good case in point, for without benefit
of any clues to natural selection, he was preaching, before 1859,
all the worst implications of what we call social Darwinism.
When he wrote, "Man is created to fight; he is perhaps best of
all definable as a born soldier, his life a battle and a march under the right general," he was drawing upon religious as much
as natural imagery; and when he wrote concerning the Opium
War, "Our friends of China who guiltily refused to trade, had
we not to argue with them in cannon shot at last and convince
them that they ought to trade?", he was drawing all the practical conclusions of the imperial Darwinists well in advance of
their work. "After all," wrote Thomas Hughes in *Tom Brown's
School Days*, which was published the year before *The Origin
of Species*, "what would life be without fighting? From the cra-
dle to the grave fighting, rightly understood, is the business,
the real highest, honestest business, of every son of man. It
is no good for Quakers or any other body of men to uplift
their voices against fighting; human nature is too strong for
them; I am dead against crying peace when there is no peace."
It was Charles Kingsley, the apostle of muscular Christianity
and not of muscular Darwinism, who wrote: "You Malays and
Dyaks of the Sarawak, you are the enemies of Christ the prince
of peace, you are beasts, all the more dangerous because you
have a semi-human cunning. I will, like David, hate you with

a perfect hatred even as though you were my enemies. I will blast you out with grape and rockets, I will beat you as small as the dust before the wind." What need did such fellows have of the gods of natural selection when they had the God of the Old Testament?

To realize how antihumane racism could be before Darwinian racism was possible, we need only contemplate the ugly brutality of Carlyle's *Occasional Discourse on the Nigger Question*, written in 1849. Indeed, some of the coarsest formulations of racism were given us well before 1859, in America, by apologists for slavery, most of whom invoked Biblical texts and religious sanctions at a time when naturalistic sanctions were less authoritative.

But it will be said that the point is not that Darwinism originated such views or that they could not have existed without it, but simply that Darwinism strengthened them. And I have no desire to deny that Darwinism was used to strengthen them and give them a kind of philosophical form. But before Darwinism and poor Darwin are made to carry too heavy a freight of responsibility, we should ask *why* it was so used. Was it because the social Darwinian interpretations of natural selection were correct and intellectually irresistible, or was it because nineteenth-century society was so constituted that some of its spokesmen found a convenient way of manhandling and stretching Darwin's ideas to suit various purposes we cannot condone? Did people get out of Darwin an added and specious authority for things they were already doing and preaching; or did they begin to do and preach because Darwin, as it were, put them up to it? We should not permit ourselves to forget that people made out of Darwin what they did because they already were what they were when he came along.

I am constrained to argue the case that Darwinism was intrinsically a neutral instrument, capable of being used by both sides in a moral and social debate. Interpretations of Darwinism alternative to those of the ruthless school were offered, and I think it would be conceding too much to the social Darwinians to say that their arguments were superior to those of their opponents and critics. I trust I have given some reasons for my own view that they were in fact inferior. The onus for the unhappy uses of Darwinism should not, I think, rest primarily on

Darwin or Darwinism or naturalism, but should be shared, and
shared in much the greater part, by that raw, exploitive, aggressive, industrial society that both gave birth to Darwinism and
molded social Darwinism in its own image.

We can test the assumption that the uses of Darwinism were
decided more by the social environment in which it was interpreted than by its own internal logic by asking two questions.
Was Darwinism interpreted differently in different environments? Was it interpreted differently by men in the same
environment, but of different interests and preconceptions?
Of course it was. In the Anglo-American world, individualist
Darwinism became an intellectual force. On the Continent
it never had much effect. Karl Marx, presuming to speak for
the proletariat, saw Darwinism shedding one kind of light on
industrialism. Spencer, looking at it from the standpoint of
a middle-class English dissenter, saw another. Kropotkin, the
left-wing anarchist, saw in it lessons almost directly antithetical
to those drawn by William Graham Sumner, the right-wing
anarchist. One evolutionist, Sir Arthur Keith, said that, much
as he disliked war, he could conceive of no substitute that
would serve so well for what he called "the race health of humanity" and the building of stronger races. But another biologist, David Starr Jordan, found that war is dysgenic because it
draws the healthiest young men into armies and kills them off.
The militarist and race-struggle school concluded that conflict
and war were eternal laws of progress. Bagehot and Spencer
agreed that they had fostered progress in earlier periods of
history, but that this was no longer true. Others said that it
had never been true. Spencer and Lester Ward, who agreed
on almost nothing else, felt that optimistic conclusions could
not be drawn from evolution unless one believed in the inheritance of acquired characteristics. Others said that progress
went on even without such inheritance. Still other Darwinians, like Sumner, offered little hope for progress in any case.

Darwinism has been charged with responsibility for racism
and, by extension, for much of Nazi ideology. But Darwinism,
from the very beginning, could have been interpreted, and indeed by some was interpreted, in just the opposite way. As
Gertude Himmelfarb points out in her recent book *Darwin
and the Darwinian Revolution*, Darwinism, appearing at the

climax of the debate over Negro slavery in the American Civil War was first enlisted in that argument. The only difficulty, she observes, was that Darwin's ideas could be made to favor either side. The most obvious deduction was the antiracists' one, she thinks. The theory of evolution, by denying the separateness of varieties in species, also denied the separateness and thus the intrinsic inferiority of some races. When Asa Gray, the American naturalist, first read *Origin of Species*, he blanched at being made kin to the Hottentot. Some racists opposed the book because they couldn't bear the implication that the various races of man came from a common stock. Darwin himself believed that there are higher and lower races, and did not flinch from the conclusion that many of the lower races would, as he said, be eliminated. But just to keep the matter as complicated as in historical fact it was, Darwin was an ardent abolitionist, and abolition was indeed the only social issue of his time to which he paid any attention. As to fascist racism, there would be no point in saying that it did not take cues from Darwinism or from the positivist climate of ideas, since it took cues from everything. But its racism can hardly be laid at the door of an excessive piety for science, for scientifically, Nazi racism was a pure anachronism. It was formulated after there was hardly a naturalist or ethnologist left alive in the world who still believed in racial superiority and inferiority.

The formulation, indeed, of fascist ideology is a perfect proof case of the way in which the milieu shapes the ideas. In 1863, one could have argued with at least some show of plausibility that racism was a likely deduction from Darwinism. To hold the same in 1933 was preposterous. Yet probably more than any other thing it is the experience of totalitarianism that has colored our view during the last twenty years of the social Darwinian epoch, for in its racism and its emphasis on violence and struggle, fascism appears to have overtones of social Darwinism. We thought we heard familiar voices out of an earlier era when Mussolini told us: "Strife is the origin of all things; strife will always remain at the root of human nature like a supreme fatality." Or when Hitler told us: ". . . The stronger has to rule; only the born weakling can consider this as cruel. The fight for daily bread makes all those succumb who are weak, sickly, and less determined." Of course, there is a good deal of social Darwinism in this, but I have also seen totalitarian thought traced not only to social Darwinism and positivism but to Hegelianism and German Idealism generally, to pragmatism, romanticism, traditionalism, and irrationalism. The trouble with these efforts at reconstructing intellectual genealogy is that they are all entirely misleading precisely because they are all partially correct. Styles of thought that are so eclectic and have as many filiations as fascism can also be said to have no filiations. It will not do to single out of the whole disordered fascist mélange those aspects which have to do with social Darwinism alone.

We have come, perhaps a bit abruptly, to the end, and I must summarize what I believe to be a defensible perspective on the social applications of Darwinism. I think the whole attempt to apply Darwinian theories to social affairs was a mistake, that it was a mistake quite aside from any reservations that we might have about the adequacy of natural selection as an attempt to account for development. I believe the attempt failed not because it was done in the wrong way, but because the task was impossible in the first place. The principles and terms governing the natural world are not those that govern the life of man in society. I believe that man acquires knowledge of the ways of nature, not to follow them or subordinate himself to them, but to manipulate them and, in a sense, to surmount them. Natural science may help us in innumerable ways, but it cannot generate for us an adequate ethic or an adequate scheme of sociology, economics, or history. Moreover, I consider the search for absolutely universal principles or rules, or terms, by which our knowledge of nature and our theories of society can be wrought into some kind of comprehensive interlocking unity, fruitless. To achieve the unity of knowledge is not merely a chimerical goal in itself but one which, if taken seriously, may impede the pursuit of that partial knowledge in which it is always possible for us to engage fruitfully. At the same time, I cannot agree with some modern interpreters in laying an excessively heavy burden of responsibility for our ills upon the men who made this mistake in the closing decades of the nineteenth century. Still less can I accept the conclusion that since nineteenth-century positivism was wrong, we can become right by swinging to the opposite extreme and insisting that all naturalistic views of the world are inconsistent with the formulation of a humane and acceptable ethic. For if we recognize that the findings of science cannot in any case yield us an ethic, we may also recognize that the limitations and failures of science will not deprive us of an ethic, much less deprive us of our morals. Our good behavior, so far as we can control it, rests not upon inferences from science but upon the humane and rational interpretation of the world about us, to which science can contribute only in a humble and marginal way. It will be objected that to invoke such vague and fallible guides as humanity and rationality does not promise us conclusiveness or finality. And this is true; but it is precisely as a warning against the effort to be conclusive and final that the whole experience of the social Darwinian generation stands.

1962

The Revolution in Higher Education

IN DISCUSSING the revolution that took place in American higher education between 1870 and 1910, it is impossible to meet the expectations created by the currently fashionable set of mind, which demands that the cultural situation be portrayed as constantly in a state of decline. One is obliged to report that this era was one of impressive achievement. We take for granted, as elements in our cultural inheritance, the existence of universities and an academic profession. But before the Civil War the United States had neither, in any respectable degree. They were created within one generation, in a country that previously had not much more than a scattered brood of small colleges in various stages of inanition.

To assess this academic revolution, it is necessary first to look at the old college without sentimentality or illusion. Troubled as we are by our present sense of educational failure, we may be too ready to imagine the old college to have been far better than it was. We think of the impersonality of so much contemporary college instruction, and long for that log with Mark Hopkins at one end and a student at the other; we think of the disorders of the modern curriculum, and long for the old classical course; we contemplate the half-literate products of many modern colleges, and long for graduates reared on Horace, Demosthenes, Cicero, and Tacitus. We tend to forget that the college that offered its undergraduates President Hopkins (himself on some counts intellectually retrograde)[1] offered them otherwise all too little; that the great writers of antiquity were commonly taught as exercises in grammar; and that students were frequently bored into disorderly reaction against the picayune discipline and unimaginative pedagogy of the old regime.

If the graduate of the old-time college sometimes turned out to be a well-educated man it was only in small part because of the contents of the college curriculum itself. Obsolescent mathematics, a smattering of science, and poorly taught classics no doubt had their disciplinary values; but whatever the typical old-time college student may have learned of modern literatures, including English, of modern languages (except in some colleges a little French), or of history or political economy came to him either through informal and extracurricular sources or by virtue of some rare local accident. The status of history may serve to illustrate this curricular poverty. As late as 1884, even after leaders of the university movement had begun to overhaul the undergraduate colleges, Charles William Eliot pointed out that "the great majority of American colleges . . . make no requirements in history for admission, and have no teacher of history whatever."[2] Nor can it be imagined that this was the case only with the inferior colleges; Eliot remarked that Dartmouth had no teacher of history—not so much as a temporary instructor—and that Princeton had only one professor of history (who doubled in political science), as compared with three professors of Greek.

On occasion the old-time colleges were sentimentalized by their alumni; but rarely by their teachers or their presidents. Most of the serious literature of college reminiscence is a literature of complaint: the mordant criticisms of Harvard College in the 1850's that have been etched on the memories of countless readers by Henry Adams's *Education* were exaggerated and unfair; but they were no more than hyperbolic statements of what dozens of other graduates and many educators had to say of their schools. As to the educators themselves, one must of course remember that a large portion of the writing in their field has always been an expression of discontent; but when this allowance has been duly made, one is still impressed by the volume and the cogency of their criticisms. Outstanding pre–Civil War teachers and presidents—men like George Ticknor, Francis Wayland, Philip Lindsley, Henry P. Tappan, F. A. P. Barnard, and others—echo in their educational writings the reminiscent complaints of graduates and anticipate the tart critiques of later university-builders like Charles William Eliot, Andrew D. White, and Daniel Coit Gilman.

With the exception of a few so-called universities, feebly maintained by the states, the colleges of the old regime were creations of various religious denominations. Sectarian competition, compounded by local competition, had prevented the educational energies of the country from being concentrated in a limited number of institutions of adequate size and adequate sustenance. Instead, the country was dotted with tiny colleges, weakly founded; only one out of five created before the Civil War survived—it is an incredible rate of failure. Those that did survive were frequently too small to be educationally effective; they lacked complexity; they lacked variety. We are too much tempted to think of the old college as being represented by the larger, better, and more famous institutions like Harvard, Yale, and Dartmouth, that had, by the 1850's, faculties ranging from fifteen to twenty-five officers and student bodies of from three to four hundred. But much smaller and more obscure and inefficient schools with faculties of six or eight and student bodies of 50 to 100 are far more typical of the 200-odd colleges of 1860, many of them inferior in quality to the best academies. Sectarian competition kept such institutions small and inadequate; the indifference of parents to good instruction, so long as their sons could emerge with degrees, made it unnecessary for these schools to do better than totter along from year to year. "What has heretofore been the idea of an University with us?" asked Longfellow. "The answer is a simple one:—Two or three large brick buildings,—with a chapel, and a President to pray in it!"[3] This was in 1829; a generation later the situation was but slightly changed, except in a few fortunate institutions.

Diversity of performance in the old-time college makes it difficult to make a universally fair appraisal of its work. Of course there were, as there always are, exceptional teachers with a gift for arousing the minds of the young. The classical curriculum, competently taught, could develop the capacity for work, instill a feeling for rhetoric, and inspire passion for learning. A not inconsiderable number of learned men came out of the old colleges, among them the leaders and scholars of the postwar university movement itself. The undergraduate literary and debating societies, whose libraries were often better and always more accessible than the college libraries, made it possible for the self-education and the mutual education of the undergraduates, always one of the most fruitful aspects of college life, to be carried on to good effect. Sometimes the capstone course in moral philosophy, given to seniors by the college president, was a source of genuine intellectual illumination.

But in good part, the old-college classroom was a dreary place. The students were subjected to a curriculum which rarely gave them any choice of courses, hardly ever a choice of teachers. They were submitted to a teaching routine consisting almost entirely of tedious daily recitations, and governed in detail by disciplinary rules that were excessively demanding. Since their instructors were set over them as policemen,[4] outbursts of mutual hostility were a perennial motif. Term time was frequently punctuated by student riots, and putting the cow in the chapel was a standard college prank. In the atmosphere of tension and irritation created by rigid discipline and nagging boredom, the instructor who achieved an affectionate or inspiring relationship with his charges represented a triumph of personal kindliness and ingenuity over poor institutional arrangements.

It was neither gratifying nor particularly useful to go to college. Earlier, in the latter half of the eighteenth century, the American colleges, still few in number, had done a bit to modernize their curricula, to put education into step with science and the thought of the Enlightenment, and to surmount the limitations of sectarian control. Their achievements in educating the revolutionary generation had been considerable. But in the early decades of the nineteenth century, the excessive diffusion of the nation's educational resources and the tightening grip of the sects crippled the colleges' capacity for further advances. They became less and less related to the intellectual life of the country; or, after the rise of industrialism, to its vocational and practical life. To be sure, for those interested in the ministry a college degree was always of vocational value; and the accoutrements of a college education, not least the formality of the degree itself, continued to give cachet to anyone in the professions and to confer social prestige. But a college degree was not necessary for law or medicine, and most of the engineers in the country were trained at West Point. Some parents, resigned to the modest accomplishments of the colleges, took them cynically as inexpensive custodial institutions—for it must be conceded to the colleges that they charged even less for their services than they were worth. Francis Wayland, the president of Brown, remarked in 1842: "Parents have assured me that they were obliged to send their sons to college because they could not afford to bring them up in a good counting house."

Cheap though they were, the colleges had ceased by the time of the Civil War to attract students in proportion to the growth of the population. In 1826 one in 1,513 young men of college age went to college. By 1855 it was down to one in 1,689; by 1869 to one in 1,927. The colleges were falling behind the birth rate, and at an accelerating pace. "The sad fact stares us in the face," said Charles Kendall Adams, "that the training which has long been considered essential to finished scholarship has been losing ground from year to year in the favor of the people."[5] But even as he spoke, the university revolution was under way, and the educational scene was undergoing drastic transformation.

II

After years of what seemed to be fruitless agitation, the university era began abruptly. It is true that some preparation had been made in the 1850's, a decade notable for lively educational criticism and new plans; and that a few leading institutions, notably Yale and Harvard, had made prewar gains that brought them to a stage of development something like that of the smaller German universities. But nothing could have prepared observers of the educational scene for the sudden explosive change of the post–Civil War years. The years 1868 and 1869 stand out—the first for the opening of Cornell under Andrew D. White, the second for the election of Charles William Eliot to the presidency of Harvard. Seven years after Eliot's inauguration, instruction began at Johns Hopkins under the presidency of his friend Daniel Coit Gilman. These men led the university revolution, created its models, and set its tone; and while they were rapidly building modern universities and fostering advanced studies in the East, James Burrill Angell was working, though with less success, to carry the impetus of the university idea into the largest of the state universities at Michigan.

The first surge of reform, represented by these four men and institutions, was followed by others. Minnesota and Wisconsin made marked progress in the 1880's. Between 1889 and 1891, G. Stanley Hall, William Rainey Harper, and David Starr Jordan launched Clark, Chicago, and Stanford. Around the turn of the century Arthur Twining Hadley, Woodrow Wilson, and Nicholas Murray Butler, taking over Yale, Princeton, and Columbia, helped to bring these older institutions more fully into the swing of the university revolution.

Harvard, though not quite so innovative as Cornell or Johns Hopkins, was the leading institution of the university movement, partly because it brought the prestige that no newly founded school could bring. The achievements of Eliot were a measure of what a great administrator could do with adequate support. When Eliot became president, Harvard, consisting of the College, the Divinity, Law, Medical, Dental, and Scientific schools, had about a thousand students and sixty teachers. At the close of his reign in 1909 it had added the graduate schools of Arts and Sciences, Applied Science, and Business Administration, had some 4,000 students and about 600 teachers, and had increased its endowment from $2,500,000 to more than $20,000,000. Size is no measure of quality; but Harvard had also developed advanced study and had transformed and immensely improved undergraduate and professional studies— had grown, in short, from a small fledgling university to a great one. Other institutions, less daring, began to imitate her.[6]

No doubt the Civil War, by giving an impetus to science and technology, had something to do with quickening the university movement. In 1861 the legislature of Massachusetts chartered M.I.T., and the following year the Morrill Act made millions of acres available as a subsidy to state universities and agricultural and mechanical colleges. But it was mainly private funds, supplied on an unprecedented scale, that touched off the movement, and private institutions that showed the way. The work of sponsoring universities in which the states had failed and the sects had been no better than a hindrance, was at last taken over successfully by the postwar millionaires.

The contrast between the massive postwar donations and the poverty of the old college can hardly be overstated. When Princeton, for instance, had been revivified by her alumni in the middle 1830's, the largest single gift was $5,000, and the overall goal of this unprecedented drive was only $100,000. Williams was founded on $14,000, Amherst on $50,000. The largest single cash bequest received by Columbia before the Civil War was $20,000. With these figures one must compare

Ezra Cornell's $500,000 for his new university at Ithaca, which
was augmented to $2,500,000 in twenty years by the sale of
land scrip allotted to New York under the Morrill Act; Johns
Hopkins's $3,500,000; Vanderbilt's $1,000,000; Rockefeller's
$30,000,000 for Chicago; Stanford's $20,000,000; or the
endowment of over $20,000,000 that Harvard had built up
at the close of Eliot's regime. In the twenty years after 1878,
private donors gave at least $140,000,000 to all branches of
higher education.

When the rich began to give their money, the people began
to send their children, and the relative numerical decline of students before the year 1869 was at last reversed. Between 1870
and 1910, while the nation's population doubled, the number
of students enrolled in higher education nearly quintupled.
American parents were taking greater interest in sending their
sons to college, and were beginning to send their daughters.[7]
Graduate education, as well as coeducation, was entirely the
creation of this forty-year period: the first Ph.D. was granted
by Yale in 1861; total graduate enrollment rose from 198 students in 1871 to 2,382 in 1890 and 9,370 in 1910. The sources of
undergraduate recruitment also grew, as the number of public
high schools rose from about 1,000 in 1870 to 6,000 in 1900.
In 1898 there were five times as many pupils enrolled in secondary schools as there had been twenty years earlier.

The great universities were launched with generous minds as
well as generous purses. For decades farsighted educators had
pleaded with very little success to get the yoke of sectarianism
lifted from American higher education. Suddenly, within the
span of a few years, it was lifted; almost, it seemed, without
effort. In the main, the new donors, though far from impious
men, were content to let the work of inquiry go on untrammeled by sectarian restraints. They were prepared to give away
immense sums without interfering unduly with the manner
in which their money was spent. Abruptly, the paternalism
of the small college was abandoned, along with its sectarian
atmosphere.

The same generosity of mind was brought to bear upon the
debate over the curriculum and the competing claims of the
disciplines. One thinks of Ezra Cornell's famous statement,
"I would found an institution in which any person can find

instruction in any study"; or of the opening of Eliot's inaugural address:

> The endless controversies whether language, philosophy, mathematics, or science supplies the best mental training, whether general education should be chiefly scientific, have no practical lesson for us to-day. This University recognizes no real antagonism between literature and science, consents to no such narrow alternatives as mathematics or classics, science or metaphysics. We would have them all, and at their best. . . .
>
> It were a bitter mockery to suggest that any subject whatever should be taught less than it now is in American colleges. The only conceivable aim of a college government in our day is to broaden, deepen, and invigorate American teaching in all branches of learning. It will be generations before the best of American institutions of education will get growth enough to bear pruning.[8]

III

The university revolution broke the institutional grip of sectarianism on American education; at the same time the Darwinian revolution broke its intellectual grip. While the needs of postwar industry gave science practical prestige, Darwinism gave it a preeminent prestige in the realm of thought. The response of American scientists to Darwinism was prompt and hearty. By 1873, when Louis Agassiz, the last major scientist who opposed evolution, went to his grave, Darwinism had swept the scientific profession. Darwin himself was accorded the honor of election to the American Philosophical Society as early as 1869; it was ten years from that date before his own university, Cambridge, gave him an honorary degree.

The flexibility of the more enlightened clergy before the Darwinian challenge was impressive. However, insofar as clerics active in academic life resisted Darwinism, their resistance only discredited their old dominion over education, and underlined the truth of Eliot's observation, "A university cannot be founded upon a sect." That scientists found occasion to attack the conservative ministers was not so fatal as the fact that they began to laugh at them.

Scientists and ministers alike had moved into an altogether different intellectual milieu. In the old-time sectarian college, orthodoxy had been a major test of the eligibility of an academic to his job. A professor had to be, in many places, a Christian of the right denomination or theological persuasion. For instance, in 1854 Oliver Wolcott Gibbs, a distinguished chemist, had been denied appointment at Columbia because the Episcopalian trustees, including several ministers, could not stomach his Unitarianism. This incident, one of many such throughout the country, caused the few enlightened trustees to despair of making Columbia into a genuine university. But all of this was quick to change. In the postwar decades, evolutionary science and the dominant scientific ideal enlarged and aggrandized the claims of *competence* as a criterion for faculty appointments. As competence displaced orthodoxy, the new university promoters began quietly to ignore sectarian criteria in choosing professors, and they found themselves upheld by their boards of trustees. Enlightened men knew that there was only one way to realize the dream of creating great universities equal to those of Europe—above all, those of Germany—and that was to recruit men on the basis of distinguished learning, without regard to other considerations.

The strategy of such promoters of the secular university as Gilman, White, and Eliot was not one of militancy but of quiet persistence and partial accommodation. These men were not interested in making the tension between science and religion the source of unnecessary antagonism and struggle. Being administrators and promoters rather than agitators, they went on their way firmly and steadily, avoiding polemics, quietly ignoring religious interests or thrusting them into the background, counting upon the passage of time and the undeniable usefulness of their enterprises to carry them through. They preferred by-passing the major religious strongholds rather than carrying them by assault—and not surprisingly, for they were themselves by no means devoid of religious feeling. It is true, of course, that Andrew D. White wrote a two-volume *History of the Warfare of Science with Theology*, but to him the last word of this title was essential: it was not, as he saw it, true religion but dogmatic theology that had stood in the way of science. In any case, the book was not published until 1896, when White's university-building work had been done and he had been eleven years retired from

Cornell's presidency. In practice, White had not been excessively bold. For instance, he had brought Felix Adler (later the founder of the Society for Ethical Culture) to lecture on Hebrew and Oriental literature; but when Adler's latitudinarian ideas aroused widespread criticism in the local religious press, the university refused to renew an expired three-year appointment. White seems to have interposed no objection when Vice-President William C. Russel cashiered Adler.

The secularization of the new and more dynamic institutions proceeded from the top down, beginning with the donors. It is significant that of the three vanguard institutions in the university revolution, two were endowed by millionaires with Quaker backgrounds, who well understood the evils of sectarian oppression, while the third was Harvard with its relaxed Unitarian tradition. Moreover, donors of large fortunes preferred to have their gifts and bequests managed by businessmen and men of affairs rather than by clergymen. As the universities came to be less concerned with matters on which the clergy were deemed authoritative, the ministers seemed less competent to run them. The development of institutions large enough to be considered great enterprises suggested the need for business and promotional skills. Quietly, with the passage of time, clergymen began to disappear from governing boards. At Harvard the combined boards, Overseers and Corporation, had seven clergymen out of thirty-six members in 1874; by 1894 there was only one. Earl McGrath's study of the boards of fifteen private institutions shows that while in 1860 39 per cent of the trustees were clergymen, the figure had dropped to 23 per cent by 1900 and to 7 per cent by 1930.

Boards increasingly dominated by men with an eye to the needs of business and the development of research began to think naturally of laymen for college presidencies. By solemn tradition, the presidential office had gone to clergymen, and it was secularized at the same time as the trusteeships themselves. Columbia, choosing the chemist and naturalist F. A. P. Barnard in 1864, was one of the pioneers; and took as his successor in 1889 Seth Low, a businessman and politician. Harvard, which had already had two nineteenth-century lay presidents—Josiah Quincy in 1829 and Cornelius C. Felton in 1860—turned from a minister, Thomas Hill, to a scientist, Eliot, in 1869. Cornell

and Johns Hopkins began their existence with laymen as their
presidents, as did Clark with G. Stanley Hall, a psychologist,
and Stanford with David Starr Jordan, a biologist. Yale's first
lay president was Arthur Twining Hadley, an economist, in
1899; Princeton's was Woodrow Wilson, a political scientist,
in 1902.

A final phase in the induced secularization of the colleges
came only after the turn of the century. The Carnegie Foundation for the Advancement of Teaching, established in 1906
to provide retirement allowances for professors in private, *non-
sectarian* colleges, excluded from its bounty all colleges having
intimate relations to religious denominations or requiring that
trustees be members of a stated church. Many good colleges
suffering from sectarian affiliations were happy to use their
need for the foundation's bounty as an excuse to throw off
church control. A number renounced their sectarian connections and revised their charters or by-laws to qualify for aid.
At first only fifty-one institutions satisfied the foundation that
they were nondenominational; but within four years twenty
more managed to qualify, and others did so soon afterwards.
Several hundred colleges still held the sectarian line, to be sure,
but by and large these were the weakest colleges at the bottom
of the educational ladder. Sectarianism was left mainly with the
rearguard of American education.

IV

If we look for the educational convictions underlying the university revolution, we find ideas that may now seem so obvious
as to have little compelling interest—ideas, moreover, so clearly
anticipated by men like Jefferson, Ticknor, Wayland, Tappan,
and others that they could hardly have been considered new
in the years after 1869. The novelty lay in the means and the
determination to implement them. Still, the convictions had
to be reasserted in the university era and to be established
against a tenaciously held counter-philosophy. During his first
twenty years of service as Harvard's president, Eliot once said,
he was "generally conscious of speaking to men who, to say
the least, did not agree with me." President Hyde of Bowdoin

remembered him as having been "misunderstood, misrepresented, maligned, hated," for his first twenty-five years.[9]

As education had been understood in the Anglo-American college tradition, the formation of character was held to be more important than the development of intellect, the transmission of inherited knowledge more important than the search for new knowledge, and discipline more important than stimulation. Of course these are not necessary antinomies. Few spokesmen either of the old or the new regimes would have been prepared to say that there is some inevitable antagonism between character and intellect, or between conserving past knowledge and acquiring new knowledge. But there was an undeniable difference in emphasis, a difference that, carried far enough, aroused real antagonism. For this reason men like Eliot, Gilman, and White could not simply assert their ideas, but had to campaign for them. If cultivating intellect was to become their central business, colleges devoted to character and discipline must undergo important changes. Again, to foster research was not to challenge the importance of conserving the past; but it did lead to an upheaval in a curriculum and in teaching methods that had been based almost entirely upon the ideal of conserving knowledge. To exalt the ideal of secular knowledge in the age of Darwinian science constituted, whether one was looking for controversy or not, a subversive movement against institutions reared upon sects.

The new generation had a strikingly untraditional sense of what higher education should be, derived in the main from their experience with the German universities.[10] Since the early nineteenth century, American students returning from Germany had brought with them a conception of university work altogether at odds with their American college experience. In the German university two things were central: scholarship and freedom. Scholarship was specialized and advanced, so that it was possible for students and faculties to go beyond the elementary stages and reach depth of understanding in special subjects. Freedom for the students meant not only the chance for a choice in one's studies, but also the opportunity to form one's habits and goals of conduct independently. The German idealization of scholarship gave to the professor a position of

social importance unheard of in America. The German ideal
of educational freedom (not to be confused with the modern conception of political-academic freedom) stressed the free
pursuit by the professor of his scholarly interests without regard to curricular limitations. Where the American college had
fitted its faculty to a curriculum, the German university tended
to fit the curriculum to its faculty. The established German
professor taught what he wished. The student too was free to
choose among professors and even among universities in the
pursuit of a self-determined and specialized scholarly goal. The
German emphasis on *Lehrfreiheit* and *Lernfreiheit* was translat-
able (though in the process of translation it was substantially
altered) in the Anglo-American conceptions of democracy,
competition, and laissez-faire.[11] As the new open curriculum
crept into the American college, all academic subjects were
thought to have been created equal, and all teachers and pupils
entitled to the pursuit of intellectual happiness by exercising
their free choice among subjects. Professors and curricular offerings were to engage in a measure of open competition, thus
realizing more closely the model of economic behavior portrayed in classical economics. It would be exaggerating to suggest that this is what was done, but this was the ideal toward
which changes were directed.

The canons of university education were, then, in some
sense new. They embraced the following propositions. First,
education must be freed from sectarian and political domination. Moreover, it must be freed from paternalistic domination:
trustees must leave educational, curricular, and disciplinary
matters almost entirely to the faculties. Trustees should consider themselves business managers and general overseers; but
must largely forgo control of the educational process itself.[12]

Secondly, the faculties were now recognized, not in law but
surely in fact, to constitute the universities. Not grand buildings, not imposing presidents, not respectable church sponsorship, not large and well-behaved student bodies—none of these
was any longer assumed to be the important thing. A university was an aggregate of intellectual talents. Illustrious teachers
—recruited from at home or abroad without serious concern
for anything but their scholarly or scientific achievements—
were understood to be the heart and soul of the university. To

attract them an institution must be prepared to pay well, and the whole community must be willing to make the academic profession roughly commensurate with other professions in salaries, in dignity, and in freedom.

Thirdly, a university must make advanced study its main concern. The graduate school was not an afterthought or an adornment, but a necessity and a model. Not only must advanced scholars be recruited to teach in graduate schools, but good students must, in effect, be hired to attend them—i.e., fellowships must be provided. It was assumed that *all* instruction, including professional and undergraduate instruction, would be improved in the atmosphere created by advanced research and experimentation. When opponents of a graduate school at Harvard suggested that it was useless to compete in this respect with Johns Hopkins, and that a graduate school would weaken the College, Eliot replied: "It will strengthen the College. As long as our teachers regard their work as simply giving so many courses for undergraduates, we shall never have first-class teaching here. If they have to teach graduate students as well as undergraduates, they will regard their subjects as infinite, and keep up that constant investigation which is necessary for first-class teaching."[13]

Fourthly, the resistance of the old college to the scientific and vocational demands of the community gave way. Scientific and technical education were no longer frowned at, or isolated in separate "scientific" schools, but were made an integral part of the educational process.

Finally, undergraduate teaching and the undergraduate curriculum were overhauled. Science was given an increasingly important part in the course of studies. But even more drastic was the enlarged place of the social sciences and modern languages and literature, hitherto but slightly represented. Under the elective system the undergraduate was given a high degree of freedom to choose his course of studies. Now the disciplines had to compete with each other for enrollment—which could put a premium upon fresh and interesting teaching (as it could also, unfortunately, upon the easy course). The tedious recitation session lost favor, and ultimately disappeared, in favor of more imaginative methods of instruction: the lecture, the small discussion group (borrowed from the graduate seminar), and,

in science, demonstrations and laboratory work. The elective
system, while making more specialized courses available to undergraduates, made it possible for teachers to teach subjects
of vital interest to themselves. The consequent improvement
in the morale of instructors contributed substantially to the
liveliness of teaching.

The greatest single weakness of the old colleges had been
neither their curriculum, however archaic, nor their faculties,
however limited, but their hopelessly dull recitation method
of teaching, which could deaden the most interesting subjects
and convert faculty men of genuine intellectual and scholarly
distinction into drillmasters.[14] James Freeman Clarke's ironic
remark at the Harvard commencement dinner of 1886 may be
taken with entire seriousness: "Formerly, the only business of
a teacher was to hear recitations, and make marks for merit.
Now, he has the opportunity of teaching. This is one of the
greatest educational discoveries of modern times,—that the
business of a teacher is to teach."[15]

V

Before the university era, men had spent their lives teaching
in colleges, but there was nothing that could be called an academic profession. There were no well-recognized and generally maintained standards of competence in scholarly subjects;
professional and intellectual specialization was not generally
recognized as a prerogative of the college teacher; there was
no lively academic marketplace in which competing institutions could or would regularly bid for the skills of eminent
men; there were few opportunities or facilities for specialized
research or experimentation; there were few scholarly organizations or publications. With these elementary prerequisites of
professional life so conspicuously lacking, there could be no
such spirit of professional solidarity as began to manifest itself
in informal ways after 1870 and finally found formal expression
in 1915 in the organization of the American Association of University Professors.

The lack of specialization was only slowly overcome in
the university era, except in the vanguard institutions. We
need not, perhaps, concern ourselves overmuch with such

institutions of the educational underworld as Florida State College of Agriculture, with its professorship in agriculture, horticulture, and Greek. But distinguished men were often reduced to drillmasters and petty disciplinarians, tormented by the tedium of underspecialization. James Burrill Angell, president of the University of Vermont in the 1860's, finding that the institution lacked the funds to round out its faculty, taught all the missing subjects himself—including rhetoric, German, history, and international law. David Starr Jordan, as late as the 1870's when he taught at Lombard University in Illinois, had classes in natural science, political economy, evidences of Christianity, German, Spanish, and literature, and pitched for the baseball team. Eliot well knew the costs of this system—or lack of system—for he had suffered from it as a young assistant professor at Harvard in the 1850's. To Charles Eliot Norton he wrote in 1860:

> I generally experience a slight disgust at recitations at the beginning of a term, particularly at Mathematical recitations. I wish I could teach the science in which I am most interested, and in which I work during leisure hours, but at present I have four recitations in Mathematics for one in Chemistry, and I see no reasonable hope of any change. . . . And yet the College demands so much of my time that I can do original scientific work only by working up to the very limit of physical endurance and sometimes going a little beyond it.[16]

The feebleness of the libraries was almost as great an obstacle to professional work in the old colleges. A privileged scholar like George Ticknor might build a private library, mainly in his own specialty, of 13,000 volumes; but it was upon such efforts, or upon inconvenient resort to general libraries not maintained by their own schools, that American academics did what important scholarly work was done. Ticknor had pointed out when he joined Harvard that its library, then 20,000 volumes, was only one-tenth the size of Göttingen's. By 1839, when Harvard's library had grown to 50,000, Yale's was the only other college library with more than half as many; and in the country at large there were only sixteen colleges that could claim more than 10,000 books. As late as 1873 the library of the University of Pennsylvania, with 20,000 volumes, was dwarfed by the Philadelphia Mercantile Library with 125,000. This poverty persisted into the post-Civil War period. In 1869 Gilman, who had only recently ceased being Yale's librarian, pointed out that "Yale College has not a dollar on hand to buy books for the next two years, its scanty library income having been expended two years in advance."[17] To scholars familiar with these conditions of the pre-university era, the growth of libraries was immensely heartening. By 1900 Harvard's, the leading library, had 560,000 volumes and 150,000 pamphlets. Such lesser libraries as that of Pennsylvania had grown to respectable size with about a third as many.

The situation of laboratory science in the old colleges had been still worse. American colleges provided no laboratories for teaching, or even, normally, for the experiments of faculty members. At Yale, pre-eminent in science, Benjamin Silliman, Sr., could do no more for his students in this respect than perform some experiments for them in the lecture room. He disliked having students in his private laboratory for fear they would "hinder me and my trained assistants, [or] derange or break the apparatus."[18] The younger Silliman, as his father's assistant, was able to get a room at Yale in 1842, in which he could give practical laboratory instruction to a few students, but this was an unofficial arrangement having no functional connection with college instruction. The foundation in 1847 of Sheffield Scientific School at Yale and Lawrence at Harvard represented a step toward academic laboratories, but adequate support for scientific teaching and research had to await the more substantial endowments of the period after 1870.

Professionalism moved from the institutions to the disciplines. There had been professional organizations before the Civil War, but usually they had been either local organizations, like the Massachusetts Historical Society, the American Academy of Arts and Sciences, and the American Antiquarian Society, or comprehensive and unspecialized, like the American Association for the Advancement of Science. Now the various disciplines, many of them being taught for the first time in the universities, began under the stimulus of Gilman and Johns Hopkins to form their own specialized societies. Learned societies began to proliferate with rapidity in the 1870's and 1880's; by 1908 there were 120 national societies and countless local

ones besides. Again spurred by Johns Hopkins, professional
journals began to develop, led by the mathematicians, chemists, and philologists. Chicago followed the example of Johns
Hopkins in becoming a major center for the publication of
professional journals.

The development of graduate studies and professional standards spread from academic studies to the professional schools.
Legal and medical education, as they had been carried on in
the United States during the nineteenth century, were hardly
professional. Law schools had little to offer that was better
than the informal apprentice training available in the office
of a good lawyer. Eliot found the law school at Harvard in
disgraceful condition, unchanged for the past twenty years,
staffed by three lawyers busy with their own private practices,
and attended by students less than half of whom were college graduates, and none of whom had to pass examinations
in order to get the LL.B. degree. The new president forced
Christopher C. Langdell into the deanship in 1870, and thus
instituted a series of changes that in good time set the pace for
legal education throughout the country. A capable faculty was
recruited, law study was extended from eighteen months to
three years, written examinations were required, and the case
method of study replaced the old textbook method. These reforms, much resisted at first, paid off within a little more than
a dozen years. By then the student body had doubled, and the
Harvard Law Review had been founded. After 1893 none but
college graduates were admitted. Harvard set a pattern that
was widely imitated.

Where legal education had been lax, medical education had
been lethal. The old proprietary medical schools were essentially profit-making institutions, devoid of laboratories and
hospital connections, in which teaching was done by lecture
and a rare dissection. The course of study was normally one
academic year; the tuition income was divided among the local
medical practitioners who did the teaching. "Chairs" in medicine were sold to their occupants. Examinations were brief
and oral. Even at Harvard the candidate who could pass with
five out of nine examiners was qualified for medicine. There
were no state boards to impose standards. Eliot considered
that "the ignorance and general incompetency of the average

graduate of American Medical Schools, at the time when he receives the degree which turns him loose on the community, is something horrible to contemplate."[19]

Harvard Medical School began its reforms under Eliot simultaneously with the reforms in the law school. A three-year course of study was set up, and written examinations established, with the requirement that all fields be passed by those who were to receive their M.D.'s. Johns Hopkins opened its great medical school in 1893 requiring a bachelor's degree for admission. When Abraham Flexner made the famous investigation in 1910 that launched a general reform in medical education, he took Johns Hopkins as the model of what an American medical school should be, and graded other institutions by measuring their distance from the Johns Hopkins standard. Twenty years earlier there had been no school in America good enough to serve as a standard.

But quite as important as the effects of the university revolution on the other professions was its effect on the academic profession itself. Now, for the first time, the profession developed the capacity both for large-scale innovative work in scholarship and for social criticism and practical contribution to the political dialogue of American society. If one considers only philosophy and the social sciences, the roster of men reared in the university movement is impressive enough: Oliver Wendell Holmes (one of Langdell's first recruits) and Roscoe Pound in law; Thorstein Veblen and John R. Commons in economics; John Dewey and William James in philosophy; Charles A. Beard, Carl Becker, James Harvey Robinson, Frederick Jackson Turner in history. The important and original movements in thought and scholarship—pragmatism, legal realism, institutional economics, the "new history," which are all products of this era, stand in refreshing contrast to the earlier borrowings from Scottish realism and classical economic doctrine.

Pragmatism itself, the most significant product of American academic work, was in part the result of applying to philosophical problems certain insights derived from Darwinian evolution and from Anglo-American case law. It became, in a sense, almost the official philosophy of American liberalism. It was ideally adapted to a time when the academic man was beginning to overcome his traditional civic passivity and take an active part in the shaping of political events. A long-standing estrangement between the life of the mind and the life of politics was overcome at the turn of the century, and in the new synthesis of academic life and politics, scholars like John Dewey, J. Allen Smith, and Charles A. Beard were to play a signal part. Among the consequences of the empirical special-ized skills that had been fostered by the university movement, academic men had not only prestige but some real marketable advice to bring to public life. It was not surprising that they played an important part in the Progressive era, both on the national level and in the states. In Wisconsin, under La Follette, the idea of the university in the service of the reformist state received a remarkable consummation. In the nation at large, the participation of professors in government had become a thing familiar enough not to cause exceptional notice. In 1918, when Woodrow Wilson, himself a product of the university movement, took to Paris a team of about 150 scholars to give technical advice on the making of the peace, the employment of experts seems to have been sufficiently taken for granted to elicit only faint hostile comment.

VI

Every revolution has its excesses, its disappointments, its Ther-midor; the university revolution was no exception. Its lead-ers, who were familiar only with the underspecialization and impracticality they had to surmount, could not very well an-ticipate or prevent the new evils of overspecialization and ex-cessive vocationalism. The modern university brought with it the defects of its merits. If the old college had preserved too much of what was dead in the past, the new university became in time all too responsive to trivial innovations of the present. Limited though it had been in the quality and range of its achievement, the old college had had a clear form and mold and a firm sense of purpose. The university often lost its cen-ter and became a diffuse federal union whose parts seemed to work at cross purposes. It replaced underspecialization with overspecialization, overdiscipline of the young with excessive indulgence, archaism with a restless and sometimes indiscrimi-nate passion for novelty, impracticality with a crass surrender to vocationalism, neglect of science with obtrusive scientism and crude positivism, stubborn resistance to change with complaisant response to the demands of an anti-intellectualist society.

The history of the elective system is a perfect case of the difficulties of change. By 1910 it was recognizable that those institutions which had made the elective experiment too fast and carried it too far had invited curricular chaos. Students, freed from set courses of study, sometimes chose courses largely because they were easy or entertaining; some were capable of devising for themselves strange collections of courses aggregating enough credits to earn the B.A. but hardly constituting a liberal education. Much of the curricular planning of the twentieth-century college has been an attempt to surmount this tendency toward formlessness, to devise meaningful core curricula, and to conform once again to the old-college ideal of giving the student a minimum base in general education preliminary to specialization.

Although the old college subordinated intellect to character and discipline, it never doubted that education was basically concerned with the mind. The modern university, with its multiple concerns and its effort to meet a variety of needs, has at times degenerated into a kind of cultural filling-station. This tendency has reached its peak among the state universities, one of whose presidents once declared: "The state universities hold that there is no intellectual service too undignified for them to perform."[20] By 1930, when Abraham Flexner published his famous survey, *Universities: American, English, German,* his account of the trivialities to which the universities at their worst had descended—the correspondence courses, the offerings in advertising, judo, food etiquette, and home laundering, the graduate theses on ways of washing dishes, on the bacterial content of cotton undershirts, or on "the origin and nature of common annoyances"—matched in scorn his earlier account of the inadequacies of the medical schools.

These things must be said as a caution against claiming too much for the university revolution. But no one who looks carefully into the old college and the work of the university reformers would propose that we simply set the clock back. We go on, trying to strike a balance between the vocational and the intellectual, between the general and the specialized, between the "two cultures" of science and humanities with an uneasy awareness that the problem is not susceptible to perfect solution. No doubt there is something missing and something wrong in every educational dispensation. Education is a field in which everyone is, in his own mind, an expert; a field in which everyone cherishes a Utopia which he imagines to be realizable. We think of men or women whom we consider well educated, and we demand that somehow institutions be created that will turn out such products wholesale; but a good education depends upon an uncommon, happy conjunction between institutional excellence and personal capacity and desire.

1963

Notes

1. In his excellent book, *Mark Hopkins and the Log* (New Haven, 1956), Frederick Rudolph examines the myth of the old college, as exemplified by Mark Hopkins and Williams College, judiciously but with disillusioning results.

2. Charles William Eliot, *Educational Reform* (New York, 1898), p. 105.

3. Quoted in Orie W. Long, *Literary Pioneers* (Cambridge, Mass., 1935), p. 166.

4. Cf. Andrew White: "I had, during my college life, known sundry college tutors seriously injured while they were doing police duty. I have seen a professor driven out of a room, through the panel of a door, with books, boots, and bootjacks hurled at his head; and even the respected president of a college, a doctor of divinity, while patrolling buildings with the janitors, subjected to outrageous indignity." *Autobiography* (New York, 1922), I, 348.

5. *Representative Phi Beta Kappa Orations*, ed. Northrup, Lane, and Schwab (Boston, 1915), pp. 160–161.

6. The size and wealth of an institution were in fact of vital importance to the quality of its achievement. George W. Pierson has pointed out that Harvard in this period was working with endowments that made even such rivals as Princeton and Yale "plain and poor." "American Universities in the Nineteenth Century: the Formative Period," in Margaret Clapp, ed., *The Modern University* (Ithaca, 1950), p. 80.

7. Practically all the new state universities of the West and South adopted a coeducational policy more or less as a matter of course. In 1880 fifty-one per cent of the colleges were mixed; in 1898, it was seventy per cent. The number of women students rose from about 2,700 to more than 25,000. By the turn of the century four out of five colleges, universities, and professional schools admitted women.

8. Eliot, *Educational Reform*, pp. 1–2.

9. Samuel Eliot Morison, *Three Centuries of Harvard* (Cambridge, Mass., 1936), p. 358.

10. Despite the clear preponderance of the German influence in the American idea of the university, some English influences persisted; they were especially strong in the better colleges and in some universities like Yale and Princeton. The English concern with the development of character in undergraduates and something that might be called atmosphere in the institutions is a noteworthy feature; as is the passion for imposing buildings, somewhat separated, if possible, from the urban community. An emphasis on teaching, as opposed to research, remains. In some institutions —notably, again, Yale and Princeton—the centrality of the college among the various parts of the university is an Anglo-American survival. So too is the aim of creating a broadly educated leadership, as opposed to a body of specialists. Finally, the English passion for undergraduate sports has survived and grown in this country—but with the unfortunate difference that the English emphasis on amateurism and broad participation has been supplanted with American commercialism and spectator sports.

11. See the account of this transformation by Walter P. Metzger in Richard Hofstadter and Walter P. Metzger, *The Development of Academic Freedom in the United States* (New York, 1955), ch. VIII.

12. Of course it should be clear that the universities were not the creations of a democracy, or of the faculties. In the main, they were created, or reformed, from the top down. They were triumphs of elite leadership, of enlightened autocracy. In the long run, they advanced academic "democracy" simply because they assembled faculties so large and so eminent that they had to be permitted in some considerable degree to govern themselves.

13. Quoted in Morison, *Three Centuries of Harvard*, pp. 335–336.

14. Cf. Andrew D. White on Yale in the 1850's: "Though the professors were most of them really distinguished men, and one at least, James Hadley, a scholar who, at Berlin or Leipzig, would have drawn throngs of students from all Christendom, they were fettered by a system which made everything of gerund-grinding and nothing of literature." *Autobiography*, I, 27.

15. Morison, p. 347.

16. Henry James, *Charles William Eliot* (Boston, 1930), I, 87.

17. Fabian Franklin, *The Life of Daniel Coit Gilman* (New York, 1910), p. 80.

18. Quoted by Dirk J. Struik, *Yankee Science in the Making* (Boston, 1948), p. 339.

19. Quoted by F. C. Shattuck and J. L. Bremer in Samuel Eliot Morison, ed., *The Development of Harvard University, 1869–1929* (Cambridge, Mass., 1930), p. 558.

20. Quoted in Logan Wilson, *The Academic Man* (New York, 1942), p. 175.

Some Comments on Senator Goldwater

B ARRY GOLDWATER is something new, very new, in our politics. As a rule, such men have flourished only in minor
parties, yet he has not only won the nomination but gained
unusually firm control over a major party. Normally a major
party nomination is won partly by establishing predominant
popularity among its voters and partly by accommodating
other party leaders. Goldwater has won without doing either,
but by arousing great intensity of conviction among a minority
of enthusiasts, and then imposing upon this minority a tight
disciplinary structure. Hitherto our major parties have not
been founded on ideologies: they have worked by arranging
continual compromises among heterogeneous interests, and
they have been led by men of much experience not merely
in organizing partisans but in meeting the practical problems
of state. Goldwater is now creating a party dominated by an
uncompromising minority faction of uncommon discipline
and dedication, and led by a millennial dreamer, a visionary
without experience in solving any of the real problems of our
public life. Despite Goldwater's apparent post-Convention
concessions to the Republican moderates, he has already made
the Republican party into a front organization for a minority
point of view.

Control of a major party brings to Goldwater and his peculiar notions a measure of respectability and legitimation that
they have not had before, and gives him a platform from which
he can maximize the effect of right-wing views. It also gives
him a strong position from which to form a new kind of political union, which will be based on jingoism, economic ultra-
conservatism, and racial animosity. Of the primary emotional
forces upon which he depends—social resentments, economic
greed, and messianic idealism—it is the last which is most dangerous, for Goldwater draws upon a deep millennial strain in
the American consciousness, and mobilizes all our impatience
with the maladies of modernity and the innumerable constraints of the contemporary world. His most ardent followers
respond not to his supposed conservatism, which is shallow

and meaningless, but to the allure of his utopian visions, embracing on one side a return to long-vanished entrepreneurial conditions and on the other a total victory (*sans* casualties and *sans* income tax) in the cold war.

I believe that Goldwater's rise to prominence, far from being a momentary thing, rests upon forces constantly at work in our society, clearly visible at least since the Korean War, and now intensified by the racial crisis, which itself seems to be unresolvable. For this reason, a defeat in the election, unless it is overwhelming, probably will not go far to dislodge Goldwater's grip on the Republican party. Such a defeat would have to be followed by an extraordinarily united and determined effort on the part of the Republican moderates, of which they do not appear today to be capable. It is still possible, then, that Goldwater, if beaten, could re-take the renomination in 1968, perhaps under circumstances more auspicious for his election. Ten years ago, assessing the impact of McCarthyism and related tendencies in an article on "The Pseudo-Conservative Revolt," I observed that, in a political culture like ours, "in which it is possible to exploit the wildest currents of public sentiment for private purposes, it is at least conceivable that a highly organized, vocal, active and well-financed minority could create a political climate in which the rational pursuit of our well-being and safety would become impossible." Today we seem a giant step closer to such an eventuality.

1964

A Long View: Goldwater in History

Early in the campaign Barry Goldwater established a firm image of himself as predictably unpredictable: no one can tell where the audacious veerings and swoopings of his mind will take him, what bizarre new sallies he will launch, what vast intellectual retreats he will find it necessary to undertake without acknowledging that he has budged an inch.

One stands in bewilderment before such a mentality. The temptation to explain the man simply as an outrageous opportunist must be resisted. There is, and indeed should be, an element of the opportunist in every political man, and Goldwater is no exception. His opportunism has grown as he has moved closer to the grand prize. But his earlier voting record, taken as a whole, is not the record of an opportunist but of a man of principle, whatever you think of his principles.

Nor is it quite satisfactory to settle for the proposition that he is not as alert or informed intellectually as we are accustomed to expect our major political figures to be. There must be many men active in our public life who are no smarter than Goldwater but who do not share his lust for banalities and absurdities. Indeed, one of Goldwater's problems is that his mind is not only more vigorous but also more pretentious than the ordinary. He yearns for profundity, and is so intent upon elaborating his ideas that he has written, or at least signed, two books that have increased his vulnerability. Much of his difficulty rests, I believe, upon the fact that his serious political education began only recently, and he has been in the unenviable position of having to conduct it in public.

It is no simple thing to account for the development and the prominence of a mind so out of key with the basic tonalities of our political life, and it would take a soothsayer to tell us what we can expect of it in the future. However, Goldwater's present difficulties in winning broader acceptance, even among the moderate voters in his own party, may blind us to the fact that up to the point of his nomination at the Cow Palace his impulsive and contradictory pronouncements were a part of his stock in trade and they were selling. His main problem now is that it is hard to create still another new image of himself. It is possible, I believe, to discern three overlapping but fairly distinct Barry Goldwaters. The chronological lines that separate them are by no means absolute, and the earlier Goldwaters can still be seen slightly below the surface of the latest Goldwater. Still, for the purpose of understanding his career, they can be roughly distinguished.

I

Goldwater I is the original, the native, the impulsive Goldwater, as he was raised in Arizona and as he regularly expressed himself up to about a year ago, before he mounted his final campaign for the nomination. To understand him one must think of the political and social atmosphere of the Southwest, where the raw views of the new millionaires count for much more than they do in other parts of the country, a region where the reforms of the New Deal, now a generation behind us, are still acutely controversial. Imagine a charming, vigorous, basically apolitical man somehow drawn out of this atmosphere into political affairs. Endowed with an active, though largely untutored, mind, he is attracted by the resonances of deep-sounding ideas, and he superimposes upon the brash conservatism of the country-club locker rooms some hasty acquaintance with the notions of our ultraconservative highbrows. Grant that you begin with a man who has a keen taste for combat—political, moral, or military—and who looks upon the necessity of countering the dominant liberal philosophy of the country as a welcome challenge to his manliness and independence. Here you have the first Goldwater, who charmed the right-wing enthusiasts in the Republican party, and whose ardent campaigning among them built up the strong cult that has made him what he is today.

Now imagine the uninhibited psychological mood in which the ideas of Goldwater I are formed and expressed. First, there is the remoteness from actual administrative, and even from legislative, responsibility; as Senator, Goldwater does not become responsible for any major positive legislation, is never thrown into a position in which he must carefully weigh the relation between legislative aims and social realities. His entire intellectual stance puts him into a negative relation to the legislative process. His contribution as a senator is not to sit, as for example, Robert A. Taft did, with other senators in committee trying to iron out the intricacies of pending legislation: it is simply to vote No. In fact, the greatest part of his political life during the years of his senatorial prominence is to make speeches—hundreds of them—before audiences already largely or entirely sympathetic to his message. He is an ideologue and a prophet; he has little need to persuade, only to exhort, and like most exhorters he hypnotizes himself with his own repetition. He luxuriates in saying what he truly believes, without having to weigh his words, before receptive and enthusiastic audiences. In the process, he makes friends and admirers throughout the country. As yet he does not really expect to be nominated for the Presidency, much less to be President; so it is hardly necessary for him to think very much about what his ideas would actually involve if they were the ideas of the man in the White House.

Goldwater I, then, spoke freely. "I don't give a tinker's damn what the rest of the world thinks about the United States as long as we keep strong militarily." "We should, I believe, announce in no uncertain terms that we are *against* disarmament." For a time he favored withdrawing recognition from the Soviets. He found the U.N. "unworkable," and urged that we "quit wasting our money on it." He denied that there is "such a thing as peaceful coexistence." He thought that Khrushchev's visit to the United States was the consequence of "a craven fear of death" that had entered the American consciousness. He attacked Eisenhower's 1957 budget as "a betrayal of the people's trust," and his administration as a "dime store New Deal," urged that the government sell TVA "even if they only get one dollar for it."

II

If Goldwater I represents the Goldwater id, Goldwater II represents the Goldwater ego, aware of the eyes of a larger world, and now making certain more rational calculations about what a major public figure ought to be saying. Goldwater II became increasingly evident about a year ago. Goldwater is here no longer the provincial prophet but an increasingly powerful party figure about to make a sustained bid for the presidential nomination, and concerned about what his ideas might sound like to a larger national audience. While he is not yet making statements that risk alienating his true believers, he is beginning to realize that some of his past utterances have discredited him. He states that he is going to process his past statements through a computer so that he will have greater mastery over what he has said. (This in itself marks a historic moment in our politics.) His statements are now often set forth within the framework of a kind of craftsmanlike equivocation.

Now it is not withdrawal of recognition of the Soviet that is demanded but the use of the threat to withdraw recognition as a means to win bargaining concessions. Withdrawal from the U.N. is no longer urged—except if Red China should be admitted. In the New Hampshire campaign Goldwater declares: "We must stay in the United Nations, but we must improve it." Again, in the same campaign, he insists that the statement that he is against social security is a "flagrant lie," but adds that he does believe that by 1970 social security beneficiaries "will be asking questions such as whether better programs couldn't be bought on the private market." More recently he has suggested threatening the Red Chinese with a show of force if they continued to supply the Viet Cong guerrillas, but he quickly added: "I'm not really recommending this but it might not be an impossible idea."

Goldwater II's increasingly experimental way with ideas may be explained in part by his previous business experience. While he has never had any administrative or legislative responsibility, he was a successful businessman in Arizona, and much of his success rested on his capacities as a merchandiser. He understands the problems of salesmanship, and appears to have transferred the salesman's pragmatic promotional techniques to politics. He once said that his political role was largely that of "a salesman of ideas," and he spontaneously used the same comparison shortly after his nomination when he said in an interview that he hoped the campaign would prove him "a better salesman" than President Johnson. Now there is a certain innocuous tentativeness about the tricks of salesmanship—like the famous "antsy pants" so successfully marketed by the Goldwater stores—and it may be both charitable and accurate to look upon Goldwater's sudden suggestions that the Marines be sent to turn on the water at Guantanamo or that the jungle in Vietnam be defoliated by nuclear devices as the experimental gestures of a man who is feeling his way into a new and larger market of public opinion. Aggressive though such proposals sound, they are put forth in an experimental way, and may be withdrawn and discarded if they do not arouse much consumer interest.

If one bears in mind that Goldwater represents a very special minority point of view, which is not even preponderant in his own party, one must grant that in capturing the Republican party he has turned in a remarkable political performance, and that Goldwater I and Goldwater II have thus far served him well. Of course, he was helped by a series of political accidents: the divorce and remarriage of Rockefeller crippled a formidable antagonist; the assassination of Kennedy and the ensuing overwhelming popularity of Johnson caused other candidates to hang back, looking to 1968 rather than 1964; an unusually large field of possible moderate candidates spread disunity among the opposition; even the fact that his prospects were greatly underrated after the New Hampshire primary worked in the end to his advantage. But what must not be discounted—quite aside from the Senator's own charisma —is that his arduous speech-making labors of the previous four years have paid off partly in putting innumerable Republican workers around the country in his debt, but largely in recruiting and inspiring a corps of fanatical workers such as no other candidate could mobilize. Above all, up to the moment of the convention in San Francisco, his equivocations and contradictions had done him more good than harm. The ideas of Goldwater I brought him his army of true believers, and the softer and more dazzling dialectics of Goldwater II suggested that he was not really in fact one of the cranks but a genuine conservative leader flexible enough to conduct a winning campaign.

III

The situation that prevailed after the convention demanded the appearance of one more Goldwater. Too many fangs had been bared in the Cow Palace and a very bad impression had been made. The national press was singularly hostile, and it is easy to believe that the Senator was wounded by his failure, even with a major-party mantle over his shoulders, to attain the full credentials of respectability. The party was still badly divided, and the extremist label seemed to be sticking. It had become necessary to make the conciliatory gestures so noticeably lacking at the Cow Palace.

Hence, at the Hershey conference, Goldwater III, an entirely new creation, was unveiled. Goldwater III is the statesman-in-the-making, building party unity and seeking the support of those middle-ground voters without whom his chances for the presidency are negligible. At the Hershey conference, Goldwater not only said most of the healing and conciliatory things that were missing from his acceptance address, but even added some gratuitous concessions. He promised to return to the "proven policy of peace through strength which was the hallmark of the Eisenhower years," and to make no appointments to the offices of Secretary of Defense or Secretary of State or other critical national security posts without first discussing his plans with Eisenhower, Nixon, and other "experienced leaders seasoned in world affairs." He reiterated his support for the U.N. and his determination to make it "a more effective instrument for peace among nations." He affirmed his support "for perhaps the one-millionth time" for the Social Security system, expressed a desire to see it strengthened, and soon afterward said he would vote to extend it. He pledged faithful execution of the Civil Rights Act. He said that he wanted to read no one out of the party, and wanted no support from extremists.

Having said all this, Goldwater told reporters: "This is no conciliatory speech at all. It merely reaffirms what I've been saying throughout the campaign. Now sometimes it hasn't gotten through quite clear. I don't know why but there are reasons, I suppose." One can readily understand the caution expressed by Nelson Rockefeller, when asked by reporters whether Goldwater's statement represented a shift of position. "I think," said Rockefeller, "it's his position as of today on these issues."

Reporters who seem to know say that there is regret in the Goldwater high command that some of these conciliatory things were not said at the Cow Palace. By letting a few weeks intervene, the image of the extremist Goldwater became fixed. To have struck the soft note earlier would have been more in the spirit of our major party politics. But one must not fail to recall that the forces that raised Goldwater to his present eminence do not share the representative major-party ethos. For Goldwater to have been soft and conciliatory at the Cow Palace would have stunned his zealots in their seats and sent them away in a state of confusion. In the nation at large the effects of such a gesture might have been good, but it would have blunted the "extremist" image only to create, at the moment of triumph, new and more urgent uncertainties about where Goldwater stands.

As it is, Goldwater's true believers can now treasure the notion that Goldwater III is a false-face created only for the purposes of the campaign, and that in his heart of hearts Barry still belongs to them. I believe that they are right in more than one sense. It is not merely that Goldwater's pulse seems to quicken when he is taking an avant-garde right-wing line, but that the hard work and the money required to nominate him were provided by zealots of a very advanced persuasion. Moderate Republicans by the millions may in the end swallow their reservations and give their votes to Goldwater, but it is only the true believers who will go on giving their hearts and their purses. If he is to be elected, or renominated in 1968, it will be only they who can do it for him.

It is their strategic importance, and the overheated ideological character of their politics, which suggest that the usual rules of political conduct are likely to be suspended. In the ordinary course of our pragmatic, non-ideological politics, party workers are moved by the desire to find a winner, to get and keep office, to frame programs on which they can generally agree, to use these programs to satisfy the major interests in our society, and to make an effort to help solve its most acute problems. If they find that they have chosen a loser, they are quick to start looking for another leader; if they see that their program is out of touch with the basic realities, they grope their way toward a new one.

It is not so with Goldwater's true believers. They seem more moved by the impulse to dominate the party than to win the country, more concerned to express resentments and punish "traitors," to justify a set of values and assert grandiose, militant visions than to solve any actual problems of state. This is one reason why they seem so little troubled by Goldwater's self-contradictory policy pronouncements. By the same token, it is not easy to predict that they will respond in the customary way to the reality of defeat. Where the conventional party worker looks upon defeat as a spur to rethink his commitments and his strategy, they are likely to see it primarily as additional evidence of the conspiracy by which they think they have been surrounded all along, and to conclude that they must redouble their efforts.

IV

The one salient thread of consistency amid Goldwater's self-contradictions is the most alarming aspect of his thinking, and that is his conception of the cold war. So far as I know, he has steadfastly repudiated the idea of peaceful coexistence. He sees the cold war as a series of relentless confrontations between ourselves and the Communists on various fronts throughout the world. He holds that if we maintain superior strength we can emerge victorious from all these confrontations; that in time the whole Communist world (which should be treated uniformly as a bloc whatever its apparent internal differences) will crack under the stress of repeated defeats; that we need not fear the likelihood that impending defeat will precipitate a counter-strike that could lead to nuclear war.

Nothing could be more disingenuous than Goldwater's attempt at Hershey to suggest that his conception of the cold war and his policies toward it are in the Eisenhower tradition of "peace through strength," as Goldwater calls it. In fact Eisenhower's policy, like that of Kennedy and Johnson, was basically the cautious one of *détente* and accommodation. What appeals to Goldwater in Eisenhower's record is not the basic circumspection that governed it but the occasional risky strokes that Eisenhower felt it necessary to make, like his move into Lebanon and his policy toward the offshore islands. Nothing could be more remote, for example, from Eisenhower's cautious abstention from interfering in Hungary in 1956 than Goldwater's belief that we should have flown in a force with tactical nuclear weapons. It will be interesting to see during the campaign how Eisenhower, even with his well-practiced gift for the vacuous and the equivocal, will be able to circumvent the fact that he is supporting a man who repudiates the best part of his own administration.

It is essential to understand that Goldwater is not merely advocating the conventional "tough" line in foreign policy, for which a rational case can be made. He goes beyond it to demand what can only be called the crusader's line. He sees it as a holy war. His goal is not merely peace, security, and the extension of our influence, but an ultimate total victory, the ideological and political extermination of the enemy. "Our objective must be the destruction of the enemy as an ideological force possessing the means of power." The ambiguous world in which we have already lived for twenty years is to Goldwater a fleeting illusion; what is ultimately real is Armageddon —total victory or total defeat. "The only alternative [to victory] is—obviously—defeat." The idea that the cold war may have somewhat changed its character in recent years is not only unacceptable, it is intolerable. Flexibility in conducting it is treasonable; and Goldwater has skirted the ideas of the paranoid right in asserting that the Democrats have led us toward unilateral disarmament in pursuit of their "no-win" policy.

This point of view, it must be clear, is very far from the old isolationism and much closer to the American missionary impulse that once sent us out to make the world safe for democracy. Although he has taken a rather dim view of most kinds of foreign aid (restoring freedom to the world must not be too expensive), Goldwater takes the broadest view of our commitments outside our own borders. It is our business to counterpose our force to that of Communism everywhere on the globe. Goldwater's accusation that President Johnson's acceptance speech was an isolationist document is in keeping with this commitment, and helps to define the difference between the two. Johnson hopes for a continuing relaxation of international tensions which will free us to renew our efforts to solve some of our pressing domestic problems. Goldwater, at least until yesterday, so to speak, proposed to dismantle our federal

apparatus in the hope that our domestic problems will somehow be solved by other means, and urged that we be lulled
by no relaxation, that we press on with that ultimate conflict
which is the true purpose of our existence on earth. In one of
his most memorable sentences, he has written: "We want to
stay alive, of course; but more than that we want to be free."

I suppose it will always remain somewhat puzzling why a
prosperous provincial merchant, speaking to a prosperous
country with unprecedented facilities at its disposal for all the
varieties of high and low enjoyment, should choose to commit
himself to such a view of the world, should prefer to see the
cold war not as the tragic burden of our epoch but as an opportunity and a challenge in which the meaning of our life can
be found. In this respect Goldwater, the nuclear gambler, takes
his place not among the conservatives of the world, but among
the millennial dreamers, the visionaries, and the inspired agitators. He belongs, it appears, to a type of man, found perhaps
in unusual numbers in this country, for whom the values to
be found in any situation arise not out of the opportunities it
offers for the peaceful arts of negotiation and persuasion but
rather out of the chances it gives to the qualities of aggression
and what is sometimes called virility.

Goldwater also appeals, of course, to a deep and widespread
strain of impatience in the American temperament, against
which thus far our sagacity and our passion for the peaceful
enjoyment of our national life have prevailed. It is difficult for
most Americans to come to terms with the situation of limited
power in which we now live. The circumstances of our historical development have encouraged a complex which D. W. Brogan once called "the illusion of American omnipotence"—the
notion that we are all-powerful in the world, and that failure
to achieve our ends arises only from unforgivable weakness of
will or from treason in high places. In our early national experience, all our military goals were realized with extraordinary
ease and at an extraordinarily low price. Our foes—Indians,
Mexicans, the decaying Spanish Empire—were easily vanquished; and while it is true that we also fought England, it
was at a time when she was fighting with Napoleon for her life
and her operations against us had the character of a sideshow.
Under these circumstances, our expansion across the continent

and our hegemony in the Western Hemisphere were achieved without great standing armies, huge military budgets, long casualty lists—in short, without those staggering costs that the peoples of Europe have always paid as the price of national security or national conquests. Even our entry into the First World War did not change this frame of expectation, for we came in when the contesting powers were bled white and our entry quickly tipped the scales.

It was only in fact after the Second World War that we began to realize that we were living in a situation which we could not fully control. This realization explains, I believe, the hysterical reaction to the Korean war which brought the era of MacArthur and McCarthy. Our policy-makers have responded soberly enough, on the whole, to the realities of limited power, but these realities remain a tormenting novelty to the public at large. Men like Goldwater cater to the impatience of people who find it inconceivable that our cold-war frustrations, in Vietnam, Cuba, Laos, or Berlin, can be the consequences of forces outside our control, and who still hope that all our problems can be solved by some simple, violent gesture. Americans yearn to go back to the days of cheap and quick triumphs, and Goldwater appeals to this wishfulness when he promises that we will at one and the same time destroy the power of the Communist world and pay much lower taxes.

While Goldwater's approach to the cold war appeals to a strong strain of aggressiveness and impatience, this appeal is more than counterbalanced by the anxieties it arouses. The public does not want to take unnecessary risks of being incinerated to further Goldwater's crusade, and the Senator has never been able to offer them satisfactory reassurance. Asked whether the attempt to press every crisis to a victorious solution will not eventually bring a general war, he can only promise that if we maintain our superiority in weapons, the Soviets will never strike. It hardly occurs to him that this is a promise on which he himself cannot deliver, and that he relies on Moscow and Peking to fulfill it for him. However, there is a curious passage in *Why Not Victory?* in which he flatly admits that they will not. The Communist world, he there asserts, is likely to resort to war only under one of two conditions. The first is, of course, if we invite their attack by political weakness and military disarmament. But the other is "if there is a decisive switch in world affairs to the point where it is obvious they are going to lose." For the moment the Senator characteristically forgets that this is precisely the point to which he is constantly urging us to press them.

V

If the polls are approximately right, as I believe they are, Goldwater starts his campaign far behind, and stands in danger of being remembered as the Republican who lost Vermont. Branded as a reckless extremist, he now has only about a month left to work a drastic change in his reputation. The technique he has always relied upon may have come to the limit of its usefulness. Goldwater has always taken advantage of the fact that the masses do not think in syllogisms but in striking images and dramatic events. In counting upon the irrationality of the public, however, he has perhaps failed to estimate the risk he has been taking of running afoul of its feeling for character. The American electorate may not try to assess its leaders by engaging in a close rational appraisal of their programs; but it does look for a certain quality and consistency in character, and seems to feel its way toward a judgment on these grounds. It does not demand that a man be wholly rational in argument, much less that he be brilliant or witty; but it asks, especially in these times, for a certain steadiness, moderation, and reliability. The process by which it arrives at a judgment is not infallible, of course, but neither is it altogether ineffective. In our own time, our more menacing public figures, such as MacArthur and McCarthy, who had very real discontents to exploit, were in the end rejected, the first because he seemed too grandiose and aggressive, the second as too sly and sinister.

Goldwater can appeal with some effect to a variety of irritations and complaints, but it is difficult for him to find a positive issue, one that does not rest in being against something or on desiring to restore something out of the unrecoverable past. In this respect he is at the same disadvantage in campaigning against Johnson and the Democrats as the moderate Republicans have been in past years. The Democrats encompass such a wide range in the American consensus that they leave little room for alternative programs. Republican issues today are made of odds and ends, and they are mainly negative. The Bobby Baker penumbra has a limited yield, and that chiefly among those already persuaded. The white backlash seems to be less portentous than a month ago, though we are certain to hear a good deal about violence and crime in the streets. The effort to disembarrass himself of the onus of nuclear reckless- ness will take up a great deal of Goldwater's time, and we may here see more of his ingenious improvisations. The charge that President Johnson authorized the discretionary use of tacti- cal nuclear weapons in the Gulf of Tonkin was another of his experiments in salesmanship, an attempt to suggest that per- haps we are really all nuclear gamblers together. It may be safer and more effective, however, simply to identify the Republican party as the party of peace and to affirm his own intention to carry on with its traditions. In Goldwater's first campaign speech at Prescott, Arizona, the word "peace" occurred twenty times.

We seem sure, then, to hear a good deal more of Goldwater III during the coming weeks. Goldwater must rely upon the hope that his appearance on the television screen, a hand- some, earnest, well-meaning man, preaching relatively famil- iar Republican doctrine, will effectively contradict the idea of the inhumane and trigger-happy extremist about whom the Democrats will be talking. But here he must thread his way rather nicely through a strategic dilemma: without a great deal of Goldwater III, Goldwater I can hardly be effaced; and yet if the true believers have to swallow too much of Goldwater III, their enthusiasm may wane and the cult will begin to fade. All this recent talk about compassion in government for example, must surely strike them as a lot of malarkey, and it was not for this thin brew that they put Goldwater where he is.

Although we have good reason to be sanguine about the re- sults of the election, the outlook for the Republican party, and hence for the health of our two-party system, is much more clouded. The events at the Cow Palace showed what an un- usual kind of control Goldwater had acquired over his party. He won his nomination not by demonstrating his popularity with the rank and file of its voters or by negotiating with its other leaders but by drawing around him a disciplined personal

following, linked to him by strong ideological ties and a messianic faith. His grip on the party apparatus is daily being tightened, and some of his most forthright Republican foes may be
defeated this fall precisely because his name leads the ticket.

One cannot therefore lightly assume that it will be as easy
to dispose of Goldwater as is usually the case with badly defeated candidates. The disaster toward which he appears to be
heading may shake his cult to the point at which it will be
possible to dislodge the Goldwaterites from the party controls,
but only at the cost of bitter struggles in many key states. The
problem confronting the moderate Republicans if and when
they retake the party from him remains inordinately difficult.
There is, after all, one point on which the right-wing Republicans have made a good case: the Republican moderates lack a
firm, separate identity. The whole spectrum of middle-ground
positions has been pre-empted by the Democrats—and never
so effectively as under President Johnson. So long as the Republican moderates are committed to keeping their party in
the American mainstream, they have had little to offer but a
choice that is only an echo.

It is always dangerous to predict the demise of a major party
in our political system, as the commentators of the 1920s discovered who persistently heralded the imminent disappearance
of the Democrats. But Goldwater may have given the Republican party the coup de grâce as a genuine major-party competitor. We may be headed for a kind of party-and-a-half system
(a situation comparable to Britain's if Labour loses this year) in
which the tasks of government normally rest in the hands of the
single major party, and in which the alternate party can expect
to return to power under, a most extraordinary combination of
circumstances. Whatever may be said about the limitations of
the two-party system in the past, it is hard to believe that such
an arrangement would be better or safer for us, especially since
in this country the minor party would always be a sitting duck
for the ultras and the cranks.

One can only sympathize, then, with the Republican moderates in the formidable double enterprise that lies ahead of them,
first of retaking the party from the cult that now runs it and
then of finding for it a program that steers clear of right-wing
ultra commitments and yet can be distinguished on sound and

significant points from what the Democrats have to offer. As one contemplates the difficulties that bestrew this course, one realizes that, come what may, Barry Goldwater has already left a deep scar on our political system: this self-proclaimed "conservative" is within a hair's breadth of ruining one of our great and long-standing institutions. When, in all our history, has anyone with ideas so bizarre, so archaic, so self-confounding, so remote from the basic American consensus, ever gone so far?

1964

Goldwater & His Party

The True Believer and the Radical Right

AT THE present writing, it seems unlikely that Barry Gold-water will be elected, at least in 1964, but his nomination is in itself a vital blow at the American political order. He has broken the usual rules of political conduct by treating a major party as a "front" organisation, capturing it neither through overwhelming popularity among its voters nor through a careful accommodation of the desires of its established national leaders, but by means of a fanatical and well-drilled minority faction organised throughout the country. He has altered the character of the party by committing it firmly to an ideology, which alone would be a minor revolution, but which is particularly remarkable here because of the extreme and reckless quality of that ideology. If he is successful, whether elected or not, in consolidating this party coup, he will have brought about a realignment of the parties that will put the democratic process in this country in jeopardy. One is loath to speculate on the consequences for the safety of the world.

In the past, the American political party has always been a consensual, accommodating, non-ideological instrument run by experienced and practical men, whose aim was to attract a coalition of interests broad enough first to win the presidency and then to make effective government possible. Goldwater's experiences have been such as to bring him to a wholly different conception. Being fundamentally a preacher and an ideologue, he draws his strength from his peculiar notions rather than from any practical achievements; and, representing a minority point of view, he has relied upon organisation and zealotry rather than negotiation and accommodation to promote his cause. For the present, his campaign plan seems to be based less vitally on reincorporating the party interests he has spurned, than on inciting resentments, asserting convictions, and developing visions, in the hope that he can weld together a mass of grievances and delusions large enough to win office. That part of the country that shows least promise of conforming is not to be appeased but is to be written off for the purposes of the campaign. Nor is this process of exclusion softened by the acceptance of outsiders into Goldwater's high command, which is staffed largely by men who, however intelligent and effective as partisan organisers, share his provincial views on the basic problems of policy.

The American political party seems to be a rather blunt instrument, notably at convention time, but it is in fact a highly sophisticated piece of apparatus, very appropriate to its vital function. Ingenious as the American constitution originally was, it would still have been inadequate for the government of this sprawling continental nation, with its wide variety of interests and its unruly and often violent people, had it not been later supplemented by the two-party system. The necessary role of parties was not only not foreseen by the Founding Fathers but was completely misapprehended. They had before them no model of a satisfactory party system, and could think of the party, which they called "faction," only as a threat to the proper balance of forces within the state, as a narrow representative of a small special interest, which might override and dominate all other interests. Our constitutional machinery, with its elaborate checks and balances, was intended to prevent any such thing from happening.

The danger in this system was that checks and balances might prevent anything at all from happening, that the federal system would fall to pieces through its inability to create an adequate governing apparatus. It is hard to see how a country so sprawling, so heterogeneous, so suspicious of power, could have been governed at all if some mechanism could not be found to bring together its hodge-podge of sections, states, and commercial interests. Perhaps the main theme of our political history in the early 19th century was the quest for a party system adequate to the task. The country had hardly evolved such a system in the era of the Jacksonians and the Whigs—the Federalist-Jeffersonian division was too irregular and impermanent to qualify as a system—when it began to break down over the slavery issue. As long as there were two intersectional parties, the Union was held together. When there was none, it broke up, and the Civil War followed.

Critics of our system have often said that our political life is dreary and unconstructive because the major parties, being two roughly similar coalitions of heterogeneous interests, cannot settle on clear principles or debate profound issues. They have often argued that a sharper division in our party ideologies along conservative and progressive lines would serve us better. They have assumed that keener ideological debate and greater intellectual clarity would be identical, and that it would be better to fight out our social issues to some kind of satisfactory finish rather than to go on smoothing them over in the inconclusive manner of our major parties. It appears that we are now about to get a sharper ideological division, and keener social conflict, and they may not like it as well as they anticipated.

The ethos and the conduct of the American major parties have always been shaped by the task of building a coalition that cuts across sections, across classes, and even across issues. The most vital demand of the system is that the factions within a party (usually there are two, and as James M. Burns has argued, in recent times these tend to be the presidential and the congressional factions) somehow avoid a fight to the death and that both conform to a series of rituals by which compromise may be achieved. The losing faction is appeased and reincorporated as an internal loyal opposition in return for its support for the national ticket.

These rituals are acted out at party conventions in a variety of ways. If there are many aspirants to the nomination, sharp two-sided feeling is avoided, and the winner finds it necessary to placate the broad range of party forces which were previously against him. A governing consideration, which tempers the ferocity of the intra-party combat and leads to a quick closing of the ranks at each convention, is that the nomination must be worth having—that is, that the party cannot be so damaged in the public eye by the spectacle of its internal conflicts that its chances in the election are ruined. A characteristic example of the cost of violating these precepts was the Democratic party convention of 1924, when the delegates wrangled ferociously over a plank condemning the Ku Klux Klan and was so deadlocked between the irreconcilable followers of Al Smith and

W. G. McAdoo that it finally after sixteen days of turmoil had
to settle on a compromise candidate, John W. Davis. The prospects of the party that year were not good to begin with but
Davis made as weak a showing as any Democrat has ever done.

Since the 1920s, the Democrats have not repeated that mistake. The achievement of the Democratic party over the past
thirty years has been testimony to the effectiveness of the consensual ethos. Since the days of FDR, for example, the Democratic party has been the chief vehicle through which the needs
of American Negroes were met and through which their political aspirations have been expressed; and yet at the same time,
it has been, despite some breaks, the party of the traditional
South. Naturally, this arrangement has not been satisfactory
to either side, and it has grown less so as time has gone on
and racial tensions have grown. At the moment it seems to be
breaking up. But in the meantime it has achieved the difficult
feat of governing peacefully and maintaining a consensus and
yet of making some progress toward racial accommodation
and justice in the face of an extremely explosive issue.

In its exceptionally delicate performance on this issue, the
Democratic party has only done what the two major parties
have tried to do with varying success on a variety of issues
over the past hundred years. There has been almost no point
at which a major party has not been significantly divided over
some major issue. Naturally, the constant task of accommodating broad differences under the same roof has regularly led to
the blurring of issues, to a great deal of juggling and about-
facing by the skilled professionals. It has also led to a built-in
pattern of hypocrisy. But the American political party is based
on the understanding that in politics hypocrisy is a minor vice
and a major virtue: its other name is tact.

The tact that must of necessity govern the conduct of our great
parties has led to certain rituals for the conduct of their conventions. When a sharp, two-sided fight takes place, it is considered
vital to have a solemn closing of the ranks. For this, several
devices are available. The defeated candidate may concede, or
present a motion to make the nomination unanimous, and he
always denounces the opposition party with renewed vigour,
and promises to support the victor with all his energy. But the

primary obligation rests on the winner himself. He may take the loser on his ticket as vice-presidential candidate—as Kennedy did with Johnson in 1960—and if he does not, he is very likely to choose someone congenial to the loser and his followers. He may make elaborate efforts to appease him and arrive at a *rapprochement*—as Eisenhower did with Taft in 1952.

The party platform provides another means for a ritual demonstration of unity. Americans themselves are often bewildered about the function of these long, tedious documents. It is sometimes said that no one reads them, and Goldwater has said that they are nothing but a lot of lies and misinformation. But writing a party platform is an important symbolic act, in which the leaders prove to themselves and to the country that they stand close enough to agree on a statement of promises and proposals. The proposals may be vague, but willingness all around to consent to their vagueness is in itself a token of capacity for compromise. When parties have been drawn into a fierce struggle over one or two planks in a platform, this is because their disunity is too great to be resolved off the floor of the convention. A possible technique for appeasement is to adopt a platform somewhat at odds with the beliefs and commitments of the candidate. In effect, this is what would have happened in San Francisco if any of the three major platform amendments proposed by the moderates—on civil rights, the condemnation of extremism, and the civilian control of nuclear weapons—had been adopted.

The Goldwater forces flouted all these conciliatory devices at San Francisco, and left the defeated faction bruised and shocked both by their manner and by the substance of what they did. Their least provocative act was in what they put in their platform, most of which can be accepted widely throughout the party. But what they left out was a source of fatal discord: an endorsement of the principle of civil rights, and an appeal for enforcement of and obedience to the existing laws. On this issue, where Senator Goldwater stands at odds with most of his party in Congress, the record of the party's liberals and moderates was first repudiated by silence, and then repudiated vocally in the rejection of the moderates' platform amendments.

A particular shock came with the rejection of the resolution calling for the condemnation of extremist groups. It became clear in the course of the debate that this proposition was not only unacceptable to the majority of the delegates but that they took it as a personal affront. Not only was Governor Rockefeller almost booed off the rostrum when he delivered an able speech arguing for this resolution, but there was a moment when the newspaper correspondents feared that a number of delegates might climb up on the rostrum and assault him. (At this point the Goldwater managers made a successful effort to control their delegates on the floor, but they were unable to check the bellowing of the true believers in the galleries.)

In the choice of a vice-presidential candidate, Goldwater could hardly have been expected to settle on Governor Scranton or any of the other moderates. The contest had been too fierce and Scranton's own controversial letter to the delegates had gone well beyond customary convention good manners. But there were possible middle-range candidates, like the convention chairman Thruston Morton, who would have added strength to the ticket and appeal to a broad middle range of the party. Instead, Goldwater chose the fiercely conservative William Miller, from upstate New York. As Chairman of the Republican National Committee, Miller is fairly well known to party leaders, but to the public he is a nonentity, who was about to retire from his own congressional seat. He adds neither dignity nor solidity, only ardent partisanship, to the ticket. The essential fact is that he can conform wholly to Goldwater's opinions.

Having given many moderates a ticket and a platform which they can hardly support in their campaigns at home without cutting their own throats, Goldwater spurned the chance to make a last conciliatory gesture in his acceptance speech. Some of the loudest brayings heard at the convention came in response to his defence of extremism: "Let me remind you that extremism in the defence of liberty is no vice. And let me remind you also that moderation in the pursuit of justice is no virtue." He also served notice that he expected no campaign help from "those who do not care for our cause." On this count he has reconsidered. At the Republican summit meeting of August 12th, Goldwater said almost all of the conciliatory things that custom demanded be said, but that could not be said from the convention platform without shrivelling the true believers in their seats. He has now won the support, however grudging and suspicious, of General Eisenhower and the other leading moderates; and while some of the faithful may be a little disturbed at the conciliatory noises he has made, the great majority will console themselves with the thought that this was all a concession to campaign strategy and that in his heart of hearts Barry still belongs to them. My guess is that they are right, and that Eisenhower now holds from Goldwater, in return for his valuable support, a handsome ideological cheque, which will be returned from the bank (if Eisenhower ever remembers to present it) marked "insufficient funds."

It would be easy to show how a series of events, each more or less accidental, was required to put a man as unrepresentative of American thinking as Barry Goldwater is, at the head of a major party. But the forces upon which his strength rests are neither accidental nor easily eradicable, and the organisation he has forged is of such character that his continued possession of power need not rest on sheer good luck.

One of the difficulties of the American party system during the period since the great depression lies in the fact that the Democratic party has been all too successful in straddling the broad middle ground, has in itself been too adequate a repository of the national consensus, and has garnered too large a proportion of the country's liberal-minded political talents. The Republican party has been starved for talents and for issues. Its right wing is, in a large degree, quite correct when it says that the moderates have been unable to give the public a very decisive choice, and that their main appeal since 1940 has been that, while they would do largely what the Democrats are doing, they would do it better. The right-wing Republicans have floundered in a state of frustration. This mood was broken only briefly by Eisenhower's administration. Eisenhower did not provide the sharp departure from the past that the right-wingers wanted. The effect of his interim was to quicken their impatience without subordinating them in the party.

In a certain sense, Goldwater has floated to the top as a result of a process of elimination. His rise to prominence dates back to the Congressional elections of 1958. In that year of disaster for the Republicans, almost the entire school of activist

ultra-conservative Republican senators who had come in during
the elections of 1946 and 1952 was wiped out—with the exception of the Senator from Arizona, who won re-election easily.
This is not to say that Goldwater's prominence in the right
wing is the consequence only of a lack of alternatives, for he
offers a very positive charisma and organisational capabilities
of his own; the point is that it left him in almost uncontested
leadership of the right wing. He had a noisy and enthusiastic
following at the Republican convention of 1960, and one of
the few direct and appealing moments at an extremely ugly
convention came with his ritual speech of withdrawal in favour
of Richard Nixon, in which he urged his followers to "grow
up," swallow their disappointments, support manfully the party's choice, and work hard to take it over at some future time.
He lived up to his own words and worked ardently for Vice-
President Nixon in the 1960 campaign. During the years that
followed, he continued to make himself available for speeches
to local groups throughout the country, campaigning tirelessly
for his "conservative" principles and addressing about 200 audiences a year. He helped scores of local Republican committees to raise funds, exposed his charms to thousands of party
workers, and put a multitude of Republican officeholders in his
debt. When his qualification for the presidency is questioned,
it is customary for his followers to cite, not his administrative
experience in government (for this he lacks), or his work in the
Senate (he is an outstanding absentee), or his association with
important legislation (he has none), but the generous ardour
of his services to the party. On this count, what he has done
can hardly be overstated, but it is a sobering thought to those
who are not enchanted by the Goldwater creed that his main
experience in political life consists in preaching a militant ideology to audiences already largely converted.

While Goldwater was thus expending himself, an organisational transformation was going on all over the country. The
party had been disorganised and demoralised by Nixon's inept campaign. When it was over, Goldwater's true believers
promptly moved in to fill the structural and moral vacuum,
while the moderate leaders rested on their oars, assuming that
they would be able to move in, as they had always done, in the

next campaign year. Goldwater men infiltrated the party much as the Communists in their days of strength infiltrated liberal organisations in order to use them as front groups. Working with highly disciplined cells or cadres, they rapidly took over county and town committees, developed their own local candidates, and prepared for battle at the national level. It was not until the San Francisco convention that anyone fully understood that they had become a highly disciplined fighting force. It is their achievement which largely explains why a candidate like Goldwater, whose showing in polls and primaries was so weak, proved so strong in the convention.

It was at this point that a series of events fortuitous for Goldwater began to occur. After President Kennedy's murder, the polls showed a great closing of the ranks of public sentiment around Lyndon Johnson. It began to look as though 1964 would be an easy Democratic year. Since the prize of the Republican nomination appeared to have diminished in value, the Republican moderates tended to lurk in the wings, wondering if they should not hold off until 1968. The only exception was Nelson Rockefeller, and his candidacy was sapped by another fortuitous occurrence—his divorce and remarriage. Among the men prominently mentioned for the nomination during the past year, he seems to have had much less appeal for the rank and file than Lodge or Nixon, and even a little less than Goldwater himself. It was this relatively weak opposition that Goldwater chiefly faced in the primaries. Both men seemed to have received a fatal blow last March in the New Hampshire primaries, when their strenuous campaigning efforts seemed only to have lost ground for them. Oddly enough, Goldwater's reverse there worked in the end to his advantage by further lulling the party moderates; at that point, when polls and primaries had demonstrated his unpopularity with the party's voters, few people took his candidacy seriously. But in the California primary it was his good fortune to draw once again as his sole opponent—the others had not filed in time —Rockefeller again. Even then, he nosed Rockefeller out with the narrowest of margins. Yet it now suddenly became clear that Goldwater had accumulated such an edge in delegates that it would require almost a political miracle to stop him.

At this point, Eisenhower's peculiar political—or apolitical

—mentality takes its place in the making of Goldwater; for in a very real sense, though he promises to undo the best work of Eisenhower's administration, Goldwater is Eisenhower's legacy to the party. What Eisenhower imagined he was doing in standing by in benevolent neutrality while Goldwater's forces advanced it is difficult to say. It is often very hard to tell what, or whether, he is thinking. His influence, unequivocally exerted, could have stopped Goldwater, certainly before California and possibly even afterward. Whatever his motives—personal vanity, unwillingness to become involved in the party scramble, misconceived notions about the way to foster party unity, or even a growing regard for Goldwater's views on domestic affairs—Eisenhower's course was curious. He had made a wholly gratuitous pledge a year earlier not to intervene in the choice of a nominee. Then he made hesitant gestures toward departing from this resolution, encouraging Scranton to enter the lists at an hour so late that success without Eisenhower's vigorous intervention was all but impossible. Finally, he withdrew and left Scranton unsupported on the firing line. He was plainly distressed at the conduct of the Goldwater forces in the convention, and by Goldwater's pronouncement on "extremism," but there is little doubt that he will campaign for the nominee, and very little chance that he will have the slightest moderating influence on Goldwater's thinking. Eisenhower's endorsement is always valuable in a campaign, but now nothing short of the threat to withhold it could have restored any of his influence. His befuddled and impotent conduct in the last few months has destroyed whatever regard party leaders on either side may still have had for him. Goldwater has already administered a calculated snub by failing to pay him a courtesy call at the close of the convention.

Barry Goldwater is a small-town politician, whose formal education ended at the close of his freshman year at the University of Arizona, and whose formative adult experiences have come from the management (now relinquished) of a substantial department store in Phoenix, his service as a flier of transport planes in the war, and his indefatigable speech-making as senator. His thinking is flavoured by a feeling for the frontier virtues and the ideas of classical economic individualism, which are the chief sources of his militant philosophy. In many ways he is like a European's caricature of the western American mind, with his cowboy virtues and old-fashioned prudential morality on one side and his love of ultra-modern gadgetry on the other. He likes to fly his own plane, is an excellent photographer, enjoys fiddling with an amateur radio transmitter, and has a flagpole at his house in Phoenix on which Old Glory is automatically elevated at dawn when the first rays of the sun strike a photoelectric cell. He is a splendid example of an American naïf, a kind of political Grandma Moses. Part of his strength rests on the fact that there are thousands of businessmen around the country, large and small, who think just as he does.

As a westerner, a flier, a horseman, an enthusiastic hobbyist, Goldwater exploits an adventurous outdoors appeal reminiscent, among our politicians, of Theodore Roosevelt's, though without T.R.'s additional appeal to progressives and intellectuals. A man of remarkable energy, he strikes resonances in the American craving for action, for movement, for aggressive utterance. Whereas his critics have found his hard-boiled statements evidence of a dangerous impulsiveness, his advocates see in them only the quality of masculine decision. "Impulsive?" one of his friends is reported to have said impatiently. "How about Teddy Roosevelt? Or Harry Truman? . . . Barry is my idea of a Teddy Roosevelt who is right for this time. He is a tough guy. I think he would make a great President if this country ever got into another war." This last incautious sentence inverts yet precisely expresses the fear of those who are most disquieted by Goldwater—that if he ever got to be President of this country, he would make another great war.

In his manner of speaking Goldwater is no demagogue or rabble-rouser. He seems happiest and most effective in small groups and more at home in expounding general principles than in analysing issues in depth. Like many men of active mind but limited formal education, he is intrigued by big generalisations that have the ring of profundity in them. His acceptance speech was almost comically vague, full of broad rhetoric about "the whole man," which at best could have been intelligible only to those who had already read and remembered his book, *The Conscience of a Conservative*, and decorated with lofty promises about the creation of an "Atlantic civilisation, the whole of Europe reunified and freed, trading openly across its borders, communicating openly across the world." One could only wonder if he could possibly not know that there is no American politician less likely to be able to do anything to realise this vision than he is.

There was a time when it seemed that Goldwater did not take his own presidential aspirations too seriously or too hopefully. It was almost as though he preferred the role of the agitator, the prophet, the ideologue, to that of the administrator, for which as yet he has shown neither taste nor aptitude. He has been quoted as saying, "I'm a salesman trying to sell the conservative view of government," and "I'm not even sure that I've got the brains to be President of the United States." The magazines have been retelling a story that is supposed to have occurred shortly after the Bay of Pigs fiasco, when Goldwater called on Kennedy, who had stepped out of his office for a few minutes. While waiting, Goldwater sat in Kennedy's rocking chair, and the President, seeing him there, asked genially, "You think you want this job?" "Good God, no!" Goldwater replied. Of course, all that is over now: the machinery has been set in motion and the dreams have been kindled. But the suspicion survives that Goldwater would rather be right-wing than President, and that he accordingly pursues the office with a less circumspect opportunism than any other politician has shown. Ironically, this might in the end prove to be an asset.

Precisely because Goldwater's ideas were not formed in the expectation that they would have to be translated into policy, they have a kind of utopian quality that is more often found in our visionary literature than in our politics. Probably everyone in public life deserves a sympathetic exposition of his ideas, but I find myself unable to enter into his mental world, which seems to be that of another century and a wholly different style of thought. Is it a gross caricature of his ideas to conclude that he proposes to dismantle, as far as possible, the federal government, and then with this enfeebled instrument to wage the cold war more aggressively than anyone has done before? Or that he proposes drastically to increase America's military strength while balancing the budget and considerably cutting back, if not abandoning, the income tax? Or that he has committed himself to bringing about a society in which urban violence is curbed and the streets are kept safe, while expounding constitutional views under which federal intervention in the sphere of urban development is strictly forbidden?

A list of Goldwater's inconsistencies could be spun out to some length, and President Johnson is reported to treasure a substantial book of provocative and jangling Goldwater quotations compiled by the Democratic National Committee. Yet I think Goldwater is probably right in thinking that his varying pronouncements gain for him more than they lose. The educated rationalist may snicker at him, but Goldwater has seized upon the fact that the masses do not think in syllogisms but in striking images and dramatic events, that they respond to promises and to strongly-worded restatements of their own feelings without demanding to be told how such promises and statements can be geared to legislative and administrative programmes.

A close analysis of Goldwater's pronouncements would show, I believe, that they were issued in two sequences. The first, which apparently represents his natural and impulsive feelings, consists of the extreme utterances with which he first won his following. The second represents a more recent phase, probably beginning when his serious presidential aspirations quickened, and in this phase he has moderated or explained away some of his earlier remarks, conceding as little as he can to the requirements of opportunism. In his first phase, with his far-out line of talk, he won the true believers who have done such hard work for him; in the second he is successfully lulling a broader, middle-ground audience which must be persuaded that he is really not so reckless as he has been pictured. By now Goldwater has evolved a rhetorical technique which enables him to cast off a policy suggestion that will strike home with the far right and yet to couple it with some kind of technical disclaimer which enables him to escape from the full odium of his position. For example, campaigning in New Hampshire, he denied that he was altogether against Social Security, and called this charge "a flagrant lie." But he added that he believed Social Security recipients by 1970 "will be asking questions such as whether better programmes couldn't be bought on the private market."

One possible explanation of Goldwater's extraordinary pronouncements, quite aside from a strain of irritability in his temperament which becomes visible when he campaigns, may lie in his characterisation of himself as "a salesman of ideas." One of his great triumphs in Phoenix, as an enterprising merchandiser, was in making men's underwear figured with red ants, which were sold widely under the catchy label, "ANTSY PANTS." Goldwater is, in this sense, an idea man, and his sudden suggestions that the Marines be sent to turn on the water at Guantanamo, or that the jungle in Vietnam might be defoliated with nuclear weapons, may in fact be not so much policy proposals as efforts to hit on formulae that the consumers will like. Such proposals are put forth, however aggressive they may sound, as tentative ideas, and may be withdrawn if they don't seem to be going down well. This frame of mind may help to explain why Goldwater is so annoyed when his statements are seized upon by newspapermen (who are indeed generally hostile to him) as indiscretions. In the case of the defoliation remark, for example, he has pointed out that it was mentioned as one possible line of procedure which he did not in fact think would be followed. After having so carefully prepared one's retreat, it is provoking to be misconstrued.

While Goldwater's shifting pronouncements on foreign policy may be the subject of much partisan discussion, it is more important, if one hopes to grasp what he is up to, to discern the thread of consistency that runs through them. What does emerge is a constantly held conception of the Cold War. Goldwater rejects the current search for security with coexistence. Writing in *The New York Times* in September 1961, he said: "Nor is there such a thing as peaceful coexistence." To him the Cold War appears rather as a series of showdowns with the Communist nations—all of which can be won if we are firm enough and have superior strength. He believes that we can go on to the end to total victory through a long series of such essays in brinkmanship without the danger of provoking a war. He is convinced that the United States is losing in such confrontations, and that this is a planned procedure. As recently as March, he asserted that this country is now engaged in unilateral disarmament, and he is firmly convinced that our weaponry is not strong enough. In discussing tight situations his mind quickly jumps to the solutions to be achieved by the use of tactical nuclear weapons, and he has proposed that regional commanders, like the commander of NATO, should have discretion in the use of such weapons.

Goldwater once advocated withdrawal from the U.N., but now only if Red China is admitted. He also once proposed withdrawing recognition from the Soviet Union, but his present position seems to be that the threat of such withdrawal could be used to gain some concessions. He voted against the nuclear test ban. He is in general opposed to foreign economic aid, though he has said that when we have to resort to it, it should be "used as a 'rifle' aimed at specific areas where we can gain an advantage over the Russians." There are times when his casual approach to the issues of the thermonuclear age is reminiscent of the sergeant in the First World War who, urging his men on into a particularly dangerous action, is supposed to have called out: "Come on, you bastards, do you want to live forever?" Characteristic of his manner of formulating and reacting to public issues was a comment he made in *The Conscience of a Conservative* about Khrushchev's visit to this country: "A craven fear of death is entering the American consciousness; so much so that many recently felt that honouring the chief despot himself was the price we had to pay to avoid nuclear destruction."

Goldwater's followers, as one saw them in action at San Francisco, make their leader seem relatively bland. The Republican moderates and the gentlemen of the press were shocked by the virulent sentiments often expressed by delegates in private, as well as by occasional outbursts during the convention proceedings. On the whole, the Goldwater delegates seem to shade off from the extremist right of the John Birch Society, the Ku Klux Klan, and the White Citizens' Councils toward a more moderate centre where ultra-conservatism and genuine conservatism meet. Newspapermen were impressed by the high proportion of new faces. These were newcomers who had just entered politics and who had only recently won places for themselves in precincts and counties throughout the country. They were neither poor, rustic, nor uneducated; they hardly seemed to be suffering great deprivation under the welfare state they detest so much; and it is one of the ironies of our situation that such fierce discontent should exist among people who are doing so well.

A newspaperman described an encounter with a young woman delegate from a Midwestern state—beautiful, elegantly dressed, and articulate. She was plainly from a very affluent family, and had attended one of the best girls' colleges in the East. There, however, she had resisted the intellectual blandishments of the professors, who, she assured my informant, were all socialists. The conversation turned to Eisenhower. It appeared that she had swallowed the John Birch line without the slightest scepticism. We had done so badly in the Cold War under Eisenhower, she explained to the baffled reporter, that it could only have been the product either of treachery or stupidity on Eisenhower's part. And since it was unthinkable, she concluded triumphantly, that the general is stupid. . . . In the light of such stories, as well as the howlings of the audience at the proposal that extremists be condemned, it becomes possible to believe the claim of a John Birch Society official that as many as a hundred members of that organisation were among the delegates.

What animates these formidable warriors? Aside from feelings aroused by the racial issue, so important for the Southern bloc but not for them alone, it is too easy to say that Goldwater is the hero of the economic troglodytes. Undoubtedly an important role is played by rich businessmen without a shred of social sympathy, who have hated the New Deal reforms for thirty years, and for whom the income tax is a major concern. They will provide the cause with funds, but there is something much deeper and more forceful behind the Goldwater movement than mere material hoggishness, which is almost always a certain loser in national politics. The Goldwater fanatics are not, and do not feel themselves to be, self-seeking. Their view of public issues may have been shaped by self-seekers, but they are themselves dedicated enthusiasts and malcontents, who

want to do something good for America and for the world.
(Those European critics who prattle mindlessly about the
menace of American materialism have probably never given
thought to the potentialities of American idealism.) I believe
that Senator Tower of Texas touched upon one of their major
concerns when he referred to the "moral decay" that we find
around us, and that Goldwater struck another in expressing
distaste for the "computer-regimented sameness" of our civilisation. The Goldwater movement is a revolt against the whole
modern condition as the old-fashioned American sees it—
against the world of organisation and bureaucracy, the welfare
state, our urban disorders, secularism, the decline of American
entrepreneurial bravura, the apparent disappearance of individualism and individuality, and the emergence of unwelcome
international burdens. Although its enthusiasts like to think of
themselves as conservatives, their basic feeling is a hatred of
what America has become and a fierce and uncompromising
insistence that it be made what they think it once was. Though
they can find very little that they want to conserve, the word
conservatism is precious to them because it conceals the wild
utopianism that emerges out of their nostalgia.

Concerning this nostalgia, James Reston wrote in *The New
York Times* at the time of the nomination:

> Mr. Goldwater may attract all the ultras and the antis—the
> forces that are anti-Negro, anti-labour, anti-foreigner, anti-
> intellectual—but he also attracts something else that is precisely
> the opposite of these vicious and negative forces. Mr. Gold-
> water touches the deep feeling of regret in American life: regret
> over the loss of religious faith; regret over the loss of simplicity
> and fidelity; regret over the loss of the frontier spirit of pugna-
> cious individuality; regret, in short, over the loss of America's
> innocent and idealistic youth.

Regret too, Reston might have said, and also anger over the
loss of what once seemed an almost magical capacity to have
our way in the world. No one has said enough about the way
in which our contemporary nationalism has been influenced
by the peculiarities of our strategic history. From our earliest
experiences with nationhood, the American mind was shaped
by the expectation that the national will could be made effective at a relatively small price. We began not as a world power
with world-wide aspirations, but as a continental power with

continental aspirations. Within our limited continental theatre of action, our ability to secure those national goals upon
which we were determined was in effect irresistible. Our foes
—Indians, Mexicans, the decaying Spanish Empire—were on
the whole easily vanquished. It is true that we also fought the
British, but only at a time when they were in mortal combat
with Napoleon. In this way we won our national expansion
without the cost of great standing armies, without great military budgets, without huge casualty lists—without, in short,
those staggering costs that the peoples of Europe have always
had to pay as the price of security or of national victories. Even
when we were first fully drawn into the world theatre of action,
in the First World War, it was only after the other combatants
were bled white and exhausted. Much as that experience was a
departure from our previous traditions, it did not put an end
to the American expectation of quick victory.

It was not until after the end of the Second World War that
we began to realise that we were living in a situation of limited
power, that even after the major effort of that war we were
living in a world that we could not fully control. This realisation came with the Korean conflict, and I believe it goes far
to explain the hysterical response aroused by that war, which
created the era of MacArthur and McCarthy. What D. W. Brogan once called "the illusion of American omnipotence" was
being shattered. On the whole, I believe our political leaders
responded realistically enough to the shattering of this illusion.
But among the public at large, the lesson has not gone down
so well. Americans still find it inconceivable that our Cold-War
frustrations and stalemates in Vietnam, Cuba, Laos, or Berlin
can be the consequence of worldwide circumstances not entirely within our control. They give their minds very readily to
men who tell them, as Goldwater does, that we are in this situation not because this is the way the world is but because we
have had irresolute and infirm leadership; or, as McCarthy and
the founder of the John Birch Society said, because we have
been the victims of constant treason in high places. Americans
want to return to the days of inexpensive triumphs. Against
this background it is a little less surprising that they listen cred-
ulously when Goldwater promises them that we will destroy
the power of the Communist world and pay smaller taxes at

the same time. As he put it in the title of one of his books, *Why Not Victory?* Why not, indeed? And while we are at it, why not victory on the cheap?

Men and women who feel so intensely about political issues are, of course, in a minority in any period short of a revolutionary one. But because they feel strongly their strength is as the strength of multitudes. The Goldwater delegates spoke for a combination of resentments and frustrations so fierce that no ordinary politics, with ordinary compromises and accommodations, will contain them. Richard Rovere has concluded from his observations at San Francisco that these smartly dressed, well-spoken delegates were "as hard as nails," and that they came to the convention not to win a nomination and then combine for the campaign with Goldwater's former enemies, but rather to achieve "total ideological victory and the total destruction of their critics." Their sense of having been long persecuted and betrayed, their impulse to retaliate and to punish, are strong. A key to their mood as significant as their endorsement of extremism was the roar of approval that went up from the crowd when Eisenhower made an unfriendly reference to press opinion, and another in response to his talk about our alleged leniency toward switchblade wielders and other criminals. The effort that Goldwater's managers had to make to restrain the ugly demonstration against Rockefeller may be a foretaste of what is to come. One cannot be sure where the true believers will stop in their passion for revenge, and Goldwater, who is himself not disposed to use McCarthy's rather special techniques, may bring us, willy-nilly, a grass-roots revival of McCarthyism.

What are Goldwater's chances?

Since Truman's feat in 1948, it has become customary to hedge carefully one's election predictions, and it is true that some unpredictable event might set off a strong national current of emotion that would overturn all the usual auguries. If one accepts the only indications now available—Goldwater's performance in the primaries and his rating in the polls—he starts very far behind. I believe it is fair to say, on the strength of public responses to issues over many years, that at the time of his nomination not more than one American in five, at a generous estimate, thought as Goldwater thought. His hope rests upon the fact that a major-party nomination is a splendid fulcrum for raising converts.

At the moment, Goldwater faces a formidable set of problems. He begins as the minority leader within the minority party. Some of the moderates are coming over to him, but he goes into the campaign with his party divided. It appears that he will be the first Republican candidate in our lifetime to have a majority of the press against him. The leaders of organised labour will be singularly hostile. While he will have the preponderance of the business community and plenty of money, surveys show that he enjoys considerably less business support than Republicans usually get. He is trying to unseat, during a period of full prosperity, a popular, formidable, thoroughly professional opponent.

Before the Republican convention, the polls showed Goldwater to have the support of about one voter in five; soon afterward it jumped, not altogether surprisingly, to about one in three. By November he seems certain to do better than this. Only four times in the last hundred years has a major-party candidate in a conventional two-party race finished with less than 40 percent of the vote. In the last two such elections, both won by F.D.R., Alf Landon had 36.5 percent in 1936 and Herbert Hoover 39.6 percent in 1932. If Goldwater is defeated, much hangs on whether he can significantly outstrip such party disasters. His chances of making further converts in the campaign seem good. Before Kennedy's murder last November, a Gallup Poll trial heat matching Goldwater and Kennedy showed a Kennedy lead of 54 to 40, with 6 percent undecided. Goldwater's popularity dropped sharply after the murder, as Johnson's rose, but in running against Johnson now, he is a good bet to pull up at least close to his previous high point in the polls, if not to surpass it.

Goldwater is almost certain to carry most of the South and a sprinkling of electoral votes from the plains and mountain states. His main concern will be to add to these a good share of the industrial Midwest, along with California. His appeal to prudential morality, individualism, and ultra-nationalism will bring him votes from the middle-class WASP (White

Anglo-Saxon Protestant) voters. His great effort must be to strike a congenial note for the industrial working class, which is so largely composed of various ethnic minorities. Hence the Catholicism of his running mate will help, as will a revival of the old demand for the "liberation" of the "captive peoples of Eastern Europe." (Goldwater thinks we should have gone into Hungary in 1956 with a force armed with tactical nuclear weapons.) Although this appeal is lethal, if it is not empty and cynical, it helped Eisenhower in 1952 and it may work again. But Goldwater's main strength will be in the "white backlash." Negro militancy has finally stimulated a strong white reaction, particularly powerful in the working class and among ethnic minorities. Today there is much to be gained by writing off the Negro vote and advancing the Republican party as the white man's party. Goldwater has said that he does not want to exploit racial tensions to win; but the convention shows that he has already found an indirect way of doing so. Without inciting racial feeling or endorsing discrimination, to which he is opposed, he can strike the necessary note by talking about violence, demonstrations, and urban crime. At the moment no one professes to know how large the backlash vote will be, but it could be decisive.

Unlike such right-wing heroes as General MacArthur, who was too grandiose for the American temper, or Joe McCarthy, who appeared sinister when the public had a good long look at him on television, Goldwater is personally appealing. Untoward events can help to put him into closer contention— more race riots in Northern cities, further disturbances in the South, disasters in Southeast Asia. No one knows how voters would respond if the President should have a recurrence of his heart trouble during the campaign. Goldwater can hardly be written off, and most of those who were disposed to do so a few weeks ago have changed their minds.

Few commentators have remarked on what seems to me the most ominous side of Goldwater's nomination, which is that he does not need to win to hold control of his party and retake the nomination in 1968; he needs only to avoid being overwhelmed, and this now seems within his grasp. Normally, of course, a defeated presidential candidate has only modest influence in his party, especially if he is altogether out of office as Goldwater would be (his Senate seat expires). But Goldwater's grip on his party is unusual. Normal candidates lead their party; he owns it. Unless his zealots are demoralised by a smashing campaign defeat and then fought, precinct by precinct, county by county, and state by state, by the Republican moderates, there is little to prevent his renomination. Even an election defeat, though it will lower his moral strength, might have the effect of increasing his grip on the party. The leading moderates are, for the most part, situated in highly competitive areas, and are more likely to be decimated in a party defeat than the Goldwater people, who occupy less hotly contested posts.

In order for the Republican moderates—Rockefeller, Romney, Scranton, and their associates and heirs—to repossess the party even from a defeated Goldwater, they will have to do what presidential aspirants have not previously been in the habit of doing. They will have to organise as a united faction long in advance of the 1968 convention, and in their private conclaves will have to make decisions that are usually made only in the convention itself. For example, they will have to agree on a single candidate to represent the moderate cause and will have to start rallying and organising moderate Republicans years in advance of the event.

There is every sign, on the contrary, that they will play the usual gentlemanly party game as though they were dealing with a typical party leader. They are, on the whole, decent and well-meaning men, who could easily produce from among their number someone capable of governing the country and keeping the peace. The question is whether they are capable of reclaiming the party from Goldwater and his true believers. By and large, the top-ranking moderates represent a privileged and moneyed class that has moved into positions of public leadership, not without effort or desire, but without the fierce partisan wrangles and tedious organisational work that has to be done by men who come up from the bottom. They have no fanatical creed that sets them sharply off from the Democrats as Goldwater's creed sets him off. Being men of judgment, and not zealots or messiahs, they are not possessed by delusions about the wonders they could accomplish if elected; and precisely because they know the difficulties of the real world, they cannot inspire the animating faith that makes Goldwater's militants so effective.

If I am right, Goldwater owns his party for the calculable future, and if he fails this year, is likely to have another try. This is one of those moments when

> *Things fall apart; the centre cannot hold . . .*
> *The best lack all conviction, while the worst*
> *Are full of passionate intensity.*

I have never been persuaded by those who see the wave of a coming apocalypse in every wrinkle on the social surface; but it is now much easier than before to believe that America is visibly sick with a malady that may do all of us in.

1964

The Goldwater Débâcle

THERE ARE times when it is a pleasure to acknowledge that one has been wrong. Writing on the Goldwater movement in the October issue of ENCOUNTER, I concluded that "it is now much easier than before to believe that America is visibly sick with a malady that may do all of us in." This was said, as the setting made clear, in the belief not that Barry Goldwater would win—which never seemed likely—but rather that he might make a respectable showing, and that if he did Goldwaterism would be entrenched in the Republican Party for the calculable future with incalculably mischievous consequences.

As it turned out, Goldwater's showing was far from respectable. The vote was unmistakably cast *against him*. Almost everywhere he ran far behind other Republicans, drawing a total 7.5 million less than Richard Nixon in 1960, a drop of 22%. Above all, the election registers a general belief that Goldwater is a threat to the peace, and it provides a stronger mandate for continuity in our foreign policies. Although we have not yet finished reckoning with what Goldwater represents, we can at least say that the malady so frighteningly displayed at San Francisco has been contained, and can hope that the Cow Palace convention may come to be seen as the high tide of the radical right.

No doubt to many observers abroad, more than 26 million votes and almost 39% of the total will seem ominously high for a candidate with Goldwater's special and dangerous view of the world. In a way it is, but this misfortune was entailed in July by the disaster of Goldwater's nomination. It must be remembered that under our party system even Jack the Ripper, with a major-party label on him, could hope to get close to 40% of the votes. If the vote exaggerates right-wing strength, it also measures its outer limits. It is a safe guess that at best not more than half of the Goldwater voters agree ardently with his ideas, and that the rest supported him out of party loyalty. The central question is whether the Goldwater cultists can hold the Republican Party, and now the odds are heavily against them.

The results make grim reading for Republican Party leaders. They lost two seats in the Senate, where they are now outnumbered 68–32, and 39 in the House where they are now outnumbered 296–139. Two of their most promising young leaders, Charles Percy in Illinois and Robert Taft Jr. in Ohio, went down under the Johnson landslide—perhaps a double misfortune, since it weakens precisely those forces which could have led the party in shedding Goldwaterism in the Midwest. Most of this can be laid to Goldwater's door, since he was dead weight on his ticket. Outside the South he tended to run close to 15% behind the more attractive Republicans on state tickets, but the margin of his disadvantage ranged higher in some states—up to an incredible 42% in Rhode Island. It probably did not surprise anyone that he got only 5% of the Negro vote or 10% of the Jewish vote, but he had only 40% in such Republican sectors of the electorate as Midwest farmers and middle-income suburbanites. Only in the upper income brackets, where Republican support is normally overwhelming, did he prevail, but even there with a slender 52%.

A noteworthy feature of the campaign was the way in which the doors of the establishment snapped shut against Goldwater, as recorded in the impressive lists of top business leaders and influential newspapers announced for Johnson. We are told, on occasion, that this country is ruled by a monolithic "power élite" which is wholly irresponsible; but faced with the fact of a recognisably irresponsible politics, the élite split, and threw its preponderant weight on the side of responsibility.

Almost everything went wrong with Goldwater's campaign. Even the Southern strategy must be counted as a failure. Although some states went Republican for the first time in history, Johnson held a majority of the popular and the electoral votes of the section; and if the polls are right, Goldwater actually ran backwards during the campaign, losing the slender margin with which he began. Outside the deep South, the "white backlash" was not significantly felt, and only a small margin of normally Democratic voters defected. Unfortunately this cannot be taken to mean that backlash sentiment is not widespread, but it is less intensive than it is extensive. With the presidency at stake, people preferred to vote on peace and bread-and-butter issues. However, in California, where they had a chance to undo a law against racial discrimination in housing, they welcomed it. We have not heard the last of the backlash effect in politics.

In contrast to the unrealised backlash, Republican defections took place on a large scale, and this may have owed less to Democratic attacks on Goldwater than to the lasting damage done to him by the Republican moderates in the primaries and at San Francisco. Governor Nelson Rockefeller's campaign in New Hampshire saddled Goldwater with the popular belief that he was "against social security," and the debate over the control of nuclear weapons at the Cow Palace confirmed the idea that he is "trigger-happy," which he considered his most serious handicap. A large portion of his campaign energy had to be spent denying that he was reactionary on social security (in fact he had voted for an extension of the system) and that he would be a reckless custodian of the Bomb. In the end these denials, especially since they did contrast with some of his earlier policy statements, had the sound of a man protesting too much. Undoubtedly the greatest single cause of Republican defections was the fear of war (though some of the aged were moved by the social security issue, and some farmers feared a complete demolition of the apparatus for price supports).

An unpredictable feature of the election was the gross ineptitude of Goldwater's campaign. At best campaigns rarely change the minds of many voters, and it would have been too much to expect even a skilful campaign to win for anyone who started as far behind as Goldwater did. But to have converted as much as 5% of the electorate would have saved many Republican candidates, and would have put a much better face on his cause; yet all the evidence indicates that, despite the unexpected boon of the Jenkins case, he had no more support in November than he had in July. Some of us were misled by the frightening efficiency shown by Goldwater's organisation up to the San Francisco convention. The Goldwater men were indeed good organisers, but as it turned out, they proved good only at organising *their own forces* for combat, and never developed a gift for conciliating or persuading other Republicans or the public at large. This too was Goldwater's responsibility. He threw away the cue given him by the party leaders at the Hershey conference in August, and he preferred to staff his campaign at national and local levels with inspired newcomers and provincials rather than to enlist the help of seasoned professionals and the more cosmopolitan figures in the party.

Some of Goldwater's brash and arrogant novices were profoundly offensive to the old Republican professionals. As the campaign went on (and as state and local Republican candidates, in the interest of their own survival, put increasing distance between themselves and the head of their ticket), the Republican campaign took on the aspect of a double effort, with separate strategies, funds, and corps of workers. The Goldwater people made no secret of their desire to rid themselves permanently of Republicans whose support of the ticket was weak or non-existent, and recriminations as to whose fault the campaign fiasco really is, which began before it was over, are now rising to a crescendo.

Goldwater's ineptitude in developing issues matched the failures of his organisation. In an election campaign a candidate who believes himself to have a commanding lead may choose to stand on generalities and not jeopardise his position with too many explicit commitments; but the man who trails faces the necessity of finding issues that will make converts. Goldwater toyed restlessly for a time with a variety of issues, tossing them out experimentally, then abandoning them without ever trying to develop them in depth. His whole stance, which was that of a man who prefers reaffirming attitudes rather than analysing issues, underlined the non-programmatic quality that has always been so characteristic of his thinking.

A typical gesture concerned the chronic crisis in Vietnam. Republican propaganda naturally referred to Vietnam with regularity. But Goldwater seems to have concluded, at least after the Tonkin counter-strike in August, that so long as he had the label of nuclear recklessness hanging around his neck, it would be dangerous for him to hit too hard on such a foreign-policy issue. His closest approach to a solution for the problem was to promise that if he was elected he would send Eisenhower to Vietnam. A similar promise apropos the Korean stalemate seemed to have helped Eisenhower in 1952—why not try it? Characteristically, Goldwater had neglected to check with the General, who at seventy-four showed an understandable reluctance to commit himself to any such junket. The matter had to be dropped. Such was the fate also of another Goldwater idea, substituting a professional army for the draft. To one who is wholly open-minded on this subject, the proposal seems not unreasonable, and it would have been interesting to see it argued in some depth. But, in his characteristic way, Goldwater let it drop after one tentative sally and nothing more was heard of it.

In the end, after several feints and forays, Goldwater settled on the morality theme, and here I think his pronouncements are of more than passing interest because they shed so much light on the nature of the movement he leads. For a number of reasons, his call for "a return to higher morality," to be inspired by nobler conduct in the White House, seemed a suitable way of synthesising a great many discontents. The morality issue could be tied in with urban disorder, juvenile delinquency, race riots, and the crime rate. It enabled Goldwater to exploit moral indignation without having to offer a positive programme, and to exploit racist sentiment without making any overtly racist utterances. Finally, it matched, at a relatively genteel level, the personal assault on President Johnson being waged by Birchist and gutter-level campaigners through many books and pamphlets. The Jenkins case seemed made to order for this appeal; but if Goldwater had any lingering doubts in October how the campaign would turn out, they must have vanished when it became clear that this incident was not moving many voters his way.

At bottom the coming effort of the Republican moderates to retake their party is an effort to recover politics from the non-political. As one who has long believed that the Goldwater cult attracts essentially non-political people who have recently been drawn into politics, I was fascinated to see the Senator openly argue for the position that politics should be pre-eminently a sphere for the realisation of fundamental moral values rather than interests, and to argue unmistakably that he thought this was the whole merit of his case. The campaign, he said, was waged "to restore to America a sense of common purpose —of moral responsibility." His fundamental approach was admittedly "unorthodox," for he had gone into Appalachia and attacked the administration's poverty programme in the very centre of its strength, had gone into Florida's old-age colonies and warned against adding "Medicare" to the social security system, had gone into the farm country and called for a transition from controlled to "free" agriculture, and had gone into an area of high urban growth and challenged the Supreme Court's decision calling for a larger share in state legislatures for the cities.

"I have done all these things *deliberately*," he went on, "for a reason that is clear in my own mind—and I want to make it clear to you tonight. *I will not attempt to buy the votes of the American people. I will not treat any of you as just so many special interests. I will not appeal to you as if you were simply pocketbooks, surrounded on all sides by self-serving concerns.*" In short, the familiar politics of interest groups is not only limited but altogether sordid. Goldwater is proud of a politics that dispenses with politics, and with the demands of interest groups —which is the kind of politics we have had since the country began—because it is an ignoble business, this trading and bartering and accommodating of interests, when we should be engaged in the pursuit of ultimate moral values.

As if to leave no doubt of what he meant in these utterances, Goldwater went on to ask: "*What place does politics have in a campaign for the Presidency?*" No place at all, he answered, for the usual politics of special interests, which calls for saying "the right thing to the right people, at the right time and place." In saying the wrong things, he felt he was giving an example of manliness and morality that is badly needed in a country where, in material terms, people always have more and more goods but where, he believes, they also have more and more evils—more crime, more juvenile delinquency, divorce, illegitimacy, mental illness, school drop-outs, drug addiction, pornography, riots and hoodlumism.

For the material prosperity of the country, he argued, we could thank the free enterprise system. But our basic social evils must be charged to something else.

> The deterioration of the home, the family and the community, of law and order, of good morals and good manners, is the result of thirty years of an unhealthy social climate. I refer to the philosophy of modern "liberalism," the dominant philosophy of the opposition party.

Among the evils charged to this philosophy were "permissiveness in the school and the home," looking upon "discipline and punishment as barbaric relics of a discredited past," the attempt to "eliminate religious sentiment from every aspect of public life." It is the modern liberal, Goldwater charged, "who is concerned for the criminal and careless about his victims, who frowns on the policeman and fawns on the social psychologist." In another speech, the candidate made it clear that he thought this liberalism was predominant in the country: "The moral fibre of the American people is beset by rot and decay."

The notion that the United States, despite its material prosperity (or perhaps because of it), suffers from some acute moral malaise is not wholly heretical—in fact many intellectuals, in a different context and for different purposes, have been saying the same thing for years. What is distinctive is Goldwater's conception of the *causes* of our social ills and the resulting notions of what to do about them. In effect he has been saying these ills are not traceable to anything in the structure of our society, and therefore that no considerable social programme is needed to cope with them. They can be met instead by changing our philosophy, girding our moral loins, steeling ourselves to a more militant posture in the cold war, getting our children to pray in school again, and finally by electing men like himself and Bill Miller whose splendid example would once again make the White House the moral centre of the nation. It is pathetic and embarrassing that a great nation should have to spend time on such twaddle, but one cannot deny that millions of people respond to it, and that a man nominated by a major party holds to it with dreadful sincerity. What is truly

significant about it is that a substantial part of the country does
not think of social and political problems as requiring social
and political solutions, but instead scorns the whole business
in favour of the idea that what is needed is only a moral reformation. In his Memphis speech Goldwater said:

> A lot of my enemies call me simple. The trouble with the so-
> called liberal today is that he doesn't understand simplicity. The
> answers to America's problems are simple.

I suppose that people who can believe this can believe anything. In any case, since the aims of the Goldwater people are
to express motives and interests other than those which we
ordinarily call "political," they are not as much discouraged
by failure as political regulars would be. Goldwater, though
he may not be prepared to try to run again, refuses to step
down from party leadership, resists suggestions that his national chairman, Dean Burch, resign, and promises to devote
all his energies to strengthening "conservatism" in the Republican Party. The "conservative" intellectuals, far from accepting the election as a fatal sign of the unpopularity of radical
rightism in the country, suggest that the campaign wasn't run
quite right, and that the cause will do better next time. To the
extremists the realities of defeat are as resistible as other realities, and they seem prepared to make a fight for their party. By
the usual party standards, their case is hopeless, since they have
produced only a momentous defeat; but men who believe they
are fighting for moral absolutes beyond the reach of usual partisan goals feel more deeply than pragmatic political regulars an
imperative to carry on.

No experienced observer would lay odds on their success,
since the genuine conservatives in the Republican Party, who
constitute in all probability its largest portion, are led mainly
by old professionals for whom the difference between victory
and defeat is still important. The present Goldwater control of
the national chairmanship and the national committee is not
as vital as it might be in a truly unified kind of party. American
political parties are loose federal unions. Their true centres of
power lie not in the national committee but primarily in the
state machines, usually led by the governors, and secondarily

in the corps of seasoned legislators on Capitol Hill. The Republican professionals are unlikely to relax their demand that the Goldwater men give up the reins of the party. The situation of right-wing Republicanism is particularly hopeless in the eight most populous industrial states of the North, whose electoral votes together are almost enough to determine a national election. In these states President Johnson's portion of the aggregate votes was 64%, ranging from 58% in California to 76% in Massachusetts. In all these states there are normally strong Republican organisations, which have produced such liberal or moderate leaders as Governors Rockefeller, Romney, and Scranton, Senators Kuchel and Case, former Ambassador Lodge, and the young hopefuls, Percy and Taft.

What now stands between these men and resumption of party control is not so much the Goldwater cult, stubborn though it is, as their own disunity and conflicting ambitions. The day after the election every princeling in the party was issuing his own manifesto as to what should be done. Vital decisions will be made at the forthcoming Conference of Republican Governors. There are seventeen of them, and though their command of their states has been impaired by the Johnson landslide, they have it within their power to make Goldwater's position untenable. My guess is that the moderates can best serve their party by taking a principled position on a few issues and by driving out of the party ranks a small fringe of extremists without alienating too many of its conservative voters. A modest defection of cranks would probably gain them more support from voters than it would cost, much as Harry Truman seemed to benefit in 1948 from what seemed at first the fatal defection of both the Wallaceite left and the racist right of the Democratic Party.

The task before the Republican moderates is formidable. Assuming that they can dispose of the Goldwater men, they still have to establish a programme for their party that will be close enough to the American consensus to be viable and yet far enough from the Democrats to stamp them with an identity they now lack. Presumably their party will survive. If the Democrats survived the Civil War and Reconstruction and then their terrible internal divisions of the 1920s, and if the Republicans survived their own split in 1912 and the Alf Landon fiasco of 1936, one can only believe that they will survive Goldwater.

For the moment, however, they do not constitute an effective or constructive opposition, and their disaster has given President Johnson a working coalition as broad as any in our history, though perhaps also as unstable. This master of consensual politics will not make the mistakes that so quickly dissolved Roosevelt's coalition in 1937. But it will be interesting to see if even his hand is sure enough to get the country off dead centre and begin a significant attack on its problems.

1964

Alexis de Tocqueville

TOCQUEVILLE MAY be best thought of as a sociologist, per-haps the first great political sociologist of the modern era. This judgment will surely provoke disagreement: there are those who prefer to think of him as a historian or a political scientist, and those who will think of Tocqueville's style as be-ing so radically unlike the style of any sociologist they can call to mind, contemporary or even classical, that the suggestion will seem bizarre. But, of course, Tocqueville was a sociolo-gist with a difference. His way of developing a theme is so characteristically that of the French literary mind, his view of society retains so much of the moralist's manner, his way of approaching his subjects remains so impressionistic. It may be useful here to contrast him with Marx. Where Marx thought he was developing a "scientific" sociology, Tocqueville was candidly intuitive—though not without system. Both of them were responding to the industrial revolution and the early rise of modern democracy. But while for Marx the concep-tion of class was the central theme—and for him a democracy could be truly achieved only after a class society was destroyed —for Tocqueville the central fact of the democratic era was the passion for status, and he saw clearly the tremendous par-adox imported into modern political and social development by the tension between the striving for status and the striv-ing for equality. "Democratic institutions awaken and foster a passion for equality which they can never entirely satisfy." Again, where Marx was the sociologist of the proletariat and of socialism, Tocqueville was the sociologist of the aristocracy and, in a certain qualified sense, of conservatism. Marx stems from the critical thought of the Enlightenment, and also, though he found a "scientific" corrective so necessary, from the utopian thought stimulated by the Enlightenment and by the French Revolution. Tocqueville owes little or nothing to utopian modes of thought: he seems rather to carry on the tra-dition of cool intelligence which we associate with Montaigne and Montesquieu. It seems important that he was a believing Catholic, since his sociological insights tend to go beyond the place and the moment and to rest on something universal in the human condition. The feeling of being embattled is alive everywhere in Marx's writing; in Tocqueville it is the sense of distance one feels most keenly, not because he has no values or commitments (far from it) but because his ears are always tuned to the music of the spheres.

One of the keys to Tocqueville's detachment, to his sense of distance, lies in the fact that he accepted the historical necessity of the values he disliked. Where Marx's "science" assured him that the future belonged to Marx, Tocqueville's intuition told him that the future most assuredly did not belong to Tocqueville. As an aristocrat, he stood for certain things—a kind of freedom, tradition, honor, and the creativity and leadership of great individuals—which his informed sense of the world told him would be replaced or diminished, perhaps in some cases eliminated, by democracy. But what distinguishes him from the reactionaries of his own era is that he wastes no time in lamentations over an *ancien régime* that cannot be restored, or in shrill denunciations of revolution. His intellectual life is an argument for accepting the pattern for the future, and for attempting only to educate, inform, and lead it. In this respect he still finds a role for a wise and flexible elite.

This explains why Tocqueville took so much trouble to see the United States at first hand, since he saw in American development the vanguard of the future, the nearest living realization of what the inevitable and unwanted democracy would be like. And this is why—with all due respect to his *The Old Régime and the French Revolution—Democracy in America* is his greatest work. It was not that he was primarily interested in the United States: he was interested in France, and in Europe. But he used the condition of America as a key to open the door to the future.

Tocqueville firmly believed that "the gradual development of the principle of equality is . . . a providential fact." "It has," he said, "all the chief characteristics of such a fact: it is universal, it is lasting, it constantly eludes all human interference, and all events as well as all men contribute to its progress. . . . To attempt to check democracy would be . . . to resist the will of God," and the nations ought to make the best of the lot meted out to them by Providence. To try to stop the advance of democracy would be not merely futile but very likely ruinous. It should not be opposed, but, while there is still time, guided. The duty of leadership is "to educate democracy, to reawaken, if possible, its religious beliefs; to purify its morals; to mold its actions; to substitute a knowledge of statecraft for its inexperience, and an awareness of its true interest for its blind instincts."

Hence, in examining America, Tocqueville was able to hold his distaste for equality in check by his regard for what Marx would have called its historic necessity, and to rein in his fears for the future by his need for hope and by his awareness that any grand historical movement that is to be guided must be understood. What he found in America, as an anchor for his hopes, was that democracy, while inelegant and chaotic, and presumably fated not to achieve the highest reaches of human creativity, was astonishingly peaceful in its mode of development and that it had a goodly variety of minor virtues to compensate for its loss of a few heroic qualities. Having experienced, as he said in his *Recollections*, two revolutions in seventeen years, he was particularly responsive to the peaceful, nonrevolutionary pattern of American politics. "I have endeavored," he wrote a friend, "to abate the claims of aristocrats and to make them bend to an irresistible future; so that the impulse in one quarter and resistance in another being less violent, society may march on peaceably toward the fulfillment of its destiny." He saw in the United States the outlines of a future in which there would be less splendor, but also less misery; fewer acutely enjoyed pleasures, but more general comfort; a less distinguished cultivation of science, but also a better-educated general public. "The nation, taken as a whole, will be less brilliant, less glorious, and perhaps less strong; but the majority of the citizens will enjoy a greater degree of prosperity, and the people will remain peaceable, not because they despair of a change for the better, but because they are conscious they are well off already."

Something should be said about the style of Tocqueville's observations. He had not only his own love of paradox but also a strong sense for the perversity of the human species and

the irregularities of conduct that this perversity engenders. He
was singularly free from those mechanical errors that follow
from the assumption that everything takes place, so to speak,
according to reason. "For my part," he wrote in his *Recollections*, "I detest these absolute systems, which represent all the
events of history as depending upon great first causes linked by
the chain of fatality, and which, as it were, suppress men from
the history of the human race. They seem narrow, to my mind,
under their pretense of broadness, and false beneath their air of
mathematical exactness." It was this freedom from mechanical
juxtapositions that made it possible for him to penetrate those
aspects of historical experience that proceed not smoothly
from point to point, but by the sudden jumps of contradiction
—"those impromptus," he called them, "which astonish and
alarm us." Though it is now a commonplace, he was one of the
first modern thinkers to prepare us to see why revolutions are
the work not of oppressed and despairing masses but rather of
classes already significantly on the rise.

This keen sense for the pattern of events is often matched by
a sense for styles of thought. See how, in recalling a conversation with Ampère, he goes to the heart of a style of thought
that not only characterizes generations of French intellectuals
but also touches perfectly upon the ways of some of the more
unthinking literary radicals of our own age: "Unfortunately,
he [Ampère] was inclined to carry the *esprit* of the salons into
literature and the *esprit* of literature into politics. What I call
esprit in politics consists in seeking for what is novel and ingenious rather than for what is true; in preferring the showy to
the useful; in showing one's self very sensible to the playing
and elocution of the actors, without regard to the results of
the play; and, lastly, in judging by impressions rather than by
reasons. . . . To tell the truth, the whole nation is a little inclined that way, and the French public very often takes a man-
of-letters' view of politics."

Certainly Tocqueville is fallible; there are, of course, some
things he misses and misinterprets, some things he exaggerates.
There are moments when he at least *seems* to contradict himself
in his comments on America. But on balance, after more than
one hundred and thirty years, one is impressed again and again
by the importance and durability of Tocqueville's insights. As

one finds one's self plodding deliberately along the muddy bottoms of uncomprehended or half-comprehended historical problems, one looks up from time to time with wonder to see how Tocqueville's mind leaps and soars. Whatever word we are to fix upon as suggesting the very opposite of pedestrian—that is Tocqueville.

1965

UNPUBLISHED ESSAYS

The Origins of the Welfare State

MY ASSIGNMENT for this occasion—accounting for the origins of the welfare state—could hardly be more generously open or more alarmingly permissive. With a little imagination, it is easy for a historian to push the origins of anything far into the past. And it is anybody's guess whether we are still living through the origins of the welfare state or whether we are at last in the era of its consummation. (There are those too who hope that it has reached its crest and will soon enter the era of its recession.) I thus know neither where the origins originate or where they can be said to stop. Moreover, the term "welfare state" itself is not a "scientific" one with a precise designation but rather a loose way of referring to a great mass of legislation and to a long-enduring historical tendency. Does it mean all governmental activity bearing on public welfare and the level of economic activity? Or does it refer more selectively to those measures, like Medicare, Social Security, and minimum-wage laws, which are intended to minister directly to the needs of the masses of people? In American usage the term is quite recent; I do not know when it was first coined, but it has gained general currency only since 1949.

In his book, *Laissez Faire and the General-Welfare State*, which is undoubtedly the most exhaustive of many histories of the welfare state idea, Sidney Fine explains that he uses the term general welfare state "to refer to a particular attitude as regards the relationship of government to the common weal and not to connote certain specific functions of government."[1] At first thought it may seem peculiar to define the term by referring to the attitude and intent behind governmental measures rather than their effects in actual operation. But on second thought one begins to see a certain point in it. Our minimum-wage laws, for example, are looked upon with a jaundiced eye today by most economists, who doubt that such laws are serving the ends for which they were meant; yet one

[1]Sidney Fine, *Laissez Faire and the General-Welfare State* (Ann Arbor, 1956), p. viii.

would not hesitate to list these laws among the various measures that constitute the welfare state. In classifying laws by the
intent behind them rather than their consequences, we do at
least avoid certain prejudgments: classify them not by their effects, which may be open to argument, but by their purposes,
which usually seem clear enough.

As one who is neither an economist nor an economic historian, I take refuge with a certain relief in pointing out that
it is not for me to measure the effectiveness of laws with an
economic purpose. Nor even as an historian of ideas and attitudes am I much tempted to try to do in a relatively brief
essay what Fine has taken 400 pages to do even for the limited
period 1865–1900—that is, to trace the course of the conflict
between laissez faire and the general-welfare idea. What I prefer to try to do—though it can be done only in a preliminary
and sketchy way here—is to lay out the advance of welfarism
in broad stages, to locate the historical trends or events that
brought about major advances in modern legislative activity,
and to give at least a tentative answer to the question, What
types or groups in the population are responsible for having
fostered the welfare state, not as a theory, but as a cumulative
body of legislation?

One of the primary aims of the American Constitution,
as enumerated in its Preamble, was to "promote the general
welfare." It is doubtful that the framers would have thought
it necessary or desirable to specify exactly what limits should
be put on the role of government, in this respect. To us the
phrase suggests a long-enduring continuity of effort. From the
beginning the needs of American enterprise and national development called forth a long series of acts of governmental
intervention, and over the generations the content of this intervention has not surprisingly changed its forms. The most
significant change that has overtaken us, however, is not a
change from laissez faire to state intervention but in the modes
of governmental action.

The working assumption that seems to lie behind most generalizations about government intervention is that American
industry and enterprise flourished during the nineteenth century under a basic regime (protective tariffs and a few such
exceptions aside) of laissez faire; and that laissez faire gave way

to government interventionism in the years after 1890. American economic history, E. L. Bogart said in 1913, "is largely the story of the achievements of a people working under free competition, untrammeled by custom, tradition, or political limitations."[2] Hence Harold U. Faulkner, contributing to the well-known Rinehart series on American economic history, entitled his book on the period 1897–1917 *The Decline of Laissez Faire*. No doubt laissez faire was in retreat during those years; it almost always is; but the question as to how much it had really prevailed in the preceding years is left open. Most of the rhetoric about American traditions has it that our economy was built up under a regime of private enterprise and rugged individualism in which state intervention was held close to a minimum. Certain major qualifications must be made in this point of view. In fact, when one penetrates beyond the veil of our federal system and considers both the state and the national governments, it is clear that the experience of the American people with state interventionism has always been extensive, and that our actual adherence to laissez faire has been vastly exaggerated. In the first place, laissez faire has been the dominant philosophy in our society only during a very limited period, during the generation from about 1865 to about 1890, and even in this period, it was neither consistently practiced nor intellectually uncontested. It is an idea that has never mustered much consistent support outside the ranks of academic economists. Above all, in our legislative practice it has been overridden with great frequency from the beginning of our national history.

All this is said not with the purpose of denying the reality of the very considerable change that has come into our economy in the past two generations, or of denying that the "welfare-state" America of 1965 is substantially different from the America of 1865. It is a prelude to re-examining the nature of government intervention in the economy, and to defining the kind of change we have had. Aid to business (as opposed to its regulation) is very frequently not taken account of by those who speak of the alleged laissez faire of the nineteenth

[2] E. L. Bogart, *Economic History of the United States* (2nd ed., New York, 1913), p. vii.

century; and the activities of the states are frequently passed by altogether. An important change is the change we had from the economic primacy of the state governments characteristic of the first half of the nineteenth century to the increasingly active role of the federal government in the twentieth. Another is the fact that the great mass of earlier legislation was directed at aid to the classes—that is, at helping entrepreneurship by one or another form of government activity—while an increasingly larger portion of government intervention in the past seventy years or so has been aimed at aid to the masses. There has been a traditional disposition to disregard the amount of government activity exerted to help American business, but to take careful note of all interventionist acts aimed to regulate it or to assist the great masses of the people.

II

The original American inheritance was that of mercantilism. As Richard B. Morris has put it: "Prior to laissez faire capitalism, both business and labor considered government regulation the normal order. This was particularly true in the age of colonial settlement, an era when business enterprise was regulated in the interest of a political program."[3] Compulsory labor for the unemployed, poor relief laws against the wrongful dismissal of employees, maximum wage laws, the regulation of prices of necessities, the regulation of terms of apprenticeship—all these were part of the English inheritance imitated in colonial laws. Such regulations were receding in the eighteenth century, but some of them were revived during the Revolution as a war measure. The institution of slavery, it need hardly be added, was underpinned by an elaborate system of legislative regulations of all kinds. The bulk of social legislation attempted by American legislatures down to 1860 is quite imposing, although it would be a mistake to assume that this legislation achieved anything like the intended effects.[4]

[3]Richard B. Morris, *Government and Labor in Early America* (New York, 1946).
[4]Henry W. Farnam, *Chapters in the History of Social Legislation in the United States to 1860* (Washington, 1938).

In early national America the real question of public policy was not whether the country should be committed to laissez faire but whether it was to be primarily the national or the state governments that would promote the general welfare. Despite the brilliant early successes of Hamilton, the dice were loaded in favor of a long-run gravitation of such prerogatives to the states. State, regional, and local jealousies, as well as constitutional scruples and ideologies, made it difficult to muster power consistently in Philadelphia or Washington and kept returning the focus of power to the state capitals. Except for the role the tariff played in the period after the War of 1812, the main story of that line of statesmen who envisaged a very positive role for the national government in directing the growth of the national economy was a story at best of brief and temporary victories but of long-run defeats. One need only think here of such men as Gallatin, John Quincy Adams, and Clay, not to speak of such non-statesmen as Nicholas Biddle.

Even the centralizing victory embodied in Hamilton's fiscal schemes had its ironic boomerang effect. He succeeded in making the national government the source of a sound capital fund and the agency of payment for the debts of the revolutionary war. But his plan to make its fiscal centrality a source of long-range power to the national government did not work quite as it was intended. By his scrupulous definition of the whole debt as a national one, and by financial devices which put the country well on the road to paying them off, he put its credit on a uniquely good footing. From this the state governments (to the ultimate regret of many foreign investors) benefited, since they shared in the general good repute of American credit. And by assuming the debts of the states, he left them relatively debt-free, with the consequence that they were much better able to launch on programs of government investment and mixed enterprise. In effect, the states assumed their priority in the promotion of the economy under a federal subsidy.

Very few people of any consequence in early national America questioned the necessity of active governmental promotion of the general welfare. Although there was a great deal of resistance to the adoption of positive economic policies by the national government during the era of Hamilton and Jefferson, very little of this hung on a steady and certain commitment to

laissez faire principles. On the whole, it had its foundations in
constitutional arguments and parochial loyalties and prejudices,
and it became increasingly informed by the South's concern for
its cotton markets and its growing fear that a strong national
government would constitute a menace to slavery.[5] Even Jefferson, who was one of the few statesmen of the era who entertained laissez-faire ideas of the classical order, receded from
them after 1805, embraced protectionism and self-sufficiency,
and finally even accepted the inevitability of the factory system.
In his second inaugural address he expressed the hope that
when the public revenue no longer had to be applied to servic-
ing the debt it could be applied "to rivers, canals, roads, arts,
manufactures, education, and other great objects within each
state"—a procedure to be executed in cooperation with the
states and upon the authority of a constitutional amendment.
As William Grampp has remarked, "His program of subsidizing domestic industry and of giving the national government
the direction of internal improvements was similar to the policy of the Federalist party"—differing from it less in substance
than in his conception of the constitutional procedure necessary to proceed with it.[6]

The drift of thought among the Jeffersonians is probably
represented by Gallatin's famous report of 1808. Unlike Jefferson, Gallatin did not think that a constitutional amendment
was necessary to what he proposed—a substantial federal program to establish a network of roads, canals, and river improvements that would knit all the sections of the country
together, and that would be constructed without quibble as to
whether they would be of primarily national or local benefit.
He estimated a program that would cost about $20 million

[5]The real issue was between national and state action. This was clear in the
constitutional debates which filled so many pages of the *Annals of Congress* and
in the works of later historians. In these the issue turned solely on the powers
given by the Constitution to the federal and state governments respectively
and not at all on the rights of private individuals and corporations. Carter
Goodrich, *Government Promotion of American Canals and Railroads* (New
York, 1960), p. 44.
[6]William Grampp, "A Re-examination of Jeffersonian Economics," *Southern
Economic Journal*, vol. XII (January, 1946), p. 280.

and that could be carried out within ten years. The plan was favorably discussed in the press and was implicitly recommended to Congress by Jefferson in his last regular message, in which he seemed to be willing to leave to Congress the question whether an amendment might be necessary.[7]

It is, of course, hardly a novel conclusion that the promoters of the American system under federal direction substantially failed. But they did so not because of a general commitment, intellectual or practical, against governmental intervention in the economy; nor did they fail because the unaided resources of private capital were adequate to the tasks of American economic development. They failed because the true centers of power in early and mid-nineteenth-century America lay not in Washington but in the state capitals. Contemporary historical investigation has shown how frequently the American voting public turned out in greater numbers to vote in state and local political contests than they did for presidential contests.[8] The picture suggests a prevalent feeling among the people that their state capitals were the centers of political activity most relevant to their interests. Before the Civil War, and perhaps to a degree even down to the 1800's, the United States was much more a *federal* union than our modern historical consciousness, shaped by economic and political centralization, is able to grasp. The state governments were focal centers of power; and it was in these governments that political action primarily shaped economic activity. The prevailing American conception between the War of 1812 and the Civil War was not that *government* should abstain from promoting, directing, or regulating economic growth. It was that the *national* government should

[7]Most of the proposals in Gallatin's report of 1808 were in fact constructed eventually, and extensive governmental assistance did prove to be necessary. Of his twenty projects for transportation improvement, sixteen were sooner or later carried out. Five were done by mixed state, local and private promotion, four were done by the states, one by the federal government, two by mixed enterprise with federal, state and private capital, one by local government and private enterprise, and three by private (or mainly private) enterprise. Goodrich, *Government Promotion*, pp. 28–35.

[8]See, for example, Richard P. McCormick, "New Perspectives on Jacksonian Politics," *American Historical Review*, Vol. LXV (January, 1960), pp. 288–301.

do relatively little of this, leaving the task mainly to the governments of the states. And when one looks at the economic functions of these governments, one becomes increasingly aware that American enterprise, at focal points, was far from being the nursling of laissez faire but was in fact the child of governmental activity.

III

This fact, although it has been amply explored only by contemporary scholarship, is in no sense a recent discovery. More than sixty years ago Guy S. Callender published a memorable article on "The Early Transportation and Banking Enterprises of the States in Relation to the Growth of Corporations" in which he set down certain general findings of central importance about economic development after the War of 1812. Callender pointed out that despite the limits placed on the federal government by American anxiety about fiscal extravagance, corruption, and centralization, "it is a fact that this country was one of the first to exhibit this modern tendency to extend the activity of the State into industry. And it advanced so rapidly and so far along this line that it became for a time almost as prominent an example of it as the Australian colonies are in our own time."[9]

It was the merit of Callender's paper to point out that the requirements of certain kinds of enterprises of absolutely essential significance to the economy—roads, canals, railroads, navigation improvements, and banks—for capital and promotional confidence were supplied by state aid, state investment, and state promotion. As Callender saw it, the central fact in the American economy in these decades was the opening of the West, the need to knit the country together, and the need for large capital sums to launch the enterprises capable of doing it:[10]

> The opening of the West gave rise to an enormous increase in the demand for capital, chiefly to provide works of internal

[9] Guy S. Callender, "The Early Transportation and Banking Enterprises of the States in Relation to the Growth of Corporations," *Quarterly Journal of Economics*, Vol. XVII (November, 1902), p. 111.
[10] Ibid., p. 153.

improvement. To construct any of the more important of these works required several millions of capital,—an amount far greater than had been brought together in any industry in this country up to that time. For corporations to secure so much capital it was necessary to bring together the many small savings of this country; and to attract the large ones of foreigners. There was no body of private individuals in the country well enough known and with sufficient influence in the business world to establish the credit of a corporation so that it could command the confidence of both these classes of investors. The only securities that could do this were public securities, or the securities of corporations which were guaranteed or assisted by the government. American public credit had been raised to the highest pitch by the debt-paying policy of the federal government; and it was inevitable that the American people should turn to the only means in their power to provide for their needs. When New York demonstrated that it was easy to secure all the capital necessary for carrying out public works by the issue of bonds on the credit of the State, the way was open for other States to pursue the same course; and only New Jersey and the smaller New England States refused to enter upon it.

Callender did not fail to point out that the authors of the early system of state intervention and mixed enterprise seemed to be quite articulate about what they were doing: no abstract principles of laissez faire interposed themselves to prevent them from openly endorsing public enterprise when it was felt to be necessary to promote the general welfare. The New York Canal Commissioners in their first report on the Erie Canal protested against a grant to private companies: "Too great a national interest is at stake. It must not become the subject of a job or a fund for speculation. . . . Such large expenditures can be more economically made under public authority than by the care and vigilance of any company." Similarly the Ohio Canal Commissioners, reporting in favor of state construction in 1825, declared: "It does not consist with the dignity, the interest, or the convenience of the State that a private company of citizens or foreigners (as may happen) should have the management and control of [navigable highways]. . . . Besides, such works should be considered with a view to the greatest possible accommodation to our citizens; as a public work, the public convenience is the paramount object; and a private company will look only to the best means for increasing their profits."[11] Such statements arose, of course, not out of any hostility to profit-making as such, or to private enterprise, but out of a pragmatic regard for the necessities of large-scale developments that were thought to promote the public interest.

Long after Callender's pioneering article, the researches of Louis Hartz, Oscar and Mary Handlin, Milton S. Heath, James Neal Primm, Harry H. Pierce, Carter Goodrich, and other scholars established the focal importance of mixed enterprise in the development of the American economy of the nineteenth century.[12] Not only was there a large story of state intervention and mixed public and private promotion to be told, but there was a great deal of mythological rubbish about laissez faire to be cleared out of the way. Writing of Massachusetts, Oscar Handlin remarked that "in the realm of the practical, there never was a period . . . when this conception [laissez faire] was of the slightest consequence." Concerning Pennsylvania, Louis Hartz found that "far from being limited, the objectives of the state in the economic field were usually so broad that they were beyond its administrative power to achieve." Concerning Georgia, Milton Heath was less positive; he found that "during the early decades there developed no

[11] Ibid., pp. 155–56.

[12] Oscar and Mary F. Handlin, *Commonwealth: A Study of the Role of Government in the American Economy: Massachusetts, 1774–1861* (New York, 1947); Louis Hartz, *Economic Policy and Democratic Thought: Pennsylvania, 1776–1860* (Cambridge, Mass., 1948); Harry H. Pierce, *Railroads of New York: A Study of Government Aid, 1826–1875* (Cambridge, Mass., 1954); Milton S. Heath, *Constructive Liberalism: The Role of the State in the Economic Development in Georgia to 1860* (Cambridge, Mass., 1954); James Neal Primm, *Economic Policy in the Development of a Western State: Missouri, 1820–1860* (Cambridge, Mass., 1954).

Among the salient discussions of the implications of these and other books are those of Robert A. Lively, "The American System," *Business History Review*, Vol. XXIX (1955), pp. 81–96; George R. Taylor, *The Transportation Revolution, 1815–1860* (New York, 1951), esp. chapter XVI, "The Role of Government"; and Stuart Bruchey, *The Roots of American Economic Growth* (New York, 1965), chapters V and VI. Henry Broude has made an effort to gauge the effectiveness of government intervention in "The Role of the State in American Economic Development, 1820–1890," H. G. J. Aitken, ed., *The State and Economic Growth* (New York, 1959), pp. 4–25.

definite philosophies defending the exclusive validity of either individual or public action."[13]

George R. Taylor summarizes the American state of mind when he describes the period 1815 as one when "the responsibility of the state for economic conditions was taken for granted." "Americans," he writes,[14]

> though much given to debates concerning the interpretation of the constitution, were not much interested in elaborate theories as to the proper role of government in economic affairs. They believed that economic conditions should constantly improve and that the government had a simple and direct obligation to take any practicable measure to forward such progress. Why should they fear the power of the state? Was it not their own creation in which the people themselves were sovereign? So issues tended to be considered on the basis of simple expediency. Or if theoretical questions were raised, nine times out of ten they dealt with constitutional interpretations having to do with whether a particular activity fell within the powers of the federal or the state government and not whether *any* action by government was theoretically defensible or desirable.

Action by the federal government was limited more by constitutional scruples than by general principles about the scope of governmental action as such. Its contributions to developments in transportation, despite such scruples, were not negligible. By 1860 it had granted about 4 million acres of the public domain to canal projects and had subscribed over $3 million to the stock of canal companies. In the 1850's it gave over 21 million acres of land to subsidize railroads, setting a precedent for the vastly greater subsidies that were to follow the Civil War. Elsewhere it did not hesitate to act where federal measures seemed necessary and proper. Since it saw a public interest in the development of the merchant marine, for example, it saw no reason not to give public subsidies to steamship lines —some $15.5 million during the 1840's and 1850's. Nor did

[13]Oscar Handlin, "Laissez-Faire Thought in Massachusetts, 1790–1880," *Journal of Economic History*, Vol. III, *Supplement* (1943), p. 55; Louis Hartz, *Economic Policy and Democratic Thought*, p. 292; Milton Heath, "Laissez Faire in Georgia, 1732–1860," *Journal of Economic History*, Vol. III, *Supplement* (1943), p. 100.

[14]*The Transportation Revolution*, pp. 552–53.

Congress hesitate, where interstate steamboat commerce was involved, to make improvements conducive to navigation—some $6 million worth from 1815 to 1860—or to pass detailed safety regulations to prevent accidents in this trade. Nor did it hesitate to pass compulsory sickness insurance for seamen or to erect 27 federal hospitals as a part of this program. Nor to construct and operate, in the interest of Morse's work on the telegraph, an experimental line from Washington to Baltimore. Nor to give large bounties to the codfish industry to be sure that it would do its bit in schooling sailors. Nor to use its procurement policies in such a way as to help build up a small-arms industry.

State aid was limited by no constitutional scruples. Where state legislatures saw a certain or probable need of public action in any line of development, they moved in with alacrity; in those areas where they saw no such need, they tended to leave development in private hands. The total amount of their intervention was indeed imposing, and because of its public character its leverage appears to have been of vital importance for turnpikes, railroads, canals, and, in some states, for banks. Outside of New England and the Middle Atlantic States, turnpike investment came in large part from state funds. Canals, though assisted by federal land grants and stock subscriptions, were mainly dependent upon the states. By the middle 1830's over $60 million of debts had been incurred by the states in the building of canals either owned outright by the public or jointly financed. Canal enterprises were characteristically state operations, railroads private ones with state aid and participation; but some states—Pennsylvania, Georgia, Virginia, Michigan, and Indiana—also built and owned railroads. Large sums were supplied. The Southern railroads, for example, that had been built by 1860 cost $245.2 million; of this the public supplied 55%, but its contribution to cash investment (since private investment often came in labor and supplies) was much closer to 75%. In New York, where private capital resources were better, state and local governments contributed investments of $47.1 million in railroads out of a total of $400 million. Pennsylvania put $101.6 million into her Main Line canal and railroad system. By 1838, when the early surge of investment was at a peak, state indebtedness of $170.8 million had been contracted for the following purposes: banking, $52.6 million; canals, $60.2 million; railroads, $42.8 million; turnpikes, $6.6 million; miscellaneous, $8.4 million.[15] After the 1830's, as a reaction to the panic and depression and as a consequence of the increasing chariness of foreign investors, this movement toward state participation received a check, but it was on the rise again in the 1850's.

The contributions of the newer states to banking enterprises were also vital. Nearly all the states invested public funds in the stock of banking corporations. In some of the older states, where capital was in adequate supply, this was motivated mainly by a desire to have the state revenues share in the substantial profits of the banking business. This motive was present in some of the newer states also, where it was supplemented by the desire to furnish a circulating medium and to improve credit facilities for commercial enterprises and for farmers. But in the rapidly expanding plantation economy of the Southwest, the interest of the states in banking was particularly vital. The large capital outlays required by plantation agriculture and slave labor created an especially urgent need for capital from the North and from Europe. To supply it, it was absolutely essential to make use of the public credit, and all states from Florida to Arkansas set up one or more banks whose capital was supplied by the sale of state bonds. In this manner the production and marketing of the cotton and sugar crops of the region was financed, and there, as Callender pointed out, where nature happily provided most of the required transportation system, state banking enterprises constituted the counterpart of the internal improvements of the North and East.[16] Thus in the Southwest as elsewhere, state-aided or state-managed enterprises suckled the thousands of individual enterprises that have given our country its reputation as the nursery of rugged individualism.

State efforts to promote development did not end with participation in enterprise through state-owned public works or mixed public and private corporations. Licensing, monopolies, bounties, subsidies, tax exemptions, price-fixing were also

[15]Taylor, *The Transportation Revolution*, p. 374.
[16]Callender, "The Early Transportation and Banking Enterprises," pp. 159–62.

resorted to. Nor did the state legislatures balk at regulation, where it was deemed necessary. Regulation and inspection of foodstuff supplies was common. Labor legislation was not neglected: eastern states passed laws for compulsory school attendance by children working in factories, prohibiting child labor before a certain age, and in some cases setting limits on hours of labor for factory workers. These laws were on the whole poorly drafted and enforced; but their presence testifies to an acceptance of the regulatory principle.[17]

Less adequately studied than state promotion, but significant was local aid, which continued in great strength after the Civil War. Carter Goodrich has counted 2,200 laws passed in 36 states by local governments interested in internal improvements.[18] Cities and counties extended themselves, sometimes in the most strenuous way. In the South, out of a total of $144 million of aid, cities and counties contributed $45.6 million. A measure of the possibilities of local enthusiasm is the case of Milwaukee, which, with a population of only 45,000 in 1860, had already lent $1.6 million to railroad companies. The movement for local aid continued with vigor throughout the nineteenth century.[19]

State aid never recovered from the revulsion from internal improvements that came along with the panic and depression of 1837. But major capital needs in transportation had not come to an end, and from 1850 to 1872 the federal government stepped in once again to subsidize the transcontinental railroads. Although loans of nearly $65 million were made available[20] the major instrument of subsidy was, of course, the land grant. In all, as much as 183 million acres seem to have been given to railroads, in the end—and the amount would have been larger if non-fulfillment of charters had not caused the reversion of some railroad lands. In all, the 286,000 square miles given to the railroads was an area larger than the state

[17]Taylor, *The Transportation Revolution*, pp. 377–83.
[18]Carter Goodrich, "Local Government Planning of Internal Improvements," *Political Science Quarterly*, Vol. LXVI (1949), pp. 412–23.
[19]On this movement, see Goodrich, *Government Promotion*, chapters VI and VII.
[20]Ibid., p. 269.

of Texas, and close to one-tenth of the area of the continental United States. It was supplemented by some 840,000 acres given by local governments and individuals, which, because of its superior location, and value, represented an increment in dollar subsidy much more material than in total acreage.[21] As Carter Goodrich puts it, "Small groups of insiders venturing very little capital of their own were able to build the roads with the money of the bondholders and the government, and to pay themselves quick and extraordinary returns out of the profits of construction."[22]

It should also be added that the revulsion from internal improvements which affected state governments did not similarly inhibit local governments. The withdrawal of the states was followed in many cases by extensive reliance on local government aid. Some programs, notably those of the city of Baltimore and of communities in Massachusetts and Virginia, were at their peak in the 1850's. State aid was resorted to extensively in the Reconstruction South and Northern post–Civil War local contributions in railroad development were very significant, either in the form of mixed enterprise or, in a few cases, municipal ones. In New York alone over 300 municipalities contributed more than $33 million to railroad building, chiefly in the form of stock subscriptions.

The point of all this is not, of course, that governmental intervention or mixed enterprise was in any sense a norm or a predominant ideal in the United States in the nineteenth century. Where the resources of private capital were adequate, as in most manufacturing, it was taken for granted that it would operate more or less independently, though benefiting in its own way from protective tariffs and from the consequences of transportation improvements. What is true is that, so far as economic convictions were concerned, American capitalists

[21]This figure is based on a survey for the Federal Co-ordinator of Transportation made in 1938. See Fred A. Shannon, *The Farmer's Last Frontier* (New York, 1945), pp. 64–67. It supplants the earlier figure, more often given, of 155 million acres, based on calculations of the Land Commissioner in 1923. See Roy M. Robbins, *Our Landed Heritage* (Princeton, 1942), pp. 222–24. Goodrich believes that the 1938 survey underestimates the amount of local aid. "Local Planning of Internal Improvements," p. 430.
[22]Goodrich, *Government Promotion*, pp. 199–200.

and legislators were entirely pragmatic and undoctrinaire about the role of the state, and had no inhibitions about resorting to it wherever they considered it necessary to facilitate some development of broad public interest, whether in transportation, banking, or other fields. The peculiar circumstances of American development—the problems of a new country with inferior capital resources developing an economy over a thinly settled continental terrain—made frequent resort to governmental aid necessary; and these objective circumstances were heightened by intense state and local rivalries. The only mystery in the development of American attitudes is not how or why interventionism was so common, but how the mythmakers of laissez faire and rugged individualism captured our image of our national past and succeeded in portraying nineteenth-century America as the home of non-interventionism and the reformers of the twentieth century as the subverters of a great national tradition.

Their success may be attributed in good part to two things —to the extent to which business for so long succeeded in shaping the national mentality and the extent to which the public eye has been focussed upon the federal government to the neglect of state and local governments. Business also has a disposition to take note of governmental actions only when they represent interferences and to ignore them when they have been intended to give aid. The rise of regulation intended to put limits on business activities has given rise to controversy, and has caught the eye of the historians. The earlier assistance to business, which on principle enjoyed the nearly unanimous consent of the community within the states, being far less controversial, has made a much less interesting history. Until the scholarship of the past twenty years finally caught up with the story of mixed enterprise, the early controversies over federal aid to internal improvements, in which relatively little was at stake and relatively little was accomplished, had far more attention in the history books than the substantial achievements of government-aided promotion and mixed enterprise within the states.

But this much can be said with a certain degree of confidence: when the reformers, toward the close of the nineteenth century and the opening of the twentieth, began to make increasing use of the powers of government at the state and federal level to regulate business and improve the condition of the masses, they were not subverting a great national tradition of government abstention. They were merely converting a tradition of governmental intervention, which had been used to some considerable effect to promote the public welfare by promoting enterprise, into a system of intervention to underwrite the general welfare in other and more direct ways.

ca. 1956

The American Right Wing
and the Paranoid Style

THE EPISODE in American history that is identified with the name of Senator Joseph R. McCarthy has made many observers acutely conscious of the strength and persistence of the extreme right wing. McCarthyism itself as a vital force in American political life no longer commands much attention. But the more obscure agitators of the radical right carry on, and in recent years have been the object of a good deal of study. I propose here to discuss some of the preoccupations of the extreme right-wing mind, with a view to portraying its intellectual style.

The American right wing is organized into an extraordinarily large number of fanatical groups of indeterminable size. These groups are far from united. They have points of co-operation and convergence, a common ideology, and mutual heroes—if they did not, it would be impossible to speak of the extreme right as a movement at all—and yet it's the pluralistic structure of the right wing that impresses most commentators. The fragmentation of the extreme right arises not quite so much from the internal quarrels and mutual disavowals that occasionally take place as from the fact that many of the right-wing groups are the *personal* organs of rather self-centered agitators, each of whom is running his own show. Although there are some independents, who seem to pick up their followings from various groups, the characteristic right-wing organization consists, at its core, of an agitator with a mailing list. The periodical, which is the agitator's fundamental vehicle, may be supplemented by local action groups or discussion circles. The leader usually writes the greater part, perhaps all, of his publication, which serves as the main organ of communication between him and his following. In some organizations the leader may travel among the members from time to time, giving speeches or small informal talks under the sponsorship of local groups.

These leaders are caught between what seems to be a sincerely felt desire to further a common cause and a driving inner need to be the center of attention. A few, though perhaps a minority, have a vested interest in their organizations because their agitational activities yield a net financial return. A very few, who have tapped the purses of rich men with cranky views, enjoy right-wing sinecures; but they hardly compare in number with those who give their lives to agitation and expect little more than intangible rewards. For some right-wing leaders, agitation seems to be a form of occupational therapy.

The extreme right wing isn't all of the same quality. It has its high-brows, represented by such savants and pundits as Russell Kirk, Willmoore Kendall, James Burnham, John T. Flynn, Max Eastman, Frieda Utley, and William Buckley—many of them converts from Communism, Socialism, Trotskyism, or fellow-travelling liberalism. It has its middle-brows, who cover a wide range, and its low-brows. The latter, who are unmitigated cranks, must be a source of embarrassment to those in the more respectable echelons of the movement, but they do shed light upon its psychological direction. Sometimes members are hard to classify. But one has little trouble classifying a lady in Chicago who represents the paranoid extremes of the movement in her journal, *Women's Voice*. This organ, presumably written entirely by herself, is against everything that the right wing is usually against, but indulges in remarkable idiosyncrasies of its own. In one of her 1957 issues, its author proposed to foster religion, circulate some of the wildest stock market tips that have ever been given to investors, solve the money question, break up land monopoly, expose invisible world government, lead a retreat from bureaucracy, distribute the Protocols of the Elders of Zion, impeach Eisenhower, repeal the income tax, destroy the Masons, persecute the Catholics, defeat Senator Bricker (a right-wing sectarian deviation here), break up the mental health movement, stop the fluoridation of water supplies, and prevent the suppression of cancer cures. Here is more than a century of American crank manias wrapped up in a single package.

It's difficult to offer more than an educated guess as to the size and influence of the extreme right. On the strength of various public opinion polls, it would appear that the characteristic views of the extreme right can normally command the assent of about 10 or 15 per cent of the voters but we have no way of estimating how many of these voters feel strongly enough about their views to join one or more of the right-wing groups. The polls also show that concerning certain issues and certain outstanding personalities, from time to time, the hard core of the extreme right finds itself in rapport with a much larger portion of the electorate. It's when these issues arise and these heroes appear that the extreme right becomes widely if sometimes fleetingly influential. Among the issues that have given the right-wingers strong points of agitation in recent years have been the Korean War, anti-Communism and the assault on civil liberties, American policy towards China, and (in the South at least) desegregation. The heroes who have rallied the extreme right have been, most conspicuously, General MacArthur and the late Senator McCarthy. It was McCarthy, of course, who really provided the political center for the extreme right, its primary point of unity. He also gave the right wing a great national sounding board. Oddly enough, I don't think McCarthy himself took most of the right-wing views very seriously. He was a complete moral nihilist, playing the political game for the fun of it: he could never understand that real moral issues were involved or that some people took seriously what for him was simply a problem in crafty maneuver: he was often amazed when men he had just insulted and slandered and accused of treason refused to speak to him. But it was in good part this lack of real feeling that gave him his strength: he never identified himself with the more vulnerable and unpopular of right-wing enthusiasms—race prejudice, for instance, or extreme laissez-faire individualism—and he avoided open entanglement with discredited right-wing sectarians. In so doing, he kept the adoration of the right-wingers and at the same time preserved—for a while—his appeal to a much larger public.

If we are to establish the outstanding political passions of the extreme right wing, I think two ideas loom over all others: first, isolationism in foreign policy, and second, a dogmatic insistence on laissez-faire liberalism in economic policy, which leads to a demand for the dismantling of the welfare state. There are, of course, a number of minor satellite characteristics that swim around these two major stars: ethnic prejudice, for instance, and a fanatically intense anti-Communism. But isolationism and laissez-faire are the two distinguishing ideas without which the right wing is meaningless. Usually they are espoused together—in spite of the many practical points at which the aggressive nationalism of the isolationists is inconsistent with the anti-statism of the laissez-faire individualists. Historically, of course, there have been a good many Americans who have been isolationist without being right-wing: indeed before 1941 there were many left-wing isolationists. Similarly, there are a number of respectable economists who believe in economic individualism and who playfully espouse abstract models of economic societies which are based upon what is commonly called "free enterprise." What distinguishes the extreme right-wingers from such people is a style of thought, behind which there lies a frame of mind. This style of thought, I choose to call the paranoid style.

The word paranoid comes from psychiatry, but it has passed into general usage. It has a layman's meaning, and it's in this sense that I use it, and as a historian of ideas who seeks to find a suitably communicative label. We speak, when we try to characterize styles, in certain shorthand terms: of baroque, of rococo, of mannerism, of cubism, and the like. In much the same spirit, I speak of the paranoid style.

One of the chief characteristics of the paranoid style is the tendency to dwell upon the failures of the past rather than to work on programmatic proposals for the future. The astute political journalist, Mr. Samuel Lubell, has remarked that American isolationism is chiefly a politics of revenge: but what is true of isolationism is true of the extreme right generally. The right-winger has always been notably bitter about the means by which the United States entered the last war—whether in 1917 or 1941. He has far less to say about avoiding the next war. He waxes violent at the thought of Roosevelt's "betrayal" of the U.S. at Pearl Harbor, but seems unconcerned about how another war could be forestalled. He's full of recriminations for the "loss" of China (which he assumes the U.S. had in its pocket and was somehow treacherously persuaded to give away to the Reds) but shows no interest in the possible defection of India. This is not to say the extreme right wing has nothing that can be called a programme. But it is to say that the programmatic side of the right wing is extremely feeble as compared with its bitterness and its demand for revenge about things that have happened in the past and cannot be undone.

Another tendency of the paranoid style is prejudice, usually directed against Negroes and Jews or both. It would be unfair to suggest that these prejudices are universal in the extreme right: and no doubt in this respect some of the more sophisticated extreme right-wingers are on occasion ashamed of the mentalities of some of their followers. But no one who has observed right wing movements in action can doubt that their appeal is strong among persons who are disposed to hate minority groups. Thirty years ago Catholics would have had to be included along with Jews and Negroes among such groups: but today the power and respectability of Catholicism in the United States is such that even those elements who may feel twinges of the old nativist feeling against Catholics suppress them. The common crusade of fundamentalist Protestantism and fundamentalist Catholicism against what they both call "godless" communism has made the old anti-Catholic nativism quite vestigial.

A general characteristic of the extreme right wing is that its spokesmen are what David Riesman calls "indignants." Their capacity for indignation is very high in proportion to their capacity for understanding of what is going on. They *do* feel that whatever is happening, it is highly immoral. In their own minds, they live in a society in which morality and fair dealing have practically ceased to exist. As Senator McCarthy once said, "The air seems to reek with intrigue." The right-wing periodical, *The Freeman*, once declared in an advertisement to its readers: "It is the tragedy of our age that moral principle is almost universally sacrificed to expediency."

There also exist among some of the extreme right-wing agitators a tremendous awareness of their own victimization by abuse, even by imaginary plots of assassination—an awareness described by two sociological observers of the right wing as the complex of "the bullet-proof martyr." "The road has been strewn with the political corpses of those who have dared to attempt an exposure of the type of individuals whom I intend to discuss today," McCarthy once announced. "Anyone who opposes American Communists becomes the object of a systematic campaign of character assassination." But: "No matter how much McCarthy bleeds, the job will continue until we have had a thorough housecleaning." One agitator, more extreme, carried on as follows: "It may cost me my life . . . Ten threats came to me within twenty-four hours here in New York City . . . I have been warned that I will not live to complete this series of articles . . . I walked into that armory alone . . . and the first thing I said was this: 'There are men in this room who would like to see me killed tonight.'" It's all rather reminiscent of *The Secret Life of Walter Mitty*.

Perhaps most important of all, the paranoid style puts a pervasive emphasis upon the idea of *conspiracy*. I do not wish to deny that in all historical experience, various groups have to resort to maneuvers that we call strategy: that some strategy demands secrecy and that wherever there is strategy-plus-secrecy an element of conspiracy actually exists. There *are* conspiracies and conspiratorial movements in history, and when those who employ the paranoid style make their accusations of conspiracy they are, on some occasions, not altogether off the mark. But what truly distinguishes the paranoid style is that its spokesmen go so far beyond merely finding an element of the conspiratorial in history. To these people, history *is* a conspiracy, or a series of conspiracies. They find universal, sinister, unbelievably evil conspiracies in almost all events—including those which have taken place in the most open and above-board manner. What they lack, then, above all is any conception of history as an objective *process*: to them history is simply a *manipulation*. The imaginative artists of the right wing, who work in the paranoid style, never feel themselves to be in the grip of history: they are always in the grip of wicked persons.

To a type of mind so obsessed with conspiracy, the "communist conspiracy" is a natural concern. Of course the entire American public is so pervasively anti-Communist that merely to be anti-Communist will not distinguish any one group. What I think is distinctive about extreme right-wing anti-Communism, aside from its sheer intensity, may be put under two headings: first, that the extreme right is usually more concerned about combating the feeble evidences of Communist sympathy *within* the United States and much less concerned than other anti-Communists with realistic techniques for checking the power of the Soviet Union in *world* affairs. Secondly, the anti-Communism of the extreme right wing differs from that of other groups in that the right-wingers, far from being interested in picking out and discriminating *actual* Communists, like to blur the distinction between Communists and non-Communist left-wing groups, even between Communists and liberals. I believe this failure of concern is, with some, simply the result of a rather cynical desire to use any weapon to discredit liberals, notably the liberal wing of the Democratic Party. But with others it's a true product of the paranoid style, one of whose features is an inability to distinguish between one aspect and another of a world which, in its totality, seems to be dominated by a sinister and all-pervasive Enemy.

The right-wingers, with their powerful emphasis on conspiracy, do not regard the involvement of the United States in the affairs of the world or the rise of the welfare state as mistakes of policy or consequences of the drift of historical events. To them, on the contrary, everything is the work of mischievous and malicious men of great power. Thus Senator McCarthy, speaking of certain alleged failures of American foreign policy in June, 1951, asked: "How can we account for our present situation unless we believe that men high in this government are concerting to deliver us to disaster? This must be the product," he said, "of a great conspiracy on a scale so immense as to dwarf any previous such venture in the history of man. A conspiracy of infamy so black that, when it is finally exposed, its principals shall be forever deserving of the maledictions of all honest men." To the right-wingers, the cold war isn't a problem that exists in its own right, but rather an artificial creation of revolutionaries who use the conditions of the cold war to subvert individualism. As one right-wing journalist, Chesly Manly, has put it: "Revolutionaries learned that a post-war external crisis would provide continued justification for the taxing and spending levels and the stifling economic controls by which they hoped to destroy the American free enterprise system."

In somewhat similar terms, the right-wing journalist and lecturer Frank Chodorov finds the development of the welfare state and the adoption of the income tax the consequences of a long-range revolutionary conspiracy. The older individualism was abandoned, he believes, not because it proved unsatisfactory, but because some of its very advocates began to exploit others through the instrumentality of the State. "The practice of privilege gave individualism a bad name and paved the way for revolutionary conspirators." Once those conspirators had legalized the income tax, they had laid the foundation for what Mr. Chodorov calls the "socialism" of the New Deal. They established the welfare state not because they were trying to remedy the sufferings caused by the Great Depression but because they hated individualism and sought to destroy it. In order to do so, it was necessary for them "to develop a slave psychology, a feeling of helpless dependence on the group," Chodorov believes. Mr. Chodorov advocates what he calls "the Return Revolution" which he hopes will repeal the income tax amendment, break up the national state, and restore a federal union, and, as he puts it, bring back the freedom from taxation "won in 1776 and lost in 1913." He hopes to propagate his views through a set of Adam Smith Clubs to be formed on American campuses. Thus far he hasn't had much success.

On the whole, indeed, the successes of the extreme right wing have been of a negative rather than a positive variety. They have succeeded in making life miserable for thousands of their favorite scapegoats, they have impaired freedom of thought in America by their pressures on teachers, writers, and librarians, and they have left their mark on American foreign policies, especially in the Far East. But their two central proposals—the Bricker Amendment, which would have crippled the President's treaty-making power, and the repeal of the income tax amendment—have come to grief. As to taking control of affairs in their own hands, they are too small a minority to dream of it. Despite certain similarities between their ideas and those of European fascists, it would be a great mistake to think of them as being fascists, or as having the fascist determination or capacity to seize power. Their failure to unite, their aimless and diffuse crankiness of mind, and their programmatic feebleness are all too symptomatic. This isn't to deny that they constitute, in a small way, a force in American politics and a problem for American policy-makers. For while they are unlikely to vault into a position from which they can govern, they are frequently in a position to hinder those who *do* govern from doing so with the wisdom and restraint that the times demand.

1959

"The Great Depression and American History: A Personal Footnote"

I SHOULD like to begin by speaking about my work in very personal and biographical terms. Behind every writer there is an individual, a personal history, a series of shaping experiences. I will try to develop those aspects of my own experiences which seem relevant to my historical writing.

There are four basic facts which will help to explain all that I have done:

First, I came of age politically during the Great Depression. I was born in 1916. The first political campaign that I can really remember was that of 1928, the first that engaged my feelings that of 1932. Moreover, I came of age in a great industrial center, Buffalo, New York, which was fast in the grip of the Depression. My mind, in common with others of my generation, was formed on the politics of the Depression and the New Deal. It was also shaped by an uncomfortable awareness of the advance of fascism in Europe, and by the threat of a great world war.

Second, all of my books have been, in a certain sense, topical in their inspiration. That is to say, I have always begun with a concern with some present reality and have been led to see the past in the light of current problems and controversies. Naturally, there are certain questions that may be raised about the value or the legitimacy of such procedures. It may be enough to say that my first two books—*Social Darwinism in American Thought*, which was written from 1940 to 1942 and published in 1944, and *The American Political Tradition*, published in 1948, refract the experiences of the Depression era and the New Deal. And that my later books, *The Age of Reform*, *The Development of Academic Freedom in the United States* (written in collaboration with Walter P. Metzger) and my most recent book, *Anti-Intellectualism in American Life*, all refract the concerns of the post-war era, of the cold war, and our experience with McCarthyism. All of these later books were conceived in the 1950s, and the first two appeared in 1955.

Third, it is important that the basic interest of my work has not been in the machinery of politics, or in the structure of political or economic power, but in ideas, moods, and atmosphere. No doubt my disposition to push the fundamental realities of power somewhat into the background is one of the weaknesses of my writing. As time goes on, however, my interest in political machinery and fundamental questions of power has grown. While I have often been referred to as an intellectual historian, or an historian of ideas, I do not think of myself in this way. I think of myself as a *political* historian whose chief contribution has been to try to tell what people thought they were doing in their political activity—that is, what they thought they were either conserving or reforming or constructing.

Fourth, my work has always been shaped by a very considerable interest in the fields adjacent to history. In the first instance, it was by philosophy, but I have found my historical writing shaped very much by my reading in literary criticism, sociology, and psychology—to a lesser degree by political science and economics. A catalogue of names may be only intermittently meaningful or helpful; but it seems only right to give some credit. I have been influenced in history by Charles A. Beard and V. L. Parrington; and some of what I have done has been in reaction against them. In literary criticism by Edmund Wilson, Van Wyck Brooks, and F. O. Mathiessen. In sociology and political science by Roberto Michels, Karl Mannheim, Thorstein Veblen, Harold Lasswell, and Thurman Arnold. I have always enjoyed and responded to a kind of sociological satire, and on this count should add to such names as those of Veblen and Arnold that of H. L. Mencken. Of course a list like this might be misleading: for example, I share almost none of the political, social, or literary views of Mencken. Much of the influence of men like Beard and Parrington has been exerted chiefly in what I have had to *un*learn. The work of Parrington, which once excited me, now seems laughably simple. Of course my list is incomplete: somewhere in the background hover the great names of Marx and Freud and an intangible residue drawn from American thinkers like John Adams and Jefferson, Dewey and James and no doubt many others. But if you were to ask me what great historians of Europe have had a formative influence—where is Gibbon or Mommsen or Macauley or Ranke or any one of a number of distinguished equivalents—I would have to plead that they have not affected me and that much of the world's great historical literature I have not read, not even sampled. Undoubtedly this is a failing, and has led to a certain American parochialism in my work. It is, I must add, a failing unlikely to be very much remedied: I do not read history for pleasure, ordinarily, and I find that I retain almost nothing that I read if the reading is not done in connection with something I am writing. Some years ago, for example, when I had occasion to spend ten days in hospital, I took with me and read through all seven volumes of Eli Halevy's *History of the English People*. I enjoyed it, and was left with an abiding sense of Halevy's great quality as an historian. But I could not remember a thing I had read, and I knew no more English history a few weeks afterward than I had known before. No doubt there are several conclusions that might be drawn from this experience, but the one I am most sure of is this: if you want to be generally educated, read voluminously when you are very young; nothing you do when you are older will be nearly so effective.

Now let me go back again to the Great Depression, which started me thinking about the world, and without which my entire generation is unintelligible. But how can anyone convey to the young student of this day and age any sense of the reality of the Depression? They are quite ready to believe that the Protestant Reformation took place, or the Crusades, or the fall of Rome, but the Depression seems altogether mythical. You can tell them that by 1933 there were, conservatively, close to 13 million unemployed in America, and that this was almost one man out of every four in the labor force. You can tell them that there was never any time from 1931 to 1940—almost a whole decade—when less than 14% of the labor force was out of work. And that there was no system of national unemployment insurance, no adequate mechanism to sustain them, during several years of this experience. The Depression remains a set of statistics, without flesh and blood reality. No one will believe anymore that people really went hungry, that they were brought by malnutrition to the brink of dreadful disease, that their morale was sapped by years of discovering in the marketplace that they were not wanted. But this was the reality faced by my generation—a reality so pervasive that it shaped all our thinking about history and all our experience of literature.

In order to get a little closer to the emotional life of the Depression generation, let me quote an article on Chicago in 1932, written by Edmund Wilson, and reprinted in his book *The American Earthquake*:

> There is not a garbage-dump in Chicago which is not diligently haunted by the hungry. Last summer in the hot weather, when the smell was sickening and the flies were thick, there were a hundred people a day coming to one of the dumps, falling on the heap of refuse as soon as the truck had pulled out and digging in it with sticks and hands. They would devour all the pulp that was left on the old slices of watermelon and cantaloupe till the rinds were as thin as paper; and they would take away and wash and cook discarded turnips, onions and potatoes. Meat is a more difficult matter, but they salvage a good deal of that, too. The best is the butcher's meat which has been frozen and has not spoiled. If they can find only meat that is spoiled, they can sometimes cut out the worst parts, or they scale it and sprinkle it with soda to neutralize the taste and smell. Fish spoils too quickly, so it is likely to be impossible—though some people have made fish-head soup. Soup has also been made out of chicken claws.
>
> A private incinerator at Thirty-fifth and La Salle Streets which disposes of the garbage from restaurants and hotels, has been regularly visited by people, in groups of as many as twenty at a time, who pounce upon anything that looks edible before it is thrown into the furnace. The women complained to investigators that the men took an unfair advantage by jumping on the truck before it was unloaded; but a code was eventually established which provided that different sets of people should come at different times every day, so that everybody would be given a chance. Another dump at Thirty-first Street and Cicero Avenue has been the center of a Hooverville of three hundred people.
>
> The family of a laid-off dishwasher lived on food from the dump for two years. They had to cook it on the gas of the people downstairs, since their own had been shut off. Their little girl got ptomaine poisoning. Two veterans of the war, who had been expelled from Washington with the bonus army and had made their homes in the fireboxes of an old kiln, were dependent on the dump for some time, though a buddy of theirs found he could do better by panhandling at people's doors.

One widow with a child of nine, who had formerly made $18 a week in a factory and who has since been living on $4 a week relief and two or three hours' work a day at fifty cents an hour, has tried to get along without garbage but has had to fall back on it frequently during a period of three years. Another widow, who used to do housework and laundry but who was finally left without any work, fed herself and her fourteen-year-old son on garbage. Before she picked up the meat, she would always take off her glasses so that she would not be able to see the maggots; but it sometimes made the boy so sick to look at this offal and smell it that he could not bring himself to eat. He weighed only eighty-two pounds.

In a world in which such things could happen, it was as clear as day that something had to change. In the 1930s you had to decide, if you were a thoughtful and humane person, not whether anything should be done about it, but along what lines action should be taken. You had to decide, in the first instance, whether you were a Marxist or an American liberal. When I was an undergraduate, I thought I was a Marxist, and I learned a great deal from the study of Marxism. But the development in the Soviet Union, starting with their terrible purges and culminating in the Nazi-Soviet pact, put me off completely. By the time I was a graduate student and beginning to do what might be called professional work in history, I knew that I was, after all, in some sense an American liberal. But it was perfectly clear that, as the world had changed, the American liberal-progressive tradition would have to change too. Our progressivism could not be any longer the progressivism of Theodore Roosevelt or Woodrow Wilson. Even the liberalism of the New Deal seemed insufficient. It seemed necessary to rethink American liberalism. And all my books have been affected by this impulse to reevaluate American liberalism, as well as to understand the failure of the older American individualism.

I cannot recall ever having made a conscious decision as to the kind of history that I wanted to write, but the drift of my work now moved in a fairly distinct direction. I consider that there are basically three kinds of history writing, though any one historical work may contain them in some combination. One, which is in the classical tradition of historiography, is simply narrative history: it seeks to tell or retell what happened, and does not blush at containing a great deal of the familiar. Often enough it has no new ideas to offer; its strength lies in the quality of its prose. It derives from the ideal of history as art. The second kind of writing derives from the scientific ideal, and is dominant in academic historiography. It is what one encounters in the typical academic monograph, the typical doctoral dissertation. Above all it rests upon the careful accumulation of detailed evidence, very often from untapped or little-used sources. If it is at all successful, it has a great deal of new information to offer us, skillfully marshalled and well presented. Sometimes it offers new ideas, in so far as its carefully gathered evidence yields new conclusions or upsets old ones. Sometimes it opens up whole new areas of awareness.

Whereas these two kinds of history derive respectively from art and science, the kind of history I have increasingly aspired to write derives from philosophy and criticism. It proceeds by examining critically the existing literature on historical events, and attempts to study the consistency of their structure of ideas, and to see if their perspectives cannot be widened by looking into new relationships. In short, it attempts to develop and state new ways of looking at historical events. Since its task is analytical, it tries to dispense with as much as possible of the apparatus of narrative history: it presumes to be written for readers who already have some grasp, so to speak, of the story. It sacrifices—at least it does in the work I have attempted—the accumulation of verifying detail also, using only enough historical detail to illustrate rather than to prove its points. Its weakness lies in its reliance upon a speculative tissue to hold it together. Its strength lies in its novelty and provocative effect, and in the play it gives to an essayistic style. Increasingly my work has been dominated by this conception of analytical history. There was some of it in my first book, and a great deal of it in *The American Political Tradition. The Age of Reform*, and my latest book on *Anti-Intellectualism in American Life*, are wholly products of analytical history.

ca. 1962

Chronology

1916 Born in Buffalo, New York, on August 6, the son of Emil Hofstadter, a furrier and the immigrant child of Polish Jews, and Katherine (Hill) Hofstadter, of German Lutheran descent, and christened in his mother's faith. The Hofstadters reside in Welmont Place, a lower-middle-class German American neighborhood on the city's East Side.

1919 Sister Betty is born.

1926 After mother dies of intestinal cancer, grandmother Mary Hill moves into family home and raises Richard in the Episcopal church, though he will cease attending services in his early teens. Betty moves across the street to live with a maternal aunt.

1929–33 Attends Fosdick-Masten Park High School, one of Buffalo's best. Popular with his classmates, he excels in his studies, graduates as class president and valedictorian, and receives the school's top award for outstanding scholarship, character, and achievement. Acquires a special admiration for H. L. Mencken and his biting mockery of rural American prudery and provincialism.

1933–36 Attends the University of Buffalo, where he majors in history and minors in philosophy. His undergraduate mentor, Julius Pratt, a specialist in the history of American imperialism, encourages him to question the prevailing Progressive interpretations of American history and advises his senior thesis, a study of the tariff and homestead issues in the 1860 election. During his sophomore year, meets and falls in love with Felice Swados, two years his senior and also from Buffalo. Active with Felice in the Communist-affiliated National Student League, serves as president of the university's chapter in 1935–36 and helps lead protests against militarism on college campuses (including mandatory Reserve Officers' Training Corps programs) and imperialism abroad. Receives his B.A. degree in February 1937.

1936 Despite opposition to the union in both families, marries Felice and moves to Brooklyn Heights. Enrolls in evening classes at New York Law School and spends days clerking in the law office of Irving Kauffman, while Felice works in a research position on the medical column for *Time* magazine, a column she soon takes over. The couple become active in the Young Communist League and befriend other young radical intellectuals, including the aspiring literary critic Alfred Kazin.

1937   After quitting law school, enrolls in the graduate program in history at Columbia University. Writes book reviews for the *New York Herald Tribune*.

1938   A revised version of his undergraduate thesis appears in the *American Historical Review* as "The Tariff Issue on the Eve of the Civil War." Travels to Mississippi with Felice to visit black sharecroppers while conducting research into the New Deal's Agricultural Adjustment Act (AAA). Completes his M.A. at Columbia under the supervision of Harry J. Carman with a thesis that harshly evaluates how the AAA supported southern planters and not poor farmers. Enlists in the Columbia graduate unit of the Communist Party with what he calls "a sense of obligation," but resigns in disgust less than a year later. "I hate capitalism and everything that goes with it," he writes to his brother-in-law, the budding leftist short-story writer and novelist Harvey Swados. "But I also hate the simpering dogmatic religious-minded Janizaries that make up the CP." A few months after his resignation, in the summer of 1939, the signing of the Nazi-Soviet non-aggression pact affirms his anti-Stalinism, although he remains strongly sympathetic to the Left.

1940–41   While researching and writing his Ph.D. dissertation under the direction of the intellectual historian Merle Curti, teaches part-time at Brooklyn College before receiving a full-time position at the downtown branch of the City College of New York. In October 1941, Doubleday publishes Felice's novel, *House of Fury* (later republished as *Reform School Girl*), which deals with racial tensions and muted lesbian relations in a girl's reformatory.

1942   Awarded Ph.D. at Columbia for dissertation on Social Darwinism in the United States. Named assistant professor of history at the University of Maryland. During his three years at College Park, joins a close circle of other rising young scholars that includes the historians Frank Friedel and Kenneth M. Stampp and the sociologist C. Wright Mills. Encouraged by Mills, he begins reading deeply in the social sciences, including works by Max Weber, Karl Mannheim, and Sigmund Freud. This will be followed in later years by readings in the work of the Frankfurt School of philosophy and social criticism, including the writings of Theodor Adorno and Max Horkheimer.

1943 Publishes article in *Political Science Quarterly* on the Jacksonian-era reform editor William Leggett, foreshadowing the biographical approach he will take in later work. Son Dan born in December.

1944 Publishes another influential article, this time in *The Journal of Negro History*, a sharp critique of Ulrich B. Phillips, then the preeminent historian of slavery and the Old South. *Social Darwinism in American Thought, 1860–1915* is published by the University of Pennsylvania Press, and wins the American Historical Association's Albert J. Beveridge Award. Begins work on a collection of portraits of American political leaders. Felice is diagnosed with cancer.

1945 In the spring, awarded Knopf History Fellowship by the publisher Alfred A. Knopf for a book tentatively entitled *Men and Ideas in American Politics*. While he continues to draft the manuscript, he devotes most of his time to caring for Felice, who dies in July.

1946 Takes up position as assistant professor of history at Columbia, where he remains for the rest of his career, rising through the ranks to full professor in 1952 and finally succeeding Allan Nevins as the DeWitt Clinton Professor of American History in 1959. Over the years, he becomes a central figure in an intensely political and predominantly Jewish community of writers and scholars that includes his longtime friend Alfred Kazin, the critic and socialist writer Irving Howe, and the sociologist Nathan Glazer, as well as his Columbia colleagues Daniel Bell, Peter Gay, Seymour Martin Lipset, Robert K. Merton, Meyer Schapiro, Fritz Stern, and Lionel Trilling.

1947 Marries the editor Beatrice Kevitt, a Buffalo native and a war widow, with whom he works closely and occasionally writes collaboratively, and whom he credits for sharpening his prose. Working as a freelancer, she goes on to edit manuscripts for, among others, C. Wright Mills.

1948   *The American Political Tradition and the Men Who Made
            It* is published by Knopf, which will remain his principal
            publisher for the remainder of his life. A departure from
            the prevailing monographic format of historical schol-
            arship, the book is well received within and beyond the
            academy, and sells well.

1949–50   Publishes essays evaluating critically the writings of
            Charles A. Beard and Frederick Jackson Turner, finding
            in Beard's work true genius compromised by the author's
            Progressive political agenda while describing Turner's as a
            regressive celebration of bygone agrarian values.

1950   Teaches at fourth session of the summer Seminar in Amer-
            ican Studies in Salzburg, Austria.

1952   Daughter Sarah is born. Delivers Walgreen Lectures at
            the University of Chicago, reevaluating the history of
            Populism and Progressivism. Joins, with Nevins, Gay, and
            others, the executive committee of an ad hoc group, Co-
            lumbia Faculty Volunteers for Stevenson, and helps draft
            an advertisement published in *The New York Times* declar-
            ing support for the Democratic presidential nominee. Co-
            lumbia's president Grayson Kirk (privately) and Columbia
            East Asian specialist William Theodore de Bary (publicly)
            protest the group's use of Columbia's name to advance
            a political cause. Publishes *The Development and Scope of
            Higher Education in the United States*, co-authored with
            C. DeWitt Hardy, sponsored by the Commission on Fi-
            nancing Higher Education, and funded by the Rockefeller
            Foundation and the Carnegie Corporation. Contributes
            chapters on American colleges before the Civil War, grad-
            uate and professional training, and the weaknesses of
            higher education in the United States. The book is the first
            of three on the history of education on which Hofstad-
            ter will collaborate, followed by *The Development of Ac-
            ademic Freedom in the United States*, written with Walter
            P. Metzger and published in 1956; and *Higher Education:
            A Documentary History*, compiled with Wilson Smith and
            published in 1963. While the volumes celebrate the virtues
            of liberal education, Hofstadter's sections pay particular
            attention to the persistent American popular distrust of
            ideas and intellectuals. His work on higher education is in-
            formed by his affiliation with the American Committee for
            Cultural Freedom, a group of liberal intellectuals opposed

to international communism that also includes Arthur Schlesinger, Jr., and John Kenneth Galbraith.

1953   Delivers the first annual Heyward Keniston Lecture at the University of Michigan in Ann Arbor, published later in the year as "Democracy and Anti-Intellectualism in America," in the *Michigan Alumnus Quarterly Review*. Participates in an interdisciplinary Columbia University Seminar on the State, involving social science faculty as well as historians, and which takes up various social research theories. Contributes a paper to the group, "Dissent and Non Conformity in the Twentieth Century" (later published as "The Pseudo-Conservative Revolt" in *The New American Right*, a 1955 essay collection edited by Daniel Bell), which examines the American Right through the lens of symbolic analysis and the concepts of status anxiety and resentment—social science categories that are coming to shape powerfully his continuing work on American reform movements. Signs a textbook deal with Prentice-Hall, in collaboration with friends and fellow scholars Daniel Aaron and William Miller.

1955   Travels to England to deliver a series of lectures on American liberalism at University College, London. Returns to spend summer as visiting professor at University of Oxford. Publishes *The Age of Reform: Bryan to FDR*. The book is awarded the Pulitzer Prize in History for 1956. Although widely praised, its strictures on both Populism and Progressivism and its broader misgivings about popular politics—influenced by the rise of the demagogic Senator Joseph McCarthy—provoke concern. Some critics, including friends and mentors, think that Hofstadter has forsaken the dissenting radical temperament of his first two books. His close friend C. Vann Woodward in time replies to the book with a respectful but firm defense of the Populists and their legacy, "The Populist Heritage and the Intellectual," published in *The American Scholar* in 1960. (Thirty years after publication, Columbia historian Alan Brinkley will call *The Age of Reform* "the most influential book ever published on the history of twentieth-century America.")

1957   Accepts a commission from the Fund for the Republic, originally contracted by the American Committee for Cultural Freedom, to write a study on the Far Right in the

United States. Completes the ninety-eight-page report, "The Contemporary Extreme Right Wing in the United States," the following year. The report begins with an epigram from Nietzsche's *Beyond Good and Evil*: "Objection, evasion, joyous distrust, and love or irony are signs of health; everything absolute belongs to pathology." Prentice-Hall textbook *The United States: The History of a Republic*, co-authored with William Miller and Daniel Aaron, is published, and will be reissued in 1959 in a two-volume version, *The American Republic*.

1958   Vintage publishes a two-volume collection of documents, *Great Issues in American History: A Documentary History*, which will be widely used in high schools and colleges and later expanded to two volumes. Spends 1958–59 academic year as the Pitt Professor of American History and Institutions at the University of Cambridge.

1961–62   Delivers the Sperry and Hutchinson Lectures at Hiram College, Hiram, Ohio, the Haynes Foundation Lectures at the University of Southern California, and the Ziskind Lectures at Smith College. His sarcastic remark made during the Haynes Lectures about the mental instability of ultraconservatives leads to a personal condemnation by California U.S. representative John H. Rousselot (who is also a member of the John Birch Society), which is published in the *Appendix of the Congressional Record*. During 1962–63 academic year he is Visiting Senior Fellow of the Humanities Council and Class of 1932 Lecturer at Princeton University.

1963   *Anti-Intellectualism in American Life* is published and is awarded the Ralph Waldo Emerson Award from Phi Beta Kappa for 1963 and the Pulitzer Prize in General Nonfiction for 1964.

1964–65   Deeply disturbed by the presidential candidacy of Barry Goldwater, writes essays for *Encounter, New York Review of Books*, and *Partisan Review* placing the Goldwater insurgency and its defeat in the November election in historical perspective.

1965   Publishes *The Paranoid Style in American Politics and Other Essays*. In March, participates with John Hope Franklin, C. Vann Woodward, and more than three dozen other concerned historians in the Selma-to-Montgomery,

Alabama, voting rights march led by Dr. Martin Luther King, Jr. Joins an informal group of Columbia professors that meets regularly at the home of Fritz Stern (and hence is known as the Stern Group, later the Stern Gang) to discuss the mounting foreign policy crisis over Vietnam. In May, cosigns letter from the group to President Lyndon B. Johnson asking for a radical reexamination of the administration's Vietnam policy; Johnson replies with a cordial and lengthy letter in defense of the war. In late December, writes to Harvey Swados about the escalating intervention, which he says fills him with a profound sense of foreboding and helplessness he had not felt since the attack on Pearl Harbor in 1941.

1966   Delivers the Jefferson Memorial Lectures at the University of California at Berkeley on the rise of the political parties in the early republic.

1968   Publishes *The Progressive Historians: Turner, Beard, Parrington*. Writes an article for *The New York Times Magazine*, published in May in response to the question "Is America by Nature a Violent Society?", expressing concern that a prolongation of the Vietnam intervention will intensify social division and inflame right-wing reaction. Continuing his interest in the social sciences, co-edits two volumes with Seymour Martin Lipset, *Sociology and History: Methods*, and *Turner and the Sociology of the Frontier*, both published by Basic Books. Delivers commencement address at Columbia in June, the only faculty member ever so honored. His speech, later published in *The American Scholar*, defends the university and the values of liberal scholarship against what he sees as the destructive excesses of the student uprising that had broken out weeks earlier and convulsed the campus. Although sympathetic to the student radicals on specific issues, he deplores what he perceives as their moralistic absolutism and contempt for open inquiry.

1969   The University of California Press publishes *The Idea of a Party System: The Rise of Legitimate Opposition in the United States, 1780–1840*, based on his 1966 Jefferson Lectures. Is dismayed when the American Historical Association considers passage of an anti–Vietnam War resolution, which he fears will threaten intellectual freedom and turn the academic association into a political organization.

1970   Despite deteriorating health, serves as vice president
        of the Organization of American Historians. Publishes
        American Violence: A Documentary History, co-edited
        with Michael Wallace. Dies in New York City of leukemia
        on October 24.

1971   The early draft chapters from a projected multivolume his-
        tory of the United States published as *America at 1750: A
        Social Portrait.*

Note on the Texts

This volume contains two of Richard Hofstadter's books, *Anti-Intellectualism in American Life* (1963) and *The Paranoid Style in American Politics and Other Essays* (1965), along with twelve essays published from 1956 to 1965. It also contains previously unpublished writings from the same period: one complete essay, an excerpt from an autobiographical reminiscence, and a radio lecture delivered on the BBC in 1959.

Hofstadter worked steadily on *Anti-Intellectualism in American Life*—a book he described as "by no means a formal history but largely a personal book"—from 1956 to 1963. This was an uncharacteristically lengthy gestation for one of his books, and at times he struggled to continue writing, even complaining of the seeming futility of his efforts in a 1962 letter to Daniel Boorstin. He published versions of chapters 7 and 14 as, respectively, "'Idealists and Professors and Sore-heads': The Genteel Reformers" in *Columbia University Forum* 5, no. 2 (Spring 1962), and "The Child and the World" in *Daedalus* 91 (Summer 1962). The 1963 Alfred A. Knopf edition of *Anti-Intellectualism in American Life* is the text printed here. In 1964 Jonathan Cape published the book in England without revision. The book was awarded the Pulitzer Prize for General Nonfiction in 1964.

Hofstadter began publishing about the phenomenon he called "pseudo-conservatism" in 1954, when his essay "The Pseudo-Conservative Revolt" appeared in the Winter 1954–55 issue of *The American Scholar*. The essay was included the following year in the anthology *The New American Right*, edited by Daniel Bell (retitled *The Radical Right* in its expanded 1963 edition), and over the next ten years Hofstadter's thinking about this current in American politics deepened and evolved. At the invitation of Robert Maynard Hutchins, the head of the American Committee for Cultural Freedom, he submitted a nearly one-hundred-page memorandum entitled "The Contemporary Extreme Right Wing in the United States" to the organization in 1958. The following year, he delivered a lecture on the BBC about conspiratorial thinking in far-right writings and rhetoric and used the phrase "the paranoid style" in its title (see "The American Right Wing and the Paranoid Style," pp. 954–61 in this volume). When invited to give a Herbert Spencer Lecture in 1963 at Oxford University, he delivered an address entitled "The Paranoid Style in American Politics"; an essay with this title was published in *Harper's* late in 1964. The version that Hofstadter included as the opening essay in his collection *The Paranoid Style in American Politics and Other Essays* (New York: Alfred A. Knopf, 1965) represents the culmination of his thinking on the subject. This Knopf edition, which also includes essays addressing the antitrust movement, free-silver populism, and other historical phenomena, contains the text printed in this volume. An English edition was published in London by Jonathan Cape without revision in 1966. Versions of the book's chapters had appeared in the following publications:

"The Paranoid Style in American Politics": *Harper's*, November 1964, 77–86.

"Pseudo-Conservatism Revisited—1965." As "Fundamentalism and Status Politics on the Right," *Columbia University Forum* 8 (Fall 1965), 18–24.

"Whatever Happened to the Antitrust Movement?" As "Antitrust in America," *Commentary*, August 1964, 47–53.

"Free Silver and the Mind of 'Coin' Harvey." Introduction to William Harvey, *Coin's Financial School* (Cambridge, MA: Harvard University Press, reprint ed., 1963).

The texts of Hofstadter's uncollected essays in the present volume are taken from the following sources:

"History and the Social Sciences": in Fritz Stern, ed., *The Varieties of History* (Cleveland: World Publishing Company, 1956), 75–95.

"American Higher Education": in College Entrance Examination Board, *College Admissions: The Interaction of School and College* (Princeton, NJ: College Entrance Examination Board, 1956), 15–24.

"The Political Philosophy of the Framers of the Constitution" and "The Economic and Social Philosophy of Franklin D. Roosevelt": in the published proceedings of the American Studies conference "America in the 20th Century," June 18–22, 1959, sponsored by the Cultural Office of the American Consulate General in Düsseldorf, the Schulkollegium Münster, and Amerika Haus Essen (Bad Godesberg, West Germany, 1959), 15–25, 47–56. "Framers" in the title of the first essay appeared as "Founders" in the source-text.

"Could a Protestant Have Beaten Hoover in 1928?": *Reporter*, March 17, 1960, 31–33.

"Darwinism and Western Thought": in Henry L. Plaine, ed., *Darwin, Marx, and Wagner: A Symposium* (Columbus: Ohio State University Press, 1962), 47–70.

"The Revolution in Higher Education": in Arthur M. Schlesinger, Jr., and Morton White, eds., *Paths of American Thought* (Boston: Houghton Mifflin, 1963), 269–90.

"Some Comments on Senator Goldwater": *Partisan Review*, Fall 1964, 590–92. Hofstadter's remarks were among several short responses by prominent intellectuals grouped under this title.

"A Long View: Goldwater in History": *New York Review of Books*, October 8, 1964, 17–20.

"Goldwater & His Party: The True Believer and the Radical Right": *Encounter*, October 1964, 3–13.

"Alexis de Tocqueville": in Louis Kronenberger, ed., *Atlantic Brief Lives: A Biographical Companion to the Arts* (Boston: Atlantic Monthly Press, 1965), 795–98.

Among the previously unpublished essays, the texts of "The Origins of the Welfare State" (ca. 1956) and the excerpts from "The Great Depression and American History: A Personal Footnote" (ca. 1962) are taken from manuscripts included in the Richard Hofstadter Papers, housed at the Rare Book and Manuscript Library, Columbia University. The text of "The American Right Wing and the Paranoid Style," which was delivered as a radio lecture on the BBC in 1959, is taken from a manuscript in the BBC Written Archives Centre at Caversham Park, Reading, U.K. The editor would like to extend sincere thanks and gratitude to John Summers, who provided valuable scholarly advice and leads, and to Andrew McKenzie-McHarg, who discovered the BBC manuscript, as well as to archivist Samantha Blake of the BBC WAC, for their assistance.

This volume presents the texts of the original printings chosen for inclusion here, but it does not attempt to reproduce nontextual features of their typographic design. The texts are presented without change, except for the correction of typographical errors. Spelling, punctuation, and capitalization are often expressive features and are not altered, even when inconsistent or irregular. The following is a list of typographical errors corrected, cited by page and line number: 35.37, Walter; 69.37, *gradem*; 87.12, condition":; 99.37, Baptists; 112.24, highbrows; 138.1, one hundred; 159.39, Gerhardt; 274.29, mid-nineteenth century; 299.37, of of; 306.34, gentleman; 307.37, gentleman; 344.27, sophists'; 344.29, meet.; 371.29, teachers; 385.23, life adjustment; 431.20, to to the; 432.8, sort or; 443.16, defer, to; 447.13, bohemian; 450.28, dessicated,; 456.26, criticism; 456.27, 1930 s,; 466.20, plan,; 475.13, persistant; 475.22, genuis; 486.3, Heyward; 535.8, sense of; 537.6, Theodore; 537.34, Theodore; 558.6, psuedo-conservative; 564.37, suggest; 587.41, "Goldwater and His;

629.3, boundry; 644.27, the the; 650.3, arrives,'"; 652.14, *Realpolitik*, and; 663.25, through; 707.2, "bandints," disloyalists,"; 707.17, its lacks; 716.19, 1870's the the; 725.4, tenacles; 728.28, This historical; 740.17–18, controlable; 755.14, Roswell H. Horr.; 760.3, twenty-three old; 765.6, eight-four.; 783.29, *gradem*; 785.27–28, eighteenth century; 789.21, Mathews; 791.24, suplemented; 806.1, thusfar; 806.14, truely; 807.4, Shay's; 809.12, aristrocracy; 810.5, and multiple centers of power (repeated); 814.1, of Constitution; 816.35, that; 817.38–39, gadgetary,; 819.10, reigns; 821.22, significant,; 821.30, men or and,; 821.33, properbooks; 822.18, rightly),; 823.14, many these; 826.16, or of financial; 827.35, it then; 843.9, Henry Simon; 848.40, Years; 852.30, optmistic; 852.36, nazi; 853.21, nazi; 884.34, dam; 885.14, poilitical; 886.6–7, noticably; 886.36, thin, said; 894.1, idealogical.

Notes

In the notes below, the reference numbers denote page and line of this volume (the line count includes headings but not blank lines). No note is made for material that is sufficiently explained in context, nor are there notes for material included in standard desk-reference works such as Webster's Eleventh Collegiate, Biographical, and Geographical dictionaries or comparable internet resources such as Merriam-Webster's online dictionary. Foreign words and phrases are translated only if not translated in the text or if words are not evident English cognates. Quotations from the Bible are keyed to the King James Version. For further biographical information than is contained in the Chronology, see David S. Brown, *Richard Hofstadter: An Intellectual Biography* (Chicago: University of Chicago Press, 2006).

ANTI-INTELLECTUALISM IN AMERICAN LIFE

11.10 Sorel] The French socialist and political philosopher Georges Sorel (1847–1922), author of *Reflections on Violence* (1908) and *The Illusions of Progress* (1908).

15.29 for Alger Hiss] Alger Hiss (1904–1996) held several positions in the administration of Franklin D. Roosevelt and worked for the State Department from 1936 to 1947. He was accused in 1948 by Whittaker Chambers (1901–1961), a former Communist, of having been a Soviet intelligence agent. Hiss was convicted of perjury in 1950 after he denied Chambers's charges before a federal grand jury and served forty-four months of a five-year sentence. Although Hiss maintained for the remainder of his life that the charges against him were false, documents made public in the 1990s, including deciphered Soviet cables, strongly suggest that he served as a Soviet intelligence agent.

16.1 Groton] Private boarding school in Groton, Massachusetts.

16.1–2 Hiss-Acheson group] High-ranking State Department officials. Dean Acheson (1893–1971) was secretary of state in the Truman administration.

17.23 Rockefeller Brothers Fund] Philanthropic organization founded in 1940.

18.22–23 Albert Schweitzer] The Alsatian-born theologian, physician, and musician Albert Schweitzer (1875–1965), who was well-known for his writing and for the hospital in Lambaréné (in present-day Gabon, Africa) where he spent most of his life working.

21.7   Arthur Bestor] Historian (1908–1994) particularly on pre-1860 communitarianism, and a critic of education in America in books such as *Educational Wastelands* (1953).

30.16–17   Jacques Barzun has said] In *God's Country and Mine* (1954) by the French-born American historian and cultural critic Jacques Barzun (1907–2012).

32.23   in one of his novels] In *L'Espoir* (1937), translated into English as *Man's Hope* (1938), by the French novelist and cultural critic André Malraux (1901–1976).

33.23–24   Voltaire describing the Calas family] Voltaire wrote *A Treatise on Intolerance* (1763) in response to the execution of the Protestant French merchant Jean Calas (1698–1762), who was falsely convicted of murdering his oldest son, a suicide. His accusers claimed that he had committed the crime to prevent his son's conversion to Catholicism. Calas's family later proved his innocence.

33.24   of Zola speaking out for Dreyfus] On January 13, 1898, the French writer Émile Zola (1840–1902) published "I Accuse," an outraged open letter to the president of the French Republic following the acquittal of Charles-Ferdinand Esterhazy (1847–1923), the army officer and spy for Germany who had falsely accused the French-Jewish artillery officer Alfred Dreyfus (1859–1935) of treason.

33.25–26   American intellectuals outraged . . . Vanzetti.] Nicola Sacco (1891–1927) and Bartolomeo Vanzetti (1888–1927) were anarchist Italian immigrants convicted of murder and armed robbery in Massachusetts on July 14, 1921, amid controversy about their case. They were executed in 1927 despite international protests that their guilt had not been proved.

34.28–29   "Man is . . . only when he plays."] From *Letters on the Aesthetic Education of Man* (1795) by the German poet and playwright Friedrich Schiller (1759–1805).

35.8–11   Harold Rosenberg . . . answers into questions] Remark made by the art critic Harold Rosenberg (1906–1978) in conversation with the editor Irving Howe (1920–1993); the statement was recalled as an "amusing improvisation" in Howe's essay "A Mind's Turnings" (1960).

35.13   Abelard's *Sic et Non*] Treatise (1125) by the scholastic philosopher Peter Abelard (1079–1142).

35.37–39   Robert Owen, Walter Rathenau . . . eminently practical] The British manufacturer and social reformer Robert Owen (1771–1858) founded New Harmony, a utopian community in Indiana, in 1825. Walther von Rathenau (1867–1922) was a German industrialist and politician who was appointed foreign minister of the Weimar Republic in 1922.

40.16 the well-publicized brain trust] Circle of advisors to President Franklin D. Roosevelt that included the political scientist Raymond Moley (1856–1935), the economist Rexford G. Tugwell (1891–1979), and the lawyer Adolf A. Berle (1895–1971).

40.18–20 Office of Strategic Services . . . Development] Office of Strategic Services (1942–45), the precursor of the CIA; the federal Office of Scientific Research and Development (1941–47) directed scientific research for military purposes.

40.20 A.E.C.] Atomic Energy Commission.

40.20–21 the Rand Corporation] RAND Corporation, think tank established in the aftermath of World War II to advise and assist the American military in research, development, and strategic planning.

42.34 Know-Nothingism] Anti-Catholic, xenophobic, and racist political movement that coalesced around the electoral efforts of the Know Nothing Party, 1844–60.

46.10 Nazi-Soviet pact] The non-aggression pact between Nazi Germany and the Soviet Union, signed in Moscow on August 23, 1939 (containing a secret protocol partitioning Poland, the Baltic states, Finland, and Romania); it was abrogated on June 22, 1941, when German forces invaded the Soviet Union.

49.10 the Scopes Trial] In 1925 the high school science teacher John Scopes (1900–1970) was tried for violation of a recently passed Tennessee law against teaching the theory of evolution in tax-supported schools. The state's case was argued in court by William Jennings Bryan, while Scopes was represented by Clarence Darrow. Scopes was convicted and fined $100; the conviction was later reversed on technical grounds by the Tennessee supreme court.

56.1–2 Parkman and Bancroft to Turner] The influential American historians Francis Parkman (1823–1893), George Bancroft (1800–1891), and Frederick Jackson Turner (1861–1932).

56.7–9 D. H. Lawrence . . . a killer."] In *Studies in Classic American Literature* (1923).

56.9–13 sexual mystique . . . theories of Wilhelm Reich] Among his other ideas, the Austrian-born psychoanalyst Wilhelm Reich (1897–1957) posited the transformative influence of a sexually potent life force, which could be harnessed by sitting in an "orgone energy" accumulator of his design.

56.15 John C. Frémont] Soldier, explorer, and politician (1813–1890), in 1856 the first Republican candidate for U.S. president.

58.2–4 of whom Edith Wharton said . . . in packs.] See the opening line of Wharton's story "Xingu" (1916): "Mrs. Ballinger is one of the ladies who pursue Culture in bands, as though it were dangerous to meet alone."

66.5   Levellers and Diggers] Radical English movements from the middle of
the seventeenth century that advocated for popular sovereignty and sought the
renewal of a corrupt society; the agrarian Diggers, a relatively small group, was
led by Gerrard Winstanley (1609–1676), quoted here.

117.5   D.D.'s] Doctors of divinity.

125.13–15   Cyrus McCormick and George Armour, Jay Cooke and John Wa-
namaker] The inventor and businessman Cyrus McCormick (1809–1884), inventor of the mechanical reaper; the businessman and investor George Armour
(1812–1881), who served as director of the Chicago Board of Trade; the financier Jay Cooke (1821–1905), who helped to fund the Union war effort and
invested heavily in railroad expansion; the merchant and department-store
magnate John Wanamaker (1838–1922).

126.4   Gamaliel Bradford] American biographer (1863–1932), author of *Confederate Portraits* (1914), *Union Portraits* (1916), *A Naturalist of Souls: Studies
in Psychography* (1917), and other books.

126.6   Lyman Abbott] Congregational clergyman (1835–1922) who joined
Henry Ward Beecher in editorship of the weekly *Christian Union* before succeeding him as editor; his many books included *The Evolution of Christianity*
(1896), *Problems of Life* (1900), and *The Spirit of Democracy* (1910).

130.11–12   egomaniac outfielders of Ring Lardner's stories] Lardner (1885–
1933) was a prolific writer of baseball fiction, of which the best known is the
comic epistolary novel *You Know Me Al* (1916).

132.10   Bruce Barton's *The Man Nobody Knows*] Best-selling book (1925), an
interpretation of the life of Jesus by the writer and motivational speaker Bruce
Barton (1886–1967).

138.23   his Northfield Conferences] Moody was the founder of the Northfield
Bible Conferences, a series of interdenominational Protestant gatherings held
from 1880 to 1902 in Northfield, Massachusetts.

150.18   John Birch Society] Extreme right-wing political organization founded
in Indiana in 1958 by candy manufacturer Robert Welch (1899–1985) and
named after John Birch (1918–1945), an American intelligence officer killed by
the Chinese Communists at the end of World War II.

153.41   *Credo quia absurdum est.*] The Latin phrase "I believe because it is
absurd," a phrase often attributed to Tertullian (cf. *De carne Christi*, V.iv).

157.9–10   converted . . . Orestes Brownson and Father Isaac Hecker] Two
well-known converts to Catholicism: Orestes Brownson (1803–1876), who
before his conversion was a Unitarian minister, and Isaac Hecker, the son
of German immigrants who after his conversion at the age of twenty-three
founded the Missionary Society of Saint Paul the Apostle, known as the
Paulist Fathers.

158.7   Robert M. Hutchins] American educator and author (1899–1977), long president of the University of Chicago.

164.15   Alien and Sedition Acts.] Four laws passed in June–July 1798 by the Federalist-controlled Fifth Congress: the Naturalization Act, the Alien Act, the Alien Enemies Act, and the Sedition Act. These laws extended the period required for naturalization from five to fourteen years, gave the president the power to expel or, in wartime, imprison dangerous aliens, and made publication of writing attacking the government a crime punishable by two years in prison.

165.7–10   Locke's impractical constitution . . . Democratic Society of Philadelphia] The English philosopher and political theorist John Locke (1632–1704) was involved in the writing of the Fundamental Constitutions of the Carolinas (1669), pertaining to a geographical area stretching from present-day Virginia to Georgia. The French mathematician and philosopher Nicolas de Condorcet (1743–1794) presented his constitutional plan to the French National Convention in 1793, which was rejected; the phrase "political follies" is taken from William Loughton Smith's pamphlet, which claims that the draft constitution contained "more absurdities than were ever before piled up in any system of government." The prominent Philadelphian David Rittenhouse (1732–1796), a mathematician, astronomer, surveyor, and inventor, was the first president of the Democratic Society of Pennsylvania.

167.17   Fisher Ames] Prominent Federalist Party politician (1758–1808), a member of the U.S. House of Representatives from Massachusetts, 1789–97.

175.17   James Kirke Paulding] Poet, playwright, and novelist (1778–1860), author of *Life of Washington* (1835).

181.18   Thurlow Weed] Journalist and politician (1797–1882), editor of the *Albany Evening Journal*, 1830–62.

186.20   Morgan Dix] Episcopal clergyman and theologian (1827–1908), son of the general, New York governor, and U.S. senator John Adams Dix (1798–1879).

187.8   Francis Bowen] American philosopher and writer (1811–1890), editor of the *North American Review*.

193.15–17   diplomatic posts . . . Charles Francis Adams, Sr., John Bigelow, George William Curtis, William Dean Howells, and John Lothrop Motley] The writer and politician Charles Francis Adams, Sr. (1807–1886), the son of John Quincy Adams, served as ambassador to Great Britain, 1861–68. John Bigelow (1817–1911) held several diplomatic posts in France during the Civil War and was appointed ambassador in 1865. The journalist, travel writer, and editor George William Curtis (1824–1892) was a staunch supporter of Lincoln but was not appointed to a diplomatic post during his presidency. The novelist and editor William Dean Howells (1837–1920) was appointed as U.S. consul in Venice in 1861. The popular historian John Lothrop Motley (1814–1877) served as U.S. minister to the Austrian Empire, 1861–67.

193.30–31   the party of men like Benjamin F. Butler and Ben Wade] Radical Republicans who had been prominent in efforts to impeach Andrew Johnson: Benjamin F. Butler (1818–1893), who served five nonconsecutive terms as U.S. representative from Massachusetts from 1867 to 1879; Benjamin Wade (1800–1878), U.S. senator from Ohio, 1851–69.

193.34   Richard Henry Dana Jr.] Lawyer, abolitionist, and author (1815–1882), best known for his autobiographical narrative *Two Years Before the Mast* (1840).

194.21   Simon Cameron] Republican politician (1799–1889), U.S. senator from Pennsylvania, 1867–77.

195.21   John Jay Chapman.] American lawyer, reformer, and essayist (1862–1933) whose books include *Emerson and Other Essays* (1898) and *Practical Agitation* (1900).

195.28   Charles Eliot Norton] Author (1827–1908) and professor of art history at Harvard, 1873–97, as well as a founder of *The Nation* in 1865.

199.15–16   James Ford Rhodes] Historian (1848–1927), author of *History of the United States from the Compromise of 1850* (7 volumes, 1893–1906).

199.17   Carl Schurz] German-born general, newspaper editor, and politician (1829–1906), Republican senator from Missouri, 1869–75, secretary of the interior, 1877–81.

200.19–20   ill-fated bolt of the Liberal Republicans in 1872.] The Liberal Republicans, a breakaway faction of Republicans opposed to the reelection of Ulysses S. Grant in 1872, nominated as their presidential candidate Horace Greeley (1811–1872), who subsequently received the endorsement of the Democratic convention.

200.24–26   appointment of such men . . . Cabinet posts.] Hamilton Fish (1808–1893), who had been a congressman, 1843–45, governor of New York, 1849–50, and a U.S. senator, 1851–57, served as secretary of state, 1869–77. The lawyer and politician Ebenezer Rockwood Hoar (1816–1895) was U.S. attorney general, 1869–70. The New York attorney William Evarts (1818–1901) was U.S. attorney general, 1868–69, and secretary of state, 1877–81. Carl Schurz, see note 199.17. The lawyer and diplomat Isaac Wayne MacVeagh (1833–1917) was U.S. attorney general in 1881.

200.28–30   election of 1884 . . . Mugwump bolt from the Republican Party . . . Blaine to Cleveland] A faction of Independent Republicans, also known as "mugwumps," supported Democratic candidate Grover Cleveland over Republican James G. Blaine in the 1884 presidential election.

201.26   Lord Macaulay] English politician, historian, and poet Thomas Babington Macaulay, 1st Baron Macaulay (1800–1859), author of *Essays*

Critical and Historical (1843) and the widely read four-volume *History of England* (1849–55).

204.25–26   battle of Chickamauga] Civil War battle fought near Chickamauga Creek in northwestern Georgia, September 19–20, 1863, a Confederate victory.

207.5   R. R. Bowker] Richard Rogers Bowker (1848–1933), editor of *Publishers Weekly* and *Harper's Magazine.*

211.14   Roscoe Conkling] Politician (1829–1888), Republican U.S. senator from New York, 1867–81.

213.12   Horace Bushnell] American Congregationalist minister (1802–1876).

214.29   Jim Fisk] The American financier James Fisk, Jr. (1834–1872).

214.30   Tweed Ring] The Tammany Hall political machine run in New York City by William Marcy Tweed (1823–1878), Democratic politician. With others, Tweed swindled millions of dollars from the city treasury and was convicted on charges related to his corrupt activities in 1873.

229.20   Mabel Dodge Luhan] Memoirist and arts patron (1879–1962) who hosted salons during her residences in Italy, New York City, and, during the latter half of her life, Taos, New Mexico.

229.24–25   "Little Renaissance"] Name given to an early-twentieth-century flourishing of modernist experimentation centered in New York City, encompassing theater, painting, photography, and poetry, as well as social and political movements such as feminism and anarchism.

231.4–5   Brander Matthews] Playwright and academic (1852–1929), professor of literature, 1892–1900, and of dramatic literature, 1900–1924, at Columbia University.

231.16–18   muckraking novelist like Upton Sinclair . . . a pure food bill] The exposé of conditions in Chicago stockyards by Upton Sinclair (1878–1968) in his novel *The Jungle* (1906) helped lead to the passage of the Pure Food and Drug Act in 1906.

232.6   Steffens] American muckraking journalist Lincoln Steffens (1866–1936), author of *The Shame of the Cities* (1904) and *The Autobiography of Lincoln Steffens* (1931).

232.6–7   found a government job for Edward Arlington Robinson] In 1905, after Roosevelt had read and admired *The Children of the Night*, a book by the poet Edward Arlington Robinson (1869–1935), he arranged for Robinson, then in financial straits, to be employed at the New York Customs Office.

232.7–9   attracted into public service . . . Robert Bacon, Charles Bonaparte, Felix Frankfurter, James Garfield, Franklin K. Lane, and Gifford Pinchot] Robert Bacon (1860–1919), a member of Roosevelt's Harvard class, was a partner at J. P. Morgan & Co., 1894–1903, then served as assistant secretary of state, 1905–9, and secretary of state, January–March 1909. Charles Bonaparte (1851–1921) was secretary of the navy, 1905–6, and U.S. attorney general, 1906–9. The Vienna-born lawyer and jurist Felix Frankfurter (1882–1965), later a U.S. supreme court justice, entered public service in 1906 as an assistant to the U.S. attorney for the Southern District of New York. James R. Garfield (1865–1950), son of President James Garfield, was secretary of the interior, 1907–9. Roosevelt appointed the Canadian-born politician Franklin K. Lane (1864–1921) as commissioner of the Interstate Commerce Commission, a post he held until 1913. Later the governor of Pennsylvania, 1923–27, 1931–35, the Republican politician Gifford Pinchot (1865–1946) was the first chief of the United States Forest Service, 1905–10.

232.15   Lord Bryce] English politician and diplomat (1832–1922), the British ambassador to the United States, 1907–13, and the author of *The American Commonwealth* (1888, revised 1910).

234.12   Bagehot] English journalist, editor, and economist Walter Bagehot (1826–1877).

239.3–4   William Allen White] White (1868–1944), known as "The Sage of Emporia," Kansas, was editor and publisher of the *Emporia Gazette*, 1895–1944, and a leader in the Progressive movement.

239.9   Ray Stannard Baker] American journalist (1870–1946), a contributor to *McClure's Magazine*, 1897–1905, and an editor of *American Magazine*, 1906–15.

239.19   Randolph Bourne] American writer and cultural critic (1886–1918).

239.19–20   *Seven Arts* magazine] Magazine founded in 1916 by Waldo Frank and James Oppenheim; in its two-year run it featured essays by Bourne as well as writers such as Van Wyck Brooks, Paul Rosenfeld, and Sherwood Anderson.

240.34   WPA and NYA] The federal Works Progress Administration and the National Youth Administration.

242.17   Henry A. Wallace] American politician (1888–1965), secretary of agriculture, 1933–40, and vice president, 1941–45. He was the Progressive candidate for president in 1948.

242.33   James A. Farley] Farley (1888–1976), chairman of the Democratic National Committee, 1932–40, and Roosevelt's campaign manager in 1932 and 1936; he served as postmaster general, 1933–40.

244.4   brain trusters] See note 40.16.

244.14   Jerome Frank . . . soon driven out] In 1935, Frank (1889–1957), a judge, legal theorist, and prolific writer, was ousted from his position as general counsel of the Agricultural Adjustment Administration, the New Deal agency responsible for the regulation of agriculture, 1933–36.

244.15   NRA] National Recovery Administration, 1933–35, agency regulating business and labor practices.

244.19–21   Moley . . . London Economic Conference] Assistant Secretary of State Moley and Secretary of State Cordell Hull (1871–1955) were part of the American delegation to the Monetary and Economic Conference, a multinational assembly convened in London in June 1933 by the League of Nations to address currency stabilization and other issues related to the Great Depression. At the conference the views of Moley, who had advocated the American abandonment of the gold standard, were passed over in favor of those of Hull. Moley resigned his position due to his conflicts with Hull in August 1933.

246.27   drunk deep, perhaps of the Pierian spring] Cf. Alexander Pope's couplet from "An Essay on Criticism" (1711): "A little learning is a dangerous thing; / Drink deep, or taste not the Pierian spring." According to ancient Greek legend, the waters of this sacred spring in Macedonia inspired those who drank from it.

246.35   Oswald Garrison Villard] American journalist (1872–1949), editor and owner of *The Nation*, 1918–32.

247.12–13   Samuel I. Rosenman] American lawyer (1896–1973), an advisor to and speechwriter for Presidents Franklin D. Roosevelt and Harry Truman.

249.11   egregious "Checkers" speech] In a televised speech on September 23, 1952, Richard Nixon, then the Republican candidate for vice president, defended himself against charges of unethically receiving $18,000 in funds from political supporters. During the speech he acknowledged receiving the gift of a dog that his daughter Tricia had named Checkers, and said: "And you know the kids love this dog and I just want to say this right now, that regardless of what they say about it, we're gonna keep it."

250.32   the Hiss case] See note 15.29.

253.25   Schlesingers, father and son] The historians Arthur Schlesinger, Sr. (1888–1965), whose books include *The New Deal in Action, 1933–1938* (1939), *Paths to the Present* (1949), and *The American as Reformer* (1950), and his son Arthur Schlesinger, Jr. (1917–2007), a speechwriter for Adlai Stevenson and John F. Kennedy, an official in the Kennedy administration, and author of *The Age of Jackson* (1945) and *The Vital Center* (1949).

253.25   Archibald MacLeish] American poet and playwright (1892–1982), Librarian of Congress, 1939–44, whose nomination to the post had been opposed by Republicans claiming he was a Communist fellow traveler.

253.27   Westbrook Pegler] American newspaper columnist (1894–1969) known for his right-wing views and vehement criticism of Franklin Delano Roosevelt, Eleanor Roosevelt, and other public figures.

255.22   Lodge] Henry Cabot Lodge, Jr. (1902–1985), the vice presidential candidate on the Republican ticket in 1960.

257.2   Pablo Casals] Spanish cellist, conductor, and composer (1876–1973).

261.27–28   Cowperwood trilogy] Novels by Theodore Dreiser (1871–1945) featuring the protagonist Frank Algernon Cowperwood: *The Financier* (1912), *The Titan* (1914), and *The Stoic* (published posthumously in 1947).

263.30   Averell Harriman, Herbert Lehman, G. Mennen Williams] American industrialist, politician, and diplomat W. Averell Harriman (1891–1986) was U.S. ambassador to the Soviet Union, 1943–45; Herbert H. Lehman (1878–1963), a partner in the Lehman Brothers investment bank, was governor of New York, 1933–42, and U.S. senator, 1949–57; G. Mennen Williams (1911–1988), from a wealthy Detroit family, served as governor of Michigan, 1949–61.

266.7–8   "radical" labor reformer like Henry George] Henry George (1839–1897), author of *Progress and Poverty* (1879) and other works, advocated a single tax on land.

272.8   those of Matthew Arnold] The English poet and critic Matthew Arnold (1822–1888) wrote disparagingly of American culture and singled out Mark Twain for criticism in "A Word About America" (1882) and (not by name, but as "the funny man") "The Spirit of Civilization" (1888).

272.20–21   his raptures over the Paige machine] Samuel Clemens suffered severe financial losses after investing in the failed Paige Compositor, a typesetting machine named after its inventor, James W. Paige (1842–1917).

273.15–16   the terrible fiasco of his Whittier birthday speech] On December 18, 1877, at a celebration of the seventieth birthday of the poet John Greenleaf Whittier (1807–1892) in Boston attended by many prominent literary figures, Clemens told a satirical tale about three drunken prospectors in Nevada whom he named after the writers Henry Wadsworth Longfellow, Oliver Wendell Holmes, and Ralph Waldo Emerson, each of whom was there in the room. After criticisms of the speech were published in newspapers, Clemens wrote letters of apology to each of the men.

277.20–21   Edward Everett, Nathaniel Frothingham, and the elder Charles Francis Adams] Politician, diplomat, and educator Edward Everett (1794–1865), who in addition to terms as U.S. congressman, U.S. senator, and Massachusetts governor served as U.S. secretary of state, 1852–53. Clergyman Nathaniel Frothingham (1793–1870), long the pastor of the First Church of Boston. Charles Francis Adams, Sr., see note 193.15–17.

287.6   Henry Ward Beecher] Henry Ward Beecher (1813–1887), prominent pastor of Plymouth Congregational Church in Brooklyn, New York.

290.4   Lord Palmerston's] Henry John Temple, 3rd Viscount Palmerston (1784–1865), British prime minister, 1855–58, 1859–65.

297.6   Russell H. Conwell's "Acres of Diamonds"] Popular inspirational speech by Baptist clergyman Russell Conwell (1843–1925), founder of Temple University.

297.7 Norman Vincent Peale] Protestant clergyman and popular author (1898–1993), best known for his inspirational book *The Power of Positive Thinking* (1952).

300.23 Bruce Barton] See note 132.10.

300.26–28 "Conduct the affairs . . . Emmet Fox.] From *Power Through Constructive Thinking* (1940), by the popular inspirational speaker and writer Emmet Fox (1886–1951).

300.28–31 "A man," . . . serve better."] From *The Soul's Sincere Desire* (1928) by the inspirational spiritual writer and entrepreneur Glenn Clark (1882–1956).

301.21–22 Horatio W. Dresser . . . New Thought] Horatio Willis Dresser (1866–1954) was a popular author as well as a historian and proponent of the New Thought, a spiritual movement originating in late-nineteenth-century America that emphasized positive thinking, healing, and personal power.

306.2 John Taylor of Caroline] Politician, Revolutionary War officer, and writer (1753–1824), U.S. senator from Virginia, 1792–94, 1803, 1822–24.

307.30 the Morrill Act] The Morrill Land Grant College Act (1862), named for Vermont U.S. senator Justin S. Morrill (1810–1898), gave federal land to individual states to be sold in order to fund the creation of agricultural colleges.

308.25 Arthur Young] English agricultural economist, farmer, and writer (1741–1820).

317.16 Greenbackism] Nineteenth-century American monetary philosophy that supported maintaining the level of paper currency in circulation or increasing it. Greenbackism was the basis of a political party and other forms of advocacy for populist and agrarian interests.

317.17–18 Henry George's single tax] See note 266.7–8.

317.22–23 Samuel Gompers and Adolph Strasser] Gompers (1850–1924), president of the American Federation of Labor, 1886–94 and 1896–1924; Strasser (1843–1939), leader of cigarmakers' unions and a founder of the American Federation of Labor.

323.33 John Spargo] English-born socialist leader and journalist (1876–1966), author of *The Bitter Cry of Children* (1906), decrying child-labor practices; later in his career he became ardently anti-Communist.

323.34–324.1 critical books . . . Louis B. Boudin, W. J. Ghent, Robert Hunter, Algie M. Simons, and William English Walling] Works such as *The Theoretical System of Karl Marx in the Light of Recent Criticism* (1907) by Louis B. Boudin (1874–1952); *Mass and Class: A Survey of Social Division* (1904) by William James Ghent (1866–1942); *Violence and the Labor Movement* (1914) by Robert Hunter (1874–1942); *Class Struggles in America* (1906) by Algie M. Simons (1870–1950); *The Larger Aspects of Socialism* (1913) by William English Walling (1877–1936).

325.7   Robert Rives La Monte] American journalist (b. 1867), an editor at the Baltimore *News* and at the New York *Call*, a Socialist newspaper.

325.14   George H. Goebel] A member of the Socialist Party's national committee from New Jersey.

328.1–2   Edward Bellamy and Henry Demarest Lloyd] Bellamy (1850–1898), Boston lawyer best known for *Looking Backward: 2000–1887* (1888), a utopian novel imagining America in the year 2000; Lloyd (1847–1903), muckraking journalist, author of *Wealth Against Commonwealth* (1894).

328.26   Paul Rosenfeld] Critic and editor (1890–1946), a member of the cultural circle surrounding Alfred Stieglitz and his "291" gallery; his books include *Musical Portraits* (1920) and *Port of New York* (1926).

329.3   John Reed] John Reed (1887–1920), journalist, poet, and political radical, best known for his eyewitness account of the Russian Revolution, *Ten Days That Shook the World* (1919).

329.15   Michael Gold] Journalist, playwright, and novelist (1894–1967), editor of the left-wing magazines *Masses* and *New Masses*, and the author of the novel *Jews Without Money* (1930).

329.17   Floyd Dell] Novelist and playwright (1887–1969), editor of *The Masses*, 1914–17, and *The Liberator*, 1918–24.

330.20–21   against Thornton Wilder] In Gold's "Wilder: Prophet of the Genteel Christ," published in *The New Republic*, October 22, 1930.

331.18   Joseph Freeman] Journalist (1897–1965), editor of *New Masses* and until 1939 a member of the American Communist Party.

331.18–19   the Foster group . . . Lovestone group] Factions in the Communist Party USA aligned, respectively, with William Z. Foster (1881–1961) and Jay Lovestone (1897–1990), the former supporting Joseph Stalin and the latter supporting Nikolai Bukharin (1888–1938) among the Soviet Communist Party leadership.

331.22–27   Malcolm Cowley . . . point. . . ."] From "The Record of a Trial" (1937) by the American writer and editor Malcolm Cowley (1898–1989), best known for his memoir *Exile's Return* (1934; revised 1951). Cowley was writing for *The New Republic* about the official Soviet report of public show trials held in Moscow, during which prominent Soviet Communists were falsely accused of conspiring with the exiled Leon Trotsky (1879–1940) to overthrow Joseph Stalin and his regime.

331.32   John Dos Passos wrote during the First World War] In a letter written while a senior at Harvard to his friend Arthur McComb.

331.37   Genevieve Taggard] Poet and anthologist (1894–1948); the quotation is from her response to a questionnaire published in *New Masses* in 1927.

332.4 N.E.P.] The Soviet Union's New Economic Policy, introduced by Lenin in 1921 as a temporary measure, ended forced food requisitions, instituted a tax in kind on agricultural production while allowing peasants to sell surplus produce, and restored private retail trade and small-scale private enterprise; under the NEP, the Soviet state retained control of heavy industry, transportation, banking, and foreign trade.

340.23–24 *Je n'ai parlé à personne*] French: I spoke to no one.

343.12–13 Jedidiah Morse's famous geography] *American Geography* (1789) by the American cartographer Jedidiah Morse (1761–1826).

343.33–35 "Little children," . . . wise."] From "Take Care," poem by the American poet Alice Cary (1820–1871).

349.6–7 *The Blackboard Jungle*] Novel (1954) by Evan Hunter (1926–2005) about a teacher confronting juvenile delinquents in an urban high school, the basis for *Blackboard Jungle* (1955), film directed by Richard Brooks (1912–1992) and starring Glenn Ford (1916–2006).

353.15–16 Washington Irving's Ichabod Crane?] The protagonist of Washington Irving's story "The Legend of Sleepy Hollow" (1820).

357.14 James Bryant Conant] Scientist, educator, and diplomat (1893–1978), president of Harvard University, 1933–53.

369.4–7 Benjamin I. Wheeler . . . James Harvey Robinson] Wheeler (1854–1927), a professor of comparative philology at Cornell; Kittredge (1860–1941), English professor at Harvard, an authority on Shakespeare and medieval literature; Cajori (1859–1930), a historian of mathematics; Newcomb (1835–1909), Canadian-born professor of mathematics and prolific writer on astronomy; Remsen (1846–1927), a chemist who served as president of Johns Hopkins University; Adams (1835–1902), president of both Cornell University and the University of Wisconsin; Bourne (1860–1908), Hart (1854–1943), and Robinson (1863–1936) were notable historians.

378.17 Edward Lee Thorndike] Psychologist (1874–1949) and professor at Teachers College, Columbia University, a pioneer in educational psychology.

379.25–28 Paraphrasing Lincoln . . . many of them.] Cf. the statement attributed to Lincoln (though without evidence that he actually said it): "God must have loved the common people: He made so many of them."

400.26 Arthur Bestor and Mortimer Smith.] Bestor, see note 21.7; Smith (1906–1981), critic of education, author of *And Madly Teach: A Layman Looks at Public School Education* (1949).

407.32 Roentgen ray] I.e., X-ray, named for the German scientist Wilhelm Röntgen (1845–1923), the physicist who discovered X-rays.

412.22 Pestalozzi, and Froebel] The Swiss educational reformer Johann Heinrich Pestalozzi (1746–1827) and the German educator and educational theorist Friedrich Wilhelm August Froebel (1782–1852), who established the first kindergarten in 1837.

414.28   The invention of Cadmus] Accounts from Greek antiquity claimed that Cadmus, the founder of Thebes, brought the alphabet from Phoenicia to Greece.

414.31–32   Cornelia, Ophelia, Beatrice] Cornelia Africana (c. 187–c. 115 B.C.E.), mother of Tiberius and Gaius Gracchus (the Gracchi), known in ancient Rome for her wisdom and virtue; Ophelia from Shakespeare's *Hamlet*; Beatrice, Dante's beloved in *The Divine Comedy*.

430.37–431.1   George H. Mead] American philosopher and social psychologist George Herbert Mead (1863–1931), longtime professor at the University of Chicago.

444.25–26   Flaubert . . . "the fatherland of my breed"] See Gustave Flaubert, "Ô Bohème! Bohème! tu es la patrie de ceux de mon sang!" *Notes de voyage*, book II, published in 1910.

447.38–39   "By dint of railing . . . oneself."] Remark attributed to Flaubert as quoted in Irving Babbitt, *Rousseau and Romanticism* (1919).

450.31   what G. K. Chesterton said] See the English writer G. K. Chesterton (1874–1936), "Modern Jargon" (1909): "The definition of a prig, I suppose, is this: one who has pride in the possession of his brain rather than joy in the use of it."

452.1   relationship of Thomas Wentworth Higginson to Emily Dickinson] The soldier, abolitionist, reformer, and writer Thomas Wentworth Higginson (1823–1911) was a friend and correspondent of Emily Dickinson (1830–1886), who sent him many of her unpublished poems; he assisted in the publication of her poems after her death.

453.4   In 1915 Van Wyck Brooks complained] In *America's Coming-of-Age* (1915) by the critic Van Wyck Brooks (1886–1963).

453.7   Philip Rahv . . . paleface and the redskin] In "Paleface and Redskin," opening essay in *Image and Idea* (1949) by the American critic Philip Rahv (1908–1973).

454.19–21   No monuments, no ruins, no Eton . . . of the word] Cf. Henry James in *Hawthorne* (1879): "One might enumerate the items of high civilization, as it exists in other countries, which are absent from the texture of American life . . . No court, no personal loyalty, no aristocracy, no church, no clergy, no army, no diplomatic service, no country gentlemen, no palaces, no castles, nor manors, nor old country-houses, nor parsonages, nor thatched cottages nor ivied ruins; no cathedrals, nor abbeys, nor little Norman churches; no great Universities nor public schools—no Oxford, nor Eton, nor Harrow; no literature, no novels, no museums, no pictures, no political society, no sporting class—no Epsom nor Ascot!"

459.38   "Little Renaissance"] See note 229.24–25.

461.28–29   Spoon River, Winesburg, and Zenith] The fictionalized midwestern settings of, respectively, *Spoon River Anthology* (1915) by Edgar Lee Masters
(1869–1950); *Winesburg, Ohio* (1919) by Sherwood Anderson (1876–1941); and
Babbitt (1922) by Sinclair Lewis (1885–1951).

462.10   Sacco-Vanzetti] See note 33.25–26.

462.10–11   Scopes trial] See note 49.10.

463.36–37   Alfred Kazin] American critic (1915–1998).

465.26–27   Milhaud, Hindemith] French composer Darius Milhaud (1892–
1974) and German composer Paul Hindemith (1895–1963).

466.7   Nazi-Soviet Pact] See note 46.10.

469.27–28   professional Jeremiahs like Vance Packard become best-sellers]
Packard (1914–1996) was the author of the best-selling *The Hidden Persuaders*
(1957), a book critical of the advertising industry, and of books warning of the
dangers of American consumerism.

472.31–34   Jack Kerouac . . . statement,"] From Kerouac's "Belief & Technique for Modern Prose," an early piece of writing that Kerouac discovered
among his papers and sent in a letter to his friend the publisher Donald Allen
in 1958, then published in *Evergreen Review* the following year.

475.26–27   discussion of the Philoctetes myth in *The Wound and the Bow*.]
In *The Wound and the Bow: Seven Studies in Literature* (1941), American critic
Edmund Wilson (1895–1972) used the story in Homer's *Iliad* of Philoctetes,
an Athenian warrior waylaid by a serpent's bite on his way to Troy, to illustrate
the dynamic between trauma (wound) and insight (bow) in literature.

476.19   *grand écrivain*] French: great writer.

477.19   Bronson Alcott's] American transcendentalist writer and reformer
(1799–1888).

478.19–20   *Masses* in Max Eastman's day.] Eastman (1883–1969) was editor of
the Socialist magazine *The Masses* from 1912 to 1917.

479.28   *Kartoffelsuppe*.] German: potato soup. The image from Mencken can
be found in his *Prejudices: First Series* (1919), ch. 10.

480.37   phrase of H. Stuart Hughes] In "Is the Intellectual Obsolete?", essay first published in *Commentary* in 1956 by the historian H. Stuart Hughes
(1916–1999).

481.10–11   ambassadors to India or Yugoslavia] During the Kennedy administration the economist John Kenneth Galbraith (1908–2006), author of *The
Affluent Society* (1958), was ambassador to India, and the historian George

F. Kennan (1904–2005), author of books about the Soviet Union's history and the architect of the Cold War policy of containment, was ambassador to Yugoslavia, 1961–63.

483.7   the jurist Holmes] Oliver Wendell Holmes, Jr. (1841–1935).

483.29–30   H. C. Lea] Henry Charles Lea (1825–1909), American historian and political activist.

THE PARANOID STYLE IN AMERICAN POLITICS

494.23   title of a well-known book] *Politics: Who Gets What, When, How* (1936) by the American political scientist and communications theorist Harold Lasswell (1902–1978).

496.5   Cassirer and Mannheim] German-Jewish philosopher Ernst Cassirer (1874–1945), author of *Philosophy of Symbolic Forms* (1923–29), and German-Jewish sociologist Karl Mannheim (1893–1947), author of *Ideology and Utopia* (1929). See also Hofstadter's discussion of Mannheim, pp. 771–72.

496.33–34   the founder of the John Birch Society] Robert Welch (see note 150.18).

509.19   Herder] German philosopher, critic, and theologian Johann Gottfried von Herder (1744–1803).

509.19   Pestalozzi.] See note 412.22.

512.8   Marat] French revolutionary leader Jean-Paul Marat (1743–1793).

512.16   Whiskey Rebellion.] Uprising in western Pennsylvania in 1794 directed against federal excise taxes on spirits.

513.9–10   Jacksonian crusade against the Bank of the United States.] During the presidential campaign of 1832, Congress passed a bill authorizing an early renewal of the charter of the Second Bank of the United States, which President Jackson vetoed. After his reelection he withdrew all federal funds from the Bank. Despite fierce resistance to Jackson's opposition to the Bank on the part of the Bank's president, Nicholas Biddle (1786–1844), as well as the emergent opposition Whig Party, the charter was permitted to expire in 1836 and the Bank ceased operations as a national institution.

514.12–13   Aaron Burr's famous conspiracy] Burr, General James Willkinson (1757–1825), and others were involved in a conspiracy to detach the western states from the Union. Wilkinson revealed the plot in a letter to President Jefferson in 1806, and the following year Burr was tried for treason and on misdemeanor charges and was acquitted.

519.30   American Protective Association] Anti-Catholic secret society established in Iowa in 1887 by Henry F. Bowers (1837–1911).

521.12–13   headed by Alger Hiss.] See notes 15.29 and 16.1–2.

523.8   Marshall Plan.] Massive economic aid plan, outlined in 1947, to help rebuild Western European economies and counter Soviet influence.

528.31–33   Stephen Shadegg, known for his success . . . campaigns] Shadegg (1909–1990) was the campaign manager for the successful U.S. Senate campaigns of Barry Goldwater (1909–1998) from 1952 onward.

532.14   Fabians] English socialists who favored incremental rather than revolutionary change.

532.16–17   work of Oswald Spengler.] *The Decline of the West* (1918–22), work arguing that Western civilization was in a state of decay, by the German historical philosopher Oswald Spengler (1880–1936).

538.24   the Bricker Amendment.] A proposed constitutional amendment introduced by John Bricker (1893–1986), Republican senator from Ohio, would have limited the power of the executive branch to enter into international treaties; a modified version of this amendment (known as the George Amendment) narrowly failed to meet the required two-thirds majority in a Senate vote on February 26, 1954.

540.27–28   six constitutional amendments brought to the floor of the U.S. Senate] In addition to the George Amendment, these amendments included proposals to reduce the voting age from twenty-one to eighteen and to limit the number of Supreme Court justices to nine; a measure prohibiting federal property seizure absent congressional authority; an equal rights amendment barring sex-based discrimination; and an authorization of state governors to name replacements to the House of Representatives in the event of a nuclear attack on Washington, D.C.

546.34–35   The election of 1928, with its religious bigotry] The Democratic presidential nominee in 1928, Governor Al Smith (1873–1944) of New York, was the first Catholic to run for president on a major party ticket; he was defeated in a landslide by Herbert Hoover. See also Hofstadter's essay, "Could a Protestant Have Beaten Hoover in 1928?" in this volume, pp. 829–36.

546.38–39   breach between Al Smith and F.D.R.] Smith was critical of Roosevelt's policies and was a founding member in 1934 of the nonpartisan American Liberty League, an anti–New Deal organization.

546.39   the rejection of Jim Farley from the New Deal succession.] The Democratic political operative James A. Farley (see note 242.33) ran Roosevelt's presidential campaigns in 1932 and 1936 and served as postmaster general, 1933–40. Seeking the Democratic nomination for president in 1940, he broke with Roosevelt when the president decided to run for a third term.

547.1   S.A.R.] Sons of the American Revolution.

552.6   Julius and Ethel Rosenberg.] Julius Rosenberg (1918–1953) and his wife Ethel Rosenberg (1915–1953), American spies for the Soviet Union, were convicted of espionage and executed on June 19, 1953. Their case was an international *cause célèbre*.

553.17   one agitator put it] Gerald Lyman Kenneth Smith (1898–1976), Christian fundamentalist preacher and extreme right-wing demagogue, at a meeting in St. Louis on March 25, 1944.

555.13   N.R.A.] See note 244.15.

558.1   Father Coughlin's] The Canadian-born Catholic priest Charles Edward Coughlin (1891–1979), known as Father Coughlin, hosted a popular radio program that began in the mid-1920s featuring mostly religious topics and later expanded to politics. Initially a supporter of Franklin Roosevelt's 1932 presidential campaign, Father Coughlin opposed Roosevelt by 1934 and broadcasted right-wing and anti-Semitic content throughout the 1930s.

558.19   Huey Long's assassination] The populist Democratic politician (1893–1935), known as "The Kingfish," was assassinated in 1935 while a U.S. senator from Louisiana; he had served as the state's governor, 1928–32.

567.16–17   *Life* magazine . . . topless bathing suit.] The July 10, 1964, issue of *Life* magazine ran an illustrated feature of the topless "monokini" created by the Austrian-born fashion designer Rudi Gernreich (1922–1985).

568.4   Whore of Babylon] Symbolic figure of corruption in the biblical Book of Revelation, ch. 17; after the Reformation the epithet was often used in Protestant churches to refer to the Roman Catholic Church.

571.5   famous speech at Wheeling] Senator Joseph McCarthy first made his accusations of widespread Communist infiltration in the State Department in a speech delivered in Wheeling, West Virginia, on February 9, 1950, and repeated them in the Senate on February 20.

575.6   Robert Merton's terminology] "Locals" and "cosmopolitans" were terms opposed to each other in the essay "Patterns of Influence" (1949) by the sociologist and Columbia University professor Robert K. Merton (1910–2003).

576.37–38   Charles A. Beard and others] Beard (1874–1948), historian and author of *An Economic Interpretation of the Constitution* (1911) and many other books; Turner, see note 56.1–2; Parrington (1871–1929), literary historian and critic who wrote the three-volume *Main Currents in American Thought* (1927); Bentley (1870–1957), philosopher and author of *The Process of Government* (1908).

577.32   George Gallup] American pollster and entrepreneur (1901–1984).

577.33–34   Paul Lazarsfeld . . . habits] Austrian-born sociologist and Columbia University professor (1901–1976), who as head of the Bureau of Applied Social Research led an empirical study of the voting habits among voters in Erie County, Ohio, in 1940, and Elmira County, New York, in 1948.

577.34–35   Elmo Roper] American pollster (1900–1971).

581.2   conservatism of Robert A. Taft] Robert A. Taft (1889–1953), U.S. senator from Ohio, 1939–53, and a prominent figure in the Republican Party who unsuccessfully sought the party's presidential nomination in 1940, 1948, and 1952.

581.7–8   two members, George Humphrey and Ezra Taft Benson] Secretaries of, respectively, the Treasury and the Department of Agriculture in the Eisenhower administration.

584.9   "the Southern strategy,"] Originating during the civil rights era, the Republican Party's electoral strategy of targeting white voters in southern states and appealing to their racism against African Americans in order, initially, to win these states' electoral college votes and ensure victory in presidential elections. Once former segregationist Democrats finally switched parties, it became the basis for turning the Deep South into a solidly Republican region by the 1980s, which in turn became the foundation of a new national party coalition.

587.35–36   Cow Palace when they circulated the famous Scranton letter] During the 1964 Republican National Convention held at the Cow Palace arena just outside San Francisco, Goldwater's opponent William Scranton (1917–2013), the governor of Pennsylvania, had a letter sent to Goldwater that attacked him, his policies, and his attitude toward delegates. Goldwater responded by distributing copies of the letter to his delegates and supporters at the convention.

587.40   my essay] Reprinted in this volume, pp. 896–918.

593.31   John Harrington] English courtier and author, also spelled Harington (1560–1612).

595.13   Hershey Conference] "Unity" conference of Republican leadership held in Hershey, Pennsylvania.

597.28   Taft-Hartley Act.] The Labor-Management Relations Act, law restricting the activities of labor unions and strengthening the position of employers in labor disputes, which was passed by Congress in 1947 over President Truman's veto.

598.32   "A Long View] See pp. 881–895.

602.35   TVA] Tennessee Valley Authority, a large New Deal public works agency.

604.18–19   such attendant lords as Bobby Baker, Billie Sol Estes, and Matt McCloskey] Associates of Johnson who exploited their positions for personal gain. Baker (1928–2017), a close aide to Johnson when he was Senate majority leader, resigned as secretary to the Senate majority on October 7, 1963, after being accused of corrupt dealings involving defense contractors, and was convicted of fraud and tax evasion charges in 1967. Estes (1925–2013), a Texas businessman and financial supporter of Johnson, was convicted in 1963 on fraud charges that involved the manipulation of federal grain storage contracts. McCloskey (1893–1973), a builder who had served as the Democratic Party's national treasurer, resigned his post as ambassador to Ireland after he was accused of bribing Baker to give his company preferential treatment in its bid to build a stadium in Washington, D.C.

606.24 test-ban treaty] The United States, Britain, and the Soviet Union signed a limited test ban treaty on August 5, 1963, that prohibited nuclear tests in the atmosphere, underwater, or in outer space, while permitting continued testing underground. Goldwater was among the minority of nineteen senators who voted against the ratification of the treaty on September 23, 1963.

610.27 Panama] In January 1964, a fight between American students and Panamanians about the flying of a Panamanian flag alongside an American flag outside a high school triggered several days of rioting in the country, resulting in the deaths of twenty-two Panamanian students and four U.S. soldiers. The crisis led the Panamanian government to sever diplomatic relations with the U.S. until the convening of diplomatic negotiations over control of the canal.

610.28 burned effigy in Greece.] On March 3, 1964, amid unrest over American policy toward the conflict between Greece and Turkey in Cyprus, demonstrators outside the U.S. embassy in Athens burned an effigy of President Johnson.

610.36 the bogus "missile gap" issue] Starting in 1958, John F. Kennedy expressed concerns that the CIA had determined that the United States was falling behind the Soviet Union in its nuclear-weapons capabilities, but not long after he took office as president it was revealed that this assessment was inaccurate; in February 1961 Defense Secretary Robert McNamara was quoted in the *Washington Post* stating "there is no missile gap today."

611.27 Yalta] Roosevelt, Stalin, and Churchill met at Yalta in the Crimea in February 1945 to work out agreements about the postwar occupation of Germany and the division of Europe, among other matters. Roosevelt's ailing health was widely regarded as having allowed the Soviets too many concessions.

612.17–18 Walter Judd or Senator Jenner.] Walter Judd (1898–1994), U.S. congressman from Minnesota, 1943–63, a staunch supporter of the Nationalists in China, where he had worked as a medical missionary; William E. Jenner (1908–1985), U.S. senator from Indiana, 1947–1959, an ally of Senator Joseph McCarthy in his anti-Communist crusade.

617.16 Knowland, Bricker, Bridges] William Knowland (1908–1974), U.S. senator from California, 1945–59, who served as the Republican majority leader; John Bricker, see note 538.24; Styles Bridges (1898–1961), Republican U.S. senator from New Hampshire, 1937–61, who served as Republican minority leader, 1952–53, and president pro tempore of the Senate, 1953–55.

619.6–7 what Fritz Stern has called . . . cultural despair."] In *The Politics of Cultural Despair: A Study in the Rise of the Germanic Ideology* (1961) by the German-born historian Fritz Stern (1926–2016).

NOTES   1003

619.10   men like Fred C. Schwarz and Stephen Shadegg] Australian anti-
Communist activist Fred C. Schwarz (1913–2009), author of *You Can Trust
the Communists (to Be Communists)* (1960) as well as the founder and leader
of the Christian Anti-Communism Crusade (CACC), organization after 1960
based in California. Shadegg, see note 528.31–33.

626.8–9   the free-silver agitation, the heated campaign of 1896] The central
plank of the 1896 presidential platform of Populist candidate William Jennings Bryan (1860–1925) was his proposal for expanding the monetary supply
through the "free and unlimited coinage of silver." Silver proponents advocated backing the currency with silver as well as gold, with their relative value
fixed at a ratio of 16:1. Opponents of "free silver" denounced it as dangerously
inflationary, since the market value of silver was well below the proposed 16 to
1 ratio, and harmful to American interests in international finance and trade,
which were conducted on a gold basis. See also Hofstadter's lengthy discussion
in his later chapter on "Coin" Harvey.

626.26   his famous paper of 1893] "The Significance of the Frontier in American History."

626.35   the Homestead and Pullman strikes] Two violent strikes of the 1890s.
The 1892 strike by the Amalgamated Association of Iron and Steel Workers and non-union steelworkers against the Carnegie Steel Company at its
plant in Homestead, Pennsylvania, led to a daylong battle between Pinkerton
agents hired by Carnegie and union members in which nine strikers and seven
Pinkertons were killed; Pennsylvania governor William Stone called in the
state militia to allow strikebreakers to resume operating the plant. The 1894
strike of Pullman railcar workers under the direction of labor leader Eugene
V. Debs (1855–1926) prompted President Cleveland to send two thousand
federal troops to Chicago. Thirteen strikers were killed, and Debs was tried
and imprisoned.

627.12   Christian social gospel] Movement in American Protestantism during
the late nineteenth and early twentieth centuries oriented toward the tackling
of social problems, especially those related to poverty. Its prominent adherents included Washington Gladden (1836–1918) and Walter Rauschenbusch
(1861–1918).

627.13–14   social settlement movement] Movement founded in England in
1884 built around the founding of "settlement houses" in urban slums for
college-educated young people interested in addressing poverty and other social problems; the most renowned American settlement was Hull-House in
Chicago, cofounded by the activist and writer Jane Addams (1860–1935).

627.21   naval theories of Captain Mahan] Captain Alfred Thayer Mahan
(1840–1914), president of the Naval War College, 1886–89 and 1892–93, wrote
about the importance of naval power in works such as *The Influence of Sea
Power upon History, 1660–1783* (1890), *The Influence of Sea Power upon the French
Revolution and Empire, 1783–1812* (1892), and *The Interest of America in Sea
Power, Present and Future* (1897).

627.37–628.1 Grant had failed miserably in his attempt to acquire Santo Domingo] In 1870 the Senate rejected President Grant's proposed treaty for the annexation of Santo Domingo (present-day Dominican Republic).

628.11 Russell A. Alger] Republican politician and cabinet member (1836–1907), secretary of war, 1897–99, and U.S. senator from Michigan, 1902–7.

628.20–21 Blaine's tart and provocative reply] On March 14, 1891, a mob in New Orleans stormed a prison holding nineteen Italian-born men who had been charged in the murder of the city's former police chief David Hennessy (1858–1890), nine of whom had been acquitted the previous day, and lynched eleven of them. The Italian government reacted by recalling its ambassador from Washington. In response to Italian demands that the lynchers be brought to justice and reparations paid, Secretary of State James Blaine (1830–1893) informed them in a letter that matters of criminal justice were not the responsibility of the federal government but of the states.

628.23 riot in Valparaíso] In 1891, the U.S. granted asylum in its Chilean embassy to supporters of President José Balmaceda (1840–1891), the losing side in the civil war won by the forces of Chile's congress, and refused to hand them over to the new government. On October 16, two Americans were killed and seventeen wounded when American sailors on shore leave in Valparaíso were attacked. The crisis brought the countries to the brink of war.

629.2–3 Venezuela boundary dispute with Britain] In 1895–96 a boundary dispute between Venezuela and British Guiana, a British colony, led to diplomatic hostilities between the United States and Britain. In a message sent to the British government on July 20, 1895, Secretary of State Richard Olney stated that the dispute fell under the Monroe Doctrine and should be settled by arbitration. After Lord Salisbury, the British prime minister and foreign secretary, rejected arbitration, President Cleveland sent a message to Congress on December 17 in which he proposed the creation of a commission to determine the boundary and warned that the United States would treat a British refusal to accept the new boundary as an act of aggression. The resulting crisis lessened when Joseph Chamberlain, the British colonial secretary, described a possible Anglo-American war as "an absurdity" on January 24, 1896. Britain and Venezuela agreed on February 2, 1897, to submit the dispute to arbitration, and a settlement was reached in 1899.

631.23 Senator Lodge] Henry Cabot Lodge (1850–1924), member of the U.S. House of Representatives, 1887–93, and U.S. senator from Massachusetts, 1893–1924.

631.27–28 Carl Schurz] See note 199.17.

632.28 Senator Proctor's] Redfield Proctor (1831–1908), Republican U.S. senator from Vermont, 1891–1908.

633.25 *reconcentrado* policy] The Spanish governor and military commander of Cuba, Valeriano Weyler y Nicolau, Marquise of Tenerife (1838–1930), instituted a "reconcentration" policy that forcibly moved Cubans to designated areas under military control as a means of denying rebels their support. Conditions in the *reconcentrado* camps were squalid and were publicized in American newspapers.

634.20   Mark Sullivan] Journalist and syndicated columnist (1874–1952), author of the six-volume *Our Times: The United States, 1900–1925* (1926–1935).

634.27   William Allen White] See note 239.3–4.

636.16   Mark Hanna] Wealthy Ohio businessman (1837–1904), chairman of the Republican National Committee, 1896–1904, and manager of McKinley's presidential campaigns in 1896 and 1900.

638.21   Brooks Adams.] American historian (1848–1927) whose books include *The Emancipation of Massachusetts* (1887), *The Gold Standard: An Historical Study* (1894), and *Law of Civilization and Decay* (1895).

640.18–19   Dewey's attack on the Spanish fleet in Manila Bay] At the Battle of Manila Bay (May 1, 1898) Commodore George Dewey (1837–1917) methodically bombarded the Spanish line of ten vessels, destroying all of them by noon; no American ships were damaged.

640.28   H. H. Kohlsaat] Newspaper owner and Chicago businessman (1853–1924), an advisor to several Republican presidents.

641.1   Aguinaldo] Emilio Aguinaldo (1869–1964), the leader of the Philippine independence movement.

649.8   walls of Jericho] In the Book of Joshua, the city of Jericho is besieged by the Israelites until its walls come tumbling down, whereupon Joshua curses the city (6:26).

649.27–28   Albert J. Beveridge] Politician (1862–1927), Republican U.S. senator from Indiana, 1899–1911.

654.19–20   *Progress and Poverty . . . School.*] Works by, respectively, Henry George (see note 266.7–8), Edward Bellamy (see note 328.1–2), and William H. "Coin" Harvey (see Hofstadter's chapter on Harvey, pp. 701–765).

657.40   Batista] Cuban general and president Fulgencio Batista (1901–1973), who ruled Cuba from 1933 to 1944 and 1952 to 1959, when he was deposed by the revolution led by Fidel Castro (1926–2016).

657.40   Machado] Gerardo Machado y Morales (1871–1939), hero of Cuba's War of Independence and the nation's president, 1925–33.

659.23   Thurman Arnold] Antitrust lawyer, reformist public official, and political analyst (1891–1969) whose books include *The Symbols of Government* (1935) and *The Folklore of Capitalism* (1937).

659.24   T.N.E.C.] The Temporary National Economic Committee, established by Congress in 1938 to investigate monopolies and economic concentration.

665.22–23   irrational assault . . . Jackson's presidency.] See note 513.9–10.

666.38   George Gunton] English-born economist and labor leader (1845–1919), editor of *Gunton's Magazine* and a proponent of a shorter workday and increased consumption.

667.18–19   Senator Orville Platt] Politician (1827–1905), Republican U.S. senator from Connecticut, 1879–1905.

668.9   Senator Hoar] George F. Hoar (1826–1905), Republican U.S. senator from Massachusetts, 1877–1904.

670.8   Richard Ely] Economist and prominent Progressive (1854–1943), a founder of the American Economic Association.

672.1   the Northern Securities case] Northern Securities, a railroad holding company established in 1901 by the financiers James J. Hill (1838–1916), J. P. Morgan (1837–1913), and Edward Henry Harriman (1848–1909), was dissolved after it was found to be in violation of the Sherman Antitrust Act in 1903.

672.12–13   Charles Van Hise, Herbert Croly, and Walter Lippmann] Van Hise (1857–1918), geologist and president of the University of Wisconsin, 1903–18; Croly (1869–1930), editor, a founder of *The New Republic*, and author of the Progressive manifesto *The Promise of American Life* (1909); Lippmann (1889–1974), journalist and author of numerous books on American politics and foreign affairs whose syndicated "Today and Tomorrow" column ran from the 1930s through the 1960s.

672.17–18   "a nation of villagers."] Chapter title in Lippmann's *Drift and Mastery* (1914).

674.24–25   Charles William Eliot] Academic (1834–1926), Harvard University's longest-serving president, 1869–1909.

677.30   William Graham Sumner] American sociologist (1840–1910) and proponent of Social Darwinism; the author of *What Social Classes Owe to One Another* (1883) and *Folkways* (1907).

681.10   Elmo Roper] See note 577.34–35.

682.13   Pujo Committee's inquiry] Report (1913) of a subcommittee of the House of Representatives' Banking and Currency Committee investigating anticompetitive practices and conflicts of interest among industrial corporations, railroads, public utilities, and insurance companies.

686.9–10   Robinson-Patman Act of 1936] Anti–price discrimination legislation aimed to help small retailers compete against chain stores.

686.10   Miller-Tydings Amendment of 1937] The Miller-Tydings Fair Trade Act, which required the setting of minimum prices so that large chains would not have a competitive advantage through practices such as loss-leading.

686.23–24   Woodrow Wilson . . . "unknown homes"] See Wilson's *The New Freedom* (1913): "The hope of the United States in the present and in the future is the same that it has always been: it is the hope and confidence that out of unknown homes will come men who will constitute themselves the masters of industry and of politics."

692.1–2   Robert La Follette] Politician (1855–1925), governor of Wisconsin, 1901–6, Republican U.S. senator, 1906–25, and the presidential candidate of the Progressive Party in 1924.

692.2   George Norris] Politician (1861–1944), a Republican (until 1936) and an independent U.S. senator from Nebraska, 1913–43.

693.1   scandal like the General Electric affair] In 1959 the Department of Justice began investigating illegal cooperation, collusion, and price conspiracies by General Electric with other companies, especially Westinghouse, which led to numerous indictments and to prison sentences for seven executives, as well as fines.

693.3–4   "gale of creative destruction"] See *Capitalism, Socialism, and Democracy* (1942) by the Austrian economist Joseph Schumpeter (1883–1950): "Every piece of business strategy . . . must be seen in its role in the perennial gale of creative destruction."

702.13   Bryan's "Cross of Gold" speech] At the Democratic National Convention in Chicago, July 9, 1896.

702.37–39   Coxey's "army" . . . Pullman strike] Ohio populist politician Jacob Coxey (1854–1951) led a protest march of unemployed men to Washington in 1894; Pullman strike, see note 626.35.

703.25   Kenesaw M. Landis] Kenesaw Mountain Landis (1866–1944), lawyer and federal judge, 1902–22, who is best known as first commissioner of Major League Baseball, 1920–44.

705.8–9   Archbishop Walsh's tract on bimetallism] *Bimetallism and Monometallism* (1893) by William J. Walsh (1841–1921), archbishop of Dublin, 1885–1921.

705.15–17   Philip D. Armour . . . Senator Shelby Cullom.] Armour (1832–1901), meatpacking entrepreneur and industrialist, the founder of Armour & Company in Chicago; Field (1834–1906), founder and owner of the department store named for him in Chicago's Loop; Kohlsaat, see note 640.28; Cullom (1829–1914), governor of Illinois, 1873–83, U.S. senator, 1883–1913.

720.1   failure of the House of Baring in 1890] Teetering on the brink of collapse, the British banking firm Baring Brothers and Company was saved through the intervention of the Bank of England, which included the establishment via subscription of a guarantee fund to cover Baring's liabilities.

720.8   As Grover Cleveland put it] In his book *Presidential Problems* (1904).

724.23   John Bull] England personified; John Bull was the title character in the satirical political pamphlets published in 1712 by the Scottish physician, mathematician, and writer John Arbuthnot (1667–1735).

728.20–22   Gertrude Stein . . . village explainer."] In Stein's *The Autobiography of Alice B. Toklas* (1933): "he was a village explainer, excellent if you were a village, but if you were not, not."

747.16   Ignatius Donnelly's *Caesar's Column*] Speculative novel (1890) set in New York City nearly a century in the future by Ignatius Donnelly (1831–1901), a farmer, editor, Populist author, orator, and politician who had served as lieutenant governor of Minnesota, 1860–63, and as U.S. congressman, 1863–69.

751.4–5   David . . . Rachel] See 2 Samuel 11 and Genesis 29.

752.40–753.2   Jewess . . . Rebecca solicitous over Ivanhoe."] Sir Walter Scott's romantic novel *Ivanhoe* (1820), set in twelfth-century chivalric England, featured a Jewish heroine, Rebecca.

753.31–33   Shylock image . . . Ezra Pound] Coughlin, see note 558.1; the writings of American poet Ezra Pound (1885–1972) are pervaded with anti-Semitism.

754.3   Redpath's *History of the World*] Eight-volume history (1894) by the American historian and biographer John Clark Redpath (1840–1900).

758.31   Mark Hanna] See note 636.16.

762.1   that General Jackson killed.] See note 513.9–10.

764.38–39   "General" Jacob Coxey] See note 702.37–39.

SELECTED ESSAYS 1956–1965

771.18   Arthur O. Lovejoy] Historian (1873–1962), author of *The Great Chain of Being* (1936) and founder of the *Journal of the History of Ideas*.

771.38–39   Mannheim] See note 496.5.

772.18–20   Harold Lasswell . . . John Dollard . . . Riesman] Lasswell, see note 494.23. Dollard (1900–1980), psychologist and social scientist whose books include *Caste and Class in a Southern Town* (1937) and, with others, *Frustration and Aggression* (1939). Riesman (1909–2002), influential sociologist best known for *The Lonely Crowd* (1950).

776.7–9   the words of Michelet . . . understand present reality."] From *The People* (1846) by the French historian Jules Michelet (1798–1874).

777.28   Buckle] English historian Henry Thomas Buckle (1821–1862), whose *History of Civilization in England* (1856, 1861) was unfinished.

778.31   *Wissenschaft*] German: science.

783.29   *ad eundem gradum*] Latin: of the same rank.

784.6–7 "illiterate ministry"] from *New England's First Fruits* (1643) by Hugh Peter (1598–1660) and Thomas Weld (1595–1661), a fundraising pamphlet for Harvard College that cites its founders' wish "to advance learning and perpetuate it to posterity, dreading to leave an illiterate ministry when our present ministers shall lie in the dust."

785.14–15 President Witherspoon . . . Princeton] John Witherspoon (1723–1794), a signer of the Declaration of Independence, served as president of the College of New Jersey (later Princeton University) and revitalized the school under his leadership, 1768–94.

785.16–17 A bigot like Thomas Clap nearly ruined Yale.] Clap (1703–1767) served as rector and as the first president of Yale College, 1740–66, but was the source of student unrest during his tenure because of strict disciplinary policies based on his Puritanism; widespread dissatisfaction with his leadership ultimately led to his resignation.

787.16 Transylvania] Transylvania University in Lexington, Kentucky.

789.6–7 George Ticknor] Scholar and Harvard professor (1791–1871) who studied literature in Romance languages, especially Spanish, and compiled a vast library; author of the three-volume *History of Spanish Literature* (1849).

789.11–12 Edward Everett] Politician, educator, and diplomat (1794–1865), who served as U.S. congressman and senator and Massachusetts governor, as well as U.S. secretary of state; he taught at Harvard and was its president, 1846–48.

789.16 Andrew D. White] Educator and diplomat (1832–1918), the founding president of Cornell University, 1868–85.

789.20 Zumpt's] German philologist Karl Gottlob Zumpt (1792–1849), author of widely used Latin grammars.

789.21 Brander Matthews] See note 231.4–5.

789.31–790.1 Professor Cooke in Chemistry and Professor Child in English] Josiah Parsons Cooke (1827–1894), scientist who taught chemistry at Harvard for more than forty years; Francis James Child (1825–1896), professor of rhetoric and oratory at Harvard, compiler of a five-volume collection of folk ballads originating in England and Scotland.

796.16–17 former President Conant of Harvard] See note 357.14.

800.3 our conference] "America in the 20th Century," conference in Bad Godesberg, Germany, June 18–22, 1959.

800.20 Harrington] English political theorist (1611–1677), author of *The Commonwealth of Oceana* (1656).

800.33 when I talk about Franklin D. Roosevelt.] In the following essay printed here, taken from a separate lecture at the "America in the 20th Century" conference.

807.4   Shay's Rebellion] Uprising in Massachusetts, 1786–87, directed against high property taxes and farm foreclosures.

807.36–40   Lincoln put . . . existence?"] In his address to Congress, July 4, 1861.

809.33   Polybius.] Ancient Greek historian (c. 208–c. 125 B.C.E.), author of *The Histories.*

815.5–6   a chapter on Franklin D. Roosevelt] "Franklin D. Roosevelt: The Patrician as Opportunist," in *The American Political Tradition and the Men Who Made It.*

817.32   Professor Current] Historian Richard N. Current (1912–2012), author of *The Lincoln Nobody Knows* (1958) and *Lincoln and the First Shot* (1963).

818.12   Professor Stavig's] Historian Richard T. Stavig (1927–2015), long a professor at Kalamazoo College.

818.15   Sacco and Vanzetti trial] See note 33.25–26.

822.34   Tammany Hall Machine] Political machine that controlled Democratic Party politics in New York City, 1850–1930, named after the headquarters of the Tammany Society on 14th Street; see also note 214.30.

825.4   Walter Lippmann] See note 672.12–13.

825.34–35   Square Deal of Theodore Roosevelt] Reformist domestic policy agenda of Theodore Roosevelt, outlined in his book *A Square Deal for Every Man* (1905) and elsewhere.

825.35–36   the New Freedom of Woodrow Wilson] Name of Woodrow Wilson's platform during the presidential campaign of 1912; also the title of a collection of his speeches published in 1913.

825.37   I quote him verbatim] From a speech delivered at the Commonwealth Club, San Francisco, September 23, 1932.

829.27   William E. Bohn] Editor of *The New Leader* and columnist (1877–1967).

831.11–13   John Maynard Keynes . . . enhanced reputation."] In *The Economic Consequences of the Peace* (1919), Keynes's book about the Paris Peace Conference that followed the cessation of hostilities in World War I, which was critical of the terms imposed on Germany by the Treaty of Versailles.

832.6   Cox] James M. Cox (1870–1957), governor of Ohio, 1917–21, the Democratic candidate for president in 1920.

832.38   Josephus Daniels] Journalist and newspaper publisher (1862–1948) who served as secretary of the navy, 1913–21.

834.2   George W. Norris] See note 692.2.

839.1   Reform Bill] An Act of Parliament (1832) that extended the electoral franchise and redistributed seats in the House of Commons.

839.4   new factory act] In 1844 the British Parliament expanded the scope of protections and regulations concerning older children and teenagers working in factories that had been established in the initial Factory Act of 1833. Later legislation continued to address conditions for young workers and for women in factories.

839.4–5   new Poor Law] The Poor Law Amendment Act (1834) updated centuries-old legislation addressing treatment of the indigent and established a system of workhouses administered locally by a board of governors.

839.6–7   1842 . . . Chartists'] Chartism was a working-class movement named for its People's Charter, which called for universal adult male suffrage in Britain and other voting-rights reforms. Chartists were involved in various acts of labor unrest in 1842, including a general strike of miners and mill and factory workers.

839.20–21   the British Fleet bombarded Alexandria.] British ships bombarded Alexandria on July 11–12, 1882, as part of their suppression of a nationalist uprising led by Ahmed Urabi (1841–1911), which was followed by the British occupation of Egypt and a continuous military presence in the country until 1956.

839.39   Malthus and Spencer] Thomas Malthus (1766–1834), English writer who studied population growth and its outpacing of the food supply, the basis for dire predictions about the future well-being of human societies if populations were not limited. Herbert Spencer (1820–1903), English philosopher, biologist, and sociologist, a champion of Darwin's ideas who coined the phrase "survival of the fittest" in 1864.

843.1–2   second famous investigation of Middletown] *Middletown in Transition: A Study in Cultural Conflicts* (1937), sociological study based on research in Muncie, Indiana, by the sociologists Robert S. Lynd (1892–1970) and Helen Merrell Lynd (1896–1982), a follow-up to their book *Middletown: A Study in Modern American Culture* (1929).

843.9–10   Hayek, von Mises, Herbert Simon, Milton Friedman] Austrian-born economist and political philosopher Friedrich Hayek (1899–1992); Austrian-born economist Ludwig von Mises (1881–1973); American economist Herbert A. Simon (1916–2001); American economist Milton Friedman (1912–2006).

844.8   a critical book on Darwinism] *Darwinism: Critical Research* (1885) by the Russian historian and philosopher Nikolay Danilevsky (1822–1885).

844.14–16   "one of the conditions . . . sleep."] In *Intellectual and Moral Reform* (1871) by the French historian, philosopher, and philologist Ernest Renan (1823–1892).

844.25–26   wrote the victorious Marshal von Moltke] In a letter to Johann Caspar Bluntschli, December 11, 1880, by the German field marshal Helmuth von Moltke the Elder (1800–1891).

844.29–30   John Fiske, James K. Hosmer, Albert J. Beveridge, and Josiah Strong] Fiske (1842–1901), philosopher and historian, the author of *Darwinism and Other Essays* (1879, 1885). Hosmer (1834–1927), historian and head of the American Library Association whose works include *A Short History of Anglo-Saxon Freedom* (1890). Beveridge, see note 649.27–28. Josiah Strong (1847–1916), Protestant pastor and adherent of the Social Gospel movement (see note 627.12), author of *Our Country: Its Possible Future and Its Present Crisis* (1885).

844.31–33   John W. Burgess . . . leadership of the world.] See *Political Science and the Comparative Constitutional Law* (1890–91) by the political scientist and Columbia University professor John W. Burgess (1844–1931), which declared that "the Teuton really dominates the world by his superior genius" and Teutonic nations "are the political nations *par excellence*."

844.33   Brooks Adams] See note 638.21.

844.34–35   Theodore Roosevelt predicted] In his 1899 speech "The Strenuous Life."

845.10–11   British Fabians] See note 532.14.

845.14   Prince Peter Kropotkin and Jacques Novikow] Kropotkin (1842–1921), Russian social philosopher and a leading advocate of anarchism; Novikow (1849–1912), Russian sociologist who lived in France and wrote largely in French.

845.17   T. H. Huxley] The English biologist and evolutionist Thomas Henry Huxley (1825–1895), known as "Darwin's bulldog" for his espousal of evolutionary theory.

845.36   "nature red in tooth and claw"] From Alfred, Lord Tennyson's *In Memoriam A.H.H.* (1850), canto 56.

846.8–9   Henry Drummond] Scottish clergyman, scientist, and lecturer (1851–1897) who addressed evolution in works such as *The Ascent of Man* (1894).

846.33   As William James put it] In "Remarks on Spencer's Definition of Mind as Correspondence" (1878).

849.1–2   St. Bartholomew's Day massacre] French Catholic violence against Huguenots that began on St. Bartholomew's Day (August 24) in 1572.

850.20–26   "Man is created . . . trade?"] From Thomas Carlyle's *Past and Present* (1843).

850.37–851.3   "You Malays . . . before the wind."] From *Charles Kingsley: His Letters and Memories of His Life*, vol. 1 (1894), posthumous collection of writings by the Anglican priest, reformer, and novelist Charles Kingsley (1819–1875).

853.35 when Mussolini told us] In a speech delivered in Trieste, September 20, 1920. In an earlier speech Mussolini had attributed "Strife is the root of all things" to the Greek pre-Socratic philosopher Heraclitus (cf. Fragment 53).

853.37 when Hitler told us] In *Mein Kampf* (1925–27).

856.8–9 log with Mark Hopkins . . . other] The saying that the ideal college is "Mark Hopkins on one end of a log and a student on the other" was attributed to President James Garfield. Hopkins (1802–1887), educator and theologian, was president of Williams College, 1836–72.

857.7 Charles William Eliot] See note 674.24–25.

857.29–31 George Ticknor . . . F.A.P. Barnard] Ticknor, see note 789.6–7. Wayland (1796–1865), president of Brown University, 1827–55. Lindsley (1786–1855), president of the College of New Jersey (later Princeton University), 1822–24, and University of Nashville, 1824–50. Tappan (1805–1881), president of the University of Michigan, 1852–63. Barnard (1809–1889), president of Columbia University, 1864–89.

860.7 Charles Kendall Adams] Educator and historian (1835–1902), president of Cornell University, 1885–92, and the University of Wisconsin, 1892–1901.

868.11 *Lehrfreiheit* and *Lernfreiheit*] German: freedom to teach and freedom to learn.

870.12 James Freeman Clarke's] Unitarian clergyman (1810–1888), minister of the Church of the Disciples in Boston and an associate of Transcendentalist authors including Margaret Fuller, whose memoirs he co-edited.

874.10–11 the famous investigation in 1910] Commissioned by the Carnegie Foundation, the report on medical education in 155 North American schools compiled by Abraham Flexner (1866–1959) was published in 1910.

875.5 J. Allen Smith] James Allen Smith (1860–1924), professor of political science at the University of Washington and the author of *The Multiple Money Standard* (1896), *The Spirit of American Government* (1907), and *The Growth and Decadence of Constitutional Government*, published posthumously in 1930.

875.11 La Follette] See note 692.1–2.

877.1 "two cultures" of science and humanities] As asserted in *The Two Cultures and the Scientific Revolution* (1959) by the English scientist and novelist C. P. Snow (1905–1980), originally delivered as the Rede Lecture at Cambridge University in 1959.

880.18 an article on "The Pseudo-Conservative Revolt"] See chapter 2 of *The Paranoid Style*, pp. 535–55.

884.39 "antsy pants"] The Goldwater department stores in Arizona marketed and sold boxer shorts adorned with red ants.

885.1–2 that the Marines be sent to turn on the water at Guantanamo] On February 6, 1964, responding to the Cuban government cutting off the water supply to the U.S. naval base at Guantanamo Bay, Goldwater declared that President Johnson should order Fidel Castro to turn the water back on "or we will march out with a detachment of Marines and turn it on ourselves." He repeated the remark at campaign rallies and in a television interview.

886.8 Hershey conference] See note 595.13.

890.29–30 what D. W. Brogan once called "the illusion of American omnipotence"] Title of essay published in *Harper's* in December 1952 by the Scottish author Dennis W. Brogan (1900–1974), who often wrote about the U.S. and American politics.

893.3 Bobby Baker penumbra] See note 604.18–19.

893.9–11 The charge that President Johnson . . . Tonkin] After reports of attacks on August 2 and 4, 1964, on American destroyers in the Gulf of Tonkin by North Vietnamese torpedo boats, Congress passed a resolution on August 7 authorizing the president to "take all necessary measures to repel any armed attack against the forces of the United States and to prevent further aggression" in Southeast Asia. (Evidence indicates that reports of the August 4 attack were probably the result of false radar contacts caused by tropical weather conditions.) On August 12, Goldwater told reporters that Johnson had told the commander of the U.S. 7th Fleet that "any weapon" could be deployed under the congressional authorization, adding "I think I know what [Johnson] means." The State Department responded with the statement that the president had given "no authorization for the use of any nuclear weapons in the course of the episode in the Gulf of Tonkin, and he made no statement which could reasonably be interpreted to suggest that any such authorization had been given. Senator Goldwater's interpretation is both unjustified and irresponsible."

898.19 as James M. Burns has argued] In *The Deadlock of Democracy: Four-Party Politics in America* (1963) by the historian, political scientist, and biographer James MacGregor Burns (1918–2014).

904.24 Lodge] Henry Cabot Lodge, Jr. (see note 255.22).

906.10 Grandma Moses] Popular name for Anna Mary Robertson Moses (1860–1961), American folk artist who began painting in her seventies and created more than 1,500 works before her death.

910.18–21 sergeant in the First World War . . . forever?"] Remark attributed to Gunnery Sergeant Daniel Daly (1874–1937) during the Battle of Belleau Wood, June 1918.

914.11 his observations at San Francisco] In "Letter from San Francisco," *The New Yorker*, July 25, 1964, by the political journalist Richard Rovere (1915–1979).

918.7–9 *Things fall apart . . . intensity.*] From "The Second Coming" (1919) by the Irish poet William Butler Yeats (1865–1939).

920.29 Southern strategy] See note 584.9.

921.12 "against social security,"] During the campaign Goldwater had made remarks suggesting that Social Security be made voluntary.

921.33 unexpected boon of the Jenkins case] Walter Jenkins (1918–1985), a top aide to Lyndon Johnson, resigned on October 14, 1964, a week after he and another man were arrested on disorderly conduct charges in the bathroom of a YMCA in Washington, D.C.

924.12–13 Supreme Court's decision] In *Reynolds v. Sims* (1964).

927.11 Romney] George Romney (1907–1995), governor of Michigan, 1963–69, later (1968) an unsuccessful candidate for the Republican presidential nomination.

927.12 Senators Kuchel and Case] Thomas Kuchel (1910–1994), Republican U.S. senator from California, 1953–69, minority whip, 1959–69; Francis H. Case (1896–1962), Republican U.S. senator from South Dakota, 1951–62.

927.13 Percy and Taft] Charles Percy (1919–2011), Republican U.S. senator from Illinois, 1967–85; Robert Taft, Jr. (1917–1993), U.S. congressman from Ohio, 1963–65, 1967–71, U.S. senator, 1971–76.

927.30–31 fatal defection . . . Democratic Party] In 1948 Henry Wallace (1888–1965), a former Democrat and vice president in the Roosevelt administration, was the presidential candidate of the newly established Progressive Party, which attracted leftist Democrats; that same year a group of segregationist southern "Dixiecrats" broke from the Democratic Party and, as the States' Rights Democratic Party, nominated South Carolina governor Strom Thurmond (1902–2003) for president.

928.1 own split in 1912] After losing the Republican presidential nomination in 1912, Theodore Roosevelt left the party and ran as a third-party candidate of the newly founded Progressive Party.

928.7–8 the mistakes . . . 1937.] Particularly Franklin D. Roosevelt's proposal to expand the membership of the Supreme Court after it had struck down several New Deal measures, which met with severe political opposition.

932.21 Ampère] Jean-Jacques Ampère (1800–1864), French literary historian.

UNPUBLISHED ESSAYS

942.16 Gallatin] Albert Gallatin (1761–1849), Swiss-born politician and diplomat, Republican U.S. congressman from Pennsylvania, 1795–1801, and secretary of the treasury, 1801–14. His "famous report" (line 954.23) was his *Report on Roads, Canals, Harbors and Rivers* (1808).

941.17 Nicholas Biddle] See note 513.9–10.

955.18–19 a lady in Chicago] Lyrl Clark Van Hyning (1892–1973), anti-Semite and founder of the extremist organization We, the Mothers, Mobilize for America.

955.27–28 Protocols of the Elders of Zion] Fraudulent document forged by Russian police officials exposing a purported plot of Jews and Freemasons to subvert Christian civilization and create a world state; published in Russia in 1902, it was translated into German, English, French, Polish, and other languages in the 1920s.

955.29–30 defeat Senator Bricker] See note 538.24.

958.19 what David Riesman calls "indignants."] In *The Lonely Crowd*.

959.7 *The Secret Life of Walter Mitty.*] Film version (1947) of comic story (1939) by James Thurber (1894–1961) about a daydreaming protagonist who imagines himself at the center of improbable adventures.

961.13 in 1913."] The year of the passage of the Sixteenth Amendment, which allowed the federal government to levy and collect income tax.

963.26 Van Wyck Brooks and F. O. Matthiessen] Brooks, see note 453.4; Matthiessen (1902–1950), American literary critic and author of *The Achievement of T. S. Eliot* (1935), *American Renaissance* (1941), and *The James Family* (1947).

963.27–28 Roberto Michels . . . Arnold.] Robert Michels (1876–1936), German Italian sociologist, author of *Political Parties* (1911); Mannheim, see note 496.5; Veblen (1857–1929), American sociologist and economist, best known as the author of *The Theory of the Leisure Class* (1899); Lasswell, see note 494.23; Arnold, see note 659.23.

964.2–3 Mommsen or Macauley or Ranke] Theodor Mommsen (1817–1903), German classicist, historian, and politician, recipient of the Nobel Prize in Literature in 1902; English historian, essayist, and poet Thomas Babington Macaulay, 1st Baron Macaulay (1800–1859), author of *Essays Critical and Historical* (1843) and the widely read four-volume *History of England* (1849–55); Leopold von Ranke (1795–1886), German historian who had a decisive impact on the field through his emphasis on "wie es eigentlich gewesen" ("how it really was").

966.22 Nazi-Soviet pact] See note 46.10.

Index

Aaron, Daniel, 328; *America in Crisis*, 623
Abbot, Abiel, 512
Abbott, Lyman, 126
Abélard, Pierre: *Sic et Non*, 35
Abingdon, Md., 114
Abolitionists, 42, 84, 197, 213, 508
Abrams, Ray H., 132
Academic freedom, 43, 868
Acheson, Dean, 16, 521, 523, 552, 554, 605, 612
Activism, 50, 66, 406
Acton, Baron (John Dahlberg-Acton), 36
Adams, Brooks, 277, 638, 844
Adams, Charles Francis, Jr., 197–99, 202
Adams, Charles Francis, Sr., 187–88, 193, 277
Adams, Charles Kendall, 369, 860
Adams, Francis, 350
Adams, Henry, 194–95, 197–99, 202–3, 269, 277, 483, 638, 702, 837; *The Education of Henry Adams*, 195, 459, 857
Adams, John, 163, 189, 485, 801, 808–9, 816, 963
Adams, John Quincy, 166, 176–81, 184–86, 188, 219, 255, 941
Adelman, M. A., 682–83, 685
Adler, Felix, 865
Adorno, T. A., 151
Adorno, Theodor W., 548–49, 551; *The Authoritarian Personality*, 537, 776–77
Adventism, 526–27
African Americans, 11, 48, 56, 359, 454, 474, 529, 551, 567, 958; and civil rights, 152, 472, 524, 584, 592, 692, 886, 900; and Democratic Party, 899; and desegregation, 152, 524, 603; and Goldwater campaign, 603, 912, 916, 920; and John Birch Society, 560; in 1950s–60s, 497–98, 551–52; in Progressive era, 236; and

Republican Party, 916; and slavery, 44, 84, 126, 494, 853, 897
Agassiz, Louis, 863
Agricultural Adjustment Act, 244
Agriculture, 449, 685; and anti-intellectualism, 305–16; and Democratic Party, 836; and education, 307–16; and free silver, 702, 715–16, 719, 738, 740, 755; and Goldwater campaign, 602, 921, 924; and New Deal, 244, 823, 833–34, 836; and science, 307–9, 311, 314–16
Agriculture Department, U.S., 235–36, 242, 756
Aguinaldo, Emilio, 641–42, 658
Air Force, U.S., 538
Alamo, 184
Albany, N.Y., 216, 281, 351
Alberty, Harold, 388, 399, 416, 430
Alcoa case, 696
Alcott, Bronson, 477
Aldington, Richard, 37
Alexandria, Egypt, 839
Alger, Horatio, 544
Alger, Russell A., 628
Alien and Sedition Acts, 164, 169
Alienation, 441–42, 444, 446–47, 456, 459–60, 462, 466–67, 470–71, 473–76, 479, 481–83
Allegheny College, 115
Allen, Leslie H., 144
Allen, William V., 721
Alsop, John, 12
Alsop, Stewart, 12
America (Jesuit publication), 159
American Academy of Arts and Sciences, 176, 872
American Antiquarian Society, 872
American Association for the Advancement of Science, 872
American Association of University Professors, 870
American Bible Society, 87
American Economic Association, 484, 669

1017

597; and New Deal, 320, 463; in
Progressive era, 626, 681, 685, 696,
702, 750; and radical organizations,
323–32; and reform, 321; right-wing
attacks on, 524
Labour Party, 532, 894
La Feber, Walter: *The New Empire*,
624, 628, 631
La Follette, Robert M., 222–23, 225–
27, 234, 692, 832, 875
Laissez-faire, 669, 839, 842–43, 868,
938–42, 944–45, 956
La Monte, Robert Rives, 325
Land-grant colleges, 307, 312–15, 861–
62
Landis, Kenesaw M., 703
Landon, Alf, 915, 928
Landon, Melville D., 706
Lane, Edward, 723
Lane, Franklin K., 232
Lane Theological Seminary, 103
Langdell, Christopher C., 873–74
Laos, 891, 913
Lardner, Ring, 130
Lasch, Christopher, 646
Lasswell, Harold, 494, 772, 963
Latimer, John F., 364, 382
Lauchner, A. H., 21
Laughlin, J. Laurence, 705, 714, 725,
728, 731, 735–36, 741–42, 744, 755;
Facts about Money, 705
Lawrence, D. H., 11, 56, 453
Lawrence, Jerome: *Inherit the Wind*,
146–47
Lawyer, Kenneth, 687
Layton, W. T., 740
Lazarsfeld, Paul F., 577, 782
Lea, H. C., 483
League of Nations, 238
Lebanon, 888
Lee, Fitzhugh, 631
Lee, Jesse, 111
Lee, Joseph, 231
Lee, Maurice, 782
Lee, Robert, 567
Lee, Robert E. (general), 204
Lee, Robert E. (playwright): *Inherit the
Wind*, 146–47
Leech, Margaret, 636
Legaré, Hugh Swinton, 185
Lehman, Herbert, 263

Leiden, Netherlands, 176
Lemaître, Georges, 37
Lenin, V. I., 655
Lenski, Gerhardt, 159
Leo XIII, 519
Lerche, Charles O., Jr., 166
Letwin, William, 670
Levellers, 66
Lewis, R. W. B., 93
Lewis, Sinclair, 330, 461, 464; *Babbitt*,
262, 465; *Dodsworth*, 261, 465
Lewis, Tayler, 269
Lewis and Clark expedition, 177
Lexington, Ky., 279
Lieberman, Myron, 348–49, 356, 358
Liebig, Justus, 307, 310–11
Life, 567
Life-adjustment education, 376, 383–
94, 399–401, 404, 416, 799
Lilge, Frederic, 434
Lilienthal, David E., 691
Lincoln, Abraham, 43, 163, 193, 195,
202, 207, 232, 252, 313, 335–36, 379,
464, 580, 588, 629, 807
Linderman, Henry R., 734–35
Lindsay, Vachel, 744
Lindsley, Philip, 352, 857
Link, Arthur, 234, 236–37
Link, Henry C.: *The Return to
Religion*, 302–3
Linn, William, 167
Lippmann, Walter, 145, 232, 239, 249,
483, 825, 833; *Drift and Mastery*,
230, 237
Lipset, Seymour M., 45, 284, 535, 551,
557, 567, 571–72, 577, 684–85
Lipton, Lawrence: *The Holy
Barbarians*, 472
Literary Digest, 643
Literature, 451–56, 461, 464–65, 477,
483, 627
Little Renaissance, 459, 462
Liverpool, England, 176
Lloyd, Henry Demarest, 328
Locke, John, 165, 800, 804; *Essay
Concerning Human Understanding*,
32
Lodge, Henry Cabot, Jr., 255, 904,
927
Lodge, Henry Cabot, Sr., 222, 231,
628, 630–31, 633, 637–39, 641, 651

THE LIBRARY OF AMERICA SERIES

Library of America fosters appreciation of America's literary heritage by publishing, and keeping permanently in print, authoritative editions of America's best and most significant writing. An independent nonprofit organization, it was founded in 1979 with seed funding from the National Endowment for the Humanities and the Ford Foundation.

*This book is set in 10 point ITC Galliard Pro, a face
designed for digital composition by Matthew Carter and based
on the sixteenth-century face Granjon. The paper is acid-free
lightweight opaque that will not turn yellow or brittle with age.
The binding is sewn, which allows the book to open easily and lie flat.
The binding board is covered in Brillianta, a woven rayon cloth
made by Van Heek–Scholco Textielfabrieken, Holland.
Composition by Dianna Logan, Clearmont, MO.
Printing by Sheridan Grand Rapids, Grand Rapids MI.
Binding by Dekker Bookbinding, Wyoming MI.
Designed by Bruce Campbell.*